Peru

Footprint Handbook

Ben Box & Alan Murphy

No more than a glow of light at first but, as the moments passed, the glow transformed into a bolt of gold. I watched transfixed and, as I did so, it struck the ancient ruins of Machu Picchu.

Tahir Shah, *Trail of Feathers* (2002)

4th edition

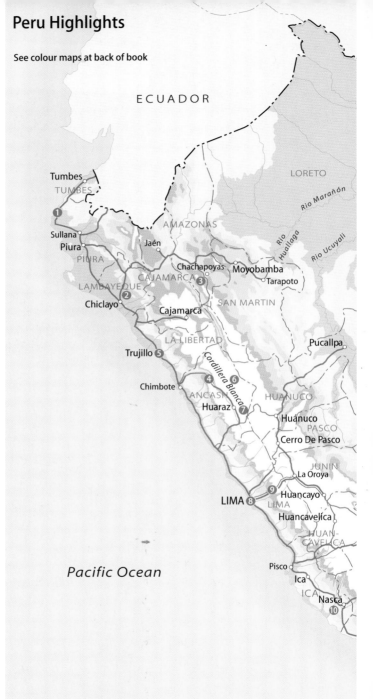

Peru Highlights

See colour maps at back of book

❶ Cabo Blanco
Inspiration for Hemingway's *Old Man and the Sea*, a major surfing spot

❷ Tucumé
Massive 1,000 year-old complex of 26 pyramids, inhabited by terrible demons

❸ Kuelap
The greatest pre-Columbian fortress in the Americas, buried high in jungle-clad mountains

❹ Cañon del Pato
Thrill-a-minute bus ride through a spectacular pass

❺ Trujillo
Colonial city, fringed by huge pyramids and the largest adobe city in the world

❻ Cordillera Blanca
Beautiful and terrifying in equal measure, these mountains offer the best trekking

❼ Chavín de Huantar
2,500 year-old fortress temple; one of Peru's most important pre-Columbian sites

❽ Lima
Bold, brash and buzzing, with the best food and nightlife in the country

❾ Lima-Huancayo railway
All aboard the most breathtaking, vertigo-inducing ride in the world

10 Nasca and Palpa Lines
Giant whales, spiders and hummingbirds, mysteriously etched in the desert

11 Iquitos
Isolated city on the banks of the Amazon, starting point for trips to the north jungle

12 Manu National Park
Home of jaguars and giant otters and one of the world's largest protected areas of rainforest

13 Machu Picchu
Peru's number one attraction remains a special place and is, quite simply, unmissable

14 Cusco
Gringo capital of South America, one of the most fascinating places you'll visit

15 Río Apurimac
The true source of the Amazon, with arguably the finest white-water rafting on the planet

16 Colca Canyon
Come face-to-face with the condor

17 Lake Titicaca
Birthplace of the Inca Empire, still the home of ancient communities

18 Santa Catalina Convent
Arequipa's 'city within a city', the most enchanting colonial structure on the entire continent

Contents

A foot in the door

8

Cusco (previous page) Standing the test of time, precision Inca stonemasonry in Cusco dwarfs a Quechua woman and her traditional beast of burden, the llama.
Tambopata National Reserve (right) The emerald, mysterious virgin rainforest, home of unknown quantities of animals, birds and plants
Sacsayhuaman (below) Spectators crowd the walls of the Inca temple-fortress for the festival of Inti Raymi

Paracas (right) Not an ideal picnic spot, these rocky islets are drenched in guano, natural fertilizer deposited by millions of marine birds
Mealy parrots (above) In Manu NP, when they take to the wing, it's a raucous cloud of green

Introducing Peru

Ever since the intrepid explorer Hiram Bingham first described Machu Picchu as a "wonderland" in a National Geographic article, the fabled Inca city has become one of the most recognized images in the world. So much so that it now virtually represents Peru – along with a certain little bear with a penchant for marmalade, of course.

But that's not even half the story. Peru boasts more ancient archaeological sites than any other country in South America; a seemingly inexhaustible supply that attract latter-day Hiram Binghams, eager to keep up with the Indiana Joneses. One of the most recent finds, at Caral, in the coastal desert, has turned the world of archaeology on its head and challenged accepted thinking on the entire theory of urban development.

There's much more to Peru than ancient stones, however. The World Resources Institute recognizes 104 life zones on the planet and Peru has 84 of them; from mangroves to cloud forest, mist-fuelled oases in the desert to glacial lakes. Amazingly, 60 percent of the country is jungle, even though less than six percent of its population lives there. The physical barrier of the Andes has prevented Peru from integrating the tropical lowlands, so much of its jungle remains intact and this vast green carpet is home to the greatest diversity of plants and wildlife on the planet. Not a year goes by without the recording of new plants and animals previously unknown to science.

In human terms, life is hard. Poverty and marginalization confront conspicuous wealth while earthquakes and El Niño storms provide great uncertainty. But people get by. Witness any one of a thousand festivals and you'll see an intense spirituality enriching daily life. Christian saints are carried through the streets as if they were the Inca emperors' sacred remains. Pachamama – Mother Earth – is offered a drop of every drink and animal spirits and old combats come alive in masquerades. Peru is a wonderland, indeed, with the uncanny knack of springing new surprises at every turn.

Highlights

Wild at heart Without doubt, Peru is the best place on earth for seeing jungle wildlife. In the southern-most department of Madre de Dios, is Manu Biosphere Reserve, over half the size of Switzerland, running from high up in the Andes down to the vast lowland rainforest of the Amazon. Its bird tally numbers over 1,000 species (more than one 10th of all the birds on earth), including countless multi-coloured macaws. It has 13 different species of monkey, turtles, capybara, tapirs, peccaries, giant anteaters, 7 metre-long black caimans, giant otters – even the occasional jaguar. A larger reserve still is Pacaya-Samiria in the northern jungle, with 130 species of mammals, 330 bird species and countless reptiles and amphibians in its lakes, swamps and watercourses. In an open boat, with guide and binoculars, you can watch Peru's wild heart to your own heart's content.

From Navel of Everyone who visits Peru inevitably comes to Cusco, one of the most fascinating cities
the World to anywhere in the world. The Spanish built their churches and houses on the original Inca
Gringo capital foundations, and this startling mix of architectural styles is still much in evidence. Cusco may have become famous as the ancient capital of the Inca Empire – the "navel of the world" – but today it is equally famous among travellers as the "gringo capital" of South America. There's more than enough here to hold the interest of even the most demanding of tourists for at least a week, and after a hard day's sightseeing or souvenir shopping, there are restaurants, cafés, bars and nightclubs aplenty in which to unwind.

Sacred sites From Cusco all the way to Machu Picchu, the Urubamba, or Sacred Valley of the Incas, is lined with a string of little Andean towns, each with its own particular appeal. There is Pisac, famous for its market and superb Inca fortress set on the mountainside high above the town. At Ollantaytambo, a flight of terraces leads up above the town to an unfinished Inca temple representing some of the finest Inca architecture in the country. The Inca plant laboratories in natural amphitheatres at Moray give a new dimension to the term crop circles. But of course, the focus is Machu Picchu, Peru's best-known archaeological site and rightly the main attraction for visitors. This remains the most spectacular sight in all the Americas, no matter how many times you see it.

Stairway to Machu Picchu can be visited in a day, by train from Cusco, but the best way to appreci-
heaven ate it is at the end of the Inca Trail, a four-day hike along a perfectly preserved Inca paved road, through tunnels and up and down huge staircases. It passes through sections of cloud forest, with an ever-present backdrop of snow-crested mountains. However, when you have recovered from the rain, sun and freezing cold nights and have exulted in reaching your goal, you realize that this is the merest cul-de-sac on a mighty highway, the Capaq Ñan or Royal Inca Road, which linked the four corners of the Incas' known universe to Cusco. For the trekker there can be no better sight than this monumental feat of engineering skill forging straight ahead, motorway-wide, paved with history.

Island highs A breathtaking train or bus ride south from Cusco leads to the sparkling sapphire waters of mystical Lake Titicaca, on the border with Bolivia, 3,856 metres above sea level. Visiting some of the islands on the highest navigable lake in the world and staying with local families is like stepping back in time. From an island peak, the sunsets have to be seen to be believed. Also in the southern Andes is the magnificent city of Arequipa, built mostly from white volcanic sillar. Inside the high walls of Santa Catalina convent is a perfectly preserved miniature colonial town which was, until recently, closed to the outside world.

Machu Picchu (left) Surely the most photographed place in South America, and yet still one of the most magical
Colca Canyon (below) Ancient agricultural terraces and condors in one of the world's deepest canyons

Santa Catalina Convent (left) Hidden from prying eyes in Arequipa for centuries, now one of Peru's colonial jewels
Lake Titicaca (above) Totora reeds are used to make boats, houses, even the floating islands of the Uros people
Urubamba Valley (next page) Ever present, the snows of the Verónica massif gleam in the rarified air of the highlands above the Urubamba river

Trujillo (top) What secrets lie
behind these colonial doorways,
window grilles and balconies?
Candelabro (above left) Etched
mysteriously onto the sandy cliffs
overlooking the Pacific Ocean for
purposes as yet unknown
Girls (above right) Shy but curious,
two young campesinas peep from a
doorway at the passing gringos
Vicuñas at El Misti (right) The
wool of the vicuña is highly prized
for its fineness and warmth
Lima (page 16) A city decked out
for the procession of Our Lord of the
Miracles, survivor of earthquakes

Arequipa is the gateway to the Colca Canyon. This remarkable chasm is twice as deep as the Grand Canyon and was thought to be the deepest canyon in the world, until 1994, when nearby Cotahuasi was discovered to be even deeper. Visitors flock to the Colca Canyon to get up close and personal with the largest bird in the world. Every morning, with alarming punctuality, condors rise on the thermals to have a good look at the latest group of awe-struck tourists.

Close encounters of the bird kind

To most people, Peruvian history starts with the Incas, but they were very much the new kids on the block in historical terms and they copied the advanced architectural and artistic styles and techniques of several equally influential earlier cultures. Most of these amazing pre-Inca sites are found along Peru's long stretch of desert coast and it is here, especially north of Lima, that tourism is now directing its attention.

Line drawings

Take the Nasca Lines for instance, nothing to do with South America's profitable cocaine industry, but huge figures of animals and geometric patterns, some of them up to 100 metres across, etched into the dust of the southern coastal desert between 200 BC and AD 600. These giant representations of a monkey, killer whale and hummingbird, among others, are visible only from the air and have puzzled scientists for many years, as well as attracting more than their fair share of new-age freaks. Only now, with new discoveries on similar designs at neighbouring Palpa, are researchers beginning to unravel one of the continent's great mysteries.

In the northern Andes is the Cordillera Blanca, home to Peru's highest mountains and a mecca for hikers the world over. However, if that's not your cup of *mate de coca*, then you can try white-water rafting, mountain biking, skiing or simply enjoy the architectural splendour of the 2,500 year-old fortress temple of Chavín de Huantar, one of Peru's most important pre-Columbian sites.

Raft of pleasures

The elegant colonial city of Trujillo, on Peru's northern coast, is the base for visiting Chan Chán, the largest adobe city in the world. The crumbling ruins cover 28 square kilometres and consist of nine great compounds built by successive dynasties which ruled this part of the country before the arrival of the Incas. Only a few kilometres from Trujillo are the massive adobe pyramids of Huaca del Sol and Huaca de la Luna, the latter with its store of fabulous, polychrome images of fierce gods and fishermen. If looking at all those old mud bricks gets too much, you can indulge in a little R'n'R at the nearby fishing village of Huanchaco, a favourite hangout for the many surfers who make the safari to the country that invented the sport.

Glorious mud

If the Trujillo area seems full of archaeological treasures, then the desert around Chiclayo, 200 kilometres further north, is positively bursting at the seams. At the twin pyramid complex of Sipán, excavations over the past decade have uncovered some of the finest examples of pre-Columbian jewellery, pottery and textiles yet found on the continent. Further north lie the mysterious and evocative ruins of Tucumé, a vast city of 26 pyramids, walled citadels and residential compounds, built over a thousand years ago. Visit them at sundown for the full eerie effect, though it may be difficult to persuade your guide to stick around as local people are very superstitious.

Desert ghosts

In the northeast, where the Andean mountains drop to meet the vast Amazonian lowlands, is the so-called *ceja de la selva* – or eyebrow of the jungle – where the towns, fortresses and cliffside tombs of the mysterious cloud people lie hidden in the forest. The most visited of these, Kuelap, is the greatest pre-Columbian fortress in the Americas, and of such immense proportions it makes the Great Pyramid at Giza look like something out of Legoland.

A raised eyebrow

Essentials

Planning your trip

Where to go

The variety which Peru can offer the visitor is enormous. It may be a tourist brochure cliché, but there really is something for everyone. The problem is, if you're on a tight schedule, how to fit it all in. Obviously people's tastes differ, but the suggested itineraries below should give an idea of what you can cover comfortably in the time available.

Getting around the country can be a difficult task and this is to be expected in a country whose geography is dominated by the Andes, one of the world's major mountain ranges. Great steps have been taken to improve major roads and enlarge the paved network linking the Pacific coast with the Highlands. This also means that there are various options, albeit on rougher roads, for the traveller wishing to go to, or from northern Peru from the centre of the country, avoiding Lima. But it is worth taking some time to plan an overland journey in advance, checking which roads are finished, which have roadworks and which will be affected by the weather. The highland and jungle wet season, from mid-October to late March, can seriously hamper travel. It is important to allow extra time if planning to go overland at this time. Peru also, unfortunately, suffers more than its fair share of natural disasters, such as the El Niño weather phenomenon. This can have dramatic effects on overland travel. Useful addresses and websites which will allow you to check up on local conditions in advance are listed under Finding out more (page 30) and Tourist information (page 49). See also Getting around (page 58) and When to go (page 21).

If you only have a couple of weeks, travelling by air is the sensible option. It allows access to most major regions and means you can spend more time at your destination and less getting there. On the downside, though, air travel reduces the amount of local colour compared with what you can see when going by bus, car or bike. But irrespective of what you choose to see and how you get there, don't attempt too much. Just take it easy and give yourself time to appreciate one of the most beautiful and fascinating countries on Earth.

The southern circuit Southern Peru offers a very rewarding circuit for those short of time. **Cusco** and **Machu Picchu**, the crown jewels of the Inca Empire, **Lake Titicaca**, **Arequipa** and **Lima** can all be visited during a two-week stay, combining air, rail and road travel. This covers the most important and popular sites in the southern part of the country. One of the main drawbacks in such an itinerary is that it allows insufficient time in the Sacred Valley of the Incas, near Cusco, where you could easily spend a week seeing archaeological sites and Quechua villages, hiking, or just relaxing.

Adding an extra week or two to the basic itinerary would allow you to see much more of Cusco (which is a difficult

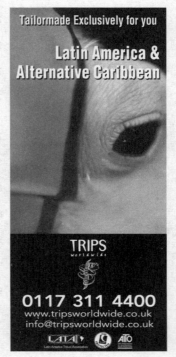

city to drag yourself away from anyway). This would also leave time to explore the **Colca Canyon** from Arequipa, or, from Puno, the shores and islands of Lake Titicaca. You could also spend a week in the jungle visiting the unique and wonderful **Manu National Park**, which is accessible from Cusco by air or road and boat. Another option would be to spend a few days in Lima visiting its fascinating museums, which give you an overview of what you'll be seeing later. And in the meanwhile, you can experience the capital's great nightlife.

Those with more than a few weeks to spare, could spend a week on the southern coast, taking in the **Paracas peninsula** (near Pisco), with its marine birdlife, and the incredible **Nasca** and **Palpa Lines**. Improved road links between Pisco and Ayacucho and Huancayo, between Nasca, Abancay and Cusco, and between Arequipa and Moquegua and Lake Titicaca are opening new routes for those who want to explore further overland.

A two-week trip is possible to a number of places, but as elsewhere in Peru, this would do scant justice to the variety on offer. **Huaraz**, in the **Cordillera Blanca**, is only seven hours by road from Lima and is the country's climbing and trekking centre. It is fast becoming one of the world's premier high altitude recreation areas, with unparalleled ease of access. Hiking or climbing in the Cordillera and neighbouring areas can easily be linked with the coastal archaeological sites near the colonial city of **Trujillo** (eg Chan Chán). **Northern routes**

Alternatively, or additionally, the **Cajamarca** area includes the pleasant city itself, plus thermal baths, archaeological and more recent historical sites and beautiful countryside. To get there from Huaraz, you have to return to the coast for flights from Lima or bus services from Lima, Trujillo or Chiclayo. Cajamarca then gives access to the more remote **Chachapoyas** region, which contains a bewildering number of prehispanic archaeological sites. Access by road is from the southwest through Celendín.

▶▶ Embassies and consulates

Australia, 40 Brisbane Av Suite 8, Ground Floor, Barton ACT 2600, Canberra, PO Box 106 Red Hill, T61-2-6273 8752, F61-2-6273 8754, www.embaperu.org.au Consulate in Sydney.

Belgium, Av de Tervuren 179, 1150 Brussels, T32-2-733 3185, F733 4819, comunicaciones@embassy-of-per.be

Bolivia, C Fernando Guachalla 300, Sopocachi, La Paz, T591-2-244 1250, F591-2-244 1240, embbol@caoba.entelnet.bo Consulate in Santa Cruz de la Sierra.

Brazil, Sector de Embaixadas Sul, Av das Nações Lote 43, 70428-900 Brasilia DF, T55-61-242 9933, F55-61-244 9344, www.embperu.org.br Consulates in Rio de Janeiro and São Paulo.

Canada, 130 Albert St, Suite 1901, Ottawa, Ontario, K1P 5G4, T1-613-238 1777, F1-613-232 3062,

emperuca@bellnet.ca Consulates in Montréal, Toronto and Vancouver.

Chile, Av Andrés Bello 1751, Providencia, Santiago, T56-2-2356451, F56-2-2358139, embstgo@entelchile.net Consulates in Arica, Iquique and Valparaíso.

Colombia, Carrera 80 A, No 6-50, Bogotá, T57-1-257 0505, F57-1-249 8581, www.embajadadelperu.org.co Consulate in Leticia.

Denmark, Trianglen 4, 4 TV, DK-2100, Copenhagen, T45-3-526 5848, F3-526 8406, www.peruembassy.dk

Ecuador, Av República de El Salvador 495, Quito, T593-2-246 8410, F2-225 2560, embpeecu@uio.satnet.net Consulates in Guayaquil, Loja, Macará and Machala.

Finland, Annankatu 31-33 C, 44, 00100, Helsinki, T358-9-693 3681, F358-9-693 3682, Embassy.peru@peruemb.inet.fi

France, 50 Av Kleber, 75116 Paris, T33-1-5370 4200, F33-1-4704 3255, www.amb-perou.fr/

There is also a more northerly road route to Chachapoyas through Bagua from **Chiclayo**, itself rich in archaeological sites (eg Lambayeque with the Brüning and Sipán Museums, Sipán itself and Túcume). If planning to explore any of these places without rushing through them, four days to a week should do, except Chachapoyas where a week minimum would be a good idea.

You can break up a tour of archaeology and mountains with some surfing at **Puerto Chicama** (north of Trujillo) and there are many more beaches in the far north near **Piura** and **Tumbes**. Tumbes also has some wildlife parks, such as coastal mangroves, unlike those in other parts of the country.

The Central Highlands A trip to the Central Andes from Lima can be done fairly quickly, calling at **Huancayo**, **Huancavelica** and **Ayacucho** in a week to 10 days. Alternatively, the route from Cusco to the Central Highlands (via Ayacucho-Huancavelica-Huancayo) is rewarding, but since there are no flights between Cusco and Ayacucho, the only, if rather demanding option is by bus. Obviously the more time you allow, the greater the variety of sights to see, especially in the **Mantaro Valley** near Huancayo, and the places of historical interest around Ayacucho. These are also two of the best places for handicrafts. Heading north from the Central Highlands is a further alternative for those with time to spare. You can travel overland from Cerro de Pasco via Oyón and Churín to **Huacho**, on the coast north of Lima, or to visit the **Cordillera Huayhuash** and make your way up to **Chiquián** and **Huaraz**. It is also possible to reach Huaraz from Huánuco, via **La Unión** and **Huallanca**.

The jungle Peru's eastern jungle include zones with some of the highest levels of biodiversity in the world. There are two distinct areas with tourism development, north and southeast, with a central zone which has little infrastructure. The southeastern jungle contains the **Manu National Park** and the **Tambopata-Candamo National Reserve**. These provide

Germany, Mohrenstrasse 42, 10117 Berlin, T49-30-206 4103, F206 4104, http://members.aol.com/perusipan Cons ulates in Frankfurt and Hamburg.
Israel, 37 Revov Ha-Marganit Shikun Vatikim, 52 584 Ramat Gan, Israel, T972-3-613 5591, F972-3-751 2286, emperu@netvision.net.il
Italy, Via Francesco Siacci N 4, 00197 Roma, T39-06-8069 1510, F39-06-8069 1777, amb.peru@agora.stm.it Consulates in Genoa and Milan.
Japan, 4-4-27 Higashi Shibuya-ku, Tokyo 150-0011, T81-3-3406 4243, F81-3-3409 7589, embperutokyo@embperujapan.org
Netherlands, Nassauplein 4, 2585 EA, The Hague, T31-70-365 3500, embperu@bart.nl
New Zealand, Level 8, 40 Mercer St, Cigna House, Wellington, T64-4-499 8087, F64-4-499 8057, embassy.peru@xtra.co.nz
South Africa, Infotech Building, Suite 201, Arcadia St, 1090 Hatfield, 0083 Pretoria,

T27-12- 342 2390, F27-12-342 4944, emperu@iafrica.co
Spain, C Príncipe de Vergara 36, 5to Derecha, 28001 Madrid, T34-91-431 4242, F34-91-577 6861, lepru@embajadaperu.es Consulate in Barcelona
Sweden, Brunnsgatan 21 B, 111 38 Stockholm, T46-8-440 8740, F46-8-205592, www.webmakers/peru
Switzerland, Thunstrasse No 36, CH-3005 Berne, T41-31-351 8555, F41-31-351 8570, lepruberna02@bluewin.ch Consulates in Geneva and Zurich.
UK, 52 Sloane St, London SW1X 9SP, T020-7235 1917, F020-7235 4463, www.peruembassy-uk.com
USA, 1700 Massachusetts Av NW, Washington DC 20036, T1-202-833 9860, F1-202-659 8124, www.peruemb.org Consulates in Los Angeles, Miami, New York, Chicago, Houston, Boston, Denver and San Francisco.

Essentials

wonderful opportunities for watchers of birds, butterflies and animals and for plant lovers. A trip to the southeastern jungle can be done as part of a visit to **Cusco** (see above) or as an item on its own. Flying both ways to **Puerto Maldonado** is the only viable option if short of time. Going overland to the Amazon Basin is possible and adventurous, either from Cusco to Puerto Maldonado (the most popular tours involve going one way by road, the other by air), or from Lima to the central jungle, via **Pucallpa** or **Oxapampa**. To travel in this area you must have a good command of Spanish. The Amazonian city of **Iquitos** is the jumping off point for the northern jungle, where there is a good network of jungle lodges on the river or its tributaries. Flying to Iquitos is one option, either from Lima, or from **Tarapoto**, which can be reached by a beautiful road which descends from the mountains just north of Chachapoyas. Alternatively, you can go overland to Pucallpa and then take a river boat downstream to Iquitos.

When to go

Peru's high season is from June to September, when the weather is most stable for hiking the Inca Trail or trekking and climbing elsewhere in the country. At this time the days are generally clear and sunny, though nights can be very cold at high altitude. The highlands can be visited at other times of the year, though during the wettest months from November to April some roads become impassable and hiking trails can be very muddy. April and May, at the tail end of the highland rainy season, is a beautiful time to see the Peruvian Andes, but the rain may linger, so be prepared.

On the coast, the summer months from December to April are best for swimming, but not in Lima or its immediate surroundings. This area is covered with *la garúa*, a blanket of cloud and mist that hangs around from approximately May to October. At this time only the northern beaches near Tumbes are warm enough for pleasant swimming.

Weather
For a more detailed description of conditions in the Cordillera Blanca, see page 85

The best time to visit the jungle is during the dry season, from April to October. During the wet season, November to April, it is oppressively hot (40° C and above) and while it only rains for a few hours at a time, which is not enough to spoil your trip, it is enough to make some roads virtually impassable.

Festivals
For a list of the major national holidays and festivals, see page 75

For a detailed list of local festival dates, see under each town in the main travelling text

Every bit as important as knowing where to go and what the weather will be like, is Peru's festival calendar. At any given time of the year there'll be a festival somewhere in the country, at which time even the sleepiest little town or village is transformed into a colourful mixture of drinking, dancing and water throwing (or worse). Not all festivals end up as massive unruly parties – some are solemn and ornate holy processions – but they all draw people from miles around. So it helps a great deal to know about these festivals and when they take place.

Many of the major *fiestas*, such as *Carnaval* (throughout February) and *Semana Santa* (March/April), take place during the wet season. June and July are also big months for *fiestas*, particularly in Cusco, which spends the whole of June in celebration. Accommodation can be very hard to find at this time in Cusco.

Check the websites of *PromPerú* and *South American Explorers* (see Finding out more page 30). For a description of some of the main festivals and their historic roots, see under Culture, on page 597.

Tour operators

UK & Ireland   *Audley Latin America*, 6 Willows Gate, Stratton Audley, Oxfordshire, OX27 9AU, T01869-276210, F276214, www.audleytravel.com *Austral Tours*, 20 Upper Tachbrook St, London SW1V 1SH, T020-7233 5384, F020-7233 5385, www.latinamerica.co.uk *Condor Journeys & Adventures*, 2 Ferry Bank, Colintraive, Argyll, PA22 3AR, T01700-841318, F01700-841398, www.condorjourneys-adventures.com Eco and adventure tourism with specially designed tours to suit your requirements. *Cox & Kings Travel*, St James Court, 45 Buckingham Gate, London, T020-7873 5000, www.coxandkings.co.uk *Dragoman*, Camp Green, Debenham, Stowmarket, Suffolk IP14 6LA, T01728-861133, www.dragoman.co.uk Overland camping and/or hotel journeys throughout South and Central America. *Exodus Travels*, 9 Weir Road, London SW12 0LT, T020-8772 3822, www.exodus.co.uk Experienced in adventure travel, including cultural tours and trekking and biking holidays. *Explore Worldwide*, 1 Frederick St, Aldershot, Hants GU11 1LQ, T01252-760000, F01252-760001, www.exploreworldwide.com Highly respected operator with offices in Eire, Australia, New Zealand, USA, Canada, Hong Kong, Belgium, Netherlands, Denmark, Norway, South Africa and Mexico, who run 2 to 5 week tours in more than 90 countries worldwide including Peru. *Guerba Expeditions*, Wessex House, 40

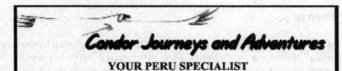

Essentials

Station Rd, Westbury, Wiltshire BA13 3JN, T01373-826611, F858351, www.guerba. com Specializes in adventure holidays, from trekking safaris to wilderness camping. *Hayes & Jarvis*, 152 King St, London W6 0QU, T0870-8989890, www.hayesandjarvis. co.uk Long established operator offering tailor-made itineries as well as packages. *Journey Latin America*, 12-13 Heathfield Terr, Chiswick, London, W4 4JE, T020-8747 8315, F020-8742 1312, and 12 St Ann's Sq, 2nd floor, Manchester, M2 7HW, T0161-832 1441, F0161-832 1551, www.journe ylatinamerica.co.uk The world's leading tailor-made specialist for Latin America, running escorted tours throughout the region, they also offer a wide range of flight options. *KE Adventure Travel*, 32 Lake Rd, Keswick, Cumbria, CA12 5DQ, T017687-73966, F74693, and 1131 Grand Av, Glenwood Springs, CO 81601, USA, T800-497 9675, 970-384 0001, F970-384 4004, www.keadventure.com Specialist in adventure tours, including three-week cycling trips in and around Cusco. *Kumuka Expeditions*, 40 Earls Court Rd, London W8 6EJ, T020-7937 8855, F202-7937 6664, and Level 4, 46-48 York St, Sydney, NSW 2000, Australia, T1800-804277, 2-9279 0491, F9279 0492, www.kumuka.com Overland tour operator for small groups, escorted or truck-based. *Last Frontiers*, Fleet Marston Farm, Aylesbury, Buckinghamshire HP18 0QT, T01296-653000, www.lastfrontiers.co.uk South American specialists offering tailor- made itineraries as well as discounted air fares and air passes. *Llama Travel*, Oxford House, 49a Oxford Rd, London, N4 3EY, www.llamatravel.com *Naturetrek*, Cheriton Mill, Cheriton, Alresford, Hants, SO24 0NG, T01962-733051, F736426, www.naturetrek.co.uk Birdwatching tours throughout the continent, also botany, natural history tours, treks and cruises. *Reef and Rainforest Tours Ltd*, 1 The Plains, Totnes, Devon, TQ9 5DR, T01803-866965, F865916, www.reefrainforest.co.uk *South American Experience*, 47 Causton St, Pimlico, London, SW1P 4AT, T020-7976 5511, F7976 6908, www.southamericanexperience.com Apart from booking flights and

Essentials

accommodation, also offer tailor-made trips. *Steppes Latin America*, 51 Castle St, Cirencester, Gloucestershire, GL7 1QD, T01285-885333, www.stepes latinamerica.co. uk *Travelbag Adventures*, 15 Turk St, Alton, GU34 1AG, T01420-593001, F544272, www.travelbag-adventures.com *Trips Worldwide*, 9 Byron Pl, Clifton, Bristol, BS8 1JT, T0117-311 4401, F311 4400, www.tripsworldwide.co.uk *Tucan Travel*, London, T020-8896 1600, london@tucantravel.com Sydney T02-9326 4557, sydney@tucan travel.com Peru, T084-241123, cuzco@tucantravel.com Offer adventure tours and overland expeditions. *Veloso Tours*, 33-34 Warple Way, London W3 0RG, T020-876 0616, F020-876 0716, www.veloso.com

Europe   *South American Tours*, Hanauer Landstrasse 208-216, D-60314, Frankfurt/M, Germany, T+49-69-405 8970, F+49-69-440432, www.southamericantours.de For holidays, business travel, or special packages. Has own office at Avenida Miguel Dasso 117, piso 14, San Isidro, Lima, T422 7254, F440 8149, satperu@terra.com.pe

North America   *4 Star South America*, 322 Se Parkhill Dr, Chehalis. WA 98532, www.4starsouthamerica. com Online tour operator. *Discover Peru Tours*, 7325 West Flagler St, Miami, Florida 33144, T305-266 5827, F266 2801, T1-800-826 4845, www.discover-chile.com *eXito*, 1212 Broadway Suite 910, Oakland, CA 94612, T1-800-655 4053 T510-655 4054 (worldwide), www.exito- travel.com *GAP Adventures*, 19 Duncan St, Suite 401, Toronto, Ontario, M5H 3H1, T1-800-465 5600, 416-260 0999, F416-260 1888, and 760 North Bedford Rd No 246, Bedford Hills, NY 10507, USA, T1-800-692 5495, 914-666 4417, F914- 666 4839, www.gap.ca *International Expeditions*, One Environs Park, Helena, AL 35080, USA, T205-428 1700, 1-800-633 4734 (toll free), F428 1714, www.ietravel.com Eight day Amazon voyages, with optional five day extension in the Sacred Valley. *Ladatco Tours*, 3006 Aviation Ave, Suite 4C, Coconut Grove, FL 33133, T305-854 8422, T1-800-327 6162, F305-285 0504, www.ladatco.com Based in Miami, run 'themed' explorer tours based around the Incas, mysticism etc. *Los Tambos Chacha poyanos Tours*, T800 743 0945, www.kuelap.org Offers tours and modern co-op lodges. *Lost World Adventures*, 112 Church St, Decatur, GA 30030, T800-999 0558, 404-373 5820, F404-377 1902, www.lost worldadventures.com *Mila Tours*, 100 S. Greenleaf Av, Gurnee, IL 60031-337, www.mila tours.com *Myths and Mountains*, 976 Tee Court, Incline Village, NV 89451, www.myths andmountains.com *South American Fiesta*, 3774 Swallow Way, Marietta, Georgia, 300 66-3031, www.southamerican fiesta.com *So*uth American Journeys, PO Box 12081, La Crescenta, CA 91214, T1-800-884 7474, T/F818 352 8289, www.southamerica exp.com Small group tours off the beaten track with Peruvian guides, involvement in ecological projects. *Tambo Tours*, T1-888-2- GO-PERU (2467378). Adventure travel and general tour specialist for areas in Peru. USA and Cusco, PO Box 60541, Houston, Texas, www.2GO

PERU.com, www.tambotours.com *Wildland Adventures*, 3516 NE 155 St, Seattle, WA 98155-7412, USA, T206-365 0868, T800-345 4453, F206-363 6615, www.wildland.com Specializes in cultural and natural history tours to the Andes and Amazon.

Southtrip, Sarmiento 347, 4th floor, of 19, Buenos Aires, Argentina, T011-4328 7075, www.southtrip.com **In Lima**: *Cóndor Travel*, Mayor Armando Blondet 249, San Isidro, T442 7305/3000, F442 0935, branch in Cusco, www.condortravel.com.pe *Coltur*, Av José Pardo 138, Miraflores, T241 5551, F446 8073, also has an office in Cusco, www.colt ur.com.pe *Dasatour*, Jr Francisco Bolognesi 510, Miraflores, T447 7772, F447 0495, also has an office in Cusco, www.dasatour.com.pe *Explorandes*, Calle San Fernando 320, T445 8683/242 9527, F242 3496, also has an office in Cusco, www.explor andes. com.pe Offers a wide range of adventure and cultural tours. *Galcruises Expeditions*, Jorge wash-ington 748 y Amazonas, Quito, ecuador, ww.galacruisesexpeditions. com *InkaNatura Travel*, Manuel Banón 461, San Isidro, Lima 27, T440 2022, F422 9225, www.inka natura.com Also at Plateros 361, mezzanine, Cusco, T84-251173. *Kinjyo Travel*, Las Camelias 290, San Isidro, T442 4000/221 6025, F442 1000, also office in Cusco, postmast@kinj yo.com.pe *Lima Tours*, J Belén 1040, Lima centre, T424 5110, F424 6269, and at Avenida Pardo y Aliaga 6908, T222 2525, F 222 5700. Recommended. *Viracocha Turismo*, Avenida Vasco Núñez de Balboa 191, Miraflores, Lima, T445 3986/447 5516, F447 2429. Cultural and mystical tours. Also hiking, rafting, birdwatching.

South America
See also individual town listings

Adventure World, 73 Walker St, North Sydney, NSW 2060, T02-8913 0755, F02-9956 7707, and 4th floor, 197 St Georges Terr, Perth 6000, T08-9226 4524, F9281 3299, www.adventureworld.com.au Escorted group tours, locally escorted tours and pack-ages to Peru and all of Latin America. *Tucan*, see above under UK. *Tempo Holidays*, 1st floor, Beach St, Port Melbourne, Vic 3207, T03-9646 0277, F99646 6722, www.yallatours.com.au Specialists in group tours to Latin America, including Peru.

Australia

Birdwatching *Kolibri Expeditions*, www.netaccessperu.net/kolibri An agency that spe-cializes in overland birdwatching tours in Peru and throughout South America, contact Gunnar Engblom. See also the Manu, Tambopata, Cusco sections.

Climbing *Andes*, 37a St Andrews St, Castle Douglas, Kirkcudbrightshire, DG7 1EN, Scotland, T01556-503929, F504633, www.andes.org.uk For climbing trips in Peru and throughout Soth America. *High Places*, Globe Centre, Penistone Rd, Sheffield, S6 3AE, T0114-2757500, F2753870, www.highplaces.co.uk Trekking and mountaineering trips.

Mountain biking *Amazonas Explorer*, in Cusco, PO Box 722, T/F084-227137/653366, www.amazonas-explorer.com In UK, *Amazonas Explorer Riverside*, Black Tar, Llangwm, Haverfordwest, Pembs, Wales, SA62 4JD, T01437-891743. In USA, *River Travel Center* (Annie Leroy), P O Box 226, Point Arena, CA 95468, annien@rivers.com Experienced in

Special interest tours
Many tour operators handle more than one type of adventure tourism Look under all types of sport for those with more than one activity on offer

Essentials

leading trekking, kayaking, rafting and mountain biking expeditions throughout South America. Also in the UK through *Journey Latin America*, *KE Adventure Travel*, *Last Frontiers*, *South American Experience*, *Trips Worldwide* (see above for addresses) and *Discover Adventure*, 5 Netherhampton Cottage, Netherhampton, Salisbury, Wiltshire, SP2 8PX, UK, T01722-741123, www.discoveradventure.com *Andean Trails*, The Clockhouse, Bonnington Mill Business Centre, 72 Newhaven Rd, Edinburgh, EH6 5QG, T0131-467 7086, www.amdeamtrails.co.uk Also for trekking and other adventure tours. *Pedal Peru and Beyond*, Cecil Lockwood, PO Box 1921, Fraser, CO 80442, T1-800-708-8604, www.pedalperu.com Multi-sport adventures. *Trailbreak Adventures*, 241 Whitley Wood Rd, Reading, Berkshire, RG2 8LD, UK, T0118-986 0652, www.trailbreak.co.uk In Lima: *Peru Bike*, Urb Nueva Castilla, Calle A, D-7, Surco, Lima 33, T449 5234/872 4021, www.peru bike.com Experienced agency leading tours, specializing in the Andes, professional guiding. Also has a mountain bike school and a workshop. In Huaraz, Julio Olaza at *Chakinani Peru - Mountain Bike Adventures* (see page 342) hires out bikes and leads tours; see website www.chakinaniperu.com In Caraz and Cusco, *Pony's Expeditions* (proprietor Alberto Cafferata) run mountain bike tours and rent mountain bikes (in Caraz); also climbing, rafting and other options. Full details under each town. In Cusco, contactable by email, *Eco Trek Peru*, ecotrekperu@hotmail.com For mountain biking and trekking. Also organizing mountain bike trips is *Peru Mountain Bike*, run from the USA. They work in conjunction with Peruvian companies in Huaraz, Caraz, Cusco and Huancayo, www.perumountainbike.com

Rafting *Amazonas Explorer*, see Mountain biking, above, for this and for other agencies who have rafting trips. *Instinct*, Procuradores 50, Cusco, T/F084-233451; C25 No 129, Córpac, San Isidro, Lima T01-2911816; Plaza de Armas s/n, Olantaytambo, T084- 204045, www.instinct-travel.com Rafting, trekking, adventure and cultural tours. *The Rivermen Inc*, PO Box 220, Lansing, WV 25862, USA, T1-800-545 7238, raftinfo@rivermen.com

Essentials

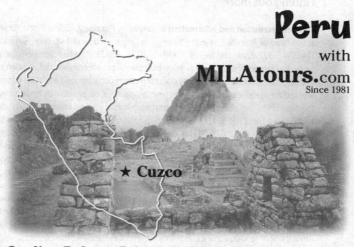

Essentials

Finding out more

Tourism promotion and information is handled by *PromPerú*, Edificio Mitinci, located at the head of Avenida Carnaval y Moreyra in Córpac, 13th and 14th floor, San Isidro, T01-224 3279/224 3118/224 3395, F224 3323, iperu@promperu.gob.pe, www.peru.org.pe They produce promotional material but offer no direct information service to individual tourists. The website does carry plenty of background and other information and they produce a monthly travel news magazine, *Kilca*, available by email: contact the press office, perudirect@Promperu.gob.pe *PromPerú* runs an information and assistance service, *i perú*, T01-574 8000 (24 hours). Its main office in Lima is at Jorge Basadre 610, San Isidro, T421 1227/1627, F421 1583, iperulima@promperu.gob.pe Hours are Monday-Friday 0900-1830 and there is a 24-hour office at Jorge Chávez airport. There are also offices in Arequipa, Ayacucho, Cusco, Iquitos, Puno and Trujillo, addresses of which are given in the text. There are also offices in most towns, either run by the municipality, or independently, which provide tourist information. The number of places with their own website is growing; these are given in the relevant part of the text. *Indecopi* is the government-run consumer protection and tourist complaint bureau. In Lima T224 7888, rest of Peru 0800-42579 (not from payphones), tour@indecopi.gob.pe In overall charge of tourism is the Ministerio de Comercio Exterior y Turismo, Calle Uno 050, Urb Córpac, San Isidro, Lima, T224 3347, www.mincetur.gob.pe (for useful links go to Turismo, then Otros Links).

Outside Peru, tourist information can be obtained from Peruvian Embassies and Consulates. An excellent source of information is *South American Explorers* in Lima (see page 101) and Cusco (see page 156).

Websites
For newspapers, radio and TV websites, see Keeping in touch, page 67 below

Destinations
www.planet.com.pe/aqpweb For Arequipa (Spanish).
www.cuscoweekly.com and www.cbc.org.pe For Cusco: the former in English (website of a recommended local English-language newspaper); the latter, in Spanish, belongs to the Centro Bartolomé de Las Casas, go to Novedades for tourist material.
www.andeanexplorer.com and www.huaylas.com For Huaraz and the Callejón de Huaylas, both available in English (latter has lots of practical information, maps, etc.).
www.machupicchu.com For Machu Picchu.
www.machupicchu.org More than just Machu Picchu, a library of all things related to the Inca region and Peru, very comprehensive.
www.yachay.com.pe/especiales/nasca, www.magicperu.com/MariaReiche Nasca lines (in Spanish).
www.perunorte.com Northern Peru (departments of La Libertad, Cajamarca and Lambayeque), in Spanish and English.
www.enjoyperu.com

Adventure travel

www.andeantravelweb.com/peru Andean adventure travel, with advice, links and more (English and Spanish).

argos.pucp.edu.pe/~airepuro Asociación de Deportes de Montaña, trekking, ice and rock climbing, mountain biking.

www.andeanexplorer.com/apotum Asociación Peruana de Operadores de Turismo de Montaña, a group of tourist operators specializing in mountain adventure.

www.geocities.com/TheTropics/Shores/8717 El Excursionismo en el Perú, details of treks in Spanish.

www.geocities.com/TheTropics/shores/8719 Perú, Ventana a la Aventura, part of the same site, dated 1997.

www.geocities.com/Yosemite/7363 Montañistas 4.0, a climbing association dedicated to going over 4,000 m.

www.geocities.com/Yosemite/4685 Nevado Rajuntay 1995, about a climb, in Spanish and English

Tourist and other information

www.conam.gob.pe The National Environmental Commission (Spanish).

www.gci275.com/peru Peruvian Graffiti, a site with politics, economics, culture and recent history

www.magicperu.com (English   and   Spanish)   and   **www.geocities.com/ perutraveller/** (English) both have information for tourists.

 www.oanda.com Currency converter and for all your financial needs.

www.peru.com/turismo Peru.com's travel page (Spanish and English).

www.perucultural.org.pe An excellent site for information on cultural activities, museums and Peruvian pre-Columbian textiles (Spanish).

www.perurail.com The website of Peru Rail (trains in the Cusco/Puno area).

www.rree.gob.pe Ministry of Foreign Relations site, which contains addresses of all Peruvian embassies and consulates.

www.SAexplorers.org South American Explorers webpage, full of useful information and advice. Recommended.

www.terra.com.pe Go to Turismo for tourist information (in Spanish).

www.traficoperu.com On-line travel agent with lots of useful information (Spanish and English).

www.yachay.com.pe Red Científica Peruana, click on Turismo to get to travel page.

Portals **www.adonde.com** and **www.perulinks.com/** The latter is in Spanish and English and is easier to use.

Essentials

Essentials

Culture http://gibbons.best.vwh.net Andean culture and Quechua (English). **www.unitru.edu.pe** The site of the Universidad de Trujillo **www.arqueologia. com.ar/peru/index.html** *Arqueología del Perú*, a site with articles and other material.

Gastronomy **www.geocities.com/TheTropics/4100/** A virtual *cevichería*, with recipes for this famous fish dish, not just from Peru.

Language

The official language is **Spanish**. **Quechua**, the language of the Inca empire, has been given some official status and there is much pride in its use, but despite the fact that it is spoken by millions of people in the Sierra who have little or no knowledge of Spanish, it is not used in schools. Another important indigenous language is **Aymara**, used in the area around Lake Titicaca. The jungle is home to a plethora of languages but Spanish is spoken in all but the remotest areas. **English** is not spoken widely, except by those employed in the tourism industry (eg; hotel, tour agency and airline staff). See page 616 for some basic Spanish for travellers.

Language courses are listed in the Essentials of each city and town. *AmeriSpan*, www.amerispan.com organizes programmes throughout Latin America from its North American and Guatemalan bases. *LanguagesAbroad.com*, 317 Adelaide St West, Suite 900, Toronto, Ontario, Canada, M5V 1P9, T416-925 2112, toll free 1-800-219 9924, F416-925 5990, www.languagesabroad.com offers Spanish and Portuguese programmes in every South American country except Colombia and Paraguay. They also have language immersion courses throughout the world. Similarly, *Cactus*, 9 Foundry St, Brighton BN1 4AT, T01273-687697, www.cactuslanguage.com For a list of Spanish schools, see www.planeta.com/ ecotravel/schools/schoolist.html Spanish Abroad, 5112N, 40th St, suite 103, Phoenix, A285018, www.spanishabroad.com

Disabled travellers

As with most underdeveloped countries, facilities for the disabled traveller are sadly lacking. Wheelchair ramps are a rare luxury and getting a wheelchair into a bathroom or toilet is well nigh impossible, except for some of the more upmarket hotels. The entrance to many cheap hotels is up a narrow flight of stairs. Pavements are often in a poor state of repair (even fully able people need to look out for uncovered manholes and other unexpected traps). Visually and hearing-impaired travellers are similarly poorly catered for as a rule, but experienced guides can often provide tours with individual attention. Disabled Peruvians obviously have to cope with these problems and mainly rely on the help of others to get on and off public transport and generally move around.

The Ministerio de la Mujer y Desarrollo Social (Ministry for Women and Social Development) incorporates a Consejo Nacional de Integración de la Persona con Discapacidad, CONADIS (National Council for the Integration of Disabled People, www.conadisperu.gob.pe – in Spanish). *CONADIS*, together with *PromPerú*, private business, *SATH* (see next paragraph) and *Kéroul* of Québec, has been involved in a project called *Peru: Towards an Accessible Tourism* and the *First Report on Accessibility in Peru for Tourists with Disabilities* was published in 2001. The report identifies many challenges in a number of major tourist sites. For instance, archaeological sites such as Machu Picchu and Chan Chán, being World Heritage Sites, may not be altered for accessibility. Specially trained personnel, however, can provide assistance to those with disabilities in these cases. The project can be accessed through the PromPerú site (see Finding out more).

Some travel companies are beginning to specialize in exciting holidays, tailor-made for individuals depending on their level of disability. For those with access to the internet, a *Global Access Disabled Travel Network Site* is www.geocities.com/Paris/1502 It is dedicated to providing information for 'disabled adventurers' and includes a number of reviews and tips from members of the public. Another informative site, with lots of advice on how to travel with specific disabilities, plus listings and links belongs to the *Society for Accessible Travel and Hospitality*, www.sath.org You might want to read *Nothing Ventured*, edited by Alison Walsh (Harper Collins), which gives personal accounts of worldwide journeys by disabled travellers, plus advice and listings. One company in Cusco which offers tours for disabled people is *Apumayo*, Calle Garcilaso 265, interior 3, T/F51-84-246018 (in Lima T/F444 2320), www.cuscoperu.com/apumayo

Gay and lesbian travellers

Movemiento Homosexual de Lima (MHOL), C Mariscal Miller 828, Jesús María, T433 5519/433 6375 (English from 1630 on), mhol@terra.com.pe Great contact about the gay community in Lima. On-line resources for gay travellers in Peru are http://gaylimape.tripod.com (a good site, in English, with lots of links and information) www.deambiente.com and www.gayperu.com/gp.htm (both in Spanish). In the Lima section we include the names of gay-friendly establishments. There are also gay-friendly places in Cusco, but the scene is not very active there (perhaps the best place to enquire is the *Café Macondo*). This does not imply, however, that there is hostility towards gay and lesbian travellers. As a major tourist centre which welcomes a huge variety of visitors, Cusco is probably more open than anywhere in Peru. Helpful general websites include *www.bluway.com*, *www.damron.com*, *www.gayscape.com*, *www.outandabout.com*

Student travellers

If you are in full-time education you will be entitled to an *International Student Identity Card*, which is distributed by student travel offices and travel agencies in 77 countries. The ISIC gives you special prices on all forms of transport (air, sea, rail etc), and access to a variety of other concessions and services. If you need to find the location of your nearest ISIC office contact: *The ISIC Association,* Herengracht 479, 1017 BS Amsterdam, Holland, T+31-20-421 2800, F+31-20-421 2810, www.istc.org

Students can obtain very few reductions in Peru with an international student's card, except in and around Cusco. To be any use in Peru, it must bear the owner's photograph. An ISIC card can be obtained in Lima from *Intej*, Av San Martín 240, Barranco, T477 2864, F477 4105, www.intej.org They can also extend student cards. In Cusco student cards can be obtained from Portal Comercio 141, p 2, T621351.

Travelling with children

People contemplating overland travel in South America with children should remember that a lot of time can be spent waiting for buses, trains, and especially for aeroplanes. You should take reading material with you as it is expensive and difficult to find. The scope for travelling by train in Peru is limited to Cusco–Machu Picchu, Cusco–Puno and Huancayo–Huancavelica. The Peru Rail services in the Cusco region are comfortable, with tables between seats, so that games can be played. Elsewhere, you must be prepared for bus or more cramped colectivo travel.

Food Food can be a problem if the children are not adaptable. It is easier to take food with you on longer trips than to rely on meal stops where the food may not be to taste. Avocados are safe, easy to eat and nutritious; they can be fed to babies as young as six months and most older children like them. A small immersion heater and jug for making hot drinks is invaluable, but remember that electric current varies. Try and get a dual-voltage one (110V and 220V). In restaurants, you can normally buy children's helpings, or divide one full-size helping between two children.

Fares On all long-distance buses you pay for each seat, and there are no half-fares if the children occupy a seat each. For shorter trips it is cheaper, if less comfortable, to seat small children on your knee. In city and local excursion buses, small children generally do not pay a fare, but are not entitled to a seat when paying customers are standing. On sightseeing tours you should *always* bargain for a family rate – often children can go free.

All civil airlines charge half price for children under 12. Note that a child travelling free on a long excursion is not always covered by the operator's travel insurance; it is advisable to pay a small premium to arrange cover.

Hotels In all hotels, try to negotiate family rates. If charges are per person, always insist that two children will occupy one bed only, therefore counting as one tariff. If rates are per bed, the same applies. In either case you can almost always get a reduced rate at cheaper hotels. Occasionally when travelling with a child you may be refused a room in a hotel that is 'unsuitable'. On river boat trips, unless you have very large hammocks, it may be more comfortable and cost effective to hire a two berth cabin for two adults and a child.

Travel with children can bring you into closer contact with local families and, generally, presents no special problems – in fact the path is often smoother for family groups. Officials tend to be more amenable where children are concerned and they are pleased if your child knows a little Spanish. Moreover, even thieves and pickpockets seem to have some of the traditional respect for families, and may leave you alone because of it! *South American Explorers* in Lima (page 101) and Cusco (page 156) can provide lots of useful information on travelling with children in Peru.

Women travellers

Generally women travellers should find visiting Peru an enjoyable experience. However, machismo is alive and well here and you should be prepared for this and try not to over-react. When you set out, err on the side of caution until your instincts have adjusted to the customs of a new culture.

It is easier for men to take the friendliness of locals at face value; women may be subject to much unwanted attention. To help minimize this, do not wear suggestive clothing and do not flirt. By wearing a wedding ring, carrying a photograph of your 'husband' and 'children', and saying that your 'husband' is close at hand, you may dissuade an aspiring suitor. If politeness fails, do not feel bad about showing offence and departing. When accepting a social invitation, make sure that someone knows the address and the time you left. Ask if you can bring a friend (even if you do not intend to do so).

If, as a single woman, you can befriend a local woman, you will learn much more about the country you are visiting as well as finding out how best to deal with the barrage of suggestive comments, whistles and hisses that will invariably come your way. Travelling with another *gringa* may not exempt you from this attention, but at least should give you moral support.

Unless actively avoiding foreigners like yourself, don't go too far from the beaten track. There is a very definite 'gringo trail' which you can join, or follow, if seeking company. This can be helpful when looking for safe accommodation, especially if arriving after dark (which is best avoided). Remember that for a single woman a taxi at night can be as dangerous as wandering around on her own. A good rule is always to act with confidence, as though you know where you are going, even if you do not. Someone who looks lost is more likely to attract unwanted attention.

Working in Peru

There are many opportunities for volunteer work in Peru (South American Explorers have an extensive database). See also the Lima section. In Cusco, *Los Niños* (at the hotel of the same name) and *Hope Foundation* (at *Marani* hotel – addresses of both are given under Cusco, Sleeping page 166) accept volunteers. For information outside Peru on voluntary work and working abroad, try *www.workingabroad.com*, 2nd floor Office Suite, 59 Lansdowne Rd, Hove, East Sussex, BN3 1FL, T01273-711406; *www.i-to-i.com*, 1 Cottage Rd, Headingley, Leeds, LS6 4DD, T0870-333 2332; *www.questoverseas.org*; *www.raleighinternational.org*; *www.projecttrust.org.uk*; *www.gapyear.com*; *www.gapyearjobs.co.uk*; *www.vacationwork.co.uk* Also contact *South American Explorers*, see above. The website *www.amerispan.com*, which is principally concerned with language learning and teaching, also has a comprehensive list of volunteer opportunities. Another site worth trying if you are looking for paid work is the the *International Career and Employment Center,* www.internationaljobs.org If you are seeking more than casual work, then there will be income tax implications which should be researched at a Peruvian consulate before departure.

Before you travel

Getting in

Visas   No visa is necessary for countries of Western Europe, Asia, North or South America or citizens of Australia, New Zealand or South Africa. Travellers from Fiji and India do need Visas. Tourist cards are obtained on flights arriving in Peru or at border crossings. The tourist card allows you up to a maximum of 90 days in Peru. The form is in duplicate and you give up the original on arrival and the copy on departure. **NB** This means you need to keep the copy as you will need to give it to the officials when you leave. A new tourist card is issued on re-entry to Peru but extensions are obtained with your current tourist card so you just take it and your passport to immigration when asking for extensions. If your tourist card is lost or stolen, apply to get a new one at *Inmigraciones*, Avenida España 700 y Avenida Huaraz, Breña, Lima, between 0900 to 1330, Monday to Friday. It shouldn't cost anything to replace your tourist card if you do it in Lima.

Tourist visas for citizens of countries not listed above cost £9.60 (approximately US$14), for which you require a valid passport, a departure ticket from Peru (or a letter of guarantee from a travel agency), two colour passport photos, one application form and proof of economic solvency.

All foreigners should be able to produce on demand some recognizable means of identification, preferably a passport. You must present your passport when reserving tickets for internal, as well as, international travel. An alternative is to photocopy the important pages of your passport – including the immigration stamp, and have it legalized by a 'Notario público', which costs US$1.50. This way you can avoid showing your passport.

An onward ticket is not usually asked for at the land frontiers at Tacna, Aguas Verdes, La Tina, Yunguyo or Desaguadero. Travellers arriving by air are not asked for an onward flight ticket at Lima airport, but it is quite possible that you will not be allowed to board a plane in your home country without showing an onward ticket.

Remember that it is your responsibility to ensure that your passport is stamped in and out when you cross frontiers. The absence of entry and exit stamps can cause serious difficulties: seek out the proper migration offices if the stamping process is not carried out as you cross.

You should always carry your passport in a safe place about your person, or if not leaving the city or town you're in, deposit it in the hotel safe. If staying in Peru for several weeks, it is worth while registering at your Consulate. Then, if your passport is stolen, the process of replacing it is simplified and speeded up.

Renewals and extensions The extension process in Lima Immigration is as follows: go to the third floor and enter the long narrow hall with many "teller" windows. Go to window number 5 and present your passport and tourist card. The official will give you a receipt for US$20 (the cost of a one-month extension) which you will pay at the Banco de la Nación on the same floor. Then go back to the teller room and buy form F007 for S/.22 (US$6.45 September 2002 price) from window 12. Fill out the form and return to window 5. Give the official the paid receipt, the filled-out form, your passport and tourist card. You have now finished your part of the process. Next, you will wait 10-15 minutes for your passport to be stamped and signed. You have just completed a not-so-painful Peruvian bureaucratic process. **NB** Three extensions like this are permitted, although it's unlikely that you will be allowed to buy more than one month at a time. Peruvian law states that a tourist can remain in the country for a maximum of six months, after which time you must leave. Crossing the border out of Peru and returning immediately is acceptable. You will then receive another 90 days and the process begins all over again.

To summarise briefly: you are given 90 days upon entering the country. You can buy 90 *more* for US$20 each (not at the same time) for a total of six months (180 days). Once your six months is completed, you must leave Peru (no exceptions). This simply means crossing into a bordering country for the day (depending on where, you can come back immediately) and returning with a fresh 90 days stamped in your passport.

Essentials

If you let your tourist visa expire you can be subject to a fine of US$20 per day, but this is up to the discretion of the immigration official so it's recommended that you are super-friendly. You can extend your visa in Lima, Cusco, Puno, Puerto Maldonado, and Iquitos, but in the provinces it can take more time than in Lima.

Business visas Visitors who are going to receive money from Peruvian sources must have a business visa: requirements are a valid passport, two colour passport photos, return ticket and a letter from an employer or Chamber of Commerce stating the nature of business, length of stay and guarantee that any Peruvian taxes will be paid. The visa costs £31 (or equivalent). On arrival business visitors must register with the Dirección General de Contribuciones for tax purposes.

Student visas To obtain a one year student visa you must have: proof of adequate funds, affiliation to a Peruvian body, a letter of recommendation from your own and a Peruvian Consul, a letter of moral and economic guarantee from a Peruvian citizen and four photographs (frontal and profile). You must also have a health check certificate which takes four weeks to get and costs US$10. Also, to obtain a student visa, if applying within Peru, you have to leave the country and collect it in La Paz, Arica or Guayaquil from Peruvian immigration (it costs US$20).

Customs **Duty-free allowance** When travelling into Peru you can bring 20 pack of cigarettes (400 cigarettes), 50 cigars or 500 g of tobacco, three litres of alcohol and new articles for personal use of gifts valued at up to US$300. There are certain items that are blacked out and therefore cannot be brought in duty-free: these include computers (but laptops are OK). The value added tax for items that are not considered duty-free but are still intended for personal use is generally 20%. Personal items necessary for adventure sports such as climbing, kayaking and fishing are duty-free. Most of the customs rules aren't a worry for the average traveller, but anything that looks like it's being brought in for resale could give you trouble. This means don't bring your tripod and 5 lenses in boxes or packages.

Export ban It is illegal to take items of archaeological interest out of Peru. This means that any pre-Columbian pottery or Inca artefacts cannot leave Peru, including various gold work and 'worry dolls' from Nasca. If you are purchasing extremely good replicas make sure the pieces have the artist's name on them or that they have a tag which shows that they are not originals. It is very important to realize that no matter how simple it seems, it is not worth your time to try and take anything illegal out of the country – this includes drugs. The security personnel and customs officials are much smarter than you and are experts at their job. It's best to understand that this is a fool-hardy idea and save yourself the wasted time, money and energy of 10 years in jail.

Before you travel make sure the medical insurance you take out is adequate. Have a check up with your doctor, if necessary and arrange your immunizations well in advance. Try ringing a specialist travel clinic if your own doctor is unfamiliar with health in Latin America. You should be protected by immunisation against typhoid, polio, tetanus and hepatitis A. A yellow fever vaccination certificate is required if you are coming from infected areas of the world. If you are going to the Peruvian jungle, especially if you will be living rough, you should be vaccinated against yellow fever. Moreover, tours to Manu and Tambopata booked outside Peru state that a yellow fever vaccination certificate is required to be allowed to enter either region. Check malaria prophylaxis for all lowland rural areas to be visited and particularly if you will be on the borders of Bolivia, Brazil, Colombia or Ecuador. Vaccination against cholera is not necessary.

Vaccinations
For a full and detailed description of necessary vaccinations and all matters relating to health, see Health section on page 88

What to take

Everybody has their own preferences, but listed here are the most often mentioned. These include an inflatable **travel pillow** for neck support and **strong shoes** (remember that footwear over 9½ English size, or 42 European size, is difficult to find in Peru). Your should also take **waterproof clothing** and **waterproof treatment** for leather footwear, and **wax earplugs**, which are vital for long bus trips or noisy hotels. Also important are **rubber-thong, Japanese-type sandals**, which can be worn in showers to avoid athlete's foot, and a **sheet sleeping-bag** to avoid sleeping on filthy sheets in cheap hotels.

A list of useful medicines and health-related items is given in the Health section, page 88)

Other useful things to take with you include: a **clothes line**, a **nailbrush**, a **vacuum flask**, a **water bottle** and a universal bath- and basin-**plug** of the flanged type that will fit any waste-pipe (or improvise one from a sheet of thick rubber); **string**, **electrical insulating tape**, a **Swiss Army knife**, an **alarm clock** for early morning departures, **candles** (for power cuts, or rural or jungle areas with limited or no electricity), a **torch/flashlight**, a **pocket mirror**, **pocket calculator**, an **adaptor**, a **padlock** for the doors of the cheapest hotels (or for tent zip if camping), a small **first aid kit**, a **sun hat**, **contraceptives** and a small **sewing kit**. The most security-conscious may wish to include a length of chain and padlock for securing luggage to bed or bus/train seat.

Useful medicines include **lip salve** with sun protection, and pre-moistened **wipes**. Always carry **toilet paper**, which is especially important on long bus trips. **Contact lens solution** is readily available in pharmacies and *boticas* in all major towns.

Money

The **Nuevo Sol** (New Sol, S/.) is the official currency of Peru. It is divided in 100 *céntimos* (cents) with coins valued at S/.5, S/.2, S/.1 and 50, 20, 10 and 5 *céntimo* pieces although the latter is being phased out as it is virtually worthless. Notes in circulation are S/.200, S/.100, S/.50, S/.20 and S/.10.

Currency

Try to break down notes whenever you can as there is a country-wide shortage of change (or so it seems) and it will make life simpler if you get change whenever you can. It is difficult to get change in shops and museums and sometimes impossible from street vendors or cab drivers. In November 2002, the exchange rate was US$1 = S/. 3.58. Prices of airline tickets, tour agency services, non-backpacker hotels and hostels, among others, are almost always quoted in dollars. You can pay in soles or dollars but it is generally easiest to pay dollars when the price is in dollars and in soles when the price is in soles. This will save you from losing on exchange rates. In major tourist centres such as Lima, Cusco and Arequipa dollars are frequently accepted.

NB Almost no one, certainly not banks, will accept dollar bills that are ripped, taped, stapled or torn (you may be able to change them on the 8th block of Jr de la Unión in the centre of Lima, at the Plaza San Martín – the rates will be poor). Do not

▶▶ Money matters

Low-value US dollar bills should be carried for changing into soles if arriving in the country when banks or casas de cambio are closed. They are also useful for shopping. In larger establishments in cities which receive many tourists, dollars are accepted instead of soles. If you are travelling on the cheap it is essential to keep in funds; watch weekends and public holidays carefully and never run out of local currency. Take plenty of local currency, in small denominations, when making trips in the provinces. There is a nationwide shortage of small change.

It's best to stick to well-known and well-accepted brands of travellers' cheques such as American Express, Visa and MasterCard. Thomas Cook cheques are reasonably well-known as well (but note that Thomas Cook has no representation in Peru). This will avoid suspicious looks or flat out "no's" from storeowners who believe you may have forged your travellers' cheques.

accept torn dollars from anyone; simply tell them you would like another bill. As well, ask your bank at home to give you only nice, crisp, clean dollars and keep your dollars neat in your money belt or wallet so they don't accidentally tear.

Warning Forgeries of dollars and soles are not uncommon. Always check the sol notes you have received, even at the bank. Money changers, especially at borders, mix fake notes with genuine bills when giving wads of soles for other currencies. Hold the bills up to the light to check the watermark. The line down the side of the bill in which the amount of the money is written should appear green, blue and pink at different angles; fake bills are only pink and have no hologram properties. There should be tiny pieces of thread in the paper (not glued on). Check to see that the faces are clear. Also, the paper should not feel smooth like a photocopy but rougher and fibrous. Try not to accept brand new notes, especially if changing on the street, slightly used notes are less likely to be forgeries. There are posters in many restaurants, stores and banks explaining exactly what to look for in forged sol notes. In parts of the country, especially Piura and the north, forged one-sol coins are in circulation. The fakes are slightly off-colour, the surface copper can be scratched off and they tend to bear a recent date.

Credit cards *Visa* (by far the most widely accepted card in Peru), *MasterCard*, *American Express* and *Diners Club* are all valid. There is often an 8-12% commission for all credit card charges. Often, it is cheaper to use your credit card to get money (dollars or soles) out of an ATM rather than to pay for your purchases. Of course, this depends on your interest rate for cash advances on your credit cards – ask your bank or card provider about this. Another option is to put extra money on your credit cards and use them as a bank card. Most banks are affiliated with Visa /Plus system; those that you will find in almost every town and city are *BCP* (formerly *Banco de Crédito*), *BBVA Continental*, *Banco Weise Sudameris* and *Banco Santander Central Hispano* (BSCH). *Telebanco 24 Horas* ATMs (eg at *BCP*) accept Visa/Plus and American Express cards. *Interbank* ATMs accept Visa, Plus, Mastercard, Maestro, Cirrus and American Express. There are also *Red Unicard* ATMs which accept Visa, Plus, Mastercard, Maestro and Cirrus. Note that not every branch of each bank offers the same ATM services (even branches within the same city).In comparison with widespread ATM use, businesses displaying credit card symbols may not accept foreign cards. Credit cards are not commonly accepted in smaller towns so go prepared with cash. Make sure you carry the phone numbers that you need in order to report your card lost or stolen. In addition, some travellers have reported problems with their credit cards being 'frozen' by their bank as soon as a charge from a foreign country occurs. To avoid this problem, notify your bank that you will be making charges in Peru (and other countries).

Credit card assistance American Express, Pardo y Aliaga 698, San Isidro, Lima, T222 2525, open Monday-Friday 0900-1700. Diners Club, Canaval y Moreyra 535, San Isidro, T01-221 2050. Mastercard, Porta 111, p 6, Miraflores, T01-242 2700/311 6000, or 0800-307 7309. Visa Travel Assistance, T108 and ask the operator for a collect call (*por cobrar*) to T410-581 9994/3836, locally phone T01-800-428 1888.

There are no restrictions on foreign exchange. Banks are the most discreet places to change travellers' cheques into soles. Some charge commission from 1% to 3%, some don't, and practice seems to vary from branch to branch, month to month. The services of the *BCP* have been repeatedly recommended. Changing dollars at a bank always gives a lower rate than with *cambistas* (street changers) or *casas de cambio* (exchange houses). Always count your money in the presence of the cashier.

US dollars are the only currency which should be brought from abroad (take some small bills). Other currencies carry high commission fees. Euros can only be exchanged at the money exchange booths at Lima airport (July 2002). For changing into or out of small amounts of dollars cash, the street changers give the best rates, avoiding paperwork and queuing, but you should take care: check your soles before handing over your dollars, check their calculators, etc, and don't change money in crowded areas. If using their services think about taking a taxi after changing, to avoid being followed. Many street changers congregate near an office where the exchange 'wholesaler' operates; these will probably be offering better rates than elsewhere on the street.

Soles can be exchanged into dollars at the banks and exchange houses at Lima airport, and you can change soles for dollars with street changers and at any border. Dollars can also be bought at the various frontiers.

American Express will sell travellers' cheques to cardholders only, but will not exchange cheques into cash. Amex will hold mail for cardholders at the Lima branch only. They are also very efficient in replacing stolen cheques, though a police report is needed. Most of the main banks accept American Express travellers' cheques and *BCP* and *BSCH* accept Visa travellers' cheques. *Citibank* in Lima and some *BSCH* branches handle Citicorp cheques. Travellers have reported great difficulty in cashing travellers' cheques in the jungle area, even Iquitos, and other remote areas. Always sign travellers' cheques in blue or black ink or ballpen.

To transfer money from one bank to another you must first find out which Peruvian bank works with your bank at home. If in fact one does, you will have to go that bank in Lima (or wherever you are) and ask them what the process is to make a transfer. Depending on the bank, transfers can be completed immediately or will take up to five working days. Another option is to use *Western Union*, which has widespread representation throughout the country. *Moneygram* also has offices throughout the capital and the provinces. It exchanges most world currencies and travellers' cheques.

Living costs in the provinces are from 20-50% below those in Lima, although Cusco is a little more expensive than other, less touristy provincial cities. For a lot of low-income Peruvians, many items are simply beyond their reach.

In 2002, the approximate budget for travelling was US$25-35 per person per day for living comfortably, including transport, or US$12-US$15 a day for low-budget travel. Your budget will be higher the longer you stay in Lima and depending on how many flights you take between destinations. Accommodation rates range from US$3-4 per person for the most basic *alojamiento* to over US$150 for luxurious hotels in Lima and Cusco. For meal prices, see Food and drink, page 70.

Essentials

Exchange

Money transfer

Cost of living

Cost of travelling

Getting there

Air

From UK & Ireland — There are no direct flights to **Lima** from London. Cheap options are available with *Avianca* via Bogotá (also the simplest connection from Paris), *Iberia* via Madrid and *KLM* via Amsterdam. Alternatively, you can fly standby to Miami, then fly the airlines shown below. A little more expensive, but as convenient, are connections via Atlanta with *Delta*, or Houston with *Continental*. Other options are *British Airways* to Caracas then change to *Aeropostal*, or *Virgin Atlantic* to New York, then change to *LanChile*. From Dublin, either fly to Paris and then on to Bogotá for connections, or use the above options via other European capitals or US hubs.

From North America — Miami is the main gateway to Peru, together with Atlanta, Dallas, Houston, Los Angeles and New York. Direct flights are available from Miami with *Aero Continente*, *American*, *Lan Perú/Lan Chile* and *Copa* (via Panama City); through New York with *Continental*, which also flies from Houston and San Diego, and *Lan Perú/Lan Chile*; from Atlanta with *Delta*; from Dallas with *American*, which also flies from Orlando and Philadelphia; and from Los Angeles with *Lan Perú/Lan Chile* and *Aeromexico*. Daily connections can be made from almost all major North American cities. From Toronto and Vancouver, there are connections in Los Angeles and New York.

From Australia & New Zealand — There are no obvious connecting flights from either Australia or New Zealand to **Lima**. One option would be to go to Buenos Aires from Sydney or Auckland (flights twice a week with *Aerolíneas Argentinas*) and fly on from there with *Lan Chile*. Alternatively, fly to Los Angeles and travel down from there. The round-the-world ticket offered by *Qantas/British Airways/American Airlines* includes 12 free stops and goes via Miami. Here you can pick up the American flight to **Lima**.

From Europe & Israel — There are direct flights to **Lima** only from Amsterdam (*KLM* via Aruba) and Barcelona and Madrid (*Iberia*). From Frankfurt, Rome or Milan, Lisbon or other European cities, connections must be made in Madrid, Caracas, Brazilian or US gateways.

The alternatives from Tel Aviv to **Lima** are with *El Al* to New York, then *Lan Chile* on to **Lima**, or *El Al* to Madrid, then *Avianca* to **Lima** via Bogotá.

From S Africa — From Johannesburg, make connections in Buenos Aires or São Paulo.

From Latin America — There are regular flights, in many cases daily, to Peru from most South American countries: Bogotá, *Avianca/Aces*, *Aero Continente* and *Aeropostal*; Buenos Aires, *Aerolíneas Argentinas*, *Taca* and *Lan Chile* (via Santiago de Chile); Caracas, *Aeropostal*, *Aero Continente* and *Taca*; Guayaquil and Quito, *Tame*, *Taca*, *Aero Continente* and *Aeropostal*; La Paz, *Lloyd Aéreo Boliviano* (LAB, also to Cochabamba and Santa Cruz), *Taca* (also to Santa Cruz) and *Aero Continente*; *Varig* to Rio de Janeiro and São Paulo (also *Taca*); *Santiago de Chile*, *Lan Perú/Lan Chile*, *Lacsa/Taca* and *Aero Continente*. From Central America: Mexico City, *Taca* and *Aeromexico*; Panama, *Copa*; San José, *Taca/Lacsa*.

From Asia — From Hong Kong, Seoul and Singapore, connections have to be made in Los Angeles. Make connections in Los Angeles or Miami if flying from Tokyo. You can also connect in New York in all cases except Singapore.

Discount flight agents

*In the UK and Ireland: **STA Travel**, 86 Old Brompton Rd, London, SW7 3LH, T0207 361 6100 , www.statravel.co.uk They have other branches in London, as well as in Brighton, Bristol, Cambridge, Leeds, Manchester, Newcastle-upon-Tyne and Oxford and on many University campuses. Specialists in low-cost student/youth flights and tours, also good for student IDs and insurance. **Trailfinders**, 194 Kensington High Street, London, W8 7RG, T020-7938 3939, www.trailfinders.co.uk They also have other branches in London, as well as in Birmingham, Bristol, Cambridge, Glasgow, Manchester, Newcastle, Dublin and Belfast.*

*In North America: **Air Brokers International**, 323 Geary St, Suite 411, San Francisco, CA94102, T01-800-883 3273, www.airbrokers.com Consolidator and specialist on RTW and Circle Pacific tickets. **Council Travel**, there are retail outlets throughout the country but in New York you will find this company at 205 E 42nd St, New York, NY 10017, 254 Greene St, NY 10003 and 895 Amsterdam Av, NY 10025. Otherwise call T1-800-2COUNCIL, or check out www.counciltravel.com A student/budget agency with branches in many other US cities. **Discount Airfares Worldwide On-Line**, www.etn.nl/discount.htm A hub of consolidator and discount agent links. **STA Travel**, 5900 Wiltshire Blvd, Suite 2110, Los Angeles, CA 90036, 1-800-781-4040, www.sta-travel.com Also branches in New York, San Francisco, Boston, Miami,*

*Chicago, Seattle and Washington DC. **Travel CUTS**, 187 College St, Toronto, ON M5T 1P7, T1-800-954-2666, www.travelcuts.com Specialist in student discount fares, IDs and other travel services. Branches in other Canadian cities as well as California, USA. **Travelocity**, www.travelocity.com Online consolidator.*

*In Australia and New Zealand: **Flight Centre**, with offices throughout Australia and other countries. In Australia call T133 133 or log on to www.flightcentre.com.au*

***STA Travel**, T1300-360960, www.statravel.com.au; 702 Harris St, Ultimo, Sydney, and 256 Flinders St, Melbourne. In NZ: 10 High St, Auckland, T09-366 6673. Also in major towns and university campuses. **Travel.com.au**, 76 Clarence St, Sydney NSW Australia, T02 9249 5232, outside Sydney: T1300 130 482, www.travel.com.au*

***NB** Using the web for booking flights, hotels and other services directly is becoming an increasingly popular way of making holiday reservations. You can make some good deals this way. Be aware, though, that cutting out the travel agents is denying yourself the experience that they can give, not just in terms of the best flights to suit your itinerary, but also advice on documents, insurance and other matters before you set out, safety, routes, lodging and times of year to travel. A reputable agent will also be bonded to give you some protection if arrangements collapse while you are travelling.*

Essentials

Baggage allowance

There is always a weight limit for your baggage, but there is no standard baggage allowance to Peru. If you fly via the USA you are allowed two pieces of luggage up to 32 kg per case. The American airlines are usually a bit more expensive but if you are travelling with a 40kg bag of climbing gear, it may be worth looking into. On flights from Europe there is a weight allowance of 20 or 23 kg, although some carriers out of Europe use the two-piece system, but may not apply it in both directions. The two-piece system is gaining wider acceptance, but it is always best to check in advance. At busy times of the year it can be very difficult and expensive to bring items such as bikes and surf boards along. Many airlines will let you pay a penalty for overweight baggage – often this is US$5 per kilo – but this usually depends on how full the flight is. Check first before you assume you can bring extra luggage. The weight limit for internal flights is often 20 kg per person, or less, so keep this in mind if you plan to take any internal flights.

Essentials

▶▶ **Airline websites**

Aerolíneas Argentinas, www.aerolineas.com.ar	*El Al,* www.elal.co.il
Aeromexico, www.aeromexico.com	*Iberia,* www.iberia.com
Aeropostal, www.aeropostal.com	*KLM,* www.klm.com
Air France, www.airfrance.com	*LAB,* www.labairlines.com
American Airlines, www.aa.com	*Lacsa,* www.grupotaca.com
Avianca, www.avianca.com.co	*Lan Chile,* www.lanchile.com
British Airways, www.britishairways.com	*Lufthansa,* www.lufthansa.com
Continental, www.continental.com	*Qantas,* www.qantas.com
Copa, www.copaair.com	*Taca,* www.grupotaca.com
Delta, www.delta-air.com	*Tame,* www.tame.com.ec
	Varig, www.varig.com.br

**Prices &
discounts**
*If you foresee
returning home at a
busy time
(eg Christmas or
Easter), a booking is
advisable on any type
of open-return ticket*

Most airlines offer discounted fares on scheduled flights through agencies who specialize in this type of fare. For a list of these agencies see box on page 43. The very busy seasons are 7 December-15 January and 10 July-10 September. If you intend travelling during those times, book as far ahead as possible. Between February-May and September-November special offers may be available. Examples of fares on scheduled airlines are: from the UK a return with flexible dates will cost about US$775, but travelling over the Christmas/New Year period can see prices rise to over US$4,000. The picture is the same from the USA: a low season return costs as little as US$250-330 from Miami, but high season is US$537. From Atlanta low season fares are US$490, but high season US$1,215; from Los Angeles low season US$410, high season US$1,470. From Sydney, Australia, a low season return is US$940-1,110, whereas a Christmas/New Year return will cost US$3,470.

Other fares on scheduled services fall into three groups. A) **Excursion (return) fares** with restricted validity. Some carriers permit a change of dates on payment of a fee. B) **Yearly fares** These may be bought on a one-way or return basis. Some airlines require a specified return date, changeable upon payment of a fee. To leave the return completely open is possible for an extra fee. C) **Student (or under 26) fares** Do not assume that student tickets are the cheapest; though they are often very flexible, they are usually more expensive than A) or B) above. Some airlines are flexible on the age limit, others strict. One way and returns are available. For people intending to travel a linear route and return from a different point from that at which they entered, there are 'Open Jaws' fares, which are available on student, yearly, or excursion fares.

If you buy discounted air tickets *always* check the reservation with the airline concerned to make sure the flight still exists. Also remember the IATA airlines' schedules change in March and October each year, so if you're going to be away a long time it's best to leave return flight coupons open. In addition, check whether you are entitled to any refund or re-issued ticket if you lose, or have stolen, a discounted air ticket. Some airlines require the repurchase of a ticket before you can apply for a refund, which will not be given until after the validity of the original ticket has expired. The *Iberia* group and *Air France*, for example, operate this costly system. Travel insurance in some cases covers lost tickets.

Rail

The only rail entry to Peru, and an erratic one at that, is from Arica in Chile to Tacna (see page 323).

Road

There are bus services from neighbouring countries to Peru. If coming from Bolivia, there are direct buses to Puno, Cusco and Arequipa from La Paz (see page 252). From Chile there is direct service from Arica to Tacna and Arequipa, where you can change for Lima. If travelling south from Ecuador, there are frequent services from Quito and Guayaquil to Lima and the major cities on the north coast. There are also new services crossing from Ecuador to Peru which do not involve a change of bus at the border, eg Loja-Piura. On rare occasions, customs officials at international borders may ask for a forward ticket out of the country. This means you'll have to buy the cheapest bus ticket out of Peru before they let you in. Note that these tickets are not transferable or refundable.

International buses

Driving **Main paved entry points for vehicles** From **Bolivia**: at Desaguadero and Yunguyo on the southeastern side of Lake Titicaca (there is also an unpaved crossing on the north shore between Moho and Puerto Acosta). From **Chile**: between Arica and Tacna. From **Ecuador**: at Aguas Verdes between Huaquillas and Zarumilla, and between Macará and La Tina (other crossings, such as Balsas – although a bridge is under construction here – and Alamor/Lalamor do not have road crossings). From **Brazil**: the crossing from Assis Brasil to Iñapari is unpaved and is only passable with ease in the dry season.

Required documents To enter Peru by private vehicle, you must have an **international driving licence**. You also need the **registration document** in the name of the driver, or, in the case of a car registered in someone else's name, a notarized letter of authorization. If renting a car, your home driving licence will be accepted for up to 6 months. To drive in Peru you must be over 21 and to rent a car over 25.

There are two recognized documents for taking a vehicle into South America: a *carnet de passages* issued jointly by the *Fedération Internationale de l'Automobile* (FIA - Paris) and the *Alliance Internationale de Tourisme* (AIT-Geneva), and the *Libreta de Pasos por Aduana* issued by the *Federación Interamericana de Touring y Automóvil Clubs* (FITAC). Officially, Peru requires either the *carnet*, or the *libreta* and, for caravans and trailers, an inventory. The consulate in London says that a *libreta* is necessary, but if you cannot obtain one a written declaration that the car will leave Peru, authorized at a Peruvian consulate before leaving your home country, will do instead.

Motorists report that a 90-day **transit permit** for vehicles is available at land borders without a *carnet de passages*, contrary to what officials may say. *Formulario 015*, which can be requested at the border, entitles visitors to bring a vehicle into Peru duty free for three months, it is not extendable, but it is free (but drivers get charged anything betweenUS$20 and US$50). In view of this confusion, contact the *Peruvian automobile club* (Avenida César Vallejo 699, Casilla 2219, Lince, T221 2432) and get their advice. In general, motorists in South America seem to fare better with a *carnet de passages* than without it.

Boat

There are passenger berths on cargo ships from European and US ports to the west coast of South America. Many of these call at **Callao**, the sea port for Lima. In the main, passage is round trip only and this is a much more expensive form of transport than flying. If you have the time and want a bit of luxury, it is a great alternative. Useful contacts for advice and tickets: *Strand Voyages*, Charing Cross Shopping Concourse, The Strand, London WC2N 4HZ, T020-7836 6363, F020-7497 0078, www.strandtravel.co.uk *Strand Voyages* are booking agents for all routes. *Cargo Ship Voyages Ltd*, Hemley, Woodbridge, Suffolk IP12 4QF, T/F01473-736265. *The Cruise People*, 88 York St, London W1H 1QT, T020-7723 2450 (reservations 0800-526313), cruisepeople@ pipex.com In Europe, *SGV Reisezentrum Weggis*, Seestrasse 7, CH-6353, Weggis, Switzerland, T041-390 1133, u.steiner@reisezentrum-weggis.ch In the USA, *Freighter World Cruises*, 180 South Lake Av, Pasadena, CA 91101, T626-449 3106, www.freighterworld.com *Travltips Cruise and Freighter Travel Association*, PO Box 580188, Flushing, NY 11358, T800-8728584, www.travltips.com On the web *www.contship.de* or the *Internet Guide to Freighter Travel*, www.geocities.com/ freighterman.geo/mainmenu.html

You can also enter Peru by **river**, on the fast launches and slower passenger boats which go upstream on the Amazon from the Peru/Colombia/Brazil border to Iquitos. A final water-borne route is across Lake Titicaca: see page 255 for *Crillon Tours'* hydrofoils and *Transturin's* catamarans between Peru and Bolivia.

Touching down

Airport information

The **Jorge Chávez Airport** is located deep in the Lima district of Callao, 16 km from the centre of the city. Passengers arriving from international flights will find the *aduana* (customs) process to be relatively painless and efficient (a push-button, red light/ green light system operates for customs baggage checks). Items such as laptops, bicycles, cameras, hiking and climbing equipment etc are exempt from taxes and should be regarded as personal effects that will not be sold or left in Peru. All customs agents should be satisfied by this and allow you to pass. Once outside and past the gate separating arriving passengers from the general public, you're subject to the mob of taxi drivers all vying to offer you their services. Fares depend on where you pick up the taxi and your bargaining skills.

Taxis No taxis use meters, so make sure you fix the price before getting in and insist on being taken to the hotel of your choice, not the driver's. It's always best to have exact change in soles to avoid having to break a large bill along the way.

Remise taxis (*Mitsui* or *CMV*) have representatives at desks outside International Arrivals and National Arrivals, US$7.25 to San Miguel, US$11.75 to the city centre, US$14.50 to San Isidro and Miraflores, US$17.50 to Barranco. This is the safest option, but also the most expensive. There are many taxi drivers offering their services outside Arrivals with similar or higher prices (more at night). If you are feeling confident and not too jet-lagged, go to the car park exit and find a taxi outside the perimeter, by the roundabout. They charge US$3 to the city centre. The security guards may help you find a taxi. **NB** All vehicles can enter the airport for 10 minutes at no charge. After that, it's S/.3.50 every 30 minutes. Taxis that have been waiting for more than the allotted free time will try to make the passenger pay the toll upon leaving the airport. Always establish who will pay before getting in.

Buses There is a service called *Urbanito*, from the airport to the centre, Breña and San Miguel US$3, Pueblo Libre, San Isidro and Miraflores US$4.35 (a slow journey, calling at all hotels), T814 6932 (24 hours)/425 1202/424 3650, urbanito@terra.com.pe Local buses (US$0.35) and colectivos run between the airport perimeter and the city centre and suburbs. Their routes are given on the front window: 'Tacna' for the centre, 'Miraflores' for Miraflores. Outside the pedestrian exit are the bus, colectivo and taxi stops, but there is more choice for buses at the roundabout by the car entrance. At busy times (which is anytime other than very late at night or early morning) luggage may not be allowed on buses. **NB** Do not take the cheapest, stopping buses which go to the city centre along Avenida Faucett. They are frequently robbed. Pay a little more for a non-stopping bus.

Car rental All hire companies have offices at the airport. The larger international chains, *Avis*, *Budget*, *Dollar*, *Hertz*, are usually cheaper and have better-maintained vehicles than local firms. The airport in Lima is the best, most cost-effective place to arrange car hire. (For addresses in Lima, see page 140.)

Hotels in the immediate airport area are generally for short-stay couples and are not appealing, especially after a long-haul flight. The larger, more expensive hotels in Miraflores and San Isidro have their own buses at the airport, and charge for transfer. Several *hostales* and *pensiones* also provide transport to and from the airport. The tourist desk inside International Arrivals can help make hotel reservations. They often say that cheaper hotels are full or unsafe and, if you allow them to make a choice for you, it will probably be more expensive than you want (they may get commission). You will

Transport into Lima

Finding hotels

▶▶ **Touching down**

Tourist Protection Bureau (Indecopi)
24-hour hotline for travellers' complaints,
T/F01-224 7777/7888, or, outside Lima, toll
free on 0800-42579 (not from pay phones),
tour@indecopi.gob.pe This is run by the
Tourist Bureau of Complaints and will help
with complaints regarding customs,
airlines, travel agencies, accommodation,
restaurants, public authorities or if you
have lost, or had stolen, documents. There
is an office in every town as well as kiosks
and information stands in airports and
public buildings. They are very effective.

Tourist Police Jr Moore 268,
Magdalena at the 38th block of Av Brasil,
T460 1060/460 0844, open daily 24 hrs.
You should come here if you have had
property stolen. They are friendly, helpful
and speak English and some German.

**Police (PNP, Policía Nacional del
Perú)** T01-475 2995 in Lima. They have
stations in every town.

Ambulance T01-225 4040 in Lima.

**Emergency medical attention
(SAMU)** T117.

Fire service T116.

IDD code 51.

Directory enquiries National T108;
International T108.

Official time 5 hrs behind GMT.

Official languages Spanish
and Quechua.

Business hours Shops; 0900 or
1000-1230 and 1500 or 1600-2000, or
1000-1900. In the main cities,
supermarkets do not close for lunch and
Lima has some that are open 24 hrs. Some
are closed on Saturday and most are
closed on Sunday. **Banks** Banks in Lima
are open 0945 to 1700. Banks outside Lima
generally close from 1200 to 1500, but
lunch hour closing varies. Many banks in
Lima and Cusco have Saturday morning
hours from 0945 to 1200. **Offices**: Many
have continuous hours 0900-1700, but
others work 0830-1230, 1500-1800 all year
round. Most close on Saturday.
Government Offices: Monday-Friday
0830-1130, January to March. The rest of
year Monday-Friday 0900-1230,
1500-1700, but this changes frequently.

General sales tax 18%, automatically
added to the bill.

Voltage 220 volts AC, 60 cycles
throughout the country, except Arequipa
(50 cycles). Most 4- and 5-star hotels have
110 volts AC. Plugs are American flat-pin.

Weights and measures The
metric system of weights and measures
is compulsory.

be bombarded as you leave the International gate by people touting for hotel business, representatives of travel agencies and taxi drivers. Be firm and don't let yourself be bullied. Closest to the **airport**, 5 minutes by taxi, is **B** *Hostal Residencial Víctor*, Manuel Mattos 325, Urb San Amadeo de Garagay, Lima 31, T567 5107/5083, F568 9570, hostalvictor@terra.com.pe Between the airport and the centre is **C** *Hostal Mami Panchita*, Av Federico Callese 198, T263 7203, F263 0749, raymi_travels@ perusat.net.pe Full details of both are given in the Lima Sleeping section, page 117.

Airport facilities There are ATMs between the national and international foyers accepting American Express, Visa, Mastercard and the Plus, Cirrus and Maestro systems. There are *Casas de Cambio* (money changing desks) in the national foyer and in the international foyer. They are open 24 hours and change all types of travellers' cheque (they claim) and most major currencies, including Euros. There are also exchange facilities for cash in the international arrivals hall. *Banco Santander Central Hispano* stands, in the national and international foyers only collect the international or domestic airport tax that must be paid in order to get through the gate. **NB** The operators of the tax collection desks change frequently.

Although public telephones are everywhere in and around the airport, there is also a *Telefónica* office in the international foyer opposite desk 20, open 0700-2300 seven

Useful addresses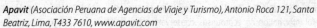

Apavit *(Asociación Peruana de Agencias de Viaje y Turismo), Antonio Roca 121, Santa
Beatriz, Lima, T433 7610, www.apavit.com*
Apotur *(Asociación Peruana de Operadores de Turismo), Bajada Balta 169, p 2,
Miraflores, Lima 18, T445 0382, F446 0422, apotur@amauta.rcp.net.pe*
Aptae *(Asociación Peruana de Operadores de Turismo de Aventura y Ecoturismo), San
Fernando 287, Miraflores, Lima 18, T241 4765, F241 4766, www.aptaeperu.com.pe*
Agotur *(Asociación de Guías Oficiales de Turismo), Baltazar La Torre 165, depto 101-D,
San Isidro, Lima, T422 8937, F365 5615, agoturlima@yahoo.com*

Essentials

days a week. Fax service is available and internet facilities at US$3 per hour (must be
one of the most expensive in the country). There are two post offices, one in the
national foyer opposite desk 26, the other at the far end of the international foyer.
Upstairs is *City Café* with fast computers for internet access at US$1.75 per hour (there
is another one in departures, once through all the gates).

The left-luggage lock-up, by the stairs between the international and national foyers, offers safe 24-hour storage and retrieval for about US$3 per bag per day, or US$1
per hour. It also has lockers.

Information desks can be found in the national foyer and in the international foyer
(opposite desk 1) and beyond the check-in area, by the stairs. There is also a helpful
desk in the international arrivals hall. It can make hotel and transport reservations. The
Zeta bookstore upstairs has a good selection of English language guidebooks. *Zeta* has
stalls in international and national departures, too.

On the second level there are other cafés besides *City Café*, some accepting major
credit cards. Food tends to be pricey and not very good. Also upstairs are toilets.

Airlines recommend that you arrive at the airport three hours before international flights **Airport**
and two hours before domestic flights. Check-in for international flights closes one hour **departure**
before departure, 30 minutes for domestic flights, after which you may not be permitted **information**
to board. Drivers of the cars entering the parking lot are subject to a document check.

There is a US$25 (or 90 soles) departure tax for international flights which is never **Airport**
included in the price of your ticket. It may be paid in dollars or soles. For national flights **departure tax**
the airport tax is 14 soles (US$4), payable only in soles (at some provincial airports the
tax is 12 soles – US$3.45). Tickets purchased in Peru will also have the 18% state tax,
but this will be included in the price of the ticket. **NB** It is very important to reconfirm
your flights when flying internally in Peru or leaving the country. This is generally done
48-72 hours in advance and can be done by phoning or visiting the airline office
directly or, sometimes, by going to a travel agent for which you may have to pay a service charge. If you do not reconfirm your internal or international flight, you may not
get on the plane. See also Customs, page 38.

Tourist information

See Tourism promotion and information, page 30, for the overall picture on tourist
offices throughout the country.

This non-profit, educational organization functions primarily as an information net- **South**
work for Peru and South America and is the most useful organization for travellers in **American**
the continent. They have offices in Lima, Cusco, Quito and the USA. Full details are **Explorers**
given in the Lima and Cusco sections (pages 101 and 156).

Essentials

The Latin American Travel Advisor

The *Latin American Travel Advisor*: this website (**www.amerispan.com/lata/**) contains a varied collection of articles offering practical advice for travellers to South and Central America. See also Ron Mader's website **www.planeta.com** which contains masses of useful information on ecotourism, conservation, travel, news, links, language schools and articles. Information on travel and language schools is available from *AmeriSpan*, one of several language school brokers in the USA (see under Language, above).

Local customs and laws

Clothing

Most Latin Americans, if they can afford it, devote great care to their clothes and appearance. It is appreciated if visitors do likewise. How you dress is mostly how people will judge you. This is particularly important when dealing with officials. Buying clothing locally can help you to look less like a tourist. Women should pack at least one medium- to long-length skirt and men might want to consider bringing a smart sweater or jacket. Nice sweaters and wool shawls can be easily purchased in Peru and make good additions to your wardrobe.

In general, clothing is less formal in the tropical lowlands, where men and women do wear shorts. In the highlands, people are more conservative, though wearing shorts is acceptable on hiking trails. Men should not be seen bare-chested in populated areas.

Courtesy

Politeness – even a little ceremoniousness – is much appreciated in Peruvian society. So much so, in fact, that business cards can prove useful. Men should always remove any headgear and say *con permiso* when entering offices, and shake hands with other men. Women or men meeting women usually greet each other with one kiss on the cheek. When introduced, Peruvians will probably expect to greet visitors in the same way. Always say *Buenos días* (until midday) or *Buenas tardes* and wait for a reply before proceeding further.

When dealing with officials, always remember to be friendly and courteous no matter how trying the circumstances. Never be impatient and do not criticize situations in public (the officials may know more English than you think and they can certainly interpret gestures and facial expressions). In some situations, however, politeness can be a liability. Most Peruvians are disorderly queuers. In commercial transactions (buying a meal, goods in a shop, etc) politeness should be accompanied by firmness, and always ask the price first.

Politeness should also be extended to street traders. Saying *no, gracias* with a smile is better than an arrogant dismissal. Whether you give money to beggars is a personal matter, but your decision should be influenced by whether a person is begging out of need or trying to cash in on the tourist trail. In the former case, local people giving may provide an indication. Giving money to children is a separate issue, upon which most agree: don't do it. There are occasions where giving food in a restaurant may be appropriate, but first inform yourself of local practice.

In Peru it is common for locals to throw their garbage, paper, wrappers and bottles into the street. Sometimes when asking a local where the rubbish bin is, they will indicate to you that it is the street. This does NOT give you the right to apply the "when in Rome" theory. There *are* rubbish bins in public areas in many centres and tourists should use them. If there isn't one around, put the garbage in your pocket. You will always find bins in bathrooms.

Time-keeping

Peruvians, as with most Latin Americans, have a fairly relaxed attitude towards time. They will think nothing of arriving an hour or so late on social occasions. If you expect to meet someone more or less at an exact time, you can tell them that you want to meet *en punto* or specify *la hora inglesa* (English time).

In most of the better restaurants a 10% service charge is included in the bill, but you can give an extra 5% as a tip if the service is good. The most basic restaurants do not include a tip in the bill, and tips are not expected. Taxi drivers are not tipped – bargain the price down, then pay extra for good service if you get it. Tip cloakroom attendants and hairdressers (very high class only), US$0.50-$1; railway or airport porters, US$0.50; car wash boys, US$0.30; car 'watch' boys, US$0.20. If going on a trek or tour it is customary to tip the guide, as well as the cook and porters.

Tipping

Responsible tourism

Travel to the furthest corners of the globe is now commonplace and the mass movement of people for leisure and business is a major source of foreign exchange and economic development in many parts of South America. In some regions (eg Machu Picchu) it is probably the most significant economic activity.

The benefits of international travel are self-evident for both hosts and travellers – employment, increased understanding of different cultures, business and leisure opportunities. At the same time there is clearly a downside to the industry. Where visitor pressure is high and/or poorly regulated, adverse impacts to society and the natural environment may be apparent. Paradoxically, this is as true in undeveloped and pristine areas (where culture and the natural environment are less 'prepared' for even small numbers of visitors) as in major resort destinations.

The travel industry is growing rapidly and increasingly the impacts of this supposedly 'smokeless' industry are becoming apparent. These impacts can seem remote and unrelated to an individual trip or holiday (eg air travel is clearly implicated in global warming and damage to the ozone layer, resort location and construction can destroy natural habitats and restrict traditional rights and activities), but individual choice and awareness can make a difference in many instances (see box) and collectively, travellers can have a significant effect in shaping a more responsible and sustainable industry.

Of course travel can have beneficial impacts and this is something to which every traveller can contribute – many National Parks are part funded by receipts from visitors. Similarly, travellers can promote patronage and protection of important archaeological sites and heritage through their interest and contributions via entrance and performance fees. They can also support small-scale enterprises by staying in locally run hotels and hostels, eating in local restaurants and by purchasing local goods, supplies and arts and crafts.

In fact, since the Responsible Travel section was first introduced in the South American Handbook in 1992, there has been a phenomenal growth in tourism that promotes and supports the conservation of natural environments and is also fair and equitable to local communities. This 'ecotourism' segment is probably the fastest growing sector of the travel industry and provides a vast and growing range of destinations and activities in South America. While the authenticity of some ecotourism operators' claims need to be interpreted with care, there is clearly both a huge demand for this type of activity and also significant opportunities to support worthwhile conservation and social development initiatives. If you are concerned about the application of the principles of ecotourism, in Peru as elsewhere, you need to make an informed choice by finding out in advance how establishments such as jungle lodges cope with waste and effluent disposal, whether they create the equivalent of 'monkey islands' by obtaining animals in the wild and putting them in the lodge's property, what their policy is towards employing and training local staff, and so on.

Organizations such as *Conservation International*, T001-202-912 1000 or 1-800-406 2306, www.ecotour.org, the *Eco-Tourism Society*, T001-802-651 9818, http://ecotourism.org, *Planeta*, www.planeta.com and *Tourism Concern*, T+44-020-7753 3330, www.tourismconcern.org.uk, have begun to develop and/or

Essentials

▶▶ How big is your footprint?

- *Where possible choose a destination, tour operator or hotel with a proven ethical and environmental commitment – if in doubt ask*
- *Spend money on locally produced (rather than imported) goods and services and use common sense when bargaining – your few dollars saved may be a week's salary to others*
- *Use water and electricity carefully – travellers may receive preferential supply while the needs of local communities are overlooked*
- *Learn about local etiquette and culture – consider local norms and behaviour and dress appropriately for local cultures and situations*

- *Protect wildlife and other natural resources – don't buy souvenirs or goods made from wildlife unless they are clearly sustainably produced and are not protected under CITES legislation (CITES controls trade in endangered species)*
- *Don't give money or sweets to children – it encourages begging – instead give to a recognized project, charity or school*
- *Always ask before taking photographs or videos of people*
- *Consider staying in local accommodation rather than foreign owned hotels – the economic benefits for host communities are far greater – and there are more opportunities to learn about local culture.*

promote ecotourism projects and destinations and their web sites are an excellent source of information and details for sites and initiatives throughout South America. Additionally, organizations such as *Earthwatch*, T+44-1865-318838 or in US 978-461 0081, or 1-800-776 0188, www.earthwatch.org, and *Discovery Initiatives*, T+44-1285-643333, www.discoveryinitiatives.com, offer opportunities to participate directly in scientific research and development projects throughout the region.

South America offers unique and unforgettable experiences – often based on the natural environment, cultural heritage and local society. These are the reasons many of us choose to travel and why many more will want to do so in the future. Shouldn't we provide an opportunity for future travellers and hosts to enjoy the quality of experience and interaction that we take for granted?

Safety

The following notes on personal safety should not hide the fact that most Peruvians are hospitable and helpful. Peru is not a highly dangerous country to travel in, but it is by no means crime free. By being aware of the possible problems you may confront and by using a mixture of common sense and vigilance you can minimize the risks.

Dangerous places   You need to take care everywhere, particularly in poor areas of cities, as this is where most theft takes place. While you should take local advice about being out at night, do not assume that daytime is safer than nighttime. If walking after dark, walk in the road, not on the pavement/sidewalk. If attacked, remember your assailants may well be armed, and try not to resist. You should also be on your guard during festivals, at markets and when streets are crowded. Care should be taken at all times and in most parts of Lima. Like any metropolis, it is subject to urban crime, with theft high on the list. Over the past couple of years there has been an alarming increase in aggressive assaults in centres along the Gringo Trail. Places like Arequipa, Puno and in particular Cusco have, at times, been plagued by waves of strangle muggings. Check with *South American Explorers* and/or the *Latin American Travel Advisor* (see page 50) for a current summary of the situation and how to keep safe. Outside the July-August peak holiday period, there is less tension, less risk of crime, and more friendliness. A friendly attitude on your part, smiling even when you've thwarted a thief's attempt, can help you out of trouble. In addition, do not be discourteous to officials. If someone tries to extract a bribe from you, insist on a receipt.

Keep all documents secure and hide your main cash supply in different places or under your clothes. The following means of concealing cash have all been recommended: extra pockets sewn inside shirts and trousers; pockets closed with a zip or safety pin; moneybelts (best worn below the waist rather than outside or at it or around the neck); neck or leg pouches; a thin chain for attaching a purse to your bag or under your clothes; and elasticated support bandages for keeping money and cheques above the elbow or below the knee.

Protecting money & valuables

Keep cameras in bags, take spare spectacles (eyeglasses) and don't wear wrist-watches (even cheap ones have been ripped off arms!) or jewellery. If you wear a shoulder-bag in a market, carry it in front of you. Small personal alarms can be bought cheaply and can be attached to hand or camera bags, with the release extended to fit securely on your person. If the bag is snatched, the alarm sounds but remains in the stolen item. It will pretty soon be dropped and you can retrieve it. Backpacks are vulnerable to slashers: a good idea is to cover the pack with a sack (a plastic one will also keep out rain and dust) with maybe a layer of wire netting between, or make an inner frame of chicken wire. It's best to use a pack which is lockable at its base. Make photocopies of important documents and give them to your family, embassy and travelling companion, this will speed up replacement if documents are lost or stolen and will still allow you to have some ID while getting replacements. An alternative, if you have an email account, is to send yourself before you leave home a message containing all important details, addresses, etc which you can access in an emergency.

Be especially careful arriving at or leaving from bus and train stations. Stations are obviously places to catch people (tourists or not) with a lot of important belongings. Do not set your bag down without putting your foot on it, even just to double check your tickets or look at your watch; it will grow legs and walk away. Daypacks are easy to grab and run with and are generally filled with your most important belongings. Take taxis to stations, when carrying luggage, before 0800 and after dark (look on it as an insurance policy). Never accept food, drink, sweets or cigarettes from unknown fellow-travellers on buses or trains; they may be drugged. Avoid staying in hotels too near to bus companies, as drivers who stay overnight are sometimes in league with thieves. Also avoid restaurants near bus terminals if you have all your luggage with you, it is hard to keep an eye on your gear when eating. Try to find a travel companion if alone, as this will reduce the strain of watching your belongings all the time.

Public transport

If someone smears mustard, or sprays paint or shampoo on to your clothes, walk on to a safe, private place to clean yourself up. Similarly, ignore strangers' remarks like "what's that on your shoulder?" or "have you seen that dirt on your shoe?" Furthermore, don't bend over to pick up money or other items in the street. These are all ruses intended to distract your attention and make it easy for an accomplice to rob you. If someone follows you when you're in the street, let him catch up with you and 'give him the eye'.

Avoiding con-tricks

Ruses involving 'plainclothes policemen' are infrequent, but it is worth knowing that the real police only have the right to see your passport (not your money, tickets or hotel room). Before handing anything over, ask why they need to see it and make sure you understand the reason. Insist on seeing identification and know that you have the right to write it all down. Do not get in a cab with any police officer, real or not, tell them you will walk to the nearest police station. Do not hand over your identification freely and insist on going to the station first. A related scam is for a 'tourist' to gain your confidence, then accomplices create a reason to check your documents.

Essentials

Hotel security It is best to leave any valuables you don't need in your hotel's safe-deposit box. But always keep an inventory of what you have deposited. If you don't trust the hotel, change to a hotel you feel safe in. If there is no alternative, lock everything in your pack and secure that in your room (some people take eyelet-screws for padlocking cupboards or drawers). If you lose your valuables, always report it to the police and note details of the report for insurance purposes.

Drugs Although certain illegal drugs are readily available, anyone found carrying even the smallest amount is automatically assumed to be a drug trafficker. If arrested on any charge the wait for trial in prison can take up to a year and is particularly unpleasant. Unfortunately, we have received reports of drug-planting, or mere accusation of drug-trafficking by the PNP (Policía Nacional de Perú) on foreigners in Lima, with US$1,000 demanded for release. If you are asked by the narcotics police to go to the toilets to have your bags searched, insist on taking a witness. See Touching down, page 47.

Tricks employed to get foreigners into trouble over drugs include slipping a packet of cocaine into the money you are exchanging, being invited to a party or somewhere involving a taxi ride, or simply being asked on the street if you want to buy cocaine. In all cases, a plain clothes 'policeman' will discover the planted cocaine – in your money or at your feet in the taxi – and will ask to see your passport and money. He will then return them, minus a large part of your cash. Do not get into a taxi, do not show your money, and try not to be intimidated. Being in pairs is no guarantee of security, and single women may be particularly vulnerable. Beware also of thieves dressed as policemen asking for your passport and wanting to search for drugs; searching is only permitted if prior paperwork is done.

Terrorism The activities of Sendero Luminoso and MRTA (Movimiento Revolucionario Túpac Amaru) appear to be a thing of the past, although it would be wrong to suggest that either organization is completely dead. In 2002 it was safe to travel to all parts of Peru, with the exception of the **Huallaga Valley**. This includes areas **near Tingo María**, as well as jungle areas **east of Ayacucho**. This is an important region for cocaine growing and trafficking, in which there remains some terrorist involvement.

Keep yourself informed and always ask locals and other travellers about the conditions up ahead, especially if you are going off the beaten track. While in Lima or Cusco, you can check in at *South American Explorers*, for latest travel updates (Lima T445 3306, Cusco T245484).

We have received new reports in 2002 of **nightclubs** denying entrance to people on the basis of skin colour and assumed economic status. This has happened in Lima and in Cusco. It is not possible to verify if this is the establishments' policy or merely that of certain doormen.

It is better to seek advice on security before you leave from your own consulate than from travel agencies. Before you travel you can contact: British Foreign and Commonwealth Office, Travel Advice Unit, T020-7238 4503, F020-7238 4545. Footprint is a partner in the Foreign and Commonwealth Office's *Know before you go* campaign www.fco.gov.uk/knowbeforeyougo US State Department's Bureau of Consular Affairs, Overseas Citizens Services, T202-647 4225, F202-647 3000, http://travel.state.gov/ travel_warnings.html Australian Department of Foreign Affairs, T06-6261 3305, www.dfat.gov.au/consular/advice.html

Police Whereas in North America and Europe, we are accustomed to law enforcement on a systematic basis; in general law enforcement in Latin America is achieved by periodic campaigns. Be aware that you are required to carry some identification even if it is just a photocopy of your passports. The tourist police in Lima are excellent and you should report any incidents to them. The office in Lima is at Jr Moore 268, Magdalena at the 38th block of Av Brasil, T460 1060/460 0844; they are open seven days a week, all hours. Dealings with the tourist police in Cusco have mixed reviews; you should double check that all reports written by the police in Cusco actually state your complaint. There have been some mix-ups, and insurance companies seldom honour claims for 'lost' baggage.

In the event of a vehicle accident in which anyone is injured, all drivers involved are automatically detained until blame has been established, and this does not usually take less than two weeks.

Never offer a bribe unless you are fully conversant with local customs. Wait until the official makes the suggestion, or offer money in some form which is apparently not bribery, eg "In our country we have a system of on-the-spot fines (*multas de inmediato*). Is there a similar system here?" Do not assume that an official who accepts a bribe is prepared to do anything else that is illegal. You bribe him to persuade him to do his job, or to persuade him not to do it, or to do it more quickly, or more slowly. You do not bribe him to do something which is against the law. The mere suggestion would make him very upset. If an official suggests that a bribe must be paid before you can proceed on your way, be patient (assuming you have the time) and he may relent.

Where to stay

Accommodation is plentiful throughout the price ranges and finding a hotel room to suit your budget should not present any problems, especially in the main tourist areas and larger towns and cities. The exception to this is during the Christmas and Easter holiday periods, Carnival, Cusco in June and Independence celebrations at the end of July, when all hotels seem to be crowded. It's advisable to book in advance at these times and during school holidays and local festivals (see Holidays and festivals, page 75).

For quick hotel price guide, see inside fornt cover

As tourism continues to grow in Peru, so the choice of accommodation increases, especially at the top end of the range. There are now many top class hotels available in Lima and the main tourist centres, such as Cusco, Arequipa, Iquitos and Trujillo. In less visited places the choice of better class hotels may be limited.

Accommodation, as with everything else, is more expensive in Lima, where good budget hotels are few and far between and, therefore, tend to be busy. The best value accommodation can be found in the busiest tourist centres, especially Cusco, which is full of excellent value hotels throughout the range. Accommodation also tends to be more expensive in the north than in the south. Remote jungle towns such as Iquitos and Puerto Maldonado also tend to be more expensive than the norm. And if you want a room with air conditioning expect to pay around 30% extra.

All hotels and restaurants in the upper price brackets charge 18% general sales tax (IGV) and 10% service on top of prices (neither is included in prices given in the accommodation listings, unless specified). The more expensive hotels also charge in dollars according to the parallel rate of exchange at midnight. Most lower grade hotels only charge the 18% sales tax but some may include a service charge.

By law all places that offer accommodation now have a plaque outside bearing the letters **H** (Hotel), **Hs** (Hostal), **HR** (Hotel Residencial) or **P** (Pensión) according to type. A hotel has 51 rooms or more, a hostal 50 or fewer, but the categories do not describe quality or facilities. Generally speaking, though, a *pensión* or *hospedaje* will be cheaper than a hotel or *hostal*. Most mid-range hotels have their own restaurants serving lunch and dinner, as well as breakfast. Few budget places have this facility, though many now serve breakfast. Many hotels have safe parking for motor cycles. Also note that in cheaper hotels water may be scarce in the middle of the day.

Prices given in the accommodation listings are for two people sharing a double room with bathroom (shower and toilet). Where possible, prices are also given per

▶▶ Hotel prices and facilities

LL *(over US$150)*, **L** *(US$100-149)* and **AL** *(US$66-99)* Hotels in these categories are usually only found in Lima and the main tourist centres. They should offer pool, sauna, gym, jacuzzi, all business facilities (including email), several restaurants, bars and often a casino. Most will provide a safe box in each room.

A *(US$46-65)* and **B** *(US$31-45)* The better value hotels in these categories provide more than the standard facilities and a fair degree of comfort. Most will include breakfast and many offer 'extras' such as cable TV, minibar, and tea and coffee making facilities. They may also provide tourist information and their own transport. Service is generally better and most accept credit cards. At the top end of the range, some may have a swimming pool, sauna and jacuzzi.

C *(US$21-30)* and **D** *(US$12-20)* Hotels in these categories range from very comfortable to functional, but there are some real bargains to be had. At these prices you should expect a reasonably sized, comfortable room with a/c (in tropical regions), your own bathroom, constant hot water, a towel, soap and toilet paper, TV, and a restaurant.

E *(US$7-11)* and **F** *(US$4-6)* Usually in these ranges you can expect some degree of comfort and cleanliness, a private bathroom with hot water (certainly in **E**) and perhaps continental breakfast thrown in. Again, the best value hotels will be listed in the travelling text. Many of those catering for foreign tourists in the more popular regions offer excellent value for money and many have their own restaurant and offer services such as laundry, safe deposit box, money exchange and luggage store. Rooms in **F** hotels may have a private bathroom, though this tends to be the exception rather than the rule. Any **F** establishment that provides these facilities, as well as being clean and providing hot water, will be recommended in our hotel listings. Breakfast is rarely included in the price.

G *(up to US$4)* A room in this price range usually consists of little more than a bed and four walls, with barely enough room to swing a cat. If you're lucky you may have a window, a table and chair. Cheap places don't always supply soap, towels and toilet paper. In colder (higher) regions they may not supply enough blankets, so take your own or a sleeping bag.

person, as some hotels charge almost as much for a single room. If travelling alone, it's usually cheaper to share with others in a room with three or four beds. If breakfast is included in the price, it will almost invariably mean continental breakfast. Prices are for the busy seasons (June-August, Christmas and Holy Week). During the low season, when many places may be half empty, it's often possible to bargain the room rate down.

Most places are friendly and helpful, irrespective of the price, particularly smaller *pensiones* and *hospedajes*, which are often family-run and will treat you as another member of the family.

Advice & suggestions The cheapest (and often the nastiest) hotels can be found around bus and train stations. If you're just passing through and need a bed for the night, then they may be okay. The better value accommodation is generally found on and around the main plaza (though not always).

Reception areas in hotels may be misleading, so it is a good idea to see the room before booking. Many hoteliers try to offload their least desirable rooms first. If you're shown a dark box without any furniture, ask if there's another room with a window or a desk. The difference is often surprising. **NB** The electric showers used in many hotels (basic up to mid-range) are a health and safety nightmare. Avoid touching any part of the shower while it is producing hot water and always get out before you switch it off.

At airports, bus or train stations, hotel representatives meet new arrivals and show them brochures of their properties. If not using their services when booking a hotel from an airport, or station by phone, always talk to the hotel yourself; do not let anyone do it for you (except an accredited hotel booking service). You will be told the hotel of your choice is full and be directed to a more expensive one.

These are ubiquitous and unpleasant, but not dangerous. Take some insecticide powder if staying in cheap hotels – Baygon (Bayer) and Boric acid have been recommended. Stuff toilet paper in any holes in walls that you may suspect of being parts of cockroach runs.

Cockroaches

Most Peruvian toilets are adequate but the further you go from main population and tourist centres, the poorer the facilities, so you may require a strong stomach and the ability to hold your breath for a long time. Almost without exception used toilet paper or feminine hygiene products should not be flushed down the pan, but placed in the receptacle provided. This applies even in quite expensive hotels. Failing to observe this custom will block the pan or drain, which can be a considerable health risk. It is quite common for people to stand on the toilet seat (facing the wall – easier to balance), as they do in Asia.

Toilets

The office of the Youth Hostel Association of Peru (*Asociación Peruana de Albergues Turísticos Juveniles*) in Lima is at Av Casimiro Ulloa 328, Miraflores, Lima, T446-5488, F444-8187. It has information about Youth Hostels all around the world. For information about International Student Identity Cards (ISIC) and lists of discounts available to cardholders contact *Intej*, see Student travellers, page 34.

Youth hostels

This presents no problems in Peru, especially along the coast. There can, however, be problems with robbery when camping close to a small village. Avoid such a location, or ask permission to camp in a backyard or *chacra* (farmland). Most Peruvians are used to campers, but in some remote places, people have never seen a tent. Be casual about it, do not unpack all your gear, leave it inside your tent (especially at night) and never leave a tent unattended.

Camping

Obey the following rules for 'wild' camping: arrive in daylight and pitch your tent as it gets dark; ask permission to camp from the parish priest, or the fire chief, or the police, or a farmer regarding his own property; never ask a group of people – especially young people; never camp on a beach (because of sandflies and thieves). If you can't get information from anyone, camp in a spot where you can't be seen from the nearest inhabited place, or road, and make sure no one else saw you go there.

Camping gas in little blue bottles is available in the main cities. Those with stoves designed for lead-free gasoline should use *ron de quemar*, available from hardware shops (*ferreterías*). White gas is called *bencina*, also available from hardware stores. If you use a stove system that requires canisters make sure you dispose of the empty canisters properly. It is very sad and unsightly to go on a hike and find blue gas canisters and toilet paper strewn about. Keep in mind as well that you are responsible for the trash that your group, guide or muledriver may drop and it is up to you to say something and pick up the rubbish. Often the garbage that is on the trails is blamed on locals and this is not usually the case – low-impact travelling is everyone's responsibility and while you are picking up your own trash, pick up other people's too.

Essentials

Getting around

Air

*See also individual
Ins and outs
or Transport sections
for each town
or area*

Peru is a big country and it can take days to cover the vast distances between some of the main tourist destinations. If you're on a tight schedule, then by far the best option is to fly. It is possible to travel by air in Peru between all major centres and many towns that are almost impossible to get to by road. The main national carriers serving the most travelled routes – Arequipa, Chiclayo, Cusco, Iquitos, Juliaca, Piura, Puerto Maldonado, Pucallpa, Tacna, Tarapoto, Trujillo and Tumbes – are *AeroContinente* and its sister airline, *Aviandina*, and *Tans*. *Lan Perú*, a subsidiary of *Lan Chile*, flies to Arequipa, Chiclayo, Cusco, Juliaca, Puerto Maldonado and Trujillo. *Grupo Taca* (the Central American airline) offers service on the Lima-Cusco route. These airlines generally cost the same, between US$39 and US$99 one-way anywhere in the country from Lima. For shorter flights it may cost a bit less (eg Cusco-Puerto Maldonado US$29). On the other hand, it is not unusual for the prices to go up at holiday times (Semana Santa, May Day, Inti Raymi, 28-29 July, Christmas and New Year), and for elections. During these times and the northern hemisphere summer seats can be hard to come by, especially on the Lima–Cusco–Lima route, so book early. *Lan Perú* and *Taca* are generally reckoned to have the better service. **NB** Low promotional tariffs are available, which are renewed monthly. Often it is best to wait to purchase internal flights until your arrival. There are no deals for round trip tickets and prices can rise within four days of the flight. For destinations in the highlands such as Andahuaylas, Ayacucho and Cajamarca flights are offered by *Aero Cóndor* (which also flies to Trujillo and Juanjui) and *LC Busre* (which also flies to Chiclayo). Huánuco and jungle airports such as Atalaya, Satipo, Tingo María and Tocache are served by *Star-Up*. Ticketing for these airlines is not possible at many travel agencies, so it is better to contact the airline direct for information and reservations (see box, page 59).

If you are interested in flying to a city or town, check with all the airlines as new routes are always being added and others deleted. Also, travel agents will often only sell tickets for certain airlines and have no information about routes other companies run; in fact, you will often be told that absolutely no one flies to the place you want to go when actually there are companies that have had regular flights for years to exactly where you are heading. Prices for tickets should be the same whether sold by the airline or an agent.

It is common for flight times to change, earlier or later, or be cancelled because of weather delays especially in the wet season. Do not be surprised or perturbed by this, often there is nothing the airline can do. Always give yourself an extra day between national and international flights to allow for any schedule changes. Flights are often

Domestic airlines

Aero Continente, Av José Pardo 6o5, Miraflores, T242 4242, www.aerocontinente.com.pe Flights to most major destinations in Peru.
Aviandina, a subsidiary of Aero Continente
Aerolca, Diez Canseco 480-B, Miraflores, T445 0859. Flights over the Nasca Lines
AeroCóndor, Av Juan de Arona 781, San Isidro, T442 5215/442 5663, F221 5783, www.aerocondor.com.pe Flights to Ayacucho, Cajamarca, Huánuco and Trujillo; also daily flights over the Nasca Lines from Lima.
Lan Perú, Av José Pardo 513, Miraflores, T213 8200/8300, www.lanperu.com Flights from Lima to Arequipa, Chiclayo,

Cusco, Juliaca, Puerto Maldonado and Trujillo.
LC Busre, Los Tulipanes 218, Lince, Lima, T421 0419, reservas@lcbusre.com.pe Fights from Lima to Chiclayo, Cajamarca and Ayacucho, also Chiclayo-Cajamarca.
Tans, Jr Belén 1015, Lima Centre, Av Arequipa 5200, Miraflores, T213 6000/6030, www.tans.com.pe Flights to most major destinations in Peru.
Taca Perú, Av Comandante Espinar 331, Miraflores, T213 7000, www.grupotaca.com Flights between Lima and Cusco
Star Up, Av José Pardo 269, Miraflores, T445 6032. Flights to Ayacucho, Cusco, Huánuco, Andahuaylas and Tingo María.

overbooked so it is **very important** to reconfirm your tickets at least 24 hours of your flight and be at the airport well in advance. By law, the clerk can start to sell reserved seats to stand-by travellers 30 minutes before the flight.

Internal flight prices are given in US dollars but can be paid in soles and the price should include the 18% general sales tax. Tickets are not interchangeable between companies but sometimes exceptions will be made in the case of cancellations. Do check with companies as to whether there are specials happening. If the price sounds too good to be true double check your ticket to make sure you are not being sold a ticket for Peruvian nationals; these tickets are often half price but you need to show Peruvian ID to get on the plane.

If you are trying to cut down travel time by flying for part of your trip, you can save a lot of money by only flying nationally. This means cross the border over land on your own and then pick up an internal flight.

To save time and hassle, travel with carry-on luggage only (48cm x 24cm x 37cm). This will guarantee that your luggage arrives at the airport when you do.

River

On almost any trip to the Amazon Basin, a boat journey will be required at some point, either to get you to a jungle lodge, or to go between river ports. Motorized canoes with canopies usually take passengers to jungle lodges. They normally provide life jackets and have seats which are not very comfortable on long journeys, so a cushion may come in handy. Being open to the elements, the breeze can be a welcome relief from the heat and humidity in the daytime, but they can also be cold in the early morning and if there is any rain about it will blow into your face. Take a waterproof to keep you dry and warm. You sit very close to the water and you soon learn to respect the driver's mate's knowledge of the river.

Public river transport cannot be regarded as luxurious by any stretch of the imagination, although on the route from Iquitos to Brazil, some posh boats do run. Boats can be extremely uncomfortable, but with patience, perseverance and a strong stomach it is still far from impossible to travel this way. Accommodation is either in a cabin, frequently tiny and dirty, which will be more expensive than slinging your hammock in the general hammock area. If you choose to sleep in a hammock, hang it away from lightbulbs (they aren't switched off at night and attract all sorts of strange insects) and away from the engines, which usually emit noxious fumes and, of course, noise. Another useful tip is not to sling your hammock near the bottom of the stairwell on double decked river boats, as this is where the cook slaughters the livestock every morning. Do try to find somewhere sheltered from the cold, damp night breeze. Take rope for hanging your hammock, plus string and sarongs for privacy. Use a double hammock of material (not string) for warmth; you may need a blanket as well. Boats have irregular schedules. Keep an eye on the departure notices (usually chalk boards) and look for a boat that other passengers have started to board. The captain will often let you embark a couple of days before departure. The captain, and only the captain, will take payment. You need to take: plenty of drinking water (the silt in the rivers will clog filters; purifying tablets may not kill giardia); decent food to relieve the appalling meals; eating utensils; plenty of prophylactic enteritis tablets; a bag to put your rubbish in (rather than doing as the other passengers do, ie chucking it all overboard); mosquito repellent and long-sleeved shirts and long trousers for after dusk. DEET is the best mosquito repellent but it will be washed directly into the river and it is lethal to most fish. Being able to speak Spanish is essential. Thieves are unscrupulous: do not leave anything out of sight, not even your shoes under your hammock at night. Women travellers can expect the usual unwanted attention, but it becomes more uncomfortable when confined to the small boat.

Road

Road network
Detailed accounts of major and minor road conditions are given in the travelling text

Peru's road network is being upgraded and better roads mean better bus services and improved conditions for drivers. Peru, however, is no different from other Latin American countries in that travelling by road at night or in bad weather should be treated with great care. It is also true that there are many more unpaved than paved roads, so extended overland travel is not really an option if you only have a few weeks' holiday.

Improving the road system is one of the Peruvian government's top priorities. More and more major routes are being paved. The Pan-American Highway runs north-south through the coastal desert and is mostly in good condition. Also paved and well-maintained is the direct road which branches off the Pan-American at Pativilca and runs up to Huaraz and on to Caraz. The Northern route from Chiclayo through to Tarapoto is almost entirely paved. It is complete to Moyobamba, plus the spur to Jaén, and is being heavily worked on to Tarapoto. Cajamarca has a smart new road connection to the coast to serve the Yanacocha mining operation. The Central Highway from Lima to Huancayo is mostly well-paved. It continues (mostly paved) to Pucallpa in the Amazon basin. There is also a paved road from La Oroya to Tarma and Satipo. South of Lima, there's the great new 'Liberatores' highway from Pisco to Ayacucho. From Nasca to Abancay is paved and only a stretch of one hour is unpaved between Abancay and Cusco. This is now the main route from Lima to Cusco. The main roads in and to the Sacred Valley from Cusco are also paved. The Cusco-Puno highway is fully paved and is a fast, comfortable journey to rival the train. The paved road continues along the south shore of Lake Titicaca to Desasguadero on the Bolivian border. In the south, the road which runs into the Sierra to Arequipa is in good condition. From Arequipa the road to Puno is newly paved. The new route to Desaguadero from the coast via Moquegua is one of the nicest highways in the country. Roads from Arequipa to Mollendo and Matarani are also excellent.

All other roads in the mountains are of dirt, some good, some very bad. Each year they are affected by heavy rain and mud slides, especially those on the eastern slopes of the mountains. Repairs can be delayed because of a shortage of funds. This makes for slow travel and frequent breakdowns. Note that some of these roads can be dangerous or impassable in the rainy season. Check beforehand with locals (not with bus companies, who only want to sell tickets) as accidents are common at these times.

Services along the coast to the north and south as well as inland to Huancayo, Ayacucho and Huaraz are very good. There are direct (*ejecutivo*) service buses to major centres (different companies use different titles for their top class or executive services, eg **Imperial, Ideal, Royal**). As well as *ejecutivo*, many bus companies have regular (local) service and the difference between the two is often great. Many buses have bathrooms, movies and reclining seats (*bus cama*); if any or all of these services are important to you, ask before you buy your ticket. **Ormeño** and **Cruz del Sur** are the two bus lines generally thought to have the best service with the most routes. *Cruz del Sur* accepts Visa cards and gives 10% discount to ISIC and Under26 cardholders (you may have to insist). **Civa** also offer extensive coverage throughout the nation, but are not in the same class as **Ormeño** and **Cruz del Sur**. There are many smaller but still excellent bus lines that run only to specific areas.

With the nicer companies or *ejecutivo* service you will get a receipt for your luggage, it will be locked under the bus and you shouldn't have to worry about it at stops because the storage is not usually opened. On local buses there will be lots of people getting on and off the buses, loading and unloading bags, so it's best to watch your luggage. It will provide you with a good excuse to get off the bus and stretch anyway. Do not put your day bag above your head inside the bus; keep it at your feet or beside you. It is too easy for someone to grab your bag and get off without your realizing. If you decide to get off the bus at a stop, take all your carry-on items with you. Tickets for *ejecutivo* service buses can cost up to double those of the local service buses. If you want to buy a return ticket from Lima, it is quite often cheaper to wait and buy the return portion when you arrive at your destination. This isn't the case always, but on the major lines things seem to cost more from the capital.

For long journeys be sure to take water and possibly a bit of food, although it is always possible to buy food at the stops along the way. **NB** See the warning under Safety, about not accepting food or drinks from fellow passengers. For mountain routes, have a blanket or at least a jacket handy as the temperature at night can drop quite low. Night buses along the coast and into main highland areas are generally fine. Once you get off the beaten track, the quality of buses and roads deteriorates and you may want to stick to the day buses.

If your bus breaks down and you have to get on another bus, you will probably have to pay for the ticket, but keep your old ticket as some bus companies will give refunds.

The back seats tend to be the most bumpy and the exhaust pipe is almost always on the left hand side of the bus.

It is best to try to arrive at your destination during the day; it is safer and easier to find accommodation. **NB** Prices of tickets are raised 60-100% during Semana Santa (Easter), Fiestas Patrias (Independence Day - July 28 and 29), Navidad (Christmas) and special local events. Prices will usually go up a few days before the holiday and possibly remain higher a few days after. Tickets also sell out during these times so if travelling then, buy your ticket as soon as you know what day you want to travel.

Combis operate between most small towns in the Andes on 1-3-hour journeys. This makes it possible, in many cases, just to turn up and travel within an hour or two. On rougher roads, combis are minibuses (invariably Japanese), while on better roads there are also slightly more expensive and much faster car colectivos. Colectivos usually charge twice the bus fare and leave only when full. They go almost anywhere in Peru. Most firms have offices. If you book one day in advance, they will pick you up at your hotel or in the main plaza. Trucks are not always much cheaper than buses. They charge 75% of the bus fare, but are wholly unpredictable. They are not recommended for long trips, and comfort depends on the load.

Bus
(For bus company addresses, see Lima, Bus companies, page 139)

Essentials

Combis, colectivos & trucks

Taxis   Taxi prices are fixed in the highland towns and cost around US$1-1.20 for anywhere in the urban areas. In Lima prices range from US$1.20-2.50, but fares are not fixed. Some drivers work for companies that do have standard fares. Ask locals what the price should be and **always** set the price beforehand.

Taxis at airports are often a bit more expensive, but ask locals what the price should be as taxi drivers may try to charge you three times the correct price. Many taxi drivers work for commission from hotels and will try to convince you to go to that hotel. Feel free to choose your own hotel and go there. If you walk away from the Arrivals gate a bit, the fares should go down to a price that is reasonable.

Another common form of public transport is the *mototaxi*, or *motocarro*. This is a three-wheel motorcycle with an awning covering the double-seat behind the driver. In some places, like Iquitos and Tarapoto, they are ubiquitous and the only way to get around. Fares are about US$1.

Car

For information about Documents, see Getting there, page 45

Toll roads   Toll roads in Peru include: Aguas Verdes-Tumbes, many on the Pan-American Highway between Tumbes and Lima, Pativilca-Huaraz, Lima-Pucusana, Ica-Nasca, Lima (highway around city), and Variante-Pacasmayo; these vary from US$1.50 to US$0.50. Ecuador to Chile/Bolivia on main roads comes to about US$20. Motorcycles are exempt from road tolls: use the extreme righthand lane at toll gates.

Motoring information   *The Touring and Automobile Club of Peru* have offices in most provincial cities offer help to tourists and particularly to members of the leading motoring associations. They give news about the roads and hotels along the way, although for the most up-to-date information try the bus and colectivo offices. Touring y Automovil Club, Avenida César Vallejo 699, Lince, Lima, T221 2432, marketing@touringperu.com.pe

Fuel   Gasoline is sold by its equivalent octane rating. Leaded, 84 octane (ochenta y cuatro); and unleaded 90 octane (noventa); 95 (noventa y cinco); and 97 (noventa y siete). Unleaded is widely available along the Panamericana and in cities with over 250,000 people. In the Central Highlands, however, unleaded fuel is rarely on sale. Diesel is referred to as "petróleo" and is marked on the price signs as D2. Prices are between US$2.50- US$ 3.50 for gasoline and around US$2 for diesel. The cost along the coast outside urban areas is slightly lower; and slightly higher in the highlands. Since the introduction in 1998 of the "Law of Amazonia" prices for fuel in the jungle are the cheapest in the country. Filling stations are called *grifos*. Always make sure that your tank is full before branching off a major highway, fill up whenever possible and make sure you put in the correct fuel for your vehicle. Gasoline, diesel and kerosene are often sold at the same filling station.

Traffic and parking   Peruvian drivers tend to regard traffic lanes and traffic lights as recommendations, at most. In Lima never trust the green light. No-parking signs are painted at the roadside and illegally parked cars are towed away. Do not leave your vehicle on the street in Lima, always put it in a car park (called *playa*), where the usual charge is US$0.75-1 per hour. If you want to sleep in your car, check with the local tourist police first. They may allow you to park near their office. Transit police in silver Landcruisers park beside the road everywhere. They check on vehicles frequently, including to see that seatbelts are being worn, so be prepared to pull over. Usually the police are friendly and helpful with dirrections.

General hints   Roads go to very high **altitudes** in Peru – make sure that the spark is properly adjusted and consider use of smaller carburettor jets if driving much at altitude. Avoid mountain travel between November and April. Take two planks of wood in case your car gets stuck in soft soil when allowing other vehicles to pass. Never travel off the main roads without being self-sufficient. If you need mechanical assistance in the mountains ask for the nearest mining or road construction camp. Four-wheel drive is not necessary, but it does give you greater flexibility in mountain and jungle territory, although you may not get far in Amazonas, where roads are frequently impassable.

Wherever you travel you should expect from time to time to find roads that are badly maintained, damaged or closed during the wet season, and delays because of floods, landslides and huge potholes. Don't plan your schedules too tightly. If you have to drive at night, do not go fast; many local vehicles have poor lights and street lighting is bad.

The disadvantages of travelling in your own vehicle include the difficulties of getting insurance, theft, finding guarded parking lots, maintenance on appalling roads and nervous exhaustion. These may outweigh the advantages of mobility and independence.

Security Apart from the mechanical aspects, spare no ingenuity in making your car secure. Use a heavy chain and padlocks to chain doors shut, fit security catches on windows, and remove interior window winders (so that a hand reaching in from a forced vent cannot open the window). All these will help, but none is foolproof. Anything on the outside – wing mirrors, spot lamps, motifs etc – is likely to be stolen. So are wheels if not secured by locking nuts.

Try never to leave the car unattended except in a locked garage or guarded parking space. Remove all belongings and leave the empty glove compartment open when the car is unattended. Also lock the clutch or accelerator to the steering wheel with a heavy, obvious chain or lock. Street children will generally protect your car fiercely in exchange for a tip. Be sure to note down key numbers and carry spares of the most important ones (but don't keep all spares inside the vehicle).

Insurance Insurance for the vehicle against accident, damage or theft is best arranged in the country of origin, but it is getting increasingly difficult to find agencies who offer this service. It is very expensive to insure against accident and theft, especially as you should take into account the value of the car increased by duties calculated in real (ie non-devaluing) terms.

If the car is stolen or written off you will be required to pay very high import duty on its value. Get the legally required minimum cover, which is not expensive, as soon as you can, because if you should be involved in an accident and are uninsured, your car could be confiscated. If anyone is hurt, do not pick them up (you may become liable). Seek assistance from the nearest police station or hospital if you are able to do so.

The minimum age for renting a car is 25. Car hire companies are given in the text. They **Car rental** do tend to be very expensive, reflecting the high costs and accident rates. Hotels and tourist agencies will tell you where to find cheaper rates, but you will need to check that you have such basics as spare wheel, toolkit and functioning lights etc.

Car rental insurance Check exactly what the hirer's insurance policy covers. In many cases it will only protect you against minor bumps and scrapes, not major accidents, nor 'natural' damage (eg flooding). Ask if extra cover is available. Also find out, if using a credit card, whether the card automatically includes insurance. Beware of being billed for scratches which were on the vehicle before you hired it.

Motorcycling
People are generally very amicable to motorcyclists and you can make many friends by returning friendship to those who show an interest in you

The motorcycle It should be off-road capable. A road bike can go most places an off-road bike can go. Get to know the bike before you go, ask the dealers in your country what goes wrong with it and arrange a link whereby you can get parts flown out to you. Get the book for international dealer coverage from your manufacturer, but don't rely on it. They frequently have few or no parts for modern, large machinery.

Security Try not to leave a fully laden bike on its own. An Abus D or chain will keep the bike secure. A cheap alarm gives you peace of mind if you leave the bike outside a hotel at night. Most hotels will allow you to bring the bike inside (see accommodation listings in the travelling text for details). Look for hotels that have a courtyard or more secure parking and never leave luggage on the bike overnight or whilst unattended.

Documents Passport, International Driving Licence, bike registration document are necessary. Riders fare much better with a *carnet de passages* than without it.

Cycling

Unless you are planning a journey almost exclusively on paved roads a mountain bike is strongly recommended. The good quality ones (and the cast iron rule is **never** to skimp on quality), are incredibly tough and rugged, with low gear ratios for difficult terrain, wide tyres with plenty of tread for good road-holding, cantilever brakes, and a low centre of gravity for improved stability. Choose a chrome-alloy frame over aluminium as it can be welded if necessary. Once an aluminium frame breaks, it's broke. End of story and trip. Although touring bikes, and to a lesser extent mountain bikes and spares are available in the larger cities, remember that in the developing world most indigenous manufactured goods are shoddy. Buy everything you possibly can before you leave home.

Bicycle equipment This should include: a small but comprehensive tool kit (to include chain rivet and crank removers, a spoke key and possibly a block remover), a spare tyre and inner tubes, a puncture repair kit with plenty of extra patches and glue, a set of brake blocks, brake and gear cables and all types of nuts and bolts, at least 12 spokes (best taped to the chain stay), a light oil for the chain (eg Finish-Line Teflon Dry-Lube), tube of waterproof grease, a pump secured by a pump lock, a Blackburn parking block (a most invaluable accessory, cheap and virtually weightless), a cyclometer, a loud bell, and a secure lock and chain. *Richard's New Bicycle Book* (Pan, £12.99) makes useful reading for even the most mechanically minded.

Luggage and equipment Many cycle tourists are opting for rugged trailers as opposed to the old rack and pannier system. The end product may look a little unwieldy but little time is necessary to get used to the new feeling. The biggest advantage is the fact that you still have a bike, instantly, not an over laden tank on two wheels. It would be a shame to ride the length of Peru and miss out on the amazing trail riding at your fingertips. BOB's (Beast of Burden) Yak Plus trailer is a great rugged choice that comes with a 90-litre bomber dry sac for your gear. The dry sac is similar to a lighter weigh climbing haul bag so it's rugged and watertight. Trailers are also much more rugged than racks, which constantly break, and are much easier to weld.

If you prefer, strong and waterproof front and back panniers are a must. When packed these are likely to be heavy and should be carried on the strongest racks available. Poor quality racks have ruined many a journey for they take incredible strain on unpaved roads. A top bag-cum-rucksack (eg Carradice) makes a good addition for use on and off the bike. A Cannondale front bag is good for maps, camera, compass, altimeter, notebook and small tape-recorder. Other recommended panniers are Ortlieb – front and back – which is waterpoof and almost 'sandproof', Mac-Pac, Madden and Karimoor. 'Gaffa' tape is excellent for protecting vulnerable parts of panniers and for carrying out all manner of repairs.

All equipment and clothes should be packed in plastic bags to give extra protection against dust and rain. Also protect all documents, etc carried close to the body from sweat. Always take the minimum clothing. It's better to buy extra items en route when you find you need them. Generally it is best to carry several layers of thin light clothes than fewer heavy, bulky ones. Always keep one set of dry clothes, including long trousers, to put on at the end of the day. The incredibly light, strong, waterproof and wind resistant goretex jacket and overtrousers are invaluable. Clipless pedals and shoes are strongly recommended for maximum power per stroke.

Useful tips Wind, not hills is the enemy of the cyclist. Try to make the best use of the times of day when there is little; mornings tend to be best but there is no steadfast rule. Take care to avoid dehydration by drinking regularly. In hot, dry areas with limited supplies of **water**, be sure to carry an ample supply. Carry an effective water filtration pump (eg Pur Explorer). For **food**, carry the staples (such as sugar, salt, dried milk, tea, coffee, porridge oats, raisins and dried soups) and supplement these with whatever local foods can be found in the markets. Give your bicycle a thorough **daily check** for loose nuts or bolts or bearings. See that all parts run smoothly. A good chain should last 5,000 miles, 8,000 km or more, but be sure to keep it as clean as possible – an old toothbrush is good for this – and to oil it lightly from time to time. Carry zap-straps to fasten components together quickly and securely when disassembled for bus or plane transport. Remember that thieves are attracted to towns and cities, so when sightseeing, try to leave your bicycle with someone such as a café owner or a priest. Country people tend to be more honest and are usually friendly and very inquisitive. However, don't take unnecessary risks; always see that your bicycle is secure (most hotels will allow bikes to be kept in rooms). In more remote regions dogs can be vicious; carry a stick or some small stones, or use a water bottle (half Coca-Cola, half water) as a spray bottle to frighten them off. Traffic on main roads can be a nightmare. It is usually far more rewarding to keep to the smaller roads or to paths if they exist. Most cyclists agree that the main danger comes from other traffic. A rearview mirror has been frequently recommended to forewarn you of vehicles which are too close behind. You also need to watch out for hazards such as oncoming, overtaking vehicles, unstable loads on trucks and protruding loads. Make yourself conspicuous by wearing bright clothing and a helmet. Dismount and move off the road when two large vehicles are passing you on a narrow, shoulderless road. You will be heartily repaid by honks, waves and even a free meal at times. Most towns have a bicycle shop of some description, but it is best to do your own repairs and adjustments whenever possible. If undertaking your own maintenance, make sure you know how to do it, and research what tyres you will need, before you go. Carry extra bearings for bottom bracket and hub repairs for local bikes, usually BMX styles. Learn to do simple overhauls and you will be generously thanked, especially in small, isolated villages.

South American Explorers have valuable cycling information that is continuously updated. The Expedition Advisory Centre, administered by the *Royal Geographical Society*, 1, Kensington Gore, London SW7 2AR, has published a useful monograph entitled *Bicycle Expeditions*, by Paul Vickers. Published in March 1990, it can be downloaded from the RGS's website (www.rgs.org). A useful website is *Bike South America*, www.e-ddws.com/bsa/ Also recommended is *Cyclo Accueil Cyclo* (CAC), 3 rue Limouzin, 42160 Andrezieux, cacoadou@netcourier.com An organization of long-haul tourers who open their homes for free to passing cyclists.

Hitchhiking in Peru is not easy, owing to the lack of private vehicles, and requires a lot **Hitchhiking** of patience. It can also be a risky way of getting from A to B, but with common sense, it's one way of travelling for free (or very little money) and a way to meet a range of interesting people.

For obvious reasons, a lone female should not hitch by herself. Besides, you are more likely to get a lift if you are with a partner, be they male or female. The best combination is a male and female together. Three or more and you'll be in for a long wait. Your appearance is also important. Someone with matted hair and a large tattoo on their forehead will not have much success. Remember that you are asking considerable trust of someone.

Positioning is also key. Freight traffic in Peru has to stop at the police *garitas* outside each town and these are the best places to try (also toll points, but these are further from towns). Make sure there is plenty of room behind you for a vehicle to stop, as well as enough distance in front for a driver to make their assessment of you. A cardboard sign setting out your destination in big letters is always helpful – and don't forget to add the word 'please' ('*por favor*').

NB Drivers usually ask for money but don't always expect to get it. In mountain and jungle areas you usually have to pay drivers of lorries, vans and even private cars; ask the driver first how much he is going to charge, and then recheck with the locals. Readers report that mining trucks are especially dirty to travel in, so avoid them if possible.

Train   Peru's national rail service was privatized in 1999. The lines of major interest to the traveller are Puno-Juliaca-Cusco, Juliaca-Arequipa (temporarily suspended in 2002) and Cusco or Urubamba-Machu Picchu. They are operated by *PerúRail SA*, which provides luxury services and a backpacker train. For information, T084 (Cusco) 238722/221992, reservas@perurail.com, www.perurail.com The other railway which carries passengers is the line from Lima to Huancayo, with a continuation to Huancavelica in the Central Highlands. The service from the capital to Huancayo, having been out of action for several years, began carrying passengers again in 2002, once every month. Huancayo-Huancavelica has daily passenger services.

There are in all 2,121 km of railway. Two rail lines run up the slopes of the Andes to the Sierra. These railways, once British owned, run from Lima in the centre and the ports of Matarani and Mollendo in the south. From Lima a railway runs to La Oroya, at which point it splits, one section going to Cerro de Pasco and the other to Huancavelica, via Huancayo. **NB** Train schedules may be cut in the rainy season.

Maps   It is a good idea to get as many as possible in your home country before leaving, especially if travelling by land. A recommended series of general maps is that published by **International Travel Map Productions** (ITM), 345 West Broadway, Vancouver BC, V5Y 1P8, Canada, T604-879 3621, F604-879 4521, compiled with historical notes, by the late Kevin Healey. Relevant to this Handbook are South America North West (1:4M) and Amazon Basin (1:4M). Another map series that has been mentioned is that of New World Edition, Bertelsmann, Neumarkter Strasse 18, 81673 München, Germany, *Südamerika Nord, Südamerika Sud* (both 1:4M).

Good maps of the Lima area and the whole country are available from street sellers in the centre of Lima, or in better bookshops (published by **Lima 2000,** Av Arequipa 2625, Lima 14, T440 3486, F440 3480, US$10, or US$14 in booklet form). Other maps can be bought from street vendors on Colmena and in the Plaza San Martín, Lima. 'Westermanns Monatshefte; folio Ecuador, Peru, Bolivien has excellent maps of Peru, especially the archaeological sites. A cheaper, less accurate, and less discreet map is published by **Cartográfica Nacional** for US$3-4. The **Instituto Geográfico Nacional** in Lima sells a selection of good, accurate country and regional maps (see page 133). **South American Explorers** stock an excellent collection of country, regional and topographical maps.

The **Touring and Automobile Club of Peru**, see page 62, sells a good road map at US$5 (Mapa Vial del Perú, 1:3,000,000, Ed 1980) and route maps covering most of Peru (Hoja de Ruta, detail maps 1:1,000,000), which are very good but have no information on road conditions. The *Guía Toyota* (Spanish), which is published annually, is one of the best guides for venturing off the beaten track. Lima 2000's *Mapa Vial del Perú* (1:2,200,000) is probably the best and most correct road map available for the country. Both can be obtained from **South American Explorers**, who will give good advice on road conditions (see page 49).

Keeping in touch

Details of organizations which can help you sort out any problems or give advice, such as **South American Explorers**, British Council and Alliance Française, or addresses of embassies and consulates, can be found in the Lima and Cusco sections (pages 101 and 156). *Stanfords*, 12-14 Longacre, London, WC2E 9LP, T020-78361321, www.stanfords.co.uk

Points of contact

You can find internet access everywhere. Centres with high tourism have internet cafés on every corner; many of them have net2phone. Internet cafés are listed in the travelling text under each town, except where there are too many to mention, like Lima. Internet cafés are incredibly cheap to use, often less than US$1 per hour. The downside of this popularity is that cafés frequently have no free terminals, so you have to pick your time carefully. When they first open in the morning is often a good time. In addition, the system is often overloaded, so getting access to your server can take a long time. Internet access is more expensive in hotel business centres and in out of the way places. *Terra* and Red Científica Peruana, *rcp* dominate the market.

Internet & email

The name of the postal system is **Serpost**.

Postal services

Parcels Sending parcels and mail can be done at any post office but Correo Central on the Plaza de Armas in Lima is the best place. The office is open Monday to Friday from 0800 to 1800. Stamps, envelopes and cloth sacks (to send bigger parcels in) can all be bought there. It costs US$1 to mail a letter up to 20 g anywhere in the Americas, US$1.50 to Europe and US$1.70 to Australia. You can also mail letters *expreso* for about US$0.55, extra to the Americas, US$0.90 to the rest of the world, and they will arrive a little more quickly. Don't put tape on envelopes or packages, wait until you get to the post office and use the glue they have. It is very expensive to mail large packages out of Peru so it is best not to plan to send things home from here. For emergency or important documents, DHL and Federal Express are also options in Lima (check in city of Lima section for addresses).

Essentials

Receiving mail To receive mail, letters can be sent to Poste Restante/General Delivery (*lista de correos*), your embassy, or, for cardholders, American Express offices. Members of the **South American Explorers** can have post and packages sent to them at either of the Peruvian offices. Remember that there is no W in Spanish; look under V, or ask. For the smallest risk of misunderstanding, use title, initial and surname only. If having items sent to you by courier (eg DHL), do not use poste restante, but an address such as a hotel: a signature is required on receipt. Try not to have articles sent by post to Peru – taxes can be 200% of the value.

Telephone services
Telephone directories found in most hotel rooms have useful city maps

The main service provider is **Telefónica** (or **Telser** in Cusco) which has offices in all large and medium-sized towns. In some cases, the **Telefónica** office is administrative and phones are provided on the street outside. Local, national and international calls can be made from public phone boxes with coins or, more commonly, prepaid phone cards. To use phone cards, remove the card from its plastic covering (which should not be broken) and, on the back, scratch off the dark grey strip to reveal the card's number. You have to dial this number when told to do so by the operator. Cards for **Telefónica** services, of which there are several, can be bought at **Telefónica** offices or the many private phone offices (could be just a counter with a phone on the street). Also on sale in larger towns are cards for a number of carriers for long distance calls: **AT&T**, **Americatel**, **Nortek** and **Perusat** (international only). Their rates are very competitive and there are usually seasonal offers to take advantage of. In some cases calls are routed through North America, so there may be a delay on the line. Each carrier has a prefix code which you must dial, as well as the card's secret code. Not every phone takes cards; **Telefónica**, for instance, has its own phones for its 147 service (national and international). So shop around for the best deal for the type of call you want to make, select a card which will give you the number of minutes you require and get dialling. The average cost for a call to Western Europe is between S/.1.75 and S/.5 per minute (US$0.50-1.40) and to the US S/.1.55 and S/.4 (US$0.45-1.10). Calls without cards from public phones cost US$1 per minute to North America, US$1.40 to Europe and US$1.50 to Australia and New Zealand. Collect calls are possible to almost anywhere by ringing the international operator (108). You can also reach a variety of countries' operators direct if you wish to charge a call to your home calling card. 108 has the 0-800 numbers for the international direct options and they speak English. Your home telephone company can give you the number to call as well. You can also receive calls at many **Telefónica** offices, the cost is usually around US$1 for 10 minutes. Net Phones are becoming increasingly popular, especially in Lima. Costs and service varies but can be as cheap as US$5 per hour to the USA. Calls to everywhere else are usually at least 50% more. Faxes cost about US$1.50 per page to North America, US$2 to most of Western Europe and US$2.50 to Israel. The cost to receive is about US$1 per page.

In smaller towns, you may have to hunt around for a phone booth that will permit international calls.

Mobile phones There are three networks in Peru, *Telefónica*, *TIM* and *Bellsouth*. *Telefónica* has the most extensive network. Mobile phones brought into Peru which operate at 800 mhz may be activated at a *Telefónica* technical services office. *TIM* phones from Europe will operate in Peru, but calls cannot be diverted to another line if the phone number dialled is unanswered. *Bellsouth* uses TDMA technology and their technical staff would have to see a foreign phone to verify its compatibility. European mobiles are not compatible with *Bellsouth*. If you need to have a mobile phone, it's best to buy one locally. All three companies sell phones, which take prepaid cards, from about US$70.

Media **Newspapers** Lima has several daily papers. The most informative are *El Comercio* and *La República*. *El Comercio* is good for international news and has a near monopoly on classified ads. It also has a good weekly tourism section. *La República* takes a more liberal-left approach and contains the *Crónica Judicial*. Its weekly tourism section, *Andares*, is recommended. Among the others are *Expreso* and *Ojo*. *Gestión* is a business daily. Very popular are the sensationalist papers, written in raunchy slang and featuring acres of bare female flesh on their pages. The main provincial cities have at least one newspaper each (details are given in the relevant sections). There are a number of websites which provide regular news updates:

El Comercio www.elcomercioperu.com.pe/
Expreso www.expreso.com.pe
Gestión www.gestion.com.pe/
La República www.larepublica.com.pe
Perú al Día news service www.perualdia.com or through www.yachay.net.pe
The following also have access to the daily news: www.terra.com.pe www.peru.com

Magazines The most widely read magazine is the weekly news magazine *Caretas*, which gives a very considered angle on current affairs and is often critical of government policy, www.caretas.com.pe A bi-monthly magazine called *Rumbos* (English and Spanish together) is a good all-round 'what's happening in Peru' magazine, www.rumbos.delperu.com Monthlies include *Business*, *Proceso Económico*, *Debate* and *Idede*. There is a weekly economic and political magazine in English, the *Andean Report*, with useful information and articles.

Radio Radio is far more important in imparting news to Peruvians than newspapers, partly due to the fact that limited plane routes make it difficult to get papers to much of the population on the same day. There are countless local and community radio stations which cover even the most far-flung places. The most popular stations are *Radioprogramas del Perú* (www.rpp.com.pe), which features round-the-clock news, and *Cadena Peruana de Noticias* (www.terra.com.pe/cpn/index.shtml).

A shortwave (world band) radio offers a practical means to brush up on the language, keep abreast of current events, sample popular culture and absorb some of the richly varied regional music. International broadcasters such as the **BBC World Service**, the **Voice of America**, Boston (Mass)-based **Monitor Radio International** (operated by *Christian Science Monitor*) and the Quito-based Evangelical station, *HCJB*, keep the traveller informed in both English and Spanish.

Compact or miniature portables are recommended, with digital tuning and a full range of shortwave bands, as well as FM, long and medium wave. Advice on models (£150 for a decent one) and wavelengths can be found in the *Passport to World Band Radio* (Box 300, Penn's Park, PA 18943, USA, £15.50). Details of local stations are listed in *World TV and Radio Handbook* (WTRH), PO Box 9027, 1006 AA Amsterdam, The Netherlands, £15.80 (www.amazon.co.uk prices). Both of these, free wavelength guides and selected radio sets are available from the BBC World Service Bookshop, Bush House Arcade, Bush House, Strand, London WC2B 4PH, UK, T020-7557 2576.

TV Many hotels include televisions in rooms, the more expensive the hotel, the more cable channels there will be on the set. There will almost certainly be US channels, often the BBC, Italian and occasionally German channels. You can find movies, sports, music, nature/discovery and news (CNN in both English and Spanish). Local channels include América Televisión (www.americatv.com.pe), Cable Mágico (www.cablemagico.com.pe), Frecuencia Latina (www.frecuencialatina.com.pe) and Panamericana (www.pantel.com.pe).

▶▶ **Restaurant prices**

Expensive *US$12 and over.*
Mid-range *US$6-12.*
Cheap *US$1-5.*

Prices for meals given in the travelling text refer to the cost of a two-course meal for one person, excluding tips or drinks.

Essentials

Food and drink

Food

Peruvian cuisine

For a glossary of food and drink terms, see page 623

Pizza is available just about everywhere

Not surprisingly for a country with such a diversity of geography and climates, Peru boasts the continent's most extensive and varied menu. In fact, Peru is rivalled in Latin America only by Mexico in the variety of its cuisine. One of the least expected pleasures of a trip to Peru is the wonderful food on offer, and those who are willing to forego the normal traveller's fare of pizza and fried chicken are in for a tasty treat.

Peruvian cuisine varies from region to region, but basically can be divided into coastal, highland and tropical.

Coastal cuisine

Not surprisingly, the best coastal dishes are those with seafood bases, with the most popular being the jewel in the culinary crown, *ceviche*. This delicious dish of white fish marinated in lemon juice, onion and hot peppers can be found in neighbouring countries, but Peruvian is best. Traditionally, *ceviche* is served with corn-on-the-cob, *cancha* (toasted corn), yucca and sweet potatoes. Another mouth-watering fish dish is *escabeche* – fish with onions, hot green pepper, red peppers, prawns (*langostinos*), cumin, hard-boiled eggs, olives, and sprinkled with cheese. For fish on its own, don't miss the excellent *corvina*, or white sea bass. You should also try *chupe de camarones*, which is a shrimp stew made with varying and somewhat surprising ingredients. Other fish dishes include *parihuela*, a popular bouillabaisse which includes *yuyo de mar*, a tangy seaweed, and *aguadito*, a thick rice and fish soup said to have rejuvenating powers.

They don't just eat fish on the coast. A favourite northern coastal dish is *seco de cabrito*, roasted kid (baby goat) served with beans and rice, or *seco de cordero* which uses lamb instead. Also good is a*ji de gallina* (see box page 71), a rich and spicy creamed chicken, and duck is excellent. People on the coast are referred to as *criollos* (see page 584) and *criollo* cooking can be found throughout the country. Two popular examples are *cau cau*, made with tripe, potatoes, peppers and parsley, served with rice, and *anticuchos*, which are shish kebabs of beef heart with garlic, peppers, cumin seeds and vinegar.

Highland cuisine

The staples of highland cooking, corn and potatoes, date back to Inca times and are found in a remarkable variety of shapes, sizes and colours. Two good potato dishes are *Causa* and *carapulca*. *Causa* is made with yellow potatoes, lemons, pepper, hard-boiled eggs, olives, lettuce, sweet cooked corn, sweet cooked potato, fresh cheese, and served with onion sauce. You will also find *causa* on coastal menus: the mashed potato is wrapped around the filling, which often contains crabmeat. Another potato dish is *papa a la huancaína*, which is topped with a spicy sauce made with milk and cheese. The most commonly eaten corn dishes are *choclo con queso*, corn on the cob with cheese, and *tamales*, boiled corn dumplings filled with meat and wrapped in a banana leaf.

Meat dishes are many and varied. *Ollucos con charqui* is a kind of potato with dried meat, *sancochado* is meat and all kinds of vegetables stewed together and seasoned with ground garlic and *lomo a la huancaína* is beef with egg and cheese sauce. A dish

Ají de gallina

This spicy chicken dish is a favourite in Lima (kindly supplied by Mónica Moreno and Leo Rovayo).
Ingredients: *One 2 kg chicken; 100 ml oil; 250 g diced onion; 1 large clove garlic, crushed; 6 green chillis, liquidized (or to taste); breadcrumbs from 4 slices of bread, crust removed; 1 can evaporated milk; 100 g parmesan cheese; 250 g ground nuts; salt and pepper. To garnish, boiled potatoes; black olives; hard-boiled egg.*
Method: *Boil the chicken in salted water*

until cooked. Drain off the stock, but do not discard it. Allow the bird to cool, then shred the meat.

Heat the oil and fry the onion, garlic and chilli. Add the breadcrumbs and a little of the chicken stock. Cook for ten minutes. Add the nuts, the parmesan cheese and the chicken.

Before serving, add the evaporated milk and combine well.
Garnish the serving dish with boiled potatoes, hard-boiled egg and black olives.

almost guaranteed to appear on every restaurant menu is *lomo saltado*, a kind of stir-fried beef with onions, vinegar, ginger, chilli, tomatoes and fried potatoes, served with rice. *Rocoto relleno* is spicy bell pepper stuffed with beef and vegetables, *palta rellena* is avocado filled with chicken or Russian salad, *estofado de carne* is a stew which often contains wine and *carne en adobo* is a cut and seasoned steak. Others include *fritos*, fried pork, usually eaten in the morning, *chicharrones*, deep fried chunks of pork ribs and chicken, and *lechón*, suckling pig. And not forgetting that popular childhood pet, *cuy* (guinea pig), which is considered a real delicacy.

Very filling and good value are the many soups on offer, such as *yacu-chupe*, a green soup which has a basis of potato, with cheese, garlic, coriander leaves, parsley, peppers, eggs, onions, and mint, and *sopa a la criolla* containing thin noodles, beef heart, bits of egg and vegetables and pleasantly spiced. And not to be outdone in the fish department, *trucha* (trout) is delicious, particularly from Lake Titicaca.

The main ingredient in much jungle cuisine is fish, especially the succulent, dolphin-sized *paiche*, which comes with the delicious *palmito*, or palm-hearts, and the ever-present yucca and fried bananas. Other popular dishes include *sopa de motelo* (turtle soup), *sajino* (roast wild boar) and *lagarto* (caiman). *Juanes* are a jungle version of *tamales*, stuffed with chicken and rice. **Tropical cuisine**

The Peruvian sweet tooth is evident in the huge number of desserts and confections from which to choose. These include: *cocada al horno* – coconut, with yolk of egg, sesame seed, wine and butter; *picarones* – frittered cassava flour and eggs fried in fat and served with honey; *mazamorra morada* – purple maize, sweet potato starch, lemons, various dried fruits, sticks of ground cinnamon and cloves and perfumed pepper; *manjar blanco* – milk, sugar and eggs; *maná* – an almond paste with eggs, vanilla and milk; *alfajores* – shortbread biscuit with *manjar blanco*, pineapple, peanuts, etc; *pastelillos* – yuccas with sweet potato, sugar and anise fried in fat and powdered with sugar and served hot; and *zango de pasas*, made with maize, syrup, raisins and sugar. *Turrón*, the Lima nougat, is worth trying. *Tejas* are pieces of fruit or nut enveloped in *manjar blanco* and covered in chocolate or icing sugar – delicious. **Desserts & fruits**

The various Peruvian fruits are wonderful. They include bananas, the citrus fruits, pineapples, dates, avocados (*paltas*), eggfruit (*lúcuma*), the custard apple (*chirimoya*) which can be as big as your head, quince, *papaya*, mango, guava, the passion-fruit (*maracuyá*) and the soursop (*guanábana*). These should be tried as juices or ice cream – an unforgettable experience.

Eating out
For a full list of restaurants, see under Eating for each individual town

The high-class hotels and restaurants serve international food and, on demand, some native dishes, but the best places to find native food at its best are the taverns (*chicherías*) and the local restaurants (*picanterías*).

Lunch is the main meal, and apart from the most exclusive places, most restaurants have one or two set lunch menus, called *menú ejecutivo* or *menú económico*. The set menu has the advantage of being served almost immediately and also usually **cheap**. The *menú ejecutivo* costs US$2 or more for a three-course meal with a soft drink and it offers greater choice and more interesting dishes than the *menú económico*, which costs US$1.50-2.50. Don't leave it too late, though, most Peruvians eat lunch around 1230-1300. There are many Chinese restaurants (*chifas*) in Peru which serve good food at reasonable prices. For really economically minded people the *Comedores populares* found in the markets of most cities offer a standard three course meal for as little as US$1 (see Health, page 88).

For those who wish to eschew such good value, the menu is called *la carta*. An *à la carte* lunch or dinner costs US$5-8, but can go up to an **expensive** US$80 in a first-class restaurant, with drinks and wine included. Middle and high-class restaurants add 11% tax and 17% service to the bill (sometimes 18% and 13% respectively). This is not shown on the price list or menu, so check in advance. Lower class restaurants charge only 5% tax, while cheap, local restaurants charge no taxes. Dinner in restaurants is normally about 1900 onwards, but choice may be more limited than lunchtime. Peruvians tend to ask guests for dinner at 2000.

The situation for **vegetarians** is improving, but slowly. In tourist centres you should have no problem finding a vegetarian restaurant (or a restaurant that has vegetarian options), especially Cusco and Arequipa and, of course, Lima. Elsewhere, choice is limited and you may find that, as a non-meat eater, you are not understood. Vegetarians and people with allergies should be able to list (in Spanish) all the foods they cannot eat. By saying *no como carne* (I don't eat meat), people may assume that you eat chicken and eggs. If you do eat eggs, make sure they are cooked thoroughly. Restaurant staff will often bend over backwards to get you exactly what you want but you need to request it.

Drink

Peru's most famous drink is *pisco*, a grape brandy used in the wonderful pisco sour, a deceptively potent cocktail which also includes egg whites and lime juice. The most renowned brands come from the Ica Valley. Other favourites are *chilcano*, a longer refreshing drink made with *guinda*, a local cherry brandy, and *algarrobina*, a sweet cocktail made with the syrup from the bark of the carob tree, egg whites, evaporated milk, pisco and cinnamon.

Some Peruvian **wines** are good, others are acidic and poor. The best are the Ica wines Tacama and Ocucaje, and both come in red, white and rosé, sweet and dry varieties. They cost around US$5 a bottle, or more. Tacama Blancs de Blancs and brut Champagne have been recommended, also Gran Tinto Reserva Especial. Viña Santo Tomás, from Chincha, is reasonable and cheap, but Casapalca is not for the discerning palate.

Peruvian **beer** is good, but is becoming pretty much the same the country over now that many individual brewers have been swallowed up by the multinational Backus and Johnson. This has happened to the *Cusqueña*, *Arequipeña*, *Callao* and *Trujillo* brands. Peruvians who had their favourites are lamenting this change. In Lima, the *Cristal* and *Pilsener* are both pretty good and served everywhere. Those who fancy a change from the ubiquitous pilsner type beers should look out for the sweetish *maltina* brown ale. A good dark beer is Trujillo Malta.

Chicha de jora is a strong but refreshing **maize beer**, usually homemade and not easy to come by, and *chicha morada* is a soft drink made with purple maize. **Coffee** in Peru is usually execrable. It is brought to the table in a small jug accompanied by a mug of hot water to which you add the coffee essence. If you want coffee with milk, a mug of milk is brought. There are many different kinds of herb **tea**: the commonest are *manzanilla* (camomile), *mate de coca* (frequently served in the highlands to stave off the discomforts of altitude sickness) and *hierbaluisa* (lemon grass).

The café section of each town, lists places that serve decent coffee

Bars as we understand them in Europe or North America are not prevalent in Peru, except in the main tourist centres. Other than in the poorer working class districts, most people seem to do their drinking in restaurants, *peñas*, discos or at *fiestas*.

Bars

Essentials

Shopping

Almost everyone who visits Peru will end up buying a souvenir of some sort from the vast array of arts and crafts (*artesanía*) on offer. The best, and cheapest, place to shop for souvenirs, and pretty much anything else in Peru, is in the street markets which can be found absolutely everywhere. The country also has its share of shiny, modern shopping centres, especially in the capital, but remember that the high overheads are reflected in the prices.

Sooner or later almost everyone has to bargain in Peru. Only the rich and famous can afford to pay the prices quoted by taxi drivers, receptionists and self-proclaimed guides. The great majority of Peruvians are honest and extremely hard working, but their country is poor and often in turmoil, the future is uncertain and the overwhelming majority of people live below the poverty line. Foreigners are seen as rich, even if they are backpackers or students. In order to bring prices down, it is extremely helpful to speak at least some Spanish and/or to convince locals that you live, work or study in Peru and therefore know the real price. See under Lima, Transport, for the box on bargaining in the capital's taxis (page 140).

Bargaining

You will not have to bargain in restaurants, department stores, expensive hotels or airline offices. However, almost all the rest is negotiable. Almost all better-class hotels have 'corporate' rates. Just say that you work for some company, that you are a journalist (they never check ID), or you are a researcher. This way you can usually get a reduction. Always see the room first – don't be reassured by the glitzy lobby.

You can negotiate the price of a tour booked through a travel agency, but not an aeroplane, bus or train ticket. In fact, you will probably get better price directly from the airline ticket office.

Bargaining is expected when you are shopping for artwork, handicrafts, souvenirs, or even food in the market. Remember, though, that most of handicrafts, including alpaca and woollen goods, are made by hand. Ask yourself if it is worth taking advantage of the piteous state of the people you are buying from. Keep in mind, these people are making a living not playing a game and the 50 centavos you save by bargaining may buy the seller two loaves of bread. You want the *fair* price not the lowest one, so bargain only when you feel you are being ripped off. Remember that some Peruvians are so desperate that they will have to sell you their goods at *any* price, in order to survive. Please, don't take advantage of it.

Essentials

What to buy
For a more detailed
look at Peruvian
arts and crafts, see
under Arts and
crafts on page 589)

It is possible to find any kind of **handicraft** in the capital. The prices are often the same as in the highlands, and the quality is high. Good buys are: silver and gold handicrafts; Indian hand-spun and hand-woven textiles; manufactured textiles in Indian designs; llama and alpaca wool products such as ponchos, rugs, hats, blankets, slippers, coats and sweaters; *arpilleras* (appliqué pictures of Peruvian life), which are made with great skill and originality by women in the shanty towns; and fine leather products which are mostly hand made. Another good buy is **clothing** made from high quality Pima cotton, grown in Peru.

The *mate burilado*, or engraved gourd found in every tourist shop, is cheap and one of the most genuine expressions of folk art in Peru. These are cheaper if bought in the villages of the Mantaro Valley near Huancayo in the Central Highlands. The Mantaro Valley is generally renowned for its folk culture, including all manner of *artesanía* (see Huancayo, page 489).

Alpaca clothing, such as sweaters, hats and gloves, is cheaper in the Sierra, especially in Puno. Another good source is Arequipa, where alpaca cloth for suits, coats, etc (mixed with 40% sheep's wool) can be bought cheaply from factories. However, although Lima is more expensive, it is often impossible to find the same quality of goods elsewhere. **NB** Genuine alpaca is odourless wet or dry, wet llama 'stinks'.

One of the best places in Peru to look for *artesanía* is Ayacucho in the Central Highlands. Here you'll find excellent woven textiles, as well as the beautifully intricate *retablos*, or Saint Mark's boxes (see page 593). Cusco is one of the main weaving centres and a good place to shop for textiles, as well as excellent woodcarvings (see page 154). Also recommended for textiles is Cajamarca. The island of Taquile on Lake Titicaca is a good place to buy *ch'uspas* (bags for coca leaves), *chumpis* (belts) and *chullos* (knitted hats).

Pre-paid Kodak slide **film** cannot be developed in Peru and is also very hard to find. Kodachrome is almost impossible to buy. Some travellers (but not all) have advised against mailing exposed films home. Either take them with you, or have them developed, but not printed, once you have checked the laboratory's quality. Note that postal authorities may use less sensitive equipment for X-ray screening than the airports do.

Developing black and white film is a problem. Often it is shoddily machine-processed and the negatives are ruined. Ask the store if you can see an example of their laboratory's work and if they hand-develop.

Exposed film can be protected in humid areas by putting it in a balloon and tying a knot. Similarly keeping your camera in a plastic bag may reduce the effects of humidity.

Entertainment and nightlife

If you want to party in Peru, head for Barranco in Lima, or Cusco. Other places like Arequipa, Puno and Huaraz have bars and discos, but with nothing like the variety or vibrancy. Barranco, an attractive seaside suburb of Lima, boasts perhaps the best nightlife in the country (see page 129). At weekends it throbs with young *limeños* out for a good time. It is also a great place for a romantic early evening drink while you watch the sun slip into the Pacific Ocean. Barranco is a short taxi ride from Miraflores suburb, which has its own fair share of trendy bars and nightclubs.

*Look out for the
flyers which give
free entry plus a
complimentary drink*

As befits its nickname of 'Gringo Capital of South America', Cusco has a staggering selection of bars and nightclubs, all within a few streets on and around the Plaza de Armas. There are British and Irish pubs, American and couch bars. Discos play Latin, techno, rock and golden oldies; some have live bands. For a less energetic evening, *peñas* offer floorshows of traditional music. Many also serve dinner.

Take it easy on the booze when you first arrive in Cusco or Puno. Having a hangover and altitude sickness at the same time is no joke. Also be aware of the dangers of trying to score drugs in nightclubs (see above).

Holidays and festivals

Two of the major festival dates are *Carnaval*, which is held over the weekend before Ash Wednesday, and *Semana Santa* (Holy Week), which ends on **Easter Sunday**. Carnival is celebrated in most of the Andes and Semana Santa throughout Peru. Accommodation and transport is heavily booked at these times and prices rise.

> **Festivals**
> *See individual towns for local festival listings*

    Another important festival is *Fiesta de la Cruz*, held on the first of **May** in much of the central and southern highlands and on the coast. In Cusco, the entire month of **June** is one huge *fiesta*, culminating in *Inti Raymi*, on **24 June**, one of Peru's prime tourist attractions.

    The two main festivals in Lima are *Santa Rosa de Lima*, on **30 August**, and *Señor de los Milagros*, held on several dates throughout **October**.

    Another national festival is *Todos los Santos* (All Saints) on **1 November**, and on **8 December** is *Festividad de la Inmaculada Concepción*.

Aside from the festivals listed above, the main holidays are: **1 January**, New Year; **6 January**, *Bajada de Reyes*; **1 May**, Labour Day; **28-29 July**, Independence (Fiestas Patrias); **7 October**, Battle of Angamos; **24-25 December**, *Navidad*.

> **National holidays**

    NB Most businesses such as banks, airline offices and tourist agencies close for the official holidays while supermarkets and street markets may be open. This depends a lot on where you are so ask around before the holiday. Sometimes holidays that fall during mid-week will be moved to the following Monday to make a long weekend. If you are going to spend a holiday in a certain area, find out what the local customs and events are. Often there are parades, processions, special types of food or certain traditions (like yellow underwear on New Year's Eve) that characterize the event. This will allow you to delve into the customs of the region you are travelling in. The high season for foreign tourism in Peru is June to September while national tourism peaks on certain holidays, Navidad, Semana Santa and Fiestas Patrias. Prices rise and accommodation and bus tickets are harder to come by. If you know when you will be travelling buy your ticket in advance.

Sport and special interest travel

Adventure sports

This is not yet widely known in Peru, but there is an organization which can provide information; *Centre of Subterranean Explorations of Peru* (Centro de Exploraciones Subterráneas del Perú, CEESPE), Av Brasil 1815, Jesús María, Lima 11, T463 4722, www.geocities.com/cespeleo/CEESPE.html Sr Carlos Morales is very helpful.

> **Cave diving**

    A cave which has attracted international expeditions is the **Gruta de Huagapo** or 'The Cave that Weeps', located in the Valle de Palcamayo 30 km northwest of Tarma in the Department of Junín, at 3,572 m (see page 508).

The attractions are obvious. The **Cordillera Blanca** is an ice climber's paradise. It takes just one or two days to reach the snowline on most mountains in this, the most intensive grouping of glaciated peaks in South America. The statistics are impressive: more than 50 summits between 5,000 and 6,000 m; over 20 surpassing 6,000 m; 663 glaciers; and there are no peak fees. It is not unusual for climbers to reach three or more 6,000-m summits, climbed Alpine style, over a three-week trip. The degree of difficulty ranges between **Pisco** (5,752 m), an excellent acclimatizer or novice's mountain, **Copa** (6,173 m), of moderate difficulty, and the tremendous challenges such as **Alpamayo**

> **Climbing**

Essentials

(5,957 m), **Artesonraju** (6,025 m), **Quitaraju** (6,036 m) and **Ranrapalca** (6,162 m). Huaraz, the main climbing centre of the Cordillera Blanca (see page 335), has a growing infrastructure and is home to the *Peruvian Mountain Guide Association* (see below).

The **Huayhuash** (see page 367) is a little more remote and Chiquián, northwest of the range, and Cajatambo to the south, have few facilities for climbers. It is possible to contact guides, *arrieros*, porters and cooks in Chiquián, although it is best to enquire in Huaraz first. Mules may need to be brought down from villages higher up. The Huayhuash has some of the most spectacular ice walls in Peru. The **Jirishancas** and **Yerupajas** (Grande and Chico) are the most popular and demanding.

The Cordilleras **Vilcabamba and Vilcanota** (see page 227) have the enticing peaks of **Salkantay** (6,271 m) and **Ausangate** (6,398 m), but Cusco is not developed for climbing. This is one of the genuine attractions of Peruvian Andinismo – there is always another mountain slightly more remote to feed the appetite. **Huagurunchu** (5,730 m), for instance in the central Andes, is barely known and **Coropuna**, Peru's third highest at 6,425 m, is hardly ever climbed.

Rock climbing In the *quebradas*, where the rock is most solid (frost-shattered higher up) this is becoming more popular, particularly in the **Quebrada de Llaca**, near Huaraz, and for beginners at **Monterrey** (see page 333). To get to Quebrada de Llaca, take a camioneta from Jirón Caraz (one block behind Raimondi) for Marian and Monterrey, US$1. At Marian, take a path leading off from the football pitch to Quebrada de Llaca. Other rock climbs in the Huaraz area are the boulders of Huanchac, the 'Sphinx', or Torre de Parón and routes in the Rurec Valley.

Equipment Technical equipment such as rope, harness, double boots, ice hammers, helmets, crampons, carabiners, pitons, chocks and ice screws can all be hired in Huaraz quite cheaply, but they can be of poor quality.

Peruvian Mountain Guide Association (AGMP) Founded in 1980, it is housed in the *Casa de Guías* and is a member of the *International Federation of Mountain Guides Association* (IFMGA). It regulates and trains guides and the three classes of porter, which are: 1) those with some ice climbing experience, who are most useful; 2) those who carry loads only on paths, who are less useful; and 3) *arrieros* (mule drivers), cooks and camp guardians.

The AGMP also sets prices and organizes rescues, though don't rely on this. One criticism of the organization is that some of the guides only have experience on the most popular mountains such as Alpamayo and Huascarán and that its influence does not extend much beyond the Cordillera Blanca and Huayhuash. However, its continued development is a positive step.

Festival Huaraz celebrates a week-long festival of *Andinismo* at the beginning of June.

Diving
The chill of the Humboldt current puts many people off diving in the Peruvian waters

Diving off the **Paracas peninsula** is rewarding, as is the warmer tropical ocean, with larger fish, off **Tumbes**. It is also practised in the **Bahía de Pucusana**. The best season for visibility is March to November because the rivers from the mountains don't deposit silt in the sea. It can be cheap to do a *PADI* course in Peru; less than US$200 for a month's course, two weeks of theory, four dives in a pool, four in the ocean (see Lima Sports page 135).

Fishing
The coastal fishing industry, including sport fishing, has been on hard times since El Niño of 1998. Opportunities still exist, but prices are higher and success can be hard to come by. There is deep-sea fishing off **Ancón**, north of Lima, and at the small port of

Cabo Blanco, north of Talara (see page 425). In that part of the Andes easily reached from **La Oroya**, the lakes and streams have been stocked with trout, and fly fishing is quite good. Some agencies have started running fishing charters to **Lago Junín**, in the Central Highlands. The unfortunate reality is that the lake is a very important and delicate habitat for many endemic and migratory birds.

Peru offers outstanding whitewater kayaking for all standards of paddlers from novice to expert. Many first descents remain unattempted owing to logistical difficulties, though they are slowly being ticked off by a dedicated crew of local and internationally renowned kayakers. For the holiday paddler, you are probably best joining up with a raft company who will gladly carry all your gear (plus any non paddling companions) and provide you with superb food whilst you enjoy the river from an unladen kayak. There is a surprising selection of latest model kayaks available in Peru for hire from about US$10-20 a day. **Kayaking**

For complete novices, some companies offer two to three day kayak courses on the **Urubamba** and **Apurímac** that can be booked locally. For expedition paddlers, bringing your own canoe is the best option though it is getting increasingly more expensive to fly with your boats around Peru. A knowledge of Spanish is indispensable.

With its amazing diversity of trails, tracks and rough roads, Peru is surely one of the last great mountain bike destinations yet to be fully discovered. Whether you are interested in a two-day downhill blast from the Andes to the Amazon Jungle or an extended off-road journey, then Peru has some of the world's best biking opportunities. The problem is finding the routes as trail maps are virtually non-existent and the few main roads (especially the Pan-American Highway) are often congested with traffic and far from fun to travel along. Recently, however, a few specialist agencies run by dedicated mountain bikers have begun to explore the intricate web of paths, single tracks and dirt roads that criss-crosses the Andes, putting together exciting routes to suit everyone from the weekend warrior to the long-distance touring cyclist, the extreme downhiller to the casual day tripper. **Mountain biking**

Here are a few tempting statistics: 80-km dirt-road downhills; 40-km single tracks from 4,200m to 2,800m in under two hours; 550-km Trans-Andean challenges and as much hill climbing as you could ever wish for! And all just a matter of hours away from the main tourist towns.

If you are considering a dedicated cycling holiday, then it is best to bring your bike from home. It's pretty easy, just get a bike box from your local shop, deflate the tyres, take the pedals off and turn the handlebars. It is worth checking first that your airline is happy to take your bike: some are, some will want to charge. Make sure your bike is in good condition before you depart as spares and repairs are hard to come by, especially if your bike is very complicated (eg: XT V-brake blocks are virtually impossible to find and rear suspension/disc brakes parts are totally unavailable). A tip from a Peruvian mountain bike guide: take plenty of inner tubes, brake blocks, chain lube and a quick release seat. Leave all panniers at home and rely on the support vehicle whenever you get tired as there will be plenty more riding later.

If you are hiring a bike, be it for one-day or longer, the basic rule is you get what you pay for. For as little as US$5-10 a day you can get a cheap imitation of a mountain bike that will be fine on a paved road, but will almost certainly not stand up to the rigors of off-roading. For US$20-25 you should be able to find something half-decent with front shocks, v-brakes, helmet and gloves. Bear in mind that there are not many high-quality, well-maintained bikes available in Peru so you should check any hire bike thoroughly before riding it.

Choosing the right tour   When signing up for a mountain bike trip, remember that you are in the Andes so if you are worried about your fitness and the altitude, make sure you get a predominantly downhill trip. Check there is a support vehicle available throughout the entire trip, not just dropping you off and meeting you at the end. Check the guide is carrying a first aid kit, at the very least a puncture repair kit (preferably a comprehensive tool kit) and is knowledgeable about bike mechanics. Bikes regularly go wrong, punctures are frequent and people do fall off, so it is essential that your guide/company provides this minimum cover.

On longer trips ask for detailed trip dossiers, describing the ups and downs and total distances of the routes, check how much is just dirt-road (suitable for just about anyone of reasonable fitness) and how much is single-track (often demanding considerable experience and fitness). Also it is good to know what support will be provided in the way of experienced bike guides, trained bike mechanics on hand, radio communications, spare bikes provided, cooking and dining facilities, toilet facilities etc.

A list of agencies in Cusco, Huaraz, Caraz and outside Peru is given in Tour operators page 27

Where to ride   Forget the Pan-American Highway, it is kilometres long, flat, full of trucks, has a strong head wind and goes through the world's driest desert. Head instead to the Andes for big descents, big hills and a maze of (often) Inca trails, seemingly designer-made for mountain bikes.

You will also find biking details in the Lima chapter, page 134

Cusco   From a half-day downhill exploring the nearby ruins to the ultimate 550-km Andes to Amazon challenge, Cusco offers a multitude of rides to suit all abilities. Here is a selection of the rides available. All ideally require a guide as its very easy to get lost in the Andes.

Cusco Ruins tour: cheat by taking a taxi to Puka Pukara and enjoying a tarmac descent (if un-guided) via Tambo Machay, Qenqo and Sacsayhuaman (don't forget your combined entrance ticket – see page 157). Alternatively, with a guide, explore some of Cusco's less-visited ruins on the mass of old Inca tracks available only to those in the know.

Chinchero-Moray-Maras-Las Salinas-Urubamba: one of the finest one-day trips in Peru, best done with a guide as it is easy to get lost. Largely downhill on a mixture of dirt road and single track, this trip takes you to the interesting circular ruins of Moray and into the spectacular salt pans of Maras on an awesome mule track (watch out for mules!)

Huchuy Qosqo: for experts only, this unbelievable trip is best described as 'trekking with your bike'. Various routes, again hard to find, are followed by what must be one of the hairiest single tracks in the world, along the top of and down into the Sacred Valley of the Incas.

Lares Valley: this offers some incredible down and uphill options on 2-3 day circuits including a relaxing soak in the beautiful Lares hotsprings.

Abra Málaga: from 4,200m, an 80-km descent to the jungle, or, alternatively a radical Inca Trail back to Ollantaytambo, both brilliant rides.

Tres Cruces to Manu: from Pisac to Manu is a 250-km, beautiful dirt road ride offering big climbs and an even bigger (two-day) descent. A side trip to Tres Cruces to see the sunrise is a must if time permits. Be warned that the road to Manu only operates downhill every other day, so be sure to check you've got it right or else beware irate truck drivers not giving way on a very narrow road!

Cusco–Puerto Maldonado: possibly the greatest Trans-Andean Challenge on a bike: 550 km of hard work up to 4,700m and down to 230m on one of the roughest roads there is (with the odd full-on single track thrown in for good measure). Be prepared to get wet as there are a lot of river crossings, sometimes up to waist deep. Either a nine-day epic, or cheat on the hills and enjoy some of the biggest downhills out (3-4 days).

Cusco–Puno (or vice-versa): now almost totally paved, this is strictly a road ride, quite pretty but nothing spectacular (but there are some interesting sites en route, especially in Cusco Department).

Cusco–Arequipa: bumpy and dusty; you're best off getting a bus than cycling this tedious and high-altitude ride.

Extreme Mule Biking: not quite yet taking off but in its planning stages this radical sport (that will never be in the Olympics) involves trekking with your bike on a mule to the top of some really high passes and descending to inaccessible places on outrageous single tracks you probably wouldn't dream of doing at home. Experts only.

Huaraz The Callejón de Huaylas offers superb variety for mountain bikers, from one-day routes to popular attractions to longer trails through agricultural land, over bridges and into traditional villages. More demanding are the routes over the Cordillera Negra to the Pacific coast and, toughest of the lot, the energy-sapping, highly exhilarating climbs over 5,000-m passes beneath the snow peaks of the Cordillera Blanca. A typical circuit is **Huaraz-Recuay-Chavín-Huari-San Luis-Chacas-Punta Olympica** which lasts two days; or returning through **Quebrada Llanganuco**, lasting six days. Camping gear is needed. Llanganuco is also a popular one-day ride from Caraz, like **Lago Parón**, the **Cañón del Pato** and the **Puya Raimondii** plants at Winchus. The **Santa Cruz Valley** forms part of another long circuit. Local agencies can supply bikes, guides and full back-up, including driving you up some of the steepest bits if your leg muscles can't cope.

Parapenting & hang gliding

Vuelo Libre is just taking off in Peru. Flying from the coastal cliffs is easy and the thermals are good. The **Callejón de Huaylas** is more risky owing to variable thermals, crosswinds and a lack of good landing sites, but there is a strong allure to flying at 6,000 m in front of the glaciers of Huascarán. Launch sites near Huaraz are the **Puca Ventana** near the Mirador, or from **Churup-Pitec**. A better site is **Cayasbamba** near Caraz, at 3,000 m.

The area with the greatest potential is the **Sacred Valley** of Cusco which has excellent launch sites, thermals and reasonable landing sites. 45 km from Cusco is **Cerro Sacro** (3,797 m) on the Pampa de Chincheros with 550 m clearance at take-off. It is the launch site for cross-country flights over the Sacred Valley, Sacsayhuaman and Cusco. Particularly good for parapenting is the **Mirador de Urubamba**, 38 km from Cusco, at 3,650 m, with 800 m clearance and views over Pisac.

From Lima, **Pasamayo** (430 m) is a good launch zone, as are the 80-m high cliffs of the Costa Verde, which are suitable for beginners. Other possibilities are flights over the **Mantaro Valley** from near **Huancayo** (580 m clearance, launching at 4,000 m), **Cumbemayo** (850 m elevation) over the Valle de Cajamarca, or from **Majes** (850 m) over the valley at the mouth of the Colca canyon, with the possibility of seeing condors.

The season in the Sierra is May to October, with the best months being August and September. Some flights in Peru have exceeded 6,500 m.

Rafting
See specialist tour operators, page 28

Peru is rapidly becoming one of the world's premier destinations for whitewater rafting. Several of its rivers are rated in the world's top 10 and a rafting trip, be it for one or 10 days, is now high on any adventurer's "must-do" list of activities while travelling in Peru. It is not just the adrenaline rush of big rapids that attract, it is the whole experience of accessing areas beyond the reach of motor vehicles, whether tackling sheer-sided, mile-deep canyons, travelling silently through pristine rainforest, or canoeing across the stark Altiplano, high in the Andes.

Rafting in Peru is undoubtedly excellent. The country has the world's deepest canyon (the Cotahuasi in Southern Peru), the source of the world's greatest river (the Apurímac is the true source of the Amazon), rivers that flow through the world's most biologically diverse region (the Amazon basin) with the world's highest bird count, as well as the world's largest macaw lick (the Río Tambopata and Río Madre de Dios) and the world's highest concentration of condors (the Río Colca).

Before you leap in the first raft that floats by, a word of warning and a bit of advice will help you ensure that your rafting 'trip of a lifetime' really is as safe, as environmentally friendly and as fun as you want it to be.

Basically, the very remoteness and amazing locations that make Peruvian whitewater rivers so attractive mean that dealing with an emergency (should it occur) can be difficult, if not nigh-on impossible. As the sport of rafting has increased in popularity over the last few years, so too have the number of accidents (including fatalities), yet the rafting industry remains virtually unchecked. How then, do you ensure your safety on what are undoubtedly some of the best whitewater runs anywhere in South America if not the whole world?

If you are keen on your rafting and are looking to join a rafting expedition of some length, then it is definitely worth signing up in advance before you set foot in Peru. Some of the rivers mentioned below will have fewer than two or three scheduled departures a year and the companies that offer them only accept bookings well in advance as they are logistically extremely difficult to organize. If it is just a day trip, or possibly an overnighter, then you can just turn up a few days in advance and chances are there will be space on a trip departing shortly.

How do you choose your operator?   It is hoped that by 2003 the Peruvian government will have put in place new regulations governing rafting operators and their river guides. If this does come into legislation, it will mean a major shake up for the companies. The new regulations demand that Class 4+ guides hold the internationally recognized qualifications of Swift Water Rescue Technician and hold current first aid certificates. All rafting equipment will be checked regularly to ensure it meets basic safety standards, eg life jackets that actually float etc. At present there are only a few companies who meet these qualifications. See Rafting in Tour operators, page 75, for recommendations.

As with many of Peru's adventure options, it simply boils down to 'You get what you pay for' and, at the end of the day, its your life. Rafting is an inherently dangerous sport and doing it in Peru with the wrong operator can quite seriously endanger your life. If price is all that matters bear in mind the following comments: the cheaper the price, the less you get, be it with safety cover, experience of guides, quality of equipment, quantity of food, emergency back up and environmental awareness.

Often on trips you will be required to sign a disclaimer and show proof that your travel insurance will cover you for whitewater rafting. If you are unsure about it, and are planning to go rafting, it is worth checking with your insurance company before you leave, as some policies have an additional charge. When signing up you should ask about the experience of the guides or even, if possible, meet them. At present there is no exam or qualification required to become a river guide, but certain things are essential of your guide. Firstly find out about his command of English (or whatever language – there are a few German speaking guides available), essential if you are going to understand his commands. Find out about his experience. How many times has he done this particular stretch of river? Many Peruvian guides have worked overseas in the off-season, from Chile to Costa Rica, Europe and New Zealand. The more international experience your guide has, the more aware he will be of international safety practices. All guides should have some experience in rescue techniques. While most guides own a rescue knife, some pulleys and a few slings, do they really know how to extract a raft safely from a rock, or a swimmer from a dangerous location? All guides must have knowledge of First Aid. Ask when they last took a course and what level they are at.

Good equipment is essential for your safe enjoyment of your trip. If possible ask to see some of the gear provided. Basic essentials include self-bailing rafts for all but the calmest of rivers. Check how old your raft is and where it was made. Paddles should be of plastic and metal construction (some locally made wooden ones have been known to snap, but ask the operator about their paddles and policy). Helmets should always be provided and fit correctly (again, home-made fibreglass copies are an accident waiting to happen). Life jackets must be of a lifeguard-recognized quality and be replaced regularly as they have a tendency to loose their flotation. Locally made jackets look the business, but in fact are very poor floaters. Does your company provide wetsuits (some of the rivers are surprisingly cold), or, at the very least, quality Splash jackets, as the wind can cause you to chill rapidly? On the longer trips, dry bags are provided – what state are these in? How old are they? Do they leak? There is nothing worse than a soggy sleeping bag at the end of a day's rafting. Are tents provided? And most importantly (for the jungle) do the zips on the mosquito net work and is it rain proof? Does the company provide mosquito netting dining tents? Tables? Chairs? These apparent excesses are very nice when camping for some time at the bottom of a sandfly infested canyon!

Back onto First Aid: ask to see the First Aid kit and find out what is in there and, most importantly, do they know how to use it? When was it last checked? Updated? Pretty basic stuff, but if someone used all the lomotil you could come unstuck.

Food and hygiene After a tough day on the river, the last thing you want to do is get sick from the food. Good, wholesome food is relatively cheap in Peru and can make all the difference on a long trip. You pay for what you get. Ask if there's a vegetarian option. On the food preparation, simple precautions will help you stay healthy but seem to be ignored by many companies. Are all vegetables soaked in iodine before serving? Do the cooks wash their hands and is there soap available for the clients? Are the plates, pots and cutlery washed in iodine or simply swilled in the river? (Stop and think how many villages up stream use that river as their main sewage outlet.) All are simple ways to avoid getting sick. **Toilet routine**. Sadly, on the Apurímac, on certain beaches, a completely uncaring attitude by many of the companies has left a string of pink toilet paper and quantities of human excrement. Certain companies are now providing septic toilets and/or removing all excrement. This is the way forward and will, it is hoped, become a legal requirement soon. At the very least your company should provide a lighter for burning the paper and a trowel to go dig a hole. Simple rules to follow are to always go below the high-water mark so at least in the rainy season it will wash clean, always bury it good and deep and watch out when burning the paper so as not to start a fire.

Rubbish and general environmental awareness. If your company does not, make it your responsibility to encourage other members of the group to keep the campsites clean. Some campsites are becoming rubbish tips. Surely all waste brought in can just as easily be taken out, save perhaps the organic waste that should be disposed of in a suitably inconspicuous way. When camping, is a campfire really necessary? On some rivers, due to rafting companies, the drift wood supplies are critically low, forcing even the locals to cut down trees. This is an environmental disaster waiting to happen. Is it really necessary for companies to cook using wood when gas or kerosene is so readily available?

Above all it is your safety on the river that is important. Some companies are now offering safety kayaks as standard as well as safety catarafts on certain rivers. This is definitely a step in the right direction but one that is open to misuse. Sometimes safety kayakers have little or no experience of what they are required to do and are merely along for the ride, sometimes they are asked to shoot video (rendering the safety cover useless). A safety cataraft is a powerful tool in the right hands, but weigh it down with equipment and it is of little use. All companies should carry at the very least a "Wrap kit" consisting of static ropes, carabiners, slings and pulleys should a raft unfortunately get stuck. But more importantly, do the guides know how to use it?

So if all this doom and gloom has not put you off, you are now equipped to go out there and find the company that offers what you are looking for at a price you think is reasonable. Bear in mind that a day's rafting in the USA can cost between US$75-120 a day. In Peru you might get the same for just US$25 but ask yourself "What am I getting for so little". After all, rafts and equipment cost the same, in fact more, in Peru.

So where are these rivers?

Cusco region   Probably the 'rafting capital' of Peru, Cusco has more whitewater runs on offer than anywhere else in Peru.

1.) **The Urubamba**: perhaps the most popular day run in the whole country, but sadly one heavily affected by pollution both from Cusco (the Río Huatanay joins the Urubamba by Huambutio and is one of the main sewage outlets of Cusco) and from the towns of the Sacred Valley of the Incas who regularly dump their waste directly into the river. A recent clean-up campaign organized by various rafting companies removed 16 tons of rubbish, predominantly plastic bags and bottles, but it just touched the surface of the problem.

Huambutio - Pisac (all year availability, Grade 2): a scenic half-day float with a few rapids to get the adrenaline flowing right through the heart of the Sacred Valley of the Incas. Fits in perfectly with a day trip to Pisac Market. A sedate introduction to rafting for all ages.

Ollantaytambo - Chilca (all year availability, Grade 3+): a fun half-day introduction to the exciting sport of whitewater rafting with a few challenging rapids and beautiful scenery near the Inca 'fortress' of Ollantaytambo. This trip also fits in perfectly with the start of the Inca Trail. Try to go early in the morning as a strong wind picks up in the late morning.

Huaran Canyon (all year, Grade 3 -4 +): a short section of fun whitewater that is occasionally rafted and used as site of the Peruvian National Whitewater Championships for kayaking and rafting.

Santa María - Quillabamba (May-Dec, Grade 3-4): a rarely-rafted two-day, high jungle trip. A long way to go for some fairly good whitewater but mediocre jungle.

Chuquicahuana (Dec-Apr, Grade 4-5, May-Dec, Grade 2-4): in the rainy season, this is a technically demanding one-day trip for genuine adrenaline junkies. In the dry season this section makes a good alternative from the now horrendously polluted sections further downstream and provides several hours of fun, technical but not-too-demanding rapids with much cleaner water and all in a very pretty canyon.

Cusipata (Dec-Apr, Grade 3-4, May-Dec Grade 2-3): often used as a warm up section in high water before attempting Chuquicahuana, this section has fun rapids and a beautiful mini-canyon, which, in low water (May-Dec), is ideal for the fun sport of inflatable canoes (duckies). Again the water purity is much better than the lower sections.

Pinipampa (all year grade 1-2): a fun and beautiful section, rarely paddled but relatively clean – no major rapids but a fun canoeing or ducky trip for beginners. Get out at the Huambutio start point, before the Huatanay disgorges Cusco's raw sewage into the Urubamba.

Kiteni-Pongo Mainique: the bit made famous by Michael Palin: an interesting jungle gorge, but logistically hard to reach and technically pretty average except in the rainy season.

2.) **The Río Apurímac**: technically the true source of the Amazon, the Apurímac cuts a 2,000-m deep gorge through incredible desert scenery and offers probably some of the finest whitewater rafting sections on the planet.

Puente Hualpachaca - Puente Cunyac (May-Nov, Grade 4-5): three (better in four) days of non-stop whitewater adventure through an awesome gorge just 5 hours drive from Cusco. Probably the most popular multi-day trip, this is one definitely to book with the experts as there have been fatalities on this stretch. Owing to the amount of people rafting this river, some of the campsites are getting overused and dirty, but the whitewater is superb with rapids with names like *U-first*, *Tooth ache* and *Last laugh* – an adventure worth doing. As seen on ITV's "Don't try this at Home".

The Abyss: below Puente Cunyac, this is a section of rarely-run whitewater. The extreme expedition involves days of carrying rafts around treacherous rapids – a total expedition that seldom gets done.

Choquequirao: another rarely-run section, this 10 day adventure involves a walk in with mules, a chance to visit the ruins of Choquequirao and raft huge rapids in an imposing sheer-sided canyon all the way to the jungle basin. Definitely only for the experts.

3.) **The Río Chalhuanca/Pachachaca** (May-Jul, Grade 2-5): a new discovery, first descended in its entirety in May 2002 by a team from *Amazonas Explorer*, this river is best accessed from the Nazca-Abancay road that parallels its course. It has excellent whitewater potential, either in inflatable canoes or, further downstream, in larger rafts. There is an unlimited supply of every grade of whitewater you could wish for. With the roads' completion due for 2003, this route could become a popular new option for those looking for an alternative river adventure. Contact Steve Cambell at *The Rivermen Inc* (address in Tour operators, page 28) for details of a new Lima-Cusco overland adventure including rafting and canoeing on the Río Chalhuanca.

4.) **The Tambopata**, wilderness, wildlife and whitewater (Jun-Oct, Grade 3-4). The Tambopata is probably the ultimate jungle adventure for those looking to get away from the standard organized jungle package. Starting with a drive from the shores of Lake Titicaca to virtually the end of the road, the Tambopata travels through the very heart of the Tambopata-Candamo national reserve, which boasts over 1,200 species of butterfly, 800 species of birdlife and many rare mammals including, jaguar, giant otter, tapir, capybara and tayra. Four days of increasingly fun whitewater followed by two days of gently meandering through virgin tropical rainforest where silent rafts make perfect wildlife watching platforms. Finally, a visit to the world's largest macaw clay lick and a short flight out from Puerto Maldonado, this once again rarely rafted river was the subject of a BBC documentary in 1998. Definitely book in advance with the experts as this is an expedition through one of the remotest places in all South America.

5.) **Arequipa**: the Río Cotahuasi (May-Jun, Grade 4-5): a recent addition to Peruvian whitewater rivers, the Cotahuasi was only first fully explored in 1994. Since then fewer than six expeditions have been led down what is now recognized as the "World's Deepest Canyon". This is a total expedition, including a long drive in past Corupuna mountain, a two-day trek around the spectacular Sipia Falls (where the river drops 150 m into an impenetrable gorge), followed by six days of non-stop technical whitewater. The scenery is out of this world, including pre-Inca Huari culture terracing and ruins all in an incredibly deep desert canyon. Probably the best whitewater river on offer in Peru, only a handful of operators offer this trip and only one or two depart each year. Once again book early and only with companies who have the experience.

The **Río Colca** (Jun, Grade 4-5): possibly even harder than the Cotahuasi, this rarely run expedition river has had its fair share of casualties in the past. Be prepared for rocks falling off the cliffs almost continuously, sandflies, storms and out of this world whitewater. Recent seismic activity around Arequipa has caused major changes to several rapids; definitely book with the local experts.

The **Río Chile** (year round, Grade 2-4): just outside Arequipa but highly water dependent and relying on dam releases to make it worthwhile, this is fun half-day out if the heat of Arequipa is getting you down. Contact Gianmarco Vellutino at *Cusipata Tours*, T054-203966.

The **Río Majes** (all year, Grade 2-3): where the Colca emerges from its gorge it becomes the Río Majes and some day trips can be organized from Arequipa. Good fresh water shrimp make up for the pretty average whitewater.

6.) **Lima**: the **Río Cañete** (Dec-Feb only, Grade 3+): the valley of Lunahuaná is home to a handful of whitewater companies that operate only during the Lima summer. A fun weekend out but watch the sandflies.

7.) **Huaraz**: the **Río Santa** (year round, Grade 2-3): not particularly special whitewater, but in pretty surroundings. Trekking is a much better option for serious adventurers here.

8.) **Tumbes**: the **Río Tumbes**, which separates Peru and Ecuador, is a new find. With only two descents so far, *Amazonas Explorer* organizes commercial descents once a year around Christmas time to take advantage of the best weather and an unforgettable New Year on the beach. It is a fun expedition that involves four-wheel drive, trekking and rafting through a spectacular canyon in the heart of the rarely visited Amotape National Park. On their 1999 expedition, they saw the incredibly rare Tumbes crocodile (the only South American crocodile as opposed to the caiman), otters, chameleons and many rare birds. It also has the advantage of ending just a few hours from the classic beach resort of Máncora that sports some of the best surfing in the whole of Peru.

Skiing Without the aid of lifts, skiing in Peru is largely for the high altitude enthusiast. **Pastoruri**, at 5,000 m, has the only piste and holds a championship during *Semana del Andinismo* at the end of the November to June season. **Pisco**, **Vallunaraju** and **Caullaraju** are also used for skiing. **Huascarán** and **Copa** have been tackled by experienced ski-mountaineers and the eastern flank of **Coropuna** also has potential. There is, however, a high possibility of crevasses on Copa and Huascarán from November to March. Those thinking of skiing the more difficult peaks should have some technical climbing experience and a guide is recommended. The *Casa de Guías* has the names of at least eight people with skiing experience; they are not instructors but have taken groups to most peaks.

The extreme ski descent craze has hit the **Cordillera Blanca** and **Huayhuash** in a big way. Since *North Face Extreme* skied and snowboarded Artesonraju in the late 1990s, the flood gates have opened. There is practically no peak that is considered out of the question.

Most agencies in Huaraz hire out equipment for between US$12-15 per day, which includes skis, boots, poles and clothing. Snowboards can be hired for US$12.

Surfing & sea bathing Peru is a top internationally renowned surfing destination. Its main draws are the variety of wave and the year-round action. Point Break, Left and Right Reef Break and waves up to 6 m can all be found during the seasons; September to February in the north and March to December in the south, though May is often ideal south of Lima.

Ocean swells are affected by two currents; the warm El Niño in the north and the cold Humboldt current in the south arriving from Antartica. **Pimentel**, near Chiclayo, is the dividing point between these two effects but a wet suit is normally required anywhere south of Piura.

The biggest wave is at **Pico Alto** (sometimes 6 m in May), south of Lima, and the largest break is 800 m at **Chicama**, near Trujillo. There are more than 30 top surfing beaches. **North of Lima** these are: Chicama and Cabo Blanco (both highly recommended); Pimentel and Puerto Etén; Pacasmayo/El Faro; and Máncora. **South of Lima** the best beaches are: Punta Hermosa, Punta Rocas (right reef break) and Pico Alto (best in May), the pick of the bunch; Señoritas (left reef break); Caballeros (right reef break); San Bartolo; La Isla (point break); El Huaico (left reef break); Los Muelles; Cerro Azul.

International competitions are held at Pico Alto (Balin Open in May) and Punta Rocas (during the summer months). A surfing magazine *Tablista* is published in December and July and there are forecasts in the US *International Surf Report*. (See also Lima Sports section, page 135).

Peru's **Pacific coastline** is more than 3,000 km long. This desert shore is crossed by 52 rivers, which rush down from the Andes to create scores of fertile oases. The desert meets the ocean via hundreds of beaches ideal for lovers of water sports and fine seafood, as well as those who simply want to lie on the beach with a good book and soak up the sun after their adventures in Peru's highlands and rainforests. There are pristine stretches of fine white sand with palm tree backdrops, while other beaches are covered with round pebbles or surrounded by exotic mangroves. Not all beaches draw surfers to the powerful waves generated by the immense Pacific. Others offer calm waters ideal for swimming. The warmest water is to be found in northern Peru, southward from **Tumbes** on the **Ecuadorean border**. There are many bathing resorts near **Lima** (do not swim at, or even visit, these beaches alone), but they are pretty quiet when the winter fog descends. In the main, though, sunny skies are guaranteed throughout the year right the way down to **Tacna** on the Chilean frontier. Note that the current off the coast can be very strong, making it too dangerous to swim in places; enquire locally.

Trekking

Peru has some outstanding circuits around the Nevados. The best known are the **Llanganuco to Santa Cruz** loop (see page 349), the **Ausangate circuit** and a strenuous trek around the Huayhuash (see page 369). See also **Treks from Caraz** (page 355), **Treks from Carhuaz** (page 347) and **Trekking in the Cordillera Blanca** (page 331).

The other type of trekking for which Peru is justifiably renowned is walking among ruins, and, above all, for the **Inca Trail** (see page 212 and the comments on new regulations on this most popular of routes). However, there are many other walks of this type in a country rich in archaeological heritage. Some of the best are: the **valley of the Río Atuen** near Leimebamba and the entire **Chachapoyas region** (see page 453); the **Tantamayo** ruins above the Marañón; the **Cotahuasi canyon** (see page 286); and beyond Machu Picchu to **Vilcabamba** (see page 221) and **Choquequirao**. People tend to think of the Inca Trail to Machu Picchu as the only stretch of Inca roadway that can be walked. It is, however, a tiny fraction of the Incas' road network and vestiges of the Capaq Ñan (the Royal Road) can be found the length of the country. In places it is well-preserved, still in use and makes for excellent trekking. In other parts it has been lost, but new interest in the road will, it is hoped, lead to its recognition as having supreme architectural and cultural value and make it accessible for walkers and Inca enthusiasts.

Most walking is on clear trails well-trodden by *campesinos* who populate most parts of the Peruvian Andes. If you camp on their land, ask permission first and, of course, do not leave any litter. Tents, sleeping bags, mats and stoves can easily be hired in Huaraz and Cusco but check carefully for quality.

Conditions for trekking and climbing May to September is the dry season in the Cordilleras. October, November and April can be fine, particularly for trekking. Most bad weather comes from the east and temperatures plummet around twilight. The optimum months for extreme ice climbing are from late May to mid July. In early May there is a risk of avalanche from sheered neve ice layers. It is best to climb early in the day as the snow becomes slushy later on.

After July successive hot sunny days will have melted some of the main support (compacted ice) particularly on north facing slopes. On the other hand, high altitude rock climbs are less troubled by ice after July. On south facing slopes the ice and snow never consolidates quite as well.

Yachting

Yacht clubs in Lima are: *Club Regatas de Lima*, García y García 494, T429 2994; *Yacht Club Ancón*, Malecón San Martín, T488 3071; *Club Regatas Unión*, Gálvez s/n, T429 0095.

Cultural tourism

For information on specialized shamanic healing and mystical tourism, see Cusco Tour operators, page 181

This covers more esoteric pursuits such as archaeology and mystical tourism. Several of the tour operators listed on page 22 offer customized packages for special interest groups. Local operators offering these more specialized tours are listed in the travelling text under the relevant location. Cultural tourism is a rapidly growing niche market. Under the umbrella heading *Al-Tur*, **PromPerú** has 31 interesting community-based tourism projects in archaeology, agro-tourism, education, jungle trips, llama trekking, nature tourism and traditional medicine. A CD-ROM (*Turismo Vivencial – Experiential Tourism*) and information are available from *PromPeru*; see Finding out more, page 30.

Federico Kaufmann-Doig is a great for information on Peruvian archaeology, for students and archaeologists. He has worked on various sites in Peru. He is the director of the **Instituto de Arqueología Amazónica**, T449 0243, or (home) T449 9103. His book, *Historia del Perú: un nuevo perspectivo*, in two volumes (*Pre-Inca*, and *El Incario*) is available at better bookshops. The **Instituto Nacional de Cultura**, in the Museo de la Nación (see page 111), should be contacted by archaeologists for permits and information. The **Museo Nacional de Antropología y Arquelogía** in Pueblo Libre (see page 111) is the centre for archaeological investigation and the Museo de la Nación holds exhibitions.

Birdwatching

Peru is the number one country in the world for birds. Its varied geography and topography, and its wildernesses of so many different life zones have endowed Peru with the greatest biodiversity and variety of birds on earth. 18.5% of all the bird species in the world and 45% of all neotropical birds occur in Peru. This is why Peru is the best destination for birds on the continent dubbed 'the bird continent' by professional birders.

A birding trip to Peru is possible during any month of the year, as birds breed all year round. There is, however, a definite peak in breeding activity – and consequently birdsong – just before the rains come in October, and this makes it rather easier to locate many birds between September and Christmas.

Rainwear is recommended for the mountains, especially during the rainy season between December and April. But in the tropical lowlands an umbrella is the way to go. Lightweight hiking boots are probably the best general footwear, but wellingtons (rubber boots) are preferred by many neotropical birders for the lowland rainforests.

Apart from the usual binoculars, a telescope is helpful in many areas, whilst a tape recorder and shotgun microphone can be very useful for calling out skulking forest birds, although experience in using this type of equipment is recommended, particularly to limit disturbance to the birds.

The birds If your experience of Neotropical birding is limited, the potential number of species which may be seen on a three or four week trip can be daunting. A four-week trip can produce over 750 species, and some of the identifications can be tricky! You may want to take an experienced bird guide with you who can introduce you to, for example, the mysteries of foliage-gleaner and woodcreeper identification, or you may want to 'do it yourself' and identify the birds on your own. Books that cover the birds of Peru are listed on page 613.

The key sites Details of the following sites are given in the main travelling text: **Paracas National Reserve** (page 299); **Lomas de Lachay** (page 376); **Huascarán Biosphere Reserve** (page 331); **Tambopata-Candamo Reserved Zone** (page 558); **Iquitos** (page 534); **Manu Biosphere Reserve** (page 546). Some of the other birding hot-spots of Peru are listed below, but there are many more. A great 3-4-week combination is about 16 days in Manu, then 2-3 days in the highlands at Abra Málaga and 2-3 days in the Huascarán

Biosphere Reserve. A trip into the Marañón Valley (Chiclayo-Cajamarca) can be substituted for Manu; this allows access to some of the most sought-after endemics, but would produce far fewer species. More information on the birds of Peru is given in the Flora and fauna section on page 608.

Maracpomacocha and the Central Highway Maracpomacocha is an area of high Puna grass-and bog-land about four hours drive east of Lima along the Central Highway. This is high altitude birding at its extreme: a giddy 4,500 m above sea-level. As well as regular high Andean species such as Ground-tyrants, Seed-snipes and Sierra-finches, the main reason for birding is twofold: Diameded Sandpiper-plover, the almost mythical wader of the mineral-rich bogs, and White-bellied Cinclodes, perhaps the prettiest and one of the rarest of the furnarids. Both can be seen here, with a little luck. Other highlights include Giant coot on the lake at Maracpomacocha and the smart Black-breasted Hillstar, a hummingbird endemic to Peru. To reach this area, a car is essential and, if you are camping overnight, make sure that your radiator has anti-freeze (something that car-hire firms in Lima tend to forget, being in the Atacama desert!). There is no accommodation at Maracpomacocha.

Along the Central Highway from the Maracpomacocha turnoff, the well-paved road continues another 120 km to **Lake Junín**, where, with prior arrangement, it is possible to hire a boat to see the endemic Junín Flightless Grebe. The lake is a fantastic place to see all the highland waterbirds and raptors, and the surrounding fields abound with Sierra-finches and Ground-tyrants. Only very basic accommodation is available at Junín, so camping is perhaps the best option. See also page 512.

188 km further along the Central Highway is **Huánuco**, the base for exploring the Carpish Tunnel area (see also page 515). About an hour's drive northeast of Huánuco, the road passes through the Carpish range, and birding either side of the tunnel can be very productive. Powerful Woodpecker, Sickle-winged Guan and large mixed feeding flocks appear out of the mist in the epiphite-laden cloud-forest.

Chiclayo-Cajamarca circuit Starting at the coastal city of Chiclayo (see page 401), a tough but rewarding trip can be made into the deep Marañón Valley and its environs. On this route, some of Peru's birds can be found: legendary species such as Marvellous Spatuletail, Marañón Crescent-chest, Long-whiskered Owlet and Buff-bridled Inca Finch, to name but a few. Many of the species to be found along this circuit have been seen by only a handful of ornithologists.

Arequipa Using the city as a base, it is possible to see many of the specialities which inhabit the arid scrub and Polylepis woodland of the Andean west slope. The best road to bird is the one to Laguna Salinas. This large salt lake regularly holds three species of Flamingo; Chilean, Andean and Puna. It is also a good place to see Andean Avocet and Puna Plover. In the dry season, you may have to hike out towards the middle of the lake, but do not forget your sunglasses as the glare from the salt is fierce.

Between Arequipa and Laguna Salinas, birding the Polylepis-clad slopes and arid scrub can produce various earthcreepers and canasteros not found elsewhere, and this is one of only two places for Tamarugo Conebill.

One of the main reasons for birders to visit the Arequipa area is to make the trip to Cruz del Cóndor, in the Colca Canyon (see page 278).

Machu Picchu and Abra Málaga Machu Picchu (see page 207) may be a nightmare for lovers of peace and solitude, but the surrounding bamboo stands provide excellent opportunities for seeing the Inca Wren. A walk along the railway track near Puente Ruinas station can produce species which are difficult to see elsewhere. This is *the* place in Peru to see White-capped Dipper and Torrent Duck.

From Ollantaytambo (see page 204), it is only two hours' drive to one of the most accessible Polylepsis woodlands in the Andes, whilst the humid temperate forest of Abra Málaga is only 45 minutes further on. In the Polylepsis some very rare birds can be located without too much difficulty, including Royal Cinclodes and White-browed Tit-spinetail (the latter being one of the ten most endangered birds on earth). The humid temperate forest is laden with moss and bromeliads, and mixed species flocks of multi-coloured tanagers and other birds are common.

Health

Written by Dr Charlie Easmon; see Acknowled-gements for his biography

It should be no surprise that the health care in the region is varied: there are some decent private and government clinics/hospitals, which more often than not follow the more aggressive American style of medicine (where you will be referred straight to a specialist) but as with all medical care, first impressions count. If a facility is grubby and staff wear grey coats instead of white ones, then be wary of the general standard of medicine and hygiene. Its worth contacting your embassy or consulate on arrival and asking where the recommended (ie those used by diplomats) clinics are. Providing embassies with information of your whereabouts can be also useful if a friend or relative gets ill at home and there is a desperate search for you around the globe. You can also ask them about locally recommended medical do's and don'ts. If you do get ill, and you have the opportunity, you should also ask your medical insurer whether they are satisfied that the medical centre or hospital that you have been referred to is of a suitable standard.

However, before discussing the disease-related health risks involved in travel within Peru remember to try to avoid road accidents. You can reduce the likelihood of accidents by not drinking and driving, wearing a seatbelt in cars and a helmet on motorbikes, but you should be aware that others on the road may think that they are in the remake of Death Race 2000.

Ideally, you should see your GP or travel clinic at least 6 weeks before your departure for general advice on travel risks, malaria and vaccinations. Make sure you have travel insurance, get a dental check (especially if you are going to be away for more than a month), know your own blood group and if you suffer a long-term condition such as diabetes or epilepsy make sure someone knows or that you have a Medic Alert bracelet/necklace with this information on it.

Vaccinations for your Peru trip

Polio Obligatory if nil in last 10 years
Tetanus Obligatory if nil in last 10 years (but after 5 doses you have had enough for life)
Typhoid Obligatory if nil in last 3 years
Yellow Fever It is best and easiest to get vaccinated. Vaccination is recommended for travelers going outside of urban areas, most notably jungle areas below 8,200 feet (2,500 m). However, it is true that the disease risk is negligible for travel to coastal areas or to Cuzco city, Machu Picchu, any intermediate tourist points in the Urubamba Valley (the only route between Cuzco and Machu Picchu), and other Andean highland destinations such as Puno, Lake Titicaca, Arequipa, and Colca Canyon but few travelers will have a trip that does not include risk areas.
Rabies Recommended if travelling to jungle and/or remote areas
Hepatitis A Recommended as the disease can be caught easily from food and water.

If you only visit the city of Lima or the highland tourist areas (Cusco, Machu Picchu, Malaria in Peru Lake Titicaca) there is no known risk. However, all other areas except the following departments carry a risk: Arequipa, Moquegua, Puno and Tacna.

The choice of malaria drug depends on where you will travel, which type of malaria you may be exposed to, and your medical and psychological history. Always check with your doctor or travel clinic for the most up to date advice.

Mosquito repellents Remember that DEET (Di-ethyltoluamide) is the gold standard. Items to take Apply the repellent every 4-6 hours but more often if you are sweating heavily. If a with you non-DEET product is used check who tested it. Validated products (tested at the London School of Hygiene and Tropical Medicine) include Mosiguard, Non-DEET Jungle formula and non-DEET Autan. If you want to use citronella remember that it must be applied very frequently (ie hourly) to be effective. If you are popular target for insect bites or develop lumps quite soon after being bitten, carry an Aspivenin kit. This syringe suction device is available from many chemists and draws out some of the allergic materials and provides quick relief.

Sun Block The Australians have a great campaign, which has reduced skin cancer. It is called Slip, Slap, Slop. Slip on a shirt, Slap on a hat, Slop on sun screen.

Pain killers Paracetomol or a suitable painkiller can have multiple uses for symptoms but remember that more than eight paracetomol a day can lead to liver failure.

Ciproxin (Ciprofloaxcin) A useful antibiotic for some forms of travellers diarrhoea (see below).

Anti-malarials Important to take for the key areas. Specialist advice is required as to which type to take. General principles are that all except Malarone should be continued for four weeks after leaving the malarial area. Malarone needs to be continued for only seven days afterwards (if a tablet is missed or vomited seek specialist advice). The start times for the anti-malarials vary in that if you have never taken Lariam (Mefloquine) before it is advised to start it at least 2-3 weeks before the entry to a malarial zone (this is to help identify serious side-effects early). Chloroquine and Paludrine are often started a week before the trip to establish a pattern but Doxycycline and Malarone can be started only 1-2 days before entry to the malarial area. NB It is risky to buy medicinal tablets abroad because the doses may differ and there may be a trade in false drugs.

Immodium A great standby for those diarrhoeas that occur at awkward times (ie before a long coach or train journey or on a trek). It helps stop the flow of diarrhoea and in my view is of more benefit than harm. (It was believed that letting the bacteria or viruses flow out had to be more beneficial. However, with Immodium they still come out, just in a more solid form.)

Pepto-Bismol Used a lot by Americans for diarrhoea. It certainly relieves symptoms but like Immodium it is not a cure for underlying disease. Be aware that it turns the stool black as well as making it more solid.

MedicAlert These simple bracelets, or an equivalent, should be carried or worn by anyone with a significant medical condition.

For longer trips involving jungle treks taking a clean needle pack, clean dental pack and water filtration devices are common-sense measures.

Essentials

Further information

Websites   **Foreign and Commonwealth Office (FCO) (UK), www.fco.gov.uk**
This is a key travel advice site, with useful information on the country, people, climate and lists the UK embassies/consulates. The site also promotes the concept of 'Know Before You Go'. And encourages travel insurance and appropriate travel health advice. It has links to the Department of Health travel advice site, see below.

Department of Health Travel Advice (UK), www.doh.gov.uk/traveladvice
This excellent site is also available as a free booklet, the T6, from Post Offices. It lists the vaccine advice requirements for each country.

Medic Alert (UK), www.medicalalert.co.uk
This is the website of the foundation that produces bracelets and necklaces for those with existing medical problems. Once you have ordered your bracelet/necklace you write your key medical details on paper inside it, so that if you collapse, a medical person can identify you as someone with epilepsy or allergy to peanuts etc.

Blood Care Foundation (UK), www.bloodcare.org.uk
The Blood Care Foundation is a Kent-based charity "dedicated to the provision of screened blood and resuscitation fluids in countries where these are not readily available." They will dispatch certified non-infected blood of the right type to your hospital/clinic. The blood is flown in from various centres around the world.

Public Health Laboratory Service (UK), www.phls.org.uk
This site has up-to-date malaria advice guidelines for travel around the world. It gives specific advice about the right drugs for each location. It also has useful information for those who are pregnant, suffering from epilepsy or planning to travel with children.

Centers for Disease Control and Prevention (USA), www.cdc.gov
This site from the US Government gives excellent advice on travel health, has useful disease maps and details of disease outbreaks.

World Health Organisation, www.who.int
The WHO site has links to the WHO Blue Book (it was Yellow up to last year) on travel advice. This lists the diseases in different regions of the world. It describes vaccination schedules and makes clear which countries have Yellow Fever Vaccination certificate requirements and malarial risk.

Tropical Medicine Bureau (Ireland), www.tmb.ie
This Irish-based site has a good collection of general travel health information and disease risks.

Fit for Travel (UK), www.fitfortravel.scot.nhs.uk
This site from Scotland provides a quick A-Z of vaccine and travel health advice requirements for each country.

British Travel Health Association (UK), www.btha.org
This is the official website of an organization of travel health professionals.

NetDoctor (UK), www.Netdoctor.co.uk
This general health advice site has a useful section on travel and has an "ask the expert", interactive chat forum.

Travel Screening Services (UK), www.travelscreening.co.uk
This is the author's website. A private clinic dedicated to integrated travel health. The clinic gives vaccine, travel health advice, email and SMS text vaccine reminders and screens returned travellers for tropical diseases.

Books

The Travellers Good Health Guide by **Dr Ted Lankester**, ISBN 0-85969-827-0. *Expedition Medicine (The Royal Geographic Society)* Editors **David Warrell and Sarah Anderson**, ISBN 1 86197 040-4. *International Travel and Health World Health Organisation Geneva*, ISBN 92 4 158026 7. *The World's Most Dangerous Places* by **Robert Young Pelton, Coskun Aral** and **Wink Dulles** , ISBN 1-566952-140-9.

The Travellers Guide to Health (T6) can be obtained by calling the Health Literature Line   Leaflets
on T0800 555 777. Advice for travellers on avoiding the risks of HIV and AIDS (Travel Safe) available from Department of Health, PO Box 777, London SE1 6XH. The Blood Care Foundation order form PO Box 7, Sevenoaks, Kent TN13 2SZ T44-(0)1732-742427.

On the road

The greater disease risk in Peru is caused by the greater volume of disease carriers in the shape of mosquitoes and sandflies. The key viral disease is Dengue fever, which is transmitted by a mosquito that bites during the day. The disease is like a very nasty form of the 'flu with 2 -3 days of illness, followed by a short period of recovery, then a second attack of illness. Westerners very rarely get the worst haemorrhagic form of the disease. Bacterial diseases include tuberculosis (TB) and some causes of the more common traveller's diarrhoea. The parasitic diseases are many but the two key ones are malaria and South American trypanosomiasis (known as Chagas Disease). The latter kills fit, young South American footballers and was recently reported to affect three donors who had received organs from a South American women in the USA.

This is almost inevitable. One study showed that up to 70% of all travellers may suffer   Diarrhoea &
during their trip.   intestinal
    Symptoms Diarrhoea can refer either to loose stools or an increased frequency;   upset
both of these can be a nuisance. It should be short lasting but persistence beyond two weeks, with blood or pain, require specialist medical attention.
    Cures Ciproxin (Ciprofloaxcin) is a useful antibiotic for bacterial traveller's diarrhoea. It can be obtained by private prescription in the UK which is expensive, or bought over the counter in South American pharmacies. You need to take one 500mg tablet when the diarrhoea starts and if you do not feel better in 24 hours, the diarrhoea is likely to have a non-bacterial cause and may be viral (in which case there is little you can do apart from keep yourself rehydrated and wait for it to settle on its own). The key treatment with all diarrhoeas is rehydration. Try to keep hydrated by taking the right mixture of salt and water. This is available as Oral Rehydration Salts (ORS) in ready-made sachets or can be made up by adding a teaspoon of sugar and a half teaspoon of salt to a litre of clean water. Drink at least one large cup of this drink for each loose stool. You can also use flat carbonated drinks as an alternative. Immodium and Pepto-Bismol provide symptomatic relief.
    Prevention The standard advice is to be careful with water and ice for drinking. Ask yourself where the water came from. If you have any doubts then boil it or filter and treat it. There are many filter/treatment devices now available on the market. Food can also transmit disease. Be wary of salads (what were they washed in, who handled them), re-heated foods or food that has been left out in the sun having been cooked

earlier in the day. There is a simple adage that says 'wash it, peel it, boil it or forget it'. Also be wary of unpasteurized dairy products, these can transmit a range of diseases from brucellosis (fevers and constipation), to listeria (meningitis) and tuberculosis of the gut (obstruction, constipation, fevers and weight loss).

Malaria & insect bite prevention

Symptoms Malaria can cause death within 24 hours. It can start as something just resembling an attack of flu. You may feel tired, lethargic, headachy; or worse, develop fits, followed by coma and then death. Have a low index of suspicion because it is very easy to write off vague symptoms, which may actually be malaria. Whilst abroad and on return get tested as soon as possible, the test could save your life.

Cures Treatment is with drugs and may be oral or into a vein depending on the seriousness of the infection. Remember ABCD: Awareness (of whether the disease is present in the area you are travelling in), Bite avoidance, Chemoprohylaxis, Diagnosis.

Prevention This is best summarized by the B and C of the ABCD, bite avoidance and chemoprophylaxis. Wear clothes that cover arms and legs and use effective insect repellents in areas with known risks of insect-spread disease. Use a mosquito net dipped in permethrin as both a physical and chemical barrier at night in the same areas. Guard against the contraction of malaria with the correct anti-malarials (see above). Some would prefer to take test kits for malaria with them and have standby treatment available. However, the field tests of the blood kits have had poor results: when you have malaria you are usually too ill to be able to do the tests correctly enough to make the right diagnosis. Standby treatment (treatment that you carry and take yourself for malaria) should still ideally be supervised by a doctor since the drugs themselves can be toxic if taken incorrectly. The Royal Homeopathic Hospital in the UK does not advocate homeopathic options for malaria prevention or treatment.

Altitude Sickness

Symptoms This can creep up on you as just a mild headache with nausea or lethargy. The more serious disease is caused by fluid collecting in the brain in the enclosed space of the skull and can lead to coma and death. There is also a lung disease version with breathlessness and fluid infiltration of the lungs.

Cures The best cure is to descend as soon as possible.

Prevention Get acclimatized. Do not try to reach the highest levels on your first few days of arrival. Climbers like to take treatment drugs as protective measures but this can lead to macho idiocy and death. The peaks are still there and so are the trails, whether it takes you a bit longer than someone else does not matter as long as you come back down alive.

Underwater health

Symptoms If you go diving make sure that you are fit do so. The British Scuba Association (BSAC), Telford's Quay, South Pier Road, Ellesmere Port, Cheshire CH65 4FL, United Kingdom, T01513-506200, F01513-506215, www.bsac.com, can put you in touch with doctors who do medical examinations. Protect your feet from cuts, beach dog parasites (larva migrans) and sea urchins. The latter are almost impossible to remove but can be dissolved with lime or vinegar. Keep an eye out for secondary infection.

Cures Antibiotics for secondary infections. Serious diving injuries may need time in a decompression chamber.

Prevention Check that the dive company know what they are doing, have appropriate certification from BSAC or Professional Association of Diving Instructors (PADI), Unit 7, St Philips Central, Albert Rd, St Philips, Bristol, BS2 0TD, T0117-3007234, www.padi.com, and that the equipment is well-maintained.

Sun protection

Symptoms White Britons are notorious for becoming red in hot countries because they like to stay out longer than everyone else and do not use adequate sun protection. This can lead to sunburn, which is painful and followed by flaking of skin. Aloe vera gel is a good pain reliever for sunburn. Long-term sun damage leads to a loss of elasticity of skin and the development of pre-cancerous lesions. Many years later a mild or a very malignant form of cancer may develop. The milder basal cell carcinoma, if detected early, can be treated by cutting it out or freezing it. The much nastier malignant melanoma may have already spread to bone and brain at the time that it is first noticed.

Prevention Sun screen. SPF stands for Sun Protection Factor. It is measured by determining how long a given person takes to "burn" with and without the sunscreen product on. So, if it takes 10 times longer to burn with the sunscreen product applied, then that product has an SPF of 10. If it only takes twice as long then the SPF is 2. The higher the SPF the greater the protection. However, do not just use higher factors just to stay out in the sun longer. 'Flash frying' (desperate bursts of excessive exposure), as it is called, is known to increase the risks of skin cancer. Follow the Australians' with their Slip, Slap, Slop campaign.

Symptoms This disease can be contracted throughout South America. In travellers this can cause a severe 'flu-like illness which includes symptoms of fever, lethargy, enlarged lymph glands and muscle pains. It starts suddenly, lasts for 2-3 days, seems to get better for 2-3 days and then kicks in again for another 2-3 days. It is usually all over in an unpleasant week. The local children are prone to the much nastier haemorrhagic form of the disease, which causes them to bleed from internal organs, mucous membranes and often leads to their death.   **Dengue fever**

Cures The traveller's version of the disease is self limiting and forces rest and recuperation on the sufferer.

Prevention The mosquitoes that carry the Dengue virus bite during the day unlike the malaria mosquitoes. Which sadly means that repellent application and covered limbs are a 24-hour issue. Check your accommodation for flower pots and shallow pools of water since these are where the dengue-carrying mosquitoes breed.

Symptoms Hepatitis means inflammation of the liver. Viral causes of the disease can be acquired anywhere in South America. The most obvious symptom is a yellowing of your skin or the whites of your eyes. However, prior to this all that you may notice is itching and tiredness.   **Hepatitis**

Cures Early on, depending on the type of hepatitis, a vaccine or immunoglobulin may reduce the duration of the illness.

Prevention Pre-travel hepatitis A vaccine is the best bet. Hepatitis B (for which there is a vaccine) is spread through blood and unprotected sexual intercourse, both of these can be avoided. Unfortunately, there is no vaccine for hepatitis C or the increasing alphabetical list of other Hepatitis viruses.

Symptoms A skin form of this disease occurs in Peru. If infected, you may notice a raised lump, which leads to a purplish discoloration on white skin and a possible ulcer. The parasite is transmitted by the bite of a sandfly. Sandflies do not fly very far and the greatest risk is at ground levels, so if you can avoid sleeping on the jungle floor, do so. There is another rarer form which is casued by a sub species of the parasite, this affects the musocal tissues such as lips and nose. Treatment and mode of transmission are the same.   **Leishmaniasis**

Cures Several weeks treatment is required under specialist supervision. The drugs themselves are toxic but if not taken in sufficient amounts, recurrence of the disease is more likely.

Prevention Sleep above ground, under a permethrin treated net, use insect repellent and get a specialist opinion on any unusual skin lesions as soon as you can.

Schistosomiasis   A fluke is a sort of flattened worm. Schistosomiasis can be acquired through wading through stagnant water and swimming in such waters.

Symptoms   The liver fluke may cause jaundice, gall stone symptoms, right-sided abdominal pain, liver test abnormalities and changes in the white cell pattern of the blood. Schistosomiasis can cause a local skin itch at first exposure, fever after a few weeks and much later diarrhoea, abdominal pain and spleen or liver enlargement.

Cures   A single drug cures Schistosomiasis. The same dug can be used for the liver fluke but this infestation is much more difficult to treat.

Prevention   Avoid infected waters, be careful with unwashed vegetables check the CDC, WHO websites and a travel clinic specialist for up-to-date information on the whereabouts of the disease.

Chagas Disease   **Symptoms**   The disease occurs throughout South America, affects locals more than travellers, but travellers can be exposed by sleeping in mud-constructed huts where the bug that carries the parasite bites and defaecates on an exposed part of skin. You may notice nothing at all or a local swelling, with fever, tiredness and enlargement of lymph glands, spleen and liver. The seriousness of the parasite infection is caused by the long-term effects which include gross enlargement of the heart and/or guts.

Cures   Early treatment is required with toxic drugs.

Prevention   Sleep under a permethrin treated bed net and use insect repellents.

Sexual Health   Sex is part of travel and many see it as adding spice to a good trip but spices can be uncomfortable. Think about the sexual souvenirs any potential new partner may have picked up or live with. The range of visible and invisible diseases is awesome. Unprotected sex can spread HIV, Hepatitis B and C, Gonorrhea (green discharge), chlamydia (nothing to see but may cause painful urination and later female infertility), painful recurrent herpes, syphilis and warts, just to name a few. You can cut down the risk by using condoms, a femidom or avoiding sex altogether. If you do stray, consider getting a sexual health check on your return home, since these diseases are not the sort of gift people thank you for.

Lima

Introducing Lima

The well-established cliché is to call Lima a city of contradictions, but it's difficult to get beyond that description. Here you'll encounter grinding poverty and conspicuous wealth in abundance. The 8,000,000 inhabitants of this great, sprawling metropolis will defend it to the hilt and, in their next breath, tell you everything that's wrong with it. The hardships of the poor are all too evident in the lives of those struggling to get by in the crowded streets and frantic bus lanes. The rubbish-strewn districts between airport and city and, even more so, the shantytowns on the outskirts emphasize the vast divisions within society. Most visitors, though, have the option of heading for Miraflores or San Isidro, whose chic shops, bars and cafés would grace any major European city. Here smart restaurants and elegant hotels rub shoulders with pre-Inca pyramids, neat parks and the Larcomar shopping centre, built into a cliff, overlook the ocean and parapenters fly on the Pacific winds.

Lima's image as a place to avoid or quickly pass through is enhanced by the thick grey blanket of cloud that descends in May and hangs around for the next seven months, seemingly perched on top of the many skyscrapers. Wait until the blanket is pulled aside in November to reveal bright blue skies and the visitor will see a very different place. This is beach weather for all Limeños, when weekends become a very crowded raucous mix of sun, sea, salsa and ceviche at the city's more popular coastal resorts.   While Lima has the ability to incite frustration, fear and despair in equal measure it can also, given the chance, entertain, excite and inform. It boasts some of the finest historical monuments and museums in the country. The colonial centre, with its grand Plaza de Armas, fine churches and beautiful wooden balconies, is one of Peru's ten UNESCO World Heritage sites. The city's cuisine has earned it the title `Gastronomic Capital of the Americas' and the bars, discos and peñas of Barranco and Miraflores ring to the sounds of techno and traditional music, and everything in between. Scratch beneath that coating of grime and decay and you'll find one of the most vibrant and hospitable cities anywhere.

Ins and outs

Getting there
Phone code: 01
Colour map 5, grid A1
& colour map 3, grid C3

Population: 8,000,000
For fuller details see
under Transport,
page 139

All international flights land at Jorge Chávez Airport, some 16 km west of the centre of the city. It is a little further to Miraflores and Barranco. Transport into town is easy if a bit expensive. There are official taxis for which tickets are bought inside the airport building, or, the cheaper option, taxis waiting outside the airport building, but within the airport perimeter fence. For details of these and of bus services, see page 47.

If you arrive in Lima by bus, it is likely you'll pull into the main terminal at Jr Carlos Zavala, just south of the historical centre of Lima. Take a taxi to your hotel even if it's close, as this area is not safe day or night. Most of the hotels are to the west.

Getting around
The Lima public transportation system, at first glance very intimidating, is actually quite good

Downtown Lima can be explored on foot in the daytime, but take all the usual precautions. The central hotels are fairly close to the many of the tourist sites. At night taxis are a safer option. Miraflores is about 15 km south of the centre. Many of the better hotels and restaurants are located here and in neighbouring San Isidro.

There are three different types of vehicles that will stop whenever flagged down: buses, *combis*, and *colectivos*. They can be distinguished by size; big and long, mid-size and mini-vans, respectively. The flat-rate fare for any of these three types of vehicle is US$0.35. **NB** On public holidays, Sun and from 2400 to 0500 every night, a small charge is added to the fare. Always try to pay with change to avoid hassles, delays and dirty looks from the *cobrador* (driver's assistant). Routes on any public transportation vehicle are posted on *windshields* with coloured stickers. Destinations written on the side of any vehicle should be ignored.

Lima

Detail maps
A Central Lima,
page 105
B Breña,
page 124
C Miraflores,
page 118
D San Isidro,
page 116

0 km 2
0 miles 2

N

■ **Sleeping**
1 Hospedaje Huaynapicchu

2 Hostal Residencial Víctor
3 Mami Panchita

Arriving at night

Barring delays, there are usually no flight arrivals between 0100 and 0530. (There are money-changing facilities and information services to meet all flights.) However, as check-in time is supposed to be three hours before an international flight, and many flights depart from 0600 onwards, the airport starts to wake up between 0300 and 0400. No matter what time of night or day, though, there are people offering taxi rides into town and, as there are no hotels in the immediate vicinity of the airport, you must take some form of transport to get a bed and somewhere to stow your bags. Your best bet is to decide on a hotel before you even get to Lima. Most will arrange to pick you up from the airport, either free as part of the room rate, or for a fee of between US$12 and US$20 (depending on the category of hotel and how many people are in the vehicle). If you haven't arranged a room, don't leave the airport perimeter to find a public taxi or bus in the dark. The expensive remises services or the official taxis are the safest option. If you wish to stay in the airport until first light, the airport has seating areas, but you will have to leave the international arrivals zone and either take the stairs between international and national concourses, or ask if you can enter the national zone to find the seating there. The airport is safe.

Buses between Lima centre and Miraflores Av Arequipa runs 52 blocks between the downtown Lima area and Parque Kennedy in Miraflores. There is no shortage of public transport on this avenue; they have "Todo Arequipa" on the windscreen. When heading towards downtown from Miraflores the window sticker should say "Wilson/Tacna". To get to Parque Kennedy from downtown look on the windshield for "Larco/ Schell/Miraflores," "Chorrillos/ Huaylas" or "Barranco/Ayacucho".

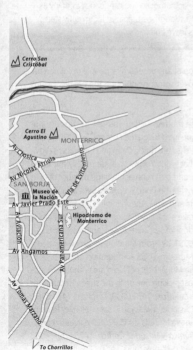

Vía Expresa Lima's only urban freeway runs from Plaza Grau in the centre of town, to the northern tip of the district of Barranco. This six-lane thoroughfare, locally known as *El Zanjón* (The Ditch), with a separate bus lane in the middle is the fastest way to cross the city. In order from Plaza Grau the 8 stops are: 1) Av México; 2) Av Canadá; 3) Av Javier Prado; 4) Corpac; 5) Av Aramburu; 6) Av Angamos; 7) Av Ricardo Palma, for Parque Kennedy; 8) Av Benavides. Buses downtown for the *Vía Expresa* can be caught on Av Tacna, Av Wilson (also called Garcilaso de la Vega), Av Bolivia and Av Alfonso Ugarte. These buses are of great interest to pickpockets who sometimes work in groups. If you're standing in the aisle, be extra careful.

Taxi Colectivos Regular private cars charging US$0.50 make this a faster, more comfortable option than municipal public transportation. There are 3 routes: 1) between Av Arequipa and Av Tacna which runs from Miraflores to the centre of Lima; 2) between Plaza San Martín and Callao; 3) between the *Vía Expresa* and the district of Chorrillos. Look for the coloured sticker

Lima

★ 24 hours in Lima

If you only have 24 hours in Lima at the beginning or end of a trip, you need to get your skates on to make the most of what the city has to offer. Don't attempt the following suggestions without taking a taxi or bus or two.

Start the day in the city centre. If your hotel doesn't do breakfast, go to the *Café Carrara* at the Hostal Roma. You will then be close to the **Plaza de Armas** with its fine, enclosed wooden balconies, great **Cathedral** and the **Government Palace**. Seek out a colonial mansion, such as the **Palacio Torre Tagle**, to see the opulence of Spanish secular architecture.

At lunchtime, you can feast royally on seafood or some other typical Peruvian dish. *El Segundo Muelle* in San Isidro is a good choice for ceviche. But you can also take the menu of the day in almost any restaurant, posh or humble, or chifa (Chinese restaurant – there are lots in Barrios Altos, like *Wa Lok*). This will set you back very little, but satisfy you well into the evening.

Lima's museums and private collections are the best in the country. Which you choose depends what you are looking for, ceramics, textiles, gold, folk art and so on. For the best overview of precolonial Peruvian history and art, visit the **Museo de la Nación**, housed in a spectacular building on Avenida Javier Prado Este, San Borja.

If you fancy a bit of a ride, take a taxi along the **Circuito de Playas**, the road at the foot of the cliffs beside the Pacific. If the sea and sky aren't merging into one on a cloudy day, late afternoon would be a good time to do this.

Las Brujas del Cachiche in Miraflores will give you a first-class blow-out for dinner, with entertainment, too. But you could do worse than spend all evening in **Barranco**. There are restaurants like *El Hornito*, where you can have pizza if you're full of local food, or *Manos Morenas*, which also has shows. The other bars, peñas and discotheques all within walking distance of each other, so you can try out as many as you choose. If you do only have a day in Lima, though, be prepared for an early start next day (or don't go to bed) as many flights leave before dawn.

posted on the windshield. These cars will stop at any time to pick people up. When full (usually 5 or 6 people) they will only stop to let someone off, then the process begins again to fill the empty space.

For prices to and from the airport, see Touching down, page 47

Taxis Meters are not used, therefore agree the fare before you get in. Tips are not expected. The South Korean company Daewoo introduced their model 'Tico' a few years back and this has become the taxi of choice. They are quick, clean and invariably yellow, but most importantly, they have seatbelts that work. Yellow taxis are usually the safest since they have a number, the driver's name and radio contact. A large number of taxis are white, but as driving a taxi in Lima (or anywhere in Peru) simply requires a windshield sticker saying "Taxi", they come in all colours and sizes. The following are taxi fares for some of the more common routes, give or take a sol. From downtown Lima to: Parque Kennedy (Miraflores), US$2. Museo de la Nación, US$2. South American Explorers, US$2. Archaeology Museum, US$2. Immigration, US$1.15. From Miraflores (Parque Kennedy) to: Museo de la Nación, US$2. Archaeology Museum, US$3. Immigration, US$2.

Official taxi companies, registered with the Municipality of Lima are without a doubt the safest option but cost much more than just picking one up in the street. Hourly rates possible. Some are *Taxi América*, T265 1960; *Moli Taxi*, T479 0030; *Taxi Real*, T470 6263; *Taxi Tata*, T274 5151; *TCAM*, run by Carlos Astacio, T983 9305, safe, reliable. Recommended, knowledgeable drivers: Hugo Casanova Morella, T485 7708 (he lives in La Victoria), for city tours, travel to airport, etc. *Mónica Velásquez Carlich*, T425 5087, T943 0796 (mob), vc_monica@hotmail.com Airport pick-ups, tours, speaks English.

i perú has offices at Jorge Chávez International Airport, T574 8000, open 24 hrs a day; **Tourist offices** Casa Basadre, Av Jorge Basadre 610, San Isidro, T421 1227/1627, Mon-Fri 0900-1830; Larcomar shopping centre, Módulo 14, Plaza Gourmet, Miraflores, Mon-Wed 1130-2000, Thu-Sun 1130-2100. *Info Perú*, Jr de la Unión (Belén) 1066, of 102, T424 7963/431 0177, infoperu@qnet.com.pe or infoperu@yahoo.com A very helpful office with lots of good advice, English, French spoken, Mon-Fri 0930-1800, Sat 0930-1400. Ask for the helpful, free, *Peru Guide* published in English by Lima Editora, T444 0815, available at travel agencies or other tourist organizations.

As much an agency as tourist office, but highly recommended nonetheless is Siduith Ferrer Herrera, CEO of **Fertur Peru**, Jr Junín 211 (main office) at the Plaza de Armas, T427 1958, T/F428 3247, fertur@terra.com.pe Open 0900-1900. Fertur also has a satellite at *Hostal España*, Jr Azangaro 105, T427 9196. Her agency not only offers up to date, correct tourist information on a national level, but also great prices on national and international flights, discounts for those with ISIC and Youth cards and *South American Explorers* members (of which she is one). Other services include flight reconfirmations, hotel reservations and transfers to and from the airport or bus stations.

South American Explorers, Piura 135, Miraflores (Casilla 3714, Lima 100), T/F445 3306 (dial 011-51-1 from USA) limaclub@saexplorers.org SAE is a non-profit educational organization which functions as a travel resource centre for South America and is widely recognized as the best place to get the most up-to-date information regarding everything from travel advisories to volunteer opportunities. Hours are Mon-Fri 0930-1700 (till 2000 on Wed) and Sat 0930-1300. A yearly membership is currently US$50 per person and US$80 per couple. Services include access to member-written trip reports, a full map room for reference, an extensive library in English and a book exchange. Members are welcome to use the SAE's PO Box for receiving post and can store luggage as well as valuables in their very secure deposit space. SAE sells official maps from the *Instituto Geografico Nacional*, SAE-produced trekking maps, used equipment and a large variety of Peruvian crafts. Note that all imported merchandise sold at SAE is reserved for members only, no exceptions. They host regular presentations on various topics ranging from jungle trips to freedom of the press. SAE also offers a discount in membership fees to researchers, archaeologists and scientists in exchange for information and/or presentations. If you're looking to study Spanish in Peru, hoping to travel down the Amazon or in search of a quality Inca Trail tour company, they have the information you'll need to make it happen. *South American Explorers*, apart from the services mentioned above, is simply a great place to step out of the hustle and bustle of Lima and delight in the serenity of a cup of tea, a magazine and good conversation with a fellow traveller. SAE has other clubhouses in Cusco, Quito (Ecuador) and Ithaca, New York. The SAE Headquarters are located in the USA: 126 Indian Creek Rd, Ithaca, NY, 14850, T607 277 0488, F607-277 6122, ithacaclub@saexplorers.org, www.saexplorers.org Official representatives in UK: *Bradt Publications*, 19 High St, Chalfont St Peters, Bucks, SL9 9QE, T01753-893444, F01753-892333, Info@bradt-travelguides.com If signing up in UK please allow 4-6 weeks for receipt of membership card.

Only 12° south of the equator, you would expect a tropical climate, but Lima has two **Climate** distinct seasons. The winter is from May-Nov, when a damp *garúa* (sea mist) hangs over the city, making everything look greyer than it is already. It is damp and cold, 8° to 15°C. The sun breaks through around Nov and temperatures rise as high as 30°C. Note that the temperature in the coastal suburbs is lower than the centre because of the sea's influence. You should protect yourself against the sun's rays when visiting the beaches around Lima, or elsewhere in Peru.

History

Lima, originally named *La Ciudad de Los Reyes*, The City of Kings, in honour of the Magi, was founded on Epiphany in 1535 by Francisco Pizarro. From then until the independence of the South American republics in the early 19th century, it was the chief city of Spanish South America. The name Lima, a corruption of the Quechua name *Rímac* (speaker), was not adopted until the end of the 16th century.

At the time of the Conquest, Lima was already an important commercial centre. It continued to grow throughout the colonial years and by 1610, the population was 26,000, of whom 10,000 were Spaniards. This was the time of greatest prosperity. The commercial centre of the city was just off the Plaza de Armas in the Calle de Mercaderes (first block of Jr de la Unión) and was full of merchandise imported from Spain, Mexico and China. All the goods from the mother country arrived at the port of Callao, from where they were distributed all over Peru and as far away as Argentina.

At this time South American trade with Spain was controlled by a monopoly of Sevillian merchants and their Limeño counterparts who profited considerably. It wasn't until the end of the 18th century that free trade was established between Spain and her colonies, allowing Peru to enjoy a period of relative wealth. Much of this wealth was reinvested in the country, particularly in Lima where educational establishments benefitted most of all.

Ever since **Francis Drake** made a surprise attack on Callao on the night of 13 February 1579, plans were made to strengthen the city's defences against the threat from English pirates. However, an argument raged over the following century between Spain and Lima as to what form the defences should take and who should pay. Finally, it was agreed to encircle the city with a wall, which was completed by 1687.

Life for the white descendants of the Spaniards was good, although *criollos* (Spaniards born in the colonies) were not allowed to hold public office in Peru. The Indians and those of mixed blood were treated as lesser citizens. Their movements were strictly controlled. They weren't allowed to live in the city centre; only in areas allocated to them, referred to as *reducciones*.

Earthquakes & wars There were few cities in the Old World that could rival Lima's wealth and luxury, until the terrible earthquake of 1746. The city's notable elegance was instantly reduced to dust. Only 20 of the 3,000 houses were left standing and an estimated 4,000 people were killed. Despite the efforts of the Viceroy, José Manso de Velasco, to rebuild the city, Lima never recovered her former glory.

During the 19th century man-made disasters rather than natural ones wreaked havoc on the capital and its people. The population dropped from 87,000 in 1810 to 53,000 in 1842, after the wars of Independence, and the city suffered considerable material damage during the Chilean occupation which followed the War of the Pacific.

Towards the 20th century Lima was built on both banks of the Rímac river. The walls erected at the end of the 17th century surrounded three sides while the Rímac bordered the fourth. By the time the North American railway engineer, Henry Meiggs, was contracted to demolish the city walls in 1870, Lima had already begun to spread outside the original limits. Meiggs reneged on his contract by leaving much of the wall intact in the poor area around Cercado, where the ruins can still be seen.

Impressions of Lima

Ever since the earthquake of 1746 all but razed the city to the ground, descriptions of Lima have tended towards the unfavourable.

Take the German naturalist and traveller, Alexander Von Humboldt, for instance, who considered life in the city to be tedious with its lack of diversions, and described touring round the capital in 1802 thus: "the filthyness of the streets, strewn with dead dogs and donkeys, and the unevenness of the ground make it impossible to enjoy." Charles Darwin, who made a short visit in 1839 during his historic research trip on the Beagle, was no less graphic in his appraisal. He found it "in a wretched state of decay; the streets are nearly unpaved and heaps of filth are piled up in all directions where black vultures pick up bits of carrion."

Rather more complimentary was Jean Jacques Tschudi, the Swiss naturalist who made extensive explorations in Peru. He wrote: "The impression produced at first sight of Lima is by no means favourable,

for the periphery, the quarter which the stranger first enters, contains none but old, dilapidated and dirty homes; but on approaching the vicinity of the principal square, the place improves so greatly that the miserable appearance it presents at first sight is easily forgotten."

The French feminist, Flora Tristan, who was Paul Gauguin's grandmother, came to Peru in 1834. She travelled extensively in the country and wrote a fascinating account of her experience, Peregrinaciones de una Paria, *in which she painted Lima in a most favourable light: "The city has many beautiful monuments," she wrote, "The homes are neatly constructed, the streets well marked out, are long and wide." Paul Gauguin himself spent his early formative years in Lima, where he was brought by his parents who were fleeing Napoleon Bonaparte's France. Towards the end of his life Gauguin wrote a collection of memoirs in which he included his impressions of Lima.*

By the beginning of the 20th century the population had risen to 140,000 and the movement of people to the coastal areas meant that unskilled cheap labour was available to man the increasing numbers of factories. Around this time, major improvements were made to the city's infrastructure in the shape of modern sanitation, paved streets, new markets and plazas. For the entertainment of the middle classes, a modern race track was opened in what is now the Campo de Marte, as well as the municipal theatre, the Teatro Segura. At the same time, the incumbent president, José Pardo, dramatically increased government expenditure on education, particularly in Lima.

Large-scale municipal improvements continued under the dictatorship of Augusto Leguía and the presidency of Oscar Benavides, who focussed on education for the masses, housing facilities for workers and low cost restaurants in the slum areas which were now growing up around Lima.

Lima, a city of over 8,000,000 people, continues to struggle to live up to its former reputation as the City of Kings. It is now very dirty and seriously affected by smog for much of the year, and is surrounded by *Pueblos Jóvenes*, or shanty settlements of squatters who have migrated from the Sierra (see box, page 145). **Modern Lima**

The city has changed drastically in the last few years. The commercial heart of Lima has begun to move away from the centre of town and has taken root in more upmarket districts such as Miraflores and San Isidro. Amid the traditional buildings which still survive soar many skyscrapers which have changed the old skyline.

▶▶ **Street names**

Several blocks, with their own names, make up a long street, a jirón (often abbreviated to Jr). You will be greatly helped by the corner signs which bear both names, of the jirón and the name of the block. The new and old names of streets are used interchangeably: remember that Colmena is also Nicolás de Piérola, Wilson is Inca Garcilaso de la Vega, and Carabaya is also Augusto N Wiese.

Sights in Central Lima

When Alberto Andrade Carmona became Mayor of Lima in 1995, he began a campaign to return the historical centre to its original beauty. This meant ejecting the *ambulantes* (street sellers), cleaning of the streets and sidewalks, and rehabilitation of the Plaza de Armas and Plaza San Martín. He also mounted a security force called *Serenazgo* to enforce public safety and order. These men are recognizable by their dark jump-suits, long night sticks, and riot gear. The municipality of Lima has also begun a time-consuming balcony restoration project, soliciting businesses and citizens to take on the financial responsibility of a balcony in need. Although many buildings in the centre are not maintained, their architectural beauty and importance is still visible and worth seeing.

Plaza de Armas

One block south of the Río Rímac lies the Plaza de Armas, which has been declared a World Heritage site by UNESCO. The plaza used to be the city's most popular meeting point and main market. Before the building of the Acho bullring in the 1760s, bullfights were traditionally held here.

Around the great Plaza de Armas stand the **Palacio de Gobierno**, the **Cathedral**, the **Archbishop's Palace**, the **Municipalidad** and the **Club Unión**. In the centre of the plaza is a bronze fountain dating from 1650. The flower beds are planted with blooms whose colours reflect the city's celebrations, eg red and white at Independence in July, purple at El Señor de los Milagros in October.

Palacio de Gobierno Palacio de Gobierno (Government Palace), on the north side of the Plaza, stands on the site of the original palace built by Pizarro. When the Viceroyalty was founded it became the official residence of the representative of the crown. Despite the opulent furnishings inside, the exterior remained a poor sight throughout colonial times, with shops lining the front facing the plaza. The façade was remodelled in the second half of the 19th century, then transformed in 1921, following a terrible fire. In 1937, the palace was totally rebuilt.

■ *The changing of the guard is at 1200. In order to take a tour of the Palace you must register at the office of public relations at Parque Pizarro, next to the Palace (ask guard for directions), a day in advance. Tours are given in Spanish and English and last 1-1½ hours, there is no charge (on a 1030 tour you get to see the changing of the guard from inside the palace).*

The Cathedral The Cathedral stands on the site of two previous buildings. The first, finished in 1555, was partly paid for by Francisca Pizarro on the condition that her father, the *Conquistador*, was buried there. A larger church, however, was soon required to complement the city's status as an Archbishopric. In 1625, the three naves of the main building were completed while work continued on the towers and main door. The new building was reduced to rubble in the earthquake of 1746 and the existing church, completed in 1755, is a reconstruction on the lines of the original.

Lima centre

Lima

Sleeping		8 Hostal España	16 Plaza Francia Inn	6 Govinda
1 El Balcón Dorado		9 Hostal Roma		7 Heydi
2 Europa		& Café Carrara	**Eating**	8 L'Eau Vive & Antaño
3 Familia Rodríguez &		10 Hostal San Martín &	1 Acllahuasy	9 Machu Picchu
Restaurant La Colmena		Restaurant San Martín	2 Chifas Fung Yen	10 Manhatten
4 Gran Hotel Continental		11 Kamana	& Capon	11 Natur
5 Gran Hotel Savoy		12 La Posada del Parque	3 Chifas Wa Lok &	12 Salon Capon
6 Granada		13 Lima Sheraton	Chun Koc Sen	
7 Hostal Belén &		14 Maury	4 Cordano	
Estrella de Belén		15 Pensión Ibarra	5 El Maurito	

Related map
A Breña, page 124

The interior is immediately impressive, with its massive columns and high nave. Also of note are the splendidly carved stalls (mid-17th century), the silver-covered altars surrounded by fine woodwork, mosaic-covered walls bearing the coats of arms of Lima and Pizarro and an allegory of Pizarro's commanders, the 'Thirteen Men of Isla del Gallo'. The assumed remains of Francisco Pizarro lie in a small chapel, the first on the right of the entrance, in a glass coffin, though later research indicates that they reside in the crypt.

There is a **Museo de Arte Religioso** in the cathedral, with free guided tours (English available, give tip), ask to see the picture restoration room. ■ *The cathedral is open to visitors Mon-Sat 1000-1430. All-inclusive entrance ticket is US$1.50. A recommended guide for the Cathedral is Patricia Cerrillo, T542 4019, English/German/French. Also Julio Torres, T475 6044.*

Archibishop's Palace & Municipalidad Next to the cathedral is the **Archbishop's Palace**, rebuilt in 1924, with a superb wooden balcony. Just behind the **Municipalidad de Lima** is **Pasaje Ribera el Viejo**, which has been restored and now is a pleasant place to hang out with several good cafés with huge terraces.

Around the centre

The Jr de La Unión, the main shopping street, runs to the Plaza de Armas. It has been converted into a pedestrian precinct which teems with life in the evening. In the two blocks south of Jr Unión, known as Calle Belén, several shops sell souvenirs and curios.

From the plaza, passing the Government Palace on the left, straight ahead is the **Desamparados** Station of the Central Railway. The name, meaning "the helpless ones", comes from the orphanage and church that used to be nearby.

The Puente de Piedra, behind the Palacio de Gobierno is a Roman-style stone bridge built in 1610. Until about 1870 it was the only bridge strong enough to take carriages across the river Rímac to the district of the same name. Though this part of the city enjoyed considerable popularity in Colonial times, it could no longer be considered fashionable.

The **Alameda de los Descalzos** was designed in the early 17th century as a restful place to stroll and soon became one of the most popular meeting places. People of all social classes would gather here for their Sunday walk, some up to the cross at the top of **Cerro San Cristóbal**. Today, however, you would be ill-advised to follow in their footsteps, as this can be a dangerous area to wander around alone. Robberies are common on Cerro San Cristóbal, so do not walk up; take a taxi (US$4.50). Worth visiting on the Alameda de los Descalzos, though, is the **Convento de los Descalzos**, founded in 1592. It contains over 300 paintings of the Cusco, Quito and Lima schools which line the four main cloisters and two ornate chapels. The chapel of El Carmen was constructed in 1730 and is notable for its baroque gold leaf altar. A small chapel dedicated to Nuestra Señora de la Rosa Mística has some fine Cusqueña paintings. Opposite, in the chapel dedicated to Señora de los Angeles, Admiral Grau made his last confession before the battle of Angamos. The museum shows the life of the Franciscan friars during colonial and early republican periods. The cellar, infirmary, pharmacy and a typical cell have been restored. The library has not yet been incorporated into the tour (researchers may be permitted to see specific books on request). ■ *Daily 1000-1300, 1500-1800, except Tue. Entrance is US$1, by guided tour only, 45 mins in Spanish, worth it. T481 0441.* Near the Alameda is the **Paseo de Aguas**, which was also popular for a Sunday stroll in days gone by. ■ *Tours can be taken by combi from in front of Santo Domingo church, through the old* barrio *of Rímac and an improved shanty town area (but still a rough area) up to the top of Cerro San Cristóbal for spectacular views over much of Lima. You pass the Inka Cola factory, too. Check the cloud level first, otherwise you will see very little. Ofistur combis depart every 15 mins, tour lasts 1 hr, Sat and Sun only, US$1.50.*

On Jr Hualgayoc is the bullring in the **Plaza de Acho**, famous for once being the largest in the world and the first in Spanish America, inaugurated on 20 January 1766. Limeños have always been great enthusiasts of bullfighting and in 1798 a royal decree had to be passed forbidding fights on Sundays as people were failing to attend mass. Next to the bullring is the **Museo Taurino**. Apart from matador's relics, the museum contains good collections of paintings and engravings, some of the latter by Goya. ■ *Hualgayoc 332, T482 3360. Mon-Sat 0800-1800. US$1; students US$0.50, photography US$2.*

July is the month when the most famous fighters come from Spain for the **Fiestas Patrias**. The season is also from October to the first week of December. Famous *toreros* practise in the Lima ring and fighting bulls are of Spanish stock.

Wedged between Avenida Abancay and Jr Ayacucho is **Plaza Bolívar**, from where General José de San Martín proclaimed Peru's independence. The plaza is dominated by the equestrian statue of the Liberator. Behind lies the Congress building which occupies the former site of the **Universidad de San Marcos**, the first University in the Americas. Founded by the Dominicans in 1551, students first began to use this building in 1574. The University now occupies other premises away from the city centre.

Plaza San Martín, south of Jr de la Unión, has a statue of San Martín in the centre. The plaza has been restored and is now a nice place to sit and relax. **Plaza Dos de Mayo** is 11/4 km to the west. About 1 km due south of this again is the circular **Plaza Bolognesi**, from which many major *avenidas* radiate.

Barrio Chino

East of the historical centre of Lima, next to the *Mercado Central* or Central Market, is Lima's Chinatown, or *barrio chino*, located within the district of Barrios Altos.

Chinese people born in Peru (referred to as "Tu-San") number more than 1,000,000

Peru is home to the largest population of first-generation Chinese in all of Latin America. The current statistic stands at around 200,000. Some of the first immigrants arrived at the port of Callao in 1849 from the Chinese provinces of Canton and Fukien to work the coastal fields, replacing the black slaves given their freedom by then-president Ramón Castilla in 1851. More Chinese began to arrive, settling in the north; Chiclayo, Trujillo and the jungle town of Iquitos.

On the seventh block of Jr Ucayali is the locally famous *Portada China*, the arch that stretches across the street and is the gateway to Chinatown. It was a gift from the Chinese government officially inaugurated by Lima mayor Alberto Andrade in July 1997. For authentic Chinese cuisine, see Eating in Central Lima, on page 127).

Gran Parque Cultural de Lima

This large park was inaugurated in January 2000 by both the mayor of Lima, Alberto Andrade, and the then President Alberto Fujimori. It has a middle-sized outdoor amphitheatre, Japanese garden, food court and children's activities. Relaxing strolls through this green, peaceful and safe oasis in the centre of Lima are recommended. ■ *At the Lima Art Museum (see Museums, page 111). 0800-2030.*

Colonial mansions

At Jr Ucayali 363, is the **Palacio Torre Tagle**, the city's best surviving specimen of secular colonial architecture. It was built in 1735 for Don José Bernardo de Tagle y Bracho, to whom King Philip V gave the title of First Marquis of Torre Tagle. The house remained in the family until it was acquired by the government in 1918. Today, it is still used by the Foreign Ministry, but visitors are allowed to enter courtyards to inspect the fine, Moorish-influenced wood-carving in the balconies, wrought iron work, and a 16th-century coach complete with commode. ■ *During working hrs, Mon-Fri, visitors may enter the patio only.* **Casa de la Rada**, or **Goyoneche**, Jr Ucayali 358, opposite, is an extremely fine mid-18th century town house in the French manner which now belongs to a bank. ■ *The patio and first reception room are open occasionally to the public.*

Another historic mansion worth visiting is the late 16th century **Casa de Jarava** or **Pilatos** opposite the San Francisco church, Jr Ancash 390. **Casa La Riva**, on Jr Ica 426, has an 18th-century porch and balconies, a small gallery with some 20th-century paintings. It is run by the Entre Nous Society. **Casa de Oquendo** or **Osambela** is at Conde de Superunda 298. It is said that José de San Martín stayed here after proclaiming independence from Spain. The house is typical of Lima secular architecture with two patios and a broad staircase leading from the first to the upper floor.

Casa de las Trece Monedas at Jr Ancash 536 was built in 1787 by Counts from Genoa, it still has the original doors and window grills.

Casa Aliaga, Unión 224, is still occupied by the Aliaga family but has been opened to the public. The house contains what is said to be the oldest ceiling in Lima and is furnished entirely in the colonial style. Don Jerónimo de Aliaga was one of the 13 commanders to arrive with Francisco Pizarro and all 13 were given land around the main square to build their own houses when Lima was founded in 1535.

AAA Theatre (Amateur Artists' Association), Jr Ica 323, is in a lovely 18th-century house with an *azaguán*, a covered area between the door and patio, a common feature in houses of this period.

Churches

La Merced The first mass in Lima was said here on the site of the first church to be built. At independence the Virgin of La Merced was made a Marshal of the Peruvian army. The restored colonial façade is a fine example of Baroque architecture. Inside are some magnificent altars and the tilework on some of the walls is noteworthy. A door from the right of the nave leads into the monastery where you can see some 18th-century religious paintings in the sacristy. The cloister dates from 1546. ■ *Church and monastery are in Plazuela de la Merced, Unión y Huancavelica. 0800-1200, 1600-2000 every day and its monastery 0800-1200 and 1500-1730 daily. T427 8199.*

Santo Domingo Built in 1549, the church is still as originally planned with a nave and two aisles covered by a vaulted ceiling, though the present ceiling dates from the 17th century. The cloister is one of the most attractive in the city and dates from 1603. The second cloister is much less elaborate. A chapel, dedicated to San Martín de Porres, one of Peru's most revered saints, leads off from a side corridor. Between the two cloisters is the Chapter House (1730), which was once the premises of the Universidad de San Marcos. Beneath the sacristy are the tombs of San Martín de Porres and Santa Rosa de Lima (see below). In 1669, Pope Clement presented the alabaster statue of Santa Rosa in front of the altar. ■ *Church and monastery is on the first block of Jr Camaná. Mon-Sat 0900-1300,1500-1800; Sun and holidays, mornings only. Entrance US$0.75. Basílica de La Veracruz is open lunchtimes. The main hall has some interesting relics. T427 6793.*

San Francisco

The baroque church, which was finished in 1674, was one of the few edifices to withstand the 1746 earthquake. The nave and aisles are lavishly decorated in the Moorish, or Mudéjar, style. The choir, which dates from 1673, is notable for its beautifully-carved seats in Nicaraguan hardwood and its Mudéjar ceiling. There is a valuable collection of paintings by the Spanish artist, Francisco de Zuburán (1598-1664), which depict the apostles and various saints.

The monastery is famous for the Sevillian tilework and panelled ceiling in the cloisters (1620). The 17th-century *retablos* in the main cloister are carved from cedar and represent scenes from the life of San Francisco, as do the paintings. A broad staircase leading down to a smaller cloister is covered by a remarkable carved wooden dome (nicknamed *la media naranja* – the half orange) dating from 1625. Next to this smaller cloister is the Capilla de la Soledad where a café is open to the public. The library contains 25,000 volumes. In the refectory, see the painting of the Last Supper in which Christ and his disciples are seated at a round table. Look for the devil at Judas Iscariot's shoulder. The Catacombs under the church and part of the monastery are well worth seeing. This is where an estimated 25,000 Limeños were buried before the main cemetery was opened in 1808. ■ *Church and monastery stand on the first block of Jr Lampa, corner of Ancash. Daily 0930-1745. Entrance US$1.50, US$0.50 children, guided tours only. T4271381.*

San Pedro

The church, finished by Jesuits in 1638, has an unadorned façade, different from any other in the city. In one of the massive towers hangs a five tonne bell called *La Abuelita* (the grandmother), first rung in 1590, which sounded the Declaration of Independence in 1821. The contrast between the sober exterior and sumptuous interior couldn't be more striking. The altars are marvellous, in particular the high altar, attributed to the skilled craftsman, Matías Maestro. The church also boasts Moorish-style balconies and rich, gilded wood carvings in the choir and vestry, all tiled throughout. The most important paintings in the church are hung near the main entrance.

In the monastery, the sacristy is a beautiful example of 17th century architecture. Also of note are La Capilla de Nuestra Señora de la O and the penitentiary. Several Viceroys are buried below. ■ *Church and monastery on the third block of Jr Ucayali. Mon-Sat 0700-1200, 1700-1800.*

Santuario de Santa Rosa

Santa Rosa is the first Saint of the Americas and Patron Saint of Lima. Born on 20 April 1586, Rosa of Lima became a member of the third Order of St Dominic and established an infirmary for destitute children and old people in her family home. She died at the age of 31 on 23 August 1617 and was beatified on 16 December 1668. 30 August is her day.

The small but graceful church was built in 1728 and contains the 'Little Doctor' image of Jesus who helped Rosa cure the sick. Beyond the church is a sanctuary where she was born and lived. There is a tiny room where she would allow herself only two hours' sleep each night on a bed of two tree trunks with stones as pillows. A chapel was later built on the site.

▶▶ A fashion for passion

A unique form of women's dress worn by Lima's upper class mestizas – women born in the colonies of Spanish origin – in the 18th century was the saya and manto. Both were of Moorish origin. The saya was an overskirt of dark silk, worn tight at the waist with either a narrow or wide bottom. The manto was like a thick, black veil fastened by a band at the back of the waist where it joined the saya. It was brought over the shoulders and head and drawn over the face so closely that only a small, triangular space was left uncovered, sufficient for one eye to peep through. This earned them the title Las Tapadas, or "covered ones".

The fashion was created by Lima's mestizas in order to compete in the flirting stakes with their Spanish-born counterparts, whose tiny waists and coquettish fan-waving was turning men's heads. The tapadas, though veiled, were by no means modest. Their skirts were daringly short, revealing their appealingly tiny feet, and necklines plunged to scandalously low levels. The French feminist, Flora Tristan, was much taken with this brazen show. She commented: "I am sure it needs little imagination to appreciate the consequences of this time-honoured practice."

One consequence of this fashion, which ensured anonymity, was that Lima's

mestizas could freely indulge in romantic trysts with their lovers. Often, however, they were content with some playful flirting – sometimes with their unwitting husbands. Another consequence of their anonymity was political. Many tapadas used their afternoon strolls to pass notes and messages to the organizers of the independence movement. This romantic and political intrigue usually took place on the Paseo de Aguas, a popular walkway of pools and gardens built by the Viceroy.

The hermitage in the garden was built by Rosa herself and she would retire there to pray alone. The well, into which she threw the key to the padlocked chain around her waist, now receives petitions from the faithful for forgiveness and thanksgivings. ■ *Santuario de Santa Rosa is on Av Tacna, first block. 0930-1300, 1500-1800 daily. Entrance to the grounds is free. T425 1279.*

Las Nazarenas Church The 18th century Las Nazarenas Church was built around an image of Christ Crucified painted by a liberated slave in the mid-16th century. In the earthquake of 1655, the church collapsed but the painting on the wall remained intact. This was deemed a miracle and the painting became the most venerated image in Lima. Together with an oil copy of El Señor de los Milagros (Lord of Miracles), the image is encased in a gold frame and carried on a silver litter – the whole weighing nearly a ton – through the streets on 18, 19, and 28 October and again on 1 November (All Saints' Day). The whole city is decked out in purple. *El Comercio* newspaper and local pamphlets give details of times and routes. ■ *On Av Tacna, fourth block. Daily 0700-1130 and 1630-2000. T423 5718.*

San Agustín's façade (1720) is a splendid example of churrigueresque archi- **San Agustín**
tecture. There are carved choir stalls and effigies, and a sculpture of Death,
said to have frightened its maker into an early grave. Since being damaged in
the last earthquake the church has been sensitively restored, but the sculpture
of Death is in storage (to protect tourists of a more nervous disposition).
■ *San Agustín is on the corner of Jr Ica and Jr Camaná, west of the Plaza de
Armas. Daily 0830-1130, 1630-1900 (ring for entry). T427 7548.*

The 18th century Jesús María on the corner of Jr Moquegua and Jr Camaná, **Jesús María**
contains some of the finest paintings and gilded Baroque altars in all of Lima.

Another church worth seeing for its two beautiful colonial doors is San **San Marcelo**
Marcelo, at Avenida de la Emancipación, fourth block. The interior is also
remarkable, particularly the 18th century gold leaf high altar and pulpit and
the religious paintings sited above attractive Sevillian tiles.

Museums

This is the anthropological and archaeological museum for the exhibition and **Museo de**
study of the art and history of the aboriginal races of Peru. There are good **la Nación**
explanations in Spanish and English on Peruvian history, with ceramics, textiles and displays of many ruins in Peru. It is arranged so that you can follow
the development of Peruvian precolonial history through to the time of the
Incas. A visit is recommended before you go to see the archaeological sites
themselves. There are displays of the tomb of the Señor de Sipán, artefacts
from Batán Grande near Chiclayo (Sicán culture), reconstructions of the
friezes found at Huaca La Luna and Huaca El Brujo, near Trujillo, and of
Sechín and other sites. Also included is the **Museo Peruano de Ciencias de la
Salud**, which has a collection of ceramics and mummies, plus an explanation
of pre-Columbian lifestyle, divided into five sections: *micuy* (Quechua for
food), *hampi* (medicine), *onccoy* (disease), *hampini* (healing) and *causay*
(life).Temporary exhibitions are held in the basement, where there is also an
Instituto de Cultura bookshop. ■ *Tue-Sun 1000-1700. US$1.75, 50% dis-
count with ISIC card. Javier Prado Este 2465, San Borja. T476 9875/9878. From
Av Garcilaso de la Vega in downtown Lima take a combi with a window sticker
that says "Javier Prado/Aviación". Get off at the 21st block of Javier Prado at Av
Aviación. From Miraflores take a bus down Av Arequipa to Av Javier Prado
(27th block), then take a bus with a window sticker saying "Todo Javier Prado" or
"Aviación". A taxi from downtown Lima or from the centre of Miraflores costs
US$2. The museum has a cafetería.*

This is the original museum of archaeology and anthropology. On display are **Museo**
ceramics of the Chimú, Nasca, Mochica and Pachacámac cultures, various Inca **Nacional de**
curiosities and works of art, and interesting textiles. The museum houses the **Antropología,**
Raimondi Stela and the Tello obelisk from Chavín, and a reconstruction of one **Arqueología**
of the galleries at Chavín. It also has a model of Machu Picchu. ■ *Tue-Sun* **e Historia**
0915-1700. US$3. Photo permit US$5. Guides are available. Plaza Bolívar in *NB Many museums*
Pueblo Libre, not to be confused with Plaza Bolívar in the centre. T463 5070. Take *are closed on Mon*
*any public transportation vehicle on Av Brasil with a window sticker saying "Todo
Brasil." Get off at the 21st block called Av Vivanco. Walk about five blocks down
Vivanco. The museum will be on your left. Taxi from downtown Lima US$2; from
Miraflores US$3. Follow the 'blue line' marked on the pavement to the Museo
Arqueológico Rafael Larco Herrera (see below), 10 mins' walk.*

▶▶ **Guilt by inquisition**

Established by Royal Decree in 1569, the Court of Inquisition was soon to prove a particularly cruel form of justice, even in the context of Spanish rule.

During its existence, the Church meted out many horrific tortures on innocent people. Among the most fashionable methods of making the accused confess their "sins" were burning, dismemberment and asphyxiation, to name but a few. The most common form of punishment was public flogging, followed by exile and the not so appealing death by burning. Up until 1776, 86 people are recorded to have been burned alive and 458 excommunicated.

Given that no witnesses were called except the informer and that the accused were not allowed to know the identity of their accusers, this may have been less a test of religious conviction than a means of settling old scores. This Kafkaesque nightmare was then carried into the realms of surreal absurdity during the process of judgement. A statue of Christ was the final arbiter of guilt or innocence but had to express its belief in the prisoner's innocence with a shake of the head. Needless to say, not too many walked free.

The Inquisition was abolished by the Viceroy in 1813 but later reinstated before finally being proscribed in 1820.

Museo Nacional de Historia is in a mansion built by Viceroy Pezuela and occupied by San Martín (1821-1822) and Bolívar (1823-1826). It is next to the Museo de Antropología y Arqueología. Take the same buses to get there. The exhibits comprise colonial and early republican paintings, manuscripts, portraits, uniforms, etc. The paintings are mainly of historical episodes. ■ *Plaza Bolívar, Pueblo Libre, T463 2009.*

Museo Arqueológico Rafael Larco Herrera Located in an 18th-century mansion, itself built on a seventh-century pre-Columbian pyramid, this museum has a collection which gives an excellent overview on the development of Peruvian cultures through their pottery. It has the world's largest collection of Moche, Sicán and Chimú pieces. There is a Gold and Silver of Ancient Peru pavilion, a magnificent textile collection and a fascinating erotica section. It is surrounded by beautiful gardens. ■ *Av Bolívar 1515, Pueblo Libre, T461 1312, www.museolarco.perucultural.org.pe Daily 0900-1800; texts in Spanish, English and French. US$4.50 (half price for students). Disabled access. Photography not permitted. Take any bus to the 15th block of Av Brasil. Then take a bus down Av Bolívar. Taxi from downtown, Miraflores or San Isidro, 15 mins, US$2-3. Follow the 'blue line' marked on the pavement to the Museo Nacional de Antropología, Arqueología e Historia (see above), 10 mins' walk.*

Museo Arqueológico Amano This very fine private collection of artefacts from the Chancay, Chimú and Nasca periods, owned by the late Mr Yoshitaro Amano, boasts one of the most complete exhibits of Chancay weaving. It is particularly interesting for pottery and pre-Columbian textiles, all superbly displayed and lit. ■ *C Retiro 160 near the 11th block of Av Angamos Oeste, Miraflores. T441 2909. Open by appointment Mon-Fri in the afternoons only. Free (photography prohibited). Take a bus or colectivo to the corner of Av Arequipa y Av Angamos and another one to the 11th block of Av Angamos Oeste. Taxi from downtown US$2; from Parque Kennedy US$1.*

This is a large collection of pottery from the Vicus or Piura culture (AD 500-600) and gold objects from Lambayeque, as well as 19th- and 20th-century paintings. Both modern and ancient exhibitions are highly recommended. ■ *Jr Ucayali at Jr Lampa, T427 6250, ext 2660. Tue-Fri 1000-1630, Sat-Sun 1000-1300. Free. Photography prohibited.*

Museo Banco Central de Reserva

This extraordinary mock Tiahuanaco façade houses a rather disjointed collection of pre-Columbian and modern artefacts, including *mate burilado* (carved gourds), *retablos*, textiles, *keros* and *huacos*. There are examples of ceramics and cloth from some Amazonian tribes and a set of watercolours by Pancho Fierro, the 19th century *costumbrista* artist. ■ *Av Alfonso Ugarte 650, Lima. T423 5892. Tue-Sun 1000-1700. US$1. Free guide in Spanish.*

Museo Nacional de la Cultura Peruana

Poli Museum is one of the best private collections of colonial paintings, silver, cloth and furniture in Peru. It also has a fine collection of pre-Columbian ceramics and gold, including material from Sipán. Guided tours are given in Spanish only and delivered rapidly by Sr Poli or his son, whose views are often contrary to long-held opinions about the symbolism of Peruvian cultures. ■ *Almte Cochrane 466, Miraflores, T422 2437. Tours cost US$10 per person irrespective of the size of the group; allow 2 hrs. Call in advance to arrange tours.*

Poli Museum

The Museo de Arte in the Palacio de la Exposición, was built in 1868 in Parque de la Exposición. There are more than 7,000 exhibits, giving a chronological history of Peruvian cultures and art from the Paracas civilization up to today. It includes excellent examples of 17th- and 18th-century Cusco paintings, a beautiful display of carved furniture, heavy silver and jewelled stirrups and also pre-Columbian pottery. ■ *9 de Diciembre (Paseo Colón) 125. T423 4732. Tue-Sun 1000-1700. US$2.30. The Filmoteca (movie club) is on the premises and shows films just about every night. See the local paper for details, or look in the museum itself. Free guide, signs in English.*

Museo de Arte

Museo de Arte Italiano is in a wonderful neo-classical building, given by the Italian colony to Peru on the centenary of its independence. Note the remarkable mosaic murals on the outside. It consists of a large collection of Italian and other European works of art, including sculpture, lithographs and etchings. The museum now also houses the Instituto de Arte Contemporáneo, which has many exhibitions. ■ *Paseo de la República 250, T423 9932. Mon-Fri 0900-1630. US$1.*

Museo de Arte Italiano

Museo de Arte Colonial Pedro de Osma A private collection of colonial art of the Cusco, Ayacucho and Arequipa schools. ■ *Av Pedro de Osma 421, Barranco, T467 0141. Tue-Sun 1000-1330, 1430-1800. US$3. Take bus 2, 54 or colectivo from Av Tacna. The number of visitors is limited to 10 at any one time.*

Museo del Tribunal de la Santa Inquisición The main hall, with a splendidly carved mahogany ceiling, remains untouched. The Court of Inquisition was first held here in 1584, after being moved from its first home opposite the church of La Merced. From 1829 until 1938 the building was used by the Senate. In the basement there is an accurate recreation *in situ* of the gruesome tortures. The whole tour is fascinating, if a little morbid. A description in English is available at the desk. ■ *Plaza Bolívar, C Junín 548, near the corner of Av Abancay. Mon-Sun 0900-1700. Free. Students offer to show you round for a tip; good explanations in English.*

Other museums

Lima

Museo de Historia Natural belongs to Universidad de San Marcos. The exhibits comprise Peruvian flora, birds, mammals, butterflies, insects, minerals and shells. ■ *Av Arenales 1256, Jesús María. T471 0117. Mon-Fri 0900-1500, Sat 0900-1700, Sun 0900-1300. US$1 (students US$0.50).*

Museo Filatélico Contains an incomplete collection of Peruvian stamps and information on the Inca postal system. There is a stamp exchange in front of the museum every Saturday and Sunday, 0900-1300. You can buy stamps here as well, particularly commemorative issues. ■ *Central Post Office, off Plaza de Armas. Mon-Sun 0815-1300, 1400-1800. No charge to enter museum.*

Museo Teatral contains a collection of mementoes and photographs of people who have appeared on the Lima stage. ■ *Teatro Segura, Jr Huancavelica 251, Lima. T426 7206. 0900-1300, 1400-1700.*

Museo de Oro del Perú y Armas del Mundo used to be on the main tourist circuit in Lima, with visitors flocking to see the huge, if chaotic collection of gold and silver pieces, as well as the collections of textiles, weaponry and military uniforms. That was until it was declared by a Congressional committee, the INC (National Institute of Culture) and Indecopi (the Tourist Protection Bureau) in 2001 that many of the objects were fakes. First estimates in July of that year said that 2,300 objects (10% of the total) were inauthentic. By September posters in the museum stated that the figure had risen to 98%. If correct, that represents fraud on a massive scale. ■ *For the record, the museum's address is 18th block of Prolongación Av Primavera (Alonzo Molina 1110), Monterrico, T345 1291.*

Lima beaches

Most beaches have very strong currents and extreme caution should be exercised. Lifeguards are not always present

Lima sits next to an open bay, with its two points at La Punta (Callao) and Punta La Chira (Chorrillos). During the summer (December-March), beaches get very crowded on weekdays as much as weekends even though all the beaches lining the Lima coast have been declared unsuitable for swimming. A stroll on the beach is pleasant during daylight hours, but when the sun goes down, the thieves come out and it becomes very dangerous. Needless to say, camping is a very bad idea.

The **Circuito de Playas**, which begins with Playa Arica (30 km from Lima) and ends with San Bartolo (45 km from Lima), has many great beaches for all tastes. If you want a beach that always is packed with people, there's **El Silencio** or **Punta Rocas**. Quieter options are **Señoritas** or **Los Pulpos**. **Punta Hermosa** has frequent surfing and volleyball tournaments.

Suburbs of Lima

San Isidro

There are many good hotels and restaurants in San Isidro (see under Sleeping, page 122 and Eating, page 125)

The district of San Isidro combines some upscale residential areas, many of Lima's fanciest hotels and important commercial zones with a huge golf course smack in the middle. Along Avenida La República is **El Olivar**, an old olive grove planted by the first Spaniards which has been turned into a beautiful park. It's definitely worth a stroll either by day or night.

See map, page 116

At Avenidas Rosario and Rivera are the ruins of **Huallamarca** – or **Pan de Azúcar** – a restored adobe pyramid of the Maranga culture, dating from about AD 100-500. There is a small site museum on the premises. ■ *US$1.75.*

North of San Isidro is the district of **Pueblo Libre** (formerly Magdalena Vieja), where the **Museo de Antropología y Arqueología**, the **Museo Arqueológico Rafael Larco Herrera** and the **Museo Nacional de Historia** are found (see under Museums, page 111). In Pueblo Libre is the church of **Santa María Magdalena**, on Jr San Martín, whose plain exterior conceals some fine ornamentation and art inside.

Parque de las Leyendas It is arranged to represent the three regions of Peru: the coast, the mountainous Sierra, and the tropical jungles of the Selva, with appropriate houses, animals and plants and children's playground. It gets very crowded at weekends. Just to the east of the park is the Universidad Católica del Perú. ■ *Daily 0900-1730. US$2. From 24th block of Av de La Marina in San Miguel, take Av Parque Las Leyendas to the entrance on Av La Mar, T464 4282. Take bus 23 or colectivo on Av Abancay, or bus 135A or colectivo from Av La Vega.*

At the intersection of Avenida Derby and Avenida Manuel Olguin in **Monterrico** is the entrance to **Daytona**, Lima's version of a North American amusement park. For *afficionados* of these types of places, Daytona will inevitably be a disappointment, but it's still a fun way to spend a weekend afternoon. There is a wide variety of fast food restaurants to choose from. The go-karts are by far the best attraction. ■ *Daily, Fri and Sat until late. US$2.*

Miraflores

Miraflores, apart from being a nice residential part of Lima is also home to a busy mercantile district full of fashionable shops, cafés, discotheques, fine restaurants and good hotels and guesthouses. In the centre of all this is the beautiful Parque Central de Miraflores – **Parque Kennedy** – located between Avenida Larco and Avenida Oscar Benavides (locally known as Avenida Diagonal). This extremely well kept park has a small open-air theatre with performances Thursday-Sunday, ranging from Afro-Peruvian music to rock'n'roll. Towards the bottom of the park is a nightly crafts market open from 1700 to 2300. Just off Avenida Diagonal across from the park is Pasaje San Ramón, better known as Pizza Street (Calle da las Pizzas). This small pedestrian walkway is full of outdoor restaurants/bars/discotheques open until the wee small hours of the morning. A very popular place to see and be seen.

See also under Sleeping, page 119, and Eating, page 125

See map page 118

At the end of Avenida Larco and running along the promenade is the renovated **Parque Salazar** and the very modern shopping centre called Centro Comercial **Larcomar**. Here the shopping centre's terraces, which have been carved out of the cliff, contain expensive shops, hip cafés and restaurants, an open-air internet café and discos. The balustrades have a beautiful view of the ocean and the sunset. The 12-screen cinema is one of the best in Lima and even has a 'cine-bar' in the twelfth theatre. Don't forget to check out the Cosmic Bowling Alley with its black lights and fluorescent balls. A few hundred metres to the north is the renovated Parque Champagnat and then, across the bridge over the gorge, the famous **Parque del Amor** where on just about any night you'll see at least one wedding party taking photos of the newly married couple. Peruvians are nothing if not romantic.

The beach, although not safe to walk at night, has a great view of the whole Lima coastline from Chorrillos to La Punta. *Rosa Náutica*, a very expensive restaurant/discotheque, see page 125, occupies a pier that juts out from the beach. A Lima dining institution for those willing to part with a nice chunk of change.

The house of the author, poet and historian **Ricardo Palma** is at Calle General Suárez 189. He is one of Peru's most famous literary figures, best known for his work *Tradiciones Peruanas*, which covers the country's colonial period (see Literature, page 598). The house is now a museum. ■ *Mon-Fri 0915-1245 and 1430-1700. Small entrance fee; photography fee US$3).*

At the intersection of Calles Borgoña y Tarapacá, near the 45th block of Avenida Arequipa, is the **Huaca Pucllana**, a 5th-8th-century AD ceremonial and administrative centre of the pre-Inca, Lima culture. The pyramid, of small adobe bricks, is 23 m high. Guided tours only in Spanish are available. It has a site museum. (See also Eating, page 125.)

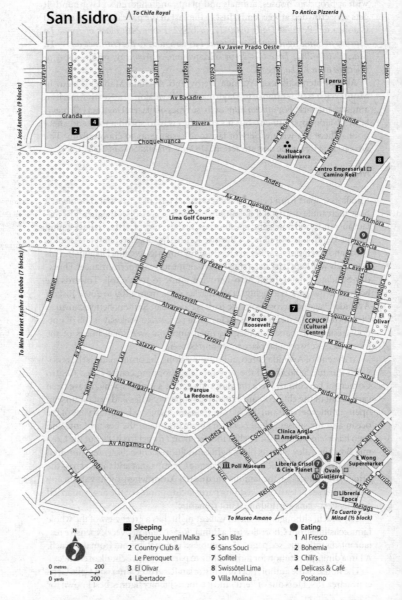

San Isidro

Sleeping ■
1 Albergue Juvenil Malka
2 Country Club & Le Perroquet
3 El Olivar
4 Libertador
5 San Blas
6 Sans Souci
7 Sofitel
8 Swissôtel Lima
9 Villa Molina

Eating ●
1 Al Fresco
2 Bohemia
3 Chili's
4 Delicass & Café Positano

Barranco

South of Miraflores is Barranco, which was already a seaside resort by the end of the 17th century. During Spanish rule, it was a getaway for the rich who lived in or near the centre. Nowadays, Barranco is something of an intellectual haven where a number of artists have their workshops.

The attractive public library, formerly the town hall, stands on the delightful plaza. Nearby is the interesting *bajada*, a steep path leading down to the beach, where many of Lima's artists live. **The Puente de los Suspiros** (Bridge of Sighs), leads towards the Malecón, with fine views of the bay.

Barranco is a quiet, sleepy suburb during the day but comes alive at night when the city's young flock here to party at weekends. Squeezed together into a few streets are dozens of good bars and restaurants (see under Eating, page 125, and Bars and clubs, page 129). No visit to Lima would be complete without a tour of Barranco's 'sights'.

An antique train wagon that discontinued its Barranco-Lima service in 1965 now offers a pleasant, albeit very short, ride (6 blocks) down Avenida Pedro de Osma to the door of the museum of the same name. There is a video on board describing the train's history. ■ *The train runs Tue-Sun from 1000 to 1700, depending on the number of passengers. Tickets can be bought at the Electricity museum (Av Pedro de Osma 105, T477 6577), US$0.70.*

Essentials

All hotels and restaurants in the upper price brackets charge **18% state tax** and **10% service** on top of prices. Neither is included in prices below, unless indicated otherwise. The central colonial heart of Lima is unsafe at night and not entirely so by day. Much safer, more comfortable and enjoyable is Miraflores, with its nostalgic streets, a good mix of places to stay, great ocean views, bookstores, restaurants and cinemas. You can then commute to the centre by bus (30-45 mins) or by taxi (20-30 mins). Consult the general Security section on page 52.

5 Le Bistrot de mes Fils
6 Matsuei
7 McDonalds
8 News Café
9 Segundo Muelle
10 TGI Friday's
11 Tierra Colombiana
12 Valentino

Lima

Miraflores

To Dino's Pizza (½ block), Ovalo
Gutiérrez (6 blocks) & C'est Si Bon
Restaurant (5 blocks)

To Madre Natura
(3 blocks)

To Museo Arqueológico
Amano & Rincón Alemán
& San Antonio Café

To Huaca
Pucllana

To Hostal Torreblanca
(1 block)

To Señorío de Sulco

To Hotel Alemán (1 block),
San Isidro & Central Lima

Santa Isabel
Supermarket

South American
Explorers

Parque
del Amor

Parque
Miranda

House of Ricardo Palma

Handicraft
Market

To Pensión Yolanda (1 block)

Mcal Oscar Benavides (Diagonal)

Parque
Kennedy

Parque
Central

Western
Union

Santa Isabel
Supermarket

Parque
Salazar

Larcomar Shopping Centre

Parque Las
Tradiciones

To Dalmacia

To Miraflores Park (4 blocks), El Rincón
Gaucho (5 blocks) & Barranco

To El Beduino
(5 blocks)

To Hotel Sipán
(2½ blocks)

Parque
Reducto

To Hospedaje José Luis
(4 blocks, turn left 3 Blocks)

0 metres   50
0 yards   50

Sleeping

1 Albergue Turístico
   Juvenil Internacional D3
2 Antigua Miraflores B1
3 Apart Hotel
   Las Américas A2
4 Ariosto D2
5 Casa de la Sra Jordan C1
6 Colonial Inn A2
7 El Carmelo &
   Restaurant Curich B1
8 El Condado C2
9 Flying Dog
   Bed & Breakfast C2

Related map
Lima, page 98

10 Friend's House C1
11 Holiday Inn C2
12 Hospedaje Atahualpa A3
13 Hostal Bellavista B2
14 Hostal El Patio C2
15 Hostal Esperanza C3
16 Hostal Huaychulo A2
17 Hostal La Castellana C2
18 Hostal Lucerna D1
19 Hostal Señorial D1
20 Imperial Inn B1
21 José Antonio C1
22 La Hacienda C1
23 La Paz Apart Hotel C2
24 Las Américas C2
25 Lex Luthor's House C1
26 Marriott D1
27 Residencial El
   Castillo Inn C3
28 San Antonio Abad D3
29 Sol de Oro C1

30 Sonesta Posada
   del Inca C2

● Eating

1 Angela's Pizzería
   y Trattoria D3
2 Astrid y Gaston C3
3 Bircher Benner C3
4 Brujas de Cachiche B1
5 Café Café B2
6 Café de la Paz B3
7 Café Voltaire B3
8 Chef's Café C2
9 Chifa Kun Fa C2
10 Dutch Sandwich Bar C1
11 El Paraíso C2
12 El Parquecito C2
13 Haiti B3
14 Heladería 4D A3
15 Il Postino B3

16 La Gloria B3
17 La Palachinke B2
18 La Tiendecita Blanca B3
19 La Tranquera B2
20 La Trattoria B3
21 Las Tejas C2
22 Pardo's Chicken D2
23 Pizza Street B2
24 Rafael C1
25 Ricota & Café Tarata C2
26 Super Rueda & Cine
   Romeo y Julieta B2
27 Tomar e Irse B2
28 Torero Sí Señor B1
29 Vivaldi B3
30 Zugatti C2

● Bars

31 Media Naranja B2
32 Murphys C2

Sleeping

LL *Las Américas*, Av Benavides 415, T444 7272, F446 0335, www.hoteleslasamericas.com Buffet breakfast included. 5-star, commercial centre, pool, gym, restaurant. **LL** *Miraflores Park*, Av Malecón de la Reserva 1035, T242 3000, F242 3393, mirapark@peruorientexpress.com.pe Price (over US$300 a night) includes tax, beautiful ocean view, excellent service and facilities, the top of the range in Lima, check with the hotel for monthly offers. Highly recommended. **LL-L** *Apart Hotel Las Américas*, C General Borgoño 116, T241 3350/3351, F447 9953. Suites equipped with kitchenette, good café, conveniently located. **LL-L** *Marriott*, Malecón de la Reserva 615, T217 7000, F217 7002, www.marriott.com Prices, which don't include tax, are 10% higher for foreigners, but buffet breakfast is included. Across from Larcomar shopping centre, wonderful views from its towers, pool, gym, two restaurants, tennis court, also has *Stellaris Casino*. **LL-L** *Sol de Oro*, Jr San Martín 305, T446 9876, F446 6676, reservas@soldeoro.com.pe Price includes tax and buffet breakfast. Secluded but central, very pleasant, with jacuzzi, sauna, room service, and laundry. **L** *El Condado*, Alcanfores 465, T444 3614, F444 1981, condado@condado.com.pe Breakfast and tax included in price. Luxury hotel with casino, sauna, gym and parking, **L** *Holiday Inn*, Av Alfredo Benavides 300, T242 3200/3191, F242 3193, www.holidayinnperu.com Price includes breakfast. A very fancy Latin version of this American chain. Some rooms have kitchenette. Gym, bar, restaurant and laundry. **L** *La Hacienda*, 28 de Julio 511 y Av Larco, T444 4346, F213 1020, reservas@bwlahacienda.com Breakfast and taxes included. English spoken, excellent service, has casino.

AL *Antigua Miraflores*, Av Grau 350 at C Francia, T241 6116, F241 6115, www.peru-hotels-inns.com A beautiful, small and elegant hotel in a quiet but central location, very friendly service, tastefully furnished and decorated, 35 rooms, gym, cable TV, good restaurant. Recommended. **AL** *Ariosto*, Av La Paz 769, T444 1414, F444 3955, ariosto@chavin.rcp.net.pe Price includes tax and buffet breakfast. Friendly, 24-hr medical assistance and all other services, airport transfer. Recommended. **AL** *Colonial Inn*, Cmdte Espinar 310, T241 7471, F445 7587, coloinn@terra.com.pe Includes breakfast and tax. Colonial style, excellent service, noisy from traffic, parking. **AL** *José Antonio*, 28 de Julio 398 y C Colón, T 445 7743, F446 8295, reservas@hoteljoseantonio.com.pe Clean, friendly, good restaurant. Recommended. **AL** *La Paz Apart Hotel*, Av La Paz 679, T242 9350, www.lapaz.com.pe Apartments with bath, kitchen, lounge, cable TV, convenient, very clean and comfortable, helpful staff. Recommended. **AL** *Sonesta Posada del Inca*, Alcanfores 329, T241 7688, F442 4345, www.sonesta.com.pe A member of this recommended chain of hotels, 28 rooms, cable TV, a/c, restaurant.

In Miraflores
■ *on map, page 118*
Price codes:
see inside front cover

Lima

A *Alemán*, Arequipa 4704, T446 4045, F447 3950, haleman@terra.com.pe No sign, comfortable, clean, friendly, quiet, garden, breakfast included, inquire about laundry service. **A** *Hostal Esperanza*, Esperanza 350, T444 2411, F444 0834, htlesperanza@terra.com.pe Breakfast and taxes included. Café, bar, TV, phone, pleasant, secure. **A** *Hostal La Castellana*, Grimaldo del Solar 222, T444 3530/4662, F446 8030. Pleasant, good value, nice garden, safe, restaurant, laundry, English spoken, 10% discount for South American Explorers (SAE) members, price includes tax. Recommended. **A** *Hostal Lucerna*, Las Dalias 276 (parallel with 12th block of Larco), T445 7321, F446 6050, hostallucerna@terra.com.pe Friendly, safe, clean, quiet, cosy, excellent value, but drinks and restaurant are expensive. Recommended. **A** *San Antonio Abad*, Ramón Ribeyro 301, T447 6766, F446 4208, www.hotelsanantonioabad.com Clean, secure, quiet, good service, welcoming, tasty breakfasts, one free airport transfer with reservation. Recommended. **A** *San Blas*, Av Arequipa 3940, T222 2601, F221 0516. Comfortable business hotel, cableTV, good restaurant. **A** *Hostal Señorial*, José González 567, T445 9724, F444 0139, senorial@viabcp.com Includes buffet breakfast, comfortable, friendly, nice garden. Recommended. **A** *Hostal Torreblanca*, Av José Pardo 1453, near the seafront, T447 0142/242 1876, F447 3363, hostal@torreblancaperu.com Includes breakfast, taxes and airport pick-u. Quiet, safe, laundry, restaurant and bar, friendly, cosy rooms, will help with travel arrangements. Recommended.

B *Hostal Bellavista de Miraflores*, Jr Bellavista 215, T/F445 7834, hostalbellavista@terra.com.pe Price includes tax, breakfast and free internet access. Excellent location, quiet, pleasant, all rooms with cable TV, can be noisy from outside at weekends. **B** *El Carmelo*, Bolognesi 749, T446 0575, carmelo@amauta.rcp.net.pe With bath and TV, great location a couple of blocks from the Parque del Amor, small restaurant downstairs. **B** *Hostal Huaychulo*, Av Dos de Mayo 494, T241 3130. Secure, helpful, German owner-manager also speaks English. **B** *Hostal El Patio*, Diez Canseco 341, T444 2107, F448 1663, hostalelpatio@qnet.com.pe Includes breakfast, reductions for long stays. Clean, comfortable, friendly, English and French spoken, convenient. **B** *Sipán*, Paseo de la República 6171, T447 0884/241 3758, F445 5298, reservas@hotelsipan.com Breakfast and tax included in price. Very pleasant, in a residential area, with bath, cable TV, fridge, security box, internet access. Free airport transfers available. **B** *Villa Molina*, B Teruel 341, T440 4018, F440 4018, villamolina@terra.com.pe Breakfast and tax included, discount for long-stay and groups. Beautiful house, quiet and friendly.

C *Hospedaje Atahualpa*, Atahualpa 646c, T447 6601. Cheaper without bath, including breakfast, long-stay rates available, parking, hot water, cooking and laundry facilities, luggage stored, taxi service. **C** *Pensión Yolanda*, Domingo Elias 230, T445 7565, pensionyolanda@hotmail.com or erwinpension@yahoo.com Price includes breakfast. English and French spoken, family house, quiet, safe, laundry, book exchange, internet and luggage store. They have travel information, can reserve flights and hotels. 25% discount for SAE members. **D** per person *Residencial El Castillo Inn*, Diez Canseco 580, T446 9501. All rooms with private bath and hot water, family home, use of lounge negotiate for longer stay. **D** per person *Casa de La Sra Jordan*, Porta 724, near Parque del Amor, T445 9840. 8 rooms, reservations required, family home, friendly, quiet. **D** *Imperial Inn*, Bolognesi 641, T445 2504, imperialinn@goalsnet.com.pe With shower, hot water, rooms are a bit dim, cable TV extra, close to Parque del Amor, good value, very friendly. Recommended. Bolognesi is a convenient street in Miraflores; opposite *Imperial Inn* are two old houses, unsigned, which serve as *hostales* in our **D** range. Just ring the bell. At weekends they are short stay, but perfectly safe and clean. **D** *Hospedaje José Luis*, Francisco de Paula Ugarriza 727, San Antonio, T444 1015, F446 7177, www.hoteljoseluis.com.pe Price

Lima

includes breakfast. Rooms with bath, hot water, safe, quiet, clean, internet, kitchen facilities, friendly, English spoken. **E** per person *Albergue Turístico Juvenil Internacional*, Av Casimiro Ulloa 328, San Antonio between San Isidro and Miraflores, T446 5488, F444 8187, hostellinginternational@terra.com.pe or www.limahostell.com.pe Youth hostel, dormitory accommodation, **C** in a double private room, US$2.50 discount for IHA card holders. Basic cafeteria for breakfasts, travel information, lounge with cable TV, cooking (minimal) and laundry facilities, swimming pool often empty, extra charge for kitchen facilities, clean and safe, situated in a nice villa. Recommended. **E** per person *Flying Dog Bed & Breakfast*, Diez Canseco 117, T445 0940, F445 2376, www.flyingdog.esmartweb.com Price includes breakfast, dormitories or private rooms, shared bath (**D** in en suite room). Central, comfortable, hot water, secure, friendly, book exchange, kitchen facilities. **F** per person *Friend's House*, Jr Manco Cápac 368, T446 6248/3521. Hot water, cable TV, use of kitchen at no cost, very popular with backpackers, near Larcomar shopping centre. Highly recommended. **F** per person *Lex Luthor's House*, Porta 550, T242 7059, luthorshouse@hotmail.com Breakfast included. Pleasant colonial house, small, basic but clean, very friendly, use of kitchen, good value.

In San Isidro
■ *on map, page 116*

LL *Country Club*, Los Eucaliptos 590, T611 9000, F611 9002, www.accesoperu.com/countryclub Excellent, fine service, luxurious rooms, safes in rooms, cable TV, free internet for guests, good bar and restaurant, classically stylish. **LL** *Sonesta El Olivar*, Pancho Fierro 194, T221 2120/2121, F221-2141, www.sonesta.com Price includes tax. Luxury, one of the top 5-star hotels in Lima, modern, restaurant, coffee shop, bar, garden, swimming pool, gym, quiet, popular with business visitors. **LL** *Swissôtel Lima*, Vía Central, Centro Empresarial Real, T421 4400, F421 4360, reservations.lima@swissotel.com Beautiful, 3 superb restaurants including *Le Café*, swimming pool, excellent 5-star service. **L** *Libertador*, Los Eucaliptos 550, T421 6666, F442 3011, www.libertador.com.pe Member of the Golden Tulip chain, overlooking the golf course, full facilities for business travellers, comfortable rooms, bar, gym, sauna, jacuzzi, fine service, good restaurant. Recommended. **L** *Sofitel Royal Park*, Av Camino Real 1050, T215 1618, www.sofitel.com Excellent rooms, charming, part of the French group, prices can be negotiated. Highly recommended.

AL *Garden Hotel*, Rivera Navarrete 450, T442 1771, F222 7175, reservas@gardenhotel.com.pe Includes tax, breakfast and internet access. Good, large beds, shower, small restaurant, ideal for business visitors, travel agency. Recommended. **A** *LimaTambo*, Av Aramburú 1025, T441 9615, F440 9584. Tax and breakfast included. Italian-owned, friendly, secure laundry service, cafetería, caters to business travellers. **B** *Sans Souci*, Av Arequipa 2670, T422 6035/441 7773, F441 7824. Breakfast and tax included. Clean, safe, friendly, good services and restaurant, garden, garage.

F *Albergue Juvenil Malka*, Los Lirios 165 (near 4th block of Av Javier Prado Este), T442 0162, T/F222 5589, hostelmalka@terra.com.pe Youth hostel, 20% discount with ISIC card, dormitory style, 4-8 beds per room, English spoken, cable TV, laundry, kitchen, nice café, climbing wall. Highly recommended.

In Barranco

D *La Quinta de Alison*, Av 28 de Julio 281, T247 1515. Breakfast extra. Lovely rooms with TV and bath, excellent value. **F** per person *Mochileros Hostal*, Av Pedro de Osma 135, 1 block from main plaza, T477 4506, www.backpackers peru.com Beautiful house but a bit scruffy, friendly English-speaking owner, shared rooms or **C** for double bed, good pub on the premises, stone's throw from Barranco nightlife. **D-E** *Safe in Lima*, Enrique Barron 440, T7282105, safeinlima.tripod.com.pe New hostal. **E** per person *Hospedaje de Osma*, Av Pedro de Osma 240, T/F251 4178, deosma@ec-red.com Exceptionally clean with comfortable rooms. **E** *The Point*, Malecón Junín 300, T247 7997, the_point_barranco@hotmail.com Popular with Israelis, internet, cable TV, backpackers' place.

B *Hostal La Posada del Parque*, Parque Hernán Velarde 60, near 2nd block of Av Petit **In Santa** Thouars, T9454260 (mob), F332 6927, www.incacountry.com Run by Sra Mónica **Beatriz** Moreno and her husband Leo Rovayo who both speak good English, a charmingly refurbished old house in a safe area, excellent bathrooms, cable TV, breakfast US$3 extra, airport transfer 24 hrs for US$14 for up to 3 passengers. Recommended as excellent value.

B *Hostal Los Q'eros*, Av Alberto Alexander 2524, T442 1224, F440 0939, **In Lince** queros@emoras.com.pe Conveniently located between centre and San Isidro, quiet area, safe, good value, discounts for long stays, price includes breakfast and transport to airport, with bath, hot water, cable TV, well-furnished, clean, English spoken (also have a house with swimming pool in Chosica). **D** *Hostal Ambassador*, Julio C Tello 650, T470 0020, cocolince@hotmail.com Clean, safe, hot water, cable TV, changes money for guests. Recommended. **E** *Hostal León Velarde*, León Velarde 210 y Mcal Miller, T471 9880. With bath and hot water, TV, parking, new.

E *Guest House Marfil*, Parque Ayacucho 126, at the 3rd block of Bolívar, T463 3161, **In Pueblo Libre** F261 1206, cosycoyllor@yahoo.com Clean and friendly, English spoken, breakfast, kitchen facilities and laundry free of charge, internet service, Spanish classes can be arranged, family atmosphere. Recommended.

C *Hostal Mami Panchita*, Av Federico Callese 198, T263 7203, F263 0749, raymi_trav- **In San Miguel** els@perusat.net.pe Dutch- Peruvian owned, English, French, Dutch, Spanish and German spoken, includes breakfast and welcome drink, comfortable rooms with bath, hot water, living room and bar, patio, email service, book exchange, have their own *Raymi* Travel agency (good service), 15 mins from airport, 15 mins from Miraflores, 20 mins from historical centre. Recommended. Several chicken places and *chifas* nearby around Mercado Magdalena.

LL *Lima Sheraton*, Paseo de la República 170, T315 5022/5023, F315 5024, **In Central Lima** reservas@sheraton.com.pe *Las Palmeras* coffee shop is good, daily buffet breakfast, ■ *on map,* good Italian restaurant, casino, all you'd expect of a 5-star hotel. *pages 3 and 105*
   A *Kamana*, Jr Camaná 547, T426 7204, F426 0790, reserva@hotelkamana.com Price includes tax. TV, comfortable, safe, French and some English spoken, very friendly staff, restaurant attached. **A** *Maury*, Jr Ucayali 201, T428 8188/8174, F426 1273, hotmaury@ amauta.rcp.net.pe Breakfast included. Fancy, secure, very clean, most luxurious hotel in the historical centre.
   B *El Balcón Dorado*, Jr Ucayali 199, T427 6028, balcondorado@hotmail.com Price includes tax, service and continental breakfast. Centrally located, very friendly, café.

B *Gran Hotel Continental*, Jr Puno 196, T427 5890, F426 1633. Price includes breakfast and is for remodelled rooms (*ejecutivo*), also basic, *económico* rooms, **C**, 24-hr room service, clean, safe. **B** *Gran Hotel Savoy*, Jr Cailloma 224, T428 3520. 210 rooms, includes taxes and breakfast. Restaurant, cafeteria, bar, laundry, airport transfer, refurbished. **B** *Hostal San Martín*, Av Nicolás de Piérola 882, Plaza San Martín, T428 5337, F423 5744, hsanmartin@goalsnet.com.pe Includes poor breakfast served in room. A/c, modern, very clean but run down, secure, friendly, helpful, safe, rooms on street very noisy, not always hot water, money changing facilities, Japanese run, good restaurant.

C *Granada*, Huancavelica 323, T/F427 9033. Includes breakfast and tax, clean, hot water, English spoken, safe, friendly, safety deposit, washing facilities. **C** *Hostal Roma*, Jr Ica 326, T/F427 7572, dantereyes@terra.com.pe With bathroom, **D** without bath, hot water all day, safe to leave luggage, basic but clean, often full, motorcycle parking (*Roma Tours*, helpful for trips, reservations, flight confirmations, Dante Reyes speaks English). Highly recommended. **D** *Estrella de Belén*, Belén 1051, T428 6462. 3-star, good service, restaurant, takes credit cards. **D-E** *Hostal de las Artes*, Jr Chota 1460, T433 0031/332 1868 (office), http://arteswelcome.tripod.com With bathroom, **F** without (no singles with bath), **G** per person in dormitory, Dutch-owned, English spoken, clean, safes in rooms and safe luggage store, friendly, nice colonial building with small garden in one patio, solar hot water system, friendly, book exchange, airport transfer US$12. Recommended.

F *Hostal Belén*, Belén 1049, just off San Martín, T4278995. Discount for groups of 3 or more but give prior notice, Italian spoken, basic breakfast extra, hot water, basic, noisy, clean, friendly. **F** *Europa*, Jr Ancash 376, T427 3351, opposite San Francisco church. Good, clean rooms with shared bathrooms, excellent hot showers, also dormitory accommodation for **G** per person, great value, friendly, popular with backpackers. Keep valuables secure. **D-E** *Hostal Iquique*, Jr Iquique 758, Breña, (discount for SAE members), T423 3699, F433 4724, http://barrioperu. terra.com.pe/hiquique With bathroom, **E** without bath, clean but noisy and draughty, friendly, use of kitchen, warm water, storage facilities, rooms on the top floor at the back are best. Repeated recommendations. **D** *Plaza Francia Inn*, Jr Rufino Torrico 1117(blue house, no sign, look for "Ecología es vida" mural opposite), near 9th block of Av Garcilaso de la Vega (aka Wilson), T330 6080, T945 4260 (mob), franciasquareinn@ yahoo.com Dormitory **E**, very clean and cosy, hot water 24 hrs, safety box in each room for each bed, kitchen and laundry facilities, airport pick up for up to 4 people US$12 (send flight details in advance), discounts for ISIC cardholders, SAE members and readers of this Handbook, same owners as *Posada del Parque*. Highly recommended.   **F** per

Breña

Map labels:
Museo de la Cultura Peruana
Turismo Chimbote
To Plaza 2 de Mayo
Cañete
Chancay
Tacna
Tinta
Zepita
Jr Quilca
Chota
Cruz del Sur Terminal
Jr Dávalos Lisson
Jr Pomabamba
Chacas
Jr Ilo
Jr Washington
Jr Carhuaz
Metro Supermarket
Av Alfonso Ugarte
Jr Chota
Av Garcilaso de la Vega Wilson
Av Venezuela
Av Uruguay
Jirón Recuay
Av Bolivia
Huanta
Quinta
Rep de Portugal
Av España
Migraciones
Paruguay
Av Arica
Breña
Plaza Bolognesi
Av 9 de Diciembre
Museo de Arte Italiano
Museo de Arte
To Hostal Machu Picchu
Don Bosco
Av Brasil
Wakrusk
Cervantes Paredes
Av Guzmán Blanco
Chota
Tarma
Huancayo
Chincha
Gregorio
Yauyos
Av 28 de Julio
To Av Arequipa, San Isidro & Miraflores

N

0 metres 100
0 yards 100

Sleeping
1 Hostal de Las Artes & Centro de Medicina Natural
2 Hostal Iquique
3 Sheraton

Eating
1 Azato
2 La Choza Náutica Cevichería

Related maps
Lima, page 98

person *Familia Rodríguez*, Av Nicolás de Piérola 730, 2nd floor, T423 6465, jotajot@terra.com.pe With breakfast, clean, friendly, popular, some rooms noisy, will store luggage, also has dormitory accommodation with only one bathroom (same price), transport to airport US$10 per person for 2 people, US$4 per person for 3 or more, good information, secure. Recommended. **F** *Pensión Ibarra*, Av Tacna 359, 14th-16th floor, T/F427 8603 (no sign), pensionibarra@ekno.com Breakfast US$2, discount for longer stay. Use of kitchen, balcony with views of the city, clean, friendly, very helpful owner, hot water, full board available (good small café next door).

  F *Hostal España*, Jr Azángaro 105, T427 9196, T/F428 5546, feertur@terra.com.pe **E** with private bath (3 rooms), **G** per person in dormitory, fine old building, shared bathroom, hot showers possible either very early or very late, friendly, run by a French-speaking Peruvian painter and his Spanish wife, English spoken, internet service, motorcycle parking, luggage store (free), laundry service, don't leave valuables in rooms, roof garden, good café, can be very busy and attention suffers. *Hostal San Francisco*, Jr Azangaro 125-127, T4262735, hostal_sanfrancisco@terramail.com.pe Dormitories with and without bathrooms, internet and cafeteria. **G** per person *Hospedaje Huaynapicchu*, Jr Pedro Ruiz 703 y Pasaje Echenique 1108, Breña, access from 11th block of Av Brazil, T431 2565, F447 9247, huaynapicc@business.com.pe Includes breakfast, shared bathroom, hot water all day, very clean, welcoming family, English spoken, internet access, laundry service, secure, great value. **G** per person *Hostal Machu Picchu*, Av Juan Pablo Fernandini 1015 (block 10 of Av Brasil), Breña, T424 3479. Family run, rooms with shared bathroom only, hot water, cheap, kitchen facilities, cable TV, laundry service, excellent value.

B *Hostal Residencial Victor*, Manuel Mattos 325, Urb San Amadeo de Garagay, Lima 31, T/F567 5107, hostalvictor@terra.com.pe 5 mins from the airport by taxi, or phone or email in advance for free pick-up, clean, large comfortable rooms, with bath, hot water, cable TV, free luggage store, American breakfast, evening meals can be ordered from local pizza or chicken places, *chifa* nearby, very helpful, owner Víctor Melgar has a free reservation service for Peru and Bolivia. Recommended. There are lots of other places to stay on Av Tomás Valle, but they are almost without exception short stay and unsafe. **Near the airport**

Miraflores: *Hostal El Patio*, see Miraflores accommodation. **Lima centre**: *Hostal de las Artes*, see Lima centre accommodation. **Barranco**: *Mochileros Backpackers*, see Barranco accommodation. **C** *Hospedaje Domeyer*, C Domeyer 296, T247 1413/1113 Friendly, clean, hot water 24 hrs, laundry service, secure. **Gay-friendly accommodation**

Eating

Expensive *Rosa Náutica*, T445 0149, built on old British-style pier (Espigón No 4), in Lima Bay. Delightful opulence, finest fish cuisine, experience the atmosphere by buying an expensive beer in the bar at sunset, open 1230-0200 daily. Highly recommended. *Astrid y Gaston*, C Cantuarias 175, T444 1496. Excellent local and international cuisine, one of the best. *Las Brujas de Cachiche*, Av Bolognesi 460, T447 1883, www.brujasdecachiche.com.pe An old mansion converted into bars and dining rooms, beautifully decorated, traditional food (menu in Spanish and English), best Lomo Saltado in town, buffets 1230-1430 daily except Sat, live *criollo* music. Highly recommended. *Café Voltaire*, Av Dos de Mayo 220, T447 4807. International cuisine with emphasis on French dishes, beautifully cooked food, pleasant ambience, good service. Closed Sun. *Cuarto y Mitad*, Av Espinar 798, T446 2988. Popular Grill. *La Gloria*, C Atahualpa 201, T446 6504, lagloriarest@terra.com.pe Very smart, excellent food and service. *Huaca Pucllana*, Gral Borgoña cuadra 8 s/n, alt cuadra 45 Av Arequipa, T445 4042. Facing the archaeological site of the same name, contemporary Peruvian fusion cooking, very good food in an unusual setting. *Rafael*, San Martín 300, T242 4149. International food, modern decor, **In Miraflores**
● *on map page 118*

nice couches. *Rincón Alemán*, Av Santa Cruz 982, T422 1562. Typical German food, authentic and good. *El Rincón Gaucho*, Av Armendáriz 580, T447 4778. Good grill. *Las Tejas*, Diez Canseco 340, T444 4360. Open 1100-2300 daily, good, typical Peruvian food. *La Tranquera*, Av Pardo 285, T447 5111. Argentine-owned steak house, very good but very expensive. *La Trattoria*, C Manuel Bonilla 106, 1 block from Parque Kennedy, T446 7002. Italian cuisine, popular, best cheesecake in Lima. *Señorío de Sulco*, Malecón Cisneros 1470, T441 0398. Excellent Creole cuisine. Recommended.

Mid-range *Angela's Pizzería y Trattoria*, Tarata 299. Excellent breakfast, lunch and dinner in nice surroundings. *Bohemia*, Av Santa Cruz 805, on the Ovalo Gutiérrez, T445 0889. Large menu of international food, great salads and sandwiches. Highly recommended. Also at Av El Polo 706, p 2, T435 9924 and at Pasaje Nicolás de Rivera 142, opposite the main post office near the Plaza de Armas, Lima centre, T427 5537. *Curich*, Bolognesi 755. Run by painter and musician Tony Curich, great home-made food, lunch specials, piano concerts nightly, poetry readings, traditional atmosphere, an institution. *Dalmacia*, C San Fernando 401, T445 7917. Spanish-owned, casual gourmet restaurant, excellent. Highly recommended. *El Beduino*, Av 28 de Julio 1301, T445 9048. Good, authentic Arabic food. *Chifa Kun Fa*, C San Martin 459 at Av Larco, T213 4200. Great Peruvian style Chinese food, excellent wan-tan soup. *Makoto Sushi Bar*, Larcomar shopping centre, T444 5030, also at Las Casas 145, San Isidro. Very good. *Il Postino*, C Colina 401, T446 8381. Great Italian food. *La Palachinke*, Av Schell 120 at the bottom of Parque Kennedy, T447 2601. Recommended for pancakes. *Torero Sí Señor*, Av Angamos Oeste 598, T446 5150. Spanish food, fun, loud. Also at Bolognesi 706, T445 3789. Mexican version of same restaurant.

Cheap *Dino's Pizza*, Av Comandante Espinar 374 (and many other branches), T242 0606, www.pizza.com.pe Great pizza at a good price, delivery service. *El Parquecito*, C Diez Canseco 150. Good cheap menu. *Pardo's Chicken*, Av Benavides 730, T446 4790. Chicken and chips, very good and popular (branches throughout Lima). *Ricota*, Pasaje Tarata 248, T445 2947. Charming café on a pedestrian walkway, huge menu, big portions, friendly. Recommended. On the same street, *Café Tarata*, No 260. Good atmosphere, family-run, good varied menu. *Sandwich.com*, Av Diagonal 234. Good, cheap sandwiches. *Super Rueda*, C Porta 133, near the Cine Julieta, T444 5609, also Av Pardo 1224. Mexican food à la Peru. *Dutch Sandwich Bar*, Grau 120. Sandwiches, not surprisingly, and Heineken beer. For cakes and sweets, *C'est si bon*, Av Comandante Espinar 663, T446 9310. Excellent cakes by the slice or whole, best in Lima. There are various small restaurants good for a cheap set meal along C Los Pinos with Av Schell, at the bottom of Parque Kennedy. C San Ramón, more commonly known as Pizza Street (across from Parque Kennedy), is a pedestrian walkway lined with restaurants specializing in Italian food. Very popular and open all night at weekends.

In San Isidro
● *on map 116*

Expensive *Antica Pizzería*, Av Dos de Mayo 728, T222 8437. Very popular, great ambience, excellent food, Italian owner. Also in Barranco at Alfonso Ugarte 242, T247 3443, and an excellent bar with a limited range of food at Conquistadores cuadra 6, San Isidro, very good value, fashionable, get there early for a seat. *Le Bistrot de mes Fils*, Av Conquistadores 510, T422 6308. Cosy French Bistrot, great food. *Chifa Royal*, Av Prescott 231, T421 0874. Excellent Sino-Peruvian food. *José Antonio*, C Bernardo Monteagudo 200, T264 0188, j-antonio@amauta.rcp.net.pe Creole and Peruvian dishes. *Matsuei*, C Manuel Bañon 260, T422 4323. Sushi bar and Japanese dishes, popular. *Le Perroquet*, *Hotel Country Club*, Los Eucaliptos 590, T211 9000. Formal and expensive, good. *Valentino*, C Manuel Bañon 215, T441 6174. One of Lima's best international restaurants.

Mid-range *Al Fresco*, C Santa Lucía 295, T422 8915. Seafood and *ceviche*, good cheap *sushi*. *Chilis*, Ovalo Gutiérrez, T222 8917. American chain with a Peruvian twist. *Segundo Muelle*, Av Conquistadores 490, T421 1206, Av Canaval y Moreyra (aka Corpac) 605, T224 3007, and Malecón Miraflores, by Parque del Amor. Excellent ceviche, younger crowd. Highly recommended. *Tierra Colombiana*, Av Conquistadores 585, T441 4705. Typical dishes from Colombia, good.

Cheap *Delicass*, C Miguel Dasso 133, T445 7917. Great deli with imported meats and cheeses, open late, slow service. Recommended. *MiniMarket Kasher*, Av Pezet 1472, T264 2187. Kosher products, excellent, cheap *chala* bread every Fri. *Qubba*, Av Salaverry 3230, next to Swiss Embassy. Delicious set lunches for US$3.30, crowded after 1300.

Snack for free by taking advantage of the free tastings at super- markets(eg Wong on Tue)

In Barranco

Canta Rana, Génova 101, T477 8934. Open daily 1200-1700, good ceviche but expensive, small portions. *La Costa Verde*, on Barranquito beach, T247 1244. Excellent fish and wine, expensive but recommended as the best by Limeños, open 1200-2400 daily, Sun buffet. *Domino's*, Av Grau 276. Open late, especially at the weekend, does 2-for-1 offer on big pizzas, Tue and Thu. *Festín*, Av Grau 323, T247 7218. Huge menu, typical and international food. *El Hornito*, Av Grau 209, on corner of the main plaza, T477 2465. Pizzería and creole food. *Manos Morenas*, Av Pedro de Osma 409, T467 0421. Open 1230-1630, 1900-2300, creole cuisine with shows some evenings (cover charge for shows). *Las Mesitas*, Av Grau 341, T477 4199. Creole food and old sweet dishes which you won't find anywhere else. Recommended. *Naylamp*, Av 2 de Mayo 239, T467 5011. Good seafood and ceviche, fashionable, expensive. Try also various smaller restaurants under the Bridge of Sighs and down towards cliff tops, open late, great cheap Peruvian food (eg *anticuchos*).

In Chorrillos

Costa Sur, Av Chorrillos 180, T251 2497. Typical Peruvian dishes, good value, try the *causa* with crab. Recommended. *El Hawaiano* Av Guardia Civil 323, T467 0317, also at Rep de Panamá 258, Barranco. Excellent daily buffet (US$16), lunch only, expensive but well worth it. *Punta Arenas*, Santa Teresa 455, 1 block from the 1st block of Av Huaylas, T467 0053. Good seafood, popular.

In Lince

Blue Moon, Pumacahua 2526, T470 1190. Open 1200-2400 daily, expensive Italian bistro, but has good value weekend buffet.

In Pueblo Libre

Taberna Quierolo, Av San Martín 1090, 2 blocks from Museo Nacional de Antropología y Arqueología. Old bar, good seafood and atmosphere, not open for dinner.

In Central Lima
● *on map, page 105*

Two places opposite the Torre Tagle Palace: *Antaño*, Ucayali 332, T426 2372, limadeantano@yahoo.com Good, typical Peruvian food, nice patio, recommended; *L'Eau Vive*, Ucayali 370, T427 5612, run by nuns, open Mon-Sat, 1230-1500 and 1930-2130, fixed-price lunch menu, Peruvian-style in interior dining room, or à la carte in either of dining rooms that open onto patio, excellent, profits go to the poor, Ave Maria is sung nightly at 2100. *El Maurito*, Jr Ucayali 212, T426 2538. Peruvian/international, good pisco sours. *Heydi*, Puno 367. Good, cheap seafood, open daily 1100-2000, popular. *San Martín*, Av Nicolás de Piérola 890, off Plaza San Martín, T424 7140. Typical Peruvian food from both coast and highlands, good value, reasonably cheap. *Machu Picchu*, near *Hostal Europa* at Jr Ancash 312. Huge portions, grimy bathrooms (to say the least), yet very popular, closed for breakfast. *Manhatten*, Jr Miró Quesada 259, T428 2117. Open Mon-Fri 0700-1900, low end executive-type restaurant, local and international food from US$5-10, good. *La Colmena*, Av Nicolás de Piérola 742. Good set lunches, open 0800-2300.

Lima

Café Carrara, Jr Ica 330, attached to *Hostal Roma*. Open daily until 2300, multiple breakfast combinations, pancakes, sandwiches, nice ambience, good. *Cafe-Restaurant Accllahuasy*, Jr Ancash 400, around the corner from *Hostal España*. Open 0700-2300, good. *Cordano*, Jr Ancash 202, T427 0181. Typical old Lima restaurant/watering hole, slow service and a bit grimy but full of character. Definitely worth the time it takes to drink a few beers. *Jimmy's Baguetería y Pastelería*, Av Abancay 298 y Huallaga. Recommended, especially for sandwiches.

Pasaje Olaya, on the Plaza de Armas between Jr de la Unión and Jr Carabaya, is a small pedestrian walkway with many nice restaurants frequented during lunch hours by executives. A bit on the pricey side but good.

On Sat and Sun, 1100-1700, traditional dishes from all over Peru are served in **Plaza Italia**, plenty of seating, music, well-organized. Highly recommended

In Breña   *La Choza Náutica*, Jr Breña 204, close to Plaza Bolognesi. Good *ceviche* and friendly service. *D'Coco*, corner of Av Bolivia and Jr Iquique. Good, cheap *ceviche*. *Azato* Av Arica 298, 3 blocks from Plaza Bolognesi, T423 4369. Excellent and cheap Peruvian dishes.

In Chinatown   There are many highly recommended *chifas* in the district of Barrios Altos. *Chifa Capon*, Ucayali 774. *Chun Koc Sen*, Jr Paruro 886, T427 5281. Open daily 0900-2300. *Fung Yen*, Jr Ucayali 744, T427 6567. *Jan Kin Sen*, Jr Andahuaylas 685, T427 1560. *Kin Ten*, Ucayali y Paruro. Excellent vegetarian options. *Salon Capon*, Jr Paruro 819 (also in Larcomar). Also has good dim-sum, though not such good cakes when you pay the bill. *Wa Lok*, Jr Paruro 864, T427 2656. Good dim-sum, cakes and fortune cookies (when you pay the bill). Owner Liliana Com speaks fluent English, very friendly.

Cafés
• *on map, page 118*

In Miraflores   *Haiti*, Av Diagonal 160, Parque Kennedy. Open almost round the clock daily, large terrace, decent food and coffee, great for people watching, frequented by politicians, journalists and artists. *Vivaldi*, Av Ricardo Palma 258, 1 block from Parque Kennedy, T446 1473. Also at Conquistadores 212, San Isidro. Good, expensive. *La Tiendecita Blanca*, Av Larco 111 on Parque Kennedy, T445 9797. One of Miraflores' oldest, expensive, good people-watching, very good cakes, European-style food and delicatessen. *Café Café*, Martín Olaya 250, near the Parque Kennedy roundabout. Very popular, good atmosphere, over 100 different blends of coffee, good salads and sandwiches, very popular with 'well-to-do' Limeños. Also at Alvarez Calderón 194, San Isidro, and in Larcomar (good sea views). *Café de la Paz*, Lima 351, middle of Parque Kennedy, T241 6043. Good outdoor café right on the park, expensive. *Chef's Café*, Av Larco 763. Nice place for a sandwich or coffee. Also has a little cart in Parque Kennedy until 2200 with good hot coffee to go. *Pin Poini*, small kiosk on Parque del Amor. Good place to watch the ocean and sip real Italian coffee. *San Antonio*, Av Angamos Oeste 1494, T421 5575, also Rocca de Vergallo 201, Magdalena del Mar and Av Primavera 373, San Borja. Fashionable *pastelería* chain, good, not too expensive. *Tomar e Irse*, Mcal Oscar R Benavides 598. Cool new place with innovative design and beans from around the world. *Café Zeta*, José Gálvez y Diagonal, past Parque Kennedy, T446 5922. American owned, excellent Peruvian coffee, teas, hot chocolate, and the best homemade cakes away from home, cheap too.

• *on map, page 116*   **In San Isidro**   *News Café*, Av Santa Luisa 110, T421 6278. Great salads and desserts, popular and expensive. Also in Larcomar. *Café Olé*, Pancho Fierro 115 (1 block from *Hotel Olivar*), T440 7751. Huge selection of entrées and desserts. *Café Positano/Café Luna*, Miguel Dasso 147. Popular with politicians, café and bistro.

In Miraflores *Bircher Benner*, Diez Canseco 487 y Grimaldo del Solar, T444 4250. **Vegetarian**
Closed Sun, natural food store inside, slow service, good cheap *menú*. *Don Champiñón*, Av Angamos Este 415, T447 3810. Excellent cheap *menús* and *ofertas*. Small food store inside. *Madre Natura*, C Chiclayo 815, T445 2522. Great natural foods shop with a café at the back, quiet, beautiful courtyard. Highly recommended. *El Paraíso*, C Alcanfores 416, 2 blocks from Av Benavides. Natural foods/snacks, fruit salads and juices. Highly recommended.

In Central Lima *Govinda*, Av Garcilaso de la Vega 1670, opposite Gran Parque de Lima. Also sells natural products, good. *Natur*, Moquegua 132, 1 block from Jr de la Unión, T427 8281. The owner, Humberto Valdivia, is also president of the South American Explorers' board of directors, the casual conversation, as well as his restaurant is highly recommended. *Centro de Medicina Natural*, Jr Chota 1462, next door to *Hostal de las Artes*. Very good.

Dove Vai, Diagonal 228. Try the *encanto* with lumps of chocolate brownie. *Heladería* **Yoghurt &**
4D, Angamos Oeste 408. Open 1000-0100 daily, good Italian ice cream, at other loca- **ice cream**
tions throughout Lima. *Mi Abuela*, Angamos 393. Open 0900-2100 daily, probably the best yogurt in Lima, large selection of natural foods, including tasty veggie burgers in wholemeal rolls, super cheap. Highly recommended. *Zugatti*, Av Larco 361, across from Parque Kennedy. Good Italian gelato.

Bars and clubs

Lima has an excellent nightlife, with many places to choose from, all with different styles and themes. Often there is a cover charge ranging from US$3-10 per person. Unfortunately, there are some nightclubs and bars that deny entrance to people solely on the basis of skin colour and assumed economic status. We **only** include here the names of the establishments that **do not** practise this policy.

Bars *Bárbaro*, Larcomar shopping center, T241-8585. *Barcelona*, also in Larcomar, **In Miraflores**
T445 4823, one of the best pubs in the city. *Barra Brava*, Av Grau 192, T241 5840. Lot's of fun, sports bar(ish). *Carlos y Charlie's*, Larcomar shopping center, T241 8585. Mexican-style bar, Tex-mex food. *Diogreeks Pub*, Av Dos de Mayo 385, T447 7958. Nice pub with Greek décor. *Media Naranja*, C Schell 130, at the bottom of Parque Kennedy. Brazilian bar with typical drinks and food. *Murphys*, C Schell 627. Great Irish pub, "a must", now doing food such as fish and chips. *The Old Pub*, San Ramón 295 (Pizza Street). Cosy, with live music most days. *Rey David*, Av Benavides 567, Centro Comercial Los Duendes. Small café/bar. *Treff Pub Alemán*, Av Benavides 571 - 11, Centro Comercial Los Duendes, T444 0148.

Clubs There are many discotheques on Pizza Street by Parque Kennedy. *Cocodrilo Verde*, Francisco de Paula 226 near corner with Bellavista, Miraflores. Relaxed, stylish bar, slightly pricey but worth it for the Wed night jazz, and live music at weekends, occasionally charges cover for music at weekends. *Downtown*, C Los Pinos 162, at the 2nd block of Av Benavides. *Ministry*, Altos de D'Onofrio, opposite Parque Kennedy, T938 9231. Good music, performances and demonstrations of dance, exhibitions, tatooing, entry US$3. Recommended. *Santa Sede*, Av 28 de Julio 441. Very popular, great music, fun crowd. Recommended. *Satchmo*, Av La Paz 538, T442 8425. Live jazz, creole and blues shows. *Teatriz*, Larcomar shopping center, T242 3084/2358. Modern, expensive entrance fee, very popular. *Tequila Rocks*, C Diez Canseco 146, a 1/2 block from Parque Kennedy. Good music, very popular, but many of the girls are prostitutes.

In Barranco Barranco is the capital of Lima nightlife. The following is a short list of some of the better bars and clubs. **Pasaje Sánchez Carrión**, right off the main plaza, used to be the heart of it all. Watering holes and discos line both sides of this pedestrian walkway, but crowds and noise are driving people elsewhere. This move has speeded up after the fatal fire in an overcrowded nightclub, *Utopia* (in another part of the city), where safety rules were ignored. Some places have been closed for safety reasons. **Av Grau**, just across the street from the plaza, is also lined with bars.

Bars *Sargento Pimienta*, Bolognesi 755. Live music, always a favourite with Limeños. Opposite is the relaxed *Trinidad* and at No 660 is *Bosa Nova*, chilled student-style bar with good music. *Juanitos*, Av Grau, opposite the park. Barranco's oldest bar, and perfect to start the evening. *El Ekeko*, Av Grau 266. *La Estación*, Av Pedro de Osma 112. Live music, older crowd. *La Posada del Mirador*, near the Puente de los Suspiros (Bridge of Sighs). Beautiful view of the ocean, but you pay for the privilege. *Kitsch Bar*, Bolognesi 743. The name says it all, decorated with flock wallpaper, dolls, religious icons, after midnight it becomes unbearably packed, but great dancing. *La Noche*, Bolognesi 307, at Pasaje Sánchez Carrión. A Lima institution and still very high standard, live music, Mon is jazz night, kicks off around 2200 (also in Central Lima – see below). Many bars around Plaza Raimondi, 1 block from Bolognesi. All are full of character and have well-priced drinks. *Backpacker's Inn*, Av Pedro de Osma 135, inside the *Mochileros Hostal*. Often has live music, such as salsa. *El Grill de Costa Verde*, part of the *Costa Verde* restaurant on Barranco beach. Young crowd, packed at weekends.

Clubs Many of the bars in this area turn into discotheques as the evening goes on. *De Parranda*, Av Grau. Once Lima's most popular discotheque, large and modern. *El Dragón*, N de Piérola near corner with Grau. Popular dancing venue. *My Place*, C Domeyer 122. *Las Terrazas*, Av Grau 290.

In San Isidro *Ceanus Piano Bar*, in *Hotel Los Delfines*, Los Eucaliptos 555. Perfect for a relaxing, if expensive, evening. *Bogart*, Av Pardo y Aliaga 456. *Palos de Moguer*, Av Emilio Cavenecia 129, T221 8363. Brews 4 different kinds of beer, typical bar food. *Punto G*, Av Conquistadores 512. Very popular, really small. Recommended.

In Central Lima *Queirolo Bar*, Jr Camaná 900 at Jr Quilca. Excellent for local colour, "a must". Opposite is the Centre's version of *La Noche* (see above). *Estadio Futbol Sports Bar*, Av Nicolás de Piérola 926 on the Plaza San Martín, T428 8866. Beautiful bar with a discotheque on the bottom floor, international football theme, good international and creole food. Recommended. *El Rincón Cervecero*, Jr de la Unión (Belén) 1045. German pub without the beer, fun. Recommended. *Piano Bar Munich*, Jr de la Unión 1044 (basement). Small and fun.

NB The centre of town, specifically **Jr de la Unión** has many discotheques. It's best to avoid the nightlife spots on and around the intersection of Av Tacna, Av Piérola and Av de la Vega. These places are on the rough side and the foreigner will most likely receive much unwanted attention.

Gay clubs *The Clash* pub and gallery, Psje Tello 269, Miraflores, T444 3376. Excellent drinks, friendly barstaff, and great décor, exclusively gay with shows and events. *Hedonismo*, Av Ignacio Merino 1700, Lince. Exclusively gay, good meeting place. *Imperio*, Jr Camaná 9th block, Lima centre. Exclusively gay, one of the older gay clubs in Lima, taxi recommended. *720 Downtown*, Av Uruguay 183, Lima centre. Exclusively gay, best in the centre, this is a rough neighbourhood so take a taxi to and from the club. *Kitsch Bar*, gay friendly, see Barranco bars. *Santa Sede*, very gay friendly, see Miraflores nightclubs.

Entertainment

Artco, Rouad y Paz Soldán 325, San Isidro, T221 3579, www.artcogaleria.com Mon-Fri 1100-2000, Sat 1030-1330, 1530-1950. *La Casa Azul*, Alfonso Ugarte 150, Mirflores, T446 6380, T8071661 (mob). Marcia Moreno and Jorge Rengifo, for advice on and sales of contemporary art and antique objects, handicrafts and furniture. *Centro Cultural Ricardo Palma*, Sala Raul Porras Barnechea, Av Larco 770, Miraflores, T446 6164/444 0540, open Mon-Sat 0900-2100. *Ediciones Wu*, Av Sáenz Peña 129, Barranco, T247 4685. Mon-Fri 1000-1300, 1400-2000, Sat 1100-1300, 1630-2000. Artist Frances Wu's studio is also a gallery of engravings, etchings and other graphics, with an emphasis on Peruvian artists. *La Quinta*, Av Grau 170, oficina C, Miraflores, T444 8816. Contemporary engravings. Old maps of Peru and South America. *Miraflores Municipal Gallery*, corner of Av Larco and Diez Canseco, Miraflores, T4440540. Mon-Sun 1000-2200. *Pancho Fierro*, Psje Nicolás de Rivera 149, centre, T426 0918. Daily 1100-2000. *Praxis Arte Internacional*, C San Martin 689, Barranco, T/F477 2822. Mon-Fri 0930-1330, 1700-2100, Sat 1700-2100. A recommended photographic gallery is *El Ojo Ajeno*, 28 de Julio 547, T444 6999/6988, http://centrofotografia.perucultural.org.pe Mon-Fri 0900-2100, Sat 0900-1800.

Art galleries
See also Cultural centres, page 143, many of which have art galleries, cinemas and theatres

There are many good cinemas throughout the city. Most films are in English with subtitles and cost US$2 in the centre and around US$4-5 in Miraflores. Cinemas in the centre tend to have poor sound quality.

The best cinema chains in the city are *Cinemark*, *Cineplanet* and *UVK Multicines*, Among the best of the other movie theatres are: *Cine Romeo y Julieta*, Pasaje Porta 115, at the bottom of Parque Kennedy, T447 5476; *Multicine Starvision El Pacífico*, on the Ovalo by Parque Kennedy, T445 6990 (both in Miraflores); *Cine Roma*, C Teniente Fernández 242, 9th block of Av Arequipa, T433 8618 (in Santa Beatriz).

Cine Clubs include: *Filmoteca de Lima*, Av 9 de Diciembre 125 (better known as Colón), T331 0126; *Cine Club Miraflores*, Av Larco 770, in the Miraflores Cultural Centre building, T446 2649.

Cinemas
The newspaper El Comercio lists cinema information in the section called 'Luces'. Tue is reduced price at most cinemas for shows throughout the day and night.

Así Es Mi Perú, Av Aviación 3390, San Borja, T476 2419. *Las Brisas de Titicaca*, Pasaje Walkuski 168, at the 1st block of Av Brasil near Plaza Bolognesi, T332 1881. A Lima institution. *Caballero de Fina Estampa*, Av del Ejército 800, Miraflores, T441 0552. *De Cajón*, C Merino 2nd block, near 6th block of Av Del Ejército, Miraflores. Good *música negra*. *Sachun*, Av Del Ejército 657, Miraflores, T441 0123/4465. Great shows on weekdays as well.

Peñas

Barranco *Del Carajo*, San Ambrosio 328, T247 7977. All types of traditional music. *Casa Vieja*, Salaverry 139. Standard *peña* in a converted theatre, nice atmosphere. *Don Porfirio*, C Manuel Segura 115, T447 3119. Traditional *peña*. Recommended. *La Estación de Barranco*, at Pedro de Osma 112, T477 5030. Good, family atmosphere, varied shows. *Las Guitarras*, C Manuel Segura 295 (6th block of Av Grau), T247 3924/ 275 0748. Recommended. *Los Balcones*, Av Grau across from main plaza. Good, noisy and crowded. *Manos Morenas*, Av Pedro de Osma 409, T467 0421. Also a restaurant, older crowd, great shows beginning at 2230. *Peña Poggi*, Av Luna Pizarro 578, T247 5790/885 7619. 30 years old, traditional. Recommended. *Perico's*, Av Pedro de Osma 1st block at the main plaza, T477 1311. *De Rompe y Raja*, Manuel Segura 127, T247 3271.

The most professional plays are staged at *Teatro Segura*, Jr Huancavelica 265, T427 9491. There are many other theatres in the city, some of which are related to Cultural centres (see page 143). The press gives details of performances.

Theatre
Theatre and concert tickets can be booked through Teleticket, T242 2823

Lima

Festivals

On **18 Jan** is the anniversary of the *founding of Lima*. **Semana Santa**, or Holy Week, is a colourful spectacle with processions. **28-29 Jul** is *Independence*, with music and fireworks in the Plaza de Armas on the evening before. **Oct** is the month of *Our Lord of the Miracles* with impressive processions (see Las Nazarenas church, above). On **3 Nov** is *San Martín de Porres*.

Shopping

Since so many artesans have come from the Sierra to Lima, it is possible to find any kind of handicraft in the capital. The quality is high. Among the many items which can be bought here are silver and gold handicrafts, Indian hand-spun and hand-woven textiles and manufactured textiles in Indian designs. However, although Lima is more expensive, it is often impossible to find the same quality of goods elsewhere. You can find llama and alpaca wool products such as ponchos, rugs, hats, blankets, slippers, coats, sweaters, etc. Note that genuine alpaca is odourless wet or dry, but wet llama stinks.

Lima is a good place to buy *arpilleras*, appliqué pictures of Peruvian life (originated in Chile with political designs). These are made with great skill and originality by women in the shanty towns. The fine leather products on sale are mostly hand made. The *mate burilado*, or engraved gourd found in every tourist shop, is cheap and a genuine expression of folk art. These are cheaper in the villages near Huancayo (see page 491). There are also bargains on offer for clothing made from high quality **Pima cotton**.

Bookshops
Finding novels in English can be a bit frustrating, as can their price once you do

Crisol, Av Sant Cruz 816 at Ovalo Gutiérrez, San Isidro, T221 1010. Book megastore with titles in English, French and Spanish, café, same building as *Cine Planet*. *Librería Cultural*, José Gálvez 124, Miraflores, T447 6223. The bookstore chain *Epoca*, with 3 locations has some nice coffee-table books as well as a decent selection of English-language books: Av José Pardo 399, T447 2149, Miraflores; Av Comandante Espinar 864 (near Ovalo Gutiérrez), T445 7430, Miraflores; and Jr Belén 1072 T424 95909, Lima centre near Plaza San Martín. *Ibero Librerías*, Diagonal 500, Miraflores. A good selection of books in Spanish. Also at Centro Comercial El Polo, Tienda B-115, Surco, T435 7597. Stocks Footprint Handbooks. *Libreria Mosca Azul*, located next to Parque Salazar on Malecón de la Reserva 713, by Larcomar, Miraflores, T241 0675, has good stock, plus some books in English. *El Sótano*, Av Nicolás de Piérola 995, Lima centre on Plaza de San Martín, T427 9364. The *Virrey* bookshop chain has a lot of great books, but few in English. If you are interested in Peruvian history and politics, this is the place to go: Larcomar Shopping Center (local 210), Miraflores, Pasaje Nicolás de Rivera, Lima centre behind the Municipalidad, T427 5080, and Miguel Dasso 141, San Isidro (next door to this branch is *Librería Sur*, No 143, also good). *Zeta*, Av Cdte Espinar 219, T446 5139 and at airport. Stocks Footprint and other guide books. For used books in English and other languages: *Bazar Gamma*, Porta 154, Miraflores. On same street, No 384, is *Eureka y Eureka*, a good place to send international fax as well as buy books. As for magazines, whether in downtown Lima or Miraflores, almost all street kiosks sell up to date magazines in English such as *Time*, *Newsweek*, *People* etc. For the most recently published magazines and newspapers, try *Mallcco's* on Av Larco 175, on the Parque Kennedy roundabout, open daily 0800-2100. They have a wide variety of magazines (expensive but the latest releases) and newspapers from England. In front of *Café Haiti* by Parque Kennedy, you'll often see the men with stacks of newspapers for sale. These are taken from arriving international flights so tend to be only a day or two old; bargain hard. The *Hotel Sheraton* sells the *New York Times* and the *Wall Street Journal*. Many cafés have various foreign newspapers to browse through while enjoying a cup of coffee or a sandwich.

Alpamayo, Av Larco 345, Miraflores at Parque Kennedy, T445 1671. Sleeping mats, boots, rock shoes, climbing gear, water filters, tents, backpacks etc, very expensive but top quality equipment. *Todo Camping*, Av Angamos Oeste 350, Miraflores, near Av Arequipa, T447 6279. Sells 100% deet, bluet gas canisters, lots of accessories, tents, crampons and backpacks. *Camping Center*, Av Benavides 1620, Miraflores, T242 1779. Selection of tents, backpacks, stoves, camping and climbing gear. *Outdoor Peru*, Centro Comercial Chacarilla, store 211, on Av Caminos del Inca 257, Surco, T372 0428. Has a decent selection of camping equipment. *Huantzan*, Jr Tarapacá 384, Magdalena, T460 6101. Equipment sales and rentals, MSR stoves, backpacks, boots. *Mountain Worker*, Centro Comercial Camino Real, level A, store 17, San Isidro, T813 8367. Quality camping gear for all types of weather, made to order products as well. Highly recommended.

Camping equipment
It is highly recommended that you bring all camping and hiking gear from home

Silvania Prints, Av Conquistadores 915, San Isidro, T422 6440, also at Av Diez Canseco 376, Miraflores. Open Mon-Sat 0930-1800. They sell modern silk-screen prints on Pima cotton with pre-Columbian designs. *La Casa de la Mujer Artesana*, Juan Pablo Ferandini 1550 (Av Brasil cuadra 15), Pueblo Libre, T423 8840, F423 4031. Cooperative run by Movimiento Manuela Ramos, excellent quality work mostly from *pueblos jóvenes* (shanty towns), open Mon-Fri 0900-1300, 1400-1700.

Handicrafts

Miraflores is a good place for high quality, pricey handicrafts. There are many shops on and around Av La Paz, and on Av Petit Thouars, blocks 51-54. *Agua y Tierra*, Av Diez Canseco 298 y Alcanfores, Miraflores, T444 6980. Highly recommended for fine crafts and indigenous art, Mon-Sat 1000-1900. *Antisuyo*, Jr Tacna 460 at 44th block of Av Arequipa, Miraflores, T241 6451. Mon-Fri 0900-1930, Sat 1030-1830, an indigenous co-operative run by an Englishwoman, sells high-quality handicrafts from all regions, reasonable prices (another outlet in Cusco). *Centro Comercial El Alamo*, corner of La Paz and Diez Canseco, Miraflores. Small shopping centre with excellent selection of jewellery and craft stores. Recommended. *Kuntur Wasi*, Ocharan 182, T444 0557. Open Mon-Sat, 1030-2000, English-speaking owner very knowledgeable about Peruvian textiles, frequently has exhibitions of fine folk art and crafts, high quality. Recommended. *Las Pallas*, Cajamarca 212, parallel to 6th block of Av Grau, Barranco, T477 4629. Open Mon-Sat 0900-1900. Good quality handicrafts. Specializes in Andean amulets, ceremonial offerings, fine textiles, masks and pottery. In Lima centre: *Artesanía Santo Domingo*, Plaza Santo Domingo, by the church of that name, T428 9860. Good Peruvian crafts.

Alpaca 111, Av Larco 671, Miraflores, T4471623. Open 1030-2030, high quality alpaca, baby alpaca and vicuña items. *Alpaca 859*, Av Larco 859, Miraflores, T447 7163. Excellent quality alpaca and baby alpaca products, English and French spoken. *Lanificio*, Av Alberto del Campo 285, San Isidro. Good value. *Royal Alpaca*, Pasaje El Suche, Av La Paz 646 no 14, Miraflores, T444 2150. *La Casa de la Alpaca*, Av La Paz 665, Miraflores, T447 6271. Open Mon-Fri 0930-2030.

Instituto Geográfico Nacional, Av Aramburú 1190, Surquillo, T475 9960/F475 3085. Mon-Fri 0830-1730. They have topographical maps of the whole country, mostly at 1:100,000, political and physical maps of all departments and satellite and aerial photographs. They also have a new series of tourist maps for trekking, eg of the Cordillera Blanca, the Cusco area, at 1:250,000. *Ingemmet* (Instituto Geológico Minero Y Metalúrgico), Av Canadá 1470, San Borja, T225 3128. Mon-Fri 0800-1300, 1400-1600. Sells a huge selection of geographic maps ranging from US$12 to US$112. Also satellite, aeromagnetic, geochemical and departmental mining maps. Enquire about new digital products. Aerial photographs are available at *Servicio Aerofotográfico Nacional*, Las Palmas Airforce Base. Mon-Fri 0800-1400. Photos from mid-1950's aerial survey available, but they are expensive. Expect a waiting period as short as one day or as long as two weeks. *Lima 2000*, Av Arequipa 2625, Lince (near the intersection with

Maps
Dress soberly and to take your passport when going to these places (except Lima 2000)

Av Javier Prado), T440 3486, F440 3480. Mon-Fri 0900-1300 and 1400-1800. Have an excellent street map of Lima (the only one worth buying), US$10, or US$14 in booklet form. Provincial maps and a country road map as well. Good for road conditions and distances, perfect for driving or cycling. *Ministerio de Transporte*, Av 28 de Julio 800, Lima centre, T433 7800. Mon-Fri 0800-1230, 1400-1600. Maps and plans of land communication routes, slow and bureaucratic. *Ministerio de Agricultura*, Av Salaverry y Húsares de Junín, Jesús María, T433 3034. Mon-Fri 0830-1300, 1400-1700. Complete set of 1:25,000 blueline maps, good service.

Markets **Parque Kennedy**, the main park of Miraflores, hosts a daily crafts market from 1700-2300. **Artesanía Carabaya**, Jr Carabaya 319 at the Plaza de Armas. There are crafts markets on Av Petit Thouars in Miraflores near Parque Kennedy. *Av Petit Thouars cuadras 51 a 54* (parallel to Av Arequipa, a few blocks from Parque Kennedy) here you'll find an unnamed crafts market area with a large courtyard and lots of small flags. This is the largest crafts arcade in Miraflores. From here to Av Ricardo Palma the street is lined with crafts markets. *La Portada del Sol*, on cuadra 54 of Petit Thouars, has a small café with reasonable prices and good coffee. All are open 7 days a week until late(ish). The *Feria Artesanal*, Av La Marina y Av Sucre, in Pueblo Libre, is smaller than it used to be but is cheaper than Av Petit Thouars. On C García Naranjo, La Victoria, just off Av Grau in the centre of town is *Polvos Azules*, the official black market of Lima. The normal connotations of a 'black market' do not apply here as this establishment is an accepted part of Lima society, condoned by the government and frequented by people of all economic backgrounds. It's good for cameras, hiking boots, music and walkmans. **NB** This is not a safe area, so be alert and put your money in your front pockets.

Lima has 3 supermarket chains: *Santa Isabel*, *E Wong* and *Metro*. They all are well-stocked and carry a decent supply of imported goods (Marmite, Tesco products etc). The *Santa Isabel* at Av Benavides 487 y Av Alcanfores in Miraflores is open 24 hrs.

Music *Music City*, Av José Larco 459, Miraflores. Probably the best, but not the cheapest, place to buy CDs and music tapes, all original, no pirated material.

Photography For camera film try *Foto Magnum*, Ocoña 190, Lima Centre, T4271599, F4272060. Mon-Fri 0900-2000. Also camera accessories. *Laboratorio Color Profesional*, Av Benavides 1171, Miraflores T446 7421/242 7575. Mon-Fri 0900-1900, Sat 0930-1300. Professional quality developing, fairly priced, touch-ups, repair services, excellent for slide developing, sells top quality equipment, film and accessories, the best you'll find in Lima. Highly recommended. Also *Metro Supermarket*, corner Alfonso Ugarte y Av Venezuela, T423 5533. Mon-Sat 0900-2200, Sun 0900-2100. Shop at Jr Cusco 592, p 4, Lima centre, T426 7920. Mon-Fri 1100-1800, good for repairs.

Sport

Association football matches and various athletic events take place at the National Stadium, in the centre of the city on ground given by the British community on the 100th anniversary of Peru's Declaration of Independence. The local soccer derby is *Universitario* against *Alianza Lima* (tickets US$2.50-25). Matches are also played at Alianza's stadium in the district of La Victoria and Universitario's new stadium in the La Molina district.

Cycling *Best Internacional*, Av Comandante Espinar 320, Miraflores, T446 4044 and Av Sucre 358, Magdalena, T470 1704. Mon-Sat 1000-1400, 1600-2000. Sells leisure and racing bikes, also repairs, parts and accessories. *Biclas*, Av Conquistadores 641, San Isidro, T440 0890, F442 7548. Mon-Fri 1000-1300, 1600-2000, Sat 1000-1300. Knowledgeable staff, tours possible, good selection of bikes, repairs and accessories, cheap airline boxes for sale. Highly recommended. *BikeMavil*, Av Aviación 4021, Surco, T449 8435. Mon-Sat 0930-2100. Rental service, repairs, excursions, selection of mountain and racing bicycles. *Casa Okuyama*, Jr Montevideo 785, Lima, T4283444/4263307. Mon-Fri 0900-1300, 1415-1800, Sat 0900-1300. Repairs, parts, try here for 28 inch tyres, excellent service. *Cicloroni*, Las Casas 019, San Isidro, 32nd block of Petit Thouars, T222 6358, F442 3936. Mon-Sat 0900-2100, for repairs, parts and accessories, good information about the Lima biking scene, ask about Sat and Sun bike rides. *Cycling*, Av Tomás Marsano 2851, Higuereta-Surco, T/F271 0247. *Neuquén*, Av Aviación 3590, San Borja, T225 5219. For Shimano parts. *Peru Bike*, Pedro de Osma 560, Barranco, T467 0757. Bike sales, repairs and accessories. *Willy Pro* (Williams Arce), Av Javier Prado Este 3339, San Borja, T346 0468, F346 4082, warceleon@misti.lared.net.pe Mon-Sat 0800-2000. Has a selection of specialized bikes and helpful staff. **Contacts**: for information about all aspects of cycling in Lima and Peru, contact Richard Fernandini at 442 1402/421 1226 during the hrs of 0900-1300, 1500-1800. He speaks English.

The Jockey Club of Peru (Hipódromo de Monterrico) has horse races every Tue and Thu at 1900 more-or-less, Sat and Sun at 1400. Bets start at US$0.75. For information about Peruvian Paso horses contact the *Asociación Nacional de Caballos de Paso* at T447 6331. **Horse racing**

Asociación de Andinismo de la Universidad de Lima, Universidad de Lima, Javier Prado Este s/n, T437 6767. Meetings on Wed 1800-2000, offers climbing courses. *Club de Montañeros Américo Tordoya*, Jr Tarapacá 384, Magdalena, T460 6101. Meetings Thu 2000, contact Gonzalo Menacho. Climbing excursions ranging from easy to difficult. Good climbing and hiking equipment shop, *Alpamayo*, at Av Larco 345, Miraflores, T4451671, F4450370. The owner of this camping shop speaks fluent English and offers information – see Camping stores, page 133. *Grupo Cordillera*, T481 6649, T917 3832 (mob). Adventure tourism, weekly excursions. *Club de Ecoturismo*, T423 3329. **Mountaineering & trekking clubs**

Fly Adventure, Jorge Chávez 658, Miraflores, T816 5461 (Luis Munarriz), T900 9150 (Eduardo Gómez). US$25 for 15-min tandem flight over the cliffs, 4 to 6-day courses US$250-350. Recommended. **Parapenting**

AquaSport, Av Conquistadores 645, San Isidro, T221 1548/7270, aquasport@ amauta.rcp.net.pe Owner is a CMAS instructor, gear for rent, tours and courses offered and quality equipment for sale. *Mundo Submarino*, Av Conquistadores 791, San Isidro, T441 7604. Sr Alejandro Pez is a professional diver, fluent in German, Italian, English, French and Portuguese and a member of the Peruvian Federation of Skin Divers, he sells new as well as second-hand diving equipment (brand names), rents equipment to certified divers only, great for general information. Mon-Fri 1100-1300, 1400-1930, Sat 1400-1930. Recommended. *Peru Divers*, Av Huaylas 205, Chorrillos, T251 6231, open Mon-Fri 0900-1900, Sat 0900-1700. Owner Lucho Rodríguez is a certified PADI instructor who offers certification courses, tours and a wealth of good information. **Scuba diving**

Focus, Leonardo Da Vinci 208, San Borja, T475 8459. Shaping factory and surf boards, some decent boards, knowledgeable about local spots and conditions, one of the better surf shops in Peru, rents boards. *Wayo Whiler*, Av 28 de Julio 287, Barranco, T247 6343 (workshop)/254 1344 (Wayo's house). For accessories, materials and repairs, can also organize excursions. *O'Neills*, Av Santa Cruz 851, Miraflores, T445 0406. One of the best surf shops in town. *Klimax*, José González 488, Miraflores, T447 1685. Sells new and secondhand boards, knowledgeable. *Tubos* is a magazine dedicated solely to the Peruvian surfing scene. It's sold at most kiosks and bookstores that carry a magazine selection. Good information given with a visit to the office, at Pasaje Los Pinos 153, near Parque Kennedy, T445 5443/242 7922, revistatubosperu@hotmail.com **Surfing**

Tour operators

Lima is busting at the seams with tour and travel agencies. Some are good and reliable, many are not. If possible, use agencies in or close to the area you wish to visit and always shop around. Bargaining ability is a plus. See also *Fertur Peru* in the Tourist Office section, page 101. **NB** We have received complaints about agencies, or their representatives at bus offices or the airport arranging tours and collecting money for companies that either do not exist or which fall far short of what is paid for. Do not conduct business anywhere other than in the agency's office and insist on a written contract.

Aracari Travel Consulting, Av Pardo 610, No 802, Miraflores, T242 6673, F242 4856, www.aracari.com Regional tours throughout Peru, also 'themed' and activity tours. *Class Adventure Travel*, Av Grimaldo del Solar 463, Miraflores, T444 1652/2220, F241 8908, www.cat-travel.com Dutch-owned and run, one of the best. Highly recommended. *Coltur*, Av José Pardo 138, Miraflores, T241 5551, F446 8073, www.coltur.com.pe With offices in Cusco and Arequipa, very helpful, well-organized. *Dasatariq*, Jr Francisco Bolognesi 510, Miraflores, T447 7772, F447 0495, www.dasa tariq.com Also in Cusco. *Explorandes*, C San Fernando 320, T445 8683/242 9527, F242 3496, www.explorandes.com.pe Wide range of adventure and cultural tours throughout the country. Also offices in Cusco (see page 182) and Huaraz (see page 342). *Fertur Perú*, Jr Junin 211, fertur@terra.com.pe *Hada Tours*, 2 de Mayo 529, Miraflores, T446 8157, F446 2714, www.hada tours.com.pe 20 years of experience. *Highland Peru Tours*, Atahualpa 197, Miraflores, T242 6292, F242 7189, www.highlandperu.com

Ideas, Ampay 036, San Miguel, T451 3603/352 0589, ideas-mz@amauta.rcp.net.pe Alternative tours of Lima, putting Inca and pre-Inca culture in its present context. *Inca Wasi*, Jr Porta 170, Miraflores, T445 9691, inkawasi@lullitec.com.pe *Lima Tours*, Jr Belén 1040, Lima centre, T424 5110, F330 4488, www.limatours.com.pe Recommended. Also office in San Isidro: Av Pardo y Alliaga 698, T222 2525, F222 5700. *Peru Expeditions*, Av Arequipa 5241-504, Lima 18, T447 2057, F445 9683, www.peru-expeditions.com Specializing in expeditions in 4x4 vehicles and Andes crossings. *Peru Travel Bureau*, Sebastián Tellería 45, San Isidro, T222 1909, F222 9250, postmast@ptb.com.pe Recommended. *Peruvian Safaris*, Alcanfores 459, Miraflores, T4478888, F2418427, www.peruviansafaris.com Reservations for the *Explorer's Inn* in Tambopata. *Queen Adventures*, Jr Callao 301, near Plaza de Armas, qtours@terra.com.pe Good for arranging tours.

Roma Tours, Jr Ica 330, next to *Hostal Roma*, T/F427 7572, dantereyes@ hotmail.com Good and reliable. Administrator Dante Reyes is very friendly and speaks English. *Servicios Aéreos AQP SA*, Los Castaños 347, San Isidro, T222 3312, F222 5910, www.saaqp.com.pe Comprehensive service, tours offered throughout the country. *Victor's Travel Service*, Jr de la

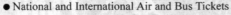

Unión (Belén) 1068, T431 4195/433 3367, F431 0046, 24 hr line 867 6341, victortravel@terra.com.pe Hotel reservations (no commission), free maps of Lima and Peru, Mon-Sat 0900-1800, very helpful. *Viracocha*, Av Vasco Núñez de Balboa 191, Miraflores, T445 3986/447 5516, F447 2429. Very helpful, especially with flights.

Private guides The following guides are certified by the MITINCI (Ministry of Industry Tourism, Integration and International Business) and most are members of AGOTUR (Asociación de Guías Oficiales de Turismo). Always book well in advance. All speak English unless indicated otherwise. *Ruben Cuneo*, T264 6092, T946 4949 (mob), ruben cuneo@yahoo.com.uk Speaks Italian. *Lorena Duharte Arias*, T/F471 3728, T963 7608 (mob), Italian and Flemish (no English). *Sra Goya*, T/F578 5937, T988 3773 (mob), speaks Japanese. *Sr Gunnar*, T/F476 5016, kolibri@netaccessperu.net or gunar_@ algonet.se Specializes in bird watching, speaks Swedish. *Tino Guzmán Khang*, T/F429 5779, T966 1363 (mob), tino@amauta.rcp.net.pe Expert in Peruvian archeology and anthropology, private tours to all parts of the country. Member of South American Explorers, US$12 per hr. Also speaks French and some Chinese. *Sra Julia Huamán*, *Lima Tours* Official Guide, T531 1839, jhuaman@tsi.com.pe *Sra Nariko de Kana*, T442 4000, guide for *Kinjyo Travel*. Speaks Japanese. *Sra Elzinha de Mayer*, T445 0676, T975 8287 (mob), elzinha@ terra.com.pe Speaks Portuguese and French. *Shoko Otani*, T221 2984, T969 2213 (mob), Shoko-o@ amauta.rcp.net.pe Speaks Japanese. *Ernesto Riedner*, T446 1082, F446 6739, T909 4224 (mob), eried@terra.com.pe Speaks German. *Nila Soto*, T452 5483, T965 0951 (mob), nilasoto@yahoo.com or nilasoto@hotmail.com Speaks Italian. *Anabella Velasco*, T/F433 7336, T993 1458 (mob). Speaks German. *Tessy Torres*, T/F422 8210, T975 8960 (mob), jctc@terra.com.pe Speaks Portuguese, Italian and French. Also recommended: *Jaime Torres*, Los Algarrobos 1634, Urb Las Brisas, T337 6953, T917 3073 (mob). Speaks English, also taxi driver, very helpful.

Transport

For all information on international flight arrivals and departures, see Touching down, **Air** page 47. For all information on domestic flights, see Getting around, page 58. Domestic flight schedules are given under the relevant destinations. To enquire about arrivals or departures, T575 1712 (international), or T574 5529 (domestic).

Although Lima is home to a seemingly never-ending list of bus companies, only a small **Bus** percentage can actually be recommended. The following is a concise, user-friendly list of the companies repeatedly recommended for either their service or professionalism. Note that some less reputable companies are included simply because they're the only ones with buses to certain destinations. It's best to buy tickets the day before travelling. Most offer daily service. Confirm that the bus leaves from same place that the ticket was purchased. For prices and approximate duration of trip, refer to the destination.

Cruz del Sur, Jr Quilca 531, Lima centre, T224 6200/424 1005, www.cruzdelsur.com.pe (The website accepts Visa bookings without surcharge.) This terminal has routes to many destinations in Peru with *Ideal* ('ee-de-al') service, meaning quite comfortable buses and periodic stops for food and bathroom breaks, a cheap option with a quality company. They go to: **Ica**, **Arequipa**, **Cusco**, **Puno**, **Chiclayo**, **Trujillo**, **Chincha**, **Cañete**, **Camana**, **Ilo**, **Moquegua**, **Pisco** and **Juliaca**. The other terminal is at Av Javier Prado Este 1109, San Isidro, T225 6163/6164. This terminal offers the *Imperial* service (luxury buses), more expensive and direct, with no chance of passengers in the aisle, and *Cruzero* service (super luxury buses). They go to: **Tumbes**, **Sullana**, **Huancayo**, **Piura**, **Chiclayo**, **Trujillo**, **Huaraz**, **Jauja**, **Camaná**, **Arequipa**, **Moquegua**, **Ilo**, **Tacna**, **Cusco** and **La Paz** (NB this service is *Imperial* only to Arequipa, where you must transfer to an *Ideal* bus for the remaining leg of the trip). *Imperial* buses stop at the central terminal when going north and *Ideal* buses stop at the Javier Prado terminal when going south.

Ormeño, depart from and arrive to Av Carlos Zavala 177, Lima centre, T427 5679; also Av Javier Prado Este 1059, Santa Catalina, T472 1710, www.ascinsa.com/ORMENO/ The following buses are all owned and operated by Ormeño: *Expreso Ancash* (routes to the **Huaraz** area), *Expreso Continental* (routes to the **north**), *Expreso San Cristóbal* (to the **southeast**), *Expreso Chinchano* (to the **south coast** and **Arequipa**) and *Expreso Internacional* (despite the name, to destinations throughout Peru). Ormeño also offers *Royal Class* and *Business Class* service to certain destinations. These buses are very comfortable with bathrooms. They arrive and depart from the Javier Prado terminal, but *Business* buses stop at both terminals. Javier Prado is the best place to buy any Ormeño ticket.

Other companies include: *Transportes Atahualpa*, Jr Sandia 266, Lima Centre, T428 7732. Direct to Cajamarca continuing on to Celendín. *Transportes Chanchamayo*, Av Manco Capac 1052, La Victoria, T265 6850/470 1189. To Tarma, San Ramón and La Merced. *CIVA*, Av Carlos Zavala 211, Lima Centre, and Av 28 de Julio y Paseo de La República, T332 1754/428 5649. To all parts of the country. Has *Servicio Imperial* (executive service), but mixed reports about this company. *Ettsa*, Paseo de la República cuadra 7. Good service to the **north**, **Chiclayo**, **Piura**, **Tumbes**. *Flores*, Paseo de la República cuadra 6. Good buses to the **south**. *Transportes León de Huánuco*, Av 28 de Julio 1520, La Victoria, T424 3893. Daily to **Huánuco**, **Tingo María** and **Pucallpa**. *Mariscal Cáceres*, Av Carlos Zavala 211, Lima Centre, T427 2844, and Av 28 de Julio 2195, La Victoria, T474 6811/7850. To: **Huancayo** and **Jauja**. Very good. Service ranges from basic to deluxe. *Expreso Molina*, Jr Ayacucho 1141, Lima Centre, T428 0617/4852. Good service to **Ayacucho** via **Pisco**. *Móvil Tours*, Av Paseo de La República 749, Lima Centre near the national stadium, T332 0024. Recommended service to **Huaraz** (

Lima

▶▶ How not to be taken for a ride

When the city of Lima tried to introduce meters in taxis, it failed. Almost anyone who puts a small sticker behind the windscreen can pass as a cabbie. 'Official taxis' were simply too expensive and despised by the locals and by now they have almost disappeared. If you flag down a taxi in Miraflores, you will be asked (depending on your language skills) to pay up to S/.25 (almost US$7) to go to the city centre. Some locals and ex-pats pay only S/.7 (about US$2). A reasonable price is

between S/.8 and S/.12 (US$2.25-3.35), depending on the destination. Bargaining is done in a friendly, almost joking fashion and always before you enter the taxi. If you don't speak Spanish, use your fingers (one for each sol) and smile. Despite the hardship, Peruvians have a great sense of humour. When you have some cash to spare and if you like the driver (some of them are professional people just trying to make extra money), contract him by the hour for the current rate of S/.15 (US$4.15).

double-decker buses at 2300 and 0100, lots of leg room, comfortable), **Chiclayo** and **Chachapoyas** (should you want to go straight through). *PerúBus/Soyuz*, Av México y Paseo de la República. To **Ica** every 8 mins, well-organized, but the buses stop frequently so don't put luggage on the overhead racks as it's easy for bags to 'walk'. *Rodríguez*, Av Roosevelt 393, Lima Centre, T428 0506, terminal at Av Paseo de La República 749, opposite national stadium. **Huaraz**, **Caraz**, **Yungay**, **Carhuaz**. Recommended to arrive in Huaraz and then use local transportation to points beyond. Good. Various levels of bus service. *Royal Tours*, Av Paseo de la República 3630, San Isidro, T440 6624. To **Huánuco**, **Tingo María** and **Pucallpa**.

Warning The area around the terminals on Av Carlos Zavala is very unsafe at any time of day but much more so at night. You are strongly advised to take a taxi to and from these terminals. Make sure you see your gear being stored on the correct bus as the place is always very busy. 'Mistakes', intentional or innocent, are not uncommon.

NB If arriving in Lima by bus from the north and heading for the airport, you do not need to go into the centre: ask to be let out at 'Fiori' (look for the sign on top of a building on the left hand side of the highway). This is by the junction of the Panamericana and Av Tomás Valle, which leads almost to Jorge Chávez. Take a taxi from Fiori.

International services *Ormeño*, Av Javier Prado 1059, Santa Catalina, T472 1710, F470 5454. To: **Guayaquil** (29 hrs, with a change of bus at the border, US$50), **Quito** (38 hrs), **Cali** (56 hrs), **Bogotá** (70 hrs), **Caracas** (100 hrs), **Santiago** (54 hrs), **Mendoza** (78 hrs), **Buenos Aires** (90 hrs). **NB** A maximum of 20 kilos is allowed per person. Depending on the destination, extra weight penalties range from US$1-3 per kilo. *El Rápido*, Av Rivera Navarrete 2650, Lince, T447 6101/441 6651. Service to Argentina and Uruguay only.

NB For international service, it's cheaper to take a bus to the border, cross and then another to your final destination. The week before and after 28 Jul (Peruvian independence day) and Semana Santa (Holy Week) are the most travelled times of the year. Bus tickets out of Lima are extremely hard to come by unless purchased in advance. Expect prices to double during these dates and check in earlier than you normally would to avoid possible problems.

Car hire Most rental companies have an office at the airport, where you can arrange everything and pick up and leave the car. It's recommended to test-drive car before signing contract as quality varies. *Avis Rent A Car*, Av Javier Prado Este 5233, T434 1111, F434 1034, www.avis.com *Budget Car Rental*, Canaval y Moreyra 569, San Isidro, T442 8703, F441 4174, www.budget.com *Inka's Rent a Car*, Cantuarias 160, Miraflores, T445 5716/447 2129, F447 2583, airport T/F575 1390, www.peruhot.com/inkas *Paz Rent A Car*, Av Diez

Canseco 319, oficina 15, Miraflores, T446 4395, F242 4306. *Hertz*, www.hertz.com, *Localiza*, www.localiza.com.br, and *National*, www.nationalcar.com, also all have representation in Peru.

At the time of going to press, service on the Central Railway to Huancayo was running **Train** once a month. Details are given under Huancayo, page 487.

Directory

Domestic *Aero Continente*, Av José Pardo 651, Miraflores; and Av Larco 123, p 2, **Airline offices** Miraflores, T242 4242. **NB** *Aviandina* is a subisidiary of Aero Continente. *Aero Cóndor*, C Juan de Arona 781, San Isidro, T442 5215/5663. *Lan Perú*, Av José Pardo 269, Miraflores, and C Paz Soldán 225, San Isidro, T213 8200. *Star Up*, Av Larco 101, oficina 1003, Miraflores, T447 7573. *Tans*, (formerly Grupo Ocho, military airline), Jr Belén 1015, Lima centre, and Av Arequipa 5200, Miraflores, T241 8510.

International *Aces*, C Jorge Chávez 400, Miraflores, T447 1311. *Aeroflot*, Av Comandante Espinar 233, Miraflores, T444 8717/8718. *Aerolíneas Argentinas*, Av José Pardo 805, p 3, Miraflores, T241 3327/444 1387. *AeroMéxico*, C Aristides Aljovín 472, Miraflores, T444 4441. *Air France*, Av José Pardo 601, Miraflores, T444 9285. *Air New Zealand*, C Aristides Aljovín 472, Miraflores, T444 4441. *Alitalia*, Mártir Olaya 129 oficina 1702, Miraflores, T447 8513. *American Airlines*, Av Canaval y Moreyra 390, San Isidro, and in Hotel Las Américas, Av Benavides y Av Larco, Miraflores, T211 7000. *Avianca*, Av Paz Soldán 225, oficina C5, San Isidro, T221 7822. *British Airways*, C Andalucía 174, Miraflores, T422 6600/1710. *Continental*, C Victor Belaúnde 147, oficina 101, San Isidro, and in the Hotel Marriott, 13th block of Av Larco, Miraflores, T221 4340/222 7080. *Copa*, Av Dos de Mayo 741, Miraflores, T444 7815/9776. *Delta*, C Victor Belaúnde 147, San Isidro, T211 9211. *Ecuatoriana*, Av José Pardo 231, Miraflores, T241 5219/241 5210. *Iberia*, Av Camino Real 390, p 9, San Isidro, T441 7801/421 4633. *KLM*, Av José Pardo 805, p 6, Miraflores, T242 1240/1241. *Lacsa*, Av Comandante Espinar 331, Miraflores, T444 4690. *Lan Chile*, Av José Pardo 269, Miraflores, T213 8200. *Lloyd Aéreo Boliviano*, Av José Pardo 231, Miraflores, T444 0510/241 5210. *Lufthansa*, Av Jorge Basadre 1330, San Isidro, T442 4466. *Taca Perú*, Av Comandante Espinar 331, Miraflores, T213-7000. *Tame*, C Andalucía 174, Miraflores, T422 6600/1710. *Varig*, Av Camino Real 456, p 8, San Isidro, T442 1449/4163.

BCP (formerly Banco de Crédito), Jr Lampa 499, Lima Centre (main branch), Av Pardo 425 **Banks** and Av Larco at Pasaje Tarata, Miraflores, Av Pardo y Aliaga at Av Camino Real, San Isidro. Mon-Fri 0900-1800, Sat 0930-1230. Accepts and sells American Express TCs only, accepts Visa card and branches have Visa ATM. *Banco de Comercio*, Av Pardo 272 and Av Larco 265, Miraflores, Jr Lampa 560, Lima Centre (main branch). Mon-Fri 0900-1800, Sat 0930-1200. Changes and sells American Express TCs only, ATM accepts Visa/Plus. *Banco Continental*, corner of Av Larco and Av Benavides and corner of Av Larco and Pasaje Tarata, Miraflores, Jr Cusco 286, Lima Centre near Plaza San Martín. Mon-Fri 0900-1800, Sat 0930-1230. TCs (American Express). Visa ATM. *Banco Financiero*, Av Ricardo Palma 278, near Parque Kennedy (main branch). Mon-Fri 0900-1800, Sat 0930-1230. TCs (American Express), ATM for Visa/Plus. *Banco Santander Central Hispano (BSCH)*, Av Pardo 482 and Av Larco 479, Miraflores, Av Augusto Tamayo 120, San Isidro (main branch). Mon-Fri 0900-1800, Sat 0930-1230. TCs (Visa and Citicorp). ATM for Visa/Plus. *Banco Wiese Sudameris*, Av Diagonal 176 on Parque Kennedy, Av José Pardo 697, Miraflores, Av Alfonso Ugarte 1292, Breña, Miguel Dasso 286, San Isidro. Mon-Fri 0915- 1800, Sat 0930-1230. TCs (American Express only), ATM for Visa/Plus. *Citibank*, in all *Blockbuster* stores, and at Av 28 de Julio 886, Av Benavides 23rd block and Av Emilio Cavenecia 175,

Miraflores, Av Las Flores 205 and in Centro Comercial Camino Real, Av Camino Real 348, San Isidro. *Blockbuster* branches open Sat and Sun 1000-1900. Changes and sells Citicorp cheques. *Interbank*, Jr de la Union 600, Lima Centre (main branch). Mon-Fri 0900-1800. Also Av Pardo 413, Av Larco 690 and in Larcomar, Mira flores, Av Grau 300, Barranco, Av Pezet 1405 and Av Pardo y Aliaga 634, San Isidro, and supermarkets *Wong* and *Metro*. Accepts and sells American Express TCs only, ATM for Mastercard.

Exchange houses and street changers There are many *casas de cambio* on and around Jr Ocoña off the Plaza San Martín. On the corner of Ocoña and Jr Camaná you'll no doubt see the large concentration of *cambistas* (street changers) with huge wads of dollars and soles in one hand and a calculator in the other. They should be avoided. Changing money on the street should only be done with official street changers wearing an identity card with a photo. Keep in mind that this card doesn't *automatically* mean that they are legitimate but most likely you won't have a problem. Around Parque Kennedy and down Av Larco in Miraflores are dozens of official *cambistas* with ID photo cards attached to their usually blue, sometimes green vest. There are also those who are independent and are dressed in street clothes, but it's safer to do business with an official money changer. There are a few places on Jr de la Unión at Plaza San Martín that will accept worn, ripped and old bills, but the exchange will be terrible. A repeatedly recommended *casa de cambio* is **LAC Dolar**, Jr Camaná 779, 1 block from Plaza San Martín, p 2, T428 8127, T/F427 3906, also at Av La Paz 211, Miraflores, T242 4069/4085. Mon-Sat 0900-1900, Sun and holidays 0900-1400, good rates, very helpful, safe, fast, reliable, 2% commission on cash and TCs (Amex, Citicorp, Thomas Cook, Visa), will come to your hotel if you're in a group. Another recommended *casa de cambio* is **Virgen P Socorro**, Jr Ocoña 184, T428 7748. Daily 0830-2000, safe, reliable and friendly.

American Express, Pardo y Aliaga 698, San Isidro, T222 2525, F222 5700, for client mail, emergency funds access and TCs. Mon-Fri 0830-1800, Sat 0900-1300. Also at Travex SA, Av Santa Cruz 621, Miraflores, T690 0900, for emergency card replacement, emergency funds access and TCs. Mon-Fri 0830-1745, Sat 0900-1300. *Mastercard*, Porta 111, p 6, Miraflores, T242 2700. *Moneygram* C Ocharan 260, Miraflores, T447 4044. Safe and reliable agency for sending and receiving money. Locations throughout Lima and the provinces. Exchanges most world currencies and Tcs. *Western Union* Main branch: Av Petit Thouars 3595, San Isidro, T422 0036/9723/440 7934. Av Larco 826, Miraflores, T241 1220 (also *TNT* office). Jr Carabaya 693, Lima centre, T428 7624.

Communications Internet Lima is completely inundated with internet cafés, so you will have absolutely no problem finding one regardless of where you are. An hour will cost you approximately S/3-5 (US$0.85-1.50).

Post office The central post office is on Jr Camaná 195 in the centre of Lima near the Plaza de Armas. Hours are Mon-Fri 0730-1900 and Sat 0730-1600. Poste Restante is in the same building but is considered unreliable. In Miraflores the main post office is on Av Petit Thouars 5201 in Miraflores (same hrs). There are many more small branches scattered around Lima, but they are less reliable. For express service, there are a few companies to choose from: *DHL*, Los Castaños 225, San Isidro, T215 7500. *UPS*, Av del Ejército 2107, San Isidro, T264 0105. *Federal Express*, Av Jorge Chávez 475, T242 2280, Miraflores, C José Olaya 260, Miraflores. *EMS*, next to central post office in downtown Lima, T533 2020/2424/2005. When receiving parcels from other countries that weigh in over 1 kg, they will be automatically sent to one of Lima's two customs post offices. Bring your passport and a lot of patience as the process can take a long time: C Teodoro Cárdenas 267, Santa Beatriz (12th block of Av Arequipa); and Av Tomás Valle, Los Olivos (near the Panamerican Highway). NB Long trousers must be worn when going to these offices.

Telecommunications There are many *Telefónica* offices all over Lima. Most allow collect calls but some don't. All offer fax services. There are payphones all over the city. Some accept coins, some only phone cards and some honour both. Phone cards can often be purchased in the street near these booths. Some Telefónica offices are: Pasaje Tarata 280, Miraflores (near Av Alcanfores); Av Bolivia 347, Lima Centre; C Porta 139, Miraflores (near the bottom of Parque Kennedy). There are also many independent phone offices all over the city. For full details on phone operation, see Telephones in Essentials, page 68.

Cultural centres

Alianza Francesa, Av Arequipa 4595, Miraflores, T241 7014. Various cultural activities, also has a library. *CCPUCP* (cultural centre of the Universidad Católica), Camino Real 1075, San Isidro, T222 6899. One of the best in Lima, with an excellent theatre (tickets US$7.15), European art films (US$1.45 Mon-Wed), galleries, good café and a bookshop selling art and literature titles. Recommended. *Centro Cultural de España*, Natalio Sánchez 181-85, Santa Beatriz, T330 0412. Has an art gallery and a cinema. *Centro Cultural Peruano Japonés*, Av Gregorio Escobedo 803, Jesús María, T463 0606. Has a concert hall, cinema, galleries, museum of Japanese immigration, cheap and excellent restaurant, lots of activities. Recommended. *Goethe Institute*, Jr Nasca 722, Jesús María, T433 3180. 0800-2000 Mon-Fri, library, German papers. *Instituto Cultural Peruano-Norteamericano*, Jr Cusco 446, Lima Centre, T428 3530, with library. Main branch at Av Arequipa 4798 y Angamos, Miraflores, T241 1940. Theatre productions and modern dance performances are just a couple of the activities the ICPNA offers. Also Spanish lessons; see Language schools, below. *Peruvian-British Cultural Association*, Av Arequipa 3495, T221 7550. English library and British newspapers. Mon-Fri 0800-1300 and 1530-1930.

Embassies & consulates

Argentine Consulate, Av 28 de Julio 828, Lima centre, T433 3381/5847 F433 0769. 1000-1200. *Australian Consulate*, Av Victor Belaúnde 147 no 1301, San Isidro, T421 4146/222 8281, F221 4996. Services are very limited and everything but the most basic information must come from the closest consulate in Santiago, Chile. *Austrian Embassy*, Av Central 643, p 5, San Isidro, T442 0503/442 1807, F442 8851. 0900-1200. *Belgian Consulate*, Angamos Oeste 392, Miraflores, T241 7566, F241 6379. 0830-1200. *Bolivian Consulate*, Los Castaños 235, San Isidro, T422 8231 (0900- 1330) F222 4594. 0900-1300. *Brazilian Consulate*, José Pardo 850, Miraflores, T421 5650, F445 2421. Mon-Fri 0930-1300. *British Embassy and Consulate*, Av Natalio Sánchez 125, p 12, at the 5th block of Av Arequipa in the Pacífico-Washington building, T433 5032/4738, F433 4735. 0830-1200. *Canadian Embassy*, Libertad 130, Miraflores, T444 4015, F444 4347. Mon, Tue, Thu, Fri 0800-1700, Wed 0800-1300. *Chilean Consulate*, Javier Prado Oeste 790, San Isidro, T221 2817, F221 1258. 0900-1300, need appointment. *Colombian Consulate*, Av Jorge Basadre 1580, San Isidro, T441 0954, F441 9806. Mon-Fri 0800-1400. *Danish Consulate General*, Av Camino Real 348, no 603, San Isidro, T441 9143, F441 9915. Mon-Fri 0830-1700. *Ecuadorean Consulate*, Las Palmeras 356, San Isidro (6th block of Av Javier Prado Oeste), T440 9991, F442 4182. 0900-1300. *French Consulate*, Arequipa 3415, San Isidro, T222 5723/215 8400, F215 8420. 0900-1300. *German Embassy*, Av Arequipa 4210, Miraflores, PO Box (Casilla) 18-0504, T422 4919, F499 6475. 0900-1200. *Guatemalan Consulate*, C Inca Rípac 309, Jesús María, T460 2078, F463 5885. 0900-1300. *Irish Consulate*, Santiago Acuña 135, Urbanización (neighbourhood) Aurora, Miraflores, T/F445 6813. 0930-1300. *Israeli Embassy and Consulate*, Natalio Sánchez 125, p 6, same building as British Embassy, Santa Beatriz, T433 4431, F433 8925. 1000-1300. *Italian Embassy and Consulate*, Av G Escobedo 298, Jesús María, T463 2727/2728, F463 5317. 0830-1100. *Japanese Embassy and Consulate*, Av San Felipe 356, Jesús María, T463 0000/9854. 0900-1200. *Netherlands Embassy and Consulate*, Av Principal 190, Santa Catalina, T476 1069 F475 6536. 0900-1200. *New Zealand*, All consular affairs handled by the British consulate, contact British Embassy, T433 8916/5032. *Norwegian Consulate*, Canaval y Moreyra 595, T440 4048, F441 6175. 0900-1200. *Paraguayan Consulate*, Av La Paz 596,

Miraflores, T444 3448, F444 2391. 0900-1300. *South African Consulate*, Vía Principal 155, Torre Real 3, San Isidro, T440 9996, F422 3881. Mon-Fri 0900-1200. *Spanish Embassy and Consulate*, Jorge Basadre 498, San Isidro, T212 5155, F440 2020. 0900-1300. *Swedish Embassy and Consulate*, Camino Real 348, p9, San Isidro, T421 3434 F212 5805. 0800-1200. *Swiss Embassy and Consulate*, Av Salaverry 3240, Magdalena, T264 0305, F264 1319. 0900-1300. *Uruguayan Consulate*, Av Miguel Dasso 117, p 11, San Isidro, T222 6252, F222 5725. 0930-1400. *US Embassy & Consulate*, Av Encalada block 17, Monterrico, T434 3000, F434 3037. Open 0800-1200, for emergencies after hours T434 3032, the Consulate is in the same building. *Venezuelan Consulate*, Av Arequipa 298, Santa Beatriz, T433 4511, F433 1191.

Language schools   *Instituto Cultural Peruano-Norteamericano*, Av Arequipa 4798, Miraflores, T241 1940/428 3530. Classes are on Mon-Fri from 0900 to 1100, US$80 per month, no private classes. *Instituto de Idiomas (Pontífica Universidad Católica del Perú)*, Av Cam- ino Real 1037, San Isidro, T442 8761/442 6419. Classes Mon-Fri 1100-1300, private lessons possible. *ESIT Idiomas de Lima*, Av Javier Prado Este 4457, Sucro, Lima 33, T434 1060, www.esit-peru.com *Euroidiomas*, Av Santa Cruz 111, Miraflores, T422 5269. US$20 per hr for private classes, 1½hr minimum per class. *Lima School of Languages*, Grimaldo del Solar 469, Miraflores, T242 7763, www.idiomasperu.com US$15 per hr for private tuition, also small groups US$11 per hr. Family homestays and volunteer programmes available. **Independent teachers** (enquire about rates): *Sra Lourdes Gálvez*, T435 3910. Also Quechua. *Sra George- lina Sadastizágal*, T275 6460. Also Sr Mariano Herrera and Sr Dante Herrera: all these can be contacted through peruidiomas@ LatinMail.com *Srta Susy Arteaga*, T534 9289, T989 7271 (mob), susyarteaga@ hotmail.com or susyarteaga@ yahoo.com *Srta Patty Félix*, T521 2559, patty_fel24@yahoo.com

Laundry   There are *lavanderías* (laundromats) all over Lima. Some charge by piece (expensive) while others by weight. Many have a self-service option. Next day service is the norm if you've left laundry for them to wash. Most of the hotels in the higher price range offer laundry service but tend to be very expensive. *Laverap*, Schell 601, Miraflores, T241 0759; Av Pardo y Aliaga 590, T422 1618, San Isidro. You can wash your own clothes or leave them to be picked up (more expensive). *Martinizing Dry Cleaning*, Av Espinar 270, T446 2406, and Av Benavides 1763, T447 5547 in Miraflores, Av Dos de Mayo 1225, T440 2911, San Isidro. Probably the best, but very expensive. *Presto*, Av Benavides 433, Miraflores, T242 9910. Good, reliable. *Cisne Blanco*, Av Santa Cruz 1318, Miraflores, T221 5234. *Lavva Queen*, Av Larco 1158, Miraflores, T444 8520.

Medical services
For hospitals, doctors and dentists, contact your consulate for recommendations

Hospitals and clinics   *Clínica Anglo Americano*, Av Salazar 3rd block, San Isidro, a few blocks from Ovalo Gutiérrez, T221 3656. Stocks Yellow Fever for US$18 and Tetanus for US$3. Dr Luis Manuel Valdez recommended. *Clínica Internacional*, Jr Washington 1471 y Paseo Colón (9 de Diciembre), downtown Lima, T433 4306. Good, clean and professional, consultations up to US$35, no inoculations. *Instituto Médico Lince*, León Velarde 221, near 17th and 18th blocks of Av Arenales, Lince, T471 2238. Dr Alejandro Bussalleu Rivera speaks English, good for stomach problems, about US$28 for initial consultation. Repeatedly recommended. *Clínica San Borja*, Av Guardia Civil 337, San Borja (2 blocks from Av Javier Prado Este), T475 4000/475 3141. *Clínica Ricardo Palma*, Av Javier Prado Este 1066, San Isidro, T224 2224/224 2226. *Instituto de Ginecología y Reproducción*, part of Clínica Montesur, Av Monterrico 1045, Monterrico parallel to Av Polo, T434 2130/434 2426. Recommended gynaecologists are *Dra Alicia García* and *Dr Ladislao Prasak*. *Instituto de Medicina Tropical*, Av Honorio Delgado near the Pan American Highway in the Cayetano Heredia Hospital, San Martín de Porres, T482 3903/482 3910. Cheap consultations, good for check-ups after jungle travel. Recommended. *Clínica del Niño*, Av Brasil 600 at 1st block of Av 28 de Julio, Breña, T330 0066/330 0033. *Centro Anti-Rabia*

Shantytowns – don't go unless you have to

Known as asentamientos humanos or pueblos jóvenes, the shantytowns of Lima are monumental reminders of racial division and social inequality, and of the poverty in which more than half of the capital's population lives. Millions of people have no access to clean drinking water. Most of the Peruvians living in these settlements came from the provinces, escaping misery and the civil war of the 1980-90s. They simply took the land on the hills surrounding Lima, only trying later to legalize their property.

There are old, 'established' shantytowns like **Villa El Salvador** with almost one million inhabitants, as well as new, rapidly expanding ones like **Mi Perú** in Ventanilla, 20 km behind the Jorge Chávez airport. Some shantytowns, like **Lurigancho** and **Canto Grande**, were controlled by Shining Path during the civil war. Others (around the Central Highway that leads towards the Andes) became famous for sheltering delinquents and drug addicts. There is even one shantytown housing Cuban exiles who escaped from the island looking for "freedom" and better life (now they wish they had stayed home). Some consist of bamboo shacks without roofs, others already have sound infrastructure including markets, shops, even small restaurants and cafés.

Social division in Peruvian society is very deep. Most of the shantytown dwellers don't even know of the existence of posh neighbourhoods like San Isidro and Miraflores. Needless to say, most inhabitants of the rich parts of Lima never visit shantytowns.

Many more voyeuristic visitors feel a fascination for Lima's poorest districts. Villa El Salvador, one of the oldest and biggest shantytowns, is the only such place that can be visited without much danger. However, the only safe way to travel is by hiring a taxi: round trip from Miraflores (including a one-hour wait) can be arranged for US$11.50. Villa El Salvador has several stores and eateries in the centre. Travel only by day, wear modest clothes and, if you walk, stick to the main street. It is not recommended that you visit any other of these towns of misery, particularly without previous planning or on your own. Almost without exception, shantytowns are dangerous, especially after dark. Every week, there are countless cases of robbery, stabbing, burglary and rape. Murder is not uncommon. Under no circumstances should you travel by public transport.

If you are planning to take a bus out of Lima, you will see many shantytowns along the highway.

---

de Lima, Jr Austria 1300, Breña, T425 6313. Mon-Sat 0830-1830. Consultation is about US$2.50. *Clínica de Fracturas San Francisco*, Av San Felipe 142 at Av Brasil, Jesús María, T463 9855. *Clínica Padre Luis Tezza*, Av El Polo 570, Monterrico, T435 6990/6991, emergency 24 hrs T437 1310. Clinic specializing in a wide variety of illnesses/disorders etc, expensive; for stomach or intestinal problems, ask for Dr Raul Morales (speaks some English, US$28 for first consultation). *Clínica Santa Teresa*, Av Los Halcones 410, Surquillo, T221 2027. Dr José Luis Calderón, general practitioner recommended. *International Chiropractors Center*, Av Santa Cruz 555, Miraflores, T221 4764.

Pharmacy When possible it is recommended to use pharmacy chains as they are modern, well-stocked, safe and very professional. They can be found in or next to supermarkets, sometimes attached to gas station mini-marts and pretty much everywhere else. Some offer 24-hr delivery service. *Boticas Fasa*, T475 7070; *Boticas Torres de Limatambo*, T444 3022/214 1998; *Farmacentro Tassara*, T251 0600/442 7301; *Superfarma*, T440 9000. *Pharmax*, Av Salaverry 3100, San Isidro, Centro Comercial El Polo, Monterrico (near the US embassy). Pharmacy/hypermarket, with imported goods (Jewish food products sometimes available at Av Salaverry branch, which is open 24 hrs). *Farmacia Deza*, Av Conquistadores 1140, San Isidro. The same as *Pharmax*, also open 24 hrs.

Places of worship

The *Union Church of Lima (Interdenominational)*, Av Angamos 1155, Miraflores, Worship in English Sun 1030, T441 1472. *Trinity Lutheran Church of Peru*, Las Magnolias 495, Urb Jardín, San Isidro. *Church of the Good Shepherd*, Av Santa Cruz 491, Miraflores (Anglican) T445 7908. Sun 0800 Holy Communion, 1000 morning service. *International Baptist Church of Lima*, Col Inclán 799, Miraflores, T475 7179. Worship Sun 1000. *Iglesia San José*, Dos de Mayo 259, Miraflores. Services in German at 0900. *Christian Science Society*, 1285 Mayta Cápac (near Av Salaverry), Jesús María. *Synagogue*, Av 2 de Mayo 1815, San Isidro, T440 0290.

Prison visits

Visits to the women's prison in the district of Chorrillos are easy and much appreciated by the inmates, both Peruvian and foreign. You must bring your passport and give the name of someone you're visiting (check with your embassy for prisoners from your own country, or ask at South American Explorers for the current list). You are permitted to bring food, magazines, books etc (up to 1 kg of fruit, but none that ferments). The *Penal de Chorrillos para Mujeres*, has its visitors day on Sat for men and Sun for women. 0900-1600 with the option to leave at 1300. **NB** This is strictly enforced. If you do not leave at 1300, you will *not* be allowed to leave until 1600. Shoes that have any kind of heel are not permitted (also no boots) and women must wear dresses which, if you don't have one, can be rented across the street from the prison. Men must wear long trousers. Visits are also possible to the men's prisons of *Callao* and *Lurigancho*.

Useful addresses

Tourist Police, Jr Moore 268, Magdalena at the 38th block of Av Brasil, T460 1060/460 0844, open daily 24 hrs. They are friendly and very helpful, English spoken. It is recommended to visit when you have had property stolen. **Immigration** Av España 700 y Jr Huaraz, Breña , open 0830-1500, but they only allow people to enter until 1300. Visa extensions on 3rd floor given the same day, usually within 30 mins (expensive). Provides new entry stamps if passport is lost or stolen. *Intej*, Av San Martín 240, Barranco, T477 2864. They can extend student cards, change flight itineraries bought with student cards. *National library*, Av Abancay 4th block, with Jr Miró Quesada, T428 7690. Mon-Sat 0800-2000, Sun 0830-1330.

The *Peruvian Touring and Automobile Club*: Av César Vallejo 699 (Casilla 2219), Lince, T221 2432. Offers help to tourists and particularly to members of the leading motoring associations. Good maps available of whole country; regional routes and the South American sections of the Pan-American Highway available (US$3.50).

Voluntary organizations

There are a number of organizations in and around Lima that welcome volunteers. Some ask the volunteer to show up when they can, other more structured projects might ask for a commitment of at least 3 months. Although some are listed below, *South American Explorers* is the best place to find out about volunteer opportunities. *Hogar San Francisco de Asis*, C Los Geranios 345, Chaclacayo, T497 1868, contact Antony Lazzera. The *hogar* is a home for abandoned and sick children. Donations of clothes, medicine, food and toys are appreciated. *Centro Anne Sullivan del Perú*, CASP, C Petromila Alvarez 180, Urbanización Pando, San Miguel, T263 6296, F263 1237, http://annsullivan. fundaciontelefonica.org.pe or annsullivan@tsi.com.pe Organization assisting mentally retarded children and those with Downs Syndrome and autism. Contact Enrique Burgos. *CARE*, Av General Santa Cruz 659, Jesús María, T431 7430, F433 4753, www.care.org.pe *Centro Educativo Especial*, Pasaje Condurcunca 118, Lince, T470 1070. Contact Olga Valdivia; works with mentally disabled children, requires strong Spanish skills. *Centro Educativo Ocupacional San Martín de Porras*, Jr Puno 412, San Martín de Porras, T427 0225. Contact Juan Torres. Trades education for children and teenagers. *Cedro*, Av Roca y Boloña 271, Miraflores, T446 6682/7046/447 0748, F446 0751, www.cedro.org.pe Contact the director Alejandro Vassilaqui, or Jorge Arnao. Substance abuse prevention programme, very large and organized. *Asociación Peruana de Mujeres*, C La Puente Olavegoya 180, Pueblo Libre, T463 3365. Contact the director Amanda de Carazas, or Mayra de Grados, or Nicida Jara de Melendes. This is a nursing home for elderly women. *La Voz de la Mujer*, Jr Conde de la Vega Baja 809, Lima centre, T330 1826. Contact Sra Rene Boluarte Zegarra. Shelter for women and childrren who have been victims off domestic violence. *Promudeh* (Ministerio de Promoción de la Mujer y del Desarrollo Humano), Jr Camaná 616, Lima centre, T428 9800, www.prom udeh.gob.pe Government-sponsored organization supporting women's issues, defending their rights and assisting in development programmes run by women.

Excursions from Lima

Callao

Lima

There is no separation between Lima and Callao, the two cities run into each other (the road between the two is lined with factories). But Callao is a city in its own right, the second largest in Peru with over one million inhabitants (much more if you include shantytown dwellers). Shipyards, far from sea, load the fishing vessels they build on huge lorries and launch them into the ocean at Callao. Jorge Chávez International Airport is located here (not in Lima) and it is the most important Peruvian port, handling 75% of the nation's imports and some 25% of its exports. Most parts of the city are ugly, unkempt, poor and dangerous. However, if you are willing to use some imagination and if you like ports, Callao is worth visiting. Some attempts are being made to restore the historical centre and port area.

Phone code: 01
Colour map 3, grid C3

Callao, founded in 1537, used to be one of the most important cities in South America, the only seaport on the continent authorized to trade with Spain during the 16th and 17th centuries. During much of the 16th century Spanish merchants were plagued by threats from English pirates such as Sir Francis Drake and Richard Hawkins who were all too willing to relieve the Spanish armada of its colonial spoils. The harbour was fortified in 1639 in order to prevent such attacks. In 1746, the port was completely destroyed by a massive wave, triggered by the terrible earthquake of that year. According to some sources, all 6,000 of Callao's inhabitants were drowned. The watermark is still visible on the outside of the 18th century church of **Nuestra Señora del Carmen de la Legua** which stands near the corner of Av Oscar Benavides and the airport road, Av Elmer Faucett.

History

In 1850, the first railway in South America was opened between Lima and Callao. It was used not only as a passenger service but, more importantly, for the growing import-export trade, transporting ore from the mines in the Central Highlands and manufactured goods from the disembarking ships.

In the heart of the city stands the enormous Spanish castle, La Fortaleza Real Felipe. It is still used by Peruvian armed forces so you will have to negotiate entry with a lethargic guard. If you succeed, you will be provided with a military guide and the tour may take anything up to two hours. There are some interesting uniforms, arms and artefacts inside the castle, also plenty of cannons. ■ *Daily 0930-1400, T429 0532. US$2 including guide, no cameras allowed.* Several houses around the **Iglesia Matriz** have been restored, but generally the centre is in a state of permanent decay. The most elegant area of Callao proper is **Plaza Grau**. It is well-maintained and from here you can see a

Sights

large part of the port and the **Palomino Islands** (inhabited by birds, seals and other marine species), including **Isla San Lorenzo**. This island has an underwater military bunker, with two famous prisoners, Abimael Guzmán, founder of Sendero Luminoso, and Víctor Polay, leader of MRTA. Trips to the islands can be arranged from the pier next to Plaza Grau. One of the agencies is called *Vientosur*. Ask around, departures are mostly unscheduled.

There is a great **Museo Naval del Perú** on Plaza Grau. Models of Peruvian and foreign ships, weapons, uniforms, torpedoes, and other relics. Interesting photographs. Recommended. ■ *Av Jorge Chávez 121, T429 4793. Tue-Sat 0900-1600, Sun 0900-1700. US$0.85.*

Essentials   It is not recommended that you **sleep** in Callao. The city centre becomes a dangerous red-light district after sunset. Good places to **eat** are: *Leo*, Jr Adolfo King 182. Local place, good food. Also try *Cebichería Mateo*, C Constitución 280. **Transport**   From Callao, **Lima** is at least 20 mins by colectivos, US$0.30, bus US$0.25, taxi US$3-4 to the centre or Miraflores. Do not take a bus back to Lima after dark.

La Punta   La Punta is a green, nostalgic peninsula next to Callao. It has the relaxed atmosphere of a beach resort, good local seafood restaurants, pleasant walks, friendly people and great views. It's an interesting place to come for lunch, but the ride back to Lima, even in a taxi, can be dangerous at night (you would have to drive through Callao proper). La Punta has only 6,800 permanent residents. Its main artery is Av Coronel Bolognesi, lined with impressive old villas. There is a well-maintained Malecón parallel to Bolognesi, a lovely walk and great views of the islands, sailing boats and Callao port. On the corner of El Malecón and Jr García y García is the **Club de Regatas Lima**, with a nice café and view from the second floor (open sporadically). Nearby is the **Club de Regatas Unión**. Along El Malecón is a pebble beach, but the water is not very clean, due to the proximity of Callao port. **Plaza Grau** is nicely restored, with a library inside the municipality building. It has no pamphlets, but you can get information about the past (La Punta was founded in 1555) and the present of La Punta there.

Boat trips   At Plaza Grau at the foot of the steps to the sea (from where the liberty boats come and go to the Peruvian Navy ships anchored out in the bay) bright pleasure boats, complete with life jackets, take trippers out to the end of La Punta beach and back. The journey is about 25 minutes and costs US$1.

Sleeping   AL-D *La Punta*, Jr Saenz Peña 486-490, T/F429 1553, info@bed-and-breakfast-la-punta.com Price includes breakfast, a variety of rooms in a recently-restored 1930s mansion, with and without bath, spacious common rooms, patio, cable TV.

Cieneguilla   Cieneguilla, about 20 km east of Lima, on the Lurín river, is a small village in the country, an easy escape from the city and cloud cover of Lima. It is a popular place on Sunday, with restaurants with gardens and swimming. All open daily for lunch. ■ *Take a combi running east on Av Prado Este, 30-45 mins, US$0.50.*

Pántanos de Villa   In the district of Chorrillos is the 396-ha wildlife sanctuary, Pántanos de Villa, an ecological wetland reserve with brackish water and abundant emergent vegetation. It provides the habitat for waterfowl typical of coastal Peru, including 17 species of migratory shorebirds. There are several species of fish, four types of reptile and over 50 species of water plants. Take binoculars. ■ *More information can be obtained from the municipal tourist office, T231 1325.*

Pachacámac is in the Lurín valley, 31 km from Lima. When the Spaniards **Pachacámac** arrived, Pachacámac was the largest city and ceremonial centre. It was a vast complex of palaces and temple-pyramids, to which pilgrims went to pay homage to the god Pachacámac, a wooden statue of whom is in the site museum.

Hernando Pizarro came to Pachacámac in 1533, having been sent by his brother to speed the delivery of gold from the coast for Atahualpa's ransom. However, great disappointment awaited Pizarro as there was no store of riches. In their desperate search for the promised gold the Spaniards destroyed images, killed the priests and looted the temples.

The ruins encircle the top of a low hill, whose crest was crowned with a **Temple of the Sun**, a large pyramid built in 1350 of sun-baked bricks, now partially restored. Slightly apart from the main group of buildings and hidden from view is the reconstructed **House of the Mamaconas**, where the 'chosen women' were taught to weave and spin fine cloth for the Inca and his court. Further to the north the Temple of Urpi-Huachac, who was reputed to be the wife of Pachacámac, is in a state of total ruin.

■ *0900 to 1700, Mon-Fri; closed 1 May. US$1.75 including the small site museum which sells soft drinks. If you plan to take public transport, go to the Pan-American Highway (south-bound) and take a combi with a sticker in the window reading "Pachacámac/Lurín" (US$0.85). Let the driver know you want to get off at the ruins. A taxi will cost approximately US$4.30, but if you don't ask the driver to wait for you (an extra cost), finding another to take you back to Lima may be a bit tricky. For organized tours contact one of the tour operators listed above.*

Near the Central Highway, in the eastern outskirts of Lima, is Puruchuco, site of **Puruchuco** a major archaeological find, announced in 2002. Under a shanty town called Túpac Amaru, over 2,000 mummy bundles have been uncovered in an Inca cemetery known as **Puruchuco-Huaquerones**. The cemetery itself is not a new discovery, but the quantity and completeness of the mummies, plus the tens of thousands of accompanying objects, should reveal a wealth of information about the last century of Inca society before the Spanish conquest. It is clear that some of the mummies are of the Inca élite and all are well-preserved. Archaeologists estimate that only 40% of the burials at the site have come to light. On the way to Chosica, up the Rímac valley, take the turn off at Km 41/2 to Puruchuco.

Also at Puruchuco is the reconstructed palace of a pre-Inca Huacho noble. There is a small museum with ceramics and textiles from the lower Rímac or Lima valley and a selection of indigenous plants and animals. ■ *Mon-Fri 0900-1700 (closed 1 May and 28 Jul). US$1.75.*

This large adobe pre-Inca city can also be visited. The turnoff (left, at **Cajamarquilla** Huachipa) is about 6 km on from the Puruchuco turn. The site cannot be seen from the road; look for a sign 'Zona Arqueológica' in the middle of a brickyard. Keep on driving through the yard, and Cajamarquilla is at the end of an ill-kept dirt road. ■ *Daily 0900-1700. US$1.75.*

Thirty kilometres northwest of Lima, Ancón is reached by a double-lane **Ancón** asphalted highway. In the 19th and early 20th centuries, this was the smart seaside resort in Peru, but has now been deserted by the wealthy and in summer is crowded with daytrippers. It has a mix of elegant 19th-century houses with wooden balconies and modern apartment blocks. There are tennis courts and a yacht club. The beaches are very small and crowded during January-March holidays, but bathing is safe with no currents and the water is "refreshing" (as Michael Fuchs of Munich puts it).

Lima

Beyond Ancón is a Chancay cemetery, from which has come much Chancay weaving and pottery (as seen in the Museo Amano).

D *Hostal del Pirata*. In Ancón, antique furniture, the building dates from the mid-19th century, good views, excellent seafood, including *ceviche*.

Canta

Phone code: 01
Colour map 3, grid B4
Altitude: 2,837 m

Canta is a popular small town on the fringes of the high Andes less than three hours from Lima by paved road. After 1½ hours, by which time the *garúa* has been left behind, you pass through **Santa Rosa de Quives**, the birthplace of the patron Saint of Lima. Her house and the adjoining Sanctuary can be visited. After two hours the petrogylphs of **Checta** are reached. Numerous, small, complex drawings cover the surface of boulders spread across a hillside 15 minutes' steep walk from the road. The path is marked.

Canta itself is not especially attractive, but there are good day walks and significant ruins nearby. The **tourist office** is on the main street, T2447013, 1000-1600 Saturday and Sunday only.

The pre-Inca ruins of **Cantamarca** (3,600 m) were probably built by the Chancay culture. They consist of large *chullpas* (burial towers) made from finely cut stone, many with roofs still supported by stone pillars. ■ *Take a steep trail from 5 km up the La Viuda road. Allow 2-3 hrs for the climb and carry water.*

A few km beyond Canta is Huaros (3,587 m) from which a long day walk can be made to the **Parque Arqueológico de Huischo** and the **Bosque de Puyos Raimondis** (4,050m). Beyond Huaros the road continues to the beautiful Lake Chuchun below the fourteen snow-capped peaks of the La Viuda cordillera.

Sleeping & eating
Arrive by lunchtime at weekends because all hotels fill up

D *Cancay Vento*, T441 5733, Friendly, clean, hot water, big bathrooms, being expanded. **E** *Alborada*. Hot water, TV, the best of several more basic ones. **E** *Hospedaje Casa Blanca*, Arica 402, T526 0282. With bath, hot water, TV, clean. **Camping**: a few km up the valley at *Huaichaullany The Hoo*, *La Casona*, just off the main street, is the best restaurant, serving local trout in an interesting old building. *Los Claveles* serves a decent *tamale* for breakfast.

Transport

Bus From/to **Lima**, 100 km, 3 hrs, US$2, *Trans El Chaparito* (Av G Unger 601, San Martin de Porres, Lima) and *Trans Cueva Santa* (Av G Unger 369) offer an hourly service between them. *Cueva Santa* buses from Lima continue to **Huaros**, **Laguna Chuchun** and **La Viuda**. A few **combis** run to La Viuda daily from Canta, 3 hrs, US$2. To **Obrajillo**, 5 km, 10 mins, US$0.50. Combis leave when full. To **Huallay and Cerro de Pasco**, only occasional vehicles cross the La Viuda pass (4,500m).

Obrajillo

At weekends Limeños flock to Obrajillo, a village set in beautiful countryside criss-crossed by fast flowing streams. You can visit the waterfall (US$0.30), or go riding (US$4 per hour). A one-hour walk runs up the south side of the valley, on the opposite side to the waterfall, to Santa Rosa de Acochaca where there is a restaurant and shop. Returning on the opposite side of the valley a detour can be made to San Miguel (1 hour), giving a bird's eye view of Obrajillo, before descending a steep path to Obrajillo (15 minutes).

Sleeping and eating Best is **D** *Hotel Cabaña*, T244 7022, on the Canta side of the village. **E** *Hostal Dodero* is the best of the *hostales*. **Camping** is possible at the waterfall (US$3 per tent) and above Santa Rosa de Acochaca. Eat in the main plaza or try the trout *chicharrones* and *pachamanca* at riverside restaurants.

Cusco and the Sacred Valley

Introducing Cusco and the Sacred Valley

Cusco stands at the head of the Sacred Valley of the Incas and is the jumping off point for the Inca Trail and famous Inca city of Machu Picchu. It's not surprising, therefore, that this is the prime destination for the vast majority of Peru's visitors. In fact, what was once an ancient Inca capital is now the 'gringo' capital of the entire continent. And it's easy to see why. There are Inca ruins aplenty, as well as fabulous colonial architecture, stunning scenery, great trekking, river rafting and mountain biking, beautiful textiles and other traditional handicrafts – all within easy reach of the nearest cappuccino or comfy hotel room.

Cusco is the centre of a magnificent Inca civilization transformed into a jewel of colonial achievment by the Spanish. Yet the city today is not some dead monument, its history

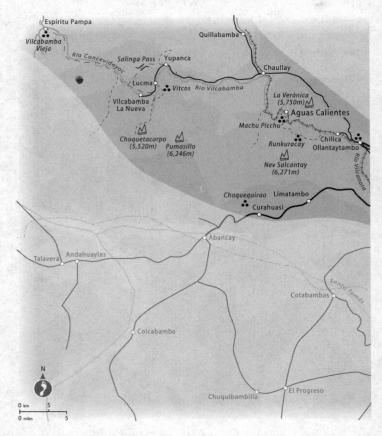

breathes through the stones. The Quechua people bring the city to life with with a combination of prehispanic and Christian beliefs and every visitor is made welcome.

Starting your visit to the Cusco region outside the city has many advantages. Staying a day or two in the **valley of the Urubamba** river will give you time to acclimatize to the shortage of oxygen at these altitudes. And as nowhere is very far from the city, you can easily nip into town for any necessities. At **Ollantaytambo**, **Pisac** and of course **Machu Picchu**, you will see Inca ruins and terraced hillsides without the overlay of the Spanish conquest. Then, when you are fit and ready, you can make your own assault on Cusco, with all the energy you need for the many churches, museums, pubs, clubs, shops and many **festivals** which are held throughout the year in this part of Peru. When you find yourself in the middle of a fiesta, try to count how many people are involved, the incredible depth of emotion and sense of participation is often overwhelming.

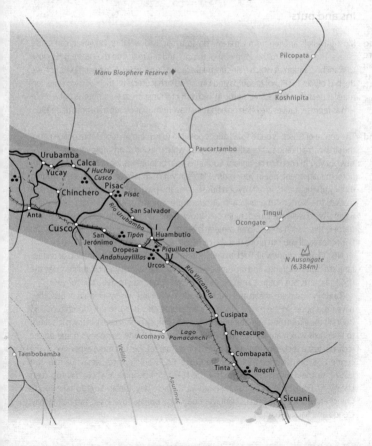

Things to do in Cusco and the Sacred Valley

- Inspect the **Inca stonework** closely, from the just-credible Stone of 12 Angles on Calle Hatun Rumiyoc in Cusco, to the frankly incredible Sacsayhuaman, and try to fathom out how it was done, page 163.
- Go **shopping** – the choice is endless; from piles of weavings to the most singular modern designs. In the markets you'll find both everyday items and weird and wonderful fruit and vegetables, page 179.
- At **Pisac**, walk up to the ruins. It's a stiff climb, but worth it. As you go higher, the views of the Urubamba Valley just get better and better, page 197.
- Take a trip to **Moray**, in the hills above Urubamba, where three large depressions were converted by the Incas into terraced crop laboratories, all under the gaze of the snow-capped Verónica mountain, page 204.
- Visit the Sistine Chapel of the Andes at **Andahuaylillas**. Nearby is the equally remarkable church at Huaro, page 226.
- Cross the last **Inca suspension bridge** at Qeswachaka, which is rebuilt annually in the only festival of its kind, page 228.

Cusco

Ins and outs

Getting there

Phone code: 084
Colour map 5, grid A5
Population: 275,000
Altitude: 3,310 m

Most travellers arriving from Lima will do so by air. Bad weather, however, can cause delays. The airport is to the southeast of the city and the road into the centre goes close to Wanchac station, at which trains from Juliaca and Puno arrive. Also near this station are the bus offices for Puno, Arequipa and Lima (Av Pachacútec e Infancia). Cusco's bus terminal is near the Pachacútec statue in Ttio district. Transport to your hotel is not a problem as representatives are often on hand. For travel information see transport, page 190.

Getting around

The centre of Cusco is quite small and is possible to explore on foot. More police patrol the streets, trains and stations than in the past, which has led to an improvement in **security**, but you still need to be vigilant. Look after your belongings, leaving valuables in with hotel management, not in your room. Places in which to take care are: when changing money on the streets; in railway and bus stations; the bus from the airport; the Santa Ana market; the San Cristóbal area and at out-of-the-way ruins. Also take care during Inti Raymi. Avoid walking alone at night on narrow streets, between the stations and the centre, or in the market areas. Stolen cameras often turn up in the markets and can be bought back cheaply. If you can prove that the camera is yours, contact the police.

NB On no account walk back to your hotel after dark from a bar, nightclub or restaurant; strangle muggings and rape are common. For the sake of your own safety pay the US$1 taxi fare, but not just any taxi. Ask the club's doorman to get a taxi for you.

Taxis in Cusco are cheap and recommended when arriving by air, train or bus. They have fixed prices: in the centre US$0.60 (a little more after dark); to the suburbs US$0.85 (touts at the airport and train station will always ask much higher fares). In town it is safest to take taxis which are registered; these have a sign with the company's name on the roof, not just a sticker in the window. Taxis on call are reliable but more expensive, in the centre US$1.25 (*Ocarina* T247080, *Aló Cusco* T222222). Trips to Sacsayhuaman cost US$10; to the ruins of Tambo Machay US$15-20 (3-4 people); a whole day trip costs US$40-70. For US$50 a taxi can be hired for a whole day (ideally Sun) to take you to Chinchero, Maras, Urubamba, Ollantaytambo, Calca, Lamay, Coya, Pisac, Tambo Machay, Qenqo and Sacsayhuaman.

48 hours in Cusco

Occupying yourself for 24 hours in Cusco will only pose problems if you are not acclimatized to the altitude. If this is your first day, you must rest. Don't worry, there is always tomorrow for trying new places. There is so much to recommend here that the following day in town is nothing more than a suggestion.

Get an early start with the breakfast buffet at La Tertulia or in the colonial splendour of El Monasterio hotel (it may cost more, but it will set you up for the day).

The Plaza de Armas is a good place to begin because it was the heart of both the Inca and Spanish cities. Just sitting here, soaking up the atmosphere and the morning sun, will get you in the right frame of mind. In the Cathedral and its neighbouring churches you can see the paintings of the Last Supper and the 1650 earthquake and other treasures. Also on the Plaza and worth a look is the main altar of La Compañía de Jesús. There may be time before lunch to visit the Inka Museum, which has the most comprehensive collection in the city.

Lunch could be a light snack at the Portal de Carnes (in Ayllu, or Bagdad), or a full Andean meal at the Inka Grill or Tunupa. Otherwise, there are also loads of places to choose from on Plateros and Procuradores. Afterwards, head downhill to see the magnificent combination of Inca and colonial architecture at Qoricancha (the Temple of the Sun) and

Santo Domingo. In the late afternoon you could go up to San Blas district, with its traditional craft shops and church with superb pulpit. On the way, look for the Stone of the 12 Angles on Calle Hatun Rumiyoc. San Blas has its share of cafés and restaurants, so if you fancy a pick-me-up, have a pastry at the Panadería El Buen Pastor, or if you're running late and want a meal, try Al Grano, Greens or Macondo.

If you fancy an afternoon alternative a little way out of the city, catch a taxi up to the huge Inca ceremonial centre of Sacsayhuaman and then watch the sunset from the nearby White Christ. Make sure you take a sweater as a chill wind can blow up at dusk and don't walk back down after dark.

Before dinner seek out which pubs have a Happy Hour. For a relaxing start try Los Perros, but if you want to be immediately re-energized brace yourself for entry to the Cross Keys Pub. Many places serve food so you could stay where you are, or move on to a restaurant.

Fit for some dancing? Here again the city won't let you down. The Ukuku's bar is a great place to dance and meet people while at Mama Africa's you'll get more dancing than talking done in a night's entertainment. If you are not up to making the moves yourself, there are just as many places with live shows, such as the peñas which have traditional music.

To organize your own Sacred Valley transport, try one of these taxi drivers, recommended by South American Explorers: *Manuel Calanche*, T227368/695402; Carlos Hinojosa, T251160; *Ferdinand Pinares*, Yuracpunco 155, Tahuantinsuyo, T225914/681519 (speaks English, French and Spanish); *Eduardo*, T231809, speaks English. Other recommended drivers are: *Angel Marcavillaca Palomino*, Av Regional 877, T251822, amarcavillaca@yahoo.com Helpful, patient, reasonable prices. *Movilidad Inmediata*, T623821 (mob), run local tours with an English-speaking guide. *Angel Salazar*, Marc avalle I-4 Huanchac, T224679 to leave messages. He is English speaking and arranges good tours, very knowledgeable and enthusiastic. *Milton Velásquez*, T222638, T680730 (mob). He is also an anthropologist and tour guide and speaks English.

If you wish to explore this area on your own, Road Map (*Hoja de ruta*) No 10 is an excellent guide. You can get it from the *Automóvil Club del Perú*, Av Sol 457, next to Banco Santander, 3rd floor. They also have other maps. Motorists beware; many streets end in

Cusco & the Sacred Valley

flights of steps not marked as such. There are very few good maps of Cusco available. Maps and guidebooks maps of the city, the Inca Trail and the Urubamba Valley are also available at tour companies.

El Tranvía de Cusco, actually a motor coach, runs on the route of the original Cusco tramway system, which operated from 1910-40. The route starts in the Plaza de Armas (except on Sunday morning when the weekly flag ceremony takes place) and ends at the Sacsayhuaman Archeological Park. There is a 10-minute stop at the mirador by the Cristo Blanco before descending to the Plaza de Armas. Departures 1000, 1150 and 1500, 1 hr 20 mins, with explanations of the city's history, architecture, customs, etc; US$2, US$1.40 for students with ID. For group reservations T740640.

Best time to visit Cusco is the most popular tourist city in Peru, but the real high season is from June to September. This also happens to be the time of year which enjoys the most stable weather for hiking the Inca Trail or trekking and climbing elsewhere. The days are generally clear and sunny, though nights can be very cold at high altitude. The highlands can be visited at other times of the year, though during the wettest months from November to April some roads become impassable and hiking trails can be very muddy. June is the highlight of Cusco's festival calendar, bringing even more people into the city. The celebrations are worth seeing, however, and there usually seems to be room for everybody.

Information & advice Cusco stands at 3,310 m, so you should respect the altitude. Two or three hours' rest after arriving makes a great difference. Also avoid smoking, don't eat meat but do eat lots of carbohydrates and drink plenty of clear, non-alcoholic liquid, and remember to walk slowly. A word of advice for those arriving in Cusco by air. It makes a lot of sense to get down to the Urubamba Valley, at 2,800 m, 510 m lower than Cusco itelf, and make the most of your first couple of days. There are good hotels in Ollantaytambo, Urubamba, Yucay and Pisac. At this relatively low altitude you will experience no headaches and you can eat and sleep comfortably.

To see Cusco and the surrounding area properly – including Pisac, Ollantaytambo, Chinchero and Machu Picchu – you need five days to a week, allowing for slowing down because of altitude. Those on a tight itinerary should note that this is a difficult city to leave and many a carefully planned travelling schedule has been revised in the face of its overwhelming attraction.

Tourist offices Official tourist information is at Portal Mantas 117-A, next to La Merced church, T263176, 0800-2000. There is also an *i perú* tourist information desk at the airport, T237364, daily 0600-1300, and another at Portal de Carrizos 250, Plaza de Armas, T252974/234498, daily 0830-1930. *Ministry of Tourism*, Av de la Cultura 734, 3rd floor, T223701/223761, Mon-Fri 0800-1300. See Visitors Ticket Box for OFEC offices and INC office for Machu Picchu.

Tourist information *South American Explorers*, Choquechaca 188, apto 4 (2 blocks behind the cathedral), T245484, cuscoclub@saexplorers.org, Mon-Fri 0930-1700, Sat-Sun 0930-1300; as Lima, an excellent resource and haven for the traveller. They also have an office at Wanchac train station. *Touring y Automóvil Club del Perú*, Av Sol 349, nivel 2, T/F224561 T/F224561. There are lots of information booklets on Machu Picchu and the other ruins at the bookshops. *Cusco Weekly* is an English language newspaper, covering local and international news; Choquechaca 188, no 3, PO Box 693, T258278, www.cuscoweekly.com For more websites, see Essentials, page 30, and for books see, page 611.

Emergency numbers: police 105; fire 133 The **Tourist Police**, Calle Saphi 5111, T249654. If you need a *denuncia* (a report for insurance purposes), which is available from the Banco de la Nación, they will type it out. Always go to the police when robbed, even though it will cost you a bit of time. The Tourist Protection Bureau (*Indecopi*), which protects the consumer rights of all tourists and will help with any problems or complaints, can be very effective in

Visitors' tickets

A combined entry ticket to most of the sites of main historical and cultural interest in and around Cusco, called the **Boleto Turístico Unificado (BTU)**, costs US$10 (S/.35) and is valid for 5-10 days. It permits entrance to: the Cathedral, San Blas, Santa Catalina Convent and Art Museum, Qorikancha or Temple of the Sun Museum (but not Santo Domingo/Qorikancha itself), Museo de Arte Religioso del Arzobispado, Museo Histórico Regional (Casa Inca Garcilazo de la Vega), Museo Palacio Municipal de Arte Contemporáneo; the archaeological sites of Sacsayhuaman, Qenqo, Puka Pukara, Tambo Machay, Pisac, Ollantaytambo, Chinchero, Tipón and Piquillacta. There is also a US$6, one-day ticket.

The BTUs can be bought at the OFEC office (Casa Garcilazo), Plaza Regocijo, esquina C Garcilazo, T226919, Mon-Fri 0745-1830, Sat 0830-1600, Sun 0800-1230, or Av Sol 103, T227037, Mon-Fri 0800-1800, Sat 0830-1300, or at any of the sites included in the ticket. There is a 50% discount for students with a green ISIC card, which is only available at the OFEC office (Casa Garcilazo) upon presentation of the student card. Take your ISIC card when visiting the sites, as some may ask to see it. There is no student reduction for the one-day card.

Note that all sites are very crowded on Sun. Many churches are closed to visitors on Sun, and the 'official' opening times are unreliable. Photography is not allowed in the Cathedral, churches, and museums.

On the back of the BTU is a map of the centre of Cusco with the main sites of interest clearly marked. It also includes a map of the tourist routes from Cusco to the Sacred Valley following the Río Urubamba towards Machu Picchu, as well as the southeastern area of Cusco on the road to Puno. The ticket includes days and hours of attention.

Entrance tickets for the Museo Inka (El Palacio del Almirante) and La Merced are sold separately. Machu Picchu ruins and Inca trail entrance tickets are sold at the Instituto Nacional de Cultura (INC), at San Bernardo s/n between Mantas y Almagro, T236061, Mon-Fri 0900-1300, 1600-1800, Sat 0900-1100.

dealing with tour agencies, hotels or restaurants. They are at the tourist office at Portal Carrizos, Plaza de Armas (see above). Toll free 0800-42579 (24-hour hotline, not available from payphones). Head office is at Av de la Cultura 732-A. P 1, T/F252987, mmarroquin@indecopi.gob.pe

The city

The ancient Inca capital is said to have been founded around 1100 AD. According to the central Inca creation myth, the sun sent his son, Manco Cápac and the Moon her daughter, Mama Ocllo, to spread culture and enlightenment throughout the dark, barbaric lands. They emerged from the icy depths of Lake Titicaca and began their journey in search of the place where they would found their kingdom. They were ordered to head north from the Lake until a golden staff they carried could be plunged into the ground for its entire length. The soil of the altiplano was so thin that they had to travel as far as the valley of Cusco where, on the mountain of Huanacauri, the staff fully disappeared and the soil was found to be suitably fertile. This was the sign they were looking for. They named this place Cusco – meaning 'navel of the earth'.

Today, the city's beauty cannot be overstated. It is a fascinating mix of Inca and colonial Spanish architecture: colonial churches, monasteries and convents and extensive pre-Columbian ruins are interspersed with countless hotels, bars and restaurants that cater for the hundreds of thousands of tourists.

Almost every central street has remains of Inca walls, arches and doorways. Many streets are lined with Inca stonework, now serving as the foundations for more modern dwellings.

Cusco has developed into a major, commercial centre of 275,000 inhabitants, most of whom are Quechua. The city council has designated the Quechua, Qosqo, as the official spelling. Despite its growth, however, the city is still

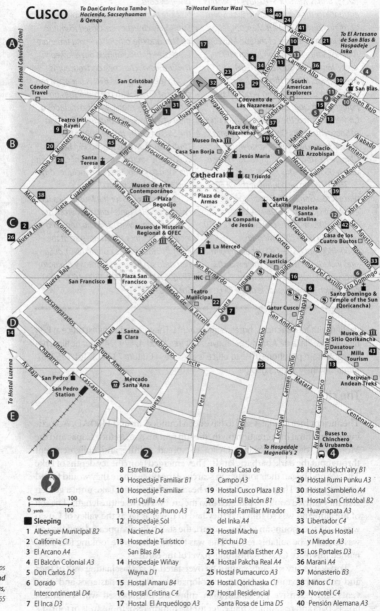

Cusco

Cusco & the Sacred Valley

Related maps
A Around
Plaza de Armas,
page 165

N

0 metres 100
0 yards 100

■ **Sleeping**
1 Albergue Municipal *B2*
2 California *C1*
3 El Arcano *A4*
4 El Balcón Colonial *A3*
5 Don Carlos *D5*
6 Dorado Intercontinental *D4*
7 El Inca *D3*

8 Estrellita *C5*
9 Hospedaje Familiar *B1*
10 Hospedaje Familiar Inti Quilla *A4*
11 Hospedaje Jhuno *A3*
12 Hospedaje Sol Naciente *D4*
13 Hospedaje Turístico San Blas *B4*
14 Hospedaje Wiñay Wayna *D1*
15 Hostal Amaru *B4*
16 Hostal Cristina *C4*
17 Hostal El Arqueólogo *A3*

18 Hostal Casa de Campo *A3*
19 Hostal Cusco Plaza I *B3*
20 Hostal El Balcón *B1*
21 Hostal Familiar Mirador del Inka *A4*
22 Hostal Machu Picchu *D3*
23 Hostal María Esther *A3*
24 Hostal Pakcha Real *A4*
25 Hostal Pumacurco *A3*
26 Hostal Qorichaska *C1*
27 Hostal Residencial Santa Rosa de Lima *D5*

28 Hostal Rickch'airy *B1*
29 Hostal Rumi Punku *A3*
30 Hostal Sambleño *A4*
31 Hostal San Cristóbal *B2*
32 Huaynapata *A3*
33 Libertador *C4*
34 Los Apus Hostal y Mirador *A3*
35 Los Portales *D3*
36 Marani *A4*
37 Monasterio *B3*
38 Niños *C1*
39 Novotel *C4*
40 Pensión Alemana *A3*

laid out much as it was in Inca times. The Incas conceived their capital in the shape of a puma and this can be seen from above, with the river Tullumayo forming the spine, Sacsayhuaman the head and the main city centre the body. The best place for an overall view of the Cusco valley is from the puma's head – the top of the hill of Sacsayhuaman.

Sights

The heart of the city in Inca days was *Huacaypata* (the place of tears) and *Cusipata* (the place of happiness), divided by a channel of the Saphi river. Today, Huacaypata is the Plaza de Armas and Cusipata is Plaza Regocijo. This was the great civic square of the Incas, flanked by their palaces, and was a place of solemn parades and great assemblies. Each territory conquered by the Incas had some of its soil taken to Cusco to be mingled symbolically with the soil of the Huacaypata, as a token of its incorporation into the empire.

As well as the many great ceremonies, the Plaza has also seen its share of executions, among them Túpac Amaru, the last Inca, the rebel conquistador Diego de Almagro the Younger, and Túpac Amaru II, the 18th century indigenous leader.

Around the present-day Plaza de Armas are colonial arcades and four churches. The early 17th century baroque **Cathedral** (on the northeast side of the square) forms part of a 3-church complex: the Cathedral itself, Iglesia **Jesús y María** (1733) on the left as you look at it and **El Triunfo** (1533) on the right. There are two entrances; the Cathedral doors are used during Mass but the tourist entrance is on the left-hand side through Iglesia Jesús y María. The Cathedral was built on the site of the Palace of Inca Wiracocha (*Kiswarcancha*) using stones from Sacsayhuaman.

The gleaming, newly-renovated gilded main altar of the Iglesia Jesús y María draws the eyes to the end of the church. However, take the time to look up at the colourful murals which have been partially restored. Walking through into the Cathedral's transept,

Plaza de Armas

As most of the sights do not have any information or signs in English, a good guide can really improve your visit. Either arrange this before you set out or grab one of those hanging around the sights' entrances – much easier to do in the low season. A tip is expected at the end of the tour

41	Posada del Sol *A3*
42	San Agustín Internacional *C4*
43	San Agustín Plaza *D4*
44	Savoy Internacional *E5*
45	Suecia II *B2*

● **Eating**
1	A Mi Manera *B3*
2	Café Manu & Manu Nature Tours *E6*
3	Chifa Sipan *D3*
4	Greens *A4*
5	Heidi Granja *B4*

6	Inkanato *C4*
7	La Bodega *A4*
8	Los Toldos *D3*
9	Macondo *A4*
10	Pacha-Papa *B4*
11	Panadería El Buen Pastor *A4*
12	Parrilla Andina *C4*
13	Pie Shop *A4*

the oldest surviving painting in Cusco can be seen. It depicts the 1650 earth-quake. It also shows how within only one century the Spaniards had already divided the main plaza in two. El Señor de los Temblores (The Lord of the Earthquakes) can be seen being paraded around the Plaza de Armas while fire rages through the colonial buildings with their typical red-tiled roofs. Much of modern-day Cusco was built after this event. The choir stalls, by a 17th-century Spanish priest, are a magnificent example of colonial baroque art (80 saints and virgins are exquisitely represented), as is the elaborate pulpit. On the left is the solid-silver high altar. In the far right-hand end of the Cathedral is an interesting local painting of the Last Supper. But this is the Last Supper with a difference, for Jesus is about to tuck into a plate of *cuy*, washed down with a glass of chicha!

Entering El Triunfo there is a stark contrast between the dark, heavy atmo-sphere of the Cathedral and the light, simple structure of this serene church. Built on the site of *Suntur Huasi* (the Roundhouse), El Triunfo was the first Christian church in Cusco. The name El Triunfo (The Triumph) came from the Spanish victory over an indigenous rebellion in 1536. It was here that the Span-iards congregated, hiding from Manco Inca who had besieged the city, almost taking it from the invaders. The Spaniards claimed to have witnessed two mira-cles in their hour of need. First, they were visited by the Virgin of the Descent, who helped put out the flames, then came the equestrian saint, James the Greater, who helped kill many indigenous Indians. The two divinities are said to have led to the Spanish victory; not only was it the triumph of the Spaniards over the Incas, but also of the Catholic faith over the Indians' religion.

El Triunfo's fine granite altar is a welcome relief from the usual gilding. Here the statue of the Virgin of the Descent resides and, above her, is a wooden cross known as the Cross of Conquest, said to be the first Christian cross on Inca land brought from Spain. ■ *The Cathedral is open until 1000 for genuine worshippers – Quechua mass is held 0500-0600. Those of a more secular inclination can visit 1000-1130 Mon, Tue, Wed, Fri and Sat or Mon–Sun 1400-1730. Entrance with the BTU tourist ticket.*

On the southeast side of the plaza is the beautiful church of **La Compañía de Jesús**, built on the site of the Palace of the Serpents (*Amarucancha*, residence of the Inca Huayna Cápac). The original Jesuit church was destroyed in the earth-quake of 1650 and the present-day building took 17 years to construct. It was inaugurated in 1668. The altarpiece is resplendent in gold leaf. It stands 21 m high and 12 m wide. It is carved in the baroque style, but the indigenous artists felt that this was too simple to please the gods and added their own intricacies. Gold leaf abounds in the many altarpieces and on the carved pulpit. ■ *Free.*

Northeast of the Plaza de Armas

The **Palacio del Almirante**, just north of the Plaza de Armas at Cuesta del Almirante 103, is one of Cusco's most impressive colonial houses. Note the pil-lar on the balcony over the door, showing a bearded man from inside and a naked woman from the outside. During the high season local Quechuan weav-ers can be seen working in the courtyard. The weavings are for sale, expensive but of very good quality. It houses the interesting **Museo Inka**, run by the Universidad San Antonio de Abad, which exhibits the development of culture in the region from pre-Inca, through Inca times to the present day. The museum has a good combination of textiles, ceramics, metalwork, jewellery, architecture, technology, photographs and 3D displays. They have an excellent collection of miniature turquoise figures and other objects made as offerings to the gods. The display of deliberately deformed skulls with trepanning is fasci-nating, as is the full-size tomb complete with mummies stuck in urns. ■ *T237380. Mon-Fri 0800-1700, Sat 0900-1600. US$1.40.*

The **Palacio Arzobispal** stands on Hatun Rumiyoc y Herrajes, two blocks northeast of Plaza de Armas. It was built on the site of the palace occupied in 1400 by the Inca Roca and was formerly the home of the Marqueses de Buena Vista. It contains the **Museo de Arte Religioso** which has a fine collection of colonial paintings, furniture and mirrors. The Spanish tiles are said to be 100 years old and each carved wooden door has a different design. The collection includes the paintings by the indigenous master, Diego Quispe Tito, of a 17th-century Corpus Christi procession that used to hang in the church of Santa Ana. They now hang in the two rooms at the back of the second smaller courtyard (see Painting and sculpture, page 602). The throne in the old dining-room is 300 years old and was taken up to Sacsayhuaman for the Pope to sit on when he visited in 1986. ■ *Mon-Sat, 0830-1130, 1500-1730. Entrance with BTU tourist ticket.*

The **Convento de las Nazarenas**, on Plaza de las Nazarenas, is now an annex of *El Monasterio* hotel. You can see the Inca-colonial doorway with a mermaid motif, but ask permission to view the lovely 18th-century frescos inside. *El Monasterio* itself is well worth a visit – ask at reception if it's OK to have a wander. Built in 1595 on the site of an Inca palace, it was originally the Seminary of **San Antonio Abad** (a Peruvian National Historical Landmark). One of its most remarkable features is the Baroque chapel, constructed after the 1650 earthquake. If you are not disturbing mealtimes, check out the dining room. This is where the monks used to sing. Also on Plaza Nazarenas is **Casa Cabrera**, which is now a gallery and used by *Banco Continental*.

The San Blas district, called Tococache in Inca times, has a large number of shops and galleries which sell local carvings, ceramics and paintings. (See Shopping, Local crafts, page 179). There are also many *hostales* and eating places on the steep, narrow streets, which are good for a day-time wander (take care after dark). The church of **San Blas**, on Carmen Bajo, is a simple rectangular adobe building whose walls were reinforced with stone after the 1650 and 1950 earthquakes. It houses one of the most famous pieces of wood carving found in the Americas, a beautiful *mestizo* pulpit carved from a single cedar trunk. ■ *Mon-Sun 1800-1130, 1400-1730, closed Thu mornings.*

The magnificent **Santa Catalina** church, convent and museum are on Arequipa at Santa Catalina Angosta. The convent was built upon the foundations of the Acllahuasi, or the House of the Chosen Women, whose nobility, virtue and beauty permitted them to be prepared for ceremonial and domestic duties – some were chosen to bear the Inca king's children. Today the convent is a closed order where the nuns have no contact with the outside world. The church has an ornate, gilded altarpiece and a beautifully carved pulpit.

Southeast of the Plaza de Armas

The museum has a wonderful collection of Cuzqueño school paintings spanning the decades of Spanish rule – a good guide can point out how the style changes from the heavy European influence to the more indigenous style. ■ *Daily 0900-1730, except Fri 0900-1500. There are guided tours by English-speaking students; a tip is expected. Church open 0700-0800 daily.*

This is one of the most fascinating sights in Cusco. Behind the walls of the Catholic church are remains of what was once the centre of the vast Inca society. The Golden Palace and Temple of the Sun was a complex filled with such fabulous treasures of gold and silver it took the Spanish three months to melt it all down. The Solar Garden contained life-sized gold sculptures of men, women, children, animals, insects and flowers, placed in homage to the Sun God. On the walls were more than 700 gold sheets weighing about 2 kg/4½ lb

Qoricancha at Santo Domingo

Cusco & the Sacred Valley

each. These the conquistadores sent back intact to prove to the King of Spain how rich was their discovery. There would also have been a large solar disc in the shape of a round face with rays and flames. This disc has never been found.

The first Inca, Manco Cápac, is said to have built the temple when he left Lake Titicaca and founded Cusco with Mama Ocllo. However, it was the ninth Inca, Pachacútec, who transformed it. When the Spaniards arrived, the complex was awarded to Juan Pizarro, the younger brother of Francisco. He in turn willed it to the Dominicans who ripped much of it down to build their church.

Walk first into the courtyard then turn around to face the door you just passed through. Behind and to the left of the paintings (representing the life of Santo Domingo Guzmán) is Santo Domingo. This was where the *Sun Temple* stood, a massive structure 80 m wide, 20 m deep and 7 m in height. Only the curved wall of the western end still exists and will be seen (complete with a large crack from the 1950 earthquake), when you later walk left through to the look-out over the Solar Garden. Still in the baroque cloister, close by and facing the way you came in, turn left and cross to the remains of the *Temple of the Moon*, identifiable by a series of niches. Beyond this is the so-called *Temple of Venus and the Stars*. Stars were special deities used to predict weather, wealth and crops. In the *Temple of Lightning* on the other side of the courtyard is a stone. Stand on this and you will appreciate how good the Incas were as stonemasons: all three windows are in perfect alignment. ■ *Mon-Sat 0800-1700, Sun 1400-1600 (except holidays). US$1.15 (not on the BTU Visitor Ticket).*

Museo de Sitio Qorikancha (formerly Museo Arqueológico) is now housed in an underground site on Avenida Sol, in the gardens below Santo Domingo. It contains a limited collection of pre-Columbian artefacts, a few Spanish paintings of imitation Inca royalty dating from the 18th century, photos of the excavation of Qoricancha, and some miniature offerings to the gods. ■ *Mon-Fri 0800-1730, Sat 0900-1700. Entrance by the BTU Visitor Ticket, or US$2. The staff will give a guided tour in Spanish, but please give a tip.*

Much **Inca stonework** can be seen in the streets and most particularly in the Callejón Loreto, running southeast past La Compañía de Jesús from the main plaza. The walls of the *Acllahuasi* (House of the Chosen Women) are on one side, and of the *Amarucancha* on the other. There are also Inca remains in Calle San Agustín, to the east of the plaza. The famous stone of 12 angles is in Calle Hatun Rumiyoc halfway along its second block, on the right-hand side going away from the plaza. The finest stonework is in the celebrated curved wall beneath the west end of Santo Domingo. This was rebuilt after the 1950 earthquake, at which time a niche that once contained a shrine was found at the inner top of the wall. Excavations have revealed Inca baths below here, and more Inca retaining walls. Another superb stretch of late Inca stonework is in Calle Ahuacpinta outside Qoricancha, to the east or left as you enter (John Hemming). True Inca stonework is wider at the base than at the top and features ever-smaller stones as the walls rise. Doorways and niches are trapezoidal. The Incas clearly learnt that the combination of these four techniques helped their structures to withstand earthquakes. This explains why, in two huge earthquakes (1650 and 1950), Inca walls stayed standing while colonial buildings tumbled down.

Southwest of the Plaza de Armas **La Merced** (on Marquéz), originally built in 1534, was razed in the 1650 earthquake and rebuilt by indigenous stonemasons in the late 17th century. The high altar is neoclassical with six gilded columns. There are a further 12 altars. Inside the church are buried Gonzalo Pizarro, half brother of Francisco, and the two Almagros, father and son. Attached is a very fine monastery. The first cloister is the most beautiful with its two floors, archways and pillars. The pictures on the first floor depict the Saints of the Order (those of the second floor have been removed for restoration). ■ *Monastery and its small museum 1430-1700. The church 0830-1200, 1530-1730, except Sun. US$0.85.*

Museo de Historia Regional, in the Casa Garcilaso, Jr Garcilaso y Heladeros, shows the evolution of the Cuzqueño school of painting. It also contains Inca agricultural implements, a Nasca mummy, colonial furniture and paintings, a photographic exhibition of the 1950 earthquake and other mementos. ■ *0730-1700. Entrance with BTU tourist ticket. A guide is recommended.*

San Francisco, on Plaza San Francisco, three blocks southwest of the Plaza de Armas, is an austere church reflecting many indigenous influences, but it has a wonderful monastery, cloister and choir. Although at the time of writing the monastery was not officially open to the public, it may be possible to visit if you approach the door to the left of the church and knock on it. The cloister is the oldest in the city, built in the Renaissance style, but with diverse influences. The ground floor has several crypts containing human bones. The fabulous high choir contains 92 detailed carvings of martyrs and saints. ■ *0600-0800, 1800-2000.*

Heading towards Santa Ana market and San Pedro station from Plaza San Francisco, you pass Santa Clara arch and the nuns' church of **Santa Clara**. It is singular in South America for its decoration, which covers the whole of the interior. Its altars are set with thousands of mirrors. ■ *Only open in the morning, 0600-0700.*

San Pedro, in front of the Santa Ana market, was built in 1688. Its two towers were made from stones brought from an Inca ruin. If you approach it through the Santa Clara arch early in the morning, you will see the street stallholders setting up at Santa Ana market. ■ *Mon-Sat 1000-1200, 1400-1700.*

Above Cusco, on the road up to Sacsayhuaman, is **San Cristóbal**, built to his patron saint by Cristóbal Paullu Inca. The church's atrium has been restored and there is a sidewalk access to the Sacsayhuaman Archaeological Park. North of San Cristóbal, you can see the 11 doorway-sized niches of the great Inca wall of the Palacio de Colcampata, which was the residence of Manco Inca before he rebelled against the Spanish and fled to Vilcabamba.

Northwest of the Plaza de Armas

Cristo Blanco, arms outstretched and brilliantly illuminated at night, stands over the town and is clearly visible if one looks north from the Plaza de Armas. He was given to the city as a mark of gratitude by Palestinian refugees in 1944. A quick glance in the local telephone directory reveals there is still a large Arab population in Cusco.

There are some magnificent Inca walls in the ruined ceremonial centre of Sacsayhuaman, on a hill in the northern outskirts. The Incaic stones are hugely impressive. The massive rocks weighing up to 130 tons are fitted together with absolute perfection. Three walls run parallel for over 360 m and there are 21 bastions.

Sacsayhuaman

Sacsayhuaman was thought for centuries to be a fortress, but the layout and architecture suggest a great sanctuary and temple to the Sun, which rises exactly opposite the place previously believed to be the Inca's throne – which was probably an altar, carved out of the solid rock. Broad steps lead to the altar from either side. Zig-zags in the boulders round the 'throne' are apparently 'chicha grooves', channels down which maize beer flowed during festivals. Up the hill is an ancient quarry, the Rodadero, which is now used by children as a rock slide. Near it are many seats cut perfectly into the smooth rock.

The hieratic, rather than the military, hypothesis was supported by the discovery in 1982 of the graves of priests, who would have been unlikely to be buried in a fortress. The precise functions of the site, however, will probably continue to be a matter of dispute as very few clues remain, due to its steady destruction.

The site survived the first years of the conquest. Pizarro's troops had entered Cusco unopposed in 1533 and lived safely at Sacsayhuaman, until the rebellion of Manco Inca, in 1536, caught them off guard. The bitter struggle which ensued became the decisive military action of the conquest, for Manco's failure to hold Sacsayhuaman cost him the war, and the empire. The destruction of the hilltop site began after the defeat of Manco's rebellion. The outer walls still stand, but the complex of towers and buildings was razed to the ground. From then, until the 1930s, Sacsayhuaman served as a kind of unofficial quarry of pre-cut stone for the inhabitants of Cusco (Peter Frost). The site is about a 30-minute walk from the town centre. Walk up Pumacurco from Plaza de las Nazarenas.

■ *Daily 0700-1730. You can get in earlier if you wish and definitely try to get there before midday when the tour groups arrive. Free student guides are available, but you should give them a tip. There are lights to illuminate the site at night.*

Other sites near Cusco
Along the road from Sacsayhuaman to Pisac, at 3,600 m above sea level, is the temple and amphitheatre of **Qenqo**. These are not exactly ruins, but rather one of the finest examples of Inca stone carving *in situ*, especially inside the large hollowed-out stone that houses an altar. The rock is criss-crossed by zig-zag channels that give the place its name and which served to course *chicha*, or perhaps sacrificial blood, for purposes of divination. The open space many refer to as the 'plaza' or 'amphitheatre' was used for ceremonies. The 19 trapezoidal niches, which are partially destroyed, held idols and mummies.

The Inca fortress of **Puka Pukara** (Red Fort), was actually more likely to have been a *tambo*, a kind of post-house where travellers were lodged and goods and animals housed temporarily. It is worth seeing for the views alone.

A few hundred metres up the road is the spring shrine of **Tambo Machay**. It is in excellent condition. There are many opinions as to what this place was used for. Some say it was a resting place for the Incas and others that it was used by Inca Yupanqui as a hunting place. There are three ceremonial water fountains built on different levels. It is possible that the site was a centre of a water cult. Water still flows by a hidden channel out of the masonry wall, straight into a little rock pool traditionally known as the Inca's bath.

For details of this and other walks in the area, see Footprint's Cusco and the Inca Trail Handbook

It is possible to walk from Sacsayhuaman to Tambo Machay, via Qenqo, **Cusilluchayoc** (Templo de los Monos, or Monkey Temple), an area of rocks and galleries with the remains of a fountain, then on a section of the Incas' Cusco-Pisac road to **Laqo** (Templo de la Luna, or Temple of the Moon), with sculptures in caves and an observatory, Chilcapuquio and Puka Pukara.

■ *Taking a guide to the sites mentioned above is a good idea and you should visit in the morning for the best photographs. Carry your multi-site ticket, there are roving ticket inspectors. You can visit the sites on foot. It's a pleasant walk through the countryside requiring half a day or more, though remember to take water and sun protection, and watch out for dogs. An alternative is to take the Pisac bus up to Tambo Machay (US$0.35) and walk back. Another excellent way to see the ruins is on horseback, arranged at travel agencies. An organized tour (with guide) will go to all the sites for US$6 per person, not including entrance fees. A taxi will charge US$15-20 for three to four people. Some of these ruins are included in the many City Tours on offer.*

Cusco & the Sacred Valley

Around Plaza de Armas

Plateros detail

Sleeping
1 El Procurador *A2*
2 Emperador Palace *C3*
3 Hostal Cáceres
   Plateros detail
4 Hostal Carlos V *A2*
5 Hostal Casa Grande *C3*
6 Hostal Corihuasi *A3*

7 Hostal Garcilaso *B1*
8 Hostal Imperial
   Palace *A2*
9 Hostal Incawasi *B2*
10 Hostal Q'Awarina *A2*
11 Hostal Qosqo *C2*
12 Hostal Resbalosa *A3*
13 Hostal Royal
   Frankenstein &
   Hostal Horeb *B1*
14 Hostal Santa María *C3*
15 Los Marqueses *B1*
16 Pensión Loreto *C2*
17 Picoaga *A1*
18 Royal Inka I *B1*
19 Royal Inka II *A1*
20 Sonesta Posada
   del Inca *C2*

Eating
1 Al Grano *C3*
2 Ama Lur
   Plateros detail
3 Blueberry Lounge *B3*
4 Café Ayllu *B3*
5 Café Bagdad *B3*
6 Café Halliy
   Plateros detail
7 Chez Maggy Clave
   de Do *A2*

8 Chez Maggy El
   Corsario *B2*
9 Chez Maggy La
   Antigua *A2*
10 Chez Maggy
   Millenium
   Plateros detail
11 El Cuate *A2*
12 El Mexicanito *A2*
13 El Truco & Taberna
   del Truco *B1*
14 Fallen Angel *B3*
15 Frutos *C3*
16 Govinda & Varayoc *B2*
17 Inka Grill *B2*
18 Keros *B2*
19 Kintaro *B1*
20 Kusikuy
   Plateros detail
21 La Barceloneta &
   La Naturaleza *B2*
22 La Dulcería *B1*
23 La Retama *B2*
24 La Tertulia *B2*
25 La Yunta *B3*
26 Los Candiles & Café
   Amaru *Plateros detail*
27 Los Tomines *C3*
28 Mesón de los
   Espaderos *B2*

29 Mesón de los
   Portales *B2*
30 Pachacútec Grill
   & Bar *B2*
31 Paititi *C3*
32 Paloma Imbil *A2*
33 Pucará
   Plateros detail
34 Spoonk
   Plateros detail
35 Trotamundos *B2*
36 Tunupa & Cross
   Keys Pub *B2*
37 Victor Victoria *A2*
38 Yaku Mama *A2*

Bars & clubs
39 Kamikaze *B2*
40 Los Perros *A2*
41 Mama Africa *C3*
42 Norton Rat's
   Tavern *C2*
43 Paddy O'Flaherty's *C3*
44 Rosie O'Grady's
   & Sky Travel *C3*
45 Templo *B2*
46 Ukuku's
   Plateros detail
47 Xcess *B3*

Related map
Cusco, page 158

Essentials

Cusco & the Sacred Valley

Sleeping
■ on map pages
158 and 165

Price codes:
see inside front cover

Prices given are for the high season in Jun-Aug and do not include 28% tax and service, unless stated. When there are fewer tourists hotels may drop their prices by as much as half. Always check for discounts. Hotel prices, especially in the mid to upper categories, are often lower when booked through tour agencies. You should book more expensive hotels well in advance through a good travel agency, particularly for the week or so around Inti Raymi, when prices are greatly increased. Be wary of unlicensed hotel agents for medium-priced hotels, they are often misleading about details; their local nickname is *jalagringos* (gringo pullers), or *piratas*. Taxis and tourist minibuses meet the train and take you to the hotel of your choice for US$0.50, but be insistent. It is cold in Cusco, and many hotels do not have heating. It is worth asking for an 'estufa', a space heater which some places will provide for an extra charge. When staying in the big, popular hotels, allow yourself plenty of time to check out if you have a plane or train to catch: front desks can be very busy.

*Assume hotels have
24-hour hot water
unless otherwise
stated. Cusco´s
low-power electric
showers often do
a poor job of
heating the water
and their safety
is sometimes
questionable*

LL *Libertador*, in the Casa de los Cuatro Bustos at Plazoleta Santo Domingo 259 (see Sights), T231961, F233152, www.libertador.com.pe Buffet breakfast is US$15 extra. This splendid 5-star award-winning hotel is built on Inca ruins (the walls can be seen in the restaurant and bar) and is set around courtyards. It has 254 well-appointed rooms; the attention to detail is so great there are even Nazca Lines drawn in the sand of the ashtrays! Enjoy Andean music and dance over dinner in the excellent *Inti Raymi* restaurant. Recommended. **LL** *Monasterio*, Palacios 136, T241777, F237111, reservas@peruorientexpress.com.pe (in Lima T01-242 3427, F242 3365 This 5-star, beautifully restored Seminary of San Antonio Abad is central and quite simply the best hotel in town for historical interest; it is worth a visit even if you cannot afford

the price tag (see Sights). There are 106 spacious rooms with all facilities, including cable TV, as well as 16 suites and a US$521 presidential suite. Staff, who all speak English, are very helpful and attentive. The price includes a great buffet breakfast (US$12 to non-residents, will fill you up for the rest of the day). The restaurant serves lunch and dinner à la carte. Email for guests (US$3 per hr) open 0930-1300, 1730-2130. Recommended. **LL** *Novotel*, San Agustín 239, T228282, F228855, www.novotel.com (in Lima T01-215 1616, F215 1617, salesjm@sofitelroyal park.com.pe). 4-star (but still **LL**) in modern section; price includes buffet breakfast. Converted from the colonial home of conquistador Miguel Sánchez Ponce (it was remodeled after the 1650 earthquake with lovely stone archways and paintings of the saints on the grand stairway). Beautiful courtyard, roofed in glass, with sofas, coffee tables and pot plants around the central stone fountain. Modern 5-storey rear extension has excellent airy and bright rooms. Rooms in the colonial section are not much different but have high beamed-ceilings and huge beds. Two restaurants.

L *Don Carlos*, Av Sol 602, T226207/224457 (Lima T224 0263, F224 8581), www.tci.net.pe/doncarlos The price includes buffet breakfast. A modern hotel, clean and bright with a friendly front desk, but it lacks character. Cable TV, safe, fridge, heating. Some rooms have facilities for the disabled. **L** *Picoaga*, Santa Teresa 344 (two blocks from the Plaza de Armas), T221269, F221246, www.computextos.com.pe/picoaga Price includes buffet breakfast. Originally the home of the Marqués de Picoaga, this beautiful colonial building has large original bedrooms set around a shady courtyard and a modern section, with a/c, at the back. Cable TV, minibar and safe, pleasant staff. Recommended. **L** *San Agustín Internacional*, Maruri 390, T221169 or 0800-43434, F221174 (also **AL** *San Agustín Plaza*, Av Sol 526, T237331, F237375), www.hotelsan agustin.com.pe Price includes continental breakfast. There is a rustic Mexican feel to the lobby with its fireplace and water feature, while Andean music is piped to the communal

Cusco & the Sacred Valley

areas. Heated bedrooms; the staff will organize tours. **L** *Savoy Internacional*, Av Sol 954, T224322, F221100 (Lima T/F446 7965), www.cusco.net/savoyhotel Price includes American breakfast. This is one of the earliest modern hotels in the city and some of the features are dated. However, bedrooms are spacious, with heating and some have good views. Bar, coffee shop, staff speak many languages. Warm, friendly atmosphere. **L** *Sonesta Posada del Inca*, Portal Espinar 142, one block from the central plaza, T227061, F248484, (Lima 01-222 4777, F422 4345), www.sonesta.com Price includes buffet breakfast but internet is US$6 an hour. Warmly decorated rooms with heating and cable TV. For best views of the Plaza, over rooftops, reserve nos 316, 318, 320 or 321 on the third floor. The restaurant serves Andean food. The all English-speaking staff provide an excellent service. Recommended.

AL *Los Apus Hostal y Mirador*, Atocsaycuchi 515 y Choquechaca, San Blas, T264243, F264211, www.losapushostal.com Price includes buffet breakfast and airport pick-up. Swiss-owned, very clean and smart with beamed bedrooms, cable TV and real radiators! **AL** *Dorado Intercontinental*, Av Sol 395, T233112, F240883, imperial_reservas@terra.com.pe (in Lima T/F01-472 1415). Price includes buffet breakfast. Modern meets colonial: the elevator shaft which dominates the central lobby is quite Gaudi-esque, while the bedrooms are decorated in colonial style. Good restaurant (*Sky Room*), serves lunch and dinner for US$10. Cafeteria is open to the public. **AL** *Royal Inka I I*, Plaza Regocijo 299, T231067, F234221, royalin@terra.com.pe Price includes buffet breakfast. A colonial house around a shady central patio, rooms with cable TV and heating. Tranquil, bar, restaurant with set menu. Recommended. **AL** *Royal Inka II*, close by, on Santa Teresa. More modern and expensive but the price includes buffet breakfast, saunas and jacuzzi (massages US$25). The colonial façade hides a modern building with a huge atrium dominated by an incongruous, three-storey high mural. Cable TV, heating. Free bus for guests to Pisac at 1000 daily, returning at 1800.

A *Pensión Alemana*, Tandapata 260, San Blas, T/F226861, pensioalemana@ terra.com.pe Price includes American breakfast; laundry and heating extra. Car parking available. Swiss-owned, modern European décor with a comfy lounge area, lovely garden with patio furniture. Recommended. **A** *Hostal Cusco Plaza 1*, Plaza Nazarenas 181 (opposite *El Monasterio*) T246161, F263842. Price includes continental breakfast. On a lovely small plaza, clean rooms with cable TV, great views (*Cusco Plaza 2*, Saphi 486, has opened in a restored colonial house, same services and conveniences, but **AL**). **A** *Emperador Plaza*, Santa Catalina Ancha 377, T227412, F263581, emperadr@ terra.com.pe Price includes buffet breakfast. Modern, light, airy, friendly and helpful English-speaking staff, gas-heated showers and electric radiators. **A** *Hostal El Balcón*, Tambo de Montero 222, T236738, F225352, balcon1@terra.com.pe Price includes breakfast. Lovingly restored 1630 colonial house, beautiful views from the balcony (but not from rooms). Ask for a TV if you want – there is no extra charge. Restaurant and kitchen for guests to use, laundry service, homely. Recommended. **A** *Hostal Garcilaso*, Garcilaso 233, T233031, F222401, hotelgarcilaso@hotmail.com Price includes continental breakfast, heater and cable TV. Services include oxygen, laundry and excursions can be organized. Modernized colonial house, spacious rooms, bar, cafeteria and dining room.

B *Hostal Cahuide*, Saphi 845, T222771, F222361. Price (discount for longer stays) includes American breakfast but ask for the free TV in your room (cable in sitting rooms only). Heating and laundry extra. Modern but plain, comfortable beds. Helpful, good value breakfasts. **B** *Hostal Casa de Campo*, Tandapata 296-B (at the end of the street), T/F243069, www.hotelcasadecampo.com (or contact via *La Tertulia* café). Price (10% discount for SAE members and Footprint Handbook owners) includes continental breakfast and free airport/rail/bus transfer with reservations. Bedrooms have fabulous views, but it's quite a climb to get to them. Safe deposit box, laundry service, meals on request and a sun terrace. Dutch and English spoken, take a taxi there after dark.

B *Hostal Corihuasi*, Suecia 561, T/F232-233, www.corihuasi.com Price includes continental breakfast and airport pick-up. Electric heaters extra; free book exchange. A tough climb up from the northernmost corner of the Plaza de Armas, tranquil, popular with tour groups. Recommended. **B** *Hostal Cristina*, Av Sol 341, T227233, F227251, hcristina@ terra.com.pe Price includes continental breakfast. Good, comfortable rooms with cable TV, friendly. Good value. **B** Hostal Monarca, C Pumapaccha 290, T226145, www.hostalesmonarca.com Breakfast included. **B** *Pensión Loreto*, Pasaje Loreto 115, Plaza de Armas (same entrance as *Norton's Rat* pub), T226352, hostal loreto@telser.com.pe Price includes continental breakfast and heater for the spacious rooms with original Inca walls. Great location; they will serve you breakfast in bed. Laundry service, will help organize travel services and guides. **B** *Los Marqueses*, Garcilaso 256, T232512, F227028, marqueseshotel@ hotmail.com Price includes breakfast, heaters extra (ask about special deals), electric showers. A splendid colonial house with a beautiful courtyard. The place is littered with antiques and the breakfast room even has its own altarpiece rescued from a church! The bedrooms are in need of renovation. **B** *Los Portales*, Matará 322, T/F223500, portales01@terra.com.pe Price includes continental breakfast and airport pickup; heaters extra. Safe deposit box, laundry, oxygen, money exchange. Modern, friendly and helpful, children welcome. Recommended. **B-C** *Hostal El Arqueólogo*, Pumacurco 408, T232569, F235126, www.hotelarqueologo.com Price includes buffet breakfast. Services include oxygen, a library and hot drinks. Colonial building on Inca foundations, rustic but stylish décor. Lovely sunny garden with comfy chairs and a small restaurant that serves interesting Peruvian food and fondue. French and English spoken. Recommended. Also has *Vida Tours*, at this address, T227750, F235126, www.vidatours.com Traditional and adventure tourism. **B** *Hostal Rumi Punku* Choquechaca 339, T221102, F242741, www.rumipunku.com Contintental breakfast included, laundry extra. A genuine Inca doorway leads to a sunny, tranquil courtyard. Large, clean, comfortable rooms, helpful staff, safe. Highly recommended.

C *Hostal Amaru*, Cuesta San Blas 541, T/F225933, www.cusco.net/amaru Price (**D** without bath) includes breakfast and airport/train/bus pick-up. Services include oxygen, kitchen for use in the evenings only, laundry and free book exchange. Rooms around a pretty colonial courtyard, good beds, pleasant, relaxing, some Inca walls. Rooms in the first courtyard are best. Recommended. **C** *Hostal Imperial Palace*, Tecseccocha 490-B, T223324, celazo@hotmail.com **D** without bath, price includes continental breakfast and heaters. Large room, comfortable beds. Café, bar and restaurant. Very friendly. **C** *El Inca*, Quera 251, T/F 221110, oscaralianza@yahoo.com Price includes breakfast; **E** in the low season, laundry extra. Heating, hot water variable, luggage store, restaurant, Wilbur speaks English and is helpful. Noisy disco in basement till 0100. Otherwise recommended. **C** *Hostal Incawasi*, Portal de Panes 147, Plaza de Armas, T223992, incawasi@telser.com.pe Rather dark, but an excellent location. Good beds, helpful staff. Good bargains for longer stays. **C** *Marani*, Carmen Alto 194, San Blas, T/F249462, marani@terra.com.pe Breakfasts available. Book exchange and information on Andean life and culture. Large rooms with heaps of character, set around a courtyard. The Hope Foundation (www.stichtinghope.org) operates here: Walter Meekes and his wife Tineke have built 20 schools in poor mountain villages and barrios, established a programme to teach teachers and set up a 30-bed burns unit in Cusco general hospital. Good value, a great cause and highly recommended. **C** *Hostal María Esther*, Pumacurco 516, T/F224382. Price includes continental breakfast, heating extra (**D** without bath). Very helpful, lovely garden and a variety of rooms. Car parking. Recommended. **C** *Niños Hotel*, C Meloc 442, T/F231424, www.targetfound.nl.ninos Cheaper without bath, excellent

breakfast for US$1.70. Services include cafeteria, laundry service, book exchange. Dutch, English, German and French spoken. Spotless, beautiful rooms in an 18th-century house, all leading onto a well-renovated courtyard. The hostal funds a charity run by Dutch couple Titus and Jolande Bovenberg, which adopts street children. Nearby are some equally well-appointed apartments (US$20) which share a kitchen, bathroom, but are cold. These help fund a restaurant in the same complex where the Niños foundation everyday feeds, cares for and helps educate 126 more street children. Highly recommended. **C** *Hostal Pakcha Real*, Tandapata 300, San Blas, T237484, pakcharealhostal@hotmail.com Price includes breakfast, the use of the kitchen (no fridge) and free airport/train/bus pick-up; heaters US$1.50. Family-run hostal with a large lounge with a fireplace and cable TV. Laundry service, spotless rooms, friendly, relaxed. **C** *Hostal Q'Awarina*, at the top of Suecia 575, T228130. Price includes continental breakfast, heating US$2 per night. No laundry service. Rooms are OK, ask for those with a view. Lovely living room with views across the city; the breakfast area upstairs is even better. Good value. **C** *Posada del Sol*, Atocsaycuchi 296, T/F246394. Includes American breakfast, heater and airport pick-up. Cheerfully decorated, sun terrace with great views, fantastic showers. Use of kitchen, laundry service, food available. Cannot be reached by taxi. Recommended.

D *El Arcano*, Carmen Alto 288, T/F232703. Breakfast and laundry available, cheaper rooms with shared bath. Lovely little communal area, small breakfast area with cable TV, book exchange. Very friendly owners (likewise their large German Shepherd dog). They will help arrange trips and own two lodges; one in the jungle and another in cloudforest. Highly recommended. **D** *Casa de la Gringa*, C Pensamiento E-3, Urb Miravalle (5-min taxi ride from the Plaza de Armas), T/F229379/241168, www.anotherplanetperu.net Price includes Andean breakfast. Large gardens surround the hostal, which has comfortable rooms, each in a distinctive style. A relaxing, spiritual place with volcanic rock sweat lodge. Kitchen facilities, lounge, luggage store, food on request, taxi to anywhere in the city for US$1; South African owner. Recommended. **D** *Hostal Familiar*, Saphi 661, T239353. **E** without bath, luggage deposit US$2.85 a day for a big pack. Popular, in a pleasing colonial house, 3 blocks from the central plaza. Most beds are comfy, hot water all day. Recommended. **D** *Hostal Familiar Mirador del Inka*, Tandapata 160, off Plaza San Blas, T261384. Cheaper without bath. Inca foundations and white colonial walls, spacious rooms, comfortable beds, hot water. Use of kitchen, laundry service. The owner's son Edwin runs trekking trips and has an agency on site. **D** *Hostal Horeb*, San Juan de Dios 260, T236775. Price includes bath. Large rooms but few have outside windows. No breakfast available. *Frankenstein* is in the same building. **D** *Hostal Kuntur Wasi*, Tandapata 352-A, San Blas, T227570. **E** without bath, services include a safe, use of the kitchen (for US$0.60 a day), laundry service. Great views from the terrace where you can breakfast. Welcoming, helpful family. **D** *Hostal Machu Picchu*, Quera 282, T231111. **E** without bath; public phone, safe, no TVs; laundry service. Central, pleasant, relaxing, but rooms without bath are dark. **D** *Hostal Royal Frankenstein*, San Juan de Dios 260 (next to *Horeb*), 2 blocks from the Plaza de Armas, T236999, ludwigroth@hotmail.com You will never forget this place with its ghoulish theme. Kitchen, cable TV in the living room, safe and laundry facilities. Rooms have good mattresses but few have outside windows. German owner. Recommended.

E *Hostal Cáceres*, Plateros 368, T232616, 1 block from the Plaza de Armas. **F** without bath, use of the kitchen US$0.30 a day, book exchange, laundry service. Well-positioned with large, if basic rooms, not all the mattresses are comfortable. Very helpful owners. Motorcycle parking in the patio. **E** *El Artesano de San Blas*, Suytuccato 790, T/F263968. Price includes use of kitchen. Large rooms in a colonial house, clean, well-decorated, friendly staff. Recommended. **E** *Hospedaje Familiar Inti Quilla*, Atocsaycuchi 281, T252659. Price includes bath, **F** without bath.

Breakfast extra. Colourfully decorated rooms around a pleasant little courtyard, on a pedestrian street. Good value, very safe, hot water. **E** *Hospedaje Jhuno*, Carmen Alto 281, San Blas, T233579. Breakfast is not included but guests can use the tiny kitchenette. Small, family-run hospedaje, clean. **E** *Hostal Qorichaska*, Nueva Alta 458, T228974, F227094. Price includes continental breakfast, use of the well-equipped kitchen and safe. Laundry service, ask for the older rooms which are bigger and have traditional balconies. Friendly, recommended. **E** *Hostal Sambleño*, Carmen Alto 114, T262979. Heating extra, breakfast available, laundry service. A lovely jumble of staircases overlooks a central courtyard, rooms of varying quality. Beds are comfortable, showers are electric. **E** *Suecia II*, Tecseccocha 465 (no bell – knock!), T239757 (it is wise to book ahead). **F** without bath, breakfast US$1.40. Warm rooms set around a glass-covered colonial courtyard. Water is not always hot or bathrooms clean, can be noisy and the luggage store is closed at night, otherwise OK. **E** *Hostal Tahuantinsuyo*, Jr Tupac Yupanqui 204, Urb Tahuantinsuyo (15-min walk from the Plaza de Armas), T/F261410. Cheaper without bath, price includes breakfast, drinks and snacks available. Warm atmosphere, very helpful. Laundry service and clothes washing facilities, secure parking for bikes and motorbikes, English, French and Italian spoken. Tours can be arranged. Recommended. **E-F** *Hostal Resbalosa*, Resbalosa 494, T224839. **F** without bath, breakfast US$1.45; laundry service. Superb views of the Plaza de Armas from a sunny terrace. Owner Georgina is very hospitable. Best rooms have a view (US$1.45 extra), others may be pokey. The electric showers are reportedly cool, but most guests love this place.

F per person *El Balcón Colonial*, Choquechaca 350, T238129. Continental breakfast included. Use of the kitchen US$1.50 per day, laundry service. Family house with basic rooms, exceptional hospitality. **F** *Chaska Wasi*, Amargura 130 (there is no sign), T622831. Cable TV and American breakfast for US$3. Guests can use the basic kitchen (no fridge), laundry service. Family house, excellent value 1 block from the central plaza. No double beds. **F** per person *Hospedaje Inka*, Suytuccato 848, San Blas, T231995. Taxis leave you at Plaza San Blas, walk steeply uphill for 5-10 mins, or phone the hostal. Price includes bath and breakfast. Wonderful views, spacious rooms and owner, Américo, is very helpful, with lots of information. **F** per person *Hospedaje Magnolia's 2*, Av Regional 898, T224898. Comfortable rooms with or without bath, quiet, safe, very clean and helpful, English spoken, laundry service, kitchen facilities, tourist information. **F** *Hostal Rickch'airy*, Tambo de Montero 219, T236606. Rooms without bath; those with cost **C**. Popular with backpackers in the cheaper part, full breakfast available (US$2), hot water in morning, family run, laundry service, nice garden with good views. **F** *Hospedaje Sol Naciente*, Av Pardo 510, T228602. Very basic but clean and comfortable, approximately 10 mins from the centre. Small fee for storing luggage and laundry can be arranged. **F** *Hospedaje Wiñay Wayna*, Vitoque 628 (at the top of Nueva Baja) T246794, miriamojeda@yahoo.com Price includes continental breakfast, no rooms have bath. Heating is available (US$1.40 a night), safe, use of kitchen, laundry extra. Fantastic value, bright, airy, comfortable rooms, cafeteria. Highly recommended.

G *Estrellita*, Av Tullumayo 445, parte Alta, T234134. Price includes breakfast and free tea and coffee all day. TV, video and old stereo in the tiny communal sitting area, basic kitchen for guests. Rooms are multiples with shared bathrooms (2 with private bath). Basic but excellent value. It's about a 15-min walk from the centre. When you arrive ring the bell several times and wait; you will be given your own keys when you register. Cars and bikes can be parked safely. Recommended. **G** *Hostal Pumacurco*, Pumacurco 336, Interior 329, T243347. In the restored part of a colonial house. Clean, secure, laundry facilities. Owner Betty is very friendly and helpful. **G** *Hostal Luzerna*, Av Baja 205, near San Pedro train station (take a taxi at night), T232762/ 237591/227768. Price includes breakfast. Nice family-run hostal with hot water and good beds, clean, safe to leave luggage. Recommended. **G** per person *Hostal San Cristóbal*, Quiscapata 242, near San Cristóbal. Dormitory hostal, next door to the youth hostel. Guests can use basic kitchen (no fridge) and wash their clothes. Showers are good. The owner is friendly and reliable – if full Sra Ema de Paredes will let you spread a sleeping bag on the floor. Recommended.

Youth hostel E per person *Albergue Municipal*, Quiscapata 240, San Cristóbal, T252506. Dormitories, very clean, helpful staff, luggage store, great views, bar, cafeteria, laundry, safe deposit, discount for members. **E-F** per person *El Procurador*, Coricalle 440, Prolongación Procuradores, T243559, hostal-procurador-cusco@hotmail.com **G** without bath, includes breakfast, hot water, laundry, motorcycle parking, friendly. Recommended.

Eating

Novo Andino cuisine is becoming a regular feature on menus It is the use of native ingredients and 'rescued' recipes

Expensive *Fallen Angel*, Plazoleta Nazarenas, beside Museo Cabrera, T258184, fallenangelincusco@hotmail.com International and Novo Andino gourmet cuisine by the same owner as *Macondo* (see below). Décor juxtaposes the modern and the kitsch with colonial surroundings (the house once belonged to one of Pizarro's relatives). Special events throughout the year. 1000-2400, at 2200 restaurant turns into a disco bar, Sun 1500-2400; DJ from 2300. *Inka Grill*, Portal de Panes 115, Plaza de Armas, T262992. According to many the best food in town, specializing in Novo Andino cuisine and innovative dishes, also homemade pastas, wide vegetarian selection, live music, excellent coffee and homemade pastries 'to go'. Visa and Mastercard ATM at the entrance. A good place to spoil yourself, recommended. 1000-2400 (Sun 1200-2400 – tables are set up under the colonial arches while the Plaza is closed to traffic). *Mesón de los Espaderos*, Espaderos y Plaza de Armas, 2nd floor with balcony overlooking the plaza. Good *parrilladas* and other typical local dishes. *Mesón de los Portales*, Portal de Panes 163, Plaza de Armas. International and Peruvian cuisine. *Paititi*, Portal Carrizos 270, Plaza de Armas. Live music and good atmosphere in a setting with Inca masonry. Excellent pizzas but service can be slow when busy. *Parrilla* Andina, Maruri 355. Good value meat-fest. Mixed grill will feed two for around US$15. Features beef, chicken, alpaca and pork. Restaurant is part of the former palace of the Inca Túpac Yupanqui. *La Retama*, Portal de Panes 123, 2nd floor, T226372, laretama@terra.com.pe Excellent new-age Andean food, buffets (main courses, salads and sweets) and service. There is also a balcony, it holds art exhibitions and has a nightly Andean music and dance show (one of the best). 1100-2300, but on Mon dinner is only served 1830-2300, after which there is jazz and Latin American music with bar till 0300. *Pachacútec Grill and Bar*, Portal de Panes 105, Plaza de Armas. International cuisine, including seafood and Italian specialities, also features folk music shows nightly. Excellent value quality *menú* for just US$2. *Spoonk*, Plateros 334. Meat, pastas and wide selection of vegetarian choices, nothing heavy, served in colonial surroundings with modern decorations. Comfortable, good views from the balconies, kitchen in full view. Also has a bar with couches and candles, DJs play excellent music, free coffee, happy hours. Daily 1200-0200. *El Truco*, Plaza Regocijo 261. Excellent local and international dishes, used a lot by tour groups, buffet lunch 1200-1500, nightly folk music at 2045, next door is *Taberna del Truco*, which is open 0900-0100. *Tunupa*, Portal Confiturías 233, 2nd floor, Plaza de Armas (same entrance as *Cross Keys*). One of the finest restaurants on the Plaza, its large restaurant is often used by tour groups. Also has the longest (glassed-in) balcony but this is narrow and best for couples only. Food is international, traditional and Novo Andino. Also a good buffet for US$15 including a pisco sour and a hot drink. From 2000-2015 there is a group plays 16th/17th century-style Cusqueñan music of their own composition accompanied by dancers.

Mid-range *Al Grano*, Santa Catalina Ancha 398, T228032. The basement has some of the finest Inca remains in the city, plus colonial arches – a superb place to eat out. The owner is a Cusqueñan, La Negra. Lunchtime menu US$2 is a good option if you are fed up with other menus (1230-1500). Evening serves Asian dishes using authentic curry ingredients for US$4.50, menu changes daily. Without doubt the best coffee in town, vegetarian choices. 1000-2100, closed on Sun. Recommended. *A Mi Manera*, corner of Triunfo and Palacio. Great tasting food and good value if you ask for a set menu (not often advertised). *Blueberry Lounge*, Portal de Carnes 236, Plaza de Armas, T221397, blueberry@yahoo.com In a beautifully restored colonial house, with open fires in the evening, cosy restaurant-bar, a good place to read, listen to music, watch cable TV or videos. The menu specializes in Asian dishes, with touches of the Novo Andino, good for breakfast, vegetarian options for lunch and dinner, excellent appetizers, desserts and coffee, has happy hours and exotic drinks. Tue-Sun 0900-2400, Mon 1200-2400. *Greens*, Tandapata 700, behind the church on Plazoleta San Blas, T243820, greens_cusco@hotmail.com Modern international food in a trendy but warm and relaxed setting with sofas to kick back in while sipping wine and reading English magazines. Famous for Sunday roasts (US$10, booking essential) as well as English breakfasts (0730-1500) and curries. Vegetarian options. Deserts and toasted sandwiches only 1500-1830, choose a video to watch; restaurant reopens 1830, closes 2300 (Mon open 1200-2300). Games, book exchange and library. Popular. *Hatunrumiyoc*, Hatun Rumiyoc y Choquechaca, T802673. Grill, pizzería and bar serving uncomplicated food including roast alpaca, pizzas, kebabs, hot sandwiches, great salads, huge juices, coffees. Informal, friendly, has games and pleasant music. Mon-Sat 1100-2300. *Inkanato*, Plazoleta Santo Domingo 279, interior 2A, T222926. Staff dressed in Inca and Amazonian outfits should not scare you off this interesting restaurant. Kitsch it may be but you can watch the staff preparing the food in the open plan kitchen that stretches into the dining area. *Keros*, Portal de Panes. Lunchtime menu for US$4.30 includes pisco sour, three courses and a tea. *Kintaro*, Heladeros 149. Japanese and vegetarian, homemade and low-fat food, good for high altitude, Japanese owner. 1200-2200, closed Mon. *Kusikuy*, Plateros 348B, T262870. Some say this serves the best cuy (guinea pig, US$10.90) in town; many other typical Cusco dishes on the menu. Set lunch is unbeatable value at only US$2. 0800-2300 Mon-Sat. Good service, highly recommended. *Macondo*, Cuesta San Blas 571, T229415, macondo@telser.com.pe A casual, arty and comfortable restaurant where sofas of iron bedsteads covered in dozens of cushions mix with chairs, tables and candles. Walls are decorated with local art. Popular, gay-friendly and a steep 3-block walk from the central plaza. Dishes use local ingredients with an artistic twist. Recommended. *Pacha-Papa*, Plazoleta San Blas 120, opposite church of San Blas, T241318. A beautiful patio restaurant in a wonderful old colonial house. Very good typical Peruvian dishes with a European influence. At night diners can sit in their own, private colonial dining room. Recommended. *Pie Shop*, Carmen Alto 254, San Blas, T237503. Sweet and savoury home-baked pies (English shepherd's pie is very popular), good range of beverages all in a relaxing atmosphere; also does take-aways. Tue-Sun 0830-2030, closed Mon. *Pucará*, Plateros 309. Peruvian and international food. Very good US$3.50 set lunch and excllent *ají de gallina* (garlic chicken) and cream of potato soup. 1230-2200, closed on Sun, pleasant atmosphere. *Los Toldos*, Almagro 171 and San Andrés 219. If you´re feeling peckish, on a budget and fancy being served by waiters in a bow tie, try the great chicken *brocheta*. Comes with fries, trip to salad bar and is enough for 2 at just US$2.30. Also *trattoria* with homemade pasta and pizza, delivery T229829. *Los Tomines*, Triunfo 384. Excellent 4-course set meal for US$5-6. Recommended. *Varayoc*, Espaderos 142, T232404. Swiss restaurant, including Peruvian ingredients (cheese fondue US$10-13 – the only place in Cusco that serves it); also has a variety of pastas, good desserts, 'tea time' beverage and pastry for US$2.80 accompanied by Andean harp music. It has a pleasant, literary atmosphere, established for 22 years and owner Oscar has a fine reputation. Daily 0800-2400 (try bircher muesli for breakfast).

Cheap Procuradores, or 'Gringo Alley' as the locals call it, is good for a value feed and takes the hungry backpacker from Mexico to Italy, to Spain and Turkey with its menus. None is dreadful, many are very good indeed, especially for the price; do not be too worried if a tout drags you into one (demand your free pisco sour) before you've reached the restaurant you have chosen from the list below.

   La Barceloneta, Procuradores 347. Spanish, Italian and Peruvian dishes, good value lunches. Has Spanish music on Thu. *Chez Maggy*, have 4 branches: *La Antigua* (the original) at Procuradores 365 and, on the same street, *El Corsario* No 344 and *Clave de Do* No 374 (open at 0700 for buffet breakfast), plus *Millenium*, Plateros 348 (opens 0700, buffet breakfast). All have good atmosphere, are popular with pizzas freshly baked in wood-burning oven, pastas, Mexican food and soups. As they share the kitchens, it's fun to sit in one restaurant and watch the waiters hurrying in from another where your food has been prepared. Hotel delivery T234861 or 246316. *El Cuate*, Procuradores 386. Mexican food, great value, big portions and simple salads. Recommended. *El Mexicanito*, Procuradores 392. Menus from US$2-3, good food. *Paloma Imbil*, Procuradores 362, has doner kebabs. The *rollo mixto* is US$2.15 and comes in delicious home-baked bread.

   Plateros, parallel with Gringo Alley but further southwest, also has good value food. Try *Ama Lur*, at No 325. This is the restaurant below *Amalu* where you go for breakfast. Clean, cheap, very good menú for US$2 as well as tasty evening meals. *La Bodega*, Carmen Alto, San Blas. Snug Dutch and Peruvian-owned café/restaurant of just 7 tables. Sip creamy hot chocolate by candlelight in the afternoons and read one of the English magazines. Pisco sour US$1.70, *pollo al vino* US$3.70. *Tallarines con pollo* are delicious! Dishes come with side trip to salad bar. *Los Candiles*, Plateros 323. Good set lunch for US$2.50. *Mao's*, Plaza Túpac Amaru 826, Wanchac. Cusco's answer to KFC, Burger King/Macdonald's, the most popular place in town for wood-oven grilled or roast chicken, crisp French fries, kebabs, huge mixed meats barbecues and salads. It's large, has a games park for kids, electronic and video games. Good value, look out for promotions, delivery service T252323 at no extra cost. *Víctor Victoria*, Tigre 130. Israeli and local dishes, highly recommended for breakfast, good value.

Seriously cheap To eat really cheaply, and if your stomach is acclimatized to South American food, make your main meal lunch and escape the Plaza de Armas. Head for the market 5 blocks southwest at Túpac Amaru and eat at one of the many stalls. Food will cost no more than US$0.70 and 3 fruit juices are just US$0.45! Otherwise, look for the set *menus*, usually served between 1200-1500, although they are no good for vegetarians. Between 1200 and 1400 every day on Puente Rosario, just off Av Sol, pick up a piece of delicious stuffed, deep-fried potato or deep-fried, battered yucca from one of the street stalls for just US$0.15.

Chinese *Chifa Sipan*, Quera 251 (better than their other branch for tourists in Plateros). Owner Carlos may not sound Chinese but he is and joins in the cooking at this excellent restaurant. There is no great ambience but it's busy at lunchtimes with locals which speaks volumes. Skip to the back of the menu for their better deals.

Vegetarian *Frutos*, C Triunfo 393, 2nd floor, tienda 202. Mon-Sat 0630-2200, Thu 0900-1500, excellent value set lunch. *Govinda*, Espaderos 128, just off the Plaza de Armas. Has set meals. *La Naturaleza*, Procuradores 351. Cheap.

Cafés *Amaru*, Plateros 325, 2nd floor. Limitless coffee, tea, (great) bread and juices served, even on 'non-buffet' breakfasts (US$1.15 for simple). Colonial balcony. Recommended. *Ayllu*, to the left of the cathedral, at Portal de Carnes 208, is probably one of the oldest cafés in Cusco and a great place to go. Fantastic breakfasts (have the special fruit salad, US$2.30), sandwiches, coffee and classical music as well as wonderful apple pastries. Very much a local venue with superb service superb. Next door upstairs is *Café Bagdad*, with a nice balcony with good views of the plaza. Cheap set lunch, good atmosphere, happy hour 1930-2130, German owner Florian Thurman speaks good English, but the service is variable. *Café Halliy*, Plateros 363. Popular meeting place, especially for breakfast, good for comments on guides, has good snacks and 'copa Halliy' – fruit, muesli, yoghurt, honey and chocolate cake, also good vegetarian *menú* and set lunch. *Café Manu* , Av Pardo 1046. Good coffee, good food in jungle decor. If the sun´s over the yard-arm it would be a sin to miss one of their liqueur coffees. *Heidi Granja*, Cuesta San Blas 525, near the bottom, T233759. German owner Carlos serves yoghurt, granolla, ricotta cheese and honey and other great breakfast options. Evening meals are US$2.15 for soup and a main course. Recommended. *Moni*, San Agustín 311, T231029, www.moni-cusco.com Peruvian/English owned, good fresh food and breakfast, British music, magazines, bright, clean and comfortable. Recommended. *The Muse*, Tandapata 682, Plazoleta San Blas. Perfect location with views over San Blas' plaza. Great for sandwiches, salads, coffee and smoothies; art exhibitions, live jazz, board games, relaxed and friendly. Daily 0900-2400. *La Tertulia*, Procuradores 50, 2nd floor. Run by Johanna and Alfredo, who also run the *Don Quijote* Language School downstairs, the breakfast buffet, served 0630-1300, includes muesli, bread, yoghurt, eggs, juice and coffee, eat as much as you like for around US$3, superb value, vegetarian buffet served daily 1800-2200, set dinner and salad bar for US$3.50, also fondue and gourmet meals, book exchange, newspapers, classical music. Open till 2300. *Trotamundos*, Portal Comercio 177, 2nd floor. This is one of the most pleasant cafés in the Plaza if a bit pricey. Has a balcony and a warm atmosphere. Good coffees and cakes, safe salads, *brochetas*, sandwiches and pancakes as well as 4 machines on the internet. Mon-Sat 0800-2400. *Yaku Mama*, Procuradores 397. Good for breakfast, unlimited fruit and coffee, good value.

Panaderías *Panadería El Buen Pastor*, Cuesta San Blas 579. Very good bread and pastries, the proceeds from which go to a charity for orphans and street children. Serves *empanadas* and endless hot drinks. Very popular with backpackers. Recommended. *La Dulcería*, Heladeros 167. Good for cakes, sandwiches, snacks and tea. *Picarones*, Ruinas and Tullumayo, is good for doughnuts. It is very small, very local and very typical for classic Peruvian sweet stuff.

Ice cream parlour: *Due Mondi*, Santa Catalina Ancha (near *Rosie O´Grady´s*). 1000-2100. At just US$0.30 per delicious Italian scoop, this is an absolute must. There´s even *chicha* flavour!

Bars & clubs

Many places have happy hours, but they change frequently Check when you get into town then you can move from happy hour to happy hour for a sozzled evening. Flyers are also handed out around the Plaza de Armas for free entry to bars which usually includes a free drink

Bars on the Plaza de Armas *Cross Keys Pub*, Plaza de Armas, Portal Confiturías 233 (upstairs). Run by Barry Walker of *Manu Expeditions*, a Mancunian and ornithologist, darts, cable sports, pool, bar meals, has happy hours, plus half price specials on certain days, great pisco sours, very popular, loud and raucous, great atmosphere. They hold a general knowledge quiz every Wed to benefit poor children. 1100-0130. *Norton Rat's Tavern*, Loreto 115, 2nd floor, is on the Plaza but has a side entrance off a road to the left of La Compañía (same entrance as *Hostal Loreto*), T246204, nortonrats@yahoo.com Pleasant pub with a fine balcony, pool table, dart board, cable TV and lots of pictures of motorbikes! Owner Jeffrey Powers loves the machines and can provide information for bikers. He has opened a juice bar inside the pub serving Amazonian specials. Happy hour and other, daily, specials. *Paddy O'Flaherty's*, C Triunfo 124 on the corner of the plaza is an Irish theme pub, serving cans of Guinness, good service. Great pub under new ownership, deservedly popular (frequently packed). 1300-0100. **Elsewhere** *Amaru Quechua Café Pub*, Plateros 325, 2nd floor, T246976. Bar with pizzería, also serves breakfast for US$2.50, games, happy hour. *Los Perros Bar*, Tecseccocha 436. Completely different vibe and a great place to chill out on comfy couches listening to excellent music. There´s a book exchange, English and other magazines and board games. Opens 1100 for coffee and pastries; kitchen opens at 1300. Jazz/blues/funk live every Mon from 2200 (free entry). Australian owner, Tammy, is really friendly, but she is not in attendance every night. *Rosie O'Grady's*, Santa Catalina Ancha 360, T247935, has good music, tasty food. English and Russian (!) spoken. 1100 till late (food served till midnight, happy hours).

Clubs *El Garabato Video Music Club*, Espaderos 132, p 3. Dance area, lounge for chilling, bar with saddles for stools, tastefully decorated in colonial setting, live shows 2300-0030 (all sorts of styles) and large screen showing music videos. Their speciality is *té piteado*, hot tea or *mate de coca* with pisco and brown sugar. Recommended. Daily 1600-0300. *Kamikaze*, Plaza Regocijo 274, T233865. *Peña* at 2200, good old traditional rock music, candle-lit cavern atmosphere, entry US$2.50 but usually you don't have to pay. *Mama Africa Pub*, Portal Belén 115, 2nd floor. Decorated in a jungle theme there is a dance floor with a large video screen, although people dance anywhere they can. The music is middle of the road, from local music through '70s classics to the latest releases. Has cybercafé with slow machines. *Templo*, Espaderos 135, 2nd floor. Sound system imported from the US, wide range of music including Latin. Entrance is free all night, has a happy hour which covers all drinks except beer. *Ukuku's*, Plateros 316. US$1.35 entry or free with a pass. This is somewhat different to the other clubs as every night there is a live local band that might play anything from rock to salsa. The DJ then plays a mixture of local and international music but the emphasis is on local. It has a good mix of locals and tourists. *White Vinyl*, Espaderos 135, p 2. Disco and lounge bar, cool atmosphere, fantastic selection of music with professional DJs. The bar serves good drinks with original appetizers. Once a month the American owner holds a fashion show of her own designs. *Xcess*, Suecia 319. Cheap, good quality drinks and excellent music. It's packed with sofas, locals and backpackers and stays open for dancing till 0600. Due to expand in 2002-03.

Don't leave drinks hanging around and don't accept drinks from strangers, spiking has been reported See Essentials, page 54 on selective entry policies

If you fancy learning a few Latin dance moves before hitting the town many of the clubs offer free lessons

Video bars   See *El Garabato Video Music Club* above. *Mama Africa*, to the right of the Cathedral, has free movies daily at 1630-1700; you must buy a drink, though. *Ukuku´s*, on Plateros, also has showings at 1600-1700, free with any purchase.

Folklore   There's a regular nightly folklore show at *Centro Qosqo de Arte nativo*, Av Sol 604, T227901. The show runs from 1900 to 2030, entrance fee US$3.50. *Teatro Inti Raymi*, Saphi 605, nightly at 1845, US$4.50 entry and well worth it. *Teatro Municipal*, C Mesón de la Estrella 149 (T227321 for information 0900-1300 and 1500-1900). This is a venue for plays, dancing and shows, mostly on Thu-Sun. Ask for their programmes. They also run classes in music and dancing from Jan to Mar which are great value.

Entertainment

On **20 Jan** is a procession of saints in the *San Sebastián* district of Cusco. *Carnival* in Cusco is a messy affair with flour, water, cacti, bad fruit and animal manure thrown about in the streets. Be prepared. **Easter Mon** sees the procession of *El Señor de los Temblores* (Lord of the Earthquakes), starting at 1600 outside the Cathedral. A large crucifix is paraded through the streets, returning to the Plaza de Armas around 2000 to bless the tens of thousands of people who have assembled there.

On **2-3 May** the *Vigil of the Cross*, which takes place at all mountaintops with crosses on them, is a boisterous affair. In **Jun** is *Corpus Christi*, on the Thu after Trinity Sunday, when all the statues of the Virgin and of saints from Cusco's churches are paraded through the streets to the Cathedral. This is a colourful event. The Plaza de Armas is

Festivals

Cusco & the Sacred Valley

The festival of Inti Raymi

The sun was the principal object of Inca worship and at their winter solstice, in June, the Incas honoured the solar deity with a great celebration known as Inti Raymi, the sun festival. The Spanish suppressed the Inca religion, and the last royal Inti Raymi was celebrated in 1535.

However, in 1944 a group of Cusco intellectuals, inspired by the contemporary 'indigenist' movement, revived the old ceremony in the form of a pageant, putting it together from chronicles and historical documents. The event caught the public imagination, and it has been celebrated every year since then on 24 Jun, now a Cusco public holiday. Hundreds of local men and women play the parts of Inca priests, nobles, chosen women, soldiers (played by the local army garrison), runners, and the like. The coveted part of the Inca emperor Pachacuti is won by audition, and the event is organized by the municipal authorities.

It begins around 1000 at the Qoricancha – the former sun temple of Cusco – and winds its way up the main avenue into the Plaza de Armas, accompanied by songs, ringing declarations and the occasional drink of chicha. At the main plaza, Cusco's presiding mayor is whisked back to Inca

times, to receive Pachacuti's blessing and a stern lecture on good government. Climbing through Plaza Nazarenas and up Pumacurcu, the procession reaches the ruins of Sacsayhuamán at about 1400, where scores of thousands of people are gathered on the ancient stones.

Before Pachacuti arrives the Sinchi (Pachacuti's chief general) ushers in contingents from the four Suyus (regions) of the Inca empire. Much of the ceremony is based around alternating action between these four groups of players. A Chaski (messenger) enters to announce the imminent arrival of the Inca and his Coya (queen). Men sweep the ground before him, and women scatter flowers. The Inka takes the stage alone, and has a dialogue with the sun. Then he receives reports from the governors of the four Suyus. This is followed by a drink of the sacred chicha, the re-lighting of the sacred fire of the empire, the sacrifice (faked) of a llama, and the reading of auguries in its entrails. Finally the ritual eating of sankhu (corn paste mixed with the victim's blood) ends the ceremonies. The Inca gives a last message to his assembled children, and departs. The music and dancing continues until nightfall.

surrounded by tables with women selling *cuy* and a mixed grill called *chiriuchu* (*cuy*, chicken, *tortillas*, fish eggs, water-weeds, maize, cheese and sausage) and lots of Cusqueña beer. In **early Jun**, 2 weeks before Inti Raymi (see below) is the highly recommended **Cusqueño beer festival**, held near the rail station, which boasts a great variety of Latin American music. The whole event is well-organized and great fun.

Also in **Jun** is *Qoyllur Rit'i*, the Snow Star festival, held at a 4,700-m glacier north of Ocongate (Ausangate), 150 km southeast of Cusco. It has its final day 58 days after Easter Sunday. To get there involves a 2 hr walk up from the nearest road at Mawayani, beyond Ocongate, then it's a further exhausting climb up to the glacier. It's a good idea to take a tent, food and plenty of warm clothing. Note that it can be very confusing for those who don't understand the significance of this ancient ritual. Many trucks leave Cusco, from Limacpampa, in the days prior to the full moon in mid-Jun; prices from US$2 upwards. This is a very rough and dusty overnight journey lasting 14 hrs, requiring warm clothing and coca leaves to fend off cold and exhaustion. Several agencies offer tours (see also page 227). Peter Frost writes: "The pilgrimage clearly has its origins in Inca or pre-Inca times, although the historical record dates it only from a miraculous apparition of Christ on the mountain, around 1780. It is a complex and chaotic spectacle, attended by hundreds of dance groups, and dominated by the character of the ukuku, the bear dancer, whose night vigil on the surrounding glaciers is the festival's best-known feature. Under the best of circumstances the journey there is lengthy, gruelling and dusty, the altitude (4,600 m at the sanctuary) is extremely taxing, the place is brutally cold, very crowded, unbelievably noisy around the clock (sleep is impossible), and the sanitary conditions are indescribable."

On **24 Jun** *Inti Raymi*, the Inca festival of the winter solstice, where locals outnumber tourists, is enacted at the fortress of Sacsayhuaman. The spectacle starts at 1000 at the Qoricancha (crowds line the streets and jostle for space to watch), then proceeds to the Plaza de Armas. From there performers and spectators go to Sacsayhuaman for the main event, which starts at 1300. It lasts 2½ hrs, and is in Quechua. Locals make a great day of it, watching the ritual from the hillsides and cooking potatoes in pits in the ground. Tickets for the stands can be bought in advance from the *Emufec* office, Santa Catalina Ancha 325 (opposite the Complejo Policial) and cost US$35. Standing places on the ruins are free but get there at about 1030 as even reserved seats fill up quickly, and defend your space. Travel agents can arrange the whole day for you, with meeting points, transport, reserved seats and packed lunch. Those who try to persuade you to buy a ticket for the right to film or take photos are being dishonest. On the night before Inti Raymi, the Plaza de Armas is crowded with processions and food stalls. Try to arrive in Cusco 15 days before Inti Raymi. The atmosphere in the town during the build up is fantastic and something is always going on.

On the last Sun in **Aug** is the *Huarachicoy festival* at Sacsayhuaman, a re-enactment of the Inca manhood rite, performed in dazzling costumes by local boys.

On **8 Sep**, the *Day of the Virgin*, is a colourful procession of masked dancers from the church of Almudena, at the southwest edge of Cusco, near Belén, to the Plaza de San Francisco. There is also a fair at Almudena, and a bull fight on the following day. **23 Sep** is *Quilla Raymi*, the Moon Festival. **8 Dec** is *Cusco Day*, when churches and museums close at 1200. And, on **24 Dec**, when all good little travellers should be tucked up in bed, is *Santuranticuy*, 'the buying of saints'. This is a huge celebration of Christmas shopping, with a big crafts market in the Plaza de Armas, which is very noisy until the early hours of the 25th.

Local arts crafts   In the Plaza San Blas and the surrounding area, authentic Cusco crafts still survive and wood workers can be seen in almost any street. A market is held on Sat. Leading artisans who welcome visitors include *Hilario Mendivil*, Plazoleta San Blas 634, who makes biblical figures from plaster, wheatflour and potatoes and *Edilberta Mérida*, Carmen Alto 133, who makes earthenware figures showing the physical and mental anguish of the Indian peasant. *Luis Aguayo Revollar*, Cuesta del Almirante 256, T248661, aguayo@latinmail.com makes fine woodcarvings.

Víctor Vivero Holgado, at Tandapata 172, is a painter of pious subjects, while *Antonio Olave Palomino*, Siete Angelitos 752, makes reproductions of pre-Columbian ceramics and colonial sculptures. *Maximiliano Palomino de la Sierra*, Triunfo 393, produces festive dolls and wood carvings, and *Santiago Rojas*, near San Blas, statuettes. Note that much of the wood used for picture frames etc is *cedro*, a rare timber not extracted by sustainable means.

Visit *Nemesio Villasante*, Av 24 de Junio 415, T222915, for Paucartambo masks.

Mercado Artesanal, Av Sol, block 4, is good for cheap crafts. *Feria Artesanacoml Tesores del Inka*, Plateros 334, open daily 0900-2300.

In their drive to 'clean up' Cusco, the authorites have moved the colourful **artisans' stalls** from the pavements of Plaza Regocijo to the main market at the bottom of Av Sol. There are, however, small markets of 10 or so permament stalls dotted around the city which offer goods made from alpaca as well as modern materials. For example, at Plateros 334, the first stall in the doorway will tailor-make reversible fleeces in two colours for US$10.

Pedazo de Arte, Plateros 334B. A tasteful collection of Andean handicrafts, many designed by Japanese owner Miki Suzuki. *La Mamita*, Portal de Carnes 244, Plaza de Armas, sells the ceramics of Pablo Seminario (see under Urubamba), plus cotton, basketry,

Shopping
Cusco has some of the best craft shopping in all Peru

Cusco is one of the weaving centres of Peru, and excellent textiles can be found at good value Be very careful of buying gold and silver objects and jewellery in and around Cusco; we have received many reports of sharp practices

jewellery, etc. A visit is highly recommended for those who do not have time to go to their studio in Urubamba (see page 199). *Maky Artesanías*, Carmen Alto 101, T653643. A great place to buy individually designed ceramics. Ask for discounts if buying several pieces. *La Pérez*, Urb Mateo Pumacahua 598, Huanchac, T232186/222137, is a big cooperative with a good selection. They will arrange a free pick-up from your hotel.

Alpaca clothing and fabrics: *El Almacén – The Warehouse*, Av Ramón Zavaleta 110, Wanchac, T256565, almacensb@terra.co.pe This is a factory outlet for genuine camelid-fibre products, which pays no commissions to guides and so no extra costs are charged to the tourist. Prices, therefore, are at least 20% cheaper than tourist shops (100% alpaca sweaters at US$55-60 compared with US$75-100 elsewhere). Alpaca 111, Plaza Regocijo 202, T243233, *Alpaca 3*, Ruinas 472, and *Cuzmar II*, Portal Mantas 118T (English spoken). *Away*, Procuradores 361, T229465. Sells handmade shoes, traditional blankets and leather goods, prices from US$15-40 for a pair, allow two days delivery for your own design. *Josefina Olivera*, Portal Comercio 169, Plaza de Armas. She sells old ponchos and antique mantas, without the usual haggling. Her prices are high, but it is worth it to save pieces being cut up to make other items. Daily 1100-2100.

The private *Miori-Bernasconi Collection of Andean Art* may be viewed by appointment, T271215, T652975 (mob), Pallay-Andean Textile website www.geocities.com/SoHo/Atrium/7785/ Quechua and Aymara pieces, 18th-, 19th-century, antique coins, wooden keros and other objects.

Traditional musical instruments: *Ima Sumac*, Triunfo 338, T244722.

Jewellery: *Joyerías Peruanas*, C del Medio 130, gold, silver and other items in pre-Columbian, Inca and contemporary designs. *Joyería H Ormachea*, Plateros 372, T237061. Handmade gold and silver. *Spondylus*, Cuesta San Blas 505, T246964. A good selection of silver jewellery and fashion tops with Inca and pre-Inca designs.

General   Markets: there are a number of options. *San Jerónimo*, just southeast of town is the location of the wholesale Sat morning fruit and vegetable market, but food which is just as good, not much more expensive and washed can be bought at the markets in town. *Huanchac* on Av Garcilaso (not to be confused with Calle Garcilaso), or *Santa Ana*, opposite Estación San Pedro, which sells a variety of goods. The best value is at closing time or in the rain. Take care after dark. Sacks to cover rucksacks are available in the market for US$0.75. Both Huanchac and Santa Ana open every day from 0700. *Plazoleta San Blas* holds a local artisans' market every Sat 0800-1800.To buy back your stolen camera, pay *El Baratillo* in the Santiago area a visit early on Sat (0700-1700), but do not take anything of value or you may become a crime statistic all over again. Just down from Santiago church (an unsafe ara at night because of drunks high on the 96% chemically produced alcohol on sale there) is a sprawling affair of stall upon stall laid out on the pavements. Everything from stolen car jacks to useless junk is for sale. It's a fascinating sight – just be sensible and leave the other camera at home. Go by taxi.

El Molino, Prolongación Av Pachacútec, opposite Terminal Terrestre in Ttío district, is for contraband goods brought in from abroad, but you get a proper bill as the vendors pay taxes on the items. Everything from computers to hi-fis, personal stereos to trekking boots, cheap camera film to wine can be bought here. It is clean and safe (but take the usual commonsense precautions about valuables). Daily 0700-2000.

Supermarkets: *D'Dinos Market*, Av La Cultura 2003, T252656 for home delivery. 24-hrs, well-supplied, takes credit cards. *Dimart*, Ayacucho 248 and Av La Cultura 742. Daily 0700-2200, credit cards accepted. They aim to open a hypermarket at Av Tomasa Titu Condemayta y Av Huayroropata, at end-2002. *Gato's Market*, Portal Belén 115. *Shop Market*, Plateros 352. Daily 1000-0300. *El Pepito*, Plaza San Francisco. Mon-Sat 0900-2000, closed lunchtime. Sells a wide variety of imported goods, delicatessen, stocks multi-packs of food (eg chocolate bars) much cheaper than other shops, a good bargain for trekking supplies.

Bookshops: *Centro de Estudios Regionales Andinos Bartolomé de las Casas*, Heladeros 129A, good books on Peruvian history, archaeology, etc. Mon-Sat 1100-1400, 1600-1900. *Jerusalem*, Heladeros 143, T235408, English books, guide-books, music, postcards, book exchange. *Special Book Services*, Av El Sol 781-A, Wanchaq, T248106. Sells Footprint Handbooks.

Camping equipment: there are several places on Plateros which rent out equipment but check it carefully as it is common for parts to be missing. An example of prices per day: tent US$3-5, sleeping bag US$2 (down), US$1.50 (synthetic), stove US$1. A deposit of US$100 is asked, plus credit card, passport or plane ticket. *Soqllaq'asa Camping Service*, owned by English-speaking Sra Luzmila Bellota Miranda, at Plateros 365 no 2F, T252560, is recommended for equipment hire, from down sleeping bags (US$2/day) to gas stoves (US$1/day) and ThermaRest mats (US$1/day); pots, pans, plates, cups and cutlery are all provided free by the friendly staff. They also buy and sell camping gear and make alpaca jackets. Mon-Sat 0900-1300, 1600-2030, Sun 1800-2030. Wherever you hire equipment, check the stoves carefully. White gas (*bencina*) costs US$1.50 per litre and can be bought at hardware stores, but check the purity. Stove spirit (*alcoól para quemar*) is available at pharmacies. Blue gas canisters, costing US$5, can be found at some hardware stores and at shops which rent gear. You can also rent equipment through travel agencies.

In general you should only deal directly with the agencies themselves. You can do this when in town, or you can raise whatever questions you may have in advance (or even in Cusco) by email. That way you will get many points answered in writing. Other sources of advice are visitors returning from trips, who can give the latest information, and the trip reports for member of the South America Explorers. Do not deal with guides who claim to be employed by agencies listed below without verifying their credentials. Beware agencies quoting prices in dollars then converting to soles at an unfavourable rate when paying and also of tours which stop for long lunches at expensive hotels. Check what the cancellation fee will be. Students will normally receive a discount on production of an ISIC card.

The agencies are divided into their respective categories. Those listed under general tours (well-established, more recently established and economical) offer a wide range of different tours, including Machu Picchu.

Well-established, expensive and mid-range (in alphabetical order): most of these agencies have their main offices away from the centre, but have a local contact or hotel contact downtown, cellular phone, or internet/email address. *Andes Nature Tours*, Garcilaso 210, Casa del Abuelo, oficina 217, T245961, F233797, ant@terra.com.pe Owner Aurelio speaks excellent English and has 25 years' experience in Cusco and will tailor treks "anywhere". Specializes in natural history and trekking, botany and birdwatching. *APU*

Tour operators
Most of the myriad tour operators in Cusco are packed into the Plaza de Armas. The sheer number and variety of tours on offer is bewildering and prices for the same tour can vary dramatically

General tours, including Machu Picchu

Cusco & the Sacred Valley

Expediciones, Av Sol 344, oficina 10, PO Box 24, T272442, T652975 (mob), F243453, www.geocities.com/apuexpeditions Office open 0900-1300, 1500-2000. Deals mostly through email (apuexped@yahoo.co.uk, watay71@yahoo.com, becimar@yahoo.com) and internet. Cultural, adventure, educational/academic programmes, nature tours and jungle packages to Manu and Tambopata, bilingual personnel, very knowledgeable. Andean textiles a speciality. Mariella Bernasconi Cillóniz has 18 years experience and can plan individually customized trips, as well as traditional and alternative routes to Machu Picchu. *Cóndor Travel*, C Saphi 848-A, T225961/248282, www.condor travel.com.pe (email for flights diviajes@condortravel.com.pe) A high-quality, exclusive agency that will organize trips throughout Peru and the rest of the world. They have a specialized section for adventure travel and are representatives for American Airlines, Continental and most other international airlines with ticket sales, connections, etc (contact for flights Ms Eliana Manga). *Dasatariq*, Pardo 589, T223341, F225220, www.dasatariq.com Run from a small office, offers traditional tours in the city, Sacred Valley and Machu Picchu, and runs day trips to Maras salt mines, Moray agricultural system and Chinchero in car with guide. *Explorandes*, Av Garcilaso 316-A, T/F244308, F233784, www.explorandes.com.pe In the Cusco office can book only Inca trails. Through the website you can book a wide range of trekking, rafting and cultural tours in and around Cusco and throughout Peru. Also arranges tours across Peru for lovers of orchids, ceramics or textiles. *Gatur Cusco*, Puluchapata 140 (a small street off Av Sol 3rd block), T223496, F238645, gatur@terra.com.pe Esoteric, ecotourism, and general tours. Owner Dr José (Pepe) Altamirano is knowledgeable in Andean folk traditions, excellent conventional tours. Guides speak English, French, Spanish and German. *Kantu Perú*, Portal Carrizos 258, T246372, T650202 (mob), kantuperu@ wayna.rcp.net.pe or kantikik@telser.com.pe Run by the enthusiastic, amiable Polack brothers who speak French and English. They specialize in adventure travel by trail bike

and 4-wheel drive vehicles. Trips can be as long as 16 days, or vehicles can be hired daily, with or without a guide. They have full back-up and equipment, including satellite telephones. They also offer mystic/religious tours and trips into Chile, Bolivia, Ecuador and Brazil. **Kinjyo Travel Service**, Av Sol 761, T/F231121, F244605, tes3@latinmail.com An agency that also deals with group bookings from overseas but they will arrange personalized itineraries for groups. They will book all international/national flights. Includes treks to weaving villages. **Lima Tours**, Av Machu Picchu D-24, Urb Mañuel Prado, T228431/ 235241, www.limatours.com.pe Local branch. Also Amex representative, gives TCs against Amex card, but no exchange, and DHL office, to receive a parcel you pay 35% of the marked value of customs tax. **Peruvian Andean Treks**, Av Pardo 705, T225701, F238911, www.andean treks.com Adventure tour specilaists, including the Inca Trail, using high-quality equipment and satellite phones, and Vilcanota Llama Trek to Ausangate (the mountain visible from Cusco – includes a collapsible pressure chamber for altitude sickness). Mon-Fri 0900-1300, 1500-1800, Sat 0900-1300, manager Tom Hendrickson. **Servicios Aéreos AQP SA**, Av Sol 675, T/F243229, 24hrs T620585, www.saaqp.com.pe Offers a wide variety of tours within the country, agents for American, Continental, LAB and other airlines; head office in Lima, Los Castaños 347, San Isidro, T2223312, F2225910. Tambo Tours, USA and Cusco, PO Box 60541, Houston, Texas, www.tambotours.com Adventure travel and general tour specialist for all areas around Cusco.

More recently established, all price ranges: *Andean Life*, C Plateros 341, T224227, www.andeanlife.com Tours and treks for small groups. **Another Planet**, Triunfo 120, T/F229379, www.anotherplanetperu.net Run by Lesley Myburgh (see *Casa de La Gringa*, under Sleeping), operates all kinds of adventure tours, conventional tours in and around Cusco, but specializes in jungle trips anywhere in Peru. Lesley is an expert

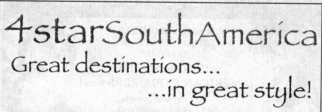

in San Pedro cactus preparation and conducts trips (see below). **Destinos Turísticos**, Portal de Panes 123, oficina 101-102, Plaza de Armas, T/F228168/624672, www.destinosturisticosperu.com The owner speaks Spanish, English, Dutch, Portuguese and specialises in package tours from economic to 5-star budgets. Individuals are welcome to come in for advice on booking jungle trips to renting mountain bikes. Very informative and helpful. **SAS Travel**, Portal de Panes 143, T/F237292 (staff in a second office at Medio 137, mainly deal with jungle information and only speak Spanish), www.sastravel.com Discount for SAE members and students. Frequently recommended for the Inca Trail. Before setting off they ensure you are told everything that is included and give advice on what personal items should be taken. They have their own hostel in Aguas Calientes, or will book other hostels for customers. Also Manu tours, mountain bike, horse riding and rafting trips. All guides speak English . They can book internal flights at cheaper rates than booking from overseas. Robyn is Australian and helpful. Responsible, good equipment and food. **Top Vacations**, Portal de Panes 109, of 6, T263278/624088, www.hikingperu.com Also highly regarded for the Inca Trail. Can also organize trekking to: Choquequirao, Ausangate, Salkantay, Vilcabamba and elsewhere, good guides and arrangements. **Trekperu**, Pumacahua C-10, Wanchac, T252899, F238591, www.trekperu.com Experienced trek operator as well as other adventure sports and mountain biking. Offers "culturally sensitive" tours.

Economical: **Carla's Travel**, Plateros 320, T/F253018, carlastravel@telser.com.pe Inca Trail trips. Will also arrange treks to Ausangate for a minimum of 7 people - excludes sleeping bag. They will book all other tours. **Liz´s** Explorer, Medio 114B, T/F246619, www.geocities.com/lizexplorer/ For the Inca Trail, Liz gives a clearly laid-out list of

what is and what is not included. If you need a guide who speaks a language other than English let her know in advance. *Naty's Travel Agency*, Triunfo 338, p 2, T/F239437, natystravel@terra.com.pe Inca Trail trips with English-speaking guides. Will organize all other trips including Puerto Maldonaldo and special fiestas. *Q'ente*, C Garcilaso 210, p 2, of 210B, T222535/247836, www.qente.com Inca Trail, private treks to Salkantay, Ausangate, Choquequirao, Vilcabamba and Q'eros. Prices depend on group size. Also horseriding to local ruins and rafting on the Urubamba. Very good, especially with children. *Sky Travel*, Santa Catalina Ancha 366, interior 3-C (down alleyway next to *Rosie O´Grady´s* pub) T240141, www.skyperu.com English spoken. General tours around city and Sacred Valley. Prides itself on leaving 30 min before other groups, thus reaching sights and the lunch spot (!) before anyone else. (For the Inca Trail the group is asked what it would like on the menu 2 days before departure.) Other trips include Vilcabamba and Ausangate (trekking only). Good service (has an office in Arequipa). *United Mice*, Plateros 351T/F221139, F238050. Another favourite for the Inca Trail, good English-speaking guides; Salustio speaks Italian and Portuguese. Discount with student card, good food and equipment.

Aerial adventures: *PerúFly*, El Comercio H11, Residencial Huancaro, T229439, T970 1547 (mob) (in Lima: Jr Jorge Chávez 658, Miraflores, T444 5004, T970 1547 (mob), www.perufly.com Bungee jumping, US$59 to see Peru upside down, jumping from a hot-air balloon! *Globos de los Andes*, Arequipa 271, T232352, T693812 (mob), www.globosperu.com Hot-air ballooning in the Sacred Valley and expeditions with ballons and 4WD lasting several days.

River rafting, mountain biking & trekking

See the rafting section under Adventure sports (page 79). Safety standards on many rafting trips from Cusco are often woefully inadequate

One-day rafting trips are available on the Río Urubamba, a good place to learn class 3 rapids. Two sections are commonly used and it's a nice way to see the Sacred Valley, with a good view of many archaeological sites. *Amazonas Explorers*, PO Box 722, Cusco, T/F 227137/653366, www.amazonas-explorer.com Experts in rafting, hiking and biking; used by BBC. English owner Paul Cripps has great experience, but takes most bookings from overseas (see Tour operators in Essentials, page 27 for other addresses). However, he may be able to arrange a trip for travellers in Cusco. *Apumayo*, C Garcilaso 265 interior 3, T/F246018 (Lima: T/F444 2320), www.apumayo.com Rafting on the Urubamba and the Apurímac. Also combine mountain biking with rafting trips. This company also offers tours for disabled people, which even includes rafting. Mon-Sat 0900-1300, 1600-2000. *Eric Adventures*, Plateros 324, T/F228475, ericadventureskayaperu.com Specialize in adventure activities. They clearly explain what equipment is included in their prices and what you will need to bring (they have no insurance so make sure your travel insurance covers you for these activities). They also rent motorcross bikes for US$45 (guide is extra). Prices are more expensive if you book by email, you can get huge discounts if you book in the office. Good guides. *Instinct*, Procuradores 50, T233451, www.instinct-travel.com Also at Plaza de Armas, Ollantay tambo, T204045. Rafting from 1 to 4 days; Inca Trail; mountain biking trips and mountain bike rental. Juan and Benjamín Muñiz speak good English and are recommended. *Loreto Tours*, Medio 111, T228264, F236331. Rafting tours on Urubamba only. Also mountain biking to Maras salt mines and Moray agricultural terracing in the Sacred Valley. *Mayuc Expediciones*, Portal Confiturías 211, Plaza de Armas, T/F232666, chando@mayuc.com (online reservations), www.mayuc.com One of the major river rafting adventure companies in Cusco. Rafting specialists on the Río Apurímac; also Tambopata jungle expedition. Qualified guides with Advanced

Swiftwater Association level 3 diplomas and first aid training. Safety-orientated and family-friendly. Also offer trekking on the Inca Trail, and an alternative route into Machu Picchu via Salcantay. A combination of horse-trekking and walking can be organized in the highlands of Peru. The helpful, English speaking staff will organize any itinerary in Peru for their clients. *Pony's Expeditions*, Santa Catalina Ancha 353, 1 block from Plaza de Armas, at *Hotel Casa Grande*, T234887, www.ponyexpeditions.com A branch of the established trekking and bike tour company from Caraz in the Callejón de Huaylas. Mon-Sat 0900-1300, 1600-2000. Organizes and provides information for trekking in Salkantay, Ausangate and Inca Trail areas. Ausangate route can include a climb (optional) on Jampa Pampa (5,200 m, rock and ice, easy) or Sorimana (5,300 m, rock, ice, easy, more interesting). Also runs mountain bike tours to rarely visited sights of Laguna Huaypo, Maras terraces and salt mines of Maras, then Urubamba in Sacred Valley and Paucartambo-Tres Cruces. Camping gear for hire or sale; bikes are all USA-made Fuji with front suspension and packages include helmet, gloves, snack and water.

Cultural   *K'uichy Light International*, Av Sol 814, of 219, T264107, F221166, T621722 (mob), kuichy@amauta.rcp.net.pe or rubenpal@yupi.mail.com Ruben E Palomino specializes in spiritual tours, good value. *Milla Tourism*, Av Pardo 689, T231710, F231388, millaturismo@amauta.rcp.net.pe Mystical tours to Cusco´s Inca ceremonial sites, such as Pumamarca and The Temple of the Moon. Guide speaks only basic English. Also private tours arranged. Mon-Fri 0800-1300, 1500-1900, Sat 0800-1300. *Mystic Inca Trail*, Unidad Vecinal de Santiago, bloque 9, dpto 301, T/F221358, ivanndp@terra.com.pe Specialize in tours of sacred Inca sites and study of Andean spirituality. This is takes 10 days, but it is possible to have shorter "experiences". *Personal Travel Service*, Portal de Panes 123, oficina 109, T225518, F244036 , ititoss@terra.com.pe Mainly deals with group bookings and package holidays. They will organize a personalized itinerary for individuals and groups including international and national flights. They specialize in cultural tours in the Urubamba valley. *Viento Sur Adventure Club*, T20 1620, www.adventurasvientosur.com

Manu
For all details on
Manu, see page 546

InkaNatura Travel, Plateros 361, mezzanine, T/F251173 (in Lima: Manuel Bañón 461, San Isidro, T440 2022/422 8114, F422 9225) www.inkanatura.com InkaNatura states that it is a non-profit organization where all proceeds are directed back into projects on sustainable tourism and conservation. Arranges trips to the Manu National Park, Manu Wildlife Centre, The Biotrip (6-day/5-night) which takes you through the Andes to lowland jungle; Sandoval Lake Lodge in Tambopata, and also a unique tour into Machiguenga Indian territory, including the Pongo de Mainique. Trips can get booked up months in advance so contact them early on in your plans. Having said that they guarantee departures even if they only have 1 passenger, so don't rule out booking with them once you are in Cusco.

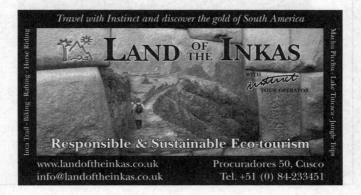

In the office they sell copies of a book called *Peru's Amazonian Eden – Manu* for US$85 where proceeds are invested in the projects, it can be found in other bookshops at a much inflated price. 10% discount on all trips for Footprint Handbook readers. **Manu Ecological Adventures**, Plateros 356, T261640, F225562, www.manuadventures.com Manu jungle tours, either economical tour in and out overland, or in by land, out by plane, giving you the longest time in the jungle, both leave on Sun. Other lengths of stay are available leaving on Mon and Tue. They operate with a minimum of 4 people and a maximum of 10 people per guide. With a minimum of 8 people they will operate specialized programmes. **Manu Expeditions**, Av Pardo 895, T226671, F236706, www. ManuExpeditions.com English spoken. Run by ornithologist and British Consul Barry Walker of the Cross Keys Pub. Three trips available: to the National Park and Manu Wildlife Centre; to the National Park only; and to the Wildlife Centre only. The first two trips visit a lodge run by Machiguenga people on the first Sun of every month and cost an extra US$150. Also runs tailor-made bird trips in cloud and rainforest around Cusco and Peru. Also has horseriding and a 9-day/8-night trip to Machu Picchu along a different route from the Inca Trail, rejoining at Sun Gate. Highly recommended. Mon-Fri 0900-1300, 1500-1900; Sat 0900-1300. **Manu Nature Tours**, Av Pardo 1046, T252721, F234793, www.manuperu.com Owned by Boris Gómez Luna. English spoken. This agency has 2 lodges in the cloud forest and reserve. Various options available. **Pantiacolla Tours**, Plateros 360, T238323, F252696, www.pantiacolla.com Manu jungle tours: 5- and 7-day trips include return flights, 9-day trip is an overland return. Guaranteed departure dates regardless of number, maximum 10 people with 1 guide. The trips involve a combination of camping, platform camping and lodges. All clients are given a booklet entitled, *Talking About Manu*, written by the Dutch owner, Marianne van Vlaardingen, who is a biologist who studied Tamarind monkeys at the biological station of Manu. She is extremely friendly and helpful. If you are lucky you may get her as a guide. Marianne and her Peru-

vian husband are working with the Yine Indians to open a lodge in Manu. In 10 years time the aim is for the Yine to run the lodge independently, but in the meantime they are looking for professional and/or mature volunteers who can dedicate 2 months to the project. For further details contact Marianne. **Peruvian Field Guides**, Plateros 362, T/F243475, www.peruvianfield guides.com Only organizes trips to Manu. Group size to 1 guide is between 5-10 people. Three days are in a lodge and the rest are platform camping. They use 4-man tents for 2 people and provide thick mattresses. Well-organized and professional. Guides speak English and office staff speak English and German. **Expediciones Vilca**, Plateros 363, T244751, F251872, www.cbc. org.pe/manuvilca/ Manu jungle tours: 8-day/7-night, other lengths of stay are available. Will supply sleeping bags at no extra cost. Minimum 5 people, maximum 10 per guide. They give clients a copy of the full-colour, *Manu Nature's Paradise*, by Finnish author Arto Ovaska. He works as a guide for *Vilca* so if you want a Finnish guide – ask! This is the only tour which camps at the Otorongo camp, which is supposedly quieter than Salvador where many agencies camp. There are discounts for students and members of SAE. In the low season they will organize other tours.

Tambopata
For all details on Tambopata, see page 558

Peruvian Safaris, Plateros 365, T/F235342, www.peruviansafaris.com For reservations for the *Explorer's Inn* – excluding park entrance fees and flights. Also see *Explorandes*, *Apu Expeditions*, *Mayuc* and *IncaNatura* above.

Shamans & drug experiences

San Pedro and Ayahuasca have been used since before Inca times, mostly as a sacred healing experience. The plants are prepared with special treatments for curative purposes; they have never been considered a drug. If you choose to experience these incredible healing/teaching plants, only do so under the guidance of a reputable agency or shaman and always have a friend with you who is not partaking. If the medicine is not prepared correctly, it can be highly toxic and, in rare cases, severely dangerous. Never buy from someone who is not recommended, never buy off the streets and never try to prepare the plants yourself. We suggest the following, whom we know to be legitimate.

Casa de la Serenidad, T222851, www.shamanspirit.net It's a shamanic therapy centre run by a Swiss-American healer and Reiki Master who uses medicinal 'power' plants. It also has bed and breakfast accommodation and has received very good reports. *Eleana Mollina*, T2636647, who has been recommended for both plants. *Lesley Myburgh* (address above under *Another Planet*, in 'More recently established, all price ranges' is very knowledgeable and experienced in the preparation of San Pedro, as well as guiding trips. She arranges San Pedro journeys for healing at physical, emotional and spiritual levels in beautiful remote areas. The journeys are thoroughly organized and safe, a beautiful, unforgettable experience.

Private guides
All of those listed are bilingual.
Set prices: city tour US$15-20 per day; Urubamba/Sacred Valley US$25-30, Machu Picchu and other ruins US$40-50 per day

Classic standard tours *Mireya Bocángel*, mireyabocangel@ latinmail.com Recommended. *Boris Cárdenas*, boriscar@telser.com.pe Esoteric and cultural tours. *José Cuba and Alejandra Cuba*, Urb Santa Rosa R Gibaja 182, Urb Santa Rosa R Gibaja 182, T226179/685187, alecuba@Chaski.unsaac.edu.pe both speak English, Alejandra speaks German and French, very good tours. *Roberto Dargent*, Urb Zarumilla 5B-102, T247424, M 622080, dargenttravelperubolivia@hotmail.com Very helpful. *Mariella Lazo*, T264210/241318, speaks German, experienced, also offers river rafting. *Haydee Mogrovejo*, T221907, Aymoa@hotmail.com *Victoria Morales Condori*, San Juan de Dios 229, T235204. *Juana Pancorbo*, Av Los Pinos D-2, T227482. *Satoshi Shinoda*, T227861 and *Michiko Nakazahua*, T226185, both Japanese-speaking guides. **Adventure trips:** *Roger Valencia Espinoza*, José Gabriel Cosio 307, T251278, F235334, vroger@qenqo.rcp.net.pe

Transport

Air The airport is at Quispiquilla, near the bus terminal, 1.6 km from the centre. For flight information T222611. There are regular daily flights to **Lima**, 55 mins, with *Aero Continente/Aviandina*, *Tans*, *Taca* and *Lan Perú*. *Grupo Ocho* (military) flies every Wed in a Hercules transport plane, US$55, T221206. Flights are heavily booked on this route in the school holidays (May, Jul, Oct and Dec-Mar) and national holidays. To **Arequipa**, 30 mins daily with *Lan Perú* and *Aero Continente*. To **Puerto Maldonado**, 30 mins, daily with *Tans* and *Aviandina*, 3 a week with *Lan Perú*. *Grupo Ocho* has 2 flights a month via Iberia from which there is a dry season route to Brazil (see under Iñapari, page 562). To/from **La Paz**, *LAB* and *Aero Continente* each fly twice a week.

Airport information T222611/222601. A taxi to and from the airport costs US$2-3 (US$3.50 by radio taxi). Colectivos cost US$0.20 from Plaza San Francisco or from outside the airport car park to the centre. You can book a hotel at the airport through a

A market for beads

⏪

A major feature of Pisac's popular market is the huge and varied collection of multi-coloured beads on sale. Though commonly called 'Inca beads', this is something of a misnomer. For although the Incas were highly talented potters and decorated their ware with detailed geometric motifs, they are not known to have made ceramic beads.

These attractive items have become popular relatively recently.

They used to be rolled individually by hand and were very time-consuming to produce. Now, in a major concession to consumerism, they are machine-made and produced in quantity, then hand-painted and glazed.

Today, the clay beads are produced in countless, often family-run, workshops in Cusco and Pisac. Some are made into earrings, necklaces and bracelets, but many thousands are sold loose.

travel agency, but this is not really necessary. Many representatives of hotels and travel agencies operate at the airport, with transport to the hotel with which they are associated. Take your time to choose your hotel, at the price you can afford. There is a post office, phone booths, restaurant and cafeteria at the airport. Also a Tourist Protection Bureau desk, which can very helpful if your flight has not been reconfirmed (not an uncommon problem). Do not forget to pay the airport tax (US$4) at the appropriate desk before departure.

NB On the Cusco-Lima route there is a high possibility of cancelled flights during the wet season; tourists are sometimes stranded for several days. It is possible for planes to leave early if the weather is bad.

Make sure you reconfirm at least 72 hrs before your flight departure. Check-in is 2 hrs before departure (3 hrs for international flights).

Sit on right-hand side of the aircraft for the best view of the mountains when flying Cusco- Lima; it is worth checking in early to get these seats

Bus The bus terminal, Terminal Terrestre, is at Av Vallejo Santoni, block 2, T224471 (Prolongación Pachacútec). A colectivo from centre costs US$0.15, taxi US$0.60. There is a platform tax of US$0.30. To **Juliaca**, 344 km, 5-6 hrs, US$8.75, *Imexso* (Av Sol 818, T240801, terminal T229126), 0830, 2030. Also *Cisnes, Civa, Julsa, Libertad*, US$4.40, *Sur Oriente*, US$5.85-7.35, and *Ormeño* Royal class, US$14.70. All Juliaca buses continue to **Puno**. The road is fully paved, but after heavy rain buses may not run. To **Puno**, 44 km from Juliaca, new service with *First Class* (Garcilaso 210, of 106, T240408, www.firstclassperu.com) and *Inka Express* (pick up at hotel, T/F247887, inkaex@yahoo.com), daily, 0700 or 0800, 9½ hrs, interesting stops *en route*, US$25; *Tour Perú* morning and evening service, brief stop at **La Raya**, US$8.75, 6½-8 hrs. See under Puno for routes to La Paz. For services between Peru and Bolivia, call *Litoral*, T248989, which runs buses between the two countries, leaving Cusco at 2200, arriving La Paz 1200, US$30, including breakfast on bus and a/c. Travel agencies also sell this ticket. **NB** This bus does not go to Copacabana; you will be transferred to a colectivo to get to the border and then make your own way from there to Copacabana.

To **Arequipa**, 521 km, 10-12 hrs direct, US$6-7.50 (eg *Carhuamayo*, 3 a day). Some bus companies take the road that leaves the Cusco-Puno road at Sicuani and runs close to the Colca Canyon, via Puente Callalli for Chivay; it is very rough in parts. Buses travel mostly at night and it's a very cold journey, so take a blanket. For **Chivay**, alight at 0400-0500 and wait till 0600-0700 (there is shelter) for first colectivo, US$1.20, 3 hrs. Most of the major bus companies, eg *Cruz del Sur*, use double-decker buses, which go via **Juliaca** and **Puno**, and then down the new highway to **Moquegua**, from where they loop back to Arequipa. The fare is about US$8.75.

All direct buses to Lima (20 hrs) go via **Abancay**, 195 km, 5hrs (longer in the rainy season), paved to within an hour of Abancay, and **Nasca** (14 hrs). If prone to carsickness, be prepared on the road to Abancay, there are many, many curves, but the scenery is magnificent. From Abancay to Nasca via Puquío, the road is paved; a safe journey with some stunning scenery. At Abancay, the road forks, the other branch going to **Andahuaylas**, a further 138 km, 10-11 hrs from Cusco, and **Ayacucho**, another 261 km, 20 hrs from Cusco. On both routes at night, take a blanket or sleeping bag to ward off the cold. All buses leave daily from the Terminal Terrestre. *Molina*, who also have an office on Av Pachacútec, just past the railway station, and *Expreso Wari* have buses on both routes. *Molina* twice a day, *Wari* 3 a day to Abancay, Nasca and Lima, both at 1900 to Abancay, Andahuaylas and Ayacucho (Andahuaylas-Ayacucho leg may be cancelled, requiring the purchase of a new ticket on another service, no refunds – it's best to buy ticket to Andahuaylas, then another). *San Jerónimo* has buses to Abancay and Andahuaylas at 1800. *Turismo Ampay*, *Turismo Abancay* and *Expreso Huamanga* go to Abancay. *Cruz del Sur* and *Ormeño* both run to Nasca and Lima. Fares: Abancay US$4.30, Andahuaylas US$5.75-7.20 (*Molina*), Ayacucho US$14.40, Nasca US$20, US$27 (*Imperial*), Lima US$21.60. After 2½ hrs buses pass a checkpoint at the Cusco/Apurímac departmental border. All foreigners must get out and show their passport. In Cusco you may be told that there are no buses in the day from Abancay to Andahuaylas; this is not so as *Señor de Huanca* does so. If you leave Cusco before 0800, with luck you'll make the onward connection at 1300, which is worth it for the scenery. For more information on buses in Abancay, see page 505.

Buses to the Sacred Valley: to **Pisac**, 32 km, 1 hr, US$0.85, from Calle Puputi on the outskirts of the city, near the Clorindo Matto de Turner school and Av de la Cultura. Colectivos, minibuses and buses leave whenever they are full, between 0600 and 1600; also trucks and pick-ups. Buses returning from Pisac are often full. The last one back leaves around 2000. An organized tour can be fixed up anytime with a travel agent for US$5 per person. Taxis charge about US$20 for the round trip. To **Pisac**, **Calca** (18 km beyond Pisac) and **Urubamba**, buses leave from Av Tullumayo 800 block, Wanchac, US$1. Combis and colectivos leave from 300 block of Av Grau, 1 block before crossing the bridge, for **Chinchero**, 23 km, 45 mins, US$0.45; and for **Urubamba** a further 25 km, 45 mins, US$0.45 (or US$1 Cusco-Urubamba direct, US$1.15 for a seat in a colectivo taxi). To **Ollantaytambo**, 0745 and 1945 direct, or catch a bus to Urubamba from Av Grau. Tours can also be arranged to Chinchero, Urubamba and Ollantaytambo with a Cusco travel agency. To Chinchero, US$6 per person; a taxi costs US$25 for the round trip. Usually only day tours are organized for visits to the valley; see under Tour operators above. Using public transport and staying overnight in Urubamba, Ollantaytambo or Pisac will allow much more time to see the ruins and markets.

Car hire *Avis*, Av El Sol 808, and at airport, T248800, avis-cusco@terra.com.pe

Rail There are 2 stations in Cusco. To **Juliaca and Puno**, trains leave from the Estación Wanchac on C Pachacútec, T221992/238722. The office here offers direct information and ticket sales for all PerúRail services. Look out for special promotional offers. When arriving in Cusco, a tourist bus meets the train to take visitors to hotels. **Machu Picchu** trains leave from Estación San Pedro, T221313, opposite the Santa Ana market. To Ollantaytambo and Machu Picchu, see page 207.

The train to **Juliaca and Puno** leaves at 0800, on Mon, Wed, Fri and Sat, arriving in Juliaca at 1635 (10 mins' stop) and Puno at 1800 (sit on the left for the best views). The train makes a stop to view the scenery at La Raya, where handicrafts are on sale. Trains return from Puno on Mon, Wed, Thu and Sat at 0800, arriving in Cusco at 1800.

Schedules may be increased or decreased according to demand. Fares: Tourist class, US$12, Inka US$60. A glass-sided observation carriage makes sightseeing easier and, for Inka class passengers, a three-course dinner is served in this car. An oxygenation system helps to relieve the problems of altitude sickness.

Tickets can be bought up to 5 days in advance. The ticket office at Wanchac station is open Mon-Fri 0700-1700, Sat 0700-1200 and sells tickets for trains to Puno and Machu Picchu. San Pedro station is only open 0500-0900.You can buy tickets through a travel agent, but check the date and seat number. Meals are served on the train. Always check on whether the train is running, especially in the rainy season, when services can be reduced or cancelled.

Airline offices *AeroCondorPerú*, at airport, T652162/693595, F252774, accuzco@terra.com.pe Regional, national and international charters. *Aero Continente/Aviandina*, Portal de Carnes 254, Plaza de Armas, T235666, airport 235696 (toll free 0800-42420). *LAB*, Santa Catalina Angosta 160, T224715, F222279, airport 229220. *Lan Perú*, Av Sol 627-B, T225552-54, F255555, airport 255550, F255551. *Taca*, Av Sol 226, T249921/249926, airport 246858 (national and international reservations 0800-48222), good service. *Tans*, San Agustín 315-17, T251000.

Directory

Banks Most of the banks are along Av Sol and all have ATMs from which you can with-draw dollars or soles. Whether you use the counter or an ATM, choose your time carefully as there can be long queues at either. Most banks are closed between 1300 and 1600. *BCP*, Av Sol 189. Gives cash advances on Visa and changes TCs to soles with no commis-sion, 3% to dollars. It has an ATM for Visa. It also handles Amex. Other branches with ATM: Av Diagonal 120, Wanchac, and Av La Cultura in Santa Mónica suburb, on road out to Puno. *Interbank*, Av Sol y Puluchapata, charges no commission on TCs and handles Mastercard, with an ATM which gives dollars as well as soles for Visa and Mastercard. Next door is *Banco Continental*, also has a Visa ATM and charges US$5 commission on TCs. It has another branch with ATM on Av Garcilaso, on the corner opposite Wanchac market. *BSCH*, Av Sol 459, changes Amex and Thomas Cook TCs at reasonable rates. Has an ATM for Visa/Plus. *Banco Wiese*, on Maruri between Pampa del Castillo and Pomeritos, gives cash advances on Mastercard, in dollars. *Western Union* at Sta Catalina Ancha 165, T233727, money transfers in 10 mins; also at *DHL*, see Communications.

Many travel agencies and *casas de cambio* change dollars. Some of them change TCs as well, but charge 4-5% commission. There are many *cambios* on the west side of the Plaza de Armas (eg Portal Comercio Nos 107 and 148) and on the west side of Av Sol, most change TCs (best rates in the *cambios* at the top of Av Sol).

The street changers hang around Av del Sol, blocks 2-3, every day. Some of them will also change TCs. In banks and on the street check the notes.

Communications Internet: there are thousands of places in the area around the Plaza de Armas. All offer the same price (US$0.75/hour) except for *Ukuku´s*, which has machines for US$0.60 in the morning. *@Internet*, Portal de Panes 123, Plaza de Armas at C Procuradores, oficina 105. *Internet Perú*, Portal de Comercio 141, Plaza de Armas. 10 computers, fast connection, helpful, spacious. *Internet Cusco*, at Galerías UNSAAC, Av Sol s/n beside Banco de Crédito, T238173. Daily 0800-2400, 20 machines, no prob-lem if you want more than an hour. *Los Togas*, Portal de Carnes 258, Plaza de Armas, lostogas@latinmail.com Internet and coffee bar. *Telser*, at Telefónica del Perú, C del Medio 117, T242424, F242222. 15 machines, popular, lower prices after 2100, difficult to get more than an hour, they have a café if you have to wait; also at Plazoleta Limacpampa, at Av Tullumayo and Arcopunco, T245505. *DSI-Cyber Café*, Av Sol 226, daily 0800-2400. *Worldnet*, Santa Catalina Ancha 315. 0800-2200. Café, bar, music, net to phone, games, etc. Many more south of Plaza de Armas. **Post office**: Av Sol at the bottom end of block 5, T225232. Mon-Sat 0730-2000, 0800-1400 Sun and holidays. *Poste restante* is free and helpful. Sending packages from Cusco is not cheap. For sending packages or money overseas, *DHL*, Av Sol 627, T244167.

Telephone: *Telefónica*, Av del Sol 386. This is the main office, for the sale of telephone cards. To make long distance calls and to send or receive faxes, *Telser*, Calle del Medio 117 and at Plazoleta Limacpampa, Av Tullumayo. International calls can be made by pay phone or go through the operator – a long wait is possible and a deposit is required. To send a fax costs about US$2-3 per page. **Radio messages**: *Radio Tawantinsuyo*, Av del Sol 806. Mon-Sat 0600-1900, Sun 0600-1600. Messages are sent out between 0500 and 2100 (you can choose the time), in Spanish or Quechua, price per message is US$1. This is sometimes helpful if things are stolen and you want them back. *Radio Comercial*, Av del Sol 457, oficina 406, T231381. Daily 0900-1200, 1600-1900, for making contact with other radio-users in Cusco and the jungle area. This is helpful if you wish to contact people in Manu and costs US$1.50 for 5 mins.

Phone consuls in advance for an appointment if no hours of attention given

Consulates *Belgium*, Av Sol 954, T221098, F221100. Mon-Fri 0900-1300, 1500-1700. *France* Jorge Escobar, C Micaela Bastidas 101, p 4, T233610. *Germany*, Sra Maria-Sophia Júrgens de Hermoza, San Agustín 307, T235459, Casilla Postal 1128, Correo Central. Mon-Fri, 1000-1200, appointments may be made by phone, it also has a book exchange. *Ireland*, Charlie Donovan, Santa Catalina Ancha 360 (*Rosie O'Grady's*), T243514. *Italy*, Sr Fedos Rubatto, Av Garcilaso 700, T224398. Mon-Fri 0900-1200, 1500-1700. *Netherlands*, Sra Marcela Alarco Zegarra, Av Pardo 854, T264103. *Spain*, Sra Juana María Lambarri, T650106 (mob). *UK*, Barry Walker, Av Pardo 895, T239974, F236706, bwalker@amauta.rcp.net.pe *US Agent*, Dra Olga Villagarcía, Apdo 949, Cusco, T222183, F233541, or at the Binational Center (ICPNA), Av Tullumayo 125, Wanchac.

Language classes *Academia Latinoamericana de Español*, Av Sol 580, T243364, latinocusco@goalsnet.com.pe Graduate teachers with groups or individual tuition, all levels catered for. The school offers tours, dance classes and a volunteer programme. Lodging is with Cusqueña families. Recommended. *Acupari*, the German-Peruvian Cultural Association, San Agustín 307, T242970, acupari@terra.com.pe Spanish classes. *Amerispan*, reservations: *Casa de Lenguas*, Albert Aguilera 26, p 2, Madrid, T0034-91-591 2393, www.casadelenguas.com *Amigos Spanish School*, Zaguán del Cielo B-23, T242292, A non-profit school from which the proceeds go to a programme for poor youth, *Nuevo Día del Cusco*. Family stays can be arranged, flexible schedules and a volunteer programme available. *Cusco al Mundo Language Center*, Siete Diablitos 222, San Blas, T237918, pukllas@terra.com.pe Conversational and written Spanish classes, associated with a project called *Pukllasunchis*. *Cusco Spanish School*, Garcilaso 265, oficina 6, T226928, www.web cusco.com/cuscospan or www.geocities.com/cuscospan School offers homestays, optional activities including dance and music classes, cookery courses, ceramics, Quechua, hiking and volunteer programmes. Also offer courses on a *hacienda* at Cusipata in the Vilcanota valley, east of Cusco. *Don Quijote*, Suecia 480, p 2, T/F262 345, PO Box 1164, www.donquijote.com Same owners as *La Tertulia* and *Hostal Casa de Campo*. Spanish classes, one-to-one or in small groups, also Quechua classes and workshops in Peruvian cuisine, dance and music, US$6 per hr one-to-one, US$175 per week including accommodation. They have apartments to rent, arrange excursions and can help find voluntary work. They also have a school in Urubamba.

English School, Purgatorio 395 esq Huaynapata, T235830/235903. US$5 per hour for one-to-one Classes. Recommended. *Excel*, Cruz Verde 336, T235298, F232272, www.excel-spanishlanguageprograms-peru.org Professional, US$3.50-7 per hour depending on group size, can arrange accommodation with local families. *Inca's Language School*, Saphi 652, http://orbita.starmedia.com/~incaslanguage Reliable and professional, can arrange lodging with families, salsa classes and other extras. *Stephen Light*, an English-born translator and journalist, offers Spanish classes to individuals and small groups. For more details: newworldnews_int@hotmail.com

Laundry *Dana's Laundry*, Nueva Baja y Unión. US$2.10 per kg, takes about 6 hrs. *Lavandería Louis*, Choquechaca 264, San Blas. US$0.85 per kg, fresh, clean, good value. *Lavandería T'aqsana Wasi*, Santa Catalina Ancha 345, T226651. Same day service, they also iron clothes, US$1 per kg, good service, speak English, German, Italian and French. Mon-Sat 0730-2030, Sun 0730-1400. *Lavandería* at Saphi 578. 0800-2000 Mon-Sat, 0800-1300 Sun, good, fast service, US$1 (S/.3) per kg. String markers will be attached to clothes if they have no label. There are several cheap laundries on Procuradores (eg No 351), and also on Suecia and Tecseccocha.

Medical services *Dr Eduardo Franco*, Av de la Cultura, Edif Santa Fe, of 310, T242207, T650179 (mob). 24-hr attention. **Health**: *Clínica Panamericana*, Urb Larapa Grande s/n, between San Sebastián and San Jerónimo districts (10 mins by taxi from centre), T222644, T651552 (mob). 24-hr emergency and medical attention. *Clínica Pardo*, Av de la Cultura 710, T240387, T930063/624186 (mob), www.clinicapardocusco.com 24-hr emergency and hospitalization/medical attention, international department, trained bilingual personnel, handles complete medical assistance coverage with international insurance companies, free ambulance service, visit to hotel, discount in pharmacy, dental service, X-rays, laboratory, full medical specialization. The best regarded and highly recommeded clinic in Cusco. Director: Dr Alcides Vargas. *Clínica Paredes*, C Lechugal 405, T 225265. Newly expanded premises and medical attention. Director: Dr Milagros Paredes, whose speciality is gynaecology. *Hospital Regional*, Av de la Cultura, T227661, emer-

Cusco & the Sacred Valley

gencies 223691. *Dr Ilya Gomon*, Av de la Cultura, Edif Santa Fe, of 207, T651906 (mob). Canadian chiropractor, good, reasonable prices, available for hotel or home visits. *Dr Gilbert Espejo* and *Dr Boris Espejo Muñoz*, both in the Centro Comercial Cusco, oficina 7, T228074 and T231918 respectively. If you need a yellow fever vaccination (for the jungle lowlands, or for travel to Bolivia or Brazil where it is required), it is available at the paediatric department of the *Hospital Antonio Lorena* from 0830 on Mon, Wed and Fri; they are free and include the international vaccination certificate.

Public conveniences Desperate for the loo and can´t face that in the internet café? There are good conveniences at the top of Plateros, at its junction with Saphi, US$0.50.

Useful information **Immigration**: Av Sol s/n, block 6 close to post office, T222740. Mon-Fri 0800-1300. **ISIC-Intej office**, Portal Comercio 141, p 2, T251208/621351. Issues international student cards. You have to provide documentary evidence from your school or university to certify that you are a full time student and over 12. You also need one passport-size photograph and US$10. The card is also available for teachers. Also available is an International Youth Travel Card. In Cusco the ISIC attracts discounts for entry to cultural and historical sites, on international flight tickets, bus and train fares, car rental and discount rates at hotels and lodgings. **Motorcycle mechanics**: Eric and Oscar Antonio Aranzábal, Ejercícios 202, Tahuantinsuyo, T223397. Highly recommended for repairs. **Bicycle repair**: A good mechanic is Eddy, whose workshop is off Av Garcilaso (street between Tacna and Manco Inca). He welds, builds wheels, etc, but has no spares. For parts, cyclists must go to Arequipa or Lima, or try to use local parts.

The Urubamba Valley

The Río Urubamba cuts its way through fields and rocky gorges beneath the snow-capped peaks of the Cordillera. Brown hills, covered in wheat fields, separate Cusco from this beautiful high valley, which stretches from Sicuani (on the railway to Puno) to the gorge of Torontoi, 600 m lower, to the northwest of the city. That the river was of great significance to the Incas can be seen in the number of strategic sites they built above it, Pisac, Ollantaytambo and Machu Picchu among them. Upstream from Pisac, the river is usually called the Vilcanota, downstream it is the Urubamba.

Getting there The road from Cusco which runs past Sacsayhuaman and on to Tambo Machay (see page 163) climbs up to a pass, then continues over the pampa before descending into the densely populated Urubamba valley. There are two viewpoints above Pisac, Mirador C'orao and Miradaor Taray, over the plain around Pisac and, beyond, the Pitusiray and Sawasiray mountains. This road then crosses the Urubamba river by a bridge at Pisac and follows the north bank of the river to the end of the paved road at Ollantaytambo. It passes through Calca, Yucay and Urubamba, which can also reached from Cusco by the beautiful, direct road through Chinchero (see below, page 203). For details of transport, see under Cusco (page 154).

Best time to visit For the visitor, a paved road, plentiful transport and good hotels and eating places make this an easy place to explore, either on a quick visit from the city or, better still, lingering for a few days. The best time to visit this area is Apr-May or Oct-Nov. The high season is Jun-Sep, but the rainy season, from Dec-Mar, is cheaper and pleasant enough.

Pisac

Pisac, 30 km north of Cusco, is well worth a visit for its superb Inca ruins, high above the town, on the mountainside. Most visitors come to Pisac, though, for its Sunday morning market.

Phone code: 084
Colour map 5, grid A5

The **market** contains sections for the tourist and sections for the local community. Traditionally, Sunday is the day when the people of the highlands come down to sell their produce (potatoes, corn, beans, vegetables; weavings; pottery; etc). These are traded for essentials such as salt, sugar, rice, noodles, fruit, medicines, plastic goods and tools. The market comes to life after the arrival of tourist buses around 1000, and is usually over by 1500. However, there is also an important ceremony every Sunday at 1100 sharp, in which the Varayocs (village mayors) from the surrounding and highland villages participate in a Quechua Catholic mass in Pisac church.

Pisac has other, somewhat less crowded, less expensive markets on Tue and Thu morning

It's best to get there before 0900

On the **plaza**, which has several large *pisonay* trees, are the church and a small interesting **Museo Folklórico**. There are many souvenir shops on Bolognesi. On the same side of the plaza as the museum are the municipal building with a computer centre (email and internet US$0.75 per hour, closed Sunday morning) and a public phone booth. If you need to change money, there is a shop on M Castilla, heading away from the Plaza, near where the road bends; it will change travellers' cheques. A local fiesta is held on 15 July.

Pisac is usually visited as part of a tour from Cusco, but this usually allows only 1½ hours here, not enough time to take in the ruins and splendid scenery.

The **ruins of Inca Pisac** stand on a spur between the Urumbamba river to the south and the smaller Chongo to the east. It provides an ideal vantage point over the flat plain of the Urumbamba and the terraced hillsides. This is one of the largest Inca ruins in the vicinity of Cusco and it clearly had defensive, religious and agricultural functions, as well as being an Inca country estate.

Inca Pisac

The walk up to the ruins begins from the plaza, passing the Centro de Salud and a control post. The path goes through working terraces, giving the ruins a context. The first group of buildings is *Pisaqa*, with a fine curving wall. Climb up to the central part of the ruins, the *Intihuatana* group of temples and rock outcrops in the most magnificent Inca masonry. Here are the *Reloj Solar* ('Hitching Post of the Sun') – now closed because thieves stole a piece from it, palaces of the moon and stars, solstice markers, baths and water channels. From *Intihuatana*, a path leads around the hillside through a tunnel to *Q'Allaqasa*, the 'military area'. Across the valley at this point, a large area of Inca tombs in holes in the hillside can be seen. The end of the site is *Kanchiracay*.

Pisac

Path to Archaeological Site

Sleeping
1 Hospedaje Familiar Kinsa Ccocha
2 Parador de Pisac
3 Pisaq
4 Residencial Beho

Eating
1 Bakery
2 Café Restaurante Doña Clorinda

At dusk you will hear, if not see, the *pisaca* (partridges), after which the place is named. If lucky you will also see deer.

■ *The site is open 0700-1730. If you go early (before 1000) you'll have the ruins to yourself. To appreciate the site fully, allow 5 or 6 hrs if going on foot. Even if going by car, do not rush as there is a lot to see and a lot of walking to do. Road transport approaches from the Kanchiracay end. The drive up from town takes about 20 mins. Walking up, although tiring, is recommended for the views and location. It's at least one hour uphill all the way. The descent takes 30 mins on foot. Horses are available for US$3 per person. Combis charge US$0.60 per person and taxis US$3 one way up to the ruins from near the bridge. Then you can walk back down (if you want the taxi to take you back down negotiate a fare). Overnight parking is allowed in the parking lot. Entry is by multi-site ticket. Guides charge US$5, but the wardens on site are very helpful and don't charge anything to give out information.*

Sleeping
■ *on map*

AL *Royal Inca Pisac*, Carretera Ruinas Km 1.5, T203064/65/66, F203067, royalin@terra.com.pe In the same chain as the *Royal Incas I* and *II* in Cusco, with the hotels' own bus service. On the road that goes up to the ruins, a taxi ride after dark. Price includes taxes and breakfast. Camping available for US$5 per person. Will provide guide for ruins, very pleasant, converted hacienda with pool, sauna and jacuzzi (US$7), tennis court, horse riding, bicycle rental, restaurant and bar. Popular with day-trippers from Cusco. Has a rescued owl and deer on the property, also a puma in a cage. **E** per person *Pisaq*, at the corner of Pardo, on the Plaza in front of the church and marketplace, Casilla Postal 1179, Cusco, T(084) 203062, hotelpisaq@terra.com.pe **D** in the only room with bath, all others share bathrooms, which are spotless. Breakfast is extra, excellent brownies, pizza served on Tue, Thu, Sat and Sun, very clean, hot water 24 hrs, pleasant decor, sauna, friendly, knowledgeable, English, German and French. Recommended. **F** *Residencial Beho*, Intihuatana 642, 50 m uphill from the Plaza, T/F203001. Ask for a room in the main building, good breakfast for US$1, has a shop selling local handicrafts including masks, the owner's son will act as a guide to the ruins at the weekend. **G** per person *Parador*, on the Plaza, T203061. Shared bathrooms with hot water, breakfast is extra, but the restaurant serves other meals. **G** per person *Hospedaje Familiar Kinsa Ccocha*, on the Plaza. Basic rooms with shared bath, cheaper without hot water.

Eating
● *on map*

Good, cheap trout is available in many restaurants. Good, cheap food can be bought on market day. *Doña Clorinda*, on the Plaza opposite the church, doesn't look very inviting but cooks very tasty food, including vegetarian dishes, very friendly. The bakery at Mcal Castilla 372 sells excellent cheese and onion *empanadas* for US$0.25, suitable for vegetarians, and good wholemeal bread. The oven is tremendous! *Valle Sagrado*, just along from the bridge going towards Urubamba. Not cheap, but huge portions and good value. Recommended, especially for the fish.

Lamay

Near Lamay, the second village on the road from Pisac towards Urubamba, are **warm springs**, which are highly regarded locally for their medicinal properties. There is a pleasant little *hostal* beside the springs called *Jerseyhuasi* (**F** per night including breakfast, with generous portions of good food at other meals, clean and comfortable rooms). They also have camping possibilities.

Calca

Colour map 5, grid A5

Eighteen kilometres beyond Pisac is Calca at 2,900 m. The plaza is divided in two parts. Urubamba buses stop on one side, and Cusco and Pisac buses on the other side of the dividing strip. Look out for the *api* **sellers** with their bicycles loaded with steaming kettle and assortment of bottles, glasses and tubs. The municipal library has internet connection.

There are mineral baths at **Machacanch**a, 8 km east of Calca. These springs are indoors, pleasantly warm and will open at night for groups. They are half an hour by taxi from town. Three kilometres beyond Machacancha are the Inca ruins of **Arquasmarca**.

The ruins of a small Inca town, **Huchuy Cusco**, are across the Río Urubamba, and up a stiff climb, 3-4 hours. Huchuy Cusco (also spelt Qosqo), which in Quechua means "Little Cusco", was originally called Kakya Qawani, "from where the lightning can be seen". It is dramatically located on a flat esplanade almost 600 m above the villages of Lamay and Calca. The views are magnificent. The ruins themselves consist of extensive agricultural terraces with high retaining walls, and several buildings made from both finely-wrought stonework and adobe bricks. The INC began restoration work in 2001.

The easiest route to the site is to follow the steep trail behind Lamay, which is reached by crossing the bridge over the river. There is also a clearly marked trail from Calca. Another longer route leads from Tambo Machay near Cusco, a magnificent one- or two-day trek along the route once taken by the Inca from his capital to his country estate at Huchuy Cusco, where some sections of the original Inca highway remain intact. There are many places to camp, but take water.

E *Hostal Pitusiray*, on the edge of town. **G** *Hostal Martín*, opposite the market place, 1 block from the plaza, , dirty, cold water only. Restaurant *El Emperador*, Av Vilcanota 810. It serves trout, good service. Recommended. Other basic restaurants around the plaza.

Sleeping & eating

Yucay

A few kilometres east of Urubamba, Yucay has two large, grassy plazas divided by the restored colonial church of **Santiago Apóstol**, with its oil paintings and fine altars. On the opposite side from Plaza Manco II is the **adobe palace** built for Sayri Túpac (Manco's son) when he emerged from Vilcabamba in 1558.

Colour map 5, grid A5

L-AL *Sonesta Posadas del Inca*, on Plaza Manco II de Yucay 123, T201414, F201345 (Lima T222 4777, F422 4345), www.posadas.com.pe Price includes taxes and buffet breakfast. A converted 300-year-old monastery which is like a little village with plazas, lovely gardens, chapel, and many different types of room. As well as rooms in the old part, there are recent additions, which are comfortable and well-appointed. The restaurant serves an excellent buffet lunch. Recommended. **AL** *Sonesta Posada del Inca Yucay II*, on same plaza, T201107, F201345. In this colonial house Simón Bolívar stayed during his liberation campaign in 1825. The price includes taxes and breakfast. Rooms have heating and, outside, there are 2 patios and gardens. There is a restaurant and pizzería. Canoeing, horse riding, mountain biking and guided treks and tours can be arranged.

Sleeping

Urubamba

Like many places along the valley, Urubamba is in a fine setting with views of the Chicón snowpeaks and glaciers and enjoys a mild climate. The main plaza, with a fountain capped by a maize cob, is surrounded by buildings painted blue. Calle Berriózabal, on the west edge of town, is lined with pisonay trees. The large market square is one block west of the main plaza. The main road skirts the town and the bridge for the road to Chinchero is just to the east of town.

Altitude: 2,863 m
Colour map 5, grid A5

A visit to the **Seminario-Behar Ceramic Studio** is highly recommended. Founded in 1980, the studio is in the beautiful grounds of the former *Hostal Urpihuasi*, Calle Berriózabal 111, a right turn off the main road to Ollantaytambo. Seminario has investigated the techniques and designs of pre-Columbian Peruvian cultures and has created a style with strong links to the past. Each piece is hand made and painted, using ancient glazes and minerals, and is then fired in reproduction pre-Columbian kilns. The resulting pieces are very attractive. Reservations to visit the studio and a personal appointment with the artists (Pablo and Marilú) are welcomed. ■ *The art gallery and shop are open every day, just ring the bell. T201002, F201177, kupa@terra.com.pe*

Five kilometres west of Urubamba is the village of **Tarabamba**, where a bridge crosses the Río Urubamba. If you turn right after the bridge you'll come to **Pichingoto**, a tumbled-down village built under an overhanging cliff. Also, just over the bridge and before the town to the left of a small, walled cemetery is a salt stream. Follow the footpath beside the stream and you'll come to **Salinas**, a small village below which are a mass of **terraced Inca salt pans** (*salineras*), which are still in production after thousands of years. It's a very spectacular sight as there are over 5,000. These are now a fixture on the tourist circuit and can become congested with buses. The walk to the salt pans takes about 30 minutes. Take water as this side of the valley can be very hot and dry.

Sleeping
■ *on map*

Out of town **LL-AL** *Sol y Luna*, west of town, T/F201620, www.hotelsolylu na.com Attractive bungalows set off the main road in lovely gardens, pool, excellent buffet in restaurant, French-Swiss owned. Has *Viento Sur* adventure travel agency, for horse riding,

	Sleeping	3 Hostal Urubamba	Eating	4 Pizzonay
1 Capulí	4 Incaland	1 Chez Mary	5 Quinta los
2 Hospedaje Perla	5 Las Tres Marías	2 El Maizal	Geranios
de Vilcanota	6 Macha Wasi	3 Pintacha	

0 metres 100
0 yards 100

mountain biking, trekking and paragliding, www.aventuras vientosur.com **AL** *Incaland Hotel and Conference Center*, Av Ferrocarril s/n, 5 mins' walk from the centre, T/F201126/201117, www.incalandperu. com Special rates are also available. 65 comfortable, spacious bungalows set in extensive gardens, English- owned, good restaurant serving buffet meals, bar, disco, 2 pools, also horse riding (eg to Moray), mountain biking, kayaking and rafting. The staff are helpful and service is good.

AL *K'uychi Rumi*, Km 73.5 on the road to Ollantaytambo, 3 km from town, T201169, www.urubamba.com 6 cottages for rent with 2 bedrooms, fully equipped, fireplace, terrace and balcony, surrounded by gardens. Price is for 1-2 people, each house can accommodate 6 (**L**). **AL** *Río Grande Club Hotel*, Rumichaca s/n, at Km 75 on the main road Urubamba-Ollantaytambo, T/F201528, jotacha@hotmail.com Beautiful old farm of the Chávez family, all rooms with bath, country-style breakfast included, 24-hr hot water, swimming pool is solar heated, children's play grounds, natural eucalyptus sauna, hikes in the area, horse riding, birdwatching. Recommended. **AL-A** *San Agustín Urubamba*, Km 71, T201443-44, F201025 (or at *San Agustín Internacional* in Cusco), 20 mins' walk from town, towards Yucay. Comfortable, small pool, restaurant serving a buffet on Tue, Thu and Sun for US$3.50. **B** *Perol Chico*, Km 77 on the road to Ollantaytambo, office Grau 203, Casilla postal 59, Correo Central, Urubamba, T201694, stables 624475, www.perolchico.com Dutch/Peruvian owned, private bungalows with fireplace and kitchen on a ranch, specializes in horse riding (see below). Recommended. **D** per person *Las Chullpas*, 3 km west of town in the Pumahuanca Valley, T685713, www.chullpas.com Very peaceful, includes excellent breakfast, vegetarian meals, English and German spoken, Spanish classes, natural medicine, treks, riding, mountain biking, camping US$3 with hot shower. Mototaxi from town US$0.85, taxi (ask for Querocancha) US$2.

In town C *Las Tres Marías*, Zavala 307, T201004 (Cusco 225252). New, with beautiful gardens, hot water, welcoming. Recommended. **D** *Macha Wasi*, Jr Nicolás Barre, T201612, www.unsaac.edu.pe/machawasi Canadian owned guesthouse with comfortable rooms and a dormitory, delicious breakfast extra, safe, lovely garden, laundry. Spanish courses and treks can be arranged. Recommended. **F** per person *Capulí*, Grau 222. With bath, hot water and TV, or **G** per bed with shared bath. **F** *Hostal Urubamba*, Bolognesi 605. Basic but pleasant, rooms with bath and cold water, **G** without bath. **G** *Hospedaje Perla de Vilcanota*, on 9 de Noviembre, T201135. Price is per bed, without bath, but hot water in the shared bathrooms, there are even cheaper rooms.

La Casa de la Abuela, Bolívar 272, 2 blocks up from the Plaza de Armas, T622975. Excellent restaurant with rooms grouped around a small courtyard. The trout is fantastic and food is served with baskets of roasted potatoes

Eating
● *on map*

9 de Noviembre

2

□ Coliseo Municipal

2

5

To San Agustín Urubamba, Yucay & Cusco via Calca

To Cusco via Chinchero

and salad. Recommended. *Chez Mary*, Comercio y Grau, corner of main Plaza, T201003/201190. Mary Cuba, the owner, is a local Urubambina, very pleasant and helpful, she speaks good English. She serves excellent food, good pasta and pizzas, and the atmosphere is very cosy and comfortable, with smart decor and good music. At night the bar has live music. *El Fogón*, Parque Pintacha, T201534. Traditional Peruvian food, large servings, great atmosphere. Recommended. *Pintacha*, Bolognesi 523. Pub/café serving sandwiches, burgers, coffees, teas and drinks. Has games and book exchange, cosy, open till late. *Pizzonay*, Av Mcal Castilla 2nd block. Pizzas, excellent lasagne. Mulled wine served in a small restaurant with nice decor. Clean, good value. Recommended. *Tequila*, Av Mcal Castilla 3rd block. The door is always closed so you must ring the bell. Disco, drinks, good coffee, open till late. On the main road, before the bridge, are: *Quinta los Geranios*, T201043. Regional dishes, excellent lunch with more than enough food, average price US$13. *El Maizal*, T201454. Country-style restaurant with a good reputation, buffet service with a variety of typical Novo Andino dishes, plus international choices, beautiful gardens with native flowers and fruit trees. Recommended (they also have a hotel of the same name, **B**).

In **Tarabamba**, *Tunupa*, on left side of the road on the riverbank, in a new, colonial-style hacienda (same ownership as *Tunupa* in Cusco), zappa@ terra.com.pe Excellent food served indoors or outdoors, bar, lounge, library, chapel, gardens, stables and an alpaca-jewellery shop. Outstanding exhibition of pre-Columbian objects and colonial paintings, and *Seminario´s* ceramics feature in the décor. Valley tours (Tue, Thu, Sun) are served a varied buffet including Novo Andino cuisine; buffet lunch US$15, 1200-1500. Lunch and dinner (1800-2030) is available daily.

May and Jun are the *harvest months*, with many processions following mysterious ancient schedules. Urubamba's main festival, *El Señor de Torrechayoc*, takes place during the **first week of Jun**.

Horse riding   *Perol Chico Tours*, Casilla postal 59, Correo Central, T695188/ 624475, www.perolchico.com   Owned and operated by Eddy van Brunschot (Dutch/Peruvian), 1 to 12-day trips out of Urubamba, good horses, riding is Peruvian Paso style; 1-day trip to Moray and the salt pans costs US$60 (6 hrs). See also Sleeping, above. Recommended. Also contact through *SAS Travel* in Cusco.

Bus   The bus and combi terminal is just west of town on the main road. Buses run from Urubamba to Calca, Pisac (US$0.80, 1 hr) and Cusco (2 hrs, US$1), from 0530 onwards. Also buses to Cusco via Chinchero, same fare. Colectivos to Cusco can be caught outside the terminal and on the main road, US$1.15. Combis run to Ollantaytambo, 45 mins, US$0.30. Hotels such as the *Incaland* and *Posadas del Inca* (Yucay) run a twice-daily shuttle between Cusco airport and Urubamba for US$10. There are buses to Quillabamba. **Rail**   See under Machu Picchu for the Sacred Valley Railway from Urubamba to Aguas Calientes.

Banks   *Banco de la Nación* is on M Castilla at the start of the 2nd block. **Communications**   *Serpost*, post office, is on the Plaza de Armas. There are several phone booths around the centre. The one outside *Hostal Urubamba* can make international calls.

Chinchero

Chinchero is northwest from Cusco, just off the direct road to Urubamba. The streets of the village wind up from the lower sections, where transport stops, to the **plaza**, which is reached through an archway. The great square appears to be stepped, with a magnificent Inca wall with tall niches separating the two levels. From the lower section, which is paved, another arch leads to an upper terrace, upon which the Spaniards built their **church**. The ceiling, beams and interior walls are covered in beautiful floral and religious designs, restored to reveal their full glory. The altar, too, is fine. The church is open on Sunday for mass and at festivals. Opposite the church is a small local **museum**. Excavations have revealed many Inca walls and terraces. ■ *The site is open daily, 0700-1730, on the combined entrance ticket (see page 157).*

Altitude: 3,762 m
Colour map 5, grid A5

The local produce **market** on Sunday morning is fascinating and very colourful, and best before the tour groups arrive. It's on your left as you come into town. There's also a small handicraft market, also on Sunday, up by the church. The town celebrates the **day of the Virgin**, on 8 September.

Chinchero to Huayllabamba hike: there is a scenic path from Chinchero to Huayllabamba, a village on the left bank of the Río Urubamba, or Vilcanota, between Yucay and Calca (see above). The hike is quite beautiful, with fine views of the peaks of the Urubamba range, and takes about three to four hours. Follow the old Chinchero-Urubamba dirt road, to the left of the new paved road. Ask the locals when you are not sure. It runs over the pampa, with a good view of Chinchero, then drops down to the Urubamba valley. The end of the hike is about 10 km before the town of Urubamba. You can either proceed to Urubamaba or back to Cusco.

An alternative hike from Chinchero follows the Maras-Moray-Pichingoto salt mines route.

Sleeping   **F** *Hotel Restaurant Antabaraj*, just beyond ticket control, T/F306002 (Patricia Cagigao), antabaraj@hotmail.com Basic rooms, take sleeping bag, kitchen facilities, good views, food at reasonable prices.

Moray

Colour map 5, grid A5   This remote but beautiful site lies 9 km to the west of the little town of **Maras** and is well worth a visit. There are three 'colosseums', used by the Incas, according to some theories, as a sort of open-air crop nursery, known locally as the laboratory of the Incas. The great depressions contain no ruined buildings, but are lined with fine terracing. Each level is said to have its own microclimate. It is a very atmospheric place, which, many claim, has mystical power. The scenery around here is absolutely stunning, especially in late afternoon, when the light is wonderful; but for photography it's best to arrive in the morning. ■ *Entry to Moray costs US$1.45.*

Getting there   There is a paved road from the main road between Chinchero and Urubamba to Maras and from there an unmade road in good condition leads to Moray, 9 km. Ask in Maras for the best route to walk, other than on the main road. There is public transport from Chinchero to Maras and regular pick-up trucks which carry people and produce in and out. Transport stops running between 1700 and 1800; it costs between US$0.60-1. The most interesting way to get to Moray is from Urubamba via the Pichingoto bridge over the Río Urubamba. The climb up from the bridge is fairly steep but easy, with great views of Nevado Chicón. The path passes by the spectacular salt pans (see above), which are about 1½ km below Maras. Moray is about 1½ hrs further on. If you cannot get transport into Maras, take any combi going between Urubamba and Chinchero, get out at the junction for Maras and walk from there. It's 30 mins to Maras; once through the village, bear left a little, and ask directions to Moray. It's 1½ hrs walk in total. Hitching back to Urubamba is quite easy, but there are no hotels at all in the area, so take care not to be stranded. The *Hotel Incaland* in Urubamba can arrange horses and guide and a pick-up truck for the return, all for US$30-40 per person (see page 201).

Ollantaytambo

Altitude: 2,800 m
Colour map 5, grid A5   The attractive little town of Ollantaytambo, at the foot of some spectacular Inca ruins and terraces, is built directly on top of the original Inca town, or Llacta. The Inca canchas (blocks) are almost entirely intact and can be clearly seen. It's an impressive sight and one that shouldn't be missed, even though many people only visit the ruins above the town.

When Manco Inca decided to rebel against the Spaniards in 1536, he fell back to Ollantaytambo from Calca to stage one of the greatest acts of resistance to the *conquistadores*. Hernando Pizarro led his troops to the foot of the Inca's stronghold and, on seeing how well-manned and fortified the place was, described it as a "horrifying sight". Under fierce fire, Pizarro's men failed to capture Manco and retreated to Cusco, but Manco could not press home any advantage. In 1537, feeling vulnerable to further attacks, he left Ollantaytambo for Vilcabamba.

Entering Ollantaytambo from Urubamba, the road is built along the long wall of 100 niches. Note the inclination of the wall: it leans towards the road. Since it was the Incas' practice to build with the walls leaning towards the interiors of the buildings, it has been deduced that the road, much narrower then, was built inside a succession of buildings. The road leads into the main plaza, where public transport congregates in the centre. The original Inca town is behind the north side of the plaza. The road out of the northwest corner of the plaza looks straight up to the Inca temple, but to get there you have to cross the river bridge and go down to the colonial church with its enclosed *recinto*. Beyond is a grand plaza (and car park) with entrances to the archaeological site.

Ins & outs

There is a direct bus service from Ollantaytambo to Cusco at 0715 and 1945, US$2.85. The station is 10-15 mins walk from the plaza (turn left at the sign that says 'Centro de Salud' between the Plaza de Armas and the ruins). There are colectivos at the plaza for the station when trains are due. Also, a bus leaves the station at 0900 for Urubamba and Chinchero, US$1.50. Check in advance the time trains pass through here (see also under trains to and from Machu Picchu, page 207). You won't be allowed on the station unless you have previously bought a ticket for the train. The gates are locked and only those with tickets can enter. For those travelling by car and intending to go to Machu Picchu, it is recommended to leave the car at Ollantaytambo railway station, which costs US$1 a day, or at suitable hotels (see Sleeping, below).

Sights

Great walled terraces of fine masonry climb the hillside, at the top of which is an unassailable sanctuary. The ceremonial sector is dominated by six, pinkish monoliths, each over 3 m high, which comprise one side of the base of a platform. Below this so-called Temple of the Sun are examples of perfect stonework, the dark grey stone embellished today with bright orange lichen.

You can either descend by the terraces you came up, or follow the terracing round to the left (as you face the town) and work your way down to the valley of the Patacancha. Here are more Inca ruins in the small area between the town and the temple fortress, behind the church. Most impressive is the **Baño de la Ñusta** (Bath of the Princess), a grey granite rock, about waist high, beneath which is the bath itself. The front of the boulder, over which the water falls, has been carved in a three-stepped pyramid, making a relief arch over the pool. ■ *0700-1730. Admission is by combined entrance ticket, which can be bought at the site. If possible arrive very early, 0700, before the tourists. Guides at the entrance charge US$2. Avoid Sun afternoons, when tour groups from Pisac descend in their hundreds. Ask for Dr Hernán Amat Olazábal, a leading Inca expert, at the community museum for further explanation.*

El Museo Catcco is one block from the plaza, in the Casa Horno on Patacalles. It has good displays of textiles as well as ethnographic and archaeological information and findings from local ruins, run by Sra Rosa de Alamo. ■ *Tue-Sun 1000-1300, 1500-1800. US$1.75 (children free). Internet access US$2.85 per hr. T084-204034.* **Tourist information** *is available in the museum. Information on the museum and other aspects of Ollantaytambo can be found in Spanish on www.cbc.org.pe/rao the site developed from the Ollantaytambo Pilot Project, which was undertaken by Prom Perú and the European Union. The project, aimed at delevoping the town, its tourism and community participation, has produced much useful material and we recognise here our debt to it in researching this section.*

A **two-dimensional 'pyramid'** has been identified on the west side of the main ruins of Ollantaytambo. Its discoverers, Fernando and Edgar Elorietta, claim it is the real Pacaritambo, from where the four original Inca brothers emerged to found their empire, contrary to the more popular legend (see page 570). Whether this is the case or not, it is still a first-class piece of engineering with great terraced fields and a fine 750-m wall creating the optical illusion of a pyramid. The wall is aligned with the rays of the winter solstice, on 21 June. People gather at mid-winter dawn to watch this event.

The mysterious 'pyramid', which covers 50-60 ha, can be seen properly from the other side of the river. This is a pleasant, easy one-hour walk, west from the Puente Inca, just outside the town. You'll also be rewarded with great views of the Sacred Valley and the river, with the snowy peaks of the Verónica massif as a backdrop.

Sleeping
● *on map*

AL *Pakaritambo*, C Ferrocarril s/n, T204104, F204105, www.pakaritampu.com Modern 3-star hotel in lovely surroundings, with bath, breakfast included, stylish local decorations, TV room, restaurant and bar, internet service for guests, laundry, safe and room service. Adventure sports such as rafting, climbing, trekking, mountain biking and riding can be arranged. Excellent quality and service, but meals, which are extra, are not as good. **C** *Albergue Kapuly*, at the end of the station road, T204017. Quiet, spacious rooms with and without bath, cheaper in low season, garden. Recommended. Also on the road to the station is **C** *Hostal Munay Tika*, T204111, tika@latinmail.com Breakfast included, dinner by arrangement, sauna US$3 with prior notice, nice garden, good. **D** per person *El Albergue Ollantaytambo*, within the railway station gates, T/F204014 (or in Cusco at *Manu Expeditions*, T226671, Casilla 784, Cusco). Owned by North American Wendy Weeks, 6 rooms full of character set in buildings around a courtyard, shared bathrooms, "wonderful showers", charming, very relaxing, homely, with eucalyptus steam sauna, breakfast US$3, box lunch US$5, full dinner available on request at US$10, good place for information. See the office-cum shop-cum-exhibition where interesting handicrafts can be bought. Private transport can be arranged to the salt mines, Moray, Abra Málaga for birdwatching and taxi transfers to the airport. Highly recommended. **E** per person *Las Orquídeas*, near the start of the road to the station, T204032. Good accommodation, meals available. **E** *Hostal La Ñusta*, T204035/077, up side street on right on way from Plaza de Armas towards ruins, T204035/077. Very good, hot showers, knowledgeable proprietor, good view from terrace and some rooms, parking US$1.50 per day for those going to Machu Picchu. **F** *Hostal Chuza*, just below the main plaza in town, T204038. Very clean and friendly with safe motorcycle parking. Recommended. **F** *Hostal Miranda*, between the main plaza and the ruins, T204091. With shower, basic, clean.

Eating
● *on map*

Mid-range *Café Sol del Oriente*, esquina Plaza de Ruinas, T204009. Soups, salads, vegetables, fish and meat, "from Peruvian to pizza", open for breakfast, lunch and dinner. Recommended. *Fortaleza Pizzería*, north corner of Plaza de Armas. Good pizza, pasta dishes and traditional food. *Kusi Coyllor*, Plaza Ruinas, T246977 for delivery. Nice atmosphere, café and bar. *Mayupata*, Jr Convención s/n, across the bridge on the way to the ruins, on the left, T204083. International and a selection of Peruvian dishes, desserts, sandwiches, coffee, bar with fireplace, opens at 0600 for breakfast, also lunch and dinner, river view, relaxing atmosphere. **Cheaper places** *Alcázar Café*, C del Medio. Has a good tourist menu, reasonable prices, English spoken. On the Plaza de Armas, *Ollantaytambo*, next to police station. Has *menú*, à la carte and public phone. Also *La Ñusta*, good. *La Puzunga*, C del Medio. Good little bar serving homemade herbal tonics, nice atmosphere.

Festivals

On **6 Jan** there is the *Bajada de Reyes Magos* (the Magi), with traditional dancing, a bull fight, local food and a fair. **End-May/early-Jun:** *Pentecostes*, 50 days after Easter, *Fiesta del Señor de Choquekillca*, patron saint of Ollantaytambo, with several days of dancing, weddings, processions, masses, feasting and drinking (the last opportunity to see traditional Cusqueño dancing). On **29 Jun**, following *Inti Raymi* in Cusco, there is the colourful *Ollanta-Raymi*, at which the Quechua drama, *Ollantay*, is re-enacted. **29 Oct**, *Aniversario de Ollantaytambo*, with dancing in traditional costume and many local delicacies for sale. (With thanks to Wendy Weeks for additional information on festivals.)

Directory **Useful addresses Police**: *PNP*, southwest corner of the Plaza de Armas.

Around Ollantaytambo

The stone quarries of **Cachiccata** are some 9 km from Ollantaytambo. Standing to the left of the six monolithic blocks of the Temple of the Sun, you can see them, looking west-south-west across the valley. The stones that the Inca masons chose here had to be quarried, hewn into a rough shape, and hauled across the valley floor and up to the temple by means of a ramp, which can still be seen. Between the ruins and the quarries more that 50 enormous stones that never reached their destination lie abandoned. They are known as the *las piedras cansadas*, or "the tired stones". It takes about a day to walk to the Inca quarries on the opposite of the river and return to Ollantaytambo.

At **Pinkuylluna** hill, on the western edge of Ollantaytambo, is an impressive collection of storehouses, or *qolqas*, sometimes referred to as prisons. It's a relatively straightforward climb up the mountain, although there are some difficult stretches. Allow 2-3 hours going up. The path is difficult to make out, so it's best not to go on your own.

Machu Picchu

There is a tremendous feeling of awe on first witnessing this incredible sight. The ancient citadel (42 km from Ollantaytambo by rail) straddles the saddle of a high mountain with steep terraced slopes falling away to the fast-flowing Urubamba river snaking its hairpin course below in the valley floor. Towering overhead is Huayna Picchu, and green jungle peaks provide the backdrop for the whole scene.

Altitude: 2,380 m
Colour map 5,
grid A5

Ins and outs

The only true way to get to Machu Picchu is to sling your rucksack on your back, and follow in the footsteps of the Incas. This way you are making a true pilgrimage and the sweat and struggle is all worth it when you set your eyes on this mystical site at sunrise from the Inca sun gate above the ruins. See the Inca Trail, page 212, for more information.

Getting there

Rail The *PerúRail* trains to Machu Picchu run from San Pedro station in **Cusco**. They pass through Poroy and Ollantaytambo to **Aguas Calientes** (the official name of this station is 'Machu Picchu'). There is a new train station for the tourist trains here in Aguas Calientes on the outskirts of town, 200 m from *Machu Picchu Pueblo Hotel* and 50 m from where buses leave for Machu Picchu ruins. The ticket office is open 0630-1730; there is a guard on the gate. (Trains do not go on to Machu Picchu station, officially called 'Puente Ruinas'. The railway continues to Quillabamba, but this section has been closed since 1998.) There is a paved road in poor condition between Aguas Calientes and 'Puente Ruinas' station, which is at the foot of the road up to the ruins.

There are three classes of tourist train which depart from Cusco. *Vistadome* is the quickest and most comfortable service. The carriages have panoramic windows in the ceiling. Passengers can forego the initial winding climb out of Cusco at the beginning of the journey by driving to Poroy and boarding the train there (train Cusco-Poroy takes over an hour, minibus 20 mins). The full train trip lasts 3¼ hours one way. Snacks and hot and cold refreshments are included in the price of US$73 return. *Vistadome* services also run three times a day from Ollantaytambo and from Urubamba (see below, *The Sacred Valley Railway*).

Inca, slightly more leisurely than the *Vistadome*, has comfortable seats and tables for continental breakfast or afternoon tea. The fare is US$70 return. These trains have toilets, video, snacks and drinks for sale.

The *Backpacker* is a considerably renovated version of the classic Machu Picchu train of yore, with seats re-upholstered in indigenous fabrics and additional storage space for baggage. The fare is US$35 return.

The *Sacred Valley Railway (SVR) Vistadome* service runs daily from the newly refurbished station at Urubamba. It passes through Ollantaytambo (where passengers can also board, and alight on the return journey) and is the first train to arrive at Aguas Calientes, giving an hour-and-a-half or more at the ruins before the crowds and a full seven hours at the site. The service is a code share with PerúRail. Going down one day and returning on another is permitted, as is travelling one-way on the SVR and returning on one of PerúRail's services. Bookings paid 15 or more days in advance receive special deals, including either a free box lunch or a buffet lunch at the *Incaland Hotel*, which is 80 m on foot from the station. Package deals are also available. SVR Cusco office is at Av El Sol 803, T249076, or Casa Estación, Av Ferrocarril s/n, Urubamba, T/F201126/27, www.sacredvalleyrailway.com Several Urubamba and Yucay hotels offer free transport to and from the Urubamba station. Visitors can also arrange to travel on to Cusco in the evening by bus to arrive there around 2000. Return tickets cost US$58 either from Urubamba or Ollantaytambo, one way tickets US$29.

Schedules The *Vistadome* leaves **Cusco** daily at 0600, stopping at **Poroy** at 0640 and **Ollantaytambo** at 0805, arriving at Machu Picchu at 0930. It returns from Machu Picchu at 1500, passing Ollantaytambo at 1625 and Poroy at 1750, reaching Cusco at 1850. The *Inca* leaves at **Cusco** 0615, passing **Poroy** at 0700 and **Ollantaytambo** at 0830, reaching Machu Picchu at 1000. It returns at 1525, passing Ollantaytambo at 1655 and Poroy at 1827, getting to Cusco at 1925. The *Backpacker* leaves **Cusco** at 0630, passing **Poroy** at 0720 and **Ollantaytambo** at 0900, arriving in Machu Picchu at 1030. It returns at 1610, passing Ollantaytambo at 1750 and Poroy at 1930, getting to Cusco at 2030.The *Sacred Valley Railway Vistadome* leaves **Urubamba** at 0625, reaching Machu Picchu at 0800, returning at 1625, reaching Urubamba at 1830. The *Ollantaytambo Vistadomes* leave at 1010 and 1510, arriving at 1118 and 1630, returning from Machu Picchu at 0825 and 1330, reaching Ollantaytambo at 0952 and 1444. Seats can be reserved even if you're not returning the same day. Tickets for PerúRail's trains should be bought at Wanchac station in Cusco, on Av Pachacútec or through PerúRail's website, www.peru rail.com

Tourist tickets Many people return by bus from Ollantaytambo, leaving the trains emptier for the return trip to Cusco. Those trains that arrive in Cusco at night give a magical view of the city lights. Tour agencies in Cusco sell various tourist tickets which include transfer to station, train fare, round trip by bus up to the ruins, entrance fee and guide (about US$80), but day trips (except those commencing in Urubamba) can be rather rushed.

Local trains The *Tren Local* or *Servicio Social* from Cusco and the *Cerrojo Social* from Ollantaytambo, are only for people who live along the route of the

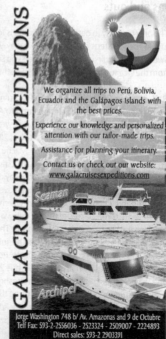

railway, Peruvian students and retired Peruvians. Tourists cannot buy tickets for these trains. If they do and are found on board they will be removed from the train at the first opportunity and will have to get back to Cusco at their own expense. These trains are run by PerúRail as a public service, to support the local communities, and tourists purchasing seats will be depriving local people of their only means of transport.

Local buses Leave **Aguas Calientes** for Machu Picchu every 30 mins from 0630 to 1300 and cost US$9 return, valid for 48 hrs. Buses run down from the ruins from 1200 to 1730. It is also possible to take a bus down between 0700 and 0900. The office for buying bus tickets is opposite the bus stop.

The site is open from 0700 to 1730. Entrance fee is US$20, half price with an ISIC card. It is possible to pay in dollars, but only clean, undamaged notes will be accepted. You can deposit your luggage at the entrance for US$0.50. Guides are available at the site, they are often very knowledgeable and worthwhile, and charge US$30 for 2 hrs. Site wardens are also informative, but give information in Spanish only. **Admission & best time to visit**

It takes at least a day to appreciate the ruins and their surroundings fully. Mon and Fri are bad days because there is usually a crowd of people on guided tours who are going or have been to Pisac market on Sun. The hotel is located next to the entrance, with a restaurant serving buffet lunch. Beside the entrance and luggage store is a snack bar. Neither place is cheap so it's best to take your own food and drink, and take plenty of drinking water. Note that food is not officially allowed into the site.

The ruins are at their busiest in the morning, after the buses arrive bringing tourists up from the first Cusco train 0925. It is quieter in the afternoon, but a lot of people stay on to see the sun setting behind the mountains. A good time to visit is before 0830, when the views are at their best. Permission to enter the ruins before 0630 to watch the sunrise over the Andes, which is a spectacular experience, can be obtained from the *Instituto Nacional de Cultura* (INC) in Cusco, but it is also often possible if you talk to the guards at the gate. The ruins are also quieter after 1530, but don't forget that the last bus down from the ruins leaves at 1730. The walk up takes 2-2½ hrs, following the Inca path. Walking down to Aguas Calientes, if staying the night there, takes 30 mins-1 hr.

NB You cannot take backpacks into Machu Picchu; leave them at ticket office. In the dry season sandflies can be a problem, so take insect repellent and wear long clothing.

The site

For centuries the site was buried in jungle, until Hiram Bingham stumbled upon it in July 1911. It was then explored by an archaeological expedition sent by Yale University. Machu Picchu was a stunning archaeological find. The only major Inca site to escape 400 years of looting and destruction, it was remarkably well-preserved. And it was no ordinary Inca settlement. It sat in an inaccessible location above the Urubamba gorge, and contained so many fine buildings that people have puzzled over its meaning ever since.

Once you have passed through the ticket gate you follow a path to a small complex of buildings which now acts as the main entrance to the ruins. It is set at the eastern end of the extensive terracing which must have supplied the crops for the city. Above this point, turning back on yourself, is the final stretch of the Inca Trail leading down from Intipunku (see below). From a promontory here, on which stands the building called the **Watchman's Hut**(9), you get the perfect view of the city, laid out before you with Huayna Picchu rising above the farthest extremity. This is an ideal place to spend the last few minutes of daylight. Go round the promontory and head south for the Inca bridge (see also below). The main path into the ruins comes to a **dry**

Numbers in brackets refer to the map, page 210

moat(3), which cuts right across the site. At the moat you can either climb the long staircase which goes to the upper reaches of the city, or you can enter the city by the **baths**(4 and 5) and **Temple of the Sun**(6).

Machu Picchu

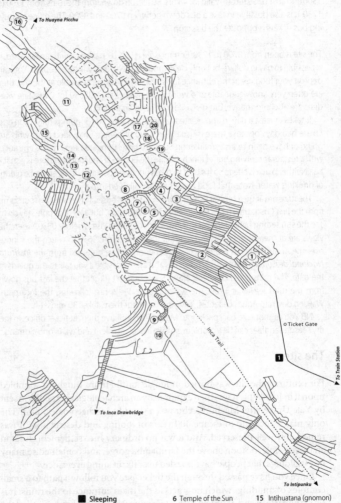

To Huayna Picchu

To Inca Drawbridge

Inca Trail

Ticket Gate

To Train Station

To Intipunku

N

| 0 metres | 50 |
| 0 yards | 50 |

■ Sleeping
1 Machu Pichu Sanctuary Lodge

○ Sights
1 Main entrance
2 Agricultural sector
3 Dry moat
4 Ceremonial baths
5 Principal bath

6 Temple of the Sun
7 Two fountains
8 Royal sector
9 Watchman's hut
10 Funerary rock
11 Main plaza
12 Temple of the 3 Windows
13 Principal temple
14 "Sacristry"

15 Intihuatana (gnomon)
16 Sacred rock
17 Living quarters & workshops
18 Mortar buildings
19 Prison Group or Condor Temple
20 Intimachay

Cusco & the Sacred Valley

The more strenuous way into the city is by the former route, which takes you past quarries, on your left as you look down to the Urubamba on the west flank of the mountain. To your right are roofless buildings where you can see in close up the general construction methods used in the city. Proceeding along this level, above the main plazas, you reach the **Temple of the Three Windows**(12) and the **Principal Temple**(13), which has an associated smaller building called the **Sacristy**(14). The two main buildings are three-sided and were clearly of great importance, given the fine stonework involved. The wall containing the three windows is built onto a single rock, one of the many instances in the city where the architects did not merely put their construction on a convenient piece of land. They used and fashioned its features to suit their conception of how the city should be tied to the mountain, its forces and the alignment of its stones to the surrounding peaks. In the Principal Temple, a diamond-shaped stone in the floor is said to depict the constellation of the Southern Cross. Continue on the path behind the Sacristy to reach the **Intihuatana**(15), the `hitching-post of the sun'. The name comes from the theory that such carved rocks (gnomons), found at all major Inca sites, were the point to which the sun was symbolically `tied' at the winter solstice, before being freed to rise again on its annual ascent towards the summer solstice. The steps, angles and planes of this sculpted block appear to indicate a purpose beyond simple decoration and researchers, such as Johan Reinhard in *The Sacred Center*, have sought the trajectory of each alignment. Whatever the motivation behind this magnificent carving, it is undoubtedly one of the highlights of Machu Picchu.

Climb down from the Intihuatana's mound to the **Main Plaza**(11). Beyond its northern end is a small plaza with open-sided buildings on two sides and on the third, the **Sacred Rock**(16). The outline of this gigantic, flat stone echoes that of the mountains behind it. From here you can proceed to the entrance to the trail to Huayna Picchu (see below). Returning to the Main Plaza and heading southeast you pass, on your left, several groups of closely-packed buildings which have been taken to be **Living Quarters**(17) and **Workshops**(18), **Mortar Buildings**(19) (look for the house with two discs let into the floor) and the Prison Group, one of whose constructions is known as the **Condor Temple**(19). Also in this area is a cave called **Intimachay**(12).

A short distance from the Condor Temple is the lower end of a series of **Ceremonial Baths**(4) or **fountains**. They were probably used for ritual bathing and the water still flows down them today. The uppermost, **Principal Bath**(5), is the most elaborate. Next to it is the **Temple of the Sun**(6), or Torreón. This singular building has one straight wall from which another wall curves around and back to meet the straight one, but for the doorway. From above it looks like an incomplete letter P. It is another example of the architecture being at one with its environment as the interior is taken up by the partly worked summit of the outcrop onto which the building is placed. All indications are that this temple was used for astronomical purposes. Underneath the Torreón a cave-like opening has been formed by an oblique gash in the rock. Fine masonry has been added to the opposing wall, making a second side of a triangle, which contrasts with the rough edge of the split rock. But the blocks of masonry appear to have been slotted behind another sculpted piece of natural stone, which has been cut into a four-stepped buttress. Immediately behind this is a two-stepped buttress. This strange combination of the natural and the manmade has been called the **Tomb** or **Palace of the Princess**. Across the stairway from the complex which includes the Torreón is the group of buildings known as the **Royal Sector**(8), reckoned from the grandness of the construction to have been where the nobles had their quarters.

The famous **Inca bridge** is about 45 minutes along a well-marked trail south of the Royal Sector. The bridge – which is actually a couple of logs – is spectacularly sited, carved into a vertiginous cliff-face.

Huayna Picchu The mountain overlooking the site (on which there are also ruins), has steps to the top for a superlative view of the whole site, but it is not for those who are afraid of heights and you shouldn't leave the path. The climb takes up to 90 minutes but the steps are dangerous after bad weather. The path is open 0700-1300, with the latest return time being 1500; and you must register at a hut at the beginning of the trail.

The other trail to Huayna Picchu, down near the Urubamba, is via the **Temple of the Moon**, in two caves, one above the other, with superb Inca niches inside, which have sadly been blemished by graffiti. To reach the Temple of the Moon from the path to Huayna Picchu, take the marked trail to the left; it is in good shape. It descends further than you think it should. After the Temple you may proceed to Huayna Picchu, but this path is over-grown, slippery in the wet and has a crooked ladder on an exposed part about 10 minutes before reaching the top (not for the faint-hearted). It is safer to return to the main trail to Huayna Picchu, although this adds about 30 minutes to the climb. The round trip takes about four hours. Before doing any trekking around Machu Picchu, check with an official which paths may be used, or which are one way.

Sleeping
■ *on map*

LL *Machu Picchu Sanctuary Lodge*, for reservations the details are the same as for the *Hotel Monasterio* in Cusco, which is under the same management (Peru Orient Express Hotels, see page 166). At the entrance to the ruins, completely refurbished in 2001 with some environmentally-friendly features. They will accept American Express traveller's cheques at the official rate. Comfortable rooms, good service and helpful staff. Food in the restaurant is well-cooked and presented; the restaurant is for residents only in the evening, but the buffet lunch is open to all.

Recommended reading

Lost City of the Incas by Hiram Bingham. *A Walking Tour of Machu Picchu* by Pedro Sueldo Nava – in several languages, available in Cusco. The Tourist Hotel sells guides, although at a rather inflated price. South American Explorers in Lima and Cusco have detailed information on walks here.

The Inca Trail

The wonder of Machu Picchu has been well-documented over the years. But equally impressive is the centuries-old Inca Trail that winds its way from the Sacred Valley near Ollantaytambo, taking three to four days to walk. What makes this hike so special is the stunning combination of Inca ruins, unforgettable views, magnificent mountains, exotic vegetation and extraordinary ecological variety. The government acknowledged this uniqueness in 1981 by including the trail in a 325 sq-km national park, the Machu Picchu Historical Sanctuary.

Machu Picchu itself cannot be understood without the Inca Trail. Its principal sites are ceremonial in character, apparently in ascending hierarchical order. This Inca province was a unique area of elite access. The trail is essentially a work of spiritual art and walking it was formerly an act of devotion.

Ins and outs

In 2000 it was decided that the Inca Trail was becoming too seriously degraded because of the number of people allowed access. The authorities therefore introduced limits on the number of people using it. The regulations are detailed under Tours below, but the main change is that no one may walk the Inca Trail independently. Access is therefore only permissable with a licensed agent. This ruling applies wherever you decide to start.

An entrance ticket for the trail must be bought at the *INC* office in C San Bernardo, Cusco: no tickets are sold at the entrance gates. Furthermore, tickets are only sold on presentation of a letter from a licensed tour operator on behalf of the visitor. There is a 50% discount for students, but note that officials are very strict, only an ISIC card will be accepted as proof of status.

General
information
& advice
*See page 216
for information
about tours
and equipment*

Leave all your valuables in Cusco and keep everything inside your tent, even your shoes. Security has improved in recent years, but robberies still occur. Avoid the Jul-Aug high season and the rainy season from Nov-Apr (note that this can vary). In the wet it is cloudy and the paths are very muddy and difficult. Also watch out for coral snakes in this area (distinguished by black, red, yellow bands).

Please remove all your rubbish, including toilet paper, or use the pits provided. Do not light open fires as they can get out of control. *The Earth Preservation Fund* sponsors an annual clean-up Jul-Aug: volunteers should write to EPF, Inca Trail Project, Box 7545, Ann Arbor, Michigan 48107, USA. In Cusco, different agencies organize the clean-up each year. **The main Trail was due to be closed for 'ecological reasons' in Feb 2003**.

Those concerned about the working conditions of the porters on the trail should contact *Porteadores Inka Ñan*. The co-ordinator for this new project, associated with the International Porter Protection Group, is Alison Crowther, T084-245021, F232603, www.peruweb.org/porters (site under construction Oct 2002). They are always looking for volunteer helpers and for any equipment you'd care to donate to the porters.

The trek and the sights

The trek to the sacred site begins either at Km 82, **Piscacucho**, or at Km 88, **Qorihuayrachina**, at 2,600 m. In order to reach Km 82 hikers are transported by their tour operator in a minibus on the road that goes to Quillabamba. You can depart as early as you like and arrive at Km 82 faster than going by train. The tour operator's equipment, food, fuel and field personnel reach Km 82 for the Inrena staff to weigh each bundle before the group arrives. Km 88 can only be reached by train, subject to schedule and baggage limitations. The train goes slower than a bus, but you start your walk nearer to Llaqtapata and Huayllabamba.

The first ruin is **Llaqtapata**, near Km 88, the utilitarian centre of a large settlement of farming terraces which probably supplied the other Inca trail sites. From here, it is a relatively easy three-hour walk to the village of **Huayllabamba**. Note that the route from Km 82 goes via **Cusichaca**, rather than Llaqtapata. (See below for details of variations in starting points for the Inca Trail.)

A series of gentle climbs and descents leads along the Río Cusichaca, the ideal introduction to the trail. The village is a popular camping spot for tour groups, so it's a better idea to continue for about an hour up to the next site, **Llulluchayoc** – 'three white stones' – which is a patch of green beside a fast-flowing stream. It's a steep climb but you're pretty much guaranteed a decent pitch for the night. If you're feeling really energetic, you can go on to the next camping spot, a perfectly flat meadow, called **Llulluchapampa**. This means a punishing 1½-hour ascent through cloud forest, but it does leave you with a much easier second day. There's also the advantage of relative isolation and a magnificent view back down the valley.

For most people the **second day** is by far the toughest. It's a steep climb to the meadow, followed by an exhausting 2½-hour haul up to the first pass – aptly named **Warmiwañusqa** (Dead Woman) – at 4,200 m. The feeling of relief on reaching the top is immense and there's the added, sadistic pleasure of watching your fellow sufferers struggling in your wake. After a well-earned break it's a sharp descent on a treacherous path down to the Pacamayo valley, where there are a few flat camping spots near a stream if you're too weary to continue.

Halfway to the second pass, comes the ruin of **Runkuracay**, which was probably an Inca tambo, or post-house. It is no longer permitted to camp here. A steep climb up an Inca staircase leads to the next pass, at 3,850 m, with spectacular views of Pumasillo (6,246 m) and the Vilcabamba range. The trail then desends to **Sayacmarca** (Inaccessible town), a spectacular site overlooking the Aobamba valley. Just below Sayacmarca lies **Conchamarca** (Shell town), a small group of buildings standing on rounded terraces – perhaps another tambo.

A blissfully gentle two hours climb on a fine stone highway, leads through an Inca tunnel and along the enchanted fringes of the cloud forest, to the third pass. This is the most rewarding part of the trail, with spectacular views of the entire Vilcabamba range, and it's worth taking the time to dwell on the wonders of nature. Then it's down to the extensive ruins of **Phuyupatamarca** (Cloud-level town), at 3,650 m, where adjacent Inca observation platforms offer awesome views of nearby Salkantay (6,270 m) and surrounding peaks. There is a 'tourist bathroom' here, where water can be collected, but purify it before drinking.

Inca Trail

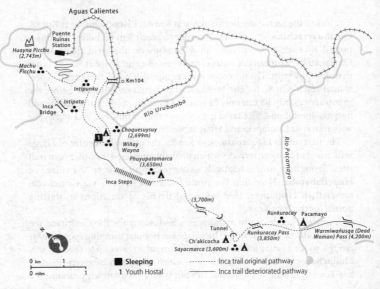

From here an Inca stairway of white granite plunges more than 1,000 m to the spectacularly sited and impressive ruins of **Wiñay-Wayna** (Forever Young), offering views of newly uncovered agricultural terraces at **Intipata** (Sun place). A trail, not easily visible, goes from Wiñay-Wayna to the newly-discovered terracing. There is a **youth hostel** at Wiñay-Wayna, with bunk beds (**G** per person), showers and a small restaurant, but the place is often fully booked. You can sleep on the floor of the restaurant more cheaply, but it is open for diners until 2300. There are also spaces for a few tents, but they get snapped up quickly. The hostel's door is closed at 1730. A gate by Wiñay-Wayna is locked between 1530 and 0500, preventing access to the path to Machu Picchu at night.

After Wiñay-Wayna there is no water, and no place to camp, until Machu Picchu

From here it is a gentle hour's walk through another type of forest, with larger trees and giant ferns, to a steep Inca staircase which leads up to **Intipunku** (Sun gate), where you look down at last upon Machu Picchu, basking in all her reflective glory. Aching muscles are quickly forgotten and even the presence of the functional hotel building cannot detract from one of the most magical sights in all the Americas.

Alternative Inca routes

A short Inca trail, the **Camino Real de los Inkas**, starts where a footbridge gives access to the ruins of Chachabamba. The trail, which ascends above the ruins of Choquesuysuy, connects with the main trail at Wiñay-Wayna. This first part is a steady, continuous ascent of three hours (take water) and the trail is narrow and exposed in parts. About 15 minutes before Wiñay-Wayna is a waterfall where fresh water can be obtained (best to purify it before drinking).

The Inca Trail from Km 104

A three-night trek goes from Km 82 to Km 88, then along the Río Urubamba to Pacaymayo Bajo and Km 104, from where you take the trail described above to Wiñay Wayna and Machu Picchu.

Three-night trek

A trek from Salkantay joins the Inca Trail at Huayllabamba, then proceeds as before on the main Trail through Wiñay Wayna to Machu Picchu. There is no checkpoint at Salkantay for verifying that the relevant fees have been paid, but you will get checked at Huayllabamba. To get to Salkantay, you have to start the trek in Mollepata, northwest of Cusco in the Apurímac valley. Buses of the *Ampay* company run from Arcopata on the Chinchero road, or you can take private transport to Mollepata (3 hours from Cusco). It is down an unpaved road which turns off the main road after Limatambo. From Mollepata it's an all-day trek to Salkantay Pampa, also called Soraypampa. Camp below Apu Salkantay (6,250 m). From Salkantay Pampa a very demanding ascent

Trek from Salkantay

leads to the Incachiriaska Pass (4,900 m). Descend to camp at Sisaypampa. From there, trek to Pampacahuana, an outstanding and seldom-visited Inca ruin. The remains of an Inca road then go down to the singular Inca ruins of Paucarcancha. This entire section is done with mules and/or horses. There is an obligatory change from animals to porters before you reach Huayllabamba. Salkantay to Machu Picchu takes 3 nights.

Trek from Paucarcancha A 4-night trek from Paucarcancha to Huayllabamba, then on the traditional Trail to Machu Picchu. Paucarcancha is an abandoned set of ruins on the descent from Pampacahuana, before the village of Huayllabamba on the main Inca Trail. Paucarcancha is also shown as Incarakay on some maps. Nearby there are some hot springs. Paucarcancha is an important camping site on the trek from Salkantay.

Equipment It is cold at night, and weather conditions change rapidly, so it is important to take not only strong footwear, but also rain gear and warm clothing (this includes long johns if you want to sleep rather than freeze at night) – dress in layers. Also take food, water, water purification tablets, insect repellent, sunscreen, a hat and sunglasses, a supply of plastic bags, coverings, a good sleeping bag filled with down, a torch/flashlight and a stove for preparing hot food and drink to ward off the cold at night. A stove using paraffin (kerosene) is preferable, as fuel can be bought in small quantities in markets.

Walkers who have not taken adequate equipment have died of exposure – check all hired equipment before you set off

A tent is essential, but if you're hiring one in Cusco, check carefully for leaks. Caves marked on some maps are little better than overhangs and are not sufficient shelter to sleep in. You could also take a first-aid kit; if you don't need it the porters probably will, given their basic footwear.

All the necessary equipment can be rented in Cusco (see page 156 under Tour agencies). Good maps of the Trail and area can be bought from South American Explorers in Lima or Cusco. If you have any doubts about carrying your own pack, porters/guides are available through Cusco agencies. Carry a day-pack, water and snacks in case you walk faster or slower than the porters and you have to wait for them to catch you up or you have to catch them up.

Tours Tour Agencies in Cusco will arrange transport to the start, equipment, food, etc, for an all-in price, generally around US$250-290 per person for a good quality, 4-day/3-night trek. All agencies are subject to strict rules and all must be licensed. Groups of up to 10 independent travellers who do not wish to use a tour operator are allowed to hike the trails if they contact an independent, licensed guide to accompany them, as long as they do not contract any other persons such as porters or cooks. There is a maximum of 500 visitors per day allowed on the Trail. Operators pay US$15 for each porter and other trail staff; porters are not permitted to carry more than 25 kg. Littering is banned, as is carrying plastic water bottles (canteens only may be carried), or metal-tipped walking poles. Pets and pack animals are prohibited, but llamas are allowed as far as the first pass. Groups have to use approved campsites. **Prices** On all hiking trails (Km 82 or Km 88 to Machu Picchu, Salkantay to Machu Picchu, and Km 82 or 88 to Machu Picchu via Km 104) adults must pay US$50, students and children under 15 US$25. On the Camino Real de los Inkas from Km 104 to Wiñay Wayna and Machu Picchu the fee is US$25 per adult, US$15 for students and children.

With the enforcement of the new rules, it is necessary to book at least two days in advance. Because there is a quota for agencies and groups to use the Trail, the earlier you can book (eg by email), the better chance you have of getting a trip on your preferred dates. Cheaper agencies pool their clients together, so shop around for the best value (but remember that you get what you pay for – the cheapest, under US$200, say, tend not to pay the environment the respect the new rules were designed to instil).

You can save a bit of money by arranging your own transport back to Ollantaytambo in advance, either for the last day of your tour, or by staying an extra night in Aguas Calientes and taking the early morning train, then take a bus back to Cusco. If you take your own tent and sleeping gear, some agencies offer an 'umbrella service', which means that you walk with their group, but you do all your own carrying and cooking.

Aguas Calientes

One-and-a-half kilometres back along the railway from Puente Ruinas, this is *Colour map 5, grid A5* a popular resting place for those recovering from the rigours of the Inca Trail. It is called Aguas Calientes after the hot springs above the town. It is also called the town of Machu Picchu.

The **baths** consist of a rather smelly communal pool, 10 minutes' walk from the town. ■ *0500-2030, and entry is US$1.50 (less for Peruvians). You can rent towels and bathing costumes for US$0.65 at several places on the road to the baths. There are basic toilets and changing facilities and showers for washing before entering the baths; the price of the guardaropa (where you can leave your belongings) is included in the ticket price. Take soap and shampoo.*

LL *Machu Picchu Pueblo Hotel*, Km 110, 5 mins walk along the railway from the town. **Sleeping** For reservations: *Inkaterra*, Andalucía 174, Lima 18, T01-610 0404, F422 4701, Cusco ■ *on map* T084-245314, F244669, www.inkaterra.com Beautiful colonial-style bungalows set in a village compound surrounded by cloud forest. Lovely gardens with are many species of birds, butterflies and orchids, pool, expensive restaurant. Campsite with hot showers at good rates. It offers tours to Machu Picchu, several guided walks on the property. The buffet breakfasts for US$12 are great. It also has the *Café Amazónico* by the railway line. Recommended, but there are a lot of steps between the public areas and rooms. **L** *Hatuchay Tower*, Carretera Puente Ruinas block 4, T211200, F211202 (in Lima 447 8170, in Cusco 244272), www.hatuchaytower.com.pe Smart modern hotel below the old station, price includes American breakfast, but not tax and service, standard and luxury rooms. **AL-A** *Machu Picchu Inn*, Av Pachacútec 101, T211057, mapiinn@peruhotel.com.pe With bathroom, includes breakfast, cold, functional.

B *Gringo Bill's* (*Hostal Q'oñi Unu*), Colla Raymi 104, T/F211046, gringobills@ yahoo.com With bathroom, cheaper without, friendly, relaxed, hot water, fairly basic but very clean, laundry, money exchange, good but expensive meals served in *Villa Margarita* restaurant, breakfast from 0530, they offer a US$2 packed lunch to take up to the ruins, luggage stored, good beds. Don't stay in the rooms nearest the entrance as they flood during heavy rain.

Cusco & the Sacred Valley

C *Presidente*, at the old station, T211034 (Cusco T/F244598). Adjoining *Hostal Machu Picchu*, see below, more upmarket than its neighbour, rooms without river view cheaper, price includes breakfast and taxes.

D *La Cabaña*, Av Pachacútec M20-3, T/F211048. With bath, hot water, café, laundry service, popular with groups. **D** *Hostal Continental*, near the old train station, T211065. Very clean, good beds, hot showers. **D** *Las Orquídeas*, Urb Las Orquídeas A-8, T211171.

Aguas Calientes

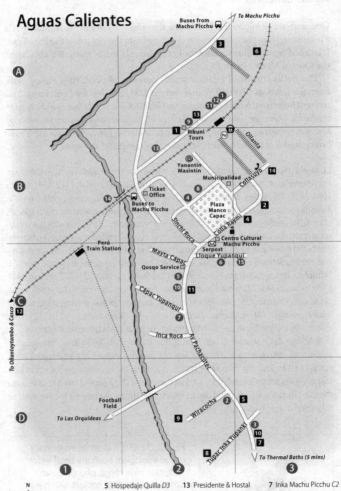

N
Not to scale

■ Sleeping
1 El Tambo *B2*
2 Gringo Bill's (Qoñi Unu Hostal) *B3*
3 Hatuchay Tower *A2*
4 Hospedaje Las Bromelias *B3*
5 Hospedaje Quilla *D3*
6 Hostal Continental *A3*
7 Hostal Pachakúteq *D3*
8 Hostal Samana Wasi *D2*
9 Hostal Wiracocha Inn *D2*
10 La Cabaña *D3*
11 Machu Picchu Inn *C2*
12 Machu Picchu Pueblo *C1*
13 Presidente & Hostal Machu Picchu *A2*
14 Rupa Wasi Hostal *B3*

● Eating
1 Aiko *A2*
2 Clave de Sol (Chez Maggy) *D2*
3 Govinda *D3*
4 Illary *B2*
5 Inca Wasi *C2*
6 Indio Feliz *C2*
7 Inka Machu Picchu *C2*
8 Inka's Pizza Pub *B2*
9 Las Qenas *A2*
10 Machu Picchu *C2*
11 Pizzería La Chosa *A2*
12 Pizzería Samana Wasi 1 *A2*
13 Pizza Samana Wasi 2 *B2*
14 Toto's House *B1*
15 Waisicha Pub *C3*

From Av Pachacútec, cross the bridge over the river to the football pitch, find a small dirt path on the right. Rooms with bath, hot water, clean, quiet, pleasant. **D** *Hostal Machu Picchu*, at the old station, T211212. Clean, functional, quiet, friendly, especially Wilber, the owner's son, with travel information, hot water, nice balcony over the Urubamba, grocery store, price includes breakfast and taxes. Recommended. **D** *Hostal Pachakúteq*, up the hill beyond *Hostal La Cabaña*, T211061. With bathroom, hot water 24 hrs, good breakfast, quiet, family-run. Recommended. **D-E** *Rupa Wasi Hostal*, Collasuyo 110, T211101, rupawasi@hotmail.com Rooms and dormitories, hot water, traditional breakfasts, packed lunches and other meals, flexible, helpful, rooftop terrace, laundry, internet. Can arrange tours with a shaman. Recommended. **D** *Hospedaje Quilla*, Av Pachacútec between Wiracocha and Tupac Inka Yupanki. Price includes breakfast, bath, hot water, rents bathing gear for the hot springs. **D** *Hostal Wiracocha Inn*, C Wiracocha, T211088. With bath, hot water, breakfast and soft drinks available, small garden, friendly and helpful, popular with groups.

F *Hospedaje Las Bromelias*, Colla Raymi, just off the plaza before *Gringo Bill's*. With bath, hot water, cheaper without bath. **E** per person *El Tambo*, at the old station, T211054. 4 rooms, with bath and hot water, breakfast included, also bar, *cambio*, restaurant serving pizzas and pasta. **E** *Hostal Samana Wasi*, C Tupac Inka Yupanki, T211170, quillavane@hotmail.com With bath, hot water 24 hrs, **F** without bath, friendly, pleasant place.

Camping The only official campsite is in a field by the river, just below Puente Ruinas station. Do not leave your tent and belongings unattended.

● on map

Eating

Pizza seems to be the most common dish in town, but many of the pizzerías serve other types of food as well. The old station and Av Pachúcet are lined with eating places

At the station (where staff will try to entice you into their restaurant), are, among others: *Aiko*, recommended; *La Chosa Pizzería*, pleasant atmosphere, good value; *Las Quenas*, café and baggage store (US$0.30 per locker); and two branches of *Pizza Samana Wasi*. *Toto's House*, Av Imperio de los Incas. Good value and quality *menú*. *Café Inkaterra*, next to train station. Biffet restaurant with views of river. *Clave de Sol*, Av Pachacútec 156. Same owner as *Chez Maggy* in Cusco, Italian food for under US$4, changes money, has vegetarian menu. 1200-1500, 1800-whenever. Also on this street: *Govinda*, by corner with Tupac Inka Yupanki. Vegetarian, cheap set lunch. Recommended. *Machu Picchu*. Good, friendly. *Inca Wasi*, very good; *Inka Machu Picchu*, No 122, including vegetarian. *Inka's Pizza Pub*, on the plaza. Good pizzas, changes money, accepts traveller's cheques. Next door is *Illary*, popular. On C Lloque Yupanqui are *Waisicha Pub*, good music and atmosphere, and *Indio Feliz*, T/F211090, great French cuisine, excellent value and service, set 3-course meal for US$10, good pisco sours. Highly recommended.

Cusco & the Sacred Valley

Directory   **Banks** **Exchange**: there are no banks in Aguas Calientes. Those businesses that change money will not do so at rates as favourable as you will find in Cusco. **Communications**   Internet: At *Yanantin Masintin* (US$3 per hr), which is part of the *Rikuni* group, as is *Tea House*, which is opposite, Av Imperio de los Incas 119. Both serve coffees, teas, snacks etc. The town has electricity 24 hrs a day. Post: *Serpost* (Post Office): just off the plaza, between the Centro Cultural Machu Picchu and *Galería de Arte Tunupa*. **Telephone**: office on Calle Collasuyo and plenty of phone booths around town. *Qosqo Service*, at the corner of Av Pachacútec and Mayta Cápac, has postal service, *cambio* and guiding service. The travel agency, *Rikuni Tours*, is at the old station, Av Imperio de los Incas 123, T/F211036, rikuni@chaski.unsaac.edu.pe Nydia is very helpful. They change money, have a postal service and sell postcards, maps and books (expensive).

Quillabamba

Phone code: 084
Colour map 5,
grid A5
Population: 10,000

La Cuidad de Eterno Verano (the city of eternal summer), as it is known, was once a prosperous town from the sale of coffee. It has now become the overnighting spot for those travelling to Vilcabamba and Espíritu Pampa. This delightful market town now survives on the export of fruit, coffee, honey and other produce to Cusco. The tourist season is June-July, when Peruvian holidaymakers descend on the place. Although Quillabamba has plenty to offer, it is normally overlooked because of the incredibly bumpy, but beautiful ride to get there. (The railway from Machu Picchu used to continue for 79 km, through Chaullay, to Quillabamba in the Urubamba Valley, but there are no passenger services on this line any more as much of the track was severely damaged in 1998.) There is a Dominican mission here.

Getting there   As no trains run beyond Aguas Calientes, the only route is by road from Cusco via Ollantaytambo. It passes through Peña, a place of great beauty. Once out of Peña, the road climbs on endless zig-zags and breathtaking views to reach the **Abra Málaga** pass. Here are some patches of polylepis woodland at 4,00-4,300 m which contain a number of endangered birds. These include the White-browed Tit-Spinetail, the Ash-breast Tit-Tyrant and the Royal Cinclodes. Since it is so accessible, this has become a prime site for birdwatchers and conservationists are working hard to protect the area. (See the article on *Kolibri*'s website: www.netaccessperu.net/kolibri/Abra%20Malaga.htm) At Chaullay, the road meets the old railway to Quillabamba, Machu Picchu and Cusco and continues up the east bank of the river. At time of writing, owing to the roadworks at Abra Málaga, all buses leave between 1800 and 2000 from the Terminal Terrestre in Cusco. Journey time is approximately 8 hours, although expect 14 hours in the rainy season due to landslides. Three bus companies on this route are: *Valle de los Incas*, T244787, *Ben Hur*, T229193, and *Ampay*, T245734. There are two others. Purchase your ticket in advance. The bus station in Quillabamba is on Av 28 de Julio and buses depart for Cusco at 1900 daily, with extra services Sat and Sun at 1300.

Sights   For the weary traveller one of the biggest attractions is **Sambaray**, a recreation area with outdoor swimming pool, restaurant, volleyball and football field. It is about 1½ km from Quillabamba. As Sambaray is situated on the Río Alto Urubamba, you may also swim in the river or if you're feeling brave you can tube down it. Ask locals for the best place to start as the river can be quite rapid. ■ *US$0.20. Transport by combi US$0.20, taxi US$0.60.*

Siete Tinajas (seven small baths) is a beautiful waterfall some 45 minutes in combi from town. Take the bus from *Paradero El Grifo* (US$1). It is well worth it for the photos, although be careful when climbing to the top, as it can be very slippery. Another waterfall is **Mandor**, also around an hour from Quillabamba. You may go by taxi or walk, although it is advisable to take a guide. Ask at your hotel as someone is always willing to take you.

D *Quillabamba*, Prolongación y M Grau 590, just behind the main market, T281369, F281015, hostalquillabamba@latinmail.com One of the largest hotels in Quillabamba, all rooms have private bath, TV, telephone. Outdoor swimming pool, restaurant, parking and a small zoo. They also have a cockfighting school for the championship, which is held every year around 25 Jul. **D** *Hotel Alto Urubamba*, Jr 2 de Mayo 333, T281131, F281570, alturub@ec-red.com **E** with shared bath. Very clean, friendly, knowledgeable staff, local restaurant attached, one block from the Plaza de Armas. Highly recommended. **D** *Lira*, Jr La Convención 200, T281324. All rooms with bath, a bit noisy and not very clean. **E** *Hostal Don Carlos*, Jr Libertad 556, T281371. Clean, simple, private shower, generally hot water, has bar and restaurant. There is other accommodation, **G**, around the main market.

Sleeping

Pub Don Sebas, Jr Espinar 235 on Plaza de Armas. Good, great sandwiches. *El Gordito*, on Espinar. Good place for chicken, US$3. *Pizzería* Venecia, Jr Libertad 461, on the Plaza de Armas, T281582. Delivery available, good pizza. There are many *pollerías* on Av Francisco Bolognesi and many *heladerías* (much needed in the heat) mainly on the northwest corner of the Plaza de Armas.

Eating

Banks *BCP*, Jr Libertad, is good for TCs. *Banco Continental*, Av F Bolognesi, accepts Visa and Cirrus.

Directory

Pongo de Mainique

Cascading waterfalls on arms of the Río Urubamba have carved their way through the last of the most eastern edge of the Andes, pouring into the jungle. The Machiguenga Indians who live further down the river believe this to be the portal to the afterlife. For others, travellers mostly, this area is one of the most beautiful places on the planet and well worth a visit for the adventurous. The Machiguengas, however, are very private people and do not take kindly to strangers, so if you wish to visit them on their reserve take someone who has contact with them.

Colour map 5, grid A5

From Quillabamba take a bus to **Ivochote** from behind the main market. Buses take around 14 hrs and cost US$4. In Ivochote there is basic local accommodation. This is where you need to secure passage on a canoe (*lancha*) down through the Pongo. This costs US$30-40 per person, although you can hire the whole canoe if there is a group of you. If you are feeling very adventurous, it is possible to continue on to Pucallpa and even Iquitos.

Getting there

There are 2 agencies in Cusco that specialize in tours to the Pongo: *Eco Trek Perú*, contact ecotrekperu@hotmail.com, and *InkaNatura Travel*, Plateros 361, mezzanine, T/F251173 (in Lima: Manuel Bañón 461, San Isidro, T440 2022/422 8114, F422 9225) www.inkanatura.com

Huancacalle

At Chaullay, the historic Choquechaca bridge, on Inca foundations, was wiped out by a landslide in 1998. Reconstruction is under way. When reopened, it will allow drivers to cross the river to get to the village of Huancacalle. A temporary bridge allows foot passengers across, but vehicles

Altitude:3,000m

The Vilcabamba mountains

Peru's rugged and largely unexplored Vilcabamba mountains lie to the north and east of the main Andean chain, situated between the canyons of the mighty Apurímac and Urubamba rivers. Extending a mountainous tongue into the Amazon Basin they rise from tropical rainforest to the freezing glaciers of Nevado Salcantay at 6,271 m, covering an area of approximately 30,000 sq km.

Vilcabamba lies in an area of immense biological diversity known as the Tropical Andes Eco-region, the meeting of Andes and Amazon, which supports the greatest range of animal and plant life on the planet. This diversity is a result of the massive variation in altitudes, climates and habitats within a relatively small area, thus forcing flora and fauna to specialize and evolve along divergent paths. Vilcabamba's isolation adds to this 'ambient wealth' – high mountains, surrounded on all sides by deep canyons means that many high altitude species have been cut off from other populations for thousands, perhaps millions of years, developing separate characteristics and eventually becoming new species, endemic to the region.

As with many other areas in South America, Vilcabamba is almost unknown to biologists. In the face of growing threats from oil and gas companies and settlement from the more densely populated mountain regions of Peru, Conservation International and the Smithsonian Institute conducted a 'rapid assessment programme' to determine the areas biological richness and undiscovered species. Carried out in two sites and packed into less than a month the programme nevertheless provided a snapshot of the riches in this cloud-wreathed wonderland. Among others, 12 previously unknown species of amphibian and reptile where recorded, along with a very large rodent, discovered by Louise Emmons, perhaps the foremost authority on South America's mammals.

In addition to this wealth of species is a wealth of human culture. In the foothills of the mountains themselves and in the river valleys surrounding live four indigenous groups, the Yora, Nanti, Kirineri and Machiguenga. Some of these people live in voluntary isolation from the 'outside world'; a few are possibly unaware of the outside world's existence. This is one of the last places on earth, in these days of cellular phones and computers, where groups of people live unmolested by our culture of capitalism and 'progress'.

Sadly, both the people and wilderness are under threat. It's an all to familiar story. US oil giants Shell, Mobile and Chevron explored the area and now US and Argentine companies are constructing of a natural gas pipeline from the small village of Camisea on the Río Urubamba, across the Vilcabamba Range and on to Lima. The pipeline will cut a swathe of destruction across the mountains and possibly open the area to colonization. Deforestation of the range's western slope began in Inca times, but recent population pressure and cultivation is accelerating the process. The east, on the other hand, has remained a wild and pristine wilderness. Will it stay this way? Conservationists and, increasingly, ecotourism interests are fighting to preserve the treasures of this region (eg the Pongo de Mainique, Vilcabamba Vieja and Espíritu Pampa, the Machiguenga Center Lodge, plus almost unlimited trekking and nature tourism prospects). Can they succeed? Only time will tell.

go 30 minutes downstream to Maranura, where a new bridge crosses the river. Then you have to backtrack down on the other side to get to Huancacalle, a two-street village 5 hours from Quillabamba and the start of many treks in the area. Nearby are the Inca ruins of **Vitcos**. Here is the palace of the last four Inca rulers from 1536 to 1572, and **Chuquipalta**, the sacred White Rock of

The last Incas of Vilcabamba

After Pizarro killed Atahualpa in 1532 the Inca empire disintegrated rapidly, and it is often thought that native resistance ended there. But in fact it continued for 40 more years, beginning with Manco, a teenage half-brother of Atahualpa.

In 1536, Manco escaped from the Spanish and returned to lead a massive army against them. He besieged Cusco and Lima simultaneously, and came close to dislodging the Spaniards from Peru. Spanish reinforcements arrived and Manco fled to Vilcabamba, a mountainous forest region west of Cusco that was remote, but still fairly close to the Inca capital, which he always dreamed of recapturing.

The Spanish chased Manco deep into Vilcabamba but he managed to elude them and continued his guerrilla war, raiding Spanish commerce on the Lima highway, and keeping alive the Inca flame. Then, in 1544, Spanish outlaws to whom he had given refuge murdered him, ending the most active period of Inca resistance.

The Inca line passed to his sons. The first, a child too young to rule named Sayri Túpac, eventually yielded to Spanish enticements and emerged from Vilcabamba, taking up residence in Yucay, near Urubamba in 1558. He died mysteriously – possibly poisoned – three years later.

His brother Titu Cusi, who was still in Vilcabamba, now took up the Inca mantle. Astute and determined, he resumed raiding and fomenting rebellion against the Spanish. But in 1570, Titu Cusi fell ill and died suddenly. A Spanish priest was accused of murdering him. Anti-Spanish resentment erupted, and the priest and a Spanish viceregal envoy were killed. The Spanish Viceroy reacted immediately, and the Spanish invaded Vilcabamba for the third and last time in 1572.

A third brother, Túpac Amaru was now in charge. He lacked his brother's experience and acuity, and his destiny was to be the sacrificial last Inca. The Spanish overran the Inca's jungle capital, and dragged him back to Cusco in chains. There, Túpac Amaru, the last Inca, was publicly executed in Cusco's main plaza.

The location of the neo-Inca capital of Vilcabamba was forgotten over the centuries, and the search for it provoked Hiram Bingham's expeditions, and his discovery of Machu Picchu. Bingham did also discover Vilcabama the Old, without realizing it, but the true location at Espíritu Pampa was only pinpointed by Gene Savoy in the 1960s, and was not confirmed irrefutably until the work of Vincent Lee in the 1980s.

the Incas (also referred to as Yurac Rumi). Once the most sacred site in South America, the White Rock is very large (8 m high by 20 m wide), with intricate and elaborately carvings. Lichens now cover its whiteness.

You can also hike up to **Vilcabamba La Nueva** from Huancacalle. It's a three-hour walk through beautiful countryside with Inca ruins dotted around. There is a missionary building run by Italians, with electricity and running water, where you may be able to spend the night.

Getting there & sleeping From Quillabamba buses (combis) depart daily from Jr San Martín, nr Plaza Grau, at 0900 and 1200, US$2.50. On Fri they go all the way to Vilcabamba. There are a few restaurants, shops and basic places to stay at Huancacalle. There is a hostal, **G** *Sixpac Manco* (opened by Vincent R Lee). Villagers will let you stay on their floor, or you can camp near the river below the cemetery. Allow plenty of time for hiking to, and visiting the ruins. It takes 1 hr to walk from Huancacalle to Vitcos, 45 mins Vitcos-Chuquipalta, and 45 mins Chuquipalta-Huancacalle. Horses can be hired if you wish.

Espíritu Pampa

In 1536, three years after the fall of the Inca empire to the Spanish *conquistadores*, Manco Inca lead a rebellion against the conquerors. Retiring from Cusco when Spanish reinforcements arrived, Manco and his followers fell back to the remote triangle of Vilcabamba, where they maintained the Inca traditions, religion and government outside the reach of the Spanish authorities. Centuries after the eventual Spanish crushing of Inca resistance, it was difficult to locate and identify Manco's capital of Vilcabamba. See the box, The last Incas of Vilcabamba, page 223.

Travellers with plenty time can **hike** from Huancacalle to Espíritu Pampa, the remote site of the **Vilcabamba Vieja** ruins, a vast pre-Inca ruin with a neo-Inca overlay set in deep jungle at 1,000 m. The jungle in the area of Vilcabamba Vieja is full of wildlife and worth the trip on its own. At Espíritu Pampa is a sister stone of the Yurac Rumi.

Getting there & information

From Huancacalle a trip will take 5-8 days on foot. It is advisable to take local guides and mules. Insect repellent is essential, there are millions of mosquitoes. Also take pain-killers and other basic medicines; these will be much appreciated by the local people should you need to take advantage of their hospitality.

Maps Available from the South American Explorers in Cusco and Lima. Before leaving don't forget to register with the tourist representative in Huancacalle. Ask around in Huancacalle for guides. The *Sixpac Manco* hostal has various guides and other people in the village will offer their services. Distances are considerable – it is at least 100 km from Chaullay to Espíritu Pampa – and the going is difficult.

Reading If you intend to attempt this trip, you should first read *Sixpac Manco: travels among the Incas*, by Vincent R Lee, which is available in Cusco. It contains accurate maps of all the archaeological sites in this area, and describes two expeditions into the region by the author and his party in 1982 and 1984, following in the footsteps of Gene Savoy, who first identified the site in the 1960s. His book, *Antisuyo*, which describes his expeditions here and elsewhere in Peru, is also recommended reading. See also Lee's book *Forgotten Vilcabamba*. (We are grateful to Fiona Cameron, formerly manager of the South American Explorers clubhouse in Cusco, for much new information on Quillabamba, Pongo de Mainique and Vilcabamba.)

Best time to visit

The best time of year is May-Nov, possibly Dec. Outside this period it is very dangerous as the trails are very narrow and can be thick with mud and very slippery.

Vilcabamba

© Peter Frost

East from Cusco

Along or near the main road that now links Cusco with Lake Titicaca and Peru's major southern city, Arequipa, are a number of archaeological sites, some fascinating colonial churches, beautiful lakes and the Ausangate massif, where you can do some serious high-altitude trekking. Off this route is also the gateway to Peru's southeastern jungle in the Department of Madre de Dios.

A newly paved road runs southeast from Cusco to Sicuani (see page 229), and on to Puno, on the shores of Lake Titicaca. Combis run every 15-20 minutes between Cusco and Sicuani (US$1.25), and more frequently to the villages and towns in between. **Getting there**

Leaving Cusco, you will soon pass the six-storey high condor monument by the poor district of San Sebastián, then enter San Jerónimo, home to Cusco's wholesale Saturday morning food market. Porters struggle past carrying loads of up to 70 kg and there is a huge array of colourful fruit and vegetables. Get there for 0800, but take no valuables. **San Jerónimo**

Tipón ruins, between the villages of Saylla and Oropesa, are extensive and include baths, terraces, irrigation systems and a temple complex, accessible from a path leading from just above the last terrace – all in a fine setting. It is thought to have been an agricultural laboratory because a great variety of potatoes and corn were found here. The terracing and agricultural areas extend from 3,000 m to 3,800 m. ■ *From Tipón village it's a 5 km climb on a road to the ruins. To get to Tipón you can either take a combi from the Post Office in Cusco to Oropesa, then a taxi, or take a taxi all the way, US$6. There are also tours from Cusco.* **Tipón & Oropesa** *17 km from Cusco*

Oropesa church contains a fine ornately carved pulpit. The town is the national bread capital; try the delicious circular loaves.

At Huambutío, north of Huacarpay, the road divides; northwest to Pisac (see page 197) and north to Paucartambo, on the eastern slope of Andes. **Huambutío & around**

The road from Huambutío northwest to Pisac (about 20 km) is fully paved. This is an access road for the first **river-rafting** section on the **Río Urubamba**, which also connects with another rafting route from **Piñipampa**. In the rainy season, and for less-experienced rafters, the Huambutío (Piñipampa) to Pisac river section is safer to run. The rapids are class 2 to 3. The length of the rafting trip is 30-35 km with spectacular views of the Urubamba valley that are not seen in a conventional Valley tour. This part of the river offers views of the **Sanctuary of El Señor de Huanca**, an image painted on a rock around which the sanctuary (church) has been built. The rock and surroundings date back to pre-Inca times as a *huaca*, or sacred place. This another example of religious synthesis, the pre-Columbian sacred place being taken over by the Catholic church with a consequent merging of cultures. The month of pilgrimage to the Sanctuary of Huanca is September and it is visited by the faithful not only from the surrounding highlands, but also the more distant departments in southern and northern Perú, as well as Bolivia, Chile and Argentina. The main day is 14 September.

Cusco & the Sacred Valley

Paucartambo

Colour map 5, grid A6 This once remote town, 80 km east of Cusco, is on the road to Pilcopata, Atalaya and Shintuya. This is the overland route used by tour companies from Cusco into Manu National Park. Consequently, it has become a popular tourist destination. It has a famous **17th-century stone bridge**, built on the orders of King Carlos III of Spain. On 15-17 July, the festival of the *Virgen del Carmen* is a major attraction and well worth seeing. Masked dancers enact rituals and folk tales in the streets.

From Paucartambo, in the dry season, you can go 44 km to **Tres Cruces**, along the Pilcopata road, turning left after 25 km. Sr Cáceres in Paucartambo will arrange this trip for you. Tres Cruces gives a wonderful view of the sunrise in June and July: peculiar climactic conditions make it appear that three suns are rising. Tour operators in Cusco can arrange transport and lodging.

Getting there Private car hire for a round trip from Cusco on 15-17 Jul costs US$30; travel agencies in Cusco can arrange this. A minibus leaves for Paucartambo from Av Huáscar in Cusco, every other day, US$4.50, 3-4 hrs; alternate days Paucartambo-Cusco. Trucks and a private bus leave from the Coliseo, behind Hospital Segura in Cusco; 5 hrs, US$2.50.

Sleeping There are 2 basic places to stay: **G** *Quinta Rosa Marina*, near the bridge; and **G** *Albergue Municipal Carmen de la Virgen*.

To Andahuaylillas and Huaro

Piquillacta Further on from Huacarpay, on the road southeast to Puno, are (on the left) the Huari (pre-Inca) adobe wall ruins of Piquillacta, which translates rather irritatingly, as the City of Fleas, and the wall and gate of Rumicolca.

Piquillacta was an administrative centre at the southern end of the Huari empire. The whole site is surrounded by a wall, there are many enclosed compounds with buildings of over one storey and it appears that the walls were plastered and finished with a layer of lime. ■ *Daily, 0700-1730, entry by BTU tourist ticket. Buses to Urcos from Av Huáscar in Cusco will drop you at the entrance on the north side of the complex, though this is not the official entry. Walk through to the official entry and continue to Rumicolca on the other side of the highway.* The **Piquillacta Archaeological Park** also contains the Laguna de Huacarpay and the ruins that surround it: Kañarakay, Urpicancha and Rumicolca. It's good to hike or cycle and birdwatch around the lake.

The huge gateway of **Rumicolca** is on the right of the main road to Sicuani, shortly after the turn-off to Piquillacta. You can walk around it for free. This was a Huari aqueduct, built across this narrow stretch of the valley, which the Incas clad in fine stonework to create this gateway. If you look at the top you can see the original walls, four tiers high.

Andahuaylillas Next down the road, 32 km southeast from Cusco, is Andahuaylillas with a fascinating 17th-century church. This is a simple structure, but it has been referred to as the Andean Sistine Chapel because of its beautiful frescoes and internal architecture. Go in, wait for your eyes to adjust to the darkness, to see on the right of the splendid door the path to heaven, which is narrow and thorny, and on the left the way to hell, which is wide and littered with flowers. Above is the high choir, built in local wood, where there are two organs. The carved ceiling is painted, too. The main altar is gilded in 24-carat gold leaf and has symbols from both the Quechua and Christian religions. Ask for Sr

Eulogio; he is a good guide, but speaks Spanish only. Taxis go to Andahuaylillas, as does the Oropesa bus (from Av Huáscar in Cusco) via Tipón, Piquillacta and Rumicolca.

Sleeping E per person *La Casa del Sol*, on Garcilaso. Well-decorated rooms set around a courtyard, excellent value. Owned by Dr Gladys Oblitas, the hostel funds her project to provide medical services to poor campesinos. In Cusco, Procuradores 42, T227264, medintegral@hotmail.com

At the quiet village of Huaro (turn left off the main road) the **church** on the ugly main plaza is stunning inside, but likely to be locked. For the giant key, ask for Sr Pablo Ticuña at 2 de Mayo 367, a block away. He will show you around for US$0.85 (he only speaks Spanish). The walls are plastered with graphic, grim frescoes used to evangelize the illiterate. Grinning skeletons compete with dragons and devils ushering the living into the afterlife and punishing them thereafter. They are now mostly in a sad state of repair.

Huaro

Urcos to Tinqui

Beyond Huaro is Urcos, from where a spectacular road crosses the Eastern Cordillera to Puerto Maldonado in the jungle (see page 554). 47 km after passing the snow-line Hualla-Hualla pass, at 4,820 m, the super-hot thermal baths of **Marcapata**, 173 km from Urcos, provide a relaxing break (entry US$0.10). 82 km from Urcos, on the road to Puerto Maldonado, at the base of **Nevado Ausangate** (6,372 m, the highest mountain is southeastern Peru), is the town of **Ocongate**, which has two hotels on the Plaza de Armas.

Beyond Ocongate is Tinqui, the starting point for hikes around Ausangate and in the Cordillera Vilcanota. On the flanks of the Nevado Ausangate is *Q'Olloriti*, where a church has been built close to the snout of a glacier. This place has become a place of pilgrimage (see Cusco Local festivals, page 178).

Tinqui

Getting there and sleeping Buses to Tinqui leave Cusco Mon-Sat at 1000 (6-7 hours, US$3.50) from C Tomasatito Condemayta, near the Coliseo Cerrado. There is accommodation in Tinqui at **G** *Hostal Tinqui Guide*, on the right-hand side as you enter the village, friendly, meals available, the owner can arrange guides and horses. **G** *Ausangate*, very basic but warm, friendly atmosphere. Sr Crispin (or Cayetano), the owner, is knowledgeable and can arrange guides, mules, etc. He and his brothers can be contacted in Cusco on F227768. All have been recommended as reliable sources of trekking and climbing information, for arranging trips and for being very safety-conscious.

The hike around the mountain of Ausangate takes five to six days. It is spectacular, but quite hard, with three passes over 5,000 m, so you need to be acclimatized. Alternatively, a shorter and easier return trek can be made from Ausangate down the beautiful **Pitumarca Valley** to the town of the same name and the Sacred Valley. It is recommended to take a guide or *arriero*. *Arrieros* and muleteers have formed a union and as such they are much more organized than in recent years. An *arriero* charges US$7 per day, US$6 per day for each mule, but more for a saddle horse. A chief *arriero* takes along one to two assistants (US$5 per day per assistant). *Arrieros* expect foodstuffs (noodles, sugar, rice, coca leaves), plus cigarettes, alcohol, and kerosene to be provided for a well-planned expedition. *Arrieros* and mules can be hired in Tinqui. A recommended *arriero* is Enrique Mandura, who also rents out equipment. South

Hiking around Ausangate

American Explorers, who can provide information, recommend Theo. Make sure you sign a contract with full details. Buy all food supplies in Cusco. Maps are available at the IGM in Lima or South American Explorers (who can supply all the latest advice). Some tour companies in Cusco have details about the hike.

From Tinqui you can hike in 3-5 hours to **hot springs** at Upis and Pachanta.

Acomayo and Qeswachaka

Southeast from Urcos, the main road passes through **Cusipata**, with an Inca gate and wall. Here the ornate bands for the decoration of ponchos are woven. Close by is the Huari hilltop ruin of Llallanmarca.

Between Cusipata and Checacupe a road branches west up what soon becomes a dirt road. At the first fork, just before a beautiful mountain lake, Lago Pomancanchi, turn right to travel past a small community and on to **Acomayo**, a pretty village which has a chapel with mural paintings of the 14 Incas. From Acomayo, you can walk to the canyons of the upper Apurímac, vast beyond imagination, and to Inca ruins in astonishing locations. You must take camping equipment, plenty of water, or purification, and warm clothing for night-time. This area is best visited by four-wheel drive vehicle. Alternatively, hire a vehicle with a driver or go with a tour company from Cusco. You can also cycle in this area.

Getting there and sleeping Accommodation in Acomayo: *Pensión Aguirre*. To get to Acomayo, take a Cusco-Sicuani bus or truck (US$1, 1½ hours), then a truck or bus to Acomayo (3 hours, same price). Or get off at Checacupe and take a truck on to Acomayo.

If you turn left at Lago Pomancanchi, the road passes three more beautiful lakes. Stop awhile by the fourth. Set against the pale-green grass banks, serene waters reflect the red soil of the hills behind. The only sound is the occasional splash and hoot of a white-beaked Andean Coot. From February to May there are lots of birds in the area. You can camp wild here.

Altitude: 3,200 m   The road continues to Yanaoca, from where it is possible to continue to Sicuani, but a side trip to **Qeswachaka** and the **grass Inca bridge** 30km away is well worth the effort. Take a right just before you leave the village to join a road which, at times, is very rough. The way is marked with kilometre signs and you must turn right just after Km 22 where another road begins, marked with a Km 0. You will find steps down to the bridge shortly before Km 31, two bends from the bright orange road bridge. The footbridge has been rebuilt every year for the past 400 years during a **three-day festival**. This starts on June 10 and is celebrated by the three communities who use the bridge. It is built entirely of *pajabrava* grass, woven and spliced to make six sturdy cables which are strung across the 15-m chasm.

The work lasts five months, after which the fibres deteriorate and you should not attempt to cross! The bridge can also be reached from Combapata on the main Cusco-Sicuani-Puno road. Combis and colectivos leave for the 30 km trip when full from the plaza for Yanaoca (US$0.50) where there are restaurants and basic accommodation. Then hitchhike either to Quehue (no accommodation), a 1½-hour walk from Qeswachaka, or to Qeswachaka itself, which is on the road to Livitaca. Be prepared for long waits on this road. On Wednesday and Saturday there are direct buses to Livitaca from Cusco with the *Warari* and *Olivares* companies which pass the site, returning on Monday and Thursday. There is good camping downstream, but take water.

About 120 km southeast of Cusco, in a fertile tributary valley of the Vilcanota, is **Raqchi** the colonial village of **San Pedro de Cacha**, which stands within one of the most important archaeological sites in Peru, Raqchi. A few hundred metres beyond the village are the principal remains, the once great temple of Viracocha, the pan-Andean creator of all living creatures. This is one of the only remaining examples of a two-storey building of Inca architecture. It was 90 m long and 15 m high and was probably the largest roofed building ever built by the Incas. Above walls of finely-dressed masonry 3-4 m high rise the remains of another 5-6 m high wall of adobe brickwork of which only isolated sections remain. Similarly, of the 22 outer columns, which supported great sloping roofs, just one or two remain complete. There are numerous other constructions, including Acllahuasi (houses of chosen women), granaries, reservoirs, baths and fountains. The burial site includes round *chullpa* tombs of the sort found around Lake Titicaca. Much of it was damaged in search of treasure during or after the Spanish conquest. ■ *Entrance to the site is US$1.75. There is a basic shop at the site. The school next door greatly appreciates donations of books and materials.*

The *Wiracocha* festivities in San Pedro and neighbouring San Pablo start on 24 June. Dancers come to Raqchi from all over Peru and through music and dance they illustrate everything from the ploughing of fields to bull fights. This leads into the feast of San Pedro and San Pablo on 29 June.

Sicuani

Sicuani at 3,690 m is an important agricultural centre and an excellent place for items of llama and alpaca wool and skins. They are sold on the railway station and at the excellent Sunday morning **market**. Around Plaza Libertad there are several shops selling local hats.

Colour map 6, grid A1

Sicuani is 137 km from Cusco (bus, US$1.25) and 250 km from Puno. 38 km beyond the **Getting there** town is La Raya pass. The bus terminal is in the newer part of town, which is separated **& around** from the older part and the Plaza de Armas by a pedestrian walkway and bridge. It is impossible to buy unleaded petrol in this town.

E *Royal Inti*, Av Centenario 116, T352730, on the west side of the old pedestrian bridge **Sleeping** across the river is modern and clean. **E** *Obada*, Jr Tacna 104, T351214, has seen better days. Large rooms with hot showers. **E** *Samariy*, Av Centenario 138 (next to Royal Inti), T352518. Good value rooms with bathroom. **F** *Manzanal*, Av 28 de Julio 416. Basic and noisy with cold showers. **G** *Hostal Obada*, 2 de Mayo, close to hotel of the same name. Basic dormitory accommodation with separate bathrooms. **G** per person *José's Hostal*, Av Arequipa 143, T351254. Rooms with bath. There are others near the bus terminal.

Pizzería Ban Vino, 2 de Mayo 129, 2nd floor, off the east side of the plaza, is good for an **Eating** Italian meal, while *Viracocha*, on the west side of the plaza, left of the purple concrete and mirror-glass monstrosity, is also OK. On Calle Zevallos, the main drag down from the plaza, there are many *pollerías*. A good one is *El Fogón* (smart, painted pink, on the left heading down), chicken and chips US$1.70. There are also several *picanterías*, eg *Mijuna Wasi*, Jr Tacna 146 (closed Sun), with a run-down but atmospheric courtyard. Recommended. On 2 de Mayo, running northeast from the plaza, there are several cafés which are good for snacks and breakfasts. *Piano Bar*, just off the first block of 2 de Mayo, is the best nightspot in town.

Banks *Banco de la Nación* has a branch on the plaza as does *BCP*, but the one cash **Directory** machine takes only local cards.

West from Cusco

Anta
Colour map 5, grid A5

The Cusco-Machu Picchu train follows the road west from the city through the Anta Canyon for 10 km, and then, at a sharp angle, the Urubamba canyon, and descends along the river valley, flanked by high cliffs and peaks. In the town of Anta felt **trilby hats** are on sale.

Sleeping, eating and transport G *Hostal Central*, Jr Jaquijahuanca 714, basic, friendly, motorbike parking. Restaurant *Tres de Mayo* is very good, with top service, popular. Bus to Anta from Cusco is US$0.30.

Tarahuasi

Seventy-six kilometres from Cusco, beyond Anta, on the Abancay road, 2 km before Limatambo at the ruins of Tarahuasi, a few hundred metres from the road, is a very well-preserved **Inca temple platform**, with 28 tall niches, and a long stretch of fine polygonal masonry. The ruins are impressive, enhanced by the orange lichen which give the walls a beautiful honey colour.

Dr Ken Heffernan of Australia, writes: "The ruins at Tarahuasi were part of of the Inca *Tanpu* called 'Limatambo' in the 16th century, along the road to the famous Apurímac bridge (see below). The lands immediately surrounding the *tanpu* were then claimed by a son of Huayna Cápac, Cristóbal Paullu Inca and his wife, Doña Catalina Tocto Usica. The extent of Inca agricultural terraces in the valley of Limatambo and Mollepata exceeds 100 ha."

Sleeping and eating   There is accommodation in Limatambo at **G** *Hostal Rivera*, near the river, an old stone house built round a courtyard, clean, quiet, full of character. There is also a nice restaurant hidden from the road by trees.

Apurímac Canyon & Curahuasi

One hundred kilometres from Cusco along the Abancay road is the exciting descent into the **Apurímac Canyon**, near the former **Inca suspension bridge** that inspired Thornton Wilder's *The Bridge of San Luis Rey* (see Books, page 611). The bridge itself was made of rope and was where the royal Inca road crossed the river. When the *conquistadores* reached this point on their first march to Cusco, they found the bridge destroyed. But luck was on their side since, it being the dry season, the normally fierce Apurímac was low enough for the men and horses to ford. In colonial times the bridge was rebuilt several times, but it no longer exists.

Also along the road to Abancay from Cusco, near Curahuasi (126 km from Cusco), famous for its anise herb, is the stone of **Saihuite**, carved with animals, houses, etc, which appears to be a relief map of an Indian village. Unfortunately, 'treasure hunters' have defaced the stone. There are other interesting carvings in the area around the Saihuite stone. ■ *US$1.45*.

Sleeping and eating   In Curahuasi is **G** *Hostal San Cristóbal*, clean, nice decor, pleasant courtyard, shared bath with cold shower. Camping is possible on the football pitch, but ask the police for permission. The best restaurant in town is *La Amistad*, popular, with good food and moderate prices, but poor service.

Choquequirao

Choquequirao is another 'lost city of the Incas', built on a ridge spur almost 1,800 m above the Apurímac. Its Inca name is unknown, but research has shown that it was built during the reign of Inca Pachacútec. Although only 30% has been uncovered, it is reckoned to be a larger site than Machu Picchu, but with fewer buildings. The stonework is different from the classic Inca construction and masonry, simply because the preferred granite and andesite is not found in this region. Peter Frost in *Exploring Cusco* describes it thus: "Its utterly spectacular location...reminds one of Machu Picchu itself. The buildings around its central plaza represent extremely fine ceremonial and high-status residential architecture. There is a chain of ritual baths, an enormous, curving bank of fine terraces, numerous intriguing outlier groups of buildings – a large group of buildings whose existence was hitherto unsuspected was discovered buried in forest on a ridge spur below the main site during the 1990s – and a vast area of irrigated terracing on a nearby mountain slope, evidently designed to feed the local population."

A number of high-profile explorers and archaeologists, including Hiram Bingham, researched the site, but its importance has only recently been recognized. Cusco tour companies are now offering this adventure and the tourist authorities are planning to make Choquequirao more easily accessible so that it will become eventually a mainstream tourist attraction.

There are three ways in to Choquequirao. None is a gentle stroll. The shortest way is from **Cachora**, a village on the south side of the Apurímac, reached by a side road from the Cusco-Abancay highway, shortly after Saihuite. It is four hours by bus from Cusco to the turn-off, then a three-hour descent from the road to Cachora (from 3,695 m to 2,875 m). Buses run from Abancay to Cachora, but there is none arriving after 1100. **Accommodation** (eg *Hospedaje Judith Catherine*, T084-320202, **G** per bed), guides (Celestino Peña is the official guide) and mules are available in Cachora. From the village you need a day to descend to the Río Apurímac on a newly made trail. You camp at a beach called Rosalina in the canyon by the suspension bridge across the river (take insect repellent). It then takes seven hours to climb up to Choquequirao, where you camp for two nights, allowing a full day at the site. You then return the way you came in one or two days. This route is increasingly being used by tour groups.

Three ways to Choquequirao: from Cachora (shortest), from Huancacalle or from San Teresa (both minimum 8 days)

The second and third routes take a minimum of eight days and require thorough preparation. You can start at **Huancacalle** (see page 221) and cross the watershed of the Cordillera Vilcabamba between the Urubamba and Apurímac rivers. The pass of Choquetacarpo is 4,600 m high. You reach Choquequirao on the seventh day. Alternatively start the hike at **Santa Teresa**, between Machu Picchu and Chaullay and pick up the second route at the village of Yanama, one of the most remote in the area. Both routes pass the mines of La Victoria and both involve an incredible number of strenuous ascents and descents. In each case you end the trail at Cachora (you could start from here if you wish). You should be acclimatised for altitudes ranging from 2,400 m to between 4,600 and 5,000 m and be prepared for extremes of temperature. During the day in full sun, temperatures can exceed 25ºC. At night, the temperature can fall well below freezing. It is only possible to do these treks safely in the dry season, as during the rainy season tracks turn to slippery, potentially dangerous mud. The paths in some parts are nothing more than mule tracks, very narrow, overgrown and perched on the side of mountains. The views of snow peaks and deep canyons are fabulous. You can see condors and meet very friendly people.

To much fanfare, the discovery of an Inca site near Choquequirao briefly fuelled stories of a new 'lost city'. **Corihuayrachina**, on Cerro Victoria (hence the nickname, 'Victoria's Secret') lies near an Inca road from Choquequirao to the interior of Vilcabamba, about 1½ days' hard walk from either Choqequirao or Santa Teresa. Controversy surrounded the announcement

New discoveries

of the discovery (the 2001 expedition was led by Gary Ziegler, Peter Frost and Alfredo Valencia, with backing from the National Geographic Society), but it appears that the site was a support community for nearby mining operations, with a fluctuating population and no monumental structures.

Gary Ziegler also led the expedition, with Hugh Thomson (see *The White Rock* in Books, page 611), which uncovered another Inca site in the Vilcabamba mountains, **Cota Coca**. About 30 stone buildings surround a central plaza at a city in an isolated valley by the Río Yanama. Erosion of the canyon has made the site unapproachable along the river bank, so the team was forced to descend from the mountain above. It is likely, though, that when the city was occupied a road linked Cota Coca with Choquequirao.

Lake Titicaca

Introducing Lake Titicaca

Straddling Peru's southern border with landlocked Bolivia are the deep, sapphire-blue waters of mystical Lake Titicaca, everyone's favourite school geography statistic. This gigantic inland sea covers up to 8,500 square km and is the highest navigable lake in the world, at 3,856 m above sea level. Its shores and islands are home to the Aymara and Quechua, who are among Peru's oldest peoples, predating the Incas by a thousand years. Here you can wander through old traditional villages

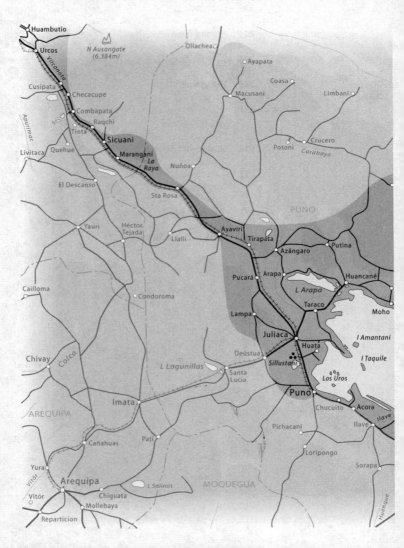

where Spanish is a second language and where ancient myths and beliefs still hold true.

The main town on the lake is Puno, where chilled travellers gather to stock up on warm woollies to keep the cold at bay. The high-altitude town is the departure point for the islands of Taquile and Amanataní, as well as the floating reed islands of Los Uros. But while the latter may not be to everyone's taste, having acquired a reputation for tourism overkill, a trip to Taquile and Amanataní gains a real insight into traditional Andean life, especially during one of the their festivals. Taquile is also a good place to find those essential souvenirs.

Apart from the obvious attraction of the lake's islands Puno is also well-placed to visit the remarkable funeral towers of Sillustani. Even if you're feeling a bit ruined-out by this stage in your Peruvian odyssey, Sillustani is well worth the effort. There's also the beautiful train ride from Puno to Cusco, and the opportunity to reach the parts of Peru that other travellers rarely reach, by exploring the remote eastern shore of the lake, an area that is only just beginning to welcome curious visitors.

N

0 km 20
0 miles 20

S Juán del Oro

Sandia

Yanahuaya

Ananea

BOLIVIA

Cojata

Rosapata

Tilali

I Soto

Lake Titicaca

Juli

Pomata

Yunguyo

Lago de Huiñaimarca

Zepita

Desaguadero

★ Things to do in Lake Titicaca

- Watch the **sun set**. The lake scenery is magnificent, particularly on the north shore, with its cliffs and bays. The quality of the light and the brilliance of the sunsets, in this age of so many types of pollution, are out of this world.
- Tourism has had an adverse effect on some of the islands in the lake, so visit some of the lesser-known attractions such as **Llachón** and **Suasi**, page 250 .
- Wonder at the unique architectural quality of the funerary towers at **Sillustani**, emphasized all the more by the barrenness of the surroundings, page 244.
- Visit the beautiful churches in the towns of **Juli** and **Pomata**, page 251.
- Get a blast of Victorian determination at **The Yavari**, moored near one of Puno's upmarket hotels, and a reminder of how shipping once was on Titicaca, page 237.
- Immerse yourself in the extensive folklore of the region, which expresses itself in textiles, ceramics, music and dance. Of the umpteen festivals, the **Fiesta de la Virgen de la Candelaria** in Puno is a must, page 242.

Phone code:
054
Colour map 6, grid B2
Population: 100,170
Altitude: 3,855 m

On the northwest shore of Lake Titicaca, Puno is a major folklore centre and a great place to buy handicrafts, particularly those amazingly tactile alpaca jumpers, hats and gloves. It also boasts a rich tradition of music and dance and is a good place to enjoy a number of Andean festivals, some wild, some solemn. Puno is capital of its Department and while it isn't the most attractive of cities, it has a certain vitality, helped by the fact there is a large student population.

Ins and outs

Getting there The railway station for trains from Cusco is quite central and within walking distance of the centre, but if you've got heavy bags, it's a good idea to hire a 3-wheel cycle cart, trici-taxi, which costs about US$0.20 per km. The new bus station and the depots for local buses are further away, southeast of the centre, but trici-taxis and conventional taxis serve this area.

Getting around The centre of town is easy to walk around, but as said above, a trici-taxi can make life a lot easier, even if this is not your first stop at high altitude. Colectivos (buses) in town charge US$0.15.

Climate Being so high up, Puno gets bitterly cold at night, especially in Jun-Aug, when the temperature at night can plummet to -25°C. Days are bright and the midday sun is hot, but you can never be quite sure what weather is going to come off the lake. The first two weeks in Feb, when the Fiesta de la Candelaria takes place, and 4-5 Nov, the pageant of the emergence of the founding Incas, are good times to visit, but crowded, too.

Tourist *i perú*, Lima y Deústua, T365088, near Plaza de Armas, open Mon-Fri 0830-1930. They
information are friendly and helpful with general information, they sell a city guide and map for US$1.20. **Indecopi**, the tourist protection bureau, has an office at Lima y Fermín Arbulú, p 2, T/F366138, sobregon@indecopi.gob.pe www.punored.com is a portal for the Puno area. www.punonet.com has some information, with links to a number of establishments. Visit also www.titicacaalmundo.com, which has good information on Puno, sponsored by several local businesses (they also distribute a free CD-Rom).

Sights

Puno sits on a bay at the northwest end of the lake. The Bahía de Puno is only

A load of bulls

The village of Pucará, north of Juliaca, is famous for its distinctive pottery, a detailed style dubbed grotesque because the figures' features are wildly exaggerated. The figures are usually left unpainted and unglazed, and the earth colour and rough surface play a part in the overall effect. Among the figures produced, the best known is the Pucará bull.

The llama was a votive symbol for the Incas, often carved out of stone and used for burning incense and other sacred purposes, until the bull, introduced to the Americas by the invading Spanish, took its place as a symbol of strength and virility. In some fiestas in the surrounding area, bulls are cut on the neck and their blood offered to Pachamama, the mother earth. Flowers are then thrown at the animal and coca leaves placed on its wounds to cure the pain.

Coca leaves are even painted on the ceramic versions of the popular Pucará bull, which gained fame with the introduction of the Puno-Cusco railway.

---

3 m deep and a channel is dredged to the exit into the open water of Titicaca. The port and lakeside quarters are several blocks from the centre, whose focus is the Plaza de Armas. The impressive baroque exterior of the **Cathedral**, completed in 1657, belies an austere interior. Just across the street from the Cathedral is the famous **Balcony of the Conde de Lemos**, on the corner of Deústua and Conde de Lemos, where Peru's Viceroy stayed. Also here is the **Museo Municipal Dreyer**, which combines municipal collections with the private collection of pre-Columbian artefacts bequeathed to the city by their owner, Sr Carlos Dreyer. ■ *Mon-Fri 0730-1330. US$1. Conde de Lemos 289.*

A short walk up Independencia leads to the **Arco Deústua**, a monument honouring those killed in the battles of Junín and Ayacucho. Nearby, is a mirador giving fine views over the town, the port and the lake beyond. The walk from Jr Cornejo following the Stations of the Cross up a nearby hill, with fine views of Lake Titicaca, has been recommended, but be careful and don't go alone. The same applies to any of the hills around Puno: Huajsapata is best known for music and folklore gatherings; Azoguine and Cancharani are higher, with good views and sacred associations. To get to Azoguine you have to go through Barrio Las Cruces, which is very dangerous.

The historic ship, **Yavari**, which is the oldest ship on Lake Titicaca, used to be berthed in the port of Puno while it was being restored and turned into a Museum. In 2002 it was moved to a berth near the entrance to the *Sonesta Posada del Inca Hotel* (see below). The iron-hulled ship, now painted in her original livery of black, white and red, was built in England in 1862 and, together with her twin, the *Yapura* (now the Peruvian Navy's Hospital ship and called the *BAP Puno*), was shipped in kit form to Arica. From Arica, the two ships went by rail to Tacna from where the 2,766 pieces were carried by mule to Lake Titicaca. The journey took six years. The *Yavari* was eventually launched on Christmas Day 1870 and on 14 June 1871 sailed on her maiden voyage. The *Yapura* followed in 1873. For those interested in steam engines, the Bolinder four-cyclinder hot bulb semi-diesel engine on view today replaced the original dried llama dung steam engine in 1913. From after the War of the Pacific until the nationalization of the Railways and Lake Fleet in 1975, the *Yavari* was operated as a passenger/cargo vessel by the London-based Peruvian Corporation. The ship was bought in 1987 and is being restored by an Anglo-Peruvian Association. Visitors are very welcome on board the *Yavari* and will be shown over the ship and its exhibition of archival documentation and memorabilia on the Lake Fleet by the Captain, Carlos Saavedra, or a volunteer. ■ *0800-1700, then illuminated till 2300 for 'Happy Hour' managed by the hotel staff. Entrance is free in the daytime, but donations are most welcome to help with maintenance costs. To get there you can go by taxi or bus, but the most charming way is by boat from the port, about US$2 return, including wait.* **Project addresses**: *61 Mexfield Rd, London, SW15 2RG, England, T44-20 8874 0583, F20 8871 0723, yavari.larken@virgin.net In Lima: Giselle Guldentops, T0051-1-998 5071, yavari.gulden@dwp.net In Puno: Asociación Yavari, c/o Capitán Carlos Saavedra, T0051-54-369329, M054-622215, yavaricondor@terra.com.pe For general information, volunteering, donations, etc, visit www.yavari.org*

In the harbour, moored at the jetty near which boats to the islands collect, is Hull (UK)-built **MS Ollanta**, which sailed the lake from 1926 to the 1970s. *PerúRail* has restored the vessel with a view eventually to starting cruises.

Puno

Essentials

Puno sometimes suffers from power and water shortages. Check if breakfast is included in the price. Note also that some hotels are full of dubious street tour sellers. Others are linked to tour operators which may or may not belong to them, so are not above pressurized tour selling (see Tour operators, page 242).

Sleeping
■ *on map*
Price codes:
see inside front cover

These 3 hotels are outside town: **L** *Libertador Isla Esteves*, on an island linked by a causeway 5 km northeast of Puno (taxi US$3, or red colectivo No 16, or white Nos 24 and 33), T367780, F367879, www.libertador.com.pe Built on a Tiahuanaco-period site, the hotel is spacious with good views. Bar, good restaurant, disco, good service, electricity and hot water all day, parking. **L** *Sonesta Posada del Inka*, Av Sesquicentenario 610, Huaje, 5 km from Puno on the lakeshore (take same transport as for *Isla Esteves*), T364111, www.sonesta.com/peru_puno/ 62 rooms with heating, in similar vein to other hotels in this group but with local touches, such as the textile decorations and the Andean menu in the *Inkafé* restaurant. Has facilities for the disabled, good views, folklore shows.

AL *Eco Inn*, Av Chulluni 195, Huaje (same transport as the above), T365525, F365526, www.ecoinnpuno.com Price includes taxes and buffet breakfast. Comfortable, brightly-decorated rooms with bath, safe, luggage store, internet,parking, nice view of the lake from the front. Has alpacas in the grounds.

AL *Plaza Mayor*, Deústua 342, T366089, reservas@plazamayorhostal.com Price includes buffet breakfast. New, comfortable, well-appointed and decorated, the nearest hotel to the Plaza (and the smartest). The aim is to extend it and become 5-star; prices will rise. Good big beds, hot water, TV, laundry, safe. Recommended. **A** *Colón Inn*, Tacna 290, T351432, www.titicaca-peru.com Price includes tax and buffet breakfast. Colonial style, good rooms with hot shower, good service, safe, internet for guests, restaurant *Sol Naciente* and pizzería *Europa*, the Belgian manager Christian Nonis is well known, especially for his work on behalf of the people on Taquile island. Recommended. **A** *Hostal Hacienda*, Jr Deústua 297, T/F356109, hacienda@latinmail.com Price includes breakfast. Refurbished colonial house, comfortable rooms with bath and hot water, TV, café. Recommended. **A** *Joya del Titicaca*, Arequipa 522, T/F351823, joyadeltiticaca_hotel@hot mail.com Price includes breakfast. Rooms are bright, with bath, firm beds, TV, hot water, laundry, safe. Café on 5th floor, has lake view. **A** *Sillustani*, Jr Lambayeque 195, T351881, sillustani@punonet.com Price includes breakfast and taxes. Hot water, cable TV, safety deposit, heaters, internet, very good.

Puno centre

Lake Titicaca

To Los Uros, Taquile & Amantaní

Lake Titicaca

errestre (Bus ocks, turn left **5**

6

B *Balsa Inn*, Cajamarca 555, T363144, www.balsainn.punored.com With breakfast (no other meals except for groups by arrangement). See the Nativity collection on display; comfortable lobby. Rooms are comfy, too, with big bathrooms, hot water, TV, safe, heating. Very helpful. **B** *Hostal Pukara*, Jr Libertad 328, T/F368448, pukara@terra.com.pe Includes good American breakfast. Popular, with bath, hot water and heating. English spoken, central, quiet, free coca tea in evening. Under same ownership is **B** *Tikarani*, Independencia 143, T365501, also includes breakfast. Similar facilities. Both are recommended. **B-C** *Hostal Italia*, Teodoro Valcarcel 122, T352521, hitalia@peru-perured.net 2 blocks from the station. With continental breakfast, cheaper in low season. Good, safe, hot water, good food, small rooms, staff helpful. **B-C** *El Buho*, Lambayeque 142, T/F354214, hotel_elbuho@yahoo.com Breakfast included. Hot water, nicely decorated rooms with heaters, TV, restaurant, safe, special discount to Footprint Handbook owners, travel agency for excursions and flight reconfirmations. Recommended.

C *Posada Don Giorgio*, Tarapacá 238, T363648, dongiorgio@titicacalake.com New, breakfast included. Large, comfortable, pleasantly decorated rooms with bath, hot water, TV. **C** *Hostal Imperial*, Teodoro Valcarcel 145, T352386. **D-E** (low season), breakfast extra, US$1.85. With bath, hot water, helpful, stores luggage, comfortable, safe. **C-D** *Hostal Rubi 'Los Portales'*, Jr Cajamarca 152-154, T/F353384, hostalrubi@punonet.com Breakfast US$2 extra, hot water, safe, TV, good, tours arranged.

D *Internacional*, Libertad 161, T352109, h_internacional@latinmail.com **E** without shower, hot water, TV, safe. Restaurant has a varied menu. **D** *Hostal Monterrey*, Lima 441, T351691, www.hostalmonterrey.com **E** without bath, better rooms with good showers, hot water, breakfast extra, restaurant, laundry, secure for luggage, motorcycle parking US$0.50. **D** *Hostal Tumi*, Cajamarca 237, T353270, with *Tumi 2* next door. Both hotels are secure, with warm water, breakfast available, some rooms are a bit dark and gloomy but most are big and comfortable, tours sold. **D** *Vylena*, Jr Ayacucho 505, T/F351292, hostalvylena@hotmail.com Breakfast extra, with bath and hot water, quiet, safe, cheaper in low season. **D-E** *Hostal Arequipa*, Arequipa 153, T352071. With bath, hot water, will change TCs at good rates, stores luggage, secure, arranges tours to the islands, OK. **D-E** *Manco Cápac Inn*, Av Tacna 227, T352985, mancocapacinn@punonet.com With bath and hot water, luggage store, safe, average breakfast extra, as are heating and cable TV. **D-E** *Hostal Nesther*, Deústua 268, T351631. Also has triples, with bath, hot water, clean. Recommended. **D-E** *Hostal Q'oñiwasi*, Av La Torre 135, opposite the rail station, T365784, qoniwasi@mundomail.net **E** without bath and in low season. Heating is extra, but hot water available all day, laundry facilities and service, luggage store, breakfast extra from 0600-0900, lunch on request, safe, very helpful. Recommended.

E *Hostal Europa*, Alfonso Ugarte 112, near the train station, T353023. Very popular, cheaper without bath, luggage may be stored, but don't leave your valuables in the room, hot water sometimes, garage space for motorcycles. **E** *Hostal Illampu*, Av La Torre 137-interior, T353284. With bath and warm water, breakfast and TV extra. Has a café, laundry, safe, exchanges money, arranges excursions (ask for Santiago). **E** *El Inti*, Av La Torre 137, is on the same passage, T351594. Cheaper with shared bath. Has a café/restaurant, Las Brujas del Cachiche. **E** *Los Uros*, Teodoro Valcarcel 135, T352141. Cheaper without bath. Hot water, plenty of blankets, breakfast is available (at extra cost), quiet at the back, good value. They make a small charge to leave luggage, laundry, often full, changes TCs a reasonable rate. Recommended. **E-F** *Hostal Los Pinos*, Tarapacá 182, T/F367398, hostalpinos@hotmail.com Cheaper without bath. Family run, hot showers, good breakfast, safe, luggage store, laundry facilities, helpful, cheap tours organized. Recommended. **F** *Hospedaje Don Julio*, Av Tacna 336, T363358. New, pleasant. **F** pp *Hospedaje Residencial Margarita*, Jr Tarapacá 130, T352820. Large building, family atmosphere, hot water most of the day, stores luggage, tours can be arranged.

◀◀

Pot luck

One of the most intriguing items for sale in Andean markets is Ekeko, the god of good fortune and plenty and one of the most enduring and endearing of the Aymara gods and folk legends.

He is a cheery, avuncular little chap, with a happy face to make children laugh, a pot belly, because of his predilection for food, and short legs so he can't run away.

His image, usually in plaster of Paris, is laden with sacks of grain, sweets, household tools, baskets, utensils, suitcases, confetti and streamers, rice, noodles and other essentials. Dangling from his lower lip is the ubiquitous lit cigarette. Believers say that these little statues only bring luck if they are received as gifts, and not purchased.

Lake Titicaca

Recommended. Near the station and market are several *hospedajes*, ranging from **E** *San Carlos*, Ugarte 161, T351862, with bath, hot water, TV and phone, to **F** *Santa Rosa*, Los Incas 208, T356733, cheaper without bath, with hot water, helpful, but not very clean.

Youth Hostel F-G pp *Albergue Juvenil Virgen de Copacabana*, Ilave 228, T354129 (no sign). Huge rooms, well-furnished, "awesome bathroom" with hot water, good location, quiet, helpful owners, will wash your clothes for a reasonable fee, full breakfast for US$1.30, a real bargain. The passageway leading to the hostel is very dark and robbery has occurred; take great care at night (the hostel is as helpful as it can be).

On or near Jr Lima (all up to US$5 for a main dish) *Fontana*, No 339. *Pizzería and trattoria*, good food. *Pizzería El Buho*, No 349 and at Jr Libertad 386. Excellent pizza, lively atmosphere, open 1800 onwards, pizzas US$2.35-3. *IncAbar*, No 356-A. Open for breakfast, lunch and dinner, interesting dishes in creative sauces, fish, pastas, curries, café and couch bar. *Apu Salkantay*, No 357 and in 400 block. Wide menu of meats, fish (more expensive), pastas, sandwiches, pizza, coffee, popular. *Don Piero*, No 360. Huge meals, live music, try their 'pollo coca-cola' (chicken in a sweet and sour sauce), slow service, popular, tax extra. *El Dorado*, No 371. Good for local fish, large portions. *La Casona*, No 521. Good for typical food, also Italian and pizzas. *Panq'arani*, Grau casi Lima. Closed Sat and some evenings, excellent typical dishes, breakfasts US$1.50-2, main dishes US$3.50-4. *Keros*, Lambayeque 131. Bar/restaurant with very good food, mostly Peruvian, good service, pleasant surroundings, good drinks.

Others mid-range *La Plaza*, Puno 425, Plaza de Armas. Good food, including fish. *Internacional*, Moquegua 201. Very popular, excellent trout, good pizzas, service variable. **Cheap** *Adventista*, Jr Deza 349. Good, closed after lunch. *Chifa Fon Seng*, Arequipa 552. Good food, service and value, Chinese, popular.

Vegetarian *Sabor y Vigor*, Arequipa 508. Delicious meals. *Sol Interior*, Libertad 466, and *Vida Natural*, Libertad 449 (open for breakfast, salads, fruits, yoghurts). *El Milagro*, Arequipa 336. Natural food shop.

Eating
● *on map, page 238*
Very cheap places in Jr Deústua for lunch or dinner. Many places on Lima, too many to list here, catering for the tourist market

Casa del Corregidor, Deústua 576, aptdo 2, T355694. In restored 17th century building, sandwiches, good snacks, coffee, good music, nice surroundings with patio (exhibition space, library, handicrafts and internet planned). *Café Delisse*, Moquegua 200 corner with Libertad. Open from 0600 (closed Sat), espresso coffee, good vegetarian food, excellent set lunch US$1.50, but disorganized and slow. *Cafetería Mercedes*, Jr Arequipa 351. Good *menú* US$1.50, also breads, cakes, snacks, juices and tea. *Ricos Pan*, Jr Lima 424. Café and bakery, great cakes, excellent coffees, juices and pastries, good breakfasts and other dishes, reasonable prices, great place to relax, open 0600-2300, closed Sun. Branches of their *panadería* at Av Titicaca 155 and Moquegua 330. *Panadería Una*, Lima 317 and Arequipa 144. For croissants, fresh bread and cakes.

Cafés

Bars & clubs *Dómino*, Libertad 443. "Megadisco", happy hour 2000-2130 Mon-Thu, good. *Peña Hostería*, Lima 501. Good music, also restaurant. Recommended. *Positive Vibrations*, Lima 445 y Grau. Good late night place (opens early evening) which serves food. Recommended. *Pub Ekeko's*, Jr Lima 355, p 2. Live music every night, happy hour 2000-2200.

Festivals The very colourful *Fiesta de la Virgen de la Candelaria* takes place during the first 2 weeks in **Feb**. Bands and dancers from all the local towns compete in this *Diablada*, or Devil Dance, with the climax coming on Sun. The festival is famous for its elaborate and grotesque masks, which depict characters in local legends as well as caricatures of former landowners and mine bosses. The festivities are better at night on the streets than the official functions in the stadium. Check in advance on the actual date because Candelaria may be moved if pre-Lenten carnival coincides with it. This festival is great fun and shouldn't be missed if you're in the vicinity around this time.

Other festivals include a candlelight procession through darkened streets, which takes place on **Good Friday**, with bands, dignatories and statues of Jesus. On **3 May** is *Invención de la Cruz*, an exhibition of local art. On **29 Jun** is the colourful festival of 0, with a procession at Zepita (see page 252). Another takes place on **20 Jul**. In fact, it is difficult to find a month in Puno without some sort of celebration.

Finally, remember, remember **5 Nov**, when there's an impressive *pageant* dedicated to the founding of Puno and the emergence of Manco Cápac and Mama Ocllo from the waters of Lake Titicaca. The royal couple sail from a point on the lake (it varies annually) and arrive at the port between 0900 and 1000. The procession from the lake moves up Av Titicaca to the stadium where a ceremony takes place with dancers from local towns and villages. If you buy an entrance ticket, US$0.60, you can watch from the top tier as the float carrying the Incas, followed by the local dancing groups, enters the stadium. Many of the groups continue dancing outside. This is not the best time to visit Taquile and Amantaní since many of their inhabitants are at the festival. This date coincides with the anniversary of the founding of Puno, celebrated with parades at night and a full military parade on the Sun.

Shopping The markets between Av Los Incas and Arbulu (*Ccori Wasi*) and on the railway between
Alpaca goods are the Av Libertad and Av El Puerto are two of the best places in Peru (or Bolivia) for **llama and**
best buy here **alpaca wool** articles, but bargain for a good price when buying in quantity (and you
Beware of pickpockets will!), especially in the afternoon. In the covered part of the market (bounded by Arbulu,
in the market Arequipa, Oquendo and Tacna) mostly **foodstuffs** are sold (good cheeses), but there are also model **reed boats**, attractive **carved stone amulets** and *Ekekos* (**household goods**). This central market covers a large area and on Sat it expands down to the stadium (mostly fruit and vegetables) and along Av Bolívar (potatoes and grains). You will be hassled on the street and outside restaurants to buy woollen goods, so take care.

Tour operators Agencies organize trips to the Uros floating islands and the islands of Taquile and Amantaní, as well as to Sillustani, and other places. Make sure that you settle all details before embarking on the tour. Alternatively, you can easily go down to the lake and make your own arrangements with the boatmen. **NB** Watch out for the many unofficial street tour sellers – or *jalagringos* – who offer hotels and tours at different rates, depending on how wealthy you look. Once you realize they have charged more than the going rate, they'll be gone. They are everywhere: train station, bus offices, airport and hotels. Ask to see their guide's ID card. Only use agencies with named premises and compare prices.

The following agencies have been recommended as reliable and helpful and offer good value. *Allways Travel*, Tacna 234, T/F355552, awtperu@terra.com.pe Very helpful, kind and attentive to visitors' needs. Reliable, staff speak German, French, English and Italian. They offer a unique cultural tour to the islands of Anapia and Yuspique in Lake

Wiñaymarka, beyond the straits of Tiquina, 'The Treasuer of Wiñaymarka'. *Arcobaleno*, Jr Lambayeque 175, T/F351052, arcobaleno@titicacalake.com Local tours, Western Union representative and agent for *Crillon Tours* of La Paz, Bolivia. *Edgar Adventures*, Jr Lima 328, T/F353444 (office)/354811 (home), edgaradventures@terra.com.pe Run by Edgar Apaza F and Norka Flórez L who speak English, German and French, very helpful. *Ecoturismo Aventura*, Jr Lima 458, T355785. Very helpful. *Käfer Turismo*, Arequipa 179, T354742, F352701, kafer@inkanet.com.pe For local tours. *Kolla Tour*, Jr Moquegua 679, T352961, F354762. Sell airline tickets and have their own boat for tours on the lake. *Pirámide Tours*, Jr Deza 129 (at side of *Hotel Ferrocarril*), T/F367302, www.titikakalake.com Out of the ordinary and classic tours, flexible, personalized service, modern fast launches, very helpful. *Turpuno*, Lima 208, stand 8-II, upstairs in Gallery, T352001, F351431, http://turpuno.com Very good service for local tours, transfers and ticketing, DHL and Western Union agent. Most agencies will go and buy train tickets for you, at varying rates of commission, similarly for bus tickets.

Boats on Lake Titicaca Boats to the islands leave from the terminal in the harbour; *trici-taxi* from centre, US$1.

Transport

Buses All long-distance buses, except some Cusco services and buses to La Paz (see below), leave from the new Terminal Terrestre, which is between Av Simón Bolívar and the lake, southeast of the centre. It has a tourist office, snack bars and toilets. Platform tax US$0.30.

Bus prices to Cusco and La Paz have seasonal variations

Daily buses to **Arequipa**, 6 hrs via **Juliaca**, 297 km, most buses are taking this route now, US$6. Or 11 hrs via **Desaguadero** and **Moquegua**, US$6-10, sit on left for views of the lake and altiplano (*Cruz del Sur* - office also at Lima 442, *Best Way*, *Destinos*, *Julsa* - office also at Melgar 232, T369447, *Señor de Milagros*, or *Sur Oriente*, T368133, most have a morning and evening bus – better quality buses go at night). To **Moquegua**, US$4.50, and **Tacna**, US$5.30, *San Martín*, *Latino*, Sagitario, *Roel*. To **Lima**, 1,011 km, US$18, all buses go through **Arequipa**, sometimes with a change of bus.

Small buses and colectivos for **Juliaca**, Ilave and towns on the lake shore between Puno and Desaguadero, including **Yunguyo**, leave from Av Bolívar between Jrs Carabaya and Palma. To **Juliaca**, 44 km, 45 mins, US$0.45. For **Yunguyo** and the **Bolivian border** see page 252.

To **Cusco**, 388 km, 5-6 hrs, *Imexso*, Jr Libertad 115, T363909, 0800, 1930 (good buses), *Tour Perú*, at Terminal and Tacna 282, T352991, tourperu@mixmail.com, 0830, 2000, both US$8.75 (less in low season); *Libertad*, at Terminal, T363694, 4 a day, *Cisnes*, at Terminal, T368674, 2 a day, *Pony Express* and others, US$4.40. *First Class* (Jr Puno 675, T365192, www.firstclassperu.com) and *Inka Express* (pick up at hotel, T/F365654, inkaex@yahoo.com), 0830 arriving 1800, US$25, daily, recommended. This service, while higher in price than the *turismo* train, leaves a little later and is comfortable, with a good lunch stop and visits to Pukará, La Raya, Raqchi and Andahuaylillas en route.

If you wish to travel by bus and cannot get on a direct bus, it is no problem to take separate buses to Juliaca, then to Sicuani, then to Cusco

Trains The railway runs from Puno to **Juliaca** (44 km), where it divides, to **Cusco** (381 km) and **Arequipa** (279 km; no passenger service, 2002, expected to resume in 2003). To **Cusco** on Mon, Wed, Thu and Sat at 0800, arriving in Juliaca at 0910 and in Cusco at about 1800 (try to sit on the right hand side for the views). The train stops at **La Raya**. In the high season (Jun especially), tickets sell well in advance. In the wet season services may be cancelled for short periods. Always check. **Fares** Puno-Cusco, *turismo*, US$12; *Inca* class, US$60 including meal. The ticket office is open from 0630-1030, 1600-1900 Mon-Sat, and on Sun in the afternoons only. Tickets can be bought in advance, or 1 hr before departure if there are any left. The station is well-guarded by police and sealed off to those without tickets.

Directory   **Airline offices** *Aero Continente*, Tacna y Libertad, T354870. *LanPerú*, also Tacna y Libertad. **Banks** *Banco de Crédito*, Lima y Grau. Changes TCs before 1300 without commission, cash advance on Visa and Visa ATM. *Banco Continental*, *Interbank* (Lima y Libertador, changes TCs morning and afternoon, 0.5% commission), and *BSCH* have branches in town, but only *Continental*, Lima y Libertad, has an ATM (Visa). No bank in Puno accepts Mastercard. For cash go to the *cambios*, the travel agencies and the better hotels. Best rates with money changers on Jr Lima, many on 400 block, and on Tacna near the market, eg Arbulu y Tacna. Check your Peruvian soles carefully. Exchange rates from soles to bolivianos and vice versa are sometimes better in Puno than in Yunguyo; check with other travellers. **Communications** Internet: there are offices everywhere in the centre, upstairs and down. Many raise their prices from US$0.50/hr in the morning to US$0.75 in the afternoon; many have overnights. Good ones include *CompuRed*, Jr Moquegua 189, 24 hrs; above *Fontana* restaurant, Lima 339; at *Pizzería Café Giorgio*, Lima 430; *Impacto's@net*, next to *Hostal Qoñi Wasi*, on Av La Torre (another one in the same block). **Post office**: Jr Moquegua 267. **Telephone**: *Telefónica* at Puno y Moquegua for local and international calls. Another phone office is at Lima 489. **Consulates** *Bolivia*, Jr Arequipa 120, T351251. Issues a visa on the spot, US$10, open 0830-1330 Mon-Fri. **Laundry** *Don Marcelo*, head office at Ayacucho 651, T352444, has agencies in several places in the centre and will collect and deliver laundry. US$1.45 per kg, good service. **Useful addresses** Immigration, Ayacucho 240, T352801. For renewing entry stamps, etc. The process is very slow and you must fill in 2 application forms at a bank, but there's nothing else to pay. **Ministry of Tourism**, Jr Deústua 351, T352811. Helpful with complaints. *Touring y Automóvil Club del Perú*, Arequipa 457.

Around Puno

Sillustani

Colour map 6, grid B2   A highly recommended trip is to the *chullpas* (pre-Columbian funeral towers) of Sillustani in a beautiful setting on a peninsula in **Lago Umayo**, 32 km from Puno on an excellent road.

'Most of the towers date from the period of Inca occupation in the 15th century, but they are burial towers of the Aymara-speaking Colla tribe. The engineering involved in their construction is more complex than anything the Incas built – it is defeating archaeologists' attempts to rebuild the tallest 'lizard' *chullpa*. Two are unfinished: one with a ramp still in place to raise blocks; the other with cut stones ready to go onto a very ambitious corbelled false dome. A series of stone circles to the east of the site are now thought to be the bases of domed thatch or peat living huts, rather than having any religious meaning. The quarry near the towers is also worth seeing.' (John Hemming). Other Inca remains can be seen in the shape of square buildings, a temple of the Sun and a temple of the Moon. Underground burials at the site predating the Colla have been found from the Pukara and Tiahuanaco periods.

Lago Umayo, at 3,890 m, is higher than Titicaca. On its island is a vicuña breeding programme.

There is a museum and handicraft sellers in traditional costume wait at the exit. Guides are also available here. Photographers will find the afternoon light best, though this is when the wind is at its strongest and can kick up a mini-sandstorm. It's also best not to wear contact lenses. The scenery is barren, but nonetheless impressive. On the lake before the ruins there are flamingos and ducks. Take warm clothing, water and sun protection.

The sacred lake

Lake Titicaca has played a dominant role in Andean beliefs for over two millenia. This, the highest navigable body of water in the world, is the most sacred lake in the Andes.

From the lake's profound, icy depths emerged the Inca creator deity, Viracocha. Legend has it that the sun god had his children, Manco Cápac and his sister, Mama Ocllo, spring from the its waters to found Cusco and the Inca dynasty.

The name Titicaca derives from the word 'titi', an Aymara mountain cat and the Quechua word 'caca' meaning rock. The rock refers to the Sacred Rock on the Isla del Sol (on the Bolivian side) which was worshipped by the pre-Incan people on the island. The mountain cat inhabited the shores of the lake and is said to have visited the Isla del Sol occasionally.

The link between the rock and the cat comes from the legend that the ancient indigenous people saw the eyes of a

mountain cat gleaming in the Sacred Rock and so named it Titicaca, or Rock of the Mountain Cat. It was this that gave rise to the idea of the sun having its home there.

The titi has characteristics – such as its aquatic ability and the brilliance of its eyes – that conceptually link it with a mythological flying feline called ccoa. The role of the ccoa was (and in some parts still is) important throughout the Andes. It is believed to have thrown lightning from its eyes, urinated rain (hence the expression), spit hail and roared thunder. It was generally associated with the gods that coolled the weather.

Among indigenous people today the ccoa is believed to be one of the mountain god's servants and lives in the mountains. It is closely involved in their daily life and is considered the most feared of the spirits as it uses lightning and hail.

Lake Titicaca

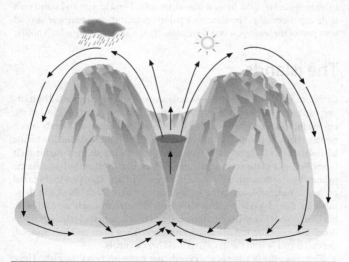

■ *US$2.25. Take an organized tour, which lasts about 3 to 4 hrs and leaves at 1430, US$5. Tours usually stop at a Colla house on the way, to see local products, alpacas and guinea pigs. Alternatively, take a Juliaca bus to the Sillustani turnoff (US$0.35); from here a 15-km paved road runs across the altiplano to the ruins. Moto-taxis and some combis run to Atuncolla (4 km away with a lovely colonial church), US$0.40, or US$0.85 to Sillustani (out of season you may have to walk the 4 km from Atuncolla). Go early to avoid tour groups at the site. A taxi from Puno costs about US$25. Camping possible outside the museum (tip the guardian).*

Lake Titicaca

▶▶ A lasting tradition

One of the most enduring textile traditions in Peru is found among the people of Taquile. Each family possesses at least four different types of costume: for work; leisure; weddings and festivals.

For weddings, which all take place on 3 May, when the planet Venus – Hatun Chaska – is visible, the bridegroom wears a red poncho provided by the best man. As a single man he wore a half red, half white cap, but to signify his married status he wears a long red hat and a wide red wedding belt, or chumpi. His bag for coca leaves, ch'uspa, is also filled.

The bride wears a wide red hat (montera) and her hands are covered with a ritual cloth (katana-oncoma). A quincha, a small white cloth symbolizing purity, is hidden in her skirt. With her red wedding blouse, or gonna, she wears a gathered skirt or pollera, made from 20 different layers of brightly coloured cloth. She also wears a belt (faja) and black cloak known as a chukoo.

The wool used for weaving is usually spun by the women, but on Taquile men spin wool, as well as knitting their conical hats (chullos). In fact, only the men on Taquile know how to knit. By the age of 10, a boy can knit his own Chullo Santa María, which is white-tipped to show single status. When he marries, or moves in with a woman, he adopts the red-tipped chullo, which is exclusive to the island. Today, much of the wool for knitting is bought ready-spun from factories in Arequipa.

Another place where *chullpas* can be seen is **Cutimbo**, 34 km south of Puno in the district of Pichacani, between Puno and Laraqueri on the old road to Moquegua. Here the funeral towers are round and square and stand on a table-top mountain. There are rock paintings on the mountain side. A road goes part of the way up. A taxi there costs US$14.50, including wait, 3 hours.

The islands

Los Uros
Colour map 6, grid B2

Of the estimated 32 floating islands, only some 15 are regularly visited by tourists, and today we can talk about two kinds of Uros people; those close to the city of Puno and easily accessible to tourism, and those on islands which remain relatively isolated. The Uros' islanders fish, hunt birds and live off the lake plants, most important of which are the totora reeds they use for their boats, houses and the very foundations of their islands. (See the box, *Like the fish and birds of the water*.) Their diet is very rich in fats. This, plus the high red corpuscle content, leads to the saying that they have black blood. On those more far-flung islands, reached via narrow channels through the reed beds, the Uros do not like to be photographed and continue to lead relatively traditional lives outside the monetary economy. They hunt and fish and still depend on trade with the mainland for other essentials.

Visitors to the floating islands encounter more women than men. These women wait every day for the tour boats to sell their handicrafts. The few men one does see might be building or repairing boats or fixing their nets. The rest are to be found out on the lake, hunting and fishing. The Uros cannot live from tourism alone, and the extra income they glean from tourists merely supplements their more traditional activities.

Many tourists find that, though the people are friendly, they are very poor and some subject visitors to a hard-sell approach for handicrafts and demands for sweets and money. The islands visited by tour boats are little more than 'floating souvenir stalls'. All the same, this form of tourism on the

Uros Islands is now well-established and, whether it has done irreparable harm or will ultimately prove beneficial, it takes place in superb surroundings. There is no drinking water on the floating islands and you need to be careful where you walk, as the surface can be unsteady underfoot.

■ *Motorboats charge US$2.85 per person to take tourists to the islands for a 2-hr excursion. Boats leave from the harbour in Puno about every 30 mins from about 0630 till 1000, or whenever there are 10 or more people to fill the boat. The earlier you go the better, to beat the crowds of tourists. Almost any agency going to the other islands in the lake will stop first at Los Uros.*

Isla Taquile, some 45 km from Puno, has numerous pre-Inca and Inca ruins, and Inca terracing. At the highest point is a ruin from which to view the sunset (the path is signed). The island is quiet and hospitable, but at the height of the season and at Sunday lunchtime it gets busy and touristy.

Taquile

The island is only about 1 km wide and 6-7 km long. On the north side of the island is the warmest part of Lake Titicaca. Ask for the (unmarked) **museum of traditional costumes** and also where you can see and photograph local weaving. It is on the plaza and is free. There is a co-operative shop on the plaza that sells exceptional woollen goods which are not cheap, but of very fine quality. They are cheaper in the market at Puno. You need to spend a night on Taquile fully to appreciate its beauty and, therefore, it may be better to travel independently and go at your own pace.

Every Sunday, the island's four *suyos* (districts) coordinate their activities with a reunion in the main plaza after Quechua mass. Numerous **festivals** take place on the island. These include: *Semana Santa*, a festival from 2 to 7 June, the *Fiesta de Santiago*, held over two weeks in mid-July, and on 1 and 2 August, the principal festival days, with many dances in between. Weddings take place each May and August. The priest comes from Puno and there is a week-long party.

The influx of tourists unfortunately prompts persistent requests by children for sweets or to have their photo taken. They whisper, quite politely, *caramelo* or *foto*. This irritates many travellers. When you arrive, boys tie friendship bracelets to your wrist, or give you *muña* (a herb used for infusions) for a sol. Above all, stay good-humoured. Buy their handicrafts instead of handing out sweets indiscriminately. Recordings of traditional music have been made and are on sale as an additional source of income for the islanders. **Gifts** of fruit, torches/flashlights (there is no electricity), moisturizer or sun block (the children suffer sore cheeks), pens, pencils or notebooks are appreciated.

You are advised to take with you some food, particularly fruit, bread and vegetables, water, plenty of small-value notes, candles and a torch/flashlight. Take precautions against sunburn and seasickness. If staying the night, take warm clothes, a sleeping bag and a hot water bottle. The same applies to Amantaní. Tourism to both islands is community-based: the less you pay, the smaller the amount that goes to the islanders. Bear this in mind when you shop around for a good value tour (there is not much variation at the lower end of the price range).

There are two main entry points. The Puerto Principal at the south end has a very steep climb up many steps; the northern entry is longer but more gradual (remember you are at 3,800 m). Visitors pay US$0.30 to land. Plentiful **accommodation** can be found in private houses and, on arrival, you are greeted by a *jefe de alojamiento*, who oversees where you are going to stay. There used to be a system of assigning accommodation to visitors by rota, but this has fallen into disuse. You can either say where you are going, if you (or

Lake Titicaca

▶▶ Like the fish and birds of the water

Titicaca's waters nourished great civilizations like the Tiahuanaco and Pukará and drew the Incas south in search of new lands and the origin of their own creation legend. But very little is known about a third people who made Titicaca their home. They were the Uros, the people of the floating islands. The ephemeral nature of their totora reed constructions and the watery world they inhabit make archaeological study impossible, and only their myths remain to teach us something of their history.

In their oral histories, the Uros say that their forefathers came from the south. We cannot know with any certainty when the Uros first arrived at Lake Titicaca, but it is thought that a great drought around 1200 AD provoked a series of massive migrations of entire peoples across the altiplano. In a scenario similar to the one predicted for many parts of the world in the 21st century, conflicts arose as competition increased for water and fertile land.

The Uros found the fertile shores of the great lake occupied by other, much larger ethnic groups. According to Uro tradition, facing inevitable defeat by their more established rivals, the Uros escaped to the reed beds. It is said that they hid in the water among the reeds. Tired and cold, they cut the totora and, by binding the reeds together, made a number of rafts on which they slept.

Legend has it that when the Inca Pachacútec arrived to conquer the lake region he asked the Uros who they were. These people who had hunted and fished in the same way for generations replied as they always had, saying: "We are the founders of the world, the first inhabitants of the planet. Our blood is black and we cannot drown. We are like the fish and birds of the water".

With the arrival of the Spanish in the 16th century, the Uros isolated themselves even more from the mainland. Persecuted by the invaders, the Uros began to meld themselves more than ever to their lake environment and their only outside contact was with other ethnic groups onshore, with whom they exchanged fish and birds for agricultural products.

Recalling their childhood, some old Uros islanders still remember when the first tourists arrived. Fearing that the Spanish had returned, their grandparents told them to run and hide.

Times have changed on some of the floating islands. There the Uros smile, pose for photographs, and then ask for a tip. After generations of intermarriage with their Aymara neighbours, what was once one of South America's most ancient tribal groups is in fact now ethnically extinct. The last Uro died in 1959, and the Uros' language died with her.

your guide) know where you want to stay, or the *jefe* can find you a room. Guides have been instrumental in this change as large groups wish to stay close together, rather than be separated. The average rate for a bed is **G**, plus US$1.50 for breakfast. Other meals cost extra. Several families now have size-able *alojamientos* (eg Pedro Huille, on the track up from the north entry, with showers under construction, proper loos, no sign). There are many small **restaurants** around the plaza and on the track to the **Puerto Principal** (eg Gerardo Hualta's *La Flor de Cantuta*, on the steps; *El Inca* on the main plaza). Meals are generally fish (the island has a trout farm), rice and chips, tortilla and *fiambre* – a local stew. Meat is rarely available and drinks often run out. Breakfast consists of pancakes and bread. Shops on the plaza sell film, post-cards, water, chocolate bars and dry goods.

■ *Boats leave Puno harbour daily at 0700-0800. The journey takes 3 hrs. Boats return at 1430, arriving in Puno at 1730. It costs US$5.80 one way. This doesn't leave enough time to appreciate the island fully in one day. Organized tours can be arranged for about US$10-16 per person, but only give you about 2*

◀◀

Mother Earth

Pachamama, or Mother Earth, occupies a very privileged place in Aymara culture because she is the generative source of life. The Aymara believe that man was created from the land, and thus he is fraternally tied to all the living beings that share the earth. According to them, the earth is our mother, and it is on the basis of this understanding that all of human society is organized, always maintaining the cosmic norms and laws.

Women's and men's relationship with nature is what the Aymara call ecology, harmony and equilibrium. The Aymara furthermore believe that private land ownership is a social sin because the land is for everyone. It is meant to be shared and not only used for the benefit of a few.

Vicenta Mamani Bernabé of the Andean Regional Superior Institute of

Theological Studies states: "Land is life because it produces all that we need to live. Water emanates from the land as if from the veins of a human body, there is also the natural wealth of minerals, and pasture grows from it to feed the animals. Therefore, for the Aymaras, the Pachamama is sacred and since we are her children, we are also sacred. No one can replace the earth, she is not meant to be exploited, or to be converted into merchandise. Our duty is to respect and care for the earth. This is what white people today are just beginning to realize, and it is called ecology. Respect for the Pachamama is respect for ourselves as she is life. Today, she is threatened with death and must be liberated for the sake of her children's liberation."

hrs on the island. Make sure you and the boatman know exactly what you are paying for. The book, Encuentro con los hijos del sol/Encounter with the Children of the Sun/Rencontre avec les fils du soleil, by Christian Nonis of the Colón Inn, has been recommended.

Another island well worth visiting is Amantaní. It is very beautiful and peaceful, and many say is less spoiled, more genuine and friendlier than Taquile. There are six villages and ruins on both of the island's peaks, Pacha Tata and Pacha Mama, from which there are excellent views. There are also temples and on the shore there is a throne carved out of stone, the Inkatiana. It is rather eroded from flooding. It's a 30 minutes' walk west of El Pueblo, the village on the north end. Turn right down the steep slope after the last house on the right.

Amantaní
Colour map 6, grid B2

On both hills, a **fiesta** is celebrated on 15 January (or thereabouts). The festivities in January have been reported as spectacular, very colourful, musical and hard-drinking. There is also a festival on the first Sunday in March with brass bands and colourful dancers. Another fiesta is the *Aniversario del Consejo* (of the local council), which might not be as boring as it sounds.

The residents make beautiful **textiles** and sell them at the **Artesanía Cooperativa**, at the east end of El Pueblo. They also make **basketwork** and **stoneware**. The people are Quechua speakers, but understand Spanish.

Ask your boat owner where you can stay; families living close to the port tend to receive tour company business and more tourists. Accommodation is in our **F** range. This includes three meals of remarkable similarity (eg *Hospedaje Jorge Wasi*, basic, but nice family, great view of lake from room). It's a great deal for visitors, but the prices have been forced down to unrealistically low levels, from which the islanders benefit hardly at all. There is one restaurant, *Samariy*. Islanders arrange dances for tour groups (independent travellers can join in), visitors dress up in local clothes and join the dances. Small shops sell water and snacks, but more expensive than Puno.

Lake Titicaca

■ *Boats from the harbour in Puno leave at 0700-0800 daily, and return at 0800, arriving in Puno around 1200. The trip costs US$5.80 one way. The journey takes 4-5 hrs - take water. A one-day trip is not possible as the boats do not always return on the same day. Several tour operators in Puno offer two to three day excursions to Amantaní, Taquile and a visit to the floating islands. These cost from US$12 per person upwards, including meals, depending on the season and size of group. This gives you one night on Amantaní and three or four hours on Taquile. There is little difference in price visiting the islands independently or on a tour, but going independently means that the islanders get all the proceeds, with no commission paid to Puno tour companies, you can stay as many nights as you wish and you will be able to explore the islands at your own pace. When not taking a tour, do not buy your boat ticket from anyone other than the boat operator at the harbour, do not believe anyone who says you can only visit the islands on a tour and do not be pressurized by touts. If you wish to visit both Taquile and Amantaní, it is better to go to Amantaní first. From there boats go to Taquile at around 0800, costing US$2.50 per person. There is no regular service – boats leave if there are enough passengers. You would then take the 1430 boat from Taquile to Puno.*

Llachón   At the eastern end of the Península de Capachica, which encloses the northern side of the Bahía de Puno, is Llachón, a farming village (population: 1,300) which is introducing community-based tourism. It has electricity and one phone. The scenery is very pretty, with sandy beaches, pre-Inca terracing, trees and flowers. The view of the sunset from the Auki Carus hill is reckoned to be better even than from Taquile. It is a charming area and new arrivals are given a necklace of cantuta flowers in welcome. Visitors share in local activities and 70% of all produce served is from the residents' farms. The peninsula is good for hiking and mountain-biking and sailing boats can be hired. Neither Taquile nor Amantaní are far away. Twelve families offer accommodation on a rotational basis (**G** per bed). Most meals are served in the house of Valentín Quispe, the organizer of tourism in Llachón: breakfast US$1.20, other meals US$2. There is a campsite towards the end of the peninsula. To contact Don Valentín, T360226/7, T680796 (mob), llachon@yahoo.com or visit www.titicaca-peru.com/capachicae.htm

■ *Public boats leave Puno for Llachón on Fri, Sat and Sun only. Road transport runs on Wed and Sun; the unpaved road to the peninsula branches east from the main road half way between Puno and Juliaca. Tour operators in Puno arrange visits, about US$25 per person staying overnight, in groups of 10-15.*

Anapia &   In the Peruvian part of the Lago Menor are the islands of Anapia, a friendly,
Yuspique   Aymara-speaking community, and Yuspique, on which are ruins and vicuñas. The community has organized committees for tourism, motor boats, sailing boats and accommodation with families (*All Ways Travel* arranges tours). This is part of PromPerú's *Al Tur 'Turismo Vivencial'* scheme. Visitors are involved with community projects during their visit and there is always a celebration at the end of the stay. It's highly worthwhile. On the island ask for José Flores, who is very knowledgeable about Anapia's history, flora and fauna. He sometimes acts as a guide. ■ *To visit Anapia independently, take a colectivo from Yunguyo to Tinicachi and alight at Punta Hermosa, just after Unacachi. Boats to Anapia leave Punta Hermosa on Sunday and Thursday at 1300 (they leave Anapia for Yunguyo market on the same days at 0630). It's two hours each way by boat.*

Villages on the western shore of Lake Titicaca

Anybody interested in religious architecture should go from Puno to visit the villages along the western shore of Lake Titicaca. They are all on the main road to Bolivia; only Zepita is beyond the turn-off to Yunguyo (see page 252).

An Inca sundial can be seen near the village of Chucuito (19 km), which has an **Chucuito** interesting church, La Asunción, and houses with carved stone doorways. Visits to Chucuito usually include the Templo de la Fertilidad, **Inca Uyo**, which boasts many phalli and other fertility symbols. The authenticity and original location of these objects is the subject of debate. The locals tend to expect a tip for every and any thing. Nearby, are cave paintings at **Chichiflope**.

Sleeping There is accommodation 1 km north of town on the road from Puno at **C** *Hostal Chucuito*, includes breakfast, nice rooms, clean, new furniture but lacks atmosphere, courtyard can be used for parking bicycles, hot water, negotiable in low season, T054-352108, leave message for Alfredo Sánchez. Also **E** *Albergue Juvenil Las Cabañas*, T054-351276. Great wee cottages, meals, will collect you from Puno. Highly recommended.

On the road to Juli is Ilave, where the old road for Tacna branches off. It is typ- **Ilave** ical of a gaunt *altiplano* town, with a good Sunday market where you can buy woven goods. Many buses and colectivos go there from Puno (US$1.40).

The main road then by-passes the little town of Juli, 83 km southeast, which **Juli** has some fine examples of religious architecture in its four churches.

  San Pedro on the plaza, designated as the Cathedral, has been extensively restored. It contains a series of paintings of saints, with the Via Crucis scenes in the same frame, and gilt side altars above which some of the arches have baroque designs. No opening hours are displayed. **San Juan Letrán** has two sets of 17th century paintings of the lives of St John the Baptist and of St Teresa, contained in sumptuous gilded frames. San Juan is a museum. ■ *Open mornings only; US$1.15; under restoration in late 2001-2002.* It also has intricate *mestizo* carving in pink stone. A long flight of shallow steps leads past the Centro Comunal and schools to **Santa Cruz**. The church is partly roofless, with scaffolding and a shelter protecting what remains of the tower. It is completely closed to visitors, but there is a view of the lake from the plaza in front. The fourth church, **La Asunción**, is also a museum. The great nave is empty, but its walls are lined with colonial paintings with no labels. The original painting on the walls of the transept is fading. Its fine bell tower was damaged by earthquake or lightning. Outside is an archway and atrium which date from the early 17th century. ■ *US$0.85.* Needlework, other weavings, handicrafts and antiques are offered for sale in town. Near Juli is a small colony of flamingoes. Many other birds can be seen from the road.

Colectivos from Puno to Juli cost US$0.75. They stop in the main plaza before going to **Transport** the *paradero* outside market, at Ilave 349, from where they return to Puno. The main **& sleeping** road passes a park with odd buildings-cum-sculptures and arches (good views of the town and lake). You could get out of a Puno-Desaguadero bus and walk down from there to the market or plaza. **F** per person *Municipal*, Jr Ilave 312, opposite market, **G** without bath, cold water, no restaurant. **G** per person *Hostal San Pedro*, on main plaza, basic, cold water, shared bath, restaurant.

Lake Titicaca

Pomata A further 20 km along the lake is Pomata (US$0.30 from Juli), whose church of Santiago Apóstol is built of red sandstone (1532, started by the Jesuits, finished by the Dominicans). It stands on a promontory above the main road and has wonderful carvings in Andean *mestizo* baroque of vases full of tropical plants, flowers and animals in the window frames, lintels and cornices. The windows and font are of alabaster. The beautiful interior contains statues, painted columns, a Spanish tiled floor, paintings of the Cusqueña school and a cupola decorated with figures whose florid, stylized bodies have linked arms. Beneath the Altar of El Señor del Sepulcro is an altarpiece covered in all the tools used in the construction. ■ *Entry free, but give a donation for upkeep and lighting, and a tip to the guardian. Open daily 0700-1200, 1330-1600. If the colectivo does not enter town, get out by the barracks – cuartel – and walk up.*

At **Zepita**, near Desaguadero, the 18th-century Dominican church is also worth a visit.

Border with Bolivia

Peruvian time is 1 hr behind Bolivian time

There are two principal routes across the border, both of which are fairly straightforward. The one listed first is by far the more popular of the two. There is a third and rarely travelled route (see under Juliaca), and, finally, it is possible to cross the border by hydrofoil or catamaran as part of a tour.

Puno to La Paz via Yunguyo and Copacabana

Leaving Peru
Don't take a taxi Yunguyo-Puno without checking its reliability first, driver may pick up an accomplice to rob passengers

The road is paved from Puno to Yunguyo (the border) and the scenery is interesting. The views are also good on the Bolivian side. In Puno three companies sell bus tickets for the direct route from Puno to La Paz, taking 6-8 hours (the fare does not include the Tiquina ferry crossing, US$0.25): *Colectur*, Tacna 221, T352302, 0730, US$6.50, combines with *Galería* in Bolivia; *Panamericano*, Tacna 245, T354001, 0700, US$7.35, combines with *Diana Tours*; *Tour Perú* (address under Puno Transport, page 243), 0800, US$8.75, combines with *Combi Tour* (fares rise at holiday times). They stop at the borders and one hour for lunch in Copacabana, arriving in La Paz at about 1700. Passengers change buses at Copacabana and it seems that the Bolivian bus may not be of the company indicated and may not be of the same standard as the Peruvian bus. This can cause discomfort and delays. You only need to change money into Bolivianos for lunch on this route. Bus fare Puno-Copacabana US$4.40-5.80. There are local buses and colectivos all day between Puno and Yunguyo, 3 hours, US$1.20; they leave from Avenida Bolívar in Puno. From Yunguyo to the border (Kasani), colectivos charge US$0.25 per person. From the border it is a 20-minute drive to Copacabana. Colectivos and minibuses leave from just outside Bolivian immigration, US$0.50 per person. A taxi from Yunguyo to Copacabana costs about US$1.50 per person.

At the border **Peruvian immigration** The office is five minutes' drive from **Yunguyo** and 100 m from the Bolivian post. It is open 24 hours a day (but Bolivian immigration is only open 0830-1930). When leaving you must get an exit stamp before crossing the border and a tourist visa on the other side. 90 days is normally given when entering Peru (30 days for Bolivia). Be aware of corruption at customs and look out for official or unofficial people trying to charge you a fee on either side of the border (say that you know it is illegal and ask why only gringos are approached to pay the 'embarkation tax').

Sleeping In **Yunguyo G** per person *Hostal Isabel*, San Francisco 110, at Plaza de Armas, T350233, ext 19. Shared bathroom, hot water, good value, will change money and arrange transport. There area couple of other basic places in our **G** range.

Directory *Bolivian Consulate*, Jr Grau 339, T856032, near the main plaza in Yunguyo. Mon-Fri 0830-1500, for those who need a visa. Some nationalities have to pay, the fee varies per nationality. **Exchange** Good rates are available for dollars or bolivianos at the two *casas de cambio* in the main plaza in Yunguyo, cash only. Travellers' cheques can be exchanged though rates are poor. Exchange rates for cash are reasonable at the border.

The Bolivian border town of **Copacabana** is famous for its Dark Virgin of the Lake, La Virgen de Candelaria. From the town, excursions can be made to Isla del Sol and Isla de la Luna on Lake Titicaca. There is a wide variety of hotels, restaurants and other services. All road transport from Copacabana to La Paz has to take the ferry across the Straits of Tiquina.

Into Bolivia

Puno to La Paz via Desaguadero

This is the most direct road route, which continues 41 km beyond the turn-off to Yunguyo, all paved for the 150 km to the border. **Desaguadero** is a scruffy, unscrupulous place, with poor restaurants and dubious accommodation. There is no need to stopover in Desaguadero as all roads to it are paved and if you leave La Paz, Moquegua or Puno early enough you should be at your destination before nightfall.

Leaving Peru for Bolivia

Lake Titicaca

Transport *Tricitaxis* carry people and their baggage around for US$0.30, but they'll probably ask for more at some point in the ride. Colectivos and buses run every 30 minutes between **Puno** and Desaguadero; 2¼ hours, US$1.50. The last bus from the border to Puno leaves at 1930. There are minibuses to **La Paz** (105 km from Desaguadero), 1½ hours, US$1.50. The last one leaves at 1700, though buses may leave later if there are enough passengers. See page 318 for the road from **Moquegua**. *Mily Tours*, Av Panamericana 321, run colectivos to Moquegua, US$10, 3½ hours. Several bus companies do the route for US$6, 4 hours (*Ormeño* US$11.75), continuing to **Arequipa**. 3 km off this route is **Tanka Tanka**, where there are *chullpas* in the Inca *lupaca* style, both round and square, cave paintings, a large fortress and a church with a surrounding wall.

Immigration offices Peruvian immigration is beside the bridge. It is open 0830-1230 and 1400-2000. Bolivian immigration is open the same hours, except closes at 2100. Both offices are usually closed for dinner around 1830-1900. 30 days is normally given on entering Bolivia, ask for more if you need it, or get an extension in La Paz.

At the border

Sleeping and eating The best of a poor lot is **D-E** *Hostal Corona*, Av Panamericana 248, T851120. **F** without bath, TV, hot water, parking, luggage store, no meals. **F** San Carlos. Without bath, extra for hot shower, basic, tiny rooms. There is accommodation on the Bolivian side at **G** per person, eg *Hostal Barrientos*, Residencial San Francisco. Most places have rooms for sleeping and lock-ups in which to put all the goods you are going to sell on in Peru or Bolivia. There are several restaurants, mostly *pollerías*, on both sides of the bridge. On the Peruvian side *Panamericano*, *Así Es Mi Tierra* and *Perú Criollo* advertise a bit more variety.

Exchange It is better to change money (even bolivianos) on the Peruvian side. Money changers are just before the bridge, opposite immigration.

Lake Titicaca

The road as far as Guaqui (22 km) and on to La Paz is paved. This particular border crossing allows you to stop at the archaeological site of **Tiahuanaco** en route. It is possible to do a round trip to the site from Puno in about 12-13 hours. Take an early colectivo to Desaguadero, cross the border and take another colectivo towards La Paz. Pay the full fare, but ask to be let out at the junction for Tiahuanaco; walk or hitch the 1½ km to the ruins (entry US$2.10).

There are luxury services from Puno to La Paz by *Crillon Tours* hydrofoil and *Transturin*'s catamarans.

Crillon's services can be booked at their office at *Arcobaleno Tours* (see Tour operators), Puno (or all Puno travel agents have details), or their head office at Avenida Camacho 1223, PO Box 4785, La Paz, T591 2-233 7533, F211 6481, www.titicaca.com (in USA: 1450 South Bayshore Drive, Miami, FL 33131, T305-358 5353, F372 0054, darius@titicaca.com). The Puno office will take care of all documentation for crossing the border into Bolivia. The main itinerary is: Puno-Copacabana by bus; Copacabana-Isla del Sol-Huatajata (Bolivia) by hydrofoil; Huatajata-La Paz by bus; 13 hours. Visits to Pomata, Juli and reed-boat builders are included. At Huatajata *Crillon* has the **AL** *Inca Utama Hotel and Spa*, 5-star accommodation, health facilities, together with the Andean Roots cultural complex (4 museums representing 7 cultures), restaurants and observatory. *Crillon* also has *La Posada del Inca*, a hotel in a restored colonial hacienda on the Isla del Sol. They run a tour which can start at Juliaca airport (for new arrivals in the region), thence to Copacabana, then to Isla del Sol, back to Puno by hydrofoil, continuing to Cusco and Machu Picchu. Visits to their establishments can be incorporated into *Crillon's* tours covering many options.

Similar services, by more leisurely catamaran, are run by *Transturin*, whose dock is at Chúa, Bolivia: Puno to Copacabana by bus, Copacabana to the Isla del Sol (including a land tour) and on to Chúa by catamaran, then bus to La Paz. The trip can be done in one day, or with a night on board the catamaran, moored at the Isla del Sol. It is also possible to go Puno (depart 0630)-Isla del Sol-Puno (arrive 1930). On the Isla del Sol, *Transturin* has the *Inti Wata* cultural complex, with restored Inca terraces, an Aymara house and the underground *Ekako* museum. Extensions from Cusco to Puno by train are available. *Transturin* also run buses between Puno and La Paz, with no change of bus at the border. Bookings can be made through *Transturin*'s offices in La Paz, C Alfredo Ascarrunz 2518, Sopocachi, Casilla 5311, T591 2-242 2222, F241 1922, www.travelbolivia.com (this office offers economical, last minute bookings,

Into Bolivia

To La Paz by hydrofoil or catamaran

Lake Titicaca

24 and 48 hours in advance); Avenida 6 de Agosto s/n, T/F08-622284, Copaca-bana (stand-by tickets are available here); Avenida Libertad 176, Puno, T352771, F351316, leontours@terra.com.pe

North and east Titicaca

The opposite shores of Lake Titicaca are quite different. Between Desaguadero and Puno the plain is intensively worked. The tin roofs of the communities glint everywhere in the sun. Heading north from Puno, the road crosses a range of hills to another coastal plain, which leads to Juliaca. North of Puno is the first sector (29,150 ha) of the **Reserva Nacional del Titicaca**. The smaller, Ramis sector (7,030 ha) is northeast of Juliaca, at the outflow of the Río Ramis which floods in the wet season. The reserve protects extensive totora reed beds in which thousands of birds live. On the flat, windy altiplano between Juliaca and Huancané (see below) you will see small, square houses with conical roofs, all made of blocks of earth, *putukus de champa*. After Huancané, the lakeshore becomes mountainous, with cliffs, bays and fabulous vistas over the water.

Juliaca

Phone code: 054
Colour map 6, grid B2
Population: 134,700
Altitude: 3,825 m

As the commercial focus of an area bounded by Puno, Arequipa and the jungle, Juliaca has grown very fast into a chaotic place with a large impermanent population, lots of contraband and counterfeiting and more tricitaxis than cars. Monday, market day, is the most disorganized of all. Other than waiting for a plane or a train, there is not much reason to stop here. If you do have to hang around, it's freezing cold at night. So make sure you're wrapped up well in your recently purchased alpaca clothing.

Sights
You can buy wool and alpaca goods at the large Sunday **market** in the huge Plaza Melgar, several blocks from the centre. On the same plaza is an interesting colonial **church**. Another good place to find cheap alpaca sweaters is the **Galería Artesanal Las Calceteras**, on Plaza Bolognesi. **Túpac Amaru market**, on Moquegua, seven blocks east of the railway line, is a cheap black market. The **Plaza de Armas** is mostly lined with modern buildings. On it stands the grey-stone cathedral, sombre inside and lit by candles and the yellow light through the windows. If you're unlucky enough to fall ill here, there's a first class hospital run by the Seventh Day Adventists.

Sleeping
■ *on map*
Price codes:
see inside front cover

There are water problems in town, especially in the dry season.

AL *Suites Don Carlos*, Jr M Prado 335, on the outskirts of town, T321571/327270, dcarlosjuliaca@terra.com.pe 45 rooms, including a presidential suite. Prices include taxes, good facilities, quite central, continental breakfast US$6.50, lunch/dinner US$13. **B** *Hostal Don Carlos*, Jr 9 de Diciembre 114, Plaza Bolognesi, T323600, F322120. Breakfast and taxes included. Owned by the same group, comfortable, modern facilities, hot water, TV, heater, good service, restaurant and room service. Recommended. **B** *Royal Inn*, San Román 158, T321561, Hotel_royal_inn@latinmail.com Decent accommodation with hot water, TV, safe, laundry, good restaurant *La Fonda del Royal* with *menú* US$1.50. Recommended. **D** *Karlo's Hostal*, Unión 317, T321817, lanzap@hotmail.com Comfortable, firm beds, hot water, TV, laundry, restaurant *Che Karlín* attached. **D** *Hostal Luquini*, San Román 409, Plaza Bolognesi, T321510. **E** without bath, breakfast included. Comfortable, hot water, restaurant for all meals, *menú* US$1.50. Recommended. **E** *Hostal Sakura*, San Román 133, T322072. Rooms with bath and hot water, TV extra. Also has rooms without bath, **F**. Breakfast is extra. **E** *Yarur*, Jr M Núñez 414, T 321501.

F without bath, hot water, safe, no breakfast. **F-G** *Hostal Ferrocarril*, San Martín 249. Shared and private rooms, shared bath, basic.

Trujillo, San Román 163. Extensive menu, daily specials, US$3-5.50 for main dishes, US$7.50 for fish. *Trujillo 2*, at No 175, serves chicken, sandwiches and snacks. Next door is *Ricos Pan*, bakery with café. There is a vegetarian restaurant, *La Fuente de la Salud*, at 8 de Noviembre 167. There are many chicken places on Calles M Núñez, Cusco and Unión, some of which are quite upmarket.

Eating
● *on map*

Air connections The airport is small but well-organized. There are daily flights to/from Lima (21/4 hrs) with *Aero Continente* and *Aviandina*, *Tans*, and *Lan Perú* all via **Arequipa** (30 mins). *Lan* Perú also flies to Cusco. Minibuses 1-B, 6 and 14 to airport from 2 de Mayo at either Núñez or San Román, US$0.15; from airport to town they take you to your hotel. Taxi from Plaza Bolognesi, US$1.75. **Tourist buses** run direct from Puno to the airport and vice versa; US$1.50 pp, 1 hour. Also taxis, US$11.75. If taking a public colectivo from Puno to Juliaca for a flight, allow plenty of time as they drive around Puno looking for passengers to fill the vehicle first.

Transport

Lake Titicaca

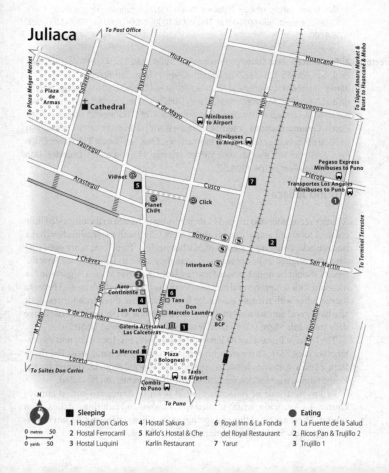

Juliaca

Sleeping					Eating
1 Hostal Don Carlos	4 Hostal Sakura		6 Royal Inn & La Fonda		1 La Fuente de la Salud
2 Hostal Ferrocarril	5 Karlo's Hostal & Che		del Royal Restaurant		2 Ricos Pan & Trujillo 2
3 Hostal Luquini	Karlín Restaurant		7 Yarur		3 Trujillo 1

N

0 metres 50
0 yards 50

Bus The new Terminal Terrestre is at Jr Mantaro y San Agustín: go down San Martín 10 blocks and cross Av Circunvalación. Lots of companies serve Desaguadero, Moquegua, Arequipa (US$5.80), Lima (US$10-17.65) and Cusco (US$4.40). *Cruz del Sur*, T322011; *Julsa*, T331952; *Ormeño*, T321181. To **Cusco**, 344 km, 5-6 hrs, with *Imexso* (in Terminal, T326389) and *Tour Perú* (tourperu@mixmail.com), day and night buses, prices as from Puno. *First Class* (www.firstclassperu.com) and *Inka Express* (inkaex@yahoo.com) have pullman tourist buses which stop for sightseeing and lunch, with guide, see under Puno. The road is paved and in good condition. To **Puno**, 44 km, 1 hr, US$0.45; small buses leave from Piérola y 18 de Noviembre, 2 companies, *Pegaso Express* and *Los Angeles*. Combis to Puno leave from another Terminal Terrestre on Plaza Bolognesi, also US$0.45. To **Huancané** (on the north side of Lake Titicaca), 51 km, 40 mins and Moho, a further 31 km, *Santa Cruz* and *Joyas del Sur* companies, Moquegua 1019, at the corner with Ballón near the Túpac Amaru market, US$1.75, 3 hrs to Moho. It is a bumpy ride on a poor road, but the views are wonderful. See below on how to get to the Bolivian border.

Rail The station at Juliaca is the junction for services between **Arequipa** (no passenger services in 2002), **Puno** and **Cusco**. See under Puno (page 243) and Cusco (page 192) for more information. Fares to Cusco are the same as for Puno.

The ticket office, whose entrance is on Plaza Bolognesi, opens 0700-1100, 1400-1800, except Tue 1400-1800, Thu 0600-1000, 1400-1800, Sat 0700-1100, Sun 0600-1000.

Directory **Airline offices** *Aero Continente/Aviandina*, San Román 139, T328440/327857. *Lan Perú*, San Román 125, T322228 (airport 324441). *Tans*, San Román 152, T321272. **Banks** *Interbank*, M Núñez 231. With *Red Activa 24* ATM for Visa/Plus, Mastercard/Cirrus and Amex. *BCP*, M Núñez entre Chávez y 9 de Diciembre, changes cash and TCs but has no ATM. *Cambios* are mostly around the junction of M Núñez with Bolívar and San Martín. **Communications** Internet: there are many places in the centre, all charging US$0.60 per hr (some charge less in the morning). *Click*, San Román 338; *Planet Ch@t*, Pje C Arestegui 111, also has café; *Vi@net*, Jauregui 117; and others. **Laundry** *Don Marcelo*, San Román 104, T324052.

Around Juliaca

A highly recommended trip is 34 km northwest of Juliaca to the unspoiled little colonial town of Lampa, known as the 'Pink City', with a splendid church, La Inmaculada, containing a copy of Michelangelo's 'Pietà' (the story goes that when the original in Rome was damaged, they came to Lampa to see how the repairs should be done). Also of interest is the Kampac Museo, Ugarte 462, a museum with sculptures and ceramics from the Lampa and Juli areas. There is a tourist office with friendly guides for free. Nearby are three Inca fortresses. It also has a good Sunday market. There is a basic *hostal*, **G** per person. Buses leave daily from 2 de Mayo (take a tricycle to get there), one hour, US$0.70.

The town of **Pucará** lies 63 km to the north, with pre-Inca ruins and its pottery (see page 237). There are some restaurants along the main road. The sheep farm of San Antonio, between Ayaviri and Chiquibambilla, owned by the Prime family, who are descendants of British emigrants, can be visited.

71 km northeast of Juliaca is the old town of **Azángaro** with a famous church, La Asunción, which is filled with *retablos* and paintings of the Cusco school. There are good thermal springs at the village of **Putina**, 84 km northeast of Juliaca, 51/2 hours by bus or truck, US$2.50.

Some tours from Cusco to Lake Titicaca have the Isla de Suasi (see below) as their initial destination. The route taken goes through Pucará, Azángaro and Muñani and two nights are spent at **Mallkini**, an alpaca farm owned by the Michell family, the largest alpaca textile group in Peru. If you wish to see an altiplano farm, this is a first-class set-up, rustic, guests are well-looked after and can take part in various activities. Head office is Juan de la Torre 101, San Lorenzo, Arequipa, T054-202523, ext 154, F202727, www.michell.com.pe

Juliaca to Cusco

The road Puno-Juliaca-Cusco is now fully paved and in good condition. Bus services are consequently an acceptable alternative to the train, which runs at an average altitude of 3,500 m. There is much to see on the way, but neither the daytime buses nor the trains make frequent stops. You would have to be using your own transport, or taking buses from town to town to sample what the places en route have to offer. The road climbs steadily after Juliaca, passing Pucará (see above) then running through the villages of Ayaviri and Santa Rosa (where knitted alpaca ponchos and pullovers and miniature llamas are sold, rooms are available). It then rises further, up to the pass at La Raya.

Ayaviri is a lively town with a daily market. In the pleasant plaza are two *puya raimondi* plants. There are three hotels including **G** *Paraíso*, Jr Leoncio Prado 254 (about 3 blocks from the plaza), T863024. Hot showers, clean, friendly. **G** Hostal Ayaviri, Grau 180. Basic and unfriendly. *Restaurante La Mundial*, Jr Tacna 465, T863375. Cheap local food, friendly. The local speciality is lamb.

The road and railway cross the altiplano, climbing to **La Raya**, the highest pass on the line; 210 km from Puno, at 4,321 m. Up on the heights breathing may be a little difficult, but the descent along the Río Vilcanota is rapid. To the right of **Aguas Calientes**, 9 km from La Raya, are steaming pools of hot water. The temperature of the springs is 40°C, and they show beautiful deposits of red ferro-oxide. Several communal bathing pools and a block of changing rooms have been opened. Entrance US$0.15. At **Maranganí**, the river is wider and the fields greener, with groves of eucalyptus trees. At Km 147, next to a colonial house, is the *Maranganí Fábrica Tejidos* (T352215), a textile manufacturer using alpaca wool. Although only 10 years old, some of the machines are much older than that and all use punch cards (no computerization here). The textiles are exported all over the world. The administrator, Sr Walter Chung Valdez, is happy to show interested travellers around.

The Vilcanota plunges into a gorge, but the train winds above it and round the side of the mountain. At **Huambutío** the railway turns left to follow the Río Huatanay on the final stretch to Cusco. The Vilcanota here widens into the great Urubamba canyon, flanked on both sides by high cliffs, on its way to join the Ucayali, a tributary of the Amazon. (For more information about places between La Raya and Cusco, see page 225.)

Along the east side of Lake Titicaca

This is the most remote, but nevertheless highly recommended route for crossing from Peru into Bolivia, via Huancané, and Moho (the last town of any size in Peru). As the road leaves Juliaca, it crosses a single track-bridge, which can get congested if opposing drivers do not give way. To Huancané the road is paved across the altiplano. In town is **F** *Hostal Conquistador*, Puno y Castilla. The road then deteriorates, badly in places. There are two possibitle way of getting to Moho (40 km): inland, over the hills, the route the buses take

Via Huancané & Moho

Lake Titicaca

as it is shorter; or clinging to the lakeshore, with lots of bends, but beautiful views. Moho is known as the 'Garden of the Altiplano'. Maximizing the climatic benefits of the lake, they grow roses and many other flowers. The plaza has rosebushes, topiary hedges and a colourful fountain. The large, green Consejo Municipal is totally out of keeping with the rest of the plaza, but it is supposed to have a hotel when finished. Other places to stay (all **F-G**): *Hostal Moheño*, blue, across from the church, basic but clean; *Señor Exultación*, on the plaza; *Albergue de la Parroquia*, run by nuns, separate facilities for men and women. Buses for Juliaca collect on the plaza. From Juliaca there are several daily buses to Huancané and Moho.

Beyond Moho, some walking may be involved as there is little traffic onwards to **Puerto Acosta**, the first town on the Bolivian side. Make sure you get an exit stamp in Puno, post-dated by a couple of days. From Moho, hitchhike to **Tilali**, the last village in Peru (three hours on foot, basic accommodation). Night buses serve Tilali direct from Juliaca (6 hours, only for certain on Mon, Tue, Fri and Sun), but you miss the scenery. From Tilali it is 15 minutes' walk to the **Peruvian immigration** post, the border a further 30 minutes (38 km from Moho) and **Puerto Acosta** is a further 10 km (possible on foot, two hours, or bike, not by car – the road is bad). From there take a bus for 2½ hours to Chaguaya, where there is a control post and immigration next door. Leave the bus to get a Bolivian entry stamp; the officials help you get transport to continue your journey. The road is good (paved from Escoma), several buses daily to La Paz.

The only tourist project on the north shore is **AL** *Albergue Rural Isla de Suasi*, T054-622709, or Puno T/F365968 (office, albergue@suasi.com) or 351417 (owner, Martha Giraldo, martha@suasi.com), or Lima 01-973 1404, www.suasi.com The hotel is the only house on this tiny, tranquil island. There are beautiful terraced gardens, which are at their best January-March. The non-native eucalyptus trees are being replaced by native varieties. You can take a community rowing boat around the island to see birds (US$1.50) and the island has four vicuñas, a small herd of alpacas and one vizcacha. The sunsets from the highest point are out of this world. Facilities are spacious, comfortable and solar-powered. Rooms have bath and hot water and hot water bottles are put between your sheets at bedtime. Price includes breakfast but other meals are extra, US$10-15; good food, lots of vegetables, all locally-produced. Private boats from Puno are expensive and take four to six hours (2½ hours by fast boat, US$450 up to 15 passengers), but you can call at the islands or Llachón en route. A car for four people will cost US$75. Otherwise take public transport from Juliaca to Moho and on to Cambría, near Conima, walk down to the shore and take a rowing boat to Suasi, 10 minutes, US$1.50 per person.

Rinconada At 5,200 m, Rinconada is a cold, isolated town near Ananea and Culijón mountain. Its population of about 25,000 is involved entirely in gold mining and the mines are all under a glacier. A glacier lake below the town is marred by the rock and sand dug out of the mines. You can see all the processes in extracting, refining and selling the gold (which can be found pretty cheaply in the local shops). There is no infrastructure for tourists: there are four or five basic *hostales*, countless basic restaurants serving good food and, apart from gold, shops sell mainly mining equipment. Wrap up warm as it is cold by day and bitter at night (it is hard to sleep in the thin air). ■ *Buses leave Juliaca at 0600-0700, taking 5-6 hrs, and the road is very bumpy after Huancané, but was being improved in 2001. Buses return from Rinconada at 0500-0700, taking about 30 mins less on the downhill journey; US$3.50 one way. Also in 2001 a border crossing to Bolivia was opened (no details available, other than a Friday bus).*

Arequipa

Introducing Arequipa

The distinctive volcanic sillar used in the building of the city of Arequipa, has given it its nickname of the 'White City'. Spanish churches, mansions and the 19th-centruy Plaza de Armas all shine with this stonework. In contrast, the city's most famous colonial jewel, the **Santa Catalina convent**, is painted in bright colours, a gorgeous little city within a city. This is only one of the attractions in a region of volcanoes, deep canyons and terraced valleys. The perfect cone of **El Misti** and its companions **Chachani** and **Pichu-Pichu** overlook Arequipa itself. Active **Sabancaya** and frequent earth tremors are reminders that this is a very unstable region. As recently as 2001 the city lost one tower of its cathedral in an earthquake.

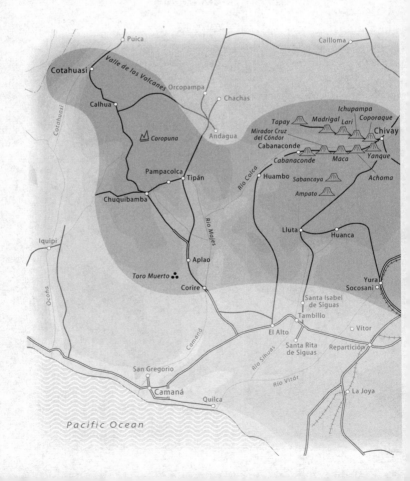

Two famous canyons are within relatively easy reach. To arrive at these great gorges, you must take rough roads at high altitudes. **Cotahuasi Canyon** is the deepest in the world at 3,354 m, but it has not yet achieved the same popularity as its neighbour, **Colca**. And it was only recently that the ancient peoples here, the Cabana and Collagua, had their villages and farms exposed to the gaze of tourism. There is excellent trekking and riding on the terraces of Colca, accommodation is improving all the time and the calendar is full of festivals. Above all, Colca also happens to be the best place in the whole country to get up a close up view of the majestic condor, but it is worth more of your time than a short visit just to see the birds rising on the morning thermals. On the altiplanos of this region there are herds of **alpaca** and **vicuña** and, at **Toro Muerto**, the largest field of petroglyphs in the world.

There's an individual feeling to this southwestern corner of Peru which, in part, stems from the stubborn pride of its people who have continuously attempted to gain more independence from Lima. Fellow Peruvians will jokingly refer to this region as the 'Independent Republic of Arequipa', but don't believe them when they kindly inform you of the need for a visa. Forget the politics and savour the difference over a spicy arequipeña meal in a *picantería*, in the quality of the alpaca clothing and the light of the setting sun on the snows of El Misti.

Things to do in Arequipa

- Soak up the atmosphere of the **Santa Catalina Convent**, the beauty and variety of flowers in vases, and the touching quality of some of the rooms make it a must on anyone's itinerary, page 266.
- Stop off at the **Museo Santuarios Andinos** to see the mummy of Juanita (if she is not jet setting off on some foreign exhibition), page 267.
- Before it gets dark, go to the mirador at Yanahuara suburb to see the setting sun light up **El Misti** volcano, page 267.
- Go shopping for alpaca goods in Arequipa having seen these animals in the wild, for instance in the Colca Canyon, page 273.
- Take a trip to **Cotahuasi Canyon**, more adventurous than Colca because it has not yet acquired major tourist status, page 286.
- Try to catch one of **Colca's festivals** and experience the traditional way of life that extends throughout the entire canyon, page 280.

Arequipa

Phone code: 054
Colour map 5,
grid C6
Population 1 million
Altitude: 2,380 m

The city of Arequipa stands in a beautiful valley at the foot of El Misti volcano, a snow-capped, perfect cone, 5,822 m high, guarded on either side by the mountains Chachani (6,057 m), and Pichu-Pichu (5,669 m). The city was re-founded on 15 August 1540 by an emissary of Pizarro, but it had previously been occupied by Aymara Indians and the Incas. It has since grown into a magnificent city – fine Spanish buildings and many old and interesting churches built of sillar, a pearly white volcanic material were almost exclusively used in the construction of Arequipa – exuding an air of intellectual rigour and political passion. Among its famous sons and daughters are former President Fernando Belaúnde Terry and novelist and failed presidential candidate, Mario Vargas Llosa. Now, Arequipa is the main commercial centre for the south and its fiercely proud people resent the general tendency to believe that everything is run from Lima.

Ins and outs

Getting there Rodríguez Ballón airport is 7 km from town. For transport to and from the airport, see page 275. The bus terminal is a 10-15 min drive south of the centre. The train station is a 15-min walk from the centre (see map on page 266).

Getting around Arequipa is a compact city with the main places of interest and hotels within a few blocks of the Plaza de Armas. Take a bus or taxi if you want to the visit the suburbs. Taxis (can be shared) charge US$4-5 from the airport to the city. Fares around town are US$0.70-0.85, including to bus terminal. Radio taxis: *Nova Taxi*, T252511; *Taxi 21*, T212121; *Telemóvil*, T221515; *Taxitur*, T422323; *Henry Málaga*, T655095, Spanish only.

Tourist information *i perú*, is in the Municipalidad on the south side of the Plaza de Armas, T221228, iperuarequipa@ptomperu.gob.pe 0830-1930 daily. They are very helpful and friendly and give free street plans. Also an office in the airport, 2nd floor, T444564. 0630-1730 daily. *Indecopi*, the tourist protection bureau, has two offices: Moral 316, T212054, mcornejo@indecopi.gob.pe and Quezada 104, Yanahuara, T270181, rneyra@indecopi.gob.pe Or T0800-42579, 24 hrs, toll-free. *Tourist Police*, Jerusalén 315, T251270/239888, helpful with complaints or giving directions. *Ministry of Tourism*, La

Merced 117, T213116, handle complaints. *Touring y Automóvil Club del Perú*, Av Goyeneche 313, T289868, mechanical assistance T215640, arequipa@ touringperu.com.pe

Arequipa enjoys a wonderful climate, with a mean temperature before sundown of **Climate** 23°C, and after sundown of 14°C. The sun shines on 360 days of the year. Annual rainfall is less than 150 mm.

Theft can be a problem in the market area, especially after dark, in the park at Selva **Security** Alegre and on Calles San Juan de Dios and Alvarez Thomas, but the police are conspicuous, friendly, courteous and efficient.

Sights

The elegant **Plaza de Armas**, beautifully laid-out with palm trees, gardens and fountain, is faced on three sides by arcaded colonial buildings (rebuilt after an earthquake in 1863) with many restaurants, and on the fourth by the **cathedral**. Behind the cathedral there is a very attractive alley, Pasaje Catedral, with handicraft shops and places to eat.

The central **San Camilo market**, between Perú, San Camilo, Piérola and Alto de la Luna, is worth visiting, as is the **Siglo XX market**, to the east of the rail station. At **Selva Alegre** there is a shady park in front of the *Hotel Libertador*, which is within easy walking distance of all the famous churches and main plaza (see Security, above).

Arequipa is said to have the best-preserved colonial architecture in Peru, apart from Cusco. The oldest district is **San Lázaro**, a collection of tiny climbing streets and houses quite close to the *Hotel Libertador*, where you can find the ancient **Capilla de San Lázaro**.

A cheap tour of the city can be made in a Vallecito bus - 1½ hours for US$0.30. It is a circular tour going down Calles Jerusalén and San Juan de Dios.

The massive **cathedral** on the Plaza de Armas was founded in 1612 and **Churches** largely rebuilt in the 19th century. It is remarkable for having its façade along *Because of the* the whole length of the church and takes up one full side of the plaza. Inside *ever-present danger of* is a fine Belgian organ and elaborately carved wooden pulpit. Despite the *earthquakes, churches* care taken in building techniques, the June 2001 earthquake caused one of *in the city were built* the cathedral's twin towers famously to collapse. Repairs are continuing and *low. They are usually* will not be completed until 2004. Visiting is fairly unaffected, other than the *open 0700-0900* obvious annoyance of the outer scaffolding in photos! The entrance to the *and 1800-2000* Cathedral is on the plaza.

A visit to the church and cloister of **La Compañía**, at General Morán y Alvarez Thomas, is recommended. The main façade (1698) and side portal (1654) are striking examples of the florid Andean *mestizo* style. Also of note is the **Capilla Real** (Royal Chapel) to the left of the sanctuary, and its San Ignacio chapel with a beautiful polychrome cupola. The stark cloister is impressive. ■ *Mon-Sat 0900-1240, 1500-1945, Sun 1700-1945. US$0.50.*

Also well worth seeing are the churches of **San Agustín** (corner of San Agustín y Sucre), the early 17th century **La Merced** (La Merced 303), **Santo Domingo**, also 17th century (Santo Domingo y Piérola), and **San Francisco**, 16th century (Zela 103, also has a convent and library, open 0900-1230, 1500-1830). Opposite San Francisco is the interesting **Museo Histórico Municipal** with much war memorabilia. ■ *Plaza San Francisco 407. Mon-Fri 0800-1800. US$0.50.*

Santa Catalina Convent By far the most interesting place to visit is to the Santa Catalina Convent, opened in 1970 after four centuries of mysterious isolation. This is the most remarkable sight in Arequipa and a complete contrast to what you would expect from nuns who had taken vows of poverty. The convent has been beautifully refurbished, with period furniture, pictures of the Arequipa and Cusco schools and fully equipped kitchens. It is a complete miniature walled colonial town of over 2 ha in the middle of the city. About 450 nuns lived here in total seclusion, except for their women servants.

Arequipa

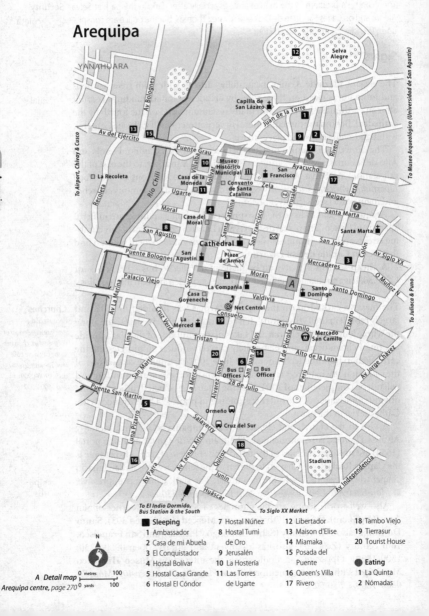

A *Detail map*
Arequipa centre, *page 270*

■ Sleeping	7 Hostal Núñez	12 Libertador	18 Tambo Viejo
1 Ambassador	8 Hostal Tumi	13 Maison d'Elise	19 Tierrasur
2 Casa de mi Abuela	de Oro	14 Miamaka	20 Tourist House
3 El Conquistador	9 Jerusalén	15 Posada del	
4 Hostal Bolívar	10 La Hostería	Puente	● Eating
5 Hostal Casa Grande	11 Las Torres	16 Queen's Villa	1 La Quinta
6 Hostal El Cóndor	de Ugarte	17 Rivero	2 Nómadas

The few remaining nuns have retreated to one section of the convent, allowing visitors to see a maze of cobbled streets and plazas bright with geraniums and other flowers, cloisters and buttressed houses. These have been finely restored and painted in traditional white, orange, deep red and blue.

■ *Santa Catalina 301. T229798. 0900-1600 daily. US$7.25. The tour they offer you at the entrance is worthwhile and lasts 1½ hours; there's no set price and many of the guides speak English or German (a tip of US$2.85 is expected). There is a good café, which sells cakes made by the nuns and a special blend of tea.*

La Recoleta La Recoleta, a Franciscan monastery built in 1647, stands on the other side of the river, on Recoleta. It contains several cloisters, a religious art museum, a precolumbian museum, an Amazon museum, a library with many rarities, and is well worth visiting. ■ *The monastery was closed to visitors after the 2001 earthquake, but ask the staff if you can visit the library.*

Colonial houses Arequipa has several fine seignorial houses with large carved tympanums over the entrances. Thanks to their being one-storey structures, they have mostly withstood the earthquakes which regularly pound this city. They are distinguished by their small patios with no galleries, flat roofs and small windows, disguised by superimposed lintels or heavy grilles.

One of the best examples is the 18th century **Casa Tristán del Pozo**, better known as the **Gibbs-Ricketts house** with its fine portal and puma-head waterspouts. It is now the main office of Banco Continental, at San Francisco 108. ■ *0915-1245, 1600-1830, Sat 0930-1230.*

Other good examples are: the **Casa del Moral**, or Williams house, with a museum, in the Banco Industrial, at Calle Moral 318 y Bolívar. ■ *Mon-Sat 0900-1700, Sun 0900-1300, US$1.40 or US$0.90 for students.* The **Casa Goyeneche**, La Merced 201 y Palacio Viejo, is now an office of the Banco Central de la Reserva. Ask to see the courtyard and fine period rooms. Also see Casa de la Moneda, at Ugarte y Villalba; **La Casona Chávez de la Rosa**, at San Agustín 104, part of the Universidad San Agustín (art and photography exhibitions).

Museums The **archaeological museum** at the Universidad de San Agustín, Avenida Independencia between La Salle and Santa Rosa, has a good collection of ceramics and mummies. Apply to Dr E Linares, the Director, T229719. ■ *Mon-Fri 0800-1400. US$1.*

The **Museo Santuarios Andinos** contains the frozen mummies recently found on Ampato volcano. The mummy known as 'Juanita' is particularly fascinating (see page 281). ■ *The museum is at Santa Catalina 210, on the corner with Ugarte, opposite the convent, T200345, www.ucsm.edu.pe/santury Mon-Sat 0900-1800, Sun 0900-1500. The US$4.40 entry fee includes a 20 min video of the discovery in English followed by a guided tour in English, French, German, Italian or Spanish (tip the guide), discount with student card.*

Arequipa suburbs
When El Misti has its full covering of snow (in August), they say it is wearing its poncho

Northwest of the city (2 km) is the district is **Yanahuara**, where there is a 1750 *mestizo*-style church (opens 1500), with a magnificent churrigueresque façade, all in *sillar*. The church stands on a plaza, at the end of which is a *mirador*, through whose arches there is a fine view of El Misti with the city at its feet. There's live music at *Peña El Moro*, on Parque Principal. A score of *picanterías* specialize in piquant foods such as *rocoto relleno* (hot stuffed peppers), *cuy chactado* (seared guinea-pig), *papas con ocopa* (boiled potatoes with a hot spicy yellow sauce) and *adobo* (pork stew). ■ *To get there cross the Puente Grau and turn right up Av Bolognesi.*

Arequipa

In the hillside suburb of **Cayma**, 3 km northwest of the city, is a delightful 18th-century church (open until 1700), and many old buildings associated with Bolívar and Garcilaso de la Vega. ■ *Many local buses go to Cayma.*

Beyond the airport, at **Las Canteras de Sillar**, you can see the quarries where the *sillar* blocks are cut for buildings in the city. They are worth a brief visit if passing, but not a special detour.

The **thermal baths** of Jesús are 30 minutes by car, on the slopes of Pichu-Pichu. ■ *0500-1230.*

Tingo, which has a very small lake and three swimming pools, should be visited on Sunday for local food such as *anticuchos* and *buñuelos*. ■ *Take bus 7, US$0.20.*

Three kilometres past Tingo, beside the Sabandía river on the Huasacache road, is **La Mansión del Fundador**. Originally owned by the founder of Arequipa, Don Garcí Manuel de Carbajal, in 1540, it has been open to the public since 1897 and restored as a museum with original furnishings and paintings. ■ *US$2.50, with cafeteria and bar.* Nearby is the **Mirador Sachaca** with fine panoramic views, best between 0630 and 0730 before the smog obscures the view. ■ *US$0.35. Take a bus marked 'Sachaca' from C La Merced.* In the district of Sachaca, 4 km from the centre, is the **Palacio Goyeneche**.

Southeast of Arequipa (8 km) is the **Molino de Sabandía**, the first stone mill in the area, built in 1621. It has been fully restored and the guardian diverts water to run the grinding stones when visitors arrive. The well-kept grounds have old willow trees and the surrounding countryside is pleasant; a worthwhile trip. ■ *US$1.50, ring the bell for admission. A round trip by taxi costs US$4.* Nearby is **L-AL** *El Lago Resort*, Camino al Molino de Sabandía s/n, T448383, F448344, about 20 minutes from the city, with swimming pool and horseriding. Recommended. Adjoining Sabandía is **Yumina**, with many Inca terraces which are still in use and between Sabandía and Arequipa is Paucarpata, with an old church and views of terraces, El Misti and Chachani.

Essentials

Sleeping
■ *on map*
Price codes:
see inside front cover

LL-L *Libertador*, Plaza Simón Bolívar, Selva Alegre, T215110, F241933, www.libertador.com.pe Safe, large comfortable rooms, good service, swimming pool (cold), gardens, good meals, pub-style bar, cocktail lounge, squash court. Recommended. **L-AL** *Posada del Puente*, Av Bolognesi 101, T253132, F253576, beside Puente Grau, alongside Río Chili. Attractive, small, friendly, good, restaurant. Recommended. **AL** *Portal*, Portal de Flores 116, T215530, F234374. 4-star, on the plaza, good views, rooftop swimming pool, *El Gaucho* restaurant (very good, huge portions) and *Chifa Portal*, a bit dated. **AL-A** *Hostal La Gruta*, La Gruta 304, Selva Alegre, 5 mins from the centre, T224631, F289899, www.lagrutahotel.com Price includes breakfast, cable TV, garden, laundry, 24-hr café, fax service, parking. **AL-A** *Maison d'Elise*, Av Bolognesi 104, T256185, F271935. Attractive Mediterranean-style village with pool, large rooms, also suites and apartments, helpful staff, pricey restaurant. **A** *Hostal Casa Grande*, Luna Pizarro 202, Vallecito, T214000, F214021. Includes taxes, small, cosy, well-furnished, quiet, friendly, good services and restaurant. Recommended. **A** *El Conquistador*, Mercaderes 409, T212916, F218987. Clean, safe, lovely colonial atmosphere, owner speaks English, thin walls. **A** *Maison Plaza*, Portal San Agustín 143, T218929, F218931, maisonplaza@planet.com.pe With breakfast, bathroom and TV, comfortable, clean, friendly, good value, older and newer rooms. **A** *La Plazuela*, on Plaza Juan Manuel Polar 105, Vallecito (5 mins' walk from the centre), T222624, F234625. A lovely old house next to a small park some distance from centre, nicely furnished, hot water, cable TV, laundry service, cafeteria, restaurant, owners speak English. **A** *La Posada del Monasterio*, Santa Catalina 300, T/F283076.

(sidebar) Arequipa

Colonial building opposite Santa Catalina, breakfast included, garden. **A** *Samana*, Av Ejército 704, Yanahuara, F254194, samana-hotel @terra.com.pe Comfortable rooms, TV, good views. Recommended. **A-B** *Jerusalén*, C Jerusalén 601, T244441/81, F243472. Hot water, comfortable, modern, good restaurant, safe, with breakfast, pleasant, car parking. Also has more expensive suites.

B *Casa de Melgar*, Melgar 108, T/F222459. Excellent rooms, all different, delightful 18th century building, with bathroom, hot water all day (solar panel), safe, clean, friendly, nice courtyard, good breakfast in café open in the morning and 1730-2100. **B** *Casa de Mi Abuela*, Jerusalén 606, T241206, F242761, casadmiabuela@LaRed.net.pe Very clean, friendly, safe, hot water, laundry, cable TV, swimming pool, rooms at the back are quieter and overlook the garden, **D** without bathroom, self-catering if desired, English spoken, internet access US$3 per hr, tours and transport organized in own agency (*Giardino*, T221345, F as above, giardinotours@chasqui.LaRed.net.pe), which has good information (expensive), small library of European books, breakfast or evening snacks on patio or in beautiful garden, parking, **A-B** for apartment for 4. Recommended. **B** *Crismar*, Moral 107, T215290, F239431, opposite the main Post Office. With bathroom, modern, safe, noisy, central, good restaurant. **B** *Queen's Villa*, Luna Pizarro 512, Vallecito, T235233, jrowlands@terra.com.pe With bath, hot water, breakfast, safe, parking, laundry. **B** *Hostal Solar*, Ayacucho 108, T/F241793, solar@rh.com.pe Nice colonial building, TV, bath, hot water, includes good breakfast served in nice patio, sun lunge on roof, very secure, quiet.

C *Hostal Bolívar*, Bolívar 202. Colonial-style, recently renovated, breakfast served in patio. Recommended. **C** *La Hostería*, Bolívar 405, T/F289269. Small, friendly, comfortable and attractive. Recommended. **C** *Los Balcones de Moral y Santa Catalina*, Moral 217, T201291, F222555, losbalcones@hotmail.com Convenient, 1 block from Plaza de Armas and close to Santa Catalina, large rooms, comfortable beds, with bath, hot water, laundry, café, tourist information. **C** *Miamaka*, San Juan de Dios 402, T241496, F227906. Excellent service, cable TV, helpful, English spoken. Recommended. **B** *Tierrasur*, Consuelo 210, T227132, F286564, www.tierrasur.com Modern 3-star, convenient for centre, clean, comfortable, safe, very helpful staff, English spoken, gym. Recommended.

D *Hostal Le Foyer*, Ugarte 114 y San Francisco, T286473. Comfortable, very hot water 24 hrs, laundry, luggage store, safe, helpful. Recommended. **D** *Lluvia de Oro*, Jerusalén 308, T214252, F235730. Cheaper without bath, English-speaking, breakfast US$2, good views, laundry service, friendly. Recommended. **D** *Las Torres de Ugarte*, Ugarte 401, T/F283532, hlastorres@hotmail.com www.hotelista.com Next to Santa Catalina convent, hot water all day, cable TV, roof terrace, laundry service, parking, safe, luggage store, friendly. **D** *Hostal Tumi de Oro*, San Agustín 311A, 2 blocks from the Plaza de Armas, T/F281319. With bathroom, French and English spoken, hot water, roof terrace, book

exchange, tea/coffee facilities, safe. Recommended. **D** *Posada de Sancho*, Santa Catalina 213 A and 223 A, near the convent, T/F287797, posadasancho@terra.com.pe Hot showers, cheaper without bath, clean, safe, nice patio and terrace with a view of El Misti, good breakfast extra, very friendly owners, English, French and German spoken, information on travel and Spanish classes, offer cheap tours. **D** *Tambo Viejo*, Av Malecón Socabaya 107, IV Centenario, T288195/206140, F284747, tamboviejo@yahoo.com, www.home.zonnet.nl/pcueva 5 blocks south of the plaza near the rail station. In high season and rooms with garden view are **C**. **D-E** with shared bath, **F** pp in dormitory. Family home, quiet, very friendly, English and Dutch spoken, walled garden, hot water, expensive laundry service, cable TV, safe deposit, coffee shop, bar book exchange (2 for 1), money changed, tourist information for guests, use of kitchen, internet, phone for international calls, bike rental, popular with young travellers, luggage store extra, tours arranged. For a small fee, you can use the facilities if passing through. When arriving by bus or train, do not believe taxi drivers who say the hotel is closed or full; ring the door bell and check for yourself. Better still, telephone the hostal and they will pick you up free of charge form 0500-2100. *Hotel Premier*, Av Quiroz 100, T241091, reservas@hostalpremier.com Good value hostal also a travel agency.

E *Ambassador*, Jerusalén 619, T281 048. With bathroom, cheaper without, hot water, TV, laundry, café, helpful, English-speaking staff. **E** *Hospedaje El Caminante Class*, Santa Catalina 207-A, 2nd floor, T203 444. With bathroom, cheaper without, hot water, clean, laundry service and facilities, sun terrace, very helpful owners, new in 2001. Recommended. **E** *Hostal Núñez*, Jeru- salén 528, T233268. With bathroom, cheaper without, hot water, TV, laundry, safe, small rooms, breakfast on roof terrace overlooking the city. **E** *Hostal Rivero*, Rivero 420, T229266, www.ciudadblanca. net/ hostalrivero Cheaper with shared bath, hot water, cable TV extra, medical assistance, laundry facilities, very helpful, good value. **E** *Hostal Santa Catalina*, Santa Catalina 500, T233705. Clean, hot water, TV, friendly, upper rooms quiet but elsewhere noisy, safe, luggage stored. **E** *The Tourist House*, Alvarez Tomás 435, T211752. In an unsafe area, hot showers, clean, safe hotel, friendly, kitchen, TV lounge, offers tours.

F *Casa Itzhak*, Av Parra 97, T204596, M 946643. With and without bath, includes breakfast, cable TV, laundry service, restau- rant, free transport to bus station, very

Related map
Arequipa, page 266

Arequipa centre

Sleeping
1 Casa de Melgar
2 Colonial House Inn
3 Crismar
4 Hospedaje El
   Caminante Class
5 Hostal La Portada del
   Mirador
6 Hostal La Reyna
7 Hostal Le Foyer
8 Hostal Posada de
   Sancho
9 Hostal Regis
10 Hostal Santa Catalina
11 Hostal Solar
12 La Casita de Ugarte
13 La Fiorentina
14 La Posada del
   Monasterio & Le Café
   Art Montreal
15 Lluvia de Oro
16 Los Balcones de Moral
   y Santa Catalina
17 Maison Plaza
18 Portal

Eating
1 Anushka
2 Ary Quepay
3 Bonanza
4 Bóveda San Agustín
5 Café Capriccio
6 Café El Buho
7 Café Manolo
8 Casa Vegetariana
9 Challwa
10 El café
11 El Fogón
12 El Rincón Norteño
13 El Turko
14 El Turko II
15 Gianni
16 Govinda
17 La Canasta
18 La Casita de José
   Antonio
19 Lakshmivan
20 La Rueda
21 Mandala
22 Pizzería Los Leños
23 Pizzería San Antonio
24 Pushkin
25 Zig Zag

Bars
26 Forum & Dejá Vu

helpful. F *La Casona de Romana*, Quinta Romana 122, T235917. Central, hot water, cable TV in the dining room, laundry service, very hospitable, family-run (daughter speaks English), very good. F *Colonial House Inn*, Puente Grau 114, T/F223533, colonialhouseinn@hotmail.com or casos.@ec-red.com Hot water, quieter rooms at the back, laundry facilities and service, kitchen facilities, roof terrace, good choice of breakfasts, owners speak English. F *Hostal El Cóndor*, San Juan de Dios 525, T206166. Most rooms with bath, hot showers, cable TV, free luggage store, no breakfast, very friendly, tours arranged. F per person *El Indio Dormido*, Av Andrés Avelino Cáceres B-9, T427401, the_sleeping_indian@yahoo.com Close to bus terminal, free transport to centre, some rooms with bath, TV, clean, very helpful. F *La Fiorentina*, Puente Grau 110, T202571. **G** without bath, hot water, comfortable, ask for a good room, family atmosphere, tours arranged, laundry facilities, use of kitchen extra. F *Hostal La Portada del Mirador*, Portal de Flores 102, Plaza de Armas, T201229. Basic, shared bath, hot water, clean, safe, friendly, will store luggage, great views from the roof. F *Hostal Regis*, Ugarte 202, T226111. Colonial house, French-style interior, clean, hot water all day, cooking and laundry facilities (good laundry service), sun terrace with good views, safe deposit, luggage store, video rental, book exchange, very helpful, tours arranged. Recommended. F *Hostal La Reyna*, Zela 209, T286578. With or without bath, two more expensive rooms at the top of the house, hot water 24 hrs, clean, the daughter speaks English, laundry, breakfast for US$1.15, pizza available at any hour, rooftop seating, will store luggage and arrange trips to the Colca Canyon and volcanoes. Do not believe taxi drivers who say the hotel is closed or full; ring the door bell and check for yourself.

G *La Casita de Ugarte*, Ugarte 212, T204363. English/Peruvian run, large basic rooms in a colonial building, new, good value.

Youth hostels D *Premier*, Av Quiroz 100, T/F241091, www.hostalpremier.com HI-affiliated, F per person form HI members or in dormitory, cultural, archaeological and adventure trips offered. F *Youth Hostel Arequipa*, Zela 313, T669253. Dormitory accommodation, kitchen, cosy lounge, cable TV, laundry facilities, very helpful, luggage stored.

Camping Overnight vehicle parking at *Hostal Las Mercedes*, Av La Marina 1001, T/F213601. US$6 for 2 including use of toilet and shower.

Expensive *Anushka*, Santa Catalina 204. Open 1700-2100, or later if busy, occasional live music, German specialities, handicrafts for sale. *Ary Quepay*, Jerusalén 502. Excellent local meat and vegetarian dishes, open 1000-2400, slow service. *Picantería La Cantarilla*, Tahuaycani 106-108, Sachaca, T251515, southwest of the centre. Good Arequipeña and Peruvian dishes, including ostrich. *La Rueda*, Mercaderes 206. Excellent *parrilladas*. *Tradición Arequipeña*, Av Dolores 111, Paucarpata, T246467. Restaurant serving excellent food, popular with tourists and locals alike, also dance hall. There are many other restaurants and discos on this avenue, some distance from the centre.

Eating
● *on map*
Several restaurants overlook the Plaza de Armas; their staff may pounce on you good-naturedly as you pass

Mid-range *Le Bistrot*, Santa Catalina 208. Excellent crepes, good value set lunch, also snacks, cocktails, coffee. *Café-Restaurante Bóveda San Agustín*, Portal San Agustín 127-129. Attractive, good value breakfasts and lunches, evening specials, opens at 0700. *El Camaroncito*, San Francisco y Ugarte. Recommended for seafood, with a good fixed-price lunchtime menu. *La Casita de José Antonio*, Plaza San Francisco 401 y Zela. *Cevichería*, fish and seafood. *Challwa*, Moral 113. Peruvian dishes, including *ceviche*, burgers, pasta, seafood, owner speaks English, tourist information. *El Fogón*, Santa Marta 112. Serves large steaks and chops, good. *Gianni*, San Francisco 304. Good value for pasta and pizza. *Nómadas*, Melgar 306. Swiss and South American owned, breakfasts, wide menu including vegetarian, sandwiches. *Pizzería Los Leños*, Jerusalén 407. Excellent, good atmosphere, evenings only, popular, especially with tourists. *Pizzería San Antonio*, Jerusalén y Santa Marta. Popular. *La Quinta*, Jerusalén 522. Excellent food, large portions, quiet garden. *El Rincón Norteño* , San Francisco 300 B.

Recommended for seafood. *El Turko II*, San Francisco 315. Turkish, local and international. Recommended. *Zig Zag*, Zela 210, zigzagfood@mailcity.com In a colonial house, European (including Swiss) and local dishes, meats include ostrich and alpaca.

Cheap *Bonanza*, Jerusalén 114. Western-style food. *Café El Buho*, in Casona Chávez de la Rosa (UNSA), San Agustín. Evenings only. Recommended. *El Turko*, San Francisco 216. Kebabs, coffee, breakfasts recommended, good sandwiches, open 0700-2200.

Vegetarian *Casa Vegetariana*, Moral 205. Asian, typical local food and western dishes. *Govinda*, Santa Catalina 120, T285540. Set meal for US$1.25, themed each day, eg, Hindu, Italian, Arequipeño (mixed reports), good yoghurt and muesli. Mon-Sat 0700-2100. *Lakshmivan*, Jerusalén 402. Set lunch for US$1.25 (small portions), pleasant courtyard. *Mandala*, Jerusalén 207, mandala26@correoweb.com Good value, breakfast, 3 set menus for lunch, buffet, dinner, friendly staff. Recommended.

Cafés *El Café*, San Francisco 125. Popular meeting place. *Café Capriccio*, Mercaderes 121. Not that cheap, but excellent coffee, cakes, stuffed baked potatoes, pastas, sandwiches and juices. *La Canasta*, Jerusalén 115. Bakes excellent baguettes twice daily, also serves breakfast and delicious apple and brazil nut pastries. *Café Manolo*, Mercaderes 107 and 113. Great cakes and coffee, also cheap lunches. *Pushkin*, Ugarte 121B. Good for set breakfasts, crêpes, burgers, very friendly and pleasant.

Typical Arequipeño food is available at the San Camilo market. A good local speciality is Mejía cheese. You should also try the *queso helado*, which is frozen fresh milk mixed with sugar and a sprinkling of cinnamon. The local chocolate is excellent: *La Ibérica*, Jerusalén y Moral, is top quality, but expensive. The toffee and the fruit drinks called *papayada* and *tumbada* are also local specialities in the market and restaurants. Try *Casa Tropical*, on the first block of Rivero for a huge selection.

Bars & clubs *Le Café Art Montreal*, Santa Catalina 300B-1. Atmospheric Canadian-run jazz/blues restaurant/bar with live music Wed and Sat. *La Casa de Klaus*, Zela 207. German bar and restaurant, foreign beers, expensive but popular. *Forum*, San Francisco 317. Rock café, live music Thu-Sat 1800-0400, disco, pool tables, US$5 cover if band is playing, includes 1 drink, drinks US$1.50. *Déjà Vu*, San Francisco 319-B. Café/restaurant and bar, good food, DJ evenings, shows movies, 2000-2400. *Cactus*, Moral 223, caktus@terra.com.pe Good coffee, drinks, live music at weekends, piano concerts. Recommended. *Branighan's*, Jerusalén 522A. Blues bar, good music, live shows Sat, very friendly.

Clubs *Qashwa*, Santa Catalina 200, below *Hospedaje Los Balcones Moral y Santa Catalina*. Fri and Sat 2200 live music. There are many good dancing spots on Av Ejército in Yanahuara.

Festivals In Jan is *El Día del Reyes* in the district of Tiabaya, traditionally celebrated by shaking the fruit from pear trees. On **10 Jan** *Sor Ana de Los Angeles y Monteagudo* is a festival for the patron saint of Santa Catalina monastery. On **2-3 Feb** the *Fiesta de la Virgen de la Candelaria* is celebrated in the churches of Cayma, Characato, Chiguata and Chapi with masses, processions of the Virgin through the streets, and fireworks.

On **3 Mar** the *Fiesta de La Amargura* is a movable feast in Paucarpata, during which the Passion Play is enacted in the main plaza. *Domingo de Cuaresma*, in the district of Tiabaya, is also dedicated to Jesus Christ. Residents gather in the plaza and carry the cross from there up to a nearby hilltop, crossing the Río Chili.

The *Semana Santa* celebrations in Arequipa are carried out *Sevillano* style, with the townsfolk turned out in traditional mourning dress. There are huge processions every night, culminating in the burning of an effigy of Judas on **Easter Sunday** in the main plazas of Cayma and Yanahuara, and the reading of his 'will', containing criticisms of the city authorities. Afterwards, people retire to the *picanterías* to partake of a little *Adobo a la Antaño* with some *pan de tres puntas*.

On **1 May** the *Fiesta de la Virgen de Chapi* is a great pilgrimage to the sanctuary of Chapi and one of the most important religious ceremonies in the region. May is known as the *'Month of the Crosses'*, with ceremonies on hilltops throughout the city. On **15 May** the popular fiesta of **San Isidro Labrador** takes place in Sachaca, Chuquibamba and other towns and villages in the valley, and lasts for 7 days.

On **13 Jun** a remembrance of *San Antonio de Padua*, patron of hopeless cases, is held in the churches of Tingo Grande and San Francisco, among others. On **29 Jun**, in Yanahuara, the *Fiesta de San Juan*, the local patron saint, is held with mass and fireworks.

On **6-31 Aug** is the *Fiesta Artesanal del Fundo del Fierro*, a sale and exhibition of artesanía from all parts of Peru, taking place near Plaza San Francisco. At the same time, **6-17 Aug** is the celebration of the *city's anniversary*; various events are held, including music, dancing and exhibitions. On the eve of the actual day, the 15th, there is a splendid firework display in the Plaza de Armas and a decorated float parade. There is also a mass ascent of El Misti from the Plaza de Armas. It is virtually impossible to find a hotel room during the celebrations. On **30 Aug** *El Día de Santa Rosa* is celebrated in the churches of Tomilla, Cayma and Huancarqui in the Majes Valley.

In Arequipa **Nov** is also the month of the traditional *guaguas*, which are *bizcochos* (sponge cakes) filled with *manjar* (caramel made from boiling milk and sugar).

Shopping

Bookshops *Librería El Lector*, San Francisco 221. Wide selection, including of Peruvian authors, book exchange in various languages. *Librerías San Francisco* has branches at Portal de Flores 138, San Francisco 102-106 and 133-135. Books on Arequipa and Peru, some in English. For international magazines, look along San Francisco, between Mercaderes and San José. Old books and magazines are bought and sold at *Compra y Venta de Libros y Revistas*, on Calle Puente Grau.

Markets There are markets which are good for general handicrafts. The covered market opposite the Teatro Municipal on Mercaderes is recommended for knitted goods, bags, etc. Also worth a try is the market around Valdivia and Nicolas de Piérola. The large *Fundo del Fierro* handicraft market behind the old prison on Plaza San Francisco is also worth a visit. Shop 14 sells alpaca-wool handicrafts from Callalli in the Colca Canyon.

Casa Secchi, Av Víctor Andrés Belaunde 124, in Umacollo (near the aeroplane statue), sells good arts, crafts and clothing. *Sombrería El Triunfino*, N de Piérola 329-331, has a good selection of hats, but is expensive.

Leather Arequipa is also noted for its leather work. The main street of saddlers and leather workers is Puente Bolognesi. The handicraft shop in the old prison opposite San Francisco is particularly good for bags.

Photography *Foto Esparza*, Mercaderes 321-A-6132-2, T992783 (home 253125). Cameras mended. *Foto Mundo Color*, San Francisco 218-A, will develop good quality prints in 1 hr, US$3.50 for 24. *Sandy Color*, Santa Catalina 118D.

Wool Arequipa is an excellent place to buy top quality alpaca knitwear. *Alpaca 111*, Zela 212, T223238. Recommended for high-quality alpaca and wool products, also in Claustros del Compañía, local 18, T205931. *Alpaca 21*, Jerusalén 115, of 125, T213425. Also recommended. *Colca Trading Company*, Santa Catalina 300B, T283737, pakucho@terra. com.pe Sells a wide variety of naturally-coloured cotton and alpaca clothing for adults and children. *Lanificio*, La Pampilla sin número, T225305, is a factory selling high-quality alpaca cloth at better prices than Lima outlets.

Tour operators

These agencies have been recommended as helpful and reliable. Most run tours to the Colca Canyon (see page 278)

Castle Travel, Santo Domingo 302, castle@castletravel.com.pe Arrange all kinds of local tours, friendly. *Conresa Tours*, Jerusalén 409, T285420/247186 (24 hrs T602355), conresa tours@rch.com.pe *Holley's Unusual Excursions*, T/F258459 (home) any day 1700-0700, or all day Sat and Sun, or Mon-Fri 0800-1600 T222525/225000 and leave a message, angocho@terra.com.pe, http://barrioperu.terra.com.pe/angocho Expat Anthony Holley runs trips in his Land Rover to El Misti, Toro Muerto, the desert and coast. *Ideal Travels SAC*, Urb San Isidro F-2, Vallecito, T244439, F242088, idealperu@ terra.com.pe Mon-Fri 0800-1900, Sat 0830-1300, tours to Colca Canyon (2 days, 1 night, US$45-75, depending on accommodation, private service, all meals, rafting US$33), Cotahuasi Canyon, Andagua Volcanic valley, Majes River, Cotahuasi River, Toro Muerto, jeep and microbus rentals, excellent bilingual guides, international ticket reservations, accepts credit cards. *Illary Tours*, Santa Catalina 205, T220844. English-speaking guides. Daily 0800-1300, 1500-1930. *Inca Trail Tours*, Jerusalén 203. OK. *Naturaleza Activa*, Santa Catalina 211, T204182, naturactiva@yahoo.com Experienced guides, knowledgeable, climbing and trekking. *Santa Catalina Tours*, Santa Catalina 219-223, T216994. Offer unique tours of Collagua communities in the Colca Canyon. Daily 0800-1900. Recommended. *Servicios Aéreos AQP SA*, T/F281800, airport T443466, 24hrs T650206. Head office in Lima, Los Castaños 347, San Isidro, T01-222 3312, F01-222 5910, www.saaqp.com.pe Offers tours to Arequipa, Colca and to all parts of the country. *Transcontinental Arequipa*, Puente Bolognesi 132, oficina 5, T213843, F218608, transcontinental-aqp@terra.com.pe Cultural and wildlife tours in the Colca Canyon. *Volcanyon Travel*, C Villalba 414, T205078, mario-ortiz@terra.com.pe Trekking and some mountain bike tours in the Colca Canyon, also volcano climbing. Guide Jorg Krosel, T997971, joergkrosel@hotmail.com or contact through *Wasi Tours*, Santa Catalina 207. German guide who also speaks English, enthusiastic, efficient, trekking, oxygen carried on high-altitude trips, including Colca. A recommended guide for climbing, trekking, mountain biking and river rafting in the Colca Canyon is Vlado Soto, Campamento Base, Jerusalén 401 B, T2027687, jbustios@ ucsm.edu.pe He is knowledgeable and helpful and also rents equipment. Another climbing guide recommended as experienced is Julver Castro, who has an agency called *Mountrekk*, T601833, julver_mountrekk@hotmail.com For general tours, *Gerardo J Pinto Abraca*, geratour@yahoo.com Speaks good English, helpful, lots of information.

Many agencies on Jerusalén, Santa Catalina and around Plaza de Armas sell air, train and bus tickets and offer tours of Colca, Cotahuasi, Toro Muerto, Campiña and city. Prices vary greatly so shop around. As a general rule, you get what you pay for, so check carefully what is included in the cheapest of tours. Always settle the details before starting the tour and check that there are enough people for the tour to run. Many tourists prefer to contract tours through their hotel. If a travel agency puts you in touch with a guide, make sure he or she is official. It is not advisable to book tours to Machu Picchu here. Make these arrangements in Cusco.

Climbing *Zárate Expeditions*, Santa Catalina 204, of 3, T202461/263107. Run by Carlos and Miguel Zárate of the Mountaineering Club of Peru. They are mountaineers and explorers, who have information and advice and rent some equipment. Carlos also runs trips to the source of the Amazon.

Air Airport information T443464. At the airport are two desks offering hotel reserva- **Transport** tions (not always accurate) and free transport to town, a travel agency (*Domiruth*) and *Avis* car rental. To and from **Lima**, several flights daily with *LanPerú, Aero Continente/ Aviandina* and *Tans*. These airlines also serve **Juliaca**. Also daily flights to **Cusco** with *Aero Continente* and *Lan Perú*.

A reliable means of transport to and from the airport to the hotel of your choice is with *King Tours*, T243357/283037, US$1.30 per person. You need to give 24 hrs notice for the return pick-up from your hotel. The journey takes 30-40 mins depending on the traffic. **Transport to the airport** may be arranged when buying a ticket at a travel agency, for US$1 per person, but it's not always reliable. **Local buses** go to about 500 m from the airport.

Bus All buses leave from one of the two terminals at Av Andrés A Cáceres s/n, Parque Industrial, opposite *Inca Tops* factory, south of the centre; 15 mins by colectivo US$0.20, or taxi US$1.75. The older terminal is called Terminal Terrestre, which contains a tourist office, shops and places to eat. The newer terminal is Terrapuerto, the other side of the carpark, also with a tourist office (which makes hotel reservations with free transfer to affiliated hotels) and its own hostal (**E** without breakfast), T421375. A terminal tax of US$0.30 must be paid on entry to the platform. Check which terminal your bus will leave from as it may not depart from the terminal where you bought your ticket ('*¿Por dónde me embarco, Terminal o Terrapuerto?*') All the bus companies have their offices in the Terminal Terrestre and several also have offices in Terrapuerto. Some companies also have offices around C San Juan de Dios (5-6 blocks from the Plaza de Armas), where tickets can be bought in advance, saving a trip to the terminal. Addresses are given below. **Warning** Theft is a serious problem in the bus station area. Take a taxi to and from the bus station and do not wander around with your belongings. No one is allowed to enter the terminal 2100-0500, so new arrivals cannot be met by hoteliers between those hours; best not to arrive at night.

To **Lima**, 1,011 km, 16-18 hrs, 'normal' service US$8.70, 'imperial' US$17.40 (video, toilet, meals, comfortable seats, blankets), 'crucero' US$23-29 several daily; *Enlaces* (T430333, office only in Terrapuerto), *Flores* (T238741), *Ormeño* (T423975, or San Juan de Dios 657, T218885) and *Cruz del Sur* (T216625, or Av Salaverry 121, T213905) are recommended (prices quoted are of Cruz del Sur). The road is paved but drifting sand and breakdowns may prolong the trip. Buses will stop at the major cities en route, but not always Pisco. The desert scenery is spectacular.

To **Nasca**, 566 km, 9 hrs, US$7.25-10 (US$30 on *Ormeño Royal* service), several buses daily, mostly at night and most buses continue to Lima. Beware, some bus companies to Nasca charge the Lima fare. To **Moquegua**, 213 km, 3 hrs, US$3-5.85, several buses and colectivos daily. To **Tacna**, 320 km, 6-7 hrs, US$3.85-4.40, several buses daily, most with *Flores*.

To **Cusco**, 521 km, 12 bumpy hrs direct, eg with *Carhuamayo* at 0700, 1700 and 1800, US$6-7.50. Otherwise go via Juliaca or Puno, US$8.75. There is a new, quick paved road to **Juliaca**, via Yura amd Santa Lucía, cutting the Arequipa-Juliaca journey time to 5 hrs, US$5.80, and **Puno**, 6 hrs, US$6. Most buses and colectivos continue to Puno. Just about all bus companies are now using the new route, with double-decker buses (bath, TV, hostess, etc). Another paved route runs Arequipa-Moquegua-Desaguadero-Puno-Juliaca: 12 hrs to **Puno** and 13 hrs to **Juliaca**, US$6-10.

Arequipa

Car hire *Avis*, Palacio Viejo 214, T282519, or at the airport T443576. *Transjesa*, Jr Victoria 122, Urb Manuel Prado, Paucarpata, T655594, F460403, transjesa@rh.com.pe Also at the airport. Good value and new vehicles. **Car repairs**: *FCI, Fidel Condorvilca*, Cacique Alpaca 205, Cayma, T271175. **Bicycle repairs and equipment**: *Andes Bike*, Villalba 414, T205078 (see *Volcanyon Travel*, above).

Trains The railway system goes from Arequipa to Juliaca, where it divides, one line going north to Cusco, the other south to Puno. With the opening of the new Arequipa-Juliaca highway, the decreased demand for rail travel led to the suspension of regular passenger services on this route. *PerúRail* runs trains for private charter of for groups of over 40. There are plans to reopen the route in 2003, although this has not been confirmed. The service Puno-Juliaca-Cuzco is running as usual.

Directory **Airline offices** All airline offices are on the Plaza de Armas: *Aero Continente/ Aviandina*, Portal San Agustín 113, T207294. *LanPerú*, Santa Catalina 118-C, T 201100. *Tans*, Portal San Agustín 143A, T205231. For private hire and tourist flights to the Colca Canyon. Most tour agencies sell air tickets. Prices are quoted in dollars but payment is in soles so check exchange rate carefully.

   Banks *Interbank*, Mercaderes 217. Mastercard representative and ATM. *BCP*, San Juan de Dios 125, also at Santo Domingo y Jerusalén. Accepts Visa Card (has ATM) and gives good rates, no commission. Recommended. *BBV Continental*, San Francisco 108. Visa ATM. *BSCH*, C Jerusalén, close to the Post Office. Changes Visa and Citicorp TCs, low rates, accepts Mastercard, has Visa ATM. *Banco Wiese*, Mercaderes 410. Change money at *cambios* on Jerusalén and San Juan de Dios, and several travel agencies. *Sergio A del Carpio D*, Jerusalén 126, T242987, good rates for dollars. *Via Tours*, Santo Domingo 114, good rates. *Casa de Cambio*, San Juan de Dios 109, T282528, good rates. It is almost impossible to change TCs on Sat afternoon or Sun; try to find a sympathetic street changer. Better rates for cash dollars in banks and *casas de cambio*.

   Communications Internet: *C@tedr@l*, Pasaje Catedral 101, T220622, internetcatedral@hotmail.com 0800-2400, fast machines, international calls. *Chips Internet*, San Francisco 202-A, chips@chips.com.pe *La Red Café Internet*, Jerusalén 306, café@LaRed.net.pe 0830-2200, US$0.45 per hr, good for netphone. Also on Jerusalén: *Tienes un Email*, No 306B, and *Tr@vel Net*, No 218, US$0.75 per hr and international phone calls. *Líder Tours*, Portal San Agustín 105, Plaza de Armas, www.lider.lared.net.pe, US$0.75 per hr. *Net Central*, Alvarez Thomas 219, netcentral@netcentral. lared.net.pe 0900-2300, fast machines. *Cybercafé.com*, Santa Catalina 115-B, at Easy Market. US$0.75 per hr. Another at Puente Bolognesi 108. 0700-2300.

   Post office: (central) is at Moral 118, opposite *Hotel Crismar*. Letters can only be posted at the post office during opening hrs. Mon-Sat, 0800-2000, Sun 0800-1400. *DHL*, Santa Catalina 115, T234288/250045, for sending documents and money. Also Western Union representative. *World Courier*, T241925, F218139. **Telephone and fax**: at Alvarez Thomas y Palacio Viejo.

   Cultural centres *Instituto Cultural Peruano-Norte Americano*, in the Casa de los Mendiburo, Melgar 109, T243201. Has an **English Library**. *Instituto Cultural Peruano Alemán*, Ugarte 207, T228130. *Instituto Regional de Cultura*, Gen Morán 118 (altos), T213171. *Instituto Nacional de Cultura*, Alameda San Lázaro 120, T213171. *Alianza Francesa*, Santa Catalina 208, T215579, F286777, aptdo 2724, www.ambafrancia.com.pe With *Le Bistrot*, see Eating.

   Consulates *Bolivia*, Mercaderes 212, of 405, T205703. Mon-Fri 0900-1400, 24 hrs for visa (except those needing clearance from La Paz), go early. *Chile*, Mercaderes 212, p 4, Of 401-402, Galerías Gameza, T/F233556/933556, entrance to lift 30m down passageway down Mercaderes on left. Mon-Fri 0900-1300, present passport 0900-1100 if you need a visa. *France*, Estadio Oeste 201-A, IV Centenario, T232119 (Sun T224915).

Mon-Fri 1530-1900. *Germany*, in Colegio Max Uhle, Av Fernandini s/n, Sachaca. Mon-Fri 0900-1300, Casilla 743, T232921. *Italy*, La Salle D-5, T221444. 1130-1300, in the afternoon T254686 (home). *Netherlands*, Mercaderes 410 (Banco Wiese), Sr Herbert Ricketts, T219567, F215437, Casilla 1. Mon-Fri 0900-1300, 1630-1830. *Spain*, Ugarte 218, p 2, T214977 (home T224915). Mon-Fri 1100-1300, Sat 0900-1300. *Sweden*, Av Villa Hermosa 803, Cerro Colorado, T259847/252868. Mon-Fri 0830-1300, 1500-1730. *Switzerland*, Av Miguel Forga 348, Parque Industrial, T232723/229998. *UK*, Mr Roberts, Tacna y Arica 156, T241340, gerencia@roberts.rh.com.pe Mon-Fri 0830-1230, 1500-1830, reported as very friendly and helpful.

Language courses *Centro de Intercambio Cultural Arequipa (CEICA)*, Urb Universitaria G-9, T/F231759. Classes at US$5 per hr, accommodation with families arranged, with board (US$70 per week) or without (US$30), also excursions. Recommended. *Silvana Cornejo*, 7 de Junio 118, Cerrito Los Alvarez, Cerro Colorado, T254985. US$6 per hr, negotiable for group, she speaks German fluently and is recommended. Her sister Roxanna charges US$3 per hr. Fidelia and Charo Sánchez, T224238, are recommended, Fidelia speaks French, and Charo speaks English. Classes are also available at the Instituto Peruano-Norte Americano and Instituto Cultural Peruano Alemán (see Cultural Centres).

Laundry *Lavanderías Chick*, Ugarte 101. *Magic Laundry*, Jerusalén 404B and La Merced 125. Coin-operated, open daily. *Lavendería del Pueblo*, Ejercicios 558. *Don Marcelo*, T421411 (morning), T229245 (afternoon). Delivery service.

Medical services Hospitals: *Regional Honorio Delgado*, Av A Carrión s/n, T238465/233812/231818 (inoculations). *General Base Goyeneche*, Av Goyeneche s/n, T211313. *Nacional del Sur*, Filtro y Peral s/n, T214430 in emergency. Clinics: *Clínica Arequipa SA*, esquina Puente Grau y Av Bolognesi, T253424/416. Fast and efficient with English-speaking doctors and all hospital facilities, consultation costs US$18, plus US$4 for sample analysis and around US$7 for a course of antibiotics. *Monte Carmelo*, Gómez de la Torre 119, T231444, T/F287048. *Paz Holandesa*, Av Jorge Chávez 527, T/F206720, www.pazholandesa.com Dutch foundation dedicated to helping impoverished, which also has a travel clinic for tourists. Dutch and English spoken, 24-hr service. Highly recommended (see their website if you are interested in volunteering). *San Juan de Dios*, Av Ejército 1020, Cayma, T252256/255544. **Ambulance**: T289800 (24 hrs). **Pharmacy:** *Farmacia Libertad*, Piérola 108. Owner speaks English.

Around Arequipa

Yura, is a pleasant town, 29 km from Arequipa in a small, interesting valley on the west slopes of Chachani. It is popular with Arequipeños for its **thermal baths** and verdant riverside picnic spots. To reach the baths, walk down to the river from the main road by the *Yura Tourist Hotel* (see below). The first set of baths contains four small pools which are not suitable for swimming. Follow the river to the next one, which is bigger. Note that the water is not very hot. ■ *Tue-Sat, until 1500. US$1.50. To return to Arequipa, catch a colectivo on the main road by the hotel.*

Yura
Colour map 5, grid C6

Sleeping D *Yura Tourist Hotel*, with bath, meals available. There's also an unsigned hotel opposite, **F**, which is good. A bus to Yura leaves every 3 hrs from C San Juan de Dios in Arequipa, US$0.40.

At 5,822 m, El Misti volcano offers a relatively straightforward opportunity to scale a high peak. Start from the hydroelectric plant, after first registering with the police there, then you need one day to the Monte Blanco shelter, at 4,800 m. Start early for the 4-6 hours to the top, to get there by 1100 before the mists

El Misti
Colour map 5, grid C6

obscure the view. If you start back at 1200 you will reach the hydroelectric plant by 1800. Take a jeep at 3,300 m to the end of the rough road, then 4-5 hrs hike to the campground at 4,600 m. Only space for 3 tents (2-3 person tents).

Alternatively, buses leave Arequipa for Baños Jesús, then on to Chiguata, from where you can walk to the base of El Misti. Guides may be available at Cachamarca. Be sure to take plenty of food, water and protection against the weather; it takes two days to reach the crater. Remember that the summit is at a very high altitude and that this, combined with climbing on scree, makes it hard going for the untrained. Recent reports of hold-ups of climbers make it inadvisable for you to go alone. Join a group or take a guide. Further information is available from travel agencies and Miguel and Carlos Zárate (address under Tour Operators, Climbing, page 274).

The Colca Canyon

Colour map 5, grid B6   *The Colca Canyon is twice as deep as the Grand Canyon and was thought to be the deepest canyon in the world – until the nearby Cotahuasi Canyon was found to be all of 163 m deeper. This is an area of astounding beauty. Giant amphitheatres of pre-Inca terracing become narrow, precipitous gorges, and in the background looms the grey, smoking mass of Sabancaya, one of the most active volcanoes in the Americas, and its more docile neighbour, Ampato. Unspoiled Andean villages lie on both sides of the canyon, inhabited by the Cabana and Collagua peoples.*

Background

The Río Colca snakes its way through the length of this massive gorge, 3,500 m above sea level at Chivay (the canyon's main town) falling to 2,200 m at Cabanaconde, at the far end of the canyon. The roads on either side of the canyon are at around 4,000 m and Nevado Ampato, a short distance to the south, rises to 6,288 m.

The name Colca derives from the Inca practice of storing harvested crops in sealed vaults which they called *colcas*, carved into the canyon walls. Now, though, the name has become associated with a rather large bird. Would-be David Attenboroughs flock here for a close encounter with the giant Andean condor at the aptly-named *Cruz del Cóndor*. But the canyon has much more to offer than this, notably its culture and its magnificent landscapes.

Despite its history, this part of southern Peru was practically unknown to the outside world until the late 1970s when a Polish team made the first descent by raft and canoe. The canyon appears on 19th century maps and the first aerial reconnaissance was made in 1929 by US Navy Lt George R Johnson (published as *Peru from the Air* by the American Geographical Society, 1930). In 1931 Johnson returned by land with Robert Shippee and the account of their Shippee-Johnson Peruvian Expedition was reported in the *Geographical Review* of the American Geographical Society in October 1932 ('Lost Valleys of Peru') and the *National Geographic* of January 1934.

The Colca Canyon was 're-discovered' from the air again in 1954 by Gonzalo de Reparaz. Two good studies of the region are *El Valle del Colca. Cinco Siglos de Arquitectura y Urbanismo*, by Ramón Gutiérrez (Buenos Aires, 1986) and *Discovering the Colca Valley*, by Mauricio de Romaña, with photographs by Jaume Blassi and Jordi Blassi (Barcelona, 1987). (With thanks to Daniel Buck, Washington DC.)

Camelid fibre

Four-thousand years before the Spanish conquistadors set foot on Peruvian soil, the indigenous peoples excelled at the textile arts. This age-old weaving tradition would not have been possible, however, without the necessary raw materials.

While cotton was cultivated for this purpose on the arid coast, up on the high Andean plain there was a ready supply of weaving fibre in the shape of the native camelids – llamas, alpacas, vicuñas and guanacos – which are distant cousins to the camel. The alpacas and llamas are thought to have been domesticated as early as 4,000 BC.

The fibres and skins of the wild camelids – guanacos and vicuñas – were used prior to domestication of their cousins. In fact, guanaco skins were used as clothing by the early hunters who roamed the bleak, high Andean plateau, or altiplano, before 4,000 BC.

By 1,500-1,000 BC there is evidence of domesticated camelids on the coast while llamas were being used for ritual burial offerings, indicating their increasing prestige. Thus, the importance of camelids to Andean man, both in practical and ideological terms, was probably a long-established tradition by this time.

Because camelid fibre is so easy to spin and dye, the ancient weavers developed extraordinarily fine spinning techniques. The precolumbian peoples prized the silky-soft fibre of the alpaca, in particular. Living at altitudes of 4,000 m, where temperatures can drop to -15°C, these animals have adapted to the extreme conditions and developed a coat that not only has thermal properties but is also soft and resistant.

It is these qualities that have led to worldwide demand. Production of alpaca fibre, however, remains low owing to the fact that more than 75% of Peru's alpacas are in the hands of small breeders and peasant communities who still herd and manage their animals in much the same way as their ancestors.

Ins and outs

Getting there Most buses follow the new road via Yura following the railway, which is being developed as a new route to Cusco from Arequipa. This is longer, but quicker, than the old route through Cayma. *Cristo Rey*, *La Reyna* and *Andalucia* (recommended) have 7 departures daily from Arequipa to **Chivay**, continuing to **Cabanaconde**; a further 75 km, 2 hrs, US$1. *La Reyna* has the quickest service, about 6 hrs, US$3.85, others US$3. Buy a ticket in advance to ensure a seat. It is a rough route and cold in the morning, reaching 4,825 m at the Pata Pampa pass, but the views are worth it. In the rainy season it is better to travel by day as the road can get icy and slippery at night. Buses return to Arequipa from the market. Buses all leave from the main terminal in Arequipa but you can get your ticket the previous day at the bus company offices in C San Juan de Dios.

For **Cabanaconde** and **Cruz del Cóndor** catch the 0500 bus from Chivay which stops briefly at the Mirador at 0700 (if this doesn't seem likely, ask), US$0.75. Combis run infrequently in each direction, none on Sun. You could also try hitching a lift with a tour bus.

Combis and colectivos go from near the central market in Chivay to any village in the area. Ask the drivers. *Combis* leave from beside the market for **Achoma** (every ½ hr), **Maca** (every hr), **Ichupampa** (every hr) and **Puente Callalli** (every hr). It is difficult to go to Cusco from Chivay: you can take a colectivo to Puente Callalli, but the police there are unwilling to let passengers wait for a passing Cusco-bound bus, which may not stop anyway. Best to go back to Arequipa.

Best time to visit From Jan-Apr is the rainy season, but this makes the area green, with lots of flowers. This is not the best time to see condors. May-Dec is the dry, cold season when there is more chance of seeing the birds.

Tours of the   Travel agencies in Arequipa arrange a 'one-day' tour to the **Cruz del Cóndor** for
Colca Canyon   US$18-20. They leave Arequipa at 0400, arriving at the Cruz del Cóndor at 0800-0900,
followed by an expensive lunch stop at Chivay and back to Arequipa by 2100. For
many, especially for those with altitude problems, this is too much to fit into one day
(the only advantage is that you don't have to sleep at high altitude). Two day tours start
at US$20-30 per person with an overnight stop in **Chivay**; more expensive tours range
from US$45 to US$75 with accommodation at the top of the range. You should allow
at least 2-3 days, more if planning to do some trekking, when visiting the Colca Canyon. Travel agents frequently work together in a 'pooling' system to fill buses (even the
more expensive agencies may not have their own transport) and there are lots of touts.
This can mean that a busload of tourists will come from different agencies, all paying
different prices, but all expecting the same level of service. On occasion the company
providing the transport may not have the same high standards as the operator
through whom the tour was booked.

Festivals   This is a region of wild and frequent festivals. On **2-3 Feb** *Virgen de la Candelaria* is celebrated in the towns of Chivay and Cabanaconde, with dancing in the plaza, and over 5
days in Maca and Tapay. *Semana Santa* is celebrated with particular gusto in the villages of the Colca Canyon.

   27 Apr is the celebration of the apostle Santiago. During **Apr** and **May** many festivals
are held in the Colca canyon: *La Cruz de Piedra* is celebrated over 5 days in **May** in the
main plaza in Tuti, near Chivay. On **13 Jun** *San Antonio* is celebrated in the villages of
Maca, Callalli and Yanque. On **14 Jun**, in Sibayo and Ichupampa, the *Fiesta de San Juan* is
held over 5 days. On **21 Jun** is the anniversary of the district of Chivay in Cailloma.

   On **14-17 Jul** the *Fiesta de la Virgen del Carmen* is held in Cabanaconde and
Pampacolca, when folk dancing takes place in the streets. Of particular interest is the
dance of *Los Turcos*, which represents the indigenous peoples' struggle against the
conquistadors. This fiesta is also held in the churches of Yura, Carmen Alto, Congata,
Tingo Grande and the Convent of Santa Teresa in Arequipa city. On **25 Jul** in
Coporaque and Madrigal, in the Colca canyon, is the *Fiesta de Santiago Apostol*. From
26 Jul to 2 Aug various religious ceremonies, accompanied by dancing, are held in
honour of the *Virgen Santa Ana* in Maca.

   On **15 Aug** in Chivay is the fiesta of the *Virgen de la Asunta*, the town's patron saint,
which lasts 8 days. In **Sep** in Tisco, the *Virgen de la Natividad* is held over 5 days. On **8
Dec**, *Inmaculada Concepción* is held in Chivay and Yanque, when groups of musicians
and dancers present the traditional dance, the *Witite*, lasting 5 days. On **25 Dec** once
again in Yanque, just in case you haven't had enough, the *Witite* is held over 6 days.

Arequipa to Chivay

Colour map 5,   A poor, very bumpy dirt road runs north from Arequipa, over the altiplano,
grid B/C6   to Chivay, the first village on the edge of the Canyon. The road affords fine
views of the volcanoes Misti, Chachani, Ampato and the active Sabancaya.
■ *US$2 entrance fee to the Colca Canyon (not included in agency prices).
Despite being the main road from Arequipa to Chivay, this is not suitable for
ordinary cars: 4-wheel drive is best. Cyclists should use the new road via Yura; it is
in better condition and there is less of a climb at the start. Paving is under way on
the road to Chivay.*

   About an hour out of Arequipa, on the road to Chivay, is the **Aguada
Blanca National Vicuña Reserve**. If you're lucky, you can see herds of these
rare and timid camelids near the road. If taking a bus to the reserve to
vicuña-watch, there should be enough traffic on the road to be able to hitch a
ride back to Arequipa in the evening.

Appeasing the Gods

To the Incas, Nevado Ampato, in the Colca region, was a sacred god who brought life-giving water and good harvests and, as a god claimed the highest tribute, the sacrifice of one of their own.

In September 1995, anthropologist, Johan Reinhard, of Chicago's Field Museum of Natural History, accompanied by Peruvian climber, Miguel Zárate, whose brother, Carlos is a well-known Arequipa mountain guide, were climbing Ampato when they made a startling discovery, at about 6,000 m. They found the perfectly preserved mummified body of an Inca girl. Wrapped tightly in textiles, this girl in her early teens must have been ritually sacrificed and buried on the summit.

Mummies of Inca human sacrifices have been found before on Andean summits, but the girl from Ampato, nicknamed Juanita, is the first frozen Inca female to be unearthed and her body may be the best preserved of any found in the Americas from pre-Columbian times. The discovery is considered of worldwide importance, as the body is so well-preserved. The intact body tissues and organs of naturally mummified, frozen bodies are a storehouse of biological information. Studies will reveal how she died, where she came from, who her living relatives are and even yield valuable insights about the Inca diet.

Juanita's clothes are no less remarkable. The richly patterned, dazzling textiles will serve as the model for future depictions of the way noble Inca women dressed. Her lliclla – a bright red and white shawl beneath the outer wrappings – has been declared "the finest Inca woman's textile in the world".

Ampato, with its icy summit, may seem an unlikely Inca ceremonial site. However, the mountain was described as one of the principal deities in the Colca Canyon region. The Incas appeased the mountain gods, who were said to supply water to their villages and fields, with children as sacrifices. The Cabana and Collagua people even bound their children's heads to make them look like the mountains from which they believed they were descended.

A subsequent ascent of Ampato revealed a further two mummies at the summit. One is a young girl and the other, though badly charred by lightning, is believed to be a boy. If so, it may mean that these children were ritually sacrificed together in a symbolic marriage.

Nowadays, villages in the Colca continue to make offerings to the mountain gods for water and good harvests, but thankfully the gods have modified their tastes, now preferring chicha to children.

Chivay is the main linking point between the two sides of the canyon. A road heads northeast to **Tuti**, where there is a small handicrafts shop, and **Sibayo**, with a *pensión* and grocery store. A long circuit back to Arequipa heads south from Sibayo, passing through **Puente Callalli** (where Arequipa buses can sometimes be caught for Cusco), **Chullo** and **Sumbay**. This is a little-travelled road, but the views of fine landscapes with vicuña, llamas, alpacas and Andean duck are superb.

Arequipa

Another road from Sibayo goes northwest, following the northern side of the Colca mountain range to **Cailloma**, **Orcopampa** and **Andagua** (see page 289). Water from the Colca river has been diverted through a series of tunnels and canals to the desert between Repartición and Camaná, to irrigate the Majes pampa.

Crossing the river at Chivay going west to follow the canyon on the far side, you pass the villages of **Coporaque**, **Ichupampa** (a footbridge crosses the river between the two villages and foot and road bridges connect the road between Coporaque and Ichupampa with Yanque), **Lari**, **Madrigal** (a footbridge connects to Maca) and **Tapay** (connected by a footbridge to Cabanaconde).

Chivay

Colour map 5, grid B6

Chivay is the gateway to the canyon and the overnight stopping point for two-day tours run by agencies in Arequipa. At 3,600 m, the nights are cold.

The hot springs of **La Calera** are 4 km away. To get there take one of the regular colectivos (US$0.25) from beside the market or it's a pleasant hour-long walk. There are several large hot pools and showers but only one pool is open to tourists; entry US$1.25. The hot springs are highly recommended after a hard day's trekking. From La Calera you can trek through the Canocota canyon to Canocota (4-5 hours), or take a colectivo to Canocota and hike to La Calera), a beautiful trip, but ask directions. A reconstructed *chullpa* on the hilltop across Puente Inca gives good views over the town. There is a very helpful **tourist office** in the Municipalidad on the west side of the plaza which gives away a useful map of the valley. The tourist police, also on the plaza, can give advice about locally trained guides.

Sleeping
Ask if your hotel can provide heating

C *Rumillacta*, 3 blocks from the plaza off the Arequipa road, T521098. Attractive cabins with hot showers and a cosy bar/dining area serving good alpaca steaks. Recommended. **C** *Wasi Kolping*, 10 blocks south of the town, opposite the Plaza de Toros, T521076. Comfortable cabins with hot shower, very clean and quiet, good views.

D *El Posada del Inca*, Salaverry 330, T521032. Modern, with hot showers, carpeted rooms, safe, clean and friendly. **E** *Hostal Anita*, on the north side of the plaza. Clean, with bathroom, rooms look onto a small garden, friendly. Recommended. **E** *Inca*, on Salaverry. Spacious rooms, good restaurant, vehicle parking. **F** *La Casa de Lucila*, M Grau 131, T054-607086, with bath, comfortable, coffee, guides available. **F** *Hospedaje Jessy*, Zarumilla 218, 1 block from market. Simple, clean, excellent showers, **G** without bath, helpful, parking. **F** per person *Los Leños*, on Bolognesi, 1 block from the plaza and 1 block to the left. Clean, safe, very friendly, excellent breakfast and tomato soup. Recommended. **F** *Hospedaje Restaurant Los Portales*, Sucre, T521101. Good accommodation, breakfast US$0.75, same price for dinner in restaurant. **G** pp *Rumi Wasi*, C Sucre, 6 blocks from plaza (3 mins' walk). New, good rooms, breakfast included, hot water, helpful.

Many of the better hotels are regularly used by tour groups. There are several other hotels and family homes where you can stay; ask around.

Eating

There are several good, attractively decorated restaurants in Chivay, which are both cosy and friendly. They serve good value set meals for around US$3 which offer a choice of dishes. Not all restaurants are open at night. *Casa Blanca*, on the main plaza, good, main dishes US$2.50-7.50. *Fonda del Cazador*, on the north side of the plaza, serves delicious alpaca steaks. *Farren's*, bar run by a Peruvian and an Irishman, handmade Guinness sign outside, warm, friendly, good selection of drinks, sandwiches and music, also bikes for hire. Other good places to eat include *Ricardito* and *Posada del Cóndor*, both on Salaverry. The latter hires out traditional local costumes at US$2 per hr, for both men and women, but only in smaller sizes. Local food can be found at *Don Angel*, near the health centre, and *La Pascana*, near the Plaza de Armas, both cheap.

For bike hire and rafting tours, *Colca Adventures*, 22 de Agosto 101, T531137, **Tour operators**
rcordova@terra.com.pe Or T531081, jonyma@terramail.com.pe Good machines and
equipment, very helpful. The owner is Oscar Vela and the guide is Miguel Rumaldo
Mamani Huanca.

Banks The *Banco de la Nación* on the plaza in Chivay will change dollars cash. Travel- **Directory**
lers' cheques and credit cards are seldom accepted so take plenty of cash.

Treks from Chivay

From Chivay you can hike to **Coporaque** (1¾ hrs) and **Ichupampa** (a further
1½ hrs), cross the river by the footbridge and climb up to **Yanque** (1 hr), from
where it's an 8-km hike back to Chivay. It's better to follow the road, which
seems longer, or you'll end up lost in a maze of terraced fields. Half an hour
above Coporaque there are interesting **cliff tombs** and just beyond the village
the Huari ruins of **Ullu Ullu**. The foot and road bridges to Yanque (see below)
are between Coporaque and Ichupampa. If you feel too tired to walk back to
Chivay, catch a colectivo from the plaza in Yanque for US$0.25. It takes two
days to walk from Chivay to Cabanaconde (70 km), you can camp along the
route. You will have to walk all day in the sun – there is no shade. You'll need
plenty of drinking water and sun block.

To visit the source of the Amazon and the Río Carhuasanta (at about **To the source**
5,000 m), take a colectivo from Chivay to Tuti (50 mins, US$0.60). In Tuti ask **of the Amazon**
for the guide Emeterio Quicano, T280365, who is very experienced and will
take you there and back in three days. You will need a tent, sleeping bag, all
food, etc. The scenery is astonishing. (See also Carlos Zárate under Climbing,
Arequipa, page 274.)

Chivay to Cabanaconde

From Chivay, the main road goes west along the Colca Canyon. The first village **Yanque**
encountered, after 8 km, is Yanque – excellent views. There's an interesting
church and a bridge to the villages on the other side of the canyon. Beside the
renovated Inca bridge on the Yanque to Ichupampa road, a 20-minute walk
from Yanque plaza, is a large, warm **thermal swimming pool**. ■ *US$0.75.*

Yanque A *Tradición Colca*, on main road. Contact Carelia and Emmanuel Derouet, **Sleeping**
Jerusalén 300C, T205336, F424926, www.tradicioncolca.8m.com Price includes **outside Chivay**
breakfast, with gardens, restaurant, bar, games room, new; they also have a travel
agency. **F** *Posada de Yanque*, run by Remi and Vitaliana Suyco. Nice rooms, traditional
meals, guiding to local sites. Recommended. One other *Hostal*, **AL** *Parador del Colca*,
paradorcolca@chasqui.lared.net.pe 3½ km from Yanque, 10 km from Chivay Built of
local materials, with solar power, on an old estate, the hotel offers lots of activities;
comfortable suites, typical food, meals extra. Recommended.

In **Coporaque**, Sr Mejía offers lodging in his *Casa del Turista Mayta Cápac*, on the
plaza. Ask to see Sr Mejía's collection of old pictures; he also knows some good excursions. **Between Coporaque and Ichupampa** is **AL** *Colca Lodge* (in Arequipa Jerusalén
212, T202587, F220407, www.colca-lodge.com/index.htm). Very pleasant and relaxing,
with beautiful hot springs beside the river, trekking, cycling, riding, rafting, spend at least

Arequipa

a day there to make the most of what's on offer. Recommended. In **Ichupampa** is *Casa del Turista Inca*, family lodging where Lourdes can act as a guide; in the morning, watch the bread being made, and don't miss the chance to taste it.

West from Yanque

The next village after Yanque is **Achoma**, 30 minutes from Chivay along the Cabanaconde road. There is an old settlement where you can camp.

The road continues to **Maca**, which barely survived an earthquake in November 1991. New housing has been built. Then comes the tiny village of **Pinchollo**, with a basic *hostal* on the plaza (a room full of beds and one shared bathroom). There are no restaurants but you can eat at the *comedor popular*. You can walk from here to the Sabancaya geyser in approximately seven hours. Boys offer to guide you there. For information, ask for Eduardo, who acts as a guide. He lives next to the plaza. *El Día de San Sebastián* is celebrated over five days from 20 January in Pinchollo.

Cruz del Cóndor

From Pinchollo the road winds its way on to the Mirador, or Cruz del Cóndor at the deepest point of the canyon. The view from here is wonderful but people don't come for the view. This is where the immense Andean vulture, the condor, can be seen rising on the morning thermals.

The reason this particular spot is so unique is that the condors swoop by in startling close up, so close, in fact, that you feel you can reach out and touch them. It is a breathtaking and very humbling experience. The best time to arrive in the morning is a matter of some dispute, though the consensus is around 0900. Arrive by 0800 for a good spot, any earlier and you may be faced with a long, chilly wait (this may be unavoidable by public transport – buses from Chivay stop here very briefly). The condors fly off to look for carrion on the higher slopes of the surrounding peaks at 0900-1000. The condors can also be seen returning from a hard day's food searching at around 1600-1800. Just below the Mirador is a rocky outcrop, which allows a more peaceful viewing but take great care on the loose scree (or you'll end up on the menu). Binoculars are recommended. Snacks and drinks are available. Camping here is officially forbidden, but if you ask the tourist police in Chivay they may help. ■ *You may have to pay a US$1.45 entry fee. To get to the Mirador from Cabanaconde, take one of the return buses which set off at around 0730, and ask to be dropped off at the Mirador, just in time for the morning performance. Or you can walk along the road, which takes about three hours. Horses can be hired to save you the walk; arrange the night before in Cabanaconde. To walk from the Mirador to Cabanaconde, follow the road until Cabanaconde is in sight, then turn off the road 50 m after a small reservoir down a walled track. After about 1 km turn left on to an old Inca road and continue down to rejoin the road into Cabanaconde.*

Cabanaconde

Colour map 5, grid B5

Local women are very camera-shy. If you really must intrude, then at least ask permission first

From the Mirador it is a 20-minute bus ride to this friendly village at 3,287 m, the last in the Colca Canyon. The indigenous people of this part of the canyon are Cabanas and the women wear round, embroidered hats. The plaza is brimming with life. Women squat on their haunches, selling bruised fruit and a few knobbly root crops. Their distinctive flower-patterned hats, voluminous skirts and intricately embroidered blouses bring a splash of colour to the uniform brown adobe buildings. Children tend sheep, goats and llamas; old men lead burdened mules while pigs laze in the sun and chickens peck at the ground. At dusk large groups of animals wander back into the village to the corrals adjoining most houses.

The views into the canyon are excellent and condors can be seen from the hill just west of the village, a 15-minute walk from the plaza, which also gives views of the amazing terraces, arguably the most attractive in the valley, to the south of the village. The hill is surrounded by a 2 km long Huari wall, 6 m high and 4 m wide in places. It also encompasses the village football field where it is possible to see condors overflying a late afternoon game.

Cabanaconde suffered badly during the earthquake in April 1998. Many buildings collapsed and many people were injured.

Sleeping & eating

C *Posada del Conde*, C San Pedro, T440197, F441197, M 936809. Cheaper in low season, new, with hot shower, excellent value, very good restaurant. *Hostal San Pedro*, 2 blocks from the plaza. Bright rooms, no shower. **G** *Hostal Valle del Fuego*, 1 and 2 blocks from the plaza, T280367 (Arequipa 203737). Good but basic, has two places, both with restaurants serving good meals for around US$3. The owner and his son, both Pablo Junco, is a wealth of information. They usually meet the incoming buses but otherwise turn left facing the church on the plaza and the first place is 1 block along on the right. **G** *Virgen del Carmen*, 5 blocks up from the plaza. Clean, hot showers, friendly, may even offer you a welcoming glass of *chicha*. Recommended. There are several basic restaurants around the plaza, including *Rancho del Colca*, which is mainly vegetarian, and *Don Piero*, signposted just off main plaza, excellent choice and good information.

Transport

See under Chivay for buses on the Arequipa-Chivay-Cabanaconde route. The buses leave Cabanaconde for **Arequipa** at between 0730 and 1200.

Trekking in the Colca Canyon

There are many hiking possibilities in the area. Make sure to take enough water as it gets very hot and there is not a lot of water available. Moreover, sun protection is a must. Some treks are impossible if it rains heavily in the wet season, but most of the time the rainy season is dry. Check beforehand. Ask locals for directions as there are hundreds of confusing paths going into the canyon. Buy food for longer hikes in Arequipa. Topographical maps are available at the *Instituto Geográfico Militar* in Lima, and good information can be obtained from South American Explorers. Henry López Junco, is a guide in Cabanaconde, T280367. US$7.15 per day for two people.

Two hours below Cabanaconde is **Sangalle**, an 'oasis' of palm trees and swimming areas and two campsites with toilets, US$1.50-3 (3-4½ hours back up, ask for the best route in both directions, horses can be hired to carry your bag up, US$5.85), recommended. A popular hike involves walking east on the Chivay road to the Mirador de Tapay (before Cruz del Cóndor), then descending to the river on a steep track (4 hours, take care). At the village of San Juan you can stay and eat at **G** *Hostal Roy*, dinner US$1.85, breakfast less than US$1, good. From there you go to the oasis, spend the night and return to Cabanconde on the third day.

Tapay is another two hours above the 'oasis', on a good trail with great views. It's possible to stay overnight in Tapay, or camp at the houses just before the bridge. There is running water in a supply channel in the morning and evening; ask the locals.

A longer hike from Cabanaconde goes to **Chachas** and takes four or five days. Follow a small path to the west, descending slowly into the canyon (three hours); ask locals for directions to **Choco**. Then cross the Río Colca by the Puente Colgado (an Inca bridge) and go up to Choco, 2,473 m (5-6 hours).

From Choco climb high above the village to the pass at 4,500 m and then down to Chachas, at 3,100 m (8-12 hours). Sometimes there is transport from Chachas to **Andagua** in the valley of the volcanoes. Otherwise it is a day's hike. (For more details, see page 289). This is a superb walk through untouched areas and villages. You need all camping equipment, food and plenty of water, as there is hardly any on this trek.

Toro Muerto

The world's largest field of petroglyphs at Toro Muerto is near **Corire**, which lies north of the Pan-American Highway between Camaná and Repartición). You can make a return day trip from Arequipa, if you leave really early, but it's better to allow two days.

■ *To reach the petroglyphs, there's a turn-off on the right heading back out of Corire. It's about a one hour walk. Alternatively, ask to be let off the bus at the big sign to 'Toro Muerto' beside a small church. A track leads through the fields; at the end, turn right. Ask directions en route. Just before the site is a tiny settlement of very basic wattle and daub huts. From here follow the most worn track which veers right between the hills. There are two signposts on the track leading up from here into the desert valley.*

The higher you go, the more interesting the petroglyphs, though many have been ruined by graffiti. The designs range from simple llamas to elaborate human figures and animals. The sheer scale of the site is awe-inspiring (it's on the UNESCO World Heritage list) and the view back down the arid desert valley against the backdrop of the distant lush, green irrigated fields is wonderful. Allow several hours to appreciate the place fully and take plenty of water and protection against the fierce sun, including sunglasses.

Sleeping & eating   There are several restaurants around the plaza in Corire and a *Banco de Crédito*. There's accommodation at **E** *Hostal Willys*, on the Plaza de Armas, which is clean and helpful. Also *Hostal Manuelito*, 3 blocks from the plaza, is good and friendly. There's another *Hostal*, one block from the plaza, which is OK, has hot water but is noisy.

Transport   **Bus**   Buses (*Empresa Del Carpio*) to Corire leave from Arequipa main terminal hourly from 0500 onwards, 3-4 hrs, US$3. Ask to be let out at the beginning of the track to Toro Muerto. You can also hire a taxi from the plaza in Corire, US$6-10, including a 2-hour wait. A guide is recommended if short of time because they guide you to some of the more interesting carvings. It takes 2 hrs to walk around the site, a lot in the heat.

Cotahuasi Canyon

Colour map 5, grid B5   *North of Corire, on the same road that branches off the Pan-American, is Aplao, traversing the western slopes of Nevado Coropuna, Peru's third highest peak at 6,425 m, before winding down into Cotahuasi. Considered one of the most beautiful canyons in the world, as well as the deepest (about 1,850 m deeper than the Grand Canyon in the USA), Cotahuasi has several traditional communities where ancient customs persist. The river, cutting its way through steep walls, is the focus of some tremendous scenery and top-quality rafting or kayaking. Once part of an Inca route from coast to Cusco, it is now a great place for hiking.*

The area

The canyon, in the northwest of the Department of Arequipa, has been cut by the Río Cotahuasi, whose waters are formed by the Río Huayllapaña flowing from the north, above Pampamarca, and the Río Huarcaya from the west, above Tomepampa. The river cuts its way westwards and then southwards through the deepest parts of the canyon, below Quechualla. It flows into the Pacific as the Río Ocuña, having joined with the Río Marán along the way.

At its deepest, at Ninochaca (just below the village of Quechualla), the canyon is 3,354 m deep, 163 m deeper than the Colca Canyon and the deepest in the world. From this point the only way down the canyon is by kayak and it is through kayakers' reports since 1994 that the area has come to the notice of tourists. It was declared a Zona de Reserva Turística in 1988.

The vertiginous gradient of the canyon walls and the aridity of its climate allow little agriculture but there are several charming citrus-growing villages downstream, among them **Chaupa**, **Velinga** and **Quechualla**.

In Inca times the road linking Puerto Inca on the Pacific coast and Cusco ran along much of the canyon's course. It was used for taking fish to the ancient Inca capital. Parts of the road are still intact and there are numerous remains of *andenes*, or terraces, which supported settlement along the route. There are also Huari and other pre-Inca ruins. A website with pictures and some information on Cotahuasi is www.lared.net.pe/cotahuasi Information can also be obtained at *Hotel Corregidor*, San Pedro 139, Arequipa, T288081, F239803, corregidor@LaRed.net.pe (which is an **A** hotel).

NB The Cotahuasi region was affected by the June 2001 earthquake.

Rafting in the canyon

It is possible to raft or kayak from a point on the Upper Cotahuasi, just past the town, almost to the Pacific (boats are usually taken out of the water at the village of Iquipi), a descent of 2,300 m. The season is May-August; rapids class three to five; some portaging is unavoidable. (See the Rafting section on page 79.)

Cotahuasi

Cotahuasi town nestles in a sheltered hanging valley beneath Cerro Huinao, several kilometres away from the erosive action of the Río Cotahuasi. Though above the citrus zone itself, it has fertile, irrigated environs. The name Cotahuasi derives from the Quechua words 'Cota' (union) and 'Huasi' (house), literally translating as united house or close-knit community.

Population: 4,000
Altitude: 2,600 m

It is a peaceful, colonial town of narrow streets and whitewashed houses with gently subsiding balconies. The main street, Jirón Arequipa becomes a part of the plaza on busy Sunday mornings. The only traffic seen is the occasional glimpse of the mayor's car, the odd tractor and the infrequent comings and goings of the two buses (see below).

F *Hostal Villa*, just off the plaza. **G** *Alojamiento Chávez*, Jr Cabildo 125, T210222. Has rooms around a pleasant courtyard, friendly, Sr José Chávez is helpful on places to visit, if a little vague on timings. Recommended. *Restaurant El Pionero*, Jr Centenario. Clean, good *menú*. Three small restaurants/bars on Jr Arequipa offer basic fare. There are many well-stocked *tiendas*, particularly with fruit and vegetables.

Sleeping & eating

Arequipa

Transport   **Bus** Three bus companies leave daily from **Arequipa** bus terminal, 12 hrs, US$9: *Alex*, *Cromotex*, at 1730; *Reyna* at 1700; all return from the plaza in Cotahuasi in the afternoon. On arrival in Cotahuasi you may sleep on the bus till dawn. All companies stop for refreshments in **Chuquibamba**, about halfway.

Directory   There is no place to change money. The **PNP** are on the plaza; it is advisable to register with them on arrival and before leaving. Some survey maps are available in the Municipalidad and PNP. They may let you make photocopies at the shop on the corner of the plaza and Arequipa. Sr Chávez has photocopies of the sheets covering Cotahuasi and surroundings.

Trekking in the Cotahuasi Canyon

One of the main treks in the region follows the Inca trade road from **Cotahuasi to Quechualla**. The path starts next to the football pitch beside the airstrip. It heads downhill to **Piro**, which is almost a satellite of Cotahuasi and the gateway to the canyon (the path heads round to the right of the village, just above it). The path then crosses the river twice as it follows its course to **Sipia** (three hours), near which are the tremendously powerful, 150 m high **Cataratas de Sipia**. Climb to the bluff just beyond the mouth of the black hole and you'll have a superb view downriver. Take care near the falls if it is windy. Water is a problem further down the canyon, if continuing, fill up your water bottles near the falls.

The next three hour stretch to **Chaupo** is not for those of a nervous disposition as the path is barely etched into the canyon wall, 400 m above the river in places. The towering cliffs are magnificent reds and browns and dissected by near vertical water channels.

An opportunity to camp comes at Chaupo, which lies on the pampa, 100 m above the river. Water is available. Ask permission to camp in the citrus groves and do not pick the fruit. Llamas are herded on the pampa.

Next is **Velinga**, a village which was almost wiped out by Chagas disease. Now only six families remain. Take the path down to the river before the village and cross over the bridge to the right bank. Half a km further on you may need to wade for about 15 m at the foot of a cliff to regain the path. Stay on the same side of the river.

If it rains, Quechualla can be cut off for days as sections where the river has to be waded become too deep and treacherous (eg just past Velinga)

Before Quechualla are the extensive ruins of **Huña**. They are dilapidated but the remains of terraces and houses give a good idea of the importance of this route in precolumbian times. There is an almost intact 100 m stretch of Inca road above a bend in the river on the approach to **Quechualla**. It can be a bit scary in parts but the alternative is to wade waist deep through the river.

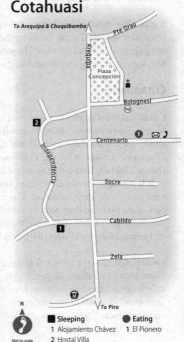

Cotahuasi

To Arequipa & Chuquibamba
Pre Grau
Arequipa
Plaza
Concepción
Botognesi (Pol)
Centenario
Independencia
Sucre
Cabildo
Zela
To Piro

N
Not to scale

■ **Sleeping**
1 Alojamiento Chávez
2 Hostal Villa

● **Eating**
1 El Pionero

Arequipa

Quechualla is a charming village and administrative capital of the district. It sits up on a cliff above the river. The church and school overlook the wooden bridge and the short climb up to the citrus groves. Trellised vines provide some welcome shade in the street. Though the village is populated by only eight families, you may be able to sleep in the schoolhouse. Ask Sr Carmelo Velásquez Gálvez for permission. Below the village, on the opposite side of the river are the ruined terraces of **Maucullachta**.

A 16 km hike continues to the ruins of **Marpa**, which are in better condition than Maucullachta. The canyon walls, however, are too steep to continue along the river. You need to climb 8 km, on a path at right angles to the river, to Huachuy, then descend a further 8 km to the ruins near the river. There is no water en route; allow four more days.

Other treks from Cotahuasi

It is a three hour walk to the ruins of **Pampamarca**, north of Cotahuasi. The ruins are impressive, as is the high waterfall. The village is well-known for rugmaking.

The thermal baths of **Luicho** lie between Tomepampa and Alca. Take a bus to Tomepampa; the first leaves at 0600, there are several more. A days' walk beyond Tomepampa is the spectacular rock forest of **Santo Santo**. Start the trek from Huaynacotas, near Luicho.

Towards the Valley of the Volcanoes

A road goes to the east from the Cotahuasi road to **Andagua**, a village lying at the head of the valley of the volcanoes. There are several hotels in Andagua and on the plaza *Restaurant Sarita* will cook good, cheap meals for you. No petrol/gasoline is available here.

A bus leaves from Arequipa on Sunday, Wednesday and Friday at 1530, with *Empresa Delgado*. To Arequipa: *Trans Alianza* leaves at 1300 and goes the long way via Cailloma, US$9; *Trans Trébol* leaves at 1600 or 1700 and takes the shorter route via Aplao and Corire, 9½ hours, US$8. Both buses arrive in Arequipa in the very early morning, but you can sleep on the bus until daybreak.

The Arequipa-Andagua bus goes on to **Orcopampa**, from which the thermal springs of Huancarama can be visited.

From Andagua there is a road to **Chachas**, a picturesque little village on the edge of a lake. A truck leaves for Andagua around 1000, usually on Saturday, Tuesday and Thursday (ask the locals, they know when it's leaving). A woman in the village will let you sleep in a spare room next to her house. She also provides an evening meal. The cost is not fixed and is left up to you - around US$2 per person should be okay.

The area is heavily cultivated and there are perfect views of the valley of the volcanoes from the top of the hill above Chachas. It is possible to hike from Chachas to Choco and on to Cabanaconde via the Río Colca in four or five days (see page 285).

If you have a four-wheel drive vehicle, this is a superb area for driving some rough roads through stunning scenery, for instance a circuit Arequipa-Aplao-Andagua-Orcopamba-Cailloma-Chivay-Arequipa.

Arequipa

Toward the Valley of the Volcanoes

South Coast

Introducing the South Coast

The Pan-American Highway runs all the way south from Lima to the Chilean border and the desert coast has some distinctive attractions, the most famous, and perhaps the strangest, are the enigmatic **Nasca Lines**, whose origin and function continue to puzzle scientists. More designs on the desert, plus tomb finds at neighbouring **Palpa** are casting new light on the mystery. The **Paracas** peninsula is one of the world's great marine bird reserves and was home to one of Peru's most important ancient civilizations. As you bob in a boat to the Ballestas Islands to watch the seabirds, look for the giant Candelbra, drawn on the

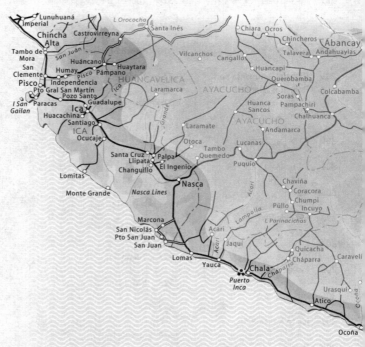

cliffs by unknown hands. Further south, the **Ica Valley**, with its wonderful climate, is home to that equally wonderful grape brandy known as pisco. South of Nasca, on a small bay, is **Puerto Inca**, the seaport and fishing harbour for Cusco in pre-colonial times. The road from here through the canyons to the Sierra was a major Inca artery. That route may have fallen into disuse, but new roads are making it much easier to climb up from the coast with its ramshackle fishing villages and brief flashes of green irrigated valleys. One is the newly paved highway from Nasca to Abancay which passes the **Pampas Galeras** vicuña reserve. Further south the stunning road from the port of Ilo to Lake Titicaca can be picked up in the oasis town of **Moquegua**.

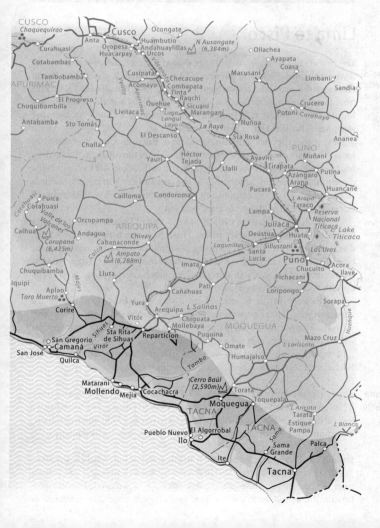

South Coast

Things to do on the South Coast

- Visit the 'guano' producers of the **Ballestas Islands**, off the Paracas Peninsula. Cormorants, boobies, pelicans and terns as well as penguins and sealions inhabit the rocks and arches of the islands, page 300.
- Sample table wines, sweet wines and, above all, pisco at one of the **bodegas** in the river valleys south of Lima. The owners are usually pretty generous with their measures, page 303.
- Take a Gods' eye view of the **Nasca Lines**, one of the great archaeological enigmas of South America. As the small plane circles and banks over the designs, you will be truly impressed by the artistry and endeavour of the people who sent their creators such long-lasting messages, page 312.
- Take advantage of **new roads inland**: Pisco to Ayacucho, Nasca to Abancay via the Pampas Galeras vicuña reserve and Moquegua to Desaguadero.

Lima to Pisco

El Silencio
San Bartolo
Pucusana
Chilca
Colour map 5, grid A1

The first 60 km south from Lima are dotted with a series of seaside resort towns and clubs. First is **El Silencio**, at Km 30, which is good, then **Punta Hermosa** at Km 35, and **Punta Negra** at Km 40. **San Bartolo** is 43 km south from Lima. Accommodation is available at *Posada del Mirador*, Malecón San Martín 105, T290388, **C** in bungalows or **A** full board, *Handbook* users are welcome. A further 2 km is **Santa María**.

Next comes the charming fishing village of **Pucusana**, 60 km south from Lima. There are excellent views from the cliffs above the village. You can hire a boat for an hour, but fix the price beforehand and stick to it. Don't sail in the direction of the smelly factory, but to the rocks where you can see seabirds close at hand. There is a compulsory police checkpoint before the turning to Pucusana. The *Hotel Bahía* has good seafood.

Most beaches have very strong currents and can be dangerous if swimming. If you're unsure, ask the locals

The small beach resort of **Chilca**, 14 km south of Pucusana, is 30 minutes by colectivo from the market place. There isn't much to see, but a long, deserted beach does present camping possibilities. You can walk along the beach from Chilca to Salinas (5 km), which has mineral baths. There are a few restaurants and *pensiones*. In summer (December-February), these places fill up with holidaymakers from Lima.

Chepeconde beach is reached by a dirt road from Km 120 of the Panamericana. It has fine sand and rocky outcrops which divide it into three sections. The northernmost is the safest and most visited. It's very popular with Peruvian campers in the summer months.

If driving south from Lima, you can make a detour to visit the ruins of **Pachacámac** on the way. See Lima, Excursions, page 149.

San Vicente de Cañete

About 150 km south of Lima, on the Río Cañete, this prosperous market centre is set amid desert scenery. It is commonly called Cañete. The town hosts a festival during the last week in August. At Cerro Azul, 13 km north of Cañete, is a unique Inca sea fort known as **Huarco**, which is now badly damaged.

Sleeping, eating and transport Hotels include **D** *Hostal San Francisco*, Santa Rosa 317, 2 blocks north of the plaza, T912409. With bathroom, **E** without, clean, friendly, quiet. Recommended. There are cheaper places. A recommended restaurant is *Cevichería Muelle 56*, Bolognesi 156. There are also several good Chinese restaurants.

The main bus stop is on the highway; wait for the service you want going north or south and hope there are free seats. To **Pisco**, US$1.30. To **Lunahuaná**: unless you are on a Lima-Cañete-Imperial bus, take a combi from the highway to Imperial, then a bus to Lunahuaná.

A paved road runs inland, mostly beside the Río Cañete, through **Imperial**, which has a market on Saturday, Sunday and Monday (good for every type of household item), and **Nuevo Imperial** to the Quebrada de Lunahuaná. After the town of Lunahuaná (40 km from Cañete), the road continues unpaved to Huancayo up in the sierra; bus US$9 (see page 486).

Lunahuaná

Lunahuaná consists of the town of the same name and several districts (*anexos*) strung along the valley. They are totally dependent on the Río Cañete, for irrigation and for its chief tourist attraction of rafting and kayaking. Beyond the reach of the water, the surrounding countryside is completely barren, but not without its own appeal. In early morning and at dusk the hills are painted in infinite shades of grey and brown, framed by the clear blue sky, fertile green valley and rushing water.

Phone code: 01
Colour map 5, grid A2

Eight kilometres before Lunahuaná is **Incawasi**, the ruins of an Inca city. A new road cuts right through the middle of the site which dominates the valley and *quebradas* that run down into it. Incawasi is said to have been a replica of Cusco, with its divided trapezoidal plaza. The site was built outside the fertile zone of the valley and its rough walls blend in perfectly with the barren hills.

Paullo is the first of the *anexos* reached after Incawasi. Here stand the ruins of the first church of Lunahuaná. In summer, when the river is high, rafting trips start from just below the plaza. In the low river season a temporary footbridge crosses the river to **Lúcumo**.

Two kilometres further on is **San Jerónimo**, the area's white-water rafting centre; there are several agencies to choose from (see below). Other adventure tourism activities include paragliding and there is an artificial wall for climbing.

Lunahuaná town has an **18th-century church** on the plaza. Opposite the west door, at the top of the plaza, are the *Banco de la Nación* and *Municipalidad*.

Beyond Lunahuaná are **Condoray** and **Uchupampa**. Past Uchupampa the road paving ends before the road crosses the Río Cañete to **Catapalla**. A little further on is a *puente colgante* (suspension bridge). Across the road bridge turn right to the village or left to the pre-Inca remains of **Cantagallo**. The site is not signposted; ask directions. Miguel Casas Sánchez in Catapalla can guide to these ruins.

It is interesting to visit the *bodegas* (wine cellars) in the valley and try the wine. The best-known is *Los Reyes* (T437 3187/434 0872), in **Condoray**, where you can try their *pisco*, wine, *manzanilla* and *arope* (a grape juice concentrate). A good time to visit is during February and March when you can see the traditional methods of treading the grapes by foot to the beat of the drum.

Bodegas

Other *Bodegas* in the area include: *El Olimpo*, in Uchupampa, beside the *Hotel Embassy*, T460 7698; *Viña Santa María*, in Condoray, beside *Hostal Río Alto*, T437 8892. Also in Condoray are *Del Valle*, by *La Laguna* restaurant, and *Viñas del Sur*, T437 3187. In Catapalla are *Bodegas Reina de Lunahuaná*, a 5-minute walk from the suspension bridge. It is the most rustic and authentic *bodega* in the valley and it produces an excellent pisco. They have a free tour and restaurant, open at weekends. Recommended.

Sleeping & eating	There are hotels ranging from: **A-B** *Embassy* and *Embassy Río*, in **Uchupampa**, T472 3525. With all facilities, restaurants, disco, gardens, rafting, large property, good, popular with families. **B** *Regina*, in CondorayT/F284 1147. Hot water, TV, swimming pool, cafetería, attractive, with good views over the valley. **B** *Río Alto*, T841125 (in Lima 463 5490), just outside Lunahuaná. Rooms or bungalows for 7, pool, with bathroom, hot water, restaurant, disco, rafting, very nice. At the lower end: **D** *Hostal Lunahuaná*, , in **Lunahuaná** itself, T424 0624, with restaurant and disco, and **D-E** *Grau*, Grau 205. Shared bathroom, clean, all meals available. There are various **camping** possibilities. There are several restaurants in town and in the surrounding *anexos*, some offering rafting.
Festivals	*Fiesta de la Vendimia*, a grape harvest festival, is held in first weekend in **Mar**. At the end of **Sep/beginning Oct** is the lively *Fiesta del Níspero* (medlar fruit harvesting festival).
Rafting & kayaking *See also page 79*	Several places in San Jerónimo and Paullo offer rafting and kayaking. From Nov-Apr the river is high (highest from Dec) and during those months the white-water rafting is at levels four to five. May-Oct is the low water season when only boat trips are possible (levels 1-2). Excellent kayaking is 2½ hours upriver. Rafting costs US$15 per person for 1½ hours. Annual championships and a festival of adventure sports are held every Feb.

Chincha Alta

Colour map 5, grid A2
Population: 110,016

Thirty-five kilometres north of Pisco, near Chincha Baja, is **Tambo de Mora**, the old port, with nearby archaeological sites at Huaca de Tambo de Mora, La Centinela, Chinchaycama and Huaca Alvarado. **Chincha** itself is a fast-growing town where the negro/criollo culture is still alive. For more details, see the sections on People (page 584), Food (page 70) and Music (page 594). Chincha is a good place to sample locally produce wine and pisco. One of the best **bodegas** is the 100-year old *Naldo Navarro*, Pasaje Santa Rosa, Sunampe, 100 m west of the Panamericana (free guided tours, including tasting). Other bodegas have guided tours. The third Saturday in September is national pisco day.

Sleeping	**AL** *Hacienda San José*, is a 17th-century sugar and cotton estate ranch-house, 9 km south of town in El Carmen district, turn off at Km 203, T034-221458 (or book in Lima at Juan Fanning 328, of 202, Miraflores, T444 5242, www.peru-hotels.com/chinsanj.htm credit card payment only). The price is for full board (cheaper Mon-Thu), beautiful buildings but overpriced, with pool, garden, small church, colonial crafts, underground from the basement runs a labyrinth of tunnels believed to link up with Tambo de Mora in order to facilitate the contraband trade in black slaves from Africa. The catacombs, where many of those slaves are interred, can be visited, US$3 per person. In Chincha are **C** *El Valle*, Panamericana in town centre, with excellent *Palacio de los Mariscos* restaurant. **F** *Hostal La Rueda*, near the plaza. Breakfast is extra, hot showers, pool, lounge. There are several other hotels and restaurants.
Festivals	Among other things (olives, for one) Chincha is famous for its many festivals. On **6 Jan** is the *Celebración del Nacimiento de la Beata Melchorita Saravia*. The *Verano Negro*, or Black Summer, is at the **end of Feb**. During this time the black culture of the area, repressed for so many centuries, is freely expressed in the dancing competitions, though black participation in the festival is still somewhat limited. In the **second week of Mar** is the *Festival de la Vendimia*. In mid-Jul is the *Virgen del Carmen* festival and the tourist week takes place during the **end of Oct/beginning of Nov**. Also in Nov, the *Festival de Danzas Negras* is held in the black community of El Carmen, 10 km south. Not enough? Well, on **4 Dec** there's the *Peregrinación a la Ermita de la Beata Melchorita*.

Pisco

Despite being christened as San Clemente de Macera by the Spanish in 1640, the town had already been unofficially named after the famous local brandy and always would be known as Pisco. Now the largest port between Callao and Matarani, 237 km south of Lima, it serves a large agricultural hinterland.

Phone code: 034
Colour map 5, grid B2
Population: 82,250

Ins and outs

All the bus terminals are in the centre. However, if arriving by bus, make sure it is going into town and will not leave you at the Repartición, which is 5 km from the centre, a 10-min taxi (US$1) or combi ride (US$0.50), and not a particularly safe area after dark.

Getting there

The town is small and compact. All you want to do and see is contained within a 300-m radius of the Plaza de Armas. Taxis can be caught here. Combis from the Repartición (see above), stop at *Hostal Comercio* by Plaza Belén. If staying by the beach, it will cost US$0.50 to get to the Plaza de Armas, but drivers try to charge US$1.50.

Getting around

Sights

Pisco lies a short distance to the west of the Pan-American Highway. The town was originally divided into two: Pisco Pueblo with its colonial-style homes, patios and gardens; and Pisco Puerto, which, apart from fisheries, has been replaced as a port by the deep-water Puerto General San Martín, beyond Paracas. The two have now expanded into one fairly unattractive town. If the wind is in the wrong direction, the smell of fish can be pretty bad.

In **Pisco Pueblo**, half a block west of the quiet Plaza de Armas, with its equestrian statue of San Martín, is the **Club Social Pisco**, at Avenida San

South Coast

Pisco

To Hostal San Isidro (1½ blocks)
To Hostal La Portada (1½ blocks)
To Pisco Puerto
To As de Oro Restaurant (1½ blocks)
To Pan-American Highway & Cemetery (1 block)

Sleeping
1 Colonial
2 El Condado
3 Embassy
4 Embassy Suites
5 Hostal Belén
6 Hostal Candelabro
7 Hostal Pisco
8 Hostal San Jorge
9 Posada Hispana
10 Regidor

Eating
1 Don Manuel
2 El Dorado

Transport
1 Buses from Repartición
2 Empresa General San Martín Buses
3 Ormeño Buses
4 Soyuz
5 Transportes Saky

N
0 metres 50
0 yards 50

Martín 132, the HQ of San Martín after he had landed at Paracas Bay. There is an old Jesuit church on San Francisco, one block from the plaza, separated from the Municipalidad by a narrow park. The newer **Cathedral** is on the main plaza. Avenida San Martín runs from the Plaza de Armas to the sea.

Essentials

Sleeping
The town is full at weekends with visitors from Lima
Mosquitoes are a problem at night in the summer

■ *on map page 297*
Price codes:
see inside front cover

B *Regidor*, Arequipa 201, T/F535220/219, regidor@mail.cosapidata.com.pe With bath, TV, fan, jacuzzi, café and restaurant, sauna, very good, price negotiable at quiet times. **C** *Hostal Candelabro*, Callao y Pedemonte, T532620. TV, fridge, fax service, hot water, café, bar on roof, laundry, safe, clean. **D** *Embassy*, on Jr Comercio just off the Plaza de Armas, T532809. With bathroom, clean, noisy, nice bar on roof, has disco, trips to Ballestas Islands, under the same ownership as *Embassy Suites* on Bolognesi and the *Embassy Beach*. **D** *Posada Hispana*, Bolognesi 236, T536363, F461 4907 (Lima), andesad@terra.com.pe, www.posadahispana.com Rooms each with loft and bathroom, also rooms with shared bath (**G** per person), hot water, TV, can accommodate groups, comfortable, clean, breakfast extra, information service, email, laundry facilities, luggage store, English, French, Italian and Catalan spoken. Recommended, but check what is included in the price. **E** *Hostal Belén*, Arequipa 128, Plazuela Belén, T533046. Comfortable, hot water, recommended. **E** *El Condado*, Arequipa 136, Plazuela Belén, T533623. Hot water, cable TV, laundry, breakfast available, tours to Ballestas arranged. **E** *Hostal Pisco*, Plaza de Armas, T532018, vonlignau@LatinMail.com Lower prices Nov-Mar. With bathroom, **F** without, hot water, clean, breakfast US$1.75 from 0600-1100, bar, good tour company adjoining hotel, parking for motorcycles. **E** *Hostal La Portada*, Alipio Ponce 250, T532098. Clean, free coffee, hot water, bath, recommended. **E** *Hostal San Isidro*, San Clemente 103, T/F536471, hostalsanisidro@lettera.net With bath, cheaper without, hot water, safe, laundry facilities, use of kitchen, English spoken, parking. **F** *Colonial*, on the pedestrianized part of Jr Comercio. Shared bathroom, large rooms with balcony overlooking plaza, very clean.

Pisco Puerto F per person *Hostal Pisco Playa* (Youth Hostel), Jr José Balta 639, Pisco Playa, T532492. Quite nice, clean, kitchen, washing facilities, breakfast US$1.50.

Eating
● *on map, page 297*

As de Oro, San Martín 472. Good food at reasonable prices, closed on Mon. *El Dorado*, main plaza opposite Cathedral, good value local dishes, popular. *Don Manuel*, Comercio 187. US$2-4 for a main dish. There are other restaurants on the pedestrianized block of Comercio. Seafood restaurants can be found along the shore between Pisco and San Andrés, and in San Andrés itself (buses from Plaza Belén, near *Hostal Perú*).

Festivals

San Pedro is at the end of **Jun**. The second week of **Sep** is designated tourist week, and on **21 Nov** is the grandly titled *Peregrinación a la Hermita de la Beata de Humay*.

Transport

Bus To Lima, 242 km, 3-4 hrs, US$3 with *Ormeño* (San Francisco, 1 block from the plaza), *San Martín* (San Martín 199), and *Soyuz*, Callao on the Plaza (bus ticket includes taxi from Plaza to Highway to catch the bus). Buses leave almost hourly 0715-1800. Also colectivos. For buses from Lima, see under Lima, Transport, page 139.

To **Ayacucho**, 317 km, 8-10 hrs, US$7-10, several buses daily (*Expresos Molina* recommended), leave from San Clemente 10 km north on Panamericana Sur, take a colectivo (20 mins), book in advance to ensure seat and take warm clothing as it gets cold at night. The road is completely paved. To **Huancavelica**, 269 km, 12-14 hrs, US$7, with *Oropesa* (Conde de la Monclova 637) coming from Ica; also a few trucks. There is regular transport to **Ica**, US$2 by colectivo, US$0.70 by bus, 45 mins, 70 km; with *Ormeño* and *Saky* (Pedemonte y Arequipa). To **Nasca**, 210 km, US$5, 3 hrs by bus, via Ica, at 0830 with *Oropesa* and 3 daily with *Ormeño*. To **Arequipa**, US$12, 10-12 hrs, 3 daily.

South Coast

Banks *BCP* on the Plaza de Armas. Gives good rates for Amex TCs and cash, Visa ATM. **Directory**
Also on Plaza is *Interbank*, Mastercard agent. **Communications** Internet: at *Bill Gates* computer school, C San Francisco next to the church. US$3 per hr. **Telephone and fax office** is on the Plaza de Armas between Av San Martín y Callao. **Hospitals and medical services** *Dr Carlos Alfonso Bonilla Flores*, at C San Francisco 219, T523373. Doesn't speak English but is very helpful and will make hotel visits.

Paracas Peninsula and Ballestas Islands

Fifteen kilometres down the coast from Pisco Puerto is the bay of Paracas shel-   *Colour map 5, grid B2*
tered by the Paracas peninsula. It is named after the Paracas winds – sandstorms that can last for three days, especially in August. The wind gets up every after- noon, peaking at around 1500.

Paracas National Reserve

The whole peninsula, a large area of coast to the south and the Ballestas Islands   *It's advisable to see*
are all part of a National Reserve, created in 1975, which covers a total of   *the peninsula as part*
335,000 ha, on land and sea. It is one of the most important marine reserves in   *of a tour it is not safe*
the world, with the highest concentration of marine birds. The region also is   *to walk alone and*
economically important, being a major producer of guano.   *it is easy to get lost*

The **fauna** on view also includes a wide variety of sea mammals and rare and exotic birds. Condors can even be seen in February and March from the rough road between Paracas and Laguna Grande. These massive vultures feed on the ready supply of sea lion carcasses.

Paracas Peninsula

Rather more delicate are the fla- mingos which feed in Paracas bay, a short walk from the museum (see below). Boat trips do not go to see the flamingos and that from January to March the birds head for the sierra. It is said that these graceful red and white birds inspired General San Martín to design Peru's red and white flag of independence. ■ *Entrance to the reserve is US$1.70 per person.*

By private transport it takes about 50 **Getting there**
mins to Lagunilla from the park entrance, 45 mins to La Mina and 1 hr to Mirador de los Lobos. Make sure your car is in good condition, never leave it unattended, and travel in a group as robbery has been a problem in the past. The reserve can be reached by the coast road from San Andrés, passing the fishing port and a large proportion of Peru's fishmeal indus- try. Alternatively, go down the Pan-American Highway to 14½ km past the Pisco turning and take the road to

Paracas across the desert. After 11 km turn left along the coast road and 1 km further on fork right to Paracas village. Return to the main road for the entrance to the reserve, where you can ask for a map.

Around the peninsula　The **Julio Tello site museum** is at the entrance to the Reserve. The exhibits are from the burial sites discovered by the Peruvian archaeologist, Julio C Tello, under the Paracas desert in 1925. The best examples of textiles and funerary bundles can be found in the Museo de la Nación and archaeological museum, Pueblo Libre, in Lima. ■ *Daily 0900-1700, with a shop which sells guide books, film and drinks, and a visitors' centre. US$1.*

The tiny fishing village of **Lagunilla** is 5 km from the museum across the neck of the peninsula. It has beaches which are free from sting rays, but not very clean, and eating places which tend to be overpriced (*Rancho de la Tía Fela* is recommended). A network of good dirt roads, reasonably well-signed, crosses the peninsula. Details of **walking routes** are available from the Park Office or ask for 'Hoja 28-K' map at Instituto Geográfico Nacional in Lima. Note that it is not safe to walk if alone and that it is easy to get lost in the hot, wide desert area.

Other sites on the peninsula include **Mirador de los Lobos** at **Punta El Arquillo**, 6 km from Lagunilla, which looks down on a raucous mob of sea lions. **La Catedral** is a rock formation in the cliffs, 6 km from Lagunilla in the opposite direction. Some guides may tell you that this was the site for the filming of *Planet of the Apes*.

Nearby, is a monument which marks the spot where San Martín landed in Peru, on 8 September 1820, after liberating Argentina. Soon after, a shipload of British troops, led by Lord Cochrane, arrived to help the General plan his strategy to break the Spanish stranglehold in the region.

About 14 km from the entrance to the Reserve is the pre-Columbian **Candelabro** (or Candelabra) traced in the hillside. At least 50 m long, it is best seen from the sea (see below). Approaching it by land is not a good idea as disturbance of the sand around it is beginning to destroy the monument. Some idiots have even driven over it. There are differing theories as to its exact purpose. Some believe it to be linked to the Nasca Lines (see page 312), 200 km to the south, others that it is related to the Southern Cross constellation and was used to help guide ancient sailors. Still others contend that it represents the cactus used by the ancient high priests for its hallucinogenic powers. A few cruel cynics have even suggested – God forfend – that it was the work of some opportunistic local guides.

Ballestas Islands

The Ballestas islands, dubbed the "poor man's Galápagos" by many, are nonetheless spectacular in their own right and well worth visiting. They are eroded into numerous arches and caves, hence their name – *ballesta* means bow, as in archery. These arches provide shelter for thousands of seabirds, some of which are very rare, and countless sea lions. A former guano factory can be seen on one of the islands and several others have installations. The book *Las Aves del Departamento de Lima* by Maria Koepcke is useful. Trips to the Islas Ballestas leave from the jetty at El Chaco, the beach and fishing port by Paracas village.

Getting there　Boat trips to the islands usually start at 0730, returning at 1100 to avoid rougher seas in the afternoon. Tours may be cancelled if the sea is too rough. Few tours include Isla San Gallán, where there are thousands of sea lions. All boats are speedboats with life jackets, but some are very crowded. Wear warm clothing, but also take protection against the

The Paracas Necropolis Culture

*The Paracas Necropolis culture inhabited this region between 1300 BC and AD 200 and is renowned for its finely woven textiles, in particular their **mantos** (large decorated cloth) embroidered with anthropomorphic, zoomorphic and geometric designs. These mantos were used to wrap mummified bodies in their funerary bundles, the discovery of which gave anthropologists and archaeologists vital clues into this civilization. The bodies were often found to have trepanned skulls. Trepanation was a form of brain surgery performed by the Paracas people in which metal plates were inserted to replace broken sections of skull – a common injury among warring factions at that time. The Paracas culture also practised the intentional deformation of infants' skulls for aesthetic reasons.*

sun and wear sunglasses. You will see, close up, sea lions, guano birds, pelicans, penguins and, if you're lucky, dolphins swimming in the bay. The boats pass Puerto San Martín and the Candelabra en route to the islands. Tours to the islands cost US$9-10 per person, and to the peninsula US$20 per person, but are a lot cheaper out of season.

Tours

For trips to Islas Ballestas: *Ballestas Travel Service*, San Francisco 249, T533095, jpachecot@terra.com.pe *Blue Sea Tours*, C Chosica 320, San Andrés, Pisco; also at El Chaco. Guides Jorge Espejo and Hubert Van Lomoen (speaks Dutch) are frequently recommended and there is no time limit on tours. *Paracas Islas Tours*, Comercio 128, T665872. *Paseo Turístico Islas Ballestas*, C San Francisco 109. *Paracas Tours*, San Francisco 257. *The Zarcillo Connection*, San Francisco 111, T262795, zarcillo@terraplus.com.pe (also good for the Paracas National Reserve). Recommended. The main hotels in Pisco and Paracas will also arrange tours, eg *Hotel Paracas*, US$18 in their own speed boat, 0900-1700. Operators usually go to Ballestas in the morning and the Paracas Reserve in the afternoon.

Beware scams, only book tours in company offices not in hotels, nor on the street

Sleeping

A *Paracas*, T Pisco 545100, hparacas@terra.com.pe Bungalows on the beach, good food, not cheap, good buffet lunch on Sun US$25, fine grounds facing the bay, TCs can be changed here at good rates. It is a good centre for excursions to the Peninsula and flights over Nasca, it has tennis courts and an open-air swimming pool (US$2 for non-residents), it also houses the Masson ceramics collection, which is worth seeing. Dune-buggy trips of 2 hrs can be arranged at the hotel for US$25 per person; you decide how many stomach-churning descents you want to do, or how much gentle viewing, good fun. Next door is the *Hostería Paracas*, Av Paracas 169, reasonably priced, comfortable. **C** *El Mirador*, at the turn-off to El Chaco, no phone, reservations in Lima, T445 8496, ask for Sra Rosa. Hot water, good service, boat trips arranged, meals available, sometimes full board only. **D** *Alojamiento El Amigo*, 5 rooms, nice view from first floor, with bathroom. Also *Hostal El Cóndor*, T545080. At El Chaco, the beach-cum-jetty area.

Camping is possible on the beach near the *Hotel Paracas* at a spot called La Muelle. There are no facilities and the sea is polluted. Ask for permission to camp in the reserve, but note that there is no water. Do not camp alone as robberies occur.

Eating

There's excellent fried fish at the open-sided restaurants at El Chaco (see below), eg *Jhonny y Jennifer*, friendly; and *El Chorito*, close to *Hotel Paracas*.

Transport

A taxi from Pisco to Paracas costs about US$3-4. Combis to/from El Chaco beach (marked 'Chaco-Paracas-Museo') leave when full, US$0.50, 25 mins. Some of them continue to the museum Lagunilla. The last one returns at around 2200. There is no public transport on the peninsula.

South Coast

An economic mess

The islands lying off the coast of Peru are the breeding grounds for millions of sea birds, whose droppings have accumulated over the centuries. These piles of mineral-rich excrement were turned into piles of cash during the last century.

Though the ancient Peruvians knew of the benefits of guano – the name given to the natural fertilizer – and used it on their crops, it wasn't until 1840 that the vast deposits of the stuff were exploited for commercial purposes. It was at this time that Peru first began to trade abroad, particularly with France and England. Almost simultaneously, guano began to replace rare metals as the country's main export.

However, with the economy heavily based on the sales of bird droppings, Peru was caught in a vicious circle of borrowing money on future sales, then having to repay loans at vastly inflated rates. This unhealthy state of affairs was exacerbated in 1864 when Spain, in a petulant show of aggression towards her ex-colony, decided to occupy the guano islands of Chincha, to the south of Lima, thereby leaving the Peruvian government really up to its neck in it.

The main producers of guano are the Guanay Cormorant and the Peruvian Booby. They gather in colonies on the islands, attracted by the huge shoals of anchovy which feed on the plankton in the cold water of the Humboldt current.

Inland from Pisco

From the Pan-American Highway near Pisco, a paved road runs 317 km up to Ayacucho in the sierra, with a branch to Huancavelica. At Castrovirreyna it reaches 4,600 m. The scenery on this journey is superb.

Tambo Colorado   Tambo Colorado, one of the best-preserved Inca ruins in coastal Peru, is 48 km from Pisco. It includes buildings where the Inca and his retinue would have stayed. On the other side of the road is the public plaza and the garrison and messengers' quarters. The caretaker will act as a guide, and he has a small collection of items found on the site. Entrance is US$1.50.

From Humay, go to Hacienda Montesarpe, and 500 m above the hacienda is the line of holes known as '*La avenida misteriosa de las picaduras de viruelas*' (the mysterious avenue of smallpox spots) which stretches along the Andes for many kilometres. Its purpose is still unknown.

■ *There's a bus from Pisco which leaves at 0800 from near the Plaza (ask for directions); US$1.60, 3 hrs. Also colectivos, US$1.20 per person. Get off 20 mins after the stop at Humay. The road passes right through the site. Return by bus to Pisco in the afternoon. For the bus or truck back to Pisco wait at the caretaker's house. A taxi from Pisco is US$25. Tours from Pisco agencies cost US$10 with guide, minimum 2 people.*

Huaytará & Incahuasi   The town of Huaytará is four hours by bus from Pisco. The whole side of the church is a perfectly preserved Inca wall with niches and trapezoidal doorways. 20 minutes from town are the ruins of Incahuasi with thermal baths. On 24 June is the Fiesta of San Juan Bautista, which involves a week of processions, fireworks, bullfights and dancing day and night (and probably the occasional drink). There's accommodation at **D** *Hotel de Turistas*, which also offers food and tours; and **E** *Municipal*, which has warm water. A bus from Pisco is US$2.25 (rising to US$5.50 for the festival!). A *Molina* bus goes from Lima, taking six hours.

South Coast

From Pisco the Pan-American Highway runs 70 km south to Ica. At Km 245 a dirt road runs to Paracas. If coming from the south you could try your luck, avoiding the detour via Pisco, but there is little traffic along this road.

Ica

Ica is Peru's main wine centre. Most travellers will only pass through en route to the oasis at Huacachina. The city is on the Río Ica, which is almost permanently dry and rubbish-strewn. As well as wine, the city is also famous for its tejas, a local sweet of manjarblanco.

Phone code: 034
Colour map 5, grid B2
Population: 161,406
Altitude: 410 m

Ins and outs

Buses from Lima travel along the Av Municipalidad nearly into the centre of town. Most hotels though are on the far side of the Plaza de Armas. Beware of thieves at the bus stations, even in daylight, especially when transferring between buses to or from Nasca, Pisco or Lima. Also watch out for bogus hotel or tour agents.

Getting there

Ica is much more spread out than Pisco. You will need a taxi to get around especially if you intend to visit the bodegas. **Tourist offices** Some information is available at travel agencies. Also try *Touring y Automóvil Club del Perú*, Fermín Tangüis 102, Urb San Miguel, T219393, F235061, ica@touringperu.com.pe

Getting around

Sights

The waters of the Choclacocha and Orococha lakes from the eastern side of the Andes are tunnelled into the Ica valley and irrigate 30,000 ha of land. The lakes are at 4,570 m and the tunnel is over 9 km long. The **San Jerónimo church** at Cajamarca 262 has a fine mural behind the altar.

   Museo Regional houses mummies, ceramics, textiles and trepanned skulls from the Paracas, Nasca and Inca cultures. There's a good, well-displayed collection of Inca counting strings (*quipus*) and clothes made of feathers. Also good and informative displays with maps of all sites in the Department. Behind the building there is a scale model of the Nasca lines with an observation tower. It's a useful orientation before visiting the lines. The kiosk outside sells copies of motifs from the ceramics and textiles (small selection, US$2). It also sells good maps of Nasca for US$1.65. ■ *Mon-Sat 0800-1900, Sat-Sun and holidays 0900-1800. US$1.15, students US$0.65. To get there, take bus 17 from the Plaza de Armas (US$0.50).* On the Plaza de Armas itself is the controversial museum of **Dr Javier Cabrera Darquea** (who died in 2001). It contains his collection of about 11,000 stones, 'La Piedras de Ica', which are engraved with a multitude of symbols. Dr Cabrera claimed that the stones' drawings were prophetic, showing the passing of comets, cures for cancer, and so on, but the scientific community gives no credence to his beliefs, saying that they are all fakes. It's "very interesting and fun place, well worth a visit, even if you don't believe in his conclusions", say Verena Stammbach and Christoph Bigler. ■ *The tourist office doesn't recognise this museum; ask travel agents for directions. Entry US$3.*

The **Bodega El Carmen** is on the right-hand side when arriving from Lima. This pisco distillery has an ancient grape press made from a huge tree trunk and is worth a visit.

Bodegas

Ten kilometres outside Ica, in the district of Subtanjalla, is José Carrasco González, **Bodega El Catador**, a shop selling home-made wines and pisco, and traditional handicrafts associated with winemaking. It is also a restaurant-bar serving lunch and, in the evening, with dancing and music. The best time to visit is during harvest – late February to early April – when wine and pisco tasting is usually possible. Try *Cachina*, a very young white wine 'with a strong yeasty taste', which is drunk about two weeks after the grape harvest. ■ *1000-1800. Take a combi from the second block of Moquegua, 20 mins, US$0.40. Taxi takes 10 mins, US$1.50*

Near Bodega El Catador is **Bodega Alvarez**. The owner, Umberto Alvarez, is very hospitable and won the gold medal for the best pisco in Peru in 1995. Ask about their *pisco de mosto verde* and the rarer, more expensive, *pisco de limón*, which will set you back US$40 per bottle.

In Ocucaje, 30 km south of Ica, a very good, strong *moscatel* is made by Sr Luis Chipana and sold in unlabelled bottles. He is always short of bottles so it's best to take your own. A visit is recommended, but you'll need good Spanish. Sr Chipana lives on the main plaza of Ocucaje beside his bodega. Ask for him in the bar on the plaza. The town is a popular excursion from Ica for tours of the *Ocucaje* winery which makes wines and pisco. There is a hotel at the winery, which also has a collection of fossilized whale and other sea creatures' bones in the garden. (See under Huacachina, page 307, for tours.)

Ica

Sleeping ■
1 Hostal Christian
2 Hostal El Aleph & Hostal Siesta I & II
3 Hostal Palacios
4 Hostal Paraíso
5 Hostal Silmar
6 Hostal Tumi de Oro
7 Konfort
8 Sol de Ica
9 Tucaranda

Eating ●
1 Café Mogambo
2 El Otro Peñoncito
3 La Bruja de Cachiche
4 Pastelería Velazco
5 Pizzería Venecia
6 Tejas Helena
7 Viña Mejía

South Coast

Pisco: a history in the making

A visit to Peru would not be complete without savouring a pisco sour. Peruvians are mighty proud of their national tipple, which has turned out to be one of the few positive results of conquest.

Peru was the first conquered territory in Spanish America to produce wines and brandies. The cultivation of grapes began with the import of vinestalks from the Canary Islands which were planted on the outskirts of Lima. The crop later reached as far as Cusco and Ayacucho in the Andes, but it was in Ica that the enterprise really took off, owing mainly to the region's exceptional climate.

A hundred years after the conquest, the wine and pisco trade had grown considerably. Ica sent its wine to Huamanga, Cusco, Lima and Callao. And from Pisco ships left for other important ports like Guayaquil, Santa Fe, Panamá, Realejo and Sonsonate (in Central America), as well as Valparaíso and Buenos Aires. Reports of maritime trade in the 16th and 17th centuries reveal the growing prestige of grape brandy as pisco exports eventually displaced those of wine.

Pisco trade surged in spite of royal bans to halt the vineyard explosion that endangered the Spanish wine industry. In 1629, the prohibition included the transport of Peruvian wines aboard Atlantic-bound ships. But despite the restrictions, the industry continued to expand during most of the 18th century.

Though a few firms utilize modern procedures to manufacture and market larger quantities, pisco is still mostly made by small, independent producers using mainly traditional techniques. The traditional method of crushing the grapes by foot can still be found and the fermented grape juice is emptied into traditional Peruvian stills, called falcas, which are crucial to the process of true pisco production. Also more conventional wineries still rely on wood from the carob tree. This slow-burning fuel is said to provide a constant source of heat that makes for a finer flavour, rather like food cooked over a charcoal fire.

Another important factor in pisco production is the type of grape. The unscented quebranta grape, brought to the Americas by the Spaniards, lends its unique characteristics to the making of the renowned "pure pisco". There are also fragrant piscos from Moscatel and Albilla varieties, "creole piscos" made with prime fragrant grapes and green piscos made with partially fermented grape juice.

The Ica valley still ranks as Peru's foremost producer of pisco, followed by the nearby valleys of Pisco, Chincha and Lunahuaná and Moquegua further south. Other production centres include Vitor in Arequipa, Locumba in Tacna and Surco in Lima.

Essentials

AL Las Dunas, Av La Angostura 400, T231031, F231007. Prices don't include 18% tax and service, about 20% cheaper on weekdays, located in a complete resort with restaurant, swimming pool, horse riding and other activities, it has its own airstrip for flights over the Nasca Lines, 50 mins. Highly recommended. Lima offices: Ricardo Rivera Navarrete 889, Oficina 208, San Isidro, Casilla 4410, Lima 100, T/F442 4180. **C-D Hostal Siesta I**, Independencia 160, T233249. With bathroom, hot water, friendly owner, but very noisy. Also **Siesta II**, T234633, which is similar. **C Hostal Silmar**, Castrovirreyna 110, T235089. Hot water, TV, carpets. **C Sol de Ica**, Lima 265, T236168 F470 8455, 1 block from Plaza de Armas, soldeica_hotel@peru.com Clean rooms, reasonably comfortable, breakfast extra, swimming pool, tour agency. **E Hostal El Aleph**, Independencia 152. Good. **E Konfort**, La Mar 251, 4 blocks from the plaza, T233672. Clean, motorcycle parking. **E Princess**, Urb Santa María D-103, T/F215421, princesshotelos@yahoo.com A taxi ride from the main plaza, with hot

Sleeping
Hotels are fully booked during the harvest festival & prices rise greatly

■ *on map*
Price codes: see inside front cover

water, TV, pool, tourist information, helpful, peaceful, very good. **E** *Tucaranda*, Lambayeque, next to the Ormeño bus terminal. With private bathrooms. **E** *Hostal Tumi de Oro*, Independencia y Castrovirreyna. New, clean, friendly. **F** *Hostal Cristian*, Ayacucho 352, T218048. Large, clean, friendly. **F** *Hostal Palacios*, Tacna 177. Modern, clean, good value. **F** *Hostal Paraíso*, Bolívar 418, T215457. Clean, quiet, basic. **G** *Salaverry*, Salaverry 146, T214019. Basic but clean, shared bathroom, cold water.

Eating
● *on map*
There's a good restaurant at the Ormeño bus terminal

La Bruja de Cachiche, Cajamarca 118. Serves local dishes such as *chicharrones con pallares* (butter beans). *Chifa Karaoke Central*, Urb Los Viñedos de Santa María E-25, T221294. Excellent Chinese food. *Café Mogambo*, Tacna 125. A good place for breakfast. *El Otro Peñoncito*, Bolívar 255. Set lunch US$2, friendly, clean, good toilets. *Pastelería Velazco*, on Plaza de Armas. Clean, good service. Recommended. *Pizzería Venecia*, Lima 252. Best pizzas in town. *Viña Mejía*, Callao 179. A rustic bar where local wines can be tried. The best *tejas* are sold at *Tejas Helena*, Cajamarca 137. *Tejas Ruthy*, Cajamarca 122, are also good and a bit cheaper.

Festivals
The wine harvest festival (*Festival Internacional de la Vendimia*) is held in **early Mar** as is the *Concurso Nacional de Marinera*. In the **first week of May** is *Fiesta de la Cruz*. Also in **May, the third Sun**, is *Día Internacional del Pisco* (you don't need to be told what happens – use your imagination). In the **third week of Jun** is *Ica Week* and the **last week of Sep** is *Tourist Week*. In the **first 2 weeks of Oct** the image of *El Señor de Luren*, in a fine church in Parque Luren, draws pilgrims from all Peru, when there are all-night processions.

Transport
To **Pisco** (70 km), 45 mins, US$0.70 with *Saky* buses from opposite the Ormeño terminal. *Ormeño* is at Lambayeque 180. Most bus offices are on Lambayeque blocks 1 and 2 and Salaverry block 3. To **Lima** (302 km), 4 hrs, US$5, several daily including *Soyuz* (Av Manzanilla 130 – every 8 mins 0600-2200) and Flores (see also Lima, Buses). To **Nasca** (140 km), 2 hrs, US$2; several buses and colectivos daily, including *Ormeño*, and *Trans Sr de Luren*, hourly on the hour 0600-2200. To **Arequipa** the route goes via Nasca, see under Nasca; most reliable buses with *Ormeño, ECS* and *Flores*. **Taxis** For trips in and around Ica, *Luis Andrade*, T222057, BETOSOUL812@hotmail.com US$4 per hr in an old Chevrolet.

Directory
Banks Avoid changing TCs if possible as commission is high. If you need to, though, *BCP* is reasonable. **Communications** Post Office: at Callao y Moquegua. **Telephone**: at Av San Martín y Huánuco.

Huacachina

Colour map 5, grid B2

Five kilometres from Ica, round a palm-fringed lake and amid impressive sand dunes, is the attractive oasis and summer resort of Huacachina. Its green sulphur waters are said to possess curative properties and attract thousands of visitors. **Sandboarding** on the dunes has become a major pastime here, attracting fans from Europe and elsewhere. Board hire is US$1 per hour. **NB** For the inexperienced, sandboarding can be dangerous on the big dunes. Take a taxi from Ica for less than US$1.

Sleeping & eating
A *Hotel Mossone*, at the eastern end of the lake, T213630, F236137, otorres@derramajae.org.pe A great place to relax, full board available, with bath, pool (US$4 including snacks, US$15 including meals, for non-residents), bicycles and sandboards for guests' use. End the day with a *Perú libre* in the majestic bar overlooking the lake. **C** *Hostería Suiza*, Malecón 264, T238762, hostessuiza@yahoo.com

Overlooking lake, quiet, friendly, clean, includes breakfast. **F** *Cas de Arena*, T215439. Basic rooms, **G** without bath, bar, small pool, laundry facilities, board hire, popular with backpackers. **F** *Hostal Rocha*, T222256. Rooms with bath, hot water, family run, kitchen and laundry facilities, board hire, small pool, popular with backpackers, but generally run-down and dirty. **G** *Hostal Titanic*, T229003. Small rooms, clean, pool and café, clothes washing, board hire, good value. *La Sirena* is the best place to eat, the big *corvina* fish steaks are excellent. *Morrón*, beside the lake, is also good but is closed in the evening. *Curahuasi* and *Mayo* at the entrance to the settlement are the other 2 options.

Tours *Robert Penny Cabrera*, at *Hostales Rocha* or *Casa de Arena*, icadeserttrip@yahoo.es Speaks English, runs trips to the desert at Ocucaje, 30 km south of Ica, in 4-wheel drive pick-up. Day trips US$14.50 (minimum 4, maximum 6), can arrange overnight trips, bring your own food.

Ica to Nasca

Palpa
Population: 15,000

Known as the 'Capital de la Naranja' (the Orange Capital), Palpa is a hospitable town 97 km south of Ica. The Plaza de Armas, on which the Municipalidad and church stand, is bordered by arches. Some colonial-style buildings survive. The climate is hot and dry (average annual temperature 21.4°C) and the main crops, besides oranges, are other fruits (eg plums, bananas) and cotton. There is also fishing for shrimp in the river. The **Fiesta de la Ciruela y Vendimia** (plum harvest) is in March/April. The town's tourist week is in the last week of July. The main *fiesta* is on 15 August.

Sleeping **F** *San Francisco*, 2 blocks from the plaza. Other hotels include the *Palpa*. There are also several *pensiones*, including *El Sol*, which is not recommended. Most restaurants are along the Pan-American Highway.

Sights around Palpa
There are several archaeological sites, of different periods, not far from the town. The **Ciudad Perdida de Hualluri**, on the west side of the Panamericana Sur, 16 km from Palpa, 5 km from the Highway (Distrito Santa Cruz), is a ruined pre-Inca city. At the entrance to the site is a huarango tree which is over 1,000 years old. In Sector Sacramento, 2 km from the Highway, is the **Puente Colgante del Inca**, built during the reign of Pachacútec.

On the desert near Palpa there are drawings similar to those found at Nasca: a sun dial, the Reloj Solar, measuring 150 m across, a whale (35 m), a pelican (45 m), the so-called Familia Real, a man, woman and child (30 m tall) and another 1,000 or so lines and figures. Two Nasca culture centres have been excavated at **La Muña** and **Los Molinos**. At the former, the tomb of **El Señor de Palpa** forms part of a laberinthine funerary complex. Ceramics, necklaces, spondylus sea shells and gold objects have been found, despite earlier sacking by grave robbers. Los Molinos is a monumental complex where more burials have been uncovered. See under the **Nasca Lines**, below, for the relationship of these markings on the desert with those at Nasca.

Guides & information
Seek information from the Consejo Municipal. There are no travel agencies in town. Otherwise ask for information and guides in Nasca.

South Coast

Nasca

Phone code: 034
Colour map 5, grid B3
Population: over
50,000
Altitude: 598 m

Set in a green valley surrounded by mountains, Nasca would be just like any other anonymous desert oasis (the sun blazes the year round by day and the nights are crisp) were it not for the 'discovery' of a series of strange lines etched on the plain to the north. Tourists in their thousands now flock to the town to fly over the famous Nasca Lines, whose precise purpose still remains a mystery. Overlooking the town is Cerro Blanco (2,078 m), the highest sand dune in the world, which is popular for sandboarding and paragliding.

Ins and outs

Getting there   There is no central bus station, but offices are at the western end of town, close to the Panamerica Sur after it has crossed the Río Tierras Blancas.

Getting around   Most of the hotels are spread out along Jr Lima and around the Plaza de Armas and are within easy walking distance of the bus stations.

Sights

Nasca was badly damaged by an earthquake in 1996. Among the buildings destroyed was the municipality's museum on the main plaza. There are no plans to rebuild it, but the large, new **Museo Antonini**, at Avenida de la Cultura 600, at the eastern end of Jr Lima, next to the municipal swimming pool, was opened in 1999. It houses the discoveries of Professor Orefici and his team from the huge pre-Inca city at Cahuachi (see below), which, Orefici believes, holds the key to the Nasca Lines. Many tombs survived the *huaqueros* and there are displays of ceramics, textiles, amazing *antaras*

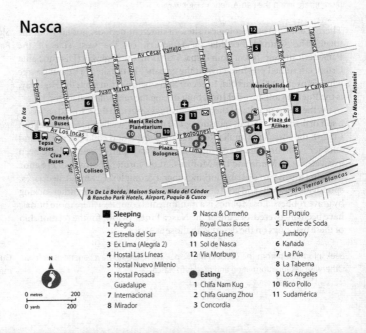

Nasca

■ Sleeping
1 Alegría
2 Estrella del Sur
3 Ex Lima (Alegría 2)
4 Hostal Las Líneas
5 Hostal Nuevo Milenio
6 Hostal Posada
   Guadalupe
7 Internacional
8 Mirador

9 Nasca & Ormeño
   Royal Class Buses
10 Nasca Lines
11 Sol de Nasca
12 Via Morburg

● Eating
1 Chifa Nam Kug
2 Chifa Guang Zhou
3 Concordia

4 El Puquio
5 Fuente de Soda
   Jumbory
6 Kañada
7 La Púa
8 La Taberna
9 Los Angeles
10 Rico Pollo
11 Sudamérica

0 metres 200
0 yards 200

(panpipes) and photos of the excavations and the Lines. ■ *0900-1900, ring the bell to get in. Entry is US$3, including a local guide. A video is shown in the Conference Room. T523444. It is a 10-mins' walk from the plaza, or a short taxi ride. Recommended.*

The **Maria Reiche Planetarium**, at the *Hotel Nasca Lines*, was opened in May 2000 in honour of Maria Reiche (see below). It is run by Edgardo Azabache, who speaks English, Italian and French, and Enrique Levano, who speaks English and Italian. Both give lectures every night about the Nasca Lines, based on Reiche's theories, which cover archaeology and astronomy. The show lasts about 45 minutes, after which visitors are able to look at the moon, planets and stars through sophisticated telescopes. ■ *Shows are usually at 1845 and 2045 nightly; entry US$6 (half price for students). Very good. T522293.*

Sights around Nasca

The Nasca area is dotted with over 100 cemeteries and the dry, humidity-free climate has preserved perfectly invaluable tapestries, cloth and mummies. *For Nasca Lines, see page 312*

At the cemetery of **Chauchilla**, 30 km south of Nasca, grave robbing *huaqueros* ransacked the tombs and left remains all over the place. Bones, skulls, mummies and pottery shards litter the desert. ■ *A tour is worthwhile and takes about two hours. It should cost about US$7 per person with a minimum of three people. On the Panamericana Sur, heading south from Nasca, Chauchilla is on the left, unsigned, 12 km from the highway.*

There are other cemeteries in the vicinity. Some, like Poroma, have been so desecrated that there is nothing left to see. A good cemetery, with mummies still to be seen, is in the valley of **Jumana**, one hour west of Nasca in the river bed. Cemetery tours usually include a visit to a gold shop. Gold mining is one of the main local industries and a tour includes a visit to a small family processing shop where the techniques used are still very old-fashioned.

Some tours also include a visit to a local **potter's studio**. That of Sr Andrés Calle Benavides, who makes Nasca reproductions, is particularly recommended. He is very friendly and takes time to explain the techniques he uses although his small gallery is a bit on the expensive side. Anyone interested in pre-Columbian ceramics is welcome to make an appointment to visit him independently. He is very knowledgeable on the coastal desert cultures.

The Paredones ruins, also called Cacsamarca, are Inca on a pre-Inca base. They are not well-preserved. The underground aqueducts, or *puquios*, built 300 BC-AD 700, still provide water for the local people. They are beautifully built and even have S-bends to slow down the flow of water, and they're very cool. 33 aqueducts irrigate 20 ha each and, to this day, local farmers have the job of cleaning the section for which their group has been responsible for as long as they can remember. ■ *By taxi it is about US$10 round trip, or go with a tour.*

Cantalloc is a 30 minutes to an hour walk through Buena Fe, to see markings in the valley floor. These consist of a triangle pointing to a hill and a *tela* (cloth) with a spiral depicting the threads. Climb the mountain to see better examples. There are also aqueducts here. This is best done with a guide, or by car. ■ *To visit costs US$8, minimum 3 people.*

Cahuachi, to the west of the Nasca Lines, comprises several pyramids and a site called **El Estaquería**. The latter is thought to have been a series of astronomical sighting posts, but more recent research suggests the wooden pillars were used to dry dead bodies and therefore it may have been a place of mummification. ■ *To visit the ruins of Cahuachi costs US$8, minimum 3 people. See also the Museo Antonini, above.*

South Coast

Essentials

Sleeping
■ *on map*
Price codes:
see inside front cover
*Those arriving by bus
should beware being
told that the hotel
of their choice is
closed, or full*

L-A *Maison Suisse*, opposite the airport, T/F522434. Nice, comfortable, safe car park, expensive restaurant, pool, rooms with jacuzzi, accepts Amex, good giftshop, shows video of Nasca Lines. Also has camping facilities. **A** *Nasca Lines*, Jr Bolognesi, T522293, F522293. With a/c, comfortable, rooms with private patio, hot water, peaceful, restaurant, good but expensive meals, safe car park, pool (US$2.50 for non-guests, or free if having lunch), they can arrange package tours which include 2-3 nights at the hotel plus a flight over the lines and a desert trip for around US$250. Recommended. **A** *De La Borda*, an old hacienda at Majoro about 5 km from town past the airstrip, T522750. Gardens, pool, pricey restaurant, quiet, English-speaking manageress.

C *Nido del Cóndor*, opposite the airport, Panamericana Sur Km 447, T522424, acnasca@terra.com.pe Large rooms, hot water, good restaurant, bar, shop, videos, swimming pool, camping US$3, parking, English, Italian German spoken, free pick-up from town, reservation advised. **C-D** *Hostal Las Líneas*, Jr Arica 299, T522488. Cheaper without bath, clean, spacious, restaurant. Recommended, but ask for a room away from the street. **D** *Estrella del Sur*, Callao 568, T522764. Small, clean rooms with shower, price includes breakfast. **D** *Internacional*, Av Maria Reiche, T522166. With bathroom, hot water, garage, café and newer bungalows. **D** *Mirador*, Tacna 436, T523121, F523714. On main plaza, comfortable rooms with shower, cheaper with shared bath, hot water (unreliable at peak times), TV, modern, clean. Recommended.

E per person *Alegría*, Jr Lima 166, T22702, T/F522444, www.nazcaperu.com Continental breakfast and tax included. Rooms with bathroom, carpet and a/c, hot water, cafeteria, rose garden, English, Italian, German and Hebrew, laundry facilities, safe luggage deposit (including for bus passengers not needing a hotel), book exchange, email facilities for US$2 per hr, netphone also US$2, free video on the lines at 2100, very popular. Recommended. Efraín Alegría also runs a tour agency and guests are encouraged to buy tours (see Tour operators), flights and bus tickets arranged. Don't listen to anyone who says that *Alegría* is closed, or full, and no longer runs tours; if you phone or email the hotel they will pick you up at the bus station free of charge day or night (*Alegría* gives 1 hr free internet use to those who email in advance). **E** per person *ex-Lima (called Alegría)*, Av Los Incas 117, opposite Ormeño bus terminal, T522497. More basic than *Alegría* (above) with which it is unrelated, cheaper without bathroom, hot water, clean. **E** *Rancho Park*, on Panamericana 1 km from town towards the airport, T521153. Hotel on farmland with two swimming pools (one for children), entry to pools US$1, popular at weekends, good restaurant. **E** *Sol de Nasca*, Callao 586, T522730. Rooms with and without hot showers, TV, also has a restaurant, pleasant, don't leave valuables in luggage store. **E** *Hostal Restaurant Via Morburg*, JM Mejía 108, 3 blocks from Plaza de Armas, T/F522566 (in Lima T479 1467, F462 0932). With bathroom, fan, hot water, small swimming pool, TV room, free pisco sour on arrival, excellent and cheap restaurant on top floor. Recommended.

F *Posada Guadalupe*, San Martín 225, T522249. Family-run, lovely courtyard and garden, **G** without bath, hot water, good breakfast, relaxing (touts who try to sell tours are nothing to do with hotel). **F** *Nasca*, C Lima 438, T/F522085, hot water, noisy, clothes washing facilities, luggage store, hard sell on tours and flights, bargain hard for better price, mixed reports, safe motorcycle parking. **G** *Hostal Nuevo Milenio*, Arica 582. Hot water, use of kitchen, owner can book flights, tours and buses.

Eating
● *on map*

Concordia, Lima 594. Good, also rents bikes at US$1 an hour. *Farita*, Bolognesi 388, 1 block from plaza. Typical Nasca breakfast (*tamales*, *chicharrones*, etc). *Chifa Guang Zhou*, Bolognesi 297, T522036. Very good. *Kañada*, Lima 160, nazcanada@yahoo.com Cheap *menú*, excellent pisco sours, nice wines, popular, display of local artists' work, email service, English spoken, owner Juan Carlos Fraola is very helpful.

Los Angeles, Bolognesi 266. Good, cheap, try *sopa criolla*, and chocolate cake. *Chifa Nam Kug*, on Bolognesi near Plaza Bolognesi. Recommended. *La Púa*, Jr Lima, next to *Hotel Alegría*. Good. *El Puquio*, Bolognesi 50 m from plaza. Good food, especially pastas, pleasant atmsophere, good for drinks, popular. *Rico Pollo* opposite *Hotel Alegría*. Good local restaurant, cheap. *Sudamérica*, Lima 668. Good local food, especially meat. *La Taberna*, Jr Lima 321, T521411. Excellent food, live music, popular with gringos, it's worth a look just for the graffiti on the walls. *The Grumpys*, Bolognesi 282. Despite its name, really friendly, salads, fish and chicken dishes, cocktails. *Fuente de Soda Jumbory*, near the cinema. Good *almuerzo*. *Panadería*, Bolognesi 387, opposite *Farita*.

There is a market at Lima y Grau, and the Mercado Central is between Arica and Tacna. For work by local artists, contact *Asociación Cultural Cahuachi*, T522393, Sr Orlando.

Shopping

The *Virgen de la Guadelupe* festival is held on **Aug 29-Sep 10**.

Festivals

All guides must be approved by the Ministry of Tourism and should have an official identity card. As more and more touts (*jaladores*) operate at popular hotels and the bus terminals, they are using false ID cards and fake hotel and tour brochures. They are all rip-off merchants who overcharge and mislead those who arrive by bus. Only conduct business with agencies at their office, or phone or email the company you want to deal with in advance. Some hotels are not above pressurising guests to purchase tours at inflated prices. *Alegría Tours*, Lima 186, T523775, F522444, T621673 (mob), info@alegriatoursperu.com www.alegriatoursperu.com Run by Efraín Alegría, offer inclusive tours (see Sleeping above) which have been repeatedly recommended. Guides with radio contact and maps can be provided for hikes to nearby sites. They have guides who speak English, German, French and Italian, with tours to Palpa, Puerto Inca, Sacaco and the San Fernando Reserve to see the marine wildlife, to Chauchilla, Cantalloc, etc. Tours go as far as Ica, Paracas and the Ballestas Islands. In the high Andes they have birdwatching, visits to Pampas Galeras vicuña reserve, visits to the village of Andamarca and downhill mountain biking trips. Also sandboarding on Cerro Blanco. *Alegría* run a bus from Nasca to Pisco every day at 1000 (returns at 1000 from Pisco's Plaza de Armas), via Ica, Huacachina and *bodegas*. The *Fernández* family, who run the *Hotel Nasca*, also run local tours. Ask for the hotel owners and speak to them direct. Also ask Efraín Alegría or the Fernández family to arrange a taxi for you to one of the sites outside Nasca (eg US$50 to Sacaco, 30 mins at site). Also recommended are: *Jesús Erazo Buitrón*, Juan Matta 1110, T523005, T699607(mob). Very knowledgeable, he speaks a little English but his Spanish is easy to follow. Juan Tohalino Vera of *Nasca Trails*, Bolognesi 550, T522858, nascatrails@terra.com.pe He speaks English, French, German and Italian. Also *Nanasca Tours*, Jr Lima 160, T/F522917, T622054 (mob), nanascatours@yahoo.com Juan Carlos Iraola is very helpful. *Tour Perú*, Arica 285, Plaza de Armas. Efficient. *Viajes Nasca*, Jr Lima 185, T521027, guide Susi recommended.

Tour operators
Do not take just any taxi on the plaza for a tour as they are unreliable and can lead to robbery

It is not dangerous to visit the sites if you go with a trustworthy person. Taxi drivers usually act as guides, but most speak only Spanish

Bus To **Lima** (446 km), 6 hrs, several buses and colectivos daily. Recommended companies include: *Ormeño*,T522058, *Royal Class* at 1330 US$25, from *Hotel Nasca Lines*, Jr Bolognesi, normal service from Av Los Incas, 6 a day, US$5; *Civa*, Av Guardia Civil, T523019, normal service at 2300, US$8. Ormeño's *Royal Class* arrives in Santa Catalina, a much safer area of Lima (see page 98).

Transport
It is worth paying the extra for a good bus. Reports of robbery on the cheaper services

Ormeño to **Ica**, 2 hrs, US$2, 3 a day, and to **Pisco** (210 km), 3 hrs, US$5, also 3 a day. *Royal Class* to **Paracas**, 23/4 hrs, and Pisco, both at 1330, US$15. Note that buses to Pisco don't go into the centre, but stop 5 km outside town; change to a colectivo.

Overbooking is common

To **Arequipa**, 623 km, 9 hrs: *Ormeño* 1530, 2000, 2300, from Av Los Incas, US$7.25, with *Royal Class* at 2130, US$30, 8 hrs. *Civa*, 1100, 1500, 2300, US$10, 9 hrs, with *Imperial* service at 1200, 9 hrs, US$20. Delays are possible out of Nasca because of drifting sand across the road or because of mudslides in the rainy season. Travel in daylight if possible. Book your ticket on previous day.

Buses to **Cusco**, 659 km, 14 hrs, via **Chalhuanca** and **Abancay**. On the **Lima-Nasca-Abancay-Cusco** route *Expreso Wari* have normal services at 1600, 1800, and 2200, US$17, and *Imperial* service at 1200, US$20 (bus may run if not enough passengers). Their offices are at the exit from Nasca on the road to Puquío. Also buses to Cusco with *Ormeño*, US$27, *Cruz del Sur*, 1630, 2400, US$20, and *Molina*.

Directory   **Banks**   *BCP*, Lima y Grau. Changes cash and Visa TCs at decent rates, also cash advance on Visa, Visa ATM. *Interbank*, on the Plaza de Armas. Changes cash, Mastercard agent. Some street changers will change TCs, but at 8% commission. **Communications**   Internet: many places on Jr Bolognesi. *Lucy@com*, Bolognesi 298. US$0.75 per hr. *Migsu Net*, Arica 295, p 2. Daily 0800-2400, good, fast machines, US$1 per hr. Facilities at *Hotel Alegría* and *Nasca Trails*. **Post Office**: at Fermín de Castillo 379, T522016. Also at *Hotel Alegría*. **Telephone**: *Telefónica del Perú* for international calls with coins on Plaza Bolognesi. Also on Plaza de Armas and at Lima 359 where you can send or receive faxes and make international collect calls. **Useful addresses**   Police: at Av Los Incas.

Nasca Lines

Colour map 5, grid B3   *Cut into the stony desert are large numbers of lines, not only parallels and geometrical figures, but also designs such as a killer whale, a monkey, birds (one with a wing span of over 100 m), a spider and a tree. The lines, which can best be appreciated from the air, were etched on the Pampa sands by the Nasca people. It's estimated that they were begun around 400 BC and continued to be made for perhaps another thousand years. The famous lines are above the Ingenio valley on the Pampa de San José, about 22 km north of Nasca, and across the Ingenio river, on the plain around Palpa. The Pan-American Highway passes close to, even through, the Lines.*

The mystery of the lines   Since the Nasca Lines were first spotted from the air 70 years ago, their meaning, function and origin have tormented scientists around the world.

Dr Paul Kosok, a North American scientist, gave the first scientific explanation in 1941, when he observed a line pointing towards the place where the sun would have risen on the midwinter solstice in ancient Nasca times. So impressed was he, that he described the Nasca pampa as "the biggest astronomy book in the world".

By the 1950s Maria Reiche (see below), inspired by Kosok, was mapping the area and discovered giant animals too vast to be appreciated from the ground. Her many years of research led her to the conclusion that they were a huge astronomical calendar.

There are those who disagree with the German mathematician's hypothesis. The International Explorers Society, for example, was convinced that the desert artists would not have drawn something they themselves could not see. They set out to prove that the ancient Peruvians could fly, based on the fact that the lines are best seen from the air, and that there are pieces of ancient local pottery and tapestry showing balloonists as well as local legends of flying men. In 1975, they made a hot-air balloon of cloth and reed, called it *Condor I* and attempted to fly it for 15 minutes over the pampa. Unfortunately for them, the flight lasted only 60 seconds, thereby leaving the issue unresolved.

Some of the competing theories as to the function of the Nasca lines are rather far-fetched. Erich Von Daniken, in his book *Chariots of the Gods*, posited that the pampa was an extraterrestrial landing strip. This idea, however, only succeeded in drawing to the site thousands of visitors who tore across the lines on motorbikes, four-wheel drives, horses and whatever else they could get their hands on, leaving an indelible mark. It is now an offence to walk or drive on the pampa, punishable by heavy fine or imprisonment.

Other theories are that the Nasca designs were part of a giant running track (George A Von Breunig – 1980; also proposed by the English astronomer Alan Sawyer). Another suggestion is that they represent weaving patterns and yarns (Henri Stirlin), or that the plain is a map demonstrating the Tiahuanaco Empire (Zsoltan Zelko). Dr Johan Reinhard brings together ethnographic, historical and archaeological data, including the current use of straight lines in Chile and Bolivia, to suggest that the Lines conform to fertility practices throughout the Andes.

Recent research

The BBC series 'Ancient Voices' pointed to yet another theory. The clues to the function of the lines are found in the highly advanced pottery and textiles of the ancient Nascans, which relate directly to the subject matter of the lines. Some pots and tapestries show a flying being emitting discharge from its nose and mouth. This is believed to portray the flight of the shaman. The shaman consumes certain psycho-active drugs that convince him he can fly and so enter the real world of spirits in order to rid sick people of evil spirits.

In this way, the lines were not designed to be seen physically from above, but from the mind's eye of the flying shaman. This also explains the presence of incongruous creatures such as a monkey or killer whale. They were chosen because they possess the qualities admired and needed by the shaman in his spirit journeys.

But this does not explain the spectacular geometric figures. These straight lines are a feature of ancient Peruvian ritual behaviour, much like ley lines in Europe. They represent invisible paths of perceived energy. The Pampa's most remarkable features are the trapezoids, which are thought to have been ritual spaces where offerings were made to the gods, in the hope of favours in return.

Scientists have discovered evidence of a terrible 40-year drought around AD 550 or 600. This coincides not only with the abandonment of the nearby Cahuachi temples but also with a period of increased bloody warfare and increased line-making in the desert sands. This would seem to indicate that the Nascans grew increasingly desperate in the face of continued drought, abandoned traditional religious practices, and instead made more and more sacrificial offerings to the gods.

The results of six years' work by Peruvian archaeologist Johny Isla and Markus Reindel of the Swiss-Liechtenstein Foundation threw new light on the Lines in 2002. It ties together some of the earlier ideas and discredits both the astronomical calendar and extraterrestrial theories. Working at La Muña and Los Molinos, Palpa (see above) and with photogrammetry (mapping using aerial photographs), they have deduced that the lines on both the Palpa and Nasca plains are offerings dedicated to the worship of water and fertility. These two elements were paramount to the coastal people in this arid environment and they expressed their adoration not only in the desert, but also on their ceramics and on the engraved stones of the Paracas culture. Isla and Reindel believe that the Palpa lines predate those at Nasca and that the lines and drawings themselves are scaled up versions of the Paracas drawings, made at a time when the Nasca people were becoming independent of Paracas. In addition, objects in the shape of drops of water, whales and chilis, found in the grave of El Señor de Palpa, are repeated in the desert. This

South Coast

new research proposes the theory that the Nasca culture succumbed not to drought, but to heavy rainfall, probably during an El Niño event.

In 1976 Maria Reiche had a platform called the mirador put up at her own expense, from which three of the huge designs can be seen – the Hands, the Lizard and the Tree. Her book, *Mystery on the Desert*, is on sale for US$10 (proceeds to conservation work) at the hotel. In January 1994 Maria Reiche opened a small **museum**. Victoria Nikitzhi, a friend of Maria Reiche, gives lectures about the Nasca Lines, with a scale model, at 1900 at Jr San Martín 221; donations of US$2.85 requested. ■ *US$1), 5 km from town at the Km 416 marker, take a micro from in front of Ormeño terminal, US$0.70, frequent. See www.magicperu.com/MariaReiche/* See also the **Planetarium**, page 309.

Tours of the Nasca Lines

By land Taxi-guides to the mirador, 0800-1200, cost US$4.35 per person, or you can hitch, but there is not always much traffic. Travellers suggest the view from the hill 500 m back to Nasca is better. An *Ormeño* bus leaves for the lines at 0900 (US$1.75); hitch back, but have patience. Go by an early bus as the site gets very hot. Better still, take a taxi and arrive at 0745 before the buses.

By air Small planes take 3-5 passengers to see the Nasca Lines. Flights last 30-35 mins and are controlled by air traffic personnel at the airport to avoid congestion. Reservations should be made at the airport for flights with *Aerocóndor*, Panamericana Sur Km 447, T522424, F522404 (or their office in *Hotel Las Dunas* in Ica, T256230 – see below for Lima), www.aerocondor.com.pe Flights can also be booked at *Hotel Alegría* with *Alas Peruanas*, T522444/523775 (24 hours), info@alasperuanas.com, alegriatours@hotmail.com (experienced pilots fluent in English), *Hotel Nasca*, *Aero Montecarlo*, *AeroParacas* (T667231, F522688) or *Aero Ica* in Jr Lima and at the airport. These companies are well-established and recommended. There are others. The price for a flight is US$35 per person (special deals are sometimes available, eg, *hostal* included; touts charge US$50; shorter flights on sale for US$25). You also have to pay US$2 airport tax. It is best to organize a flight direct with the airlines at the airport. Flights are bumpy with many tight turns – many people are airsick. If you fly first thing it may be best not to eat or drink anything for breakfast. Best times to fly are 0800-1000 and 1500-1630 when there is less turbulence and better light. *Alas Peruanas* usually include other features in their 35-min flight over the Lines, such as the spiral ventilation holes of the aqueducts. They also offer 1-hr flights over the Palpa and Llipata areas, where you can see human figures,

Maria Reiche – Guardian of the lines

The greatest contribution to our awareness of the lines is that of Maria Reiche, who lived and worked on the Pampa for over 50 years. The young German mathematician arrived in Peru in the early 1930s and would dedicate the rest of her life to removing centuries of windswept debris and painstaking survey work. She even used to sleep on the Pampa.

Maria Reiche's years of meticulous measurement and study of the lines led her to the conclusion that they represented a huge astronomical calendar. She also used her mathematical knowledge to determine how the many drawings and symbols could have been created with such precise symmetry. She suggested that those responsible for the lines used long cords attached to stakes in the ground. The figures were drawn by means of a series of circular arcs of different radius.

Reiche also contended that they used a standard unit of measurement of 1.30 m, or the distance between the fingertips of a person's extended arms.

As well as the anthropomorphic and zoomorphic drawings, there are a great many geometric figures. Reiche believed these to be a symbolic form of writing associated with the movements of the stars. In this way, the lines could have been used as a kind of calendar that not only recorded celestial events but also had a practical day-to-day function such as indicating the times for harvest, fishing and festivals.

Whatever the real purpose of the Nasca Lines, one fact remains indisputable: that their status as one of the country's major tourist attractions is largely due to the selfless work of Maria Reiche, the unofficial guardian of the lines. Maria Reiche died in June 1998.

birds, geometric designs and other rare patterns (US$60 per person, minimum 3). They can also organize flights from Pisco (US$130) and Ica (US$120). All *Alas Peruanas* flights include the BBC film of Nasca.

Aerocóndor (in Lima T442 5215/5663) and *Aero Ica* (Lima T445 0839) both offer flights over the lines from Lima in a 1-day tour (lunch in Nasca) for US$260 per person; or flights from Ica for US$130 per person. *Aero Ica* also offers a night in *Maison Suisse* plus flight for US$65, but book 48 hrs in advance. A taxi to the airport costs US$1.35; bus, US$0.10. Make sure you clarify everything before getting on the plane and ask for a receipt. Also let them know in advance if you have any special requests.

Nasca to Cusco

The highway from Nasca to Cusco is paved and safe. Two hours out of Nasca is the **Reserva Nacional Pampas Galeras** at 4,100 m, which has a vicuña reserve. There is an interesting Museo del Sitio, also a military base and park guard here. It's best to go early as entry is free. At Km 155 is **Puquio**, which has **F** *Hostal Central*, Avenida Castilla 625, with shared bath, hot water and restaurant (motorcycle parking available). It's then another 185 km to **Chalhuanca**. There are wonderful views on this stretch, with lots of small villages, valleys and alpacas. In Chalhuanca is **F** *Hostal Victoria*, Jr Arequipa 305, T321301, shared bath, clean and comfortable, and one other on the main road between the plaza and the Wari bus stop, cheaper, very basic, dirty, but has parking. From Chalhuanca to Abancay the road is paved. Fuel is available in Puquio and Chalhuanca. For the route from Abancay to Cusco, see page 230.

South Coast

South of Nasca

Sacaco One-hundred kilometres south of Nasca is Sacaco, which has a museum built over the fossilized remains of a whale excavated in the desert. The keeper lives in a house nearby and is helpful. Take a bus from Nasca, C Bolognesi, in the morning (check times in advance) towards Puerto de Lomas. Ask the driver where to get off and be ready for a 2-km-walk in the sun. Return to the Pan-American Highway no later than 1800 for a bus back. Do not go two to three days after a new moon as a vicious wind blows at this time.

Puerto de Lomas Lying 7 km off the Pan-American Highway, on the coast 98 km from Nasca, is Puerto de Lomas, a fishing village with safe beaches which are popular in February and March. It is 1½ hours by bus from Nasca, US$1.75 (one hour by car). **C** *Hostal Capricho de Verano*, T210282. Beautifully situated on the cliffs, bungalows with bathroom, clean, very friendly, special rates for young travellers. Recommended. There are several fish restaurants.

From Puerto de Lomas the highway heads south through **Yauca** to **Chala**. The Yauca valley is almost entirely devoted to olive trees, so have a few soles ready to buy some when the bus stops.

Chala
Phone code: 034
Chala, 173 km from Nasca, is a friendly fishing village with nice beaches but it is only safe to swim near the harbour. The town has expanded greatly in recent years on the back of gold-mining in the nearby hills. It now consists of 'old' Chala and Chala Norte, spread out along 3 km of the Panamericana. Good fresh fish is available in the morning and it may be possible to go fishing with the local fishermen.

Sleeping, eating and transport All the better hotels are in old Chala. **C** *Turistas*, T551111, with bathroom, **D** without, large rooms, good beds, friendly, hot water, restaurant, great sea view. **F** *Hostal Grau*, T551009, rooms facing the ocean, use of kitchen, cheap meals on request. Next door is *Hostal Evertyth*, T551095, also clean, comfortable and friendly with rooms facing the ocean. There are dozens of restaurants, most catering for passing buses. Try *chicharrones de pulpo* (octopus) and *lenguado* (fried fish).

Colectivos leave daily from Nasca in the morning, US$3.50 per person, 2 hrs. Buses stop in **Chala Norte**, a 10-min walk north of the hotels. If heading south, the night buses from **Lima** arrive at 0600-0700, and there are others in the early evening. Buses heading north come through nearer 0500, or in the early afternoon.

Puerto Inca Ten kilometres north of Chala are the large **pre-Columbian ruins** of Puerto Inca on the coast in a beautiful bay. On their discovery in the 1950s, the ruins were misunderstood and thus neglected. It is now recognized that this was the port for Cusco. The site is in excellent condition. The drying and store houses can be seen as holes in the ground (be careful where you walk). On the right side of the bay is a cemetery, on the hill is a temple of reincarnation, and the Inca road from the coast to Cusco is clearly visible. The road was 240 km long, with a staging post every 7 km so that, with a change of runner at every post, fish for the Inca's table and messages could be sent in 24 hours.

In the two small bays the water is always calm and clear and the **fishing** and **diving** are excellent. There is a good two-hour **walk** from Puerto Inca to Chala. Take one of the paths going up behind the ruins on the south side of the bay and swing slightly inland to cross a deep *quebrada*. The path then continues through spectacular rock formations with dramatic views of the coast towards the road.

Sleeping, eating and transport C *Puerto Inka*, at Km 603 on the Panamericana Sur (for reservations T551055 - Chala, or Av Ejército 506, oficina 202, Arequipa, T/F272663). A great place to relax, with bungalows on a superb beach, boats and diving equipment for hire, disco, hammocks outside, highly recommended but used by tour groups and busy in the summer months. Also **camping** for US$2 per person. The restaurant has not received the same consistently favourable reports as the hotel. A Chala colectivo can be picked up just north of the town. A taxi from Chala costs US$5, or take a Yauca colectivo to Km 603 (US$0.50 per person) and walk down the track to the bay (3 km).

South of Chala the Pan-American passes **Atico** (**F** *Hostal La Unión*, basic) and **Ocoña** before reaching **Camaná** (392 km from Nasca).

On 23 June 2001, southern Peru was devastated by an earthquake measuring 7.9 on the Richter scale, whose epicentre was in the Pacific Ocean about 82 km from Ocoña. A tidal wave three-storeys high hit the coast, devastating resorts and agricultural land and causing severe damage inland. For this reason we do not include the section of coast around Camaná.

The Pan-American Highway swings inland from Camaná to **El Alto** where a road branches left off the Pan-American Highway and leads to **Corire**, Aplao and the valley of the Río Majes (see page 286). The Pan-American then runs along the top of a plateau with strange ash-grey **sand dunes**. These are unique in appearance and formation. All are crescent shaped and of varying sizes, from 6 to 30 m across and from 2 to 5 m high, with the points of the crescent on the leeward side. The sand is slowly blown up the convex side, drifts down into the concave side, and the dunes move about 15 m a year. If plans to extend the Majes project are completed, the irrigation of a further 60,000 ha of land will destroy a large portion of these unique sand dunes.

Inland from Camaná

The road suddenly descends into the canyons of the Siguas and Vitor rivers. There is an *hostal* (**F**) and restaurants 5 km south of **Siguas** and a *hostal* in the village of **Vitor**.

At Repartición, 42 km southwest of Arequipa, 134 km from Camaná, a branch of the Panamericana Sur leads south through Moquegua to Tacna and Arica on the Chilean border. Cyclists warn that the road to Moquegua is very hilly. From this latter road a branch leads off from **La Joya** west to Mollendo and Matarani.

Repartición

Mollendo

Since Matarani, 14½ km to the northwest, has replaced it as a port, Mollendo depends partly upon the summer attraction of its beaches, despite the presence of a smelly oil refinery. Hotels can be full during the high season, which starts on 6 January, the first day of summer and anniversary of the district, and lasts to April. Out of season, Mollendo has the appearance of an abandoned wild west town, with its ramshackle wooden houses, some painted in gaudy colours. It still houses the port workers and has the main customs agencies for the harbour.

*Phone code: 054
Colour map 6, grid C1
Population:
approximately 30,000
130 km south
of Arequipa*

Three sandy **beaches** stretch down the coast. The small beach nearest town is the safest for swimming. The swimming pool on the beach is open January-March. Out of season the beaches are littered with rubbish.

On the coast, a few kilometres southeast by road (US$0.40 by colectivo), is the summer resort of **Mejía**. The small national reserve at the lagoons has 72 resident species of birds and 62 visiting species. Arrive early in the morning to see the birdlife at its best. ■ *US$1.50.*

South Coast

The road into Mollendo goes down the fertile **Valle de Tambo**, which is full of rice paddies, sugar cane and fields of peppers and onions. Tambo is famous for its *alfajores de Tambo*, small round pastries filled with cane syrup or *manjar blanco*. The very best are made in **La Curva**, 10 km from Mollendo. Ask in the Palacio de Municipalidad for directions on where to buy them direct from the señoras who make them.

Sleeping & eating   C *Hostal Cabaña*, Comercio 240. A wooden building with huge balconies, with bathroom, **F** per person with shared bathroom, clean, good. **D** *Hostal Willy*, Deán Valdivia 437-443. Hot water, modern, spacious, noisy disco nearby. Recommended. There are several other cheap options in the **E-F** range on Arica. **F** *Hostal California*, Blondel 541, T535160. Best rooms at top, restaurant. Recommended. Several restaurants including *Cevichería Tío*, Comercio 208, excellent, cheap set meals. Others can be found on Comercio (eg *Tambo, Hong Kong Express*).

Bars & clubs   *El Observatorio*, Comercio y Deán Valdivia. A massive, booming, semi-open-air disco, "has to be seen to be believed", no cover charge.

Transport   **Bus** To **Arequipa**, 129 km, buses and **colectivos** daily, 2 hrs, US$3, many companies on Comercio opposite the church. To **Moquegua**, 156 km, 2 hrs, US$2-3, several buses and colectivos daily. To **Tacna**, 315 km, direct transport does not go daily, best to take a colectivo early in the morning to **El Fiscal** (restaurant), US$0.40, about 100 km before **Moquegua**, where you can connect with Arequipa-Tacna buses.

Moquegua

Phone code: 054
Colour map 6, grid C2
Population: 110,000
Altitude: 1,412 m

Moquegua is a peaceful town in the narrow valley of the Moquegua River and enjoys a sub-tropical climate. The town was formerly known as Santa Catalina de Guadalcazar, but thankfully reverted to its original name, which means 'silent place' in Quechua. This could be due to the rather taciturn nature of its inhabitants.

The Inca Emperor, Mayta Capac, sent his captains to carry out a pacifying occupation of the fertile valleys around Moquegua. They founded two settlements, Moquegua and Cuchuna, which is thought to be the site of present-day Torata. Today, most of the valley below the city grows grapes and the upper part grows avocados (paltas), wheat, maize, potatoes, some cotton, and fruits. Northeast from Moquegua is Cuajone, one of the most important copper mines in Peru.

Ins and outs

Getting there   There is no bus station. All bus companies are on Av Ejército, 2 blocks north of the market at Jr Grau, except *Ormeño*, Av La Paz casi Balta. The road into town runs along Av La Paz. It joins the main street (Av Balta) at the large roundabout.

Getting around   A nicely compact town, the main street is Av Balta running two blocks north of Plaza de Armas. On Sat nights Jr Moquegua west from the plaza to Jr Piura, becomes the centre of activity. The town was severely damaged by the earthquake of June 2001, but by the end of the year all services were operating. Taxi fare in town US$0.60, US$0.85 going outside the city. **Tourist offices** Jr Callao 121, in the Prefectura, is more administrative than service oriented, open 0830-1600.

Sights

Moquegua is not a pretty sight from the Pan-American Highway, but the old centre, a few blocks above Av Balta, is well worth a look for its quiet, winding, cobbled streets and historic buildings. The **Plaza de Armas**, with its mix of ruined and well-maintained churches, colonial and republican façades and fine trees, is one of the most interesting small-town plazas in the country. The fountain is said to have been designed by Eiffel, though there is some debate on the matter. The decadent statuary of the fountain in front of the Santo Domingo church (three twin-tailed mermaids with linked hands and bare breasts) is seen by some as a challenge to the traditional Catholic religious iconography within the church. Inside **Santo Domingo** itself is the body of the city's saint, Santa Fortunata, who lies in a glass-sided casket. She died in the 17th century, but her hair and nails are reputed to continue to grow miraculously. The roofs of many of the old houses are built with **sugar-cane thatch** and clay and are of an unusual design, with semi-rounded gables, a little reminiscent of the 18th-century Dutch gables. This type of construction is called *mojinete* and is also found in the Valle de Tambo. The houses' sculpted door surrounds are particularly notable. See also the balconies, for example on 700 block of Moquegua.

There are several interesting colonial houses which make a good, short walking tour. **Casa de Regidor Perpetuo de La Ciudad** or **Casa Conde de Alastaya**, is an 18th century house at Jr Moquegua 404-414 (just the portal remains after the 2001 earthquake). **Casa de Fernández Cornejo y Córdova** is at Jr Ayacucho 540, beside the post office on the plaza. It has a fine 18th-century wooden balcony. Also on the south side of the Plaza is the office of the INC (corner of Ancash) and a museum of regional ethnography is being established. At Jr Lima 849 is **Casa de Samuel Ordóñez**, which stands empty. **Casa de Díaz Fernández Dávila**, at Jr Ayacucho 828, has a collapsed interior but baroque elements can be seen in the ornate portal.

Also worth seeing are: **Casa de Don Pacífico Barrios**, Jr Moquegua 820-848, and opposite, the façade at No 831; **Casa de Diez Canseco**, esquina Tarapacá y Ayacucho; and **Casa de la Serpiente**, Tarapacá 390, the former

Moquegua

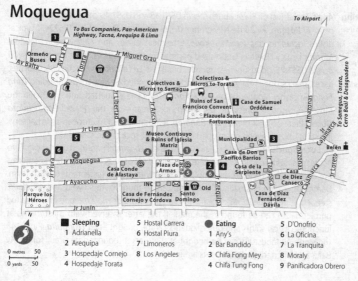

Sleeping		5 Hostal Carrera	Eating	5 D'Onofrio
1 Adrianella		6 Hostal Piura	1 Any's	6 La Oficina
2 Arequipa		7 Limoneros	2 Bar Bandido	7 La Tranquita
3 Hospedaje Cornejo		8 Los Angeles	3 Chifa Fong Mey	8 Moraly
4 Hospedaje Torata			4 Chifa Tung Fong	9 Panificadora Obrero

South Coast

offices of Essalud (the health service). Some of these houses are private, but the owners may allow entry. On Jr Lima, between Callao and Tacna, are the ruins of the convent of San Francisco. There is little to see and nothing inside except an open-air chur5ch with an awning roof.

Outside town in the direction of the airport are some interesting **bodegas**. Moquegua is famous for its pisco. *Biondi* is the best known brand. Another is *Bodega Villegas*, which is at the corner of Jr Ayacucho and Puno. You can also find wine from Omate in town, eg *Bodegas Quinistaquillas*.

Museums   **Museo Contisuyo** on the Plaza de Armas, is within the ruins of the Iglesia Matriz, which was rebuilt after many earthquakes over the centuries, but finally left as a ruin in 1868. It covers the cultures which thrived in the Moquegua and Ilo valleys, including the Huari, Tiahuanaco, Chiribaya and Estuquiña, who were conquered by the Incas. Artefacts from the area are well-displayed and all the exhibits are clearly explained in Spanish and English. ■ *Mon-Sun 1000-1300, 1500-1730, except Tue 1000-1200, 1630-2000, US$0.45, T761844, http://members.aol.com/contisuyo/MuseoC.html*

Essentials

Sleeping   **D** *Hostal Adrianella*, Miguel Grau 239, T/F763469. Modern, hot water, TV, safe, helpful,
● *on map*   tourist information, group discounts available, close to market and buses. Recom-
Price codes: mended. **D** *Limoneros*, Jr Lima 441, T761649. With bathroom, hot water, **E** without
see inside   bath, car park, discount for groups of more than 10, pool (usually empty), old house
front cover   with basic rooms, nice garden (the hotel suffered earthquake damage in 2001). **D** *Los*
Hotels do not   *Angeles*, Jr Torata 100-A, T762629. Cheaper without, hot water, TV, large comfortable
serve breakfast   rooms, market right outside, close to buses. Recommended. **E** *Arequipa*, Jr Arequipa
360, T761338. Clean, hot water sometimes. **E** *Hostal Carrera*, Jr Lima 320, T762113.
With bath and hot water (**F** shared bath, cold water), laundry facilities on roof. Recommended. **E** *Hostal Piura*, Piura 225, T763974. With bath, hot water, TV, friendly. **F** per
person *Hospedaje Cornejo*, Tarapacá 281-A, T761034. Shared bath, hot water. **F** per
person *Hospedaje Torata*, Arequipa 3443, T761697. With bath and warm water.

Eating   *Any's*, Tacna, just off Plaza. Lunch *menús* US$1.15 and US$1.45, other dishes expensive,
● *on map*   *peña*. *El Bosque*, Av 25 de Noviembre s/n, beyond La Villa bridge., T762245. Typical
The old market beside   dishes including *cuy*, *lomito saltado*, fish, meat dishes and *chifa*. Recommended.
Sant Domingo has a   *Moral y*, Lima y Libertad. Good sized portions, moderate prices, "best in town", *menú*
fine entrance but not   *del día* US$1.75, good lunches, open for breakfast. *La Oficina*, Ayacucho 685. Lunches,
much inside   juices, snacks, opens early for breakfast. Recommended. Several *chifas*, including *Tung*
Fong, Ancash y Moquegua on Plaza, *Fong Mey*, Lima y Libertad, and another in the
Museo Contisuyo precinct. *D'Onofrio* ice cream on the Plaza. *Panificadora*
Obrero,Piura 270. For breads. *Bar Bandido*, Jr Moquegua 333. European-style bar serving spirits, pizzas, wood oven, opens around 1930, rock music, videos.

Local specialities: the best-known dish is *cuy chactado*, pan-fried guinea pig. Two
of the most famous places to try it are Samagua and Los Angeles, both a few kilometres
out of town (taxi US$0.50, or combi, 10 mins), with several restaurants in each town.
Damascos, a type of small, yellow plum, can be found both stewed and *remojado*,
steeped in pisco (delicious). *Chicha de jora* and *chicha de maíz morado* (from malted
purple maize) can be found in the market; the latter is served with most *menús* at
lunchtime. Local spirits and other liqueurs can be bought at *La Tranquita*, Piura 148
(no sign). All foodstuffs can be bought at the market (bounded by Grau, Torata, Av
Balta and Libertad) and the streets around.

On **14 Oct** is *Santa Fortunata*. The main celebration is *Día de Santa Catalina* on 25 **Festivals**
Nov, which is the anniversary of the founding of the colonial city.

Ledelca Tours, Ayacucho 625, T763890, opposite Santo Domingo. For local tours, eg to **Tour operators**
bodegas to taste pisco, city tours and archaeological sites.

All bus companies are on Av Ejército, 2 blocks north of the market at Jr Grau, except **Transport**
Ormeño, Av La Paz casi Balta. From **Lima**, US$23.50-11.75, 5 companies with executive
and regular services. To **Tacna**, 159 km, 2 hrs, US$2, several buses and colectivos daily.
To **Arequipa**, 3 hrs, US$3-5.85, several buses daily. To **Desaguadero**, 4 hrs, US$6 (11.75
Ormeño), and **Puno**, 5-6 hrs, US$7.35, several companies on the new road (see below).
Mily Tours, Ev Ejército, T764000, run colectivos to Desaguadero, 3½ hrs, US$10. *Ormeño*
continues to **La Paz**, US$30, and to **Cusco**, US$23.50, as does *Cruz del Sur*, US$17.65.

Banks *BCP*, esquina Moquegua y Tarapacá. The only bank that changes TCs, will also **Directory**
advance money on Visa. 0915-1315, 1630-1830, *Telebanco 24 Horas* ATM (Visa). **Communications** Internet: several places on Jr Moquegua 400 block, just off Plaza de
Armas, US$0.70 per hr. Also *Viv@net* on Plaza de Armas. **Post office**: on the Plaza de
Armas in a colonial house. **Telephone**: there is a public phone office at Jr Moquegua 617.

Around Moquegua

Samegua, 4½ km from Moquegua, is known as **avocado town**, with many **Samegua**
restaurants. To get there take a micro from Avenida Balta, between Tacna and
Ancash. It takes 10 minutes.

Twenty-four kilometres northeast from Moquegua is Torata, a quiet, small **Torata**
town with a nice, shaded plaza. Above the town, on a hill above the right of the
two crosses which overlook the town, are the **Huari ruins** of Torata Alta, a
30-minute walk away. The ruins are in a poor state but you can still get a good
idea of their extent and the shape and size of the houses from the low surviving
walls. The site enjoys good views over to Cerro Baúl. ■ *To get there take a micro
or colectivo from Avenida Balta, between Jr Arequipa y Tacna, US$1.70, 30 mins.*

A highly recommended trip is to Cerro Baúl, 2,590 m. This can be combined **Cerro Baúl**
with the ruins at Torata to make a full day's excursion. The mountain is like a
tepuy, with sheer sides and flat top, hence its name, which means trunk. There
are excellent views for miles around from the summit. In the 7th century AD it
was a Huari citadel and at the end nearest the path are extensive **Huari ruins**.
The mountain became famous in legend as the place of refuge for the
Cochunas, who resisted the peaceful invasion of the Incas. Eventually the
Cochunas were starved off the mountain, but the refuge had lasted for a considerable time as their children regularly made nocturnal food raids into the
Inca camps below. Covering the entire flat summit, which is 1½ km long and
200 m wide, are hundreds of modern arrangements of stones and miniature
fields and houses, a mixture of pagan and Christian, which, together with
looting, is destroying the place.

To get to Cerro Baúl, take a micro for Torata, or for Cuajone, and get off at
the crossroads for Torata, at the top of the pass beneath the northern end of
the mountain. The path leads up the gradual slope from the road. There is a
steep section for the last 200 m, on which cement steps have been built. It takes
an hour or so from the road to the top. The path leads to a Christian shrine
(two crosses). Take water and protect against the sun.

South Coast

Omate

Population: 3,000
Altitude: 2,160 m

Omate is a small town, 146 km to the north of Moquegua on an unpaved road, and 129 km to the south of Arequipa (five hours). The town is important for its famed **Semana Santa processions**. It is also known for growing grapes, *damascos* and other fruits, and for its shrimp farms. Nearby are the thermal baths at **Ulucán**.

Moquegua to
Desaguadero

The Carretera Binacional, from Ilo to La Paz, has a breathtaking stretch from Moquegua to Desaguadero at the southeastern end of Lake Titicaca. It skirts Cerro Baúl and climbs through zones of ancient terraces at Camata to its highest point at 4,755 m. At 4,610 m is lonely *Restaurant Humajalso*. On the altiplano there are herds of llamas and alpacas, watery *bofedales*, lakes with waterfowl, strange mountain formations and snow-covered peaks. At Mazo Cruz there is a PNP checkpoint where all documents and bags are checked. Approaching Desaguadero the Cordillera Real of Bolivia comes into view. The road is fully paved and should be taken in daylight.

Ilo

Phone code: 054
Colour map 5, grid C6
Population: 95,000

Moquegua's exports – avocados and wine – go by an excellent 96 km road to the port of Ilo. Its main industries are copper refining, fishing, fish oil products and tourism. There are many beaches nearby. In 1992, Bolivia was given part of the beach south of Ilo, now called Bolivia Mar, and half of the tax free industrial zone, for the import and export of Bolivia's goods.

In pre-Columbian times, between 900 and 1300 AD, Ilo was the centre of the Chiribaya culture. Exhibits can be seen in the **Museo Eduardo Jiménez Lazo**, on the Plaza de Armas; it also houses more recent exhibits. There are, in fact, three Ilos: Ilo Viejo was founded by the French as a port for their ships. It has seafront gardens, an amphitheatre for theatre productions, a gazebo (La Glorieta) at the end of a short pier, an old fishing pier (Muelle Fiscal), old port buildings and a sheltered fishing harbour. **Museo Naval**, in the Capitanía building at the harbour, is good on local nautical history and includes some of Admiral Grau's manuscripts and a good explanation of the War of the Pacific. The **Casa de Cultura**, on Avenida Grau s/n, on the seafront, doubles up as a source of tourist information, with leaflets on pre-Columbian culture. It is a very distinctive, red and white building, with very friendly and helpful staff.

The present town is pretty ugly, with a fishmeal factory, oil tanks, and dusty cobbled streets and 'half-door' saloons. Uglier still is the third Ilo, Ilo Nuevo, a breezeblock town built by the Southern Peru Copper Corporation for its engineers and their families on a plateau out of sight of Ilo Viejo. The *Festival del Olivo* takes place in September.

Valle de los Olivares, also known as Valle Ilo, lies 15 km to the north. The main attraction is the **Museo de Sitio El Algarrobal,** which is dedicated to the local Chiribaya culture and displays mummies, ceramics and some textiles. There are petroglyphs in the garden. Ask for the director Gerardo Carpio to show you around; he speaks slowly and clearly in Spanish. Recent discoveries, including 18 mummies found in 2000 by archaeologists led by Sonia Guillén, are beginning to reveal more about this mysterious culture. ■ *Tue-Fri 0730-1400 and Sat 0900-1300, closed Mon. US$0.80. There are two buses daily from the main plaza. A taxi costs US$6 return including 1 hr at the museum. The museum was seriously damaged in the 2001 earthquake.*

Sleeping
& transport

The city has a good range of hotels in our **C** range and below, and a selcetion of restaurants. **Buses** to Moquegua, US$1.15 with *Cruz del Sur, Flores Hnos* and *Ormeño*.

Tacna

Tacna was in Chilean hands from 1880 to 1929, when its people voted by plebiscite to return to Peru. It is an important commercial centre and the local authorities have been struggling to gain free-trade status from the government. There are good schools, housing estates, a stadium to seat 10,000 people, an airport, many military posts and one of the best hospitals in Peru. Chileans cross the border for cheap medical and dental treatment.

Around the city the desert is gradually being irrigated. The local economy includes olive groves, vineyards and fishing. The waters of Laguna Aricota, 80 km north, are now being tapped for further irrigation and hydroelectric power for industry.

Phone code: 054
Colour map 6, grid C2
Population: 174,366
Altitude: 550 m

Ins and outs

Getting there

With the peak of Tacora in the distance, Tacna is 156 km south of Moquegua by the Pan-American Highway, 36 km from the Chilean frontier, and 56 km from the international port of Arica, to which there is a railway. It is 1,292 km from Lima by road.

As this is the nearest town to Chile, transport links are good with the rest of the country. The airport is some way out of town to the southwest; taxis run to the border but it's cheaper to go to town and take a colectivo from the international bus station. The two bus stations are on Hipólito Unánue, 1 km from the plaza (colectivo US$0.25, taxi US$0.60 minimum). One terminal is for international services, the other for domestic, both are well-organized, local tax US$0.30, baggage store, easy to make

Tacna

To Bus Station, Panamericana Norte & Alto de la Alianza
To Panamericana Norte & Stadium

Chilean Consulate
Presbitero Andía
Zarumilla
Julio Mac Lean
Museo Ferroviario
2 de Mayo
Touring y Automóvil Club
Cnl Albarracín
P Meléndez
Gral Deústua
Arias Araguez
de la Barca
Teatro Municipal
Modesto Basadre
Centro Cultural Miculla
Hipólito Unánue
28 de Julio
Fco de Zela
Museo Zela
Gral Blondel
Fco Lazo
Cnl Inclán
Cathedral
Plaza de Armas
Callao
Moquegua
Arequipa
Ugarte
Casa de la Cultura
Aero Continente
Tans
San Martín
Junín
Municipalidad
Simón Bolívar
Lan Perú
Parque de la Locomotora
Av Bolognesi
Pallardelli
Ayacucho
Av Restauración

To Panamericana Sur, Airport & Arica (Chile)

South Coast

N
0 metres 400
0 yards 400

Sleeping
1 Alameda
2 El Mesón
3 Hostal Bon Ami
4 Hostal HC
5 Gran Hotel Central
6 Gran Hotel Tacna
7 Lido
8 Lima & Phone Office

Eating
1 Delfín Azul
2 Le Petit, El Sabor Criollo & Shaffie's House
3 Margarita's Café
4 Sociedad de Alimentación Vegetariana
5 Sur Perú
6 Vida y Salud

connections to the border, Arequipa or Lima. Tickets can be purchased several days before departure and buses fill up quickly. **NB** Beware of touts selling bus tickets at inflated prices. The railway station is closer into town in the west on Crnl Albarracín. It is still a taxi drive into the centre though.

Getting around   The town is quite spread out although there are several hotels around the Plaza de Armas. You will need to catch a bus or taxi to see much. **Tourist offices** *Dirección Regional de Indistria y Turismo*, Gral Blondell 50, by the Centro Cultural Miculla, corner of Francisco Lazo, T722784. *Touring y Automóvil Club del Perú*, Av 2 de Mayo 55, T744237, F723121, tacna@touringperu.com.pe

Sights

Above the city (8 km away, just off the Panamericana Norte), on the heights, is the **Campo de la Alianza**, scene of a battle between Peru and Chile in 1880. The cathedral, designed by Eiffel, faces the Plaza de Armas, which contains huge bronze statues of Admiral Grau and Colonel Bolognesi. They stand at either end of the Arca de los Héroes, the triumphal arch which is the symbol of the city. The bronze fountain in the Plaza is said to be a duplicate of the one in the Place de la Concorde (Paris) and was also designed by Eiffel. The **Parque de la Locomotora**, near the city centre, has a British-built locomotive, which was used in the War of the Pacific. There is a very good railway museum at the station. ■ *0700-1700, daily. US$0.30; knock at the gate under the clock tower on Jr 2 de Mayo for entry.* The house of Francisco Zela, who gave the Cry of Independence on 20 July 1811 is a museum (**Museo de Zela**). ■ *Zela 542, Mon-Sat 0830-1230, 1530-1900.* At Bolognesi 721 is *Feria La Caplina*, a shopping mall-cum-market selling jewellery, a few musical instruments, but mostly clothes. The main market is at Bolognesi y Pallardelli.

Essentials

Sleeping   **A** *Gran Hotel Tacna*, Av Bolognesi 300, T724193, F722015. Gardens, 2 swimming
Accommodation is   pools, safe car park, good breakfast for US$3-4, *menú* US$6, English spoken. **C** *Gran*
hard to find in the   *Hotel Central*, San Martín 561, T712281, F726031. With breakfast, central, secure, Eng-
centre, especially at   lish spoken. Recommended. **C** *El Mesón*, Unánue 175, T725841, F721832,
Christmas-time,   mesonhotel@terra.com.pe With breakfast, TV, central, modern, comfortable, safe,
when Chileans go   internet service. Recommended. **D-E** *Lima*, San Martín 442, T711912, on Plaza de
on shopping sprees   Armas, american_tours@hotmail.com With breakfast, TV, hot water, bar, good restau-
Everything closes   rant, stores luggage. **E** *Alameda*, Bolognesi 780, T744978. **F** without bath or TV, good
1300-1600   food. Recommended. **E** *Hostal Bon Ami*, 2 de Mayo 445, T711873. **F** without bath, hot
water, secure. **E** *Hostal HC*, Zela 734, T742042. Hot water, TV, discounts available,
Beware of pickpockets   cafetería next door, laundry service, videos. Recommended. **E** *Lido*, San Martín 876-A,
in the market area   near Plaza de Armas, T741598. With hot showers, no breakfast. Recommended.

Eating   One recommended eating place is *Sur Perú*, Bolívar 380. Popular for lunch are *Shaffie's House*, Ayacucho 84-B, *El Sabor Criollo*, No 86-C, and *Le Petit*, No 88-A, US$2 *menú*. *Delfín Azul*, Zela 375. Good. *Margarita's Café*, Unánue 145, T711481. Excellent French pastry and desserts, nice inviting ambience, cheap. 1600-2130. Recommended. Vegetarian: at *Vida y Salud*, Bolívar 335. Swiss-Peruvian owned and run, German, French and English spoken, yoghurts and juices, natural products for sale, also serves meat, good, open 0730-2030. *Sociedad de Alimentación Vegetariana*, Zela 495, T711037. Mon-Fri and Sun with reservation. *La Espiga*, San Martín 431. Good bakery and pastry shop.

Air To **Lima**, 1½ hrs; daily flights with **Aero Continente**, **Lan Perú** and **Tans**. To **Transport**
Arequipa, 40 mins with Lan Perú and Tans. A taxi to town and the bus terminal costs
US$3. It is possible to take a taxi from the airport to Arica, US$30 (can be shared), but
the cheapest way is to take a taxi to the bus station, then take a colectivo.

Bus To **Moquegua**, 159 km, 2 hrs, US$2, several buses and colectivos daily (colectivos
also leave from the town exit, uphill from the terminal, eg *El Buen Samaritano*, 5 passengers, US$3, less than 2 hrs). There are no direct buses to **Mollendo**, so catch one of
the frequent buses to El Fiscal (US$4, 4 hrs, see above), then a colectivo to Mollendo.

To **Arequipa**, 6 hrs, US$3.85-4.40, several buses daily, most with *Flores*, T725376. To
Nasca, 793 km, 12 hrs, US$9, several buses daily, en route for Lima. Several companies
daily to **Lima**, 1,239 km, 21-26 hrs, US$9-27, eg *Flores, Cruz del Sur* and *Ormeño*, rec-
ommended. To **Puno**, 395 km, go to Moquegua or Arequipa and change there.

At Tomasiri, 35 km north of Tacna, passengers' passports and luggage are checked, *Do not carry anything*
whether you have been out of the country or not. There is also a police control 10 km *on the bus for a*
after the Camiara bridge (being rebuilt, near a military base), just before the *Peruvian, just your*
Tacna/Moquegua departmental border (also called Camiara, 59 km from Tacna, 61 km *own belongings*
from Moquegua).

To **La Paz**, the best route is via Moquegua and Desaguadero. The most direct service is
Ormeño's Royal service, 1930, US$35, but you have to change buses in Moquegua.
Samericano colectivos go direct to Desaguadero, otherwise take transport from
Moquegua (see above). To **Santiago**, *Pullman Bus Internacional*, 6 a day, 28 hrs, US$25,
semi cama with meals, to **Antofagasta**, 14 hrs, US$15. *Tramaca* also runs to Santiago.

Airline offices *Aero Continente*, Apurímac casi San Martín, T747300. *Lan Perú*, **Directory**
Apurímac y Bolívar, T743252. *Tans*, San Martín 611, T747002. **Banks** *BCP*, San Martín
574, no commission for TCs (Amex, Citicorp) into soles. Similarly at *Banco Wiese*, San
Martín 476. *Banco Santander*, Apurímac, with exchange and ATM for Visa/Plus,
Mastercard/Cirrus. *Interbank*, San Martín 646, has ATM for Visa/Plus, Mastercard/Cirrus
and Amex. *Cambios Tacna* and *MoneyGram*, San Martín 612, T743607. Street changers
stand outside the Municipalidad. **Communications** Internet:, Internet:, several on San
Martín: *UPT Net*, on Plaza, *Infored*, No 735, *Vi@com* at P Meléndez, *Vi@net 24 horas*, No
832, *Jay's*, No 854, 24 hrs, and *Explorer*, No 858. *F@stnet.com*, 2 de Mayo 380. 0800-2400.
Also international phone calls, cheaper than others. *Metro Line*, Junín 94.
N@vig@tor.com, Av Bolognesi y Ayacucho. *Tacna Net*, Av H Unánue at Plaza de Armas.
Average price US$0.45/hr, US$0.60 overnight. **Post office:** Av Bolognesi y Ayacucho.
Mon-Sat 0800-2000. **Telephone:** public *locutorio* on Plaza de Armas, in same building as
Hostal Lima. **Consulates** *Chile*, Presbítero Andía block 1, T 723063. Mon-Fri 0800-1300,
closed holidays. **Laundry** *Lavamatic*, Av Bolognesi 954, reliable and cheap.

Border with Chile

There is a checkpoint before the border, which is open 0900-2200. Peruvian *Peruvian time is one*
immigration is closed on public holidays. You need to obtain a Peruvian exit *hour earlier than*
stamp and a Chilean entrance stamp; formalities are straightforward (see *Chilean time Mar-Oct;*
below). If you need a Chilean visa, you have to get it in Tacna (address above). *two hours earlier*
Crossing by private vehicle For those leaving Peru by car buy *relaciones de* *Sep/Oct-Feb/Mar*
pasajeros (official forms, US$0.45) from the kiosk at the border or from a book- *(varies annually)*
shop; you will need four copies. Next, return your tourist card, visit the PNP *No fruit or vegetables*
office, return the vehicle permit and finally depart through the checkpoints. *are allowed into Chile*
or Tacna (even if
  Exchange Money changers are given under **Banks**, above. They can also be *arriving by air on an*
found at counters in the international bus terminal; rates are similar in town. *internal flight)*

Transport   **Road**   56 km, 1-2 hrs, depending on waiting time at the border. Buses to Arica charge US$1.50 and colectivo taxis US$3 per person. All leave from the international terminal in Tacna throughout the day. Colectivos (old Fords and Chevrolets which carry 5 passengers) only leave when full. As you approach the terminal you will be grabbed by a driver or his agent and told that the car is "just about to leave". This is hard to verify as you may not see the colectivo until you have filled in the paperwork. Once you have chosen a driver/agent, you will be rushed to his company's office where your passport will be taken from you and the details filled out on a Chilean entry form. You can change your remaining soles at the bus terminal while this is being done. It is 30 mins to the Peruvian border post at Santa Rosa, where all exit formalities are carried out. The driver will hustle you through all the procedures. A short distance beyond is the Chilean post at Chacalluta, where again the driver will show you what to do. All formalities take about 30 mins. It's a further 15 mins to Arica's bus terminal. A Chilean driver is more likely to take you to any address in Arica. **Train**   At 0900 and 1600, US$1, Tacna-Arica (service frequently cancelled).

Into Chile   **Arica**, Chile's most northerly city, is 20 km south of the border (*Population*: 174,064). It has road and rail links with La Paz, Bolivia, road links with the rest of Chile and is a good starting place for visits to Andean national parks, such as Lauca. It has a wide selection of hotels, restaurants and services. The tourist office, *Sernatur*, is at San Marcos 101, in the centre, T252054, a kiosk next to the Casa de la Cultura.

Cordillera Blanca

Introducing Cordillera Blanca

The Cordillera Blanca is a region of jewelled lakes and sparkling white mountain peaks which attract mountaineers, hikers, cyclists and rafters in their thousands. Even the archaeologist is catered for in the shape of the ruins of **Chavín de Huantar**. This fortress-temple belonged to one of the earliest and most influential cultures in pre-Inca Peru and it has some fine carvings and stonework.

Among the highest mountains in South America, the Cordillera Blanca offers some of the finest scenery, as well as the best climbing and trekking in the country. The region's main centre is **Huaraz**. Here you can see nearly two dozen snow-crested peaks of over 5,000 m including Huascarán, the highest mountain in Peru at 6,768 m.

This area contains the largest concentration of glaciers found in the world's tropical zone: a source of both beauty and danger. The turquoise-coloured lakes (*cochas*) which form in the terminal moraines are the jewels of the Andes and you should hike up to at least one during your stay. **Laguna Churup** is a day's walk from Huaraz, **Lago Parón** is close to Caraz, while the beautiful twin lakes of **Llanganuco** are within easy reach of Yungay and are on the route of the long-distance Santa Cruz trek. The tranquility of these glacial lakes masks a frightening history. They have caused much death and destruction when dykes have broken, sending tons of water hurtling down the canyons wiping out everything in their path. The levels of some have been artificially lowered for flood control and to feed the huge Cañon del Pato dam. Earthquakes, too, have scarred the high valleys and the mass grave which was once the old town of **Yungay** is a very humbling place.

Communities are close to each other in the **Callejón de Huaylas**, so there is little sense of isolation until you are right up in the mountains, or in the remoter areas beyond this valley. Huaraz is undoubtedly at the heart of things, catering for miners and for the mountain sports market, plus all the befores and afters that go with some days in the wilds. Only an hour away, **Caraz** has the same mix of engineers (for the hydroelectric scheme) and tourism, but on a much smaller scale. Above all, though, the waters coming off the mountains make this a fertile area and it is agriculture which dictates the pace of life.

Cordillera Blanca

Things to do in Cordillera Blanca

- To visit the Cordillera Blanca without doing just one of the fantastic treks on offer is really missing the point of coming here at all. Consider the lesser-known **one-day hikes**, or the **Huayhuash circuit**, page 367.
- If you are a whitewater virgin, take a rafting trip on the **Río Santa**, available all year round and with some stunning background scenery, page 342.
- There are many plants in the mountains, but keep an eye out for the remarkable **Puya Raimondi** with its century-long lifespan, page 333.
- Take a moment to study the bark of the **quenoal trees** (polylepis), like shreds of the finest paper, rich browns and oranges against the blue of the lakes and sky and the white of the snow, page 350.
- Don't leave without visiting the 2,500 year-old fortress temple of **Chavín de Huantar**, page 361.
- The markets, say Carhuaz on a Wednesday or Yungay on Thursday, are good places to see the local wares (nothing touristy).

The area

Colour map 3, grid B3

The snow-capped Cordillera Blanca runs north to south for almost 200 km. Alongside it to the west lies its alter ego, the bare and dry Cordillera Negra, which rises to 4,600 m. The valley of the Río Santa, known as the Callejón de Huaylas, separates the two ranges. The Santa arises in Laguna Conococha, at the south end of the two mountain chains and flows due north between them, before turning west to enter the spectacular Cañón del Pato and making it's way to the Pacific.

To the east of the Cordillera Blanca lies another set of valleys, the Callejón de Conchucos, containing the archaeological treasures of Chavín de Huantar (see page 360). Both the Callejones de Huaylas and Conchucos are well-populated areas with picturesque villages, narrow cobblestone streets and odd-angled house roofs. This is an agricultural centre – potatoes and barley are grown at the higher altitudes and maize, alfalfa, fruits and flowers lower down.

These valleys also provide road access to the region's wonders. Many excellent trekking routes and approaches to climbers' base camps cross from one callejón to the other, over the high passes of the Cordillera Blanca. Further south lie the Cordilleras Huayhuash and Raura, offering more spectacular climbing and hiking in a less-visited area (see page 367).

Ins and outs

Getting there There are three main routes to reach the Cordillera Blanca. Probably the easiest is the paved road which branches east off the Pan-American Highway north of Pativilca, 187 km from Lima (see page 377).

A second route is via the Callán pass from Casma to Huaraz (see page 379), a rough but beautiful trip through the heart of the Cordillera Negra.

The third alternative is from Chimbote to Caraz via the Cañón del Pato (see page 383), also a very scenic journey, with magnificent views of this spectacular canyon.

When to go The dry season (May-Sep) is the best time to visit the region, and the only time for climbing most summits. Trekking is also possible at other times of the year, but conditions are less amenable and the views are less rewarding. Christmas to New Year is a popular time for foreigners seeking an exotic location to spend the holidays.

Cordillera Blanca

Huascarán National Park

Established in July 1975, the park includes the entire Cordillera Blanca above *Colour map 3, grid B3*
4,000 m. It covers a total area of 3,400 sq km and is 180 km from north to south
and 20 km from east to west. It is a UNESCO World Biosphere Reserve and
part of the World Heritage Trust. The park's objectives are to protect the
unique flora, fauna, geology, archaeological sites and extraordinary scenic
beauty of the Cordillera. Please make every attempt to help by taking all your
rubbish away with you when camping. The park office is in the Ministry of
Agriculture, at the east end of Av Raymondi in Huaraz (T722086). It is open
only in the mornings. It provides limited general information but is useful for
those planning specific research activities. ■ *US$1.25 for a day visit. For visits
of up to 7 days (ie for trekking and climbing trips) a permit costing US$20 must be
bought. If you stay longer than 7 days, you will need another permit. These fees
will be collected at Llanganuco (see page 350), Santa Cruz, Cashapampa and
Huascarán (see page 349 for the Llanganuco to Santa Cruz trek), and at Collón
on the way up the Quebrada Ishinca.*

Trekking and climbing in the Cordillera Blanca

*The Cordillera Blanca offers the most popular backpacking and trekking in Peru,
with a network of trails used by the local people and some less well-defined mountaineers' routes. There are numerous possibilities for day-hikes, trekking and
climbing. Of these only a very few routes are currently used by most visitors, and so
they have accumulated trash and other signs of impact. While these favourite treks
(notably Santa Cruz-Llanganuco and Olleros-Chavín) are undeniably interesting, you should consider the various excellent alternatives if you want to enjoy a less
crowded experience and help conserve the area's great natural beauty.*

The many other options include: **Laguna Parón**, with its impressive cirque of **Trekking**
surrounding summits (access from Caraz, see page 352); **Hualcayán to** **options**
Pomabamba, traversing the northern end of the Cordillera Blanca with fine
views of Alpamayo and many other peaks (access from Caraz); Laguna 69 at
the end of Llanganuco valley (access from Yungay); the **Ulta Valley** and
Laguna Auquiscocha, between the massifs of Huascarán, Ulta and Hualcán
(access from Carhuaz, see page 346); to name but a few. There remains a good
deal to be discovered in the area and your creativity in choosing a route is certain to be rewarded. See also Adventure sports, page 75.

The height of the mountains in the Cordillera Blanca and nearby ranges and **Advice to**
their location in the tropics create conditions different from the Alps or even **climbers**
the Himalayas. Fierce sun makes the mountain snow porous and the glaciers **& hikers**
move more rapidly. In 2000 the local Unidad de Salvamento de Alta Montaña
(high mountain rescue unit – see below), run by the PNP, reported a greater
incidence of fatal accidents on the mountains as a result of climbers thinking
that their experience on other ranges would be sufficient for the Cordillera
Blanca. First-timers here should take a guide for safety. (A South African
climber died on Huascarán in 2000. His parents requested that he be left
hanging from his rope on the mountainside because that is 'how he would
have wanted to go'.) The British Embassy advises climbers to take at least six

days for acclimatization (the PNP suggests 10-15 days), to move in groups of four or more, reporting to the **Casa de Guías** (see page 332) or the office of the guide before departing, giving the date at which a search should begin, and leaving the telephone number of your Embassy with money. **Rescue operations** are limited. Insurance is essential (cannot be purchased locally), since a guide costs US$50-70 a day and a search US$2,000-2,500. A search by helicopter costs US$10,000 (up to 4,500 m only).

In 1999 the Policía Nacional de Perú established a 35-member rescue team (two of whom are women) in Yungay, with 24-hour phone service and vhf/uhf radio dispatch. They have two helicopters and trained search-and-rescue dogs. They respond and effect rescues, 'no questions asked', for anyone, at any time, but the service is not free. T044-793327/333/327/291, F793292, usam@pnp.gob.pe

Be well-prepared before setting out on a climb. Wait or cancel your trip when weather conditions are bad. Every year climbers are killed through failing to take weather conditions seriously. Climb only when and where you have sufficient experience.

Most circuits can be hiked in five days. Although the trails are easily followed, they are rugged and the passes very high – between 4,000 and nearly 5,000 m – so backpackers wishing to go it alone should be fit and properly acclimatized to the altitude, and carry all necessary equipment. Essential items are a tent, warm sleeping bag, stove, and protection against wind and rain (climatic conditions are quite unreliable here and you cannot rule out rain and hail storms even in the dry season). Trekking demands less stamina since equipment can be carried by donkeys.

NB Check locally on public safety conditions. A few robberies of hikers have taken place. Do not camp near a town or village, never leave a campsite unattended and always hike with others when heading into the remote mountain districts.

On all treks in this area, respect the locals' property, leave no rubbish behind, do not give sweets or money to children who beg and remember your cooking utensils, tent, etc, would be very expensive for a campesino, so be sensitive and responsible.

Hiring guides & muleteers The Dirección de Turismo issues qualified guides and *arrieros* (muleteers) with a photo ID. Always check for this when making arrangements; note down the name and card number in case you should have any complaints. Prices for specific services are set so enquire before hiring someone. Prices in 2002: *arriero*, US$10 per day; donkey or mule, US$5 per day; trekking guides US$30-50 per day; climbing guides US$60-90 per day, depending on the difficulty of the peak. In the low season guides' prices are about 20-30% less. You are required to provide or pay for food and shelter for all porters, guides, cooks and *arrieros*. **NB** Some guides speak English and are friendly but lack technical expertise; others have expertise but lack communicative ability. You may have to choose between the former and the latter.

Casa de Guías, Plaza Ginebra 28-g in Huaraz, T721811, F722306, agmp@terra.com.pe or casa_de_guias@hotmail.com   This is the climbers' and hikers' meeting place. It is useful with information, books, maps, arrangements for guides, *arrieros*, mules, etc. There is a notice board, postcards and posters for sale, a language school and lecture hall. They provide rescue facilities (may be very expensive) and you can register here free of charge before heading out on your climb or trek. Be sure to advise of your return or any delay. Mon-Sat 0900-1300, 1600-1800, Sun 0900-1300.

The Casa de Guías has a full list of all members of the *Asociación de Guías de Montaña del Perú* (AGMP) throughout the country.

A blooming century

The giant Puya Raimondi, named after Antonio Raimondi, the Italian scholar who discovered it, is a rare species, considered to be one of the oldest plants in the world.

Often mistakenly referred to as a cactus, it is actually the largest member of the Bromeliad family and is found in only a few isolated areas of the Andes. One of these areas is the Huascarán National Park, particularly the Ingenio and Queshque gorges, the high plateaus of Cajamarquilla, along the route leading to Pastoruri in the Pachacoto gorge and by the road from Caraz to Pamparomas.

At its base, the Puya forms a rosette of long, spiked, waxy leaves, 2 m in diameter. The distinctive phallic spike of the plant can reach a height of 12 m during the flowering process. This takes its entire lifespan – an incredible 100 years – after which time the plant withers and dies.

As the final flowering begins, usually during May for mature plants, the spike is covered in flowers. As many as 20,000 blooms can decorate a single plant. During this season, groups of Puya Raimondi will bloom together, creating a spectacular picture against the dramatic backdrop of the Cordillera Blanca.

Ted Alexander, *Skyline Adventures*, Jr José de San Martín 637, T722301, skylineadventures@hotmail.com American, Outward Bound instructor, very knowledgeable, lots of information. **Koky Castañeda**, T721694, or through *La Casa de Zarela*. Speaks English and French, AGMP certified. **Aritza Monasterio**, through *Casa de Guías*. Speaks English, Spanish and Euskerra. **Augusto Ortega**, Jr San Martín 1004, T724888, is the only Peruvian to have climbed Everest. **Filiberto Rurush Paucar**, Sucre 1240, T722264, speaks English, Spanish and Quechua. **Hugo Sifuentes Maguiña** and his brother **César** (speaks English and a little French), at *Trekperu*, Av Centenario 687, T728190/682616, trekperuhuaraz@terra.com.pe, or in the *Casa de Guías*.

Recommended mountain guides *Not necessarily members of AGMP*

Several of the agencies, independent guides and **Casa de Guías** run rock climbing courses at Monterrey (behind *Hotel Baños Termales Monterrey*, see page 344), Chancos, Recuay and Huanchac (30 mins' walk from Huaraz). Also ice climbing cna be arranged at Vallanaraju and Pastururi, for example. Ask for details from the *Casa de Guías* and tour agencies in Huaraz.

Climbing courses

Irma Angeles, T722205, speaks some English, knows the Huayhuash well. *Christopher Benway*, T721203/692814, cafeandino@hotmail.com American, leads treks in the Huayhuash. *Vladimiro Hinostrosa*, at *Mountain Shop Chacraraju*, T692395, is a trekking guide with knowledge of the entire region. *Tjen Verheye*, Jr Carlos Valenzuela 911, T722569, is Belgian and speaks Dutch, French, German, and reasonable English, runs trekking and conventional tours and is knowledgeable about the Chavín culture. *Genaro Yanac Olivera*, T722825, speaks good English and some German, also a climbing guide. See also under Tour operators in Huaraz for organized trips.

Recommended trekking guides

Many trekking agencies sell camping gaz cartridges. White gas (called *bencina blanca*) is available from *ferreterías*, but shop around to avoid overcharging. *Galaxia Expeditions*, Jr Leoniza Lescano 630, galaxia_expedition@hotmail.com Also offer mountain bike hire and guiding services. For trekking provisions see Shopping, page 341.

The following agencies are recommended for hiring gear: **Andean Kingdom; Anden Sport Tours; Monttrek; Kallpa** (see under Tour operators in Huaraz for their addresses); also **Skyline** (see above) and **Montañero**, Parque Ginebra 30-B, T726386, andeway@terra.com.pe And **MountClimb**, Jr Mcal Cáceres 421, T726060, mountclimb@yahoo.com *Casa de Guías* rents equipment and sells dried food. Also **Lobo**,

Hiring camping gear

Cordillera Blanca

Mining the mountains

The department of Ancash contains important mineral deposits including copper, zinc, silver, gold and perhaps uranium (the latter is not discussed openly). 12,000 different sites have been prospected in the Cordillera Negra alone. An open pit mine and smelter, 12 km north of Huaraz has brought major changes to the Callejón de Huaylas. The cost of accommodation and other services has been rising and unemployed from all over Peru have come to the area in search of jobs. The US/ Canadian consortium operating the mine has promised to minimize environmental impact, but there can be little doubt that this large-scale project will leave its mark on the economic and social environment, as well as the natural environment of the Callejón de Huaylas.

Similar developments are taking place east of San Marcos, near Chavín in the Callejón de Conchucos, where a huge underground mine and concentrator at Antamina has come on stream. Hundreds of kilometres of good roads, thousands of jobs for Peruvians and a resident ex-pat community near Huaraz have undoubtedly had a significant effect on the local economy.

In the Cordillera Huayhuash, a Japanese corporation began a major mining project in 1997, in the vicinity of Pocpa and Laguna Jahuacocha, the jewel of the entire region. Other mines are under consideration and some local residents have proposed the creation of a Huayhuash National Park to protect the region's unique natural beauty, as well as its economically important tourist potential.

Luzuriaga 557, T724646. On the 2nd floor of the *Hotel Residencial Cataluña*, Av Raymondi 622, T722761, José Valle Espinosa, 'Pepe', hires out equipment, organizes treks and pack animals, sells dried food, and is generally helpful and informative.

Check all camping and climbing equipment very carefully before taking it. Gear is usually of poor quality and mostly second hand, left behind by others. Also note that some items may not be available, so it's best to bring your own. All prices are standard, but not cheap, throughout town. All require payment in advance, passport or air ticket as deposit and will only give 50 % of your money back if you return gear early. Campers have complained that campsites are dirty, toilet pits foul and guides and locals do not take their rubbish away with them.

Maps   Alpenvereinskarte *Cordillera Blanca Nord* 0/3a at 1:100,000 is easily the best map; it is available in Huaraz for US$12 (also in Lima – stocks locally are small, best to get it before you arrive). The south sheet, 0/3b, should be available by 2003. The Alpine Mapping Guild's 2002 *Cordillera Huayhuash* map, 1:80,000, is also recommended (available from *Café* Andino, US$15). A good tourist map of the Callejón de Huaylas and Cordillera Huayhuash, by Felipe Díaz, is available in many shops in the region and at Casa de Guías in Huaraz; it's not accurate enough for hiking the less-travelled trails. Maps of the area are available from the IGN in Lima. *Hidrandina*, the state hydroelectric company, at 27 de Noviembre 773, has dye-line maps of the Cordillera Blanca; open in the morning only. Several guides and agencies have their own sketch maps of the most popular routes. Maps are also available by international mail-order from **Latin American Travel Consultants**, PO Box 17-17-908, Quito, Ecuador, F593-2 562566, www.amerispan.com/lata/

South American Explorers publishes a good map with additional notes on the popular Llanganuco to Santa Cruz loop, and the *Instituto Geográfico Nacional* has mapped the area with its 1:100,000 topographical series. These are more useful to the mountaineer than hiker, however, since the trails marked are confusing and inaccurate. For guide books, see Books in Background, page 611.

Cordillera Blanca

Huaraz

The main town in the valley, Huaraz is expanding rapidly as a major tourist centre but it is also a busy commercial hub, especially on market days (Monday and Thursday). The region is both a prime destination for hikers and international climbers, as well as a vacation haven for Peruvian urbanites seeking clean mountain air and a glimpse of the glaciers. School groups flock to the city from mid-September to mid-December (the 'época de promociones colegiales'). The city was half destroyed in the earthquake of May 1970 so don't expect red-tiled roofs or overhanging eaves. However, the Plaza de Armas has been rebuilt, with a towering, white statue of Christ and a new Cathedral is still being built. What the reconstructed city lacks in colonial charm, it makes up by its spectacular setting between the mountains of the Cordilleras Blanca and Negra. The peaks of Huamashraju, Churup, Rima Rima and Vallunaraju loom so close as to seem almost a part of the architecture while, in the distance, the giants Huascarán and Huandoy can be seen.

Phone code 044
Colour map 3, grid B3
Population: 80,000
Altitude: 3,091 m

Ins and outs

Getting there See Getting there, page 330. The bus offices are in the centre of town and are conveniently close to many of the hotels and hostels.

Getting around Small enough to get around by foot providing sensible precautions are taken especially at night (see below). The standard fare for a taxi in town is about US$0.60, US$0.70 at night. The fare to Monterrey or Huanchac is US$1.45. Radio taxis T721482 or 722512.

Tourist office Basic tourist information is available from the *Policía de Turismo*, in an alley between the post office and the Municipalidad, T721341, ext 315. Report all crimes and mistreatment by tour operators, hotels, etc, to them. Mon-Fri 0900-1300, 1600-1900, Sat 0900-1300.

Security Huaraz has its share of crime, especially since the arrival of mining in the area (see Box Mining the mountains) and during the high tourist season. Muggings have been reported on the way to the Mirador Rataquenua and Pukaventana. A minimum group size of three is recommended for this walk; on no account should women go alone. Also avoid the area by the river and deserted streets at night, be careful near the market and keep a close eye on your luggage at the bus stations.

Sights

For good panoramic views go to the *Mirador Rataquenua* at the cross (visible from Huaraz). It's a one hour walk from the town - turn left past the cemetery and head uphill through a small forest. To get a truly amazing view of the whole valley, continue past the *Mirador* up to *Pukaventana*. (See above regarding safety for both these excursions.)

Museo Regional de Ancash, Instituto Nacional de Cultura, on Plaza de Armas, contains stone monoliths and *huacos* from the Recuay culture. The exhibits are well labelled and laid out. ■ *Mon-Fri 0900-1700, Sat 0830-1700, Sun 0830-1400. US$1.45.*

The **Museo de Miniaturas del Perú** is at the Gran Hotel Huascarán. It has models of Huaraz and Yungay before the earthquake, plus an interesting (honest!) collection of Barbie dolls in Peruvian dress.

The **Sala de Cultura** in *Banco Weise*, Sucre 766, often has interesting art and photography exhibitions by local artists. ■ *Free.*

Cordillera Blanca

Huaraz

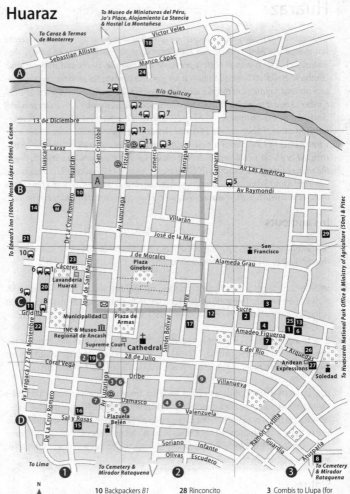

Cordillera Blanca

N

| 0 metres | 100 |
| 0 yards | 100 |

Detail map
A Huaraz centre, page 338

■ Sleeping
1 Albergue Churup C3
2 Alojamiento El Jacal C3
3 Alojamiento Marilla C3
4 Alojamiento Nemys C3
5 Alojamiento Norma D2
6 Alojamiento Soledad C3
7 Alojamiento Sra Tomaza Huarato C3
8 Andino Club D3
9 Angeles Inn & Sol Andino D2
10 Backpackers B1
11 Casa de Jaimes C1
12 Casa Jansy's C2
13 Casa Sucre C3
14 Casablanca B1
15 El Tumi I D1
16 El Tumi II D1
17 Grand Huaraz C2
18 Hostal Colomba A2
19 Hostal Continental C1
20 Hostal Galaxia C1
21 Hostal Los Andes B1
22 Hostal Mi Casa C1
23 Hostal Quintana C1
24 Hostal Yanett A2
25 La Cabaña C3
26 La Casa de Zarela C3
27 Olaza Guesthouse C3
28 Rinconcito Huaracino A2
29 San Sebastián B3

● Eating
1 Café Central C1
2 El Conquistador D1
3 Extreme D1
4 Huaraz Querido D2
5 La Estación D2
6 Las Kenas D1
7 Limón, Leña y Carbón D1
8 Pizza Bruno D1

🚌 Transport
1 Chavín Express C1
2 Combis to Caraz A1, A2
3 Combis to Llupa (for Laguna Churup) B2
4 Combis to Wilcawain A2
5 Cruz del Sur B2
6 El Rápido C1
7 Los Andes & Turismo Huaraz A2
8 Terminal Terrestre Transportistas Zona Sur C1
9 Trans Rodríguez C1
10 Trans Sandoval C1
11 Virgen de Guadalupe B2
12 Yungay Express & Trans Huandoy A2

Essentials

The main thoroughfare, Av Luzuriaga, is bursting at the seams with travel agencies, climbing equipment hire shops, restaurants, cafés and bars. For those seeking a quieter ambience, there are many other options a block or two away from the main drag. A small cluster of cafés and restaurants offers a pleasant, tranquil, atmosphere on Jirón Julián de Morales, one block east of Luzuriaga.

Hotels are plentiful (there are many more than those listed below) but fill up rapidly during the high season (May-Sep), especially during public holidays and special events (such as the Semana de Andinismo in Jun) when prices rise. Lodging in private homes is common during these periods.

Sleeping
■ on map
Price codes:
see inside front cover

AL *Andino Club*, Pedro Cochachín 357, some way southeast from the centre (take a taxi after dark), T721949, T/F722830, www.hotelandino.com The best in town, expensive restaurant, free internet for guests, safe parking, Swiss run, friendly, 2nd floor rooms with balconies and views of Huascarán are more expensive, climbing and hiking gear for hire. Recommended.

B *Grand Huaraz*, Larrea y Loredo 721, T722227, F726536. Modern (1998), with cafetería. **B** *San Sebastián*, Jr Italia 1124, T726960, F722306, andeway@net.telematic.com.pe 2-star, very helpful, breakfast included, good views. Recommended. **C** *Hostal Colomba*, Francisco de Zela 278, on Centenario across the river, T721501/727106, F722273, colomba@terra.com.pe Lovely old hacienda, bungalow, family-run (German), garden, friendly, safe car parking. **C** *Edward's Inn*, Bolognesi 121, T/F722692. Cheaper without bathroom, clean, not always hot water, laundry, friendly, food available, insist on proper rates in low season, popular, Edward speaks English and knows a lot about trekking and rents gear (not all guides share Edward's experience). Highly recommended. **C** *El Tumi I*, San Martín 1121, T/F721784, in Lima T/F346 2725, hottumi@terra.com.pe Good restaurant (serves huge steaks), fairly good, advance reservations advised. **C** *Hostal Los Portales*, Raymondi 903, T/F728184. With bathroom, hot water, parking, a pleasant place to stay. **C** *Hostal Montañero*, Plaza Ginebra 30-B (ask at Casa de Guías), T/F722306. Hot water, very clean, modern, comfortable, friendly, climbing equipment rental and sales.

D *Casablanca*, Tarapacá 138, which is near the market, T722602, F724801, cashotel@telematic.edu.pe Clean, pleasant, modern. **D** *Residencial Cataluña*, Av Raymondi 622, T722761. With bathroom, hot water, TV, **E** for more basic rooms, restaurant open only in the high season, clean, safe, noisy. **F** per person *El Pacífico*, Luzuriaga 630, T721683, F724416. With bathroom, not always hot water, friendly, helpful good restaurant. **D** *El Tumi II*, San Martín 1089, T721784. With bathroom, reasonable value, beds not too comfortable. **D** *Hostal Raymondi*, Raymondi 820, T721082 (in Lima T427 9016). With bathroom, cheaper without, hot water only in the mornings in the ground floor shower, comfortable, charges for left luggage, café serves good breakfast. **D** *Hostal Yanett*, Av Centenario 164, at the north end of town across the river, T727150. Friendly, hot water, clean, large rooms, restaurant for breakfast. Recommended. **D** *Samuel's*, Bolívar 504, T/F726370. Cheaper without bathroom, clean, modern, small rooms. **D** *Schatzi*, Bolívar 419, near Raimondi, T723074. Clean, nice courtyard, with bath, hot water, breakfast extra.

E *Hostal Copa*, Jr Bolívar 615, T722071, F722619. Cheaper without bathroom, hot water, laundry facilities, clean, owner's son Walter Melgarejo is a well-known guide, popular with trekkers, restaurant, travel agency with local tours. **E-F** *Casa Jansy's*, Jr Sucre 948. Hot water, meals, laundry, owner Jesús Rivera Lúcar is a mountain guide. Recommended. **E** *Hostal Estoico*, San Martín 635, T722371. Cheaper without bathroom, friendly, clean, safe, hot water, laundry facilities, good value. Recommended. **E** *Hostal Gyula*, Parque Ginebra 632, opposite the Casa de Guías, T721567,

Cordillera Blanca

hotelperu@infoweb.com.pe With bathroom, hot water, clean, very friendly and help-ful, has good information on local tours, stores luggage. Noisy at weekends but recom-mended. **E** *Hostal Galaxia*, Jr de la Cruz Romero 638, T722230. Cheaper without bathroom, hot water, laundry facilities, basic, friendly. Recommended. **E** *Jo's Place*, Jr Daniel Villayzan 276, T725505. Safe, hot water, kitchen facilities, nice mountain views, garden, terrace, warm atmosphere, English owner. Highly recommended. **E** *Hostal Los Andes*, Tarapacá 316, T724700. Cheaper without bathroom, warm water, clean, laun-dry facilities, noisy, not very comfortable but friendly. **E** *Oscar's Hostal*, La Mar 624, T/F722720, marciocoronel@hotmail.com With bathroom, hot water, cheap breakfast next door, good beds, helpful, cheaper in low season. Recommended. **E** *Hostal Quintana*, Mcal Cáceres 411, T726060. Cheaper without bathroom, hot shower, laun-dry facilities, clean, basic, stores luggage, friendly, popular with trekkers.

Huaraz centre

Cordillera Blanca

Sleeping
1 El Pacífico *C1*
2 Familia Meza & Café Andino *C2*
3 Hostal Copa *C3*
4 Hostal Estoico *C1*
5 Hostal Gyula *D2*
6 Hostal Imperio *B1*
7 Hostal Los Portales *A3*
8 Hostal Montañero *C2*
9 Hostal Raymondi *A2*
10 Hostal Tany *B2*
11 Oscar's Hostal *B2*
12 Residencial Cataluña *A1*
13 Samuel's *C3*
14 Schatzi *A3*

Eating
1 Baby Donkey & Skyline Adventures *C1*
2 Bistro de los Andes *C3*
3 Chifa Jim Hua *C1*
4 Créperie Patrick *A1*
5 Euskalerria *A1*
6 Fuente de Salud *B1*
7 La Placita: Rinconcito Minero, Hoja Sagrada, Querubin's, Vagamundo *C2*
8 Las Puyas *C1*
9 Makondo's *B2*
10 Monte Rosa *B2*
11 Pepe's Place *A1*
12 Piccolo *C1*
13 Pizza B & B *B2*
14 Pizzería Landauro *D2*
15 Sabor Salud & Avance *D1*
16 Siam de Los Andes *C3*

Bars
17 Amadeus *D2*
18 Monttrek Disco *D2*
19 Neo *B2*
20 Pachamama *D1*
21 Taberna Tambo *B2*

N

0 metres 20
0 yards 20

Recommended. **E** *Hostal Tany*, Lúcar y Torre 468A, T722534. With bathroom, cheaper without, hot water at night, spotlessly clean, money exchange, tours, café/restaurant.

F per person *Caroline Lodging*, Urb Avitentel Mz D – Lt 1, T722588, T691896 (mob), trojas@viabcp.com or terrori@latinmail.com Price includes breakfast, free pick-up from bus station (phone in advance), hot water, kitchen facilities, tourist information and guides, laundry, very helpful. Frequently recommended. **F** *La Casa de Zarela*, J Arguedas 1236, T721694, zarelaz@hotmail.com With bath, hot water, popular with climbers and trekkers, owner Zarela organizes groups and is very knowledgeable. **F** *Lodging Casa Sucre*, Sucre 1240, T722264, F721111. Private house, with bath, kitchen, laundry facilities, friendly, clean, hot water, English and French spoken, mountaineering guide, Filiberto Rurush, can be contacated here. **F** per person *Albergue Churup*, Jr Figueroa 1257, T722584, www.churup.com Ring bell and wait for them to come from Jr Pedro Campos 735. Double rooms and shared rooms, with and without bath, more rooms being built, nice garden and fire in sitting room, internet access, use of kitchen at Pedro Campos where they serve breakfast, lots of information, luggage store, laundry, book exchange, English spoken, Spanish classes, helpful, motorcycle parking. Recommended. **F** *Hostal Continental*, 28 de Julio 586 near Plaza de Armas, T724171. With bath, clean, hot water, friendly, cafeteria serving good breakfasts. Recommended but avoid the rooms overlooking the street as there are 2 noisy *peñas* nearby. **F** *Alojamiento El Jacal*, Jr Sucre 1044, blue house with no sign, cheaper without shower, hot water, very nice family. **F** *Albergue El Tambo*, Confraternidad Internacional Interior 122-B. Clean, laundry and cooking facilities, 3 rooms with 12 beds, friendly, good meeting place. **F** *Familia Meza*, Lúcar y Torre 538, T726367, lacima_peru@hotmail.com Popular with trekkers, mountaineers and bikers. **F** *Hostal Imperio*, José de la Mar 528 y San Martín. With private electric shower, clean, good beds, ask for hot water. **F** *Hostal López*, Prolongación Alberto Gridilla s/n, Huarapampa, behind *Edward's Inn*, ask near the Estadio just off Av Bolognesi at the Santa river end. Lukewarm showers, washing facilities for clothes, beautiful garden and restaurant, good views, luggage stored, very friendly. **F** per person *Hostal Mi Casa*, Tarapacá 773 (Av 27 de Noviembre), T723375, F729273, bmark@ddm.com.pe Includes breakfast, cheaper in low season, hot water, English spoken, very friendly and pleasant, owner Sr Ames is an expert on glaciers, his son is a climbing and rafting guide. **F** *Alojamiento Norma*, Pasaje Valenzuela 837, near Plaza Belén, T721831. Includes breakfast, cheaper without bathroom, hot water. Recommended. **F** per person, *Olaza Guest house*, J Arguedas 1246, T722951, info@andeanexplorer.com.pe Safe, comfortable, luggage stored, discount for bikers. **F** *Hostal Rinconcito Huaracino*, Fitzcarrald 226, T727591. Cheaper without bathroom, hot water, modern, clean, front rooms are noisy. **F-G** *Angeles Inn*, Av Gamarra 815, T722205, solandperu@yahoo.com No sign, look for *Sol Andino* travel agency in same building (www.solandino.com) New, kitchen and laundry facilities, small garden, hot water, owners Max and Saul Angeles are official guides, helpful with trekking and climbing, rent equipment.

G per person *Backpackers*, Av Raimoondi 510, T721773, http://huaraz.com/backpackers Includes breakfast, spacious, hot showers, good views, friendly, a real bargain. **G** per person *La Cabaña*, Jr Sucre 1224, T723428. Shared and double rooms, hot showers, laundry, kitchen, computer, very friendly, popular (especially with Israelis), safe for parking, bikes and luggage. **G** per person *Lodging House Ezama*, Mariano Melgar 623, Independencia, T723490, 15 mins' walk from Plaza de Armas (US$0.50 by taxi). Light, spacious rooms, hot water, safe, helpful. **G** per person *Casa de Familia Gómez Díaz*, Jr Eulogio del Río 1983, T723224. Hot water, quiet, family atmosphere, good beds. **G** *Alojamiento La Stancia*, Jr Huaylas 162, Centenario, T723183. With bath or shared shower, luggage store, safe motorcycle parking, good value. **G** *Alojamiento Marilla*, Sucre 1123, T728160/691956, alojamaril@latinmail.com Good views, modern, rooms with and without bath, also dormitory accommodation, hot water, laundry and

There are usually people waiting at the bus terminals offering cheap accommodation in their own homes

breakfast available, kitchen facilities, luggage store, knowledgeable owners. **G** per person *Alojamiento Nemys*, Jr Figueroa 1135, T722949. Secure, hot shower, breakfast US$2.40, good for climbers, luggage store. Recommended. **G** per person *Alojamiento Soledad*, Jr Amadeo Figueroa 1267, T721196 (in Lima 242 8615), ajsoled@terra.com.pe Breakfast extra, shared bath, not the best beds, intermittent hot water, kitchen, family-run and very friendly, cafeteria, secure, trekking information. Recommended for value. **G** *Alojamiento Sra Tomaza Huarato*, Jr Amadeo Figuera 1194, T721915. With patio, hot shower, safe, quiet, clean, luggage store, run by an elderly couple and their family. **G** per person *Casa de Jaimes*, Alberto Gridilla 267, T722281, 2 blocks from the main plaza. Clean dormitory with hot showers, washing facilities, has maps and books of the region, use of kitchen, popular with Israelis. Noisy but recommended.

Youth Hostels **F** per person *Alojamiento Alpes Andes*, at *Casa de Guías*, Plaza Ginebra 28-g, T721811, F722306. Member of the Peruvian Youth Hostel Association, 1 dormitory with 14 beds and another with 6 beds, hot water, with very good restaurant (open 0700-1100, 1700-2300), laundry, free luggage store, the owner Sr López speaks English, French and German and is very helpful, he is the mountain guides administrator. **F** per person *Hostal la Montañesa*, Av Leguía 290, Centenario, T711217. Member of the Peruvian Youth Hostel Association.

Eating
● *on map*

Expensive *Pizza Bruno*, Luzuriaga 834. 1600-2300. Excellent pizzas, crepes and pastries, good service. French owner Bruno Reviron also has a 4-wheel drive with driver for hire. *Euskalerria*, Luzuriaga 406. Basque cuisine, good food and service, trekking information, owner is a top mountain guide. *Huaraz Querido*, Bolívar 981. Excellent *cevichería*. *Monte Rosa*, J de la Mar 661. 1000-2300. Pizzería, also fondue and other Swiss specialities. Swiss owner is Victorinox representative, offering knives for sale and repair service, also Suunto (altimeters, GPS), sells mountaineering gear and excellent postcards, rents skiis and snowboards and has climbing and trekking books to read. *Créperie Patrick*, Luzuriaga 422. Excellent crepes, fish, quiche, spaghetti and good wine. *Siam de Los Andes*, Gamarra corner J de Morales. Authentic Thai cuisine. Recommended.

Mid-range *Alpes Andes*, Plaza Ginebra in *Casa de Guías*. Muesli, yoghurt etc in the morning, pastas and pizzas in the evening. *Baby Donkey*, San Martín (next to *Skyline Adventures*). Mexican, all-you-can-eat place, very popular. *Bistro de los Andes*, J de Morales 823, T/F726249. Great food, owner speaks English, French and German. Recommended. *Fuente de Salud*, J de la Mar 562. Vegetarian, also meat and pasta dishes, good soups, breakfast, recommended. *Hoja Sagrada*, J de Morales 747. Good *menú*, pleasant. *Limón, Leña y Carbón*, Av Luzuriaga 1002. Typical dishes in the day, local grills at night, also seafood and fish dishes, bar, excellent food and value. Recommended. *Monttrek Pizza Pub*, Luzuriaga 646 (upstairs from the agency). Good pizzas and pastas, indoor climbing wall, shows videos. *Pachamama*, San Martín 687. Bar, café and restaurant, concerts, art gallery, garden, nice place to relax, good toilets, pool table and table-tennis, information on treks, Swiss-owned. Recommended. *Pepe's Place*, Raymondi 624, good pizza, chicken, meat, warm atmosphere, run by Pepe from *Residencial Cataluña*. *Pizza B&B*, La Mar beside laundry of same name. Recommended for its traditional sauces for pizza and pasta, and deserts. *Pizzería Landauro*, Sucre, on corner of Plaza de Armas. Very good for pizzas, nice atmosphere. *Rinconcito Minero*, J de Morales 757. Breakfast, lunch (including vegetarian), coffee and snacks, popular and good. *Querubín's*, J de Morales 767. Clean, friendly, good breakfast and set meals, also vegetarian, snacks and à la carte. Recommended. *Sabor Salud*, Luzuriaga 672, upstairs. Restaurant and pizzería specializing in vegetarian and Italian food.

Cordillera Blanca

Cheap *La Estación*, 2 locations on Plazuela Belén. Video pub which serves a good lunch for only US$1, also good steaks, nice atmosphere, very friendly owner. Recommended. *Chifa Jim Hua*, Luzuriaga 645, upstairs, large, tasty portions, *menú* US$1.15. Mon-Sat 0900-1500, 1800-2400, Sun 1800-2200. *Piccolo*, J de Morales 632. Pizzería, very popular with gringos. *Pico de Oro*, San Martín 595. Good value Peruvian food.*Las Puyas*, Morales 535. Popular with gringos, serves an excellent *sopa criolla* and very good trout, also serves breakfast. *Vegetarian Food*, Sucre y Av Bolívar. Excellent vegetarian, 3-course meal US$1. *Panadería Ancash*, Raymondi cuadra 7. Different types of bread, including *integral*, cakes, ice cream.

Café Andino, Lúcar y Torre 538, T721203, cafeandino@hotmail.com American run café **Cafés** and book exchange, extensive lending library in many languages, a nice place to relax and write postcards, great atmosphere, good meeting place, occasional movies, new Huayhuash maps for sale, owner guides treks in Cordillera Huayhuash, lots of advice offered. *Café Central*, 28 de Julio 592. Good breakfast for US$1.30, great chocolate cake and apple pie. *Comedor 14*, San Martín 525. Good value breakfasts, sandwiches, teas, etc.

Las Kenas, Jr Gabino Uribe near Luzuriaga. Live Andean music, happy hr 2000-2200, **Bars & clubs** good pisco sours. Next door, upstairs, is *Extreme*, bar popular with *gringos*. 1900-0200. *Vagamundo*, J de Morales 753. Popular new bar with snacks and football tables.

Clubs and peñas *Amadeus*, Parque Ginebra, bar-disco. *La Cascada*, Luzuriaga 1276, disco tavern. *El Conquistador*, 28 de Julio 570. Excellent *peña* with good fixed-price lunches. *Makondo's*, José de la Mar, opposite *Tambo*. Disco, bar, nightclub and restaurant, safe, popular. *Monttrek Disco*, Sucre just off Plaza de Armas, in converted cinema, reasonable prices. *Neo*, Lúcar y Torre 460, disco pub.*Taberna Tambo*, José de la Mar 776, folk music daily, disco. 1000-1600, 2000-0200, knock on door to get in.

Semana Santa, or Holy Week, is widely celebrated and always colourful and lively. The **Festivals** town's Patron saints' day is *El Señor de la Soledad*, during the week starting **3 May**, with parades, dancing, music, fireworks and much drinking. The *Semana del Andinismo* is an international climbing and skiing week, held in **Jun**. The festivals of *San Juan* and *San Pedro* are celebrated throughout the region during the last week of **Jun**. On the eve of *San Juan* fires are lit throughout the valley to burn the chaff from the harvest. The following day the entire valley is thick with smoke.

Handicrafts Local sweaters, hats, gloves, ceramics, and wall hangings can be bought **Shopping** from stalls on Pasaje Mcal Cáceres just off Luzuriaga, in the stalls off Luzuriaga between Morales and Sucre, also on Bolívar cuadra 6 and elsewhere. *Andean Expressions*, Jr J Arguedas 1246, near La Soledad church, T722951, olaza@qnet.com.pe 0800-2200, run by Lucho, Mauro and Beto Olaza, and recommended for hand-printed T-shirts and sweatshirts with unusual motifs. Handmade boots, cowboy-style can be made to fit in 3 days at *La Perla*, Sr Enrique Salazar Salas, Jr San Martín 574, about US$80.

Groceries and trekking provisions Two well-stocked supermarkets are *Ortiz*, Luzuriaga 401 corner Raymondi (good selection) and *Militos*, Sucre 775. Other shops include *Bodega Chong Roca*, Jr J de Morales 661 and *Comercial Anita*, Jr San Cristóbal 369. The central market offers a wide variety of canned and dry goods, including nuts and dried fruit, as well as fresh fruit and vegetables. Be sure to check expiry dates. *Panadería Robles*, Bolívar 479, has good bread that keeps well on treks. Local cheese and *manjarblanco* from *Rosa Rosita*, Jr San Martín, ½ block from Morales.

Photography *Foto Galería Andes*, at Pasaje Cayetano Requena, near the market, is good for camera repairs and sells professional photos of the Cordillera Blanca.

Motorcycle shop *Ying*, Gamarra 1136, T722443. Ask for Chino, also has workshop, good equipment. Recommended.

Cordillera Blanca

Sports   **Horseriding**   Contact *Sr Robinson Ayala Gride*, T723813, well in advance for half-day trips (enquire at *El Cortijo* restaurant – see page 345). He is a master *paso* rider. *Posada de Yungar*, at Yungar (about 20 km on the Carhuaz road), T721267, M 679836, Swiss run. Ask for José Flores or Gustavo Soto. US$4.50 per hr on nice horses; good 4-hr trip in the Cordillera Negra with fabulous views.

    Mountain biking   Contact Julio Olaza at *Mountain Bike Adventures*, Lúcar y Torre 530, T724259, julio.olaza@terra.com.pe, or www.chakinaniperu.com   US$20 for 5 hrs, various routes (see page 77). Julio speaks excellent English and also runs a book exchange, sells topo maps and climbing books. *La Casa de Zarela* (see Sleeping, above), rents good quality mountain bikes (no guides). See also Tour operators below and *Galaxia Expeditions* under Hiring camping gear, above.

    River rafting and canoeing   Contact Carlos Ames, *River Runners*, via *Monttrek*, Av Luzuriaga 646, see Tour operators below (also see page 79).

Tour operators   Huaraz is overflowing with agencies and quality varies. Try to get a recommendation from someone who has recently returned from a tour, climb or trek. All agencies run conventional tours to Llanganuco, Pastoruri (both US$8.50 per person) and Chavín (US$10 per person), entry tickets not included. Many hire equipment (see Trekking and climbing in the Cordillera Blanca, page 331) and also offer rafting on Río Santa (US$15 for half a day), climbing and trekking tours and ski instruction. Most agencies provide transport, food, mules and guides. Prices are generally 20% lower during the low season, which is from Oct-Apr. **NB** Tour agencies shouldn't recommend Pastoruri as a first trip. It's best to go to Llanganuco first to acclimatize. The following are recommended: *Andean Kingdom*, Luzuriaga 522. Free information, maps, climbing wall, rock and ice climbing, treks, equipment rental, very helpful, English and some Hebrew spoken. *Anden Sport Tours*, Luzuriaga 571, T721612. Have a basic practice wall behind the office. They also organize mountain bike tours, ski instruction and river rafting. *Baloo Tours*, Bolívar 471, T723928. Organizes tours and rents gear. *Chavín Tours*, Luzuriaga 502, T721578, F724801 (Willy Gordillo can also be found at *Hostal Casablanca*, see above, T722602). *Cordillera Blanca Adventures*, run by the Mejía Romero family, T724352. Experienced, quality climbing and trekking trips, good guides and equipment. *Explorandes*, Av Centenario 489, T721960, F722850, postmast@exploran.com.pe   *Hirishanka Sport*, Sucre 802, T722562. Climbing, trekking, horse riding, 4-wheel drive hire, they also rent rooms, **E** per person, with bath, hot water, breakfast. *Kallpa*, Luzuriaga 479, T727868, kallpaperu@terra.com.pe   Organizes treks, rents gear, arranges *arrieros* and mules, very helpful. *Monttrek*, Luzuriaga 646, upstairs, T721124, F726976. Good trekking and climbing information, advice and maps, run ice and rock climbing courses (at Monterrey), tours to Laguna Churup and the 'spectacular' *Luna Llena* tour; they also hire out mountain bikes, run ski instruction and trips, and river rafting. Next door in the Pizzería is a climbing wall, good maps, videos and slide shows. For new routes and maps contact Porfirio Cacha Macedo, 'Pocho', at *Monttrek* or at Jr Corongo 307, T723930. *Pablo Tours*, Luzuriaga 501, T721142/721145. All local tours.

Transport   **Bus**   To/from Lima: 420 km, 7 hrs, US$5.75-10. The road is in good condition. There is
Many bus companies a large selection of buses to Lima, both ordinary service and luxury coaches, with
have offices selling departures throughout the day. Many of the companies have their offices along Av
tickets in the centre, Raymondi and on Jr Lúcar y Torre. Some recommended companies are: *Cruz del Sur*,
but buses leave from Raymondi just east of Gamarra, T723532; *Transportes Rodríguez*, Tarapacá 622,
the edge of the centre T721353; *Civa Cial*, Morales opposite Lúcar y Torre; *Móvil Tours*, Bolívar 468, T722555; *Empresa 14*, Fitzcarrald 216, T721282, terminal at Bolívar 407.

    Other long distance buses: To **Casma** via the Callán pass and Pariacoto (150 km) 6-7 hrs, US$4.25, the lower section of the road is very poor, landslides and closures are common (sit on the left for best views): *Transportes Huandoy*, Fitzcarrald 261, T727250 (terminal at Caraz 838), daily at 0800, 1000 and 1300. *Yungay Express*, same office and terminal, 3 a day. They continue to **Chimbote**, 185 km. To Chimbote via Caraz and the Cañon del Pato (sit on the right for the most exciting views; see page 383) *Yungay Express*, daily, US$7, 10 hrs. Other companies go to **Chimbote** via Pativilca; US$6, 7 hrs (to **Pativilca**, 160 km, 4 hrs, US$3.50). Most continue to **Trujillo**, all buses go at night, 8-9 hrs, US$7.15-8.65: *Chinchaysuyo* (Lúcar y Torre 487, T726417), *Línea* (Simón Bolívar 450, T726666), *Empresa 14* and, *Móvil Tours*, addresses above.

Within the Cordillera Blanca area: Several buses and frequent minivans run daily, 0500-2000, between Huaraz and **Caraz**, 1 hr, US$1. They stop at all the places in between. They depart from the parking area under the bridge on Fitzcarrald and from the open space beside the bridge on the other side of the river (beware of thieves here). To **Chavín**, 110 km, 4 hrs (sit on left side for best views), US$3: *Chavín Express*, Mcal Cáceres 338, T724652, daily at 0730, 0830, 1100 and 1400, Sun 1500; *Trans Sandóval*, 27 de Noviembre 582, T726930, 0800 and 1300; *Trans Río Mosne*, Cáceres 275, T726632, 0700 and 1300. All 3 companies have buses that go on to Huari, 6 hrs, US$5, and Llamellín, 8 hrs, US$7. To **Chacas** (US$3.75) and **San Luis** (US$5.75), at 0700 with *Virgen de Guadalupe*, Caraz 607, also to La Unión, US$4.35 at 0700. *Renzo*, Raymondi 821, T724915, runs to Chacas and San Luis (1300 Mon-Sat, 1500 Sun), Yanama, Piscobamba and Pomabamba (0630, best service). *Los Andes*, 13 de Diciembre 201, T727362, goes daily at 0700 to Yungay, US$0.75, Lagunas de Llanganuco, US$3.45, Yanama, US$3.45, Piscobamba, US$5.20 and Pomabamba, US$6 (8 hrs). Also to **Pomabamba** via **Yungay**, Lakes **Llanganuco** and **Yanama**, *Transvir* and *La Perla de Altamayo*, 0630, 8 hrs, US$6. To **Sihuas**, *Chavín Express*, twice a week, and *Perú Andino*, once a week, 8 hrs, US$7. Colectivos to **Recuay**, US$0.45, **Ticapampa** and **Catac**, US$0.55, leave daily at 0500-2100, from Gridilla, just off Tarapacá (Terminal Terrestre Transportistas Zona Sur). To **Chiquián** for the Cordillera Huayhuash, see page 370. To **Huallanca** (Huánuco), via Pachacoto (see page 357), US$3.50. A fantastic journey which offers the option of travelling south, through the Sierra towards Cuzco avoiding Lima. The route follows the Pastoruri valley passing through the Puyo Raimondi forest and offers glimpses of the Pastoruri glacier. The rough road then climbs up above the glacier to 5,000 m and there are even more spectacular views of several other snow-capped massifs, including the Cordillera Huayhuash in the distance. In winter this route may be blocked by snowfalls. The road then descends to the Vizcarra valley and briefly coincides with the impressive Antimina highway (wide and paved) before passing through several mining settlements. Between Huallanca and La Unión the road follows the river in the beautiful Vizcarra gorge. *Trans El Rápido*, Mcal Cáceres 312, T726437 (next to Chavín Express), 4½ hrs, US$3.50, at 0630 and 1300; *Yungay Express* also at 1300. Good views on both sides. Some *El Rápido* buses continue to La Unión, 6 hrs, US$4.50. There are regular colectivos from Huallanca to La Unión from the corner of Comercio y 28 de Julio, 1 hr, US$0.75.

Directory

Banks *BCP*, on the Plaza de Armas. Closed 1300-1630, changes cash, 3.25% commission on TCs into soles, good rates, 5% commission charged on TCs into dollars, cash advance on Visa, very long queues, *Telebanco 24 Horas* ATM (Visa). *Interbank*, on Plaza de Armas. Cash and TCs (no commission into soles), Mastercard ATM. *Banco Wiese*, Sucre 766. Changes cash and cheques. *Casa de Cambio Oh Na Nay*, across the street from Interbank. Gives good rates for cash dollars, but poor rates for other currencies. There are several other *casas de cambio* and many street changers (be careful) on Luzuriaga.

Communications Internet: *Universidad Nacional (UNSAM)*, Av Centenario 200. 0800-2200 daily, but sometimes closes at weekends, US$2 per hr, minimum 30 mins. *Avance SRL*, Luzuriaga 672. 0700-2300 daily, US$3 per hr, US$1.75 per email message, US$1.75 to read or write a diskette, good equipment but expensive. There are several places with internet access in the centre, eg: one next to *Casa de Guías*, another opposite at Plaza Ginebra 630; *Portalnet*, Luzuriaga 999; *The H@ckers*, Luzuriaga y Pasaje Coral

Cordillera Blanca

Vega; *Net Computer*, Av Fitzcarrald 320, interior, T728088, cgmacedo@latinmail.com, telephone office downstairs; *Fantasynet*, Caraz 601, of 102, fatasynet@lanet.com.pe Average price US$0.75 per hr. **Post**: *Serpost* is on Luzuriaga opposite the Plaza de Armas. 0800-2000 daily. **Telephone**: *Telefónica*, Sucre y Bolívar, corner of Plaza de Armas. National and international phone and fax. 0700-2300 daily. There are many other private calling centres along Luzuriaga, plus coin phones everywhere.

Laundry *B & B*, La Mar 674. US$1.20 per kg, special machine for down garments and sleeping bags, French run. Recommended. *Huaraz*, on the plaza on Mcal Cáceres, next to *Galaxia Mountain Shop*. *Lavandería Liz*, Bolívar 711. US$2 per kg. Also at the Casa de Guías (see page 332) and *Laundry Express* at *JM Expediciones*, on the lane between Luzuriaga and Plaza Ginebra.

Useful services Public showers on Raymondi between Gamarra and Bolívar, hot water especially good around 1500.

Around Huaraz

Willkawain
A good grasp of Spanish will greatly enhance the pleasure of this experience as the locals are very welcoming

The Willkawain archaeological site lies about 8 km to the northeast of Huaraz. The ruins date from AD 700-1000, which was the second and imperial phase of the Huari empire. During this period, the Huari influence spread north from the city of the same name near Ayacucho. The Huari empire was remarkable for the strong Tiahuanaco influence in its architecture and ceramics. The Huari introduced a new concept in urban life, the great walled urban centre.

The site consists of three large two-storey structures with intact stone slab roofs and several small structures. The windowless inner chambers can be explored with the help of a torch/flashlight, though most of the rooms are inaccessible. A few, however, have been opened up to reveal a sophisticated ventilation system and skilful stone craftsmanship. About 500 m past Willkawain is Ichiwillkawain with several similar but smaller structures.

Even if you're not an archaeology buff, the trip is worth it for a fascinating insight into rural life in the valley. Take a colectivo up to the ruins and walking back down to Huaraz is thoroughly recommended (about a two-hour walk).

■ *Entrance to the site is US$1.50. Take a combi from 3 de Diciembre y Comercio, US$0.55 direct to Willkawain. If walking, go past the Hotel Huascarán. After crossing a small bridge take a second right (well-signposted), from where it's about a 2-hr uphill walk. Ask frequently as there are many criss-crossing paths. Beware of dogs en route (and begging children). Alternatively, the purple city bus (line 2B) will take you to Marian, a 15-min walk from the ruins.*

Monterrey
Colour map 3, grid B3
Altitude: 2,780 m

North of Huaraz, 6 km along the road to Caraz, are the thermal baths at Monterrey. It's a good place for a day trip to soak in the **thermal baths** and an alternative place to stay for those seeking peace and quiet. The baths are run by the *Hotel Baños Termales Monterrey* and, owing to the high iron content, the water is dark brown but not dirty. ■ *There are 2 pools: the lower pool is US$0.85; the upper pool, which is nicer is US$1.35. There are also individual and family tubs which cost US$1.35 per person for 20 mins. The upper pool is closed on Mon for cleaning. It gets crowded at weekends and holidays.*

Sleeping **B** *Baños Termales Monterrey*, Av Monterrey, at the top of the hill, T/F721717. Slightly run down but classic old spa, price includes breakfast and use of pools, restaurant, bar, good location for walking, there is a rock face behind the hotel which is used for climbing practice. **B** *El Patio*, Av Monterrey, 250 m downhill from the baths, T724965. Includes breakfast, meals on request, bar, friendly, colonial-style. Recommended.

Cordillera Blanca

Eating There are several country style restaurants in Monterrey which are popular with locals and busy at weekends, serving trout, *pachamanca* and other regional specialities. Along the Huaraz-Caraz road at Km 6.5 is *El Cortijo*, which serves very good food, eg chicken and barley stew, and *anticuchos*. At Km 5.5 *El Viejo Molino*, T721268, along the Río Santa. There are several cheaper restaurants and stands along Av Monterrey.

Transport City buses along Av Luzuriaga go as far as Monterrey (US$0.22), until 1900. A taxi costs US$2-3.

Laguna Churup

To the east of Huaraz, off the road between Unchus and Pitec is a trail to **Laguna Churup**, which makes a good one-day excursion from Huaraz. Take a colectivo from Caraz y Comercio early in the morning for the 40-minute ride along the Río Quilcay to Llupa (US$0.60), then hike one hour to Pitec and, from the National Park entrance, a further three hours up to the lake, which is surrounded by high mountains. The last part involves scrambling over rocks. It's about three hours back to Llupa, where colectivos run until about 1800.

From Pitec there are **three-day hikes** up the Quebrada Quillcayhuanca to Cayesh or to Lagunas Tullpacocha and Cuchilacocha. From the latter you can cross a pass to the Cojup valley and desccend to Llupa (a further two days). You have to pay a national park entrance fee in Pitec to do these treks.

Punta Callan walk

This is an excellent day walk from Huaraz, with superb views of almost the whole of the Cordillera Blanca and some nice rural scenery. It is best to leave Huaraz early in the morning, ideally about 0800, for the best light on the mountains. A taxi to Punta Callan will cost about US$25 and take about one hour, or take a Casma bus and get off at the pass. From the pass at 4,200 m walk northwards (the right hand side of the road) to a small hill of 4,600 m for the best views. Then head directly back down to Huaraz, which you'll see in the valley below you. Follow various trails and farm tracks, with several routes being possible. It takes about four hours walking to reach the first places where you'll get return minibus transport. Add another hour or so if you want to, or have to walk all the way back to Huaraz.

North from Huaraz

Huaraz to Carhuaz

Colour map 3, grid B2/3

The main road north from Huaraz through the **Callejón de Huaylas** goes to **Taricá** (not to be confused with Tarica at the north end of the Cordillera Blanca), where there is a home pottery industry. Good value purchases can be made from Francisco Zargosa Cordero.

The next town is **Marcará**, 26 km from Huaraz (one hour, US$0.45). There area couple of hotels, basic restaurants and shops.

Pick-ups and colectivos go east from Marcará along a branch road 3 km to **Chancos**, a little settlement with hot baths. There is accommodation in the shape of two very basic *alojamientos*, several basic restaurants and food stalls.

There is an uninviting lukewarm pool (US$0.45), as well as some none too clean private tubs (US$0.90) and very popular natural steam baths in caves (US$1.35 per person). The caves are interesting and worth a try, with locked changing rooms (cave 5 is the smallest and hottest). Buy eucalyptus leaves and other aromatic herbs from the local children to add some fragrance to your steam bath.

Cordillera Blanca

From Chancos the road and transport continue to **Vicos**, 3 km further up the Huandoy valley. Vicos is 7 km from Marcará (US$0.30). Vicos is in superb surroundings with views of Nevados Tocllaraju and Ranrapalca. To hike from Chancos to Vicos takes about two hours up the valley through farmland. A trail leads from Vicos to Laguna Lejíacocha, taking four hours.

There are archaeological sites at **Copa**, **Kekepampa** and **Joncopampa**. The last named is considered to be second only to Chavín in the region. From Vicos, cross the river on a footbridge, and it's about one hour further to Joncopampa.

From Vicos, you can walk through the Quebrada Honda, over the Portachuelo de Honda pass at 4,750 m, to **Chacas**, an excellent, not difficult hike, which takes about four days.

Carhuaz

Colour map 3, grid B2   Carhuaz, a friendly, quiet mountain town with a pleasant plaza with tall palm trees and lovely rose bushes is 7 km further on from Marcará. There is very good trekking in the neighbourhood (outlined below). Market days are Wednesday and Sunday. The latter is much larger, and *campesinos* bring their produce to town. Good peaches are grown locally, among other crops. The local fiesta in honour of the **Vírgen de las Mercedes** is celebrated from 14 to 24 September and rated as the best in the region. The locals are renowned for their lively celebrations, hence the town's nickname, *Carhuaz alegría*.

Sleeping   **C** per person *Casa de Pocha*, 1½ km out of town towards Hualcán, at foot of Nevado Hualcán, ask directions in town, T613058 (mob). Nice country setting, price includes breakfast and dinner, entirely solar and wind energy powered, hot water, sauna and pool, home-produced food (vegetarian available), horses for hire, camping possible, Spanish, Portuguese, English, French and Italian spoken. Recommended. **D** per person *El Abuelo*, Jr 9 de Diciembre y Tumbes, T794149. Modern, 3-star, comfortable, cafeteria, parking, ask at *Heladería El Abuelo* on main plaza. **E** *Hostal Residencial Carhuaz*, Av Progreso 586, T794312, just off the plaza. Cheaper without bathroom, varying standards of rooms (check first), basic but pleasant, hot water, nice courtyard and garden. **F** *Hostal La Merced*, Ucayali 724, T794241 (in Lima T442 3201). 'Like going back to the 1950s', clean, friendly, hot water (usually), some rooms with private bathroom, luggage store.

Eating   *El Palmero*, Av Progreso 490. Good value and friendly. There are several other restaurants on the plaza. *Café Heladería El Abuelo*, on the Plaza de Armas, sells local ice-cream, sweets and snacks, is clean and friendly, and also sells regional maps and guides and has the Información Turística Kuntur, T794149.

Transport   All transport leaves from the main plaza. There are one or two trucks daily and one minivan (0800) going up the **Ulta valley** to **Chacas** (see page 364), 87 km, 4-5 hrs, US$4.50. The road works its way up the Ulta valley to the pass at Punta Olímpica from where there are excellent views. The dirt road is not in a very good condition owing to landslides every year (in the wet season it can be closed). The trucks continue to **San Luis** (see page 364), a further 10 km, 1½ hr. Each Thu, a bus (*Trans Huandoy*) does the trip from Carhuaz to **Chacas** and returns; US$6 one way, 5 hrs. To **Huaraz**, colectivos and buses leave 0500-2000, US$0.75, 40 mins. To **Caraz**, 0500-2000, US$0.75, 1 hr.

Treks from Carhuaz

Trek 1 to Yanama The trek up to the **Ulta valley** over the Punta Yanayacu pass to Yanama is little used but offers impressive views of Huascarán and other peaks. It takes three days. If you catch a truck up the valley to where the road begins to zig-zag up to the pass, it will shorten the trek by one day. If not, start hiking from Shilla, 13 km east of Carhuaz, or Huaypan. There are combis to Shilla when full (early morning) from Jr 9 de Diciembre y La Merced, one block northeast of the Plaza, US$0.30. A taxi to Shilla costs US$3 (sharing possible). Transport Shilla-Carhuaz is scarce. Combis go to Huaypan on Wednesday and Sunday only, US$0.50, one hour.

Trek 2 to hot springs Seven kilometres east of Carhuaz, near the village of Hualcán, are the Baños de Pariacaca, which were badly damaged by a landslide in 1993. The hot springs can be seen bubbling between the rocks by the river's edge and there are some small rock pools in which the enthusiastic can bathe.

From the plaza in Carhuaz follow Comercio to the top of the hill, turn right as far as *cinco esquinas* (five corners), turn left and follow the road uphill. When you reach the bridge, cross it left to Hualcán and ask directions from there. There is transport to Hualcán leaving from the plaza in Carhuaz on Wednesday and Sunday.

Trek 3 to Laguna 513 Half an hour beyond Baños de Pariacaca (see Trek 3 above) is the village of **Pariacaca** (no facilities) from where a trail continues into the mountains. In three hours you can reach **Laguna Rajupaquinan** and, 45 minutes beyond, the imaginatively named **Laguna 513**, with beautiful views of the surrounding peaks. If you continue, you will see the Auquiscocha lakes which you can reach in another three hours. Laguna 513 can also be reached directly from Hualcán in about four hours, along the north side of the river. This latter trail has fewer rocks to negotiate. Make sure to take adequate gear and a map if you plan to go beyond Pariacaca.

Mancos
Colour map 3, grid B2

From Carhuaz it is a further 14 km to Mancos, at the foot of Huascarán. There's accommodation at *La Casita de mi Abuela*, Barrio Huascarán (a nice dormitory), *Pukio*, Jr Comercio 110, and *La Plazza*, on the Plaza de Armas, can provide meals. There are also some basic shops and restaurants.

Climbers of Huascarán can go to **Musho** to reach the base camp. You can do a strenuous 30-km, one-day walk which gives great views of Huascarán. From Mancos follow the road east and take the branch for Tumpa, about 13 km away. Ask directions as the road branches several times. Continue north to Musho for about 1 km. You can descend via Arhuay to Ranrahica, which is between Mancos and Yungay on the main road. ■ *There are daily colectivos from Mancos to Musho. Transport to Ranrahica and Arhuay is on Wed and Sun only.*

Cueva Guitarreros is a cave in the Cordillera Negra which contains rock paintings dating back some 12,000 years. Access is either through Mancos, from where it is about 30 minutes walking along an overgrown trail (with many spines!), or through Tingua and Shupluy further south, from where it takes about one hour.

The **Chirpas thermal springs**, which have a high lithium content, are near the caves. There are good views of Huascarán from around this area.

Cordillera Blanca

Yungay

Colour map 3 grid A2

The original town of Yungay was completely buried during the 1970 earthquake by a massive mudslide caused when a piece of Huascarán's glacier was pried loose by the quake and came hurtling towards the town. It was a hideous tragedy in which 20,000 people lost their lives. The earthquake and its aftermath are remembered by many residents of the Callejón de Huaylas and the scars remain part of the local psyche.

The original site of Yungay, known as **Yungay Viejo**, has been consecrated as a *camposanto* (cemetery). It is a haunting place, with flower beds and paths covering the 8-12 m of soil under which the old town lies. Of the four palm trees from the old Plaza de Armas that protrude through the landslide, only one remains alive. Five pine trees and a monument mark the site where five policemen died. Nearby, on top of a hill, is the old cemetery with a large statue of Christ, where a handful of residents managed to escape the disaster. Many of the town's children also escaped as they were in the stadium watching the circus. There are a few monuments marking the site of former homes. ■ *The site is officially open 0800-1800. If you enter through the main entrance, which has a café, toilets and shops, off the Huaraz-Yungay road, there is a fee of US$0.75.*

The **new settlement** is on a hillside just north of the old town, and is growing gradually. It has a pleasant modern plaza and a concrete market, busiest on Wednesday and Sunday, which is good for stocking up on supplies for hiking. The predominant colour in the town is celeste (sky blue). One part of town is called the Barrio Ruso, where typical, Russian wooden houses, erected temporarily in the 1970s as a gift from the USSR, are still in use. The **tourist office** is on the corner of the Plaza de Armas.

Excursions from Yungay

A day walk from Yungay to **Mirador de Atma** gives beautiful views of Huascarán, Huandoy and the Santa valley. ■ *From town, follow a new dirt road east for 3 km (about one hour). You can return via the Quebrada Ancash road which runs further north, between the Río Ancash and Cerro Pan de Azúcar. This will bring you to the Yungay-Caraz road about 1 km north of Yungay. It is about a three hours round trip.*

Matacoto, 6 km from Yungay, is in the Cordillera Negra at 3,000 m, with excellent views of Huascarán,

Yungay

To Caraz

A Graziani

Evitamiento

Ancash Express

Combis to Caraz

M

Yungay Express

Municipalidad

Rosario

Combis to Lagos Llanganuco

Los Andes

Combis to Yanama (Santa Cruz loop)

Ica Tours

Combis & Buses to Huaraz

To Yungay Viejo & Huaraz

To Lagos Llanganucos, Santa Cruz loop & Pomabamba

N

0 metres   20
0 yards   20

■ **Sleeping**
1 Blanco
2 Gledel
3 Las Rocas
4 Mery
5 Sol de Oro
6 Suiza Peruana
7 Yungay

● **Eating**
1 Alpamayo
2 Pilar

Huandoy and other major peaks. ■ *The turn-off is at Huarazcucho (Km 251), 3 km south of new Yungay. It is another 3 km from here, across the bridge over the Río Santa to Matacoto (a new road has been started, but work is temporarily stalled). Trucks go daily 0700-1300, US$0.50. On other days transport costs US$8. Matacoto can also be reached in 3 hrs from Mancos. There is no tourism infrastructure in the town.*

Sleeping

E per person *COMTURY*, Complejo Turístico Yungay, Prolongación 2 de Mayo 1019, 2½ km south of the new town, 700 m east of the main road in Aura, the only neighbourhood of old Yungay that survived, T691698/722578. Nice bungalows with space for up to 10, in a pleasant country setting, hot water, fireplace, friendly, restaurant with regional specialities, camping possible. **E** *Hostal Gledel*, Av Arias Grazziani, north past the plaza, T793048. A few cheaper rooms are available (**G**), owned by Sra Gamboa, who is hospitable and a good cook, very clean, shared bathroom, hot water, no towels or soap, excellent meals prepared on request, nice courtyard. Highly recommended. **E** *Hostal Las Rosas*, T793673. New, clean, friendly, hot water. **E** *Hostal Yungay*, Jr Santo Domingo on the plaza, T793053. Clean, basic, shared bathroom. **F** *Hostal Blanco*, follow the hospital street at north end of plaza and continue up hill, there are signs, T793115. Shared bathroom, basic, nice views. **F** *Hostal Mery*, T793252. Hot water, rooms at front noisy. **F** *Hostal Sol de Oro*. New, clean, shared bathroom.

The following **casas de alojamiento** have been set up as part of a pilot project of family run guest houses. Prices are in the **F** range: *La Suiza Peruana*, Av Arias Grazziani s/n, Familia Sullca, T793321, small rooms, clean, shared bath, hot water.

Eating

Alpamayo, Av Arias Grazziani s/n, at the northern entrance to town. Best in town serving excellent value local dishes such as trout, cuy, tamales and pachamanca at weekends. Open lunch only. *Café Pilar*, on the main plaza. Good for juices, cakes and snacks. There are several small *comedores* in and around the market and by the plaza (eg *El Sabroso*, but better is *El Rosario*).

Festivals

On Oct 17 is *Virgen del Rosario*. On Oct 28 is the *anniversary of the founding of the town*, celebrated with parades, fireworks and dances.

Transport

Yungay is 8 km north of Mancos on the main road. Most transport leaves from Jr 28 de Julio. Buses, colectivos and trucks run all day to **Caraz** (12 km, US$0.30), and **Huaraz** (54 km, 1½ hrs, US$1). To lakes **Llanganuco**, combis leave when full, especially 0700-0900, from Av 28 de Julio 1 block from the plaza, 1 hr, US$1.25. To **Yanama**, via the Portachuelo de Llanganuco Pass, 4,767 m, 58 km, 3 hrs, US$3; stopping at María Huayta, after 2 hrs, US$2. To **Pomabamba**, via Piscobamba, *Trans Los Andes*, daily at 0800, the only company with a ticket office in Yungay; *Transvir* and *La Perla de Altamayo* buses coming from Huaraz, 0730, stop if they have room, 6-7 hrs, US$6. After passing the Llanganuco lakes and crossing the Portachuelo the buses descend to Puente Llacma, where it is possible to pick up buses and combis heading south to San Luis, Chacas and Huari.

Huaraz travel agencies organize trips to Llanganuco for about US$7.25 (see page 342)

Llanganuco to Santa Cruz trek

For trekkers this is one of the finest and most heavily used walks in the Cordillera Blanca. It usually takes three to five days depending on your starting point. It is considered somewhat easier in the opposite direction (Santa Cruz to Llanganuco), requiring three to four days, depending where you start or finish (see Treks from Caraz, page 355 for details). **Please take all your rubbish with you**; the 'servicios higiénicos' are reported to be the "among the foulest in the hemisphere".

Note that the following numbers correspond to the numbers on the map

Cordillera Blanca

Lagunas de Llanganuco   The Lagunas de Llanganuco are two lakes nestling 1,000 m below the snowline beneath Huascarán and Huandoy. The first you come to is Laguna Chinancocha (3,850 m), the second Laguna Orconcocha (3,863 m). The story goes that in times gone by, when the water levels were higher, each evening the day's snow melt and rainfall would raise Orconcocha sufficiently for it to flow into Chinancocha. By dawn they had separated. Hence the lakes' other names, Laguna Macho (male - Orconcocha) and Laguna Hembra (female - Chinancocha). The rise and fall of the waters, in legend, is also related to the tears of Huáscar and Huandy, the prince and princess of enemy tribes whose forbidden love was discovered, causing them to be turned into the mountains Huascarán and Huandoy. A nature trail, Sendero María Josefa (sign on the road), takes 1½ hours to walk to the western end of Chinancocha where there is a control post, descriptive trail and boat trips on the lake (a popular area for day-trippers). Walk along the road beside the lake to its far end for peace and quiet among the quenoal trees. These trees (*polylepis*, or paper bark) are the symbol of the Huascarán national park; they provide shelter for 75% of the birdlife found in the park.

1 Arrive in Yungay early for transport to the lakes or Yanama.

2 Entry point to the **Huascarán National Park**. The park office is situated here below the lakes at 3,200 m, 19 km from Yungay. Accommodation is provided for trekkers who want to start from here, US$2 per person. The entrance fee to the park for trekkers and climbers who will camp is US$20 (US$1.25 for a day pass, free if travelling through). All vehicles stop at the park office. Although you can start hiking up the Llanganuco valley from the park office, most hikers continue by bus or truck to **María Huayta** (see below). From the park office to Laguna Chinancocha is 1½ hours (a steep climb).

3 There is a campsite beyond Laguna Orconcocha, at Yurac Corral. From the lakes to the pass will take a further two to three hours, with perfect views on a clear day of the surrounding peaks. Walkers have the choice of a steep zig-zag path or the longer road to the pass. Just before the zig-zag climb, there is a trail heading north, up to the Pisco base camp and the Demanda valley where, to the left, Laguna 69 is situated and, to the right, the Broggi glacier. There is a doorless *refugio* by the Broggi glacier, so you can spend the night after hiking up from the lakes, continue next day to Laguna 69 and catch a truck to Yanama.

4 From the Portachuelo de Llanganuco down to **Vaquería** at 3,700 m, is about 9 km but the gradient is less steep. Some trekkers prefer to reduce the trek time by taking a Yanama combi and getting off at **María Huayta** (Km 66), though it is possible to get off at any point during the descent. From María Huayta there is a clear trail leading down in to the valley and then up the other side and round in to the next valley, Quebrada Ranincuray, entering it just above Colcabamba, 4km, 2 hours.

5 **Colcabamba** is a small village with basic lodging and food, should you decide to stay there. Familia Calonge is recommended, friendly, good meals. You can arrange an *arriero* and mule for about US$15 per day.

6 From Colcabamba the trail goes up the **Huaripampa valley**. As you enter the valley, you cross a bridge. There is a trail to the left which you should not follow. As you climb up to a curve you'll see another trail leading off to the right; do not follow this.

7 Push open the gates and continue through.

8 The trail starts again but it is best to keep close to the river to avoid the swamps. There are good camping spots from here to Punta Pucaraju.

9 **Quebrada Paría**: here you'll see a signpost. The trail continues up to the right.

10 From **Paría** you'll find a forest of quenoales. The trail crosses the river here; look for a wide spot which has rocks to use as stepping stones.

11 After 15 minutes you'll reach some large boulders on your right. Here you'll find the trail on your left. Start climbing and look for markers (piles of stones) on the way.

12 Once you reach the wall of the morraine begin the climb to the highest point at **Punta Unión**, 4,750 m. The views are wonderful. Look for the markers.

13 Go through the pass and a few metres ahead you'll see a marker to the right. Follow the track down to the pampa. From here it is downhill through the Santa Cruz valley to Cashapampa. You can camp anywhere on the way.

Llanganuco to Santa Cruz Trek

14 Cross the pampa and you'll reach a swamp from where you can see a signpost across the river. Follow the river; on the right you'll see a quenoal forest. In the middle of the river is a large rock. Five m before the rock is a natural bridge to cross the river. A bit further on is a good side trek up to the Alpamayo base camp.

15 Recrossing the river, you'll see a signpost. Follow the trail until you reach a large boulder. On the left is a cave; head towards it to get back on the right trail, otherwise you'll end up in the middle of the swamp.

16 Once you reach **Jatuncocha**, the trail goes up to the left through the rock avalanche.

17 About 45 minutes further on you reach another swamp. The trail continues on the left.

18 At the end of the Santa Cruz valley you reach a eucalyptus forest. Don't cross the bridge but follow the trail and in 15 minutes you'll be in **Cashapampa** (2,800 m). Trucks from Cashapampa to Caraz leave at 0600, 1200, 1300 and 1400; two hours, US$1.35. Alternatively, hike via the little village of Santa Cruz to Caraz, in about five hours. You can stay overnight in a basic *hospedaje* **G**, two meals US$2.

Caraz

Population: approximately 4,000
Altitude: 2,250 m
Phone code: 044
Colour map 3, grid A2

The pleasant town of Caraz is a good centre for walking and the access point for many excellent treks and climbs. It is increasingly popular with visitors as a more tranquil alternative to Huaraz. In July and August the town has splendid views of Huandoy, Huascarán from its lovely plaza filled with rose bushes, palms and jacarandas. In other months, the mountains are often shrouded in cloud. Caraz has a milder climate than Huaraz and is more suited to day trips. The sweet-toothed will enjoy the excellent locally produced *manjar blanco*, a sort of toffee, from which the town derives its nickname, Caraz dulzura. The **tourist office** is on Plaza de Armas, in the municipality, T791029. Limited information.

Sights The ruins of **Tunshukaiko** are in the suburb of Cruz Viva, to the north before the turn-off for Parón. This is a poor area so be discreet with cameras etc. There are seven platforms from the Huaraz culture, dating from around BC 500. Minimal excavations have taken place and only the tops of a couple of the structures are accessible, some of which are estimated to have been up to 50 m in height. There isn't much to see, but walking around will give you some idea of just how large these structures are. They are on a promontory with a panoramic view of the farms, fields, eucalyptus and other trees between the Cordilleras Blanca and Negra.

■ *To get there, from the plaza in Caraz follow San Martín uphill, turn left on 28 de Julio, continue about 400 m past the bridge over the Río Llullán. Look for a wide track between houses on your left (it's about 300 m before the turn-off for Lago Parón); ask the way.*

Museo del Traje Típico y Arte Religioso explains the significance of traditional clothing. It is part of the Colegio Dos de Mayo. ■ *Av Noé Bazán, continuation of Sucre. US$0.30.*

C *O'Pal Inn*, at Km 265.5 outside town set back from the road to Yungay, T/F791015 (Lima 476 4857). With bath, scenic. Recommended. **D** *La Alameda*, Av Noé Bazán Peralta 262, T791177 (Lima 461 0541), jtorres@viabcp.com.pe Comfortable rooms, hot water, breakfast, parking, gardens. Recommended. **D** *Hotel Restaurant Chamanna*, Av Nueva Victoria 185, 25 mins' walk from the centre of town, from the plaza follow San Martín uphill, turn left at 28 de Julio, continue past the turnoff to Lago Parón. Run by Germans Ute Baitinger and Reiner Urban, clean cabañas set in beautiful gardens, hot water, secure, excellent French and international cuisine. Recommended. **D** *La Perla de los Andes*, Plaza de Armas 179, T/F792007. Comfortable rooms with bath, hot water, TV, helpful, good restaurant. Has a large new annex 1 block up San Martín. Recommended.

E *Caraz Dulzura*, Sáenz Peña 212, about 10 blocks from the town centre, follow San Martín uphill north from the plaza to 3rd block, at the statue at Av N Bazán Peralta turn left and take the right fork on to Sáenz Peña, T791523 (Lima 287 1253). Modern building in an old street, 6 double rooms, hot water, with bathroom and TV, cheaper without, very comfortable, great service, clean and airy rooms, breakfast extra. Highly recommended. **E** *Chavín*, San Martín 1135 just off the plaza, T791171, F791529, hostalchavin@latinmail.com With bathroom, warm water, good service but a bit grubby, breakfast extra, guiding service, tourist information (adventure and conventional), owner can arrange transport to Lago Parón. **E** *Hostal La Casona*, Raymondi 319, 1 block east from the plaza, T791334. **F** without bathroom, hot water, clean, lovely little patio. **E** *Regina*, Los Olivos s/n y Gálvez, at the south end of town, 1 block west of road to Yungay, T791520. Modern, with bathroom, hot water, clean, quiet, good value.

F *Alojamiento Caraz*, Sucre 1305, T791084. Clean, basic, cold water, some rooms with bigger beds, best of the cheaper options. **F** *Alojamiento Retama*, Sucre 712, T/F791932/715. 4 rooms, **G** in low season (Nov-Mar), with bath, hot water (towel, soap,

Caraz

Footpath to Tunshukaiko Ruins, Hotel
Restaurant Chamanna & Hotel Caraz Dulzura

To Hostal La Alameda, Laguna
Parón & Tunshukaiko Ruins

To Cañón del Pato, Pueblo Libre & Chimbote

Santa Cruz
La Mar
Jr Córdova
San Francisco
La Merced
Av Santa Rosa
Jr Daniel Villar
M Cáceres

Cathedral
Plaza de Armas
Municipalidad
Pony's Expeditions & Café de Rat

San Martín
Sucre
Grau
Jr Bolognes
Jr Alfonso Ugarte
Manco Capac
Raymondi
L Prado
José Gálvez

To O'Pal Inn, Yungay & Huaraz

Importaciones América

0 metres 50
0 yards 50

Sleeping	
1	Alojamiento Caballero
2	Alojamiento Retama
3	Chavín
4	Familia Aguilar
5	Hostal La Casona
6	La Perla de los Andes
7	La Perla de los Andes Annex
8	La Suiza Peruana
9	Los Pinos
10	Ramírez
11	Regina

Eating & drinking	
1	Bar Kuchy
2	Caraz Dulzura
3	Cevichería Oasis
4	El Mirador
5	El Turista
6	Esmeralda
7	Huandy (Club)
8	Jeny
9	La Alameda
10	La Punta Grande
11	Olla de Barro
12	Taberna Tabasco (Club)

Transport	
1	Ancash Express
2	Cars to Huallanca
3	Chinchaysuyo
4	Combis to Huaraz & Yungay
5	Coop Ancash
6	El Huaralino
7	Móvil
8	Transportes Rodríguez
9	Turismo Huaraz
10	Yungay Express

toilet paper provided), patio, laundry facilities, safe for bicycles, breakfast extra, friendly. **F** *La Suiza Peruana*, San Martín 1133 by the plaza, T791166. With bathroom, cheaper without, not clean, has *comedor*. **G** per person *Alojamiento Caballero*, D Villar 485, T791637, or ask at *Pony's Expeditions* on the plaza. Shared bathroom, hot water, washing facilities, stores luggage, basic, family run. **G** per person *Ramírez*, D Villar 407, T791368. Basic, shared bathroom, cold water. **G** *Familia Aguilar*, San Martín 1143, next to *Chavín*, T791161. Basic, shared bathroom, owner is Prof Bernardino Aguilar Prieto.

Youth Hostel **G** per person *Los Pinos*, Parque San Martín 103, 5 blocks from plaza, T791130, lospinos@terra.com.pe All rooms shared, except one, all with bath except one (which is cheaper), hot water, a member of the Peruvian Youth Hostel Assoc, discount for HI members, camping on the premises costs US$2 per person, use of internet US$2.75 per hr, clean, safe, book exchange, information.

Eating	*Caraz Dulzura*, D Villar on the plaza, next to *Perla de los Andes*. Excellent home made ice cream, good value meals and set lunches (US$1), pastries. *Esmeralda*, Av Alfonso Ugarte 404. Good set meal, breakfast, friendly, recommended. *Jeny*, Daniel Villar on the plaza between cathedral and phone office. Good food at reasonable prices. *El Mirador*, Sucre 1202 on the plaza. Nice view from terrace, set lunch and BBQ chicken at night. *Cevichería Oasis*, Raymondi, just off the plaza. Meals for about US$1-1.50, also has rooms (**F**). *La Olla de Barro*, Sucre 1004. Good set meal. *La Punta Grande*, D Villar 595, 10 mins' walk from centre. Best place for local dishes, good, open for lunch only till 1700. *Café de Rat*, Sucre 1266, above *Pony's Expeditions*. Serves breakfast, vegetarian dishes, pizzas, drinks and snacks, darts, travel books, nice atmosphere, recommended. *El Turista*, San Martín 1117. Small, popular for breakfast, ham omelettes and ham sandwiches are specialities. *Establo La Alameda*, D Villar 420. Excellent *manjar blanco* (they let you try it first), cakes and sweets. Good *manjar blanco* is also sold by the Lúcar family, Villa Luisa brand, in a house next to the phone office on Raymondi.

● on map
Many restaurants give pensión to engineers working at the Cañon del Pato hydroelectric scheme, so may be very busy

Bars & clubs	*Bar Kuchy*, adjoining *Cevichería Oasis*. Small intimate bar and disco. *Taberna Disco Huandy*, Mcal Cáceres 119. Reasonable prices, good atmosphere. Fri-Sat. *El Tabasco Taberna*, 3 blocks from the plaza.
Festivals	*Virgen de Chiquinquirá* is held on **20 Jan**. *Holy Week* features processions and streets carpeted with flower petals. *Semana Turística* takes place during the last week in **Jul**, with sports festivals, canoeing, parasailing and folkloric events.
Shopping	Shop for camping supplies, such as fresh food, in the market. Some dried camping food is available from *Pony's Expeditions*, who also sell camping gaz canisters and white gas (see below).
Sports	**Horse-riding** *La Almeda* bakery offers horse-riding at Km 264.5, 5 mins by combi towards Yungay, T791935. A variety of routes through flower fields, across the Río Santa and up in to the Cordillera Negra to give fine views of the peaks are possible, US$5 per hr, with guide. Horses for both experienced and inexperienced riders are available.
	Parasailing Parasailing is practiced at Km 259 on the road to Huaraz but you must supply all your own equipment.
	Swimming There is a cold water pool at the southern entrance to town. Adults US$0.45, children US$0.20.
Tour operators	*Apu Expeditions*, D Villar 215, T792159, apuaventura@terra.com.pe Offer a wide range of trips in the surrounding area. *Pony's Expeditions*, Sucre 1266, near the Plaza de Armas, T/F791642, mobile 682848, www.ponyexpeditions.com Open daily 0900-1300 and

1600-2100, English, French and Quechua spoken, reliable information about the area. Owners Alberto and Haydée Cafferata are very knowledgeable about treks and climbs. Local tours and trekking with guides are arranged, maps and books for sale, also equipment for hire, mountain bike rental (from US$5 for 1 hr up to US$25 for a full day), use of internet US$2.30 per hr. Highly recommended. Another trekking guide is Mariano Araya, who is also keen on photography and archaeology. Ask at the municipality.

Long distance buses From Caraz to Lima, 470 km; several buses (5 companies, on D Villar and Jr Córdova) leave daily, fares ranging from US$5.20 (eg *El Huaralino*) to US$5.75 (*Expreso Ancash*, T791509, *Móvil*, and *Rodríguez*, T791184), 10-11 hrs. All buses go via Huaraz and Pativilca. Most buses on the Lima-Huaraz route continue to Caraz. To **Chimbote**, with *Yungay Express* (D Villar 318), via Huaraz and Pariacoto, 3 a day, US$5.50, 8-10 hrs; *Yungay Express*, also goes via Huallanca and Cañón del Pato 0900 every day, US$5.50, 8 hrs. Sit on the right for best views. To **Trujillo**, via Huaraz and Pativilca, with *Chinchaysuyo* (D Villar 230, T791930), at 1830 daily, US$8, 11-12 hrs, stops in Casma (US$5.20) and Chimbote (US$5.75).

Regional buses From Caraz to **Huaraz**, frequent combis leave daily, 0400-1900, 1 hrs, US$1, the road is in good condition. They leave from all along Jr José Gálvez. A taxi costs US$10, a minivan US$17.50. By combi to **Yungay**, 12 km, 15 mins, US$0.30. To the village of **Parón** (for trekking in Laguna Parón area) pickups leave from the corner Santa Cruz and Grau by the market, from Mon to Sat 0500 and 1300, and Sun 0300 and 1300, 1 hr. They return from Parón at 0600 and 1400. To **Cashapampa** (Quebrada Santa Cruz) buses leave from Bolognesi (terminal terestre), near the market, hourly from 0830 to 1530, 2 hrs, US$1.30. To **Huallanca** (Caraz)(for the Cañón del Pato, see page 383), several buses leave daily from Manco Cápac corner Grau, near the market (cars leave from the same place, 0600-1800, leave when full, US$3).

Transport

Banks *BCP*, D Villar 217. Cash and TCs at good rates, no commission. Mon-Fri 0915-1315, 1630-1830, Sat 0930-1230. *Pony's Expeditions* (see above) cash only, good rates. *Apu Expeditions* also change cash. *Importaciones América*, Sucre 721, T791479 (Esteban). Good rates and service, open weekends and evenings. **Communications** Internet: See *Los Pinos* and *Pony's Expeditions*, above. Also at San Martín 1088, 0900-2300, and Av 1 de Mayo 189, T791819. **Post office**: at San Martín 909. **Telephone**: national and international phone and fax service at Raymondi y Sucre. Also several others, eg at Sucre y Santa Cruz, and on Plaza de Armas next to *Jeny*. No collect calls can be made except from private lines. Very few of the coin boxes take phone cards.

Directory

Cordillera Blanca

Treks from Caraz

A good day hike with nice views of the Cordillera Blanca is to Pueblo Libre. Follow Jr D Villar east across the Río Santa bridge and turn south to Tunaspampa, an interesting desert area with cacti and hummingbirds. Continue through the villages of Shingal, Tocash and Rinconada on to Pueblo Libre. It is about a four hour round trip, or you can take a colectivo back to Caraz.

A longer walk – 6-7 hours – with views of Huandoy and Huascarán follows the foothills of the Cordillera Blanca, south from Caraz. Leave town on Bolognesi up to 28 de Julio, turn right, go past the 2 de Mayo (Markham) High School and climb Cerro San Juan; about 45 minutes. Continue south to the main local summit in an area known as Ticrapa (two hours). Head down to Pata-Pata, from where a track goes down beside the Río Ancash to Puente Ancash on the Caraz-Yungay road (two to three hours), where you can take transport back to Caraz. The hike can be done the other way by getting out of a combi from Huaraz or Caraz at Puente Ancash. Tourist offices have a map of this hike.

To Pueblo Libre
Colour map 3, grid A2

To Laguna Parón From Caraz a narrow, rough road goes east 32 km to Laguna Parón, in a cirque surrounded by several, massive snow-capped peaks, including Huandoy, Pirámide Garcilazo and Caraz. The water level has been lowered to protect Caraz, and the water from the lake is used for the Cañon del Pato hydroelectric scheme. The gorge leading to it is spectacular.

It is a long days' trek for acclimatized hikers (25 km) up to the lake at 4,150 m, or a five to six hour walk from the village of Parón. Where possible follow the walking trail which is much shorter than the road. By climbing up the slippery moraine to the south of the lake towards Huandoy, you get a fine view of Artesonraju. If there is room, you might (at the discretion of the guard) be able to stay at the refuge run by EGENOR (has kitchen and bathroom). Otherwise, camping is possible, but rough.

A trail follows the north shore of the lake to a base camp on the north side of the inflow, about two hours past the refuge. Beyond this point, the trail divides, one branch goes towards Pirámide Garcilazo (5,885 m) and Pisco (5,752 m), another to Laguna Artesoncocha at the base of an enormous glacier, and a third towards Artesonraju (6,025 m).

There are camping possibilities along these trails. Try to find shelter in the quenoal stands or behind a ridge, as the wind can be very strong and the nights are cold. The views are magnificent as you are always surrounded by many beautiful peaks. When you ford a river, remember that the flow increases in the afternoon with the meltdown, so make sure you can get back to your camp early. On the route to Artesonraju there is a moraine camp, just before reaching the glacier. You will need a map if you are going past Laguna Parón.

A taxi from Caraz costs US$20 for four, with four hours wait (but less to go back to town if you catch one after it has deposited a new set of trekkers), or from Huaraz, US$50 return.

Santa Cruz Valley The famous Llanganuco-Santa Cruz hike is done most easily starting in the Santa Cruz valley. Take a vehicle from Caraz in the morning up to Cashapampa (see Caraz regional buses page 355). It takes three to four days, up the Santa Cruz Valley, over the pass of Punta Unión, to Colcabamba or Vaquería (see Llanganuco to Santa Cruz trek on page 349 for details). In this direction the climb is gentler, giving more time to acclimatize, and the pass is easier to find.

Three km north of Cashapampa, or a one to two hour hike, are the hot-baths of **Huancarhuas**. These have been improved, with a pool (entry fee payable).

It is almost impossible to hitch from the end of the trail back to Yungay. Yanama to Yungay combis can be caught at Vaquería between 0800-0900, US$4, three hours. Also frequent combis Vaquería-Yungay US$2.25. Travellers describe this journey down to Yungay as exhilarating and terrifying.

Alpamayo valley This offers a beautiful, but difficult, 10 day trek from Cashapampa to Pomabamba, which is for the experienced only. From Cashapampa head up to the Cullicocha lake, passing the first pass at Los Cedros (4,850 m), down the Mayobamba valley and up the third pass at 4,500 m. Then into the Tayapampa valley, on to the village of Huillca, up the fourth pass at 4,280 m and down to Collota, Yanacollpa and Pomabamba. **NB** Please carry out *all* your rubbish.

Cordillera Negra For hikes in the Cordillera Negra, a truck leaves from Caraz market at 1000 to Huata at 2,700 m, where there is a religious sanctuary and a dirty hotel (**F**). From here you can climb to the Quebrada de Cochacocha (3,500 m) at the top of which is the Inca ruin of Cantu (excellent views), and on to the Inca lookout, **Torreón Andino** (5,006 m).

Take water, food and tent with you. Allow three days for the hike, as there are lagoons near the peak. 6 km down a track off the Caraz-Huata road are the Inca ruins of Chonta. Seek advice from Prof Bernardino Aguilar Prieto in Caraz, San Martín 1143, T791161. Also refer to his Torreón Andino Information book before climbing it.

A large stand of **Puya Raimondi** can be seen in the Cordillera Negra west of Caraz. Beyond Pueblo Libre (see above), the road which continues via Pamparomas and Moro joins the coastal highway between Casma and Chimbote. After 45 km (two hours) are the Puya Raymondi plants at a place called Wuinchus, with views of 120 km of the Cordillera Blanca and to the Pacific. To get there, hire a combi in Caraz for US$42.50 for eight people, plus US$7.20 for a guide. Alternatively take a public combi heading for Pamparomas from Grau y Ugarte between 0800 and 0900 and get out at the Yuashtacruz pass at 4,300 m (also known as *La Punta*), US$2, 2½ hours. From the pass it is a short walk to the plants.

Check that the plants are in flower before going, usually May or Oct

There is usually transport five days a week, ask beforehand. There are buses returning to Caraz only on some days. If there is no bus, you can walk back to Pueblo Libre in four hours, to Caraz in six to eight hours, but it is easy to get lost and there are not many people to ask directions along the way. Take warm clothing, food and water. You can also camp near the puyas and return the following day.

South of Huaraz

South of Huaraz on the main road (27 km, 30 minutes) is Recuay, one of the few provincial capitals which survived the 1970 earthquake and conserves its colonial features. There is a sizeable cave with stalagmites and stalagtites on the main road, entry free. On 11-16 September is the **Festividad Señor de Burgos de Recuay**. D *Hostal Pastoruri*, Bolognesi 240, T744139.

Recuay & Olleros

The road passes the turn-off for **Olleros** at 3,450 m, the starting point for the spectacular three-day hike to Chavín, along a precolumbian trail (see below). Some basic meals and food supplies are available here. C *Altas Montañas*, at edge of village, T722569, altasmont@yahoo.es Small 3-star lodge, Belgian-run, with hot showers, good breakfast included, dinner available, bar, birdwatching, guided treks, information, laundry, recommended for start or end of trek, phone 24 hours in advance, preferably at 2000, to arrange free pick-up from Huaraz.

An alternative trek from Olleros is to **Quebrada Rurec** via **Huaripampa**, a small village with a few *bodegas* which will sell or prepare food. Public transport is available to Huaripampa. There are granite walls of up to 600 m at Rurec, the highest in the Cordillera Blanca, which are recommended for rock climbing. The trek itself is also worthwhile.

Olleros to Chavín trek

You can get off at the main road and walk the 2 km to Olleros, or catch a truck or minibus from Huaraz (at Tarapacá y Jr Cáceres, near *Edward's Inn*) to the village, 29 km, US$0.30.

1 If you take a Huaraz-Catac minibus, get off at the cross before the Bedoya bridge. As you start uphill take the shortcut to Olleros to avoid the main road.

Note that the numbers in the text relate to the numbers on the map

Cordillera Blanca

2 About 50 m past the main plaza in Olleros take the street on the right heading towards the bridge.

3 When you reach Canray Chico, turn right to keep on the road which follows the Río Negro. Keep the river on the left. The track is not always clear but it's difficult to get lost.

4 At this point a track branches off to the left into the Quebrada Rurec (see above); continue straight ahead.

5 Here you'll see a corral and, on the right, two small hills with houses. Head for the houses; don't follow the road with the bridge.

6 Once you pass the swamps and the corrals you'll climb up to some houses. A big stick would be useful here to fend off the resident canines.

7 Head towards the trees, at which point you start the climb towards the pampas that will lead to the **Punta Yanashallash**. This is a good spot to camp for the night. At the top of the valley, it divides into four valleys. The path swings right to avoid the marsh then heads up the second valley on the left, often with a ridge between the path and the river, to the highest point. It is quite easy to lose the track here, but keep heading in the direction of the pass and you'll pick it up eventually. It's a slow, gradual climb to the pass.

8 Here you reach the **Punta Yanashallash**, which is marked by great piles of rocks. From here you start going downhill.

9 Here you'll find a collection of houses or huts and a good camping spot.

10 Cross the swampy area and river before the trail starts again.

11 Follow the narrow trail which takes you down to another swampy area. Stay on the right side of the swamp and cross a small wooden bridge with some houses at the other end.

12 Follow the river until a large wooden bridge; cross it to continue the trail, which leads to the village of **Chichucancha**. Note that the valley leading down

Olleros to Chavín Trek

© Trekking & Backpacking Club Lima

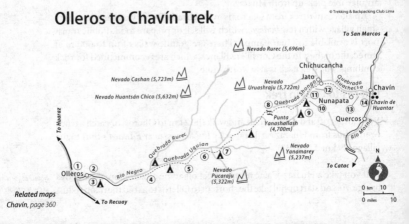

Related maps
Chavín, page 360

to Chavín is much more cultivated and populated. It may be better to camp near the foot of the descent from the pass in order to avoid beggars.

13 Head down into the Quebrada Huachecsa till you reach Punta Huancayo where you can see the ruins of **Chavín de Huantar**.

14 Go through the village of Nueva Florida to reach the road. The town of Chavín is on the left and the archaeological ruins are straight ahead (see below).

Recuay to Chavín

The main road continues 11 km south from Recuay to **Catac**, where a road branches east for Chavín (first 10 km paved, then 20 km good gravel, then 40 km fair gravel). There's accommodation in Catac at *Hostal Central* and *Hostal Catac*, both are basic. *Restaurant La Familia* is good. *Servicios Turísticos Mel's*, opposte *Hsotal Catac*, serves meals.

Colour map 3, grid B3

From Catac to Chavín is a magnificent, scenic journey, if frightening at times. There's currently a lot of road building in progress between Catac and Laguna Querococha. Beyond Laguna Querococha, there are good views of the Yanamarey peaks and, at the top of the route, the road is cut through a huge rock face, entering the Cahuish tunnel at 4,550 m. On the other side it descends the Tambillo valley, then the Río Mosna gorge before Chavín. The road beyond Laguna Querococha is not suitable for ordinary cars, especially in the wet.

South from Catac

Several kilometres south of Catac on the main road is **Pachacoto** from where a road goes to **Huallanca** (Huánuco) on the other side of the Cordillera Blanca (133 km, 4½ hours), not to be confused with the town of the same name by the Cañón del Pato. See under Huaraz, Transport, for buses to Huallanca; *El Rápido* returns to Huaraz at 0600 and 1300.

In this southern part of the Cordillera there are few high, snow-covered peaks, but the glacier of **Pastoruri** is used as the only skiing area in Peru. It is nothing compared to other skiing areas in South America, there aren't even ski lifts, but it is a place to get in a little practice. **NB** Pastoruri receives many large groups, and rubbish is a serious problem here. The glacier is receding rapidly and a famous ice cave (still sold as an excursion by Huaraz tour operators) has melted away to almost nothing.

A good place to see the impressive **Puya Raimondi** plants is the Pumapampa valley. 14 km gravel road from Pachacoto to park entrance (4,200m), then 2 km to plants. Daily tours from Huaraz run to the Pastoruri valley, which is now a reserve with baisc tourist facilities, to see the Puya Raimondi plants, lakes and the glacier, a steep one hour walk up from the car park, US$7 per person,) 0900-1800. Take extra clothing. You can hike up the trail from Pachacoto to the park entrance – 2½ hours – where there is a park office. You can spend the night here. Walking up the road from this point, you will see the gigantic plants. Another good spot, and less visited, is the **Queshque Gorge**. Follow the Río Queshque from Catac (see above); it's easy to find.

Cordillera Blanca

Chavín

The town of Chavín, just north of the famous ruins, is the commercial centre for the nearby potato and corn growing area. Carved stone replicas are produced for the tourist trade.

Chavín has a pleasant plaza with palm and pine trees. Day tours from Huaraz last 10-12 hours, an exhausting day, so if you have time it is definitely worth considering staying the night. That way you avoid the midday crowds, too. There are several good, simple hotels and restaurants, the shops are well stocked with basic supplies and there is a small market. There is nowhere to change money in town. Gasoline is available at the north end of town. The local *fiesta* takes place on July 13-20.

There are hot sulphur baths (Baños Termales de Chavín) about 2 km south of Chavín at Km 68 in the village of **Quercos**. They consist of one small pool and four individual baths in a pleasant setting by the Río Mosna. Camping is possible here. ■ *US$0.30; tip the boy who cleans the bath for you (he doesn't get paid).*

Sleeping
Accommodation is better value in Chavín than in Huaraz; outside the main holiday seasons it is possible to negotiate rates lower than those displayed at many places. **E** *La Casona*, Wiracocha 130, Plaza de Armas, T754020. In an old house with attractive courtyard, private bathroom, **F** with shared bath, warm water, friendly, no double beds (*matrimoniales*), motorcycle parking. Recommended. **E** *Hotel Chavín*, Tello y Inca Roca, T754009, F754055. Modern, clean, hot water, all rooms with bath and TV. Recommended. **E** *Inca*, Wiracocha 160. In a renovated house, with bathroom, **F** without, good beds, hot water on request, garden, friendly. **E** *Ri'kay*, on 17 de Enero 172N (north), T754068, F754027. Set around two patios, modern, best in town, all rooms with private bathroom and TV, hot water, restaurant serving Italian food in the evening. **F** per person *Montecarlo*, 17 de Enero 101S (south), T754014. Shared bathroom, cold water, cold at night, member of the Peruvian Youth Hostel Association. **F** *Hostal Chavín*, Jr San Martín 141-151, half a block from the plaza, T/F754055. Set around a pleasant courtyard, hot water, provides breakfast for groups, best of the more basic hotels. **F** *Gantu*, Huayna Capac 135. Basic, shared bathroom, cold water. **Camping** inside park gates for vehicles.

Chavín

To San Marcos & Huari

Transportes
Cóndor de
Chavín & others

Municipalidad

Chavín
Express

Inca Roca

17 de Enero

Julio Tello

Wiracocha

Río Huachecsa

✤ *Chavín Ruins*
∨ *To Thermal Baths (2 km) & Huari*

■ **Sleeping**
1 Chavín
2 Gantu
3 Hostal Chavín
4 Inca
5 La Casona
6 Montecarlo
7 Ri'Kay

● **Eating**
1 Chavín Turístico
2 La Ramada
3 Los Portales

N

Not to scale

Eating
From north to south along the main street, 17 de Enero, are: *La Ramada*, regional dishes, also trout and set lunch. *Chavín Turístico*, the best in town, good *menú* and à la carte, delicious apple pie, clean, nice courtyard, internet. *Los Portales*, in an old house with tables set around a garden. *Ri'kay*, see above, pasta and pizza dishes in the evenings. It is possible to eat very well in the better restaurants where specialities include rabbit stew, trout ceviche and *llunca*, a solid, wheat-based soup.

Bus For buses from **Huaraz**, see under Huaraz; 110 km, 4 hrs, US$3. To Huaraz: Only **Transport** *Chavín Express* has buses direct from Chavín to Huaraz, at 1730 and 2130. However, these buses are often full and need to be booked the day before. Several other companies such as *Transportes Sandoval* and *Río Mosna* as well as *Chavín Express* have buses coming from destinations further east, such as Huari, which pass through Chavín at 2200-2300. This makes visiting Chavín in a day by public transport very difficult. There are also other buses passing through from these towns heading for Lima which can drop you in Catac, 3 hrs, US$2.50, from where there are frequent combis to Huaraz, 1 hr, US$0.50. These buses also mainly pass through Chavín 2100-2400; avoid *Huari Express* (old buses, bad drivers). Huaraz travel agencies organise daily tours to the ruins and sometimes sell the spare seats when they return at 1500-1700, US$5, 4 hrs.

To **Lima**: 438 km, 12 hrs, US$9, with *Trans El Solitario* and *Perú Andino* daily. Most companies use older, uncomfortable buses and many locals prefer to travel first to Huaraz and then take one of the more reputable companies from there.

To other destinations in the Callejón de Conchucos it is necessary either to use buses coming from Huaraz or Lima, or to hop on and off combis which run between each town. To **San Marcos**, 8 km, and **Huari**, 38 km, it is easiest to take one of the combis which leave regularly from the main plaza in Chavín, 20 mins and 30 mins respectively. There are buses during the day from Lima and Huaraz which go on to Huari, with some going on to **San Luis**, a further 61 km, 3 hrs; **Piscobamba**, a further 62 km, 3 hrs; and **Pomabamba**, a further 22 km, 1 hr; such as *El Solitario* which passes through Chavín at 1800. Other buses from Huaraz and Lima terminate in Llamellín, 120 km, 4 hrs, US$3.

Communications Internet: at *Restaurante Chavín Turístico*. Post office and tele- **Directory** phone service: at 17 de Enero 365N (north). 0630-2200.

Chavín de Huantar

Chavín de Huantar, a fortress temple, was built about 800 BC. It is the only *Colour map 3,* large structure remaining of the Chavín culture which, in its heyday, is *grid B3* thought to have held influence in a region between Cajamarca and Chiclayo in the north to Ayacucho and Ica in the south. In 1985, UNESCO designated Chavín a World Heritage Trust site.

The site is in good condition despite the effects of time and nature. The easternmost building was damaged in 1993 when the Río Mosna burst its banks, while in 1945 a major landslide along the *Río Huachecsa* completely covered the site with mud. It took many years to remove the rubble and some structures remain hidden. Investigations are going on which suggest an extensive tunnel system beyond the boundaries of the current site which has yet to be excavated. This may lead to the Huaraz road, which cuts across this area, being moved to the other side of the valley some time in the future.

The main attractions are the marvellous carved stone heads and designs in relief of symbolic figures and the many tunnels and culverts which form an extensive labyrinth throughout the interior of the structures. The carvings are in excellent condition, though many of the best sculptures are in Huaraz and Lima. The famous Lanzón dagger-shaped stone monolith of 800 BC is found inside one of the temple tunnels. Excavations in 2001 uncovered a collection of 20 *pututos* (wind instruments) dating from the site's origins.

In order to protect the site some areas are closed to visitors. All galleries open to the public have electric lights. The guard is also a guide and gives excellent explanations of the ruins. There is a small museum at the entrance, with carvings and some Chavín pottery.

Cordillera Blanca

■ *Daily 0800-1700. US$3, students US$1.50, US$5 for a group with Span-ish-speaking guide. Camping is possible with permission from the guard. The site is busiest between 1200-1700 in the main holiday periods with tourist buses from Huaraz. Go early to avoid the crowds (another good reason for staying overnight in town). You will receive an information leaflet in Spanish at the entrance. The guard also sells other reference material including Chavín de Huantar by Willhelm and Nancy Hoogendoorn, an English/Spanish guide to the ruins which includes a description of each building and an historical overview. From Chavín you can return to Huaraz by road, via Huari, San Luis, Yanama and Yungay (see page 348) but travel along this route can be very slow as the bus service is infrequent.*

Callejón de Conchucos

Along the east side of the Cordillera Blanca, which is known as the Callejón de Conchucos, runs a good, but narrow, dirt road, subject to rapid deterioration when it rains. Public transport is less frequent and less reliable here than in the Callejón de Huaylas, with some towns getting only two buses per week, direct from Lima. Private vehicles, usually large trucks, are few and far between. The region has also seen less foreign tourists and some discretion, as well as responsible behaviour, is called for. If you plan to travel in this area, allow plenty of time, especially in the rainy season.

San Marcos   The road north from Chavín descends into the dry Mosna river canyon. After 8 km it reaches San Marcos, a small, friendly town with a nice plaza and a fancy modern church. It is known as 'City of the Magnolias', but there are few in evidence around the town. There are several basic *hostales*, but much the best is **F** *La Rinconada*, La Merced 325. There are also several basic restaurants of which *Las Magnolias* and *Crillón Chico*, in the main plaza, are best. Gasoline is available 24 hours.

Combis run from San Marcos to the large, Canadian-run mine, high on the puna, at **Antamina**, two hours. Unfortunately, the impressive mine road from Antamina, via Huallanca, to Conococha is privately owned and it is not possible to travel direct from Chavín to Huallanca without returning to Huaraz at present.

Twenty kilometres beyond San Marcos, at the junction of the Huari and Mosna rivers, is the village of **Pomachaca** (Las Tunas), where a road branches northeast to **Llamellín**. The main road continues north and climbs, criss-crossing the Huari river amid dry hills, to reach Huari 12 km further on.

Huari

Colour map 3, grid B2   The town, perched on a hillside at 3,150 m, has steep streets and enjoys good views of the surrounding mountains. The Plaza de Armas and cathedral are modern, having been rebuilt after the 1970 earthquake. It has a small fruit and vegetable market, which is quite busy on Sunday, and well-stocked shops. The water supply can be intermittent. The local fiesta of **Nuestra Señora del Rosario** is held during the first two weeks of October.

Sleeping   **F** *El Dorado*, Bolívar 341. Basic, comfortable, sunny patio, shared bathroom, hot water. **F** *Añaños*, Alvarez 437, next to the market. Very basic but clean. There are a few others which are very basic, all **F**.

The stone gods of Chavín

Archaeologists have learnt very little about the Chavín culture, whose architecture and sculpture had a strong impact on the artistic and cultural development of a large part of the coast and central highlands of Peru. Based on physical evidence from the study of this 17-acre site, the temple of Chavín de Huantar is thought to have been a major ceremonial centre.

What first strikes visitors upon arrival at Chavín is the quality of the stonework found in the temple walls and plaza stairways. The sculptures have three functions: architectural, ornamental and the third is purely cultist and includes the Lanzón, the Tello obelisk and the Raimondi stela. The latter two currently grace the Museum of Anthropology and Archaeology in Lima.

At 5 m high, the Lanzón is the crowning glory of the Chavín religion and stands at the heart of the underground complex. Its Spanish name comes from the lance, or dagger-like shape of the monolith which appears to be stuck in the ground. Carved into the top of the head are thin, grooved channels and some speculate that animals, or even humans, may have been sacrificed to this god. Others suggest that the Lanzón was merely the dominant figure for worship.

Named after the Peruvian scientist, Julius C Tello, the Tello obelisk belongs to the earliest period of occupation of Chavín (ca 100 BC). It represents a complex deity – perhaps a caiman-alligator – connected with the earth, water and all the living elements of nature. Carved on the body are people, birds, serpents and felines which the divine beast has consumed.

The Raimondi stela was named after the Italian naturalist, who also gave his name to the famous plant, not to mention a fair percentage of the streets in the region. It shows a feline anthropomorphic divinity standing with open arms and holding some sort of staff in each hand.

Together, the figures carved on the stones at Chavín indicate that the resident cult was based principally on the feline, or jaguar, and secondarily on serpents and birds.

The Raimondi Stela

Cordillera Blanca

Los Angeles, Ancash 669, off the main plaza. Mainly chicken, popular. *Rinconcito Huaracino*, Bolívar 530. Good menú, open till 2100. *Centro Virgen del Rosario*, San Martín by Parque Vigíl. Serves coffee, sweets and snacks, very clean and friendly, open evenings and Sun, run by an Italian nun and her students. **Eating**

Bus Bus companies have their offices around Parque Vigil. To **Huaraz**, 5-6 hrs, US$3.75; departures through the day. To **San Luis**, buses leave on Tue and Sat: with *El Solitario* at 0600, *Perú Andino* at 0830. Buses heading north pass through Huari between 2200 and 2400, but not every day. To **Lima**, 13 hrs, US$10: with *Turismo Huari* on Sun, Wed and Fri at 0630, *Perú Andino* on Sun and Wed at 0800. On the other days, except Thu, buses bound for Lima originating further north pass Huari between 1000 and 1200. **Transport**

Directory **Communications** The **post office** is at Luzuriaga 324 by Parque Vigíl. The **telephone office** is at Libertad 940. 0700-2200 daily.

Huari to Chacas trek

There is a spectacular two to three days walk from Huari to Chacas via Laguna Purhuay, as described by John Myerscough from Derbyshire in England: 'The route is clearly shown on the IGM map, sheet 19. The walking is very easy, over a 4,500-m pass and through two of the best valleys I've ever been in. Plenty of streams and lots of good places for camping. Amazing rock strata.'

To get to Laguna Purhuay, climb the stairs at the end of Jr Luzuriaga, in Huari, to the main road, turn right, or north, and walk for about 3 km to the village of Acopalca, which has a fish farm where you can buy trout. Turn left after crossing the bridge in town (ask directions). It is a 1½-walk up to the lake. The path to Chacas forks left just before the lake. Another good trail crosses the outflow and climbs above the eastern shore to a good lookout, then divides: the left fork descends to the inflow, which is a narrow gorge called La Cola (the tail); the right fork climbs to the village of Cachitzin (no facilities). There are no good trails along the shore of the lake.

Alberto Cafferata of *Pony's Expeditions*, Caraz (see page 354), writes: 'The Purhuay area is beautiful. It has splendid campsites, trout, exotic birds and, at its north end, a 'quenoal' forest. This is a microclimate at 3,500 m, where the animals, insects and flowers are more like a tropical jungle, fantastic for ecologists and photographers.' A day walk to Laguna Purhuay is recommended for those who don't want the longer walk to Chacas.

Chacas to Pomabamba

Chacas
Colour map 3, grid A3

Ten kilometres south of San Luis, off the main road, is Chacas, with its fine church. The local fiesta patronal is in mid-August, with bullfights, a famous carrera de cintas and fireworks. Seek out the Taller Don Bosco, a woodcarving workshop run by an Italian priest.

There are a few basic shops, restaurants, a small market and two or three basic hostals, including Hostal de Pilar.

It is a two-day hike from Chacas to **Marcará** (see page 345) via the Quebradas Juytush and Honda (lots of condors to be seen). The **Quebrada Honda** is known as the Paraíso de las Cascadas because it contains at least seven waterfalls.

San Luis
Colour map 3, grid A3

From Huari the road climbs to the Huachacocha pass at 4,350 m and descends to San Luis at 3,130 m. There is accommodation at **G** *Hostal Rotta*, also a few basic restaurants, shops and a market. Buses run to Chavín on Wednesday and Sunday, five hours, US$6. To Huaraz via Yanama and the pass at 4,730 m under Huascarán takes eight hours, but public transport is scarce on this route (Virgen de Guadalupe and Renzo buses go to Huaraz via Chacas). You may have to hire a minibus to take you to Puente Llacma, 28 km north, the junction of the roads for Yanama and Pomabamba (US$15 for the vehicle). From there you can hitchhike to Yanama and Yungay. Trucks also provide transport in this area.

A large sanctuary to **Nuestro Señor de Pumayukay**, built by Italian priests, is a 15-minute ride from San Luis towards Pomabamba and then a turn-off to the east.

The road which branches left at Puente Llacma goes to Yanama, 45 km from **Yanama**
San Luis, at 3,400 m. It has one marked hotel outside and one unmarked *Colour map 3, grid A3*
hotel, **G**, on the plaza; ask at the pharmacy. Food is available, but no electricity
in the village, which is beautifully surrounded by snow-capped peaks. A day's
hike to the ruins above the town affords superb views. There are several
combis a day, especially in the early morning and late afternoon, between
Yungay and Yanama over the 4,767m Portachuelo de Llanganuco (three
hours, US$2), continuing to Pomabamba. Trucks also go along this route.

The main road through the Callejón de Conchucos continues north from San **Piscobamba**
Luis for 62 km to Piscobamba (the pampa of the birds, from the quechua *Colour map 3, grid A3*
'Pishco Pampa'). There are spectacular views across the heavily wooded valley
to the Cordillera Blanca, from the Alpamayo massif to the north to beyond
Huascarán to the south. *Hostales San Pedro* and *Yomara* are both basic, **F**.
There are also a few shops and small restaurants. Twenty-two kilometres
beyond Piscobamba is Pomabamba.

Known as 'City of the Cedars', though only two very old specimens remain in **Pomabamba**
the centre of the plaza, surrounded by roses and jacarandas, Pomabamba (the *Colour map 3, grid A3*
pampa of the pumas, quechua 'Puma Pampa') is worth a visit on several counts.
There are very hot natural springs across the river, a five-minute walk down a
steep path from the main plaza. There are three different bathing establishments, all with private baths, US$0.30 per person, no time limit. Ask for the
baths to be cleaned before you use them. There is a small museum and tourist
office at Huaraz 515, variable opening hours. The main **festival** is 24 June.

Sleeping and eating **F** *Hostal Estrada Vidal*, Huaraz 209, T751048. Run by friendly
Sra Estrada Vidal, rustic, rooms around a pleasant courtyard, clean, cold water. Recommended. **G** *Hostal Pomabamba*, on the main plaza. Basic, safe for luggage. **G** *No nos
Ganan*, block from the plaza. Basic but OK. Also: **F** *Alpamayo*, on the plaza, *Anny* (**F**),
new but dirty, and *San Martín de Porres*, off the smaller plaza, all basic. Family lodging,
F, at the house of *Sr Alejandro Vía*, on Jr Primavera s/n. There is a limited choice of
places to eat and most close by 2100. *Davis-David*, Huaraz 269, offers the best *menú*
and can prepare soups to order; *Los Cedros*, Huaraz 531, is good for breakfast; *El Rey*,
Chávez 360, offers trout *ceviche*.

Transport To **Piscobamba**, combis depart regularly when full, 1 hr, US$0.75. To
Sihuas, a combi departs at 0600 and 1600 daily but best to reserve your seat by arriving
at least an hr before, 3 hrs, US$2.75. Occasionally, other combis and camionetas may
travel this route. To **Yungay**, *Trans Los Andes, Transvir* and *La Perla de Altamayo*, daily,
6-7 hrs, US$6, continuing to Huaraz. To **San Luis** combis depart from Piscobamba
when full, about hourly, 2 hrs, US$2.50. Pomabamba to **Lima** buses also stop in San
Luis and then Huari but they mainly run at night. To **Huaraz** via San Luis and Chacas,
Trans Renzo is the best of several companies operating this route, 0700, 7 hrs, US$6.

From Pomabamba back to the Callejón de Huaylas, a road beyond Palo Seco **Pomabamba**
(see above) goes through Andemayo to the mining town of **Pasacancha**. **to Yuramarca**
Daytime trucks run from Pasacancha, through Tarica (not to be confused
with Taricá, 16 km north of Huaraz) and Yanac, past pre-Inca chullpas to Tres
Cruces (basic friendly restaurant, no accommodation). Buses from Tres
Cruces go to Yuramarca, north of the Cañón del Pato, and on to Caraz (and
from there to Yungay and Huaraz).

Cordillera Blanca

Treks from Pomabamba Several good walks into the Cordillera Blanca start from near Pomabamba. You can go via Palo Seco or Laurel to the Lagunas Safuna, from where you can go on, if you're fit enough, to **Nevado Alpamayo**, dubbed 'the most beautiful mountain in the world'. The glacier of Alpamayo is an incredible sight. From there, continue down to Santa Cruz and Caraz for several days' hard walking in total.

For the less energetic, a good day trip can be made to the quite large and extensive, though sadly dilapidated, Huari ruins of **Yaino**, on top of a very steep mountain and visible from the main plaza of Pomabamba. The walls are beautifully built and there are two very large buildings, a square one and a circular one. The site commands excellent views of the many peaks of the Cordillera. To get there take a combi to Huaychao, one hour, US$1. Take the path to Garhuay, smaller Huari ruins, two hours, and continue upwards to Yaino, two hours. An alternative return route is to walk down to Huayllan, on the Pomabamba/Huaychao road, and catch a combi (30 minutes). Take food and lots of water; you can get very dehydrated climbing and perspiring in the thin dry air. It's also very cold high up if the sun goes in, so go with warm, waterproof clothes.

Another good day walk leaves Pomabamba from the **Curayacu** fountain. The path runs to **Pueblo Libre**, two hours, where there are good remains of the Camino Real de los Incas and then on to Mesa Rumi, another two hours, to see a remarkably precise and unique metre-square block of Inca stone with ceremonial holes in its upper surface.

A shorter walk (three to four hours) begins from the bridge over the river and runs up a side valley, past a trout farm, to the beautiful **Jancapampa** valley below the Alpamayo massif. Camping is possible there.

Sihuas
Colour map 3, grid A2

From Pomabamba a dusty road runs up the wooded valley crossing the *puna* at Palo Seco, 23 km. The road then descends steeply in to the desert like Sihuas valley, passing through the village of Sicsibamba. The valley is crossed half an hour below Sihuas.

The small town of **Sihuas** itself is divided into three sections spreading over a kilometre up the valley. The lowest district is the oldest with a fine colonial interior to the church. All the bus company offices, hotels and restaurants are in the middle district. The town is a major connection point between the Callejón de Conchucos, Callejón de Huaylas, the upper Marañón and the coast. Other than as a stopover while travelling between these areas there is little to do in the immediate surrounding area.

Sleeping and eating F *Hostal Don César*, Av 28 de Julio 309. Clean, friendly, basic. **F** *Hostal Liliana*, in a newer building, large rooms some with bath. **F** *Hostal Los Milagros*. The best in town with rooms set around a patio, rustic, clean. There are few good places to eat. *La Estación* on the plaza is the best and offers the local speciality *ceviche de pollo* as well as trout. *Chosas Nauticas* is also good for breakfast.

To **Huaraz**, *Trans Chavín Express*, via Huallanca, Wed and Sat, and *Perú Andino* on Tue, 1100, 8 hrs, US$7. To **Chimbote**, *Trans La Perla de Altamayo* on Tue, Thu and Sun, 10 hrs, US$9. To **Tayabamba**, *Trans Garrincha* on Mon and Thu passing through from Chimbote at 0800-0900, and *La Perla de Altamayo* on Mon, Wed and Sat, passes through at 1300-1400, 8 hrs, US$7. To **Huacrachuco**, *Trans Andina*, daily at 1000. To **Trujillo** via Chimbote, *Garrincha* on Mon and Thu, 2200, 12 hrs, US$10. To **Pomabamba**, combis at 0600 and 1600, 3 hrs, US$3.

From Sihuas it is now possible to travel, via Huancaspata, Tayabamba, Retamas and Chahual, to Huamachuco along a road which is very poor in places and involves crossing the river Marañón twice. The building of a new bridge over the river means that it is now possible to travel from Cusco to Quito through the Andes entirely by public transport. This journey is best undertaken in this direction though the road may be almost impassable in the wet season. A detour up the Marañón valley leads to **Huacrachuco**, where there are several basic hostals. The significant Inca ruins of **Mamahuagay** are nearby and a five-day walk down to Uchiza in the Huallaga valley can be made.

Cordilleras Huayhuash and Raura

Colour map 3, grid B3/4

Lying south of the Cordillera Blanca, the Cordillera Huayhuash has been dubbed the 'Himalayas of America' and is perhaps the most spectacular in Peru for its massive ice faces which seem to rise sheer out of the contrasting green of the Puna. Azure trout-filled lakes are interwoven with deep quebradas and high pastures around the hem of the range. You may see tropical parakeets in the bottom of the gorges and condors circling the peaks.

Although the area may well have been inhabited for thousands of years, the Huayhuash only became known to the outside world following a plane crash at Jahuacocha in 1953. Since then the number of visitors has grown steadily, with a hiatus during the era of insurgency in the 1980s. Although less touristy than the Cordillera Blanca, it nonetheless receives significant numbers of trekkers and climbers every year.

Trekking in the Cordillera Huayhuash is generally considered difficult, and certainly requires stamina (10 to 12 days for the complete loop, see page 369) but the trails are good and most gradients are relatively gentle. There are up to eight passes over 4,600 m, depending on the route.

Cordilleras Huayhuash & Raura

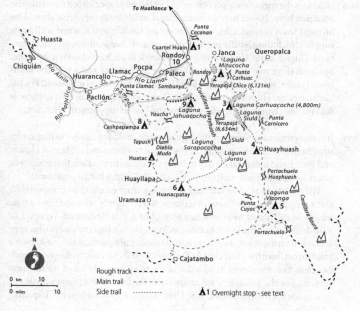

Rough track	- - - - -
Main trail	— — —
Side trail	··········

▲1 Overnight stop - see text

Cordillera Blanca

There are two traditional trekking routes in the Huayhuash, (see below): a complete loop around the range; and a half-circuit, starting from the trail head at Cuartel Huain and ending in Cajatambo. These are but two of very many excellent options however, and hikers are urged to be creative in choosing their routes and camp sites, both to enjoy more pristine surroundings and to allow over-used areas to recover.

Both the Huayhuash and Raura ranges are approached from **Chiquián** in the north, **Oyón**, with links to Cerro de Pasco to the southeast, **Churín** in the south or **Cajatambo** to the southwest. The area is remote and the local villagers are generally herdsmen, tending flocks of cattle, sheep and alpacas.

Safety & conduct Remember that you must be entirely self-sufficient and that evacuation in the event of illness or accident may require several days.

The residents of the region are poor and the presence of visitors has had its impact. Children beg for sweets, pencils or money and adults may also ask for handouts; be polite but firm in your refusal. Do not leave your gear unattended at any time and stow everything in your tent overnight.

Fortunately armed robberies are rare. The eastern side of the range, in the Department of Huánuco, has a reputation for more aggressive behaviour, be especially cautious in this area (see Central Highlands, page 515).

You will encounter many cattle and dogs guarding them throughout the trek. It's best to give both a wide berth. Carrying a walking stick or crouching to pick up a stone will usually discourage the canines. Throwing stones has been known to provoke an attack.

Garbage is an important problem at the usual camp sites and you should personally pack out everything you bring in; you cannot trust muleteers in this regard. Much of the area is above tree-line, the remainder has been badly deforested. Make sure you have a reliable stove and enough fuel for cooking and resist the temptation to use what little firewood remains.

Provisions Huaraz is the region's supply centre, all but the most specialized items may be obtained here. If you require freeze-dried meals however, these should be brought from abroad. Chiquián's shops are usually well stocked with basic supplies, including locally produced butter and cheese, although prices may be a bit higher here. Almost nothing is available in the hamlets along the route, but fresh trout may be purchased by some of the lakes and a very few items (mostly beer, soft drinks and potatoes) might be purchased in Llamac, Pocpa, Carhuacocha, Huayllapa and Pacllón. Take coins and small bills as there is seldom any change. Bring a fishing line and lure to supplement your diet.

Mule hire It is sometimes a problem in the high climbing/trekking season to hire mules straightaway. This is because all the ones at the northern end are kept at Llamac and Pocpa and it may take a day to bring the mules to your starting point. For prices for donkeys and muleteers see page 332. Bargain but be reasonable.

The muleteers are a mixed bunch, ranging from excellent to irresponsible. Get a recommendation from someone who has recently returned from a trek, otherwise call ahead to Hostal San Miguel or ask at Restaurant Yerupajá or Panadería Santa Rosa (see Chiquián, below). Do not hire muleteers who approach you on the street, there have been a number of rip-offs. Always ask to see a valid carnet from the Dirección de Turismo. You should also make your priorities clear to the muleteer in advance of the trek (pace, choice of route, camp sites, etc.) or else you will be led around with the line, 'all the gringos do this'.

A guide for the Huayhuash is Sr Delao Callupe. Ask for him in Chiquián.

The Huayhuash Circuit

The trail head is at **Cuartel Huain** (1 - figures indicate usual camping sites), between Matacancha and the **Punta Cacanan** pass (the continental divide at 4,700 m). This northernmost point on the trek gives access to the village of **Janca**, **Laguna Mitucocha** (2) and the eastern flank of the Cordillera.

A very steep short cut on scree is through the gap in the northern spur of the range above Matacancha and Janca village on the other side. This could save two or three hours.

The eastern side of the Cordillera is a chain of passes, lakes and stunning views of **Jirishanca Chico**, **Yerupajá Chico**, **Yerupajá** (Peru's second highest peak at 6,634 m) and **Siulá Grande**. From Janca, a small side valley leads off **Quebrada Mitucocha** to **Punta Carhuac** (4,650 m) and beyond to **Laguna Carhuacocha**, with magnificent camping (3) and views. Following on from there are **Punta Carnicero** (4,600 m, a section of Inca road and petroglyphs are found nearby), the twin lakes of **Azulcocha** and **Atoqshaico** (just beyond the pass) and **Huayhuash village** (4 - one house). This is the regular route, but a new route is also open, following round Laguna Carhaucocha, passing Laguna Siulá and emerging on the regular route just before Huayhuash village. This trail has gained popularity thanks to *Touching the Void*, the book by Joe Simpson; there are no maps and it is advisable for experienced trekkers only. A guide is recommended. The weather can change very suddenly.

The next pass, **Portachuelo Huayhuash** (4,750 m, the continental divide) overlooks the superb southward line of pyramidal peaks and rounded ice caps of the **Cordillera Raura**. A path leads from **Laguna Viconga** below (5 - near the dam), over a pass and hugs the western flank of the Raura all the way to **Oyón**. Transportes Javier run a daily bus from Raura to Cerro de Pasco, seven hours, US$5.50, to which there are also daily buses from Oyón.

Four hours away from Oyón is **Churín**, which boasts the 'best thermal baths in Peru'. There is also a small thermal pool 1 km past the outflow of Viconga, along the trail to Cajatambo. Note that water is released from the Viconga dam daily 0500-1100, and you cannot ford the outflow during this time.

If you are bailing out at **Cajatambo** (6), it is downhill all the way from Laguna Viconga, apart from a short sting in the tail at the end. Those continuing the circuit must cross the **Punto Cuyoc** (5,000 m), sometimes snowbound, with outstanding 360° views. The highpoint of the circuit in every sense of the word.

There follows a long, gentle descent into the **Quebrada Huanacpatay** (6 on the full circuit) and an optional one day side trip up the valley of the **Río Huayllapa** to **Laguna Jurau** and **Laguna Sarapococha**, both beautiful lakes.

The route continues downhill to the village of **Huayllapa**, just before town it turns north to begin climbing to the **Tapush Pass** (4,800 m) below the summit of **Diablo Mudo** (also known as **Suerococha**), via **Huatac** (7).

After the pass you reach **Cashpapampa** (8), from where you head east to the **Yaucha Pass** (4,800 m, outstanding views), then north, by way of the **Quebrada Huacrish**, to **Laguna Jahuacocha**, which lies beneath **Yerupajá** and Nevados **Jirishanca** and **Rondoy**. The lake offers the most idyllic campsite (9) in the Cordillera. It can also be reached from Llamac over the Punta Llamac pass at 4,300 m, southeast of that town. First head southwest along a path just beneath the cemetery and zig-zag up above the town.

A 4,800-m pass, Sambunya, beneath Rondoy, leads to the descent to the town of Rondoy (10), Matacancha and the trail head.

Chiquián
Population: approximately 5,000
Altitude: 3,400 m
Phone code: 044

Chiquián is is a town of narrow streets and overhanging eaves. An interesting feature is a public television mounted in a box on a pedestal which sits proudly in the Plaza de Armas, around which folks gather every evening. There is a Semana Turística during the first week of July and the local fiesta is celebrated on 30 August in honour of Santa Rosa.

Sleeping E *Gran Hotel Huayhuash*, Figueredo esquina 28 de Julio, T747049/ 747183. Private bathroom, hot water, TV, restaurant, laundry, parking, modern, great views. **E** *Hostal San Miguel*, Jr Comercio 233, T747001. Nice courtyard and garden, clean, many rooms, popular. **G** per person *Los Nogales de Chiquián*, Jr Comercio 1301, T747121 (in Lima T460 8037), hotel_nogales_chiquian@yahoo.com.pe With bath, cheaper without, hot water, new, cable TV, cafetería, parking. Recommended.

Eating *Yerupajá*, Jr Tarapacá 351; and *El Refugio de Bolognesi*, Tarapacá 471. Both offer basic set meals. There are several others. *Panificadora Santa Rosa*, Comercio 900, on the plaza. For good bread and sweets, has coin-operated phones and fax.

Transport Coming from Huaraz, the road is now paved from Conococha to within 23 km of Chiquián. More paving around Chiquián is in progress, including from the town towards Llamac and from Llamac towards Huallanca. Four bus companies run from Huaraz to Chiquián, 120 km, 2 hrs: *El Rápido*, at Cáceres 312, T726437, at 0600 (very crowded), 1330, 1900; *Virgen del Carmen*, around the corner from Huascarán on Raymondi; *Chiquián Tours*, on Tarapacá behind the market; and *El Amigo del Milenio*, opposite the Frigorífico de Huaraz on Bolognesi. From Chiquián to Huaraz: all buses leave the plaza at 0500 daily, and *El Rápido*, Jr Figueredo 216, T747049, at 0500 and 1500. The companies have pretty good buses, US$1.75 (except El Rápido, US$2). There is also a connection from Chiquián to Huallanca (Huánuco) with buses coming up from Lima in the early morning and combis during the day, which leave when full, 3 hrs, US$2.50. From Huallanca there are regular combis on to La Unión, 1 hr, US$0.75, and from there transport to Huánuco.

Cajatambo

The southern approach to the Cordillera Huayhuash is a small, developing market town, with a beautiful 18th century church and a lovely plaza. **F** *Hostal Miranda*, Jr Tacna 141. Homely, friendly, small rooms, cold shower, basic. Recommended. **G** *Hostal Cajatambo*, on the plaza. Basic, cheap, not for the squeamish as the courtyard is a chicken slaughterhouse. **G** *Hostal Tambomachay*, just off the plaza on Grau (same street as bus office), ask for directions. Nice courtyard and restaurant. **G** *Hostal Trinidad*, Jr Raimondi 141. Basic. *Restaurant Andreita*, is at Av Grau 440. Buses to Lima leave daily at 0600, US$8.80, with Empresa Andia (office on plaza next to Hostal Cajatambo) and Tour Bello, one block off the plaza. The only way back to Huaraz is via Pativilca on the coast, a long detour. Buses from Cajatambo arrive in Pativilca around midday; wait for Lima-Huaraz buses to pass between 1330 and 1400 and arrive in Huaraz about 1700. Turismo Cajatambo, Jr Grau 120 (in Lima, Av Carlos Zavala 124 corner of Miguel Aljovin 449, T426 7238, in Barranca, Prologación Sáenz Peña 139).

Cordillera Blanca

North Coast

Introducing the North Coast

This part of Peru is well known to those heading overland to or from Ecuador, but compared to the likes of Cusco, Arequipa or Lake Titicaca in the south, it receives relatively few short-term visitors. This lack of attention is undeserved as the thin belt of coastal desert that runs north from Lima to the Ecuadorean border is home to some of the country's greatest treasures. Peru's north coast could well be described as the Egypt of South America. This is a region of numerous monumental ruins, built by the many highly-skilled pre-Inca cultures that once thrived here. In the vicinity of Trujillo, Chan Chán was the capital of the

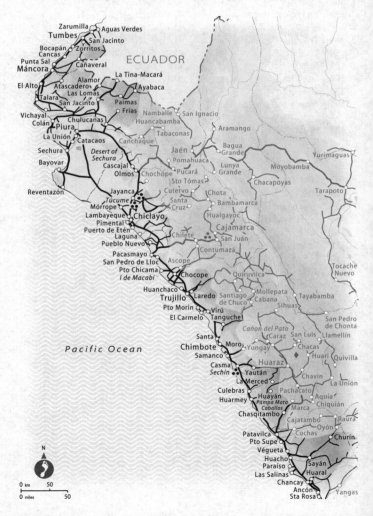

Chimú kingdom; its crumbling remains still represent the largest adobe city in the world. The Huaca de la Luna of the Moche empire is revealing fabulous, multicoloured friezes of gods from the first millenium AD. Further north, near Chiclayo, the adobe brick pyramids of Túcume, Sipán and Batán Grande rise massively from the coastal plains. The wealth from some of their tombs is now displayed in new, state-of-the-art museums. But it's not all pyramids and royal tombs. The elegant city of Trujillo is one of the finest examples of colonial architecture in the country. There are charming towns such as Huanchaco, with its bizarre-looking reed fishing rafts, and Chulucanas, with its famous pottery. Lambayeque Department has umpteen festivals; you can visit witchdoctors or simply buy their potions; up and down the coast the seafood is wonderful and the hospitality unrivalled. In addition, the northern seaboard enjoys a rain free climate all year, and sports Peru's finest beaches for bathing and surfing. Around Tumbes, the most northerly provincial capital, three reserves protect mangroves, equatorial dry scrub and rain forest, each of which contains endangered species, ranging from crocodiles to eagles.

Things to do on the North Coast

- Visit **El Brujo** archaeological complex at the end of the day and wonder at the lives of people who created this place as their bones and pottery crunch under your feet, page 397.
- See the Sunday morning flag-raising ceremony in the **Plaza Mayor** in **Trujillo**, with its statue to Liberty, surrounded almost completely by colonial buildings painted in strong, traditional colours, page 384.
- Watch the fishermen who work from **totora-reed boats-cum-surfboards** in towns like Hanchaco or Santa Rosa. You can even ride the waves with them.
- Buy your fish, your soap powder and your cat's claw all under one roof at **Chiclayo's Mercado Modelo** – for all your shamanic shopping needs, page 405.
- In **Lambayeque**, two fascinating museums detailing the prehispanic cultures of the north coast should not be missed, the Brüning and the new Royal tombs of Sipán museum, page 408.
- On long **bus journeys** through a mostly barren landscape play the 'guessing which hump in the distance is a pyramid and which a hill' game.

Lima to Chimbote

Between Lima and Pativilca there is a narrow belt of coastal land deposited at the mouths of the rivers and, from Pativilca to the mouth of the Río Santa, north of Chimbote, the Andes come down to the sea. The Pan-American Highway parallels the coast all the way to the far north, and feeder roads branch from it up the various valleys. Just north of Ancón (see page 149), the Pasamayo sand dune, stretching for 20 km, comes right down to the seashore. The old road which snakes above the sea is spectacular, but is now closed except to commercial traffic and buses. The new toll road (US$0.85), which goes right over the top, is safe and gives spectacular views over the nearby coast and valleys.

Chancay Valley
Colour map 3, grid C3

Just inland from the coastal town of Chancay is **Huaral** (C *El Parque II*, good facilities), which gives access to the Chancay Valley, up which are the extraordinary, little-visited ruins of **Chiprac**, **Rupac** and **Añay**.

Chiprac is a 2½-hour climb from **Huascoy** (see below). The Salvador family have accommodation and Carlos is a recommended guide for the ruins, though a guide is not strictly necessary. It is a good day's walk there and back with time to take photographs and eat. Huascoy celebrates the **Fiesta de San Cristóbal** in the week before Independence (28 July), with a procession, masses, dancing, fireworks and football matches.

Rupac is best reached from La Florida. Its ruins are the best preserved of the group, though less extensive than Chiprac. All the ruins have complete roofs, which is unique in Peru.

For Añay, go to Huaral as for the other ruins, then get transport to Huayopampa (basic accommodation) or La Perla from where the ruins can easily be reached. Get a guide to take you there from either village.

Transport Take a bus to Huaral from Plaza de Acho, by the bullring, in Lima (beware of thieves). Then take the Juan Batista bus, on Tue and Fri, to Huascoy (US$2), 2 km beyond San Juan, which is up beyond Acos: a "hair-raising, breath-taking and bone-shaking ride, up to 3,500 m above sea-level".

At Km 101 is Huacho, where you can turn off the Pan-American and head west to Puerto Huacho, which is the outlet for cotton and sugar grown in the rich Huaura valley. There are cotton-seed oil and other factories. The port and sea are sometimes alive with huge jellyfish. A turn-off at Km 135 leads to **El Paraíso**, where endless, empty beaches and calm, clear waters attract campers in summer. There is good fishing and windsurfing. Birdwatchers should go to the nearby lagoon, formed by run-off from an irrigation project, where over 100 species have been recorded.

Huacho
Colour map 3, grid B3
Population: 35,900

Sleeping and transport There are several basic hotels at Huacho and **camping** at *El Paraíso*. Bus, 2½ hours, US$2, or Comité 18, daily colectivos, US$2.50. Buses north usually arrive full. They can be caught at the roundabout on the Pan-American. There are regular combis to **Sayán** (see next page). There is a toll post at El Paraíso Huacho, US$0.75 for cars. There is a sign for a tourist office.

The journey inland from Huacho, up the Huaura valley, is spectacular. **Sayán**, 30 km inland, is an attractive agricultural town at the base of the Andean foothills. It is a nicer place to stay en route to Churín than the coastal towns. There is only one reasonable place to stay, *Hotel Tolentino*, Balta 541, T371018, small rooms, shared bath, but wake in the morning to delicious smells from the bakery beneath. *Jalisco*, Balta 342, is the best place to eat and sometimes has local river shrimp and wine on the menu. Combis go every half hour to Huacho from Avenida Balta. Buses from Lima for Churín stop at the bridge.

Huacho to Churín

Churín

Beyond Sayán the road, which was badly damaged in the 1998 El Niño, follows the Huaura valley which narrows almost to a gorge before climbing steeply to Churín, one of Peru's best-known spas, with hot, sulphurous springs which are used to cure a number of ailments. The climate is dry, temperatures ranging from 10° to 32°C. The area is famous for cheese, yoghurt and other natural products. Churín is very popular with Limeños. Accommodation and buses are fully booked at holiday times.

Colour map 3, grid B3
Population: 2,000
Altitude: 2,080 m

A highly recommended excursion can be made up a side valley, 5 km below Churín, to **Huancahuasi**. The new Huancahuasi baths include a pool that ex-President Fujimori swam in (hot, US$0.70 per person), while on the opposite side of the river the new **Picoy** baths include excellent private pools carved out of the rock (hot, US$0.30 per person). Snacks such as 'pachamanca' are available at riverside stalls. The trip also includes a stop-off at Picoy, which has a remarkable colonial church with a highly carved façade, and at **Chiuchin** (E *Hostal Doña Hermina*, set in attractive grounds). The Chiuchin baths (hot, US$30 per person for pool; US$0.50 per person for private baths) are now rather neglected and run down. ■ *Combis leave from beside the church in Churín for the two-hour trip (0800-0900, US$3 round trip fare, returning 1500-1700).*

Excursions

B *Santa Rosa*, T373014, international T373015. Modern with the usual facilities. **C** *Las Termas*, T373005. Has rooms with a pool in the town centre and others up at the La Meseta baths. **D** *Hostals Beatriz and Danubio*, T373028. Modern, clean, quiet, friendly. **E** *Hostal La Cabaña*. Clean, with attractive courtyard.

Sleeping
All hotels are within a couple of blocks of each other. Prices double at peak holiday periods

North Coast

Eating Churín is full of restaurants and cafés offering healthy portions and a wide range of 'dulces' (desserts). Local delicacies include honey, *alfajores*, flavoured *manjar blanca*, cheeses and *calabaza* (a delicious pudding made from squash).

Transport *Trans Estrella Polar*, *Espadín* and *Beteta* each have several buses a day to **Lima**, 4-5 hrs, US$5. Some buses from Lima continue to **Oyón**, 1 hr. From Oyón it is possible to continue over the sierras to **Cerro de Pasco** on a very rough high altitude road, *Trans Javier*, 0800, 5 hrs, US$3.50.

Loma de Lachay National Reserve One kilometre north of the turn-off to Sayán (see above) is a sandy track which leads to the **Loma de Lachay National Reserve**, 3 km further on. A four-wheel drive vehicle is recommended to get there.

This small reserve is a typical example of '*loma*' habitat, and it holds several important species. *Loma* vegetation is formed during the winter months, when fog caused by the Humboldt Current drives inland, rises and condenses, and forms a dew on the surrounding landscape. This dew is sufficient to sustain the seasonal *loma* or 'fog vegetation' that is the home of birds such as the endemic Raimondi's Yellow-finch and Thick-billed miner.

In September-October the plants are in bloom and very beautiful. There is a visitors' centre, trails, camping and picnic areas. The reserve is very popular with Lima residents at the weekend.

Huacho to Barranca Just across the river from Huacho, is **Huaura** where the balcony is still preserved from which San Martín declared the country's independence from Spain. Try *guinda*, the local cherry brandy.

The road passes from the wide valley of Mazo through the irrigated valley of San Felipe. Midway between Huaura and Supe, on the coast road, is **Medio Mundo**, with a lake between the village and the sea. It is a good camping spot, with tents for rent, which is guarded at weekends. Bring food and water - there is none for bathrooms or drinking. The turn-off is outside the village on the Pan-American Highway, to the left; look for the sign, 'Albufera de Medio Mundo'. It is hot and busy in summer.

There is more desert and then the cotton-fields of San Nicolás lead to **Supe** (**F** *Hostal Grau*) at Km 187, a small busy port shipping fishmeal, cotton, sugar and minerals. At **Aspero**, near Supe, is one of the earliest prehistoric sites in Peru (see History section, page 570).

Barranca
Phone code: 034

At Barranca (Km 195) the beach is long and not too dirty, but windy. *Banco de la Nación*, accepts TCs but at poor rates. A few km before Barranca (158 km from Lima) a turning to the right (east) leads to **Caral**, a city 20 km from the coast in the Supe Valley whose date (about 2,600 BC) and monumental construction are overturning many of the accepted theories of Peruvian archaeology. It appears to be easily the oldest city in South America. The only way to get there without your own transport would be to negotiate with a colectivo driver. For details of the excavation project contact: Proyecto Arqueológico Caral-Supe/UNMSM, T(Lima)332 5380/424 5110 ext 296, caral@terra.co.pe

Sleeping and eating D *Chavín*. With bathroom, warm water, clean, good value and recommended, though the front rooms are noisy, it also has a restaurant on the 1st floor for lunch and dinner (try *arroz con conchas*), breakfast bar and café opens onto the street by the main entrance. **F** *Casanova*, on the main street. With bathroom, clean but unwelcoming, safe motorcycle parking. **F** *Jefferson*, Lima 946. Clean, friendly.

F *Pacífico*. With bathroom, clean, good value. **G** *Colón*, Jr Gálvez 407. Friendly, basic. There are many other hotels on the main street, and plenty of bars and restaurants. *Cevichería Fujino*, Arica 210. Good for fish. Try the *tamales*.

Transport Buses stop opposite the service station (*el grifo*) at the end of town. From **Lima** to Barranca, takes 3½ hrs, US$3. As bus companies have their offices in Barranca, buses will stop there rather than at Pativilca or Paramonga. Several buses leave daily from Barranca to **Casma**, 155 km, 2½ hrs, US$3. Also daily buses and trucks to **Huaraz**; 4 hrs, US$6.

The straggling town of Pativilca (Km 203), has a small museum and a good, cheap restaurant, *Cornejo*. Just beyond town, a good paved road turns east for Huaraz in the Cordillera Blanca (see page 335). **Pativilca to Huaraz**

The road at first climbs gradually from the coast. At Km 48, just west of the town of **Chasquitambo** (*Restaurante Delicias*) it reaches *Rumi Siki* (Rump Rock), with unusual rock formations, including the one that gives the site its name. Beyond this point, the grade is steeper and at Km 120 the chilly pass at 4,080 m is reached. Shortly after, **Laguna Conococha** comes into view, where the Río Santa rises. Delicious trout is available in Conococha village. A dirt road branches off from Conococha to **Chiquián** (see page 370) and the Cordilleras Huayhuash and Raura to the southeast.

After crossing a high plateau the main road descends gradually for 47 km until **Catac** (see page 359), where another road branches east to Chavín and on to the Callejón de Conchucos (see page 362). Huaraz is 36 km further on and the road then continues north through the Callejón de Huaylas.

Four kilometres beyond the turn-off to Huaraz, beside the highway, are the well preserved ruins of the Chimú temple of Paramonga. Set on high ground with a view of the ocean, the fortress-like mound is reinforced by eight quadrangular walls rising in tiers to the top of the hill. It is well worth visiting. ■ *US$1.20. No buses run to the ruins, only to the port (about 15 mins from Barranca). A taxi from Paramonga and return after waiting costs US$4.50, otherwise take a Barranca-Paramonga port bus, then it's a 3-km walk.* **Paramonga** *Colour map 3, grid B2*

The town of Paramonga is a small port, 3 km off the Pan-American Highway, 4 km from the ruins and 205 km from Lima.

Between Pativilca and Chimbote the mountains come down to the sea. The road passes by a few very small protected harbours in tiny rock-encircled bays - **Puerto Huarmey**, **Puerto Casma** and **Vesique**. Between Paramonga and Huarmey there are restaurants at Km 223 and 248. In Huarmey, on the Pan-American Highway is: **C-D** *Hotel de Turistas*. Small, clean, good service, restaurant, noisy from road traffic. **D** *Hostal Santa Rosa*, on the plaza.

Casma

The town, largely destroyed by the 1970 earthquake, has since been rebuilt, partly with Chilean help. It has a pleasant Plaza de Armas, several parks and two markets including a good food market. Sechín ruins are only 5 km away and it is a much nicer place to stay than Chimbote. The weather is usually sunny, hence its title *Ciudad del Sol Eterno* (City of Eternal Sun). *Colour map 3, grid B2 Population: about 40,000*

Most of the following hotels are on the Panamericana so rooms at the back will be quieter. **D** *Hostal El Farol*, Tupac Amaru 450, T711064, hostalfaro@yahoo.com Ask for the cheaper rate in the low season, with bathroom, breakfast extra, hot water, swimming **Sleeping** pool, good restaurant, pleasant garden setting, parking, good local information. **E** *Gregori*, Luis Ormeño 530, T711073. Cheaper without bathroom, clean, friendly, café downstairs. **E** *Monte Carlo*, Nepeña 370, T711421. Clean, friendly, TV, internet, laundry, good value. **E** *Rebeca*, Huarmey 377, T711258. Modern, with bath, clean. Recommended. **E** *Hostal Celene* Ormeño 595, T711065. Large new rooms, clean, friendly. **F** *Las Dunas*, Ormeño 505, T/F711057. A converted family home, friendly, being upgraded and enlarged in 2002.

Eating   *Cevichería Henry's*, G de la Vega 295. New, good *ceviche*, popular. *Sechín*, Nepeña esquina Mejía, near the plaza. Friendly, good set meal and chicken. *Tío Sam*, Huarmey 138. Specializes in excellent fresh fish dishes, such as *lenguado sudado*, decorated with photos of Sechín. *Venecia*, Huarmey 204. Serves local dishes such as goat stew, popular with locals. *Café Gregori*, under the hotel. Good for juices and cakes, especially in the afternoon. *Café Lucy*, Mejía 150. Opens early for breakfast, which includes fried fish and soups. There are several *cevicherías* on Av Ormeño 600 block and cheap restaurants on Huarmey. The famous locally made ice-cream, *Caribe*, includes some delicious flavours such as lúcuma and maracuyá. Available at the *panadería* at Ormeño 545.

Tour operators   *Sechín Tours*, in *Hostal Monte Carlo*, T711421. Organize tours in the local area. The guide, Renato, only speaks Spanish but has knowledge of local ruins and can be contacted on T712528, renatotouts@yahoo.com   US$3 per hr, including use of mototaxi.

Transport   There are half hourly buses from Lima to Chimbote which can drop you off in Casma, 370 km, 6 hrs, US$5. If going to **Lima** many of the buses from Trujillo and Chimbote stop briefly opposite the petrol station, block 1 of Ormeño or, if they have small offices, along blocks 1-5 of Av Ormeño. To **Chimbote**, 55 km, it is easiest to take a *Los* Casmeños colectivo, huge old Dodge cars, which depart when full from in front of the petrol station, block 1 of Ormeño, or from plaza Poncianos, 45 mins, US$1.20. To **Trujillo** it is best to go first to Chimbote bus station and then take an *América Express* bus (see Chimbote, **Transport** section). To **Huaraz** (150km), via Pariacoto, buses come from Chimbote, 6-7 hrs, US$4.25 (for a description of the route see below). *Transportes Huandoy*, Ormeño 166, T712336, departs at 0700, 1100 and 1400, while *Yungay Express*, Ormeño 158, departs at 0600, 0800 and 1400. Most Huaraz buses go via Pativilca, which is further but the road is better, 6 hrs, US$5, *Móvil Tours* and *Trans* Chinchaysuyo, all run at night.

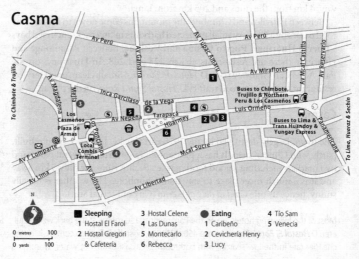

Casma

Sleeping ■		Eating ●	
1 Hostal El Farol	3 Hostal Celene	1 Caribeño	4 Tío Sam
2 Hostal Gregori	4 Las Dunas	2 Cevichería Henry	5 Venecia
& Cafetería	5 Montecarlo	3 Lucy	
	6 Rebecca		

0 metres 100
0 yards 100

Banks Good rates for cash and TCs, no commission, at *BCP*, Bolívar 181. Dollars can be   Directory
changed at Ormeño 529 and Nepeña 384. **Communications** Internet: café on west
side of Plaza. 0900-2100. **Post office**: Fernando Loparte, ½ block from Plaza de Armas.

From Casma a road runs inland over the **Callán pass** (4,224 m) 150 km to   **Casma to**
Huaraz. It's a difficult but beautiful trip, and worth taking in daylight. Few   **Huaraz via**
buses take this route, so check before leaving (see Casma Transport, above).   **Pariacoto**
   From Casma the first 30 km are paved, then a good dirt road follows for
30 km to **Pariacoto**. From here to the pass the road is rough, with landslides
in rainy season, but once the Cordillera Negra has been crossed, the wide,
gravel road is better with spectacular views of the Cordillera Blanca. To catch
the best views, before the Cordillera Blanca becomes covered in cloud (usually in the afternoon), take the earliest bus possible. Sit on the righthand side
of the bus.

Sleeping and eating in Pariacoto **F** *Hostal Eddier*, on the plaza. Basic but nice.
G *Alojamiento Sáenz Peña*, Gonzalo Salazar, cuadra 5. Basic. *Restaurant Iris* is good.

Sechín

This is one of the most important ruins on the Peruvian coast. It consists of a   *Colour map 3, grid B2*
large square temple completely faced with carved stone monoliths - probably
over 500 of them - representing two lines of warriors marching towards the
principal entrance from opposite sides. Between each warrior are carvings of
men being eviscerated, heads with blood gushing from eyes or mouths, dis-
membered legs, arms, torsos, ears, eyes and vertebrae.
   The mural is thought to narrate the results of a battle, with the fates of the
conquerors and the conquered graphically depicted. The style is unique in
Peru for its naturalistic vigour. The importance of the site lies in the fact that it
is one of the oldest centres in the country to demonstrate the development of
warlike activity and the extent to which extreme violence was a part of life.
   Within the stone temple is an earlier, pre-ceramic mud temple with painted
walls. The complex as a whole forms a temple-palace associated with the
development of the local pre-Chavín Sechín culture, dating from about 1500
BC. Three sides of the large stone temple have been excavated and restored.
You cannot see the adobe buildings inside the stone walls, which belong to an
earlier period. They were later covered up and used as a base for a second
storey which unfortunately has been completely destroyed.
   Some experts think the temple and surroundings were buried on purpose.
Others believe it was engulfed by natural disaster. The latter theory is supported by finds of human skeletons. Tombs have been found in front and at
the same level as the temple. A wall of a large adobe building under excavation
can be seen and runs round the sides and back of the temple.
   There is an attractive, shady picnic garden. Photography is best around
midday. The **Max Uhle Museum** by the ruins has an interesting display of
Sechín artefacts and a replica of the façade of the inner adobe temple. If you
need a guide ask in advance for Wilder León or Carlos Cuy, who speaks English and French. Outside the museum is an orientation map showing the location of the different archaeological sites in the Casma area.
   ■ *0800-1800 daily. US$1.50, children half price; the ticket is also valid for the*
museum and Pañamarca (see page 383). Frequent colectivos leave from in front
of the market in Casma for US$0.30 per person, but leave early in the morning; or
take a moto-taxi for US$1 per person.

North Coast

Two kilometres further along is **Sechín Alto**, two pyramids of the late Chavín period, but these have not yet been extensively excavated. Follow the track to the west (left) at the Km 4 post past the first, smaller pyramid and the farm house. The second pyramid is huge, measuring 300 x 250 x 25 m, covering 50 ha, and once consisted of three levels. Though most of the stone façade has turned to rubble, small sections of the exterior wall and huge entrance stones on the north side are visible. Recent investigations have uncovered some storage chambers and adobe platforms built from unusual conical adobes atop the pyramid.

Among numerous other sites in the area, there are two of particular interest, but a mototaxi is needed to visit them. At Km 15 on the Pariacoto road there are several lines and figures etched in the desert surface, as at Nasca. Though nowhere near as impressive as the Nasca Lines, the figure of a 'warrior' is clearly visible from a nearby hill-top. The lines are up to 25 m long, 20 cms wide and have been dated to 1,000BC. Archaeologists are uncertain as to their purpose.

Chanquillo, located off the Panamericana at Km 361, is a 2,300-year old fortress on a hill-top. It consists of three concentric stone walls with rectangular and circular buildings inside the interior wall. Some of the original *algarrob* tree supports remain.

Playa Tortugas   Located 2 km east of the Pan-American Highway at Km 391, 18 km north of Casma, Playa Tortugas is a fishing village on a nice bay with calm water and a rocky beach. Colectivos leave Casma when full from Plaza Poncianos between the Plaza de Armas and the market, 0500-2000, US$0.75, 15 minutes. There are several hotels (**C**), including *Las Terrazas*, T619042, www.lasterrazas.com and *Mi Relax*, T619904, but they are only open November-April. The **C** *Hotel Farol Beach Inn*, sister to the one in Casma, is open all year. One of the best seafood restaurants for fried fish or *ceviche* is *Costa Azul*, on the seafront as you enter the settlement. From the north end of the bay the road continues to **Playa Huayuna**, a windy, closed bay with a sandy beach and a scallop farm. From the south end of Tortugas a road goes to **Rincón de Piños**, a beach with wild surf. To the south of Casma, at Km 345, are the sandy beaches of **La Gramita** and **Las Aldas**.

Chimbote

Phone code: 044
Colour map 3, grid A2
Population: 296,600

In one of Peru's few natural harbours, a port has been built to serve the national steel industry. Chimbote is also Peru's largest fishing port; fishmeal is exported and the smell of the fishmeal plants is very strong. There are no tourist attractions as such, but the city has become increasingly important as an access to the Cordillera Blanca. The city also carries the dubious honour of being the spot where cholera first appeared in South America.

Ins and outs

Warning   Chimbote is neither a pleasant nor a safe city by day or night. Many travellers are attacked and robbed here. You should take extensive precautions, always use taxis from the bus station to your hotel and preferably not venture far from the hotel. In addition, cyclists are warned not to ride in the area.

Getting there   The airport is at the south end of town, but there are no scheduled flights. The bus station is 4 km south of the city centre on Av Meiggs. Some buses to/from places north of

Chimbote will drop people off in the centre if they only have hand luggage, but not in a safe area. Always go to the terminal and, under no circumstances, walk from there to the centre: a colectivo costs US$0.30, taxi US$1. There are no hotels near the terminal, but some bus companies have ticket offices in the centre.

If arriving from Caraz via the Cañón del Pato there is usually time to make a connection to Casma or Trujillo/Huanchaco and avoid overnighting in Chimbote. If travelling to Caraz, however, overnighting in Chimbote is almost unavoidable. Casma is near enough to stay in but you will need to buy your Caraz ticket the day before; the bus station is on the Casma side of Chimbote.

Getting around

Although Chimbote is small enough to walk around, don't: take a taxi instead, except for going out to eat near your hotel. Radio taxis from T334433, T327777 and T322005. www.laindustria.com   (website of the local newspaper) has a section on Chimbote.

Sights

The city was damaged by the 1970 earthquake. Today, it has a spacious **Plaza de Armas**, the cathedral and several public buildings have since been rebuilt, and the modern Municipal building has a small **art gallery** downstairs. ■ *0900-2000*. Bathing is forbidden on the bay, though there is a public **swimming pool** at Vivero Forestal. Flocks of brown pelicans and masked boobies can be seen from the beach. At weekends two-hour boat trips go around the bay to visit the cliffs and islands to see the marine birdlife and rock formations. Take suntan lotion.

Note that the main street, Avenida Victor Raul Haya de la Torre is more commonly known as José Pardo.

Chimbote

To Trujillo, Caraz & Northern Peru

North Coast

To New Bus Terminal, Casma & Lima

Pacific Ocean

0 metres 50
0 yards 50

Sleeping ■
1 Cantón & Chifa Cantón
2 D'Carlo
3 El Parque
4 Felic
5 Gran Hotel Chimú
6 Hostal Antonio's
7 Hostal Augusto
8 Hostal Karol Inn & Chifa Jin Lon
9 Hostal Persia
10 Hostal San Felipe
11 Hostal Tany
12 Ivansino Inn

Eating ●
1 Aquarius
2 Recutecu

Essentials

Sleeping

● on map
Price codes:
see inside front cover
There are plenty of
hotels in Chimbote so
it is often possible to
negotiate a lower rate

A *Cantón*, Bolognesi 498, T344388. The most modern, luxury hotel in the city, has a good but pricey *chifa* restaurant. **B** *Gran Hotel Chimú*, José Gálvez 109, T/F321741. Price includes breakfast, minibar, safe parking. **B** *Ivansino Inn*, Haya de la Torre 738, T321811, F321927, ivansino@hotmail.com Includes breakfast, comfortable, clean, modern, cable TV, minibar. **C** *D'Carlo*, Villavicencio 376, on the plaza, T/F321047. Spacious, friendly, TV, mini-bar, restaurant. **C** *San Felipe*, Haya de la Torre 514, T323401. With bathroom, hot water, clean, friendly, comfortable, restaurant. **D** *Hostal Antonio's*, Bolognesi 745, T/F32 5783. Clean, hot water, minibar. **D** *Augusto*, Aguirre 265, T324431. With bathroom, clean, front rooms noisy, overpriced. **D** *Felic*, Haya de la Torre 552, T325901. **E** without bathroom, clean, quiet. Recommended. **D** *Hostal Karol Inn*, Manuel Ruiz 277, T/F321216. Clean, with bathroom, hot water, a good place to stay, family run, laundry service, cafeteria. **D** *Residencial El Parque*, E Palacios 309, on the main plaza, T323963. A converted old home, with bathroom, hot water, clean, nice, friendly. **E** *Hostal El Ensueño*, Sáenz Peña 268, 2 blocks from Plaza Central, T328662. **F** without bath, very good, safe, welcoming. **E** *Tany*, Palacios 553, T/F323411. Includes breakfast, friendly, clean, TV, good value. **F** *Hostal Persia*, L Prado 623, T/F342540. Clean, friendly, TV, cheap, but nearer market.

Eating

● on map

Aquarius, Haya de la Torre 360. Vegetarian. *Buenos Aires*, Aguirre near the beach. *Chifa Jin Lon*, adjoining *Hostal Karol Inn*. Well-prepared Chinese food, popular and convenient. *Pollo Gordo*, Prado y Aguirre. Good chicken and cold beer. *Recutecu*, L Prado 556. Good set lunch with a wide choice. There are several cheap restaurants on Haya de la Torre by the plaza. An excellent bakery is *Delca*, at Haya de la Torre 568.

Tour operators

Chimbote Tours, Bolognesi 801, T324982, F324792. Helpful, friendly, English spoken.

Transport

Bus From **Lima** to Chimbote, 420 km, 6 hrs, US$7-9. Buses depart every 30 mins, *Trans Isla Blanca* has the most frequent service, *Línea* (T322416), *ECS* (T318132) and *Oltursa* (T328275). To **Trujillo**, 130 km, 2 hrs, US$1.50, *América Express* have buses every 20 mins. To **Huaraz** most companies, with the best buses, go the 'long way round', ie down the Panamericana to Pativilca, then up the paved highway, 7 hrs, US$6. The best companies are *Móvil Tours* and *Chinc haysuyo*; both start in Trujillo, their buses continue on to **Caraz**. To **Huaraz** via Pariacoto, 7 hrs, US$5.50, *Trans Huandoy* (Etseturh), T354024, at 0600, 1000 and 1300, 7 hrs, US$5.50, and *Yungay Express* at 0500, 0700 and 1300. (See below for a description of this route). To **Caraz** via Cañón del Pato, 7-8 hrs, US$5.50, *Yungay Express* at 0830 (for a description of this route see below). To **Sihuas**, 10 hrs, US$7, *Trans Andino* is the only company with a daytime bus at 0800 on Wed, Fri and Sun.

Directory

Banks *BCP* and *Interbank*, both on Bolognesi and M Ruiz. For TCs and cash. *Casa Arroyo*, M Ruiz 292. For cash only. There are other *casas* and street changers along M Ruiz between Bolognesi and VR Haya de la Torre. **Communications** Internet: At Palacios 518, Aguirre 278 and J.Pardo 660. **Post**: *Serpost*, Jr Tumbes behind market. Also at Palacios 441. **Telecommunications:** *Telefónica* main office, Tumbes 356. National and international fax and phone. Also at Haya de la Torre 420 and M Ruiz 253.

Around Chimbote

About 25 km south of Chimbote, at Km 405 on the Pan-American Highway, a paved road leads east to the **Nepeña Valley**, where several pre-Columbian ruins including Cerro Blanco, Pañamarca and Paredones can be found. The valley is dominated by the vast San Jacinto sugar plantation.

North Coast

The village of Capellanía is 11 km from the crossroads. Just beyond are the ruins of **Pañamarca**. The site includes a two-storey stone structure, built on a hill, dating from the formative period (2000 BC-AD 100) and many adobe structures from the Moche period, including three pyramids. Remains of polychromatic murals and animal sculptures can also be seen.

Twenty kilometres from Pañamarca, via the villages of San Jacinto and Moro, is the site of **Paredones**, a large stone structure, with 4-m high granite walls and a very impressive gateway known as 'Portada de Paredones' or 'Puerta del Sol'. It is believed to have been a Chavín palace.

The route from Chimbote to Huaraz passes through the **Santa Valley** and the spectacular Cañon del Pato, one of the most thrilling bus trips in all of Peru.

Chimbote to Huaraz

Just north of Chimbote, a road branches northeast off the Pan-American Highway and, joining another road from the town of Santa, goes up the Santa valley following the route, including tunnels, of the old Santa Corporation Railway. This used to run as far as **Huallanca** (Ancash - not to be confused with the town of the same name southeast of Huaraz), 140 km up the valley, but the track was largely destroyed by the 1970 earthquake. At Chuquicara, 3 hours from Chimbote, some 60 km before Huallanca, is *Restaurante Rosales*, a good place to stop for a meal (US$1-1.30 - you can sleep here, too, but it's very rough). The road goes between barren hills and passes poor mining camps. The geology is fantastic, with ravines, whorls, faults and strata at all angles to each other. The colours are also amazing, with rock in various shades. The next village is **Yuramarca** where there is lodging, places to eat, fuel and a police station.

At Huallanca is an impressive hydroelectric plant, built into a mountain, which cannot be visited. There is accommodation at the *Hotel Huascarán*, which is good and friendly; also *Koki's Hostal* and *Fantasy's Pollería*. Fuel is available. Everything closes early.

At the top of the valley by the hydroelectric centre, the road turns right to go through the very narrow and spectacular **Cañon del Pato**. You pass under tremendous walls of bare rock and through 36 tunnels, but the flow of the river has been greatly reduced by the hydroelectric scheme which takes the water into the mountain at the Bocatoma. After this point the road is paved for all but a few kilometres around Cooperativa Chiquinquirá. Soon you reach the Callejón de Huaylas and the road south to Caraz and Huaraz.

An alternative road for cyclists (and vehicles with a permit) is the private road known as the 'Brasileños', used by the Brazilian company Odebrecht which has built a water channel for the Chavimochic irrigation scheme from the Río Santa to the coast. The turn-off is 35 km north of the Santa turning, 15 km south of the bridge in Chao, on the Pan-American Highway. It is a good all-weather road to Tanguche, 22 km from the turn-off, where it continues up the north bank of the Río Santa, crosses a bridge 28 km from Tanguche, to meet up with the public road (which is in worse condition).

The highway crosses the valleys of Chao and Virú, and after 137 km reach the first great city of Northern Peru, Trujillo. The Virú valley contains the largest single sand dune in South America. Between Virú and Trujillo the desert is being turned 'green' with asparagus and other crops, thanks to the huge Chavimochic project. It is hard to believe that the irrigated land was once as lifeless as the desert that surrounds it. There is basic lodging available and places to eat in both Chao and Virú. The best is *Hostal Santa Rosa*, Alameda 315, Virú, T641008. **G** per person *La Posada*, Carretera Virú con Panamericana, is simple, with cold water; cheap, good restaurant downstairs.

North of Chimbote

North Coast

Trujillo

Phone code: 044
Colour map 3, grid A1
Population: 850,000

Trujillo, capital of the Department of La Libertad, disputes the title of second city of Peru with Arequipa. Founded by Diego de Almagro in 1534 as an express assignment ordered by Francisco Pizarro, the city was named after the latter's native town in Spain.

There is enough here to hold the attention for several days. The area abounds in pre-Columbian sites, there are beaches and good surfing within easy reach and the city itself still has many old churches and graceful colonial homes built during the reigns of the viceroys. Besides the Cathedral it has 10 colonial churches as well as convents and monasteries.

Ins and outs

Street names   Trujillo has confusing double street names: the smaller printed name is that generally shown on maps, in guide books and in general use. **NB** Tourists may be approached by vendors selling *huacos* and necklaces from the Chimú period. The export of these items is strictly illegal if they are genuine, but they almost certainly aren't.

Getting there
See also Transport, page 392
Not surprisingly communications with the rest of the country are good. The airport is a little way out of town to the west – you will come into town along Av Mansiche. There is no central bus terminal and none of the bus stations is in the centre. They are spread out on three sides the city, beyond the inner ring road, Av España. Companies are now moving to new premises north and south along the Panamericana. There is little in the way of accommodation near them but there are lots of taxis and colectivos to get you to your hotel (insist on being taken to the hotel of your choice).

Getting around   With its compact colonial centre and mild, spring-like climate, Trujillo is best explored on foot. Take care beyond the inner ring road, Av España and in the Sánchez Carrión district at night. Bus and colectivos, on all routes, cost US$0.15-0.30; colectivos are safer as there are fewer people and fewer pick-pockets. Taxis, of which there are thousands, charge US$0.60 within the Av América ring road (drivers may ask for more at night). To Chan Chán US$3 per car, to the airport is US$4; to Huanchaco, US$4-5. Beware of over-charging, check fares with locals. A taxi can be hired from in front of the *Hotel Libertador* for US$7 an hr about the same rate as a tour with an independent guide or travel agent for 1-2 people. Always use official taxis, which are mainly yellow. The major sites outside the city, Chan Chán, the Moche pyramids and Huanchaco beach are easily reached by public transport, but care is needed when walking around. A number of recommended guides run expert tours to these and other places.

Tourist offices   *i perú*, Plaza Mayor, T294561, Mon-Sat 0800-1900, Sun 0800-1400. Useful websites: www.xanga.com/TrujilloPeru Michael White and Clara Bravo's site, with loads of links and information (click on 'reviews'). www.laindustria.com/industria local newspaper in Spanish (click on 'ecoturismo'). www.bcrp.com/Espanol/Sucursales/trujillo Banco Central de Reserva site with information on colonial houses, folklore and economy in Spanish. Maps available from **Touring and Automobile Club**, Av Argentina 258, Urb El Recreo, T290736, F223983, trujillo@touringperu.com.pe; also from **Librería Ayacucho**, Ayacucho 570. **Instituto Nacional de Cultura**, Independencia 572. **Tourist Police** have an office at Independencia 630, Casa Ganoza Chopitea, T291705. Open 365 days a year. They provide useful information. The *Indecopi* tourist complaints office is at Junín 454, T242422, F242888, ldiaz@indecopi.gob.pe Or contact the Dirección Regional de Turismo, Av España 1801, T245345/245794.

Sights

The focal point is the pleasant and spacious **Plaza Mayor** (used more commonly than Plaza de Armas here). The prominent sculpture represents agriculture, commerce, education, art, slavery, action and liberation, crowned by a young man holding a torch depicting liberty. Fronting it is the **Cathedral**, dating from 1666, with its museum of religious paintings and sculptures next door (closed in 2002). Also on the plaza are the *Hotel Libertador*, the colonial style Sociedad de Beneficencia Pública de Trujillo and the Municipalidad.

The **Universidad de La Libertad**, second only to that of San Marcos at Lima, was founded in 1824. Two beautiful colonial mansions on the plaza have been taken over. The Banco Central de Reserva is in the Colonial-style **Casa Urquiaga (or Calonge)**, Pizarro 446, which contains valuable pre-Columbian ceramics. ■ *Mon-Fri, 0900-1500, Sat-Sun 1000-1330. Free guided tour lasts 30 mins, take passport.* The other is **Casa Bracamonte (or Lizarzaburu)**, at Independencia 441, with occasional exhibits. Opposite the Cathedral on Independencia, is the **Caja Rural** (officially known as Casa Garci Olguín), recently restored but boasting the oldest façade in the city and Moorish-style murals. The buildings that surround the Plaza, and many others in the vicinity, are painted in bright pastel colours. Street lamps are on brackets, adding to the charm of the centre.

Las Delicias is a clean beach with good surf, about 25 minutes by colectivo (US$0.30) and 15 minutes by taxi from Trujillo. Colectivos leave from Las Incas y Atahualpa.

Colonial houses Near the Plaza de Armas, at Jr Pizarro 688, is the spacious 18th century **Palacio Iturregui**, now occupied by the **Club Central**, an exclusive social centre of Trujillo. It houses a private collection of ceramics. ■ *Mon-Sat 1100-1800. To enter the patio is free, but to see more of the palace and the ceramics collection costs US$1.45.*

Other mansions, still in private hands, include **Casa del Mayorazgo de Facalá**, Pizarro 314, which is now the Banco Wiese. Its former owner was Don Pedro de Tinoco whose wife embroidered the first Peruvian flag to be hoisted following Trujillo's independence from Spanish rule in 1820. The **Casa de la Emancipación**, Jr Pizarro 610 (Banco Continental), is where independence from Spain was planned and was the first seat of government and congress in Peru. The first room on the right as you go in displays plans and the history of the building. There are exhibits on the life of the poet César Vallejo and Bishop Martínez Compagñon (1737-97), whose tours took him all round northern Peru. There are waterclours of life in the 18th century. ■ *Daily 0900-1300 and 1700-2000.*

The **Casa del Mariscal de Orbegoso**, Orbegoso 553, named after the ex-President, General Luis José de Orbegoso, is the Museo de la República, owned by Banco de Crédito. It holds temporary exhibitions and cultural events most Thursday evenings. ■ *Daily 0930, during banking hrs. Free.* **Casa Ganoza Chopitea**, Independencia 630 opposite San Francisco church, is architecturally the most representative house in the city and considered the most outstanding of the viceroyalty. It combines Baroque and Rococo styles.

Churches Many churches were damaged in the 1970 earthquake. One of the best, the 17th century **La Merced** at Pizarro 550, with picturesque moulded figures below the dome, has been restored, but part of the dome has collapsed because of building work next door. It has a mock rococo organ above the choir stalls and retablos

Trujillo

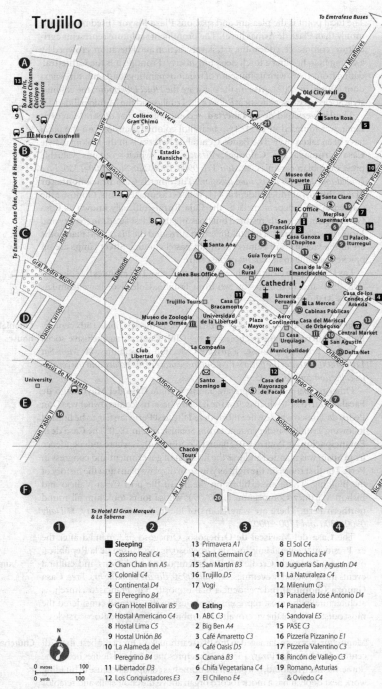

To Emtrafesa Buses

To Arco Iris, Puerto Chicama, Chiclayo & Cajamarca

To Esmeralda, Chan Chán, Airport & Huanchaco

Old City Wall

Santa Rosa

Coliseo Gran Chimú

Estadio Mansiche

Museo Cassinelli

Museo del Juguete

Santa Clara

EC Office
Merpisa Supermarket

San Francisco
Casa Ganoza Chopitea

Palacio Iturregui

Central Market

Santa Ana

Guía Tours

Casa de la Emancipación

Línea Bus Office

Caja Rural

INC

Cathedral

Librería Peruana

La Merced

Casa de los Condes de Aranda

Trujillo Tours
Casa Bracamonte

Museo de Zoología de Juan Ormea

Universidad de la Libertad

Plaza Mayor

Aero Continente
Cabinas Públicas

Casa del Mariscal de Orbegoso

Casa Urquiaga

San Agustín

Delta Net

La Compañía

Municipalidad

Club Libertad

University

Santo Domingo

Casa del Mayorazgo de Facalá

Belén

Chacón Tours

To Hotel El Gran Marqués & La Taberna

Sleeping
1 Cassino Real *C4*
2 Chan Chán Inn *A5*
3 Colonial *C4*
4 Continental *D4*
5 El Peregrino *B4*
6 Gran Hotel Bolívar *B5*
7 Hostal Americano *C4*
8 Hostal Lima *C5*
9 Hostal Unión *B6*
10 La Alameda del Peregrino *B4*
11 Libertador *D3*
12 Los Conquistadores *E3*
13 Primavera *A1*
14 Saint Germain *C4*
15 San Martín *B3*
16 Trujillo *D5*
17 Vogi

Eating
1 ABC *C3*
2 Big Ben *A4*
3 Café Amaretto *C3*
4 Café Oasis *D5*
5 Canana *B3*
6 Chifa Vegetariana *C4*
7 El Chileno *E4*
8 El Sol *C4*
9 El Mochica *E4*
10 Juguería San Agustín *D4*
11 La Naturaleza *C4*
12 Milenium *C3*
13 Panadería José Antonio *D4*
14 Panadería Sandoval *E5*
15 PASE *C3*
16 Pizzería Pizzanino *E1*
17 Pizzería Valentino *C3*
18 Rincón de Vallejo *C3*
19 Romano, Asturias & Oviedo *C4*

from the 17th century which, unusually, are painted on the walls, from the time before free-standing altars were used. ■ *Entry US$2.* **El Carmen** church and monastery at Colón y Bolívar, has been described as the 'most valuable jewel of colonial art in Trujillo'. It has five gilt altars, balconies and religious paintings. Next door is the Pinacoteca Carmelita, with more paintings. It includes a room on picture restoration. ■ *The church and pinacoteca open Mon-Sat 0900-1300. Entry US$0.85. The church is open for mass at 0700-0730 Sun.* **La Compañía**, the former Jesuit church near Plaza de Armas, is now an auditorium for cultural events.

In **San Francisco**, on the corner of Gamarra and Independencia, is the pulpit which survived the earthquake of Saint Valentine's Day in 1619. It has three golden altars and others inside. Other churches include: **Belén** on the 6th block of Almagro; **Santa Clara** on the 4th block of Junín (Sunday only); **San Agustín,** Bolívar at the 6th block of Mcal Orbegoso; **Santa Ana** on the 2nd block of the same street (one of the three 'iglesias menores', the others were San Lorenzo and Santa Rosa); and **Santo Domingo** on the 4th block of Bolognesi.

Plazuela El Recreo, at the north end of Pizarro, was known as El Estanque during the colonial period as it housed a pool from which the city's water was distributed. A marble fountain by Eiffel now stands in the square, transferred from the Plaza de Armas, fronted by restaurants.

Museo de Arqueología, houses a large collection of thematic exhibits from prehispanic cultures of the area. ■ *Mon 0930-1400, Tue-Fri 0915- 1300, 1500-1900, Sat and Sun 0930-1600. US$2.85. Guided tours in Spanish available. www.unitru.edu. pe/arq/indice.html for good information.* Casa Risco, Junín 682 y Ayacucho, T249322.

Museums

20 Romano-Rincón Criollo *F3*
21 Sol y Pimienta *B3*
22 Taverna Chelsea *B5*

🚌 **Transport**
1 Agreda *B6*
2 América Express, El Sol *F5*
3 Buses to Cruz del Sur *A5*
4 Buses to Huaca del Sol y de la Luna *D6*

5 Buses to Huanchaco, Chan Chán, Huaca Arco Iris & Huaca La Esmeralda *D6*
6 Chinchaysuyo *B2*
7 Civa *A5*
8 ITTSA
9 Turismo Díaz *B1*
10 Olano & Flores *A5*
11 Ormeño *A5*
12 Línea North Terminal *C2*

North Coast

The basement of the **Cassinelli** garage on the fork of the Pan-American and Huanchaco roads contains a superb private collection of Mochica and Chimú pottery and is highly recommended. The caretaker sometimes gives a thorough explanation including demonstrations of the whistling *huacos* and is knowledgeable on any subject you care to discuss (in Spanish). ■ *0915-1230, 1515-1830. US$1.50.*

Museo del Juguete, the toy museum, contains examples from prehistoric times to 1950, collected by painter Gerardo Chávez. Downstairs is the Espacio Cultural Angelmira with a café bar; in a restored *casona*, worth a visit. ■ *Independencia 705 y Junín, www.angelmira.com Tue-Sat 1000-1800, Sun 1000-1300, 1500-1800. US$0.85, children US$0.30. Café open 0800-2100.*

Museo de Zoología de Juan Ormea, has interesting displays of Peruvian animals. ■ *Jr San Martín 368. Mon-Fri 0700-1900. US$0.60.*

Essentials

Sleeping
■ *on map*
Price codes:
see inside front cover

L *Libertador*, Independencia 485 on Plaza de Armas, T232741, F235641, trujillo@libertador.com.pe Price includes tax, pool (can be used by non-guests if they buy a drink), cafeteria and restaurant, continental breakfast US$5, excellent buffet lunch on Sun. Recommended. **AL** *El Gran Marqués*, Díaz de Cienfuegos 145-147, Urb La Merced, T/F249366, F249161, www.elgranmarques.com Price includes tax and breakfast, modern, free internet connection in rooms, pool, sauna, jacuzzi, restaurant. Recommended. **A** *Los Conquistadores*, Diego de Almagro 586, T203350, F235917, losconquistadores@viabcp.com Price includes tax and American breakfast, bar, restaurant, very comfortable. **A-B** *Gran Bolívar*, Bolívar 957, T222090, F262200, www.granbolivarhotel.com Price includes tax, breakfast, airport transfer and welcome drink, in converted 18th century house, internet, café, bar, parking.

B *La Alameda del Peregrino*, Jr Pizarro 879, T470512, www.perunorte.com/ alamedaperegrino Includes breakfast, cable TV, internet service, restaurant, bar, café, safe, money exchange. Recommended. Also *El Peregrino*, Independencia 978, T203990, www.elperegrinohotel.com which is convenient for the Lima buses. **B** *Cassino Real*, Pizarro 651, T/F257416, crealh@viabcp.com Includes tax and American breakfast, cable TV, restaurant, disco, casino (can be noisy), car rental provided and expensive tours. **B** *Saint Germain*, Junín 585, T208102, www.perunorte.com/ saintgermain Voted best in town, price includes breakfast. With bath, hot water, TV, internet, laundry, safe, parking.

C *Continental*, Gamarra 663, T241607, F249881. Opposite the market, includes tax and breakfast, clean, good, safe. Restaurant recommended. **C** *Vogi*, Ayacucho 663, T243574. Includes tax, with bath, TV, clean, safe, quiet. Recommended. **D** *Colonial*, Independencia 618, T258261, F223410. Clean, attractive, friendly, rooms are a bit small, good restaurant. Recommended. **D** *San Martín*, San Martín 749, T/F252311. Good value, with bath and TV, small restaurant, good for breakfast, clean but noisy from neighbouring establishments. Recommended. **D-E** *Primavera*, Av N de Piérola 872, Urb Primavera, T231915, F257399. With bathroom, hot water, restaurant, bar, pool.

E *Hostal Americano*, Pizarro 764, T241361. A vast, rambling old building, rooms without bathrooms are noisy and very basic, most rooms don't have window (Nos 134 and 137, and those either side of 303, have windows, balconies and good views), safe, a good meeting place as all backpackers seem to end up here, but mixed reports. **E** *Hostería El Sol*, Brillantes 224, Urb Santa Inés, T231933, near bus terminals on Av Nicolás de Piérola. With hot shower, restaurant, all meals available for US$2.60. **E** *Trujillo*, Grau 581, T243921, F244241. With bathroom, **F** without bath or TV, hot water at times, good value but can be noisy. Recommended. **E** *Hostal Unión*, La Unión 122. Well-located for buses, clean, fairly basic. **E** per person *Hostal Wyllie's*, Raimondi 318, T205671. Hot water, good service, negotiate price.

F per person *Chan Chán Inn*, Av Ejército 307, T/F294281, mocheperu@hotmail.com Close to several bus terminals, price includes breakfast (cheaper without), popular with backpackers, luggage store, café, laundry, internet, money exchange and information. **F** per person *Clara Bravo and Michael White*, Cahuide 495, T243347, M 662710, T/F299997, microbewhite@yahoo.com With bath, groups can be accommodated, meals on request, very helpful and friendly, loads of information available, many languages spoken (see Guides, below). Recommended. **G** *Hostal Lima*, Ayacucho 718, T244751. Popular with gringos, dirty, terrible bathrooms.

Mid-range *El Mochica*, Bolívar 462. A typical restaurant with a good reputation, the food is good and, on special occasions, has live music. There is another branch on the road to Las Delicias beach. *Big Ben*, Av España 1317. Good seafood, open 1000-1630. *Romano*, Pizarro 747. International food, good *menús*, breakfasts, coffee and cakes, but slow service. *Romano-Rincón Criollo*, Estados Unidos 162, Urb El Recreo, a 10-min walk from the centre, T244207. Specializes in northern Peruvian cuisine and has a good value lunch *menú* for US$2 in smart surroundings. In the same group: *Pizzería Pizzanino*, Av Juan Pablo II 183, Urb San Andrés, opposite the University, T263105. Recommended for pizzas, also pasta, meats and desserts, open in evening only. *Pizzería Valentino*, Orbegoso 224. Very good.

Cheap *ABC*, Orbegoso 290 y San Martín. Good for chicken. *Asturias*, Pizarro 741. Nice café with excellent meals, good juices and snacks. *PASE*, Gamarra 353, T/F234715. Hotel and restaurant school, very good *menú* US$1.45, buffet for US$2.85 on Fri, opens 1300, closed weekends. Recommended. *Café Oviedo*, Pizarro 737. With vegetarian options, good salads, helpful. *Rincón de Vallejo*, Orbegoso 303. Good *menú*, typical dishes, very crowded at peak times. *Juguería San Agustín*, Bolívar 526. Good juices, good *menú*, popular, excellent value. *La Selecta*, Pizarro 870. Set lunch for US$1.75, good value, also *heladería*. *Sol y Pimienta*, Colón 201. Very popular for lunch, US$1, close to buses for Huanchaco and Chan Chán. **Vegetarian** (not exclusively): *El Sol*, Pizarro 660. The original and best, cheap set meals, also serves other dishes. *Milenium*, Gamarra 316. *La Naturaleza*, Gamarra 455. Vegetarian dishes, unfriendly. *Chifa Vegetariana*, Pizarro 687. Also vegetarian, with yoghurts and fruits. **Cafés**: *Café Amaretto*, Gamarra 368. Good selection of coffees, sweets, snacks and drinks. *El Chileno*, Ayacucho 408. Café and ice cream parlour, popular. *Kasumy*, Pizarro 857. Good value food and beer, beware overcharging. *Cafetería Oasis*, Gamarra y Grau. Good for breakfasts.

There are five cheap seafood restaurants at Plazuela El Recreo, at the end of Pizarro. For really cheap meals try the central market at Grau y Ayacucho. Good selection of breads at *Fitopán*, Bolívar 406, *Panadería Sandoval*, Orbegoso 822, and *Panadería José Antonio*, Ayacucho 561-65, in the Mercado Central. On Orbegoso are shops selling dairy products, yoghurts, fruits, etc, *Productos Lácteos Rodriguito* at No 716, and *Lácteos Daisy* at No 719.

Canana, San Martín 791. Bars and restaurant, disco, live music at weekends (US$1.50-3 depending on the show), video screens (also has travel agency). Recommended, but take care on leaving. *Taverna Chelsea*, Estete 675, T257032. Bar, restaurant, live Salsa at weekends (US$4 entry), exclusive and lively. Highly recommended. *Luna Rota*, América Sur 2119, at the end of Huayna Capac. Very popular with locals. *La Taberna*, Av Húsares de Junín, Urb La Merced. Good for Andean folk music. *Las Tinajas*, Pizarro y Almagro, on Plaza Mayor. A pub-disco with live rock music and *peña* on Sat.

The two most important festivals are the *National Marinera Contest* and the *Festival Internacional de La Primavera*. The former is held at the end of **Jan** for 2 weeks and consists of hundreds of couples competing in six categories, from children to seniors

Eating
• *on map*

It's difficult to find a meal before 0800. A Mon speciality is shambar, a thick minestrone made with gammon

Bars & clubs

Festivals

North Coast

(see Música criolla, page 596). This event is organized by the *Club Libertad* and has taken place since 1960. The *Festival de la Primavera* is held in the last week in **Sep**. Organized by the *Club de Leones*, it is a celebration of the arrival of Spring and has grown over the years to become one of Peru's most important tourist ev ents. The final parade (*corso*) has plenty to enjoy, with many local dancers, dog owners' clubs, schools parades, and so on. Those who are strongly opposed to beauty pageants may want to give it a miss as there are floats with beauty queens from South and North America participating (but it's all very decorous). Other days feature cultural events (some philanthropic/charitable), and, above all, Trujillo's famous *Caballos de Paso*, a fine breed of horses with a tripping gait that has made them renowned worldwide. These horses, a Spanish legacy, have been immortalized in Peruvian waltzes. Riders still compete in their own form of the Marinera dance and buyers from around the world congregate to see them shown at the Spring Festival (see www.rcp.net.pe/rcp/caballos).

Other major festivals include the *Feria de San José* held in Las Delicias on **19-22 Mar**. *Festival de la Música* takes place on **18 Jun**.

Shopping   **Bookshops** *Librería Peruana*, Pizarro 505, just off the Plaza Mayor. Has the best selection in town, ask for Sra Inés Guerra de Guijón. **Camera repairs** *Fotolab*, Av España 2755, T295590. Hugo Guevara repairs all makes, film developing. *Fotovisión Para Tí*, Pizarro 523, also repairs cameras. **Markets** *Mercado Central* on Gamarra, Ayacucho and Pasaje San Agustín. *Mercado Mayorista* between Sinchi Roca and Av Los Incas (not a safe zone). The best **supermarket** is *Merpisa*, Pizarro y Junín. **Pharmacies** Several pharmacy chains in the centre (on Pizarro and Gamarra) and others on either side of Belén hospital on Bolognesi. There are places for spectacles/eye glasses repair here.

Sports   **Swimming** *Academia Berendson*, Bolognesi 231, heated pool. There's an outdoor swimming pool next to Mansiche stadium, where buses leave for Chan Chán and Huanchaco. It's open 0900-1300 and 1600-1800, entry US$0.50.

Tour operators
Prices vary and competition is fierce so shop around for the best deal Few agencies run tours on Sun and often only at fixed times on other days

Chacón Tours, Av España 106-112, T255212. Open Sat afternoon and Sun morning. Recommended. *Guía Tours*, Independencia 580, T234856, F246353. Also Western Union agent. Recommended. *Trujillo Tours*, San Martín y Almagro 301, T233091, F257518, ttours@pol.com.pe Work with *Lima Tours*. To **Chan Chán**, **El Dragón** and **Huanchaco**, 3 hrs for US$15 per person. To **Huacas del Sol** and **de la Luna**, 2 hrs for US$13 per person. To **El Brujo**, US$20-25 per person. **City tours** cost US$6.50 per person (minimum of 2 people; discounts for 4 or more).

Guides: many hotels work on a commission basis with taxi drivers and travel agencies. If you decide on a guide, make your own direct approach. *Clara Bravo*, Cahuide 495, T243347, T09-662710 (mob), T/F299997, www.xanga.com/TrujilloPeru, http://communities.msn.com/TrujilloPeru/pictures   An experienced tourist guide

The Moche culture

One of the most remarkable pre-Inca civilizations was that of the Moche people, who evolved during the first century AD and lasted until around AD 750. Though these early Peruvians had no written language, they left a vivid artistic record of their life and culture in beautifully modelled and painted ceramics.

Compared with the empires of their successors, the Chimú and Inca, the realm of the Moche was very small, covering less than 250 miles of coast from the valleys of Lambayeque to Nepeña, south of present-day Chimbote. Though a seemingly inhospitable stretch of coast, the Moche harnessed rivers spilling from the Andean cordillera, channelling them into a network of irrigation canals that watered the arid coastal valleys. The resultant lush fields produced plentiful crops, which, along with the sea's bountiful harvest of fish and seafood, gave the Moche a rich and varied diet. With the leisure allowed by such abundant food, Moche craftsmen invented new techniques to produce their artistic masterpieces. It is these ancient pottery vessels that have made the greatest contribution to our understanding of this great civilization.

These masters of sculpture used clay to bring to life animals, plants and anthropomorphic deities and demons. They recreated hunting and fishing scenes, combat rituals, elaborate ceremonies and sexual intercourse (sometimes with contraception). They depicted the power of their rulers as well as the plight of their sick and invalid.

The violence and death of war is a common theme in their work; prisoners of war are apparently brought before congregations where their throats are cut and their blood offered to those present. Decapitation and dismemberment are also shown.

Moche potters were amazingly skilled at reproducing facial features, specializing in the subtle nuances of individual personality. In addition to these three-dimensional sculptures, the Moche potter was skilled at decorating vessels with low-relief designs. Among the most popular scenes are skeletal death figures holding hands while dancing in long processions to the accompaniment of musicians. The potters also developed a technique of painting scenes on ceramic vessels. Over a period of several centuries the painters became increasingly skillful at depicting complex and lively scenes with multiple figures. Because of their complexity and detail, these scenes are of vital importance in reconstructing Moche life.

The early introduction of moulds and stamps brought efficiency to the production of Moche ceramics. By pressing moist clay into the halves of a mould, it was possible to produce an object much more rapidly than by hand. Similarly, the use of stamps facilitated the decoration of ceramic vessels with elaborate low-relief designs. Mould-making technology thus resulted in many duplications of individual pieces. Since there were almost no unique ceramic objects, elaborate ceramics became more widely available and less effective as a sign of power, wealth and social status of the élite.

Although among the most sophisticated potters in Spanish America, the Moche did not use ceramics for ordinary tableware. Neither do their ceramics show many everyday activities, such as farming, cooking and pottery making. This is because Moche art expresses the religious and supernatural aspects of their culture and nothing of everyday life is illustrated for its own sake. See also under History, on page 568.

Drawing of the decoration of a Moche pot, depicting a warrior holding a naked prisoner

North Coast

▶▶ The Chimú culture

Chimú was a despotic state which based its power on wars of conquest. Rigid social stratification existed and power rested in the hands of the great lords. These lords were followed in the social scale by a group of urban courtiers who enjoyed a certain amount of economic power. At the bottom were the peasants and prisoners for sacrifice. The Chimú economy was based on agriculture supplemented by fishing, hunting and craft production. They were renowned metalsmiths, who, like the Moche, alloyed and plated copper with gold and silver. The burial mounds of the Chimú nobles at Chan Chán were despoiled of all their gold and silver statuettes and ornaments by the Spaniards.

with her own transport, who speaks Spanish, German and understands Italian. She takes tourists on extended circuits of the region and is good for information (archaeological tour US$16 for 6 hrs, city tour US$7 per person, US$53 per car to El Brujo, with extension to Sipán, Brüning Museum and Túcume possible). Clara works with English chartered accountant *Michael White* (same address, microbewhite@yahoo.com, speaks German, French and Italian), who provides transport. He is very knowledgeable about tourist sites. They run tours any day of the week; 24-hr attention. They can also arrange tours to see and possibly ride *caballos de paso*.

Zaby Miranda Acosta, Camelias 315, Huanchaco, T461246, T601102 (mob), Zaby_miranda@hotmail.com Works at the tourist office, speaks German, Italian, US$10 per day. *Jannet Rojas Sánchez*, T401184, T380047 (mob), jannarojas@hotmail.com Speaks English, enthusiastic, works independently and for *Guía Tours*. *José Soto Ríos*, Atahualpa 514, dpto 3, T251489. He speaks English and French. Other experienced guides are *Oscar and Gustavo Prada Marga*, Miguel Grau 169, Villa del Mar, or at Chan Chán. *Pedro Puerta* T609603 (mob), works with *Guía Tours* and independently. *Celio Eduardo Roldán*, celioroldan@hotmail.com Helpful and informative taxi driver. The tourist police (see above) has a list of official guides; average cost is US$7 per hr.

Caballos de paso: *La Asociación de Criadores de Caballos de Paso Peruanos* has an enclosure with plots for each member's house anbd stables on the Vía de Evitamiento, just north of its junction with Av Larco. Owners may be prepared to show visitors around. *El Palmar*, stables, on the Vía de Evitamiento near *Hotel El Golf*, charges US$12 per person to see and maybe ride the horses at its stables. Book the day before at the office on Pizarro, next to the Municipalidad on the Plaza Mayor. For group visits to *Manucci* stables, just south of the Huaca del Sol, and *Vásquez Nacarino* at Paijan, contact Clara Bravo and Michael White.

Transport **Air** There are daily flights to and from **Lima** with *Aero Cóndor, Aero Continente, Lan Perú* and *Tans* to **Tarapoto** and **Iquitos**, 2 a week, with *Tans*. To **Cajamarca** daily with *Aero Cóndor* and **Tumbes** daily with *Aero Continente*. Taxi to airport costs US$4; or take a bus or colectivo to Huanchaco, get out at airport turn-off then walk 2 km (US$0.25).

Bus To and from **Lima**, 561 km on a good road, 8 hrs in the better class buses, average fare US$14.30-18.50 in luxury classes, 10 hrs in the cheaper buses, US$7.15-11.50. There are many bus companies doing this route, among those recommended are: *Ormeño*, Av Ejército 233, T259782, 3 levels of service, 5 daily; *Cruz del Sur*, Amazonas 437 near Av Ejército (see map), T261801; *Turismo Díaz*, Nicolás de Piérola 1079 on Panamericana Norte, T201237, leaves at 2230; *Línea*, Av América Sur 2857, T297000, ticket office at San Martín y Orbegoso, T245181, 3 levels of service, also to Chimbote and Chiclayo hourly, Huaraz 2100, 9 hrs, US$8.65, Cajamarca 4 a day, US$5.75-8.60, 0, and Chiclayo, US$2.85 (from Carrión by Av Mansiche, T235847, on the hr), and Piura,

2300, US$5.75. Also *Flores* (Av Ejército 346, T208250), *Ittsa* (Av Mansiche 145, T251415; No 431 for northern destinations, T 222541), *Móvil Tours* (Av América Sur 3959 – Ovalo Larco, T286538). *Trans Olano* (Oltursa), Av Ejército 342, T263055, offer a *bus cama* service to Lima, with full reclining seats, a/c, heating, meals and drinks, depart at 2200, with connection at Lima for Arequipa.

Small *Pakatnamú* buses leave when full, 0400-2100, from Av Mansiche 1092, T206564, to **Pacasmayo**, 102 km, 1¼ hrs, US$2. To **Chiclayo**, another 118 km, 3 hrs from Trujillo, US$2.85, several companies. Among the best are *Emtrafesa*, Av Túpac Amaru 285, T471521, on the ½-hr every hr; to **Piura**, 278 km beyond Chiclayo, 6 hrs, US$5.75; and **Tumbes**, a further 282 km, US$7.15, 8 hrs. Other companies include: *Transportes Dorado*, Av América Norte 2400, T291778, leave at 1245, 2220 to Piura and Sullana, US$4.30/5.75; and *Olano, Civa, Ormeño*, US$8.60; *Ormeño* also has US$14.35 (2215) and US$8.65 (1915) services to Tumbes. *Móvil*'s Lima-Chiclayo-Chachapoyas service passes through Trujillo at 0130.

Direct buses to **Huaraz**, 319 km, via Chimbote and Casma (169 km), with *Móvil* and *Línea* (see above), 8 hrs, US$8.60 special. Also *Chinchaysuyo*, Av Mansiche 391, at 2030; US$7.15, 10 hrs. There are several buses and colectivos to **Chimbote**, with *América Express* from Lloque 162, 135 km, 2 hrs, US$1.50, departures every 30 mins from 0530 (ticket sales from 0500); then change at Chimbote (see above - leave Trujillo before 0600 to make a connection from 0800). *Turismo Huaraz/Expreso Yungay* depart at 0830 for Huaraz via the Cañon del Pato on Sun, Tue, Thu, sometimes daily, US$7, 8 hrs. Ask Clara Bravo and Michael White (see Guides, page 390) about transport to Caraz avoiding Chimbote (a very worthwhile trip via the Brasileños road and Cañon del Pato).

To **Cajamarca**, 300 km, 7-8 hrs, US$5.75-8.60: with *Línea* (see above); *Emtrafesa*, see above, at 2230, and *Tur Díaz* 6 a day. To **Huamachuco**, 170 km, 8 hrs, *Trans Agreda*, La Unión 149, 0800, and *Trans Gran Turismo*, Prol Vallejo 1368, T425391, 0830.

To **Tarapoto**, via Moyobamba, *Turismo Tarapoto*, Av N de Piérola 1221, T221493, at 2230, US$14.30, also to Yurimaguas at 2330, US$20, and *Ejetur* Av N de Piérola 1238, T222228, at 0030, US$15.70, and to Jaén at 1600, US$7.15. To **Tayabamba** (see page 441) via Sihuas with *Trans Garrincha*, Prol Santa 1919, T214025, 1800 Sun and Wed, US$25, 18 hrs on a very rough road.

From the Santa Cruz terminal at Av Santa Cruz y Av América Sur, **microbuses**, **combis** and **colectivos** depart for **Puerto Malabrigo/Puerto Chicama**, **Cartavio**, **Casagrande**, **Paijan**, **Ascope**, **Chao** and **Virú**.

Airline offices *Aero Continente*, Pizarro 470, Plaza de Armas, T244042. *Aero Cóndor*, **Directory**
T255212. *Lan Perú*, Pizarro 340-42.

Banks *BCP*, Gamarra 562. No commission on cash into soles, but US$12 fee on TCs or changing into dollars, cash advance on Visa card, ATM (Visa). *Interbank*, Pizarro y Gamarra. Good rates for cash, no commission on Amex TCs into soles, reasonable rate, Visa cash advance, quick service, also has Mastercard ATM. Mon-Fri 0900-1815, Sat 0900-1230. *Banco Wiese Sudameris*, Pizarro 314, *Casa de Mayorazgo de Facalá*. Good rates for Amex TCs, 2% commission into soles or dollars, ATM for Visa/Plus. *BBV Continental*, Pizarro 620. Amex TCs and Visa card accepted, US$10 commission up to US$500. *Banco Santander Hispano*, Junín 479. Visa ATM. Note that banks close 1300-1615. There is little difference between the rates for cash dollars given by banks and street changers, *casas de cambio* and travel agencies. There are many *casas de cambio* and street changers on the plazoleta opposite the Casa de Condes de Aranda and all along the 600 block of Bolívar. *Western Union*, Almagro 579, España y Huayna Cápac, see also *Guía Tours*, above.

Communications Internet: there are internet offices all over the centre, mostly on Pizarro. Many others on Ayacucho, but most of these are slow or "stationary". Standard fee US$0.75 per hr, but can be as low as US$0.45 at night and weekends.

North Coast

Post office: Independencia 286 y Bolognesi. 0800-2000, Sun 0930-1300, stamps only on special request. *DHL*, Almagro 579. **Telephone**: *Telefónica*, headquarters at Almagro 744. Private call centre at Pizarro 561, others on 5th block of Bolívar for national and international phone calls and faxes and Av España 1530.

   Cultural centres *Alianza Francesa*, San Martín 858-62, T204504/231232. *Instituto de Cultura Peruano Norteamericano*, Av Venezuela 125, Urb El Recreo, T261944, F261922.

   Consulates *European Community*, Independencia 630, behind Caretur office. *UK*, Honorary Consul, Mr Winston Barber, Jesús de Nazareth 312, T235548, F245935, winstonbarber@terra.com.pe Mon-Fri 0900-1700.

   Laundry *American dry cleaners*, Bolognesi 782, US$1.45 wash only, ironing extra. 24-hr service. *Aquarelas*, Bolívar 355, laundry and dry cleaner. *Lavandería El Carmen* , Pizarro 759. *Lavanderías Unidas*, Pizarro 633. *Lavandería Japonesa* Grau 417. *Lavandería y Tintorería Luxor*, Grau 637. 0800-2000, cheap, charges per item, next day service, "a bit hectic but all clothes were found eventually". *La Moderna*, Orbegoso 270, US$1.75 per kg.

   Medical services Hospital: *Hospital Belén* Bolívar 3rd block. *Clínica Peruano Americana*, Av Mansiche 702, T231261. English spoken, good.

   Useful addresses **Immigration**: Av Larco 1220, Urb Los Pinos. Entrance is at the back of the building on Los Torcazos. Mon-Fri 0815-1230, 1500-1630. Gives 30-day visa extensions, US$20 (proof of funds and onward ticket required), plus US$0.80 for *formulario* in Banco de la Nación (fixers on the street will charge more).

Chan Chán

Colour map 3, grid A1
You need at least an hour to gain a full explanation of Chan Chán and Huaca La Luna; many tours only allow 20 mins each

Perhaps Trujillo's greatest attraction are the impressive ruins of Chan Chán. This crumbling imperial city of the Chimú is the largest adobe city in the world and lies about 5 km from the city. Heavy rain and flooding in 1925 and 1983 damaged much of the ruins and although they are still standing, eight palaces are closed to visitors. Thankfully, UNESCO donated US$100,000 and protection work ensured that the 1998 *El Niño* had little effect. Conservation work has uncovered more friezes since then.

Ins & outs   **Getting there** Buses and combis leave from Zela, on the corner of Los Incas, near the market (No 114A) inTrujillo, but it's safer to catch bus at north corner of Huayna Cápac y Avenida Los Incas or from the corner of España and Manuel Vera (114B); US$0.35, 20 minutes; US$0.25 to Chan Chán entrance. A taxi is US$5 from Trujillo, US$0.85 from museum to ruins, US$2.85 to Huanchaco from ruins.

Admission A ticket which covers the entrance fees for Chan Chán, the site museum, as well as Huaca El Dragón and Huaca La Esmeralda (for 2 days) costs US$2.85 (half price for students with an official ISIC card – tickets can be bought at any of the sites, except Esmeralda). A guide at the site costs US$5.80 per hour. The price is the same for a small group. Sometimes a singer waits in the Plaza Principal of the Ciudadela to show the perfect acoustics of the square (she expects a tip). A map and leaflet in English is on sale for US$0.75.

Safety It is relatively safe to walk on the dirt track from turn-off to the site (20 minutes) but preferably go in a group. If alone, contact the Tourist Police in Trujillo to arrange for a policeman to accompany you. **Warning** On no account walk the 4 km to, or on Buenos Aires beach near Chan Chán as there is serious danger of robbery, and of being attacked by dogs.

The ruins consist of nine great compounds built by Chimú kings. The 9-m **The site**
high perimeter walls surrounded sacred enclosures with usually only one narrow entrance. Inside, rows of storerooms contained the agricultural wealth of
the kingdom, which stretched 1,000 km along the coast from near Guayaquil,
in Ecuador, to beyond Paramonga.

Most of the compounds contain a huge walk-in well which tapped the
ground water, raised to a high level by irrigation higher up the valley. Each
compound also included a platform mound which was the burial place of the
king, with his women and his treasure, presumably maintained as a memorial.
The Incas almost certainly copied this system and transported it to Cusco
where the last Incas continued building huge enclosures. The Chimú surren-
dered to the Incas around 1471 after 11 years of siege and threats to cut the
irrigation canals.

The dilapidated city walls enclose an area of 28 sq km containing the
remains of palaces, temples, workshops, streets, houses, gardens and a canal.
Canals up to 74 km long kept the city supplied with water. What is left of the
adobe walls bears well-preserved moulded decorations showing small figures
of fish, birds and various geometric motifs. Painted designs have been found
on pottery unearthed from the debris of a city ravaged by floods, earthquakes,
and *huaqueros*.

The **Ciudadela of Tschudi** has been restored. It is a 15-minute walk from
the main road. It is open 0900 to 1630 (but it may be covered up if rain is
expected); arrive well before 1600 as you will not be allowed in much after
that. Besides, you need more than 30 minutes to see the site. The **site museum**
on the main road, 100 m before the turn-off, has a son-et-lumière display of
the growth of Chan Chán as well as objects found in the area. It also has a good
table showing Peruvian archaeology in the context of world history.

Other archaeological sites near Trujillo

The partly restored temple, **Huaca El Dragón**, dating from Huari to Chimú
times (1000-1470 AD), is also known as **Huaca Arco Iris** (rainbow), after the
shape of friezes which decorate it. It is on the west side of the Pan-American
Highway in the district of La Esperanza. ■ *0900-1630. Take a combi from Av
España y Manuel Vera marked 'Arco Iris/La Esperanza'; a taxi costs US$2.*

Around Trujillo

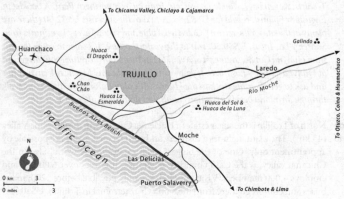

North Coast

The poorly preserved **Huaca La Esmeralda** is at Mansiche, between Trujillo and Chan Chán, behind the church (not a safe area). Buses to Chan Chán and Huanchaco pass the church at Mansiche.

Huacas del Sol & de la Luna   A few kilometres south of Trujillo are the huge Moche pyramids, the Huaca del Sol and Huaca de la Luna. The Huaca del Sol was once, before the Spanish diverted the nearby river and washed half of it away in a search for treasure, the largest man-made structure in the western hemisphere, reaching a height of 45 m. Built from 100 million adobe bricks, it was the political centre of the site. The ceremonial platforms have been further eroded by the weather and visitors, but climbing on them is prohibited. Today, about two-thirds of the pyramid have been lost.

The Huaca de la Luna, 500 m away, was a 'religious pyramid'. It received relatively little attention compared to its larger neighbour until more than 6,000 sq m of remarkable mural paintings and reliefs were uncovered throughout 1990s. In fact, this is the only site where the fascinating brightly coloured moulded decorations found on the interior walls of huacas can be easily viewed. The yellow, white, red and black paint has faded little over the centuries and many metres of the intricate geometric patterns and fearsome feline deities depicted are virtually complete. It has now been established that the pyramid once consisted of six levels, each pertaining to a different ruler-priest. When each priest died he was buried within the huaca and a new level was built covering up entirely the previous level. The number of levels suggests that there were six ruler-priests over a period of approximately 200 years. It is now possible to view impressive brightly coloured moulded friezes of the upper 4 levels on the northern exterior wall of the huaca. The highest mural is a 'serpent' which runs the length of the wall, beneath it there are repeated motifs of 'felines' holding decapitated heads of warriors, then repeated motifs of 'fishermen' holding fish against a bright blue background and, finally, huge 'spider/crab' motifs, discovered in mid-2002. Archaeologists hope to uncover the final two levels in 2004. Combined with intricate, brightly painted two-dimensional motifs in the sacrificial area atop the huaca, Huaca de la Luna is now a truly significant site well worth visiting.

Between the two huacas lie the remains of a once sizeable settlement, now mainly lost beneath the sands, though some excavations are taking place.

■ *0830-1600. US$3, with a professional guide, some of whom speak European languages (students half price, children US$0.30). The visitors' centre has good toilets and café and an artesanía shop selling attractive, high quality ceramics, T-shirts, woven bags, wooden boxes, etc, from all over northern Peru. A booklet in English or Spanish is sold for US$2.85. A taxi to the site costs US$2.50 (there are plenty at the site for the return). Colectivos (blue and yellow) every 15 minutes from Suárez y Los Incas, US$0.30, run to the visitors' centre. It's safer to catch the bus from Huayna Cápac, southeast of Avenida Los Incas. On the return you can get out at Huayna Cápac y Los Incas. If you want a walk take any Moche colectivo or bus and ask to get off at the track to the Huacas. It's about an hour's interesting walk through farmland beside irrigation canals, but don't walk after dusk.*

Hacienda Cartavio   North of Trujillo is the sugar estate of Hacienda Cartavio, in the Chicama Valley (43 km). The plant includes a distillery and rum factory. Visits are possible by appointment only. One of the biggest sugar estates in the world, also in the Chicama valley, is the Casa Grande cooperative. It covers over 6,000 ha and employs 4,000 members. Visits (guided) are only possible before 1200; many buses and combis go there from the Santa Cruz terminal in Trujillo, US$0.75.

Sixty kilometres north of Trujillo, is considered one of the most important **El Brujo**
archaeological sites on the entire north coast. The complex, covering 2 sq km,
consists of Huacas Prieta, Cortada and Cao Viejo. This complex is collectively
known as El Brujo and was a ceremonial centre for perhaps 10 cultures,
including the Moche.

Huaca Cortada (or El Brujo) has a wall decorated with high-relief, stylized
figures. Huaca Prieta is, in effect, a giant rubbish tip dating back 5,000 years,
which once housed the very first settlers to this area. Huaca Cao Viejo has
extensive friezes, polychrome reliefs up to 90 m long, 4 m high and on five different levels, representing warriors, prisoners, sacrificer gods, combat and
more complex scenes, with a total of seven colours in reliefs. In front of Cao
Viejo are the remains of one of the oldest Spanish churches in the region. It
was common practice for the Spaniards to build their churches near these
ancient sites in order to counteract their religious importance.

The excavations at the site will last many years, but part is already open to the
public (entry US$1.85). On view, but extensively sheltered by awnings to pre-
vent further fading of the colours, is the sacrificer god, warriors and prisoners
and what may be a line of priests. Photography is allowed. As the nearest public
transport stops 5 km away at Magdalena de Cao and individuals especially, but
also tour groups, may not be allowed in without specific permission, it is best to
go with a local tour guide. A guide may be able to arrange with the site guardian
to view recent excavations, but it depends on the time of day and what work is in
progress. Tip the guardian if this opportunity arises; it will not be offered to lone
visitors. Permission should be sought from The Wiese Foundation, The
Regional Institute of Culture, *INC* (Trujillo), or the University of Trujillo. The
Director of Excavations may also deny access on windy days. The exhibition
formerly at *Banco Wiese*, Trujillo, has been moved to the Chan Chán site
museum but (2002) is not yet on display. There are other exhibitions at *Banco
Wiese* and *Museo de la Nación* in Lima, or visit a number of websites, including
www.unitru.edu.pe/arq/index.html and www.research.ibm.com/peru/brujo.
htm Road access is tricky, there are no public transport services to it and there
are no tourist facilities other than the ticket office.

■ *The complex can be reached by taking one of the regular buses from Trujillo
to Chocope and then a colectivo (every 30 minutes) to Magdalena de Cao from
where it is a 5 km walk to the site. You may be able to hitch, or persuade a passing
combi to take you. The roads are a mixture of paved and unpaved and there are
no signposts at all.*

Huanchaco

A cheaper alternative to staying in Trujillo is the fishing and surfing village of   *Phone code: 044*
Huanchaco, which is full of hotels, guest houses and restaurants. It has great   *Colour map 3, grid A1*
beaches to the south; to the north are marshes good for birdwatching. The vil-
lage is famous for its narrow pointed fishing rafts, known as **caballitos** (little   *The strength of the
sun is deceptive.*
horses), made of totora reeds and depicted on Salinar, Gallinazo, Virú, Moche,   *A cool breeze off the
sea reduces the*
Lambayeque and Chimú pottery. These are still a familiar sight in places along   *temperature, but
you can still be*
the northern Peruvian coast. Unlike those used on Lake Titicaca, they are flat,   *badly sunburned*
not hollow, and ride the breakers rather like surfboards. You can see the reeds
growing in sunken pits at the north end of the beach. ■ *Fishermen offer trips on
their caballitos for US$1.50, be prepared to get wet; groups should contact Luis*   *For information, see
www.huanchaco.net*
*Gordillo, El Mambo, T461092. Fishermen will give demonstrations for US$2.85;
groups should give more. You can see fishermen returning to shore in their reed rafts
about 0800 and 1600 when they stack the boats upright to dry in the fierce sun.*

North Coast

The village, now developed with the beach houses, is overlooked by a huge **church**, one of the oldest in Peru, from the belfry of which are extensive views. ■ *Entry to the pier, which also gives good views, costs US$0.15; the Municipalidad has an expensive cafetería on the pier.*

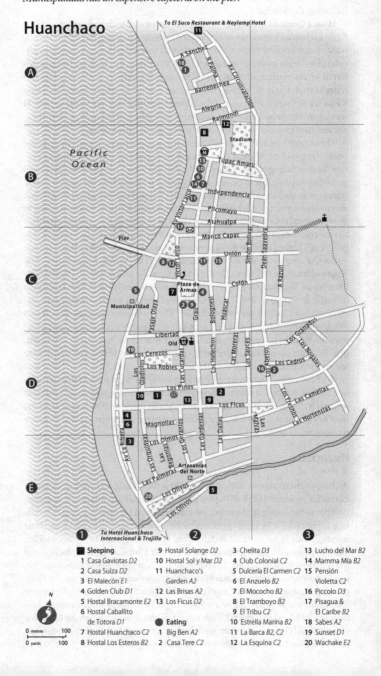

Huanchaco

North Coast

0 metres   100
0 yards   100

Sleeping		9 Hostal Solange *D2*	3 Chelita *D3*	13 Lucho del Mar *B2*
1 Casa Gaviotas *D2*	10 Hostal Sol y Mar *D2*	4 Club Colonial *C2*	14 Mamma Mía *B2*
2 Casa Suiza *D2*	11 Huanchaco's	5 Dulcería El Carmen *C2*	15 Pensión
3 El Malecón *E1*	Garden *A2*	6 El Anzuelo *B2*	Violetta *C2*
4 Golden Club *D1*	12 Las Brisas *A2*	7 El Mococho *B2*	16 Piccolo *D3*
5 Hostal Bracamonte *E2*	13 Los Ficus *D2*	8 El Tramboyo *B2*	17 Pisagua &
6 Hostal Caballito		9 El Tribu *C2*	El Caribe *B2*
de Totora *D1*	● Eating	10 Estrella Marina *B2*	18 Sabes *A2*
7 Hostal Huanchaco *C2*	1 Big Ben *A2*	11 La Barca *B2, C2*	19 Sunset *D1*
8 Hostal Los Esteros *B2*	2 Casa Tere *C2*	12 La Esquina *C2*	20 Wachake *E2*

C *Caballito de Totora*, Av La Rivera 219, T/F651828, totora@terra.com.pe Includes taxes, **D** in low season, surfers' room **F**, pool, friendly, English spoken, nice garden, clean, restaurant with good food and coffee, parking, good value. Recommended. Owners Elvira and Walter are very friendly and knowledgeable. **C** *Hostal Bracamonte*, Los Olivos 503, T461162, F461266, hostalbracamonte@yahoo.com Comfortable, good, chalets with private bathroom **B**, you can camp on the grass (US$4.30), pool, secure, good restaurant, English spoken. Highly recommended. **C** *Hostal Huanchaco*, Larco 287 on the plaza, T461272, F461688, huanchaco_hostal@terra.com.pe With bath and breakfast, TV, hot water, clean and friendly, pool, car park, expensive cafeteria with home-made cakes and other good meals, video, pool table, back door is ½ block from beach. Recommended. **C** *Huanchaco Internacional*, Autopista a Huanchaco Km 13.5 (Playa Azul), T461754, F461753, huancacoint@pmail.net Some distance from town, **B** in bungalows, also has bunk rooms, breakfast included, comfortable, clean, hot water, TV, internet, pool (open to non-residents in summer), airport pick-up, restaurant. **C-D** *El Malecón*, Av La Rivera 320, T461275, overlooking the sea. Some rooms with terrace, clean.

D *Hostal Sol y Mar*, Los Pinos 570, T461120, F206647. With pool, restaurant, friendly owner, garden. Recommended. **D** *Hostal Los Esteros*, Av Larco 618, T461300, los esteros@trujillobusiness.com. With bathroom, hot water, cable TV, restaurant, friendly, safe car and motorcycle parking, can arrange surfing and caballitos de totora trips. **D** *Las Brisas*, Raymondi 146, T461186, F461688, lasbrisas@hotmail.com 20 rooms with bathroom, hot water, cafeteria, cable TV, comfortable. **E** *Naylamp*, Prolongación Víctor Larco 3, at the northern end of the seafront in El Boquerón, T461022, naylamp@terra. com.pe Rooms set around a courtyard, also dormitories **F** per person, hammocks, nice garden, kitchen, very clean, with bath, hot water 24 hrs, camping US$1.45 with own tent, US$2.30 to hire tent, laundry facilities, safe, good views of the sunset from the campsite and terrace restaurant, Italian food, good breakfasts. Recommended.

F *Casa Hospedaje Los Ficus*, Los Ficus 516, T461719, www.huanchaco.net/ losficus Cheaper with shared bath. Family run, hot water, use of kitchen, breakfast, laundry. Recommended. **F** per person *Golden Club*, Av La Rivera 217, T461306. 8 rooms, gym, pool, restaurant, use of kitchen, popular with surfers, very laid back atmosphere, excellent value, rooms on 1st floor cheaper. Recommended. **F** per person *Huanchaco's Garden*, Av Circunvalación Mz U, Lote 3, El Boquerón, T461980, huanchacosgarden@huanchaco.zzn.com Family-run, bungalows, hot water, use of kitchen, friendly and helpful, garden with small pool, parking, laundry. Frequently recommended. **F** *Hostal Solange*, Los Ficus 484, 1 block from the beach, T461410, hsolange@yahoo.es With bathroom, hot water, good food, laundry facilities, limited use of kitchen. Highly recommended. **G** per person *La Casa Suiza*, Los Pinos 451, T461285, www.huanchaco. net/casasuiza 3 blocks from the beach, run by Heidi and Oscar Stacher, speak German and English, cheaper with shared bathroom, 4 rooms with bath, others share bathroom, hot water, nice roof balcony, excellent breakfast for US$1.50, friendly, family home (no drugs), surf boards to rent, book exchange, internet access. Highly recommended.

Accommodation with families: **F** per person *Casa Gaviotas*, Los Pinos 535, T461858, small, comfortable, snacks, restaurant and cocktails, run by a responsible and honest old couple. **G** per person *Sra Mabel Díaz de Aguilar*, Túpac Amaru 248, T461232, mabel_minerva@hotmail.com near the football ground. Shared bath, hot water, Sra Mabel speaks English, very friendly. Also *Hospedaje Okey*, Sra Fanny Valente, Atahualpa 147. 4 rooms with bath, 6 without, hot water all day. The very friendly *Señora Nelly Neyra de Facundo* offers accommodation at Las Palmeras 425, and is recommended.

Sleeping
■ *on map*
Price codes:
see inside front cover
Many other
hotels in town

North Coast

Eating

● *on map*
*There are about
30 restaurants on
the beachfront
Many close in the
low season*

El Anzuelo, next to *Estrella Marina*. Good *ceviche*, offers 'taster' dishes at lower prices. *La Barca*, Unión 320 (and two other branches). Very good seafood, well-run, popular. *Big Ben*, Víctor Larco 836, near A Sánchez, T461869. Seafood and international menu, most expensive but very good. *Club Colonial*, Grau 272 on the plaza. Reputedly the best restaurant, though expensive, serving fish, chicken or meat, has atmosphere of a traditional colonial dining club, but with private zoo. *El Tramboyo*, on the little plaza opposite the pier, is good, helpful and friendly. Next door is *La Esquina*, Unión 299, T461081, recommended (also has accommodation **G** per person). *Lucho del Mar*, serves excellent sea food. Next door is *Estrella Marina*, which is great value. Good fish also at *Pisagua*, just past the pier, and *El Caribe*, just around the corner at Atahualpa 291. *Mamma Mia*, on the seafront. Good value Italian food and delicious home-made ice-cream, English spoken by owner Fernando, good lodging (**F** per person, shared showers) available next door, rents surfboards. *El Mococho*, Bolognesi 535. Said to be one of the best seafood restaurants, expensive, caters for groups. *El Tribu*, Pasaje M Seoane 140, Plaza de Armas. Atmospheric bar in an old house, live musice on Fri, opens 1900 *Sabes?*, V Larco 920, T461555, ysabes@yahoo.com Pub with food, internet café, popular, American run (closed till early 2003). *Wachake*, southern end of seafront road. Owned by Edgar who lived in the US for many years, speaks English, good food, also has good value sleeping space for backpackers.

Cheap *Casa Tere*, Víctor Larco 280, Plaza de Armas. For best pizzas in town, also pastas, burgers and breakfasts. *Chelita*, Los Abetos 198. Good value *menú* with choices, fish dishes are best, very popular. *Dulcería El Carmen*, Av La Rivera 269. Open 0800-2100 for breakfasts and sandwiches. *Piccolo*, Los Abetos 142, 5 blocks from the plaza. Cheap, friendly, live folk music weekend evenings, excellent, also has a surf and art shop. Good seafood, including *ceviche*, at *El Suco*, at the north end of the beach, cheaper than those in the centre. *Sunset*, Av La Rivera 600. Also has *hospedaje*, good food, popular with young crowd. *Violetta*, a private house on Unión – 4 blocks directly inland from the pier. Good meals provided for US$1.

Festivals

In the first week of **May** is the *Festival del Mar*, a celebration of the disembarkation of Taycanamo, the leader of the Chimú period. A procession is made in Totora boats. **30 Jun**, *San Pedro*, patron saint of fishermen: his statue is taken out to sea on a huge totora-reed boat. Also the annual *Olímpiadas Playeral* and *El Festival Internacional de la Primavera* (see Trujillo). There are also surf competitions. *Carnival* and *New Year* are also popular celebrations.

Shopping

A small market selling a wide range of artesanía is on the seafront beside the pier. *Artesanías del Norte*, Los Olivos 504, T461220, marycortijo@usa.net Sells mostly items of her own design, using prehispanic methods and motifs,primarily ceramics, but also cotton and alpaca goods and hand-painted products in wood. Food in the shops is a bit more expensive than Trujillo. There is a small fresh food market on Pilcomayo, ½ block from Deán Saavedra.

Sports

Surfing *Un Lugar*, Pilcomayo next to the market, T921371. Ask for English-speaking Juan Carlos. *Surf School*, Los Ficus 545, T461327. Instruction, rent wet suits and boards.

Transport

Combis between Trujillo and Huanchaco are routes A, B and Crun 0500-2100 every 5-10 mins. A and B do an anti-clockwise circuit of Huanchaco and enter Trujillo by the roundabout on Av Mansiche, 3 blocks northwest of Av España in front of the Cassinelli museum, then A goes round the west side of Trujillo onto Av 28 de Julio, while B goes round the east side on Av Manuel Vera, España as far as Bolívar. At night they go only to España y Grau. Fare is US$0.30 for the 20-min journey. Slower 'micros', B and H, follow similar routes to América; leaving Trujillo B goes north of the centre on España, H goes south (convenient stops are shown on the Trujillo map), in daylight only. There are also colectivo cars and taxis, minimum fare US$2, more likely US$4-5.

Communications Internet: *Beach Internet*, Jr Los Pinos 533, T673016. US$0.70-0.85 per hr. 1100 (more likely 1300)-1800. *JEC Café Internet*, Pasaje M Seoane 235 ,Plaza de Armas. 1400-2400, US$0.70 per hr. **Post office**: at Manco Cápac 306. 1300-1800.

Directory

North of Trujillo

Seventy kilometres north of Trujillo this is a real surfers' hang-out, as it's the best surf beach in Peru, claiming that it has the longest left-hand point-break in the world. There are several basic places to stay and eat. Combis and colectivos go there from the Santa Cruz terminal in Trujillo.

Puerto Malabrigo (Chicama)

Pacasmayo, port for the next oasis north, is 102 km north of Trujillo, and is the main road connection from the coast to Cajamarca. The paved 180 km road to Cajamarca branches off the Pan-American Highway soon after it crosses the Río Jequetepeque. There are four *hostales*, including *Pacatnamú* on the seafront. ■ *Bus Pacasmayo-Cajamarca US$4.30, 5 hrs; to Chiclayo US$1.70, 2 hrs).*

Pacasmayo
Population: 12,300

A few kilometres northwest on the other side of Río Jequetepeque are the ruins of Pacatnamú, comparable in size to Chan Chán. It consists of pyramids, cemetery and living quarters of nobles and fishermen, possibly built in the Chavín period. There is evidence also of Moche and Chimú occupation. No explanations at the site. ■ *To get there, take a taxi bus to Guadalupe, 10 km from the ruins, and a taxi is possible from there for US$20. Micros run in summer.*

Pacatnamú & Farfán

   Where the Pan-American Highway crosses the Jequetepeque are the well-signed ruins of Farfán, separate from those of Pacatnamú, but probably of the same period.

Sleeping and eating **F** *Panamericano*, Leoncio Prado 18, T522521. With private cold shower, small, basic, friendly, safe, reasonable restaurant downstairs. **F** *San Francisco*, at No 21,opposite the *Panamericano*, T522021. Basic, cleaner, OK. There are other places to stay, from 3-star down, and several cheap restaurants on the main street.

North Coast

Chiclayo

Chiclayo, founded in the 1560s as a rural Indian village by Spanish priests, has long since outgrown other towns of the Lambayeque Department. Sandwiched between the Pacific Ocean and the Andes, Lambayeque is one of Peru's principal agricultural regions, and its chief producer of rice and sugar cane. It is also the outlet for produce from the northern jungle, which comes by road over the comparatively low Porculla Pass. Chiclayo is the major commercial hub of the zone, but also boasts distinctive cuisine and musical tradition (Marinera, Tondero and Afro-indian rhythms), a famous witch doctors' market and an unparalleled archaeological and ethnographic heritage (see Archaeological sites). Chiclayo is dubbed 'The Capital of Friendship', and while that tag could equally apply to most of the north coast of Peru, there is an earthiness and vivacity about its citizens that definitely sets it apart.

Phone code: 074
Colour map 1, grid C2
Population: 411,536

Ins and outs

Getting there José Abelardo Quiñones González airport is 1 km from the town centre; taxi from centre costs US$1. There is no *terminal terrestre*; most buses stop outside their offices on Bolognesi, which is south of the centre. Confusingly many of the buses leaving for the surrounding area are to the north of the centre. It is difficult to find decent cheap accommodation in Chiclayo. Also note that hotels in Chiclayo are often full.

Getting around Calle Balta is the main street but the markets and most of the hotels and restaurants are spread out over about 5 or 6 blocks from the Plaza de Armas. Mototaxis are a cheap way to get around. They cost US$0.50 anywhere in city, but are not allowed in the very centre.

Chiclayo

12 Lido *B2*	8 Kaprichos *A3*	5 Colectivos to Monsefú *A3*
13 Mochicas *C2*	9 La Panadería *B2*	6 Colectivos to Puerto Etén *A3*
14 Paracas *A3*	10 La Parra *C3*	7 Combis to Pimentel *A2, B1*
15 Paraíso *A3*	11 La Plazuela *B2*	8 Cruz de Chalpón & Paredes Estrella *C3*
16 Royal *B3*	12 Las Américas *B3*	9 Cruz del Sur *C3*
17 Sicán *C2*	13 Mi Tía *B2*	10 Emtrafesa *C3*
18 Sol Radiante *C2*	14 Pollo Campero *B2*	11 Flores/Cial *C3*
19 Tumi de Oro *B3*	15 Roma *C3*	12 Línea *C2*
	16 Romana *C3*	13 Olano Oltursa *B1*
■ Sleeping		14 Tepsa *C2*
1 América *B2*	**● Eating**	15 Transportes Chiclayo *B1*
2 Aristi *C1*	1 Boulevar *B2*	
3 El Sol *B1*	2 Brasa Roja *B3*	
4 Europa *B2*	3 Café Astoria *C2*	
5 Garza *C3*	4 D'Onofrio *C3*	
6 Gran Chiclayo *B1*	5 El Rancho *B3*	
7 Hostal Adriático *B3*	6 Govinda *B3*	
8 Hostal San José *A2*	7 Hebron *C3*	
9 Hostal Santa Rosa *B2*		
10 Inca *B2*	**🚍 Transport**	
11 Kalu *A3*	1 Brüning Express to Lambayeque *B1*	
	2 Buses to Chonoyape *B3*	
	3 Civa *C3*	
	4 Colectivos to Lambayeque *A2*	

Centro de Información Turística, CIT, Sáenz Peña 838, T238112. *Indecopi*, Av Balta 506, **Tourist offices**
T209021, F238081, ctejada@indecopi.gob.pe Mon-Fri 0800-1300, 1630-1930, for
complaints and tourist protection. The tourist police, Av Sáenz Peña 830, T236700 ext
311, 24 hrs a day, are very helpful and may store luggage and take you to the sites
themselves. There are tourist kiosks on the Plaza and outside *El Rancho* restaurant on
Balta. For local news and occasional tourist information on specific places in Spanish,
www.laindustria.com (website of the local newspaper). Another site to try is
http://bcm.notrix.net/lambayeque

Sights

On the Plaza de Armas is the 19th-century neoclassical **cathedral**, designed
by the English architect Andrew Townsend, whose descendants can still be
identified among the town's principals. The **Palacio Municipal** is at the junction of Avenida Balta, the main street and the Plaza. The private **Club de la
Unión** is on the Plaza at the corner of Calle San José.

Where Avenida Balta meets Bolognesi, a Paseo de Las Musas has been
built, with pleasant gardens, statues of the Greek Muses and imitation Greek
columns. A similar Paseo de Los Héroes is being built at the opposite end of
town. Another newish plaza is Parque Leonardo Ortiz, with a statue of
Ñaymlap, buildings in the Lambayeque style and fountains.

Essentials

AL *Gran Hotel Chiclayo*, Villareal 115, T234911, F223961, granhotel1@terra.com.pe   **Sleeping**
Refurbished to a high standard, price includes taxes and breakfast, pool, jacuzzi, enter-   ■ *on map*
tainments, restaurant, safe car park, changes dollars, casino. Recommended.   *Price codes:*
AL-A *Garza*, Bolognesi 756, T228172, F228171, garzahot@chiclayo.net Excellent bar   *see inside front cover*
and restaurant, a/c, pool, car park, tourist office in lobby provides maps, information in
English, vehicle hire. Highly recommended, but it is close to the bus stations so there is
activity at all hours.

B-C *Inca*, Av L González 622, T235931, F227651, incahotel@cpi.udep.edu.pe With
TV and a/c, restaurant, garage, comfortable and helpful. **C** *América*, Av L González
943, T229305, F270664, americahotel@latinmail.com Comfortable, friendly, restaurant, good value (except for the expensive breakfast and the laundry). Recommended. **C** *Aristi*, Francisco Cabrera 102, T228673. With TV, fan, parking costs US$1
per day extra, clean, comfortable, reasonable value. **C** *Hostal Santa Victoria*, La
Florida 586, Urb Santa Victoria, T225074. Hot water, restaurant, free parking, cash
dollars exchanged, quiet, 15-20 mins' walk from the centre. **C- C-D** *El Sol*, Elías
Aguirre 119, T232120, F231070, hotelvicus@hotmail.com Price includes taxes, with
bathroom, hot water, restaurant, pool, TV lounge, clean, free parking, good value.
There are 3 hotels in a row, near the Mercado Modelo: **D** *Kalu*, Pedro Ruíz 1038,
T/F229293, HOTELKALU@terra.com.pe Comfortable, with bath and TV, laundry, safe,
good. **D** *Paracas*, Pedro Ruíz 1046, T221611. With bathroom, TV, good value. Recommended. **D** *Paraíso*, Pedro Ruíz 1064, T/F222070, hotelparaiso@ terra.com.pe Also
comfortable and well-appointed, but can be noisy. Recommended. **D** *Europa*, Elías
Aguirre 466, T237919, F222066. With bath (**F** without, single rooms can be small),
hot water, restaurant, good value. **D** *Mochicas*, Torres Paz 429, T237217,
mochcas1@hotmail.com Fan, TV, helpful, good service. **D** *Santa Rosa*, L González
927, T224411, F236242. With bathroom, clean, laundry service, international phone
service, good breakfast downstairs in snack bar. Recommended. **D** *Hostal Sicán*,
Izaga 356, T237618. With bath, TV, clean, comfortable, welcoming. Recommended.

North Coast

E *Lido*, Elías Aguirre 412A, T237642. With bathroom, fairly clean, safe, rooms near reception are noisy. **E** *Sol Radiante*, Izaga 392, T237858, robertoiza@mixmail.com With bath and TV, cold water, comfortable, pleasant, but noisy at the front.

F *Royal*, San José 787, on the Plaza, T233421. With bathroom, a big, rambling old building, a bit seedy and rundown, the rooms on the street have a balcony but are noisy. **F-G** *Hostal San José*, on Juan Cuglievan 1370, 1 block from the Mercado Modelo, T273394. Basic, clean, acceptable, cold water. There are many other cheap hotels near the Mercado Modelo, especially on Arica.

There are several cheap hotels on Av Balta, near the bus offices, which range from basic to hygienically-challenged. Most have only cold water: **F-G** per person *Adriático*, Av Balta 1009. The best of a bad bunch, fairly clean but basic, cold water.

Eating:
● on map

Expensive *Fiesta*, Av Salaverry 1820 in 3 de Octubre suburb, T201970. Local specialities, first class. *El Huaralino*, La Libertad 155, Santa Victoria, wide variety, international and creole.

Mid-range *Las Américas*, Aguirre 824. Open 0700-0200, good service. Recommended. For more upmarket than average chicken, but also local food and *parrilla*, are *Hebrón*, Balta 605, and *El Rancho*, Balta 1115 at Lora y Cordero. *Bar/Restaurante Roma*, Izaga 706. Wide choice. *Romana*, Balta 512,T223598. First-class food, usually good breakfast, popular with locals. *Kaprichos*, Pedro Ruíz 1059, T232721. Chinese, delicious, huge portions. *La Parra*, Izaga 752, Chinese and creole, *parrillada*, very good, large portions.

Cheap *Café Astoria*, Bolognesi 627, breakfast, good value *menú*. *Boulevar* Colón entre Izaga y Aguirre. Good, friendly, *menú* and à la carte. *La Plazuela*, San José 299, Plaza Elías Aguirre. Good food, seats outside. *Mi Tía*, Aguirre 650, just off the plaza. Huge portions, great value *menú*, very popular at lunchtime. Recommended. There are many cheap *pollerías* everywhere: two good ones in the centre are *Pollo Campero* and *La Brasa Roja* on Vicente de la Vega 800 block, the latter is very popular. *Govinda*, Balta 1029. Good vegetarian, open daily 0800-2000. *La Panadería*, Lapoint 847. Good choice of breads, including *integral*, also snacks and soft drinks. *Snack Bar 775*, Ugarte 775. Good breakfast, US$0.85. For great ice cream try *D'Onofrio*, Balta y Torres Paz, and *Greycy*, Elias Aguirre y Lapoint.

Local food & drink

Local specialities include *Ceviche* and *chingurito* (a *ceviche* of strips of dried guitar fish, which is chewy but good). For delicious and cheap ceviche, go to the *Nativo* stall in the Mercado Central, a local favourite. *Cabrito* is a spiced stew of kid goat. *Arroz con pato* is a paella-like duck casserole. *Humitas* are *tamale*-like fritters of green corn. *King Kong* is a baked pastry layered with candied fruit and milk caramel, appealing to those with a very sweet tooth (of whom there would appear to be a great many as there are countless shops selling the stuff). *Chicha* is the fermented maize drink with delicious fruit variations.

Festivals

This is an area rich in traditional customs and beliefs. Among the many festivals held in and around the city is *Reyes Magos* in Mórrope, Illimo and other towns on **6 Jan**. This is a recreation of a medieval pageant in which pre-Columbian deities become the Wise Men. On **4 Feb** are the *Túcume devil dances*. On **14 Mar** in Monsefú is *Festividad Señor Cautivo*. During **Holy Week** are traditional Easter celebrations and processions in many villages. *Fiesta de la Cruz* is held in Pimentel from **1 May**, and in the last week of **Jun** is *Festividad de San Pedro* in Morrope. In the first week of **Jun** is the Divine Child of the Miracle, in Villa de Etén. Also in Monsefú, on **27-31 Jul**, is *Fexticum*, with traditional foods, drink, handicrafts, music and dance. On **5 Aug** is the pilgrimage from the mountain shrine of Chalpón to Motupe, 90 km north of Chiclayo. The cross is brought down from a cave and carried in procession through the village. On **24 Sep** is *Virgen de las Mercedes* in Incahuasi, 12 hrs by truck east of Chiclayo. Indians still sing in the ancient Mochica language in this post-harvest festival. At **Christmas** and **New Year**, processions and children dancers (*pastorcitos* and *seranitas*) can be seen in many villages, eg Ferreñafe, Mochumi, Mórrope.

Shopping

Five blocks north of the main plaza on Balta is the *Mercado Modelo*, one of northern Peru's liveliest and largest daily markets. Don't miss the colourful fruits, handicrafts stalls (see *Monsefú*) and the well-organized section of ritual paraphernalia used by traditional curers and diviners (*curanderos*), which is just off Calle Arica on the south side.

James Vreeland, a North American anthropologist, considers the Chiclayo *mercado de brujos* (witch doctors' market) to be one of the most comprehensive in South America, filled with herbal medicines, folk charms, curing potions, and exotic objects used by *curanderos* and *brujos* to cure all manner of real and imagined illnesses. The stallholders are generally very friendly and will explain the uses of such items as monkey claws, dried foetuses and dragon's blood! *Casa La Cabalonga*, stand 43, near the corner of Arica and Héroes Cíviles, has been recommended as particularly helpful and informative. **NB** As in all markets, take good care of your belongings.

Paseo de Artesanías, 18 de Abril at the end of Colón, stalls sell woodwork, basketwork and other handicrafts in a quiet, peaceful, custom-built open-air arcade. *Supermercado El Centro* at Aguirre y González has good stock, good value. There is a Mercado Central in the city centre, smaller than the Mercado Modelo.

Photography *J&M Color*, Av Balta 801, T224096. Repairs all kinds of photographic and electrical equipment.

Tour operators

The Brüning Museum, Sipán and Túcume can easily be done by public transport. Expect to pay US$18-25 per person for a 3-hr tour to Sipán, and US$25-35 per person for Túcume and the *Brüning Museum* (5 hrs). Batán Grande is US$45-55 per person for a full-day tour including Ferreñafe and Pomac. To Zaña and the coastal towns is US$35-55 per person. These prices are based on 2 people; there are discounts for larger groups. *Indiana Tours*, Colón 556, T222991, F225751, indianatours@terra.com.pe Daily tours to Sipán (US$15), Thor Heyerdahl's *Kon Tiki museum*, archaeological excavations in Túcume, *Brüning Museum* in Lambayeque, Batán Grande and a variety of other daily and extended excursions with 4WD vehicles, as well as reservations for national flights and hotels. English and Italian spoken and Handbook users welcome. Recommended. *Tambo Tours*, USA and Peru, www.2GOPERU.com, www.tambotours.com Adventure and general tour operator

North Coast

Transport
Air connections Daily flights to and from **Lima** with *Aero Continente/Aviandina*, *Lan Perú* and *Tans*. Also daily flights to **Piura** with *Aero Continente/Aviandina* and *Tans* and to **Trujillo** with *Lan Perú*. To **Cajamarca** with *LC Busre* Sat and Sun, US$20.

Bus To **Lima**, 770 km, US$11.50 and US$17.15 for *bus cama*: *Civa*, Av Bolognesi 714, T223434; *Cruz del Sur*, Bolognesi 888, T225508; *Ormeño*, Bolognesi 954A; *Las Dunas*, Bolognesi block 1, luxury service with a/c, toilet, meals, leaves at 2000; *Línea*, Bolognesi 638, T233497, especial and *bus cama* service; *Olano Oltursa*, ticket office at Balta e Izaga, T237789, terminal at Vicente de la Vega 101, T225611, full range of services; *Transportes Chiclayo*, Av L Ortiz 010, T237984. Most companies leave from 1900 onwards.

To **Trujillo**, 209 km, with *Emtrafesa*, Av Balta 110, T234291, almost hourly from 0530-2015, US$2.85, and *Línea*, above. To **Piura**, US$2.85, *Línea* leaves all day; also *Emtrafesa* and buses from the *Cial/Flores* terminal on Bolognesi 751, eg *Flores*, T239579. To **Sullana**, US$4.35. To **Tumbes**, US$5.75, 9-10 hrs; with *Cial*, or *Transportes Chiclayo* (see above); *Oltursa* has an overnight service which leaves at 2015 and arrives at 0530 (this is a good bus to take for crossing to Ecuador the next day), seats can be reserved, unlike other companies which tend to arrive full from Lima late at night.

Many buses go on to the **Ecuadorean border** at **Aguas Verdes**. Go to the *Salida* on Elías Aguirre, mototaxi drivers know where it is, be there by 1900. All buses stop here after leaving their terminals to try and fill empty seats, so it's possible to get a substantial discount on the fare to the border. **NB** Bear in mind that the cheapest buses may not be the most secure.

Direct bus to **Cajamarca**, 260 km; with *Línea* (Bolognesi 638), normal 2200, US$4.85, *bus cama* 2245 US$7.15; many others from Tepsa terminal, Bolognesi y Colón, eg *El Cumbe*, T272245, 3 a day, *Días*, T224448. To **Chachapoyas**, 230 km: with *Civa* at 1630 daily, 10-11 hrs, US$5.75; *Turismo Kuelap*, in Tepsa station, 1830 daily, US$7. To **Jaén**, US$4.35-5.15: *Línea* at 1300 and 2300, 8 hrs; *Señor de Huamantanga*, in Tepsa station, T274869, 1145 and 2230 daily; *Turismo Jaén*, in Tepsa station, 7 a day. To **Tarapoto**, 18 hrs, US$11.50, with *Ejetur*, Bolognesi 536, T209829; also *Turismo Tarapoto*, Bolognesi 751, T636321. To **Huancabamba**, with *Etipthsa*, on Mon and Fri from the Tepsa terminal, T229217; at 1700, 12 hrs, US$8.65.

Directory
Beware of counterfeit bills, especially among street changers on the 6th block of Balta, on Plaza de Armas and the 7th block of MM Izaga

Airline offices *Aero Continente*, Elías Aguirre 712, T209916/17. *LC Busre*, Elias Aguirre 830, T275340. *Tans*, T226546/226669. **Banks** *BCP*, Balta 630, no commission on Amex TCs for US$100 or more (US$12 commission if less), cash on Visa, also Telebanco 24 Horas ATM for Visa. Opposite, at Balta 625, is *Banco Wiese Sudameris*, changes Amex TCs, cash advance on Visa card, ATM for Visa/Plus. *Banco Santander*, Izaga y Balta, changes Amex TCs. *Interbank*, on the Plaza de Armas, no commission

North Coast

on TCs, OK rate, good rates for cash, Visa cash advance, Mastercard ATM. *NBK*, Elías Aguirre 275 on Plaza, Unicard ATM but no exchange facilities. You may have to wait for a while in the banks. It's much quicker and easier to use the ATMs. Banking hrs 0915-1315, 1630-1830, Sat 0930-1230. *Western Union* is at *Tumi Tours*, Elías Aguirre 560, also *DHL*. **Communications** Internet: lots of places, particularly on San José and Elías Aguirre, average price US$0.60 per hr. *Africa Café*, San José 473, T229431, with café downstairs. Another at San José 389. *Internet 20*, San José y Luis González. On MM Izaga: *Ciber Café Internet*, No 716. **Post office:** on the first block of Aguirre, 6 blocks from the Plaza. **Telephone:** *Telefónica*, headquarters at Aguirre 919; bank of phone booths on 7th block of 7 de Enero behind Cathedral for international and collect calls. Phone card sellers hang around here. **Cultural centres** *Instituto Peruano Británico*, Av 7 de Enero 256. T227521. *Instituto Nacional de la Cultura*, Av L González 375, T237261. Has occasional poetry readings, information on local archaeological sites, lectures, etc. It sells a combined entrance ticket for US$4.35 to Sipán, the Brüning Museum, San Pedro church and Casa Montjoy in Lambayeque, Túcume, Sicán, Zaña and other sites. *Instituto de Cultura Peruano-Norteamericana*, Av MM Izaga 807, T231241. *Alianza Francesa*, Cuglievan 644, T236013. **Hospitals and medical services** Ambulance: *Max Salud*, 7 de Enero 185, T234032, F226501, maxsalud@telematic.edu.com **Useful addresses** *Touring y Automóvil Club del Perú*, San José 728, T231821, F237848, chiclayo@touringperu.com.pe Also a travel agency selling air tickets.

Chiclayo area

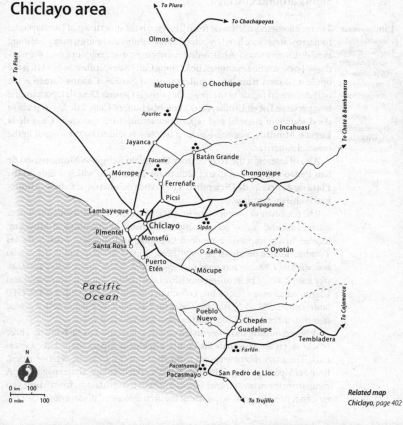

Related map
Chiclayo, page 402

The legend of Ñaymlap

Like much else along this stretch of the Peruvian coast, the exact origin of the people's forebears is something of a mystery. The Spaniard, Cabello de Balboa, in 1578, is said to be the first outsider to hear of a local folk legend referring to a person named Ñaymlap who arrived on the coast of Lambayeque along with his court, his servants and his many concubines in numerous balsa rafts.

He then built residential buildings near the coast and a temple called Chota, or Chotuna, where he placed an idol called Yampallec, from which Lambayeque is supposed to derive its name.

The name Ñaymlap came to occupy an important place in the religious imagery of later civilizations through the designs of

tumis, or ceremonial knives, funerary masks and countless other objects. In the ancient Muchik language spoken by the Moche, ñam means bird and lá means water, and the figures on Moche ceramics, jewellery and temple walls often have bird-like features and eyes shaped like wings. On his death, the people were told that Ñaymlap had grown wings and flown away.

Ñaymlap had many children but only three are known of: Cium, Nor and Cala, who founded the present site of Túcume. This dynasty is said to have ended with the death of the last governor, Fempellec, as a result of his illicit relationship with a demon in the shape of a beautiful woman. With catastrophic consequences, she tricked him into moving Yampallec away from Chota.

Sights around Chiclayo

Lambayeque
Population: 20,700
A multisite entrance ticket is available for US$4.35 covering most of the sites mentioned below. It can be bought at the INC in Chiclayo or any of the sites themselves

Twelve kilometres northwest from Chiclayo is the quiet town of Lambayeque. Its narrow streets are lined by colonial and republican houses, many retaining their distinctive wooden balconies and wrought iron grill-work over the windows. For some fine examples, head along Calle 8 de Octubre: at No 410 is the opulent **Casona Iturregui Aguilarte** and, at No 328, **Casona Cuneo** is the only decorated façade in the town. Opposite is **Casona Descalzi**, perhaps the best preserved of all Lambayeque's colonial houses. Calle 2 de Mayo is also a good source of colonial and republican architecture, especially **Casa de la Logia o Montjoy,** whose 64-m long balcony is said to be the longest in the colonial Americas.

Also of interest is the 16th-century **Complejo Religioso Monumental de San Pedro** and the baroque church of the same name which stands on the **Plaza de Armas 27 de Diciembre**. The French neo-baroque **Palacio Municipal** is also on the plaza.

The reason most people come to visit is to see the two museums: the longer established and highly recommended **Brüning Archaeological Museum**, located in an impressive modern building, and the new **Museo de las Tumbas Reales de Sipán** (■ *0900-1200, 1600-1900 Tue-Sun. Visitors who arrive before 1200 can stay until 1300, likewise those who arrive before 1900 can stay until 2000*). The **Brüning** specializes in Mochica, Lambayeque/Sicán and Chimú cultures, and has a fine collection of Lambayeque gold. ■ *0900-1700 daily; entry US$2.85 (if you don't have the INC multiple entry ticket), a guided tour costs an extra US$2.85, most exhibits labelled in English.*

A board outside shows Peruvian cultures in relation to each other. Three blocks east is the **Museo de las Tumbas Reales de Sipán**, shaped like a pyramid. The magnificent treasure from the tomb of a Moche warrior priest, found at Sipán in 1987, is displayed here (see Archaeological sites page 410). A ramp from the main entrance takes visitors to the third floor, from where you descend, mirroring the sequence of the archaeologists' discoveries.

Sleeping and eating E *Hostal Karla*, Av Huamachuco 758, opposite the museum, T282930. *Jopami*, Grau 143, T282367. *Lambayeque*, Tarapacá 261, T283474. **F** per person *La Posada Norteña*, Panamericana Norte Km 780, T282602. With bath, quiet, safe, clean, cold water, more expensive with TV. There are several good restaurants. *El Cántaro*, on the 1st block of 2 de Mayo, serves excellent traditional local dishes cooked by Juanita. *La Huaca*, on the 3rd block of Calle Junín, and *La Cabaña*, on the 4th block of Calle Libertad, are both good for *ceviche*.

Transport Colectivos from Chiclayo; US$0.50, 20 mins. They leave from Pedro Ruíz at the junction with Av Ugarte. Also *Brüning Express* combis from Vicente de la Vega between Angamos and Av L Ortiz, every 15 mins, US$0.20.

Colonial & traditional towns

The traditional town of **Monsefú**, 16 km to the southwest, is worth a visit. The town's **music** is nationally famous, and there are many popular orchestras. It is also known for **handicrafts** and has a good **market** on Avenida Venezuela, four blocks from the plaza. Handicraft stalls open when potential customers arrive. (See also Local festivals under Chiclayo.) The **Feria de Monsefú**, at the end of September, has market stalls around the plaza selling *artesanía*, bread, plastic toys and ceramics. The town market covers one block, entered off the plaza (with your back to the church, on the left side). At the entrance are bread sellers with huge baskets of breads and buns. ■ *Combis to Chiclayo cost US$0.45; from Chiclayo they leave from Amazonas y 7 de Enero, beyond the Mercado Modelo. Colectivos to Monsefú leave from 7 de Enero y Arica.*

The colonial town of **Ferreñafe**, 18 km northeast of Chiclayo, is worth a visit, especially for its new **Museo Nacional Sicán,** designed to house objects of the Sicán (Lambayeque) culture from Batán Grande (excellent exhibits, knowledgeable staff, but little English spoken). ■ *www.xanga.com/TrujilloPeru Tue-Sun 0900-1800. From the colectivo terminal ask the driver to take you to the museum.*

At **Mórrope**, on the Pan-American Highway north of Chiclayo, craftsmen still produce pottery for the towns of northern Peru using prehispanic techniques. Using a *paletín* (paddle) the potter manipulates the coil of clay into shape. Sometimes the *paletín* has a pattern on it, which is transferred onto the clay. Step inside the 16th century **Capilla de la Ramada Las Animas** on the plaza and you'll know how Jonah felt inside the whale. The pillars and rafters were hewed from the local *algarrobo* tree, giving the church interior the appearance of the skeleton of some enormous beast. Poor restoration work converted the crown and keys of Saint Peter into a skull and crossbones.

The ruined Spanish town of **Zaña** (also spelt Saña), lies 51 km south of Chiclayo. Zaña was destroyed by floods in 1726, and sacked by English pirates on more than one occasion. The ruins of five colonial churches and the convents of San Agustín, La Merced and San Francisco bear witness to the former splendour of this town which, at one time, was destined to become the country's capital. ■ *Zaña is on the multiple entry ticket sold by the INC in Chiclayo.*

Further south, on the Pan-American Highway to Trujillo, lies **Chepén**. The town itself is not particularly fascinating but **Cerro Chepén**, towering over it, is the site of an ancient fortress from the Middle Horizon (late Moche/Huari). The fortress contains the ruins of what may be a palace, surrounded by other buildings. The as yet unexcavated site could have been the main station in a chain of lookout posts along the north coast. ■ *Take any Trujillo bus, US$1.10.* Outside town on the Panamericana is **F** *Hotel Puente Azul*, which is pleasant, clean, with bath and cold water. The restaurant is open in the afternoon only, not for dinner.

North Coast

Coastal towns **Pimentel**, 8 km from Chiclayo by a new highway, is the closest beach resort to
There are three the city. It gets very crowded on Sundays. The **surfing** between Pimentel and
ports serving the the Bayovar Peninsula is excellent, reached from Chiclayo (14½ km) by road
Chiclayo area branching off from the Pan-American Highway. Sea-going reed boats
(*caballitos de totora*) are used by fishermen and can be seen returning in the
late afternoon. The old, decaying pier, from which huge quantities of cotton
and sugar were once exported, can be visited to watch the fishermen unloading their catches. ■ *Entry US$0.25.* There is a **Casa/Museo** dedicated to **José
Quiñones**, hero of the 1942 war with Ecuador, at Quiñones 448.

A more traditional and authentic fishing village is nearby **Santa Rosa**,
where fishermen use two groups of boats *caballitos* and *bolicheros* – pas-
tel-painted craft which line the shore after the day's fishing. Take a combi
between the two towns.

The most southerly is **Puerto Etén**, a quaint port 24 km by road from
Chiclayo. In the adjacent roadstead, **Villa de Etén**, panama hats are the
local industry.

Sleeping, eating and transport In Pimentel: **F** *Hostal Garuda*, Quiñones 120 (basic
but OK), and 2 others. *Restaurant Angustino* on the seafront serves good food. *Bar
Cevichería El Yate*, on the plaza, is one of many places serving good *ceviche*. In Santa
Rosa: there is a small hostal, *Puerto Magnolia*, which is basic, and a restaurant *Bello
Horizonte*. The seafood is superb. Two specialities are *tortilla de rayo* (manta ray) and
chingurito. The 3 ports can all be visited on a pleasant half day trip from Chiclayo.
Combis leave from Vicente de la Vega 200 to Pimentel; others leave from González y L
Prado. Both take 20 minutes, US$0.25. Colectivos Etén leave from 7 de Enero y Arica.

Sipán

Colour map 2, At this imposing twin pyramid complex 35 km southeast of Chiclayo, exca-
grid C2 vations since 1987 in one of the three crumbling pyramids have brought to
light a cache of funerary objects considered to rank among the finest examples of pre-Columbian art.

The Peruvian archaeologist Walter Alva, leader of the dig, continues to
probe the immense mound that has revealed no less than 12 royal tombs filled
with 1,800-year-old offerings worked in precious metals, stone, pottery and
textiles of the Moche culture (circa AD 1-750). In the most extravagant
Moche tomb discovered, **El Señor de Sipán**, a priest was found clad in gold
(ear ornaments, breast plate, etc), with turquoise and other valuables. A site
museum was opened in 1992 featuring photos and maps of excavations, technical displays and replicas of some finds.

In another tomb were found the remnants of what is thought to have been a
priest, sacrificed llama and a dog, together with copper decorations. In 1989
another richly- appointed, unlooted tomb contained even older metal and
ceramic artefacts associated with what was probably a high-ranking shaman
or spiritual leader, called '**The Old Lord of Sipán**'.

Three tombs are on display, containing replicas of the original finds. Replicas
of the Old Lord and the Priest are awaited. You can wander around the previously excavated areas of the Huajada Rajada to get an idea of the construction of
the burial mound and adjacent pyramids. For a good view, climb the large pyramid across from the excavated Huaca Rajada. There is a path, but it looks as
though it should be closed off to prevent erosion of the pyramid.

The old Lord of Sipán

The excavations at Sipán by the archaeologist Walter Alva have already revealed a huge amount of riches in the shape of 'El Señor de Sipán'. This well-documented discovery was followed by an equally astounding find dating from AD 100. The tomb of the 'Old Lord of Sipán', as it has come to be known, predates the original Lord of Sipán by some 200 years, and could well be an ancestor of his.

Some of the finest examples of Moche craftsmanship have been found in the tomb of the Old Lord. One object in particular is remarkable; a crab deity with a human head and legs and the carapace, legs and claws of a crab. The gilded piece is over half a metre tall – unprecedented for a Moche figurine. This crab-like figure has been called Ulluchu

Man, because the banner on which it was mounted yielded some of the first samples yet found of this ancient fruit.

The ulluchu fruit usually appears in scenes relating to war and the ritual drinking of a prisoner's blood. One theory is that the ulluchu is part of the papaya family and has anticoagulant properties which are useful to prevent clotting before a man's blood is consumed.

■ *Site and museum: 0900-1700. Entrance for the tombs and museum is US$2, students half price (the site is also on the multiple entry ticket sold by the INC in Chiclayo). A guide at the site costs US$2.85 (may not speak English). Small boys offer to guide you (other kids hang around the handicraft stalls and pester for a tip for doing nothing). Allow about 3-4 hrs in total. Take mosquito repellent. Buses to Sipán leave from Terminal Este Sur-Nor Este on C Nicolás de Piérola, east of the city (take a taxi there, US$1; it can be a dangerous area), US$0.40, 1 hr. Colectiovs leave from 5-6 blocks east of Mercado Modelo, take care here, too. The way to the village is well-signed through fields of sugar cane. Once you get to the village, the signs end: turn left, then right and go through the village to get to the site.*

Pampagrande and Chongoyape

Twenty-five kilometres from Sipán is Pampagrande, a Mochica settlement interpreted by Canadian archaeologists in the 1970s as the first true northern coast city, circa AD 550. **Pampagrande**

This was the largest Moche complex 1,400 years ago, at which time as many as 10,000 people may have lived here. Pampagrande was a ceremonial centre, possibly including ritualoffering of human blood as represented in the Sipán exhibits. These were presided over by a lord who also directed production and distribution, including precious materials to the artisans. Some experts believe that a prolonged drought around AD 562-594 displaced large groups of Moche people living to the south who moved to Pampagrande, which become the centre of a state holding sway over the Lambayeque and Jequetepeque valleys.

The reason for the downfall of this once-powerful city remains in dispute. The structures associated with the rich and powerful ruling class appear to have been selectively burned and then abandoned leading some to conclude

North Coast

A tale of demons and fish

Just one of the many legends that abound in this part of Northern Peru pertains to the hill which dominates the pyramids at Túcume and the precise origin of its name. The hill is known locally as 'El Purgatorio' (purgatory), or more commonly, Cerro La Raya.

The former name derives from the conquering Spaniards' attempts to convert the indigenous people to the Christian faith. The Spanish invaders encountered fierce local resistance to their new religion and came up with the idea of convincing the people of Túcume that the hill was, in fact, purgatory. They told the locals that there lived on the hill a demon who would punish anyone not accepting the Roman Catholic faith.

In order to lend some credence to this tale, a group of Spaniards set out one dark, moonless night and built a huge bonfire at the foot of 'El Purgatorio', giving it the appearance of an erupting volcano and frightening the townsfolk half to death. Thus they came to accept the Spaniards' assertion that any unbelievers or sinners

would be thrown alive into the flames of this diabolical fire.

As if that wasn't enough to terrify the local populace, the Spanish also concocted the fiendish tale of 'El Carretón', or waggon. This was an enormous waggon pulled by four great horses which supposedly would speed forth from the bowels of 'El Purgatorio' on the darkest of nights. Driven by a dandily-dressed demon boss, and carrying his equally dandy demon buddies, this hellish vehicle careered round the town of Túcume making a fearsome racket. Any poor unbelievers or sinners unfortunate enough to be found wandering the streets would immediately be carted off and thrown into the flames of purgatory.

The alternative name of Cerro La Raya refers to the local legend of a Manta Ray that lived in a nearby lake. The local children constantly tormented the fish by throwing stones at it, so, to escape this torment, the poor creature decided to move to the hill and become part of it. The lake then disappeared and ever since, the hill has been enchanted.

that a peasant revolution may have been the cause. Others (eg Moseley) believe that an earthquake, El Niño events and drought combined to lead to the demise of the Moche.

Chongoyape A minor road runs to Chongoyape, a pleasant old town 70 km to the east (3 km before the city, turn left/west to the Chavín petroglyphs of Cerro Mulato). Nearby are the vast Taymi and Pampagrande pre-Columbian and modern irrigation systems (the modern are also called Taymi). Also near Chongoyape are the aqueduct of Racarrumi, the hill fort of Mal Paso and the ruins of Majín (12-14 pyramids). ■ *Buses from Chiclayo leave from the corner of Leoncio Prado and Sáenz Peña; US$1, 1½ hours.*

Túcume

Colour map 1, grid C2 About 35 km north of Chiclayo, beside the old Panamericana to Piura, lie the ruins of this vast city built over a thousand years ago. This mysterious and evocative site is worth visiting around sundown, not only to avoid the fierce sun, but to add to the eerie thrill that it induces. It may be difficult to persuade anyone to accompany you, though, as local people are very superstitious.

A short climb to the two *miradores* on **Cerro La Raya**, or **El Purgatorio**, as it is also known, offers an unparalleled panoramic vista of 26 major pyramids, platform mounds, walled citadels and residential compounds flanking a ceremonial centre and ancient cemeteries.

Combis go from Chiclayo, Angamos y Manuel Pardo, US$1.50, 45 mins. A combi from **Getting there**
Túcume to the village of Come passes the ruins hourly. You cannot miss the town of
Túcume with its huge sign. Soon after the sign take a right turn on the paved road
which leads to the museum and site. Don't be fooled by the pyramid close to the sign;
it's part of the group, but some distance from the entrance. A combi from Túcume to
Lambayeque is US$0.35 and takes 25 mins.The entire complex covers well over 200 ha
and measures 1.7 km from east to west and 2 km from north to south. One of the pyramids, Huaca Larga, where excavations were undertaken from 1987-92, is the longest
adobe structure in the world, measuring 700 m long, 280 m wide and over 30 m high.

There is no evidence of occupation of Túcume previous to the Lambayeque **History**
people who developed the site between AD 1000 and 1375 until the Chimú
came, saw and conquered the region, establishing a short reign until the
arrival of the Incas around 1470. The Incas built on top of the existing structure of **Huaca Larga** using stone from Cerro La Raya. Among the tombs excavated so far is one dating from the Inca period. It is thought to be that of a
warrior, judging by the many battle scars. The body is heavily adorned and
was interred along with two male compatriots and no less than 19 females
aged between 10 and 30. Beside the Huaca Larga is the shrine known as the
Templo de la Piedra Sagrada (Temple of the Sacred Stone), which was clearly
very holy to the Lambayeque, Chimú and Incas.

Among the other pyramids which make up this huge complex are: **Huaca El** **Sights**
Mirador, Huaca Las Estacas, Huaca Pintada and **Huaca de las Balsas,**
which is thought to have housed people of elevated status such as priests.
  Excavations at the site, led by the late Norwegian explorer-archaeologist,
Thor Heyerdahl of *Kon-Tiki* fame, challenge many conventional views of
ancient Peruvian culture. Some suspect that it will prove to be a civilization
centre greater than Chan Chán. There is also evidence, including art and
remains of navigation gear, that the people of Túcume were intrepid seafarers.
A 5-year excavation project was undertaken by Thor Heyerdahl, since when
there has been no further excavation work for lack of funds.
  The **site museum**, with three halls, is built from adobe and mezquite logs in
prehispanic style. The collections show architectural reconstructions, photographs and drawings, highlighting the finds, which include weaving paraphernalia, a ceremonial oar and a fabulous bas relief and mural depicting
maritime scenes suggesting former sea trade and interregional contact. Traditional dishes and drinks are available at the site. ■ *US$2 (also on the INC mul-
tiple-entry ticket). Guides at the site charge US$2.85. Museum open 0900-1700.*

This typical north coast town is a 15-minute walk from the site, or a US$0.85 **The town**
mototaxi ride. On the plaza is the interesting **San Pedro Church**, a mixture of **of Túcume**
baroque, churrigueresque and neo-classical styles. There are no hotels in town.
The surrounding countryside is pleasant for walks and swimming in the river.
  The present site of the town is not the original one but dates from 1720.
Local legend has it that the town was moved following an apparition of the
Virgin. The icon of the Virgin mysteriously disappeared but was later seen on
top of Cerro Cueto, having her long hair combed by a native girl while gazing
over pasture lands below. This was taken as a sign to relocate the church and
the rest of the town with it.
  Túcume celebrates the **Fiesta de la Purísima Concepción**, the town's
Patron Saint, eight days prior to Carnival in February, and also in September.
This is the most important festival, with music, dancing, fireworks,

cockfights, sports events and, of course, much eating and drinking. During the Dance of the Devils (which is common in northern Peru), the participants wear horned masks, forked tails and long capes and are said to represent the diabolical drunken Spanish priests from colonial times. It also features a song and dance dedicated to the native girl who was seen combing the Virgin's hair.

Batán Grande

Colour map 1, grid C2 This site, 50 km from Chiclayo, has revealed several sumptuous tombs dating to the middle Sicán period, AD 900-1100. The ruins comprise some 50 adobe pyramids, where some of the best examples of pre-Columbian gold artefacts, notably the 915-g Tumi (ceremonial knife), were found. Many gold objects have been removed to private collections and museums, such as the *Gold Museum* in Lima.

In the ancient Muchik language, Sicán means 'house or temple of the moon' and Batán Grande, or Poma, as it was also known, was the centre of the mid-Sicán culture which shares many stylistic similarities with the later Chimú culture.

Getting there Colectivos (US$1.20) leave Chiclayo from 7 de Enero block 15 and J Fanning to the main square of the sugar cane cooperative (in which the ruins are set). You must get permission to visit the site from the cooperative and go with site archaeologist. You need to speak Spanish and to pay to visit the site, which is open Monday-Friday only. A private car (taxi) from the cooperative to the site costs US$7-9 (bargain hard). You'll need a full day to visit. This is impossible in the wet season, from Jan-Mar. Seek sound advice before you go, otherwise go with a tour company.

The site Professor Izumi Shimada has worked here for more than 15 years researching a culture which has, to a large extent, been forgotten. He has excavated **Huaca Loro**, one of five monument temples that make up the vast rectangle known as the Great Plaza. Research points to the existence of a well-structured theocracy led by a small class of priest-lords. Political, economic and religious dominance of the Sicán theocracy stretched over most of the north coast, from Sullana in the north to Trujillo in the south. Their dominion lasted from about 700 AD to the 14th century and the Chimú conquest. It appears that Batán Grande suffered a devastating flood in about 100, after which it was burnt. Some archaeologists use the term Lambayeque as the name of the culture which Professor Shimada calls Sicán.

The site, in 300 ha of desert-thorn forest of mezquite (*Prosopis pallida*), known locally as Pomac forest, is now a national sanctuary and is protected by police. Both Batán Grande and the Bosque Pomac are on the INC multiple entry ticket sold in Chiclayo.

North on the Old Pan-American Highway

Apurlec Sixty kilometres north of Chiclayo is the site of Apurlec beside the old
Colour map 1, grid C2 Panamericana. It comprises a stone wall surrounding a hill and pyramids dating from the Tiahuanaco period, as well as irrigation canals and reservoirs. The system was enlarged during Moche, Chimú and Inca occupation of the site. The ruins are overgrown, but climb the Cerro Viejo to get an idea of its size. To get there from Chiclayo, take a bus from Pedro Ruíz block 5. The bus continues to Motupe (10 km).

Further north on the old Pan-American Highway 885 km from Lima, is the **Olmos**
peaceful town of Olmos. During the last week of June the **Festival de Limón** is
celebrated here. **G** *Hospedaje San Martín*, very dirty, bargain hard. **E-F** *Hotel
Remanso*, is in a restored farmstead, beautiful, all rooms different, good food,
friendly, discounts for cyclists.

At Olmos, a road runs east over the Porculla Pass for Jaén and Bagua (see
pages 477 and 476). The old Pan-American Highway continues from Olmos
to Cruz de Caña and on to Piura.

North on the New Pan-American Highway

At Lambayeque the new Pan-American Highway, which is in good condition,
branches off the old road and drives 190 km straight across the Sechura Desert
to Piura. There is also a coast road, narrow and scenic, between Lambayeque
and Piura, via Bayovar and the town of Sechura. The fine 17th-century cathedral has a lovely west front which has been under renovation for a long time
and is normally closed to the public. There is a restaurant at the junction to
Bayovar, where you can sleep.

A large area of shifting sands separates the cities of Chiclayo and Piura. Water   **Sechura Desert**
for irrigation comes from the Chira and Piura rivers, and from the Olmos and   *Colour map 1, grid B2*
Tinajones irrigation projects which bring water from the Amazon watershed by
means of tunnels (one over 16 km long) through the Andes to the Pacific coast.

The northern river – the Chira – has usually a superabundance of water.
Along its irrigated banks large crops of Tangüis cotton are grown. A dam has
been built at Poechos on the Chira to divert water to the Piura valley. In its
upper course the Piura – whose flow is far less dependable – is mostly used to
grow subsistence food crops, but around Piura, when there is enough water,
the hardy long-staple Pima cotton is planted.

In the 1870s, the government of Manuel Pardo decreed that all native cotton, including kapok, should be destroyed because it was believed that it gave
parasites to the favoured, imported varieties. This was not the case and the
value of Peruvian cotton is now recognized. It grows on a tall bush, unlike the
short, Egyptian variety, and comes in seven colours, each of which was given a
name by the Moche.

NB Solo cyclists should not cross the Sechura Desert as muggings have
occured. Take the safer, inland route. There are several restaurants between
Km 845 and 848, and another midway between Mórrope and Piura, but there
are no hotels. Do not camp out if possible. Heading south, strong headwinds
may make camping unavoidable. Do not attempt this alone.

Piura

A proud and historic city, 264 km from Chiclayo, Piura was founded as San Miguel   *Phone code: 074*
at Tangarará in 1532, three years before Lima, by the conquistadores *left behind*   *Colour map 1, grid B1*
by Pizarro. It was relocated, first as Pirwa, then with its current name, in   *Population: 324,500*
1534. There are two well-kept parks, Cortés and Pizarro (with a statue of the con-
quistador, also called Plaza de las Tres Culturas), and public gardens. Old build-
ings are kept in repair and new buildings blend with the Spanish style of the old city.

Ins and outs

Getting there   A taxi to the airport costs US$1.85 by day, more by night. Most bus companies are on Av Sánchez Cerro, blocks 11, 12 and 13 in the northwest of the town. There are some hotels in this area, but for central ones take a taxi: Radio Taxis, T324509/324630.

Getting around   From the Plaza de Armas, some of the hotels and bus companies are too far to walk, but many of the sights and places to stay can be reached on foot. Three bridges now cross the Río Piura to Castilla, the oldest from C Huancavelica, for pedestrians (Puente San Miguel), from C Sánchez Cerro, and the newest from Av Panamericana Norte, at the west end of town. A fourth bridge, from C Bolognesi, was lost in El Niño of 1997-98. Taxis in town charge US$1, mototaxis US$0.50.

Piura

North Coast

Information at the tourist office on the Plaza de Armas, next to Municipio, open **Tourist offices**
Mon-Fri 0900-1300, 1600-2000, Sat 0900-1300. *Dirección Regional de Turismo*, Av
Fortunato Chirichigno, Urb San Eduardo, T327351, at the north end of town; *Indecopi* is
also here, T304045, helpful when there are problems. *Touring y Automóvil Club del
Perú*, Sánchez Cerro 1237, T325641, has little information.

The winter climate, May-Sep, is very pleasant although nights can be cold and the wind **Climate**
piercing, while Dec-Mar is very hot. It is extremely difficult to find a room in the last week
of Jul because of Independence festivities. The city suffers from water shortages.

Sights

Standing on the **Plaza de Armas** is the **cathedral**, with gold covered altar and
paintings by Ignacio Merino. A few blocks away at Lima y Callao is the **San
Francisco** church, where the city's independence from Spain was declared on
4 January 1821, nearly eight months before Lima. The church was being completely rebuilt in 2002.

The of **María Auxiliadora** stands on a small plaza on Libertad, near
Avenida Sánchez Cerro. Across the plaza is the **Museo de Arte Religioso**. **San
Sebastián**, on Tacna y Moquegua, is also worth seeing. The birthplace of
Admiral Miguel Grau, hero of the War of the Pacific with Chile, is **Casa
Museo Grau**, on Jr Tacna 662, opposite the Centro Cívico. It has been
opened as a museum and contains a model of the *Huáscar*, the largest Peru-
vian warship in the War of the Pacific, which was built in Britain. It also con-
tains interesting old photographs. ■ *0800-1300, 1600-1900. Free.*

Interesting local craftwork is sold at the **Mercado Modelo**. **Museo Municipal Vicús**, with archaeological and art sections, is open on Sullana, near
Huánuco, and though small it is very interesting.

Essentials

AL *Costa del Sol*, Loreto 649, T/F302864, www.costadelsolperu.com Luxury, pool, **Sleeping**
casino, internet facilities, restuarant. **AL** *Los Portales*, Libertad 875, Plaza de Armas, ■ *on map*
T323072, F321161, www.acceso.peru.com/countryclub Price includes breakfast, tax *Price codes:*
and welcome cocktail. This ex-government hotel, in the *Country Club* group, has been *see inside*
attractively refurbished and is the city's social centre, elegant, a/c, hot water, pleasant *front cover*
terrace and patio, nice pool.

C *Esmeralda*, Loreto 235, T/F327109, www.hotelesmeralda.com.pe With bathroom, hot water, fan (**B** with a/c), clean, comfortable, good, restaurant. **C** *Hostal
Latino*, Huancavelica 720, T335123, http://hostallatino.tripod.com.pe All rooms with
bath, a large, slightly gloomy concrete building, with restaurant (breakfast extra).
C *San Miguel*, Lima 1007, Plaza Pizarro, T305122. Modern, comfortable, with bath, TV,
café. **C** *Vicus*, Av Guardia Civil B-3, in Castilla 2 blocks across the river on the Sánchez
Cerro bridge, T343186, F343249. With bathroom, hot water, fan, clean, quiet, parking.

D *El Almirante*, Ica 860, T/F335239. With bathroom, fan, clean, modern, owner is
knowledgeable about the Ayabaca area (see page 422). **D** *El Sol*, Sánchez Cerro 411,
T324461, F326307. With bathroom, hot water, small pool, snack bar, parking, accepts
dollars cash or TCs but won't change them. Recommended. **D** *Perú*, Arequipa 476,
T333421, F331530. With bathroom and fan, clean, safe, friendly, laundry service, cold
water, modern small rooms, all meals in restaurant extra.

E *La Capullana*, Junín 925, T321239. With bath, some cheaper single rooms, welcoming. **E** *Continental*, Jr Junín 924, T334531. Some rooms with bathroom, clean,
comfortable, no breakfast. **E** *Hostal Moon Night*, Junín 899, T336174. Comfortable,

modern, spacious, with bath, **F** without bath or TV, clean, good value. **E** *San Jorge*, Jr Loreto 960, T327514. With bathroom and fan, cheaper without cable TV, hot water, clean. **F** *Hospedaje Aruba*, Junín 851, T303067. Small rooms but clean and comfortable, shared bath, fan on request, very friendly. Recommended. **F** per person *California*, Jr Junín 835, upstairs, T328789. Shared bath, own water-tank, mosquito netting on windows, roof terrace, clean, brightly decorated, the owner is very friendly. Recommended (some short stay, though). **F** *Oriental*, Callao 446, T304011. Cheaper without bathroom and fan, clean, good value but very noisy, TV in reception.

Convenient for buses B *Algarrobo Inn*, Av Los Cocos 389, T307450, algarrobo@compunet.com.pe With bath, hot water, TV, safe, everything works OK but it needs doing up, good breakfast, very friendly, overpriced. **E** *Hostal Los Jardines*, Av Los Cocos 436, T326590. With bath, hot water, TV, laundry, parking, good value. There are 3 2-star hotels on Av Sánchez Cerro 1300 block, and **E** *Hostal Peony*, Mártires de Uchuruccay E2, T322127, with bath and TV.

Eating
● *on map*

Expensive *Carburmer*, Libertad 1014. Very good lunches and dinners, also pizza. In the same precinct is *Picantería Los Santitos*, lunch only, wide range of traditional dishes in a renovated colonial house. *La Cabaña*, Ayacucho 598, esquina Cusco. Pizzas and other good Italian food.

Mid-range *Alex Chopp's*, Huancavelica 538. A la carte dishes, seafood, fish, chicken and meats, beer, popular at lunchtime. *Brosti Chopp*, Arequipa 780. Similar, but with lunch *menú* for US$1.45. *Grand Prix*, Loreto 395. Good food, reasonable prices. *La Carreta*, Huancavelica 726. One of the most popular places for roast chicken. *Chef R*, Sánchez Cerro 210, near the bridge. Seafood restaurant *Romano*, Ayacucho 580. Popular with locals, extensive menu, excellent set meal for US$1.55. Highly recommended. *Las Tradiciones Peruanas*, Ayacucho 579. Regional specialities, also an art gallery.

Cheap *Chalán del Norte* has several branches for sweets, cakes and ice cream, Tacna 520 on Plaza de Armas, Grau 173 and 450 (*Chalán de la Avenida*). *D'Pauli*, Lima 541. Also for sweets, cakes and ice-cream, good. *Frutilandia*, Jr Tacna 376. Good *menú*, good for breakfast, juices, ices and desserts. *Italia*, Grau 172. For breakfasts, snacks, desserts and juices. *Ganímedes*, Lima 440. A good vegetarian restaurant, very popular set lunch, à la carte is slow but well worth it, try the excellent yoghurt and fruit.

Local specialities Piura's special dishes include *Majado de Yuca*, manioc root with pork; *Seco de Chavelo*, beef and plantain stew; and *Carne Seca*, sun-dried meat. Its best-known sweet is the delicious *natilla*, made mostly of goats' milk and molasses. Its local drink is *pipa fría*, chilled coconut juice drunk from the nut with a straw.

Bars & clubs Many of the nightspots are concentrated on Ayacucho, and some of them are also restaurants. In addition are: *Bloom Moon*, at 522; and *Café R & B Zelada*, at 562.

Festivals 26-28 Jul *Festival Internacional de Tunas*. 27 Aug to 2 Sep *Semana Turística de Piura*. 7 Oct *Festival Nacional de Marinera y Tondera*.

Shopping There are delicatessens around Plaza de Armas. The market on *Sánchez Cerro* is good for fruit. **Chulucanas pottery** (see page 421) can be bought at two shops on Libertad and from *Milagros García de Linares*, who lives in Urbanización Santa Inés, T327322. **Supermarkets**: *Cossto*, Arequipa y Sánchez Cerro, and *Don Vito*, Arequipa y Callao.

Tour operators *Piura Tours*, C Ayacucho 585, T328873, F334379, piuratours@mail.udep.edu.pe The manager Mario speaks very good English.

North Coast

Air There are daily flights to and from **Lima** with *Aero Continente/Aviandina* and
Tans. Also daily flights to and from **Chiclayo** with *Aero Continente*, who also fly to
Tumbes 5 days a week.

Bus Most companies are on Av Sánchez Cerro, blocks 11, 12 and 13. To **Lima**, 1,038
km, 14-16 hrs, from US$7 (eg *Tepsa*), on the Panamericana Norte. Most buses stop at
the major cities on route; *Flores*, Av Libertad 1210, T306664; *Ittsa*, Sánchez Cerro 1142,
T333982 (US$17.15 on top floor, US$21.50 on lower floor); *Línea*, Sánchez Cerro 1215,
T327821; *Tepsa*, Loreto 1198, T323721. To **Chiclayo**, 190 km, 3 hrs, US$2.85, several
buses daily. Also several daily buses to **Trujillo**, 7 hrs, 487 km, US$5.75, to travel by day
change in Chiclayo. To **Tumbes**, 282 km, 4½ hrs, US$4.80, several buses daily, eg
Cruz del Sur (La Libertad 1176, T337094, also to Lima), *Cial* (Bolognesi 817, T304250)
and *Emtrafesa* (Los Naranjos 235, T337093, also to Chiclayo and Trujillo); also
colectivos, US$5.75. To **Talara**, US$2, 2 hrs, with *Eppo*, T331160. To **Paita**, *Trans Dora*,
Sánchez Cerro 1391, every 20 mins, 1 hr, US$0.75; also from Paita terminal on Av
Gullman, just off Sánchez Cerro. To **Máncora**, US$3.15, 3 hrs, with *Eppo*.

  Crossing to Ecuador: go to Tumbes and travel on from there for the Aguas Verdes
crossing. There are frequent buses to **Sullana**, 38 km, 30 mins (US$0.45), *Eppo, Sullana
Express* and *Turismo del Norte*, all on 1100 block of Sánchez Cerro; also colectivos
(US$1). To **La Tina** on the Ecuadorean frontier, is a further 128 km, 1¾ hrs, US$2.85. It's
best to take an early bus to Sullana (start at 0430, leave when full), then a colectivo (see
under Sullana). *Coop Loja*, Av Prol Sánchez Cerro 228-58, 1-B, T309407 (mototaxi
US$0.70 from centre), direct buses to Loja, 3 a day, 9 hrs, US$7.15. The route is
Sullana-La Tina-Macará (US$3.40)-Loja. There is also a connecting colectivo to
Vilcabamba from Loja. *Coop Loja* also have a direct bus to Machala via Aguas Verdes at
2230, US$7., US$7.20 in total. Try not to arrive in Sullana or Piura after dark, it's unsafe.

Airline offices *Aero Continente*, Libertad 951, T325635. *Tans*, Libertad 442, T302432.
Banks *BCP*, Grau y Tacna. Cash and Visa and Amex TCs (US$12 commission), cheques
changed in the mornings only, has ATM. *Banco Continental*, Plaza de Armas. Changes
Amex TCs with US$10 commission. *Interbank*, Grau 170, changes Visa TCs, ATM for Visa,
Mastercard and AmEx. *Casas de cambio* are at Arequipa 722, and Ica 429 and 460. Street
changers can be found on Grau outside *BCP*. **Communications** Internet: at Arequipa
728 and others in the centre. 10 machines in the Biblioteca Municipal, Urb Grau, US$0.60
per hr. **Post office**: on the corner of Libertad and Ayacucho on Plaza de Armas is not too
helpful. Perhaps it's better going to *Hotel Los Portales*. **Telephone:** Loreto 259, national
and international phone and fax. Also at Ovalo Grau 483. **Consulates** *Honorary British Consul*, c/o American Airlines, Hancavelica 223, T305990, F333300. *Honorary German Consul*, Jutta Moritz de Irazola, Las Amapolas K6, Urb Miraflores, Casilla 76, T332920,
F320310. **Laundry** *Lavandería Liz-to*, Tacna 785. Charges by weight.

Around Piura

This small town is famous for its *chicha* (maize beer) – though be careful as the
quality is not always reliable – and *picanterías*, which are local restaurants, some
with music. *La Chayo*, San Francisco 439, is recommended for its local dishes
and *chicha*. There are several others on and close to Calle San Francisco. The village is also noted for its **artesanía** such as tooled leather, gold and silver filigree
jewellery, wooden articles and straw hats, though prices are relatively high and
streets are lined with shops, including some jewellers more suited to a shopping
mall. Inside the large church are vivid murals and, in 2000, a miracle was said to
have occurred when an image of Christ appeared in the paintwork on an exterior wall. The village is also renowned for its celebrations in **Holy Week**, Good

Friday especially (when all of Piura seems to be there). There is a procession at 1800 and the town centre is closed to traffic. ■ *Colectivos leave Piura from the far side of Puente San Miguel, US$0.20, 15-20 mins; also combis from the bus terminal, block 12 Av Sánchez Cerro, US$0.25.*

Narihualá Two kilometres south of Catacaos is the Narihualá archaeological site. It includes a large adobe pyramid, 40 m high, from the Tallán culture which populated the Chira and Piura valleys before it was conquered by the Chimús.

Paita

Colour map 1, grid B1
Population: 51,500

The port for the area, 50 km from Piura, Paita exports cotton, cotton seed, wool and flax. Built on a small beach, flanked on three sides by a towering, sandy bluff, it is connected with Piura and Sullana by paved highways.

It is a very old fishing port. Several **colonial buildings** survive, but they are in poor condition. Bolívar's mistress, Manuela Sáenz, lived the last 24 years of her life in Paita, after being exiled from Quito. She supported herself until her death in 1856 by weaving and embroidering and making candy after refusing the fortune left her by her husband. The house can be visited if you ask the people living in it, but there's not much to see. It is on the main road into town, after the market, just before and overlooking a petrol station. Fishing and fish-meal are prosperous industries.

On a bluff looming over Paita is a small colonial **fortress** built to repel pirates. Paita was a port of call for Spanish shipping en route from Lima to Panama and Mexico. It was a frequent target for attack, from Drake (1579) to Anson (1741).

Sleeping **E** *El Faro*, Junín 322, T611076. Small and clean. **E** *Miramar*, Malecón J Chávez 418, opposite Credicoop Paita, T611083. A filthy old wooden mansion on seafront. **E** *Las Brisas*, Av Ugarte. The best, with bathroom but little cold water, safe. **F** *El Mundo*, on 300 block of Bolívar. Not bad but short-stay. There are others but none is recommendable and mostly full anyway.

Eating The restaurant on 2nd floor of Club Liberal building, Jorge Chávez 161, serves good fish, seafood and crêpes, and is good value. *Chifa Hong Kong*, Junín 358. Considered by locals to offer really authentic Peruvian Chinese food. *El Mundo*, Jr Junín. Quite good. There are others on the Plaza de Armas.

Transport See above under Piura Transport, for details. All drop off and collect passengers in the market area in Paita.

Colán
Phone code: 074
Colour map 1, grid B1

Twenty-five kilometres up the coast is Colán, reached by driving down a large, sandy bluff (turn off at Km 989). Near the base is a striking and lonely **colonial church**, with breath-taking architecture and beautiful paintings in good condition. It is claimed by some to be the oldest church in Peru, if not South America. The key-holder can be found by asking in the adjoining village of San Lucas de Colán. The seafront houses in the holiday resort stand on wooden stilts and are surrounded by palms. The seawater is clear and warm (but beware stingrays – drag your feet when entering the water) and sunsets are spectacular.

Sleeping All the hotels are pricey, eg **B** *Hotel Sol de Colán*, on the promenade, T321784, with pool, bar, games room, restaurant and bungalow accommodation with en-suite facilities. **D** *Frente al Mar*, T615465, owner Alfred Leigh is of English descent, 4

North Coast

rooms, damp, sea terrace, friendly. Its seafood restaurant is quite cheap and will cook vegetarian pasta if you wish. There are other hotels and excellent seafood restaurants. By public transport, go to Paita and change buses there.

East from Piura

Fifty km northeast of Piura and 10 km off the old Pan-American Highway is the small town of Chulucanas, centre of the lemon and orange growing area.

Chulucanas

An ancient **pottery** technique has been discovered and revived here since the 1960s. The local potters formerly produced only large, utilitarian terracotta pots, until the 1960s when graverobbers brought to light examples of pottery from the Vicus and Tallane cultures dating from the second half of the first millennium BC. A group of Quechua pottery specialists researched and experimented with forms and techniques based on the pre-Columbian finds. These produce a very subtle and unusual effect. At first, the potters imitated the forms of the Vicus pieces but gradually they began to develop their own stylized figures. The most popular form is now the *Chichera*, a fat lady who makes and sells chicha. The most highly prized pieces are signed and sold in galleries and shops in Lima and abroad. Excellent ceramics can also be bought in the town, at a shop on the plaza and three others are within one block. ■ *Combis leave from Piura; US$1.50.*

Huancabamba

From Chulucanas the paved road heads southeast. A turn-off east to Morropán leads to a dirt road to **Canchaque**, a delightfully situated small centre for coffee, sugar-cane and fruit production (basic lodging available). The difficult and tiring road, impossible for ordinary vehicles in the wet season, continues over a pass in the Andes of more than 3,000 m for 69 km to Huancabamba.

Colour map 1, grid B2

This very pretty town in a wonderful setting has three claims to fame. First, the predominance of European features, due to the fact that it was an important Spanish settlement in colonial times. Second, it is called 'the walking town', *la ciudad que camina*, as it is built on irregularly slipping strata which cause much subsidence. Evidence for this includes the fall of the bridge over the Río Huancabamba.

The third, and by far the most remarkable claim to fame, is that Huancabamba is the base for reaching **Las Guaringas**, a series of lakes at about 4,000 m. Around here live the most famous witch doctors of Peru, to whom sick people flock from all over the country and abroad. "The shamanic ceremony is definitely off the gringo trail and is an unforgettable trip. To take part in the ceremony, arrive in town and prepare to be approached almost immediately by a shaman's "agent". As dodgy as this sounds, this person can help you by doing all preparations. Go to the tourist centre in the plaza beforehand and double check if the agent's witch doctor is trustworthy. You'll then hop in a van, travel to the doctor's house, agree on a price and commence the ceremony immediately. It is an outdoor affair involving light hallucinogenic *San Pedro* cactus juice that is quite vile. The ceremony lasts all night and participants dance, reveal and predict the future. The entire ceremony is very mellow and most witch doctors have the disposition of concerned uncles. A spartan meal is provided so bring snacks. The next day involves a three-hour horseback ride to a high mountain lagoon where near-skinny dipping and more ceremonies take place. You're back in Huancabamba (tired and cold) by late afternoon" (Tom Gierasimczuk).

North Coast

Buses to the lakes leave at 0400 from the main plaza. Horses to the lakes can be hired for US$5. There are also trips to the village of **San Antonio** below Lago Carmen, and the village of Salalá below Lago Shumbe, where there is accommodation at G *Hotel San José* (very basic, take your own food). Ignacio León, who owns a *bodega* opposite *El Dorado* (see below) runs an early pick-up service to the outlying villages and takes trips at negotiable prices.

Local specialities include *rompope*, a rich and strong drink made of egg, spices and *cañazo* (sugar-cane spirit), roast *cuy* (guinea-pig) and local cheeses. The town hosts a tourist week in early July and the *Virgen del Carmen* festival in mid-July.

Sleeping & transport   F *Hotel El Dorado*, on the main plaza. Good, clean, informative owner, with restaurant. There are also a couple of others on the plaza. A bus from Piura to Canchaque and Huancabamba leaves daily at 0900 and 1000 (at least 10 hrs, US$9), from Avenida Ramón Castilla 196. Buy your ticket early on the day before travelling. It returns from Huancabamba at 0700 and 1000. A truck costs US$11.50. If driving, take the Pan-American Highway south of Piura for 66 km where there is a signpost to Huancabamba.

Ayabaca
Colour map 1, grid B2
Altitude: 2,850 m

225 kilometres northeast of Piura in the highlands is the pleasant town of Ayabaca. This is the access point for the **Aypate** archaeological site and the **Samanga** hieroglyphics. It is also the home of **El Señor Cautivo de Ayabaca** (the captured Christ on his way to crucifixion). Many devotees make pilgrimages to his shrine, the most famous in northern Peru, especially on 12 October. Some leave from Piura, taking months over the journey. ▪ *There are several hostales in town. Buses leave from Piura in the morning, starting at 0800, from the Mercado Modelo; 6 hours, US$7.*

To Ecuador   From Ayabaca it's 2 hours to Samanguilla, or 2½ to the frontier bridge near the village of Espíndola (US$3 by public transport). Over the bridge it's 4 km to the Ecuadorean village of Jimbura, from where you can get a pick-up to Amaluza (45 mins). There are two basic hotels in Amaluza (best is F *El Rocío*, on the plaza), from where a daily bus runs to Quito, taking about 24 hours.

Sullana

Colour map 1, grid B1
Population: 147,361

Sullana, 39 km north of Piura, is built on a bluff over the fertile Chira valley and is a busy, modern place. Avenida José de Lama, once a dusty, linear market, has a green, shady park with benches along the centre. Many of the bus companies have their offices along this avenue. San Martín is the main commercial street. Parks and monuments were added in 1994/5, which greatly improved the city's appearance. At the entrance, on the Pan-American Highway is an interesting mosaic statue of an iguana. There are lookouts over the Chira valley at Plaza Bolognesi and by the arches near the Plaza de Armas. The local fiesta and agricultural fair is *Reyes*, held on 5-29 January.

NB Although the city is safer than it once was, you should still take great care by the market. Do not arrive in the town after dark.

Sleeping
▪ *on map*
Price codes:
see inside front cover

A *Hostal La Siesta*, Av Panamericana 400, T/F502264, at the entrance to town. Hot water, fan, cable TV, **B** with cold water, pool, restaurant, laundry. **D** *Hostal Turicarami*, San Martín 814, T502899. With bathroom, fan, some rooms have hot water, clean, **E** without bathroom or fan. **D** *El Churre*, Tarapacá 501, T/F507006. With bath, TV, laundry, café. Recommended. **E** *Hostal Lion's Palace*, Grau 1030, T502587. With bathroom, fan, patio, pleasant, quiet, no breakfast. **E** *Hospedaje San Miguel*, C J Farfán 204,

T502789. **F** without bathroom, all rooms open off a central passageway, basic, helpful, good showers, staff will spray rooms against mosquitoes, cafeteria. **F** *Hospedaje Hugo*, San Martín 1022, T504016. Basic, small rooms. **F** *Hostal Príncipe*, Espinar 588. Clean and friendly.

Café Café, Tarapacá 484. Sandwiches, *tamales*, lunch *menú* US$1, juices and drinks. **Chifa El Dorado**, on the Plaza, and *Chifa Kam Loy*, San Martín 925, are the most authentic of several *chifas*. *Due Torri*, E Palacios 122. Italian and regional, popular with locals. *Monterrico*, Plaza de Armas. Set menu for US$1, popular. *Pollos La Cabaña*, Sucre y Palacios. Offers the standard grilled chicken. On 400 block of Sucre are *La Carreta*, No 419, for chicken, *Cebichería Rincón de Alejo*, No 423, *D-licia*, No 434, snacks, and *Chifa Nuevo Dorado*, No 438, Chinese.

Eating
● *on map*

Mototaxis charge US$0.30. **Taxis** Radio Taxis, T502210/504354. There are several daily buses to and from **Tumbes**, 244 km, 4-5 hrs US$5. To **Piura**, 38 km, 30 mins, US$0.45, there are frequent buses and colectivos, US$1, taxi US$2. *Eppo, Transportes del Norte* and *Cial* buses are at Terminal Turismo del Norte, Callao y Av José de Lama. If you have time, it is worth continuing to Piura rather than staying in Sullana. To **Chiclayo** and **Trujillo** see under Piura. To **Lima**, 1,076 km, 14-16 hrs, US$9-18, several buses daily, most coming from Tumbes or Talara. A luxury overnight bus via Trujillo with *Ittsa* (Av José de Lama 481, T501710) is US$18: with *Cruz del Sur*, at Av José de Lama 100 block; and *Continental (Ormeño)*, Tarapacá 1007. To Paita colectivos leave from the market, 2 blocks from Av Lama, US$1, 1 hr. To **Talara**, *Eppo* and *Emtrafesa*, C Comercio, 1 block from Av Lama, each leave hourly. *Eppo* are faster but more expensive, 1 hr, US$1.25. To **Máncora**, *Eppo*, 5 a day, 2½ hrs, US$3, or travel to Talara and then on from there via Los Organos.

Transport

Sullana

North Coast

Sleeping
1 El Churre
2 Hospedaje Hugo
3 Hospedaje San Miguel
4 Hostal Lion's Palace
5 Hostal Turicarami
6 Príncipe

Eating
1 Café Café
2 Cebichería Rincón de Alejo
3 Chifa El Dorado
4 Chifa Kam Loy
5 Chifa Nuevo Dorado
6 D-licia
7 Due Torri
8 La Cabaña
9 La Carreta
10 Monterrico

0 metres 100
0 yards 100

Directory   **Banks** *BCP*, San Martín 685. Changes cash and TCs. There are *casas de cambio* and street changers on San Martín by Tarapacá. **Communications** Internet: at San Martín 798 and 847 (*World Net*, US$0.60 per hr), and at Av José de Lama 125 and corner with Tarapacá. **Post office**: at Farfán 326. **Telecommunications**: telephone and fax at Miró Quesada 213. **Tour companies and travel agents** *Pesa Tours*, Espinar 301 y Tarapacá, T/F502237. For airline tickets (flights from Piura) and information. *Pola Tours* on the main plaza. Aero Continente and Tans agency. **Useful addresses** Immigration: Grau 939.

Border at La Tina-Macará

Leaving Peru   At Sullana the Pan-American Highway forks. To the east it crosses the Peru-Ecuador border at La Tina and continues via Macará to Loja and Cuenca. The road is scenic and paved to the border, 128 km. The more frequently used route to the border is the coastal road which goes from Sullana northwest towards the Talara oilfields and then follows the coastline to Máncora and Tumbes.

Transport to the border Combis leave from Sullana to the international bridge from Terminal Terrestre La Capullana, off Av Buenos Aires, several blocks beyond the canal. They leave when full, US$2.85 per person, 13/4 hrs. It's best to take a taxi or mototaxi to and from the terminal. From the border to Macará is 4 km: walk over the bridge and take one of the pick-ups which run from the border (10 mins, US$0.30, or US$1.25 for whole car). Frequent buses leave the Ecuadorean side for Loja (5-6 hrs, US$5), so if you are not taking the through bus (see under Piura), you can go from Sullana to Loja in a day. From the border to Sullana, cars may leave before they are full, but won't charge extra.

At the border   **Peruvian immigration** The border crossing is problem-free, open 24 hrs and officials are helpful. Go to Peruvian immigration at the end of the bridge, get a stamp, walk across and then go to Ecuadorean immigration. There are no customs searches (vehicles, including colectivos, are subject to full searches, though). There are banks at each side for changing cash only, Mon-Fri; rates are a little better in Macará.

Sleeping There is one *hospedaje* and several eating places on the road down to the bridge. At Suyo, 1½ hrs from Sullana (a pretty place), there are 2 *hospedajes*.

Into Ecuador   **Macará** is a dusty town in a rice-growing area (*Population*: 11,500. *Altitude*: 500 m). There are plenty of hotels and a few restaurants in town.

Border at Alamor

Colour map 1, grid B2   Colectivos run from Sullana for 3 dusty, bumpy hrs to Alamor, a rather remote, but official border crossing west of La Tina (US$3, or US$18 for whole car). A rowing boat crosses the Río Lalamor to Lalamor in Ecuador (US$0.20), or you can wade across. Peruvian **immigration** is a short walk from the ferry and there are money changers offering regular rates. On the Ecuadorean side immigration is by the church, a long walk from the crossing (ask directions). Officials on both sides have to leave their post once a fortnight to register their documents. If you are unlucky enough to arrive on one of these days (as was the author), you can't cross because you cannot get the right stamps. From Lalamor trucks run to the riverside town of Zapotillo (21 km, dirt, 40 mins, US$1), also on the border, but not an official crossing.

Sleeping in Zapotillo It has 3 hotels (**D** *Los Charanes* is best), eating places and buses to Loja, 7 hrs, and Quito. A paved road goes to Macará.

Coastal Route to Ecuador

Talara

Talara, the main centre of the coastal oil area, with a state-owned 60,000 bar-rel-a-day oil refinery and a fertilizer plant. Set in a desert oasis 5 km west of the Panamericana, the city is a triumph over formidable natural difficulties, with water piped 40 km from the Río Chira. La Peña beach, 2 km away, is unspoilt.

Phone code: 074
Colour map 1, grid B1
Population: 44,500
135 km from Piura
and 1,177 km
from Lima

Paved highways connect the town with the Negritos, Lagunitos, La Brea and other oilfields. Of historical interest are the old tarpits at La Brea, 21 km inland from Punta Pariñas, south of Talara, and near the foot of the Amotape moun-tains. Here the Spaniards boiled the tar to get pitch for caulking their ships. Surfers will love the empty swell north and south of town, especially near Negritos where a gentle beach break and rolling thunder are separated by Punta Balcones, the western-most point of South America. The impressive sea lion colony and the occasional dolphin make this an interesting spot.

Sleeping **NB** All hotels in Talara have problems with the water supply. Hotels include: **A** *Gran Pacífico*, Av Aviación y Arica, T/F385450. The most luxurious in town, suites, hot water, pool, restaurant, bar, parking, pay in dollars. **D** *Residencial Grau*, Av Grau 77, T382841, near the main plaza. Clean, friendly, possible to park one motor bike, owner changes dollars. **E** *Hostal Talara*, Av del Ejército 217, T382186. Clean and comfortable.

Eating The better restaurants can be found in the main hotels. There are many cheap restau-rants on the main plaza.

Transport **Bus** See under Sullana. To and from **Tumbes**, 171 km, 3 hrs, US$3.50, several daily. Most come from Piura and most stop at major towns going north. To **Piura**, 111 km, 2 hrs, US$1.75. To **El Alto** (Cabo Blanco), 32 km, 30 mins, US$0.75.

To **Máncora** take a combi from beside the Tepsa terminal to Los Organos (an oil workers town on the Panamericana with a windy beach and good seafood restaurants on the plaza), US$1, 1 hr; change combis there and continue to Máncora, 28 km, 20 mins, US$0.50.

Beaches north of Talara

Thirty-two kilometres north of Talara, is the small port of Cabo Blanco, famous for its excellent sea-fishing and surfing. The scenery has, unfortu-nately, been spoilt by numerous oil installations. The turn-off from the Pan-American Highway is at the town of **El Alto**, where many oil workers are housed. There are several basic hotels here. Camping is permitted free of charge at Cabo Blanco, on the beach or by the Fishing Club overlooking the sea, at least in the off-season, June-December. The film of Ernest Heming-way's *The Old Man and the Sea* was shot here.

Cabo Blanco
Colour map 1, grid B1

Marlin grew scarce in the late 1960s owing to commercial fishing and to cli-matic and maritime factors but in the last few years the Marlin have returned. The old Fishing Club, built in the 1950s, has been remodelled in the shape of the *Fishing Club Lodge Hotel*. A launch also provides all the necessary facilities for deep-sea fishing. Now, would-be Ernest Hemingways can return to Cabo Blanco in search of their dream catch.

▶▶ The old man and the marlin

Though Ernest Hemingway's famous novel, The Old Man and the Sea, was set in a Cuban fishing village, the people of Cabo Blanco, on the north coast of Peru, claim that the great writer was inspired by their own fishing waters.

The protagonist of the book, the old fisherman, Santiago, was perhaps the product of Hemingway's own obsession with the idea of catching a marlin weighing more than 1,500 pounds. One of the very few places where such a feat is possible is off the coast of Cabo Blanco. Here, in the 1950s, the marlin were abundant and reached extraordinary sizes. Indeed, during that decade Cabo Blanco became a sort of world sport fishing capital and fishermen the world over congregated there to chase the great black marlin, the largest and the most difficult to catch owing to its tremendous strength.

So it was that when Hollywood producers decided to make a film based on Hemingway's novel they realized that the only place they could find a

suitably large fish was in the waters off Cabo Blanco. In April 1955, the shooting team arrived with the writer, who was there to help them locate the fish that would appear in the movie.

Hemingway wasn't too interested in the movie, he was along for the fishing and quickly struck up a rapport with the down-to-earth local fisherfolk. In one particularly poignant anecdote they made him a gift of a bottle of pisco, a popular grape brandy, with a note saying "As long as the grapevines cry, I will drink their tears". The following morning, before going out to fish, the writer met those who had given him the pisco, smiled and said to them in Spanish, "I have drunk the tears".

Hemingway did not realize his dream of the 1,500 pound marlin during almost two months on the Peruvian coast, though he did manage to catch one weighing a little over 900 pounds. It was one of the largest black marlin he had ever caught and probably the last one of that size he would catch during the few remaining years of his life.

Sleeping **B** *Fishing Club Lodge*, clean, restaurant, pool, watersports, likely to be full in the New Year period. Recommended. **C-D** *El Merlín*, right on the beach, huge rooms.

Las Arenas At Las Arenas resort, 4 km south of Máncora, the beach is completely unspoiled, with armies of small crabs and abundant bird life, including frigates and masked and brown pelicans.

Máncora

Phone code: 074
Colour map 1, grid B1

A small, attractive resort stretching along 3 km of the Highway, Máncora is parallel to a long, sandy beach with safe bathing. It is a popular stop-off for travellers on the Peru-Ecuador route. The water here is warm enough for bathing and the town has some of the friendliest local surfers on the planet. **Surfing** is best November-March (boards and suits can be hired from *Gondwanaland Café*, Avenida Piura block 2, US$1.50 each per hour). This stretch of coast is famous for its excellent *mero* (grouper).

The Pan-American Highway runs through the centre of town and is the main street, called Avenida Piura. At the north end of town the beach is inaccessible and dirty, and this is not a safe area. South of Máncora along the coastal road (old Pan-American Highway) are some excellent beaches which are being developed, for example Las Pocitas (a resort ideal for families, or just for relaxing). There are several hotels (see below) and many beach homes of well-to-do Limeños.

Fresh water is piped into the area, producing the incongruous but welcome sight of green lawns and lush gardens between the sea and desert cliffs. There is a line of rocks parallel to the beach, which form interesting bathing pools at low tide, though these can be dangerous at high tide.

All places to stay are to be found along the Panamericana between the main plaza at the north end of town and the bridge at the south end. The better hotels are at the southern end of town. **B-C** *El Mar* and *Las Olas* (T858109), both on the beach in block 1 of Piura, offer smart, cabin-style rooms with bath, hammocks and gardens, half and full-board rates available. **D** *Punta Ballenas*, south of Cabo Blanco bridge at the south entrance to town, T4470437 (Lima), **B** in high season, lovely setting on beach, garden with small pool, expensive restaurant, recommended. **D** *Sausalito*, Piura block 4, T858058, comfortable, quieter rooms at back, breakfast included. **E** *Sol y Mar*, Piura block 2, on beach, T858106 (ask for Coqui Quiroga). With bath, fan and mosquito repellent extra, basic, restaurant, popular with surfers, shop, internet café (very slow connection), occasionally host parties, recommended but noisy disco next door till 0600. **E** per person *El Angolo*, Piura 262, on the beach. With bathroom, basic, nice terrace, friendly, restaurant, camping permitted in garden. Recommended. **E-F** *Hospedaje Crillon*, Paita 168, 1 block back from Panamericana in centre, T858001, basic rooms with 4 or more beds, shared bath, plenty of water, recommended.

The following places are along the old Pan-American Highway south of town (10 mins by mototaxi, US$1.45): **L** *Las Arenas*, 3½ km south of Máncora, T858104. Full board, 8 luxury bungalows, pool, lush gardens, trampoline, playground, kayaks for use, free transport from Tumbes airport. **B** *Puerto Palos*, T858199, www.puertopalos.com Excellent, small, nice pool overlooking the ocean. Restaurant is good but expensive. Recommended. Other options: **B** *Bungalows Playa Bonita*, T858113 (Lima 326 1263), very nice; *Máncora Beach Bungalows*, T858125.

Sleeping
Prices can increase by up to 100% in high season (Dec-Mar)

Stephanie's, adjoining *Sol y Mar* overlooking beach, serves *fuentes*, huge plates big enough for two. *Café La Bajadita*, is the best place in the evening to hang out, eat chocolate cake or *manjarblanco* and listen to rock and reggae. Also good are the two *La Espada* restaurants and *Cebichería Costa Azul* on the highway. Take-away food from *Sunset*, T858111.

Eating

To **Sullana and Piura** with *EPPO*, Grau 470, 1 block north of plaza, 5 a day, US$2.50 and US$3, 2½ and 3½ hrs respectively. Other buses stop en route from Tumbes in the main plaza. To **Tumbes** (and points in between), combis tour the length of Av Piura all day as far as the bridge until sufficiently full to depart, US$1.50, 2 hrs.

Transport

Banks *Tienda Marlón*, Piura 613. Changes US$ cash at poor rates. **Communications Internet**: several internet cafés on the highway. **Telephone**: at Piura 509, opposite the church. National and international calls, also collect.

Directory

East of Máncora are hot mud baths (*baños del barro*), which are nice after a day in the surf. There is no infrastructure, but the landscape, desert foothills and shrub lands, is beautiful. The access is north of town, at Km 1,168, from where you head for Quebrada Fernández. Beyond is **El Angolo game reserve**, which extends as far south as the Río Chira. Take a mototaxi from Máncora, 20 minutes, and pay US$5.75 for the return journey and an hour's wait while you bathe.

North Coast

Playa Punta Sal

Phone code: 074
Colour map 1, grid B1

At Km 1,182 is an enormous customs house for checking southbound traffic. 22 km north of Máncora, at Km 1,187 (El Arco – or arch), is the turn-off for **Punta Sal Grande**, a posh resort town at the southern end of beautiful Playa Punta Sal, a 3 km long sandy beach, with calm surf. It's a favourite of well-to-do Lima businessmen and politicians.

Sleeping

The only restaurants are in the hotels

The hotels in town are listed running from north to south

C per person *Hospedaje El Bucanero*, new Dec 2002, with pool, bar, restaurant and great view. **C** *Los Delfines*, T320251, near the beach. Shared bathroom, clean, nice rooms, restaurant open in high season, meals on request in low season, vegetarian available, Canadian-run, very friendly, full board **AL**, more during high season for full board, **A** for a room only in high season. **D** per person *Sunset Punta Sal*, T540041 (Lima 475 2739), puntasunset@hotmail.com **C** with full board (low season price), small pool with jacuzzi, fishing trips, wonderful place. Opposite is **E** per person *Las Terrazas*, only open a few months a year, small restaurant. **B** *Caballito de Mar*, at the southern end of the bay, T800814 (Lima 4463122, F4476562), caballito@amauta.rcp.net.pe With bathroom, nice location overlooking the ocean, all rooms have ocean view, comfortable, friendly, pool, restaurant, full board available. Recommended. **C** *Huá*, on the beach, T608365 (Lima 461 2031), huapuntasal@yahoo.com A rustic old wooden building, rooms with bath, pleasant terrace overlooking ocean, discount for IYHF card holders, camping permitted on the beach beside the hotel, meals available, **B** in the high season.

The north end of the beach is known as **Punta Sal Chica**: **A** per person *Punta Sal Club Hotel*, access road at Km 1,193, T608878. 18 bungalows, 12 rooms, solar heated water, relaxing, private beach, watersports, pool, horse riding, deep-sea fishing, transport to Tumbes airport US$10 per person. Recommended.

Transport

From Máncora combis will drop you at El Arco, US$0.25, or at **Cancas**, just north of Punta Sal Chica (Km 1,193), US$0.50. In Cancas mototaxis can be hired to go to Punta Sal Grande for US$3, 20 mins, and Punta Sal Chica, US$1.50, 10 mins. Colectivo from Piura US$8.50-11.50, 3-3½ hrs.

Punta Sal to Los Pinos

Colour map 1, grid B1

The fishing village of **Cancas** has a few shops, restaurants and a gas station. From Punta Mero (Km 1,204) north, the beach is used by *larveros*, extracting shrimp larvae from the ocean for use in the shrimp industry, and is no longer considered safe for camping.

Sleeping

Several new resorts are being built between Punta Mero and Tumbes. **C** *Hotel Playa Florida*, at Km 1,222, pleasant bungalows on the ocean (look for the red roofs), food available, T/F(074)320251, T428 9110 (Lima). *Hotel Punta Camarón*, at Km 1,235, T608007. With secluded private beach, swimming pool, restaurant. Recommended. **E** per person *Casa Grillo Centro Ecoturistico Naturista*, Los Pinos 563, between Bocapán and Los Pinos, 30 km from Tumbes, T/F(074)525207, T/F446 2233 (Lima). To get there take a colectivo from Tumbes market to Los Pinos, or get off bus on Pan-American Highway at Km 1,236.5. Youth Hostel with excellent restaurant including vegetarian meals, very friendly, great place to relax, 6 rustic-style rooms for up to 4 people, shared bath, hot water, laundry, also surfing, scuba diving, fishing, cycling, trekking, horse riding (US$4 per hr), camping available. Recommended.

Zorritos, 27 km south of Tumbes, is an important fishing centre, with a good beach. Several new hotels and resorts have been built. A good restaurant is *Sunset Beach*, Km 1,245, T542243, seafood.

This is the only part of the Peruvian coast where the sea is warm all year. There are two good beaches near Tumbes, one is at Caleta La Cruz 16 km southwest, where Pizarro landed in 1532. The original Cruz de Conquista was taken to Lima. Regular colectivos run back and forth from Tumbes, US$0.80 each way.

Tumbes

Tumbes, about 141 km north of Talara, and 265 km north of Piura, is the most northerly of Peru's provincial capitals. It is not the most beautiful, but it does have some interesting historic wooden buildings in the centre. Tumbes is also a garrison town, so watch where you point you camera.

Ins and outs

A taxi to the airport costs US$4, 20 mins. Combis charge US$1.50. Taxis meet flights to take passengers to the border for US$7-9. There are no combis from the airport to the border. Beware of overcharging. All bus companies have offices on Av Tumbes.

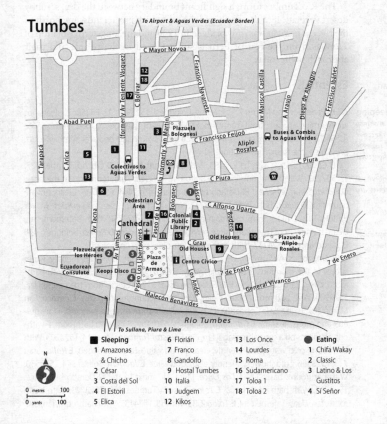

Tumbes

To Airport & Aguas Verdes (Ecuador Border)

To Sullana, Piura & Lima

Río Tumbes

■ Sleeping		6 Florián	13 Los Once	● Eating
1 Amazonas		7 Franco	14 Lourdes	1 Chifa Wakay
& Chicho		8 Gandolfo	15 Roma	2 Classic
2 César		9 Hostal Tumbes	16 Sudamericano	3 Latino & Los
3 Costa del Sol		10 Italia	17 Toloa 1	Gustitos
4 El Estoril		11 Judgem	18 Toloa 2	4 Sí Señor
5 Elica		12 Kikos		

N

0 metres 100
0 yards 100

Getting around Everything is fairly conveniently located close to the Plaza de Armas, although transport to the Ecuadorean border is a little bit farther out. Hotels are mostly central to the north of the river either side of Av Tumbes and Bolívar.

Tourist offices *Centro Cívico*, Bolognesi 194, 1st floor, on the plaza. 0800-1300, 1400-1800. Helpful, provides map and leaflets. *Pronaturaleza*, Av Tarapacá 4-16, Urb Fonavi, T523412. *Touring y Automóvil Club*, Huáscar 330, T523475, F522690, tumbes@touringperu.com.pe

Sights

The long promenade, the Malecón Benavides, beside the high banks of the Río Tumbes, gives good views of the river. It is decorated with arches and a monstrous statue called El Beso (the Kiss), has several cafés, but is rather dilapidated. Old houses are best seen on **Calle Grau**, particularly at the junction with C Los Andes, and a colonial public library with a small museum stands in the **Plaza de Armas**. The **cathedral**, dating in its present incarnation from 1903, was restored in 1985. There are two pedestrian malls, arranged with benches and plants, Paseo de Los Libertadores on Bolívar and Paseo de la Concordia on San Martín, both leading north from the Plaza de Armas. In the main Plaza and the Paseo de la Concordia there are several ornate, brightly-coloured mosaic statues giving the city a slightly more exotic, tropical feel than anywhere else on the Peruvian coast.

The Río Tumbes forms a significant boundary between the dry, scrubby desert vegetation to the south and the more lush green landscape north of the river. The river was only bridged in 1930 and the long-term isolation of Tumbes from the rest of Peru is still reflected in the people and their approach to life today.

Essentials

Sleeping **A** *Costa del Sol*, San Martín 275, Plazuela Bolognesi, T523991/92, F525862. Clean, hot
■ *on map* water, minibar, fan, front rooms noisy, restaurant has good food and service
Price codes: (US$5.75-7), parking extra, has nice garden with swimming pool, racquetball court,
see inside provides some tourist information.
front cover

   D *César*, Huáscar 311, T/F522883. With bathroom, fan, TV. **D** *Chicho*, Tumbes 327,
Av Tumbes is still T/F522282. With bathroom, fan, mosquito net, TV, clean, quieter rooms at the back.
sometimes referred **D** *Florián*, Piura 414 near El Dorado bus company, T522464, F524725. Clean, private
to by its old name bath, fan. **D** *Kikos*, Bolívar 462, T523777. With bathroom, basic. **D** *Lourdes*, Mayor
of Teniente Vásquez Bodero 118, 1 block from the main plaza, T522966, F522758. With bathroom, fan,
The water clean, friendly, roof restaurant, slow service. Recommended. **D** *Roma*, Bolognesi 425
supply is poor Plaza de Armas, T524137. With bathroom, fan, pleasant, convenient.

   E *Amazonas*, Av Tumbes 317, T520629. With bathroom, fan, clean, friendly, water supply in the mornings is unreliable, noisy. **E** *Elica*, Tacna 319, T523870. With bathroom, clean, fan, quiet, good. **E** *El Estoril*, Huáscar 317, 2 blocks from the main plaza, T524906. With bathroom, good, clean, friendly, discount for long stay. **E** *Franco*, San Martín 107, Paseo de la Concordia, T525295. With bathroom, fan, upper rooms are quieter and more pleasant. **E** *Gandolfo*, Bolognesi 420, T522868. With bathroom, **F** without, all rooms off a central passage, fan, OK. **E** *Hostal Tumbes*, Grau 614, T522203. With bathroom, cold water, fan, friendly, clean, good value. Recommended. **E** *Italia*, Grau 733, T523396. Cold showers, friendly, also good value. **E** *Judgem*, Bolívar 344, T523530. With bathroom, basic, OK. **E** *Los Once*, Piura 417, next to the El Dorado bus office, T523717. With bathroom, basic. **E** *Toloa 1*, Avda Tumbes 430, T523771. With bathroom, fan, clean, safe, helpful. **E** *Toloa 2*, Bolívar 458, T524135. With bathroom, fan, OK.

F *Sudamericano*, San Martín 110, Paseo de la Concordia. Shared bathroom, basic but good value. There are many other cheap hotels by the market. At holiday times it can be very difficult to find a vacant room.

Classic, Tumbes 185. Popular and recommended.*Latino*, Bolívar 163, on Plaza de Armas. Good set meals and à la carte, also *peña* most evenings. *Los Gustitos*, same address, next door-but-one. Excellent *menús* and à la carte. *Chifa Wakay*, Huáscar 417. Smart, good, recommendedThere are other inexpensive restaurants on the Plaza de Armas, Paseo de la Concordia and near the markets. For example, *Sí Señor*, Bolívar 119 on the plaza. Good for snacks. Also *Pizzería Studio* on the plaza. Good pizza and desserts.

Eating
● *on map*

    Heladería La Suprema, Paseo Libertadores 298. Good ice cream, sweets and cold drinks. Next door at 296 is *Bam Bam*, for breakfast and snacks.

    Try *bolas de plátano*, soup with banana balls, meat, olives and raisins, and *sudado*, a local stew.

Pub Discoteca Keops, Bolívar 121 on the plaza. Sometimes has live groups at weekends.

Bar & clubs

There's a well-stocked supermarket *Anilu*, on Bolívar.

Shopping

Most companies offer day tours of the local area for US$20 per person, minimum 2, and US$35-50 per person to the hinterland. *Flamenco Travel*, Av Tumbes 819, T522771. *Preferencial Tours*, Grau 427. Knowledgeable and friendly. *Rosillo Tours,* Tumbes 293, T/F523892. Information, tickets, Western Union agents.

Tour operators

Air connections Daily flights to and from **Lima** and **Trujillo** with *Aero Continente*; also 5 days a week via **Piura**, US$70-90. It is essential to reconfirm flights 24 hrs before departure. It is better to buy tickets in Tumbes rather than at the airport.

Transport

Bus Daily buses to and from **Lima**, 1,320 km, 18-20hrs, US$12 (normal service), US$25 (*Cruz del Sur*), US$34 (*Cruz del Sur* VIP service).

    Most bus companies have offices on Av Tumbes: *Civa*, No 518, T525120; *Cruz del Sur*, 519 (T522627); *Ormeño*, Av Tumbes s/n, T522228; *Trans Chiclayo*, 466 (T525260). Cheaper buses usually leave 1600-2100, and more expensive ones 1200-1400. Except for luxury service, most buses to Lima stop at major cities en route. Tickets to anywhere between Tumbes and Lima sell quickly, so if arriving from Ecuador you may have to stay overnight. Piura is a good place for connections in the daytime.

    To **Talara**, 171 km, US$3.50, 3 hrs. To **Sullana**, 244 km, 3-4 hrs, US$4.50, several buses daily. To **Piura**, 4-5 hrs, 282 km, US$4.50; with *Trans Chiclayo, Cruz del Sur, El Dorado* (Piura 459, T523480, also to Máncora and Trujillo) 8 a day. *Comité Tumbes/Piura* colectivos (Tumbes 308, T525977) costs US$5.75, fast cars, leave when full, 3½ hrs. To **Chiclayo**, 552 km, 6 hrs, US$5.75, several each day with *Cruz del Sur, El Dorado*. To **Trujillo**, 769 km, 10-11 hrs, US$7.15-14.35, *Ormeño, Cruz del Sur, El Dorado* and *Emtrafesa*, Tumbes 581. To **Chimbote**, 889 km, 13-14 hrs, US$10. For transport to the border, see Border with Aguas Verdes (Ecuador), page 433.

Airline offices *Aero Continente*, Tumbes 217, T522350. **Banks** *BCP*, Paseo de los Libertadores 261, for cash only, poor rates. *Banco Continental*, Bolívar 121, changes cash and Amex TCs only, US$5 commission. *Banco Regional*, 7 de Enero, Plaza de Armas, ATM, TCs exchanged. *Cambios Internacionales*, Av Bolívar 161, Plaza de Armas. Cash only, good rates. Money changers on the street (on Bolívar, left of the Cathedral), some of whom are unscrupulous, give a much better rate than the banks or *cambios*, but don't accept the first offer you are given. Street changers don't change cheques. All banks close for lunch. Rates offered at the airport are bad. If you are travelling on to

Directory

Ecuador, it is better to change your Soles at the border as the rate is higher. **Communications** Internet: widely available in many cheap cafés and major hotels. Around the Plaza de Armas, *El Mundo* and *Planet.com* are open late, and there is a good place between *Latino* and *Los Gustitos*. Post office: San Martín 208. **Telephone office**, San Martín 210. Both on Paseo de la Concordia. **Consulates** *Ecuadorean Consulate*, Bolívar 155, Plaza de Armas, T523022, 0900-1300 and 1400-1630. Mon-Fri. **Laundry** *Lavandería Flash* at Piura 1000. Pay by weight.

Around Tumbes

The remains of the Cabeza de Vaca cult centre of the Tumpis Indians can be found at **Corrales**, 5 km south of Tumbes, but were heavily damaged by the 1983 and 1997/98 rains. The Incas built their fort of San Pedro on the site of the Tumpis settlement. The fort was visited by Pizarro on his way from the coast along the Inca coastal highway up to Cajamarca.

Three protected areas consisting of three distinct environments form the UNESCO Biosphere Reserve of northwest Peru. It is an area rich in wildlife and flora, but little visited by travellers passing by en route between Peru and Ecuador. In a single day it is possible to visit all three areas and sample the rainforest, dry scrub and mangrove swamps.

Santuario Nacional los Manglares de Tumbes
Mosquito repellent is a must for the Tumbes area

The Santuario Nacional los Manglares de Tumbes is a national reserve, created to protect the mangrove ecosystem in the northernmost part of the Peruvian coast. It extends between the border with Ecuador in the north and Puerto Pizarro (see below) in the south. 4,750 ha remain, of which 2,988 ha are protected. There are 5 species of mangrove, the main one being the red mangrove on whose roots the *conchas negras* live. At least 200 bird species have been recorded, eight of which are endemic, including the mangrove eagle. The mangroves are under threat from fresh water brought down by the rivers during El Niño and the expanding shrimp farming industry, though at 3,000 ha it's small compared to that of Ecuador.

The mangrove swamps are full of pelicans; best to visit them at high tide. A few tame birds beg for fish on the beaches.

Ins & outs The best access to the mangrove reserve is via the Pan-American Highway north as far as Zarumilla. Combis leave every few minutes from Tumbes, US$0.50, 30 mins. Then hire a motorbike in Zarumilla to go to CEDECOM (Centro de Conservación para el Desarrollo de los Manglares), 7 km, US$1.50 each way but you must arrange for the bike to return to collect you. The standard tour price is US$12 for a boat that takes up to 6 passengers, 2½ hrs, and includes the mangrove walkway and a trip up several creeks by boat, subject to tide levels. Book with Pronaturaleza, in Tumbes, who can also arrange a Sanctuary visitors permit from Inrena. There is no entry fee.

Puerto Pizarro Puerto Pizarro, a small, rubbish-strewn fishing port 13 km northeast of Tumbes, is another access point for the mangroves. Worth visiting from here is the research station where the **Río Tumbes crocodile**, a UN Red-data species, is protected. The crocodile is found at the river's mouth, threatened by shrimp farming, and in the Río Tumbes' upper reaches, threatened by gold-mining. Boats from *Comité de Transporte Acuático*, Malecón Turístico, T543019 go to: **Isla de Amor** (bars, restaurants, camping, windsurfing, hammocks for rent, overnighting 'homeless lovers', US$4.30); **Isla Hueso de Ballena** (open ocean and quiet bay, swimming, no services, US$5.75); **crocodile farm** (US$7.15); **Isla de los Pájaros** (best to see birds 1700-1800, US$8.55); **full tour including**

mangroves, 2 hours, US$12.85 (price per boat, maximum 8 people). The **Festival of San Pedro y San Pablo** takes place on 29-30 June.

Sleeping, eating and transport   E per person *Hospedaje Bayside*, by the Malecón, bungalows with bath, pool, food available. *Restaurante Playa Hermosa*, by the Malecón. To get there, take colectivo No 6 from the small plaza on C Piura in Tumbes; US$0.50, 20 mins.

The Parque Nacional Cerros de Amotape was created to protect an area representative of the equatorial forest. It extends southeast from the south bank of the Tumbes river, towards the El Angolo game preserve northeast of Máncora. It covers 90,700 ha comprising seven different habitats, including the best preserved area of dry forest on the Pacific coast. Some of the endemic species are the Tumbes crocodile, the river otter and white-winged turkeys. Other species to be seen are black parrot, puma, deer, tigrillo and white-backed squirrels.

Parque Nacional Cerros de Amotape

Ins and outs   Access is via the road which goes southeast from the Pan-American Highway at Bocapán (Km 1,233) to Casitas and Huásimo, it takes about two hours by car from Tumbes, and is best done in the dry season (Jul-Nov). Also access via Quebrada Fernández from Máncora and via Querecotilo and Los Encuentros from Sullana. Permission to enter is needed from Inrena, which *Pronaturaleza* can arrange. There is no entrance fee. All water must be carried which is why most visitors choose to visit by tour.

The Zona Reservada de Tumbes, formerly Bosque Nacional de Tumbes (75,000 ha), lies to the northeast of Tumbes, between the Ecuadorean border and Cerros de Amotape National Park. It was created to protect dry equatorial forest and tropical rainforest. The wildlife includes monkeys, otters, wild boars, small cats and crocodiles.

Zona Reservada de Tumbes

Access from Tumbes is via Cabuyal, Pampas de Hospital and El Caucho to the Quebrada Faical research station or via Zarumilla and Matapalo. The best accessible forest is around El Narango, which lies beyond the research station.

Border at Aguas Verdes (Ecuador)

The main Peruvian immigration and customs complex is outside Zarumilla, about 4 km before the international bridge. The frontier is open 24 hrs a day and passports can be stamped on either side of the border at any time.

Peruvian Immigration

Police officers on either side of the international bridge sometimes ask for bribes. Try to avoid them if possible but if approached be courteous but firm. Porters on either side of the border charge exorbitant prices, but don't be bullied. If you wish to photograph the border, ask the Ecuadorean immigration officers first.

There are virtually no **customs** formalities at the border for passengers crossing on foot, but spot-checks sometimes take place.

Having obtained your exit stamp, proceed across the bridge into Huaquillas. Passports are stamped 3 km north of town along the road to Machala. There's no urban transport; inter-city buses charge US$0.20 from Huaquillas; taxis US$1.50.

Entering Ecuador

When driving into Peru vehicle fumigation is not required, but there is one outfit who will attempt to fumigate your vehicle with water and charge US$10. Beware of officials claiming that you need a carnet to obtain your 90-day transit permit. This is not so; cite Decreto Supremo 015-87-ICTI/TUR (but check that rules have not changed). There are frequent road tolls between Tumbes and Lima, approximately US$0.75 each.

Crossing by private vehicle

North Coast

Sleeping If stuck overnight in the border area there is a hotel in **Aguas Verdes**: **E** *Hostal Francis*, Av República del Perú 220, T561177. OK. There are 4 hotels in **Zarumilla**, at Km 1,290 on the Pan-American Highway, 5 km south of Aguas Verdes. There is a signpost on the highway and the main plaza is only a few blocks away from the turn-off: **E** *Imperio*, on the plaza, T565178. Small, modern, very basic, cold water turned off at night, very clean, mosquito nets, very friendly. Recommended. *Hospedaje Karibiam*, Tumbes 310, T565409.

Transport **From Tumbes to border** Colectivos leave from block 3 of Av Tumbes. US$1 per person or US$6 to hire a car, but overcharging of gringos is very common, especially from the border to Tumbes. Make sure the driver takes you all the way to the border and not just as far as the complex 4 km south of the bridge. Combis leave from the market area along Mcal Castilla across the Calle Alipio Rosales, US$0.50 (luggage on the roof). Run down city buses ply the same route as combis, US$0.40, but are slower. All vehicles only leave when full, 30-45 mins to Aguas Verdes on the Peruvian side of the international bridge. They pass the turn-off for the airport from which it is a 500-m walk to the terminal. Colectivos to the airport charge US$1.50 per person, but often ask for much more. From the border to Zarumilla by moto-taxi costs US$0.50 per person. Colectivos can cross the bridge, taxis cannot (so don't hire a Peruvian taxi to take you into Ecuador).There is an *Aero Continente* office in Aguas Verdes, good for booking flights from Tumbes or Piura.

Directory **Banks** Money can be changed on either side of the border, but note that, since 2000, Ecuador has been using the dollar as currency. Beware sharp practices by money changers using fixed calculators and passing false bills (examine ALL notes). Do not change money on the minibus in Aguas Verdes, very poor rates.

Into Ecuador **Huaquillas** is a small city with a reasonable selection of hotels and other services. Transport links to other parts of Ecuador (Machala – 80 km, 1 hr, Quito, Guayaquil, Cuenca, Loja) are good. Transit Police, Customs and the Military have checkpoints on the road north so keep your passport to hand.

Northern Highlands

Introducing the Northern Highlands

This vast area stretches from the western foothills of the Andes right across the mountains and down to the fringes of the Amazon jungle. It contains Peru's most spectacular pre-Columbian ruins, some of them built on a massive scale unequalled anywhere in the Americas. A good road rises from the coast to the city of **Cajamarca**, where the Inca Atahualpa was captured by the Spanish. Only one Inca building remains, the so-called Ransom Chamber, but the city has a pleasant colonial centre with comfortable hotels and good restaurants. Change is coming fast as a huge gold mine is bringing new investment to the area. Close by are the **hot springs** where Atahualpa used to bathe, still very much in use today, and a number of pre-Inca sites. Beyond Cajamarca, a tortuous road winds its way east to the functional town of **Chachapoyas**. This is a friendly place, opening its doors

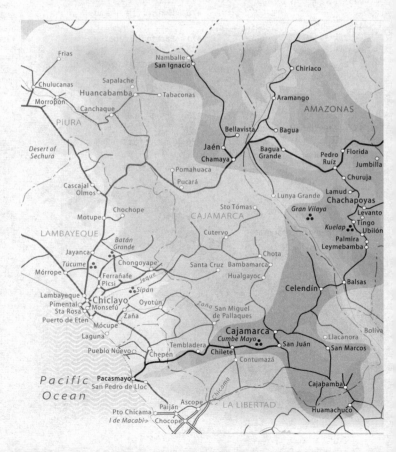

to visitors as it lies at the centre of a region full of fantastic archaeological treasures whose mysteries are just being uncovered. There are **fortresses**, **mysterious cities** and strange **burial sites** replete with mummies and giant sarcophagi.

From Chachapoyas there are three options: carry on eastwards on one of Peru's most beautiful roads to the tropical lowland town of **Tarapoto** passing waterfalls and high moors before dropping down to the jungle zone; return to the coast at Chiclayo; or you can head north to Ecuador on a new route via Jaén and San Ignacio for the crossing to Zumba and Vilcabamba. With new roads and bridges in operation, a great adventure is opening up. It's possible now to travel from Ecuador, through Chachapoyas and Cajamarca on to the Cordillera Blanca, even to Cusco, without touching the coast and all by public transport. It may be a slow route, but it will take some beating. All these possibilities are getting easier as the area becomes the focus of tourism development to rival the Lima-Cusco-Arequipa axis.

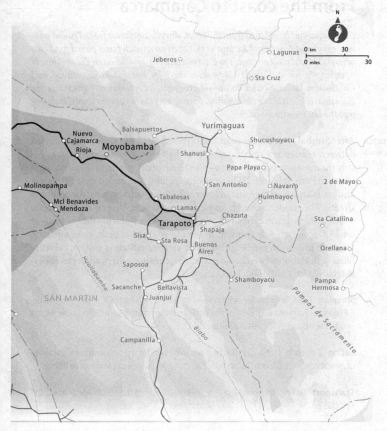

Northern Highlands

> ## Things to do in the Northern Highlands
>
> • For an out-of-the-way archaeological experience, go to **Marca Huamachuco**, in its trategic location on the Royal Inca Road, page 439.
>
> • If you are in Cajamarca and fancy a quick dip, the **Baños del Inca** are just outside town. The municipal hot springs have just been restored and are clean and definitely hot. It will be a quick dip, too, as the waters are so potent you are advised not to say in for long, page 450.
>
> • In need of refreshment? Try one of the exotic fruit-flavoured ice creams at *Heladería Holanda* on the Plaza in Cajamarca. For more dairy delights there are plenty of shops selling the local cheeses and *manjar blanco*, page 448.
>
> • Hike up to **Kuelap** (or take the long and twisty road by car). The vast fortress will take your breath away. Seeing it in sunshine gives the clearest view, but on a misty day the Cloud People's citadel is truly atmospheric, page 461.
>
> • Make **Tarapoto** your gateway to the **jungle**. From the high passes, follow the waters as they rush down to the lowlands, passing colonists' towns and weekend resorts called *recreos*. Introduce yourself to tropical fruits, the local sausage (*chorizo*) and fried green bananas (*tocacho*), page 473.

From the coast to Cajamarca

Cajamarca can be reached from the coast, directly northeast from Trujillo on a very rough road, or from Chiclayo via Chepén on a much faster paved road (see below). The old road northeast to Cajamarca from Trujillo is terrible and lonely – especially for cyclists. It takes three days by bus via Huamachuco and Cajabamba because buses do not interconnect, as opposed to eight hours via Pacasmayo, but it is more interesting, passing over the bare puna before dropping into the Huamachuco valley.

Otuzco
Colour map 3, grid A2

After **Simbal** (just off the road itself) there is a 17 km stretch of new road between Hacienda Concon and Casmiche before reaching Otuzco, arguably the most accessible sierra town, in terms of proximity to the coast, anywhere in Peru. It is only 2½ hours from Trujillo. 'La Ciudad de la Fe', as it is known, is an attractive Andean town at 2,200 m with some narrow cobbled streets. The modern church houses the important **Virgen de la Puerta**, which attracts devotees from all over Peru, especially during the big **festival** on 15 December. Adjoining it, in the old colonial church, is an amazing museum filled with public gifts for the Virgen, including endless cabinets filled with elaborately embroidered capes, cheap jewellery and even shoes. ■ *0830-1230, 1400-1600. US$0.25.*

Sleeping **E** *Los Portales*, Santa Rosa 680. Hot water, with bath, TV, clean, good value. **F** *Progreso*, Progreso 653. Best of the basic hostales, shared bathroom, some rooms without windows. All hotels are full in mid-Dec.

Eating *Zagitario*, Tacna 769. The best place in town for the delicious local speciality of *jamón con yuca*. *Otuzco*, Tacna 608. Also good for guinea pig and turkey dishes.

Transport To **Trujillo**, hourly buses leave when full from the south side of town, 2½ hrs, US$2.

In **Agallpampa** there is one, unsigned *hostal*. Further on is the mining town of **Shorey**, 5 km beyond which, at **Quiruvilca**, there is one hotel. In Shorey a road branches off to **Santiago de Chuco**, birthplace of the poet César Vallejo (see Literature, page 598), where there is the annual festival of Santiago El Mayor in the second half of July. The main procession is on 25 July, when the image is carried through the streets. Buses to Santiago de Chuco from Trujillo: *Horna*, Avenida América del Sur 1368, and *Agreda*, Unión 149, 8 hours, US$6, only at night. **Otuzco to Huamachuco**

From **Cachicadan**, where there are good hot baths, the *Transportes Horna* and *Agreda* buses continue from Santiago, 2 hours. Combis also depart frequently, when full, from Santiago de Chuco, US$1.50, 1½ hours. **E** *Hostal Silita Star*, in Cachidan is attractive and rustic with hot water, TV and restaurant. Recommended.

Huamachuco

The road, formerly on the royal Inca Road, runs on to this colonial town, 181 km from Trujillo. The main reason for visiting Huamachuco is to see the spectacular, but little known ruins of **Marca Huamachuco**, which are located on the summit (3,600 m) of one of the mountains that surround the town. The town also has the largest main plaza in Peru and a controversial modern **cathedral**. There is a colourful **Sunday market** and **Museo Municipal Wamachuko**, Libertad 100, displays artefacts found at Cerro Amauta and Marca Huamachuco. ■ *Free*. *Colour map 3, grid A2 Altitude: 3,180 m*

The Marca Huamachuco ruins surely rank in the top 10 archaeological sites in Peru. It is an extensive site, 3 km long, dating back to at least 300 BC though many structures were added later. Its most impressive features are: El Castillo, a remarkable circular structure with walls up to 8 m high located at the highest point of the site. This and other structures are the oldest-known buildings in Peru to extend to more than two storeys and may have reached five storeys. The outer defensive wall, which is accessible where it bisects the hill halfway along, also reaches up to 8 m in height. It consists of two parallel walls with gallery rooms in between. El Convento complex consists of five circular structures of varying sizes located towards the northern end of the hill. These are later constructions dating back to AD 600-800. The largest one has been partially reconstructed by the Instituto Nacional de Cultura (INC) and provides an interesting insight into how they must once have appeared, with two or three parallel outer walls, gallery rooms between them and several other internal structures. It has been suggested that these buildings housed the privileged members of an elite class. (The guardian should be tipped, US$1.) **Marca Huamachuco**

Three km before the ruins you will pass the remarkable **Cerro Amauta** on the left. It would seem that the whole of this relatively small hilltop was adapted to store water by placing an impermeable layer of clay around it. Wells on the summit, which can still be viewed, then provided access to the water within. Almost certainly the hill acquired major religio-cultural significance within the Huari-Tiahuanaco empire and became a place of pilgrimage and sacrifice in times of drought.

It seems likely that Marca Huamachuco existed for many centuries as the centre of an autonomous religious cult, separate from the activities of the Chachapoyans to the north and east. The site was certainly used as much as a ceremonial centre as it was for defensive purposes. Latest theories suggest that the the Huari-Tiahuanaco culture (AD 600-1100) may have developed from the north out of places such as Marca Huamachuco and Yaino and then spread south, rather than the other way round. Apparently, the chronology of sites fits much better on this basis, but, if correct, this would require a complete reassessment of the Huari-Tiahuanuco culture.

■ *The ruins are a 3-hr walk, 9 km, from town along a clear track. A driver for those not wanting to walk is Alexis Rebaza, T441082, who has a 4-wheel drive vehicle, US$5 per hour. A minimum of 2 hrs is needed at the site, four hours to really know it. There is no entry fee. Carry all food and drink with you.*

Wiracochapampa is an extensive Huari site, 3 km, 45 minutes' walk, to the north of the town. Much of the site is overgrown and poorly conserved, but walls up to 3 m high can still be found. It is believed that the complex was never completed, possibly because the principal builder was taken south to construct Piquillacta, near Cusco, with which it has many similarities.

Also worth seeing in the Huamachuco area is **Laguna Sausacocha**, surrounded by low hills. There are several restaurants and it is possible to go rowing on the lake.

Sleeping **E** *Hostal Noche Buena*, San Román 401 on the main plaza. Clean, with hot showers and TV. **E** *Huamachuco*, Castilla 354, on the plaza, T441393. Clean, with hot showers (**F** without), friendly. **F** *Kaseci*, San Martín 756. Rustic, cold, sometimes holds art exhibitions. **F** *Casa de hospedaje Las Hortensias*, Castilla 130, T441049. A variety of rooms in a ramshackle family home, very friendly, shared bath, *cuyes* in the kitchen. **F** *Hostal San José*, Balta 310. Clean, friendly, basic. **F** *Hostal Viracocha*, Carmen La Troya, behind the market, safe, water problems.

Eating *La Casona*, Balta 850. Serves reasonable local dishes. *Café Noche Buena*, good food, open late. *Pollería Pollón*, Balta 320. The best of several chicken eateries around the plaza. *Café Sebastián*, on upper side of plaza. Open early for breakfast. *El Túnel*, on the Trujillo road at the entrance to town. With tables outside, good for typical dishes and a game of 'sapo'. *Café Venezia*, Castilla 687. Serves excellent, coffee, cakes and pies. *Peña Catequil*, 5 Esquinas, 2 blocks from the plaza along the Trujillo road. Weekends only, attractive décor, good food and dance floor. *Bar Michi Wasi*, San Román 461, on the plaza. An attractive, atmospheric bar and a good place to meet locals who know the area. Recommended.

Festivals On the **second Sun in Aug** is *Waman Raymi*, a major festival held in the ruins of Wiracochapampa (see above), a northern version of *Inti Raymi* in Cusco. A week of festivities begins on **15 Aug** to mark the *founding of Huamacucho* and features spectacular fireworks and the remarkable *Turcos* – aggressive male dancers from a nearby village who wear at least 10 layered skirts when dancing.

Transport **Air** *Air Líder* flies **Trujillo-Huamachuco** daily, 45 mins, US$45, T204470, Trujillo; Balta 264, T441248, Huamachuco. **Bus** From **Trujillo**, 170 km, poor road, dusty in places, 8 hrs: *Agreda* (Unión 149, Trujillo; Balta 865, Huamachuco) at 0800 each way, also 1800, and *Gran Turismo* 0830 from Trujillo (Prol Vallejo 1368, T425391), 1245 from Huamachuco (Balta 798), the only buses in daylight. To **Cajabamba**, *Trans Anita*, Psje Hospital off Av.10 de Julio, have combis at 0500 and 1230, 3 hrs, US$3.

Directory **Communications** There is internet access at S Carrión 740.

The Yanasara **thermal baths** are a 30-minute walk from the village of Palla **Yanasara**
set in a beautiful valley at 2,300 m. The hot, clean baths consist of a pool and **& Palla**
four individual baths, all US$0.30 per person. Recommended. Close to the
baths is a hotel (**F**), clean and friendly, with restaurant, run by local and
Spanish priests. A pleasant two-hour walk can be made up the Río Grande
valley to the hacienda of **Cochabamba**, once the Andean retreat of the owners of the Laredo sugar plantation, near Trujillo. To Yanasara, combis
depart when full, 0500-0700 and at 1300, from Avenida 10 de Julio, for El
Convento and can drop you in Palla, two hours, US$1.50. Or *Trans Mi
Joyce*, Suárez 720, departs daily at 0700 and returns at 1500.

Huamachuco to the Cordillera Blanca

It is now possible to travel, via Retamas and Tayabamba (see below), to *Colour map 3, grid A2*
Sihuas (see page 366) and the Cordillera Blanca along a road which is very
poor in places and involves crossing the Río Marañón twice. The building of
a new bridge over the river means that it is feasible to go from Cusco to Quito
entirely by public transport, though few travellers have made this journey. It
is most easily undertaken coming from the south. Note that the road may be
almost impassable in the wet season.

At **Chahual**, a small hot settlement straddles the Río Marañón and the
hillsides are covered in cactuses, mango and avocado trees. The road divides
here for Tayabamba and Pataz. **G** *Hostal Oasis*, is clean and friendly and has
a restaurant. Chahual is reached after eight hours, US$7. There is a small air-
port 5 km down the valley (Air Líder have daily flights to Trujillo, US$75,
one hour).

Pataz is a small gold-mining town, about 100 km from Huamachuco. From **Pataz &**
here you can reach the World Heritage Site of **Pajatén**, with its circular **Pajatén**
pre-Inca ruins. The ruins lie within the Río Abiseo National Park, but an
INRENA permit is needed to visit it. These are only issued to archaeologists and researchers, though day passes to enter the Park can also be
obtained. Pataz is one hour by road from Chahual but there is no regular
transport. Your best chance of finding a *camioneta* going up is early in the
morning.

After Chahual the road climbs steeply past Laguna Pías and through the **Tayabamba**
hectic and scarred mining communities of **Retamas** (a couple of basic
hostales), Marsa and Buldibuyo, bordering the Río Abiseo National Park,
before dropping down to Tayabamba. In this small Andean town, most
buildings in the centre are early 20th-century, giving the place a very traditional feel. **F** *Hostal Gemini* is new and clean but has limited hot water,
while **F** *Hostal Caballero* has hot water and is friendly but some rooms
smell. **G** *Hostal Sol y Sombra* is the most basic option, rooms are small.
Juan Baptista is the only proper restaurant in town but has a limited menu.
Otherwise the restaurants in the entrance to the market are the best bet.
Almost all eating places close by 2100.

From Huamachuco to Retamas, at least 3 combis daily from Av 10 de Julio, 12 hrs, **Transport**
US$10, and *Trans Garrincha*, Balta 850, buses coming from Trujillo on Mon, Thu and
Sat (returning on Wed, Fri and Sun), 0600, if there are spare seats, 12 hrs, US$8. This is
a challenging journey involving rough roads, tremendous changes in temperatures
between the *puna* and Marañón valley, and vertical drops of 1,000 m from hair-pin

Northern Highlands

bends. There is rarely space to board in Yanasara. To Tayabamba, *Trans San Antonio de Padua* buses from Lima may have spare seats, 18 hrs, US$12. If you decide you need to return to Lima, *Trans San Antonio de Padua* have a direct bus, 40 hrs, US$30, at least there are 2 drivers! *Trans El Patacino* combis between Retamas and Tayabamba 0600-0800, 4 hrs, US$3.50.

Huancaspata   Huancaspata is a very small Andean town with extensive views over the surrounding valleys and a well-kept plaza dominated by a large golden statue of a farmer and bull. *Hostales Roldán and Paraíso* (G) are both rustic, with rooms set around courtyards, cold water and shared baths. *Restaurant Kananga* (apparently named after a Japanese cartoon character!) is the best place to eat and serves an excellent *caldo*.

Huamachuco to Cajamarca

Via Cajabamba   From Huamachuco the road runs on 48 km past Laguna Sausacocha
Colour map 1, grid C4   through impressive eucalyptus groves to Cajabamba, which lies in the high part of the sugar-producing Condebamba valley. It has an attractive Plaza de Armas. **F** *Hostal Flores*, Leoncio Prado 137, on the Plaza de Armas, T851086. **G** without bath, hot water in morning, friendly and clean, nice patio. There are a couple of other basic places to stay: *Hostales Caribe* and *Amílcar*. Restaurants are *Cajabambino II*, Martínez 1193, offering local trout and a variety of chicken dishes, and *Café Grau*, Grau 133, serving big fresh fruit salads and cakes. *Trans Anita* have two combis a day to Huamachuco, three hours, US$3. To Cajamarca, via San Marcos (below) *Atahualpa*, *Rojas* (T851399) and *Trans Días*, among others, have daily buses, US$2.85, six hours. Some have buses to Trujillo or Lima.

The road continues from Cajabamba through **San Marcos** to Cajamarca. There is a short section of asphalt road to the south of San Marcos, which is important for its Sunday cattle market. Both it and Cajabamba are on the Inca Road. There are three hotels including **G** per person *Nuevo*, with bath, water shortages, but clean and quiet. There's are buses to Cajamarca (124 km); three hours, US$2.50.

To Cajamarca via Pacasmayo

The port of Pacasmayo is the main road connection from the coast to Cajamarca (see page 401). The paved 180 km road branches off the Pan-American Highway soon after it crosses the Río Jequetepeque.

Chilete   Some 103 km east of Pacasmayo is the mining town of Chilete. 21 km from
Colour map 1, grid C3   Chilete, on the road north to San Pablo, are the pyramid and stone monoliths of **Kuntur Wasi**. The site, which was devoted to a feline cult, is undergoing new development under a Japanese archaeological team. It now has an on-site museum, making a visit worthwhile. There's accommodation in Chilete at *Hotels Amazonas* and *San Pedro*, both **G**, both with filthy bathrooms. Rooms are hard to find on Tuesday because of the Wednesday market. Further along the road to Cajamarca is Yonán, where there are petroglyphs.

Cajamarca

Cajamarca is a beautiful colonial town and the most important in the northern highlands. It sits at the edge of a green valley which is ideal for dairy farming. Around the Plaza de Armas are many fine old houses, which are being converted into tasteful hotels, restaurants and galleries to cater for engineers and incomers from a major mining project and in anticipation of the expansion of tourism. This can only grow once the extension of the airport is complete (late 2002). The mine is far enough away not to intrude on the provincial calm, or upset the sense that this city is closely tied to its pastoral surroundings. It's a great place to buy handicrafts, but lest you forget where the money now lies, you can find soapstone carvings of miners with power drills alongside more traditional figures. Outside town are several good haciendas which offer bed, board and rural pursuits, while at the Baños del Inca, just up the road, you can unwind as the steam from the thermal waters meets the cool mountain air. Not that there is much pressing to escape from.

Phone code: 044
Colour map 1, grid C3
Population: 117,500
Altitude: 2,750 m

Before Cajamarca became an Inca religious centre and favoured haunt of the nobility in 1456, it had been at the heart of a culture known as Caxamarca, which flourished from 500 to 1000 AD. The violent events of 1532-33 are today belied by the city's provincial calm. It was named provincial capital in 1855 and Patrimonio Histórico y Cultural de las Américas by the Organization of American States in 1986. In addition to its historical associations, Cajamarca is best known for its dairy industry, textiles and intricately worked mirrors (see Shopping, below). Change is coming, though, in the form of the *Circuito Turístico Nororiental*, which is opening up the Chiclayo-Cajamarca-Chachapoyas tourist route, and in the effect on the town from the Yanacocha gold mine. This has brought many foreign mining engineers and economic benefits, but also debates over ecological impact. The mine's public relations office is at Amazonas 725, T821684, F821685, www.yana cocha.com.pe Only groups are allowed to visit.

Ins and outs

The airport is 3 km from town; taxi US$1.50, mototaxi US$0.75. It is to the northeast: take the Cerrillo road. Extension of the airport in 2002 will make the city much more accessible. The bus offices on the other hand are to the southeast of the centre, on the Baños del Inca road past La Recoleta church; a 20-min walk from the Plaza de Armas.

Getting there

All the main sights are clustered around the Plaza de Armas. With its many old colonial buildings it is an interesting town to wander around although the climb up Santa Apollonia hill is quite demanding. The district around Plaza Francia (Amazonas y José Gálvez), the market area and east of Amazonas are not safe at night because of prostitution. Buses in town charge US$0.20. Taxis US$0.60 within city limits. Mototaxis US$0.30. Radio taxi: *El Sol*, T828897/827123, 24 hrs.

Getting around

Cajamarca has a pleasant climate the year round, with warm days and chilly nights. The wettest months are Dec-Mar. Depending on your point of view, Carnival (Feb or Mar) is the time to be there, or the time to avoid – it is a riotous, messy affair. Hotels are also booked up at this time. More sedate festivals are Holy Week, especially Palm Sunday at nearby Porcón, and Corpus Christi in May. During Oct there are numerous school trips to this area, so most of the budget hotels are full at this time.

Best time to visit

Northern Highlands

Tourist offices   *Dirección Regional de Turismo* and *Instituto Nacional de Cultura*, in the Conjunto Monu-mental de Belén, Belén 631, T822997, F822903, cajamarca@mitinci.gob.pe, Mon-Fri 0730-1300, 1415-1900. *Cámara Regional de Turismo (Caretur)*, José Gálvez 771, T831579, careturcajamarca@regionalcaj.zzn.com *Cenfotur*, José Gálvez 767, T829714, cenfocaj@enfoturcajamarca.org.pe, is the organization overseeing the *Circuito Turístico Nororiental*. The University tourist school's office is at Del Batán 289, T821546, open 0700-1345 daily. The *Indecopi* office is at 2 de Mayo 359, T823315, caraujo@indecopi.gob.pe

Cajamarca

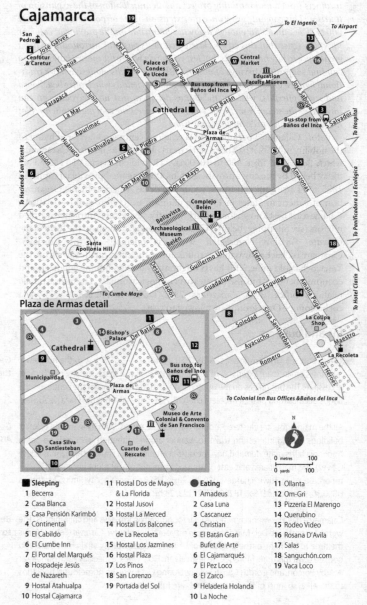

Plaza de Armas detail

■ Sleeping	11 Hostal Dos de Mayo	● Eating	11 Ollanta
1 Becerra	& La Florida	1 Amadeus	12 Om-Gri
2 Casa Blanca	12 Hostal Jusovi	2 Casa Luna	13 Pizzería El Marengo
3 Casa Pensión Karimbó	13 Hostal La Merced	3 Cascanuez	14 Querubino
4 Continental	14 Hostal Los Balcones	4 Christian	15 Rodeo Video
5 El Cabildo	de La Recoleta	5 El Batán Gran	16 Rosana D'Avila
6 El Cumbe Inn	15 Hostal Los Jazmines	Bufet de Arte	17 Salas
7 El Portal del Marqués	16 Hostal Plaza	6 El Cajamarqués	18 Sanguchón.com
8 Hospadeje Jesús	17 Los Pinos	7 El Pez Loco	19 Vaca Loco
de Nazareth	18 San Lorenzo	8 El Zarco	
9 Hostal Atahualpa	19 Portada del Sol	9 Heladería Holanda	
10 Hostal Cajamarca		10 La Noche	

Northern Highlands

Sights

The **Complejo Belén** comprises the tourist office and Institute of Culture, a beautifully ornate church, considered the city's finest, and two museums. The arches, pillars and walls of the nave of Belén church are covered in lozenges (*rombos*), a design picked out in the gold tracery of the altar. See the inside of the dome, where eight giant cherubs support an intricate flowering centrepiece. The carved pulpit has a spiral staircase and the doors are intricately worked in wood. In the same courtyard is the **Museo Médico Belén**, which has a collection of medical instruments. Across the street is a maternity hospital from the colonial era, now the **Archaeological and Ethnological Museum** (Junín y Belén). It has a wide range of ceramics from all regions and civilizations of Peru. ■ *0900-1300, 1500-1730, 0900-1230 Sat-Sun. US$0.85, valid for more than one day. A ticket is also valid for the Cuarto de Rescate. A guide for all the sites costs US$2.85 (US$5.75-8.50 for guides in other languages).*

The **Cuarto de Rescate** is not the actual ransom chamber but in fact the room where Atahualpa was held prisoner. A red line on the wall is said to indicate where Atahualpa reached up and drew a mark, agreeing to have his subjects fill the room to the line with gold treasures. The chamber is roped off and can only be viewed from the outside. Pollution and weather have had a detrimental effect on the stone. ■ *The entrance is at Amalia Puga 750.*

The plaza where Atahualpa was ambushed and the stone altar set high on **Santa Apollonia hill** where he is said to have reviewed his subjects can also be visited. There is a road to the top or, if you are fit, you can walk up from Calle 2 de Mayo, using the stairway. The view from the top, over red-tiled roofs and green fields, is worth the effort, especially very early in the morning for the beautiful sunrises. ■ *US$0.30. Take bus marked Santa Apolonia/Fonavi.*

The **Plaza de Armas**, where Atahualpa was executed, has a 350-year-old fountain, topiary and gardens. The impressive **Cathedral**, opened in 1776, is still missing its belfry, but the façade has beautiful baroque carving in stone. Many belfries were left half-finished in protest against a Spanish tax levied on the completion of a church. The altar is covered in original gold leaf.

On the opposite side of the plaza is the 17th century **San Francisco Church**, older than the Cathedral and with more interior stone carving and elaborate altars. A side chapel has an ornate ceiling. The attached **Museo de Arte Colonial** is filled with colonial paintings and icons. The guided tour of the museum includes entry to the church's spooky catacombs. ■ *Mon-Sat 1430-1800. US$0.85, entrance is unmarked on far left corner of church. Tickets are sold from an unmarked office on right of courtyard as you walk towards the church.*

Other churches worth seeing are **La Recoleta**, at Maestro y Avenida Los Héroes, and **San Pedro**, at Gálvez y Junín. The city has many old colonial houses with garden patios, and 104 elaborately carved doorways: see the **Bishop's Palace**, across the street from the Cathedral; the **palace of the Condes de Uceda**, at Jr Apurímac 719 (now occupied by BCP bank); and the **Casa Silva Santiesteban** (Junín y 2 de Mayo).

The **Education Faculty of the University** has a museum at Del Batán 283 with objects of the pre-Inca Cajamarca culture, not seen in Lima. The attendant knows much about Cajamarca and the surrounding area. ■ *Mon-Sat 0900-1200, 1430-1700. US$0.20 (guided tour).* The University maintains an experimental **arboretum** and agricultural station.

Northern Highlands

Essentials

Sleeping
■ *on map*
Price codes:
see inside front cover
Many good mid-range
hotels cater for the
mining market

In the outskirts L *Posada del Puruay*, 5 km north of the city, T827928, F(Lima) 336-7835, postmast@p-puruay.com.pe A 17th-century *hacienda* which has been converted into a 'hotel museum' with all rooms appointed to a high standard and containing beautiful pieces of colonial furniture. All rooms en suite. Recommended. **A** *El Ingenio*, Av Vía de Evitamiento 1611-1709, T/F827121. With bathroom, solar-powered hot water, spacious, very relaxed, fax service, helpful. Highly recommended. **A-B** *Hostal Hacienda San Vicente*, 2 km beyond Santa Apollonia, T/F822644, www.cajamarca.net In an old hacienda, totally remodelled in the style of Gaudi, with bath, hot water, TV, gardens, bar, restaurant and laundry. At **Baños del Inca**: **L-AL** *Laguna Seca*, Av Manco Cápac 1098, T894600, F894646, www.lagunaseca.com.pe In pleasant surroundings with thermal streams (atmospheric misty mornings), private hot thermal baths in rooms, swimming pool with thermal water, good restaurant, bar, health spa with a variety of treatments (US$10-48), disco, horses for hire. Recommended. **B** *Hostal Fundo Campero San Antonio*, is 2 km off the Baños road (turn off at Km 5), T/F838237, http://hsanantonio.cjb.net An old *hacienda*, wonderfully restored, with open fireplaces and gardens, 15 mins walk along the river to Baños del Inca. All rooms en suite. The price includes breakfast and a ride on the hotel's caballos de paso. Restaurant serves the hotel's own dairy produce, fruit and vegetables, catch your own trout for supper; try the *licor de sauco*. Recommended. **F** per person *Hospedaje La Posada de Atahualpa*, Manco Cápac 205, T838229, before bridge going into town. OK. For accommodation at the municipal baths, see Around Cajamarca, Los Baños del Inca, below.

In town A-B *Continental*, Jr Amazonas 760, T822758, F823024. Very clean, hot water, modern, good restaurant (popular for lunch, specializes in *cuy frito*), often full. Recommended. **B** *Hostal El Portal de Marqués*, Del Comercio 644, T/F828464, portalmarques@terra.com.pe Located in an attractive converted colonial house, all rooms carpeted, en suite, with TV, laundry, safe, parking, restaurant *El Mesón Colonial*. Recommended.

C *Hostal Cajamarca*, in a colonial house at Dos de Mayo 311, T822532, F821432. Sizeable rooms, clean, hot water, food excellent in *Los Faroles* restaurant (T825113) which also has good local music and disco/pub, *Cajamarca Tours* next door. Recommended. **C** *Casa Blanca*, Dos de Mayo 446 on Plaza de Armas, T/F822141. Room service, clean, safe, nice old building with garden, good restaurant. **C** *Clarín*, Amazonas 1025, T831274, F831277, Hotel_clarin@hotmail.com Prince includes tax. New, modern hotel with pleasant decoration, with bath, good beds, laptop connection, 5th floor terrace with view, car park, *panadería* next door. **C** *El Cabildo*, Junín 1062, T/F827025, cabildoh@latinmail.com Includes breakfast. In a historic monument with patio and modern fountain, some rooms dark as no new windows allowed, but full of character, wooden balconies, elegant, local decorations, comfortable, breakfast served, gym, massage if booked in advance. Recommended. **C** *El Cumbe Inn*, Pasaje Atahualpa 345, T826858, elcumbeinn@terra.com Includes breakfast and tax. Comfortable, bright rooms, with bath, hot water, personal service, two patios, small gym, well-kept, will arrange taxis. Recommended. **C** *Los Balcones de la Recoleta*, Amalia Puga 1050, T/F823003, luchi92000@yahoo.com A beautifully restored 19th-century house, with a pleasant central courtyard full of flowers; some rooms with period furniture but all are en suite, breakfast extra. Recommended. **C** *Hostal Los Pinos*, Jr La Mar 521, T/F825992, pinoshostal@yahoo.com Price includes breakfast. Lovely colonial house with a new extension, decorated in old style, comfortable, other meals on request, very nice. **C** *Hostal Portada del Sol*, Pisagua 731, T823395, PortadadelSol@terra.com.pe Good rooms, tastefully decorated, with bath, hot water, comfortable beds. Also has *Portada del Sol Hacienda* at Km 6 on road to Cumbe Mayo (**B**). Recommended.

D *Hospedaje Los Jazmines*, Amazonas 775, T821812, assado@hotmail.com In a converted colonial house with a pleasant courtyard and café, 3 rooms with bath, 2 without, all funds go to handicapped children, some staff are handicapped, guests can visit the project's school and help. Owner Christa Stark from Germany also has *Fundo Ecológico El Porongo* on road to Baños del Inca, bunk beds, **G** per person. Ask about tourist possibilities off the beaten track. Recommended. **D** *Hostal Jusovi*, Amazonas 637, T822920. With bathroom (**F** without TV), comfortable, modern, hot water, safe. **D** *Hostal Plaza*, Plaza de Armas 669, T922058. An old building with handmade wood furnishings, mainly large rooms with many beds, private bathroom and balcony, **E** with shared bath, hot water but poor water supply, quiet, recommended (especially rooms 4 and 12). **D** *Hostal San Lorenzo*, Amazonas 1070, T/F826433. With bathroom, hot water, modern, clean, friendly, helpful, meals available at extra cost.

E *Hostal Atahualpa*, Pasaje Atahualpa 686, T827840. Hot water 0700-0900, 1900-2100, clean, good value, meals extra, restaurant open 0800-2200. **E** per person *Hostal Becerra*, Del Batán 195 (unsigned), T827867. With hot water and TV, **F** per person without shared hot shower, modern, clean, friendly, they'll let you leave your luggage until late buses depart. **E** *Hostal San Carlos*, Av Atahualpa 324, T822600, and **E** *Hostal Pepe*, opposite at No 343, T821887, are the most convenient for bus offices on Atahualpa. Both are cheaper without bath, hot water, no breakfast, noisy from all-night traffic.

F per person *Colonial Inn*, Av Los Héroes 350, T825300, F827249. Hot water, cheaper with shared bath, English spoken, 24-hr attention, meals extra, convenient for buses. **F** *Hostal Dos de Mayo*, Dos de Mayo 585, T822527. Shared bathroom, hot water, simple, quite dark, good value *menú* in the restaurant. Recommended. **F** per person *Casa pensión Karimbó*, Dos de Mayo 700, T829888. Full board, shared rooms, some with bath. **F** *Hostal La Merced*, Chanchamayo 140, T822171. Small, friendly, hot water on request, set around a courtyard, laundry facilities, good value, but not a safe area. **F** *Hospedaje Jesús de Nazareth*, Jr 5 Esquinas 328 (no sign), T822949. Shared bath, warm water, family run, quiet, owner runs good tours.

Expensive *El Cajamarqués*, Amazonas 770, T922128. Excellent, also has good value *menú*, elegant colonial building with garden full of exotic birds. *El Batán Gran Bufet de Arte*, Del Batán 369, T826025. Great food, international dishes, good wine list and wide choice of drinks, local dishes on non-tourist menu, some of the staff speak English, live music at the weekend, art gallery on the 2nd floor, closed Mon. Recommended. *Querubino*, Amalia Puga 589. Mediterranean-style decoration with American and French influence inthe cooking, specializes in fish, but lots of choice, breakfasts, cocktails, coffees, expensive wines.

Eating
● *on map*

Mid-range *Amadeus*, 2 de Mayo 930. Peruvian and international dishes, including salads, pizzas, pastas, daily specials, recommended for cocktails. *Om-Gri*, San Martín 360, near the Plaza de Armas. Good Italian dishes, small, friendly, French spoken, opens at 1300 (1830 Sun). *Ollanta*, Amalia Puga 726, opposite San Francisco. Clean, with main dishes, lunch *menú*, sandwiches, burgers, juices and yoghurts. *El Pez Loco*, San Martín 333. Recommended for fish, also on road to Baños del Inca. *Pizzería El Marengo*, Junín 1201. Good pizzas and warm atmosphere, T828045 for delivery. *Salas*, Amalia Puga 637, on the main plaza. Fast service, good local food (try their *cuy frito*), best *tamales* in town; also has a branch in Baños del Inca (1100-1600, Fri-Sun and holidays). Both serve the same food at same prices, own production. *El Zarco*, Jr Del Batán 170, T823421. Very popular with local residents, also has short *chifa* menu, good vegetarian dishes, excellent fish, popular for breakfast; also *El Zarco Campestre*, off road to airport. Both are closed Sat, use own produce, recommended for pork.

Northern Highlands

There are cheap eating places on Del Comercio and 2 de Mayo y Sabogal

Cheap *La Florida*, 2 de Mayo next to *Hostal Dos de Mayo*. Popular, serves good ceviche. *Pizzería Vaca Loca*, San Martín 330. Popular, the name doesn't seem to put the locals off. *Rosana D'Avila's* restaurant, Del Batám 368. Good value, tasty buffet, set lunches, open for dinner too. For early breakfasts go to the market.

Cafés *Casa Luna*, 2 de Mayo 334. Lots of activities here, *Akaesh* café with couches, grill at night in the evening (bring your own meat Sat-Sun), art gallery, craft shop, book exchange, no TV, no internet. *Cascanuez Café Bar*, Amalia Puga 554, near the Cathedral. Great cakes, extensive menu including *humitas*, breakfasts, ice creams and coffees. *Christian*, Del Comercio 719. Snacks, juices, set lunch for US$1.10. *Heladería Holanda*, Amalia Puga 657 on the Plaza de Armas, T830113. Dutch-owned, easily the best ice-creams in Cajamarca, 50 flavours (but not all on at the same time), try *poro poro, lúcuma* or *sauco*, 'sit back and indulge' (John Pilkington, Winchester, UK), also serves coffee. *Sanguchón.com*, Junín 1137. Best burgers in town, sandwiches, also popular bar. *Panificadora La Ecológica*, Cinco Esquinas 741. Good selection of breads, including *integral*, especially in afternoon.

Bars & clubs *El Brujo*, Apurímac 519. Disco bar, popular with younger set. *La Noche*, San Martín y Junín. Popular nightspot for young crowd. *Rodeo Video*, San Martín 352. Pub and disco.

Festivals Cajamarca is known as the Carnival capital of Peru. It hosts a messy, raucous *carnival week* in **Feb** with many processions and dances. But note that the level of water and paint-throwing would put Laurel and Hardy to shame. This is not for the faint-hearted. You have been warned!

In Porcón, 16 km to the northwest, the *Domingo de Ramos* (Palm Sunday) processions are worth seeing. *Corpus Christi* is held in **May** or **Jun** and is a solemn religious affair. On **24 Jun** is *San Juan* in Cajamarca, Chota, Llacanora, San Juan and Cutervo. An agricultural fair, *Feria Fongal*, is held in **Jul** at Baños del Inca. It coincides with *Fiestas Patrias* and besides agricultural displays, has *artesanía* and caballos de paso. On the **first Sun in Oct** is the *Festival Folklórico* in Cajamarca. Also in **Oct**, in the second week, is the city's *'Tourist Week'*.

Shopping Cajamarca is an excellent place to buy handicrafts. They're cheap and the quality is good. Specialities include cotton and wool saddlebags (*alforjas*). Handwoven woollen items can be made to order. Other items include painted ceramic masks and soapstone figures (including miners with power drills).The market on Amazonas is good for *artesanía*. There are stalls in the street on block 7 of Belén every day. There are several shops on 300 block of Dos de Mayo. All offer a good range of local crafts. A different selection at *Textiles y Artesanías Paredes*, 2 de Mayo 264, up the steps.

Cajamarca is famous for its **gilded mirrors**. The *Cajamarquiña* frames are not carved but decorated with patterns transferred onto pieces of glass using the silk-screen process. This tradition lapsed during the post-colonial period and present production goes back less than 20 years.

Look for the Asociación de Productores Lácteos sticker for quality

The area is renowned for its **dairy produce**. Many shops sell cheese, butter, honey, etc. *La Collpa* (see below) has a shop at Romero 124, sells some of the best cheese and butter. Try the *queso mantecoso*, which is full-cream cheese, or sweet *manjar blanco*, or *humitas*, which are ground maize with cheese. *El Porcón* has a shop on Chanchamayo (hard to find). It sells excellent *queso suizo*. *El Tambo*, 2 de Mayo 576. Has a good selection of cheeses. Eucalyptus honey is sold in the market on C Amazonas and is said to be a cure for rheumatism.

Several travel agencies around the Plaza de Armas offer trips to local sites and further **Tour operators**
afield (eg Kuntur Wasi, Kuelap), trekking on Inca and other trails, riding caballos de
paso and handicraft tours. Average prices of local tours: Cumbe Mayo, US$5.75,
Ventanillas de Otusco US$3.30, Porcón US$5.75. Recommended are: *Cajamarca Tours*,
Dos de Mayo 323, T/F822813 (also DHL, Western Union and flight reconfirmations).
Clarín Tours, Del Batán 161, T/F826829, clarintours@yahoo.com *Cajamarca Travel*, 2
de Mayo 570, T/F828642, cajamarcatravel@si.computextos.net *Cumbemayo Tours*,
Amalia Puga 635 on the plaza, T/F822938. Guides in English and French.. *Inca
Atahualpa Tours*, Amazonas 770, T822495 (in *Hotel Continental*). *Inca Baths Tours*,
Amalia Puga 655, T/F821828. *Sierra Verde*, 2 de Mayo 448, on Plaza, T830905,
sierraverde_2000@yahoo.es *Variservice*, Silva Santisteban 134, T822228. A small office
where flights can be reconfirmed.

Air To/from **Lima** (US$89) daily with *Aero Cóndor* (Dos de Mayo 323, at *Cajamarca*   **Transport**
Tours, T825674), via **Trujillo**, *Atsa* (at *Cajamarca Travel*, T828642), daily except Sun, and
LC Busre, Comercio 1004-C, T821098, Mon-Fri (daily Cajamarca-Lima; also to Chiclayo
Sat-Sun). **NB** When the new airport is open, schedules will change.

Bus To **Lima**, 856 km, 12-14 hrs, *económico* US$10-11.45, to US$14.30-20 on *Cial*'s dou-
ble-deckers, to US$20-26 for *Cruz del Sur*'s luxury service (includes taxi to your lodging in
Lima), several buses daily (see below). The road is paved. To **Pacasmayo**, 189 km, 5-6 hrs,
US$7, several buses and hourly colectivos. To **Trujillo**, 296 km, 6½ hrs, US$4.30-8.55, regular buses daily 0945-2230 most continue to Lima. To **Chiclayo**, 260 km, 4½ hrs, US$4.85-
7.15, several buses daily; you have to change buses to go on to Piura and Tumbes. To
Celendín, 112 km, 4 hrs, US$2.85, at 0700 and 1300 (*Atahualpa*), 0800 and 1200
(*Palacios*, poor minibuses). The route follows a fairly good dirt road through beautiful
countryside. *Atahualpa*, *Trans Días* and *Rojas* go to **Cajabamba**, 75 km, US$2.85, 6 hrs,
several daily. These buses, and *Palacios*, also go to **Bambamarca, Chota and Cutervo.**
  Among the bus companies are: *Atahualpa*, Atahualpa 299, T823060 (Lima,
Celendín, Cajabamba, Bambamarca, Chota); *El Cumbe*, Sucre 594, T823088 (to
Chiclayo and Jaén); *Trans Días*, San Martín y Av Atahualpa, T831283 (Lima, Trujillo,
Chimbote, Bambamarca, Cajabamba); *Turismo Días*, Sucre 422, T828289 (to Lima,
Chimbote, Trujillo, Chiclayo); *Emtrafesa*, Atahualpa 315, T829663 (to Trujillo); *Línea*,
Atahualpa 318, T823956 (Lima, Trujillo, Chiclayo). *Trans Mendoza*, Atahualpa 179,
T828233 (to Chiclayo); *Ormeño*, Vía Evitamiento 474, T829885; *Trans Palacios*,
Atahualpa 339, T825855 (Lima, Trujillo, Celendín and Bambamarca); *Rojas*, Atahualpa
409, T823006 (to Cajabamba, buses not coming from Lima); Companies which serve
only Lima include: *Cial*, Av Atahualpa 300, T828701; *Civa*, Ayacucho 753, T821460;
Cruz del Sur, Atahualpa 600, T822488.

Banks *BCP*, Apurímac 719. Changes Amex TCs, cash advance on Visa, US$11.50 com-   **Directory**
mission, Visa ATM. *Banco Wiese*, Amazonas 750. Accepts Amex and Mastercard TCs,
US$3 commission, cash advance on Visa, Mastercard and Diners Club, but no ATM for
foreign cards. *Interbank*, 2 de Mayo 546, on Plaza. US$5 commission on dollar TCs,
Mastercard and Visa ATM. There is a *Telebanco 24 Horas* ATM (Visa) at the gas station
next to *Cial* buses on Av Atahualpa. Dollars can be changed in most banks and travel
agencies on east side of Plaza. *Casa de cambio* in musical and electrical store at
Amazonas 137. Good rates, cash only. **Street changers** on Jr Del Batán by the Plaza de
Armas and at Del Batán y Amazonas. **Communications** Internet: *@tajo*, Comercio
716. Mon-Sat 0830-0100 daily, US$0.85 per hr, good machines, also for phone calls.
CyberNet, Comercio 924 on Plaza de Armas. US$0.70 per hr. On 2 de Mayo, *Efe@net*, No
568, and *Maniacos Net*, No 693, US$0.85 per hr. **Post office:** *Serpost*, Amazonas 443.
0800-2045. **Telephone:** *Telefónica* offices at Amalia Puga 1022, and Amazonas 518,

for national and international calls. On Plaza, by *Casa Blanca*, is a phone office for national and international calls, phone cards on sale. **Laundry** *Lavandería Dandy*, Jr Amalia Puga 545. Pay by weight. **Medical services Hospital**: Av Mario Urteaga. *Clínica Limatambo*, Puno 265, T824241, and *Clínica San Francisco*, Av Grau 851, T822050. Both private and recommended.

Around Cajamarca

Colour map 1, grid C3 The surrounding countryside is worth exploring. You can either do this on your own or choose from the many tours on offer in town.

Los Baños del Inca Six kilometres away are the sulphurous thermal springs known as Los Baños del Inca, where there are baths whose water temperature is 78ºC. Atahualpa tried the effect of these waters on a festering war wound and his bath is still there. The entire complex was renewed in 2002, with gardens and various levels of accommodation: **B** bungalows with thermal water, TV, fridge; **C** in less luxurious bungalows; **G** per person *Albergue Juvenil*, bunk rooms. ■ *0500 (best water then)-1930 daily. In the thermal baths section, baths cost US$0.85 in units A, B and C, US$1.15 in the Turistas and US$1.45 in the Imperial, US$2.85 for the sauna (with designated times for men and women), US$0.55 for the hot shower or large swimming pool (closed Mon and Fri, take your own towel; soaps are sold outside). The Isla, or small pool, complex has showers, a park and thermal swimming pool, US$0.85 (0500-0800, 0830-1100, 1200-1500, 1530-1830). Only spend 20-30 mins maximum in the water; obey instructions. Combis marked Baños del Inca leave every few mins from Amazonas (at junction with Del Batán or 2 de Mayo, or Cinco Esquinas), US$0.30, 15 mins. Taxis US$1.50.*

Llacanora & La Collpa Llacanora is a typical Andean village in beautiful scenery (13 km southeast). La Collpa, a *hacienda* which is now a cooperative farm of the Ministry of Agriculture, breeds bulls and has a lake and gardens (11 km southeast). The cows are handmilked at 1400, not a particularly inspiring spectacle in itself, but the difference here is that the cows are called by name and respond accordingly.

Around Cajamarca

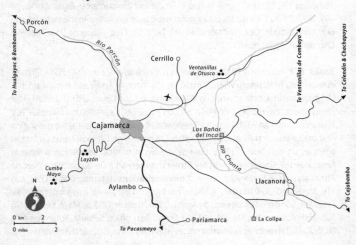

Ventanillas de Otusco, part of an old pre-Inca cemetery, has a gallery of sec- **Ventanillas**
ondary burial niches. ■ *US$1. A 1-day round trip can be made: take a bus from* **de Otusco**
Del Batán to Ventanillas de Otusco (30 mins) or a colectivo leaving hourly from
Revilla 170, US$0.15, then walk to Baños del Inca (1½ hrs, 6 km), from there
walk to Llacanora (1 hr, 7 km), passing the caves and rock art at Callacpuma,
and then a further hour to La Collpa.

Another typical Andean village from which you can walk to Baños del Inca
is **Pariamarca**. ■ *Take a micro from Ovalo Bolognesi heading towards the coast.*
Ask to be let out at the turn-off to Pariamarca and walk from there.

A road goes to Ventanillas de Combayo, some 20 km past the burial niches of **Ventanillas**
Otusco. These are more numerous and more spectacular, being located in a **de Combayo**
rather isolated, mountainous area, and are distributed over the face of a steep
200-m high hillside. ■ *There are occasional combis on weekdays, but more*
transport to the site on Sun when a market is held nearby, 1 hr.

Cumbe Mayo, a *pampa* on a mountain range, is 20 km southwest of **Cumbe Mayo**
Cajamarca. It is famous for its extraordinary, well-engineered pre-Inca chan- *Altitude: 3,600m*
nels, running for 9 km across the mountain tops. It is said to be the oldest
man-made construction in South America. The sheer scale of the scene is
impressive and the huge rock formations of Los Frailones ('big monks') and
others with fanciful names are strange indeed. It is worth taking a guided tour
since the area offers a lot of petroglyphs, altars and sacrificial stones from
pre-Inca cultures. On the way to Cumbe Mayo is the Layzón ceremonial centre from 500-200 BC (7 km).

■ *There is no bus service. A guided tour costs about US$5.75 per person and*
runs from 0900-1300, and a taxi US$15. It may be possible to go with the milk
truck leaving at 0400 from C Revilla 170; ask Sr Segundo Malca, Jr Pisagua 482.
There's a small charge, and dress warmly. To walk up takes 3-4 hrs (take a guide,
or a tour, best weather May-Sep). The trail starts from the hill of Santa Apollonia
(Silla del Inca), and goes to Cumbe Mayo, straight through the village and up the
hill. At the top of the mountain, leave the trail and take the road to the right to the
canal. The walk is not difficult and you do not need hiking boots. Take a good
torch/flashlight. The locals use the trail to bring their goods to market.

This rural cooperative, with its evangelical faith expressed on billboards, is a **Porcón**
popular excursion (morning or afternoon), 30 km northwest of Cajamarca. It *Altitude: 3,400 m*
is tightly organized and has a bakery, cheese and yoghurt-making, zoo and
vicuñas. Its carpentry utilizes wood from extensive pine plantations. ■ *A good*
guide helps to explain everything. If not taking a tour, contact Cooperqtive
Agraria Atahualpa Jerusalén, Chancahmayo 1355, Fonavi 1, T/F825631,
granjaporcon@yahoo.com

Celendín

East from Cajamarca, the first town of note is Celendín, whose residents are *Phone code: 044*
known as Shilicos. It is a clean and tranquil place, with warm friendly people *Colour map 1, grid C4*
but a decidedly chilly climate. The **plaza** and **cathedral** are both appealing. *Population:*
There is also an interesting local **market** on Sunday. Walk up the hill to the *approximately 15,000*
chapel of San Isidro Labrador for views of town and surroundings. Note the *Altitude: 2,625 m*
huge hats worn by the townsfolk. These are woven from fine straw and can
be bought, along with other straw handicrafts, at Artesanías San José de
Pilco, 2 de Mayo 319.

Northern Highlands

Sleeping
■ *on map*
Price code:
see inside front cover

E-F *Celendín*, Jr Unión 305, Plaza de Armas, T855041, F855239. Colonial, with bathroom, very limited hot water, nice patio, clean, friendly, good but noisy restaurant, best value. **E** *Loyer's*, José Gálvez 410, T855210. With bathroom, cheaper without, patio, nice. **F** *Amazonas*, Dos de Mayo 316. With bathroom, cheaper without, cold water, basic, helpful. **F** *Maxmar*, Dos de Mayo 349. With bathroom, cheaper without, hot shower extra, basic, clean, parking, good value, owner Francisco is very helpful. **F** *José Gálvez*, Dos de Mayo 344. With bathroom, cheaper without, cold water, basic, friendly.

Celendín

● **Eating**
1 Bella Aurora
2 Jalisco
3 La Reserve
4 Santa Isabel

🚍 **Transport**
1 Atahualpa
  (to Cajamarca)
2 Días (to Cajamarca)
3 Palacios
  (to Cajamarca)
4 Virgen del Carmen
  (to Chachapoyas)

■ **Sleeping**
1 Amazonas
2 Celendín
3 José Gálvez
4 Loyer's
5 Maxmar

0 metres 50
0 yards 50

Eating
● *on map*

La Reserve, José Gálvez 313. Good quality and value. Recommended. *Bella Aurora*, Grau y José Gálvez. Good. *Jalisco*, Jr Unión, Plaza de Armas. Good value breakfasts and other meals, but beware overcharging. *Santa Isabel*, Jr José Gálvez 512. Clean, OK. There are several other places to eat. *Panadería El Carmen*, Dos de Mayo 332. Good bakery.

Festivals
The town hosts its *Virgen del Carmen* festival on **16 July**. Bullfights with *matadores* from Spain and cock fighting are all part of the well-attended celebrations.

Transport
To **Cajamarca**, 107 km, 4-5 hrs: with *Atahualpa*, 2 de Mayo 707, Plaza de Armas, T855256, at 0700 and 1300 daily, US$2.85; *Palacios*, Jr Unión 333, Plaza de Armas, at 0645 and 1300 daily, poor minibuses, US$3. To **Chachapoyas** via Balsas and Leymebamba, 12-14 hrs (may be much longer in the rainy season, take warm clothing, food and water): *Virgen del Carmen*, Cáceres 117, on Sun and Thu at 1100, US$7.20. Other local transport leaves from the market area.

Directory
Banks There are no banks or *casas de cambio*, but try the local shops. **Communications** Post office: Jr Unión 415. **Phone office:** José Gálvez 600 y Pardo, Plaza de Armas.

To Chachapoyas
The rough narrow road from Celendín to Chachapoyas (226 km) follows a winding course, crossing the wide and deep canyon of the Río Marañón at Balsas (*Altitude*: 950 m). It then climbs steeply, over countless hair-raising hairpin bends, with superb views of the mountains and the valleys below, to reach the Barro Negro pass at 3,680 m, before descending to Leymebamba in the upper Utcubamba valley (see page 464). The journey takes 12-14 hours in the dry season. It can be much longer and more dangerous when it rains. Take warm clothing, food and water. The route is generally safe but a couple of bus and private vehicle robberies were reported in 2001.

Chachapoyas Region

The Chachapoyas region contains so many archaeological riches that you need at least a week to begin to appreciate the remarkable legacy of the Chachapoyans, also known as 'The Cloud People'. Great pre-Inca cities, immense fortresses such as Kuelap and ancient effigies which gaze over a dramatic landscape reward the visitor to a region which is due to become a major tourist destination as soon as regular air service begins..

The area

Theories about the Chachapoyan Empire show that their cities, highways, terracing, irrigation, massive stonework and metalcraft were all fully developed. The culture began about AD 800 and covered an area bounded by the rivers Marañón and Huallaga, as far as Pataz in the south and Bagua in the north. Socially the Chachapoya were organized into chiefdoms, which formed war-alliances in the case of external aggression. Mark Babington and Morgan Davis write: "This is surely a region which overwhelms even Machu-Picchu in grandeur and mystery. It contains no less than five lost, and uncharted cities, the most impressive of which is Pueblo Alto, near the village of Pueblo Nuevo (25 km from Kuelap). By far the majority of these cities, fortresses and villages were never discovered by the Spanish. In fact many had already returned to the jungle by the time they arrived in 1532... On a recent map of the area, no less than 38 sites can be counted". (See Books page 611.)

This region is called *La Ceja de la Selva* (the eyebrow of the jungle), whose beautiful scenery includes a good deal of virgin cloud-forest (although other sections are sadly deforested), as well as endless deep dry canyons traversed by hair-raisingly dangerous roads. The temperature is always in the 20s (70s Farenheit) during the day, but the nights are cool at around 3,000 m. Many ruins are overgrown with ferns, bromeliads and orchids and easily missed.

The central geographic feature of the department, and its boundary with neighbouring Cajamarca, is the great Río Marañón, one of the major tributaries of the Amazon.

Running roughly parallel to the mighty Marañón, one range to the east, is the gentler valley of the Utcubamba, home to much of the area's ancient and present population. Over yet another cordillera to the east, lie the isolated subtropical valleys of the province of Rodríguez de Mendoza, the origin of whose inhabitants, has been the source of much debate (see page 468).

Ins and outs

Getting there The city of Chachapoyas is the best base for visiting this region. Regular, twice-weekly flights from Lima resumed in Oct 2002, but service has frequently been discontinued in the past. If the service doesn't last, or if you don't want to fly, Chachapoyas can be reached overland from Chiclayo, Cajamarca or Tarapoto. *Transcarh, Civa* and *Móvil Tours* all offer reasonably comfortable bus services from Lima, travelling Chiclayo-Chachapoyas by day. Bus schedules starting from Chiclayo all involve an overnight journey, missing the fine scenery along the way. An alternative is to go by bus from Chiclayo to Jaén, continuing the next day to Chachapoyas, via Bagua Grande and Pedro Ruíz, using combis (see the corresponding sections for details). From Cajamarca, you can go first to Celendín (see page 451) and then on to Chachapoyas, crossing the Marañón at Balsas between descents and climbs of thousands of vertical metres. The journey is an

Northern Highlands

entirely unforgettable experience in its own right, but half of it is done at night. Also beautiful is the route from Tarapoto via Moyobamba and Pedro Ruíz, especially since the highway has been paved for the most part. It is possible to do this journey in one day, leaving Tarapoto at 0800 or 0900, but the last part will be done in darkness. Break the journey in Moyobamba or Pedro Ruíz and take combis on some stretches.

When to go The dry season is infinitely preferable (normally May-Sep, but the seasons are less stable than in the past; in the last few years it has been sunny and dry well into Dec). During the rains, roads may become impassable due to landslides and access to the more remote areas may be impossible, or involve weeks of delay. Likewise, trekking in the area can be very pleasant in the dry season, but may involve too much wading through waist-deep mud on some routes during the rainy season. Other places are still accessible in the wet, but rubber boots are essential. Good hiking gear is always a must; also a sleeping bag, tent and canned goods.

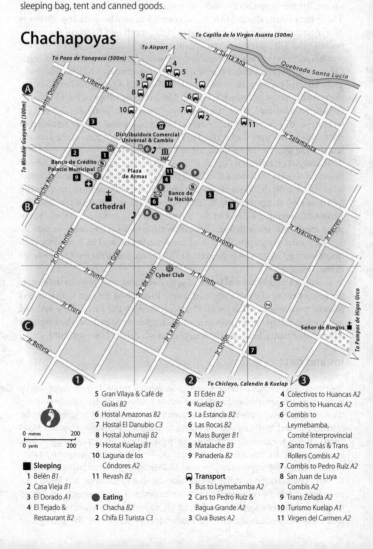

Chachapoyas

Sleeping	
1 Belén *B1*	
2 Casa Vieja *B1*	
3 El Dorado *A1*	
4 El Tejado & Restaurant *B2*	
5 Gran Vilaya & Café de Guías *B2*	
6 Hostal Amazonas *B2*	
7 Hostal El Danubio *C3*	
8 Hostal Johumaji *B2*	
9 Hostal Kuelap *B1*	
10 Laguna de los Cóndores *A2*	
11 Revash *B2*	

Eating
1 Chacha *B2*
2 Chifa El Turista *C3*
3 El Edén *B2*
4 Kuelap *B2*
5 La Estancia *B2*
6 Las Rocas *B2*
7 Mass Burger *B1*
8 Matalache *B3*
9 Panadería *B2*

Transport
1 Bus to Leymebamba *A2*
2 Cars to Pedro Ruíz & Bagua Grande *A2*
3 Civa Buses *A2*
4 Colectivos to Huancas *A2*
5 Combis to Huancas *A2*
6 Combis to Leymebamba, Comité Interprovincial Santo Tomás & Trans Rollers Combis *A2*
7 Combis to Pedro Ruíz *A2*
8 San Juan de Luya Combis *A2*
9 Trans Zelada *A2*
10 Turismo Kuelap *A1*
11 Virgen del Carmen *A2*

To Chiclayo, Calendín & Kuelap

Northern Highlands

The Valley of the Whites

The tiny villages in the Guayabamba valley could be any other sleepy, sub-tropical settlements. A collection of wooden houses on a fertile plain where oranges, bananas, guava and yucca grow, where colourful butterflies and mesmerizing birdsong fill the warm, humid air. But the people of this remote region are very different from your average jungle dweller. They are blond-haired, blue-eyed and fair-skinned and could easily have just stepped off the 1700 flight from Stockholm.

The population of the Guayabamba valley themselves don't know where they came from and opinions among experts vary. Some posit the theory that they originate from warring conquistador factions in the early 16th century. This view hasn't satisfied those who point to the rarity of this phenomenon. It's true that the Spanish chronicler Garcilaso de la Vega described the fair-skinned people resisting the Incas before the conquest, but evidence tends to show that it is unlikely that the people of Guayamba have anything to do with the Chachapoyas cloud people.

Dr Jacques de Mahieu of Buenos Aires believes the latter to be descendants of the Vikings, who came to Peru in the 11th century. He supports such a theory with evidence on Easter Island, west of Chile, of drawings showing Viking longships, as well as linguistic parallels between the Quechua language and Scandinavian tongues.

The romantic theories are countered by research showing that the pre-conquest peoples did not speak Quechua in this region and that the Spanish chroniclers have been misunderstood: the phrase "the Chachapoyas were of fair complexion" has been taken to mean, wrongly, that they were blond. Perhaps the mystery will be solved by investigation into the DNA of the mummies found at Laguna de Cóndores and Scandinavian bog people and other European mummies. Moreover, in Guayamba DNA samples can be traced back to one Spanish family who lived in the region for a long time and there is evidence that the people of Chirimoto were originally Italian and Spanish settlers in the 1820s.

Whatever the explanation, the incongruous presence of these fair-skinned people in such a remote part of the country will continue to attract the attention of ethnologists.

Guides & contacts

Robert Dover is a British guide to sites throughout the Chachapoyas region and is recommended. Contact him through the *Vilaya Tours* in Chacha, or the *Café de Guías*, see Eating and Tour operators, below. Carlos Burga, proprietor of *Hostal Revash* (see Sleeping below) organizes and sometimes guides groups. He is knowledgeable, helpful and friendly, and also recommended.

The German ethnologist, **Dr Peter Lerche** (F778438), is the resident expert regarding Chachapoyan cultures and trekking. He is very knowledgeable, speaks English, sometimes guides groups and may be contacted for information on anthropology and history. He is the author of *Los Chachapoyas y los Símbolos de su Historia* and the trekking guide *Chachapoyas: Guía de Viajeros*. They are out of print. In an article in *National Geographic*, September 2000, "Quest for the Lost Tombs of the Peruvian Cloud People", Dr Lerche writes about the discovery of a Chachapoya tomb named the 'White House' and gives a good general introduction to the history and archaeology of the region (he has also provided information for this section). **Gumercindo 'Gumer' Zegarra** is the proprietor of the *Gran Hotel Vilaya* and knowledgeable about happenings in and around Chachapoyas.

Charles Motley, 1805 Swann Ave, Orlando, FL 32809, USA, in Chachapoyas at Grau 534, T778078, www.kuelap.org, is directing a long-term project with volunteers, called *Los Tambos Chachapoyanos (LTC)*. LTC have lodges at Choctámal and Levanto. They are ancient in style, with modern utilities, jointly built, owned and run by the villages on their tribal land. LTC also have one English-speaking Peruvian guide and an American on the staff who can sometimes guide.

Northern Highlands

Morgan Davis (see The area, above), a Canadian, has written about Chachapoyan archaeology and collaborated with Motley. He visits the area regularly and is well known among the locals.

The town

Phone code: 044
Colour map 1, grid C4
Population: 25,000
Altitude: 2,335 m

Chachapoyas, or 'Chacha', as it is known among locals, is the capital of the Department of Amazonas. It was founded on 5 September 1538, but retains only some of its colonial character, in the form of large old homes with their typical patios and wooden balconies.

Sights

The city's importance as a crossroads between the coast and jungle began to decline in the late 1940s, with the building of the road through Pedro Ruíz. However, archaeological and ecological tourism have grown gradually since the 1990s and there are hopes that these will bring increasing economic benefits to the region.

The modern **cathedral** faces a spacious plaza which fills with locals for the evening *paseo*. Other interesting churches are the **Capilla de la Virgen Asunta**, the city's patroness, at Asunción y Puno, and **Señor de Burgos**, at Amazonas y Santa Lucía. The **Instituto Nacional de Cultura (INC)** has a small, sad museum at Ayacucho 675, with a few decaying mummies and artefacts (not so much a museum as a storage facility).

The **Mirador Guayamil** offers fine views of the city, especially at early dusk. Nearby is the **Pozo de Yanayacu**, also known as the *fuente del amor*, at the west end of Avenida Salamanca. Legend has it that those who visit this well will fall in love and remain in Chachapoyas (though it obviously doesn't work every time). A decisive battle for independence from Spain took place at the **Pampas de Higos Urco**, at the east end of town, a 20-minute walk, with great views of lush Andes to the east.

Tour to Kuelap

Most hotels will organize tours to Kuelap and other archaeological sites when there are sufficient people. Those run by *Gran Hotel Vilaya* and *Hostal Revash* are recommended. Expect to pay around US$8.65 per person for a full-day trip to Kuelap, not including lunch, US$11.50 including guide and lunch. Tours leave at 0800 and, after a spectacular, if not disconcerting, three-hour drive, you arrive at Kuelap. The tours usually allow a sufficient three to four hours for exploration before returning to Chachapoyas, with a possible stop along the way for a late lunch. A less expensive option and, in many ways, the recommended one since it allows you to see Kuelap wrapped in early-morning mist, is to take the local combi at 0300 (see below). Please be ready to go. This is a public bus and locals have better things to do than wait for a tardy gringo.

Sleeping
■ *on map*
Price codes:
see inside front cover

C *Gran Vilaya*, Ayacucho 755, T777664, F778154, vilaya@wayna.rcp.net.pe The best in town, comfortable rooms with firm beds, parking, English spoken, all services. **D** *Casa Vieja*, Chincha Alta 569, T777353, casavieja@terra.com.pe In a converted old house, very nicely decorated, all rooms different, family atmosphere, hot water, cable TV, living room and *comedor*, continental breakfast, internet and library. Recommended. **D** *El Tejado*, Grau 534, Plaza de Armas. On first floor, same entrance as restaurant, good, laundry. **D** *Revash*, Grau 517, Plaza de Armas, T777391, F777356, revash@tsi.com.pe With private bathroom, plenty of hot water, clean, patio, friendly, helpful, laundry, good local information, restaurant, sells local items. Recommended. **E** *Belén*, Jr Ortiz Arrieta, on Plaza next to the bank. With bath, hot water, nicely furnished, new in 2002. **E** *El Dorado*, Ayacucho 1062, T777047. With bathroom, hot water, clean, helpful. **F** *Hostal Amazonas*, Grau 565, Plaza de Armas, T777199. With private bathroom, cheaper with shared bathroom, large rooms often filled with shrieks of local amorous couples, nice patio, no breakfast, friendly, basic. **F** *Hostal El Danubio*, Tres Esquinas 193 y Junín 584, Plazuela Belén, some distance from centre, T777337. With private bathroom, hot water, cheaper with shared bath and cold water, clean, friendly, meals can be ordered in advance. **F** *Hostal Johumaji*, Ayacucho 711, T777279, F777819, olvacha@ddm.com.pe With bathroom, hot water, TV, cheaper without TV, meals extra. **E** *Hostal Kuelap*, Amazonas 1057, T777136. With private bathroom, hot water and TV, cheaper without TV, cheaper still with shared bathroom and cold water, parking. Recommended. **G** *Laguna de los Cóndores*, Salamanca 941, T777492. Very basic, shared bathroom, cold water.

There are many good, simple and cheap restaurants. Slightly upscale is *El Tejado*, **Eating** upstairs at Grau 534, Plaza de Armas. Good quality, nice view and atmosphere. Recom- • *on map* mended. The *Café de Guías*, in *Hotel Gran Vilaya*, serves snacks, meals and organic coffee from the area, also has lots of local information, good. It is run by Tom Gierasimczuk, a Canadian guide, journalist and part-owner of *Vilaya Tours*. *Chacha*, Grau 541, Plaza de Armas. Especially popular with locals, clean, serves good, huge portions, friendly. Recommended. *Chifa El Turista*, Amazonas 575. Reasonable, friendly and helpful. *El Edén*, Amazonas 828, p 2. Very good vegetarian, large helpings, open by 0830, closed Sat afternoon/evening. *La Estancia*, Amazonas 861. Grill and video pub. *Las Rocas*, Ayacucho 932 on Plaza. Popular, good local dishes, open Sun evening. *Kuelap*, Ayacucho 832. Good, friendly. Recommended. *Mass Burger*, Ortiz Arrieta, Plaza de Armas. Excellent juices, cakes, fruit salads. *Matalache*, corner of Amazonas and Grau. Also good and very popular. Huge portions. After a hard trek, try the massive *bistek a lo pobre* (tenderised steak) piled high with fried plantains, fries and egg. Recommended. The *Panadería* at Ayacucho 816 does good breakfasts, open Sun evening when many other places are shut. *Patisserie*, Jr 2 de Mayo 558. Good pastries. Try *Dulcería Santa Elena*, at Amazonas 800, for sweets.

Among the town's festivals are *Semana Turística de Amazonas*, held in the first week of **Festivals** **Jun**. *Virgen Asunta* takes place in the second week of **Aug**.

Comercial Tito, Libertad 860, is a good place for supplies. Also *Rojasa*, Amazonas 821. **Shopping**

Tours in the surrounding area include: city tour, Levanto, Yalape (0800-1530, **Tour** US$8.65), Kuelap, Karajía, La Jalca, Leymebamba (all full day, US$11.50 including **operators** guide and food), Revash (by vehicle to Santo Tomás, then 2-hr hike), Gran Vilaya or Laguna de los Cóndores (4-5 days each, depending on size of group), Mendoza

Northern Highlands

(groups of 6 to 8). *Chachapoyas Tours SAC*, Grau 534, Plaza Armas, p 2, T778078 www.kuelapperu.com or in the USA T(1-800)743-0945/(407)851-2289. *Vilaya Tours*, c/o *Gran Hotel Vilaya*, Jr Grau 624, T777506, F778154, www.vilayatours.com Or internationally T(1-416) 535-1163. Robert Dover, all-inclusive area treks throughout northern Peru catering to international clientele. Excellent guides (eg Luis, speaks good English). They have a regular newsletter and also work in conjunction with commuity projects. Recommended.

Transport   **Air** *Tans* from **Lima** at 0700 on Mon and Thu, via Chiclayo. The airport is 20 mins from town. A taxi costs US$3.

Bus To **Chiclayo** with *Civa* (Ortiz Arrieta 368), at 1600 daily, 10 hrs (may be longer in the rainy season), US$5.75 (US$4.35 to Chamaya junction for Jaén); to **Lima** 0800, 22 hrs, US$30; *Turismo Kuelap* (Ortiz Arrieta 412, T778128), at 1500 daily, except Mon and Fri at 1700, US$7; *Transcarh* (La Libertad between La Merced and La Unión) and *Móvil Tours*, also have buses to Chiclayo and Lima, 0800, 20 hrs, US$30. To **Celendín**, from which there are connections on to Cajamarca: with *Virgen del Carmen* (Av Salamanca y 2 de Mayo, in *El Aguila*), on Tue and Fri at 0700, 12-14 hrs (may be much longer in the rainy season, an unforgettable journey, take warm clothing, food and water), US$7.20. To **Pedro Ruíz**, for connections to Chiclayo or Tarapoto, combis (US$1.75, 0600-2000) and cars (US$2.60, US$5.20 to Bagua Grande) leave from either side of the corner of Grau and the small street between Salamanca and Libertad, 3 hrs. To **Mendoza** (86 km), *Trans Zelada* buses leave from Ortiz Arrieta 310 (also to Chiclayo, Trujillo and Lima); combis (1000 and 1400, 4½ hrs, US$3.45) and cars (leave when full, 3 hrs, US$5.20) leave from *Comité Interprovincial Santo Tomás*, Grau, by the cul-de-sac between Salamanca and Libertad.

For **Kuelap**: if intending to walk up to the fortress, combis leave daily to **Tingo** between 0900 and 1600 *Comité Interprovincial Santo Tomás*, 2 hrs, US$1.45; alternatively, *Transportes Rollers*, Grau 300 y Salamanca, have combis to **Choctámal** at 0300 (`dirección Yumal') and 0400 ('dirección María') daily, 3½ hrs, US$2, and to **Lónguita** and **María** at 0400, US$2.85, ask the María combi if it will take you to Quizango, the last village before the Kuelap carpark. To **Leymebamba**, bus leaves from Grau y Salamanca (vehicle parks on west side, if no one around knock on door opposite), at 1200 daily, 0300 Sun, 4 hrs, US$2. Cars for Leymebamba leave from next to *Rollers* 1300 daily, except Sun, 2½ hrs, 3½ hrs in the wet. To **Jalca Grande**, *Comité Interprovincial Santo Tomás*, departures about 1300 onwards (few if any on Sat), US$1.75 (return in morning). To **Lamud**, from *Comité Interprovincial Santo Tomás* between 0600 and 1600, 1 hr, US$1.15, or from *San Juan de Luya*, Ortiz Arrieta 364, also to Luya, throughout the day till 1800, US$1.45. Taxis may be hired from the Plaza for any local destination, eg US$35 per vehicle to Kuelap, US$14.50 to Levanto, return.

NB If driving your own vehicle, Chacha is the last petrol for a long way (84 octane only), though small amounts can be bought in Leymebamba. Note also that there are two roads out of Chachapoyas, one for heavy vehicles, one for light vehicles.

Directory   **Banks** *BCP*, Ortiz Arrieta 576, Plaza de Armas. Gives cash on Visa card, changes cash and TCs, ATM (Visa/Plus). *Hostal Revash* changes cash only, as do *Distribuidora Comercial Universal*, Ayacucho 940, Plaza de Armas, and the *Librería* at Amazonas 864. Communications **Internet:** *Cyber Club*, Triunfo 761, T778419. 2 terminals, closed Sun. *Lili@n's Explorer*, Jr 2 de Mayo 445, T778420, US$0.85 per hr. Also at Ortiz Arrieta 520, Plaza de Armas, formerly *Amazon Tours* (they can still organize tours). **Post office:** Grau on Plaza de Armas. **Telephone offices:** Ayacucho 926, Plaza de Armas. Also at Grau 608. **Laundry** *Lavandería Speed Clean*, Ayacucho 964 on Plaza, T777665.

Around Chachapoyas

Huancas, a picturesque village, stands on a hilltop north of Chacha. It's a two-hour walk starting on the airport road. The town is developing a reputation as an artisans' centre and local pottery can be bought. Walk uphill from Huancas for a magnificent view into the deep **canyon** of the Río Sonche. There is good walking in the area, which also has Inca and pre-Inca ruins.

Huancas

Sites around Chachapoyas

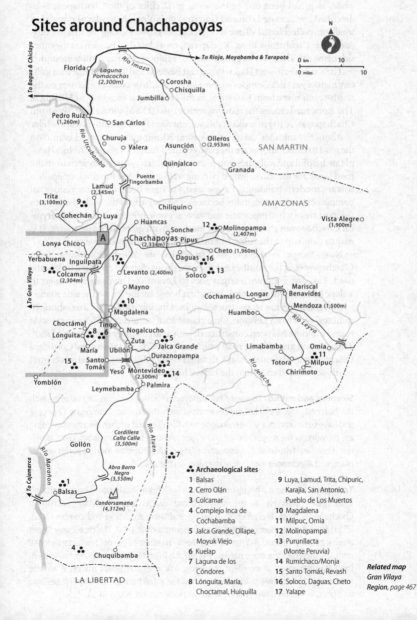

·· Archaeological sites

1 Balsas
2 Cerro Olán
3 Colcamar
4 Complejo Inca de Cochabamba
5 Jalca Grande, Ollape, Moyuk Viejo
6 Kuelap
7 Laguna de los Cóndores
8 Lónguita, María, Choctamal, Huiquilla

9 Luya, Lamud, Trita, Chipuric, Karajía, San Antonio, Pueblo de Los Muertos
10 Magdalena
11 Milpuc, Omia
12 Molinopampa
13 Purunllacta (Monte Peruvia)
14 Rumichaco/Monja
15 Santo Tomás, Revash
16 Soloco, Daguas, Cheto
17 Yalape

Related map
Gran Vilaya
Region, page 467

Northern Highlands

■ *Colectivos for Huancas leave from Jr Ortiz Arrieta y Salamanca; 20 minutes, US$0.45. A large prison complex has been built nearby and all colectivos go there on the way to the village.*

Levanto
Colour map 1, grid C4

The Spaniards built this, their first capital of the area, in 1538, directly on top of the previous Chachapoyan structures. Although the capital was moved to Chachapoyas a few years later, Levanto still retained its importance, at least for a while, as it had been one of the seven great cities of the Chachapoyans as described by Cieza de León and Garcilaso de la Vega. Nowadays Levanto is a small, unspoilt colonial village set on flat ground overlooking the massive canyon of the Utcubamba River. Kuelap can, on a clear day, be seen on the other side of the rift. The town is a good centre for exploring the many ruins around.

The Kuelap east-west Highway starts at Levanto and links with the Inca military highway at Jalca Grande (see page 463). Levanto was about mid-way on the north-south route from Colombia to the Huari, then Inca hub, at Huánuco. This stone road crosses the modern vehicle road at La Molina, about 5 km from Chachapoyas. A 10 km walk on this ancient road from Levanto is worthwhile.

About five minutes' drive, or a pleasant 30-minute walk, from Levanto on the road to Chachapoyas are the partly cleared ruins of **Yalape**. The local people are helpful and will guide you to the ruins which can be easily seen from the road (look for the three, linked curving walls just above the road, opposite a solitary modern building). Yalape seems to have been a massive residential complex extending over many hectares. The majority of the walls visible from the road are of white limestone and there are well-preserved examples of typical Chachapoyan architecture and masonry with quite elaborate friezes. It is easy to climb up to the ruins, but many of the structures are overgrown.

Near Yalape is the site of **San Pedro de Wushpu**: coming from Chachapoyas, at the point where the road drops over the crest, is a fork in the road. Take the left branch (right goes to Levanto). The ruins are similar to Yalape but easier to get to; ask at the first house on the left on the side road.

Morgan Davis has reconstructed an Inca building at **Colla Cruz**, about 20 minutes' walk from Levanto. On a classic Inca stone terrace, a regional-style round building has been constructed, with a three-storey high thatched roof. This garrison guarded the road which ran past Colcamar, over the Cordillera Oriental on a 1½-km-staircase, through Gran Vilaya, to Cajamarca's central north-south road and on to the coastal highway.

Sleeping and eating *Tambos Chachapoyanos'* hostal, two circular buildings with tall thatched roofs, stand behind Levanto's church; they can accommodate 12 people and have bathroom, hot shower, lounge with fireplace and kitchen. Beds and bedding are provided in the mayor's office and village meeting hall for small groups of travellers. There are two small *bar-bodegas* selling drinks, but little food), **Laurita** on the plaza, and **Alexsandra**, just before the plaza on the road in.

Transport Levanto is 2 hrs by truck or a 6-hr walk from Chachapoyas by a very rough road (barely passable in the rainy season). Trucks leave from the market in Chachapoyas most days at 0600, US$0.90, and there are trucks and combis (2 hrs, US$1) from outside *Bodega El Amigo* on Jr Hermosura at 1400. The nicest way to get there is by the Inca Road, 4-5 hrs. Take the heavy transit road out of Chachapoyas for 40 minutes, then take the stone path on the left. It is in pretty good shape, with one 15-m long stone stairway in excellent condition. Ask in Chachapoyas market if anyone returning to Levanto will guide you for a small fee. A taxi from Chachapoyas to Levanto and back, including driver waiting while you look around, is US$14.50.

South of Chachapoyas

To visit the sites south of Chacha, you have to descend to the road in the Río Utcubamba valley, cross the bridge to the west bank and head to Tingo. Near the bridge is *Casa Hospedaje Villa Consuela Fundo Hidalgo*. At Shipamarca there is a Sunday *feria* of handicrafts. Before Tingo is a sign to Kuelap, but this is a poor road. It's better continue to Tingo itself where the new road to Kuelap starts beside the river. Between these two roads, look for the ruins of **Macros** above the east bank of the river. Tingo is about 37 km south of Chachapoyas. Much of the village was washed away in the floods of 1993. In the hills above Tingo, 3½ km away, is **Tingo Nuevo**, with its plaza of flowers and topiary in front of the church. There is no running water or electricity. **Market** day is Sunday.

Tingo
Colour map 1, grid C4
Altitude: 1,800 m

Sleeping F pp *Albergue León*, Jr Saenz Peña s/n, no sign, walk 50 m from the police checkpoint to the corner and turn left, it's the third house on the left (righthand door), T999390. Basic, shared bathroom, cold water, friendly, run by Lucho León, who is very knowledgeable.

Eating *Kuelap*, at the junction of the main road with the road on the south bank of the Río Tingo, is clean and OK. Two other eating places.

Local guides *Oscar Arce Cáceres* based at 'El Chillo' near the Río Utcubamba, 4½ km outside Tingo. He owns a farm and knows the area very well. He is a very reliable guide but only speaks Spanish. He also has accommodation with bath, provides good meals and stores luggage. The trek into this area, like the walk up to Kuelap, starts from Tingo – the way is all mule track. The walk from El Chillo to Kuelap is shorter than from Tingo. The return to El Chillo can be made via the village of Nogalcucho (ask for directions). El Chillo is one of the places where the marvellous spatule tail hummingbird, unique to the Río Utcubamba, may be seen.

Transport For transport from Chachapoyas to Tingo, see above. There are several combis (from 0500) daily to Chachapoyas.Tingo to Leymebamba takes 2 hrs, US$1.75.

Kuelap

Kuelap (3,000 m) is a spectacular pre-Inca walled city which was rediscovered in 1843 by Juan Crisótomo Nieto. Morgan Davis writes that though successive explorers have attempted to do justice to the sheer scale of this site even their most exaggerated descriptions have fallen short. Kuelap was built over a period of 200 years, from AD 900-1100 and contained three times more stone than the Great Pyramid at Giza in Egypt.

Colour map 1, grid C4

Ins and outs

There are 4 options for visiting Kuelap:
1) Take a tour from Chachapoyas, as described above, page 456.
2) Hire your own vehicle with driver in Chachapoyas. Check at Salamanca on the corner with Grau. Also Sr Victor Torres, T777688.
3) Take a combi from Chachapoyas to Choctámal, María or Quizanga, see Chachapoyas Transport, above. You can spend the night in Choctámal village (no hotels, accommodation may be available in local homes) or at the *Tambos Chachapoyanos* Choctámal

Getting there

Northern Highlands

Lodge, known locally as 'el hotel', 3 km past the town (see Sleeping below). The next day, it is a relatively gentle 19 km, 4-5 hr, walk along the vehicle road to Kuelap. It's best to visit the site at your leisure and spend the night here (see sleeping above), then walk down the steep path (3-4 hrs) to Tingo the next day.

4) Take a combi from Chachapoyas to Tingo, see above. You should consider spending the night in Tingo to start climbing at dawn the next day. The strenuous 3½-4 hr hike (with a 1,200 m vertical gain) to Kuelap begins on the right hand side of the bridge, past the police station. At first the track follows the west bank of the Utcubamba, before turning right and climbing steeply into the mountains. The route is intermittently marked with red arrows painted on the rocks. It can get very hot and there is no water whatsoever until the top, but the trail may be muddy in the rainy season. Take water, food, adequate clothing and footwear, etc. You reach tThe small village of Kuelap first, the walls of the fortress become visible only at the very end of the climb. To walk down takes about 3 hrs.

Admission & facilities Open 0800-1700. US$3 (50% discount for students with identification). A small Centro de Interpretaciones is open 0800-1630; it has a good model of the site. There is a toilet block. The ruins are locked. The guardian, Gabriel Portocarrero, has the keys and accompanies visitors. He's very informative and friendly. Guides are available; pay them what you think appropriate. Beside the interpretation centre is a drinks and snacks stall. They will prepare hot coffee and food (boiled potatoes and eggs – make sure they are thoroughly cooked).

The site

The site lies sprawled along the summit of a mountain crest, more than a kilometre in length. It is divided into three parts: at the northwest end is a small outpost; at the southeast end of the ridge is a spread out village in total ruin; and the cigar-shaped fortress lies between the two, 585 m long by 110 m wide at its widest. The walls are as formidable as those of any pre-Columbian city. They vary in height between 8 and 17 m and were constructed in 40 courses of stone block, each one weighing between 100 and 200 kg. It has been estimated that 100,000 such blocks went into the completion of this massive structure.

The majority of the main walls on all four levels are original. Also original is the inverted, cone-shaped structure, long assumed to be a dungeon, although recent studies claim it to be a giant solar calendar , known as *el tintero* (the inkwell). There are a number of defensive walls and passageways as well as very many houses. Some reconstruction has taken place, mostly of

Kuelap

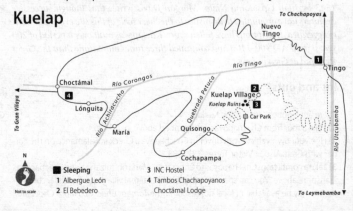

small houses and walls, but only one building has been completely restored. The remainder have been left in their cloud forest setting, the trees covered in bromeliads and moss, the flowers visited by hummingbirds. Although there are no carvings, some structures are adorned with simple geometric friezes which represent the eyes of animals and birds. An interesting feature is that almost all the buildings (about 420 in number) are circular. Recent archaeological findings indicate that the buildings were public spaces and served as kitchens, toilets and storage areas, rather than warriors' barracks as was first thought. It is estimated that up to 3,500 people lived in Kuelap at its zenith. The fortress was built, some believe, as the first large Chachapoya city in the region. Defence was vital for the developing culture against the constant raids from the Huari armies. With the Huari defeated, the Chachapoya moved out of Kuelap and into lower, less fortified altitudes where the farming was better. Kuelap was never mentioned in Inca chronicles, meaning that by the time of the Inca invasion in the 1470s, it was of little significance to the Chachas. The five rectangular structures indicate that the Incas occupied the fortress.

Sleeping When walking up from Tingo, the last house to the right of the track (*El Bebedero*, just above a small spring) offers accommodation: bed, breakfast and evening meal for US$6; good meals, friendly and helpful. A bit further, on the left, 100 m below the ruins, is the ***Instituto Nacional de Cultura (INC)*** hostel. It's a clean dormitory with room for about 12 people, in a lovely setting, US$1.75 per person, no running water (please conserve the rainwater in the buckets), simple meals may be available from the caretaker for US$1. There is free camping outside the hostel. Outside Choctámal the ***Tambos Chachapoyanos*** project operates a lodge with space for 35 people in 7 rooms with private bath, US$5 per person if you have a sleeping bag, US$7 per person if you want sheets and towels. It's in a lovely setting with great views, but cold at night. The facilities are not always open. Check beforehand at the address given above, or ask in Choctámal for whoever has the key.

Jalca Grande The town of Jalca Grande (or La Jalca as it is known locally), at 2,600 m, lies between Montevideo and Tingo, up on the east side of the main valley. There is a market on Saturday. In the town itself, one block west of the Plaza de Armas, is the **Choza Redonda**, the remains of a Chachapoyan roundhouse which was inhabited until 1964.

Half an hour west of the town are the ruins of **Ollape**, a series of platforms with intricate fretwork designs and wide balconies. A much larger site, though more primitive, is **Moyuk Viejo**, a 2½-hours' walk to the North.

A strenuous but rewarding three to four day trek can be made from La Jalca to Huambo or Limabamba (see page 468), over the cordillera and through cloud forests to the subtropical valleys. Part of the route follows an ancient road and there are undeveloped ruins along the way. Trekking experience and self-sufficiency are indispensable.

Sleeping and transport There is a *hostal* in La Jalca, one block from the plaza, passing the church, where the phone is, very basic. You may be able to find a room through the Alcaldía. Don't expect too much privacy, however, as it is used until 2200, after which time there is no electricity. So bring a torch (and a pack of cards; there isn't much in the way of nightlife, other than drinking). *Comité Interprovincial Santo Tomás* combis from Chachapoyas (see above) depart from about 1300 daily (except Sat); 3½ hrs, US$1.85. They return from La Jalca to Chachapoyas at 0500 daily.

Northern Highlands

Ubilón   Jalca Grande can also be reached from Ubilón, on the main road north to Tingo. Lots of transport passes Ubilón, but there is only one daily bus direct to the village. It's a strenuous three hour walk uphill to La Jalca. There is not much in Ubilón itself, save for a few shops selling next to nothing. Cheap, basic accommodation is available at *Bodega Irmita*.

Revash   Further south are the towns of **Yerbabuena** and **Puente Santo Tomás**, which is at the turn-off for the vivid burial *chullpas* of **Revash**, belonging to the Revash culture (around AD 1250). In Yerbabuena the Sunday market is the largest in the area, with animals, local produce, including cheeses, farming implements, etc on sale or for barter. There is one unnamed basic *hospedaje*, **G**, with running water but no electricity. There is also *Restaurant Karina*, which is cheap.

The **ruins** of Revash are roughly three hours' walk from Puente Santo Tomás. Follow the dirt road towards **Santo Tomás**, then cross the wooden bridge on the right and take the dirt track towards the mountains; it is a steep climb up. Eventually small adobe houses can be seen in the cliff face, covered by an overhang. The houses are buff coloured with red roofs and resemble tiny Swiss cottages with crosses in the form of bricked-up windows. They are, in fact, small tombs. There are lots of human bones lying around and cave paintings. The tombs have long since been looted. To get close, climb up a small goat track and walk along a ledge. Please do not climb on the houses as they are incredibly fragile. Examine the cliff face to the left of the houses and you'll notice several more tombs, peeking out from the limestone face. It is about an hour's walk back downhill from Santo Tomás to Puente Santo Tomás, from where there is transport north towards Chachapoyas.

Rumichaco/   Beyond Puente Santo Tomás there is a turn-off which heads east beyond
Monja   **Duraznopampa** to the small town of **Montevideo**. An hour's walk southeast of Montevideo is the ruined complex of **Rumichaco/Monja**, spread along a ridge above the town. The upper Rumichaco sector consists of massive undecorated platforms while the lower Monja sector is better preserved with some intricate fretwork on the platforms. Local guides can be hired; ask for Tito Rojas Calla in Montevideo. There are no hotels in the town but ask the owner of the only restaurant if you can sleep there.

Cerro Olán   Another Chachapoyan site is Cerro Olán, reached by colectivo to **San Pedro de Utac**, a small village beyond Montevideo, then a 30 minutes' walk. From the plaza a clear trail rises directly into the hills east of town to the ruins, which can be seen from the village. Here are the remains of towers which some archaeologists claim had roofs like mediaeval European castles.

According to Morgan Davis this was essentially a military installation and once a small city of considerable luxury, similar in construction to La Congona (see page 466) but on a grander scale. Ask the *alcalde* for accommodation.

The road south from Chachapoyas crosses the Utcubamba River then passes through **Palmira** and heads to Leymebamba.

Leymebamba

Colour map 1, grid C4   This pleasant town derives its name from a visit in around 1475, by the Inca Túpac Yupanqui, who stayed to celebrate the Fiesta de Inti-Raymi. From that moment, the town came to be known as the Field of the Festival of The Sun, or **Raymi-Pampa**, which in turn became Leymebamba. The city was moved from its original location, 3 km south, following an epidemic of yellow fever in the 1600s. The local fiesta is held in honour of the Virgen del Carmen on the week preceeding July 16.

The town's market is very limited; try the one at Yerbabuena on Sunday morning (see above). The young Spanish priest, Padre Diego, is very helpful, especially to Europeans. He is involved in the new museum project (see below). Water is sporadic and should be boiled to within an inch of its life. The Centro de Salud is helpful and will even visit your hotel if you're too ill to move. The *Comité Turístico* on the plaza is the place to go for all information on how to reach sites, including Laguna de los Cóndores (see below), for guides and horse hire.

E *Laguna de los Cóndores*, Jr Amazonas, half a block from the plaza. Cheaper without bath, warm water. **F** *Didogre*, 16 de Julio 320. Basic, cold water, shared bathroom, friendly. **F** *Escobedo*, 16 de Julio 518. Cold water, very basic, doors locked at 2130. — **Sleeping**

Cely Pizza's, Amazonas, Plaza de Armas. Good value, 2-course set meals for US$2.50, will cook vegetarian meals at 24 hrs notice, great for breakfast (no pizzas though), very clean, has fridge for cold beer, friendly. Recommended. *El Sabor Tropical*, 16 de Julio. Good chicken and chips, friendly. Try breakfast at the restaurant a few doors down. *El Caribe* on the plaza. Basic meals. — **Eating**

Bus Buses from Chachapoyas to Celendín (see page 458) pass through Leymebamba about 4 hrs after departure and make a lunch stop here. There's no guarantee of a seat, but you might have a better chance if you purchase your ticket in advance in Chachapoyas, advising that you will get on in Leymebamba. Combis to Chachapoyas leave the plaza 0200-0400 daily, except Sun, when they depart 0500-0600 to Yerbabuena only, where you can get other vehicles on to Chachapoyas. Inquire locally. The road between Chachapoyas and Leymebamba takes only 2½ hrs by car, but both car and bus take longer in the rainy season. — **Transport**

In 1996 a spectacular site consisting of six burial *chullpas*, containing 219 mummies and vast quantities of ceramics, textiles, woodwork, *quipus* and everyday utensils from the late Inca period, was discovered at Laguna de los Cóndores, a beautiful lake in a jungle setting, south of Leymebamba. — **Laguna de los Cóndores**

In order to protect this material from *huaqueros*, who had already done considerable damage, all the material was moved to town. It is, without doubt, a major discovery. A spectacular new **museum** was opened in 2001, with Austrian financial assistance, at San Miguel (3 km south), the site of the original Leymebamba town. Over 5,000 artefacts are on display, the great majority of them saved from the Laguna de los Cóndores site. The museum and its materials were entirely made by hand, a true artisan construction. There is a café, a great place to admire the architecture and lush surroundings. For further information contact Dr Sonia Guillén, Director, Centro Mallqui Bioanthropology Foundation, Av A Márquez 2014, Jesús María, Lima 11, T261 0095, F463 7875, mallqui@amauta.rcp.net.pe ■ *Mon-Sat 0900-1200, 1400-1700. Entry fee US$4.35 (S/15), but anything over that amount is most welcome. From the town it's a 30-40 mins' walk, take the footpath and ask directions constantly, the road is much longer.*

The **trip to Laguna de los Cóndores from Leymebamba** takes 10-12 hours on foot and horseback, nine hours return. Fran Cole (Surrey) writes: 'It is not for the fainthearted. Everyone who makes the trip agrees that it is the trip of a lifetime. Funnily enough, very few people want to do it twice!' Note that

Northern Highlands

the route climbs to 3,700 m before descending to the laguna where there is a basic lodge, US$5. Bring all food and cook it there or pay the family to prepare it. Make sure your horse is in good condition as the track is often knee deep in mud. Also take food and warm clothes. It is best done during the dry season (May to September); hire a local guide and horses. Three-day tours cost about US$70 per person. Unfortunately, the impressive funerary site overlooking the river has been stripped of artefacts and even some of its colourful plaster. Please do not climb on the houses or remove anything from the site.

La Congona There are many ruins around Leymebamba, many of which are covered in vegetation. The most spectacular is the Chachapoyan site of La Congona.

The site is a brisk three hours' walk along a clear trail which starts at the lower end of 16 de Julio. The path climbs steeply from the town, then levels off before descending to a large flat pasture. Turn left at the end of the pasture and follow the white sand, then bear right where the trail divides, to reach the middle of three peaks, identified by a white limestone cliff. The ruins are clustered in a small area, impossible to see until you are right among them. The views are stupendous and the ruins worth the effort. This is the best preserved of three sites, with 30 decorated round stone houses and a watch tower. 'It is supposed to be the only site displaying all three Chacha friezes – zigzag, rhomboid and Greek stepped.' (Richard Robinson, Newbury, England.)

There are two other sites, **El Molinete** and **Pumahuanyuna**, nearby. All three can be visited in a day but a guide is essential to explain the area and show the way to the ruins as it is easy to get lost.

Gran Vilaya

Colour map 1, grid C4 The name Gran Vilaya was created by US explorer, Gene Savoy, one of the candidates for the original 'Indiana Jones', who discovered this extensive set of ruined complexes in 1985. There are about 30 sites spread over this vast area, 15 of which are considered important by Morgan Davis. Among the sites are Pueblo Alto, Pueblo Nuevo, Paxamarca and Machu Llacta.

The whole area stretches west from the Río Utcubamba to the Río Marañón. Moist air pushing up from the Amazon Basin creates a unique biosphere of clouds and mist in which bromeliads and orchids thrive. Being near to the equator and over 3,000 m above sea level, the daytime temperature is a constant 22° C. While the Marañón valley is a desert, the peaks are always misted from June to September and drenched in rain the rest of the year. This creates a huge variety of mini-ecological zones, each with its own flora and fauna, depending on altitude and which flank of the mountain they are on.

Getting there Head north from Tingo or south from Chachapoyas as far as the Huinchuco bridge across the Río Utcubamba. On the west bank of the river a road leads to the left, if heading north, to the town of Colcamar, which is the starting point for exploring this area. A road from Choctámal to the Yumal pass into the Gran Vilaya region facilitates access but also places the area's cloud-forests at considerable risk of destruction. The Inca Roads in this region make for incredible trekking. Three villages are possible starting points, Cohechán, Inguilpata or Colcamar. Trails all lead to Belén, a gigantic silted-in glacial tarn with a spectacular panorama of the river meandering below. This is above the nightly freeze line and the only large flat spot in the zone. From here you cross the spine of the Andes on a 1.6-km Inca stairway, dropping into Gran Vilaya. You pass many ruins near Vista Hermosa (3½-4 hrs from Belén). You can lodge with Sr Cruz. The Kuelap East-West ancient road takes you over the Abra Yumal pass with a climb of

1,600-1,700 m ('a killer'), from where the trail thankfully descends to Choctámal. The Choctámal Lodge is therefore a good finishing (or starting) point for treks in the Gran Vilaya. It is recommended to take a letter of introduction from the *Instituto Nacional de Cultura* in Chachapoyas, or ask Los Tambos Chachapoyanos for assistance in finding a guide (essential), accommodation, meals and perhaps horses. Also ask local *alcaldes* for help. Padre Juan Castelli, an English priest who has been living in the area for many years, is very knowledgeable.

East of Chachapoyas

Forty kilometres east from Chachapoyas, on the road to Mendoza, are the pre-Inca ruins of Monte Peruvia (known locally as **Purunllacta**). They consist of hundreds of white stone houses with staircases, temples and palaces. The ruins have been cleared by local farmers and some houses have been destroyed. A guide is useful as there are few locals of whom to ask directions. The area is currently undergoing initial excavation by archaeologist Jorge Ruiz (ask for him in the *Café de Guías* in Chachapoyas). He believes that the entire structure is one of the largest in the Chachapoyas realm.

If you're stuck in **Pipus**, ask to sleep at restaurant *Huaracina* or at the police station next door. There are no hotels in **Cheto** but a house high up on the hill above the town with a balcony has cheap bed and board. The same family also has a house on the plaza. There are two small shops selling very little and a small house with one room serves basic but good meals.

Gran Vilaya Region

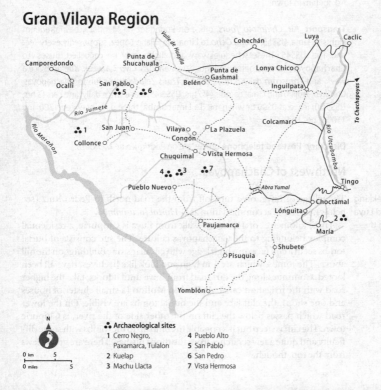

.: Archaeological sites

1 Cerro Negro, Paxamarca, Tulalon
2 Kuelap
3 Machu Llacta
4 Pueblo Alto
5 San Pablo
6 San Pedro
7 Vista Hermosa

Transport There is no direct transport from Chachapoyas. Take a combi at 0930 and 1500 from Jr Salamanca, fourth block down from the market, to Pipus, which stands at the turn-off to Cheto; 1½ hrs, US$1.35. You may have a long wait in Pipus for transport to Cheto; a camioneta leaves early in the morning, US$0.90. Or it's a 2-hour walk on a rough road.

Mendoza
Colour map 1, grid C4
Altitude: 1,500 m

The road east from Chachapoyas continues through Pipus to **Molinopampa**, two hours' drive from Chachapoyas, it then carries on, passing a forest of palms, to Mendoza, capital and supply centre of the subtropical province of the same name (Rodríguez de Mendoza), which reportedly produces the best coffee in Peru. Organically grown coffee from the area is exported directly to Europe.

Mendoza is also the starting point for an ethnologically interesting area in the Guayabamba Valley where there is a high incidence of fair-skinned people. There are roads and public transport to the small towns of Huambo, Santa Rosa, Totora, Limabamba, Chirimoto Viejo and Milpuc; and horse trails to other remote villages. Visitors going beyond Mendoza should be self sufficient.

Sleeping and eating F *Altiplano*, Rodríguez de Mendoza 321. With bathroom, cheaper without, cold water, very basic. F *Grandez*, Pje Hilario López 110. With bathroom, cheaper without, cold water, very basic. There are several simple restaurants on Rodríguez de Mendoza.

Guides Augustus Grandez Loja is a local guide and hunter and can take travellers around the little known environs of Mendoza. He can provide horses for longer treks. Ask for him in town.

Transport Air *Chirimoto Tours*, office on Rodríguez de Mendoza, has infrequent flights to Lima, US$55; *Grupo Ocho* to Lima, Pje Hilario López, supposedly every second Tue, US$45. These schedules vary and flights may be cancelled. **Buses** To **Chachapoyas**, from Jr Toribio Rodríguez de Mendoza, *Civa* 3 a week, *Kuelap* twice a week, and *Transcarh* daily, 5 hrs, US$3.50; *Trans Zelada* buses run to Chachapoyas, Chiclayo, Trujillo and Lima; combis (4½ hrs, US$3.45) leave twice daily, and cars (3 hrs, US$5.20) leave at 0500 or when full. To **Limabamba**, three daily between 1300 and 1500, 2 hrs, US$1.20.

Directory Post and telephone offices are on Rodríguez de Mendoza.

Northwest of Chachapoyas

Trekking around Luya

The village of Luya, on a turn-off from the road north to Pedro Ruíz (see below), has basic accommodation at **G** *Hostal Jucusbamba*.

Three kilometres or 1½ hours' walk from Luya is **Chipuric**, a residential complex belonging to the Chachapoyas culture. The site consists of burial tombs set in a cliff face on a high ledge with circular stone buildings on the hill above. The tombs, which are 1 m high and look like beehives, have all been looted. Continue along the dirt road from Luya until it forks; take the higher road with the irrigation canal. At **Pueblo Molino** (a small cluster of houses and one shop), the cliff face and the burial tombs are visible. On the lower road which passes below the cliff on the other side of the river, is Chipuric town. The cliff is steep but it's possible to climb up to the tombs with some difficulty and quite a few scratches from the thorn bushes. There are great views from the top, though.

Karajía, also known as Solmol, is 2½ hours' walk from Luya but more accessible from **Trita**. A short walk from Trita, in the valley behind the village, are the remarkable, 2½-m high sarcophagi, which date from 1200 AD, set into an impressive cliff face. Just below these inscrutable figures are plenty of human bones, if you look carefully. Study the cliff face for a dozen more, smaller sarcophagi. The main figures have been looted long ago by tourism-minded grave robbers who broke in via holes in the back, thus preserving the striking effigies. Ask for directions in Luya. It's best to take a local guide. Expect to pay around US$3.50-5 a day. In dry weather a short way to get there is from Cohechán (see below) to Cruzpata. At other times the road can be very muddy.

A good way to get to know the local people and to appreciate fully the magnificent scenery of this region is a three to four day trek starting from Luya. Walk 2-2½ hours to **Shipata** and from there to Karajía (30-40 minutes). Ask around for directions. You cannot get to the sarcophagi, but can view them from the other side of the valley (the same view point as from Trita), with binoculars preferably. At Shipata you can stay with Sra Rosa Zota, who will cook you dinner and breakfast. A better option, however, is to continue 1-1½ hours to **Cohechán**. To get there from Karajía, you have to go back to Shipata. Continue from Cohechán to **Belén** (four to five hours) and **Vista Hermosa,** thence to Yumal and Choctámal (see under Gran Vilaya).

Ten minutes north of Luya, 37 km northwest of Chachapoyas, is Lamud, a convenient base for several interesting archaeological sites. The local fiesta of **Señor de Gualamita** on 14 September is well-attended.

Lamud

At **San Antonio**, half an hour from Lamud, is a sandstone cliff face with several groups of burial tombs high on a ledge. They are difficult to see unless you know what you're looking for (there are sarcophogi and other tombs, but you need binoculars to see them). The ruins, set on the hill above, are a residential complex, thought to form part of a group of people belonging to the Chipuric. The main nucleus is almost completely ruined, but the ruins are unusual in that the stucco is still in place. A guide is not necessary, but ask for directions. On the bottom of the hill, where the road ends, a colonial-era tunnel and water-wheel can be explored.

Ten kilometres from Lamud are the mind-boggling ruins of **Pueblo de los Muertos**, circular stone houses overlooking the valley a thousand m below. A road goes to within 40 minutes of the site and then you have a steep, 40-minute walk on loose rock. The view is spectacular and the ruins are difficult to find as they are overgrown. Since being brought to public attention by Gene Savoy in the mid-1960s, the site has been largely destroyed by local grave robbers. Despite this, it is unmatched for location and scenery in the area. Ask directions before setting out.

Sleeping and eating In Lamud: **D** *Hostal Kuelap*, Garcilaso de la Vega 452, on the plaza. Clean, basic, friendly, hot water, **E** with cold water and shared bathroom. A few doors down is restaurant *María*, which is cheap, friendly and obliging, steak and chips is recommended, ask for *pension* which is 3 meals for US$1.80, excellent value, popular.

Guides Photographer Angel Mestanza Bobadilla, Garcilaso de la Vega 458, near the hotel on the plaza, T044-780213/780223, amesbo@latinmail.com , is recommended. His prices are reasonable. One trip is to local caves (be prepared to get muddy, take a torch); also to waterfalls.

Northern Highlands

Transport Buses and combis from Chachapoyas to Luya and Lamud are detailed above under Chachapoyas, Transport. The road is unpaved but in reasonable condition.

North of Chachapoyas

Pedro Ruíz
Colour map 1, grid B4
Altitude: 1,370 m

The road north from Chachapoyas heads through the beautiful Utcubamba River canyon with steep mountains on either side. In places the road is cut into the canyon wall. In the rainy season landslides may occur, especially near Pedro Ruíz, the town at the crossroads where you can either head west to Chiclayo on the coast or east to Tarapoto, Yurimaguas and the jungle. This is a small but important junction at the confluence of the Río Ingenio and the Utucubamba.

Sleeping and eating E per person *Casablanca*, on the main road, close to the Chachapoyas turning. Private bathroom, comfortable, the best in town. E *Amazonense*, near Policía Nacional on the main road. Cheaper with shared bathroom, basic, clean, friendly, helpful. Recommended. F *Marginal*. Shared bathroom, basic. There are several restaurants. *Shilico* is recommended.

Transport Many buses to and from **Chiclayo**, **Tarapoto** (8-9 hrs) and **Chachapoyas** all pass through town, mostly at night from 2000-2400. There is no way to reserve a seat and buses are usually full. Combis (US$1.75) and cars (US$2.30) go to **Bagua Grande**, 1½ hrs. Combis (US$1.75) and cars (US$2.60) also go to Chachapoyas, 3 hrs, and to Nuevo Cajamarca, US$3.45 (combi), 4½ hrs. Combis to Moyobamba, US$5.75, 4 hrs. One side of the junction for Chachapoyas, by the bridge, is the *Trans Kuelap* office; on the other side is *Transcarh*. Opposite the turning, in *Restaurante Gissela* (breakfasts and lunches) is the *Civa* office. Cars to Bagua Grande stop outside the restaurant. For cars and combis to Chachapoyas, from the junction walk down the main road towards Bagua and turn left a short way down a side street.

Directory Banks *Banco de la Nación* changes cash only. **Telephone office**, on the main road between *Casablanca* and *Policía Nacional*.

Around Pedro Ruíz

There are many interesting options for walking in the surrounding hills, covered with patches of cloud-forest and a good deal of undeveloped archaeology.

Catarata Chinata is a lovely 150-m waterfall which can be reached by walking along the trail to the village of San Carlos, about two hours uphill. Continue uphill past San Carlos then turn left along a smaller track to the waterfall, a further two hours. Ask the locals for directions. It's a very nice full-day hike through sections of cloud-forest.

Pomacochas lake, at 2,150 m above sea level, is near the town of Florida. The blue-green water is surrounded by *totora* reeds. Take a combi to Florida or Balsapata along the road to Rioja (one hour, US$1.75); there are good views of the lake from the road. Where the buses stop in Florida, women sell cheese and bread spread with *dulce/manjar*. There are a couple of hotels in the town and it is a popular day excursion from Chachapoyas.

Near Florida is the **Río Chido** trail, a famous birdwatching site with some rare species, including the marvellous spatule tail hummingbird. Access is five minutes before the high point on the road to Florida, at San Ignacio. A highly recommended guide is young Dilberto Faustino, who is very enthusiastic and knowledgeable.

East to the Amazon

The eastern branch of the road at Pedro Ruíz runs all the way to Yurimaguas. The road has been paved as far as Tarapoto. All sections are still prone to landslides in the wet season. This is a very beautiful journey where the high Andes tumble into the Amazon Basin before your eyes.

After Florida, the road winds down then up through Buenos Aires to a cultivated zone around the villages of La Esperanza, El Progreso and Oso Perdido. A further descent through forested mountains leads to the new town of Nuevo Cajamarca (with a few thousand inhabitants), 152 km east of Pedro Ruíz. There is a large market for local produce. There are frequent colectivos to Rioja (US$1.15, 45 minutes) and to Pedro Ruíz (they usually continue to Bagua Grande). There is accommodation on the main road.

Nuevo Cajamarca
Colour map 1, grid B4

Just beyond Nuevo Cajamarca is Rioja. There are a number of caves (Diamante, Cascayunga) and river sources (Tioyacu, Negro) nearby and the chief local tourist attractions are *complejos* and *recreos turísticos* with accommodation, local foods and swimming pools. The best is the *Yacumama Lodge*, where the owner gives guests tours of his property and can arrange local excursions.

Rioja
Colour map 1, grid B5

Sleeping and eating *Hostal San Martín*, Grau 540; *San Ramón*, Jr Faustino Maldonado 840; and *Carranza*, Jr Huallanga. All basic. *Restaurante Los Olivos*, recommended.

Transport There are regular combis to **Moyobamba** (US$0.85, 45 mins).

Moyobamba

Moyobamba, a pleasant town in an attractive valley, was founded in 1540 as the original capital of Maynas. It then became capital of Loreto before the establishment of the department of San Martín, of which it became capital in 1906. This area has to cope with lots of rain in the wet season and in some years the whole area is flooded. In the last week of June the town celebrates its annual tourist week festival, in the last week of July is the **Fiesta de Santiago** and in November (a different week each year) is the **Semana de la Orquídea**. The valley, including both Moyobamba and Rioja, is renowned for its orchids.

Phone code 094
Colour map 1, grid B5
Population: 14,000
Altitude: 915 m

Puerto Tahuishco is the town's harbour on the Río Mayo, where locals sell their produce at weekends. From **Morro de Calzada**, there is a good view of the area. ■ *Take a truck to Calzada (30 mins), then walk up for 20 mins.* There are Baños Termales at **San Mateo**, 5 km from Moyobamba, which are hot and worth a worth a visit on weekends when the entire town seems to be there, and sulphur baths at **Oromina**, 6 km from town.

Sights

The more adventurous can hike to the **Gera waterfalls**, 21 km from Moyobamba in the jungle. Take a micro to Jepelacio. From there, take a good path through a well-populated valley, crossing two bridges on the way, then head along the river through dense jungle. There are three more river crossings but no bridges, so access may be tricky, even dangerous when the rivers are high. **Tourist offices** *Dirección Regional de Turismo*, is at Jr San Martín 301, on the plaza, T562043, dritinci-ctarsm@ddm.com.pe Information on excursions and hikes is available from the *Instituto Nacional de Cultura*, Jr Benavides 352, which also has a small departmental museum, entry US$0.35.

Northern Highlands

Sleeping **A** *Puerto Mirador*, Jr Sucre, 1 km from the centre, T/F562050 (in Lima T4423090, F4424180, Av R Rivera Navarrete 889, of 208, San Isidro). Includes breakfast, nice location, pool, good restaurant. **C** *Marcoantonio*, Jr Pedro Canga 488, T/F562045/319. Smartest in town centre, with bath and hot water, TV, restaurant. **E** *Hostal Atlanta*, Alonso de Alvarado 865, T562063. With bathroom, hot water, TV, fan, clean, good but noisy, no breakfast. **E** *Hostal Country Club*, Manuel del Aguila 667, T562110. With bath, hot water, clean, comfortable, friendly, nice garden. Recommended. **E** *Hostal Royal*, Alonso de Alvarado 784, T562662, F562564. With bath, hot water, TV (cheaper without), laundry, cafeteria. **G** pp *Hostal Cobos*, Jr Pedro Canga 404, T562153. With bathroom, cold water, simple but good, friendly.

Eating *La Olla de Barro*, Pedro Canga y S Filomeno. Typical food, expensive compared with other places in town but still good value. *Rocky's*, Pedro Canga 402. Also typical food, good but cheaper. Both open for breakfast. Also on Pedro Canga, No 451, is *Chifa Kikeku*. *Edén*, 3rd block of Callao. Vegetarian. There are many other places in town, especially *pollerías*. *Panaderías*: *América*, San Martín y Alonso de Alvarado, and *Las Orquídeas*, San Martín 421.

Transport
Be careful travelling at night in this region; buses tend to travel in convoy

Bus Buses leave from the Terminal Terrestre, about a dozen blocks from the centre on Av Grau, which leads out of town to the main highway (mototaxi to the centre US$0.30). Several companies to **Tarapoto** (eg *Turismo Tarapoto*, T563307, *Paredes Estrella*, *Sol Peruano*, *Guadalupe*), US$2.85, 3¼ hrs. Buses heading west, en route from Tarapoto to **Pedro Ruíz**, **Chiclayo** and **Lima**, arrive at about 1400 or later, except *Mejía*, which has a departure to Pedro Ruíz and Chiclayo at 1100. **Combis** leave from *Transportes y Turismo Selva* terminal, Jr Callao between Benavides and Varacadillo. To **Tarapoto** US$2.85, **Yurimaguas** US$6.35, **Rioja** US$0.85, **Pedro Ruiz** US$5.75; departures between 0530 and 1900, leave when full. **Cars** to **Tarapoto** (3 hrs, US$6) and **Rioja** (30 mins, US$1.30) leave when full from Jr Pedro Canga.

Directory **Banks** *BCP*, Alonso de Alvarado 903 y San Martín. ATM (Visa/Plus). *BBV Continental*, San Martín 494.

Moyobamba

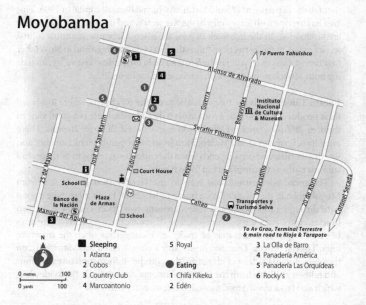

Sleeping
1 Atlanta
2 Cobos
3 Country Club
4 Marcoantonio
5 Royal

Eating
1 Chifa Kikeku
2 Edén
3 La Olla de Barro
4 Panadería América
5 Panadería Las Orquídeas
6 Rocky's

To Puerto Tahuishco

Alonso de Alvarado

Instituto Nacional de Cultura & Museum

Serafín Filomeno

Court House

School

Banco de la Nación

Plaza de Armas

School

Transportes y Turismo Selva

To Av Grau, Terminal Terrestre & main road to Rioja & Tarapoto

25 de Mayo
José de San Martín
Pedro Canga
Guerra
Benavides
Reyes
Gral
Varacadillo
20 de Abril
Coronel Secada
Callao
Manuel del Aguila

0 metres 100
0 yards 100

Tarapoto

Rioja, Moyobamba and Tarapoto are growing centres of population, with much forest clearance beside the Carretera Marginal de la Selva. The 109 km from Moyobamba to Tarapoto has been greatly improved and is almost entirely paved. It is heavily used by trucks, with fuel and meals available. You can stop at Tabalosas to buy fresh fruit from women at the roadside. Tarapoto is a busy town, founded in 1782, with a good local market 1½ blocks from the Plaza Mayor on Avenida Raimondi. It is a very friendly place, eager to embrace tourism and agricultural development now that the threat of terrorism and drug-trafficking has receded from the area. It competes with Iquitos for the record number of motorcycle taxis per square metre of road. There are three parts to the town: Tarapoto itself, Morales to the west and La Banda de Shilcayo to the east. The **Museo Regional de la Universidad Nacional de San Martín**, on Maynas, half a block from the Plaza, behind the church, contains a little of everything, paleontology, geology, ethnography, stuffed animals, and so on, but it's rather faded and dusty. ■ *Mon-Fri 0800-1200, 1230-2000, US$0.35.* In the second week of July is the town's rowdy **tourist week festival**, but between May and September, it seems like every weekend celebrates something. It doesn't take much for the *Tarapoteños* to party. Some tourist information can be found at the *Casa del Turista*, Moyobamba on the Plaza Mayor, which is mostly a handicrafts shop, and at the *Cámara de Comercio*, Moyobamba y Manco Cápac.

Phone code: 094
Colour map 1, grid C5

Tarapoto

Sleeping
1 Alojamiento Tarapoto
2 Edinson
3 El Mirador
4 July
5 La Posada
6 Lily
7 Los Angeles
8 Nilas
9 San Antonio

Eating
1 Chifa Lug Ming
2 Las Terrazas
3 Pizza Selecta
4 Real & El Camarón

Northern Highlands

Sleeping **A** *Nilas*, Jr Moyobamba 173, T527331, F525175, nilas-tpto@terra.com.pe Modern, the best in the centre, with bath, hot water, a/c, TV, fridge, internet access, pool, jacuzzi, gym, airport transfer, very well-appointed, also has conference facilities. **A** *Río Shilcayo*, Pasaje Las Flores 224, 1 km east of town in La Banda de Shilcayo, T522225, F524236 (in Lima T4479359). With bathroom, excellent meals, non-residents can use the swimming pool for a fee. **B** *Lily*, Jiménez Pimentel 405-407, T523154, F522394. With bath, hot water, a/c, TV, price includes breakfast and tax, laundry, sauna, restaurant. **C** *La Posada Inn*, San Martín 146, T522234, F526768, laposada@ terra.com. pe Another good central hotel, comfortable, with bath, hot water, fridge, TV, some rooms with a/c, nice atmosphere, breakfast and lunch, small library of books in Spanish on the region. **D** *El Mirador*, Jr San Pablo de la Cruz 517, T522177. 5 blocks uphill from the plaza, with bath, cold water, fan, TV, very welcoming, clean, laundry facilities, breakfast (US$2) and hammocks on roof top terrace with good views, also offers tours. Recommended. **E** *Edinson*, Av Raimondi y Maynas, 10 m from Plaza Mayor, T523997, T/F524010. With bathroom, a/c, cheaper without, cold water, breakfast, clean and comfortable, also has karaoke bars and disco. **E** *July*, Jr Alegría Arias de Morey 205, T522087. With bath, cold water, TV, fridge, no breakfast. **E** *Alojamiento Tarapoto*, Jr Grau 236, T522150, F524942, alojatarapoto@mixmail.com With bath, cold water, TV, fan, clean, nice rooms, no breakfast. **F** *Hostal San Antonio*, Jr Jiménez Pimentel 126, T522226. With private bathroom and TV, fan, courtyard, no breakfast. Noisy but recommended. **F** *Los Angeles*, Jr Moyobamba, near the Plaza, T525797. Good value, **G** without bath, laundry facilities, restaurant. There are several other *hostales* and *alojamientos* in the 300 block of Jiménez Pimentel. **G** pp *Alojamiento Santa Juanita*, Av Salaverry 602, Morales (20 mins from centre). New, good beds, fan, spotless, family run, owner speaks English, safe.

Eating The best are *Real* and *El Camarón*, which are both in the same building on Moyobamba on the Plaza and are expensive. *Las Terrazas*, Ramírez Hurtado, also on the Plaza, serves typical food and is recommended. There are many others, such as *Chifa Lug Ming*, San Pablo de la Cruz, Chinese, and *Pizza Selecta*, J Vargas 185, for pizza, lasagne and chicken. Regional specialities, which can also be found in Moyobamba, include *cecina* (dried pork), *chorizo* (sausage – good and tasty), both ususally served with *tocacho* (see under Iquitos, Eating), also *juanes, inchicapi* and *ensalada de chonta* as in Iquitos. Interesting juices are *cocona*, made with cloves and cinnamon, and *aguajina*, from the *aguaje* fruit (deep purple skin, orange inside, sold on street corners). Regional fruits include grapes and pineapples, and many more besides.

Entertain-ment There are many bars and pubs around the centre. The adventurous can try any of Tarapoto's many local inebriators, made from sugarcane liquor and a host of fruit juices. For local discos, check out the neighbourhood of **Morales**, about 10 mins west of town on the highway. Popular local discos include *El Papillon* and *Las Pumas*. They sometimes charge a US$1.50 cover at weekends.

Tour operators *Quiquiriqui Tours*, Jiménez Pimentel 314, T527863, F524016. Sells flight tickets, *Turismo Tarapoto* bus tickets (see below) and tours.

Transport **Air** Flights to **Lima** with *Aviandina* (Moyobamba y San Pablo de la Cruz, T524332), daily, and *Tans* Plaza Mayor 491 (T525339), daily except Tue and Fri, who also fly to **Iquitos**. *Saosa*, M de Compagñón 468, has flights in small planes to **Pucallpa**, **Tocache**, **Contamaná** and other places. Book in advance, particularly in the rainy season. A taxi to the airport is US$1.75, mototaxi US$1.45. There's no bus service, but it's no problem to walk.

Bus Buses to destinations to the west all leave from Av Salaverry, Morales, about 10 mins by mototaxi from the Plaza, except *Turismo Ejecutivo/Ejetur*, whose office is on Cabo A Leveau in the centre. The following companies have buses to **Moyobamba**, 116 km, US$2.85, 3¼ hrs, **Pedro Ruíz**, US$7.20 (US$8.65 *Turismo Tarapoto* and *Paredes Estrella*), 9 hrs, **Chiclayo**, 690 km, 22 hrs, US$11.50, **Trujillo**, 25 hrs, and **Lima**, US$20: *Paredes Estrella* (T523681) at 0800 and 1400, *Turismo Tarapoto* (T523259), at 1230 and 1300, *Turismo Ejecutivo*, *Trans Guadalupe* at 0900 and 1300, *Sol Peruano* at 1100, *Expreso Huamanga* at 1230 and 1400 and *Guadalupe Express* at 0900 and 1300. Combis to Moyobamba leave from *Turismo La Selva*, Av Salaverry, closer to the centre than the bus offices. Cars also run to *Moyobamba*, US$5.75. To *Yurimaguas*, US$3.45, 5-6 hrs, several bus companies (same price by combi); pick-ups, daily, charge US$5.75 in the front, US$2.85 in the back; cars charge US$7.20 (see next page for road conditions). Buses to Yurimaguas leave from the eastern side of Tarapoto. Truck/pick-up leaves for Yurimaguas (usually 0800-0900, and in the afternoon) from Jorge Chávez 175, down Av Raimondi 2 blocks, then left along Av Pedro de Urzua.

Banks *BCP*, Maynas 134. Changes TCs, ATM for Plus/Visa. *BBV Continental*, Ramírez Hurtado, Plaza Mayor, with Visa/Plus ATM. *Interbank*, Grau 119, near the Plaza. No commission on changing TCs for soles, handles Mastercard. Street changers near the corner of Maynas and Jiménez Pimentel, on the Plaza Mayor. **Communications** Internet: 4 places close to each other: at San Martín y Arias de Morey, Arias de Morey 109 (*C@binas Internet*) and 136 (*Club Internet*) and San Martín 129 (also *C@binas Internet*).   **Directory**

Around Tarapoto

There are petroglyphs at **Demor** and **Pólish** east of the city, 4 and 5 km respectively. **Laguna Azul** (or Laguna Sauce as it is also known) is a big lake 52 km south of Tarapoto, with *cabañas* for rent on the shore. They cost US$80 per night for four beds and a shower. They are very basic and no fresh water or food is available. A colectivo takes 2½ hours and costs US$3.45. You can go river rafting on the Río Mayo for US$10 per person.

Twenty-two kilometres from Tarapoto, on the road to Moyobamba, a road leads off to **Lamas** where there is a small but highly recommended museum, with exhibits on local Indian community, the Lamistas. ■ *US$0.60, custodian will show you round "in garbled Spanish".* Turn right out of the museum and walk a couple of blocks uphill, then down into the part of town where the Lamistas live. There's a **market** in the morning. In town, *Rolly's*, San Martín 925, just off the plaza, serves good food. ■ *Colectivo from Tarapoto; 30 mins, US$0.85, from Paradero Lamas on road to Moyobamba (take mototaxi from centre, US$0.45). There are infrequent combis.* From Lamas you can visit the waterfalls at **Chapawanqui** (taxi US$7, 15 minutes) and many others.

About 14 km from Tarapoto on the spectacular road to Yurimaguas are the 50-m falls of **Ahuashiyacu**. A walkway leads up to a pool at the foot of one of lower parts of the falls. You can swim here, but wait until after the sun has warmed the water; before 0900 it's freezing. This is a popular place at lunchtimes and weekends. ■ *The falls can be visited by tour from Tarapoto (US$14.50 by mototaxi). Entry is US$0.30 (toilets US$0.15).* The entire falls can be seen from the *recreo turístico El Paraíso Verde*, with a restaurant serving typical food, drinks, toilets, swimming pool (US$0.60), also popular. About 300 m beyond Ahuashiyacu is *El Mono y La Gata* restaurant, beyond which is El Pozo, a manmade pool for swimming and washing. Carry on along the road to Yurimaguas for 22 km and you come to the **Baños Termales de San José y Cascada de Carpishoyacu**.

Northern Highlands

Tarapoto to Yurimaguas

The journey from Tarapoto to Tingo María (see page 524) is not advisable. In the rainy season the roads are impossible and it is a drugs-growing area. From Tarapoto it is 129 km to Yurimaguas on the Río Huallaga (see page 526). The spectacular road can be very bad in the wet season, taking six to eight hours for trucks (schedules above). Once the plains are reached, the road improves and there is more habitation. It is not advisable to take the road to Yurimaguas very early in the morning or in the evening as hold-ups may occur. **Shapaja** is the port for Tarapoto, 14 km from town, served by colectivos. At Shapaja cargo boats can be caught to Yurimaguas. There's plenty of birdlife and river traffic to be seen. From Yurimaguas on the Río Huallaga, launches go to Iquitos.

To the Coast

The road from Pedro Ruíz (see page 470) goes west for 65 km to Bagua Grande, at first through a narrow gorge, the ridges covered with lush cloud-forest, then along the broad and fertile lower Utcubamba valley. It then crosses the Marañón at Corral Quemado. From the confluence of the Marañón with the Río Chamaya, the road follows the latter, past bare cliffs covered by dry scrub, towering over the deep river canyons. It reaches the Abra de Porculla (at 2,150 m, the lowest pass through the Peruvian Andes) in 60 km, before descending to join the old Pan-American Highway at Olmos (see page 415). From here you can go southwest to Chiclayo, or northwest to Piura. The road from Pedro Ruíz west to Olmos is paved, but prone to landslides in the rainy season.

Bagua Grande
Colour map 1, grid B3

The the first town of note heading west from Pedro Ruíz is Bagua Grande. It's a hot and dusty place, sprawled along its main street, Avenida Chachapoyas, where all the hotels and restaurants are located. Bagua Grande is not very safe. If arriving late, ask to sleep on the bus until daybreak. Police may ask to see travellers' documents here. The town celebrates the **Fiesta de Santiago** over the last week in July and in September holds its tourist week festivities. *BCP*, Avenida Chachapoyas 1978. Cash only.

Transport Many buses pass through Bagua Grande en route from Chiclayo to Tarapoto and Chachapoyas and *vice-versa*, mostly at night. Cars (US$2) and combis (US$1) to Jaén leave from the west end of Av Chachapoyas, 1 hour. From the east end of Av Chachapoyas, cars (US$2.30) and combis (US$1.75) leave to Pedro Ruíz, 1½ hrs. Taking a mototaxi (US$0.30) between the two stops is a good alternative to walking in the heat.

Bagua Chica
Colour map 1, grid B2

Near Bagua Grande, along a side road is Bagua Chica, also referred to as just Bagua, a garrison. Pay careful attention to the names when arranging transport, so you are not taken to the wrong Bagua. ■ *Marañón or Cenepa buses Chiclayo-Bagua Chica, six hours, US$4.50, at 1030 and 2100 or 2130. Between Bagua Grande and the turning for Bagua Chica is a toll post, US$0.75 for cars. By the 24 de Julio bridge over the Río Marañón is a forestry control post.*

Northeast to Sameriza

Collour map 1, grid B4

From Bagua Grande the road continues northwest, then forks: southwest to **Chamaya**, for Jaén and the coast, and northeast to **Sameriza**, the first port on the Marañón. The northeast branch passes through **Aramango** and **Chiriaco** and continues to another fork, northeast to **Oracuza** and **Santa María de Nieve**, and east to Sameriza and **Puerto Delfus**, both on the Río Marañon.

Santa María de Nieve is a welcoming place, typical of a small riverside town with a mixed community. It has a zoo, good swimming in the river, fishing and trips to indigenous villages and downriver to the Pongo de Manseriche. From Bagua Chica, take a car or combi to Imaza (also called Imacita), six hours, US$8.60. From Imaza boats go to Santa María, four hours, US$13 (*Civan* or *Riomar* companies, none after 1500). In Santa María ask to be taken to Inigo's house then contact the Torres family who have rooms (**F**), serve meals, do laundry and offer guiding service. The house, with garden and hammocks on the balcony, has great views of the river. Contact luidelrio@hotmail.com

Travelling beyond Bagua Chica, even though some birdwatching groups do go here, is not recommended unless you have permission from the Aguaruna Indian communities and take local guides who know each community that you will pass through. The road is in very bad condition and it is not advisable to stop en route. The Aguaruna have shown some hostility towards foreigners as a result of oil exploration on their lands and the local political situation is very sensitive. There have also been robberies and sexual assaults on desolate parts of road.

Fifty kilometres west of Bagua Grande, a road branches northwest at Chamaya (one basic hostel, El Volante) to Jaén (15 minutes). This is the best place to break the journey from Chachapoyas or the jungle to Chiclayo and vice-versa. **To Jaén**

Jaén

Although it was founded in 1536, Jaén retains little of its colonial character. Rather, it is the modern and prosperous centre of a rich agricultural region producing rice, coffee, and cocoa. From 1563 to 1789 it was governed by the Real Audiencia de Quito and it is close to territory that used to be disputed by the two countries, hence its former designation 'Corazón de la Peruanidad'. The local festival of **Señor de Huamantanga** on 14 September is widely attended. It is a friendly place, but Jaén is currently developing the dubious reputation as the centre for Peruvian opium poppy production.

Phone code: 044
Colour map 1, grid B3
Population: approximately 25,000
Altitude: 740 m

A colourful modern **cathedral** dominates the large plaza around which most services of interest to the visitor are clustered. A **museum** at the Instituto 4 de Junio, Hermógenes Mejía s/n, displays pre-Columbian artifacts from the Pakamuros culture. **Sights**

C *El Bosque*, Mesones Muro 632, T/F731184. With fridge, pool, parking, gardens, best in town. **C** *Prim's*, Diego Palomino 1353, T731039, hotel prims@terra.com.pe Good service, comfortable, hot water, friendly, full internet and computer service for guests and non-guests, US$1.50 per hr, small pool. Recommended. **D** *Hostal Cancún*, Diego Palomino 1413, T733511. Clean and pleasant, with bath, hot water, fan, restaurant, pool. Recommended. **D** *Hostal Diana Gris*, Urreta 1136, T732127. Family run and friendly, with bath, TV, fan, laundry service, café. **E** Hostal César, Mesones Muro 168, T731277, F731491. Fan, phone, TV (cheaper without), parking, restaurant, nice. **E** Hostal Bolívar, Bolívar 1310, Plaza de Armas, T/F734077, cel 992232. Clean, with fan, TV, no breakfast. **E** Santa Elena, San Martín 1528, T732713. With bath, basic. **F** *San Martín*, San Martín 1642. With bathroom, hot water, basic, negligent staff.

Sleeping
■ *on map*
Price codes: see inside front cover

Northern Highlands

Eating *La Cueva*, Pardo Miguel 304. Recommended. There are many others around the plaza.

Transport **Bus** To **Chiclayo** with *Civa*, Mariscal Ureta 1300 y V Pinillos (terminal at Bolívar 936), at 1030 and 2130 daily, 8 hrs, US$3.75. To **Lima** (US$17) on Mon, Wed and Fri, 1500, US$13-14.50. Many others to Chiclayo including *Ejetur*, Mesones Muro 410, at 2030, US$4.35, continuing to **Trujillo**, US$7.20; several from a terminal in the middle of the 4th block of Mesones Muro (eg *Transcade*, *El Cumbe* – also to Cajamarca), and *Línea*, Mesones Muro 475, T733746, 1300 and 2300, US$4.35. To **Moyobamba** via Pedro Ruiz (the crossroads for Chachapoyas, 4 hrs), Nuevo Cajamarca and Rioja: *Turismo Jaén*, R Castilla 421, T731615, US$7.20. Continuing to **Tarapoto**: *Ejetur*, address above, US$3.75 to Pedro Ruíz, US$5.75 to Nuevo Cajamarca, US$7.20 to Rioja and Moyobamba, US$10 to Tarapoto and US$14.40 to Yurimaguas; *Jaén Express* and *Guadalupe*, Mesones Muro first block, and *Transportes Mejía* and *Jaén Express*, from terminal on fourth block of Mesones Muro, all have the same prices to Moyobamba and Tarapoto. (Jaén Express also has an office at Túpac Amaru 109). Cars (US$2) run in the early morning and when full from *San Agustín*, Av Mesones Muro y Los Laureles to **Bagua Grande** (1 hr), where connections can be made for Pedro Ruíz. Combis do the same route (US$1.30) from Servicentro San Martín de Porras, Mesones Muro 4th block.

Directory **Banks** *BCP*, Bolívar y V Pinillos. Cash only; ATM (Visa/Plus). *Banco Continental*, Ramón Castilla y San Martín. Cash, US$5 commission for TCs. *Cambios Coronel*, V Pinillos 360 (Coronel 2 across the street at 339). Cash only, good rates. *Ceymar* and *John Lennon*, V Pinillos on plaza, next to public phones. Cash only. **Communications** Internet: at *Foto center Erick*, Pardo Miguel 425. US$1.15 per hr. **Post office**: Pardo Miguel y Bolívar. **Telephone office**: V Pinillos, on the plaza.

Around Jaén There is no organized tourism around Jaén. To **bathe in the Marañón**, take a combi from the corner of Cajamarca and Eloy Ureta to Bellavista (40 minutes, US$0.50). From here it is a 45-minute walk beside rice paddies to the river, ask for directions. Swim- ming is possible but mind the strong current. Many locals go there on Sundays. A motorboat across the Marañón costs US$0.45 one way.

To Ecuador

Colour map 1, grid B3 A road runs north from Jaén to **San Ignacio** (107 km), near the frontier with Ecuador. It passes the valley of the Chinchipe, renowned for its lost Inca gold. San Ignacio has a *fiesta* on 31 August. Combis run from the *paradero* at the northern exit of Jaén for the 2½-hour journey on a good, unmade road (US$3, from 0330 till the afternoon). **F** per person *La Posada*, clean, OK. There are a couple of restaurants on the main street, eg *Oliver*, US$1 for set meal, and one internet café. From San Ignacio colectivo taxis run to Namballe (one new, concrete *hotel*, **G** pp), US$2.30, and on to the border at La Balsa, two hours, US$3. This new, official border post has a vehicle bridge under construction (late 2002), but until it's ready you cross the river on a raft made from oil drums, US$0.25. To leave Peru, go first to the PNP police office, then knock loudly on the door of the new immigration building to summon the officer. It may be possible to change money in the immigration posts. Allow one hour of formalities. Once through Ecuadorean immigration, you can take a *chiva* to Zumba, 1230 and 1730, 1½ hours on a bad road, US$1.50, and then a bus to Vilcabamba and Loja, a further seven hours, eight a day, US$4. It may be necessary to stay the night in Zumba (**E** *Oasis*, next to Banco de Fomento, modern, bath; **F** *Chinchipe*, shared bath, cold water; **F** *Hostal La Choza*, Avenida 12 de Febrero, with restaurant, shared bath, cold water. Two restaurants serve set meals).

Central Highlands

Introducing the Central Highlands

Stretching from the southern end of the Cordillera Blanca right up to Cusco department, this area of stunning mountain scenery and timeless Andean towns and villages is a must for those who appreciate traditional, good quality textiles and ceramics. The main highlights include the cities of Huancayo, Ayacucho and the surrounding villages – the main production centres of handicrafts. The people of **Ayacucho**, shrugging off the area's reputation as former home of the Maoist terrorist movement, Shining Path (see page 578), are relieved to see tourists return to their towns and cities. Visitors are treated with great friendship

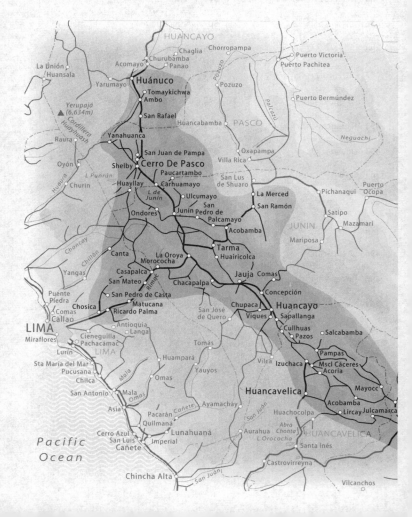

Central Highlands

and hospitality and Ayacucho also hosts one of the largest and most impressive Holy Week celebrations in Latin America. Those who enjoy a lively festival will not be disappointed in the **Mantaro Valley** – it almost doesn't matter when you go, there is usually some celebration afoot. More good news is that the **Central Railway from Lima to Huancayo** has started up passenger services again, so one of the outstanding train rides in South America can be experienced again.

More than just fabulous landscapes, this area hides important pre-Inca sites, such as **Kotosh**, near Huánuco, and **Huari**, outside Ayacucho, two early examples of Andean urban civilizations. Stretches of the **Royal Inca Road** run from the temple fortress of Huánuco Viejo and up the Yanahuanca Valley, reminders of this

great imperial causeway. The Spaniards, too, left their mark, with fine churches and mansions in **Ayacucho**, a beautiful altar in **Huancavelica** and the missionary training-centre of **Santa Rosa de Ocopa**.

Nature lovers shouldn't feel left out as **Lago Junín** has some of the best birdwatching in the Andes and, east of Tarma, the **central jungle** (Selva Central) is just waiting to be explored. The fertile Chancamayo Valley leads down to isolated communities, like the German-Austrian outpost at **Pozuzo**, and distant river towns from where you can head north to Pucallpa. West of the Sierra, there are good new roads to the coast, and southwards an exciting route to Cusco runs through **Abancay**, a typical Andean town which is now the junction for the Cusco-Nasca road.

Central Highlands

★ Things to do in the Central Highlands

- Go shopping in the **Mantaro Valley** near Huancayo. It's a souvenir-hunter's paradise. Each village specializes in its very own variety of artesania – everything from silver filigree jewellery to blankets, and from gourd carvings to hats. In Ayachucho, don't miss the artists' quarter of Santa Ana, page 491.
- **Party** at any number of the area's spread of festivals. Especially worth waiting for are the Easter celebrations at **Muquiyauyo**, page 491.
- Don't miss **Ayacucho**, with its fine array of colonial churches, spectacular processions and carpets of flowers decorating the streets at Easter time, pre-Columbian ruins and the site of the final battle in the liberation of Peru from Spanish rule, page 496.
- Time your arrival (or departure) with the monthly running of the **train from Lima to Huancayo**. One of the engineering marvels of South America, page 490.
- Go for a hike along the **Royal Inca Road** which will lead you right back to times before the Spaniards arrived. One fine section goes to the temple-fortress of **Huánuco Viejo** near La Unión, page 518.

Lima to Huancayo

The Central Highway between Lima and Huancayo more or less parallels the course of the railway. The roads from Lima to Huancayo and Pisco to Ayacucho are paved, but all the other roads in this region are in poor condition, especially when wet. At La Oroya (see page 484), the central highway divides. Its southern branch follows the valley of the Río Mantaro, to Huancayo, and on to Huancavelica or Ayacucho. The northern branch runs to Cerro de Pasco and on to Huánuco, Tingo María and Pucallpa.

Chosica

Phone code: 01
Colour map 3,
grid C3
Population: 31,200
Altitude: 860 m

Chosica is 40 km from Lima and the real starting place for the mountains. It is a popular winter resort because it is above the cloudbank covering Lima in winter. Beyond the town looms a precipitous range of hills almost overhanging the streets. There are four basic *hostales* in Chosica, two are off the main road near the market, and the other two up the hill on the left. All have water problems. Recommended is **F** *Hospedaje Chosica*, Av 28 de Julio 134, T361 0841. It has rooms with and without bath and the family that runs it is friendly. **F** *La Posada*, Jr Trujillo y Salaverry, just off main road, is comfortable, with hot water. ■ *Colectivo minibuses for Chosica leave from Av Grau, Lima, when full, between 0600 and 2100, and cost US$0.60. Colectivo taxis leave from the* Sheraton *hotel, behind the Centro Cívico on Av Garcilaso de la Vega, charging US$1.50 for a seat or US$6 for the whole car. A regular taxi will charge US$6-10 Lima-Chosica. Most buses on the Lima-La Oroya route are full; colectivo taxi to La Oroya US$3.60, 3 hrs, very scenic, passing the highest railway in the world (see below).*

In the mountains above Chosica is **Callahuanca**. Sitapati Das (resident in Lima) writes: "It could feature first in an 'anti-tour guide' as one of the least interesting places to go if you want fast-paced action, but it is definitely off the gringo trail. It's an unpretentious place, great for getting fresh air and avoiding the *vendedores* of Lima's streets. Visit on 29-31 August for the anniversary festival, when the town fills up over three nights with people from the surrounding communities for music and dancing. The local people are very friendly and helpful. The town is clean and has rubbish bins that don't have holes in the bottom and well-maintained municipal toilets. If they are locked, the local Club de Madres is more than happy to let you use theirs." ■ *Colectivos leave from Chosica's Parque Central to Callahuanca, US$0.30, 20 mins' journey.*

San Pedro de Casta

Around 40 km beyond Chosica, up the picturesque Santa Eulalia valley, is the village of San Pedro de Casta, which has some interesting sights nearby. **Marcahuasi** is a table mountain about 3 sq km, at 4,200 m, nearby. The *meseta* has been investigated by the late Daniel Ruzo. There are three lakes, a 40-m high 'monumento a la humanidad', and other mysterious lines, gigantic figures, sculptures, astrological signs and megaliths which display non-American symbolism. Ruzo describes this pre-Incaic culture in his book, *La Culture Masma*, Extrait de l'Ethnographie, Paris, 1956. Others say that the formations are not man-made, but the result of wind erosion. The trail starts behind the village of San Pedro, and bends to the left. About halfway you have to choose between the longer trail (the easier of the two) and the shorter tail, which is better for views of the valley below. ■ *It's a minimum of three hours to the meseta. Guides cost about US$3 a day, and are advisable in misty weather. Mules for carrying bags cost US$4 to hire, a horse costs US$4.45 (standard prices from the tourist office). Tours can be arranged with travel agencies in Lima. Entry to the meseta US$3 (US$0.90 for students).*

Colour map 3, grid C4

San Pedro de Casta celebrates a *fiesta* on 25-26 March called **The Cleaning of the Chullpas** in which local families participate.

The best hotel in San Pedro is **E** *Marcahuasi*, just off the plaza (**F** per person without bath), which is clean and has a restaurant. There are two other restaurants. Locals in town will put you up for US$0.60 per person; ask at tourist information at the municipality on the plaza, T01-571 2087; buy a map of the plateau here for US$1.50, otherwise you will not find the monuments. If you speak good Spanish, ask in town for Manuel Olivares, who worked with Dr Ruzo and knows a lot about the plateau. He also sells maps for US$0.20. Take all necessary camping equipment: you can camp anywhere, there are many good spots. At a shop on the plaza in San Pedro you can buy everything for the trip to Marcahuasi, including bottled water. On the plateau (at the *Anfiteatro*) locals have set up three little tents where they sell drinks, coca tea, and basic food (rice, eggs, soup etc). There is also water, but only for cooking; everything is very cheap. Buses to San Pedro de Casta leave **Chosica** from Parque Echenique, opposite the market, at 0900 and 1500, 4 hrs, US$2; return 0700 and 1400. The road is in a reasonable condition until the Callahuanca hydroelectric station.

Sleeping, eating & transport

Chosica to La Oroya

Beyond Chosica each successive valley looks greener and lusher, with a greater variety of trees and flowers. **Matucana**, Km 84, at 2,390 m, is set in wild scenery, where there are beautiful walks. The road continues to climb to **San Mateo** (Km 95, 3,215 m), where the San Mateo mineral water originates. There is basic accommodation in both towns. Beyond San Mateo is **Infiernillo** (Little Hell) Canyon, at Km 100. Car excursions can be made from Lima.

Colour map 3, grid C4

Between Río Blanco and **Chicla** (Km 107, 3,733 m), Inca contour-terraces can be seen quite clearly. After climbing up from **Casapalca** (Km 117, 4,154 m, accommodation), there are glorious views of the highest peaks, and more mines, at the foot of a deep gorge.

Central Highlands

The road climbs to the Ticlio Pass, before the descent to **Morococha** (Km 169, altitude 4,600 m) and **La Oroya**. A large metal flag of Peru can be seen at the top of Mount Meiggs, not by any means the highest in the area, but through it runs Galera Tunnel, 1,175 m long, in which the main line of the Central Railway reaches its greatest altitude, 4,782 m (see box).

Ticlio, at Km 132, the highest passenger station in the world, is at 4,758 m. It lies at the mouth of the tunnel, on one side of a crater in which lies a dark, still lake. There are still higher points on the railway on the branch of the line that goes through **Morococha** – 4,818 m at La Cima, and 4,829 m on a siding. At Morococha is the Centromín golf course, which welcomes playing visitors. It stands at 4,400 m and disputes the title of the world's highest with Mallasilla, near La Paz, in Bolivia.

La Oroya
Phone code: 064
Colour map 3, grid C4
Population: 36,000
Altitude: 3,755 m

La Oroya is the main smelting centre for the region's mining industry. It can seem a dreary place with its slag heaps, but is nevertheless full of vitality. It stands at the fork of the Yauli and Mantaro rivers, 196 km from Lima by a road. (For places to the east and north of La Oroya, see pages 505 and 512 respectively.)

Asthmatics beware, the pollution from the heavy industry can cause severe problems

Sleeping **F** *Hostal Inti*, Arequipa 117, T391098. Shared bathroom, warm water, clean but basic. **F** *Hostal Chavín*, Tarma 281. Shared bathroom, cheap restaurant. **G** per person *Hostal Regional*, Lima 112, T391017. With bathroom, basic, hot water in the morning.

Eating *El Tambo*, 2 km outside town on the road to Lima. Good trout and frogs. The *Chanchamayo* bus stops here en route Lima-Tarma; the trout at the stop on the return journey, at *Las Américas* restaurant, is said to be even better. *La Caracocha*, Lima 168. Cheap, good *menú*. *Punta Arenas*, Zeballos 323. Good seafood, chifa. There are lots of *pollerías* in front of the train station in C Lima.

Transport For buses to the Central Highlands see under Lima, Buses (page 139). To **Lima** from La Oroya takes 4½ hrs and costs US$5.20. To **Jauja** (80 km), takes 1½ hrs and costs US$1. To **Tarma**, 1½ hrs, US$1.35. To **Cerro de Pasco**, 131 km, 3 hrs, US$2.20. To **Huánuco**, 236 km, 6 hrs, US$4.35. Colectivos also run on all routes (see under Lima). They are quicker but only leave when full and prices are double that of the bus fares.

Jauja

Phone code: 064
Colour map 3, grid C5
Population: 105,000
Altitude: 3,330 m

Eighty kilometres southeast of La Oroya is the old town of Jauja, Pizarro's provisional capital until the founding of Lima. It has a very colourful Wednesday and Sunday market. Jauja is a friendly, unspoilt town, in the middle of a good area for walking.

Sights There is a good **archaeological museum**, with artefacts from the Huari culture. A modernized church retains three fine 17th-century altars. The **Cristo Pobre** church is claimed to have been modelled after Notre Dame and is something of a curiosity. Sr Loayza, a local teacher, is a passionate fossil collector. You ca see his collection at Jr Cusco 537. ■ *Free, but donations welcome.*

On a hill above Jauja is a fine line of Inca storehouses, and on hills nearby, the ruins of hundreds of circular stone buildings from the Huanca culture. There are also ruins near the **Laguna de Paca** 3½ km away. The western side of the lake is lined with restaurants which are good for lunches, such as *La Sirena de Oro*, which prepares delicious *ceviche de trucha* and, at weekends, *pachamanca*. It is possible to walk around the lake in about 3 hours. Many of the restaurants have launches which offer half-hour boat trips at weekends, US$0.75 per person. ■ *Colectivos leave regularly from Av Pizarro, 10 mins, US$0.30.*

E per person *Hostal Manco Cápac*, Jr Manco Cápac 575, T361620. Central, with good **Sleeping** rooms and a beautiful patio, pleasant, relaxing, good breakfast and coffee, German run. **E** *Hostal Francisco Pizarro*, Bolognesi 334 (opposite the market), T362082. Shared bathroom, hot water, rundown, noisy. **E** *Santa Rosa*, on main plaza. Modern, big rooms with bathroom, restaurant. **F** *Ganso de Oro*, R Palma 249, T362165. **G** without bath, hot water, good value, good restaurant, US$2-4 per meal. **F** *Hostal Los Algarrobos*, Huancayo 264, T362633. Shared bathroom, hot water in the morning, very clean, good value.

There are several good restaurants on the main plaza serving local dishes such as pork **Eating** and lentils in wine. *Centro Naturista*, Huarancayo 138. Serves fruit salad, yoghurt, granola, etc. *Marychris*, Jr Bolívar 1166, T362386. For lunch only, *menú* US$1.55, excellent food. *La Rotunda*, Tarapacá 415. Tables in a pleasant courtyard or dining rooms, good lunch *menú* and pizzas in the evening.

Festival '*La Tunantada*' is held on **22 Jul**. **Festivals**

Bus To **Lima**: with *Mcal Cáceres*, daily at 0800 and 2300, *Etucsa* at 0815 and 1345, **Transport** US$6, 6 hrs. Also *Sudamericano*. Most companies have their offices on the Plaza de Armas, but their buses leave from Av Pizarro. *Cruz del Sur*, Pizarro 220, direct to Lima, 5 hrs, US$8. **Jauja to Huancayo**, 44 km, takes 1 hr and costs US$1.

To **Cerro de Pasco**, *Oriental* leave from 28 de Julio 156, and *Turismo Central* from 28 de Julio 150, 5 hrs, US$3.55. *Oriental* and *Turismo Central* also go to **Huánuco**, 7 hrs, US$5.35. To **Tarma**, US$2.25, hourly with *Canary tours* and *ET San Juan* from Jr Tarma; the latter continues to **Chanchamayo**, US$4.50. To **Satipo**, with *Turismo Central*, 12 hrs, US$6.25.

Banks No TCs are accepted at the *BCP*. *Dollar Exchange Huarancayo*, on Jr **Directory** Huarancayo, gives a much better rate than *BCP*. **Communications** Internet: *CSI*, Bolognesi 512. US$0.75 per hr. **Post office**: Jr Bolívar. **Telephone**: *Telefónica* at Bolognesi 546, T(064)362020, T/F361111. Also at Ricardo Palma, opposite the *Hotel Ganso de Oro*, T/F362395, gives better service and prices.

Concepción, 18 km to the south of Jauja, on the road to Huancayo, has a mar- **Concepción** ket on Sunday as well as a colourful bullfight later in the day during the season. *Altitude: 3,251 m*

From Concepción a branch road leads for 6 km to the **Convent of Santa** *Colour map 3,* **Rosa de Ocopa**, a Franciscan monastery set in beautiful surroundings. It *grid C5* was established in 1725 for training missionaries for the jungle. It contains a fine library with over 20,000 volumes and a biological museum with animals and insects from the jungle. The Convent also contains a large collection of paintings, including copies by the priests of many works by masters such as Murillo and Ribera. ■ *0900-1200 and 1500-1800, and closed Tue. Tours start on the hour and last 45 mins. US$1.10. Colectivos run from the market in Concepción, 15 mins, US$0.25.*

A road to **Satipo** branches off near the Convento de Santa Rosa de Ocopa. The scenery is spectacular, with snow-capped mountains in the Paso de la Tortuga, followed by a rapid drop to the Caja de Silva in Satipo (see page 511). Buses do not use this route, preferring instead to go via Tarma and La Merced.

Huancayo

Phone code: 064
Colour map 3, grid C5
Population: over
500,000
Altitude: 3,271 m

The large, sprawling departmental capital of Huancayo is a functional kind of place. As the main commercial centre for inland Peru it has had to eschew the tourist trappings in favour of the no-nonsense comings and goings of everyday trade. The city's attractions are outwith its boundaries. It lies in the beautiful Mantaro Valley, surrounded by villages that produce their own original crafts and celebrate festivals all year round (see page 489). The city has its own important festivals, however, when people flock from far and wide with an incredible range of food, crafts and music. At this height, nights are chilly and altitude can be a problem for those arriving straight from the coast.

Ins and outs

Getting there Most of the bus offices of the better companies running to Lima are 2-3 blocks north of the main plaza, while those of the cheaper companies are located to the north of the Río Shullcas, a 10-15 min walk from the centre. The offices of bus companies operating to destinations to the south of Huancayo, such as Huancavelica and Ayacucho, are 4-5 blocks south of the main plaza. A new bus terminal for all buses, to all destinations, is planned 3 km north of the centre. The railway station for Huancavelica is in the suburb of Chilca to the southwest of the city (15 mins by taxi).

Getting around Huancayo is quite spread out with all the main sights as well as the Sunday market quite a way from the centre. The station for trains from Lima is over 6 blocks east of the Plaza Constitución. Take the bus or a taxi. Plaza de Armas is called Plaza Constitución.

Tourist offices *Ministry of Tourism*, C Real 481, to the right of the *Casa de Artesano*, T214192, junin@mitinci.gob.pe It has information about the area and is helpful; open Mon-Fri 0900-1400, 1600-2000. There is a less informative office by the post office between Calles Real and Ancash (no English spoken here). *Touring y Automóvil Club del Perú*, Jr Lima 355, T231204, F216377, huancayo@touringperu.com.pe

Sights

Keep an eye out for bagsnatchers and pickpockets
Beware of overcharging by taxi drivers and shopkeepers

The Sunday **market** gets going after 0900 (giving a little taste of Huancayo at festival time) every week even though it has been described as expensive and offering little choice. It is better to go to the villages for local handicrafts. The stalls on Jirón Huancavelica, 3 km long, still sell typical clothes, fruit, vegetables, hardware, handicrafts and, especially, traditional medicines and goods for witchcraft. There is also an impressive daily market behind the railway station.

The museum at the **Salesian school** has over 5,000 pieces, including jungle birds, animals and butterflies, insects, reptiles and fossils. ■ *Tue, Thu, Fri and Sun 0815-1100, 1415-1700, Wed 0815-1100, and Sat 1415-1600. US$0.60.*

The **Parque de Identidad Wanka**, on Jr San Jorge in the Barrio San Carlos, northeast of the city, is a fascinating mixture of surrealistic construction interwoven with indigenous plants and trees and the cultural history of the Mantaro Valley. ■ *Entry is free, but contributions are appreciated. It can get crowded at weekends.* Opposite are the *Misti Wasi* and *Pacaywasi* restaurants serving traditional meals.

On the outskirts of town is **Torre-Torre**, eroded sandstone towers on the hillside. Take a bus to Cerrito de la Libertad and walk up. Not far from here is a large park with a zoo and good swimming pool. ■ *US$0.25.*

Essentials

B *Turismo*, Ancash 729, T231072, hotelhyo@correo.dnet.com.pe In an old building. Rooms with bathroom, some rooms are small, quiet. Restaurant serves good meals for US$3.50. **B** *Presidente*, C Real 1138, T231736, 231275, same email address as *Turismo*. With bathroom, clean, friendly, helpful, safe, breakfast only. Recommended. **C** *Kiya*, Giráldez 107, Plaza Constitución, T214955, F214957. With bath, hot water, restaurant does not serve breakfast, avoid noisy rooms on Av Real. **C** *Santa Felicita*, Giráldez 145,

Sleeping
Prices may be raised in Holy Week
■ *on map*
Price codes:
see inside front cover

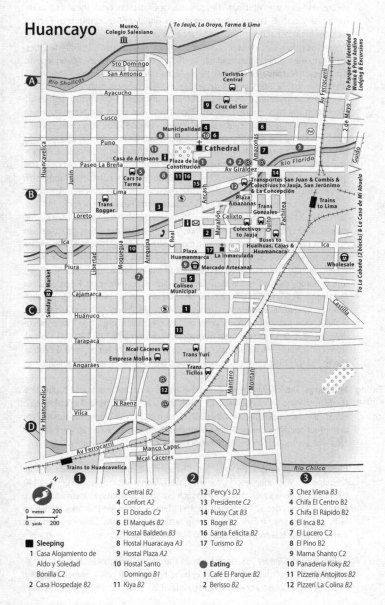

Huancayo

Sleeping
1 Casa Alojamiento de Aldo y Soledad Bonilla *C2*
2 Casa Hospedaje *B2*
3 Central *B2*
4 Confort *A2*
5 El Dorado *C2*
6 El Marqués *B2*
7 Hostal Baldeón *B3*
8 Hostal Huaracaya *A3*
9 Hostal Plaza *A2*
10 Hostal Santo Domingo *B1*
11 Kiya *B2*
12 Percy's *D2*
13 Presidente *C2*
14 Pussy Cat *B3*
15 Roger *B2*
16 Santa Felicita *B2*
17 Turismo *B2*

Eating
1 Café El Parque *B2*
2 Berisso *B2*
3 Chez Viena *B3*
4 Chifa El Centro *B2*
5 Chifa El Rápido *B2*
6 El Inca *B2*
7 El Lucero *C2*
8 El Pino *B2*
9 Mama Shanto *C2*
10 Panadería Koky *B2*
11 Pizzería Antojitos *B2*
12 Pizzerí La Colina *B2*

Central Highlands

Plaza Constitución, T235285. With bathroom, hot water, good. **D** *El Dorado*, Piura 452, T223947. With bathroom, hot water, friendly, clean, some rooms with TV are in the **C** category. **D** *El Marqués*, Puno 294, T219026, F219202. Rooms with bathroom and TV, good value. **D** *Hostal Plaza*, Ancash 171, T214507. Clean, hot water, ask for a room at the front. **D** *Roger*, Ancash 460, T233488. With bathroom, hot water, basic, clean.

E per person *Casa Alojamiento de Aldo y Soledad Bonilla*, Huánuco 332, no sign, half a block from Mcal Cáceres bus station, T232103 (Lima 463-1141). **D** per person full board, beautiful colonial house, some hot water, owners speak English, laundry, secure, relaxing, nice courtyard, they can arrange local tours, book ahead to guarantee a reservation. **E** *La Casa de La Abuela*, Av Giráldez 691. Dormitory at **F**, price includes breakfast and hot pisco drink at *La Cabaña* (see below) and 30-mins' free internet voucher. Hot shower, some rooms with antique beds, laundry facilities, good breakfast, other meals available at US$1, nice garden, games. Mixed reports. **E** per person *Hospedaje César Ada*, Pasaje Santa Teresa 294, El Tambo-3 Esquinas, 5 km from centre, T235615 for pick-up, wadaycesar@latinmail.com Quiet, shared bath, garden, meals available, use of kitchen, breakfast included. **E** *Confort*, Ancash 231, 1 block from the main plaza, T233601. Rooms with hot water are nicer, but more expensive than those with cold water, all rooms are good value, very clean, ask for a room not facing the street for peace and quiet, safe for bicycles, car parking costs US$1. **E** *Hostal Huaracaya*, Amazonas 323. Hot water and TV, good value. **E** *Percy's*, Real 1399, T231208. Shared bathroom, hot water in morning, TV, basic but clean and good value. **E** *Pussy Cat*, Giráldez 359, T231565. Not what the name might suggest, **F** with shared bathroom, hot water, safe, friendly, luggage stored, comfortable beds.

F per person *Peru Andino Lodging and Excursions*, Pasaje San Antonio 113-115, San Carlos, 3 blocks from Av Centenario, 15 mins' walk from the centre, T223956 (be patient waiting for an answer at the door; if taking a taxi, stress that it's *Pasaje* San Antonio). Price includes breakfast, clean rooms with hot showers, several with private bathroom, safe area, cosy atmosphere, run by Sra Juana, her daughter speaks some English, friendly, they also organize trekking and mountain bike tours, Spanish classes (run by Jorge), cooking and laundry facilities. Highly recommended. **F** *Hostal Santo Domingo*, Ica 655, T235461. Set around two pleasant patios, clean, basic, good value. **G** per person *Hostal Baldeón*, Amazonas 543, T231634. Friendly, kitchen and laundry facilities, nice patio, good hot shower on request, basic rooms, good value, security-conscious. **G** per person *Casa hospedaje*, Huamanmarca 125, T219980. Central, small, comfortable, hot water, shared showers, family run, nice atmosphere. **G** *Central*, Loreto 452, T211948. Large place, basic, shared bath, hot water in the morning.

Eating
● *on map*

Mid-range The following restaurants serve typical dishes for about US$4-5, plus 18% tax. *El Inca*, Puno 530. Good value for meals and salads. *La Cabaña*, Av Giraldez 652. Pizzas, ice-cream, *calentitos*, and other dishes, folk music at weekends (see *Incas del Perú* under Tour operators, below). *Pizzería Antojitos*, Puno 599. Attractive, atmospheric pizzeria with live music some nights. *Pizzería La Colina*, Lima 151. Recommended.

Cheap *Chifa El Centro*, Giráldez 238. Chinese food, good service. *Chifa Rápido*, Arequipa 511. Authentic, good value and quality. *Mama Shanto*, Coliseo Cerrado 140 (Real block 8). Serves typical local dishes such as *papa a la huancaína* and *ají de gallina*, clean, beautifully decorated. *El Pino*, Real 539. Serves typical food for about US$2-3 a dish, and fixed price *menú*. Lots of cheap restaurants along Av Giráldez serving set *menú*. Breakfast is served in the Mercado Modelo from 0700.

Cafés *Berisso*, Giráldez 258. Good for cakes and quiche, friendly. *Gustitos*, Real at corner of Plaza Constitución. Good service, huge burgers, real coffee. *Panadería Koky*, Ancash y Puno. Good for breakfasts and pastries during the day, pricey. Smart places to take coffee and cake: *Café El Parque*, Giráldez y Ancash, on the main plaza; and *Chez Viena*, Puno 125. Good, small, unnamed café at Puno 209, serves breakfast. *El Lucero*, Arequipa 929, very good vegetarian food, good value and service.

Bars *Café Billar*, Paseo de Breña 133. 0900-2400, serves beer and snacks, pool tables. **Bars & clubs**
La Cereza, Puno just below Plaza, near *Fuente de Soda El Inca*, good for late-night drinks, sandwiches, music videos, popular.
    Clubs *A1A*, Bolognesi 299. Most discos open around 2000 and close at 0200. Some charge an entrance fee of US$3-4.
    Peñas All the *peñas* have folklore shows with dancing, open normally Fri, Sat and Sun from 1300 to 2200. Entrance fee is about US$2 per person. *Taki Wasi*, Huancavelica y 13 de Noviembre. *Ollantaytambo*, Puno, block 2.

Cinemas *Ciné Mantaro*, Real 950, El Tambo. Tickets cost US$2.   **Entertainment**

Festividad del Tayta Niño is held on **19-31 of Jan**. *Festividad de la Virgen de*   **Festivals**
Cocharcas is held on **8 Sep** (see also Mantaro Valley page 491). *Festividad de San Jerónimo de Tunan* takes place on **30 Sep**. In **Oct: 4**, *San Francisco de Asís*; **18**, *San Lucas*; **28-30** is the culmination of month-long celebrations for *El Señor de los Milagros*. The *Semana Turística de Huancayo* begins on **16 Nov**.

All handicrafts are made outside Huancayo in the many villages of the Mantaro Valley   **Shopping**
(see page 491), or in Huancavelica. The villages are worth a visit to learn how the items *Thieves in the market*
are made. *Casa de Artesano*, on the corner of Real and Paseo La Breña, at Plaza *hand out rolled up*
Constitución, has a wide selection of good quality crafts. There is a large handicrafts mar- *pieces of paper whilst*
ket between Ancash and Real, block 7, offering a wide selection of local handicrafts. *picking your pocket*

Turismo Huancayo, C Real 517 oficina 6, T233351. Organizes local tours and is recom- **Tour operators**
mended. *Incas del Perú* information office next to *La Cabaña* restaurant (Av Giráldez
652) offers artesan and archaeological day tours, walking tours and mountain biking
trips, US$35, which can include visits to Huamancaca prison. Inmates' handicrafts are
sold, they cook meals and will discuss politics (many are ex-Sendero Luminoso). Incas
del Perú also have maps and a book exchange, bicycle hire (US$15 per day),
www.incasdelperu.com *Wanka Tours*, Real 550, T231743, and *Peruvian Tours*, Puno
488, on the main plaza, T213069, are both reputable organizers of tours to a variety of
places in the Mantaro Valley.

Bus There are regular buses to **Lima**, 6-7 hrs on a good paved road, costing US$10. **Transport**
Travelling by day is recommended for the fantastic views and, of course, for safety. If
you must travel by night, take warm clothing. Recommended companies: *Mcal
Cáceres*, Real 1247, T216633, 1000 and 2230; *Cruz del Sur*, Ayacucho 281, T235650, 4 a
day; *Transportes Rogger*, Lima 561, T212687, *cama* and *semi-cama* at 1300 and 2330,
comercial at 2230. Many other companies ply this route, many are cheaper but also less
comfortable and less safe. Small buses for Lima congregate 15 blocks north of Plaza
Constitución on C Real; there is much competition for passengers.
    To **Ayacucho**, 319 km, 11 hrs, US$5.70. *Empresa Molina*, C Angaráes 334, T224501, *If driving to Ayacucho*
0700 and 3 in the evening, recommended. Also *Turismo Central*, Ayacucho274, *and beyond, roads are*
T223128, leave at 2030, and *Transportes Ticllos*, Ancash y Angaráes, at 1830. The road *"amazingly rough"*
is in poor condition and is very difficult in the wet. Take warm clothing. After Izcuchaca, *Don't go alone*
on the railway to Huancavelica, there is a good road to the Quichuas hydroelectric *Count kilometres*
scheme, but thereafter it is narrow with hair-raising bends and spectacular bridges. *diligently to keep*
The scenery is staggering. *a record of where*
you are: road signs
are poor

Central Highlands

To **Huancavelica**, 147 km, 5 hrs, US$2.85. Many buses leave daily, including *Transportes Yuri*, Ancash 1220, 3 a day, *Transportes Ticllos*, 10 a day, also *Turismo Central, Molina, Turismo Nacional, Selva Tours*, and *Mcal Cáceres*. The road is in poor condition but being improved, and takes longer when wet. The scenery is spectacular.

To **Cerro de Pasco**, 255 km, 5 hrs, US$4. *Turismo Central* at 1400. Alternatively, take a bus to La Oroya, *Gonzales*, Calixto y Amazonas, at 1630, US$1.45, or buses leave when full, about every 20 mins, from Av Real about 10 blocks north of the main plaza. From La Oroya there are regular buses and colectivos to Cerro. The road to La Oroya and on to Cerro is in good condition, although roadworks between Huancayo and La Oroya were causing some delays in mid-2002.

To **Huánuco**, 7 hrs, *Turismo Central* have a direct bus at 2115, US$6, good service.

To **Chanchamayo**: *Empresa San Juan*, Ferrocarril 161 and Plaza Amazonas, and *Canary Tours* each have an hourly service via Jauja to Tarma, 3 hrs, US$2.50, some of which continue on to La Merced, 5 hrs, US$4. The only company with a direct day service to **Satipo** is *Selva Tours*, Giráldez block 3, at 0800, US$6, 229 km, 12 hrs, on a very difficult road, which is impossible in the wet.

Some trucks and a few buses travel to **Cañete**, 289 km, 10 hrs, US$4. It is a poor road, with beautiful mountain landscapes before dropping to the valley of Cañete.

To **Jauja**, 44 km, 1 hr. Colectivos and combis leave every few mins from Huamanmarca y Amazonas, and Plaza Amazonas, US$1.50. Ones via San Jerónimo and Concepción have 'Izquierda' on the front. Most buses to the Mantaro Valley leave from several places around the market area. Buses to **Hualhuas**, **Cajas** and **Huamancaca** leave from block 3 of Pachitea. Buses to **Cochas** leave from Amazonas y Giráldez.

Ask the driver if he'll let you ride in the engine **Rail** There are 2 unconnected railway stations. The Central station serves Lima, via La Oroya (298 km). Service on the Lima-Huancayo railway recommenced in 2002, once a month, usually coinciding with public holidays. The fare is US$15 one way, US$25 return (the train returns a day or two later). Information on forthcoming departures can be obtained from *Incas del Perú*, see above

From the small station in Chilca suburb (15 mins by taxi, US$1), trains run 128.7 km to **Huancavelica**, on a narrow gauge track (3 ft). There are 2 trains: the *autovagón* leaves at 1300 daily. It costs US$3.70 and has 1st class and Buffet carriages. The journey takes 4 hrs, and is a spectacular one with fine views, passing through typical mountain villages. There are 38 tunnels and the line reaches 3,676 m. Meals, drinks and snacks are served on the train, and at the village stations vendors sell food and crafts.

The local train leaves at 0630 daily and takes 5 hrs. There are 1st, US$2.55, 2nd, US$2.20, and Buffet, US$3.70, classes. Tickets can only be bought on the day of travel; get in the queue at 0600 at the latest. Services are often suspended, especially when rainy.

Directory **Banks** *BCP*, Real 1039. Changes TCs with no commission, cash advance on Visa. *Banco Wiese*, Real casi Ica. ATM does not accept international cards, poor rates for TCs. *Interbank* and *Banco Continental* are on block 6 of Real. *Western Union Money Transfer*, Ancash 440, T224816/235655. Mon-Fri 0900-1300 and 1600-2000, Sat 0900-1300. There are several *casas de cambio* on Ancash. Street changers hang out in front of *Hotel Kiya*. **Communications** Internet: numerous places round Plaza Constitución on Giráldez, eg *Alph@net*, No 288, and *LaRed*, No 304, Paseo La Breña, eg *Cyberwanka*, No 173, very good, and Real 1300 block. Average price under US$0.75 per hr. **Post office**: on Plaza Huamanmarca. **Cultural centres** *Peruvian-North American Cultural Institute*: Jr Guido 740. **Language classes** *Katia Cerna* is a recommended teacher, T225332, katiacerna@hotmail.com She can arrange home stays; her sister works in adventure tourism. *Incas del Perú* (see Tour operators) organize Spanish courses for beginners for US$100 per week, 3-hrs a day, including 5 nights' accommodation at *La Casa de La Abuela* and all meals, also homestays, and classes in weaving, playing traditional music, Quechua and gourd carving. See also *Peru Andino Lodging* above.

Laundry Good *lavandería* on Paseo La Breña behind *Casa de Artesano*.

Mantaro Valley

The main attraction in the area is the Mantaro Valley, which is rich in culture, music, local food, dances and handicrafts and plays host to numerous festivals.

Colour map 3, grid C5

To the west of the Río Mantaro, 19 km from Huancayo, is **Viques**, which is known for the production of belts and blankets. Sra María Magdalena Huzco, Calle San Martín, two blocks from the Plaza Principal, offers **weaving lessons**, US$34 for 15 hours, plus the cost of materials. Other weavers may also give lessons. It's a worthwhile experience, not just for learning how to weave, but also for an insight into the life of this part of Peru. **Huayucachi**, 7 km away, organizes festivals with dancing and impressive costumes in January and February and also makes embroidery.

The ruins of **Warivilca**, 15 km from Huancayo, are near **Huari**, with the remains of a pre-Inca temple of the Huanca culture. There is a museum in the plaza, with deformed skulls, and modelled and painted pottery of successive Huanca and Inca occupations of the shrine. The ruins and museum are under the supervision of a local archaeologist and are slowly being restored. ■ *1000-1200, 1500-1700. US$0.15. The museum is open in the morning only. To get there, take one of the micros for Chilca, which leave from Calle Real.*

Between Pilcomayo and Huayo (15 km) is the **Geophysical Institute of Huayo**, on the 'Magnetic Equator' - 12½ degrees south of the geographical equator. Here meteorological, seismic and cosmic-ray observations are made. A visit is recommended and the best time is in the morning, or when the sun is shining. ■ *Take bus from Jr Giráldez to Chupaca, but get out by bridge before Chupaca, where the road splits, then take a colectivo to Huayao. The Institute is on the left of the road.*

Chupaca is a picturesque village with a good Saturday market. A colectivo leaves from the fruit and vegetable market. Beyond Chupaca is the village of **Arhuac**, reached by colectivo. One block down from the Plaza de Armas, in the Colegio Amauta, is a museum with items found at the nearby Huanca ruins of **Arhuaturo** (Quechua for 'burned bones'). The site is in two parts, civil and religious, on adjacent hills and was occupied from the 13th to the 15th centuries. The first, civil set of ruins is a 45-minute walk from Arhuac; great views of the Mantaro Valley. There is a small restaurant on the plaza in Arhuac, which serves a set lunch for US$1.

Also west of the river, 17 km from Huancayo, is **Laguna Ñahuinpuquio**, a lake with pleasant surrounding countryside. You can walk there from Arhuac or take a taxi for US$1.80. **Sicaya**, 8 km away, holds festivals in August and has an 18th century church. The ruins of **Guaqui-Guaqui** are just outside the village of **Matahulo**. **Muquiyauyo** is famous for its Semana Santa celebrations.

The villages of **Cochas Chico** and **Cochas Grande**, 11 km away on the east side of the river, are both well worth visiting. This is where the famous *mate burilado*, or gourd carving, is done (see page 594). You can buy them cheaply direct from the manufacturers, but ask around. You can also enjoy beautiful views of the Valle de Mantaro and Huancayo. ■ *Micros leave from Plaza Hunamarco or by the market near the railway line, US$0.25.*

Hualahoyo (11 km from Huancayo) has a little chapel with 21 colonial canvases. **San Agustín de Cajas** (8 km) makes fine hats, and **San Pedro** (10 km) makes wooden chairs. In the village of **Hualhuas** (12 km) you can find fine alpaca weavings, which you can watch being made. The weavers take

Central Highlands

Lima-Huancayo railway

This masterpiece was the project of the great American railway engineer, Henry Meiggs, who supervised the construction from 1870 until his death in 1877. It was built by the Pole Ernesto Malinowski, with imported Chinese labour, between 1870 and 1893.

The ruling grade of the Central Railway is about 4½°. Along the whole of its length (335 km to Huancayo) it traverses 66 tunnels, 59 bridges, and 22 zig-zags where the steep mountainside permits no other way of negotiating it.

During its years of operation, this was a tough journey, with altitude sickness an ever-present problem. This discomfort was more than compensated, though, by the spectacular views during the ascent which are beyond compare. Railway buffs may like to know that the last Andes type 2-8-0 steam locomotive, No 206, is still in working order, although usually locked in a shed at Huancayo. It was built specifically for this route in 1953 by Beyer Peacock of Manchester.

special orders; small items can be finished in a day. Negotiate a price. One particularly recommended place to buy them is *Tahuantisuyo*, run by Familia Faustino Maldonado y Agripina, on a side road on the way to the San Jerónimo junction. *Hostal La Llamita*, Jr Huancayo 445. New, 30 rooms with bath, also dormitories, hot water, friendly owner, swimming pool, laundry and restaurant. It also has a handicraft shop.

The town of **San Jerónimo** is renowned for the making of silver filigree jewellery, on sale at the Wednesday market. A major fiesta is held in the town on the third Saturday in August, when one of the two plazas is converted into a temporary bullring. There are ruins two to three hours' walk above San Jerónimo, but seek advice before hiking to them.

Festivals   There are so many festivals in the Mantaro Valley that it is impossible to list them all. Practically every day of the year there is a celebration of some sort in one of the villages. We list a selection below.

La Huaconada de Mito takes place in Mito on **1-3 Jan**. *Festividad del Tayta Niño* on **19-31 Jan** in Huayucachi. As in the rest of the country, there are carnival celebrations for the whole of **Feb**, with highlights on **2**, *Virgen de la Candelaria*, and **17-19** *Concurso de Carnaval*.

Semana Santa is impressive throughout the valley, especially the **Good Friday** processions. *Fiesta de la Cruz* also takes place throughout the valley on **1 May**, as does *Fiesta de Santiago* on **24-30 Jul**. On **8 Sep** is *La Virgen de Cocharcas*, held in Concepción, Jauja and more famously in Sapallanga, 8 km south from Huancayo. Held on different dates in **Sep** is the *Semana Turística del Valle del Mantaro*.

Izcuchaca   Between Huancayo and Huancavelica, Izcuchaca is the site of a bridge over
Colour map 3, grid C5   the Río Mantaro. The name in Quechua means 'stone bridge'. The bridge was partly rebuilt in the 18th century. On the edge of town is a fascinating pottery workshop whose machinery is driven by a water turbine. There is also a small shop. There are impressive rock formatioins and tepid thermal baths 5 km back along the railway line towards Huancayo. The town celebrates the **Fiesta de la Virgen de Cocharcas** on 5-10 October. It's a nice hike to the chapel on a hill overlooking the valley (1-1½ hrs each way).

Sleeping, eating and transport   There are two hotels. One is on the plaza, **G**, with no bathroom, you have to use the public bath by the river. The other is just off the plaza, a yellow three-storey house, **G**, no shower, toilet suitable for men only, chamber pot supplied, only blankets on bed, and cold. *Restaurant El Parque* on plaza, opens 0700, delicious food. The 0630 train from **Huancavelica** arrives at 0800, then continues to **Huancayo**. The trip costs US$1.70. The train tends to be very crowded. The 1300 train passes at 1400-1430. Sit on the left for the best views. The trains from Huancayo pass at around 0900 and 1600. The direct Huancayo-Ayacucho bus passes through at 0800, alternatively take a truck, about eight hours to Ayacucho.

Huancavelica

Capital of its Department, Huancavelica is a friendly and attractive town, surrounded by huge, rocky mountains. It's not really on the tourist circuit and is slow to get going in the mornings; most places open 0900-1000. It was founded in the 16th century by the Spanish to exploit rich deposits of mercury and silver. Very few of the mines remain open, and those that do are a few hours from town. It is predominantly an indigenous town, and people still wear traditional costume.

Phone code: 064
Coloured map 3,
grid C5
Population: 37,500
Altitude: 3,680 m

Ins and outs

All bus companies have their offices at and leave from the east end of town, around Parque M Castilla, on Muñoz, Iquitos, Tumbes and O'Donovan. Just a little beyond them and about 500m from the Plaza de Armas is the train station. **Tourist offices** *Ministerio de Industria y Comercio, Turismo y Artesanías*, Arica 202, T672509, earhvca@terra.com.pe Very helpful. *Instituto Nacional de la Cultura*, Plaza San Juan de Dios. Open Mon-Sat 1000-1300, 1500-1900, director Alfonso Zuasnabar, a good source of information on festivals, archaeological sites, history, etc. Gives courses on music and dancing, and lectures some evenings. There is also an interesting but small Museo Regional.

Getting there
If you wish to visit the mines, remember that the miners consider it a bad omen if a woman enters

Sights

The **cathedral** on the Plaza de Armas has an altar considered to be one of the finest examples of colonial art in Peru. Also very impressive are the five other churches in town. The church of San Francisco, for example, has no less than 11 altars. Sadly, though, most of the churches are closed to visitors.

Huancavelica

Sleeping	Eating
1 Hostal Tahuantinsuyo	4 Santo Domingo	1 Las Magnolias
2 Mercurio	5 Savoy	2 Mochica Sachún
3 Presidente	6 Virrey	5 Pollería Joy

0 metres 100
0 yards 100

Bisecting the town is the Río Huancavelica. South of the river is the main commercial centre. North of the river, on the hillside, are the **thermal baths**. There are also hot showers, but take a lock for the doors. ■ *0600-1500. It costs US$0.15 for private rooms, but the water is not very hot, and US$0.10 for the hot public pool.*

The **handicraft sellers** congregate in front of the Municipalidad on M Muñoz and the Biblioteco on the Plaza de Armas (V Toledo). Most goods are transported directly to Lima. The **food market** at Muñoz y Barranca is being demolished so food is sold along Barranca, blocks 2-3 (not much variety). The Potaqchiz hill, just outside the town, gives a fine view. It's about an hour's walk up from San Cristóbal. Another beautiful mountain walk in the neighbourhood is to the village of Sacsaymarca.

Essentials

Sleeping
■ *on map*
Price codes:
see inside front cover

C *Presidente*, Plaza de Armas, T952760. Lovely colonial building, cheaper without bathroom, overpriced. **E** *Mercurio*, Jr Torre Tagle 455, T952773. Unfriendly, basic, cold water. **E** *San José*, Jr Huancayo, at top of Barranca (past *Santo Domingo*), T752958. With bath, hot water 1700-1900, **G** without bath, clean, comfortable beds, helpful. **F** *Camacho*, Jr Carabaya 481. Best of the cheap hotels, **G** without bath, hot shower in morning and early evening, clean and well maintained, excellent value. **F** *Hostal Tahuantinsuyo*, Carabaya 399, T952968. With bathroom, hot water in mornings, dirty and dingy. **F** *Santo Domingo*, Av Barranca 366, T953086. **F** *Savoy*, Av Muñoz 294 (no sign, difficult to find). Both are cheap, very basic, with shared bathroom and cold water. **F** *Virrey*, Av Barranca 317. Basic, cold water.

Eating
● *on map*

Expensive *Mochica Sachún*, Av Virrey Toledo 303. Great *menú* for US$1.50, otherwise expensive, popular. *Pollería Joy*, Toledo on Plaza. For chicken, popular. *La Casona*, Jr Virrey Toledo 230. Good value *menú* and *peña*. *Las Magnolias*, Manuel Muñoz a couple of blocks from the plaza. OK.

Cheap There are lots of cheap, basic restaurants on C Muñoz and Jr Virrey Toledo. All serve typical food, mostly with a set *menú* for around US$1.50. *Cami*, Barranca y Toledo. No sign, small, lively, good set menus and juices. There area also *chifas* on Toledo: *Centro*, No 275, is better than *Imperio*.

Festivals
The whole area is rich in culture with many festivals and dances

Fiesta de los Reyes Magos y los Pastores, 4-8 Jan. *Fiesta del Niño Perdido* is held on 2nd Sun in Jan. *Pukllaylay Carnavales*, celebration of the first fruits from the ground (harvest), 20 Jan-mid Mar. *Semana Santa*, Holy Week. *Toro Pukllay* festival last week of May, first week of Jun. *Fiesta de Santiago* is held in May and Aug in all communities. *Los Laygas* or *Galas* (scissors dance), 22-28 Dec.

Transport

Road To Huancayo, 147 km, 5 hrs, US$2.85, rough road. *Transportes Yuri* at 2200 and *Transportes Ticllos*, 6 a day. To Lima there are two routes: one is via Huancayo, 445 km, 13 hrs minimum, US$5.70. *Libertadores* buses to Huancayo at 1830 go on to Lima, also *Ticllos* at 1700. The other route is via **Pisco**, 269 km, 12 hrs, US$7 and **Ica**, US$8, at 1730 daily, with *Oropesa*, O'Donovon 599. Buy your ticket 1 day in advance. The road is poor until it joins the Ayacucho-Pisco road, where it improves. The views are spectacular, but most of the journey is done at night. Be prepared for sub-zero temperatures in the early morning as the bus passes snowfields, then for temperatures of 25-30°C as the bus descends to the coast in the afternoon.

Rail See under Huancayo. The *autovagón* leaves for Huancayo daily at 0630, the local train leaves at 1300, daily.

Banks *BCP*, Virrey Toledo 300 block. There is a *Multired* ATM on M Muñoz in front of the Municipalidad. **Communications** Internet: despite what they say, internet places open around 0900 till 2100-2200. There are places on V Toledo and M Muñoz. Also *Librería Municipal*, Plaza de Armas, US$0.60 per hr. **Post office**: on Ferrua Jos, at block 8 of M Muñoz. **Telephone**: Carabaya y Virrey Toledo. **Directory**

Huancavelica to Ayacucho

The direct route from Huancavelica to Ayacucho (247 km) goes via **Santa Inés** (4,650m), 78 km. Out of Huancavelica the road climbs steeply with switchbacks between herds of llamas and alpacas grazing on rocky perches. Around Pucapampa (Km 43) is one of the highest habitable *altiplanos* (4,500m), where the rare and highly prized ash-grey alpaca can be seen. Snow-covered mountains are passed as the road climbs to 4,853m at the Abra Chonta pass, 23 km before Santa Inés. By taking the turnoff to Huachocolpa at Abra Chonta and continuing for 3 km you'll reach the highest drivable pass in the world, at 5,059m. In Santa Inés are *Alojamiento Andino*, a very friendly restaurant, *El Favorito*, where you can sleep, and several others. Nearby are two lakes (Laguna Choclacocha) which can be visited in 2½ hours. 52 km beyond Santa Inés at the Abra de Apacheta (4,750m), 98 km from Ayacucho, the rocks are all the colours of the rainbow, and running through this fabulous scenery is a violet river. These incredible colours are all caused by oxides. *Colour map 3, grid C5/6*

Transport Daily direct transport from Huancavelica to Ayacucho with *Ticllos* (address above), 0500, one stop for lunch, US$5, 7 hrs. *Expreso Turismo Nacional*, Cáceres 237, combi at 0500, US$5, 9 hrs. Buy tickets the day before. The road is good and new. The journey is a cold one but spectacular as it is the highest continuous road in the world, rarely dropping below 4,000m for 150 km. Alternatives are: take the train to Izcuchaca, stay the night, or any Huancavelica-Huancayo bus to Izcuchaca (US$1.45) and then take the bus to Ayacucho (see above), or a truck. A taxi Huancavelica-Izcuchaca will cost US$22 minimum. Or: take a colectivo Huancavelica-**Lircay**, a small village with *Hostal El Paraíso*, **F** with bath, **G** without (*Transportes 5 de Mayo*, Av Sebastián Barranca y Torre Tagle, US$3, 2 hrs, leave when full). *5 de Mayo* runs from Lircay Terminal Terrestre hourly from 0430 to Julcamarca 2½ hrs, or arrange a shared taxi the day before (same price). From **Julcamarca**, which has a colonial church and *hostales* near the plaza, combis run to Ayacucho, US$1.50, 3-3½ hrs. The minibuses run from plaza and are usually packed full. The scenery is beautiful all the way, but the roads are bumpy.

There is another route to Ayacucho from Huancayo, little used by buses, but which involves not so much climbing for cyclists. Cross the pass into the Mantaro valley on the road to **Quichuas** (**G** *Hostal Recreo Sol y Sombra*, charming, small courtyard, helpful, basic). Then to **Anco** (**G** *Hostal Gabi*, appalling, but better than anything else) and **Mayocc** (lodging). From here the road crosses a bridge after 10 km and in another 20 km reaches **Huanta** (see **The Huanta Valley**, below). Then it's a paved road to Ayacucho. **Alternative route to Ayacucho**

Central Highlands

An officer and a not-so-gentle nun

One of the most bizarre tales knocking around in the annals of Ayacucho's history relates to the mysterious case of the missing nun and the gender-bending soldier.

At the beginning of the 17th century, the courageous and audacious Army officer, Antonio de Erauzo, was finally captured and brought to justice, after putting several of his adversaries to the sword up and down the length and breadth of the country. He was condemned to death and duly asked a priest to hear his last confession and give him communion.

However, seconds before the priest could administer it, the soldier took the host in his hands and fled. No one dared stop him for fear of committing an act of sacrilege. He took refuge in a nearby church (not difficult given the profusion of them in this city) where he asked for Bishop Fray Agustín de Carbajal to hear his confession.

The townsfolk, who had been eagerly watching events unfold, soon learned the astonishing truth. The officer was, in fact, a woman called Catalina, who, on being chosen by her parents for the service of God, fled from a Spanish convent, assuming the disguise of a male person.

On putting an end to the mystery of her identity, Catalina mysteriously escaped once more, assumed a new identity and spent her last days in Mexico, dressed as a man and working as an arriero, or mule-herd. To the people of Ayacucho, however, Catalina would always be known as La Monja Alferez, the officer nun.

Ayacucho

Phone code: 064
Colour map 5, grid A4
Population: 105,918
Altitude: 2,740 m

The city is built round Parque Sucre, the main plaza, with the Cathedral, Municipalidad and Palacio de Gobierno facing on to it. It is famous for its hugely impressive Semana Santa celebrations, its splendid market and, not least, a plethora of churches – 33 of them no less – giving the city its alternative name La Ciudad de las Iglesias. A week can easily be spent enjoying Ayacucho and its hinterland. The climate is lovely, with warm, sunny days and pleasant balmy evenings. It is a warm, hospitable, tranquil place, where the inhabitants are eager to promote tourism. It also boasts a large, active student population. The University, founded in 1677, and closed in 1886, was reopened in 1958.

Ins and outs

Getting there The airport is to the east of the city along Av Castilla. A taxi to the centre costs US$1; buses or colectivos leave for the Plaza de Armas. At the airport walk half a block down the street for a bus to the centre. Most of the bus offices are much nearer the centre of town, in the north and northeast.

Getting around This is a large city but the interesting churches and colonial houses are all fairly close to the Plaza de Armas. Barrio Santa Ana is further away to the south and you will probably want to take a micro or taxi to get to it. Since the reestablishment of tourist services, many new hotels have opened and the city is eager to receive more visitors.

Tourist offices *i perú*, Portal Municipal 48, on the Plaza, T818305, iperuayacucho@promperu.gob.pe. Daily 0830-1930. *Dirección Regional de Industria y Turismo*, Asamblea 481, T812548/813162. Mon-Fri 0800-1300, friendly and helpful.

Background

Ayacucho is the capital of its Department. The city was founded on 9 January 1539 by the invading Spaniards, who named it San Juan de la Frontera. This was changed to San Juan de la Victoria after the Battle of Chupas, when the king's forces finally defeated the rival Almagrist power.

Despite these Spanish titles, the city always kept its original name of Huamanga. It became an important base for the army of the Liberator Simón Bolívar in his triumphant sweep south from the Battle of Junín. It was here, on the Pampa de Quinua, on 9 December 1824, that the decisive Battle of Ayacucho was fought, bringing Spanish rule in Peru to an end. Huamanga was, therefore, the first city on the continent to celebrate its liberty. In the midst of the massive festivities, the Liberator decreed that the city be named Ayacucho – meaning 'City of Blood'.

For much of the 1980s and early 1990s, this title seemed appropriate as the Shining Path terrorized the local populace, severely punishing anyone they suspected of siding with the military. Now, though, peace has returned to this beautiful colonial Andean city.

Sights

For a fascinating insight into Quechua art and culture, a visit to **Barrio Santa Ana** is a must. The district is full of *artesanía* shops, galleries and workshops. *Galería Latina*, at Plazuela de Santa Ana 605 (wari39@hotmail.com), has been recommended. The owner, Alejandro Gallardo Llacctahuamán, is very friendly and has lots of information on weaving techniques. Also (but more expensive) *Wari Art Gallery*, run by Gregorio Sulca and his family, at Jr Mcal Cáceres 302, Santa Ana, T812529. The owners will explain the Quechua legends, weaving and painting techniques. A good grasp of Spanish is essential to appreciate the gallery fully. Next door is the Instituto de Cultura Quechua, which affords wonderful views of the city and surrounding hills form its roof.

Also worth a visit is the **Mirador Turístico**, on Cerro Acuchimay, which offers great views over the city. ■ *Take a micro or bus from the corner of Jr 2 de Mayo and Jr C F Vivanco all the way there.*

Churches The construction of Ayacucho's many colonial religious buildings is said to have been financed by wealthy Spanish mine-owners and governors. Unfortunately many have fallen into disrepair and are closed to the public. The **Cathedral**, built in 1612, has three strong, solid naves are of simple architecture, in contrast to the elegant decoration of the interior, particularly the superb gold leaf altars. ■ *Daily 1730-1845; it also has a Museo de Arte Religioso, but it is closed indefinitely.*

San Cristóbal was the first church to be founded in the city, and is one of the oldest in South America. Buried beneath its floor are the remains of some of the combatants from the Battle of Chupas. Another old church is **La Merced**, whose high choir is a good example of the simplicity of the churches of the early period of the Viceroyalty. In 1886 a flagstone was discovered with the sculpted image of a sleeping warrior, known popularly as the 'Chejo-Pacheco'. **La Compañía de Jesús** (1605), has one of the most important façades of Viceregal architecture. It is of baroque style and guarded by two impressive 18th century towers. The church also has an adjacent chapel. ■ *0900-1100.*

Central Highlands

Ayacucho

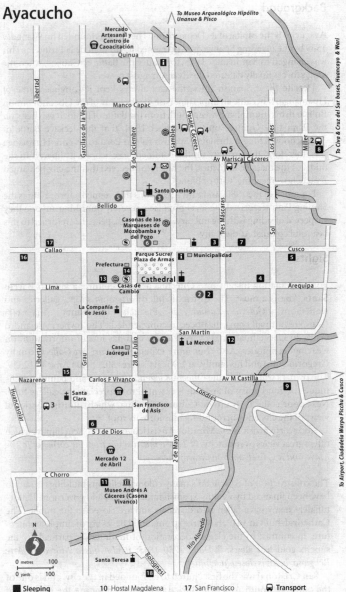

Also of note are the churches of **San Francisco de Asís** (*daily 0900-1100*), and **Santa Teresa**, 1683, (*daily 1730-1900*) with its monastery. Both have magnificent gold-leafed altars heavily brocaded and carved in the churrigueresque style. **Santa Clara** is renowned for its beautifully delicate coffered ceiling, and as the place where La Monja Alférez took refuge to avoid execution. ■ *Open only for the sale of sweets made by the nuns.* One of the city's most notable churches is **Santo Domingo** (1548). Its fine façade has triple Roman arches and Byzantine towers. ■ *Daily 0700-0800.*

To the north of the Parque Sucre, on the corner of Portal de la Unión and Asamblea, are the **Casonas de los Marqueses de Mozobamba y del Pozo**, also called Velarde-Alvarez. On the same Portal is the house of Canon Manuel Frías, where the writer and caricaturist, Abraham Valdelomar (who also used the pseudonym El Conde de Lemos after 1915), tragically died. In the Portals to the west (Portal Constitución), where the family seats of Astete and Guevara were once found, is the Casona where the chief magistrate, Nicolás de Boza y Solís, lived and which served as a prison cell for the Independence heroine, María Parado de Bellido. In this Portal is the Prefectura.

Colonial houses

Casa Jaúregui is opposite the church of La Merced on 2 de Mayo. On the 5th block of Jr Grau is the house where Simón Bolívar and José Antonio de Sucre stayed. In 1824 the house was occupied by the Flores family and is perhaps the finest example of a typical Castillian house. On the 5th block of 28 de Julio is the late 16th-century **Casona Vivanco**, which houses the **Museo Andrés A Cáceres**. The museum displays prehispanic, colonial, republican and contemporary art, as well exhibits on Mariscal Cáceres' battles in the War of the Pacific. ■ *Jr 28 de Julio 508, Mon-Sat 0900-1230, 1400-1700. US$0.45.*

Museo Arqueológico Hipólito Unanue has many Huari artefacts and a small museum of printing and art. Outside is a botanical garden featuring cactus and succulent plants. ■ *Mon-Fri 0800-1300, 1500-1700, Sat 0900-1300. US$0.75. Opposite the University Residences, on Av Independencia, at the northern end of town, T812056.*

Essentials

A *Ayacucho*, 9 de Diciembre 184, T812202. Beautiful colonial building but the rooms don't match up to the palatial splendour of the reception. It's comfortable, has TV, and some rooms overlook the plaza. **B** *Ciudadela Warpa Picchu*, Km 5 Carretera a Cusco, T819462, www.warpapicchu.com 10 mins from the city, Belgian-owned hotel, rooms with jacuzzi **A**, price includes breakfast, tax, transfers, use of pool, gym and other facilities, comfortable, restaurant, bar. Owner Sr Verbist is a knowledgeable guide (Portal Independencia 66, T815191, verbist@terra.com.pe). Recommended.

Sleeping
■ *on map*
Price codes:
see inside
front cover

C *Hostelería Santa Rosa*, Jr Lima 166, T814614. Lovely colonial courtyard, roof terrace (ask for room 40 at the top), hot water all day, friendly, car park, restaurant.

D *Colmena*, Jr Cusco 140, T811318. With bathroom (**E** without, poorer rooms), hot water 0700-0900, clean, small rooms, secure, pleasant courtyard. **D** *Florida*, Jr Cusco 310, T812565, F816029. Small, pleasant, clean, quiet, patio with flowers, all rooms with bath and TV, hot water in morning and on request. **D** *Hostal 3 Máscaras*, Jr 3 Máscaras 194, T8129217. New rooms with bath better than the old ones with shared bathroom, nice colonial building with patio, clean, basic rooms, hot water 0600-1100, car park. **D** *Samary*, Jr Callao 335, T/F812442. Discount for longer stay, safe, hot water in mornings, parking. Recommended. **D** *San Francisco*, Jr Callao 290, T912959/814501. Price includes breakfast, hot water, friendly, comfortable, nice patio. Recommended. **D** *Valdelirios*, Bolognesi 520, T813908/814014. Lovely colonial-style mansion, beautifully furnished, pick-up from the airport for US$1.30, bar, reserve at least 24 hrs in advance. Recommended.

E *Central*, Jr Arequipa 188, T812144. Rooms without bath and TV are cheaper, clean, large rooms, good value. **E** *Hospedaje Central*, Av Cáceres 1048. Rooms without bath and TV are **F**, large rooms, hot water, very clean, good value. **E** *El Mesón*, Jr Arequipa 273, T812938. Hot water on request, nice, clean, friendly, laundry service, not as close to disco as *Las Orquídeas*. **E** *Residencial La Crillonesa*, Nazareno 165, T812350. With bathroom in rooms with double bed, rooms with two singles share bathrooms (**F**), clean, friendly, hot water, washing facilities, discount for longer stay, great views from roof terrace. **E** *La Posada de Santa Inés*, Jr Chorro 139, T811670/819544. With bath, hot water 24 hrs, TV, terrace with small swimming pool (ask in advance for it to be cleaned), clean, friendly, very good value. **E** *Magdalena*, Mcal Cáceres 816, next to *Wari*, T818969. **F** without private bathroom, hot water on request, clean, basic but good. **E** *Hostal San Blas*, Jr Chorro 167, T814185/812712. With bathroom, hot water all day, clean, friendly, washing facilities, nice rooms, cheap meals available, discount for longer stay, Carlos will act as a local tour guide and knows everyone. Recommended. **E** *Hostal Wari*, Mcal Cáceres 836, T813065. **F** with shared bath, hot water in the morning, clean, basic, large rooms.

F *Hostal El Sol*, Av Mcal Castilla 132, T813069. Hot water 0800-1000, 2000-2200, **G** in rooms with cold water, clean, well-furnished large rooms. Recommended. **F** per person *Grau*, Jr San Juan de Dios 192, T812695. With bath (**G** per person without), hot water, clean, washing facilities and laundry service, good value, safe, friendly, noisy. Recommended. **F** *Guzmán*, Cusco 239, T816262. Small rooms, hot water, good restaurant, helpful owner. **F** *Hostal Las Orquídeas*, Jr Arequipa 287, T814344. With shared bath, hot water, clean, basic, very noisy from disco next door at weekends.

Eating
● *on map*
Those wishing to try cuy should do so in Ayacucho as it's a lot cheaper than Cusco

Mid-range *La Casona*, Jr Bellido 463. Regional specialities, try their *puca picante*, beef in a thick spicy sauce, rather like Indian curry. Recommended. *Lalo's Café*, Jr Lima 164. 0900-1300, 1600-2230 for coffee, teas, cakes, sandwiches and pizza. *Portales*, on plaza, Portal Unión. Popular. *Tradición*, San Martín 406. Popular, good cheap *menú*. *Urpicha*, Jr Londres 272. Recommended for typical food.

Cheap *Cameycar*, Jr Asamblea 261. Popular with locals, set menu for US$0.90, open 0900-1700. *Café Dorado*, Jr Asamblea 310. Excellent value set menu in a pleasant setting. A good bakery, *Café Libertad*, is at No 237 of the same street. *Kutimuy*, 28 de Julio 356, opposite police station. Excellent breakfasts (looks like a copy shop). *Mia Pizza*, San Martín 420. Good Italian meals. *Comedor Nueva Era*, Arequipa 170. Vegetarian, Mon-Sat 0700-1500, good. *La Pradera*, Portal Constitución 9. Vegetarian, good, cheap filling meals. Also good vegetarian meals next to *Hotel Central*. *Pollería Nino*, Jr 9 de Diciembre 205, opposite Santo Domingo church. Friendly and recommended for chicken (US$2.25). Try *mondongo*, a soup made from meat, maize and mint, at the market near Santa Clara on Jr Carlos Vivanco. Sra Gallardo has been recommended.

Bars & clubs *La Rumana Pizza-Video Pub*, Cáceres 1045. Pizzas, drinks and music videos, if there aren't many customers the owner may let you rent a video to watch on the big screen, good sound. *Peña Machi*, on Jr Grau. Peña on Fri and Sat, the rest of the week it's a disco.

Entertainment **Pool** *Salón de Billar Don César*, Jr Bellido 302, corner of Garcilaso. Has reasonably well maintained tables for US$0.90 per hr, open 1000-2200.

Festivals This area is well-known for its festivals throughout the year. Almost every day there is a celebration in one of the surrounding villages. Check with the tourist office.

Festival Internacional de la Tuna y Cochinilla is held in **Feb and Mar** (date varies, lasts for 15 days), for real 'dye' hards. Carnival in **Feb or Mar** is reported as a wild affair. Ayacucho is famous for its *Semana Santa* which begins on the Fri before **Holy Week**. There follows one of the world's finest Holy Week celebrations, with candle-lit nightly processions, floral 'paintings' on the eets, daily fairs (the biggest on Easter Sat), horse races and contests among peoples from all central Peru. All accommodation is fully booked for months in advance of Holy Week. Many people offer beds in their homes during the week. Look out for notices on the doors, especially on Jr Libertad.

On **25 Apr** is the anniversary of the founding of Huamanga province. *Vlicas Raymi* is held on **26-28 Jul**. *Virgen de las Nieves* is held on **15 Aug** in Parinacochas.

Shopping

Ayacucho is a good place to buy local crafts including filigree silver, which often uses *mudéjar* patterns. Also look out for little painted altars which show the manger scene, carvings in local alabaster, harps, or the pre-Inca tradition of carving dried gourds. The most famous goods are carpets and *retablos*. In both weaving and *retablos*, scenes of recent political strife have been added to more traditional motifs.

For carpets, go to Barrio Santa Ana, see under Sights above. In Barrio Belén, *Familia Pizarro*, Jr San Cristóbal 215, works in textiles and *piedra huamanga* (local alabaster) and produces good quality. (See also Arts and crafts, on page 589). A large new *Mercado Artesanal y Centro de Capacitación* has opened on Jr Quinua. *Mercado 12 de Abril*, Chorro y San Juan de Dios, is for fruit and vegetables.

Tour operators

Local tours with *Wari Tours*, Portal Independencia 70, T813115. Also handles Ormeño bus tickets and Western Union. *Willy Tours*, Jr 9 de Diciembre 107, T812568, F814075. Also handles LC Busre flight tickets. *Urpillay Tours*, Portal Independencia 62, T815074. Handles Tans flights tickets.

Transport

Air To **Lima**, with *Aero Cóndor*, daily, US$49-69, 45 mins, *LC Busre* daily (US$70). To **Andahuaylas**, with *Aero Cóndor*, Tue, Thu, Sat, 30 mins.

Bus To **Lima**, 9-10 hrs on a good new paved road, via Ica (7 hrs). For **Pisco**, 332 km, you have to take a Ica/Lima bus and get out at San Clemente, 10 mins from Pisco, and take a bus or combi (same fare to San Clemente as for Ica). Companies include: *Wari*, Pasaje Cáceres (opposite ReyBus), US$5.15 at 1800; *TransMar*, Av Mcal Cáceres 896 and *Reybus*, Pasaje Cáceres 166, US$5.80. More expensive are *Expreso Turismo Nacional*, Av Mcal Cáceres 886, *Libertadores*, Av Manco Cápac 295, *Trans Molina*, Jr 9 de Diciembre 458, 8 a day US$5.80-10; *Ormeño*, Jr Libertad 257, US$7.15 and US$10; *Civa*, Av Mcal Cáceres 1242, US$10, and Cruz del Sur, Av Mcal Cáceres 1264, US$11.45.

To **Huancayo**, 319 km, 8-10 hrs, US$5.70. Daily with *Trans Molina*, 3 a day, and *Central* and *Ticllos* , 1 each at night. The road is paved as far as Huanta, thereafter it is rough, especially in the wet season, but the views are breathtaking.

For **Huancavelica**, *Expreso Turismo Nacional*, direct, 0630 daily, and *Ticllos*, US$5.

To **Andahuaylas**, 261 km, takes 10 hrs (more in the rainy season). *Molina* passes through from Lima en route to Cusco at 2200, check if there is a seat; *Wari* at 0400, *ReyBus* at 1830 (not Sun), *Expreso Turismo Nacional*, 0400, 1900, *Trans Mar*, 1830 (and 0500 Sat only) and *Turismo Los Chankas*, Av Mcal Cáceres 921 and Pasaje Cáceres 144, at 0630 and 1900, all US$5.70. Only *Turismo Los Chankas'* 1900 service is direct to Cusco. To get to **Abancay**, a further 138 km, 6 hrs, you must change buses and then go on to **Cusco**, a further 195 km, 5 hrs. It takes 24 hrs to Cusco. There are no direct buses. Road conditions are terrible, and landslides a common occurrence in the wet season. The scenery, though, is stunning and makes up for it.

Central Highlands

Directory **Airline offices** *Aero Cóndor*, 9 de Diciembre 123 *LC Busre*, at *Willy* Tours, address above. *StarUp*, 28 de Julio 186, T811199. **Banks** *BCP*, Portal Unión 28. No commission on cheques, cash advance on Visa and Visa ATM. *Interbank*, opposite *Hotel Ayacucho*, Jr 9 de Diciembre 183, also has ATM for Visa, also Mastercard/Cirrus. 0915-1315, 1630-1830, Sat 0930-1230. Many street changers and *casas de cambio* can be found at Portal Constitución Nos 1 to 8 on the plaza, they offer a good rate for cash. **Communications** Internet: at Jr Lima 114, another next door. On Asamblea: *Cyberstation SAC*, No 162, and another at No 330. Also at 9 de Diciembre 213. Connections and machines are good, average price is US$0.60 per hr, some charge US$0.90 at night. All 0800-2300 daily. **Post office** and **Telefónica**: Asamblea 293. **Useful addresses** Tourist Police: at 2 de Mayo y Arequipa.

Sights around Ayacucho

Vilcashuamán These impressive Inca ruins are to the south of Ayacucho, beyond Cangallo. John Hemming writes: "There is a five-tiered, stepped *usnu* platform faced in fine Inca masonry and topped by a monolithic two-seat throne. The parish church is built in part of the Inca sun temple and rests on stretches of Inca terracing. Vilcashuamán was an important provincial capital, the crossroads where the road from Cusco to the Pacific met the empire's north-south highway." There are 3 hotels in the village of Vilcashuamán, all **G**, and all basic but clean. The **tourist office** on the Plaza in Ayacucho has a guide book, in Spanish. **Market** day is Wednesday. ■ *Tours can be arranged with Travel Agencies in Ayacucho. A full day tour includes Intihuatana, US$8. Alternatively stay overnight. Combis run from Av M Castilla, daily at 0400, 4 hours, US$2.50.*

Vischongo Near Vilcashuamán is the village of Vischongo. About an hour's walk uphill from the village are the Inca baths of **Intihuatana**, which are worth seeing as much for their superb location on a beautiful lake as for the ruins themselves. ■ *From Vilcashuamán to Vischongo takes one hour and costs US$0.45. Vischongo to Ayacucho takes 5 hrs, and costs US$2.70. It is possible to see both ruins in a day, though it's more relaxing to spend the night in Vilcashuamán, or better still, camp at the lake near Vischongo.*

Huari A good road going north from Ayacucho leads to Huari, dating from the 'Middle Horizon', when the Huari culture spread across most of Peru. This was the first urban walled centre in the Andes and was used for political, administrative, ceremonial, residential and productive purposes. The huge irregular stone walls are up to 12 m high and rectangular houses and streets can be made out. There are large areas of flat stone which may have been for religious purposes and there are subterranean canals and tunnels.

The most important activity here was artistic production. High temperature ovens were used to mass produce ceramics of many different colours. The Huari also worked with gold, silver, metal and alloys such as bronze, which was used for weapons and for decorative objects. The ruins now lie in an extensive *tuna* cactus forest. There is a museum at the site.

■ *Buses leave from the Ovalo in Barrio Magdalena. There are no specific times; they leave when full from 0700 onwards. Buses go on to La Quinua (US$1), and Huanta (US$1.35, see below). Combis pass Huari on the way to La Quinua, departing from the corner of Jr Ciro Alegría and Jr Salvador Cavero. Trips can be arranged to Huari, La Quinua village and the battlefield with travel agencies in Ayacucho.*

The Huari influence

The city of Huari had a population of 50,000 and reached its apogee in AD 900. Its influence spread throughout much of Peru: north to Cajamarca; along the north coast to Lambayeque; south along the coast to Moquegua; and south across the sierra to Cusco. Before the Inca invasion the Huari formed a chanca – a confederation of ethnic groups – and populated the Pampas river and an area west of the

Apurímac. This political agreement between the peoples of Ayacucho, Andahuaylas, Junín and Huancavelica was seen by the Incas in Cusco as a threat. The Incas fought back around 1440 with a bloody attack on the Huari on the Pampa de Ayacucho, and so began a period of Inca domination. The scene of this massacre is still known as Rincón de los Muertos.

La Quinua

This village, 37 km northeast of Ayacucho, has a charming cobbled main plaza and many of the buildings have been restored. There is a small market on Sunday. Nearby, on the Pampa de Quinua, a huge obelisk commemorates the battle of Ayacucho. The obelisk is 44 m high, representing 44 years of struggle for independence. There is also a small and poorly displayed museum. ■ *US$1.40.*

The village's handicrafts are recommended, especially ceramics. The pieces made in Quinua range from model churches and nativity figures to humorous groups of musicians and gossiping women. The rich red local clay is modelled mainly by hand and decorated with local mineral earth colours. Traditionally, the churches are set on the roofs of newly-occupied houses to ward off evil spirits. Virtually every roof in the village has a church on it - including the church itself. San Pedro Ceramics, at the foot of the hill leading to the monument, and Mamerto Sánchez, Jr Sucre, are good places to find typical local ceramics.

The village's festival, **Fiesta de la Virgen de Cocharcas** around 8 September, consists of three days of processions, dancing and bullfighting. ■ *Combis from Ayacucho (as for Huari, above) take 1 hr, US$0.75. It is a beautiful 18 km' walk downhill from La Quinua to Huari, where trucks leave for Ayacucho until about 1700.* Tombs of the Huari nobles are being excavated along the road from Ayacucho to Quinua.

The Huanta valley
Colour map 5, grid A4

This picturesque region, 48 km northeast of Ayacucho, consists of the districts of Huanta, Luricocha, Santillana, Ayahuanco, Huamanaguilla and Iguaín. The town of Huanta is one hour from Ayacucho, on the road to Huancayo. It was here that the Pokras and Chancas warriors put up their last, brave fight against the Inca invasion.

From Huanta, the lakes of Qarqarcocha, San Antonio, Chakaccocha, Yanacocha and Pampacocha can be visited (in the rainy season only the nearest lake, Chakaccocha, can be reached, and then with four-wheel drive). Also the valley of Luricocha, 5 km away, which has a lovely, warm climate. **Huanta** celebrates the **Fiesta de la Cruz** during the first week of May, with much music and dancing. Its Sunday **market** is large and interesting.

The area is notable as the site of perhaps the oldest known culture in South America, 20,000 years old, evidence of which was found in the cave of **Pikimachay**. The remains are now in Lima's museums. ■ *The cave is 24 km from Ayacucho, on the road to Huanta. It is a 30-minute walk from the road.*

Central Highlands

North to the Río Apurímac
Colour map 5, grid A4

A road runs northeast from Ayacucho to **San Francisco**, lying in the tropical lowland forests of the Apurímac valley. There are three basic hotels: **E** *Suria*, cheaper without bath; better ones are both **F** : *Pacífico*, on the east bank facing the football pitch, and *Villa*, good views over the river and town. Both are spotless and hospitable. There are many small restaurants on both sides of the bridge. Launches ply up and down the river and 15 minutes east is the village of Sampantuari, where the inhabitants still wear face paint, traditional clothing and live in bamboo huts (don't go to stare – they don't welcome outsiders). ■ *Combis leave from the paradero San Francisco in Ayacucho from 0500 till late morning, 7 hrs, US$5. The road, 143 km in all, is paved to La Quinua, then goes through Tambo.*

Ayacucho to Cusco

Chincheros
Colour map 5, grid A4

The road towards Cusco goes through Chincheros, 158 km from Ayacucho and 3 hours from Andahuaylas. It's not the most picturesque town in Peru, but the townsfolk are very friendly. Ask for the bakery with its outdoor oven (if you don't smell it first). 15 minutes before Chincheros, on the road from Andahuaylas, is **Uripa** with a good Sunday market (**G** *Hostal Zárate*). *Micros* regularly run between the two towns.

Andahuaylas

Phone code: 084
Colour map 5, grid A4
See page 230 for sites of interest between Abancay and Cusco

About 80 km further on from Chincheros, in a fertile, temperate valley of lush meadows, cornfields and groves of eucalyptus, alder and willow, stands Andahuaylas. The town offers few exotic crafts, but it has a good market on Sunday and the surrounding scenery is beautiful. A large part of the town centre has electricity. The **tourist police** have an office on Av Perú.

Sleeping

D *El Encanto de Oro*, Av Pedro Casafranca 424, T723066, F722555. Breakfast included, TV, hot water 24 hrs, laundry service, restaurant, organizes trips on request. **D** *Sol de Oro*, Jr Juan A Trelles 164, T721152/722815. Price includes breakfast, hot water 24 hrs, new rooms, TV, clean, laundry service, restaurant. **D** *Turístico Andahuaylas*, Av Lázaro Carrillo 620, T721224. With bath, hot water 24 hrs. **F** per person *Las Américas*, Jr Ramos 500 block. Hot water in the morning and on request, clean, friendly. Recommended. **F** *Wari*, Ramos 427. Cold showers, but clean. **G** *Hostal Waliman*, Av Andahuaylas 266, near where the buses leave for Cusco. Basic, cold water.

Eating

Good, cheap food can be found at *Corazón Ayacuchano*, Av Andahuaylas 145. A recommended *chifa* is at Jr Juan A Trellas 279. Excellent value. *El Ajo Parrilladas*, Jr Juan A Trelles 274. New, great for fish and meat, first class service. Good fruit juices sold in the market. *Panadería* at Av Ramón Castilla 257. *El Garabato I*, on main plaza beside Municipalidad. Video and music club, popular.

Transport

Air *Aero Cóndor* to **Lima**, daily except Sat, 1 hr 10 mins, US$54.

Bus Daily buses to **Ayacucho**, a minimum of 10 hrs, US$5.70; *Wari* at 0700; *Expreso Turismo Nacional* 2 a day, *ReyBus*, and *Turismo Los Chankas*, 2 a day, one coming from Cusco. To **Abancay**, *Señor de Huanca* at 0600, 1300 and 2000 daily, 6 hrs, US$4.30. To **Cusco**, *San Jerónimo*, via Abancay, 0630, US$7.20. On all night buses, take a blanket.

Directory

Communications Internet: J F Ramos 317, US$1.45 per hr.

Abancay

Nestled between mountains in the upper reaches of a glacial valley, this friendly town is first glimpsed when you are 62 km away. There is a petrol station. The town celebrates the *Yawar Fiesta* in July, and for lovers of blood sports there's the *Campeonata Nacional de Gallos de Navaja* on the 1-3 November.

Phone code: 084
Colour map 5, grid A5

Sleeping

B *Hotel de Turismo Abancay*, Av Díaz Barcenas 500, T321017 (Cusco, T223339). With bathroom, old-fashioned house, overpriced, run down, poor hot water supply, but it does have internet, camping permitted US$3. There are various other hotels: **D-F** *Imperial*, Díaz Barcenas 517, T321578, great beds and hot water, spotless, helpful, parking. **F** *El Dorado*, Av Arenas 131-C, T322005, is good.

Eating

Elena, on the same street as the bus companies. Good. At Av Arena 170 is the restaurant of José (Pepe) Molero Ruiz, T684397, pepe_19g@yahoo.com He is knowledgeable about the area and encouraging all forms of tourism to sites near and farther afield. *El Garabato II*, Av Arena 162, p 2. Video and music club, popular.

Transport

There are bus services from Abancay to **Cusco** (departing from Av Arenas near the market), **Andahuaylas**, and **Nasca** on the Panamericana Sur, 464 km, via Chalhuanca and Puquío, continuing to **Lima**. All buses on the Lima-Nasca-Cusco route pass through Abancay at about midnight. *Señor de Huanca* runs between Abancay and Andahuaylas, leaving Abancay at 0600, 1300, 2000. The journey Abancay-Cusco takes 5 hrs and costs US$4.30. The scenery en route is dramatic, especially as it descends into the Apurímac valley and climbs out again. There is a checkpoint at the Apurímac border. The road is paved and in good condition from Curahausi to Cusco. Coming from Cusco, after the pass it takes 1 hr to zig-zag down to Abancay.

Buses from Cusco en route either to Andahuaylas or Nasca/Lima leave Abancay 5-5½ hrs after departing from Cusco.

East of La Oroya

A paved road heads north towards Cerro de Pasco and Huánuco. A turn-off 25 km north of La Oroya branches east and drops 600 m before it reaches Tarma, which is 30 km off the Carretera Central. Beyond Tarma the road continues its steep descent. In the 80 km between Tarma and La Merced the road, passing by great overhanging cliffs, drops 2,450 m and the vegetation changes dramatically from temperate to tropical. This is a really beautiful run.

Tarma

Tarma, 'the Pearl of the Andes', was founded in 1538 and is one of the oldest towns in Peru. Though this little, flat-roofed place, with plenty of trees, is now growing with garish modern buildings, it still has a lot of charm. The **Semana Santa** celebrations are spectacular, with a very colourful Easter Sunday morning procession in the main plaza. With it's beautiful surrounding countryside, the town is also notable for its locally made fine **flower-carpets** (see Festivals, below). In 1999 it recorded the largest flower carpet in the world. **Tourist information** is available at 2 de Mayo 775 on the Plaza, T321010, Mon-Fri 0800-1300, 1600-1800. The office is very helpful and has good displays on the walls about the surrounding area.

Phone code: 064
Colour map 3, grid C4
Population: 105,200
Altitude: 3,050 m

Central Highlands

The **Odria Museum**, 2 de Mayo 755, in the library, celebrates the life of Tarma's most famous son, General Manuel Odria, who became dictator of Peru in the 1930s. The museum contains personal memorabilia. ■ *0800-1800*.

Sleeping
■ *on map*
Price codes:
see inside front cover
Accommodation is
hard to find at Easter
but you can apply
to the Municipalidad
for rooms with
local families

AL *Los Portales*, Av Castilla 512, T321411, F321410 (in Lima T421 7220). Out of town, with bathroom, hot water, heating, quiet, secluded, price includes breakfast, very good restaurant, but expensive. **A** *La Florida*, 6 km from Tarma, T341041, F341358, kreida@yahoo.com (for reservations T Lima 344 1358). 18th-century, working hacienda, 12 rooms, some furnished with antiques, with bathroom, hot water, price includes breakfast, owned by German-Peruvian couple Inge and Pepe who arrange excursions. Recommended but expensive. Also camping for US$3.

D *Hostal Internacional*, Dos de Mayo 307, T321830. With bathroom, hot water in afternoon only, clean. **E** *Albania*, Amazonas 435. Clean, small rooms with bath, hot water. **E** *Hostal Central*, Huánuco 614, T321198. Shared bathroom, hot water, friendly, laundry facilities, a bit rundown but popular with gringos, has an observatory which opens Fri at 2000. **E** *La Colmena*, Jauja 618, T321157. An old building with character, with bath, clean, convenient for Huancayo buses. **E** *Hostal Tuchu*, Dos de Mayo 561. Shared bathroom, hot water in the morning, large rooms with poor beds. **E** *Vargas*, Dos de Mayo 627, T321460. With bath, hot water in morning, clean, large rooms, TV for rent.

F *Hostal Bolívar*, Huaraz 389, T321060. An old building with character, with bathroom but shared shower, hot water. **F** *Hostal El Dorado*, Huánuco 488, T321598. **G** without bath, hot water, rooms set round a patio, first floor rooms better, clean.

Eating
● *on map*

La Cabaña de Bryan, Paucartambo 450. Good for meat dishes. *La Grima*, on Plaza de Armas. *Lo Mejorcito de Tarma*, Huánuco 190, T320685. Offers a good set *menú* with choices at US$1.50, good for local specialities, also has tourist information. *El Sabor Criollo*, Huaraz y Callao. A pleasant local restaurant, try *aji de gallina*, cheap. *Señorial/Pollería Braserita*, Huánuco 138. Good *menú*. *Café Picaflor*, opposite the Cathedral. Good for snacks. There are also several places on Lima, including a vegetarian. The *manjarblanco* of Tarma is famous, as well as *pachamanca*, *mondongo* and *picante de cuyes*. In the central market try *cachanga*, fried bread with cinnamon. A good place to buy local produce such as *manjar blanco* and honey is *El Tarmenito*, Lima 149.

Tarma

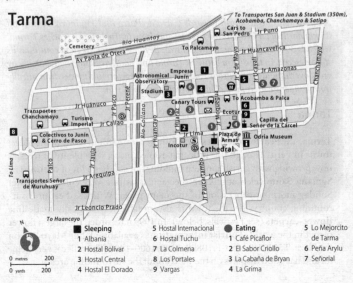

Central Highlands

Disco El Gato Pardo, Callao 227. A smart club for a small town playing the latest Latin hits. *Peña Arylu*, Paucartambo 344. Has live bands on Fri and Sat.

Bars & clubs

Aside from *Semana Santa*, Tarma hosts many other festivals. *Carnaval Tarmeño* is held on **20-25 Feb**. Also taking place during *Semana Santa* is the *Concurso de Alfombras de Flores* (flower carpet competition). Taking place throughout **May** is *Festividad Señor de Muruhuay*. On **23-24 May** is the *Circuito Turístico de Ciclismo de Montaña*. The *Festival de la Papa* is held on **23-27 Jun**. **23-29 Jul** is the *Semana Turística*. The *Fiesta de la Siembra del Maíz* is on **28-30 Sep**, in Tarma as well as Acobamba (see below). *Festival del Pan Tarmeño "La Wawa"* is held on **1-2 Nov** (the same time as All Saints).

Festivals

Incotur, Lima 481, T/F323846, and *Ecotur*, 2 de Mayo 658, and others, offer a variety of day trips to local sites.

Tour operators

Bus Direct buses leave daily to **Lima**, 231 km, 6 hrs, US$4. *Transportes Chanchamayo*, Callao 1002, T321882, is recommended as the best, 3 a day en route from Chanchamayo; *Turismo Imperial*, Callao 960, 4 a day, also coming from Chanchamayo. *Canary Tours* (0930 and 2130), *Transportes Sr de Muruhuay* (several daily) start their journey in Tarma. There is a good lunch stop at El Tambo before La Oroya, with superb fried trout. The road is paved throughout.

Transport

To **Jauja and Huancayo**, *Transportes San Juan*, buses leave from the stadium every hr departing on the ½ hr, but their buses come from Chanchamayo; and *Canary Tours*, advertised as hourly, but departing when full, 0500-2200, to Jauja 2 hrs, US$2. All buses continue to Huancayo, 3 hrs, US$2.50. Colectivos (cars) depart when full from Callao y Jauja, 2 hrs, US$4, and 3 hrs, US$6, respectively. To **Cerro de Pasco**, *Empresa Junín*, Amazonas 450, 4 a day, 3 hrs, US$2.50. Also colectivos depart when full, 2 hrs, US$4. Buses to **La Oroya** leave regularly from opposite the petrol station on Av Castilla block 5, 1 hr, US$1.25, while colectivos leave from the petrol station itself, 45 mins, US$2. To **Chanchamayo**, *Transportes San Juan* from the stadium every hr on the half ½ hr, 1½ hrs, US$1.50 to San Ramón, and 2 hrs, US$2 to La Merced. Also, colectivos, 1-11/4 hrs, US$3 and US$3.50 respectively.

To **Satipo**, *Transportes San Juan* at 0930, 6-7 hrs, US$3.50.

Banks BCP, Lima 407. Changes Amex TCs. **Communications** Internet: Internet offices can be found at Perené 292 and Paucartambo 632. **Telephone**: *Telefónica*, is on the Plaza de Armas.

Directory

Around Tarma

Eight kilometres from Tarma, the small hillside town of Acobamba has some attractive old buildings. It also has fine *tapices* made in San Pedro de Cajas which depict the Crucifixion. There are festivities during May (see Tarma festivals, above). E *Hotel Sumaq*, Chanchamayo 650, T341109, a large hotel, operated by the local council, hot water, TV, good value.

Acobamba
Colour map 3, grid B4

Two kilometres up beyond the town is the futuristic **Santuario de Muruhuay**, with a venerated picture painted on the rock behind the altar. C *Hostal Campestre Auberge Normandie*, beside the Sanctuary, T341028, or Lima 349 5440, hostalnormandie@yahoo.com 16 cabins with bath and hot water, TV, bar, restaurant, fine views over the valley. ■ *Colectivos and yellow Canary buses run from the centre of Tarma to Acobamba and up to Muruhuay every 10-20 mins, US$0.25.*

Palcamayo   The **Grutas de Huagapo**, also known as *La gruta que llora* (the cave that weeps), is 4 km from the town of Palcamayo, which is 15 km northwest of Acobamba (**F** *Hostal Municipal de Palcamayo*, on plaza, T064-343021). The caves can be entered for about 100m, at which point it is up to 30 m high and 20 m wide. Guides with torches and ropes can be hired near the entrance to reach 300 m. Beyond that wet suits and simple caving gear are needed. Even without a guide you can penetrate the cave for some way with a torch. The cave is the deepest in South America and investigations, which have penetrated up to 2,800 m, suggest that the system extends over 30 km underground. There is a small but impressive gorge, 10 minutes walk down river from the cave. ■ *Colectivos for San Pedro, which pass the cave, depart from Otera y Moquegua in Tarma, 40 mins, US$1. Combis, 1 hr, US$0.50, and colectivos, 30 mins, US$0.75, depart from Otera y Paucartambo for Palcamayo, a 30-40-min walk down river from the cave.*

San Pedro   Northwest beyond Palcamayo, the road climbs steeply for 14 km to San Pedro
de Cajas   de Cajas, a large village which is famed for its coloured sheep-wool weavings.
Altitude: 4,050 m   The principal shops are on the central plaza and the road to Palcamayo. This road joins the one from La Oroya to Cerro de Pasco below Junín. The town holds the *Festival de La Pukcha (Hilado)* on 28-30 June. There is accommodation in the village at **G** *Hotel Comercio*, in Calle Chanchamayo; also two restaurants. ■ *There are regular combis from Junín, 1 hr, US$1, while from Tarma there are fairly regular colectivos, 1 hr, US$1.50; also buses and colectivos to La Oroya.*

Three kilometres beyond San Pedro on the road to La Oroya is a **vicuña reserve** and co-operative, which is the best place to see vicuña at close range. The animals are accustomed to people and roam near the road. Every August they are sheared and the money from the sale of the fleece goes to the reserve.

On the road to   About 8 km on the road from Tarma to Huancayo, at **Tarmatambo**, is the
Huancayo   start of a good section of Inca road which runs 3 km to Huasqui on the Tarma-La Oroya road. Thirty kilometres from Tarma on the Huancayo road is **El Santuario Rupestre**, near Huairicolca. Here is the largest site of cave paintings in Peru, some 600 pictures dating back 4,000-10,000 years.

Chanchamayo

Phone code: 064   East from Tarma are the towns of San Ramón and La Merced, collectively
Colour map 3, grid B5   known as Chanchamayo.

San Ramón   San Ramón is 11 km before La Merced on the banks of the Río Tarma. It is a busy, attractive town, in the lower foothills of the Andes where the temperature is noticeably higher than in Tarma. The surrounding hills are covered in coffee plantations. ■ *From San Ramón colectivos take 15 mins to La Merced, US$0.25.*

Sleeping B *El Refugio*, Ejército 490, T/F331082, hotelrefugio@infotex.com.pe Bungalows set in a beautiful tropical garden, with pool, price includes breakfast, good value. **D** *Conquistadores*, Progreso 298, T331157, F331771. Modern, hot water, TV, parking. **E** *Chanchamayo*, Progreso 291, T331008. With hot water, TV, rooms without bathroom half the price. **D** *El Parral*, Uriate 355, T331128, F331536. Modern, with hot water, TV, clean, good restaurant serving local specialities. **F** *La Selva*, Paucartambo 247. Basic. **Camping** is possible at *Hotel Selva Alegre*, overlooking the river, 3 km east of San Ramón towards La Merced, US$3.

Eating *Café Prisci*, Progreso 456. Good for snacks, including home made lemon pie. *Mesón Francés*, Pardo 397. International cuisine, overlooking the river, with disco at weekends. *Chifa Felipe Siu*, Progreso 440, and *Chifa Conquistadores*, under the hotel, are two of the most popular restaurants in town.

Tour operators *Café Tours*, Pardo 132, T331123. They are very knowledgeable about a huge area extending as far as Satipo, Puerto Bermúdez, Oxapampa and Pozuzo. Recommended.

Transport Air: flights leave from San Ramón. There is an 'air-colectivo' service to **Puerto Bermúdez**, which continues to **Atalaya**, **Satipo**, **Puerto Inca** (see page 534) and **Pucallpa**. Air-colectivos go to Lima and to most places in the jungle region where there is an airstrip. Flights are cheap but irregular, and depend on technical factors, weather and goodwill. Aero-taxis can be chartered (*viaje especial*) to any-where for a higher price, with a maximum of five people, but you have to pay for the pilot's return to base. To find out more you have to go to the air base, across the river, on the east side of town.

Bus: to Lima *Transportes Santo Domingo de Guzmán*, Paucartambo 318, and *Transportes La Merced*, Paucartambo y Alvariño, 5 a day, 7 hrs, US$6. To **Huánuco** *Transportes León de Huánuco*, Paucartambo 380, at 2200, 6-7 hrs, US$7. To **Puerto Bermúdez** *Expreso San Ramón*, Progreso 102, at 0400, 9 hrs, a few seats are available in the cabin of the truck-bus, US$10. To **Tarma** *Transportes San Juan*, Progreso 105, hourly, 2 hrs, US$1.50, or colectivos, 1 hr, US$3. To **La Merced** there is a continuous flow of combis and colectivos from the market and main plaza, 15 mins, US$0.20 and US$0.30 respectively.

Directory Internet: next to *El Parral* on Uriate. **Post office**: Progreso 402.

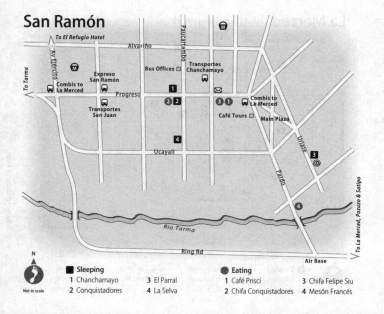

San Ramón

Not to scale

Sleeping
1 Chanchamayo
2 Conquistadores
3 El Parral
4 La Selva

Eating
1 Café Prisci
2 Chifa Conquistadores
3 Chifa Felipe Siu
4 Mesón Francés

Central Highlands

La Merced
Population: 15,000
Altitude: 775
73 km east of Tarma

La Merced, lies in the fertile Chanchamayo valley, famous for its citrus and coffee production. Campa Indians can usually be found around the central plaza selling bows, arrows, necklaces and trinkets. La Merced has two central **markets**, the Mercado Nuevo and the Mercado Viejo. At the latter you can ususally find Campa articles, exotic herbs and jungle medicines such as *uña de gato* and *sangre de grado*. The hill behind the town can be climbed up to **La Cruz** for a wonderful view of the entire Chanchamayo valley, or you can hire a mototaxi for US$1. There is a restaurant and small recreation area. A one-hour walk through the Quebrada de los Italianos leads to **Colombo**, where a distillery produces *aguardiente*. There is a **festival** in the last week of September.

There are several hotels and it is usually possible to negotiate the price

Sleeping **D-E** *Primavera*, Arequipa 175, T531433. Friendly, TV, more expensive with bathroom. Recommended. **D** *Mercedes*, Tarma 576, T531304, and *Cristina*, Tarma 582, T531276,. Modern hotels adjoining each other, with hot water, private bathrooms, TV, laundry and garage. **D** *El Edén*, on main plaza, T531183. Modern, hot water, private bathrooms, TV. **D** *Los Portales*, Jiménez 119, T532228, F531283. Hot water, with bathroom, TV, comfortable, friendly. **D** *Santa Rosa*, 3 de Mayo 447, T531012. Clean, cheaper. **F** *Hospedaje Los Víctor*, Jr Trama 373, on Plaza de Armas, T531026. With bath, cold water, good, clean and friendly. **F** *Roca*, Ayacucho 256. Basic. **F** *San Felipe*, 2 de Mayo 246, T531046. Basic.

Eating The best, and really the only restaurant is *Shambari-Campa*, on the Plaza de Armas. It has an extensive menu, an excellent set *menú* at US$3, and hundreds of interesting old photos, some dating back to the start of the century, of the local area cover the walls. Highly recommended. Try also *Ling*, Jr Junín on the Plaza, opposite BCP. Very popular with locals, better than touristy places.

Tour operators *Tsiriski Tours*, Ancash y Tarma. Offers tours of the surrounding area, including on the Río Chanchamayo (alternatively go to the river front at Canotaje).

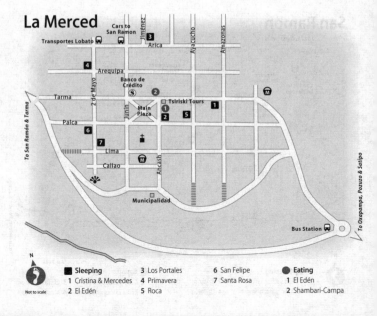

Transport There is a large bus station on the east side of town, from which most buses arrive and depart. To **San Ramón** there is a continuous flow of combis and colectivos, 15-20 mins, US$0.20-US$0.30 respectively. To **Satipo** *Transportes Lobato* at 1130 and 2330, 2½ hrs, US$2.50. Other buses coming through from Huancayo and Lima may also have room. To **Oxapampa** *Empresa Santa Rosa*, every ½ hr, 3 hrs, US$2.50. There are also regular colectivos, 2 hrs, US$5.

To **Pozuzo** *Empresa Santa Rosa* at 0430 and 0830, 6 hrs, US$4.50. The condition of the road deteriorates after Oxapampa. To **Puerto Bermúdez** *Empresa Transdife* at 0330 and 0430, 8 hrs, has some seats available in the cabin of the bus-truck, US$10. To **Lima** *Expreso Satipo, Transportes Lobato* and *Transportes Chanchamayo* (recommended) each have several buses during the day, 7½ hrs, US$6.50. To **Tarma** *Transportes San Juan*, hourly, 2½ hrs, US$2, or colectivos, just over 1 hr, US$3.50.

Banks *BCP*, Junín y Tarma.

Directory

East of Chanchamayo

Bob Cook of Encino, CA, USA, writes: "A 123-km paved road leads to Satipo. At Km 20 the confluence of the Chanchamayo and Paucartambo rivers forms the Río Perené. The road follows the river, winding through lush jungle and Asháninka villages, where Indian artifacts are often for sale." At Km 70, an expanse of palm-thatched huts signals the outskirts of Pichinaki. A few years ago this village represented the remotest of Peruvian outposts, but its fertile lands and warm climate were ideal for coffee, bananas and citrus. Tens of thousands of Andean *campesinos* flocked to the region in search of jobs and land. A paved road reached the town in 1999 and it is now the commercial hub of the region. Its long sandy beaches on the Río Perené make an ideal retreat from the encircling jungle and a jumping off point to visit the waterfalls, lakes and remote Indian villages in the area. During the dry season (April-August), the town's plaza and streets are covered with drying coffee beans. At **Playa Pescadora** (El Puerto Pichinaki) are most of the good restaurants, which serve the local delicacy, *doncella* fish (*El Bambú* is recommended).

Pichinaki
Colour map 3, grid B5
Population: 30,000
Altitude: 500 m

Beyond Pichinaki the paved road pulls away from the Río Perené and goes to the jungle town of Satipo, the main centre of this region. It is a noisy, semi-modern town. **B** *Hostal San José*, Jr Leguía 557, T545105. **D** *Hostal Majestic*, on the plaza, Jr Fundadores 408, T545015. With bathroom, electricity 1900-2300 only, noisy. **F** per person *Trujillo*, Av Grau 277. **F** *La Residencial*, four rooms, clean, garden, swimming pool. There are many other basic hotels. For good food try *La Laguna Blanca*, at Km 121 on the road to Pichinaki, nice pool and recreation area. Also *Dany's Restaurant* and *Café Yoli*, Jr Manuel Prado 224. 1 km from town is **Isla de Fantasía** and **El Lagarto**, with restaurant, nightclub and swimming in the river. Internet at Jr Francisco Irazola 359. To Satipo take a *Lobato* bus from La Merced, 1130, 2330, US$2.50. Buses from Satipo to Huancayo and Lima go at night, a very cold journey, US$9.50, 12 hours, with *Apóstol San Pedro* (more expensive but no better), *Expreso Satipo* and *Lobato*.

Satipo
Phone code: 064
Colour map 3, grid B5
Population: 22,000
Altitude: 631 m

A dirt road continues east to **Mazamari** and **Puerto Ocopa** near the confluence of the Satipo and Perené rivers. Some 10 km along this road are the **Arcoiris waterfalls**. Colectivos Satipo-Puerto Ocopa take 2 hours, US$8.50 for four. From here you can take a boat down the Río Tambo to its confluence with the Urubamba at **Atalaya** (population 8,000). It's 10 hours upstream, costing US$11.50. **F** *Hostal Denis*, Raymondi 144; several eating places on C Urubamba; internet in the Municipalidad. From Atalaya boats go to Pucallpa.

Central Highlands

North of Chanchamayo

**Puerto
Bermúdez**
Colour map 3, grid B5

The road has been extended from San Luis de Shuaro over an intervening mountain range. A turn-off east leads to Puerto Bermúdez on the Río Neguachi. There is clean accommodation in **F** *Humboldt*, good; **F** *Hostal Tania*, opposite the dock where motorized canoes tie up, and an eating house opposite the airstrip. This is a great base for exploring further into the Selva Central Peruana, with trips upriver to the Asháninca community. Boat passages are possible from passing traders.

Oxapampa
Colour map 3, grid B4
Population: 5,140
Altitude: 1,794 m

Oxapampa is set on a fertile plain on the Río Huancabamba, a tributary of the Ucayali, 81 km from La Merced. A third of the inhabitants are descendants of a German-Austrian community of 70 families which settled in 1859 at **Pozuzo**, 80 km downstream, and spread later to Oxapampa. There is much livestock farming and coffee is planted on land cleared by the timber trade. On 5 August the town hosts a festival, the **Virgen de Las Nieves**.

Sleeping and eating **F** *Hostal Jiménez*, Grau 421. Clean, cold water, shared bathroom. **F** *Hostal Liz*, Av Oxapampa 104. Clean, small, cold water. **G** *Hostal Santa Isolina*, Jr M Castilla 177. With bathroom, cold water. *Oasis*, is a highly recommended restaurant.

 Transport *Empresa Santa Rosa* buses and colectivos run from La Merced regularly (see page 511).

**North of
Oxapampa**

Twenty-five kilometres from Oxapampa is **Huancabamba**, from where it is 55 km to Pozuzo. The whole road between La Merced and Pozuzo is very rough, depending on the season. There are no less than 30 rivers to be crossed. Downstream 40 km from Pozuzo is Nuevo Pozuzo. There is no transport, it's a two-day walk. There is an interesting museum opposite the church in the town centre. The town celebrates the Semana Turística de Pozuzo during the last week in July. Website www.pozuzo.com (under construction late 2002)

Sleeping In **Pozuzo**: **E** *Frau Maria Egg*, fraumariaegg@pozuzo.com (in Lima T444 9927/441 1167). Includes breakfast, nice garden, swimming pool. Recommended. **E** *Hostal Tirol*, includes meals. Clean. Recommended. **F-G** *Hostal Maldonado*. Clean.

Transport Buses leave from Lima to Pozuzo with *La Victoria* (28 de Julio 2405, Lima) on Mon, Thu and Sat at 0800, US$12, about 16 hrs. See also under La Merced, page 511.

North of La Oroya

A paved road runs 130 km north from La Oroya to Cerro de Pasco. It runs up the Mantaro valley through narrow canyons to the wet and mournful Junín pampa at over 4,250 m, one of the world's largest high-altitude plains. An obelisk marks the battlefield where the Peruvians under Bolívar defeated the Spaniards in 1824. Blue peaks line the pampa in a distant wall. This windswept sheet of yellow grass is bitterly cold and the only signs of life are the young herders with their sheep and llamas. The road passes the eastern shores of the Lago de Junín, which is famous for its birdlife. From Junín to Cerro de Pasco the landscape is dominated by the cultivation of maca, through the Sierra Verde project – since it was declared that this tuber has strong nutritional value demand has soared. Maca juice, cake, bread, liquor, etc, is sold from roadside stalls all around the lake. It is even claimed to have aphrodisiac properties and is known locally as the "viagra chola".

San Pedro de Cajas

Twenty kilometres north of La Oroya and 30 km south of Junín is the turn-off down to Tarma and Chanchamayo. 10 km south of Junín another road leads southeast to **San Pedro de Cajas**. There are regular combis from Junín, two hours, US$1.50, but most travellers visit San Pedro from Tarma (see page 508).

Three kilometres south of the town of Junín is the **Chacamarca Historical Sanctuary**, covering 2,500 ha of the battlefield, with a large obelisk at its centre. It is a 30-minute walk from the main road.

Junín
Colour map 3, grid B4

The town of Junín lies some distance south of the lake and has the somewhat desolate feel of a high puna town, bisected by the railway. There is a small underground museum in the large new plaza with memorabilia from the battle and a large handicrafts centre at the southern entrance to the town, but little else. There is a small basic hotel on the new plaza; *El Escorpión*, also on the new plaza, is a reasonable place to eat. The regional department of tourism may be contacted on T064-200550/51, or junin@mitinci.gob.pe

The **Lago Junín National Reserve** protects one of the best birdwatching sites in the central Andes where the giant coot and even flamingos may be spotted. It is easiest to visit from the village of Huayre, 5 km south of Carhuamayo, from which it is a 20-minute walk down to the lake. Fishermen are usually around to take visitors out on the lake. Carhuamayo is the best place to stay near the lake: *Gianmarco*, Maravillas 454, and *Patricia*, Tarapacá 862, are the best of several basic *hostales*. There are numerous restaurants along the main road.

Cerro de Pasco

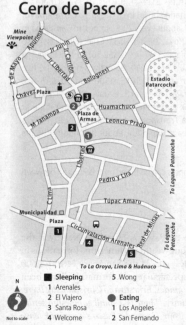

Cerro de Pasco

Sleeping
1 Arenales
2 El Viajero
3 Santa Rosa
4 Welcome
5 Wong

Eating
1 Los Angeles
2 San Fernando

This long-established mining centre is famous as the site of one of the battles of the War of Independence, on 6 December 1820, when local hero, Antonio Alvarez de Arenales, defeated Diego de O'Reilly's royalist troops. The actual battlefield is 1 km away, on Cerro Uliachin.

Phone code: 064
Colour map 3, grid B4
Population: 29, 810
Altitude: 4,330 m

Although Cerro de Pasco is not an attractive place, nevertheless the old corrugated iron buildings have a certain charm and it is very friendly. For a long time, it was known as the first settlement in South America, when the Italian explorer, Antonio Raimondi, discovered 10,000-year- old remains here. It is also interesting in that it is Peru's major mining community. Copper, zinc, lead, gold and silver are all mined here, and coal comes from the deep canyon of Goyllarisquisga, the 'place where a star fell', the highest coal mine in the world, 42 km north of Cerro de Pasco.

Central Highlands

The town is sited between Lago Patarcocha and the huge abyss of the mine above which its buildings and streets cling precariously. Not surprisingly for a place that claims to be the highest city in the world, nights are bitterly cold.

The town is a good base from which to visit the **Bosque de Piedras** of Huallay and **Lago Junín**. It is possible to connect, via Oyón, to the Cordilleras Raura and Huayhuash, and also to Churín.

Sleeping
■ *on map*
D *Wong*, Carrión 99, T721918. Modern, hot water 24 hrs, TV, clean, comfortable, friendly, attractive decorations. Recommended. **E** *Hostal Arenales*, Jr Arenales 162, near the bus station, T723088. Clean, modern, TV, friendly, hot water in the morning. **E** *Welcome*, opposite the entrance to the bus station. Some rooms without window, hot water 24 hrs, clean, friendly. **F** *El Viajero*, on the west side of the plaza, T722172. Clean, hot water morning only. **F** *Santa Rosa*, on the north side of the plaza, T722120. An old building, large, hot water all day, basic.

Eating
● *on map*
Los Angeles, Jr Libertad, near the market. Serves an excellent *menú* for US$1.50. Recommended. *San Fernando* bakery in the plaza. Opens at 0700 for first-rate hot chocolate, bread and pastries. Local specialities are trout, fried frog, *ferrocarril* (which is known elsewhere as *bistec a lo pobre*), and *maca*, the tuber, see page 512.

Festivals
Festival de La Chonguinada Cerreña takes place during the first week in **May**. On the **22-24 May** is *Semana Turística de Huarica*. On **5 Aug** is the *Virgen de Las Nieves*. In the last week of **Nov** is the *Semana Turística de Pasco*.

Transport
130 km from La Oroya by road, 8 km, 10 minutes, off the Carretera Central
All services use the large, enclosed bus station. To **Lima** there are several companies including *Paraíso Tours* at 0730 and 2100, *Carhuamayo* and *Transportes Apóstol San Pedro*, hourly 0800-1200, plus 4 departures 2030-2130, 8 hrs, US$4-5. If there are no convenient daytime buses, you could change buses in La Oroya. To **Carhuamayo, Junín** and **La Oroya**: buses leave when full, about every 20-30 mines, to Carhuamayo 1 hr, US$1; to Junín 1½ hrs, US$1; to La Oroya, 2½ hrs, US$2. Colectivos (cars) also depart with a similar frequency to all places, 1½ hrs, US$2.50, to La Oroya. To **Tarma** *Empresa Junín* at 0600 and 1500, 3 hrs, $2.50. Colectivos hourly, 1½ hrs, US$4. To **Huancayo** *Transportes Javier* at 0830, 1045, 1500 and 2015, 5 hrs, US$3.50; also *Trans Central* and *Salazar*, one each a day, US$4. To **Oyón** *Transportes Javier*, 1230, 5 hrs, US$3.50; and there is also a bus to the mine at Raura, 1100, 7 hrs, US$5. To **Yanahuanca** *Transportes Javier*, 0500, 1230, 1445, 3 hrs, US$2. To **Huánuco** buses and cars leave when full, about half hourly, 2½ hrs and 1½ hrs, US$2 and US$4 respectively.

Directory
Banks *BCP* is on Jr Bolognesi. Money changers can be found on Jr Bolognesi between the market and the Cathedral.

Around Cerro de Pasco

Huayllay
Forty kilometres southwest of Cerro de Pasco is Huayllay. Nearby is the Santuario Bosque de Piedras, with unique weathered limestone formations in the shape of a tortoise, elephant, alpaca, etc. At the Sanctuary (4,100-4,600 m), four tourist circuits through the spectacular rock formations have been laid out. ■ *US$1, but payable only if the guides, Ernesto and Christian, are there. Camping is permitted within the Sanctuary. There is a small campesino settlement nearby. Minibuses to Huallay from Cerro de Pasco's terminal leave throughout the day, about 1 hr 20 mins, US$1.50. They return until 1800-1900. The village of Huallay is 30 minutes beyond the sanctuary entrance.*

Also near Huallay are the ruins of an Inca community centre, **Bon Bón Marca**, which marks the course of a good section of Inca road, and the thermal springs of **Caleras**. Take a swimsuit; the baths are very hot and clean, ideal for a splash after a tiring day.

The Yanahuanca Valley

Sixty-five kilometres northwest of Cerro de Pasco is **Yanahuanca**, in the beautiful valley of the same name. Nearby are good **hot baths**. From the village you can reach one of the longest surviving stretches of Inca road. Two kilometres up the Yanahuanca Valley a lesser valley cuts northwards between the towering crags.

Colour map 3, grid B4

The road, its paving uneven and disturbed by countless horse and donkey convoys, leads up the smaller valley, its course sometimes shared by a stream, to the village of **Huarautambo**, about 4 km away. This village is surrounded by many pre-Inca remains. For more than 150 km the *Capaq Ñan* (the **Royal Inca road**) is not only in almost continuous existence from the Yanahuanca Valley but is actually shown on the map issued by the Instituto Geográfico Militar. The clearest stretch ends at Huari in Ancash (see under La Unión, page 518, below).

The Huallaga Valley

The Central Highway from Cerro de Pasco continues northeast another 528 km to Pucallpa, the limit of navigation for large Amazon river boats. The western part of this road (Cerro de Pasco-Huánuco) is a good paved highway. The descent along the Río Huallaga is dramatic. The road drops 2,436 m in the 100 km from Cerro de Pasco to Huánuco, and most of it is in the first 32 km. From the bleak vistas of the high ranges the road plunges below the tree line into another world of tropical beauty. The only town of any size before Huánuco is Ambo.

Huánuco

Huánuco is an attractive Andean town with an interesting market on the Upper Huallaga. The city was founded in 1539, by Gómez de Alvarado, and is one of the oldest in Peru and was originally known as 'Los Caballeros de León de Huánuco'. Its most famous son is Leoncio Prado, who refused to surrender to the Chileans at the Battle of Huamachuco in 1882 and is commemorated all over the city. There is a large main plaza fringed by enormous ficus trees, which are much more attractive than the modern cathedral. **Tourist offices** Gen Prado 716, on the Plaza de Armas. A website giving local information is www.webhuanuco.com

Phone code: 064
Colour map 3, grid B4
Population: 118,814
Altitude: 1,894 m

The two churches of **San Cristóbal** and **San Francisco** have both been much restored. The latter has some 16th century paintings. There is a natural history museum at Gen Prado 495, called **Museo de Ciencias**. It claims to have 10,000 exhibits of fauna from Peru's three regions, plus a good collection of shells and minerals. Many of the displays have multiple language signs. ■ *Mon-Fri 0900-1200, 1500-1800. Sat-Sun 1000-1200. US$0.50.*

Sights

Central Highlands

Sleeping
■ *on map*
Price codes:
see inside front cover

B *Gran Hotel Huánuco*, Jr D Beraun 775, T514222/512410. Restaurant, pool, sauna, gym, parking. Recommended. **D** *Hostal Caribe*, Huánuco 546, T513645, F513753, and adjoining it **D** *Hostal Mariño*, are large modern hotels with big rooms, bathroom and TV, as is **D** *Hostal Quintito*, 2 de Mayo 987, T512691. **D** *Cusco*, Huánuco 616, 2 blocks from the Plaza de Armas, T 513578, F514825. With bathroom, TV, friendly, cafeteria, OK. **E** *Las Vegas*, 28 de Julio 936, on Plaza de Armas, T/F512315. Small rooms, hot water, TV. Recommended. **E** *Hostal Miraflores*, Valdizan 564. Hot water, clean, TV, quiet. **F** *El Roble*, Constitución 629, T512515. Slightly cheaper without bath, clean, good value. **F** *Imperial*, Huánuco 581, T513203. With cold shower (intermittent water), reasonable value, clean and quiet.

Eating
● *on map*

La Casona de Gladys, Gen Prado 908. Good, cheap local food. *La Casona*, Ayacucho 750, overlooking Plaza Santo Domingo. Specialises in *anticuchos* and steaks. Recommended. *Pizzería Don Sancho*, Prado 645. For the best pizzas in town. There are 6 vegetarian restaurants and cafés, including at Abtao 897, 2 de Mayo 751, Prado 840, and *Govinda*, 2 de Mayo 1044, reckoned to be the best. There are several good *chifas*, especially in Beraun block 6, including the heavily decorated *Kon Wa* and *Tay Wa*. *Loockos*, Abtao 1021. An upmarket grill and burger joint. *Café Perú*, on the south side of the main plaza, is a traditional café serving good coffee, *humitas* and *tamales*. Highly recommended for breakfast. *Café Valdizan*, Valdizan y Beraun. An attractive, reasonably-priced place for breakfast or lunch. There are good bakeries in block 10 of 2 de Mayo. There are several other good value local restaurants in block 10 of 28 de Julio.

Huánuco

Central Highlands

Sleeping ■
1 Caribe
2 Cusco
3 El Roble
4 Gran Hotel Huánuco
5 Hostal Miraflores
6 Imperial
7 Las Vegas
8 Mariño
9 Quintito

Eating ●
1 Café Perú
2 Café Valdizan
3 La Casona
4 La Casona de Gladys
5 Loockos
6 Pizzería Don Sancho
7 Restaurante Vegetariano

0 metres 100
0 yards 100

On the **20-25 Jan** is the *Carnaval Huanuqueño*. On **21 Mar** is the *Festival de las* **Festivals**
Cataratas. In San Rafael, in the province of Ambo, is the festival of *El Señor de Chacos*
on **1 May**. On **3 May** is *La Cruz de Mayo*, in Huánuco. On **16 Jul**, the *Fiesta de la Virgen
del Carmen*. The *Festival de la Perricholi* is held during the last week of Jul. **12-18 Aug**
is Tourist Week in Huánuco. **15 Aug** commemorates the founding of the city. **25-27
Sep** is the *Festival del Cóndor Pasa*. **28-29 Oct** is *Fiesta del Rey y del Señor de Burgos*,
the patron of Huánuco. **25 Dec**, *Fiesta de los Negritos*.

Air From **Lima**, *Aerocóndor* (2 de Mayo 1253, T517090) Tue, Thu, Sat, 50 mins, US$70. **Transport**
There are connecting flights to **Tingo María**, **Tocache**, **Juanjui**, **Pucallpa**, **Saposoa** *Airport T513066*
and other jungle towns. Check all flight details in advance. Flights may be cancelled in
the rains or if not full.

Bus Buses to **Lima**: US$10, 8 hrs. *León de Huánuco*, Malecón Alomía Robles 821. Also
Etposa, Valdizan block 7, *Transportes El Rey*, 28 de Julio 1215 (28 de Julio 1192, La Victoria, Lima), and *Trans G & M*, Tarapacá y 28 de Julio. The majority of buses of all companies leave in the evening, 2030-2200, most also offer a bus at 0900-1000. A colectivo
to Lima, costing US$20, leaves at 0400, arriving at 1400; book the night before at Gen
Prado 607, 1 block from the plaza. Recommended.

Buses to **Cerro de Pasco**, take 3 hrs, US$2, colectivos take less than 2 hrs, US$4. All
leave when full from the roundabout, Ovalo Carhuayna, on the north side of the city,
3 km from the centre. To **Huancayo**, 6 hrs, US$5: *Turismo Central*, Tarapacá 530, at 2100.

Colectivos run to **Tingo María**, from block 1 of Prado close to Puente Calicanto,
2½ hrs, US$5. Also *Etnasa*, 3-4 hrs, US2. For **Pucallpa**, take a colectivo to Tingo María,
then a bus from there. This route has many checkpoints and robberies can occur. You
are advised to travel by day and check on the current situation regarding safety.

To **La Unión** *Transportes El Niño*, Aguilar 530, is a colectivo service, departs when
full, 5 hrs, US$7.15. This is a rough road operated by old buses of which *Transportes
Vitor*, Tarapacá 448, and *Transportes Rosario*, Tarapacá 330, 0730, 6 hrs, US$4, are the
more reliable. To **Tantamayo** *Turismo Bella*, San Martín 571, at 0630 and 0730, operate
old buses on this rough route, but are recommend by locals above *Transportes Perú*,
Tarapacá 449, 0700, 8 hrs, US$6. To **Baños** *Transportes Legionario*, Independencia
730, run buses and truck-buses on alternate days, 0830, or *Transportes Romancero*,
Tarapacá 249, 0900, 4 hrs, US$3.50.

Banks *BCP*, at Dos de Mayo 1005. **Communications** Internet: next to the Cathedral **Directory**
on the Plaza. **Post office**: 2 de Mayo on the Plaza. 0800-2000 Mon-Sat, 0800-1400 Sun.
Telefónica del Perú: at 28 de Julio 1170.

South of Huánuco

Tomaykichwa, 25 km south of Huánuco, on the edge of the Huallaga valley, is **Tomay-**
a small attractive village set among the sugar cane plantations, which once **kichwa**
supplied a substantial local aguardiente industry. It is famous as the birthplace
of 'La Perricholi'. As an 18 year old actress she rose to become the mistress of
the 62-year old Viceroy de Amat and the centre of Lima society at the end of
the 18th century. However, when he returned to Spain a few years later and
remarried, she retreated to spend the rest of her days in a convent. Her small,
recently restored, ancestral home can be visited in the village. It contains furniture and other artefacts from the 18th and 19th centuries and copies of documents relating to her life. ■ *0800-1800, US$0.25. To reach Tomaykichwa
take the Ambo colectivo that passes by Santo Domingo chuch, 20 mins, US$0.25.*

Central Highlands

West of Huánuco

Five kilometres from Huánuco on the road west to La Unión is **Kotosh** (altitude: 1,812 m), the Temple of Crossed Hands, the earliest evidence of a complex society and of pottery in Peru, dating from 2000 BC. Investigations suggest that the site was occupied for over 2,000 years. Six distinct phases of occupation have been identified the oldest of which dates back 4,000 years. It is said to be the 'oldest temple in the Americas'. There are three main temple buildings some of which have been partly reconstructed, though the original 'crossed hands' sculpture is now in the Archaeology Museum in Lima. The ruin has been sadly neglected since the original excavation in 1963. ■ *Entrance to the site is US$0.75, including a guide (in Spanish) around a marked circuit which also passes through a small botanical garden of desert plants. Beware of the vicious black flies. The site can only easily be reached by taxi, US$5 from the city centre, including a 30 min wait.*

Tantamayo
Altitude: 3,600 m
Colour map 3, grid B3

Tantamayo 50 km beyond the turn off to La Unión is a farming village surrounded by pre-Columbian ruins from the **Yarowillca** culture.

Japallan is perhaps the most scenically sited, guarding the entrance to the valley leading from the spectacular Marañón canyon. To get there, cross the river from Tantamayo and walk west to San Pedro de Pariarca. At the start of the village take the path to the right to Pariash (Upper Pariarca), and head for the ruins silhouetted on a ridge.

The ruins of **Selinin** are just above Pariash. The most elaborate ruins are **Piruru** and **Susupillu**. Piruru was occupied continuously for 1,700 years, from 3000 BC as a ceremonial, and later ceramics, centre. Both sites have high-rise stone dwellings. To reach Susupillu head northeast through the tiny village of La Florida. There are other ruins further afield.

■ *All the above mentioned ruins are visible from Tantamayo and can be reached on foot in about three to four hours; guides are available to visit the sites. The walks to the ruins are arduous; take warm clothing, a hat and suntan lotion. The scenery is stunning. Pictures and information on the sites are available from Huánuco post office.* In Tantamayo there are four basic hotels and one restaurant, *Ortega*, on the corner of the plaza. For details of transport, see under Huánuco, page 517.

La Unión
Colour map 3, grid B3

From Huánuco, a spectacular but very poor dirt road, impassable at times in the wet season, leads all the way to La Unión, capital of Dos de Mayo district. From Huánuco it climbs out of the Higueras valley to **La Corona del Inca** (the 'Crown of the Inca'), also known as Lacsahuarina, meaning 'Two Princesses' in Quechua. This distinctive rock formation is at the pass before the descent into the upper canyon of the Río Marañón. The route then follows the Marañón to its confluence with the Río Vizcarra. La Unión is a very friendly, fast-developing town which straddles the Río Vizcarra. Electricity can be a problem and it gets very cold at night. There are good **hot baths** at Tauripampa, 5 km up the Vizcarra valley, US$0.50 per person. A good section of the **Royal Inca highway**, just upriver from the baths on the north side of the valley, runs on towards Huari.

Sleeping and eating F *Hostal Gran Turístico*, Comercio 1196, has a once-grand reception area and a nice garden, rooms are small but clean, some have private bathrooms. Helpful owners provide some information about visiting Huánuco Viejo. F *Hostal Picaflor*, 2 de Mayo 840, is best of the basic ones, with shared bathroom, but wooden partitions divide up all the rooms. *Restaurante El Danubio*, near the market. Good home cooking. *Espiga de Oro*, 2 de Mayo 330, is a good bakery for breakfast. *Chifa Khon Wa*, 2 de Mayo 611, is the best in town serving large portions of authentic 'chifa' food. *Vizcarra*, beside the old bridge over the river, is the best of the local restaurants.

To **Huánuco**: *Transportes El Niño*, Jr Comercio 12, T515952, is a colectivo service, cars leave when full, 5 hrs, US$7.15; *Transportes Vitor* and *Rosario* buses leave at 0630, 5-6 hrs, US$4. To **Tantamayo**: several combis and buses daily, 5-6 hrs, US$4. However, it may be easier to take a combi first to Tingo Chico at the Vizcarra/ Marañón confluence, 1 hr, US$0.75, and then wait for the more frequent bus services from Huánuco to Tantamayo To **Huallanca**: combis leave from the market, about half hourly, when full and follow the attractive Vizcarra valley, 1 hr, US$0.75.

Transport

On the pampa above La Unión are the Inca ruins of Huánuco Viejo, a great temple-fortress with residential quarters, 2½ hours' walk from the town. To get there, take the very steep path starting behind the market and climb towards the cross, which is at the edge of a plateau (this takes one hour). Continue straight through the village on the wide path. Note that, though the locals are friendly, some of their dogs are not always well disposed to strangers. The views of the pampa, surrounded on all sides by mountains, are beautiful. Seemingly at the foot of a mountain, in front and to your right, is a silvery metallic roof of a little chapel, behind which are the ruins, 4 km from the plateau's edge.

Huánuco Viejo was a major Inca settlement on the royal highway from Cusco to Quito. The site has examples of very fine Inca stonework comparable with anything to be seen in Cusco. This includes an *usnu*, measuring 30 m by 50 m and 4 m high, encased with superb stone blocks and carved monkeys adorning the entrance and at one corner. An *usnu* was a ceremonial or judging platform, though its exact function is still uncertain. The *usnu* is surrounded by a huge central plaza, 547 m by 370 m, which, possibly, had to accommodate huge herds of animals. On the east side of the plaza are two *kallankas* (barracks), 84 m and 75 m long, nearly 10 m wide and two-storeys high, with thatched roofs. Running from the *kallankas* down to the royal Inca quarters and Inca bath are a series of six fine stone gateways adorned with beautifully carved pumas. Illa Tupac used the site as his stronghold from which he mounted resistance against the Spanish from 1536 until at least 1542. The site was then largely forgotten by the outside world and left untouched until the mid-20th century.

■ *To enter the ruins costs US$1.50; a local farmer may be available to act as a guide (US$1). Allow at least 1 hr to visit the main part of the site and at least 2 hrs for the whole site, which covers over 2 sq km and contains the remains of over 3,500 structures. Combis run from La Unión, about hourly, to El Cruce from where it is a 30-min walk to the site. The last combi down leaves El Cruce at 1800. You should take warm clothing and be prepared for some violent thunderstorms.*

Huánuco Viejo

A fine Inca road runs south from the site to the town of Baños. A major festival, Fiesta del Sol, is held at the site on 27 July each year, but lodgings in the town are almost impossible to find at this time

It is possible to get to the **Callejón de Huaylas** from here. La Unión-Huaraz direct can be done with *El Rápido*, 6 hours, US$4.50, but most transport does the route La Unión-Chiquián-Lima. Change buses in **Chiquián** (see page 335) or take a colectivo to **Huallanca** and from there take *El Rápido* or *Yungay Express* buses to Huáraz. Often known as Huallanca (Huánuco) to distinguish it from the settlement of the same name in the Cañon del Pato, this is an attractive, unspoilt small town set between four hills in the Vizcarra valley. Large-scale mining projects in the area are likely to bring rapid change to the town and are polluting the Río Vizcarra. **D** *Hotel Milán*, 28 de Julio 107,

Huánuco to Huaraz

Colour map 3, grid B3

Check local political conditions before taking this route and only travel by day

modern, TV and hot water in all rooms, best in town. **F** *Hostal Yesica*, L Prado 507, hot water, shared bathroom, the best of the basic ones. The restaurant in *Hotel Milán* is good and serves trout caught in lakes high above the town. *El Norteño*, Comercio 441, is also popular and there is a *chifa*. Combis leave when full about half hourly, from the corner of Comercio y 28 de Julio for La Unión, one hour, US$0.75. The road follows the attractive and, in places, very narrow Vizcarra gorge for most of the journey.

For cyclists, the convenient stopping places on the route Huánuco-Huaraz are: **Chavinillo** (74 km from Huánuco, lodging, restaurant, police station), **Tingo Chico** (37 km, food and lodging), **Pachas** (14 km, food and lodging), **La Unión** (17 km – see above), **Huallanca** (21 km – see above), **Mina Huanzala** (13 km, police station), then series of passes, reaching up to 4,800 m, before **Carpa** (57 km from Huanzala, there is a restaurant 17 km before Carpa), then **Pachacoto** (14 km, restaurant), **Catac** and Huaraz.

There are vigilante forces made up of local people in this area. If you're camping wild they will come to check that you are not a threat. This can be nerve-wracking at night, but if you're friendly you'll have no problems. Occasional road blocks have been reported on the route to Huánuco.

You can hike to the Cordillera Raura (see page 367) from **Laguna Lauricocha**. To reach the lake from La Unión take a camioneta to **Baños**, then take another camioneta from there to **Antacolpa**. It's half a day's walk to the lake from here. In 1959, caves were discovered by the lake with 9,500 year-old human remains and some paintings. This is where the Río Marañón rises, eventually becoming the Ucayali and then Amazon rivers, before spilling into the Atlantic Ocean, 5,800 km away to the east.

The Amazon Basin

Introducing the Amazon Basin

The immense Amazon Basin covers a staggering 4,000,000 square kilometres, an area roughly equivalent to three quarters the size of the United States. But despite the fact that 60% of Peru is covered by this green carpet of jungle, less than 6% of its population lives here. The lack of population integration with the rest of the country and the difficulty presented in getting around means that much of Peru's rainforest is still intact. The Peruvian jungles are home to a diversity of life unequalled anywhere on Earth.

It is this great diversity which makes the Amazon Basin a paradise for nature lovers, be they scientists or simply curious amateurs. This part of Peru contains some 10,000,000 living

species, including 2,000 species of fish and 300 mammals. It also has over 10% of the world's 8,600 bird species and, together with the adjacent Andean foothills, 4,000 butterfly species. This incredible biological diversity, however, brings with it an acute ecological fragility. Ecologists consider the Amazon rainforest to be the lungs of the earth – the Amazon Basin produces 20% of the Earth's oxygen – and any fundamental change in its constitution, or indeed its disappearance, could have disastrous effects for our future on this planet.

The two major tourist areas in the Peruvian Amazon Basin are the northern and southern jungles. They share many characteristics, but the main difference is that the northern tourist area is actually based on the River Amazon itself with, at its centre, a sizeable city, **Iquitos**. Although it has lost its rubber-boom dynamism, Iquitos is still at the heart of life on the river. There are jungle lodges upstream and down, each with its own speciality and level of comfort, but none more than half a day away by fast boat. To get right into the wilds, head for Peru's largest national reserve, **Pacaya-Samiria**, accessed by boat from Iquitos or the little town of Lagunas. In the south, the **Manu Biosphere Reserve** and **Tambopata National Park** are also far removed from the modern world. Most of Manu, in fact, is off limits to tourists, but those parts where visitors are allowed offer unparalleled opportunities for wildlife spotting. Parts of Tambopata, too, are remote and pristine, sharing with Manu such highlights as macaw clay licks and birdwatching on undisturbed lakes. Many lodges in this area are close to the river port of Puerto Maldonado and include local communities as part of the jungle experience.

> **Things to do in the Amazon Basin**
>
> · In Iquitos, amid the buzz of a thousand motorcycle taxis, look at the **Iron House**, or any other old mansion, and try to imagine the days of the rubber barons, when this city was more like Paris than Lima, page 536.
> · In Manu or Tambopata, make an early start to visit a *collpa* (**macaw lick**) to see the multitude of macaws and parrots getting their essential minerals: clouds of green and splashes of brilliance on the brown cliffs, pages 546 and 558.
> · Track the pink and grey **river dolphins**. If you find a school, there is no finer sight than these graceful creatures inspecting your boat, or rising from the river as they chase the current in mid-stream, pages 528 and 533.
> · Watch the bird and animal life in the **forest canopy** at first, or last light from a high-level walkway or tree-hugging tower, page 540.
> · At the end of the day, go outside and marvel at the **night sky** with its shooting stars and the fireflies in the bushes. Listen to the wild night music.

The Northern Jungle

Standing on the banks of the Amazon itself, in the northeastern corner of the country, is the city of Iquitos, made famous during the rubber boom of the late 19th century and now the main tourist attraction in this part of the Peruvian jungle. Iquitos stands in splendid isolation, accessible only by air or river, and still retains something of its frontier feel. Further south, the region's second city, Pucallpa, can be reached by road from the Central Andes.

Although this route is reported to be relatively free from terrorism, robberies do occur and it is advisable to travel only by day

The overland route from the Central Andes to Pucallpa runs from Huánuco east to Tingo María, and gives the first views of the vast green carpet of jungle. Beyond Huánuco the road begins a sharp climb to the heights of Carpish (3,023 m). A descent of 58 km brings it to the Huallaga river again; it then continues along the river to Tingo María. The road is paved from Huánuco to Tingo María, including a tunnel through the Carpish hills. Landslides along this section are frequent and construction work causes delays.

Tingo María

Phone code: 064
Colour map 3,
grid A4
Population: 20,560
Altitude: 655m

Tingo María is on the middle Huallaga, in the *Ceja de Montaña*, or edge (literally, eyebrow) of the mountains. The climate here is tropical, with an annual rainfall of 2,642 mm. (The town can be isolated for days in the rainy season.) The altitude, however, prevents the climate from being oppressive: the maximum temperature is 34ºC, minimum 18ºC, with a relative humidity of 77.5%. The Cordillera Azul, the front range of the Andes, covered with jungle-like vegetation to its top, separates it from the jungle lowlands to the east. The mountain which can be seen from all over the town is called **La Bella Durmiente**, the Sleeping Beauty, which is part of the 18,000-ha **Parque Nacional de Tingo María** (the second national park created in Peru). ■ *US$1.75. A mototaxi to the entrance costs US$0.60.*

The meeting here of Sierra and Selva makes the landscape extremely striking. Bananas, sugar cane, cocoa, rubber, tea and coffee are grown. The main crop of the area, though, is coca, grown on the *chacras* (smallholdings) in the countryside, and sold legitimately (and otherwise) in Tingo María.

The **tourist office** is on the northwest side of Plaza de Armas, in the municipal building. The staff are friendly and have lots of information on nearby attractions. They also sell T-shirts with pictures of local views (US$3.45).

NB Watch out for gangs of thieves around the buses and do not leave luggage on the bus if you get off. Note that this is a main narco-trafficking centre and although the town itself is generally safe, it is not safe to leave it at night. Also do not stray from the main routes, as some of the local population are suspicious of foreign visitors.

On a rough road, 6½ km from Tingo, is a fascinating cave, the **Cueva de las Lechuzas**, also in the national park. There are many oilbirds in the cave and parakeets near the entrance. ■ *Take a motorcycle-taxi from town, US$1.75. It's US$0.45 for the ferry to cross the Río Monzón just before the cave and entry to the cave is US$0.90. Take a torch, and do not wear open shoes. The cave can be reached by boat when the river is high.*

Sights

The small gorge known as **Cueva de las Pavas**, is 1 km from Tingo. It is good for swimming. **El Velo de las Ninfas** is a magnificent waterfall set in beautiful jungle, with lagoons where you can swim. Ten kilometres away, on the Huánuco road, are the **Cuevas de Tambillo**, with beautiful waterfalls and pools for swimming.

A small **university** outside the town, beyond the *Hotel Madera Verde (ex-Turistas)*, has a little **museum-cum-zoo**, with animals native to the area, and botanical gardens in the town. ■ *Entrance is free but a small tip would help.*

Tingo María

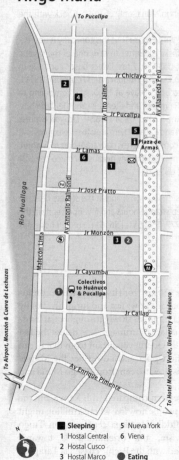

B *Madera Verde*, Av Universitaria s/n, a way out of town on the road to Huánuco, near the University, T/F561800/562047, F562774 (in Lima Jr Colina 327, Miraflores, T445 4024, F445 9005), maverde@terra.com.pe Several chalets set in beautiful surroundings, with and without bathroom, restaurant, swimming pool. **E** *Hostal Marco Antonio*, Jr Monzón 364, T562201. Quiet, restaurant of the same name next door. **E** *Nueva York*, Av Alameda Perú 553, T562406. With bath and TV, cheaper without, hot water, restaurant, laundry, good value. **F** *Hostal Central*, Av Tito Jaime 440. Central, as the names suggests, OK. **F** *La Cabaña*, Raimondi 600 block. Fairly clean, good restaurant. **F** *Viena*, Jr Lamas. With bathroom, good value, clean. **G** *Hostal Cusco*, Raimondi 671. Basic, but also very cheap.

Sleeping
■ *on map*
Price codes:
see inside front cover

Hotels are often fully booked

Amazon Basin

▶▶ The mighty Amazon

The principal means of communication in the jungle is by its many rivers, the most important of which is the Amazon, the longest river in the world. The Amazon rises high up in the Andes as the Marañón, then joins the Ucayali and winds it way east to disgorge itself finally into the Atlantic, over 6,000 km from its source. At its mouth, the Amazon is 300 km wide. This mighty waterway was so named by the Spaniard Francisco de Orellana, during his epic voyage in 1542, owing to an encounter with a hostile, long-haired indigenous group which he took to be the fearsome women warriors of Greek legend.

Eating
● *on map*

El Antojito 2, Jr Chiclayo 458. Good local food. *Girasol*, Av Raimondi 253, T562065. Chicken, burgers, cakes and fruit juices.

Tours

Tingo María Travel Tours, Av Raimondi 460, T562501. For local excursions.

Transport

Air There are no regular flights to/from Tingo María, only charters. Check with the tourist office for any departures.

Bus To **Huánuco**, 119 km, 3-4 hrs, US$2 with *Etnasa* (but this company is not recommended because of theft and drug-trafficking). Better to take one of the several micros daily, US$2 per seat, and colectivos, US$3.50, 2 hrs. Direct buses continue to Lima, 12 hrs, with *Trans Rey*, US$15 *bus cama*, *León de Huánuco* and *Transmar*, US$11. From Lima to Tingo María, *León de Huánuco* buses leave at 1900, so if continuing to Pucallpa, there is time to grab breakfast on Raimondi and then take another *León* bus, or a colectivo onwards. To **Pucallpa**, 255 km, 12 hrs, US$4.30-8.50. *Ucayali Express* colectivos leave from the corner of Raimondi and Callao. There are other colectivos and taxis, which all leave in the early morning in convoy. There is daily transport to **Juanjui**, 340 km, 15-20 hrs, US$9. This is not a recommended journey because of narco-terrorist activity. **Tarapoto** is a further 145 km; 4 hrs, US$2.

Directory

Communications Internet: several places on Raimondi and in the streets near the Plaza de Armas, fast and cheap but they keep strange hours and few open early in the morning. **Telephone:** *Catel*, Av Raimondi 272, T562551, F561611. For all phone, fax and related services, internet also.

North to Yurimaguas

*Colour map 1,
grid C5*

The Río Huallaga winds northwards for 930 km from its source to the confluence with the Marañón. The Upper Huallaga flows fast and furiously, but by the time it becomes the Lower Huallaga it moves slowly through a flat landscape. The main port of the Lower Huallaga, Yurimaguas, is below the last rapids and only 150 m above the Atlantic Ocean, yet distant from that ocean by over a month's voyage. Between the Upper and Lower lies the Middle Huallaga: that third of the river which is downstream from Tingo María and upstream from Yurimaguas.

The valleys, ridges and plateaux have been compared with Kenya, but the area is so isolated that less than 100,000 people now live where a million might flourish. The southern part of the Middle Huallaga centres upon Tingo María. Down-river, beyond Bellavista, the orientation is towards **Yurimaguas**, which is connected by road with the Pacific coast, via Tarapoto and Moyobamba (see page 473).

Lope de Aguirre

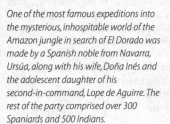

One of the most famous expeditions into the mysterious, inhospitable world of the Amazon jungle in search of El Dorado was made by a Spanish noble from Navarra, Ursúa, along with his wife, Doña Inés and the adolescent daughter of his second-in-command, Lope de Aguirre. The rest of the party comprised over 300 Spaniards and 500 Indians.

Leaving Lima in 1560, his party crossed the Andean cordillera before penetrating the dense rainforest and navigating the Huallaga river. The journey, however, was cut short for Ursúa one night when he was murdered by the mutinous Lope de Aguirre, whose loyalty to the Spanish Crown was weakening as he felt that he had not

been adequately compensated for his heroic exploits and hardship.

Lope de Aguirre took command of the group and resolved to punish any signs of loyalty to the Spanish Crown by death. He kept true to his threat, killing Doña Inés, on the pretext that her bed could no longer be supported by the deteriorating ship. He even killed his own daughter to prevent her falling into the hands of an Amazon tribe.

Despite the decimation of the expedition group, Lope de Aguirre's lust for gold drove him on down the Amazon, turning off down the Río Negro and Orinoco, before reaching the Atlantic. It is an exciting, if infamous tale, well dramatized by German director, Werner Herzog, in the film, "Aguirre, Wrath of God".

At **Tulumayo**, soon after leaving Tingo María, a road runs north down the Huallaga past **La Morada**, successfully colonized by people from Lima's slums, to **Aucayacu** and **Tocache**, which has an airport. The road has been pushed north from Tocache to join another built south from Tarapoto and has now been joined at Tarapoto to the Olmos-Bagua-Yurimaguas Transandean Highway to the coast at Chiclayo. The road is paved to 20 km past Aucayacu, thereafter it is gravel.

Sleeping

In Aucayacu E *Hotel Monte Carlo*, with bathroom, and one other hotel. Both are poor. **In Tocache** F *Hostal San Martín*; and F *Hostal Sucre*.

Transport

Air A small plane flies between Tocache and Juanjui.

Bus Colectivos run from Tingo María to **Tocache** US$13, 4½ hrs; or bus US$9.50, 6 hrs. **Tarapoto**-Tocache, US$7.50 by colectivo. Colectivos and taxis run from Tocache to **Yurimaguas**. A daily camioneta runs from Tarapoto to Yurimaguas, US$7-9, 6-8 hrs. The **Juanjui**-Tocache road has 5 bridges, but the last one across the Huallaga, just before Juanjui, was washed away in 1983 to be replaced by an efficient ferry; it costs US$9.20 per vehicle. Juanjui-Tarapoto by colectivo US$12.50.

River For the river journey, start early if you do not wish to spend a night at the river village of **Sión**. There are no facilities, but the nights are not cold. The river runs through marvellous jungle with high cliffs. Boats sometimes run aground in the river near Sión. Take food and bottled water. Balsa wood rafts also ply this stretch of river.

Yurimaguas

As one reader, Caroline Kenworthy, writes: "Yurimaguas is a wonderful town, all set up for tourism; it even has a tourist protection officer. Now all it needs is tourists." The town has a fine **church** of the Passionist Fathers, based on the Cathedral of Burgos, in Spain. A colourful **market** is held from 0600-0800, full of fruit and animals. **Tourist information** is available from the Consejo Regional building on the main plaza.

Colour map 1, grid B5
Population: 25,700

Amazon Basin

There are some interesting excursions in the area, including to the gorge of **Shanusi** and the lakes of **Mushuyacu** and **Sanango**. To organize tours, go to the Municipalidad and ask for Jorge or Samuel (who speaks English). They can take visitors to meet people in the region, for instance the villages of **Balsapuerto** (70 km west) and **Puerto Libre**. Mopeds can be hired for US$2.35 per hour, including fuel.

NB The Yurimaguas region was affected by guerrilla activity and anti-narcotics operations in the recent past. Seek the latest advice before going off the beaten track. A good contact is Luis Dalman. South American Explorers in Lima has his address and telephone number.

Sleeping **E** *Hostal Residencial El Naranjo*, Arica 318, T351560/352650, lillian@olva.com.pe or lillianarteaga@hotmail.com 'The best in town', excellent value, friendly, clean, with good restaurant. Recommended. **E** *Leo's Palace*, Plaza de Armas 104-6. Good, friendly, reasonably priced, restaurant. **F** *Camus*, Manco Cápac 201. No sign, but it does exist.

Transport **Bus** To/from **Tarapoto** (a beautiful journey), several companies, 5-6 hrs, US$3.45, same price by combi; in a camioneta it costs US$5.75 up front, US$2.90 in the back. Cars charge US$7.20.

River By ferry to **Iquitos** takes 2 days and 2 nights (upstream takes longer), take a hammock, mosquito net, bottled water – or purification, fruit and drinks. There are police inspections at each end of the trip. Fares usually include meals, US$17 for one bunk in a cabin. *Eduardo* company is best. To buy a hammock costs US$5.75-8.50 in Yurimaguas, on C Jáuregui (make sure to buy string to tie it up with). Ask at the harbour for smaller boats, which can take up to 10 days.

Directory **Banks**: *Interbank* or travel agents; poor rates. **Communications** **Internet**: on Plaza de Armas, US$1.70 per hr.

Lagunas
Colour map 1, grid B6
The river journey to Iquitos can be broken at Lagunas, 12 hours from Yurimaguas. You can ask the local people to take you on a canoe trip into the jungle where there's a good chance of seeing caiman (alligators), monkeys and a variety of birds, but only on trips of four days or so.

Sleeping and transport **F** *Hostal La Sombra*, Jr Vásquez 1121. Shared bathroom, basic, friendly, good food. The *Constante* sails from Yurimaguas to Lagunas 2-3 times a week (US$4.50). From there connections are difficult to **Iquitos**. Times of boats to Iquitos and **Pucallpa** are very vague; you should confirm departures the day before by radio. The boats pass by the villages of **Castilla** and **Nauta**, where the Huallaga joins the Ucayali and becomes the Amazon.

Jungle trips

Pacaya-
Samiria
Reserve
There are good jungle trips from Lagunas to the Pacaya-Samiria Reserve, at 2,080,000 ha, the country's largest such protected area. It is bounded by the rivers Marañón and Ucuyali (and a tributary of it, the Canal de Puinahua), narrowing to their confluence near the town of Nauta. The reserve's waterways, lakes and swamps provide habitat for mammals such as the manatee, tapir, river dolphins and giant river otters, reptile like black cayman, boas and the *charapa* (yellow-headed river turtle), 193 species of fish and some 330 bird species. Many of the animals found here are in danger of extinction. Trips are mostly on the river, sleeping in hammocks, and include fishing. To make the most of the park, a trip with a minimum of five days is recommended.

Amazon Basin

Admission Officially, you need a permit from INRENA in Lima and it is essential to visit INRENA in Lima or Iquitos before going to Pacaya-Samiria. The main part of the reserve is off-limits to tourists, who may only be taken to forest surrounding the reserve. Some guides, however, penetrate Pacaya-Samiria illegally: if caught, you may face stiff penalties for trespassing. You must make sure that your tour will not do anything that will endanger the flora and fauna in the reserve. Above all, do not join a tour that involves living off the land. Park entry costs US$20. Before entering the Reserve you pass through a village where you must pay US$4.50. When arranging a guide and boat from Lagunas, make sure you take enough fuel for the boat. Take bottled water, or purifier, and mosquito repellent.

Luiz and Edinson are recommended guides; ask for them at the *Hostal La Sombra* in Lagunas. Guides charge US$15 per day. Juan Huaycama, at Jáuregui 689, is highly recommended.

Trips to Pacaya-Samiria can also be arranged in Iquitos, for example with *Muyuna* See page 541 (whose lodge is only 80 km from the reserve) and *Paseos Amazónicos*. Expeditions must be booked in advance, all equipment and food is provided.

Tingo María to Pucallpa

From Tingo María to the end of the road at Pucallpa is 255 km, with a climb *Colour map 3,* over the watershed – the Cordillera Azul – between the Huallaga and Ucayali *grid A4/5* rivers. The road is in poor shape for most of the journey, but paving of the last stretch to Pucallpa is in progress. It is affected by mud and landslides in the rainy season. Apart from it being insecure, another reason not to travel this road at night is that you will miss the tremendous views as you go from the high jungle to the Amazon Basin. Sit on the right side of the bus to appreciate the landscape and the hairpin bends and sheer drops.

When the road was being surveyed it was thought that the lowest pass over the Cordillera Azul was over 3,650 m high, but an old document stating that a Father Abad had found a pass through these mountains in 1757 was rediscovered, and the road now goes through the pass of Father Abad, a gigantic gap 4-km long and 2,000 m deep. At the top of the pass is a Peruvian Customs house; the jungle land to the east is a free zone. Concrete stairs and metal handrails have been built for viewing the waterfalls. Coming down from the pass the road bed is along the floor of a magnificent canyon, the Boquerón Abad. It is a beautiful trip through luxuriant jungle and ferns and sheer walls of bare rock punctuated by occasional waterfalls plunging into the roaring torrent below.

East of the foot of the pass the all-weather road goes over the flat pampa, with few bends, to the village of **Aguaytía**. Here you'll find a narcotics police outpost, gasoline, accommodation in the *Hostal San Antonio* (**F**, clean), and two restaurants. From Aguaytía the road continues for 161 km to Pucallpa – five hours by bus. There is a gas station three hours before Pucallpa.

Pucallpa

The capital of the Department of Ucayali is a rapidly expanding jungle town on *Phone code: 064* *the Río Ucayali, navigable by vessels of 3,000 tons from Iquitos, 533 nautical* *Colour map 3, grid B5* *miles away. The town's newer sections have paved streets, sewers and lights, but* *Population: 400,000* *much of the frontier atmosphere still exists. Pucallpa is notable for defying the traditional rules of Spanish pronunciation – the double 'l' is pronounced as one.*

Ins and outs

Getting there   The airport is to the northwest of the town. Bus from the airport to town, US$0.25; *motos* US$1; taxi US$2-3. The floating dock at La Hoyada is about 5 km northeast of the town. Buses, colectivos and mototaxis go there. In the dry season boats dock at Pucallpillo; take a taxi for US$3, or a mototaxi for US$0.75.

Getting around   Most of the accommodation is not far from the Plaza de Armas. The office of *Ucayali Express* as well as the depot for buses to Yarinacocha are also in this quarter. You will probably want to take a taxi or mototaxi to visit the Museo Regional. **Tourist office** *Dirección Regional de Turismo* Jr 2 de Mayo 111, T571303/575110, ucayali@mincetur.gob.pe, Mon-Fri 0730-1300, 1330-1515. Information is also be available at *CTAR-Ucayali* (Consejo Transitorio de Administración Regional), Raymondi 220, T575018, oppto-ucayali@pres.gob.pe

Climate   The climate is tropical. The dry season is during Jul-Aug and the rainy seasons are Oct-Nov and Feb-Mar. The town is hot and dusty between Jun and Nov and muddy from Dec-May.

Sights

There is narcotics activity in the area. The city itself is safe enough to visit, but don't travel at night

Parque Natural Pucallpa is a zoo on the left on the road to the airport. You can see many jungle animals and most of the cages are OK, though some are inadequate. The zoo is set in parkland with a small lake. ■ *US$0.90.* **Museo Regional** has some good examples of Shibipo ceramics, as well as some delightful pickled snakes and other reptiles. ■ *0800-1200 and 1600-1800. US$0.90. Jr Inmaculada 999.*

The floating ports of **La Hoyada** and **Puerto Italia** are about 5 km away and worth a visit to see the canoe traffic and open-air **markets**. Both are reached by dirt roads. (When river levels are low, boats leave from a different port, **Pucallpillo**.) The economy of the area includes sawmills, plywood factories, a paper mill, oil refinery, fishing and boat building; timber is trucked out to the highlands and the coast. Large discoveries of oil and gas are being explored, and gold mining is underway nearby. The *Ganso Azul* oilfield has a 75-km pipeline to the Pucallpa refinery.

Essentials

Sleeping
■ *on map*
Price codes: see inside front cover

AL *Sol del Oriente*, Av San Martín 552, T575154, T/F575510, www.dhperu.net/eng/pucallpa.html Price includes breakfast and taxes. With bathroom, pool and good restaurant. The hotel also has a minizoo. **A** *Divina Montaña*, 14 km outside Pucallpa on the road to Tingo María, T571276. Bungalows for rent, restaurant, swimming pool, sports facilities. **D** *Hostal Arequipa*, Jr Progreso 573, T571348. With bathroom, good, clean. **D** *Mercedes*, Raimondi 601, T575120. Good, but noisy with good bar and restaurant attached, swimming pool. **E** *Barbtur*, Raimondi 670, T572532. With bathroom, **F** without, friendly, clean, good beds. **E** *Hostal Komby*, Ucayali 360, T571184. Comfortable, swimming pool, excellent value. **E** *Hostal Sun*, Ucayali 380, next to *Komby*. With bathroom, cheaper without, clean, good value.

Eating
■ *on map*

El Alamo, Carretera Yarinacocha 2650, T571510. Good food. *BCP Jugos Don José*, Jr Ucayali 661, T571829. One of the oldest in town. *Billy's Place*, on Arica, on the street east of Jr Mcal Cáceres. A decent bar run by an American called Rick (Billy is his pet jaguar). He only sells beer, has TV and pinball. All the locals know it; the area is very dark late at night.

Typical dishes: *patarashca* is barbecued fish wrapped in *bijao* leaves. *Zarapatera*, a spicy soup made with turtle meat served in its shell, but consider the ecological implications of this dish. *Chonta salad* is made with palm shoots, and *juanes*, is rice with chicken or fish served during the San Juan festival. *Tacutacu* is banana and sauces. The local beer 'San Juan' is good.

The city hosts its *Fiesta de San Juan* on **24 Jun**, and during **5-20 Oct** is Pucallpa's **Festivals** *Aniversario Political* and the Ucayali regional fair.

Many Shibipo women carry and sell their products around Pucallpa and Yarinacocha. **Shopping** *Artesanías La Selva*, Jr Tarapacá 868, has a reasonable selection of indigenous craftwork. For local wood carvings visit the workshop of sculptor, *Agustín Rivas*, at Jr Tarapacá 861, above a small restaurant whose entrance is at No 863 (ask for it). His work is made from huge tree roots and when Sr Rivas is in town he is happy to chat over a cup of tea. His family runs the gallery when he is in Iquitos.

Laser Viajes y Turismo, Raimondi 470, T571120, T/F573776. Recommended as helpful **Tour operators** for planning a jungle trip. Jungle tours are not very well-organized. You can negotiate a price for a group with the boatmen on the waterfront. Expect to pay around US$30 per day per person and use only accredited guides. Ask the tourist information office (see Getting around) for advice about visiting the Río Piski area, which has authentic Shibipo culture. There is no passenger traffic, so the trip may be expensive.

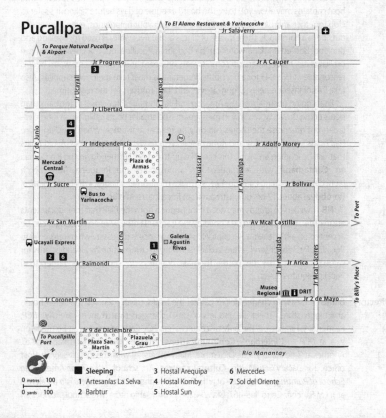

Pucallpa

Sleeping	3 Hostal Arequipa	6 Mercedes
1 Artesanías La Selva	4 Hostal Komby	7 Sol del Oriente
2 Barbtur	5 Hostal Sun	

0 metres 100
0 yards 100

Amazon Basin

Transport **Air** Daily flights to/from **Lima** (1 hr), with *Aero Continente/Aviandina* (Jr 7 de Junio 861, T575643) and with *Tans* (Arica 500, T591852). *Aviandina* and *Tans*' flights continue to/proceed from **Iquitos**. To **Atalaya** (Mon, Wed, Sat with *Omadina*, *Aero Andino*, US$56.

Bus There are regular bus services to **Lima**, 812 km, 18-20 hrs (longer in the rainy season, Nov-Mar), US$11. To **Tingo María**, 255 km, 7-9 hrs, US$4.30-8.50, combis leave at 0600, 0700 and 0800 with *Ucayali Express* (7 de Junio y San Martín). All buses have police guard and go in convoy. For road conditions see above. Take blankets as the crossing of the Cordillera at night is bitterly cold.

River To **Atalaya**, Mon, Tue, Wed, 3-4 days, US$17. To **Iquitos**The trip takes 3-4 days, and costs US$17.50 per person for hammock space, or US$20 for a bed in a cabin. See Essentials, page 79 for general hints on river travel.

You can go to Puerto La Hoyada, Puerto Italia and Pucallpillo to find boats going to Iquitos. A mototaxi to any of the ports costs US$0.75 from the Plaza de Armas, but strap all your bags on tight as things can fall off on the bumpy roads. Pucallpillo is the low water port, but there are times when all ports are in use. The large boats to Iquitos and beyond will all be docked at one of them, so you must ask around. The Capitanía on the waterfront may give you information about sailings, but this is seldom reliable. There are usually 2-3 boats in port at any given time. Quality varies, so talking to the staff can help you get a feel for the atmosphere aboard. Departure times are marked on chalk boards on the deck. Schedules seem to change almost hourly, which means that you need to keep a close eye on developments and for Peruvians in the know starting to embark.

Do not pay for your trip before you board the vessel, and only pay the captain. Some boat captains may allow you to live on board a couple of days before sailing. It's safer to club together and pay for a cabin in which to lock your belongings, even if you sleep outside in a hammock. There's a risk of illness as the river water is used for cooking and drinking. Bottled drinking water can be bought in Pucallpa, but not cheaply. You can buy crackers, toilet paper and some sweets on board at inflated prices; warm beer is reasonable at US$1.45 for a big bottle. Vegetarians must take their own supplies. Also take lots of insect repellent, long sleeves and long trousers for the night-time.

Boats going upstream on the Amazon and its tributaries stay closer to the bank than boats going down, which stay in mid-stream. The smaller boats call often at jungle villages, but otherwise the shores can only be seen at a distance. When conditions are bad boats leave in convoy and none may leave afterwards for 4-6 weeks. Avoid boats that will be loading en route, this can take up to 6 days. Further down the Río Ucayali are **Contamaná**, with a frontier-town atmosphere, and **Requena**, from which launches sail to Iquitos, taking 12 hrs. Unlike most other villages, which are *mestizo*, **Roroboya**, about 12 hrs downstream from Pucallpa, is Shipibo Indian.

NB Travellers to Iquitos may need confirmation from the PNP that their documents are in order, this must then be signed by the Capitanía otherwise no passenger can be accepted on a trip leaving Pucallpa. No such clearance is necessary when returning to Pucallpa. Passenger services are in decline owing to competition by air and priority for cargo traffic. It may be better to make journeys in short stages rather than Pucallpa-Iquitos direct.

Directory **Banks** It is easy to change dollars cash at the banks, travel agencies, the better hotels and bigger stores. There are also lots of street changers (watch them carefully). *BCP*, Raimondi y Tarapacá, is the only place to change TCs. Cash advances can be made on Visa at *BCP* and *Interbank*. **Communications** Internet: *Gibernet*, Jr Tarapacá 726. Another at 7 de Junio y 9 de Diciembre. Many others, all with cheap, fast service. **Post office**: Tarapacá y San Martín. **Cultural centres** Art school: *Usko Ayar Amazonian School of Painting*, in the house of artist Pablo Amaringo, a former *vegetalista* (healer), is at Jr LM Sánchez Cerro 465-467, www.egallery.com/pablo.html The school provides art classes for local people and is financially dependent upon selling their art. The internationally-renowned school welcomes overseas visitors for short or long stays to study painting and learn Spanish and/or teach English with Peruvian students. The painting is oriented around the Amazonian cultures, in particular the healing and hallucinogenic effects of *ayahuasca*. For more information see the book, *Wizard of the Upper Amazon*. **Useful addresses** *Policia Nacional*, Jr Independencia 3rd block, T575211.

Lake Yarinacocha

The main tourist attraction of the area, especially with Peruvians, is the picturesque Lake Yarinacocha, where you can see river dolphins. On the lake are the **Hospital Amazónico Albert Schweitzer**, which serves the local Indians, and **Summer School of Linguistics** for the study of Indian languages (callers by appointment only).

A good place to swim is at San José. Take the road out behind the power station round the lake beyond the Summer School of Linguistics.

Certain sections of Lake Yarinacocha have been designated as a reserve. The beautifully located **Jardín Botánico Chullachaqui** can be reached by boat from Puerto Callao to Pueblo Nueva Luz de Fátima. It's a 45-minute trip, then an hour's walk to the garden, entry is free. For information about **traditional medicine** contact **Mateo Arevalomayna**, San Francisco de Yarinacocha, president of the group Ametra, an organization which is working to re-establish the use of traditional remedies. T573152, or ask at Moroti-Shobo.

B *La Cabaña Lodge*, T616679, F579242. Prices include all meals and transport to and from Yarinacocha harbour, run by Ruth and Leroy from the USA, great food, jungle trips from US$50 per day including boat, guide and food. Next door is **B-C** per person *La Perla*, includes all meals, German-Peruvian owned, English and German spoken, no electricity after 2100, good, jungle tours organized. **D-E** *Los Delfines*, T571129. Rooms with bathroom, fan, fridge, some with TV, clean. **F** *El Pescador*, in Puerto Callao. The cheapest place in town, friendly, restaurant, 20 rooms and an extension. There are also some small houses for rent on a weekly basis. **Sleeping**

There are many restaurants and bars on the waterfront and near the plaza, and also stalls which barbecue fresh fish and local dishes. Among the recommended restaurants are: *El Cucharón*; *Grande Paraíso* (good view, also has a *peña* at night, popular with young people); and *Orlando's*, Jr Aguaytía. **Eating**

Yarinacocha is 20 mins by colectivo or bus from the market in Pucallpa, US$0.30, or 15 mins by taxi, US$2. **Transport**

San Francisco and Santa Clara can be visited at the far end of the lake on its western arm. Both are Shibipo villages still practising traditional ceramic and textile crafts. A canal near Santa Clara links Lake Yarinacocha with the Río Ucayali. There are a few other villages nearby, such as **Nuevo Destino** and **Santa Marta**, which are within an hour's walk. The Shibipo people are very kind and friendly and a visit is recommended. In San Francisco a good place to spend the night is in the house of Alberto Sánchez Ríos, *Casa Artesanal Shibipo*, which is very friendly and warmly recommended. **San Francisco & Santa Clara**

■ *To reach these villages take one of the motorized canoes, peke-pekes, which leave from Puerto Callao when full, US$0.90.*

Amazon Basin

Puerto Inca
Colour map 3, grid B5

You can take a colectivo from Pucallpa south to **Zungaro** (US$4.50), where a 30-minute boat ride can be taken to Puerto Inca on the Río Pachitea, about 120 km north by air from Puerto Bermúdez (see page 509), or by road on the Carretera Marginal. It is a gold-rush town, expanding quickly. *Don José's Alojamiento*, **G**, clean, safe, laundry, big rooms. Recommended.

Iquitos

Phone code: 094
Colour map 2, grid B4
Population: 600,000

Capital of the Department of Loreto and chief town of Peru's jungle region, Iquitos stands on the west bank of the Amazon. Some 800 km downstream from Pucallpa and 3,646 km from the mouth of the Amazon, the city is an urban oasis, completely isolated except by air and river. This is an active but friendly city, with the central area always busy and traders' shops up and down the streets leading north and south. It may seem, too, that Iquitos is attempting a new world record for the highest concentration of motorcycles in a built-up area.

Ins and outs

Getting there

Francisco Secada Vigneta airport, in the southwest, handles national and international flights (to/from Miami), T260147. A taxi to the airport costs US$2.85 per car. A *motocarro* (motorcycle with 2 seats) is US$2. A bus from the airport (US$0.20) goes as far as the market area, about 12 blocks from the Plaza de Armas, a taxi from there is US$1.40. The port is in the north of the town. **NB** From May-Jul the river is at its highest and the port in Iquitos moves. Boats leave from Puerto Nanay at Bellavista or from Puerto de Moronacocha. The rise and fall of the river is such that the islands off Iquitos are constantly moving (so most maps which show islands are usually wrong).

Getting around

Iquitos is well spread out and it is several blocks from the bus station into town. Hotels are dotted about all over the place. The best way to get around is by motorcycle. **Motorcycle hire**: *Rider*, Pevas 219; *Park Motors*, Tacna 579, T/F231688. The tourist office has details of other companies. Expect to pay: mopeds, US$2.60 per hr, US$35 for 24 hrs; Honda 125, US$4.50 per hr, US$44 for 24 hrs; Honda 125, US$4.50 per hr; Yamaha DT175, US$5.20 per hr, US$65 for 24 hrs.

Tourist offices

On the Plaza de Armas, in the Municipal building at Napo 226, T235621, Turismo.mpm@tvs.com.pe They have information on all legal operators offering tours to the jungle and on the 30 illegal operators on the streets. They can give good advice and a list of contacts for travelling up the Amazon, should you need help in an emergency. They are very helpful and speak five languages. They also supply maps and general tourist literature, have free baggage and valuables storage, book exchange and offer free water. The director is Gerald W Mayeaux. Mon-Fri 0800-2000, Sat-Sun 0900-1300. There is also an *i perú* office at the airport. Daily 0830-1330, 1630-2030, T260251, iperuiquitos@promperu.gob.pe If arriving by air, go first to this desk. They will give you a list of clean hotels, a map, tell you about the touts outside the airport and direct you to the office in town. The tourist office advises that all prices in Iquitos are negotiable, especially jungle lodges (see below). Always bargain for a good deal. *Indecopi*, the tourism protection service, is at C Huallaga 325, T243490, ameza@indecopi.gob.pe

History

Founded in 1757 as the mission settlement of San Pablo de los Napeanos by the Jesuits, this became in 1864 the first port of note on the great river. Rapid growth followed the Rubber Boom of the late 19th century, though the city's new-found wealth was short lived. By the second decade of this century the rubber industry had left for the more competitive Oriental suppliers. Remnants of the boom period can still be seen in the fine houses decorated with Portuguese tiles lending an air of faded beauty to the river embankment.

Iquitos has recently taken on a new lease of life as the centre for oil exploration in Peruvian Amazonia. It is also the main starting point for tourists wishing to explore Peru's northern jungle, with flights to and from Miami.

Iquitos

Sleeping
1 Acosta
2 Amazonas
3 Copoazú
4 El Dorado
5 El Dorado Plaza
6 El Sitio
7 Europa
8 Fortaleza
9 Hospedaje La Shiringa
10 Hostal Ambassador
11 Hostal Bon Bini
12 Hostal Karina
13 Hostal La Pascana
14 Hostal Rolando's Amazon River
15 Hostal Tacna
16 Internacional
17 Isabel
18 Jhuliana
19 Real Iquitos
20 Victoria Regia

Eating
1 Ari's Burger & Pollón
2 Chifa Wai Ming
3 El Nuevo Mesón
4 El Parral
5 Fitzcarrald
6 La Gran Maloca
7 La Pascana
8 Montecarlo
9 Paulina

Bars
10 Arandú
11 Teatro Café Amauta

Rubber Barons

The conquest and colonization of the vast Amazon basin was consolidated by the end of the 19th century with the invention of the process of vulcanizing rubber. Many and varied uses were found for this new product and demand was such that the jungle began to be populated by numerous European and North American immigrants who came to invest their money in rubber.

The rubber tree grew wild in the Amazon but the indigenous peoples were the only ones who knew the forests and could find this coveted tree. The exporting companies set up business in the rapidly expanding cities along the Amazon, such as Iquitos. They sent their 'slave-hunters' out into the surrounding jungle to find the native labour needed to collect the valuable rubber resin. These natives were completely enslaved, their living conditions were intolerable and they perished in their thousands, which led to the extinction of many indigenous groups.

One particularly notable figure from the rubber boom was Fitzcarrald, son of an immigrant Englishman who lived on the Peruvian coast. He was accused of spying during the 1879 war between Peru and Chile and fled to the Amazon where he lived for many years among the natives.

Thanks to Fitzcarrald, the isthmus between the basin of the Ucayali river and that of the Madre de Dios river was discovered. Before this, no natural form of communication was known between the two rivers. The first steamships to go up the Madre de Dios were carried by thousands of natives across the 8-km stretch of land which separated the two basins. Fitzcarrald died at the age of 36, one of the region's richest men, when the ship on which he was travelling sank.

The Rubber Barons lived in the new Amazonian cities and travelled around in luxurious boats which plied the great river. Every imaginable luxury was imported for their use: latest Parisian fashions for the women; finest foreign liqueurs for the men; even the best musical shows were brought over from the Old World. But this period of economic boom came to a sudden end in 1912 when rubber grown in the French and British colonies in Asia and Africa began to compete on the world market.

Sights

The incongruous **Iron House/Casa de Fierro** stands on the Plaza de Armas (at Próspero y Putumayo), designed by Eiffel for the Paris exhibition of 1889. It is said that the house was transported from Paris by a local rubber baron and is constructed entirely of iron trusses and sheets, bolted together and painted silver. It now houses a restaurant upstairs and cafeteria downstairs. Also on the Plaza, at Napo 200-12, is the **Clay House/Casa de Fitzcarrald** or **de Barro**. Built entirely of adobe, with wooden balconies, this warehouse predates the rubber boom, but the famous *cauchero*, Carlos Fermín Fitzcarrald, used it as his house and office in the early years of the 20th century. Werner Herzog's film *Fitzcarraldo* is a *cause célèbre* in the town. Next door to the tourist office on the Plaza is a **City Museum**, with items from the jungle in a lovely room with chandeliers, where rubber barons used to meet. ■ *Free*.

Also worth seeing is the old **Hotel Palace**, now the army barracks, on the corner of Malecón Tarapacá and Putumayo. Of special interest are the older buildings, faced with *azulejos* (glazed tiles). Many are along the Malecón. They date from the rubber boom of 1890-1912, when the rubber barons imported the tiles from Portugal and Italy and ironwork from England to embellish their homes.

The **Museo Amazónico** is housed in the renovated Prefetura palace on the corner of Malecón Tarapacá and Calle Morona. It has displays of Amazon art.

Belén, the picturesque, friendly waterfront district, is lively, but not safe at night. Most of its huts were built on rafts to cope with the river's 10-m change of level during the year: it begins to rise in January and is highest from May to July. Now, the cabins are built on wooden or concrete stilts. The main plaza has a bandstand designed by Alexandre Gustave Eiffel. In the high water season canoes can be hired on the waterfront to visit Belén for US$3 an hour. The **market** at the end of the Malecón is well worth visiting, though you should get there before 0900 to see it in full swing. On Pasaje Paquito, one of its side streets, there are **bars** that serve the local sugar cane rum.

Essentials

Around Peruvian Independence Day (27 and 28 Jul) and Easter, Iquitos can get crowded and excursion facilities overloaded. Prices rise at this time. At all times, hotels are more expensive than the rest of the country, but discounts of 20% or more can be negotiated in the low season (Jan-Apr).

L *El Dorado Plaza*, Napo 258 on main plaza, T222555, F224304, www.eldoradoplaza hotel.com 5 star, very good accommodation and restaurant (*Mitos*), excellent service, friendly, bar, internet access, prices inlcude service charge, breakfast, welcome drink and transfer to/from airport. The hotel offers special 3-day/2-night packages from Lima in conjunction with some of the Amazon lodges.Recommended. **AL** *El Dorado*, Napo 362, T231742, F221985, dorado@tvs.com.pe Same ownership as *El Dorado Plaza*, pool (open to restaurant users), cable TV, bar and restaurant, prices include tax and service and airport transfer. Highly recommended. **AL** *Real Hotel Iquitos*, Malecón Tarapacá, 1 block from Plaza de Armas, T231011, F236222. Includes tax and breakfast, good a/c rooms. **A** *Hostal Acosta*, Calvo de Araujo y Huallaga, T235974. Similar to *Victoria Regia* (see below) minus the swimming pool. **A** *Copoazú*, Próspero 672, T224372. 3-star. Recommended in all respects. **A** *Victoria Regia*, Ricardo Palma 252, T231983, F232499. Regarded as the second best in the city. A/c, fridge, cable TV, free map of city, safe deposit boxes in rooms, good restaurant and pool. Recommended.

B *Amazon Garden*, Pantoja 417 with Yavari, T236140, F231265, amazon@amazongardenhotel.com.pe A/c, hot water, TV, fridge, swimming pool, jacuzzi, gym, laundry, email service, price includes breakfast, relaxed atmsophere, pleasant and good value (same group as *Amazon Tours and Cruises*). **B** *Amazonas*, Plaza de Armas, Arica 108, T242431. Modern, a/c, phone, fridge bar, TV. **B** *Hostal Ambassador*, Pevas 260, T233110. Includes tax, a/c, transport to and from airport, member of Peruvian Youth Hostel Association, cafeteria, owns *Sinchicuy Lodge*. Recommended. **B** *Europa*, Brasil 222, T231123, F235483. A/c, cable TV, phone and fridge in every room, pleasant café/bar, good views from 5th floor. **B** *Jhuliana*, Putumayo 521, T/F233154. Includes tax and breakfast, friendly, nice pool, restaurant. Recommended.

C *Internacional*, Próspero 835, T/F234684. A/c, with bathroom, cable TV, fridge, phone, friendly, secure, medium-priced restaurant, good value. Recommended.

D *Hostal Bon Bini*, Arica 817, T221058. With bathroom, clean, fridge, good value. **D** *Hostal La Pascana*, Pevas 133, T231418. With cold shower, basic, fan, clean, breakfast available, luggage store, TV lounge, luxuriant garden, relaxed, popular, book exchange, ask for Coby, a Dutch lady who will take tours on her houseboat, the *Miron Lenta*.

E *El Sitio*, Ricardo Palma 541, T239878. With bathroom, very clean, fan, cafeteria. Highly recommended. **E** *Hostal Rolando's Amazon River*, Fitzcarrald y Nauta 307, T233979. With bathroom and fan, restaurant. **E** *Hospedaje La Shiringa*, Fitzcarrald 465, T243293. Comfortable, nice beds.

Sleeping
■ *on map*
Price codes:
see inside front cover

Amazon Basin

F per person *Hostal Aeropuerto*, Av Corpac block 100 y Malvinas, near the airport, clean, OK, fan in room, friendly, other 'services' available. F per person *Hostal Alfert*, García Sanz 01, T234105. Hard beds, check fan before you need it, safe but in the market area, arranges jungle trips, but not an authorized operator. F *Fortaleza*, Próspero 311, T234191. With bathroom, clean, basic, fan. F *Isabel*, Brasil 164, T234901. With bathroom, very good, clean, but plug the holes in the walls, secure, often full. F *Hostal Karina*, Putumayo 467, T235367. Water all day, fan. F *Hostal Tacna*, Tacna 516, T230714. With fan, basic but clean, rooms at front with balcony are noisy, don't leave valuables in room.

Eating
● *on map*
Many private homes offer set lunch, look for the board outside

Expensive *Fitzcarrald*, Malecón Maldonado 103 y Napo. Smart, best pizza in town, also good pastas and salads. *La Gran Maloca*, Sargento Lores 170, opposite Banco Continental. A/c, high class. *El Parral*, on Plaza de Armas, with an entrance at Napo 337. Tourist restaurant, elegant and pricey.

Mid-range *Ari's Burger*, Plaza de Armas, Próspero 127. Fast food, good breakfasts, popular with tourists. *Montecarlo*, Napo 140. Next to the casino, "best food in town". *El Nuevo Mesón*, Malecón Maldonado 153. Local specialities include wild boar, alligator, turtle, tapir and other endangered species, has lots of regular dishes, too. *La Pascana*, Ramírez Hurtado 735. Good fish and *ceviche*, try the *vientequatro raices*, 20% discount for *Handbook* users, open at lunchtimes only. *Pollón*, next to *Ari's Burger*. For chicken and chips, open in the daytime. *The Regal*, in the *Casa de Hierro*, Plaza de Armas, Próspero y Putumayo, 2nd floor. Nice location, good set lunch for US$2.30, other meals more expensive. On the first floor is *El Copoasu*, a cafetería which serves malt beer with egg and fresh milk. *Wai Ming*, San Martín at Plaza 28 de Julio. Good Chinese if a little expensive.

Cheap *Paulina*, Tacna 591.Good set lunch (US$1.75), other meals from US$4.75, popular with locals and toursists.
Heladería La Favorita, Próspero 415. Good ice-cream (try local flavour *aguaje*). *Juguería Paladar*, Próspero 245. Excellent juices.
Try the **local drink** *chuchuhuasi*, made from the bark of a tree, which is supposed to have aphrodisiac properties but tastes like fortified cough tincture (for sale at Arica 1046), and *jugo de cocona*, and the alcoholic *cola de mono* and *siete raices* (aguardiente mixed with the bark of 7 trees and wild honey), sold at *Exquisita Amazónica*, Abtao 590. You can eat cheaply, especially fish and *ceviche*, at the 3 markets. Palm heart salad (*chonta*), or *a la Loretana* dish on menus is excellent; also try *inchicapi* (chicken, corn and peanut soup), *cecina* (fried dried pork), *tacacho* (fried green banana and pork, mashed into balls and eaten for breakfast or tea), *juanes* (chicken, rice, olive and egg, seasoned and wrapped in bijao leaves and sold in restaurants). *Camu-camu* is an interesting but acquired taste, said to have one of the highest vitamin C concentrations in the world.

Bars & clubs
Sachachorro music and dance is the mythology and folklore of the Yagua culture

Bars *Snack Bar Arandú*, Malecón Maldonado, good views of the Amazon river. *Papa Dan's Gringo Bar*, Napo y Fitzcarrald, Plaza de Armas. Good set menu, US$2.85, has book exchange. *La Ribereña*, Raymondi 453. With terraced seats on a newly built plaza. *Teatro Café Amauta*, Nauta 248. Live music, open 2200-2400, good atmosphere, popular, small exhibition hall. *Tuspa*, Raimondi block 2. Light rock, lively, good place to listen to music. *Noa Noa*, Pevas y Fitzcarrald.

Festivals

On **5 Jan** is the anniversary of the *founding of Iquitos*. During *Carnival* you can see the local dance *La Pandilla*. On **24 Jun** is the *Festival of San Juan*, patron saint of Loreto. *Tourist week*, with regional music, held in the *Mercado Artesanal de San Juan*, is celebrated around the same time. On **28-30 Aug** is *Santa Rosa de Lima*, celebrated in Rumococha. On **22-25 Sep** is *Santo Tomás*, in the village of the same name (also see page 543). On **8 Dec** is *La Purísima*, celebrated in Punchana, near the docks.

Places where you can buy handicrafts are: *Amazon Arts and Crafts*, Napo block 100; *Artesanías de la Selva*, R Palma 190. *Mercado Artesanal de Productores*, 4 km from the centre in the San Juan district, on the road to the airport (take a *colectivo*). Cheapest in town with more choice than elsewhere. Good hammocks in the markets in Iquitos cost about US$5.75. *Mad Mick's Trading Post*, next to the Iron House, hires out rubber boots for those going to the jungle. *Farmacia La Loretana*, Próspero 361-3; others on Próspero and on Arica. Records and tapes at *Discotiendas Hikari*, San Martín 324. Cheap haircuts at *Barbería Jupiter*, Napo 323. A good local newspaper is *La Región*.

Shopping
Locally sold necklaces made with red and black rosary peas are extremely poisonous. Do not give them to children. They are illegal in Canada, but not in the USA

Air To **Lima**, daily with *Aero Continente*, *Aviandina*, and *Tans*. *Aviandina* flies via Pucallpa, *Tans* direct and via **Trujillo** (twice weekly), **Pucallpa** or **Tarapoto**. For *Grupo 42* flights to Santa Rosa for exit to Brazil, see page 544.

Iquitos flights are frequently delayed; be sure to reconfirm your flight in Iquitos, as they are often overbooked, especially over Christmas. Check times in advance as itineraries frequently change.

Transport

River River boats to **Pucallpa**, leave every second day, usually at 1700. The journey takes 5-6 days when river is high, and 3-4 days when it's low. The price depends on demand, eg US$17 per person in a hammock, or US$20 per person with bed and cabin. To **Yurimaguas** takes 3-4 days, longer if cargo is being carried, which is usually the case; it costs US$11 for hammock space, US$17 per bunk, and boats leave more or less daily. The *Eduardo* company is recommended.

See Essentials, page 79 for general tips on river travel

You can find information on boats and tickets at *Bellavista*, Malecón Tarapacá 596; or in the Puerto Masusa district of Puchana, at Av La Marina with Masusa (take a bus from the centre, 10 mins). Cabins are 4 berth and you have to buy both a first class ticket, which entitles you to food (whether you want it or not) and deck space to sling your hammock, and a cabin ticket if you want the 'luxury' of a berth. There are adequate washing and toilet facilities, but the food is rice, meat and beans (and whatever can be picked up en route) cooked in river water. There is a good cheap bar on board.

A monthly luxury 54-passenger boat, *Río Amazonas*, sails down-river from Iquitos and **Tabatinga (Brazil),** operated by *Amazon Tours and Cruises* (see Jungle tours below). It costs US$595 per person. Also making this trip is *M/V Arca* (US$595 per person).

There are no boats direct to Manaus. Boats to **Santa Rosa** on the border, opposite **Tabatinga** (Brazil), leave from one of two docks, Puerto de Servicio Masusa, or Embarcadero Turístico. Fast boats, *rápidos* (average speed 50 kph), leave from either, but mostly Turístico. They leave most days at 0600-0615; be at the port at 0445 for customs check. They go to Santa Rosa for immigration formalities then take passengers across to Tabatinga. *Expreso Turístico Loreto*, Próspero 441/Raimondi 384, T234084; also *Transtur* and *Transportes Pluma*. All charge the same, US$50 (but you may be able to negotiate a lower price in agencies), and include a small breakfast of a sandwich and coffee, a passable lunch and mineral water (ask for it). All carry life jackets and have clean bathrooms. Luggage limit is 15 kg. Most travel agencies sell tickets. The trip takes 11 hrs, but you will probably be told it takes 8. Hotels have details of sailings; ask around which boats are reliable. *Rápidos* leave Tabatinga for Iquitos every morning at 0600: the same price and almost the same time, 11-12 hrs.

There is no Brazilian consulate in Iquitos. If you need a visa, you must get it in Lima

Regular boats, *lanchas*, leave almost every day to **Santa Rosa**. The journey takes 2-3 days and costs US$25-30 per person with a cabin and meals (US$15-17.50 with a hammock). Passengers disembark at Santa Rosa, where immigration formalities take place (no exchange facilities), then take another US$1 boat to **Marco**, the port for **Tabatinga**. Most boats for **Manaus** depart from Marco.

If you plan to stop off along the way at small villages on the river in Peru (see below, Iquitos to the Brazilian/Colombian border), you can usually get a passing boat to make an unscheduled stop and pick you up. The best way to do this is to flag it down with a white sheet. This is what the villagers do if they want a passing boat to stop at their village. Note that this method doesn't work on the Brazilian part of the river, where boats don't make unscheduled stops. The only way to board a Brazilian boat between stops is to hire a canoe to take you out to meet it in mid-river then flag it down.

Directory

Don't change money on the streets The tourist office has the names of reliable money changers

Airline offices *Aero Continente*, Próspero 231, T233162, F233990. *Aviandina* in same office. *Grupo 42*, Sgto Lores 127, T234632. *Tans*, Próspero 215, open 0830-1300, 1530-1900, Sun 0830-1300. **Banks** *BCP*, Plaza de Armas. For Visa, also cash and TCs at good rates, has a Visa ATM around the corner on Próspero. *BBV Continental*, Sgto Lores 171. For Visa, 1% commission on TCs. *Banco de la Nación*, Condamine 478. Good rates, changes Deutschmarks. *Banco Wiese Sudameris*, Próspero 282. *Banco del Trabajo*, Próspero 223. Has Unicard ATM for Visa/Plus and Mastercard/Cirrus. *Western Union*, Napo 359, T235182. **Communications** Internet: there are lots of internet places around the Plaza de Armas, eg: *Cocon@net*, Fitzcarrald 131, T232538, with snackbar. *El Cyber*, Fitzcarrald 120, T223608. *Manguaré*, Próspero 249, T242148. All average US$1.15 per hr. **Post Office:** on the corner of C Arica with Morona, near the Plaza de Armas, open daily 0700-2000. **Telephone:** *Telefónica*, Arica 276. **Embassies and consulates** Consulates: *Britain*, Casa de Hierro (Iron House), Putumayo 189, T222732, F223607, Mon-Fri 1100-1200. *Colombia*, Nauta y Callao, T231461. **Medical services** *Clínica Loreto*, Morona 471, T233752, 24-hr attention. Recommended, but only Spanish spoken. *Hospital Iquitos*, Cornejo Portugal 1770, T264710. *Hospital Regional de Loreto*, 28 de Julio, emergency T252743. *Clínica Ana Stahl*, Av La Marina 285, T252535. **Useful addresses** Immigration: Mcal Cáceres 18th block, T235371. Quick service. *PARD*, Preservation of the Amazon River Dolphin, Pevas 253, T/F(5194)238585. Ask for Roxanne Kremer or Frank Aliaga for information. **Tourist police**: Sargento Lores 834, T242081. Helpful with complaints against tour operators. In emergency T241000 or 241001.

Jungle tours from Iquitos

All agencies are under the control of the local office of the Ministry of Tourism. They arrange one day or longer trips to places of interest with guides speaking some English. Package tours booked in Lima or abroad are much more expensive than those booked in Iquitos and personal approaches to lodge operators will often yield better prices than booking through an agency or the internet. Some agencies are reported as too easy going about their responsibilities on an organized trip, but many are conscientious. Take your time before making a decision and don't be bullied by the hustlers at the airport (they get paid a hefty commission). The tourist office in Iquitos has all the brochures and will give good advice on authorized operators, shop around and deal direct with the lodge operators themselves at their own office, not any other address you may have been told about. For an immediate response to any complaints go to the tourist office in Iquitos, who can lead you through all the relevant procedures, or contact *Indecopi* (address in Ins and outs, above). Make sure your guide has a proper licence.

Find out all the details of the trip and food arrangements before paying (a minimum of US$35 per day). Speed boats for river trips can be hired by the hour or day. Prices are negotiable, but usually about US$10-30 per hour.

Tour operators & jungle lodges

All prices are negotiable, except Muyuna, who do not take commissions

Amazon Lodge and Safaris, Av La Marina 592A, T/F251078, amazonlodge@ mixmail.com (attention Jorge and Elvira Lache); in Lima Av Alvarez Calderón 155, suite 304, San Isidro, T221 3341, F221 0974 (attention Gabriel Flores). 48 km down-river from Iquitos. Recommended as friendly and comfortable; 3 days/2 nights, US$200 per person for 2-4 people, US$50 per person for each additional night.

Amazon Tours and Cruises, Requena 336, T231611/233931, F231265, amazon@ amazoncruises.com.pe In USA, 8700 W Flagler St, suite 190, Miami, FL 33174, T305 227 2266, toll free 800 423 2791, F305-227 1880, American-owned company. Various cruises available on the M/V *Arca* Iquitos-Leticía-Iquitos, US$595 per person (ask at the tourist office if discounted cabins are available); also MV *Marcelita*; and nature cruises on the M/V *Delfín*. They also organize rugged expeditions to various jungle *tambos* (thatched shelters). They are recommended as conscientious and efficient.

Cumaceba Lodge and Expeditions, Putumayo 184 in the Iron House, T/F232229, www.manguare.com.pe/cumaceba Tours of 2-8 days to their lodges on the Amazon and Yarapa rivers, good birdwatching guides, 3 days/2 nights for US$120 per person. Very good all round.

Explorama Tours are highly recommended as the most efficient and, with over 35 years in existence, certainly the biggest and most established. Their offices are by the riverside docks on Av La Marina 340, PO Box 446, T252526/252530, F252533; in USA, SACA, Toll Free, T800-707 5275, 781-581 0844, info@saca.com, www.explorama.com They have 5 sites: *Explorama Inn*, 40 km (1½ hrs) from Iquitos, has comfortable bungalows with cold water in a jungle setting and, in the same reserve, the *Ceiba Tops* resort. This provides 'an adventure in luxury', 40 a/c rooms with electricity, hot showers, swimming pool with hydromassage and beautiful gardens. The food is good and, as in all Explorama's properties, is served communally. There are attractive walks and other excursions, a recommended jungle experience for those who want their creature comforts, US$225 per person for 1 night/2 days, US$85 for each additional night (1-2 people). *Explorama Lodge* at Yanamono, 80 km from Iquitos, 2½ hrs from Iquitos, has palm-thatched accommodation with separate bathroom and shower facilities connected by covered walkways, cold water, no electricity, good food and service. US$250 for 3 days/2 nights and US$75 for each additional day (1-2 people). *Explornapo Lodge* at Llachapa on the Sucusai creek (a tributary of the Napo), is in the same style as Explorama Lodge, but is further away from Iquitos, 160 km (4 hrs), and is set in 105,000 ha of primary rainforest, so is better for seeing fauna. Nearby is the impressive canopy walkway 35 m above the forest floor and 500 m long, 'a magnificent experience and not to be missed'. It is associated with the *ACEER laboratory* (Amazon Centre for Environmental Education and Research), a scientific station, only 10 mins from the canopy walkway; the basic programme costs US$1,135 for 5 days/4 nights (2 people), the first and last nights are spent at Explorama Lodge. A US$25 donation to the Foundation for Conservation of Peruvian Amazon Biosphere (Conapac) is included if visiting the walkway. To spend a night at the ACEER lab is US$55; each extra night to the basic programme costs US$98. Prices include transfers, advance reservations, etc. *Explor Tambos*, 2 hrs from *Explornapo*, more primitive accommodation, 8 shelters for 16 campers, bathing in the river, offers the best chance to see rare fauna. Close to Explornapo is the ReNuPeRu medicinal plant garden, run by the *curandero*, Antonio Montero. Members of South American Explorers are offered 15% discount.

Heliconia Lodge, Ricardo Palma 242, T231959. On the Río Amazonas, 1½ hrs from Iquitos, the lodge has hot water, electricity for 3 hrs a day, good guiding and staff; rustic yet comfortable. Under same management as *Zungarococha*, see below.

Loving Light, Putumayo 128, T243180, in USA 7016 248th Avenue NE, Redmond, WA98053, T425-836 9431. Near San Juan village on the Yanayacu tributary which branches off the Amazon 3 hrs upriver from Iquitos. Prices for 3-day, 2-night packages for 2 people US$300 per person, including boat transfer, all meals, guides, transfers in Iquitos. Ayahuasca ceremony is US$25 extra.

Muyuna Amazon Lodge and Expeditions, Putumayo 163, T242858, M937533, www.muyuna.com 120 km from Iquitos, also on the Yanayacu, before San Juan village. Packages from 1 to 4 nights available, US$140-250 per person for 2-3 people, but users of this *Handbook* should make reservations in person for discounted price (similarly SAE members). Everything is included in the price (transport, good food, guides, excursions), personal service, flexible, radio contact, will collect passengers from airport if requested in advance. They also arrange expeditions to the Pacaya-Samiria Reserve.

Paseos Amazónicos Ambassador, Pevas 246, T/F231618, operates the *Amazonas Sinchicuy Lodge*, US$70 per person per night. The lodge is 1½ hrs from Iquitos on the Sinchicuy river, 25 mins by boat from the Amazon river. The lodge consists of several wooden buildings with thatched roofs on stilts, cabins with bathroom, no electricity but paraffin lamps are provided, good food, and plenty activities, including visits to local villages. Recommended. They also organize visits to Lake Quistacocha.

Tahuayo Lodge, *Amazonia Expeditions*, 10305 Riverburn Drive, Tampa, FL 33647, toll free T800-262 9669, 813-907 8475, www.perujungle.com Near the Reserva Comunal de Tamshiyacu-Tahuayo on the Río Tahuayo, 145 km upriver from Iquitos, clean, comfortable cabins with cold shower, buffet meals, good food, laundry service, wide range of excursions, excellent staff. A 7-day programme costs US$1,295, all inclusive, extra days US$100. Recommended. The lodge is associated with the Rainforest Conservation Fund (www.rainforestconservation.org), which works in Tamshiyacu-Tahuayo, one of the richest areas for primate species in the world, but also amphibians (there is a poison dart frog management programme), birds, other animals and plants.

Yacumama Lodge, Sargento Lores 149, T/F235510 (Av Benavides 212, Oficina 1203, Miraflores, Lima). An excellent lodge on the Río Yarapa, 4 days/3 nights, US$389, 6 days/5 nights, US$559 (minimum 2 people), part of the fee is invested in local conservation.

Zungarococha Amazon Lodge, Ricardo Palma 242, T/F231959. A recreation centre on the Río Nanay, 35 mins from Iquitos. Comfortable lakeside bungalows reached by road (12 km), swimming pool, watersports, mini-zoo, full day US$40, 1 night/2 days US$70.

Guides   *Pedro Alava Tuesta*, Av Grau 1770, T264224, pedroalava@hotmail.com Very experienced and reliable, all types of trip arranged. Recommended. *Percy Icomena*, Diego de Almagro 555, Puchana, bekeypp@operamail.com Freelance guide who can arrange any type of tour, including jungle survival, speaks English. Recommended. His brother, Louis, is also a guide, speaks English, French, Italian, German, Japanese, contact through Percy.

General   Take a long-sleeved shirt, waterproof coat and shoes or light boots on such trips and a
information   good torch, as well as *espirales* to ward off the mosquitoes at night – they can be bought
& advice   from drugstores in Iquitos. *Premier* is the most effective local insect repellent. The dry season is from Jul-Sep (Sep is the best month to see flowers and butterflies).

Around Iquitos

Bellavista   There is a beautiful white, sandy beach at Bellavista, a suburb of Iquitos, which is safe for swimming and very popular at weekends in summer. Boats can be hired from here to see the meeting of the Nanay and Amazon rivers, and to visit beaches and villages en route. There are lots of food stalls selling typical local dishes. ■ *Take a bus from Jr Próspero to 'Bellavista Nanay'; 15 minutes, US$0.40.*

Indiana   Launches leave Iquitos (from the Mercado de Productores or Bellavista
Colour map 2, grid B4   Nanay) for the village of Indiana. Get off at the 'Varadero de Mazán' and walk through the banana plantations to the Río Mazán. A trail leads from the village of Mazán through the secondary jungle to Indiana, where there is a hotel. It's about a two-hour walk. If the hotel is full, ask at the mission or municipality for a tent for the night. From Indiana you can do several hikes of between two and four hours to little villages along the Napo river. ■ *There are daily fast boats (45-50 mins) and public boats (3 a day, 2-3 hrs), both US$2.85; cargo boats at 1000 Wed and Sat, return Mon and Thu, 15 hrs, same price.*

Thirteen-and-a-half kilometres south of the city, Lake Quistococha is beautifully situated in lush jungle, with a fish hatchery at the lakeside. The **Parque Zoológico de Quistococha** on the lake gives an example of the local wildlife, though conditions are pretty squalid (big cats in tiny cages, and so on). At the entrance are pictures and texts of local legends, which are interesting. The ticket office will supply a map of the lake and environs. There's a good two-hour walk through the surrounding jungle on a clearly marked trail. See particularly the *paiche*, a huge Amazonian fish whose steaks (*paiche a la loretana*) you can eat in Iquitos' restaurants. There are also bars and restaurants on the lakeside and a small beach. Boats are for hire on the lake and swimming is safe but the sandflies are vicious, so take insect repellent. ■ *Daily 0900-1700. US$1.30. To get to Quistacocha, combis leave every hour until 1500 from Plaza 28 de Julio. The last one back leaves at 1700. Alternatively take a motocarro there and back with a 1-hr wait, which costs US$13. Perhaps the best option is to hire a motorbike and spend the day there. The road can be difficult after rain.*

Lake Quistococha

On the road to Quistococha, is the turn-off to the village of Santo Tomás. Take a left turn just before the airport, and then another left 300 m further on. Then it's about another 4 km to the village. There are restaurants open on Sunday and dugout canoes can be hired daily. The village hosts a fiesta on 22-25 September. Trucks go there, taking passengers.

Santo Tomás

Iquitos to the Brazilian/Colombian border

The village of **Pebas**, on the north bank, is three hours from Iquitos. **Pituayac**, part of Pebas, is a military area. One of the greatest of Peru's abstract painters, Francisco Grippa, lives in Pebas. His house overlooks the river and you can stay there if you are interested in his work and art in general. Anyone in town will tell you where he lives. If you want to see his paintings, but don't want to stop in Pebas, there are several on display in the *Hotel El Dorado* in Iquitos.

Colour map 2, grid B5/6

San Pablo, a further three hours downstream, is a refuelling stop, where children swim next to the jetty. You can buy crackers and drinks during the 5-minute halt; the boat will wait for you. After another hour you reach **Chimbote**, where there is a police and customs point. Your passport will be stamped and your bags checked. Food can be bought, but it's not that hygienic.

Caballococha, 45 minutes from Chimbote is "the kind of town you always imagined when reading the books of García Márquez", writes Andre Vltchek. "Lost in the jungle and in time, Caballococha is hot, humid and nostalgic." It is built on a small arm of the river, surrounded by lush, green, tropical vegetation. There are several very basic *hostales*, including F *Hostal Internacional* (shared facilities). The best place to eat is *Restaurant El Sabroso*, next to the port (good sandwiches about US$1) and there are several cheap *comedores* around the main plaza, which is also next to the port."

Air Daily flights from/to **Iquitos** with *Grupo 42*, 1 hr 10 mins, US$50 one way; see below under Santa Rosa, Transport. The float plane lands on the river in front of the military base, 5 mins by *motocarro* from the plaza. The driver will try to charge US$1.15, but may take less. It's a 15-min walk, but it's devilishly hot. **Boat** Slow boats between **Iquitos** and **Santa Rosa** stop here. *Rápidos* between **Iquitos** and **Tabatinga** only make a brief stop so to see the town, take a *rápido* boat from **Leticia** (Colombia), 2-3 hrs depending on the number of stops, then catch a flight out or a *rápido* the next day.

Transport

Amazon Basin

Between Caballococha and Santa Rosa, the journey is beautiful, taking about two hours. To your left are rolling green hills of Colombia's Amacayacu National Park. The Iquitos-Tabatinga *rápidos* usually take the narrow, southern arm of the river, which does not give views of Colombia, so ask before you buy your ticket which route it will take. Otherwise you must take a Leticia-Caballococha boat.

Santa Rosa is the small Peruvian military base across the river from **Leticia** (Colombia) and **Tabatinga** (Brazil), in the region known as the 'tri-border'. It is the only place with a good beach, so it gets busy at weekends. It only has one very basic *hostal* next to the jetty and the large, pleasant café on the waterfront only sells *refrescos*, no water of coffee. There are no money changers.

Crossing the border

When leaving Peru, check procedures in Iquitos first at Immigration (see above) or with the Capitanía at the port

The border is open 24 hrs a day. Travelling by *rápido*, you get your exit stamp at the police station in Santa Rosa in front of the jetty. After clearing customs and getting your exit stamp, the *rápido* will take you to Tabatinga across the river (5 mins).

Immigration If you go to Brazil or Colombia from Santa Rosa, you will need a Peruvian exit stamp, which means that you will need an entry and exit stamp from either Colombia or Brazil if you want to re-enter Peru. There is an immigration office in the port of Tabatinga. Your best bet is to take a taxi and ask the driver to take you to the Polícia Federal, whose office is on the main road, some 2 km from the port. The process is very straightforward; Brazilian immigration is friendly and there is always somebody who speaks English. If you intend to stay in the border region, choose Brazilian immigration formalities over Colombian, which take more time, with more questions asked. All immigration services are free of charge. Once you have a Brazilian or Colombian entry stamp, you can move freely between Leticia and Tabatinga as there is no border between the two (for example, if you have a Brazilian entry stamp, you can stay in any hotel in Leticia – no questions asked). Nobody will check your passport if you just walk or drive (if you take a boat – for which there is no need – between Tabatinga and Leticia, the Colombians may give you a hard time). **NB** US citizens have to have a Brazilian visa. Those who don't have one should enter via Colombia.

If you go to any other destination in Brazil, you will have to get a Brazilian entry stamp. The same goes for Colombia. Peruvian immigration will give you a 30-day entry stamp in Santa Rosa. The officer is friendly and he will usually ask if you need more days.

Transport Small boats between **Tabatinga** and **Santa Rosa**, or **Leticia** and Santa Rosa are readily available and charge US$1, 2 reais, 5 soles or 2000 pesos per passenger.

Air *Grupo 42* (the Peruvian Air Force) flies between **Santa Rosa** and **Iquitos** on Mon, Wed, Sat, US$65 one way. This is a real adventure and a must for all aeroplane enthusiasts. It is the only regular float plane service in South America. Grupo 42 flies Canadian DHC-6 *Twin Otter* planes, which take off and land on the water. The plane leaves from the jetty at Santa Rosa and arrives at the military base in Iquitos (US$0.55 by *motorcarro* to the centre). Flight time is 1½ hrs. The plane flies low, some 5,000 ft above the river - great view. Santa Rosa-Iquitos flights stop at **Caballococha**. They leave Santa Rosa around 1100 and Caballococha at around 1300. To buy tickets for this flight, go to any travel agency in Iquitos. In Tabatinga, *Blue Moon*, T92-97-412 2227/412 2050; cellular in Leticia: 283 4908; andyturismo@yahoo.com.br Absurdly, you can't get tickets in Santa Rosa (Peru). **NB** The Twin Otter has a very primitive navigation system. Flights are often cancelled in bad weather. You may also get stuck in Caballococha on the way to Iquitos or Santa Rosa.

There are flights most days from Tabatinga to Manaus with *Varig* and *Rico* (expensive so ask about discounts). *Aero República* flies on Sun from **Leticia** to Bogotá.

Boat Details are given under Iquitos and Caballococha above.

Banks **Exchange**: there is no exchange office in Santa Rosa, but you can pay in reais. You can use Colombian pesos in Brazil and reais in Colombia. Peruvian soles are not accepted in Colombia, but sometimes you can pay with soles in Brazil. There are no exchange facilities in Tabatinga port, but there are several *casas de cambio* in Leticia, the best place to change money, even for reais into soles. US dollars are accepted everywhere. **Communications** **Internet**: the only place with internet is Leticia. Connection is very slow. Try the internet in the *librería*, next to the church in the centre.

The Southern Jungle

The southern selva is found mostly within the Department of Madre de Dios, created in 1902 and contains the Manu National Biosphere Reserve (1,881,000 ha) an area equivalent to a quarter of the size of Panama, the Tambopata National Reserve (254,358 ha) an area roughly the same size as Luxembourg and the Bahuaja-Sonene National Park (1,091,416 ha) which is more than four times larger than the Tambopata National Reserve.

The frontier town of Puerto Maldonado is the starting point for expeditions to the Tambopata National Reserve and is only a 30-minute flight from Cusco. (Cusco is also the starting point for trips to Manu.) The best time to visit is during the dry season when there are fewer mosquitoes and the rivers are low, exposing the beaches. This is also a good time to see birds nesting and to view the animals at close range, as they stay close to the rivers and are easily seen. A pair of binoculars is essential for wildlife viewing and insect repellent is a must.

Ecology

This area is home to black caiman, the elusive giant river otter and jaguar and the largest forest mammal the tapir - a blend of horse and rhino that crunches across the jungle floor mainly at night. Wildlife spotting chances are extremely high, although you are more likely to see large cat paws and scat than the beautiful spotted king of the jungle. However, seeing baby jaguar swimming in the Tambopata River and coming face to face with the deadliest of snakes, the Bushmaster, are not unknown.

Other rare species living in the forest are the puma and ocelot. There are also capybara, 13 species of primate and hundreds of bird species. If one includes the cloud forests and highlands of the Manu Biosphere Reserve, the bird count surpasses 1,000.

As well as containing some of the most important flora and fauna on Earth, however, the region also harbours gold-diggers, loggers, hunters and oil-men. For years, logging, gold prospecting and the search for oil and gas have endangered the unique rainforest. Fortunately, though, the destructive effect of such groups has been limited by the various conservation groups working to protect it.

The forest of this lowland region is technically called Sub-tropical Moist Forest, which means that it receives less rainfall than tropical forest and is dominated by the floodplains of its meandering rivers. One of most striking features is the former river channels that have become isolated as ox-bow lakes (*cochas*), which are home to the black caiman and giant otter and a host of other living organisms.

The climate is warm and humid, with a rainy season from November to March and a dry season from April to October. Cold fronts from the South Atlantic, called *friajes*, are characteristic of the dry season, when temperatures drop to 15-16°C during the day, and 13° at night. Always bring a sweater at this time.

Amazon Basin

Manu Biosphere Reserve

Colour map 4, grid C4 *No other rainforest can compare with Manu for the diversity of its life forms and this is one of the world's great wilderness experiences. The reserve is one of the best bird-watching spots of the world (see below) as well as offering the best chance of seeing giant otters, jaguars, ocelots and several of the 13 species of primates which abound in this pristine tropical wilderness. The more remote areas of the reserve are home to uncontacted indigenous tribes and many other indigenous groups with very little knowledge of the outside world. Covering an area of 1,881,000 ha, Manu Biosphere Reserve is also one of the largest conservation units on Earth, encompassing the complete drainage of the Manu river, with an altitudinal range from 200 m to 4,100 m above sea-level.*

Where and when to go

Visitors are not allowed inside most of the Manu National Park for reasons pertaining to indigenous groups. They can visit the lower part of the Río Manu between the confluence with the Río Madre de Dios (Boca Manu, see page 550) and the park ranger station of Pakitza (see page 550). This area was formerly known as the Manu Reserved Zone, but in August of 2002 it was elevated to National Park status. The Multiple Use Zones of the Biosphere Reserve can also be visited. The best time to visit is in the dry season from May to the end of November, but trips can also be planned during the rainy season.

The park areas

The Biosphere Reserve comprises the **Manu National Park** (1,789,000 ha), which is only accessible for government sponsored biologists, anthropologists, researchers and documentary film crews with special permits from the Ministry of Agriculture in Lima. The **Multiple Use Zone** contains acculturated native groups, colonists, and lodges. The **Nahua-Kugapakori Reserved Zone** (92,000 ha), is set aside for these two nomadic native groups, where the locals still employ traditional ways of life. It is not a part of the Reserve. Associated with Manu are other areas protected by conservationists, or local people (eg the Blanquillo reserved zone) and some cloud forest parcels along the road. The old **Manu Reserved Zone**, which is set aside for applied scientific research and ecotourism, has been recently incorporated into the **Manu National Park**.

The **Cultural Zone** is now part of the Multiple Use Zone and several lodges exist in the area (see Manu Lodges page 553). The **lower reaches of the Río Manu**, set aside for tourism and applied scientific research, are accessible by permit only. Entry is controlled and visitors must visit the area under the an authorized operator with an authorized guide. Permits are limited and reservations should be made in advance, though it is possible to book a place on a trip at the last minute in Cusco. In the former Reserved Zone of the Manu Biosphere Reserve there are two lodges: the comfortable Casa Machiguenga (see below) run by the Machiguenga communities of Tayakome and Yombebato with the help of a German NGO and the upmarket Manu Lodge (see below). In the Cocha Salvador area, several companies have tented safari camp infrastructures, some with shower and dining facilities, but visitors sleep in walk-in tents.

Birdwatching in Manu

Much of the Manu Biosphere Reserve is completely unexplored and the variety of birds is astounding: over 1,000 species, significantly more than the whole of Costa Rica and over one 10th of all the birds on earth. Although there are other places in the Manu area where you can see all the Manu bird specialities and an astonishing variety of other wildlife, the single best place for the visiting birder is the Manu Wildlife Centre.

Levelling out onto the last forested foothills of the Andes, the upper tropical zone is a forest habitat that in many parts of South America has disappeared and been replaced by tea, coffee and coca plantations. In Manu, the forest is intact, and special birds such as Amazonian Umbrellabird and Blue-headed and Military Macaws can be found.

A good place to be based for upper tropical birding and an introduction to lowland Amazon species is the *Amazonia Lodge* (see page 553), on the Río Alto Madre de Dios. From here on, transport is by river and the beaches are packed with nesting birds in the dry season. Large-billed Terns scream at passing boats and Orinoco Geese watch warily from the shore. Colonies of hundreds of Sand-coloured Nighthawks roost and nest on the hot sand.

As you leave the foothills behind and head into the untouched forests of the western Amazon, you are entering forest with the highest density of birdlife per sq km on earth. Sometimes it seems as if there are fewer birds than in an English woodland. Then a mixed flock comes through, containing maybe 70-plus species, or a brightly coloured group of, say, Rock Parakeets dashes out of a fruiting tree. For the birder who craves the mysterious and rare, this is *the* site.

Amazon Basin

This forest has produced the highest day-list ever recorded anywhere on earth and it holds such little-seen gems as Black-faced Cotinga and Rufous-fronted Ant-thrush. Antbirds and Ovenbirds creep in the foliage and give tantalizing glimpses until, eventually, they reveal themselves in a shaft of sunlight. Woodcreepers and Woodpeckers climb tree-trunks and multicoloured Tanagers move through the rainforest canopy. To get to this forest is difficult and not cheap, but the experience is well worth it.

The best place for lowland birding is the *Manu Wildlife Centre*, see page 553, which is located close to a large macaw lick and to ox-bow lakes crammed with birds. This area has more forest types and micro-habitats than any other rainforest lodge in Peru, and it has recorded an amazing 565 species of birds and boasts a walk-up canopy tower where rainforest canopy species can be seen with ease.

Manu Biosphere Reserve

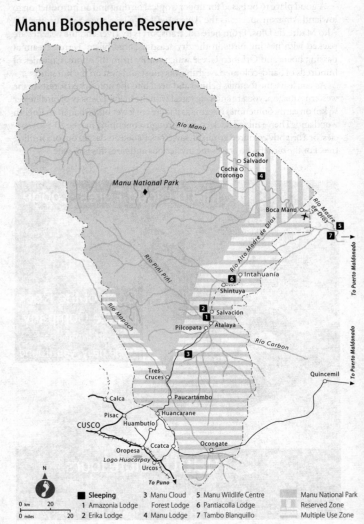

Río Manu

Cocha Salvador
Cocha Otorongo
4

Manu National Park ◆

Boca Manu ✈

Río Madre de Dios

5
7

Río Alto Madre de Dios

Río Piñi Piñi

Intahuania
6
Shintuya

2 1 Salvación
Pilcopata Atalaya

Río Mapach

Río Carbon

3

Tres Cruces

Quincemil

Calca Paucartambo

Pisac Huancarane
CUSCO Huambutio
Ccatca Ocongate
Oropesa
Lago Huacarpay
Urcos

To Puno

N

0 km 20
0 miles 20

Sleeping
1 Amazonia Lodge
2 Erika Lodge

3 Manu Cloud Forest Lodge
4 Manu Lodge

5 Manu Wildlife Centre
6 Pantiacolla Lodge
7 Tambo Blanquillo

Manu National Park
Reserved Zone
Multiple Use Zone

To Puerto Maldonado

To Puerto Maldonado

Amazon Basin

A trip to Manu is one of the ultimate birding experiences and topping it off with a macaw lick is a great way to finish; hundreds of brightly coloured macaws and other parrots congregate to eat the clay essential to their digestion in one of the world's great wildlife spectacles.

To Manu from Cusco

It is possible to visit the lodges in the Cultural Zone under your own steam. The arduous trip over the Andes from Cusco to the end of the road at Shintuya takes about 16-18 hours by local truck (20-40 hours in the wet season). It is long and uncomfortable, but, throughout, the scenery is magnificent. From Cusco you climb up to the Huancarani pass before **Paucartambo** (3½ hours), before dropping down to this picturesque mountain village in the Mapacho Valley - for details of accommodation etc in Paucartambo, see page 226). The road then ascends to the Ajcanacu pass (cold at night), after which it goes down to the cloud forest and then the rainforest, reaching **Pilcopata** at 650 m (11 hours). One hour more and you are in **Atalaya** which is the jumpoff point for river trips further into the Manu. On the way, you pass *Manu Cloudforest Lodge* and *Cock of the Rock Lodge* (see below). There are basic *hostales* in Pilcopata: **F** *Albergue Eco Turístico Villa Carmen*, www.business.com.pe/villa-carmen; **F** per person *Gallito de las Rocas* is opposite the police checkpoint and is clean. A good restaurant is *Las Palmeras*.

Colour map 5, grid A5/6

After Pilcopata, the route is hair-raising and breath-taking, passing through Atalaya, the first village on the Alto Madre de Dios river, which consists of a few houses. Basic accommodation can be found here. Even in the dry season this part of the road is appalling and trucks often get stuck. In Atalaya, meals are available at the family of Rosa and Klaus (very friendly people), where you can camp. Boats are available here to take you across the river to *Amazonia Lodge* (see page 553). The route continues to **Salvación**, where a Manu Park Office is situated. There are basic hostels and restaurants.

Amazon Basin

Shintuya
Colour map 5, grid A6

The end of the road is Shintuya, the starting point for river transport. It is a commercial and social centre, as wood from the jungle is transported from here to Cusco. There are a few basic restaurants and you can camp (beware of thieves). The priest will let you stay in the dormitory rooms at the mission. Supplies are expensive. There are two Shintuyas: one is the port and mission and the other is the native village. You can find a boat in the native village; ask for Diego Ruben Sonque or Miguel Visse. **NB** It is not possible to arrange trips to the restricted area of the Reserved Zone of the Biosphere Reserve from Shintuya, owing to park regulations. All arrangements (including permits) must be made in Cusco.

Getting there Trucks leave every Mon, Wed and Fri from the Coliseo Cerrado in Cusco at about 1000 (be there by 0800) to Pilcopata and Shintuya (passing Atalaya); US$7 to Shintuya. The journey takes at least 48 hrs and is rough and uncomfortable. They return the following day, but there is no service on Sun. There is also a bus service which leaves from the same place to Pilcopata, on Mon and Fri and returns on Tue and Sat. The journey takes 12 hrs in the dry season and costs US$8-10. From Pilcopata there are trucks to Atalaya (1 hr, US$8) and Shintuya (3 hrs, US$10). Trucks leave in the morning between 0600 and 0900. Make sure you go with a recommended truck driver. Only basic supplies are available after leaving Cusco, so take all your camping and food essentials, including insect repellent. Transport can be disrupted in the wet season because the road is in poor condition (tour companies have latest details). Tour companies usually use their own vehicles for the overland trip from Cusco to Manu.

Boca Colorado

From Shintuya infrequent cargo boats sail to the gold mining centre of **Boca Colorado** on the Río Madre de Dios, via Boca Manu, and passing *Pantiacolla Lodge* and *Manu Wildlife Centre* (see page 553). The trip takes around 9 hours, and costs US$15. Basic accommodation can be found here and is not recommended for lone women travellers. To Boca Manu is 3-4 hours, US$12. From Colorado there are plenty of boats to **Laberinto** (6-7 hours, US$20). From here there are combis to **Puerto Maldonado** (see page 554), 1½ hours.

Boca Manu

Boca Manu is the connecting point between the rivers Alto Madre de Dios, Manu and Madre de Dios. It has a few houses, an airstrip and some well-stocked shops. There is a basic municipal lodge here and, downriver on the way to the airstrip, is the *Madre de Dios Lodge* run by Sr Juan de Dios, friendly and convenient if waiting for a plane or boat. It is also the entrance to the Manu Reserve and to go further you must be part of an organized group. The entrance fee to the Reserved Zone is 100 soles per person (about US$28.75 at the time of writing) and is included in package tour prices. The Park ranger station is located in **Limonal**, 20 minutes by boat from Boca Manu. You need to show your permit here and camping is allowed if you have a permit. There are no regular flights from Cusco to Boca Manu. These are arranged the day before, if there are enough passengers. Contact *Air Atlantic*, at Maruri 228, oficina 208, Cusco, T245440; *Trans Andes* in the Cusco airport T/F224638 and *Malu Servicios* in the Cusco airport T/F242104, or check with the tour operators in Cusco.

To the National Park Zone

Upstream on the Río Manu you pass the *Manu Lodge* (see page 553), on the Cocha Juárez, three to four hours by boat. You can continue to Cocha Otorongo, 2½ hours and Cocha Salvador, 30 minutes, the biggest lake with plenty of wildlife where the *Casa Machiguenga Lodge* is located and several companies have safari camp concessions. From here it is one hour to **Pakitza**, the entrance to the restricted National Park Zone. This is only for biologists and others with a special permit.

Top of the morning

◀◀

At first sight, as the dawn comes up and the collpas's features emerge from the dark, it looks like nothing more than a long, brown, muddy cliff. But these mundane places are very special, for here macaws and parrots `lick' the clay in one of the world's great wildlife spectacles. It is believed that they do this because they need the soil's alkalis to neutralize the toxicity in fruit, especially at the end of the dry season (August-October). There is no guarantee that the birds will come, so you wait for the sun to warm the air and hope that being woken at some ungodly hour will be worth it.

A 25-minute boat ride from the Manu Wildlife Center is a floating hide (two canoes lashed together with a platform and leaves for walls) to view one important collpa. "The green parrots were already mustering as we arrived at the hide. The first shift comprised mealy and yellow-crowned parrots, which look like they have been lightly dusted with flour, and glossy blue-headed and orange-cheeked parrots. It was a riot of green, jabbering and bickering, fluttering like butterflies, then flying en masse when little more than a shadow alarmed them. After the parrots had had their fill, we spectators breakfasted on pancakes and maple syrup and waited for the macaws. Soon, in the trees, on the vines and on the lick itself, red and green macaws were putting on their show. They hung and

swivelled just like captive macaws, but with more joie-de-vivre. Individuals and pairs preened. As they spread their wings for balance while picking off lumps of the cliff, it was clear that whoever named the species was only telling half the story. Red and green, yes, but the blue in their feathers is electric." In order not to disturb the birds, you are not allowed to leave the hide before they have departed.

Another macaw clay lick is a short boat ride and walk from the Tambopata Research Center. Here you watch from the river bank, perched on small camping chairs. As at Manu, absolute silence must be maintained, but, in addition, no bright colours can be worn (those with red or yellow raincoats may get a little wet in the early morning showers). "On the first day, the blue-headed parrots were the first to `dance'. Then chestnut-fronted, blue and yellow and scarlet macaws, mealy parrots and white-eyed parakeets also turned up, but not a bird settled on the cliff. They waited in the trees, but mostly flew overhead in huge, swirling, shrieking clouds of green. Next morning, more species came: yellow-headed macaws, yellow-crowned and orange-cheeked parrots in addition to those seen the day before. To us it seemed much the same sort of day, but to the birds conditions were much more favourable for a breakfast of clay as they all settled."

Between Boca Manu and Colorado is **Blanquillo**, a private reserve (10,000 ha). Bring a good tent with you and all food if you want to camp and do it yourself, or alternatively accommodation is available at the *Tambo Blanquillo* (full board or accommodation only). Wildlife is abundant, especially macaws and parrots at the macaw lick near *Manu Wildlife Centre* (see page 553). There are occasional boats to Blanquillo from Shintuya; US$10, 6-8 hours.

Tours to Manu

There are about 15 authorized agencies in Cusco offering tours to Manu. Prices vary considerably, from as little as US$600 per person for a 6-day tour up to US$1,000-1,500 per person with the more experienced and reputable companies. The cheaper tours usually travel overland there and back, which takes at least 3 full days (in the dry season), meaning you'll spend much of your time on a bus or truck. Another important factor to consider is whether or not your boat has a canopy, as it can be very uncomfortable sitting in direct sunlight or rain for hours on end. Also the quality of guides varies a lot – you might want to meet your guide before deciding on a trip if you are in Cusco.

Amazon Basin

NB Beware of pirate operators on the streets of Cusco who offer trips to the Reserved Zone of Manu and end up halfway through the trip changing the route 'due to emergencies', which, in reality means they have no permits to operate in the area. For a full list of all companies who are allowed access to the Reserved Zone, contact the Manu National Park office (address page 554).

NB You can only enter the Reserved Zone with a recognized guide who is affiliated to an authorized tour company. Take finely-woven, long-sleeved and long-legged clothing and effective insect repellent. Note that for independent travellers, only the Cultural Zone is an option. Lodge reservations should be made at the relevant offices in Cusco as these lodges are often not set up to receive visitors without prior notice.

Tour operators   The agencies listed below are at the more expensive end of the spectrum but recommended as providing a good quality of service. *Manu Nature Tours EIRL*, Av Pardo 1046, Cusco, T252721, F234793, www.manuperu.com Owned by Boris Gómez, they run lodge-based trips and are owners of *Manu Lodge* (which is open all year), situated on an ox-bow lake, providing access to the forest. They are also part owners of *Manu Cloudforest Lodge*. Activities include river-rafting and canopy-climbing. It is highly recommended for experiencing the jungle in comfort. They offer 8-day trips with flights one way or with road/boat transport there and plane back, also 4-day trips with plane both ways. *Manu Expeditions*, Av Pardo 895, Cusco T 226671, F236706, www.ManuExpeditions.com Owned by ornithologist/British Consul Barry Walker of the *Cross Keys Pub* and his Peruvian wife Rosario Velarde, they run highly recommended 4-9 day trips in safari camps and comfortable lodges and jointly run the *Manu Wildlife Centre* (see below).

They are also highly specialized in birdwatching trips and horse-riding trips in the mountains. *Pantiacolla Tours*, Plateros 360, T238323, F252696, www.pantiacolla.com Run by Marianne Von Vlaardingen and Gustavo Moscoso. They have tours to the *Pantiacolla Lodge* (see below) and also 8-day camping trips. Pantiacolla has started a community-based ecotourism project, called the Yine Project, with the people of Diamante in the Multiple Use Zone. Among the many aspects of this project are rainforest conservation, the construction of an eco-lodge and volunteer work in conjunction with the Amauta Spanish Language School in Cusco. *InkaNatura Travel* also run tours to Manu Wildlife Centre. *Eco-tour Manu*, a non-profit making organization made up of tour operators, assures quality of service and actively supports conservation projects in the area. When you travel with an Eco-tour member you are ensuring that you support tropical rainforest conservation projects. *Eco-tour Manu* comprises *Manu Expeditions, Manu Nature Tours, Pantiacolla Tours, InkaNatura Travel,*

Manu Ecological Adventures and *Expediciones Vilca* (see Cusco, Tour operators for addresses of last two). Contact any member company for information. *Tambo Tours*, www.2GOPERU.com, www.tambotours.com Adventure travel and general tour operators for all areas of the Peruvian Amazon.

Manu Cloud Forest Lodge, located at Unión at 1,800 m on the road from Paucartambo to Atalaya, owned by *Manu Nature Tours*, 6 rooms with 4 beds. *Cock of the Rock Lodge*, on the same road at 1,500 m, next to a Cock of the Rock *lek*, 8 double rooms and 8 private cabins, run by the *ACSS* group (see below). *Amazonia Lodge*, on the Río Alto Madre de Dios just across the river from Atalaya, an old tea hacienda run by the Yabar family, famous for its bird diversity and fine hospitality, a great place to relax, contact Santiago in advance and he'll arrange a pick-up. In Cusco at Matará 334, T/F231370, amazonia1@correo.dnet.com.pe *Pantiacolla Lodge*, 30 mins down-river from Shintuya. Owned by the Moscoso family. Book through *Pantiacolla Tours* (see above). *Manu Lodge*, situated on the Manu river, 3 hrs upriver from Boca Manu towards Cocha Salvador, run by *Manu Nature Tours* and only bookable as part of a full package deal with transport. *Manu Wildlife Centre*, 2 hrs down the Río Madre de Dios from Boca Manu, near the Blanquillo macaw lick and also counts on a Tapir lick and walk-up canopy tower. Book through *Manu Expeditions* or *InkaNatura*. 22 double cabins, all with private bathroom and hot water. Also canopy towers for birdwatching. *Erika Lodge*, on the Alto Madre de Dios, 25 mins from Atalaya, offers basic accommodation and is cheaper than the other, more luxurious lodges. Contact *Aventuras Ecológicas Manu*, Plateros 361, Cusco. *Casa Machiguenga* near Cocha Salvador, upriver from *Manu Lodge*. Machiguenga-style cabins run by local communities with NGO help. Contact *Manu Expeditions* or the *Apeco NGO*.

Lodges in Manu

Amazon Basin

Useful addresses In Lima: *Asociación Peruana para la Conservación de la Naturaleza* (Apeco), Parque José Acosta 187, p 2, Magdalena del Mar. *Pronaturaleza*, Av de los Rosales 255, San Isidro. In Cusco: *Asociación para la Conservación de la Selva Sur* (ACSS), Ricaldo Palma J-1, Santa Mónica (same office as *Peru Verde*), T243408, F226392, acss@telser.com.pe A local NGO that can help with information and has free video shows about Manu National Park and Tambopata National Reserve. They are friendly and helpful and also have information on programmes and research in the jungle area of Madre de Dios. Further information can be obtained from the *Manu National Park Office*, Av Micaela Bastidas 310, Cusco, T240898, pqnmanu@cosapidata.mail.com.pe Casilla Postal 591. 0800-1400. They issue a permit for the Reserve Zone (see under Boca Manu, page 550, for the cost).

Puerto Maldonado

Phone code: 084
Colour map 6, grid A3
Population: 35,000
Altitude: 250 m

Puerto Maldonado is an important starting point for visiting the rainforest, or for departing to Brazil or Bolivia. Still, most visitors won't see much of the place because they are whisked through town on their way to a lodge on the Río Madre de Dios or the Río Tambopata. The city dwellers aren't too pleased about this and would like tourists to spend some time in town. But it's a hot, humid place, where nothing much happens.

Getting there   The vast majority of people fly (see Transport for details).

The road from Cusco   The road from the cold of the high Andes to the steamy heat of the Amazon jungle can only be described as a challenge (and is not really recommended). It is expertly described in Matthew Parris' book *Inka-Cola*. In the dry season a bus runs three times a week between Cusco and Puerto Maldonado. It takes 18 hours and costs US$15. Otherwise, from Cusco take a bus to Urcos; 1 hr, US$2.25 (see also page 227). Trucks leave from here for **Mazuko** around 1500-1600, arriving around 2400 the next day; 33 hrs, US$6.65. Catch a truck early in the morning from here for Puerto Maldonado, US$4.50, 13-14 hrs. It's a painfully slow journey on an appalling road. Trucks frequently get stuck or break down. The road passes through Ocongate and Marcapata, where there are hot thermal springs, before reaching **Quincemil**, 240 km from Urcos (15-20 hrs), a centre for alluvial gold-mining with many banks. Accommodation is available in **F** *Hotel Toni*, friendly, clean, cold shower, good meals. Ask the food-carriers to take you to visit the miners washing for gold in the nearby rivers. Quincemil marks the half-way point and the start of the all-weather road. Gasoline is scarce in Quincemil because most road vehicles continue on 70 km to Mazuko, which is another mining centre, where they fill up with the cheaper gasoline of the jungle region.

The journey takes up to 50-55 hrs in total. The road is 99 km unpaved and the journey is very rough, but the changing scenery is magnificent and worth the hardship and discomfort. This road is impossible in the wet season. Make sure you have warm clothing for travelling through the Sierra. The trucks only stop four times each day, for meals and a short sleeping period for the driver. You should take a mosquito net, repellent, sunglasses, sunscreen, a plastic sheet, a blanket, food and water.

An alternative route from Cusco goes via Paucartambo, Pilcopata and Shintuya, and from there by boat to Puerto Maldonado (see under Manu Biosphere Reserve).

Sights   Overlooking the confluence of the rivers Tambopata and Madre de Dios, Puerto Maldonado is a major logging and brazil-nut processing centre. From the park at the end of Jr Arequipa, across from the Capitanía, you get a good view of the two rivers, the ferries across the Madre de Dios and the stacks of lumber at the dockside. The brazil-nut harvest is from December to February and the crop tends to be good on alternate years. Nuts are sold on the street, plain or coated in sugar or chocolate. **El Mirador** is a 30-m high tower at the junction of Avenida Fitzcarrald and Avenida Madre de Dios, with three platforms giving fine views over the city and surrounding rainforest. There is also a toilet at the top – no curtains – from which there is an equally fine view over the city! ■ *1000-1600. US$0.30.*

Essentials

A *Wasai*, Billinghurst opposite the Capitanía, T571355, maldonado@wasai.com (or Plateros 320, Cusco T/F084-221826, cuzco@wasai.com). Price includes breakfast, a/c, TV, shower. In a beautiful location overlooking the Madre de Dios, with forest surrounding cabin-style rooms which are built on a slope down to the river, small pool with waterfall, good restaurant if slightly expensive (local fish a speciality). Recommended, although service can be stretched if hotel is full. They can organize local tours and also have a lodge on the Tambopata River (see page 558).

Sleeping
■ *on map*
Price codes:
see inside front cover

Puerto Maldonado

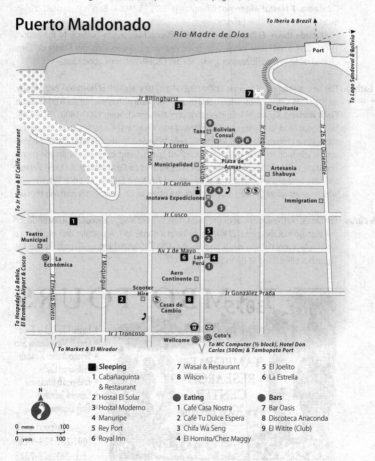

	Sleeping		7 Wasai & Restaurant		5 El Joelito
	1 Cabañaquinta		8 Wilson		6 La Estrella
	& Restaurant				
	2 Hostal El Solar		● Eating		● Bars
	3 Hostal Moderno		1 Café Casa Nostra		7 Bar Oasis
	4 Manuripe		2 Café Tu Dulce Espera		8 Discoteca Anaconda
	5 Rey Port		3 Chifa Wa Seng		9 El Witite (Club)
	6 Royal Inn		4 El Hornito/Chez Maggy		

Amazon Basin

C *Cabañaquinta*, Cusco 535, T/F571864, cabanaquinta@webcusco.zzn.com With bathroom, fan, good restaurant, friendly, lovely garden, very comfortable but could be cleaner, airport transfer. Recommended. **C** *Don Carlos*, Av León Velarde 1271, T571029, T/F571323. Nice view over the Río Tambopata, a/c, restaurant, TV, phone, good.

D *Amarumayo*, Libertad 433, 10 mins from centre, T573860. Comfortable, with pool and garden, good restaurant. Recommended. **D** *Royal Inn*, Av 2 de Mayo 333, T571048. Modern and clean, the best of the mid-range hotels, rooms at the back are less noisy.

E *Hostal El Solar*, González Prada 445, T571571. With bath (cheaper without), basic but clean, fan. **E** per person *Hostal Iñapari*, 4 km from centre, 5 mins from the airport, T572575, F572155, joaquin@lullitec.com.pe Run by a Spanish couple Isabel and Javier, price includes breakfast and dinner, excellent food, friendly, clean. They also have a rustic camping facility in the rainforest on the remote Río Pariamanu, a tributary of the Madre de Dios, upriver from Puerto Maldonado. **E** *Hospedaje La Bahía*, 2 de Mayo 710, T572127. Cheaper without bath or TV, large rooms, clean. The best of the cheaper options. **E** *Rey Port*, Av León Velarde 457, T571177. With bathroom (cheaper without), clean, fan, good value. **E** *Wilson*, Jr González Prada 355, T572838. With bathroom, basic.

F per person *Hospedaje Manuripe*, 2 de Mayo 287, T573561. Basic but clean, shared bath, has travel agency for day tours to Lago Sandoval and longer tours to Candamo. **F** *Hostal Moderno*, Billinghurst 357, T571063. Brightly painted, clean, quiet, friendly, but little privacy.

Outside town *El Brombus*, 4 km from Puerto Maldonado, halfway to the airport, T573230. A small rustic lodge with good restaurant, overlooking the Madre de Dios. Owned by Fernando Rozemberg, who speaks English and runs good tours.

Eating
● *on map*

The best restaurant in town is at the *Hotel Wasai* (see above). *El Hornito/Chez Maggy*, on the plaza. Cosy atmosphere, good pizzas, but pasta dishes are not such good value. *Chifa Waseng*, Cusco 244. Chinese (not very authentic), open 1200-1400, 1800-2300, but closed Mon lunchtime. *La Estrella*, Av León Velarde 474. The smartest and best of the *pollos a la brasa* places. *El Joelito*, Av León Velarde 328, and *El Califa*, Piura 266 (recommended) often have bushmeat, mashed banana and palm hearts on the menu. There are several cafés for snacks and cakes, such as *La Casa Nostra*, Av León Velarde 515, the best place for snacks and cakes, and *Tu Dulce Espera*, Av León Velarde 469, which serves good *tamales*, but some of the other lunch options are nothing special.

Bars & clubs

Bar Oasis, on the south side of the plaza, next to *Chez Maggy*. *Discoteca Anaconda*, on the east side of the plaza. *El Witite*, Av León Velarde 153. A popular and good disco which plays mostly latin music and charges US$1.50 after 2300, open only Fri and Sat. There is a billiard hall at Puno 520.

Amazon Basin

Artesanía Shabuya, Plaza de Armas 279, T571856. The best shop in town for handi- **Shopping**
crafts. Handicrafts are also sold at *Inotawa Expediciones*, Av León Velarde 315,
T572511 (Lima 467 4560), www.inotawaexpeditions.com This is a travel agency
which can arrange jungle trips from US$120-165.

Motorcycle hire Scooters and mopeds can de hired from *San Francisco*, and others, **Transport**
on the corner of Puno and G Prada for US$1.15 per hour or US$10 per day. No deposit is
required but your passport and driving licence need to be shown.

Air To **Lima**, daily with *Tans* and *Aviandina* at 1130 via Cusco. *Lan Perú* flies to Lima
via Cusco Tue, Thu, Sat at 1235. Combis to the airport run along Av 2 de Mayo, 10-15
mins, US$0.60. A moto-taxi from town to the airport is US$1.75. **NB** A yellow fever vaccination is offered free at the airport on arrival, but check that a new needle is used.

River To **Boca Manu and Shintuya**, via Colorado. Take a combi to Laberinto (see
Trips from Puerto Maldonando below) and take a cargo boat from there to Colorado;
several daily, US$12. You can get a daily cargo boat from there to Boca Manu and
Shintuya, 9-10 hrs, US$15. From Shintuya trucks go to Pilcopata and Cusco (see under
Manu Biosphere Reserve).

To **Puerto Heath** (Bolivian border), it can take several days to find a boat going all the
way to the Bolivian border. Motorized dugout canoes go to Puerto Pardo on the Peruvian
side, 5 hrs, US$4.50 per person (no hotels or shops); wait here for a canoe to Puerto
Heath. It is fairly hard to get a boat from the border to Riberalta (a wait of up to 3 days is
not uncommon), US$15-20. Alternatively, travel to the naval base at América, then fly.

Airline offices *Aero Continente/Aviandina*, Av León Velarde 584, T572004, F571971, **Directory**
pem@aerocontinente.com.pe *Lan Perú*, Av León Velarde y 2 de Mayo, T573677. *Tans*, Av
León Velarde 160, T571429. *Aeroregional*, Av León Velarde 525. **Banks** *BCP*, cash
advances with Visa, no commission on TCs. *Banco de la Nación*, cash on Mastercard,
quite good rates for TCs. Both are on the south side of the Plaza. The best rates for cash
are at the *casas de cambio*/gold shops on Puno 6th block, eg *Cárdenas Hnos*, Puno 605.
Communications Internet: Three on Av León Velarde 7th block, *Coto's*, *Wellcome*, and
MC Computer (No 756). *La Económica*, 2 de Mayo y E Rivero, opposite the Teatro Municipal. Another on the north side of the Plaza. All charge between US$1.15 and US$1.40 per
hr. **Serpost**: at Av León Velarde 6th block. **Telefónica**: on Puno 7th block. A phone office
on the Plaza, next to *El Hornito*, sells all phone cards for national and international calls.
Embassies and consulates Bolivian Consulate: on the north side of the plaza. **Peruvian immigration:** is at 26 de Diciembre 356, 1 block from the plaza, get your exit stamp
here. **Language schools** *Tambopata Language Centre*, T572610, tinasmith@terra.
com.pe, www.geocities.com/tambopata_language It is now possible to learn Spanish
while living close to the rainforest and this is a cheaper option than studying in Cusco.

Trips from Puerto Maldonado

The beautiful and tranquil lake is a one hour boat ride along the Río Madre de **Lago**
Dios, and then a 5-km walk into the jungle. There are two jungle lodges at the **Sandoval**
lake (see under Jungle lodges page 559). It is possible to see giant river otters
early in the morning and several species of monkeys, macaws and hoatzin. At
weekends, especially on Sundays, the lake gets quite busy. ■ *Entry to the lake
coasts US$3 (scheduled to rise to US$5 in 2003). You must go with a guide; this
can be arranged by the boat driver.*

Boats can be hired at the port for about US$20 a day – plus petrol – to go to
Lago Sandoval, but don't pay the full cost in advance. A recommended boat
owner and guide is Romel Nacimiento. (See also Tour operators page 558.)

Upstream from Lago Sandoval, towards Puerto Maldonado, is the **wreck of the *Fitzcarrald***. The steamer (a replica of Fitzcarrald's boat) lies a few metres from the Madre de Dios in the bed of a small stream. The German director, Werner Herzog, was inspired to make his famous film of the same name by the story of Fitzcarrald's attempt to haul a boat from the Ucuyali to the Madre de Dios drainage basins (this happened in what is now the Manu National Park).

Other trips   For those interested in seeing a gold rush town, a trip to **Laberinto** is suggested. There is one hotel and several poor restaurants. Combis and trucks leave from Puerto Maldonado, 1½ hours, US$2.50, uncomfortable, and returns in the afternoon daily. Boats leave from here to Manu (see Transport page 557).

At Km 13 on the Cusco road is a pleasant **recreational centre** with a restaurant and natural pools where it's possible to swim. It gets busy at weekends. It's US$2 each way by *mototaxi* from town.

Trips can be made to **Lago Valencia**, 60 km away near the Bolivian border - four hours there, eight hours back. It is an ox-bow lake with lots of wildlife. Many excellent beaches and islands are located within an hour's boat ride.

Tour operators   *Transtours*, G Prada 341, T572606. Reputable guides are *Hernán Llave Cortez* , *Celso Centeno*, the *Mejía* brothers and the *Valarezo* brothers, all of whom can be contacted on arrival at the airport, if available. Also *Javier Salazar* of *Hostal Iñapari* is a reputable guide who specializes in trips up the remote Río Las Piedras. The usual price for trips to Lago Sandoval is US$25 per person per day (minimum of 2 people), and US$35 per person per day for longer trips lasting 2-4 days (minimum of 4-6 people). All guides should have a *carnet* issued by the Ministry of Tourism (DRITINCI), which also verifies them as suitable guides for trips to other places and confirms their identity. Boat hire can be arranged through the Capitanía del Puerto (Río Madre de Dios), T573003. *Tambo Tours*, see page 553.

Tambopata National Reserve (TNR)

From Puerto Maldonado you can visit the Tambopata National Reserve by travelling up the Tambopata river or down the Madre de Dios river. The area was first declared a reserve in 1990 and is a very reasonable alternative for those who do not have the time to visit Manu. It is a close rival in terms of seeing wildlife and boasts some superb ox-bow lakes. There are a number of lodges here which are excellent for lowland rainforest birding. Explorers' Inn is perhaps the most famous, but the Posada Amazonas/Tambopata Research Centre and Tambopata Lodge are also good. In a new initiative, to try to ensure that more tourism income stays in the area, several local families have established their own small-scale 'Casas de Hospedaje'. These offer more basic facilities and make use of the nearby forest but are cheaper and may well lead to a more intimate forest experience.

Admission   The fee to enter the TNR is US$3.25 per person (it may rise to US$8 in 2003), if staying at a lodge, or US$20 per person (it may rise to US$25 in 2003) if camping. If staying at a Lodge, they will organize the payment of the fee, otherwise, you need to visit the INRENA office, formerly at Fonavi H-10, Avenida Madre de Dios, Monday to Saturday 0830-1300, 1530-1800 (the building recently burnt down in mid-2002 and it is not know if it will reopen in the same location).

The **Bahuaja-Sonene National Park** runs from the Río Heath, which forms **The park areas** the Bolivian border, across to the Río Tambopata, 50-80 km upstream from Puerto Maldonado. It was expanded to 1,091,416 ha in August 2000, with the Tambopata National Reserve (254,358 ha) created to form a buffer zone. The Park is closed to visitors though those visiting the *collpa* (macaw lick) on the Tambopata or river rafting down the Tambopata will travel through it.

Most of the lodges in the Tambopata area use the term 'ecotourism', or something **Sleeping:** similar, in their publicity material, but it is applied pretty loosely. *Posada Amazonas'* col- **Jungle Lodges** laboration with the local community is unique in the area, but fortunately no lodge offers trips where guests hunt for their meals. See Responsible tourism, page 51 in Essentials at the beginning of the book, for points to note.

Lodges on the Río Madre de Dios *Cuzco Tambo Lodge,* bungalows 15 km out on the northern bank of the Río Madre de Dios. 2, 3 and 4-day jungle programmes available, from US$90 per person in low season, tours visit Lago Sandoval. Book through Cusco-Maldonado Tour, Pasaje de Harinas 177 (T/F244054), Cusco, tamblod@ terra.com.pe *Eco Amazonia Lodge,* on the Madre de Dios, 1 hr down-river from Puerto Maldonado. Accommodation for up to 80 in basic bungalows and dormitories, good for birdwatching with viewing platforms and tree canopy access, has its own Monkey Island with animals taken from the forest, US$150 for 3 days/2 nights. Book through their office in Cusco: Portal de Panes 109, oficina 6, T236159, F225068, ecolodge@ qenqo -unsaac.edu.pe *El Corto Maltés,* Billinghurst 229, Puerto Maldonado, T/F573831, cortomaltes@terra.com.pe On the south side of the Madre de Dios river, halfway to Sandoval which is the focus of most visits. Hot water, huge dining-room, well run. Attracts a lot of French groups. **C** *Casa de Hospedaje Mejía,* an attractive rustic lodge on Lago Sandoval, with 10 double rooms, full board can be arranged, canoes are available

National Tambopata Reserve & Bahuaja-Sonene National Park

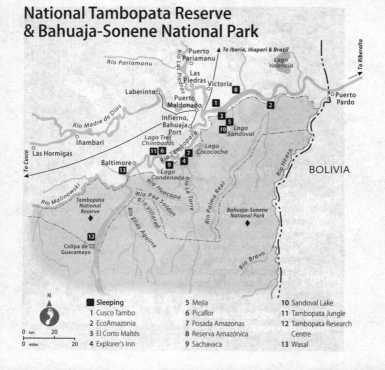

Amazon Basin

(to book T571428, visit *Mejía Tours*, L Velarde 333, or just turn up). *Reserva Amazónica Lodge*, 45 mins by boat down the Río Madre de Dios. Jungle tours available with multi-lingual guides, the lodge is surrounded by its own 10,000 ha but most tours are to Lago Sandoval, US$160 per person (double occupancy) for 2 days/1 night package, rising to US$370 for 5 days/4 nights, a naturalists programme is also provided, negotiable out of season. Has the largest number of ants recorded in a single location, 342. The lodge has a Monkey Island (Isla Rolín) for the recovery of primates. A hotel in the jungle with 6 suites and 38 rustic bungalows with private bathrooms, solar power, good food. To book: *Inkaterra*, Andalucía 174, Lima 18, T01-610 0404, F422 4701, Cusco T084-245314, F244 669, Puerto Maldonado T084-572283, F572988, www.inka terra.com.pe *Sandoval Lake Lodge*, 1 km beyond *Mejía* on Lago Sandoval, usually accessed by canoe across the lake after a 3-km walk or rickshaw ride along the trail, can accommodate 50 people in 25 rooms, bar and dining area, electricity, hot water. There is a short system of trails nearby, guides are available in several languages. Prices start at US$140 per person (double occupancy) for 2 days/1 night, to US$250 double for 4 days/3 nights. Book through *InkaNatura*, Manuel Bañon 461, San Isidro, Lima, T440 2022, F422 9225, www.inka natura.com (see also Cusco, Tour operators, page 181). They also have a small lodge on the Río Heath. *Upper Amazon Lodge*, www.geocities.com/upperamazon A small, new, rustic lodge located at the start of the trail to lake Sandoval.

Lodges on the Tambopata are reached by vehicle to Bahuaja port, 15 km up river from Puerto Maldonado by the community of Infierno, then by boat

Lodges on the Tambopata *Explorers Inn*, book through *Peruvian Safaris*, Alcanfores 459, Miraflores, Lima, T4478888, F2418427 or Plateros 365, T235342 Cusco, safaris@amauta.rcp.net.pe The office in Puerto Maldonado is at Fitzcarrald 136, T/F572078. The lodge is located adjoining the TNR, in the part where most research work has been done, 58 km from Puerto Maldonado. It's a 2½-hr ride up the Río Tambopata (1½ hrs return, in the early morning, so take warm clothes and rain gear), one of the best places in Peru for seeing jungle birds (580 plus species have been recorded here),

butterflies (1,230 plus species), also giant river otters, but you probably need more than a 2-day tour to benefit fully from the location. Offers tours through the adjoining community of La Torre to meet local people and find out about their farms (*chacras*) and handicrafts. The guides are biologists and naturalists from around the world who undertake research in the reserve in return for acting as guides. They provide interesting wildlife-treks, including to the macaw lick (*collpa*). US$180 for 3 days/2 nights, US$165 in the low season. **Picaflor Research Centre**, Casilla 105, Puerto Maldonado, T/F572589, www.picaflor.org A small lodge located just before *Tambopata Jungle Lodge*, guiding in English, visits are made to Lago Condenado. US$190 for 3 days, 2 nights with discounts for longer stays; they also offer bird-watching and researcher programmes at US$20 per night and a volunteer programme, minimum of 10 nights, US$10 per day, in return for 3 hrs assistance each day marking trails, etc. **Posada Amazonas Lodge**, on the Tambopata river, 2 hrs upriver from Puerto Maldonado. A unique collaboration between a tour agency the local native community of Infierno. Large attractive rooms with bathroom, cold showers, visits to Lake Tres Chimbadas, with good birdwatching opportunities including the Tambopata *Collpa*. Offers trips to a nearby indigenous primary health care project where a native healer gives guided tours of the medicinal plant garden. Tourist income has helped the centre become self-funding. Service and guiding is very good. Recommended. Prices start at US$190 for a 3 day/2 night package, or US$522 for 5 days/4 nights including the **Tambopata Research Centre**, the company's older, more intimate, but comfortable lodge. Rooms are smaller than Posada Amazonas, shared showers, cold water. The lodge is next to the famous Tambopata macaw clay lick. Tapir are often seen here on the bank opposite the collpa. Book through **Rainforest Expeditions**, Aramburú 166, of 4B, Miraflores, Lima 18, T421 8347, F421 8183, or Portal de Carnes 236, Cusco, T084-232772, or Arequipa 401, Puerto Maldonado, T571056, or through www.perunature.com (winners of Conservation International's Ecotourism Excellence Award in 2000). **Sachavaca Inn**, 2 bungalows for up to 20 people, located between *Explorer's Inn* and *Tambopata Jungle Lodge*. Visits are made to Lago Sachavacayoc. To book, T571045, F571297, Puerto Maldonado, www.web cusco.com/sachavacasinn **Tambopata Jungle Lodge**, on the Río Tambopata, make reservations at Av Pardo 705, Cusco, T225701, F238911, postmast@patcusco.com.pe Trips go to Lake Condenado, some to Lake Sacha vacayoc, and to the *Collpa de Chuncho*, guiding mainly in English and Spanish, package US$160 per person for 3 days/2 nights (US$145 in the low season), naturalists programme provided. **Wasai Lodge**, on the Río Tambopata, 80 km (3½ hrs) upriver from Puerto Maldonado, T571355, 1½ hrs return, same owners as *Hotel Wasai* in town; www.wasai.com Small lodge with 3 bungalows for 30 people, 15 km of trails around the lodge, guides in English and Spanish. The *Collpa de Chuncho*, one of the biggest macaw licks in the world, is only 1 hr up river; 3 day trips US$160, 7 days US$500.

Amazon Basin

Fundo Buenaventura, is part of the tourist intiative by long-term colonists living along the Tambopata river, 50-75 km upriver from Puerto Maldonado, 5-6 hrs by *peque-peque*. Accommodation for up to 10 in basic facilities, provides an insight into local lifestyles, minimum of 2 nights, from US$20-35 per person, includes transport to/from Tambopata dock, all food, mosquito net and Spanish-speaking guide, check if the package includes a trip to a *collpa*, in which case you'll also need a tent. Contact in advance, T571646, or via buenaventura50@hotmail.com There is usually a representative to meet flights at Puerto Maldonado airport. Similar in style and intention are: *Albergue Inatowa*, on the Tambopata, just downstream from *Explorer's Inn*, visits are made to the nearby Lago Tres Chimbadas. *Casa de Hospedaje Las Piedras*, T84-600109, *Casa de Hospedaje El Gato* and *Casa de Hospedaje Baltimore*, just upriver from *Tambopata Jungle Lodge*, visits are made to Lago Condenado. The *Casas* may advertise with agencies in Cusco, otherwise try to meet their representatives on arrival in Puerto Maldonado.

Long-term visitors should be aware that leishmaniasis exists in this area

Some of the lodges mentioned above also offer guiding and research placements to biology and environmental science graduates. For more details send an SAE to *TReeS: UK*- c/o J Forrest, PO Box 33153, London NW3 4DR. USA - W Widdowson, PO Box 5668, Eureka, CA 95502.

To Iberia and Iñapari

Colour map 4, grid C5

Daily public transport runs on the improved dirt road which begins across the Río Madre de Dios and runs to Iberia and Iñapari on the border with Brazil. Take one of the frequent ferries which crosses from Puerto Maldonado. In the wet season the road may only be passable with difficulty, especially between Iberia and Iñapari. In the dry, though, it is a fast road and dangerous for motorcyclists because of passing traffic. Along the road there remains no primary forest, only secondary growth and small farms (*chacras*). There are also picturesque *caseríos* (settlements) that serve as collecting and processing centres for the brazil nut. Approximately 70% of the inhabitants in the Madre de Dios are involved in the collection of this prized nut.

Iberia, Km 168, has two hotels, the best is **F** *Hostal Aquino*, basic, cold shower. Just outside the town the local rubber tappers association has set up a Reserve and Information Centre. It has a swimming pool (US$0.50).

Iñapari, at the end of the road, Km 235, has two basic hotels (the best one is **F** *Hostal Milagros*) and a restaurant, but **Assis Brasil** across the border is more attractive and has three hotels (**F**) and a good *churrascaria* on the main street.

There is a road from **Assis Brasil to Brasiléia** in Brazil (120 km, buses run in the dry season, 2½ hours, US$3.60; four-wheel drive vehicles in the wet season).

There are connections to Bolivia. It can be cold travelling this road, so take a blanket or sleeping bag. There are no exchange facilities en route and poor exchange rates for Brazilian currency at Iñapari.

Crossing to Bolivia and Brazil

Check in advance that you do not need a consular visa for Brazil or Bolivia; they are not issued at the border.

To Bolivia: take the boat to Puerto Heath (see page 557) and get a tourist visa at the Bolivian consulate in Puerto Maldonado.

To Brazil: the easiest way to reach the border is to take one of the car colectivos that leave for Iberia from the dock on the opposite side of the Madre de Dios from Puerto Maldonado between 0700-0800, three hours, US$5.50-9 (prices higher Iberia-Puerto Maldonado). From Iberia to Iñapari there are further colectivos, 1½ hours, US$2.50-3. There are also flights from Puerto Maldonado to Iberia. Exit stamps can be obtained at immigration in Iñapari, open 0800-1830. Walk across the bridge over the Rio Acre to Assis Brasil, where there is no Policía Federal office. Travel on to Brasiléia to obtain your Brazil entry stamp at Policía Federal in the Rodoviária (bus station).

Background

History and politics

Pre-Columbian history

Despite Peru's formidable geographical difficulties and frequent natural disasters, archaeologists have uncovered a pre-Columbian history of highly advanced societies that prevailed against these awesome odds. The coastal desert from Lambayeque department south to Paracas has revealed an 'American Egypt', although this has meant a bias towards the coastal region and a reliance on the contents of tombs for information. Knowledge of these tombs often only comes to light following their looting by gangs of *huaqueros* (grave robbers), incited by demand from the international antiquities market.

The Incas told the Spaniards that before they established their Tawantinsuyo Empire, the land was overrun by primitives constantly at war with one another. There were, in fact, many other civilized cultures dating back as far as 2000 BC. The most accomplished of these were the Chavín and Sechín (c 900-200 BC), the Paracas-Nasca (c 200 BC-AD 500), the Huari-Tiahuanaco (c 750 BC-AD 1000), and the Moche-Chimú (200 BC-AD 1400).

Early settlement It is generally accepted that the earliest settlers in Peru were related to people who had crossed the Bering Straits from Asia and drifted through the Americas from about 20,000 BC. However, theories of early migrations from across the Pacific and Atlantic have been rife since Thor Heyerdahl's raft expeditions in 1947 and 1969-70 (see also under Túcume, page 412).

The earliest evidence of human presence has been found at three sites: Pikimachay near Ayacucho, Pachamachay in Junín and the Guitarrero Cave in the Callejón de Huaylas. All have a radiocarbon date prior to 9000 BC. It had been thought that village settlement in Peru, on the central coast at Pampa, dated from 2500 BC. The theory was that, between these two dates, people lived nomadically in small groups, mainly hunting and gathering but also cultivating some plants seasonally. Domestication of llamas, alpacas and guinea pigs also began at this time, particularly important for the highland people around the Titicaca basin. **Caral**, however, has overturned many of the accepted tenets of Peruvian archaeology for this period. Caral is a city, 20 km from the coast in the Supe Valley whose date is about 2,600 BC. It is a monumental construction and appears to be easily the oldest city in South America, flourishing for some 500 years. The evidence points to complex urban society beginning much earlier than previously thought and the city seems to have had a primarily religious, rather than warlike purpose. If these deductions are correct, they also upset some long-held beliefs about city-building worldwide being principally bellicose rather than peaceful.

The abundant wealth of marine life produced by the Humboldt Current, especially along the north coast, boosted population growth and settlement in this area. Around 2000 BC climatic change dried up the *lomas* ('fog meadows'), and drove sea shoals to deeper water. People turned to farming and began to spread inland along river valleys.

Origins of Andean civilization From the second millennium BC to around the first century BC is known as the Formative Period (also called Preceramic Period VI and Initial Period) when the first signs of the high culture of Andean society appeared. During this period sophisticated irrigation and canal systems were developed, farming productivity increased and communities had more time to devote to building and producing ceramics and textiles. The development of pottery also led to trade and cultural links with other communities. Distribution of land and water to the farmers was probably organized by a corporate authority, and this may have led to the later 'Mit'a' labour system developed by the Incas.

Above all, this period is characterized by the construction of centres of urban concentration (Caral notwithstanding) that promoted labour specialization and the development of cultural expression. The earliest buildings built were *huacas*, adobe platform mounds, centres of cult or sacred power. Huaca Florida was the largest example of this period, near the Río Rimac, later replaced by Huaca Garagay as a major centre for the area. Similar centres spread along the north coast, such as El Aspero and Piedra Parada.

During this period, however, much more advanced architecture was being built at **Kotosh**, in the central Andes near Huánuco. Japanese archaeological excavations there in the 1960s revealed a temple with ornamental niches and friezes. Some of the earliest pottery was also found here, showing signs of influence from southern Ecuador and the tropical lowlands, adding weight to theories of Andean culture originating in the Amazon. Radiocarbon dates of some Kotosh remains are as early as 1850 BC.

Chavín & Sechín

For the next 1,000 years or so up to c 900 BC, communities grew and spread inland from the north coast and south along the northern highlands. Farmers still lived in simple adobe or rough stone houses but built increasingly large and complex ceremonial centres, such as at Las Haldas in the Casma Valley. As farming became more productive and pottery more advanced, commerce grew and states began to develop throughout central and North-central Peru, with the associated signs of social structure and hierarchies.

Around 900 BC a new era was marked by the rise of two important centres; **Chavín de Huantar** in the central Andes and **Sechín Alto**, inland from Casma on the north coast.

Chavín takes its name from the site of Chavín de Huantar in the northern highlands. This was the first of several 'horizon styles' that were of the greatest importance in Peru and had very widespread influence. The other later ones, the Huari-Tiahuanaco and the Inca, were pan-Peruvian, affecting all parts of the country. The chief importance of Chavín de Huantar was not so much in its highly advanced architecture as in the influence of its cult coupled with the artistic style of its ceramics and other artefacts. The founders of Chavín may have originated in the tropical lowlands as some of its carved monoliths show representations of monkeys and felines.

Objects with Chavín traits have been found all along the coast from Piura to the Lurin valley south of Lima, and its cult ideology spread to temples around the same area. Richard L Burger of Yale University has argued that the extent of Chavín influence has been exaggerated. Many sites on the coast already had their own cult practices and the Chavín idols may have been simply added alongside. There is evidence of an El Niño flood that devastated the north coast around 500 BC. Local cults fell from grace as social order was disrupted and the Chavín cult was snatched up as a timely new alternative.

Chavín cult

The Chavín cult was paralleled by the great advances made at this time in textile production and in some of the earliest examples of metallurgy (whose origins have been attributed to some gold, silver and copper ornaments found in graves in Chongoyape, near Chiclayo, which show Chavín-style features). But earlier evidence has been discovered in the Andahuaylas region, dating from 1800-900 BC. The religious symbolism of gold and other precious metals and stones is thought to have been an inspiration behind some of the beautiful artefacts found in the central Andean area. The emergence of social hierarchies also created a demand for luxury goods as status symbols.

Sechín The cultural brilliance of Chavín de Huántar was complemented by its contemporary, Sechín. This huge granite-faced complex near Casma, 370 km north of Lima, was described by JC Tello as the biggest structure of its kind in the Andes. According to Michael Moseley of Harvard University, Chavín and Sechín may have combined forces, with Sechín as the military power that spread the cultural word of Chavín, but their influence did not reach far to the south where the Paracas and Tiahuanaco cultures held sway.

Upper Formative Period The Chavín hegemony, which is also known as the Middle Formative Period (or Early Horizon), broke up around 300 BC. The 'unity' of this period was broken and the initial phase of the regional diversification of Andean cultures began. The process of domestication of plants and animals culminated in the Upper Formative Period. Agricultural technology progressed leading to an economic security that permitted a considerable growth in the centres of population. Among the many diverse stylistic/cultural groups of this period are: the Vicus on the north coast; Salinar in the Chicama valley; Paracas Necrópolis on the south coast; and Huarás in the Ancash highlands.

Paracas Necrópolis This was the early phase of the Nasca culture and is renowned for the superb technical quality and stylistic variety in its weaving and pottery. The *mantos* (large, decorated cloth) rank amongst the world's best, and many of the finest examples can be seen in the museums of Lima. The extreme dryness of the desert here has preserved the textiles and ceramics in the mummies' tombs which have been excavated.

Paracas Necrópolis is, in fact, a cemetery located on the slopes of Cerro Colorado, in the Department of Ica, from which 429 funerary bundles were excavated (see page 301). Each bundle is a mummy wrapped in many fine and rough textiles. Paracas Necrópolis corresponds to the last of the 10 phases into which Paracas ceramics have been divided. The previous ones, known as Paracas Cavernas, relate to the Middle Formative Period and were influenced by the Chavín cult.

Nasca culture The Regional Development Period up to about AD 500, was a time of great social and cultural development. Sizable towns of 5-10,000 inhabitants grew on the south coast, populated by artisans, merchants, government administrators and religious officials.

One of the most famous cultures of this period, or indeed of pre-Columbian history was the Nasca. The Nasca Lines are a feature of the region. Straight lines, abstract designs and outlines of animals are scratched in the desert surface forming a lighter contrast that can be seen clearly from the air. There are many theories of how and why the lines were made but no explanation has yet been able to establish their place in Peruvian history (see Nasca Lines, page 312). There are similarities between the style of some of the line patterns and that of the pottery and textiles of the same period. It is clear from the scale of the lines and quality of the work that, they were important to the Nasca culture.

In contrast to the quantity and quality of the Nasca artefacts found, relatively few major buildings belonging to this period have been uncovered in the southern desert. Dos Palmas is a complex of rooms and courtyards in the Pisco Valley, while Cahuachi in the Nasca Valley is a large area including adobe platforms, a pyramid and a 'wooden Stonehenge' cluster of preserved tree trunks. Most recently excavated are the architectural complex of Los Molinos, with large buildings, patios and passages, and the necropolis of La Muña, both near Palpa. As most of the archaeological evidence of the Nasca culture came from their desert cemeteries, little is known about the lives and social organization of the people. Alpaca hair found in Nasca textiles, however, indicates that there must have been strong trade links with highland people.

Moche culture

Nasca's contemporaries on the north coast were the militaristic Moche who, from about AD 100-800 built up an empire whose traces stretch from Piura in the north to Casma, beyond Chimbote, in the south. The Moche built their capital in the middle of the desert, outside present day Trujillo. It features the pyramid temples of the Huaca del Sol and Huaca de la Luna (see page 396). The Moche roads and system of way stations are thought to have been an early inspiration for the Inca network. The Moche increased the coastal population with intensive irrigation projects. Skillful engineering works were carried out, such as the La Cumbre canal, still in use today, and the Ascope aqueduct.

The Moche's greatest achievement, however, was its artistic genius. Exquisite ornaments in gold, silver and precious stones were made by its craftsmen. Moche pottery progressed through five stylistic periods, most notable for the stunningly lifelike portrait vases. A wide variety of everyday scenes were created in naturalistic ceramics, telling us more about Moche life than is known about other earlier cultures, and perhaps used by them as 'visual aids' to compensate for the lack of a written language (see also page 391).

Sipán A spectacular discovery of a Moche royal tomb at Sipán was made in February 1987 by Walter Alva, director of the Brüning Archaeological Museum, Lambayeque. Reports of the excavation in the *National Geographic* magazine (October 1988 and June 1990), talked of the richest unlooted tomb in the New World (see page 410). The find included semi-precious stones brought from Chile and Argentina, and seashells from Ecuador (the Moche were also great navigators).

The cause of the collapse of the Moche Empire around AD 600-700 is unknown, but it may have been started by a 30-year drought at the end of the sixth century, followed by one of the periodic El Niño flash floods (identified by meteorologists from ice thickness in the Andes) and finished by the encroaching forces of the Huari Empire. The decline of the Moche signalled a general tipping of the balance of power in Peru from the north coast to the southern sierra.

The ascendant Huari-Tiahuanaco movement, from c. AD 600-1000, combined the religious cult of the Tiahuanaco site in the Titicaca basin, with the military dynamism of the Huari, based in the central highlands. The two cultures developed independently but, as had occurred with the Chavín-Sechín association, they are generally thought to have merged compatibly. **Huari-Tiahuanaco**

Up until their own demise around AD 1440, the Huari-Tiahuanaco had spread their empire and influence from Cajamarca and Lambayeque in the north and across much of southern Peru, northern Bolivia and Argentina. The Huari introduced a new concept in urban life, the great walled urban centre, the best example of which is their capital city, 22 km north of Ayacucho (see page 502). They also made considerable gains in art and technology, building roads, terraces and irrigation canals across the country.

The Huari-Tiahuanaco ran their empire with efficient labour and administrative systems that were later adopted and refined by the Incas. Labour tribute for state projects had been practised by the Moche and was further developed now. But the empire could not contain regional kingdoms who began to fight for land and power. As control broke down, rivalry and coalitions emerged, and the system collapsed.

After the decline of the Huari Empire, the unity that had been imposed on the Andes was broken. A new stage of autonomous regional or local political organizations began. Among the cultures corresponding to this period were the Kuelap, centred in the Chachapoyas region (see page 453), and the Chimú. **Chimú culture**

The Chimú culture had two centres. To the north was Lambayeque, near Chiclayo, while to the south, in the Moche valley near present-day Trujillo, was the great adobe walled city of Chan Chán. Covering 20 sq km, this was the largest pre-Hispanic Peruvian city (see page 394).

Chimú has been classified as a despotic state that based its power on wars of conquest. Rigid social stratification existed and power rested in the hands of the great lord *Siquic* and the lord *Alaec*. These lords were followed in social scale by a group of urban couriers who enjoyed a certain degree of economic power. At the bottom were the peasants and slaves. In 1450, the Chimú kingdom was conquered by the Inca Túpac Yupanqui, the son and heir of the Inca ruler Pachacuti Inca Yupanqui.

Background

Inca Dynasty

The origins of the Inca Dynasty are shrouded in mythology. The best known story reported by the Spanish chroniclers talks about Manco Cápac and his sister rising out of Lake Titicaca, created by the Sun as divine founders of a chosen race. This was in approximately AD 1200. Over the next 300 years the small tribe grew to supremacy as leaders of the largest empire ever known in the Americas, the four territories of Tawantinsuyo, united by Cusco as the umbilicus of the Universe. The four quarters of Tawantinsuyo, all radiating out from Cusco, were: 1 Chinchaysuyo, north and northwest; 2 Cuntisuyo, south and west; 3 Collasuyo, south and east; 4 Antisuyo, east.

At its peak, just before the Spanish Conquest, the Inca Empire stretched from the Río Maule in central Chile, north to the present Ecuador-Colombia border, containing most of Ecuador, Peru, western Bolivia, northern Chile and northwest Argentina. The area was roughly equivalent to France, Belgium, Holland, Luxembourg, Italy and Switzerland combined (980,000 sq km).

The first Inca ruler, Manco Cápac, moved to the fertile Cusco region, and established Cusco as his capital. Successive generations of rulers were fully occupied with local conquests of rivals, such as the Colla and Lupaca to the south, and the Chanca to the northwest. At the end of Inca Viracocha's reign the hated Chanca were finally defeated, largely thanks to the heroism of one of his sons, Pachacútec Inca Yupanqui, who was subsequently crowned as the new ruler.

From the start of Pachacútec's own reign in 1438, imperial expansion grew in earnest. With the help of his son and heir, Topa Inca, territory was conquered from the Titicaca basin south into Chile, and all the north and central coast down to the Lurin Valley. The Incas also subjugated the Chimú, a highly sophisticated rival empire who had re-occupied the abandoned Moche capital at Chan Chán. Typical of the Inca method of government, some of the Chimú skills were assimilated into their own political and administrative system, and some Chimú nobles were even given positions in Cusco.

Perhaps the pivotal event in Inca history came in 1527 with the death of the ruler, Huayna Capac. Civil war broke out in the confusion over his rightful successor. One of his legitimate sons, Huáscar, ruled the southern part of the empire from Cusco. Atahualpa, Huáscar's half-brother, governed Quito, the capital of Chinchaysuyo. In 1532, soon after Atahualpa had won the civil war, Francisco Pizarro arrived in Tumbes with 179 *conquistadores*, many on horseback. Atahualpa's army was marching south, probably for he first time, when he clashed with Piazarro at Cajamarca.

Francisco Pizarro's only chance against the formidable imperial army he encountered at Cajamarca was a bold stroke. He drew Atahualpa into an ambush, slaughtered his guards, promised him liberty if a certain room were filled with treasure, and finally killed him after receiving news that another Inca army was on its way to free him. Pushing on to Cusco, he was at first hailed as the executioner of a traitor: Atahualpa had ordered the death of Huáscar in 1533, while himself a captive of Pizarro, and his victorious generals were bringing the defeated Huáscar to see his half-brother. Panic followed when the *conquistadores* set about sacking the city, and they fought off with difficulty an attempt by Manco Inca to recapture Cusco in 1536.

Inca society The Incas were a small aristocracy numbering only a few thousand, centred in the highland city of Cusco, at 3,400 m. They rose gradually as a small regional dynasty, similar to others in the Andes of that period, starting around AD 1200. Then in the mid-1400s, they began to expand explosively under Pachacútec, a sort of Andean Alexander the Great, and later his son, Topa. Under a hundred years later, they fell before the rapacious warriors of Spain. The Incas were not the first dynasty in Andean history to dominate their neighbours, but they did it more thoroughly and went further than anyone before them.

Enough remains today of their astounding highways, cities and agricultural terracing for people to marvel and wonder how they accomplished so much in so short a time. They seem to have been amazingly energetic, industrious and efficient – and the reports of their Spanish conquerors confirm this hypothesis. **Empire building**

They must also have had the willing cooperation of most of their subject peoples, most of the time. In fact, the Incas were master diplomats and alliance-builders first, and military conquerors only second, if the first method of expansion failed. The Inca skill at generating wealth by means of highly efficient agriculture and distribution brought them enormous prestige and enabled them to 'out-gift' neighbouring chiefs in huge royal feasts involving ritual outpourings of generosity, often in the form of vast gifts of textiles, exotic products from distant regions, and perhaps wives to add blood ties to the alliance. The 'out-gifted' chief was required by the Andean laws of reciprocity to provide something in return, and this would usually be his loyalty, as well as a levy of manpower from his own chiefdom.

Thus, with each new alliance the Incas wielded greater labour forces and their mighty public works programmes surged ahead. These were administered through an institution known as *mit'a*, a form of taxation through labour. The state provided the materials, such as wool and cotton for making textiles, and the communities provided skills and labour.

Mit'a contingents worked royal mines, royal plantations for producing coca leaves, royal quarries and so on. The system strove to be equitable, and workers in such hardship posts as high altitude mines and lowland coca plantations were given correspondingly shorter terms of service.

Huge administrative centres were built in different parts of the empire, where people and supplies were gathered. Articles such as textiles and pottery were produced there in large workshops. Work in these places was carried out in a festive manner, with plentiful food, drink and music. Here was Andean reciprocity at work: the subject supplied his labour, and the ruler was expected to provide generously while he did so. **Organization**

Aside from *mit'a* contributions there were also royal lands claimed by the Inca as his portion in every conquered province, and worked for his benefit by the local population. Thus, the contribution of each citizen to the state was quite large, but apparently, the imperial economy was productive enough to sustain this.

Another institution was the practice of moving populations around wholesale, inserting loyal groups into restive areas, and removing recalcitrant populations to loyal areas. These movements of *mitmakuna*, as they were called, were also used to introduce skilled farmers and engineers into areas where productivity needed to be raised.

The huge empire was held together by an extensive and highly efficient highway system. There were an estimated 30,000 km of major highway, most of it neatly paved and drained, stringing together the major Inca sites. Two parallel highways ran north to south, along the coastal desert strip and the mountains, and dozens of east-west roads crossing from the coast to the Amazon fringes. These roadways took the most direct routes, with wide stone stairways zig-zagging up the steepest mountain slopes and rope suspension bridges crossing the many narrow gorges of the Andes. The north-south roads formed a great axis which eventually came to be known as **Capaq Ñan** – "Royal, or Principal Road", in Quechua – which exceeded in grandeur not only the other roads, but also their utilitarian concept. They became the Incas' symbol of power over men and over the sacred forces of nature. So marvellous were these roads that the Spaniards who saw them at the height of their glory said that there was nothing comparable in all Christendom. **Communications**

Every 12 km or so there was a *tambo*, or way station, where goods could be stored and travellers lodged. The *tambos* were also control points, where the Inca state's

Background

accountants tallied movements of goods and people. Even more numerous than *tambos*, were the huts of the *chasquis*, or relay runners, who continually sped royal and military messages along these highways.

The Inca state kept records and transmitted information in various ways. Accounting and statistical records were kept on skeins of knotted strings known as *quipus*. Numbers employed the decimal system, and colours indicated the categories being recorded. An entire class of people, known as *quipucamayocs*, existed whose job was to create and interpret these. Neither the Incas nor their Andean predecessors had a system of writing as we understand it, but there may have been a system of encoding language into *quipus*.

Archaeologists are studying this problem today. History and other forms of knowledge were transmitted via songs and poetry. Music and dancing, full of encoded information which could be read by the educated elite, were part of every major ceremony and public event information was also carried in textiles, which had for millennia been the most vital expression of Andean culture.

Textiles Clothing carried insignia of status, ethnic origin, age and so on. Special garments were made and worn for various rites of passage. It has been calculated that, after agriculture, no activity was more important to Inca civilization than weaving. Vast stores of textiles were maintained to sustain the Inca system of ritual giving. Armies and *mit'a* workers were partly paid in textiles. The finest materials were reserved for the nobility, and the Inca emperor himself displayed his status by changing into new clothes every day and having the previous day's burned.

Most weaving was done by women, and the Incas kept large numbers of 'chosen women' in female-only houses all over the empire, partly for the purpose of supplying textiles to the elite and for the many deities, to whom they were frequently given as burned offerings. These women had other duties, such as making *chicha* – the Inca corn beer which was consumed and sacrificed in vast quantities on ceremonial occasions. They also became wives and concubines to the Inca elite and loyal nobilities. And some may have served as priestesses of the moon, in parallel to the male priesthood of the sun.

Religious worship The Incas have always been portrayed as sun-worshippers, but it now seems that they were mountain-worshippers too. Recent research has shown that Machu Picchu was at least partly dedicated to the worship of the surrounding mountains, and Inca sacrificial victims have been excavated on frozen Andean peaks at 6,700 m. In fact, until technical climbing was invented, the Incas held the world altitude record for humans.

Human sacrifice was not common, but every other kind was, and ritual attended every event in the Inca calendar. The main temple of Cusco was dedicated to the numerous deities: the Sun, the Moon, Venus, the Pleiades, the Rainbow, Thunder and Lightning, and the countless religious icons of subject peoples which had been brought to Cusco, partly in homage, partly as hostage. Here, worship was continuous and the fabulous opulence included gold cladding on the walls, and a famous garden filled with life-size objects of gold and silver. Despite this pantheism, the Incas acknowledged an overall Creator God, whom they called Viracocha. A special temple was dedicated to him, at *Raqchi*, about 100 km southeast of Cusco. Part of it still stands today.

Military forces The conquering Spaniards noted with admiration the Inca storehouse system, still well-stocked when they found it, despite several years of civil war among the Incas. Besides textiles, military equipment, and ritual objects, they found huge quantities of food. Like most Inca endeavours, the food stores served a multiple purpose: to supply feasts, to provide during lean times, to feed travelling work parties, and to supply armies on the march.

Ayacucho (9 December 1824). For over a year there was a last stand in the Real Felipe fortress at Callao by the Spanish troops under General Rodil before they capitulated on 22 January 1826. Bolívar was invited to stay in Peru, but left for Colombia in 1826.

Post-independence Peru

Following independence Peru attempted a confederation with Bolivia in the 1830s but this proved temporary. Then, in 1879 came the disastrous War of the Pacific, in which Peru and Bolivia were defeated by Chile and Peru lost its southern territory.

Peru's economic development since independence has been based upon the export of minerals and foodstuffs to Europe and the United States. Guano, a traditional fertilizer in Peru and derived from the manure of seabirds, was first shipped to Europe in 1841. In the three decades that followed it became an important fertilizer in Europe and by the early 1860s over 80% of the Peruvian government's revenues were derived from its export. Much of this income, though, went to pay off interest on the spiralling national debt. By the 1870s the richer deposits were exhausted and cheaper alternatives to guano were being discovered. One of these was nitrates, discovered in the Atacama desert, but Peru's defeat by Chile in the War of the Pacific ensured that she would lose her share of this wealth. **Economic change**

After the decline of guano Peru developed several new exports. In the 1890s the demand in Europe and USA for Amazonian rubber for tyres and for use in electrical components led to a brief boom in both the Brazilian and Peruvian Amazon, the Peruvian industry being based on the Amazon port of Iquitos. This boom was short-lived as cheaper rubber was soon being produced from plantations in the East Indies.

Peru's colonial mineral exports, gold and silver, were replaced by copper, although ownership was mainly under control of foreign companies, particularly the US-based Cerro de Pasco Copper Corporation and Northern Peru Mining. Oil became another important product, amounting to 30% of Peruvian exports by 1930. Further exports came from sugar and cotton, which were produced on coastal plantations (see also the Economy section, page 582).

Independence from Spanish rule meant that power passed into the hands of the Creole elite with no immediate alternation of the colonial social system. The *contribución de indígenas*, the colonial tribute collected from the native peoples was not abolished until 1854, the same year as the ending of slavery. **Social change**

Until the 1970s land relations in the sierra changed very little, as the older landholding families continued to exert their traditional influence over 'their' peones. The traditional elite, the so-called '44 families', were still very powerful, though increasingly divided between the coastal aristocracy with their interests in plantation agriculture and trade, and the serrano elite, more conservative and inward-looking.

The pattern of export growth did, however, have major effects on the social structure of the coast. The expansion of plantation agriculture and mining led to the growth of a new labour force; this was supplied partially by Chinese indentured labourers, about 100,000 of whom arrived between 1855 and 1875, partly by the migration of Indians from the sierra and partly by the descendants of black slaves.

Political developments

For much of the period since independence Peruvian political life has been dominated by the traditional elites. Political parties have been slow to develop and the roots of much of the political conflict and instability which have marked the country's history lie in personal ambitions and in regional and other rivalries within the elite. **19th century**

Background

▶▶ The War of the Pacific

One of the major international wars in Latin America since independence, this conflict has its roots in a border dispute between Chile and Bolivia. The frontier between the two in the Atacama desert was ill-defined.

There had already been one conflict, in 1836-1839, when Chile defeated Peru and Bolivia, putting an end to a confederation of the two states. The discovery of nitrates in the Atacama only complicated relations, for in the Bolivian Atacama province of Antofagasta nitrates were exploited by Anglo-Chilean companies.

In 1878 the Bolivian government, short of revenue, attempted to tax the Chilean-owned Antofagasta Railroad and Nitrate Company. When the company refused to pay, the Bolivians seized the company's assets. The Chilean government claimed that the Bolivian action broke an 1874 agreement between the two states. When Peru announced that it would honour a secret alliance with Bolivia by supporting her, the Chilean president, Aníbal Pinto, declared war on both states.

Control of the sea was vital, and this was where Chile concentrated her efforts. Following a successful naval campaign, the Chileans invaded the southern Peruvian province of Tarapacá and then landed troops north of Tacna, seizing the town in May 1880 before capturing Arica, further south. The Chilean armies were hot stuff, and in Jan 1881 they seized control of Lima.

Despite these defeats and the loss of their capital, Peru did not sue for peace, although Bolivia had already signed a ceasefire, giving up her coastal province. Under the 1883 peace settlement Peru gave up Tapapacá to Chile. Although the provinces of Tacna and Arica were to be occupied by Chile for 10 years, it was not until 1929 that an agreement was reached under which Tacna was returned to Peru, while Chile kept Arica. Apart from souring relations between Chile and her two northern neighbours to this day, the War gave Chile a monopoly over the world's supply of nitrates and enabled her to dominate the southern Pacific coast.

The early years after independence were particularly chaotic as rival caudillos (political bosses) who had fought in the independence wars vied with each other for power. The increased wealth brought about by the guano boom led to greater stability, though political corruption became a serious problem under the presidency of José Rufino Echenique (1851-1854) who paid out large sums of the guano revenues as compensation to upper class families for their (alleged) losses in the Wars of Independence. Defeat by Chile in the War of the Pacific discredited civilian politicians even further and led to a period of military rule in the 1880s.

Early 20th century Even though the voting system was changed in 1898, this did little to change the dominance of the elite. Voting was not secret so landowners herded their workers to the polls and watched to make sure they voted correctly. Yet voters were also lured by promises as well as threats. One of the more unusual presidents was Guillermo Billinghurst (1912-1914) who campaigned on the promise of a larger loaf of bread for five cents, thus gaining the nickname of "Big Bread Billinghurst". As president he proposed a publicly funded housing programme, supported the introduction of an eight hour day and was eventually overthrown by the military who, along with the elite, were alarmed at his growing popularity among the urban population.

The 1920s This decade was dominated by Augusto Leguía. After winning the 1919 elections Leguía claimed that Congress was plotting to prevent him from becoming president and induced the military to help him close Congress. Backed by the armed forces, Leguía introduced a new constitution which gave him greater powers and enabled him to be re-elected in 1924 and 1929. Claiming his goal was to prevent the rise of communism, he proposed to build a partnership between business and labour. A large programme of public works, particularly involving building roads, bridges and railways, was begun, the work being carried out by poor rural men who were forced into unpaid building work. The Leguía regime dealt harshly with critics: opposition newspapers were closed and opposition leaders arrested and deported. His overthrow in 1930 ended what Peruvians call the "Oncenio" or 11 year period.

The 1920s also saw the emergence of a political thinker who would have great influence in the future, not only in Peru but elsewhere in Latin America. Juan Carlos Mariátegui, a socialist writer and journalist, argued that the solution to Peru's problems lay in the reintegration of the Indians through land reform and the breaking up of the great landed estates. (See also the section on Literature.)

The formation of APRA   Another influential thinker of this period was Víctor Raúl Haya de la Torre, a student exiled by Leguía in 1924. He returned after the latter's fall to create the Alianza Popular Revolucionaria Americana, a political party which called for state control of the economy, nationalization of key industries and protection of the middle classes, which, Haya de la Torre argued, were threatened by foreign economic interests.

In 1932 APRA seized control of Trujillo; when the army arrived to deal with the rising, the rebels murdered about 50 hostages, including 10 army officers. In reprisal the army murdered about 1,000 local residents suspected of sympathizing with APRA. APRA eventually became the largest and easily the best-organized political party in Peru, but the distrust of the military and the upper class for Haya de la Torre ensured that he never became president.

A turning point in Peruvian history occurred in 1948 with the seizure of power by General Manuel Odría, backed by the coastal elite. Odría outlawed APRA and went on to win the 1950 election in which he was the only candidate. He pursued policies of encouraging export earnings and also tried to build up working class support by public works projects in Lima. Faced with a decline in export earnings and the fall in world market prices after 1953, plus increasing unemployment, Odría was forced to stand down in 1956.

In 1962 Haya de la Torre was at last permitted to run for the presidency. But although he won the largest percentage of votes he was prevented from taking office by the armed forces who seized power and organized fresh elections for 1963. In these the military obtained the desired result: Haya de la Torre came second to Fernando Belaúnde Terry. Belaúnde attempted to introduce reforms, particularly in the landholding structure of the sierra; when these reforms were weakened by landowner opposition in Congress, peasant groups began invading landholdings in protest.

At the same time, under the influence of the Cuban revolution, guerrilla groups began operating in the sierra. Military action to deal with this led to the deaths of an estimated 8,000 people. Meanwhile Belaúnde's attempts to solve a long-running dispute with the International Petroleum Company (a subsidiary of Standard Oil) resulted in him being attacked for selling out to the unpopular oil company and contributed to the armed forces' decision to seize power in 1968.

The 1968 coup

This was a major landmark in Peruvian history. Led by General Juan Velasco Alvarado, the Junta had no intention of handing power back to the civilians. A manifesto issued on the day of the coup attacked the 'unjust social and economic order' and argued for its replacement by a new economic system 'neither capitalist nor communist'. Partly as a result of their experiences in dealing with the guerrilla movement, the coup leaders concluded that agrarian reform was a priority.

Background

Wide-ranging land reform was launched in 1969, during which large estates were taken over and reorganized into cooperatives. By the mid-1970s, 75% of productive land was under cooperative management. The government also tried to improve the lives of shanty-town dwellers around Lima, as well as attempting to increase the influence of workers in industrial companies.

At the same time efforts were made to reduce the influence of foreign companies. Soon after the coup, IPC was nationalized, to be followed by other transnationals including ITT, Chase Manhattan Bank and the two mining giants Cerro de Pasco and Marcona Mining. After a dispute with the US government, compensation was agreed.

Understandably, opposition to the Velasco government came from the business and landholding elite. The government's crack-down on expressions of dissent, the seizure of newspapers and taking over of TV and radio stations all offended sections of the urban middle class. Trade unions and peasant movements found that, although they agreed with many of the regime's policies, it refused to listen and expected their passive and unqualified support.

As world sugar and copper prices dropped, inflation rose and strikes increased. Velasco's problems were further increased by opposition within the armed forces and by his own ill-health. In August 1975 he was replaced by General Francisco Morales Bermúdez, a more conservative officer, who dismantled some of Velasco's policies and led the way to a restoration of civilian rule.

Belaúnde returned to power in 1980 by winning the first elections after military rule. His government was badly affected by the 1982 debt crisis and the 1981-1983 world recession, and inflation reached over 100% a year in 1983-1984. His term was also marked by the growth of the Maoist guerrilla movement **Sendero Luminoso** (Shining Path) and the smaller, Marxist **Túpac Amaru** (MRTA) – see Box.

Initially conceived in the University of Ayacucho, Shining Path gained most support for its goal of overthrowing the whole system of Lima-based government from highland Indians and migrants to urban shanty towns. The activities of Sendero Luminoso and Túpac Amaru (MRTA) were effectively curtailed after the arrest of both their leaders in 1992. Víctor Polay of MRTA was arrested in June and Abimael Guzmán of Sendero Luminoso was captured in September. Although Sendero did not capitulate, many of its members in 1994-5 took advantage of the Law of Repentance, which guaranteed lighter sentences in return for surrender, and freedom in exchange for valuable information. Meanwhile, Túpac Amaru was thought to have ceased operations (see below).

APRA victory   In 1985 APRA, in opposition for over 50 years, finally came to power. With Haya de la Torre dead, the APRA candidate **Alan García Pérez** won the elections and was allowed to take office by the armed forces. García attempted to implement an ambitious economic programme intended to solve many of Peru's deep-seated economic and social problems. He cut taxes, reduced interest rates, froze prices and devalued the currency. However, the economic boom which this produced in 1986-1987 stored up problems as increased incomes were spent on imports. Moreover, the government's refusal to pay more than 10% of its foreign debt meant that it was unable to borrow. In 1988 inflation hit 3,000% and unemployment soared. By the time his term of office ended in 1990 Peru was bankrupt and García and APRA were discredited.

Modern Peru

Peru under Fujimori

In presidential elections held over two rounds in 1990, **Alberto Fujimori** of the Cambio 90 movement defeated the novelist **Mario Vargas Llosa**, who belonged to the Fredemo (Democratic Front) coalition. Fujimori, without an established political network behind him, failed to win a majority in either the senate or the lower house. Lack of congressional support was one of the reasons behind the dissolution of congress and the suspension of the constitution on 5 April 1992. The president declared that he needed a freer hand to introduce market reforms and combat terrorism and drug trafficking, at the same time as rooting out corruption.

In elections to a new, 80-member Democratic Constituent Congress (CCD) in November 1992, Fujimori's Cambio 90/Nueva Mayoría coalition won a majority of seats. Though three major political parties, APRA, Acción Popular and the Movimiento de Libertad, boycotted the elections, they satisfied many aid donor's requirements for the resumption of financial assistance.

A new constitution drawn up by the CCD was approved by a narrow majority of the electorate in October 1993. Among the new articles were the immediate re-election of the president (previously prohibited for one presidential term), the establishment of a single-chamber congress, the designation of Peru as a market economy and the favouring of foreign investment. As expected, Fujimori stood for re-election on 9 April 1995 and the opposition chose as an independent to stand against him former UN General Secretary, Javier Pérez de Cuéllar. Fujimori was re-elected by a resounding margin, winning about 65% of the votes cast. The coalition that supported him also won a majority in Congress.

The government's success in most economic areas did not appear to accelerate the distribution of foreign funds for social projects. Rising unemployment and the austerity imposed by economic policy continued to cause hardship for many, despite the government's stated aim of alleviating poverty.

Dramatic events on 17 December 1996 thrust several of these issues into sharper focus: 14 Túpac Amaru guerrillas infiltrated a reception at the Japanese Embassy in Lima, taking 490 hostages. Among the rebel's demands were the release of their imprisoned colleagues, better treatment for prisoners and new measures to raise living standards. Most of the hostages were released and negotiations were pursued during a stalemate that lasted until 22 April 1997. The president took sole responsibility for the successful, but risky assault which freed all the hostages (one died of heart failure) and killed all the terrorists. By not yielding to Túpac Amaru, Fujimori regained much popularity.

But this masked the fact that no concrete steps had been taken to ease social problems. It also deflected attention from Fujimori's plans to stand for a third term following his unpopular manipulation of the law to persuade Congress that the new constitution did not apply to his first period in office. His chances of winning looked remote as demands grew for a more open, democratic approach, though opposition to his standing for a third term of office remained fragmented. Ultimately, his chances hinged on the economy, which looked to be improving until the worst El Niño of the 20th century hit Peru in late 1997, causing chaos, many deaths and devasting damage.

Fujimori's unpopularity was further driven home by Shell-Mobil's withdrawal from the multi-million dollar Camisea natural gas project, which was supposed to pull Peru out of its energy deficit. In July 1998, a 1.4 million-name petition was presented to the National Electoral Authority, requesting a referendum on whether Fujimori should be allowed to stand for a third term. In spite of the amendment to the constitution following Fujimori's *auto golpe* in 1993, allowing presidents to run for only two successive terms, the president had, in 1996, pushed through congress a law of 'authentic interpretation' of the constitution, allowing him to run for election once more on the grounds that the new constitution did not apply to his first term. All the same, until the last month of campaigning for the 2000 presidential elections, Fujimori had a clear lead over his rivals, who insisted that he should not stand. Moreover, local and international observers voiced increasing concern over the state domination of the media. Meanwhile, the popularity of a fourth candidate, Alejandro Toledo, a former World Bank official of humble origins, surged to such an extent that he and Fujimori were neck and neck in the first poll. Toledo, a pro-marketeer given to left-wing rhetoric, and his supporters claimed that Fujimori's slim majority was the result of fraud, a view echoed in the pressure put on the president, by the US government among others, to allow a second ballot. The run-off election, on 28 May 2000, was also contentious since foreign observers, including the Organization of American States, said the electoral system was unprepared and flawed, proposing a postponement. The authorities refused to delay. Toledo boycotted the election and Fujimori was returned unopposed, but with scant approval. Having won, he proposed "to strengthen democracy".

This pledge proved to be utterly worthless following the airing of a secretly shot video on 14 September 2000 of Fujimori's close aide and head of the National Intelligence Service (SIN), Vladimiro Montesinos, allegedly handing US$15,000 to a congressman, Alberto Kouri, to persuade him to switch allegiances to Fujimori's coalition. Fujimori's demise was swift. His initial reaction was to close down SIN and announce new elections, eventually set for 8 April 2001, at which he would not stand. Montesinos was declared a wanted man and he fled to Panama, where he was denied asylum. He returned to Peru in October and Fujimori personally led the search parties to find his former ally. Peruvians watched in amazement as this game of cat-and-mouse was played out on their TV screens. While Montesinos himself successfully evaded capture, investigators began to uncover the extent of his empire, which held hundreds of senior figures in its web. His activities encompassed extortion, money-laundering, bribery, intimidation, alleged arms and drugs dealing and possible links with the CIA and death squads. Swiss bank accounts in his name were found to contain about US$70 million, while other millions were discovered in accounts in the Cayman Islands and elsewhere. In early 2001 he was eventually captured in Venezuela and returned to Peru where he is now being tried on a multitude of charges. About 2,700 'Vladivideos', films of Montesinos' dealings with public figures, continue to send shockwaves through society. Fujimori, on the other hand, is in exile in Japan from where, on 20 November 2000, he sent Congress an email announcing his resignation. Congress rejected this, firing him instead on charges of being "morally unfit" to govern. An interim president, Valentín Paniagua, was sworn in, with ex-UN Secretary General Javier Pérez de Cuéllar as Prime Minister, and the government set about uncovering the depth of corruption associated with Montesinos and Fujimori. Further doubt was cast over the entire Fujimori period by suggestions that he may not have been born in Peru, as claimed, but in Japan. His hosts certainly declared that, through his parents, he was a Japanese national and therefore exempt from extradition. If he was indeed Japanese by birth as well as ancestry, he should never have been entitled to stand for the highest office in Peru. Fujimori has not relinquished the hope of being cleared and having some part to play in Peruvian politics. You can keep up-to-date with his views on his website: www.fujimorialberto.com

In the run-up to the 2001 elections, the front-runner was Alejandro Toledo of Perú Posible, but with far from a clear majority. Other candidates included the centrist Jorge Santistevan, who had been the government ombudsman, the right-winger Lourdes Flores, ex-Economy Minister Carlos Boloña, Fernando Olivera, who had made the Montesinos video public and, ex-President Alan García, who returned to Peru in January 2001 after spending eight years in exile in Colombia. Corruption charges against García, relating to his presidency between 1985 and 1990, were dropped following a

Revolutionary movements in Peru: until the final victory?

Officially speaking, the Peruvian civil war ended in 1992. On 12 September of that year, leader of the Shining Path, Abimael Guzmán, stood after his arrest in front of the television cameras, reduced from "National Enemy Number One" to "Prisoner Number 1509". Nobody knows how many people died in the carnage that lasted for more than a decade, but the most conservative estimates speak of 35,000.

The Maoist Shining Path was officially fighting for the resurrection of the Inca state and against Western imperialism and white supremacy in this racially and economically divided society. However, its methods were brutal and counter-productive. They included intimidation and the killing of several progressive leaders and hundreds of members of other revolutionary movements (including the contemporaneous Movimiento Revolucionario Túpac Amaru - MRTA). The plan was to reduce Peru's economy to ashes by destroying its infrastructure, military and police posts, power plants, tourism and other 'strategic targets'.

Both the army and the Shining Path were responsible for the eradication of countless towns and villages in the jungle and Andes, mass executions and torture of civilians. Sandwiched between these opposing forces, villagers in the mountains were forced to migrate to the coast, settling in enormous shantytowns, doubling the population of Lima in little more than a decade. Both sides forcibly recruited children from poor neighbourhoods and both controlled the traffic in drugs (they

took it in turns to "tax" the same airstrips used by Colombian drug cartels).

During his term of office ex-president Fujimori did remove terrorism from Peru, however questionable the methods now appear. Evidence has recently come to light that many war crimes initially blamed on the Shining Path were in fact committed by the armed forces, even though it suited the guerrillas to claim responsibility at the time. And investigations into the web of intrigue surrounding Fujimori's henchman, Vladimiro Montesinos, indicate some form of 'working relationship' with Sendero Luminoso. The Fujimori-Montesinos propaganda machine managed to discredit the entire Peruvian Left by comparing it to the Shining Path. Consequently, when the war ended, there was almost no legitimate opposition in the country from this end of the political spectrum.

Both Professor Guzmán (yes, he graduated from the Philosophy Department of the University of Arequipa and was a respected expert on the German philosopher Kant) and Víctor Polay (leader of the Marxist MRTA) are now locked away in underwater cells in the navy bunker on the island of San Lorenzo (Callao). They were condemned to life imprisonment by military tribunal. Nevertheless, many Peruvian and foreign analysts believe that both Shining Path and MRTA are recruiting again, albeit with softer methods, gaining support in the jungle, the Andes and in Lima. Unless the gap between the rich and poor can be narrowed, this period of relative peace in Peru may be at risk.

---

recommendation by the Inter-American Court of Human Rights. It was García who emerged as Toledo's main opponent, forcing a second ballot on 3 June. This was won by Toledo with 52% of the vote, compared to 48% for García. Toledo pledged to heal the wounds that had opened in Peru since his first electoral battle with the disgraced Fujimori, but his first year-and-a-half in office was marked by slow progress on both the political and economic fronts. His popularity slumped as the poor and unemployed felt that he was not delivering on his election promises to create jobs and cut poverty. His standing fell further with the poor handling of the sale of electricity companies in the south of Peru, which led to riots in Arequipa and Tacna and the shelving of half the sell-off. Toledo did recoup some approval points later in the year, from 14% to 20%, after admitting paternity of an illegitimate daughter.

In March 2002, just before US President George W Bush visited Lima for a regional summit, a car bomb exploded in the city, killing several people. This led to fears of a resurgence of terrorist movements and there has been some evidence to suggest that Sendero Luminoso and Túpac Amaru have been regrouping. If this is the case, though, the groups were keeping a low profile as in late 2002, there had been no major action.

Constitution and government

Under a new constitution (approved by plebiscite in October 1993), a single chamber, 80-seat congress replaced the previous, two-house legislature. Men and women over 18 are eligible to vote, and registration and voting is compulsory until the age of 60. Those who do not vote are fined. The President, to whom is entrusted the Executive Power, is elected for five years and may, under the constitution which came into force on 1 January 1994, be re-elected for a second term.

Peru is divided into 24 Departments (divided into 150 Provinces, subdivided into 1,321 Districts).

Economy

Structure of production
Agriculture, **forestry** and **fishing** account for about 15% of gdp and employ about a third of the labour force. The coastal region is the most productive area of the country and has traditionally been the dominant economic region. Occupying 11% of the total land area, most of the export crops are grown here: cotton, rice, sugar, asparagus and fruit where the coastal desert is irrigated. Most food production is in the Sierra, where revitalization of agriculture is a government priority, with the aim of returning to the self-sufficiency of Inca times. There have been improvements in living standards, but two-thirds of the inhabitants of the Sierra still live in poverty and prices for many crops remain very low.

In 1983 and 1997-98, fishing suffered a dramatic decline as the Niño current forced the main catch, anchovy, out of Peruvian waters. On both occasions Peru had been the world's leading exporter of fishmeal before El Niño struck. A recurrence of these conditions appeared to be happening in 2002.

The government estimates that the **illegal drugs** trade generates some US$600 million a year. Efforts are being made to curb the cultivation of coca for the production of cocaine. Peru is now regarded as the second-largest grower of coca leaf in the world after Colombia. Officials are concerned, however, that opium poppies are now bringing in greater illicit revenue than cocaine.

Manufacturing contributes 22% of gdp with food processing, fishmeal and transport equipment important sectors. Manufacturing is suffering from a lack of investment and therefore performance. This posed the threat of insufficient growth to boost employment and lower poverty.

Mining has traditionally been important in Peru since pre-Conquest times. The sector contracted sharply in the 1980s because of poor world prices, strikes and guerrilla activity in mining areas, but a new Mining Law in 1992 encouraged domestic and foreign investment and the sector has since boomed. Copper and iron deposits are found on the south coast, but the Sierra is the principal mining area for all minerals, including silver, gold, lead and zinc. The largest gold mine in Latin America, Yanacocha, is in Cajamarca, producing about one million ounces annually.

Oil production comes from the northeast jungle, although some is produced on and off the northwest coast. No major new reserves of oil have been found since 1976 and proven reserves have declined to 380 million barrels. However, the Camisea gas and condensates field in the southeast jungle is huge, with reserves in two deposits estimated at 11 trillion cu ft of natural gas and 600 million barrels of condensates, equivalent to more than six times current reserves of oil.

Since the early 1990s, when the threat of terrorism had receded, numbers of foreign **tourists** to Peru have grown steadily. The total number of visitors exceeded 1 million in 2000 for the first time. Average spending per head is US$83 per day.

Society

The most remarkable thing about Peru is its people. For most Peruvians life is a daily struggle to survive in the face of seemingly insurmountable problems. Most people do get by, through a combination of ingenuity, determination and sheer hard work. Many work full time and study at night school. Those without work (and employment opportunities are few and far between) invent their own jobs.

Peru may not be the poorest country in South America, but recent estimates put the number of poor at 49% of the population, while almost a fifth of people live in extreme poverty. Over a third of homes have no electricity or running water and a third of children suffer from chronic malnutrition.

Departments

Background

Health There have been major improvements in health care in recent years, but almost a third of the population has no access to public health services. The infant mortality rate is high – 37 deaths per 1,000 births – and the figure rises steeply in some rural areas where 1 in 10 infants dies within a year of birth.

Though health services are free, people still have to pay for prescribed medicines, which are very expensive, and so rarely finish a course of treatment. As with other areas, there is a huge gulf between those who can afford to pay for health care and those who cannot. Lack of health education and limited primary health care also means that many women die in childbirth. Abortion is illegal in Peru, but those with cash can always find a private doctor. Those without the means to pay for a doctor run the risk of death or infection from botched abortions.

Education Education is free and compulsory for both sexes between six and 14. There are public and private secondary schools and private elementary schools. There are 32 state and private universities, and two Catholic universities. But resources are extremely limited and teachers earn a pittance. Poorer schoolchildren don't have money to buy pencils and notebooks and textbooks are few and far between in state schools. Furthermore, many children have to work instead of attending school; a quarter of those who start primary school don't finish. This is also due to the fact that classes are taught in Spanish and those whose native tongue is Quechua, Aymara or one of the Amazonian languages find it difficult and give up.

Migration The structure of Peruvian society, especially in the coastal cities, has been radically altered by internal migration. This movement began most significantly in the 1950s and 1960s as people from the Highlands sought urban jobs in place of work on the land. It was a time of great upheaval as the old system of labour on large estates was threatened by the peasant majority's growing awareness of the imbalances between the wealthy cities and impoverished sierra. The process culminated in the agrarian reforms of the government of General Juan Velasco (1968-75). Highland-to-city migration was given renewed impetus during the war between the state and Sendero Luminoso in the 1980s. Many communities which were depopulated in that decade are now beginning to come alive again.

Culture

People

Peruvian society today is a melting pot of Native Andeans, Afro-Peruvians, Spanish, immigrant Chinese, Japanese, Italians, Germans and, to a lesser extent, indigenous Amazon tribes, who have lived together for so long that many Peruvians can claim to have mixed blood. The total population in 2001 was 26.1 million, with an annual average growth rate of 1.7% (1995-2000). Forecast growth rate for 2000-2005 is 1.6%. The urban population in 2000 represented 73% of the total.

Criollos & mestizos The first immigrants were the Spaniards who followed Pizarro's expeditionary force. Their effect, demographically, politically and culturally, has been enormous. They intermarried with the indigenous population and the children of mixed parentage were called *mestizos*. The Peruvian-born children of Spanish parents were known as *criollos*, though this word is now used to describe people who live on the coast, regardless of their ancestry, and coastal culture in general.

A way of life

Coca leaves have long been used by the people of the Andes as a tonic. As casual as a coffee-break and as sacred as Communion, coca chewing is an ancient ritual.

The coca leaves are chewed with a piece of cal, or lime, which activates with the saliva. Some cocaine is absorbed into the bloodstream through the mouth, providing a slight numbing of cheek and tongue and more is absorbed in the stomach and intestinal tract. The desired effect is to numb the senses, which helps stave off hunger pangs and exhaustion, and to help people live at high altitude with no ill-effects.

As well as being a prerequisite for manual workers, such as miners, coca is also taken in a social context. The native population used to deny this because, in the eyes of their Spanish bosses and clergy, an increase in labour productivity was the only permissible reason for tolerating consumption of 'the devil's leaf'. The only places where coca is not chewed is in church and in the marital bed. The masticated leaves are spat out at the bedside.

Coca is also used in various rites, such as in offerings to Pachamama, or Mother Earth, to feed her when she gets hungry. Various items such as flowers and sweets, along with the coca leaves, are put together in bundles called pagos *and burned on the mountains at midnight. In Andean markets different* pagos *are sold for different purposes: to put into the foundation of a new house; for help in matters of health, business or love; or for magic, white or black. The leaves are also used for fortune-telling.*

Afro-Peruvians

Peru's black community is based on the coast, mainly in Chincha, south of Lima, and also in some working-class districts of the capital. Their forefathers were originally imported into Peru in the 16th century as slaves to work on the sugar and cotton plantations on the coast. The black community represents between 2-5% of the total population.

Asian immigrants

There are two main Asian communities in Peru, the Japanese and Chinese. Large numbers of poor Chinese labourers were brought to Peru in the mid-19th century to work in virtual slavery on the guano reserves on the Pacific coast and to build the railroads in the central Andes. The culinary influence of the Chinese can be seen in the many *chifas* found throughout the country.

The Japanese community, now numbering some 100,000, established itself in the first half of the 20th century. The normally reclusive community gained prominence when Alberto Fujimori, one of its members, became the first president of Japanese descent outside Japan anywhere in the world. During Fujimori's presidency, many other Japanese Peruvians took prominent positions in business, central and local government. The nickname 'chino' is applied to anyone of Oriental origin.

Europeans

Like most of Latin America, Peru received many emigrés from Europe seeking land and opportunities in the late 19th century. The country's wealth and political power remains concentrated in the hands of this small and exclusive class of whites, which also consists of the descendants of the first Spanish families. There still exists a deep divide between people of European descent and the old colonial snobbery persists.

Peru's indigenous people

Peru has a substantial indigenous population, only smaller as a percentage of the total than Bolivia and Guatemala of the Latin American republics. The literacy rate of the indigenous population is the lowest of any comparable group in South America and their diet is 50% below acceptable levels. The highland Indians bore the brunt of the conflict between Sendero Luminoso guerrillas and the security forces, which caused thousands of deaths and mass migration from the countryside to provincial cities or to Lima. Many indigenous groups are also under threat from colonization, development and road-building projects. Long after the end of Spanish rule, discrimination, dispossession and exploitation are still a fact of life for many native Peruvians.

Quechua According to Inca legend, the Quechuas were a small group who originally lived near Lake Titicaca. They later moved to Cusco, from where they expanded to create the Inca Empire. Their language and culture soon spread from Quito in the north through present-day Ecuador, Peru and Bolivia to northern Chile.

Predominantly an agricultural society, growing potatoes and corn as their basic diet, they are largely outside the money economy. Today, there remain two enduring legacies of Inca rule; their magnificent architecture and their unwritten language, Quechua, which has given its name to the descendants of their subjects. About two million Indians speak no Spanish, their main tongue being Quechua, but there are many more descendants of the Quechua who now speak only Spanish. Though recognized as an official language, little effort is made to promote Quechua nationally. It is only the remoteness of many Quechua speakers which has preserved it in rural areas. This isolation has also helped preserve many of their ancient traditions and beliefs. See also Festivals, on page 597.

Aymara High up in the Andes, in the southern part of Peru, lies a wide, barren and hostile plateau, the *altiplano*. Prior to Inca rule Tiahuanaco on Lake Titicaca was a highly organized centre for one the greatest cultures South America has ever witnessed: the Aymara people. Today, the shores of this lake and the plains that surround it remain the homeland of the Aymara. The majority live in Bolivia, the rest are scattered on the southwestern side of Peru and northern Chile. The climate is so harsh on the *altiplano* that, though they are extremely hard-working, their lives are very poor. They speak their own unwritten language, Aymara.

The Aymaras are a deeply religious people whose culture is permeated with the idea of the sacred. They believe that God, the Supreme Being, gives them security in their daily lives and this God of Life manifests him/herself through the deities, such as those of the mountains, the water, the wind, the sun, the moon and the *wa'qas* (sacred places).

As a sign of gratitude, the Aymara give *wax'ta* (offerings), *wilancha* (llama sacrifices) and *ch'alla* (sprinkling alcohol on the ground) to the *achachilas* (the protecting spirits of the family and community), the *Pachamama* (Mother Earth), *Kuntur Mamani* and *Uywiri* (protecting spirits of the home).

The remote mountains of the bleak altiplano are of particular importance for the Aymara. The most sacred places are these high mountains, far from human problems. It is here that the people have built their altars to offer worship, to communicate with their God and ask forgiveness. The community is also held important in the lives of the Aymara. The *achachila* is the great-great grandfather of the family as well as the protector of the community, and as such is God's representative on earth.

The offerings to the sacred mountains take place for the most part in August and are community celebrations. Many different rituals are celebrated: there are those within the family; in the mountains; for the planting and the harvest; rites to ask for rain or to ask for protection against hailstorms and frosts; and ceremonies for Mother Earth.

All such rituals are led by Aymara *Yatiris*, who are male or female priests. The *Yatiri* is a wise person – someone who knows – and the community's spiritual and moral guide. Through a method of divination that involves the reading of coca leaves, they guide individuals in their personal decision-making.

The Afro-Peruvian experience since 1532

The first person of African descent to arrive in the Americas came in 1492 with Christopher Columbus. He was a mulatto from Spain, and a free man. During the next three centuries an estimated 15 million Africans arrived in the Americas as slaves. Francisco Pizarro brought the first black slaves to Peru. They were present at the capture of Atahualpa in Cajamarca in 1532 and saved the Spanish during Manco Inca's siege of Cusco in 1536, when they put out the flames on the thatched roof of the great hall of Sunturwasi, where the embattled conquistadores had taken refuge.

When Hernando de Soto returned to Spain in 1534 bearing Atahualpa's gold and silver ransom, he asked the crown for permission to take one hundred blacks back to Peru. By 1550, their number had risen to 3,000 – half of whom lived in Lima – and by 1640 to 30,000. In total, between 1532 and 1816, an estimated 100,000 African slaves were transported to the Viceroyalty of Peru.

Africans were brought to Peru to replace an indigenous labour force ravaged by the destruction of its sociopolitical infrastructure and struck down by European diseases. Some worked in the cities as servants, artisans or porters, others were sent to the mines of Huancavelica or Potosí and the majority toiled on the coast in sugar cane plantations, cotton fields and vineyards.

Indigenous and African workers transformed Peru into the richest of all the Spanish colonies of the 16th and 17th centuries. Many fortunes, including that amassed by the Jesuits, were made using black labour. The ownership of black slaves was a status symbol and became such a powerful measure of social mobility that even some blacks who had achieved their own freedom subsequently acquired slaves.

The location of Afro-Peruvian communities today reflects the colonial distribution of black labour. They are concentrated in the coastal areas where the great haciendas once dominated Peru's feudal economy; Chincha, Cañete and Ica south of the capital, the northern departments of Piura and Lambayeque and the main cities, particularly Lima. In these places, the vibrant new culture created as a survival mechanism by slaves from diverse African heritages lives on in local art, music, dance, religious expression, folklore and food (see pages 594 and 70).

In Hispanic America, the wars of independence spread the libertarian ideal of emancipation. Promised their freedom, hundreds of Afro-Peruvians joined the republican armies, only to find their situation little changed in 1821 under a fledgling government unwilling or too weak to challenge the landowning elite. Finally, in 1854, Generals Ramón Castilla and José Rufino Echenique found themselves engaged in civil war and in need of troops. To attract black recruits Echenique offered freedom to those who would join him and in reply Castilla announced the definitive abolition of slavery, paying off the landowners with huge compensation awards raised from guano exports.

The 25,000 black slaves freed in 1854 were received by society with contempt and they remained oppressed by labour laws which still favoured the landowners. Peru has changed since 1854, but racism lives on. Colour is still identified with inferiority, from unconscious everyday attitudes to the poverty and marginalization of black communities and their lack of representation in government. 150 years after the abolition of slavery, those who shared the hardships of the first conquistadores have still not shared in their glory or wealth.

Before the arrival of the Europeans, an estimated six million people inhabited the Amazon basin, comprising more than 2,000 tribes or ethnic-linguistic groups who managed to adapt to their surroundings through the domestication of a great variety of animals and plants, and to benefit from the numerous nutritional, curative, narcotic and hallucinogenic properties of thousands of wild plants.

Amazonian peoples

Viringo

If you go to a Peruvian museum at a coastal archaeological site, you will probably see an elegant dog, with a long, thin nose and arched neck prowling around the entrance. It may be a bit shy and, if the weather is cold, it may be wearing a little woollen jacket. This is because the dog has no hair.

The Peruvian Hairless, or viringo, is a rare breed today, but in Inca times was a companion animal whose main job was to warm his master's bed. The Chavín, Moche and Chimú cultures represented it on their ceramics, but its origins are unknown. The most likely theory is that it accompanied the

first migrants to the American continent from Asia. In its most common, hairless form, it has no fleas and no smell.

Breeders note that it needs protecting against the sun and the cold, but there is also a coated variety (called 'powder puff' in the dog world).

In recognition of the importance of this dog in its history, the Peruvian government decreed in Law number 27537 that every site museum on the coast must have at least one viringo on the premises.

www.netpets.org/dogs/reference/breedi nfo/breed.desc/phairless.html

It's not easy to determine the precise origin of these aboriginal people. What is known, however, is that since the beginning of colonial times this population slowly but constantly decreased, mainly because of the effect of western diseases such as influenza and measles. This demographic decline reached dramatic levels during the rubber boom of the late 19th and early 20th centuries, as a result of forced labour and slavery.

Today, at the basin level, the population is calculated at no more than two million inhabitants making up 400 ethnic groups, of which approximately 200-250,000 live in the Peruvian jungle. Within the basin it is possible to distinguish at least three large conglomerates of aboriginal societies: the inhabitants of the *varzea*, or seasonally flooded lands alongside the large rivers (such as the Omagua, Cocama and Shipibo people); the people in the interfluvial zones or firm lands (such as the Amahuaca, Cashibo and Yaminahua) and those living in the Andean foothills (such as the Amuesha, Ashaninka and Machigvenga).

The Amazonian natives began to be decimated in the 16th century, and so were the first endangered species of the jungle. These communities still face threats to their traditional lifestyles, notably from timber companies, gold miners and multinational oil companies. There appears to be little effective control of deforestation and the intrusion of colonists who have taken over native lands to establish small farms. And though oil companies have reached compensation agreements with local communities, previous oil exploration has contaminated many jungle rivers, as well as exposing natives to risk from diseases against which they have no immunity.

Religion

The Inca religion (described on page 572) was displaced by Roman Catholicism from the 16th century onwards, the conversion of the inhabitants of the 'New World' to Christianity being one of the stated aims of the Spanish *conquistadores*. Today, official statistics state that 92.5% of the population declares itself Catholic.

One of the first exponents of Liberation Theology, under which the Conference of Latin American Bishops in 1968 committed themselves to the 'option for the poor', was Gustavo Gutiérrez, from Huánuco. This doctrine caused much consternation to orthodox Catholics, particularly those members of the Latin American church who had traditionally aligned themselves with the oligarchy. Gutiérrez, however, traced the church's duty to the voiceless and the marginalized back to Fray Bartolomé de las Casas (see *The Peru Reader*, pages 293-96; reference under Books, page 611).

Day of the Dead

One of the most important dates in the indigenous people's calendar is the 2 Nov, the 'Day of the Dead'. This tradition has been practised since time immemorial. In the Incaic calendar, Nov was the 8th month and meant Ayamarca, or land of the dead. The celebration of Day of the Dead, or `All Saints' as it is also known, is just one example of religious adaptation in which the ancient beliefs of ethnic cultures are mixed with the rites of the Catholic Church.

According to Aymara belief, the spirit (athun ajayu) visits its relatives at this time of the year and is fed in order to continue its journey before its reincarnation. The relatives of the dead prepare for the arrival of the spirit days in advance. Among the many items necessary for these meticulous preparations are little bread dolls, each one of which has a particular significance. A ladder is needed for the spirit to descend from the other world to the terrestrial one. There are other figures which represent the grandparents, great grandparents and loved ones of the person who has 'passed into a better life'. Horse-shaped breads are prepared that will serve as a means of transport for the soul in order to avoid fatigue.

Inside the home, the relatives construct a tomb supported by boxes over which is laid a black cloth. Here they put the bread, along with sweets, flowers, onions and sugar cane. This latter item is an indispensable part of the table as it symbolizes the invigorating element which prevents the spirit from becoming tired on its journey towards the Earth. The union of the flowers with the onion is called tojoro and is a vital part of the preparations. It ensures that the dead one does not become disoriented and arrives in the correct house.

The tomb is also adorned with the dead relative's favourite food and drink, not forgetting the all-important glass of beer as, according to popular tradition, this is the first nourishment taken by the souls when they arrive at their houses. Once the spirit has arrived and feasted with its living relatives, the entire ceremony is then transported to the graveside in the local cemetery, where it is carried out again, beside the many other mourning families.

This meeting of the living and their dead relatives is re-enacted the following year, though less ostentatiously, and again for the final time in the third year, the year of the farewell. It does not continue after this, which is just as well as the costs can be crippling for the family concerned.

The Catholic Church faced a further challenge to its authority when President Fujimori won the battle over family planning and the need to slow down the rate of population growth. Its greatest threat, however, comes from the proliferation of evangelical Protestant groups throughout the country. Five and a half percent of the population now declare themselves Protestant and one million or more people belong to some 27 different non-Catholic denominations.

Although the vast majority of the population ostensibly belongs to the Roman Catholic religion, in reality religious life for many Peruvians is a mix of Catholic beliefs imported from Europe and indigenous traditions based on animism, the worship of deities from the natural world such as mountains, animals and plants. Some of these ancient indigenous traditions and beliefs are described throughout this section.

Arts and crafts

Peru has a rich variety of handicrafts. Its geographic division into four distinct regions – coast, mountains, valleys and Amazon basin – coupled with cultural differences, has resulted in numerous variations in technique and design. Each province, even each community, has developed its own style of weaving or carving.

Andean mysticism

In the 1990s Andean shamanism and mysticism have attracted increasing attention, though they have always played an important part in the lives of indigenous people.

In highland cities, especially, it is common to engage a ritual specialist, called an altomisayoq, to perform a pago, or offering, when laying the foundations of a house or starting a business venture. Ritual objects for use in these ceremonies are sold at specialized stands in the local markets. Another type of ritualist, called a curandero, is summoned when someone is ill.

Some of these healers are experts in the use of dozens of medicinal plants, while others invoke spirit powers to expel illness. Sometimes eggs or guinea pigs are passed over the patient's body, and then cracked, or killed, in order to read the innards and diagnose the illness. Inevitably this field has its share of charlatans, but there are also curanderos who have many attested cures to their credit.

One thing shamans from all the Andean regions have in common is the use of a

mesa – a layout of ceremonial power objects – which is thought to attract spirit power and channel it to the shaman. Another feature running through all strains of Andean mysticism, despite the usual presence of Christian elements, is a living connection, via innumerable practices and associations, to Peru's precolombian past.

Those ritualists who seek to communicate with 'the other side' in their ceremonies often use psychoactive plants. These vary according to the region. On the coast, curanderos often take an infusion of the San Pedro cactus, a form of mescaline. The highland shamans invariably chew coca leaf, a much milder psychoactive, but with broader uses. Coca is burned with every offering, and many ritualists cast the leaves to read the fortunes of their clients. These shamans usually invoke the power of the mountain deities in their ceremonies. In the rainforest regions shamans use the powerful psychedelic vine, ayahuasca (vine of the dead – so called because it is believed to transport the user to the spirit world), as they have for millenia.

The Incas inherited 3,000 years of skills and traditions: gold, metal and precious stonework from the Chimu; feather textiles from the Nasca; and the elaborate textiles of the Paracas. All of these played important roles in political, social and religious ceremonies. Though much of this artistic heritage was destroyed by the Spanish conquest, the traditions adapted and evolved in numerous ways, absorbing new methods, concepts and materials from Europe while maintaining ancient techniques and symbols.

Textiles & costumes
Woven cloth was the most highly prized possession and sought after trading commodity in the Andes in pre-Columbian times. It is, therefore, not surprising that ancient weaving traditions have survived.

In the ninth century BC camelid fibre was introduced into weaving on the south coast. This allowed the development of the textiles of the Paracas culture which consist of intricate patterns of animalistic, supernatural and human forms embroidered onto dark backgrounds. The culture of the Chancay valleys cultivated cotton for white and beige dyed patterned cloth in preference to the camelid fibres used by the Paracas and Nasca cultures.

The Incas inherited this rich weaving tradition. They forced the Aymaras to work in *mitas* or textile workshops. The ruins of some enormous *mitas* can be seen at the temple of Raqchi, south of Cusco (see page 229). Inca textiles are of high quality and very different from coastal textiles, being warp-faced, closely woven and without embroidery. The largest quantities of the finest textiles were made specifically to be burned as ritual offerings – a tradition which still survives. The Spanish, too, exploited this wealth and skill by using the *mitas* and exporting the cloth to Europe.

A belt for every occasion

The belt plays a particularly important role in the lives of the indigenous peoples. The Incas developed a range of belts, or chumpis, *of ritual and spiritual significance which are still used today.*

Chumpis are believed to have protective and purifying qualities. In the Cusco area, some communities place chumpis *on sacred mountain tops, or* apus, *in order to communicate with the gods. Traditionally women give birth lying* on a chumpi *and the baby is wrapped in a softer version, known as a* walt'ana, *which ensures he or she will grow up properly. From adolescence, women wear a* chumpi *under their skirt to encourage a lover or deter an unwanted suitor. It is even common practice for the bridegroom to lasso his bride with one. And the age-old tradition of burying the dead with the family* chumpi *is still occasionally observed.*

Prior to Inca rule Aymara men wore a tunic (*llahua*) and a mantle (*llacata*) and carried a bag for coca leaves (*huallquepo*). The women wore a wrapped dress (*urku*) and mantle (*iscayo*) and a belt (*huaka*); their coca bag was called an *istalla*. The *urku* was fastened at shoulder level with a pair of metal *tupu*, the traditional Andean dress-pins.

Inca men had tunics (*unkus*) and a bag for coca leaves called a *ch'uspa*. The women wore a blouse (*huguna*), skirts (*aksu*) and belts (*chumpis*), and carried foodstuffs in large, rectangular cloths called *llicllas*, which were fastened at the chest with a single pin or a smaller clasp called a *ttipqui*. Women of the Sacred Valley now wear a layered, gathered skirt called a *pollera* and a *montera*, a large, round, red Spanish type of hat.

Textiles continue to play an important part in society. They are still used specifically for ritual ceremonies and some even held to possess magical powers. One of the most enduring of these traditions is found among the Aymara people of Taquile island on Lake Titicaca.

The Andean people used mainly alpaca or llama wool. The former can be spun into fine, shining yarn when woven and has a lustre similar to that of silk, though sheep's wool came to be widely used following the Spanish conquest.

Textile materials & techniques

A commonly used technique is the drop spindle. A stick is weighted with a wooden wheel and the raw material is fed through one hand. A sudden twist and drop in the spindle spins the yarn. This very sensitive art can be seen practised by women while herding animals in the fields.

Spinning wheels were introduced by Europeans and are now prevalent owing to increased demand. In Ayacucho and San Pedro de Cajas, centres of the cottage textile industry, the wheel is the most common form of spinning. Pre-Columbian looms were often portable and those in use today are generally similar. A woman will herd her animals while making a piece of costume, perhaps on a backstrap loom, or waist loom, so-called because the weaver controls the tension on one side with her waist with the other side tied to an upright or tree. The pre-Columbian looms are usually used for personal costume while the treadle loom is used by men for more commercial pieces.

Dyeing The skills of dyeing were still practised virtually unchanged even after the arrival of the Spanish. Nowadays, the word *makhnu* refers to any natural dye, but originally was the name for cochineal, an insect which lives on the leaves of the nopal cactus. These dyes were used widely by pre-Columbian weavers. Today, the biggest centre of production in South America is the valleys around Ayacucho. Vegetable dyes are also used, made from the leaves, fruit and seeds of shrubs and flowers and from lichen, tree bark and roots.

Symbolism Symbolism plays an important role in weaving. Traditionally every piece of textile from a particular community had identical symbols and colours which were a source of identity as well as carrying specific symbols and telling a story. One example is on the island of Taquile where the *Inti* (sun) and *Chaska* (Venus) symbols are employed as well as motifs such as fish and birds, unique to the island.

Animal figures dominated the motifs of the Chavín culture and were commonly used in Paracas textiles. Specimens of cotton and wool embroidery found in Paracas graves often show a puma as a central motif. Today, this and other pre-Columbian motifs are found on many rugs and wall-hangings from the Ayacucho region. Other symbols include Spanish figures such as horses and scenes depicting the execution of Túpac Amaru.

Pottery The most spectacular archaeological finds in South America have been made in Peru. The Nasca culture (100 BC-AD 900) excelled in polychrome painting of vessels with motifs of supernatural beings, often with strong feline characteristics, as well as birds, fish and animals. Many of the Nasca ceramic motifs are similar to those found in Paracas textiles.

Moche or Mochica vessels combined modelling and painting to depict details of Moche daily life. Human forms are modelled on stirrup spout vessels with such precision that they suggest personal portraits. The Moche also excelled in intricate linear painting often using brown on a cream base. (For a fuller description, see page 391.)

Inca ceramic decoration consists mainly of small-scale geometric and usually symmetrical designs. One distinctive form of vessel which continues to be made and used is the *arybola*. This pot is designed to carry liquid, especially chicha, and is secured with a rope on the bearer's back. It is believed that *arybolas* were used mainly by the governing Inca élite and became important status symbols. Today, Inca-style is very popular in Cusco and Pisac.

With the Spanish invasion many indigenous communities lost their artistic traditions, others remained relatively untouched, while others still combined Hispanic and indigenous traditions and techniques. The Spanish brought three innovations: the potter's wheel, which gave greater speed and uniformity; knowledge of the enclosed kiln; and the technique of lead glazes. The enclosed kiln made temperature regulation easier and allowed higher temperatures to be maintained, producing stronger pieces. Today, many communities continue to apply prehispanic techniques, while others use more modern processes.

Jewellery & metalwork Some of the earliest goldwork originates from the Chavín culture – eg the *Tumi* knife found in Lambayeque. These first appeared in the Moche culture, when they were associated with human sacrifice. Five centuries later, the Incas used *Tumis* for surgical operations such as trepanning skulls. Today, they are a common motif.

The Incas associated gold with the Sun. However, very few examples remain as the Spanish melted down their amassed gold and silver objects. They then went on to send millions of Indians to their deaths in gold and silver mines.

During the colonial period gold and silver pieces were made to decorate the altars of churches and houses of the élite. Metalworkers came from Spain and Italy to develop the industry. The Spanish preferred silver and strongly influenced the evolution of silverwork during the colonial period. A style known as Andean baroque developed around Cusco embracing both indigenous and European elements. Silver bowls in this style – *cochas* – are still used in Andean ceremonies.

From Pagan ritual to folk art

Retablos – *or St Mark's boxes, were introduced to Latin America by the Spanish in the 16th century. These simple, portable altars containing religious images were intended to aid in the task of converting the native population to Catholicism. Early examples often contained images of St James, patron saint of the Spanish army.*

The retablos *were made from a variety of materials and two distinct styles evolved to suit different needs. Those of clay, leather and plaster were destined for the native rural population, while those for use by the colonial hierarchy were made of gold and silver, or the famous alabaster of Ayacucho, known as Huamanga stone.*

Traditional retablos *had two floors inside a box. On the top were the patron saints of animals: St Mark, patron saint of bulls; St Agnes, patron saint of goats; and St Anthony, patron saint of mules, among others. On the lower floor was a cattle thief being reprimanded by a landowner.*

From the 17th century onwards, the native rural population used the retablo *in ceremonies accompanying cattle branding. During August, a ritual believed to have its roots in pagan fertility festivals took place in which the* retablo *was placed on a table and surrounded by offerings of food and coca leaves. People danced round the box, asking for protection for their animals and celebrating their well-being.*

In the 1940s the first retablo *reached Lima, by which time the art of making them had virtually disappeared. However, with the new-found outside interest a revival began. The traditional elements began to be varied and the magical or ritualistic value was lost as they became a manifestation of folk art. The artist Joaquín López and his family created the early examples, but today they are made in many workshops.*

The figures are made from a mixture of plaster and mashed potato, modelled or made in moulds, sealed with glue, then painted and positioned inside the brightly painted box. Some miniature versions are made in chiclet boxes or egg shells, while, at the other end of the scale, some have five floors and take months to complete.

Extracted from *Arts and Crafts of South America, by Lucy Davies and Mo Fini, Tumi.*

False filigree This was practised by some pre-Hispanic cultures. The effect of filigree was obtained with the use of droplets or beads of gold. True filigree work developed in the colonial period. Today, there are a number of centres. Originally popular in Ayacucho, the tradition continues in the small community of San Jerónimo de Tunan, near Huancayo. Here, silversmiths produce intricate filigree earrings, spoons and jewellery boxes. Catacaos near Piura also has a long tradition of filigree work in silver and gold.

Seeds, flowers and feathers These continue to be used as jewellery by many Amazonian peoples. Prehispanic cultures also favoured particular natural materials; eg the sea shell spondylus was highly revered by the Chavín and Moche. It was found only along part of the Ecuadorean coast and must have been acquired through trade. The western fashion for natural or ethnic jewellery has encouraged production, using brightly-coloured feathers, fish bones, seeds or animal teeth.

Wood is one of the most commonly used materials. Carved ceremonial objects include **Woodcarving** drums, carved sticks with healing properties, masks and the Incas' *keros* - wooden vessels for drinking chicha. *Keros* come in all shapes and sizes and were traditionally decorated with scenes of war, local dances, or harvesting coca leaves. The Chancay, who lived along the coast between 100 BC and AD 1200, used *keros* carved with sea birds and fish. Today, they are used in some Andean ceremonies, especially during *Fiesta del Cruz*, the Andean May festival.

Background

▶▶ A growing tradition

One of Peru's most popular and traditional handicrafts is gourd carving, or mate burilado. During the colonial period gourd carving decreased dramatically but limited carving continued and new European styles were developed. After independence a new style developed which incorporated traditional and narrative scenes. This made gourds more commonplace as objects and more meaningful to more people since the motifs had relevance to their own lives.

The gourds come from a creeping plant – Lagenria Vulgaris – which grows only in warm, dry regions, such as the coastal valleys. The decoration is produced by a combination of carving and burning. The outlines are carved freehand by skilled craftspeople and a red-hot stick is used to burn and blacken areas of the surface. It is a slow, laborious process and some carvers can take as long as 6 months to finish a large, finely carved gourd.

Today, carving is centred around the small communities of Cochas Grande and Chico, near Huancayo, having spread there from the earlier centres of Huanta and Mayoc in Ayacucho. The carvers now sell their art in Huancayo as well as Lima, from where it is exported.

Extracted from Arts and Crafts of South America, by Lucy Davies and Mo Fini, Tumi.

Mate Burilado

Glass mirrors were introduced by the Spanish, although the Chimú and Lambayeque cultures used obsidian and silver plates, and Inca *chasquis* (messengers) used reflective stones to communicate between hilltop forts. Transporting mirrors was costly so they were produced in Lima and Quito. Cusco and Cajamarca then became centres of production.

In Cusco the frames were carved, covered in gold leaf and decorated with tiny pieces of cut mirror. Cajamarca artisans, meanwhile, incorporated painted glass into the frames.

Gourd-carving   Gourd-carving, or *máte burilado*, as it is known, is one of Peru's most popular and traditional handicrafts. It is thought even to predate pottery – engraved gourds found on the coast have been dated to some 3,500 years ago. During the Inca empire gourd-carving became a valued art form and workshops were set up and supported by the state.

Gourds were used in rituals and ceremonies and to make *poporos* - containers for the lime used while chewing coca leaves. Today, gourd-carving is centred around the small communities of Cochas Grande and Chico, near Huancayo.

The information on arts and crafts in this Handbook has been adapted from *Arts and Crafts of South America*, by Lucy Davies and Mo Fini, published by Tumi, 1994. Tumi, the Latin American Craft Centre, specializes in Andean and Mexican products and produces cultural and educational videos for schools: at 8/9 New Bond Street Pl, Bath BA1 1BH, T01225-480470, www.tumicrafts.com Tumi (Music) Ltd specializes in different rhythms of Latin America.

Music and dance

The music of Peru can be described as the very heartbeat of the country. Peruvians see music as something in which to participate, and not as a spectacle. Just about everyone, it seems, can play a musical instrument or sing. Just as music is the heartbeat of the country, so dance conveys the rich and ancient heritage that typifies much of the national spirit. Peruvians are tireless dancers and dancing is the most popular form of entertainment. Unsuspecting travellers should note that once they make that first wavering step there will be no respite until they collapse from exhaustion.

Each region has its own distinctive music and dance that reflects its particular lifestyle, its mood and its physical surroundings. The music of the sierra, for example, is played in a minor key and tends to be sad and mournful, while the music of the lowlands is more up-tempo and generally happier. Peruvian music divides at a very basic level into that of the highlands (*Andina*) and that of the coast (*Criolla*).

When people talk of Peruvian music they are almost certainly referring to the music of the Quechua- and Aymara-speaking Indians of the highlands which provides the most distinctive Peruvian sound. The highlands themselves can be very roughly subdivided into some half dozen major musical regions, of which perhaps the most characteristic are Ancash and the north, the Mantaro Valley, Cusco, Puno and the Altiplano, Ayacucho and Parinacochas.

Highlands

Musical instruments Before the arrival of the Spanish in Latin America, the only instruments were wind and percussion. Although it is a popular misconception that Andean music is based on the panpipes, guitar and *charango*, anyone who travels through the Andes will realize that these instruments only represent a small aspect of Andean music. The highland instrumentation varies from region to region, although the harp and violin are ubiquitous. In the Mantaro area the harp is backed by brass and wind instruments, notably the clarinet. In Cusco it is the *charango* and *quena* and on the Altiplano the *sicu* panpipes.

The *Quena* is a flute, usually made of reed, characterized by not having a mouthpiece to blow through. As with all Andean instruments, there is a family of *quenas* varying in length from around 15-50 cm. The *sicu* is the Aymara name for the *zampoña*, or panpipes. It is the most important prehispanic Andean instrument, formed by several reed tubes of different sizes held together by knotted string. Virtually the only instrument of European origin is the *Charango*. When stringed instruments were first introduced by the Spanish, the indigenous people liked them but wanted something that was their own and so the *charango* was born. Originally, they were made of clay, condor skeletons and armadillo or tortoise shells.

Highland dances The highlands are immensely rich in terms of music and dance, with over 200 dances recorded. Every village has its fiestas and every fiesta has its communal and religious dances.

Comparsas are organized groups of dancers who perform for spectators dances following a set pattern of movements to a particular musical accompaniment, wearing a specific costume. They have a long tradition, having mostly originated from certain contexts and circumstances and some of them still parody the ex-Spanish colonial masters.

One of the most notable is the comical *Auqui Auqui* (auqui is Aymara for old man). The dance satirizes the solemnity and pomposity of Spanish gentlemen from the colonial period. Because of their dignified dress and manners they could appear old, and a humped back is added to the dancers to emphasize age. These little old men have long pointed noses, flowing beards and carry crooked walking sticks. They dance stooped, regularly pausing to complain and rub aching backs, at times even stumbling and falling.

Many dances for couples and/or groups are danced spontaneously at fiestas throughout Peru. These include indigenous dances which have originated in a specific region and ballroom dances that reflect the Spanish influence.

Background

One of the most popular of the indigenous dances is the **Huayno**, which originated on the Altiplano but is now danced throughout the country. It involves numerous couples, who whirl around or advance down the street arm-in-arm, in a *Pandilla*. During fiestas, and especially after a few drinks, this can develop into a kind of uncontrolled frenzy.

Two of the most spectacular dances to be seen are the **Baile de las Tijeras** ('scissor dance') from the Ayacucho/Huancavelica area, for men only and the pounding, stamping **Huaylas** for both sexes. Huaylas competitions are held annually in Lima and should not be missed. Also very popular among Indians and/or Mestizos are the Marinera, Carnaval, Pasacalle, Chuscada (from Ancash), Huaylas, Santiago and Chonguinada (all from the Mantaro) and Huayllacha (from Parinacochas).

Urban and other styles Owing to the overwhelming migration of peasants into the barrios of Lima, most types of Andean music and dance can be seen in the capital, notably on Sundays at the so-called 'Coliseos', which exist for that purpose. This flood of migration to the cities has also meant that the distinct styles of regional and ethnic groups have become blurred. One example is **Chicha music**, which comes from the *pueblos jóvenes*, and was once the favourite dance music of Peru's urban working class. Chicha is a hybrid of Huayno music and the Colombian Cumbia rhythm – a meeting of the highlands and the tropical coast.

Tecno-cumbia originated in the jungle region with groups such as Rossy War, from Puerto Maldonado, and Euforia, from Iquitos. It is a vibrant dance music which has gained much greater popularity across Peruvian society than chicha music ever managed. There are now also many exponents on the coast such as Agua Marina and Armonía 10. Many of the songs comment on political issues and Fujimori used to join Rossy War on stage.

For singing only, the mestizo *Muliza*, are popular in the Central Region, and the soulful lament of the *Yaraví*, originally Indian, but taken up and developed early in the 19th century by the hero of independence Mariano Melgar, from Arequipa (see page 598).

Coast **Música Criolla**, the music from the coast, could not be more different from that of the Sierra. Here the roots are Spanish and African. The immensely popular **Valsesito** is a syncopated waltz that would certainly be looked at askance in Vienna and the **Polca** has also undergone an attractive sea change.

Reigning over all, though, is the **Marinera**, Peru's national dance, a splendidly rhythmic and graceful courting encounter and a close cousin of Chile's and Bolivia's Cueca and the Argentine Zamba, all of them descended from the Zamacueca. The Marinera has its 'Limeña' and 'Norteña' versions and a more syncopated relative, the Tondero, found in the northern coastal regions, is said to have been influenced by slaves brought from Madagascar.

All these dances are accompanied by guitars and frequently the *cajón*, a resonant wooden box on which the player sits, pounding it with his hands. Some of the great names of 'Música Criolla' are the singer/composers Chabuca Granda and Alicia Maguiña, the female singer Jesús Vásquez and the groups Los Morochucos and Hermanos Zañartu.

Afro-Peruvian Also on the coast is the music of the small but influential black community, the 'Música Negroide' or 'Afro-Peruano', which had virtually died out when it was resuscitated in the 1950s, but has since gone from strength to strength, thanks to Nicomedes and Victoria Santa Cruz who have been largely responsible for popularizing this black music and making it an essential ingredient in contemporary Peruvian popular music. It has all the qualities to be found in black music from the Caribbean - a powerful, charismatic beat, rhythmic and lively dancing, and strong percussion provided by the *cajón* and the *quijada de burro*, a donkey's jaw with the teeth loosened.

Its greatest star is the Afro-Peruvian diva Susana Baca. Her incredible, passionate voice inspired Talking Head's David Byrne to explore this genre further and release a compilation album in 1995, thus bringing Afro-Peruvian music to the attention of the world. Another notable exponent is the excellent Perú Negro, one of the best music and dance groups in Latin America.

Some of the classic dances in the black repertoire are the Festejo, Son del Diablo, Toro Mata, Landó and Alcatraz. In the last named one of the partners dances behind the other with a candle, trying to set light to a piece of paper tucked into the rear of the other partner's waist.

Festivals

Fiestas (festivals) are a fundamental part of life for most Peruvians, taking place up and down the length and breadth of the country and with such frequency that it would be hard to miss one, even during the briefest of stays. This is fortunate, because arriving in any town or village during these inevitably frenetic celebrations is one of the great Peruvian experiences.

While Peru's festivals can't rival those of Brazil for fame or colour, the quantity of alcohol consumed and the partying run them pretty close. What this means is that, at some point, you will fall over, through inebriation or exhaustion, or both. After several days of this, you will awake with a hangover the size of the Amazon rainforest and probably have no recollection of what you did with your backpack.

Peruvian festivals also involve widespread balloons-filled-with-water fights, bags of flour and any other missile guaranteed to cause a mess. In the Amazon region various petroleum by-products are favoured ingredients, which can be bad news for smokers. Some travellers complain that they are being picked on, but to someone from the Altiplano, a 6-ft tall, blond-haired gringo makes an easier target. So, don't wear your best clothes, arm yourself with plenty of water bombs, get into the spirit and have some fun!

There are too many festivals to mention them all. The main national ones are described in Holidays and festivals, on page 75, and details of local *fiestas* are given under the listings for each town.

Among the most notable celebrations are Carnival week in Cajamarca – a raucous and messy affair, even by Peruvian standards – and the fiesta of the Virgen de la Candelaria, which takes place in the first week in February along the shores of Lake Titicaca near the Bolivian border and features dance groups from all around the region. The most famous Holy Week is held in Ayacucho, when many thousands of fervent devotees participate in daily processions. On the coast, the Spring festival in Trujillo in September is an opportunity to see the Marinera dancers, while in the black communities of Chincha, south of Lima, you can enjoy the best of Afro-Peruvian music and dance (see Music and dance above).

Meaning of fiestas It is only when they don their extravagant costumes and masks and drink, eat and dance to excess that the Peruvian Indians show their true character. The rest of the time they hide behind a metaphorical mask of stony indifference as a form of protection against the alien reality in which they are forced to live. When they consume alcohol and coca and start dancing, the pride in their origins resurfaces. The incessant drinking and dancing allows them to forget the reality of poverty, unemployment and oppression and reaffirms their will to live as well as their unity with the world around them.

The object of the fiesta is a practical one, such as the success of the coming harvest or the fertility of animals. Thus the constant eating, drinking and dancing serves the purpose of giving thanks for the sun and rain that makes things grow and for the fertility of the soil and livestock, gifts from Pachamama, or Mother Earth, the most sacred of all gods. So, when you see the Aymara spill a little *chicha* (maize beer) every time they refill, it's not because they're sloppy but because they're offering a *ch'alla* (sacrifice) to Pachamama.

The participants in the dances that are the central part of the fiesta are dressed in garish, outlandish costumes and elaborate masks, each one depicting a character from popular myth. Some of these originate in the colonial period, others survive from the Inca Empire or even further back. Often the costumes caricature the Spanish. In this way, the indigenous people mock those who erased their heritage.

Literature

Quechua The fact that the Incas had no written texts in the conventional European sense and that the Spaniards were keen to suppress their conquest's culture means that there is little evidence today of what poetry and theatre was performed in pre-conquest times. It is known that the Incas had two types of poet, the *amautas*, historians, poets and teachers who composed works that celebrated the ruling class' gods, heroes and events, and *haravecs*, who expressed popular sentiments. There is strong evidence also that drama was important in Inca society.

Written Quechua even today is far less common than works in the oral tradition. Although Spanish culture has had some influence on Quechua, the native stories, lyrics and fables retain their own identity. Not until the 19th century did Peruvian writers begin seriously to incorporate indigenous ideas into their art, but their audience was limited. Nevertheless, the influence of Quechua on Peruvian literature in Spanish continues to grow.

Colonial Period In 16th-century Lima, headquarters of the Viceroyalty of Peru, the Spanish officials concentrated their efforts on the religious education of the new territories and literary output was limited to mainly histories and letters.

Chroniclers such as Pedro Cieza de León (*Crónica del Perú*, published from 1553) and Agustín de Zárate (*Historia del descubrimiento y conquista del Perú*, 1555) were written from the point of view that Spanish domination was right. Their most renowned successors, though, took a different stance. Inca Garcilaso de la Vega was a mestizo, whose *Comentarios reales que tratan del origen de los Incas* (1609) were at pains to justify the achievements, religion and culture of the Inca Empire. He also commented on Spanish society in the colony. A later work, *Historia general del Perú* (1617) went further in condemning Viceroy Toledo's suppression of Inca culture. Through his work, written in Spain, many aspects of Inca society, plus poems and prayers have survived.

Writing at about the same time as Inca Garcilaso was Felipe Guaman Poma de Ayala, whose *El primer nueva corónica y buen gobierno* (1613-15) is possibly one of the most reproduced of Latin American texts (eg on T-shirts, CDs, posters and carrier bags). Guaman Poma was a minor provincial Inca chief whose writings and illustrations, addressed to King Felipe III of Spain, offer a view of a stable pre-conquest Andean society (not uniquely Inca), in contrast with the unsympathetic colonial society that usurped it.

In the years up to Independence, the growth of an intellectual elite in Lima spawned more poetry than anything else. As criollo discontent grew, satire increased both in poetry and in the sketches which accompanied dramas imported from Spain. The poet Mariano Melgar (1791-1815) wrote in a variety of styles, including the *yaraví*, the love-song derived from the pre-Columbian *harawi* (from *haravek*). Melgar died in an uprising against the Spanish but played an important part in the Peruvian struggle from freedom from the colonial imagination.

After Independence, Peruvian writers imitated Spanish *costumbrismo*, sketches of characters and life-styles from the new Republic. The first author to transcend this fashion was Ricardo Palma (1833-1919), whose inspiration, the *tradición*, fused *costumbrismo* and Peru's rich oral traditions. Palma's hugely popular *Tradiciones peruanas* is a collection of pieces which celebrate the people, history and customs of Peru through sayings, small incidents in mainly colonial history and gentle irony.

**After
Independence**

Much soul-searching was to follow Peru's defeat in the War of the Pacific. Manuel González Prada (1844-1918), for instance, wrote essays fiercely critical of the state of the nation: *Páginas libres* (1894), *Horas de lucha* (1908). José Carlos Mariátegui, the foremost Peruvian political thinker of the early 20th century, said that González Prada represented the first lucid instant of Peruvian consciousness. He also wrote poetry, some Romantic, some, like his *Baladas peruanas*, an evocation of indigenous and colonial history, very pro-Indian, very anti-White.

Mariátegui himself (1895-1930), after a visit to Europe in 1919, considered deeply the question of Peruvian identity. His opinion was that it could only be seen in a global context and that the answer lay in Marxism. With this perspective he wrote about politics, economics, literature and the Indian question (see *Siete ensayos de interpretación de la realidad peruana*, 1928).

20th century

Other writers had continued this theme. For instance Clorinda Matto de Turner (1854-1909) intended to express in *Aves sin nido* (1889) her "tender love for the indigenous people" and hoped to improve their lot. Regardless of the debate over whether the novel achieves these aims, she was the forerunner by several years of the 'indigenist' genre in Peru and the most popular of those who took up González Prada's cause.

Other prose writers continued in this vein at the beginning of the 20th century, but it was Ciro Alegría (1909-67) who gave major, fictional impetus to the racial question. Like Mariátegui, Alegría was politically committed, but to the APRA party, rather than Marxism. Of his first three novels, *La serpiente de oro* (1935), *Los perros hambrientos* (1938) and *El mundo es ancho y ajeno* (1941), the latter is his most famous.

Contemporary with Alegría was José María Arguedas (1911-1969), whose novels, stories and politics were also deeply rooted in the ethnic question. Arguedas, though not Indian, had a largely Quechua upbringing and tried to reconcile this with the hispanic world in which he worked. This inner conflict was one of the main causes of his suicide. His books include *Agua* (short stories, 1935), *Yawar fiesta* (1941), *Los ríos profundos* (1958) and *Todas las sangres* (1964). They portray different aspects of the confrontation of Indian society with the changing outside world that impinges on it.

In the 1950s and 1960s, there was a move away from the predominantly rural and indigenist to an urban setting. At the forefront were, among others, Mario Vargas Llosa, Julio Ramón Ribeyro, Enrique Congrains Martín, Oswaldo Reynoso, Luis Loayza, Sebastián Salazar Bondy and Carlos E Zavaleta. Taking their cue from a phrase used by both poet César Mora and Salazar Bondy (in an essay of 1964), "Lima, la horrible", they explored all aspects of the city, including the influx of people from the Sierra. These writers incorporated new narrative techniques in the urban novel, which presented a world where popular culture and speech were rich sources of literary material, despite the difficulty in transcribing them.

Many writers, such as Vargas Llosa, broadened their horizons beyond the capital. His novels after *La ciudad y los perros* encompassed many different parts of the country. An additional factor was that several writers spent many years abroad, Vargas Llosa himself, for instance, and Ribeyro (1929-1994). The latter's short stories, though mostly set in Lima, embrace universal themes of delusion and frustration. The title story of *Los gallinazos sin pluma* (1955), a tale of squalor and greed amid the city's rubbish tips, has become a classic, even though it does not contain the irony, pathos and humour of many of his other stories or novels.

Background

Other writers of this period include Manuel Scorza (1928-83), who wrote a series of five novels under the general title of *La guerra silenciosa* (including *Redoble por Rancas, El jinete insomne, La tumba del relámpago*) which follow the indigenist tradition of the Indians' struggle, and also emphasize the need to defend indigenous society with growing militancy if necessary.

Alfredo Bryce Echenique (born 1939) has enjoyed much popularity following the success of *Un mundo para Julius* (1970), a brilliant satire on the upper and middle classes of Lima. His other novels include *Tantas veces Pedro* (1977), *La última mudanza de Felipe Carrillo* (1988), *No me esperen en abril* (1995), *Dos señoras conversan* (1990), *La amigdalitis de Tarzan* (2000) and *El huerto de mi amada*, which won the Premio Planeta (Barcelona) in 2002. Other contemporary writers of note are: Jaime Bayly (born 1965), who is also a journalist and TV presenter. His novels include *Fue ayer y no me acuerdo, Los últimos días de la prensa, No se lo digas a nadie* and *La noche es virgen*. The last named is typical of his style, full of irony and slang, dealing with the lives the young and affluent in Lima, gay/bisexual, bored, dope-smoking rock-music fans. His most recent novel is *La mujer de mi hermano* (2002). See also Fernando Ampuero (born 1949), whose books include *Miraflores Melody* (1979), *Malos modales* (1994), *Bicho raro* (1996), *Cuentos escogidos* (1998) and *El enano, historia de una enemistad* (2001); Alonso Cueto (born 1954), *La batalla del pasado, El tigre blanco* and *El otro amor de Diana Abril*; and Ivan Thays (born 1968), *Escena de caza* (1996) and *Viaje interior*, as well as short stories.

20th century poetry At the end of the 19th century, the term Modernism was introduced in Latin America by the Nicaraguan Rubén Darío, not to define a precise school of poetry, but to indicate a break with both Romanticism and Realism. In Peru one major exponent was José Santos Chocano (1875-1934), who labelled his poetry "mundonovismo" (New Worldism), claiming for himself the role of Poet of South America. He won international fame (see, for example, *Alma América*, 1906), but his star soon waned.

A much less assuming character was José María Eguren (1874-1942) who, feeling alienated from the society around him, sought spiritual reality in the natural world (*Simbólicas*, 1911; *La canción de las figuras*, 1916; *Poesías*, 1929). It has been said that with Eguren the flourishing of Peruvian 20th century poetry began.

César Vallejo Without doubt, the most important poet in Peru, if not Latin America, in the first half of the 20th century, was César Vallejo. Born in 1892 in Santiago de Chuco (Libertad), Vallejo left Peru in 1923 after being framed and briefly jailed in Trujillo for a political crime. In 1928 he was a founder of the Peruvian Socialist Party, then he joined the Communist Party in 1931 in Madrid. From 1936 to his death in Paris in 1938 he opposed the fascist takeover in Spain. His first volume was *Los heraldos negros* in which the dominating theme of all his work, a sense of confusion and inadequacy in the face of the unpredictability of life, first surfaces.

Trilce (1922), his second work, is unlike anything before it in the Spanish language. The poems contain (among other things) made-up words, distortions of syntax, their own internal logic and rhythm, graphic devices and innovative uses of sounds, clichés and alliterations. *Poemas humanos* and *España, aparta de mí este cáliz* (written as a result of Vallejo's experiences in the Spanish Civil War) were both published posthumously, in 1939.

In the 1960s writers began to reflect the broadening horizons of that increasingly liberal decade, politically and socially, which followed the Cuban Revolution. One poet who embraced the revolutionary fervour was Javier Heraud (born Miraflores 1942). His early volumes, *El río* (1960) and *El viaje* (1961) are apparently simple in conception and expression, but display a transition from embarking on the adventure of life (the river) to autumnal imagery of solitude. In 1961 he went to the USSR, Asia, Paris and Madrid,

Mario Vargas Llosa

The best known of Peru's writers is Mario Vargas Llosa, born in 1936 in Arequipa and educated in Cochabamba (Bolivia), from where his family moved to Piura. After graduating from the Universidad de San Marcos, he won a scholarship to Paris in 1958 and, from 1959 to 1974, lived first in Paris then in London in voluntary exile. Much has been written about his personal life, and his political opinions have been well documented, but, as befits an author of the highest international standing and one of the leading figures in the so-called 'Boom' of Latin American writers in the 1960s, it is for his novels that Vargas Llosa the writer is best known.

The first three - La ciudad y los perros *(1963),* La casa verde *(1966) and* Conversación en la Catedral *(1969) - with their techniques of flashback, multiple narrators and different interwoven stories, are an adventure for the reader. Meanwhile, the humorous books, like* Pantaleón y las visitadoras *and* La tía Julia y el escribidor *cannot be called lightweight.* La guerra del fin del mundo *marked a change to a more direct style and an intensification of Vargas Llosa's exploration of the role of fiction as a human necessity, extending also to political ideologies. His latest novel,* La fiesta del chivo *(2000) is another fictionalized account of historical events, this time the assassination of President Trujillo of the Dominican Republic in 1961 and the intrigue and fear surrounding his period in office. It is a gripping story, widely regarded as one of his best.*

Vargas Llosa has always maintained that in Peruvian society the writer is a privileged person who should be able to mix politics and literature as a normal part of life. This drive for authenticity led to his excursion into national politics. He stood as a presidential candidate in 1990, losing to Alberto Fujimori. He has since taken up Spanish citizenship and now has homes in Lima, Paris, Madrid and London.

Websites: (in Spanish) www.mundolatino.org/cultura/vargasllosa/vargasllosa.htm (in English) www.kirjasto.sci.fi/vargas.htm

then in 1962 to Cuba to study cinema. He returned to Peru in 1963 and joined the guerrilla Ejército de Liberación Nacional. On 15 May 1963 he was shot by government forces near Puerto Maldonado.

Other major poets who began to publish in the 1960s were Luis Hernández (1941-77), Antonio Cisneros (born 1942), Rodolfo Hinostroza (born 1941) and Marco Martos (born 1942).

In the 1970s, during the social changes propelled by the Velasco regime (1968-75), new voices arose, many from outside Lima, eg the Hora Zero group (1970-73 – Enrique Verástegui, Jorge Pimentel, Juan Ramírez Ruiz), whose energetic poetry employed slang, obscenities and other means to challenge preconceptions. Other poets of the 1970s and after include Giovanna Pollarda (poet, short story writer and screenwriter, born 1952) whose collections include *Huerto de olivos*, 1982, *Entre mujeres solas*, 1996, *La ceremonia de adios*, 1997 and *Atado de nervios*, 1999, and Rocio Silva Santiesteban (born 1967) who has published short stories as well as the poetry collections *Asuntos circunstanciales* (1984), *Este oficio no me gusta* (1987) and *Mariposa negra* (1996). Younger poets of note are: Ericka Ghersi (born 1972), *Zenobia y el anciano* (1994), *Contra la ausencia* (2002), Renato Cisneros (born 1976), *Ritual de los prójimos* (1998) and *Maquina fantasma* (2002), and Oswaldo Chanove, *El héroe y su relación con la heroína* (1983), *El jinete pálido* (1994) and *Canción de amor de un capitán de caballería para una pristituta pelirroja* (2002).

Fine art and sculpture

The Catholic Church was the main patron of the arts during the colonial period. The innumerable churches and monasteries that sprang up in the newly conquered territories created a demand for paintings and sculptures, met initially by imports from Europe of both works of art and of skilled craftsmen, and later by home-grown products.

Colonial period An essential requirement for the inauguration of any new church was an image for the altar and many churches in Lima preserve fine examples of sculptures imported from Seville during the 16th and 17th centuries. Not surprisingly, among the earliest of these are figures of the crucified Christ, such as those in the Cathedral and the church of La Merced by Juan Martínez Montañés, one of the foremost Spanish sculptors of the day, and that in San Pedro, by his pupil Juan de Mesa of 1625. Statues of the Virgin and Child were also imported to Lima from an early date, and examples from the mid-16th century survive in the Cathedral and in Santo Domingo by Roque de Balduque, also from Seville although Flemish by birth.

Sculptures were expensive and difficult to import, and as part of their policy of relative frugality the Franciscan monks tended to favour paintings. In Lima, the museum of San Francisco now houses an excellent collection of paintings imported from Europe, including a powerful series of saints by Zubarán, as well as other works from his studio, a series of paintings of the life of Christ from Ruben's workshop and works from the circles of Ribera and Murillo (see Lima Churches, page 108).

The Jesuits commissioned the Sevillian artist Juan de Valdés Leal to paint a series of the life of St Ignatius Loyola (1660s) which still hangs in San Pedro. The Cathedral museum has a curious series from the Bassano workshop of Venice representing the labours of the monks and dating from the early 17th century. Another interesting artistic import from Europe that can still be seen in San Pedro (see Lima Churches) are the gloriously colourful painted tile decorations (*azulejos*) on the walls of Dominican monastery, produced to order by Sevillian workshops in 1586 and 1604.

Painters and sculptors soon made their way to Peru in search of lucrative commissions including several Italians who arrived during the later 16th century. The Jesuit Bernardo Bitti (1548-1610), for example, trained in Rome before working in Lima, Cusco, Juli and Arequipa, where examples of his elegantly Mannerist paintings are preserved in the Jesuit church of the Compañia (see Arequipa Churches, page 265).

Another Italian, Mateo Pérez de Alesio worked in the Sistine Chapel in Rome before settling in Peru. In Lima the Sevillian sculptor Pedro de Noguera (1592-1655) won the contract for the choirstalls of the Cathedral in 1623 and, together with other Spanish craftsmen, produced a set of cedar stalls decorated with vigorous figures of saints and Biblical characters, an outstanding work unmatched elsewhere in the Viceroyalty.

Native artists European imports, however, could not keep up with demand and local workshops of creole, mestizo and Indian craftsmen flourished from the latter part of the 16th century. As the Viceregal capital and the point of arrival into Peru, the art of Lima was always strongly influenced by European, especially Spanish models, but the old Inca capital of Cusco became the centre of a regional school of painting which developed its own characteristics.

A series of paintings of the 1660s, now hanging in the Museo de Arte Religioso (see Cusco Museums), commemorate the colourful Corpus Christi procession of statues of the local patron saints through the streets of Cusco. These paintings document the appearance of the city and local populace, including Spanish and Inca nobility, priests and laity, rich and poor, Spaniard, Indian, African and mestizo. Many of the statues represented in this series are still venerated in the local parish churches. They are periodically painted and dressed in new robes, but underneath are the original sculptures, executed by native craftsmen. Some are of carved wood while others use the pre-conquest technique of maguey cactus covered in sized cloth.

A remarkable example of an Andean Indian who acquired European skills was Felipe Guaman Poma de Ayala whose 1,000 page letter to the King of Spain celebrating the Andean past and condemning the colonial present contained a visual history of colonial and precolonial life in the Andes (see also above, page 598).

One of the most successful native painters was Diego Quispe Tito (1611-1681) who claimed descent from the Inca nobility and whose large canvases, often based on Flemish engravings, demonstrate the wide range of European sources that were available to Andean artists in the 17th century. But the Cusco School is best known for the anonymous devotional works where the painted contours of the figures are overlaid with flat patterns in gold, creating highly decorative images with an underlying tension between the two- and three-dimensional aspects of the work. The taste for richly-decorated surfaces can also be seen in the 17th and 18th century frescoed interiors of many Andean churches, as in Chinchero, Andahuaylillas and Huaro, and in the ornate carving on altarpieces and pulpits throughout Peru.

Andean content creeps into colonial religious art in a number of ways, most simply by the inclusion of elements of indigenous flora and fauna, or, as in the case of the Corpus Christi paintings, by the use of a specific setting, with recognizable buildings and individuals.

Changes to traditional Christian iconography include the representation of one of the Magi as an Inca, as in the painting of the Adoration of the Magi in San Pedro in Juli (see Puno Excursions, page 244). Another example is that to commemorate his miraculous intervention in the conquest of Cusco in 1534, Santiago is often depicted triumphing over Indians instead of the more familiar Moors. Among the most remarkable 'inventions' of colonial art are the fantastically over-dressed archangels carrying muskets which were so popular in the 18th century. There is no direct European source for these archangels, but in the Andes they seem to have served as a painted guard of honour to the image of Christ or the Virgin on the high altar.

Political independence from Spain in 1824 had little immediate impact on the arts of **Independence** Peru except to create a demand for portraits of the new national and continental heroes **& after** such as Simón Bolívar and San Martín, many of the best of them produced by the mulatto artist José Gil de Castro (d. Lima 1841). Later in the century another mulatto, Pancho Fierro (1810-1879) mocked the rigidity and pretentiousness of Lima society in lively satirical watercolours, while Francisco Laso (1823-1860), an active campaigner for political reform, made the Andean Indian into a respectable subject for oil paintings.

It was not until the latter part of the 19th century that events from colonial history became popular. The Museo de Arte in Lima (see Lima Museums, page 111) has examples of grandiose paintings by Ignacio Merino (1817-1876) glorifying Columbus, as well as the gigantic romanticized 'Funeral of Atahualpa' by Luis Montero (1826-1869). A curious late flowering of this celebration of colonial history is the chapel commemorating Francisco Pizarro in Lima cathedral which was redecorated in 1928 with garish mosaic pictures of the conqueror's exploits.

Of the modern movements Impressionism arrived late and had a limited impact in Peru. Teofilo Castillo (1857-1922), instead of using the technique to capture contemporary reality, created frothy visions of an idealized colonial past. Typical of his work is the large 'Funeral Procession of Santa Rosa' of 1918, with everything bathed in clouds of incense and rose petals, which hangs in the Museo de Arte, in Lima. Daniel Hernández (1856-1932), founder of Peru's first Art School, used a similar style for his portraits of Lima notables past and present.

20th century During the first half of the 20th century, Peruvian art was dominated by figurative styles and local subject matter. Political theories of the 1920s recognized the importance of Andean Indian culture to Peruvian identity and created a climate which encouraged a figurative *indigenista* school of painting, derived in part from the socialist realism of the Mexican muralists. The movement flourished after the founding of the Escuela de Bellas Artes in 1920. José Sabogal (1888-1956) is the best known exponent of the group which also included Mario Urteaga (1875-1957), Jorge Vinatea Reinoso (1900-1931), Enrique Camino Brent (1909-1960), Camilo Blas (1903-1984) and Alejandro González (1900-1984). Their work can be seen in the Museo de Arte and the Museo Banco Central de Reserva in Lima.

The Mexican muralist tradition persisted into the 1960s with Manuel Ugarte Eléspuru (1911) and Teodoro Núñez Ureta (1914), both of whom undertook large-scale commissions in public buildings in Lima. Examples of public sculpture in the indigenist mode can be seen in plazas and parks throughout Peru, but it was in photography that indigenism found its most powerful expression. From the beginning of the century photographic studios flourished even in smaller towns. Martín Chambi (1891-1973) is the best known of the early 20th century Peruvian photographers but there were many others, including Miguel Chani (1860-1951) who maintained the grandly named *Fotografía Universal* studios in Cusco, Puno and Arequipa.

From the middle of the century artists have experimented with a variety of predominantly abstract styles and the best-known contemporary Peruvian painter, Fernando de Szyszlo (1925) has created a visual language of his own, borrowing from Abstract Expressionism on the one hand and from pre-Columbian iconography on the other. His strong images, which suggest rather than represent mythical beings and cosmic forces, have influenced a whole generation of younger Peruvian artists. Look for his monument, *Intihuatana 2000*, near the sea in Miraflores.

Other leading figures whose work can be seen in public and commercial galleries in Lima include Venancio Shinki, Tilsa Tsuchiya, José Tola, Ricardo Weisse, Ramiro Llona and Leoncio Villanueva. Carlos Revilla, whose wife is his muse and principal subject of his painting, is clearly influenced by Hieronymous Bosch, while Bill Caro is an important exponent of hyperrealism. Víctor Delfín, a painter and sculptor (with beautiful work in iron) can be visited at his house in Barranco (Domeyko 366). His piece, The Kiss (*El beso*) is in the Parque del Amor in Lima. Pedro Azabache (from Trujillo) is a disciple of José Sabogal; his work is much broader in scope than the indigenism of his mentor. There are many other new artists whose work could be mentioned (Luz Letts, Eduardo Tokeshi, Carlos Enrique Polanco, Bruno Zepilli, Christian Bendayan – try to contact him in Iquitos, Flavia Gandolfo, Claudia Coca) and there are plenty of galleries in Lima with representative exhibitions. A new foundation is working towards opening a museum of contemporary art in Barranco, Lima, which is long overdue in a country where art is constantly changing.

Land and environment

Geography

Peru is the third largest South American country, the size of France, Spain and the United Kingdom combined, and presents formidable difficulties to human habitation. Virtually all of the 2,250 km of its Pacific coast is desert. From the narrow coastal shelf the Andes rise steeply to a high plateau dominated by massive ranges of snow-capped peaks and gouged with deep canyons. The heavily forested and deeply ravined Andean slopes are more gradual to the east. Further east, towards Brazil and Colombia, begin the vast jungles of the Amazon basin.

The geological structure of Peru is dominated by the Nasca Plate beneath the Pacific **Geology**
Ocean, which stretches from Colombia in the north southwards to mid Chile. Along the
coastline, this Plate meets and dives below the mass of the South American Plate which
has been moving westwards for much of the Earth's geological history. Prior to the middle of the Tertiary Period, say 40 million years ago, marine sediments suggest that the
Amazon basin drained west to the Pacific, but from that time to the present, tectonic
forces have created the Andes range the length of the continent, forming the highest
peaks outside the Himalayas. The process continues today as shown by the earthquakes
and active volcanoes and, in spite of erosion, the mountains still grow higher.

The coastal region, a narrow ribbon of desert 2,250 km long, takes up 11% of the coun- **Coast**
try and holds 44% of the population. It is the economic heart of Peru, consuming most
of the imports and supplying half of the exports. When irrigated, the river valleys are
extremely fertile, creating oases which grow cotton throughout the country,
sugar-cane and rice in the north, and grapes, fruit and olives in the south. At the same
time, the coastal current teems with fish, and Peru has on occasion had the largest
catch in the world.

Not far beyond the border with Ecuador in the north, there are mangrove swamps
and tropical rainforest, but southwards this quickly changes to drier and eventually
desert conditions. South of Piura is the desert of Sechura, followed by the dry barren
land or shifting sands to Chimbote. However, several rivers draining the high mountains to the east more or less reach the sea and water the highly productive 'oases' of
Piura, Cajamarca and Chimbote.

South of Chimbote, the Andes reach the sea, and apart from a thin strip of coastland
north of Lima, the coastal mountains continue to the Chilean border at Arica. This area
receives less rain than the Sahara, but because of the high Andes inland, over 50 Peruvian rivers reach the sea, or would do naturally for at least part of the year. As in the
north, there are oases in the south, but mostly inland at the foot of the mountains
where the river flow is greatest and high sunshine levels ensure good crop production.

The climate of this region depends almost entirely on the ocean currents along the
Pacific coast. Two bodies of water drift northwards, the one closest to the shore, known
as the Humboldt Current, is the colder, following the deep sea trench along the edge of
the Pacific Plate. The basic wind systems here are the South-East Trades crossing the
continent from the Atlantic, but the strong tropical sun over the land draws air into
Peru from the Pacific. Being cool, this air does no more than condense into mist
(known as the *garúa*) over the coastal mountains. This is sufficient to provide moisture
for some unusual flora but virtually never produces rain, hence the desert conditions.
The mixing of the two cold ocean currents, and the cloud cover which protects the
water from the strongest sunlight, creates the unique conditions favourable to fish,
notably sardines and anchovy, giving Peru an enormous economic resource. In turn,
the fish support vast numbers of seabirds whose deposits of guano have been another
very successful export for the country. This is the normal situation; every few years,
however, it is disrupted by the phenomenon known as '*El Niño*' (see page 609).

The Highlands, or *la sierra*, extend inland from the coastal strip some 250 km in the **Highlands**
north, increasing to 400 km in the south. The average altitude is about 3,000 m and
50% of Peruvians live there. Essentially it is a plateau dissected by dramatic canyons
and dominated by some of the most spectacular mountain ranges in the world.

The tallest peaks are in the Cordillera Blanca (Huascarán; 6,768 m) and the neighbour- **Mountains**
ing Cordillera Huayhuash (Yerupajá; 6,634 m). Huascarán is often quoted as the second
highest point in South America after Aconcagua, but this is not so; there are some five
other peaks on or near the Argentina-Chile border over 6,770 m.

Background

The snowline here, at nine degrees south, is between 4,500 m and 5,000 m, much lower than further south. For example, at 16° south, permanent snow starts at 6,000 m on Coropuna (6,425 m).

The reasons for this anomaly can be traced again to the Humboldt current. The Cordillera Blanca is less than 100 km from the coast, and the cool air drawn in depresses temperatures at high altitudes. Precipitation comes also from the east and falls as snow. Constant high winds and temperatures well below freezing at night create an unusual microclimate and with it spectacular mountain scenery, making it a mecca for snow and ice mountaineers. Dangers are heightened by the quite frequent earthquakes causing avalanches and landslides which have brought heavy loss of life to the valleys of the region. In 1970, 20,000 people lost their lives when Yungay, immediately west of Huascarán, was overwhelmed.

Canyons   Equally dramatic are the deep canyons taking water from the high mountains to the Pacific. The Colca Canyon, about 100 km north of Arequipa, has been measured at 3,200 m from the lower rim to the river, more than twice as deep as the Grand Canyon. At one point it is overlooked by the 5,227 m Señal Yajirhua peak, a stupendous 4,150 m above the water level. Deeper even than Colca is the Cotahuasi Canyon, also in Arequipa Department, whose deepest point is 3,354 m. Other canyons have been found in this remote area yet to be measured and documented.

In spite of these ups and downs which cause great communications difficulties, the presence of water and a more temperate climate on the plateau has attracted people throughout the ages. Present day important population centres in the Highlands include Cajamarca in the north, Huancayo in central Peru and Cusco in the south, all at around 3,000 m. Above this, at around 4,000 m, is the 'high steppe' or *puna*, with constant winds and wide day/night temperature fluctuations. Nevertheless, fruit and potatoes (which originally came from the *puna* of Peru and Bolivia) are grown at this altitude and the meagre grasslands are home to the ubiquitous llama.

Volcanoes   Although hot springs and evidence of ancient volcanic activity can be seen almost anywhere in Peru, the southern part of the *sierra* is the only area where there are active volcanoes. These represent the northernmost of a line of volcanoes which stretch 1,500 km south along the Chile-Bolivia border to Argentina. Sabancaya (5,977 m), just south of the Colca canyon, is currently active, often with a dark plume downwind from the summit. Beyond the Colca canyon is the Valle de los Volcanes, with 80 cinder cones rising 50-250 m above a desolate floor of lava and ash. There are other dormant or recently active volcanoes near the western side of Lake Titicaca – for example Ubinas – but the most notable is El Misti (5,822 m) which overlooks Arequipa. It is perfectly shaped, indicating its status as active in the recent geologic past. Some experts believe it is one of the most potentially dangerous volcanoes in South America. Certainly a major eruption would be a catastrophe for the nearby city.

Lake Titicaca   The southeastern border with Bolivia passes through Titicaca, with about half of the lake in each country. It is the largest lake in South America (ignoring Lake Maracaibo in Venezuela which is linked to the sea) and at 3,812 m, the highest navigable body of water in the world. It covers about 8,300 sq km, running 190 km northwest to southeast, and is 80 km across. It lies in a 60,000 sq km basin between the coastal and eastern Andes which spread out southwards to their widest point at latitude 18° south.

The average depth is over 100 m, with the deepest point recorded at 281 m. 25 rivers, most from Peru, flow into the lake and a small outlet leaves the lake at Desaguadero on the Bolivia-Peru border. This takes no more than 5% of the inflow, the rest is lost through evaporation and hence the waters of the lake are slightly brackish, producing the *totora* reeds used to make the mats and balsa boats for which the lake dwellers are famed.

The lake is the remnant of a vast area of water formed in the Ice Age known as Lake Ballivián. This extended at least 600 km to the south into Bolivia and included what is now Lake Poopó and the Salar de Uyuni. Now the lake level fluctuates seasonally, normally rising from December to March and receding for the rest of the year but extremes of 5 m between high and low levels have been recorded. This can cause problems and high levels in the late 1980s disrupted transport links near the shoreline. The night temperature can fall as low as -25°C but high daytime temperatures ensure that the surface average is about 14°C.

Almost half of Peru is on the eastern side of the Andes and about 90% of the country's drainage is into the Amazon system. It is an area of heavy rainfall with cloudforest above 3,500 m and tropical rainforest lower down. There is little savanna, or natural grasslands, characteristic of other parts of the Amazon basin. **Eastern Andes & Amazon basin**

There is some dispute on the Amazon's source. Officially, the mighty river begins as the Marañón, whose longest tributary rises just east of the Cordillera Huayhuash. However, the longest journey for the proverbial raindrop, some 6,400 km, probably starts in southern Peru, where the headwaters of the Apurímac (Ucayali) flow from the snows on the northern side of the Nevado Mismi, near Cailloma.

With much more rainfall on the eastern side of the Andes, rivers are turbulent and erosion dramatic. Although vertical drops are not as great – there is a whole continent to cross to the Atlantic – valleys are deep, ridges narrow and jagged and there is forest below 3,000 m. At 1,500 m the Amazon jungle begins and water is the only means of surface transport available, apart from three roads which reach Borja (on the Marañón), Yurimaguas (on the Huallaga) and Pucallpa (on the Ucayali), all at about 300 m above the Atlantic which is still 4,000 km or so downstream. The vastness of the Amazon lowlands becomes apparent and it is here that Peru bulges 650 km northeast past Iquitos to the point where it meets Colombia and Brazil at Leticia. Oil and gas have recently been found in the Amazon, and new finds are made every year, which means that new pipelines and roads will eventually link more places to the Pacific coast.

Climate

On the coast summertime is from December-April, when temperatures range from 25° to 35°C and it is hot and dry. Wintertime is May-November, when the temperature drops a bit and it is cloudy. **Coast**

The coastal climate is determined by the cold sea-water adjoining deserts. Prevailing inshore winds pick up so little moisture over the cold Humboldt current, which flows from Antarctica, that only from May to November does it condense. The resultant blanket of sea-mist (called *garúa*) extends from the south to about 200 km north of Lima. It is thickest to the south as far as Chincha and to the north as far as Huarmey, beyond which it thins and the sun can be expected to break through.

From April-October is the dry season. It is hot and dry during the day, around 20°-25°C, and cold and dry at night, often below freezing. From November-April is the wet season, when it is dry and clear most mornings, with some rainfall in the afternoon. There is a small temperature drop (18°C) and not much difference at night (15°C). **Sierra**

April-October is the dry season, with temperatures up to 35°C. In the jungle areas of the south, a cold front can pass through at night. November-April is the wet season. It is humid and hot, with heavy rainfall at any time. **Selva**

Flora and fauna

Peru is a country of great biological diversity. The fauna and flora are to a large extent determined by the influence of the Andes, the longest uninterrupted mountain chain in the world, and the mighty Amazon river, which has the largest volume of any river in the world. Of Earth's 32 known climate zones Peru has 28, and of the 104 recognized micro-climates Peru has 84. Throughout the country there are 53 protected natural areas.

Natural history This diversity arises not only from the wide range of habitats available, but also from the history of the continent. South America has essentially been an island for some 70 million years joined only by a narrow isthmus to Central and North America. Land passage played a significant role in the gradual colonization of South America by species from the north. When the land-link closed these colonists evolved to a wide variety of forms free from the competitive pressures that prevailed elsewhere. When the land-bridge was re-established some four million years ago a new invasion of species took place from North America, adding to the diversity but also leading to numerous extinctions. Comparative stability has ensued since then and has guaranteed the survival of many primitive groups like the opossums.

Coast The coastal region of Peru is extremely arid, partly as a result of the cold Humboldt current (see Climate above). The paucity of animal life in the area between the coast and the mountains is obviously due to this lack of rain, though in some areas intermittent *lomas*, which are areas of sparse scrubby vegetation caused by moisture in the sea mist. The plants which survive provide ideal living conditions for insects which attract insectivorous birds and humming birds to feed on their nectar. Cactuses are abundant in northern Peru and provide a wooded landscape of trees and shrubs including the huarango (*Prosopis juliflora*). Also common in the north is the algorrob tree – 250,000 ha were planted in 1997 to take advantage of the El Niño rains.

Andes From the desert rise the steep Andean slopes. In the deeply incised valleys Andean fox and deer may occasionally be spotted. Herds of llamas and alpacas graze the steep hillsides. Mountain caracara and Andean lapwing are frequently observed soaring, and there is always the possibility of spotting flocks of mitred parrots or even the biggest species of hummingbird in the world (*Patagonia gigas*).

The Andean zone has many lakes and rivers and countless swamps. Exclusive to this area short-winged grebe and the torrent duck which feeds in the fast flowing rivers, and giant and horned coots. Chilean flamingo frequent the shallow soda lakes.

The *puna*, a habitat characterized by tussock grass and pockets of stunted alpine flowers, gives way to relict elfin forest and tangled bamboo thicket in this inhospitable windswept and frost-prone region. Occasionally the dissected remains of a *Puya* plant can be found; the result of the nocturnal foraging of the rare spectacled bear. There are quite a number of endemic species of rodent including the viscacha, and it is the last stronghold of the chinchilla. Here pumas roam preying on the herbivores which frequent these mountain – pudu, a tiny Andean deer or guemal and the mountain tapir.

Tropical Andes The elfin forest gradually grades into mist enshrouded cloud forest at about 3,500 m. In the tropical zones of the Andes, the humidity in the cloud forests stimulates the growth of a vast variety of plants particularly mosses and lichens. The cloud forests are found in a narrow strip that runs along the eastern slopes of the spine of the Andes. It is these dense, often impenetrable, forests clothing the steep slopes that are important in protecting the headwaters of all the streams and rivers that cascade from the Andes to form the mighty Amazon as it begins its long journey to the sea.

El Niño

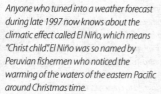

Anyone who tuned into a weather forecast during late 1997 now knows about the climatic effect called El Niño, which means "Christ child". El Niño was so named by Peruvian fishermen who noticed the warming of the waters of the eastern Pacific around Christmas time.

Every 3-7 years, for some as yet unexplained reason, the trade winds that usually blow west from South America subside. So the warm waters of the Pacific – a giant pool the size of Canada – drift eastwards towards South America. The result is worldwide weather chaos.

In 1997 El Niño made its third visit of the decade – one that made everyone sit up and take notice. The eastern Pacific heated faster than at any time in recorded history to become the most devastating climatic event of the century, surpassing even the 1982-83 El

Niño, which killed thousands and caused almost US$14 billion in damage.

The 1997 El Niño caused drought in Australia, New Zealand, Thailand, Malaysia and Papua New Guinea, the forest fires in Indonesia, famine in North Korea, hurricanes along the US Pacific coast and the failure of the fish harvest in Peru (causing the seabird population to fall dramatically). El Niño also sparked epidemics of cholera, encephalitis and bubonic plague.

But despite being implicated in all these weather crimes, scientists appear to know very little about it. The 1997 El Niño was the first major one to have been forecast. It used to arrive every 5-8 years, but recently it's been coming every 3-5 years. Supporting that hypothesis was the suspicion that El Niño was returning in 2002 (at the time of going to press, Pacific sea temperatures were rising).

This is a verdant world of dripping epiphytic mosses, lichens, ferns and orchids which grow in profusion despite the plummeting overnight temperatures. The high humidity resulting from the 2 m of rain that can fall in a year is responsible for the main-tenance of the forest and it accumulates in puddles and leaks from the ground in a constant trickle that combines to form a myriad of icy, crystal-clear tumbling streams that cascade over precipitous waterfalls.

In secluded areas orange Andean Cock-of-the-Rock give their spectacular display to females in the early morning mists. Woolly monkeys are also occasionally sighted as they descend the wooded slopes. Mixed flocks of colourful tanagers are commonly encountered as are the golden-headed quetzal and Amazon umbrella bird.

At about 1,500 m there is a gradual transition to the vast lowland forests of the Amazon **Amazon basin** basin, which are warmer and more equable than the cloud forests clothing the moun-tains above. The daily temperature varies little during the year with a high of 23-32°C falling slightly to 20-26°C overnight. This lowland region receives some 2 m of rainfall per year most of it falling from November to April. The rest of the year is sufficiently dry, at least in the lowland areas to inhibit the growth of epiphytes and orchids which are so characteristic of the highland areas. For a week or two in the rainy season the rivers flood the forest. The zone immediately surrounding this seasonally flooded forest is referred to as *terre firme* forest.

The vast river basin of the Amazon is home to an immense variety of species. The environment has largely dictated the lifestyle. Life in or around rivers, lakes, swamps and forest depend on the ability to swim and climb and amphibious and tree-dwelling animals are common. Once the entire Amazon basin was a great inland sea and the river still contains mammals more typical of the coast, eg manatees and dolphins.

Here in the relatively constant climatic conditions animal and plant life has evolved to an amazing diversity over the millennia. It has been estimated that 3.9 sq km of for-est can harbour some 1,200 vascular plants, 600 species of tree, and 120 woody plants. Here, in these relatively flat lands, a soaring canopy some 50 m overhead is the power-

The debonair dolphin

Two species of dolphin live in the Amazon, the pink Inia geoffrensis and the grey Sotalia fluvialis. The pink dolphin is mainly solitary, but small groups are often found. Instead of a dorsal fin, it has a hump on its back and it also has a long bottle nose. Because of its surfacing habits, you are unlikely to see its nose as it normally only exposes its dorsal ridge. The grey dolphin swims in groups and is a more `conventional' shape, with a dorsal fin and shorter snout. When surfacing it often jumps right out of the water. For centuries the dolphins have lived peacefully with man on the river and as a result many myths have grown up around them. Sadly, destruction of habitat and pollution have threatened this harmonious coexistence.

The best-known legend concerns the night-time exploits of the pink dolphin. Indigenous people of the Amazon have passed down stories from generation to generation about this strange animal, which they call the bufeo. They believe that the dolphins live in an underwater city in Lake Caballococha, downriver from Iquitos, near the Peru-Colombia border. By night, the bufeo can transform himself into a suave gentleman in a white linen suit and, in this guise, he preys on unsuspecting local women. Even today, unwanted pregnancies within Indian communities are sometimes blamed on this magical animal with an impressive

line in seduction techniques. There are many other stories up and down the river and its tributaries. For some communities the dolphin is a semi-divine being, for others a untrustworthy witchdoctor. Its teeth, says Alex Shoumatoff in The Rivers Amazon, are claimed to cure children's diarrhea, its ear to grant a long-lasting erection and its "grated left eye is an aphrodisiac powder."

The pink river dolphins were, until recently, a forgotten species, considered extinct. All that remained was the skeleton of one in Paris, brought back from South America as a gift to Napoleon, and a few vague scientific papers dating from the 19th century in the Natural History Museum in London. The bufeo was re-discovered by a British expedition in 1956. Then it was forgotten again until 1987, when Jacques Cousteau astounded TV viewers around the world with the first ever pictures of pink dolphins frolicking in the waters of the Amazon.

Now many Amazon lodges take travellers on dolphin-spotting expeditions. With some patience you can see one, or both types of dolphin in the flesh. The more curious pink ones circle quite close to the boat, while the grey will be further away, plunging into the river in unison – a fantastic sight. Back on land, though, women travellers should beware of a charming, smartly-dressed gentleman who doesn't raise his hat (it covers his blowhole).

house of the forest. It is a habitat choked with strangling vines and philodendrons among which mixed troupes of squirrel monkeys and brown capuchins forage. In the high canopy small groups of spider monkeys perform their lazy aerial acrobatics, whilst lower down, cling to epiphyte-clad trunks and branches, groups of saddle-backed and emperor tamarins forage for blossom, fruit and the occasional insect prey.

The most accessible part of the jungle is on or near the many meandering rivers. At each bend of the river the forest is undermined by the currents during the seasonal floods at the rate of some 10-20 m per year leaving a sheer mud and clay bank, whilst on the opposite bend new land is laid down as broad beaches of fine sand and silt.

A succession of vegetation can be seen. The fast growing willow-like *Tessaria* first stabilizes the ground enabling the tall stands of caña brava *Gynerium* to become established. Within these dense almost impenetrable stands the seeds of rainforest trees germinate and over a few years thrust their way towards the light. The fastest growing is a species of *Cercropia* which forms a canopy 15-18 m over the caña but even this is relatively short-lived. The gap in the canopy is quickly filled by other species. Two types of mahogany outgrow the other trees forming a closed canopy at 40 m with a lush understory of shade tolerant *Heliconia* and ginger. Eventually even the long-lived trees die off to be replaced by others providing a forest of great diversity.

The meandering course of the river provides many excellent opportunities to see herds of russet-brown capybara – a sheep-sized rodent – peccaries and brocket deer. Of considerable ecological interest are the presence of ox-bow lakes, or *cochas*, since these provide an abundance of wildlife which can easily be seen around the lake margins.

Jungle wildlife

The best way to see the wildlife, however, is to get above the canopy. Ridges provide elevated view points from which you can enjoy excellent views. From here, it is possible to look across the lowland flood plain to the foothills of the Andes, some 200 km away. Flocks of parrots and macaws can be seen flying between fruiting trees and troupes of squirrel monkeys and brown capuchins come very close.

The lowland rainforest of Peru is particularly famous for its primates and giant otters. Giant otters were once widespread in Amazonia but came close to extinction in the 1960s owing to persecution by the fur trade. The giant otter population in Peru has since recovered and is now estimated to be at least several hundred. Jaguar and other predators are also much in evidence. Although rarely seen their paw marks are commonly found along the forest trails. Rare bird species are also much in evidence, including fasciated tiger-heron and primitive hoatzins.

The (very) early-morning is the best time to see peccaries, brocket deer and tapir at mineral licks (*collpa*). Macaw and parrot licks are found along the banks of the river. Here at dawn a dazzling display arrives and clambers around in the branches overhanging the clay-lick. At its peak there may be 600 birds of up to six species (including red and green macaws, and blue-headed parrots) clamouring to begin their descent to the riverbank where they jostle for access to the mineral rich clay. A necessary addition to their diet which may also neutralize the toxins present in the leaf and seed diet. Rare game birds such as razor billed curassows and piping guans may also be seen.

A list of over 600 species has been compiled. Noteworthy species are the black-faced cotinga, crested eagle, and the Harpy eagle, the world's most impressive raptor, easily capable of taking an adult monkey from the canopy. Mixed species flocks are commonly observed containing from 25 to 100+ birds of perhaps some 30 species including blue dacnis, blue-tailed emerald, bananaquit, thick-billed euphoria and the paradise tanager. Each species occupies a slightly different niche, and since there are few individuals of each species in the flock, competition is avoided. Mixed flocks foraging in the canopy are often led by a white-winged shrike, whereas flocks in the understorey are often led by the bluish-slate antshrike. (For more information on the birds of Peru, see page 86.)

Books

Many general books contain information on Peru: *The Cambridge Encyclopedia of Latin America and the Caribbean*, edited by **Collier, Simon, Skidmore, Thomas E, and Blakemore, Harold** (2nd edition 1992); **Williamson, Edwin** *The Penguin History of Latin America* (1992); and **Parry, J H** *The Discovery of South America* (1979).

There are many periodicals which specialize in Peru: consult a good library for those which cover your particular interest. Consistently interesting is *South American Explorer*, published quarterly by South American Explorers. Also highly recommended is the *Peru Reader* (Stark, Degregori and Kirk, eds, 1995), Duke University Press, which, besides literature, also contains history, culture and politics and is an excellent introduction to these topics; the anthology ranges from the precolonial to the present.

History and culture For the period of the Conquest **Hemming, John** *The Conquest of the Incas* is invaluable; he refers us to **Kendall, Ann** *Everyday Life of the Incas* (1978)

Batsford. Also **Portal Cabellos, Manuel** *Oro y tragedia de los Incas*, excellent on the division of the empire, civil war and *huaqueros*. Other recommended books on Peru's history and culture are: **Alden Mason, J** *The Ancient Civilizations of Peru* (1991); **Cáceres Macedo, Justo** *The Prehispanic Cultures of Peru* (1988); **Mosely, Michael E** *The Incas and their Ancestors: The Archaeology of Peru; Peruvian Prehistory. An overview of pre-Inca and Inca Society*, edited by **Keatinge, Richard W** (1988); **Heyerdahl, Thor, Sandweiss, Daniel H, and Narváez, Alfredo** *Pyramids of Túcume* (1995), Thames & Hudson.

Cusco and Machu Picchu See Footprint's *Cusco and the Inca Trail Handbook*, Also on Cusco, the Sacred Valley, Inca Trail, Machu Picchu and other ruins is **Frost, Peter** *Exploring Cusco*. Also recommended for general information on Cusco is *Cusco Peru Tourist Guide*, published by Lima 2000. **Thomson, Hugh** *The White Rock* (2002), Phoenix, describes Thomson's own travels in the Inca heartland, as well as the journeys of earlier explorers and the history of the region. **Reinhard, Johan** *The Sacred Center* explains Machu Picchu in archaeological terms. Another recommended book on Machu Picchu, with colour photographs, is **Frost, Peter** *The Machu Picchu Historical Sanctuary*, Nuevas Imagenes. **Morrison, Tony** *Qosqo. The Navel of the World* (1997) Condor Books, describes Cusco's past and present with an extensive section of photographs of the city and its surroundings. Another beautiful book with photographs and text is **Milligan, Max** *In the Realm of the Incas* (2001) Harper Collins. **Brod, Charles** *Apus and Incas*, Inca Expeditions, describes cultural walks in and around Cusco, and treks in the Cordilleras Vilcabamba, Vilcanota and Urubamba, plus the Manu National Park. **Bingham, Hiram** *Lost City of the Incas* (2002) new illustrated edition, with an introduction by Hugh Thomson, Weidenfeld & Nicolson. **Sueldo Nava, Pedro** *A Walking Tour of Machu Picchu* in several languages, available in Cusco. **Wright, Ruth and Valnecia Zegarra, Alfredo** *The Machu Picchu Guidebook. A Self-Guided Tour* (2001) Johnson Books. **Megarry, Jacquetta and Davies, Roy** *Explore the Inca Trail* (2002) Rucksack Readers (see also Roy Davies' Inca Trail website) South American Explorers in Lima and Cusco has detailed information on walks around Machu Picchu.

Nasca **Morrison, Tony** *Pathways to the Gods: The Mystery of the Andes Lines* (1978) Michael Russell, obtainable in Lima; and *The Mystery of the Nasca Lines* (1987), Nonesuch Expeditions. **Hadingham, E** *Lines to the Mountain Gods: Nasca and the Mysteries of Peru* (1987) Random House. An account of the balloon flight is in **Woodman, Jim** *Nasca, the flight of Condor 1* (1980) Pocket Books, NY. **Reinhard, Dr Johan** *The Nasca Lines - a new perspective on their origin and meaning*, Editorial Los Pinos, Lima 18.

Chachapoyas area The whole area is full of largely unexplored ruins and some of them have been studied by the Swiss archaeologists Henri and Paula Reichlen. They surveyed 39 sites in 1948 - see *Récherches archaeologiques dans les Andes du haut Utcubamba*, in *Journal des Américanistes*, which includes an accurate map. The controversial American archaeologist Gene Savoy went further than the Reichlens; see his book *Antisuyo*. Kaufmann Doig's *Arqueología Peruana* includes a map showing the location of the '12 Cities of the Condors'. Also worth looking at are **Davis, Morgan** *The Cloud People, an Anthropological Survey*, and **Muscutt, Keith** *Warriors of the Clouds: A Lost Civilization in the Upper Amazon of Peru* (1998) New Mexico Press, an excellent coffee table book and Chachapoyas memoir; its related website (www.chachapoyas.com) is also worth consulting.

Walton, Carolyn *The City of Kings: A guide to Lima* (1987). A very readable account of the last decade of the 20th century is **Bowen, Sally** *The Fujimori File. Peru and its President 1990-2000* (2000); it ends at the election of that year so the final momentous events of Fujimori's term happened after publication.

Literature A detailed account of Peruvian literature and its finest writers is given in the Literature section on page 598. Background reading: **Higgins, James** *A History of Peruvian Literature* (1987) Liverpool monographs in Hispanic studies 7; **Franco, Jean** *Spanish American Literature since Independence* (1973) Benn; **Martin, Gerald** *Journeys through the Labyrinth* (1989), Verso; **Brotherston, Gordon** *The Emergence of the Latin American Novel* and *Latin American Poetry* (1977 and 1975) Cambridge University Press; **Villanueva, Darío, and Viña Liste, José María** *Trayectoria de la novela hispanoamericana actual* (1991). **Vallejo, César** *Selected Poems*, edited by Stephen M Hart (2000), Bristol Classical Press.

The following novels are also recommended: **Wilder, Thornton** *The Bridge of San Luis Rey* (1941) Penguin; **Matthiessen, Peter** *At Play in the Fields of the Lord* (1965); **Shakespeare, Nicholas** *The Vision of Elena Silves* (1989); **Thubron, Colin** *To the Last City* (2002) Chatto & Windus. Good travel books are: **Murphy, Dervla** *Eight Feet in the Andes* (1994); **Parris, Matthew** *Inca-Kola* (1990); **Shah, Tahir** *Trail of Feathers* (2001) Phoenix; **Wright, Ronald** *Cut Stones and Crossroads: a Journey in Peru*(1984) Viking.

Climbing, trekking and cycling **Díaz, Felipe** *Callejón de Huaylas y Cordillera Blanca* (Spanish, English and German editions), available locally. **Gómez, Antonio, and Tomé, Juan José** *La Cordillera Blanca de Los Andes* (1998) Desnivel, Spanish only, principally a climbing guide, but contains some trekking and general information, also available locally. Juanjo Tomé has also written *Escaladas en los Andes. Guía de la Cordillera Blanca* (1999) Desnivel (Spanish only), a climbing guide. Another climbing guide is **Sharman, David** *Climbs of the Cordillera Blanca of Peru*, (1995) Whizzo, available locally, from South American Explorers, as well as from Cordee in the UK and Alpenbooks in the USA. **Biggar, John** *The Andes. A Guide for Climbers* (1999) Andes Publishing, contains a chapter on the peaks of Northern Peru. **Bartle, Jim** *Parque Nacional Huascarán*, is a beautiful soft-cover photo collection with English and Spanish text. **Kolff, Helen and Kees** *Flores silvestres de la Cordillera Blanca/Wildflowers of the Cordillera Blanca* (1997) El Instituto Montaña/The Mountain Institute, is a bilingual guide, fully illustrated.

Simpson, Joe *Touching the Void* (1997) Vintage, is a nail-biting account of Simpson's almost fatal accident in the Cordillera Huayhuash. For an account of the Andean Inca road, see **Portway, Christopher** *Journey Along the Andes* (1993) Impact Books. National Geographic has published **Muller, Karin** *Along the Inca Road. A Woman's Journey into an Ancient Empire* (2000). Ricardo Espinosa, who has walked the length of the Camino Real de los Incas, from Quito to La Paz, including some of the Inca routes from the coast to the Sierra, has not yet published his account of the walk. He has, however, walked the length of Peru's coast, described in *El Perú a toda Costa* (1997) Editur. The same company has published **Zarzar, Omar** *Por los Caminos del Perú en Bicicleta*.

Rafting A recommended read is **Kane, Joe** *Running the Amazon* (1989) The Bodley Head; as is **Majcherczyk, Jerzy "Yurek"** *The Conquest of the Río Colca* (u/d) Layconsa. There are a number of magazine articles on rafting in Peru: Kurt Casey, 'Cotahuasi Canyon - an Ultimate Peruvian Adventure', in *American Whitewater* (July/August, 1995); in the same edition is 'Paddling the Inca Trail' by **John Foss**, an account of runs on the Ríos Colca, Apurímac and Urubamba; by the same author are: 'Diarios de Cotahuasi', in *Caretas* magazine, 6 July 1995; and 'Rio Cotahuasi: the World's Deepest Canyon - Really!' in *South American Explorer*, Spring 1996 edition.

Wildlife and environment Frost, Peter et al (Edited by Jim Bartle), *Machu Picchu Historical Sanctuary*, with superb text and photos on all aspects of the Inca Trail and the endangered ecosystem of the sanctuary.

Recommended for bird watchers are: **Clements, James F and Shany, Noam** *A Field Guide to the Birds of Peru* (2001) Ibis; **Krabbe, Nils and Fjeldsa, Jon** *Birds of the High Andes* (1990) University of Copenhagen, which covers all Peruvian birds that occur above 3,000 m - a large proportion of the birds likely to be seen in the Andes; **Ridgely, Robert, and Tudor, Guy** *Birds of South America* Volumes 1 & 2 (1989 and 1994) helps tremendously with the passerines, especially volume 2; **Hilty, Steve, and Brown, William** *A guide to the Birds of Colombia* (1986), covers the vast majority of the Amazonian species likely to be seen; **Parker, Ted, Parker, Susan, and Plenge, Manuel** *An Annotated checklist of Peruvian Birds* (1982), is slightly outdated but still useful, it lists all Peruvian birds by habitat type; **Koepcke, Maria** *The Birds of the Department of Lima* (1983), is useful for the coast. **Person, David L and Beletsky, Les** *Ecotraveller's Wildlife Guide: Peru* (2001) Academic Press, is recommended.

Amazon: *Birds of Colombia* by Steve Hilty, *South American Birds*, by John Dunning, *Birds of South America*, volumes 1 and 2, by Ridgeley and Tudor, *Birds of Ecuador* by Ridgeley and Greenfield, *Birds of Peru* by Jim Clements and Noam Shany and *Birds of Machu Picchu* by Barry Walker and Jon Fjeldsa give the best coverage of birds of Peru. Also *Neotropical Rainforest Mammals, A field guide*, by Louise H Emmons. *Tropical Nature*, by Adrian Forsyth and Ken Miyata, gives an explanation of the rainforest. *Manu National Park*, by Kim MacQuarrie and André and Cornelia Bartschi, is a large, expensive and excellent book, with beautiful photographs. *Madre de Dios Packet*, by South American Explorers, gives practical travel advice for the area.

The Ecology of Tropical Rainforests (republished 2001), *Tambopata - A Bird Checklist*, *Tambopata – Mammal, Amphibian & Reptile Checklist* and *Reporte Tambopata* are all published by *TReeS* (see under Tambopata-Candamo Reserved Zone for address); they also produce tapes, *Jungle Sounds* and *Birds of Southeast Peru*.

Cuisine **Lambert Ortiz, Elisabeth** *The Flavour of Latin America* Recipes and Stories (1998) Latin America Bureau, contains various Peruvian recipes in English. A comprehensive series in Spanish is produced by the Escuela Profesional de Turismo y Hotelería, Universidad San Martín de Porres (www.usmp.edu.pe) 1. *Amazonia*, 2. *Centro del Perú*, 3. *Lima*, 4. *Sur del Perú*, 5. *Norte del Perú* (all 1999, 2000). The series contains many other cookery titles. *The Silver Llama Dining Guide* (2002) Enterprise Peru Consultant, published annually, lists all the best restaurants.

Guide books For information on *Bradt Publications'* Backpacking Guide Series, other titles and imported maps and guides, contact 19 High Street, Chalfont St Peter, Bucks SL9 9QE, UK, T01753 893444, F01753 892333, www.bradt-travelguides.com Relevant to this Handbook is **Bradt, Hilary** *Backpacking and Trekking in Peru and Bolivia* (7th edition). A very useful book, highly recommended, aimed specifically at the budget traveller is **Hatt, John** *The Tropical Traveller* (1993) Penguin Books, 3rd edition.

Footnotes

Spanish words and phrases

No amount of dictionaries, phrase books or word lists will provide the same enjoyment as being able to communicate directly with the people of the country you are visiting. Learning Spanish is a useful part of the preparation for a trip to the Peru and you are encouraged to make an effort to grasp the basics before you go. As you travel you will pick up more of the language and the more you know, the more you will benefit from your stay. The following secion is designed to be a simple point of departure.

Whether you have been taught the 'Castillian' pronounciation (all z's, and c's followed by *i* or *e*, are pronounced as the *th* in *think*) or the 'American' pronounciation (they are pronounced as *s*), you will encounter little difficulty in understanding either: Spanish pronunciation varies geographically much less than English. There are, of course, regional accents and usages; but the basic language is essentially the same everywhere.

General pronunciation

The stress in a Spanish word conforms to one of three rules: **1** if the word ends in a vowel, or in **n** or **s**, the accent falls on the penultimate syllable *(ventana, ventanas)*; **2** if the word ends in a consonant other than **n** or **s**, the accent falls on the last syllable *(hablar)*; **3** if the word is to be stressed on a syllable contrary to either of the above rules, the acute accent on the relevant vowel indicates where the stress is to be placed *(pantalón, metáfora)*. Note that adverbs such as *cuando*, 'when', take an accent when used interrogatlvely; *¿cuándo?*, 'when?'

Vowels

a	not quite as short as in English 'cat'
e	as in English 'pay', but shorter in a syllable ending in a consonant
i	as in English 'seek'
o	as in English 'shop', but more like 'pope' when the vowel ends a syllable
u	as in English 'food', after 'q' and in 'gue', 'gui' **u** is unpronounced; in 'güe' and 'güi' it is pronounced
y	when a vowel, pronounced like 'I'; when a semiconsonant or consonant, it is pronounced like English 'yes'
ai, ay	as in English 'ride'
el, ey	as in English 'they'
oi, oy	as in English 'toy'

Consonants

Unless listed below consonants can be pronounced in Spanish as they are in English.

b, v	their sound is interchangeable and is a cross between the English **b** and **v**, except at the beginning of a word or after **m** or **n** when it is like English **b**
c	like English **k**, except before **e** or **i** when it is the **s** in English 'sip'
g	before **e** and **i** it is the same as **j**
h	when on its own, never pronounced
j	as the **ch** in the Scottish 'loch'
ll	as the **g** in English 'beige'; sometimes as the 'lli' in 'million'
ñ	as the 'ni' in English 'onion'
rr	trilled much more strongly than in English
x	depending on its location, pronounced as in English 'fox', or 'sip', or like 'gs'
z	as the **s** in English 'sip'

Pronouns

In the Americas, the plural, familar pronoun *vosotros* (with the verb endings - *áis*, - *éis*), though much used in Spain, is never heard. Two or more people, including small children, are always addressed as *Ustedes* (*Uds*).

Inappropriate use of the familiar forms (*tú, vos*) can sound imperious, condescending, infantile, or imply a presumption of intimacy that could annoy officials, one's elders, or, if coming from a man, women.

To avoid cultural complications if your Spanish is limited, stick to the polite forms: *Usted* (*Ud*) in the singular, *Ustedes* in the plural, and you will never give offense. Remember also that a person who address you as *tú*, does not necessarily expect to be *tuteada* (so addressed) in return.

You should, however, violate this rule when dealing with a small child, who might be intimidated by *Usted*: he/she is, after all, normally so addressed only in admonitions such as *'¡No, Señor, Ud no tomará un helado antes del almuerzo!'* 'No, Sir, you will not have ice cream before lunch!'

General hints

Note that in Peru, a common response to *¡Gracias!* is often *¡A sus ordenes!* ('Yours to command!') rather than the *'¡De nada!'* ('Tis nought!') taught in school.

Travellers whose names include *b*'s and *v*'s should learn to distinguish between them when spelling aloud as *be larga* and *ve corta* or *uve*. (Children often say *ve de vaca* and *be de burro* to distinguish between the two letters, pronounced interchangeably, either as *b* or *v*, in Spanish.)

Greetings, courtesies

excuse me/I beg your pardon	*permiso*
Go away!	*¡Váyase!*
good afternoon/evening/night	*buenas tardes/noches*
good morning	*buenos días*
goodbye	*adiós/chao*
hello	*hola*
How are you?	*¿cómo está?/¿cómo estás?*
I do not understand	*no entiendo*
leave me alone	*déjame en paz/no me moleste*
no	*no*
please	*por favor*
pleased to meet you	*mucho gusto/encantado/encantada*
see you later	*hasta luego*
thank you (very much)	*(muchas) gracias*
What is your name?	*¿Cómo se llama?*
yes	*sí*
I speak ...	*Hablo ...*
I speak Spanish	*Hablo español*
I don't speak Spanish	*No hablo español*
Do you speak English?	*¿Habla usted inglés?*
We speak German	*Hablamos alemán*
They speak French	*Hablan francés*
Please speak slowly	*hable despacio por favor*
I am very sorry	*lo siento mucho/disculpe*
I'm fine	*muy bien gracias*

I'm called_   *me llamo_*
What do you want?   *¿Qué quiere?*
I want   *quiero*
I don't want it   *No lo quiero*
long distance phone call   *la llamada a larga distancia*
good   *bueno*
bad   *malo*

Nationalities and languages

American   *Americano/a*
Australian   *Australiano/a*
Austrian   *Austriaco/a*
British   *Británico/a*
Canadian   *Canadiense*
Danish   *Danés/Danesa*
Dutch   *Holandés/Holandesa*
English   *Inglés/Inglesa*
French   *Francés/Francesa*
German   *Alemán/Alemana*
Irish   *Irlandés/Irlandesa*

Italian   *Italiano/a*
Mexican   *Mexicano/a*
New Zealand   *Neozelandés/Neozelandesa*
Norwegian   *Noruego/a*
Portuguese   *Portugués/Portuguesa*
Scottish   *Escocés/Escocesa*
Spanish   *Español/a*
Swedish   *Sueco/a*
Swiss   *Suizo/a*
Welsh   *Galés/Galesa*

Basic questions

Have you got a room for two people?
   ¿Tiene habitación para dos personas?
How do I get to_?   *¿Cómo llegar a_?*
How much does it cost?   *¿ Cuánto cuesta?*
How much is it?   *¿Cuánto es?*
When does the bus leave?
   ¿A qué hora sale el bus?

-arrive?   *-llega-*
When?   *¿Cuándo?*
Where is_?   *¿Dónde está_?*
Where is the nearest petrol station?
   ¿Dónde está el grifo más cerca?
Why?   *¿Por qué?*

Basics

bank   *el banco*
bathroom/toilet   *el baño*
bill   *la factura/la cuenta*
cash   *el efectivo*
cheap   *barato*
church/cathedral   *La iglesia/catedral*
exchange house   *la casa de cambio*
exchange rate   *la tasa de cambio*
expensive   *caro*

market   *el mercado*
notes/coins   *los billetes/las monedas*
police (policeman)   *la policia (el policia)*
post office   *el correo*
supermarket   *el supermercado*
telephone office   *el centro de llamadas*
ticket office   *la boletería/la taquilla*
travellers' cheques   *los travelers/los*
                cheques de viajero

Getting around

aeroplane/airplane   *el avión*
airport   *el aeropuerto*
bus station   *la terminal (terrestre)*
bus stop   *la parada*
bus   *el bus/el autobus etc*
minibus   *el combi*
motorcycle taxi   *el mototaxi*
bus route   *el corredor*
first/second class   *primera/segunda clase*

on the left/right   *a la izquierdo/derecha*
second street on the left
   la segunda calle a la izquierda
ticket   *el boleto*
to walk   *caminar*
Where can I buy tickets?
   ¿Dónde se puede comprar boletos?
Where can I park?
   ¿Dónde se puede parquear?

Orientation and motoring

arrival   *la llegada*
avenue   *la avenida*
block   *la cuadra*
border   *la frontera*
car used for public transport on a
   fixed route   *colectivo*
corner   *la esquina*
customs   *la aduana*
departure   *la salida*
east   *el este, el oriente*
empty   *vacío*
full   *lleno*
highway, main road   *carretera*
immigration   *la inmigración*
insurance   *el seguro*
the insured   *el asegurado/la asegurada*
to insure yourself against   *asegurarse contra*

luggage   *el equipaje*
motorway, dual carriageway   *autopista/carretera*
north   *el norte*
oil   *el aceite*
passport   *el pasaporte*
petrol/gasoline   *la gasolina*
puncture   *el pinchazo*
south   *el sur*
street   *la calle*
that way   *por allí/por allá*
this way   *por aquí/por acá*
tourist card   *la tarjeta de turista*
tyre   *la llanta*
unleaded   *sin plomo*
visa   *el visado*
waiting room   *la sala de espera*
west   *el oeste/el poniente*

Accommodation

air conditioning   *el aire acondicionado*
all-inclusive   *todo incluído*
blankets   *las mantas*
clean/dirty towels   *las toallas limpias/sucias*
dining room   *el comedor*
double bed   *la cama matrimonial*
guest house   *la casa de huéspedes*
hot/cold water   *agua caliente/fría*
hotel   *el hotel*
Is service included?   *¿Está incluído el servicio?*
Is tax included?   *¿Están incluidos los
   impuestos?*
noisy   *ruidoso*

pillows   *las almohadas*
power cut   *apagón/corte*
restaurant   *el restaurante*
room   *el cuarto/la habitación*
sheets   *las sábanas*
shower   *la ducha*
single/double   *sencillo/doble*
soap   *el jabón*
to make up/clean   *limpiar*
toilet   *el sanitario*
toilet paper   *el papel higiénico*
with private bathroom   *con baño privado*
with two beds   *con dos camas*

Health

aspirin   *la aspirina*
blood   *la sangre*
chemist/pharmacy   *la farmacia*
condoms   *los preservativos*
contact lenses   *las lentes de contacto*
contraceptive (pill)   *el anticonceptivo (la
píldora anticonceptiva)*

diarrhoea   *la diarrea*
doctor   *el médico*
fever/sweat   *la fiebre/el sudor*
(for) pain   *(para) dolor*
head   *la cabeza*
period/towels   *la regla/las toallas*
stomach   *el estómago*

Time

At one o'clock   *a la una*
At half past two/two thirty
   a las dos y media
At a quarter to three   *a cuarto para las tres*
or *a las tres menos quince*
It's one o'clock   *es la una*
It's seven o'clock   *son las siete*

It's twenty past six/six twenty
   son las seis y veinte
It's five to nine   *son cinco para las
   nueve/son las nueve menos cinco*
In ten minutes   *en diez minutos*
five hours   *cinco horas*
Does it take long?   *¿Tarda mucho?*
We will be back at ...   *Regresamos a las ...*
What time is it?   *¿Qué hora es?*

Monday *lunes*
Tuesday *martes*
Wednesday *miércoles*
Thursday *jueves*
Friday *viernes*
Saturday *sábado*
Sunday *domingo*
January *enero*
February *febrero*
March *marzo*

April *abril*
May *mayo*
June *junio*
July *julio*
August *agosto*
September *septiembre*
October *octubre*
November *noviembre*
December *diciembre*

Numbers

one *uno/una*
two *dos*
three *tres*
four *cuatro*
five *cinco*
six *seis*
seven *siete*
eight *ocho*
nine *nueve*
ten *diez*
eleven *once*
twelve *doce*
thirteen *trece*
fourteen *catorce*
fifteen *quince*

sixteen *dieciséis*
seventeen *diecisiete*
eighteen *dieciocho*
nineteen *diecinueve*
twenty *veinte*
twenty one, two *veintiuno, veintidos etc*
thirty *treinta*
forty *cuarenta*
fifty *cincuenta*
sixty *sesenta*
seventy *setenta*
eighty *ochenta*
ninety *noventa*
hundred *cien or ciento*
thousand *mil*

Family

aunt *la tía*
brother *el hermano*
cousin *la/el prima/o*
daughter *la hija*
family *la familia*
father *el padre*
fiance/fiancee *el novio/la novia*
friend *el amigo/la amiga*
grandfather *el abuelo*

grandmother *la abuela*
husband *el esposo/marido*
married *casado/a*
mother *la madre*
single/unmarried *soltero/a*
sister *la hermana*
son *el hijo*
uncle *el tío*
wife *la esposa*

Key verbs

To go *ir*
I go *voy*
you go (familiar singular) *vas*
he, she, it goes, you (unfamiliar singular) go *va*
we go *vamos*
they, you (plural) go *van*
To have (possess) *tener*
I have *tengo*
You have *tienes*
He she, it have, you have *tiene*
We have *tenemos*
They, you have *tienen*
(Also used as 'To be', as in 'I am hungry' *tengo hambre*)

(NB *Haber* also means 'to have', but is used with other verbs, as in 'he has gone' *ha ido*)
I have gone *he ido*
You have said *has dicho*
He, she, it has, you have done *ha hecho*
We have eaten *hemos comido*
They, you have arrived *han llegado*
Hay means 'there is' and is used in questions such as *¿Hay cuartos?* 'Are there any rooms?'; perhaps more common is *No hay* meaning 'there isn't any'

To be (in a permanent state) *ser*
I am (a teacher) *soy (profesor)*
You are *Eres*
He, she, it is, you are *es*
We are *somos*
They, you are *son*

To be (positional or temporary state) *estar*
I am (in London) *estoy (en Londres)*
You are *estás*
He, she, it is, you are (happy) *está (contenta)*
We are *estámos*
They, you are *están*

To do/make *Hacer*
I do *hago*
You do *haces*
He, she, it does, you do *hace*
We do *hacemos*
They, you do *hacen*

The above section was compiled on the basis of glossaries by André de Mendonça and David Gilmour of South American Experience, London, and the LatinAmerican Travel Advisor, No 9, March 1996

Food

avocado *la palta*
baked *al horno*
bakery *la panadería*
beans *los frijoles/las habichuelas*
beef *la carne de res*
beef steak or pork fillet *el bistec*
boiled rice *el arroz blanco*
bread *el pan*
breakfast *el desayuno*
butter *la mantequilla*
cassava, yucca *la yuca*
casserole *la cazuela*
chewing gum *el chicle*
chicken *el pollo*
chilli pepper or green pepper *el ají*
clear soup, stock *el caldo*
cooked *cocido*
dining room *el comedor*
egg *el huevo*
fish *el pescado*
fork *el tenedor*
fried *frito*
fritters *las frituras*
garlic *el ajo*
goat *el chivo*
grapefruit *el pomelo*
grill *la parrilla*
grilled/griddled *a la plancha*
guava *la guayaba*
ham *el jamón*
hamburger *la hamburgueso*
hot, spicy *picante*
ice cream *el helado*
jam *la mermelada*
knife *el cuchillo*
lime *el limón*
lobster *la langosta*

lunch *el almuerzo*
margarine, fat *la manteca*
meal, supper, dinner *la comida*
meat *la carne*
minced meat *el picadillo*
mixed salad *la ensalada mixta*
onion *la cebolla*
orange *la naranja*
pepper *el pimiento*
plantain, green banana *el plátano*
pasty, turnover *la empanada/el pastelito*
pork *el cerdo*
potato *la papa*
prawns *los camarones*
raw *crudo*
restaurant *el restaurante*
roast *el asado*
salad *la ensalada*
salt *el sal*
sandwich *el bocadillo*
sauce *la salsa*
sausage *la longaniza*
scrambled eggs *los huevos revueltos*
seafood *los mariscos*
small sandwich, filled roll *el bocadito*
soup *la sopa*
spoon *la cuchara*
squash *la calabaza*
squid *los calamares*
supper *la cena*
sweet *dulce*
sweet potato *la batata*
to eat *comer*
toasted *tostado*
turkey *el pavo*
vegetables *los legumbres/vegetales*
without meat *sin carne*
yam *el camote*

Drink

beer *la cerveza*
boiled *hervido*
bottled *en botella*
camomile tea *la manzanilla*
canned *en lata*
cocktail *el coctel*
coconut milk *la leche de coco*
coffee *el café*
coffee, small, strong *el cafecito*
coffee, white *el café con leche*
cold *frío*
condensed milk *la leche condensada*
cup *la taza*
drink *la bebida*
drunk *borracho*
fruit milk shake *el batido*
glass *el vaso*
glass of liqueur *la copa de licor*
hot *caliente*
ice *el hielo*

juice *el jugo*
lemonade *la limonada*
milk *la leche*
mint *la menta*
orange juice *el jugo de naranja*
pineapple milkshake *el batido de piña con leche*
rough rum, firewater *el aguardiente*
rum *el ron*
soft drink *el refresco*
soft fizzy drink *la gaseosa/cola*
sugar *el azúcar*
tea *el té*
to drink *beber/tomar*
water *el agua*
water, carbonated *el agua mineral con gas*
water, still mineral *el agua mineral natural/sin gas*
wine, red *el vino tinto*
wine, white *el vino blanco*

Glossary

Peruvian foods and dishes

Food has always played an important role in Peruvian culture. The country's range of climates has also made this South American nation internationally recognized for its diverse cuisine.

Ají (hot pepper)

Ají is found in many varieties and is used to add `spice' to everything from soup to fish to vegetable dishes. It is a staple in Peruvian kitchens from the coast to the most remote jungle villages. These peppers can be extremely spicy, so the inexperienced palate should proceed with caution!

Papa (potato)

The potato is as Peruvian as the Inca himself. There are more than 2,000 varieties of tubers although only a fraction are edible. *The International Potato Institute* is located on the outskirts of metropolitan Lima so those with a potato fetish might wish to visit. The *papa amarilla* (yellow potato) is by far the best-tasting of the lot.

Causa

A casserole served cold with a base of yellow potato and mixed with hot peppers, onion, avocado, with either chicken, crab or meat. A fantastic starter.

Estofado

A mild chicken stew, with lots of potatoes and other vegetables, served with rice.

Lomo saltado

Strips of sirloin sautéed with tomato, onion, *ají amarillo* (a spicy orange pepper) and french fried potatoes served with rice.

Papa Ocopa

A typical dish from the Arequipa region. A spicy peanut sauce served over cold potatoes with a slice of hard boiled egg.

Papa a la Huancaína

A dish which originated in the central department of Huancayo. This creamy cheese sauce served over cold potatoes is a common starter for set menus everywhere.

Papa Rellena (stuffed potato)

First baked then fried, the potato is stuffed with meat, onions, olives, boiled egg and raisins. *Camote* (yams) can be substituted for potatoes.

Choclo (corn)

Another staple in the Peruvian diet. The large kernels are great with the fresh cheese produced all over the country.

Maíz morado (purple corn)

This type of corn is not edible for humans. It's boiled and the liquid is used to make *chicha*, a sweet and very traditional Peruvian refreshment.

Chicha de Jora

A strong fermented beverage mostly found in mountain communities. The people who make it use their saliva to aid in the fermenting process.

Granos (grains)

Kiwicha and Quinoa are very high sources of protein and staples of the Inca diet. Quinoa is wonderful in soups and Kiwicha is a common breakfast food for children throughout the country.

Arroz (rice)
Another major staple in Peruvian cooking.

Anticuchos (beef heart kebabs)
Beef heart barbecued and served with cold potato and a wonderful assortment of spicy sauces. A must for all meat lovers.

Cuy (guinea pig)
Prepared in a variety of ways, from stewed to fried.

Cau Cau
Tripe and potatoes.

Rocoto relleno (stuffed hot peppers)
Stuffed with meat and potatoes, then baked.

Pachamanca
Typical mountain cuisine, so popular it's now prepared everywhere. Beef, pork and chicken mixed with a variety of vegetables, and cooked together over heated stones in a hole in the ground.

Seco de cabrito
A favorite dish from the north coast. Roasted goat marinated with fermented *chicha*, served with beans and rice.

Ají de Gallina
A rich mix of creamed, spicy chicken over rice and boiled potatoes.

Arroz con pato (duck with rice)
A dish originally from the north coast but found everywhere.

Ceviche
The national dish of Peru. Raw fish or seafood marinated in a mixture of lime juice, red onions and hot peppers usually served with a thick slice of boiled yam (*camote*) and corn. With a coastline of more than 1,800 km, the fruits of the sea are almost limitless. Sea bass, flounder, salmon, red snapper, sole and many varieties of shellfish are all in abundance. Keep in mind that *ceviche* is a dish served for lunch. Most *cevicherías* (*ceviche* restaurants) close around 1600.

Postres (desserts)

Arroz con leche
Rice pudding.

Manjar blanco
A caramel sweet made from boiled milk and sugar.

Picarones
Deep-fried donut batter bathed in a honey sauce.

Suspiro a la limeña
Manjar blanco with baked egg-white.

Turrón
This popular sweet, shortbread covered in molasses or honey, is sold everywhere during the October celebration of *Señor de los Milagros* (Lord of Miracles) in Lima.

Fruta (fruit)

There's a great selection of fruit in Peru. Aside from common fruits such as mandarins, oranges, peaches and bananas, there are exotic tropical fruits to choose from.

Chirimoya
Custard apple. In Quechua means "the sweet of the gods".
Lúcuma
Eggfruit.
Maracuyá
Passionfruit, often served as a juice.
Tuna
Prickly pear.

Bebidas (drinks)

The national beers are *Cristal, Cusqueña, Bremen* and *Pilsen*. There are also some dark beers.

Although not known as great wine producing country, there are a couple of good quality wines to choose from. *Blanco en Blanco* is a surprisingly pleasant white wine from the Tacama winery which also makes a great red wine called *Reserva Especial*. *Pisco*, a strong brandy made from white grapes is produced in the departments of Ica, Moquegua and Tacna. Pisco Sour, the national drink is made with lime juice, egg white, sugar and a dash of cinnamon.

Conversion tables

Weights and measures

Weight	1 kilogram = 2.205 pounds
	1 pound = 0.454 kilograms
Length	1 metre = 1.094 yards
	1 yard = 0.914 metres
	1 kilometre = 0.621 miles
	1 mile = 1.609 kilometres
Capacity	1 litre = 0.0220 gallons
	1 gallon = 4.546 litres
	1 pint = 0.863 litres

5 imperial gallons are approximately equal to 6 US gallons

The manzana, used in Central America, is about 0.7 hectare (1.73 acres).

Temperature

°C	°F	°C	°F
1	34	26	79
2	36	27	81
3	38	28	82
4	39	29	84
5	41	30	86
6	43	31	88
7	45	32	90
8	46	33	92
9	48	34	93
10	50	35	95
11	52	36	97
12	54	37	99
13	56	38	100
14	57	39	102
15	59	40	104
16	61	41	106
17	63	42	108
18	64	43	109
19	66	44	111
20	68	45	113
21	70	46	115
22	72	47	117
23	74	48	118
24	75	49	120
25	77	50	122

Index

Shorts

Adverts

Maps

Map symbols

Administration

- International border
- Department border
- □ Capital city
- ○ Other city/town

Roads and travel

- —— Paved road
- —— unpaved road
- ---- 4WD road, track
- ······ Footpath
- ↦▬ Railway with station

Water features

- River
- Lake
- Beach, dry river bed
- Ocean
- ⚓ Ferry

Cities and towns

- ▫ Sight
- ■ Sleeping
- ● Eating
- Building
- Main street
- Minor street
- Pedestrianized street
-)⸺(Tunnel
- → One way street
- ⊨ Bridge

Steps and symbols

- ⊪⊪⊪ Steps
- Park, garden, stadium
- ✈ Airport
- Ⓢ Bank
- ⚏ Bus station
- ✚ Hospital
- Ⓜ Market
- ⛫ Museum
- Ⓟ Police
- ✉ Post office
- ⓘ Tourist office
- ✝✝ Cathedral, church
- Ⓟ Petrol
- @ Internet
- Ⓐ Detail map
- ◀Ⓐ Related map

Topographical features

- Contours (approx), rock outcrop
- ⋀ Mountain
- ⛰ Volcano
- ⤙ Mountain pass
- Escarpment
- Gorge

Other symbols

- ∴ Archaeological site
- ♦ National park/wildlife reserve
- ✲ Viewing point
- ⋏ Campsite

Credits

Footprint credits

Text editor: Sarah Thorowgood
Map editor: Sarah Sorensen

Publishers: James Dawson and
Patrick Dawson
Editorial Director: Rachel Fielding
Editorial: Alan Murphy, Stephanie Lambe, Sarah Thorowgood, Claire Boobbyer,
Felicity Laughton, Caroline Lascom
Production: Davina Rungasamy,
Jo Morgan, Emma Bryers, Mark Thomas
Cartography: Claire Benison,
Kevin Feeney, Robert Lunn
Design: Mytton Williams
Marketing and publicity:
Rosemary Dawson, La-Ree Miners
Sales: Ed Aves
Advertising: Debbie Wylde,
Lorraine Horler
Finance and administration:
Sharon Hughes, Elizabeth Taylor,
Leona Bailey
Distribution: Pam Cobb, Mike Noel

Photography credits

Front cover: Alamy, workers in the salt pans on
terraces at Salinas Cusco
Back cover: Alamy, woman in Huaraz
Inside colour section: Alamy, Nature Picture
Library, gettyone Stone, Robert Harding Picture
Library

Print

Manufactured in Italy by LegoPrint

Publishing information

Footprint Peru Handbook
4th edition
© Footprint Handbooks Ltd
February 2003

ISBN 1 903471 51 6
CIP DATA: A catalogue record for this book is
available from the British Library

® Footprint Handbooks and the Footprint
mark are a registered trademark of
Footprint Handbooks Ltd

Published by Footprint Handbooks

6 Riverside Court
Lower Bristol Road
Bath BA2 3DZ, UK
T +44 (0)1225 469141
F +44 (0)1225 469461
E discover@footprintbooks.com
W www.footprintbooks.com

Distributed in the USA by

Publishers Group West

Acknowledgements

The preparation of the fourth edition of the Peru Handbook would not have been possible without the support of many collaborators in the UK and Peru. For their contributions to the text, warmest thanks go to the following:

John Forrest and **Julia Porturas**, who researched Tambopata, Canta, Casma, Chimbote, Trujillo, Ica and Huacachina, Yungay, Caraz and the backroads between the Cordillera Blanca and Huamachuco.

Stephen Light, for much cultural information and new material on the Uros islands, Afro-Peruvian culture and Peruvian beaches.

Andre Vltchek sent lots of practical material on Lima and Callao, including the shantytowns, sailed the Amazon from Iquitos to the Brazilian border, provided information on the northern beaches and Tumbes and wrote about political movements and bargaining (not in the same article).

As ever the **South American Explorers** have done invaluable research: **Julia Levanton** in the capital, **Tara Aleck** in Arequipa, **Sarah Kirkman** in the Central Highlands, **Andrew Genung** between Tingo María and Iquitos and **Louisa** in Marcahuasi; **Simon Atkinson** co-ordinated it all in Lima. In Cusco, **Fiona Cameron** sent new material on Quillabamba, the Sacred Valley and answered general queries.

Also in Cusco, **María Bernasconi Cillóniz** and **Alberto Miori Sanz** once again helped to keep us abreast of all the changes taking place there, right up to the last minute.

Mónica Moreno and **Leo Rovayo** in Lima helped with many factual points and sent new material on writers, artists and food.

Walter and **Frederike Eberhart** sent masses of useful material on Trujillo, Huanchaco and Cajamarca and Walter acted as my 'co-ordinador' for a great visit to Cajamarca in 2002.

On the adventure travel front, **John Biggar** updated climbing information and **Paul Cripps** did the same for mountain biking and rafting.

For their assistance around the country, many thanks to: Barry Walker (Manu), Michael White (Trujillo and its surroundings), Tom Gierasimczuk (the Chachapoyas area and northern Peru), Christopher Benway (Huaraz), Alberto Cafferata (Caraz) and Efraín Alegría and Carlos Enrique Levano (Nasca and Palpa). Stephen Frankham wrote the box on the Vilcabamba Mountains. Hugh Thomson, author of *The White Rock*, film-maker and explorer kindly gave permission for his work to be plundered for this edition. I am also grateful to Tony Morrison and Nicholas Asheshov for their expertise and experience.

For their generous hospitality in Peru in 2001 and 2002, I should like to thank *PromPerú* for the opportunity to visit Manu. I am especially grateful to Ibeth Acuña, Alessia di Paolo (and Greg), María del Rocío Vesga and María del Pilar Lazarte Conroy (and to Giovanna Salini in London). For their help on the same trip, I'd like to thank John Melton of *InkaNatura*, Jorge Quiñones, and Frida Pérez of *Inti Tour*. In similar vein *Rainforest Expeditions* made a visit to Tambopata possible and I'd like to thank Kurt Holle, Eduardo Nycander and Luis Zapater, plus all the staff in the offices and lodges, especially Aldo Durand. Blanca de Torres of *Dasatariq* provided much appreciated logistical support in June-July 2002.

In Lima, my thanks go to Cecilia Kamiche, Leo Rovayo and Mónica Moreno (Posada del Parque), Víctor Melgar (Hostal Víctor), Ricardo Espinosa, Kato, Lucho and Michael of *Fly Adventure* and Toon at *Mami Panchita*. In Puno, I am most grateful to: Víctor and Maruja Pauca and the staff of *Allways Travel*, Miguel Vera of *Pirámide Tours*, Edgar and Norka of *EdgarAdventures*, and Valentín Quispe in Llachón. At Suasi, Martha Giraldo was a wonderful hostess and thanks to Edwin Giraldo for all the driving. As well as Walter Eberhart (see above), my thanks go to the following in Cajamarca: Pim Heijster and Luz Marina (Heladería Holanda), Marco Saavedra of Cenfotur and Julio Matta of Ahora. Mike Lamb in Tambopata and, last but by no means least, thanks to Robert and Daisy Kunstaetter for a weekend of border-hopping and for their support.

For all their assistance at Footprint, I should like to thank the two Sarahs, Thorowgood and Sorensen, for their patience and all the other editorial and mapping staff who have helped to put the book together. Thanks also go to Alan Murphy, who wrote the first two editions of this Handbook. Finally, thanks to all the travellers who have written to the Peru and South American Handbooks with their recommendations, advice, tips and criticisms.

Thank you also to **Dr Charlie Easmon** who wrote the health section. His aid and development work has included: Raleigh International (Medical Officer in Botswana), MERLIN (in Rwanda his team set up a refugee camp for 12,000 people), Save the Children (as a consultant in Rwanda), ECHO (The European Community Humanitarian Office review of Red Cross work in Armenia, Georgia and Azerbaijan), board member of International Care and Relief and previously International Health Exchange. In addition to his time as a hospital physician, he has worked as a medical adviser to the Foreign and Commonwealth Office and as a locum consultant at the Hospital for Tropical Diseases travel clinic, as well as being a specialist registrar in Public Health. He now also runs Travel Screening Services (www.travelscreening.co.uk) based at 1 Harley Street.

Travellers' letters

We are very grateful to the following travellers who have written to and emailed us: **Argentina**: Juliano Golden, Herbert Levi. **Australia**: David De-Fina, Natalie Austria: Dieter Pfeifer. **Belgium**: Gert De Smedt, Harlinde Keymolen, Ilse Michielsen, Sybille Pringot, Sr y Sra Van Ibory. **Canada**: Jean-Yves Boyer, France-Éliàne Dumais, Denys Robitaille. **Denmark**: Uffe Pedersen. **Finland**: Toni Ajoksenmaki. **France**: Olivier Le Fur, François Leib, Anne Lindley. **Germany**: Jochen R Andritzky, André Bause, Stefan Beck, Cristine D'Arthuys, Christian Eckstein, Christian Faesecke, Matthias Fehrenbach, Andreas Gökeler, Ingrid Gökeler, Dagmar Graefe, Ute Keck, Andreas Kurschat, Wolfram Madlener, Thomas Mehis, Katja Nettesheim, Laura Obermiller, Sebastian Osenstetter, Albert Recknagel, Juliane Trieschmann, Hannah Völkering. **Ireland**: Helen Hanatin, Claire Hillery. **Israel**: Tamir Bazaz, Asaf Biber, Shahar Cohen, Dan Doliner, Maya Goldstein, Yael Katzin, Yonatan Klein, Roman Klotsvog, David Meidal Muskal, Hadas Nachum, Ishay Nadler, Gilad Rosenberg, Eyal Rosenfeld, Yishai Shimoni, Amit Shur, Boaz Tzur, Ran Weiss, Anat Zimmermann. **Italy**: Michelangelo Mazzeo, Fabio Spreafico, **Netherlands**: Wilbert Harmsen, Kris Kristinsson, Eppo Kuipers, Suzanne Kuipers, Hans Polane, Jakobien Renting, Jeroen Tamsma, Thomas van der Lijke, Anne van Leeuwen, Judy van Veen, Family Westra. **New Zealand**: Guy Burton, Rob Lawrence. **Norway**: Stein Morten Lund, Eric Sevrin. **Peru**: Sitapati Das, Michael Ferguson, John-Paul Kimmel, Silvia Lavalle, Jessaca Leinaweaver. **South Korea**: Gerard Paul-Clark, Hee Joung Kimmel. **Sweden**: Åsa Hasselblad, Erik Uddenbergt, Anders Wienecke, Stephen Aerni, Mirjam Barrueto, Andrea Bieder, Manuela Dosch, Maurus Dosch. **Switzerland**: Birgit Elsener, Donat Elsener, Peter Haenseler, Mirjam Humi, Simone Marzoll, Hansuedi Ruchti, Charles Sarasin, Marianne Spalinger, Reto Thalmann, Manuela Weber, Thomas Weber, Hans Zubler. **UK**: Mandy Ball, William Becker, Keith H Berry, Rachel Blair, Edith Bowman, Alice Brotherton, Hannah Brown, Annabelle Cook, Natasha Fanshawe, Lionel Ferrer, Danny Fitzpatrick, Kate Fitzpatrick, Alistair Fox, Hywel Franklin, Chris Grimwood, Maggie Hanlon, D R James, Helen King, Rachel King, Tony Lang, Nick Oliver, Ogg Olly, Jeremy Pounder, Peter Rendle, Tammy Rothenberg, Scott Saunders, Kate Smith, Kevin Spencer, Henry Stevenson, James Sturcke, Anthony Turner, Kath Vlcek, Tom Wigley, Joanne Wimble, Linda Wright, Tom Wynne-Powell. **USA**: Saul Candib, Hilary Emberton, John Embow, Gloria Fisher, Rebecca Garbett, Jorge Garzon, Lora Hish, Marc Kratzschmar, William Lavelle, Bruce Mock, Jay Rossiter, Kim Stanford, Janet Um, Chad Yarborough. **Via email**: Daniel Aderhold, Lorraine Alcock, Astrid, Uri Baruch, Vardit Baruch, Bernd, Tomas Berrin, Manuel Bichsel, Christoph Bigler, Paterson Brown, Lorraine Callery, Rob Callery, Bill Conn, Rozemarijn Cornelissen, Stefan Cornelissen, Tara Crete, Adrian Croft, Jacqueline Cullen, Charles Debakey, Yvonne Degen, Thea Devers, Felipe Dorantes, Jacqueline Feetz, David Fern, Carolynn Fischer, Michel Gagnon, Egli Hannes, Steven Hedges, Anne Hook, Patricia Houton, Manfred Imiela, Dave Katz, Joe Kopp, Bill Lee, Daniel Levy, Alex Lewandowski, Sanda Lewandowski, Geoffrey Locke, Trajan Martin, Pavel Mikhlin, Maor Moses, Russell Price, Roger Rost, Max Shenker, Yvonne Spiczynski, Verena Stammbach, David Thom, Marie Thompson, Andreas Tröndle, Tim Tucker, Sheetal Vyas, Richard and others Whitaker, Ruud Wijtvliet.

Keep in touch

Footprint feedback

We try as hard as we can to make each Footprint Handbook as up-to-date and accurate as possible but, of course, things always change. Many people write to us - with corrections, new information, or simply comments.

If you want to let us know about an experience or adventure - hair-raising or mundane, good or bad, exciting or boring or simply something rather special - we would be delighted to hear from you. Please give us as precise information as possible, quoting the edition number (you'll find it on the front cover) and page number of the Handbook you are using.

Your help will be greatly appreciated, especially by other travellers. In return we will send you details about our special guidebook offer. Email Footprint at:
per4_online@footprintbooks.com

or write to:
Elizabeth Taylor
Footprint Handbooks
6 Riverside Court, Lower Bristol Road

www.footprintbooks.com

Dip in and keep on the pulse with what Footprint are up to online.

- Latest Footprint releases
- Entertaining travel articles and news updates
- Extensive destination information for inspiration and trip planning
- Monthly competitions
- Easy ways to buy Footprint guides

What the papers say...

"I carried the South American Handbook from Cape Horn to Cartagena and consulted it every night for two and a half months. I wouldn't do that for anything else except my hip flask."
Michael Palin, BBC Full Circle

"My favourite series is the Handbook series published by Footprint and I especially recommend the Mexico, Central and South America Handbooks."
Boston Globe

"If 'the essence of real travel' is what you have been secretly yearning for all these years, then Footprint are the guides for you."
Under 26 magazine

"Who should pack Footprint-readers who want to escape the crowd."
The Observer

"Footprint can be depended on for accurate travel information and for imparting a deep sense of respect for the lands and people they cover."
World News

"The guides for intelligent, independently-minded souls of any age or budget."
Indie Traveller

Mail order
Available worldwide in bookshops and on-line. Footprint travel guides can also be ordered directly from us in Bath, via our website www.footprintbooks.com or from the address on the imprint page of this book.

HOTEL MONASTERIO

The Leading Small Hotels of the World

*You are informed that your room is oxygen-enriched
and are not surprised.....
After all, your hotel is 3,400 m (11 000 ft) up in the Andes.*

The Hotel Monasterio is located in the heart of the historic city of Cusco in the Peruvian Andes, at a height of 3,400 metres (11 000 ft) above sea level. At this altitude, there is a 30% decrease in available oxygen and consequently our guests may be at risk of altitude sickness.

Medical and Physiological Aspects of High Altitude
The effect of the decrease in inspired oxygen can lead to symptoms of acute altitude sickness. These symptoms include headache, nausea, insomnia, loss of appetite, irritability and breathlessness.

Relief ....
The Hotel Monasterio, with world experts from the Scottish Pulmonary Vascular Institute and Respiratory Medicine, have counteracted the problem of high altitude by using oxygen concentrators to enrich the atmosphere in the rooms, effectively oxygenating the rooms down to an atmospheric pressure of app 2,400 metres which is low enough to prevent altitude sickness. After sleeping in an oxygen-enriched room, the increased level of oxygen in the body declines only gradually over a period of 14 - 15 hours the following day.

We'll do whatever it takes to make you comfortable!

ORIENT-EXPRESS HOTELS, PERU

www.monasterio.orient-express.com

Discovering the Andes

PeruRail - the service comprising some of the world's most scenic railways, and linking the tourist highlights of the Andes. It operates from historic Cusco to the famous ruins at Machu Picchu and to Puno's Lake Titicaca, connecting the most spectacular attractions of Peru. The trains are comfortable, the service is splendid and the views are unmatched. It is an unparalleled way to travel within Peru.

Andean Explorer •
Cusco - Lake Titicaca

With a fleet of newly-refurbished luxury coaches including an open-air observation-bar car and decorated in the fine manner of the great Pullman trains of the 1920's, the Andean Explorer takes you across one of the highest rail routes in the world, linking two of Peru's top destinations on a journey of the utmost in romance and style.

Vistadome • Cusco - Machu Picchu
(incorporating Sacred Valley - Machu Picchu departures)

With it's panoramic windows, the Vistadome allows you to enjoy to the full the breathtaking views on the Cusco - Machu Picchu route.

Backpacker • Cusco - Machu Picchu

Created for adventure passengers seeking comfort without the extra frills, the Backpacker service has been recently reupholstered with indigenous fabrics, giving a touch of local flavour.

www.perurail.com

644

Map 1

Pacific Ocean

ECUADOR

Altitude in metres
4000
3000
2000
1000
500
200
0
Neighbouring Country
Paved road
Unpaved road
Railway
Departmental border
▲ Mountain

Tumbes · Iquitos · Rio Amazonas
Piura · Moyobamba
Chiclayo · Cajamarca
Trujillo · Pucallpa
Huaraz · Huánuco
Cerro De Pasco · Puerto Maldonado
Huancayo
Huancavelica · Machu Picchu
LIMA · Cusco · Abancay
Ayacucho · Lake Titicaca
Ica · Puno
Arequipa
Moquegua
Tacna

Pacific Ocean

Aguas Verdes
Puerto Pizarro · Zarumilla
Tumbes
Zorritos · San Jacinto
Bocapán
Cancas
TUMBES
Zona Reserva de Tumbes ▲

Máncora
Punta Sal
Los Organos
Cabo Blanco
Atascadero
Cerros de Amotape National Park ▲
Cañaveral

La Tina-Macará
Alamor
Suyo · Ayabaca
Paimas
Espíndola

Lobitos
Talara
Negritos
Vichayal · Amotape · Sullana
La Huaca
Colán
Paita
Catacaos

San Jacinto
Las Lomas
Frias
Tambo Real
Chulucanas
Morropón · Canchaque
Piura
PIURA
Chira
Piura

La Unión · Vice
Sechura · L Ramón
Desert of Sechura

Huancabamba · Sapalache · Tabaconas
Namballe
San Ignacio
Aramango
Bellavista · Bagua Chica
Jaén · Bagua Grande
Chamaya
Pomahuaca
Pucará
Lunya Grande
Sto Tómas
CAJAMARCA
Cutervo
Chota
Bambamarca
Hualgayoc

Bayovar
Reventazón
Cascajal
Olmos
Motupe · Chochope
LAMBAYEQUE
Apurlec · Batán Grande
Jayanca
Túcume · Chongoyape
Mórrope
Ferreñafe · Picsi
Santa Cruz
Lambayeque
Pimental · **Chiclayo** · Sipán
Sta Rosa · Monsefú
Oyotún
Puerto de Etén · Zaña · Zaña
Mócupe
San Miguel de
Laguna · Chepén · Tembladera
Pueblo Nuevo · Chilete · Cumbe Mayo
Reservoir · San Juán
Contumazá
Cajamarca

Pacasmayo
San Pedro de Lloc
Ascope
Chicama
Pto Chicama · Paiján
I de Macabi · Chocope
El Brujo
LA LIBERTAD

N

0 km 30
0 miles 30

① **②** **③**

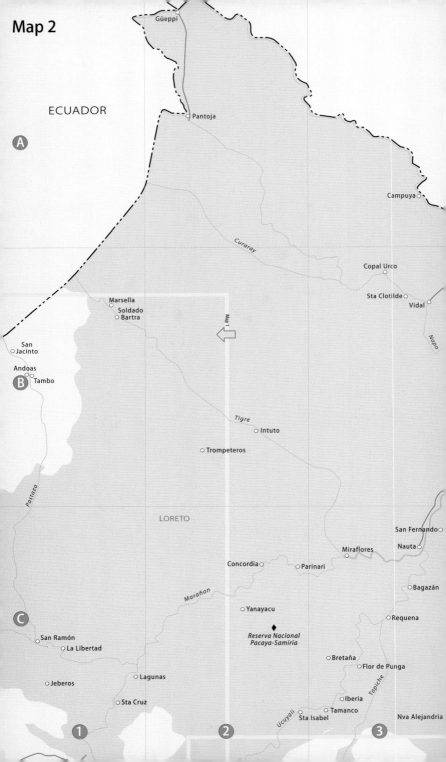

Map 2

ECUADOR

A

Güeppi

Pantoja

Campuya

Curaray

Copal Urco

Marsella
Soldado
Bartra

Sta Clotilde
Vidal

Napo

San
Jacinto

Andoas
B Tambo

Tigre

Intuto

Trompeteros

Pastaza

LORETO

San Fernando

Nauta

Miraflores

Concordia
Parinari

Bagazán

Marañón

Yanayacu

Requena

C

San Ramón
La Libertad

◆ Reserva Nacional
Pacaya-Samiria

Jeberos

Bretaña
Flor de Punga

Lagunas

Tapiche

Sta Cruz

Iberia
Tamanco

Ucuyali
Sta Isabel

Nva Alejandria

①

②

③

COLOMBIA

Flor de
Agosto

○ Puca Urco

Putumayo

Yaguas

Ipora

LORETO

B

Napo

Ampiyacu ○ Pebas

Francisco de Orellana

Mazán

○ Indiana *Amazonas*

ta Maria de Nanay

quitos

ago Quistacocha

Caballaococha

Leticia

Ramón
Castilla

San Pablo

Amelia

Yavari Mirim

Reserva
Comunal
Tamshiyacu
Tahuayo

Yavari

BRAZIL

C

Map 4   4   5   6

Map 3

LAMBAYEQUE

SAN MARTIN

Tembladera Contumazá San Marcos Campanilla

Pacasmayo Cajabamba
San Pedro de Lloc
Pto Chicama Ascope Huamachuco Pataz Río Abiseo National Park
Pto Morin Paiján Chahual Retamas Puerto Pizarro
I de Macabi Chocope Otusco Parcoy Tocache Nuevo
El Brujo Simbal Quiruvilca Marsa
Santiago de Cao Shorey Buldibuyo
Huanchaco Laredo Santiago de Chuco Mollepata Tayabamba Huancaspata
Chan Chán Huaca del Sol & de la Luna Pallasca San Pedro de Chonta
A Trujillo Salaverry Cabana Huancaspata Huacrachuco
Pto Morin Tauca Sihuas

LA LIBERTAD

El Carmelo Virú Corongo Tarica Pasacancha
Tanguche Chuquicara Tres Cruces Alpamayo (6,120m) Pomabamba Llamellín
Santa Huallanca Cañón del Pato Cashapampa Piscobamba
Chimbote Pamparomas Caraz Yanama Tantamayo
Nepeña Pueblo Libre Huascarán (6,768m) San Luis Chavín de Parlarca
Moro Mancos Yungay Chacas Llata
Samanco Marcará Chancos Huari Quivilla
Playa Tortugas Anta Huascarán NP Chavinillo
Sechín Pariacoto **Huaraz** Huantoón (6,410m) Chavín de Huantar
Casma Yaután Monterrey San Marcos Huánuco Viejo
ANCASH Olleros Chavín La Unión
Culebras Recuay Huanzala Huallanca
La Merced Catac Huanzala Baños
Pacific Ocean Aija Pachacoto Carpa
Culebras Huayán Huayllapampa Aquia Yerupajá (6,634m)
Huarmey Marca Chiquián Conococha (4,100m) Cordillera Huayhuash
B Pampa Mata Caballos Cajatambo Raura
Chasqitambo Oyón
Paramonga Cochas Churín
Patavilca Supe Cochamarca
Barranca Pto Supe
Végueta Sayán
Huaura Huacho
Paraíso Reserva Nacional Loma de Lachay
Las Salinas Huaral Chancay
Chancay Aucallama Santa Rosa de Quives
Ancón Yangas
Sta Rosa Puente Piedra **LIMA**
Ventanilla Comas Chosic
Callao Cieneguilla
LIMA Pachacáma
Miraflores Lurín
Sta María del Mar
C Pucusana
Chilc

N

0 km 30
0 miles 30

1 **2** **3**

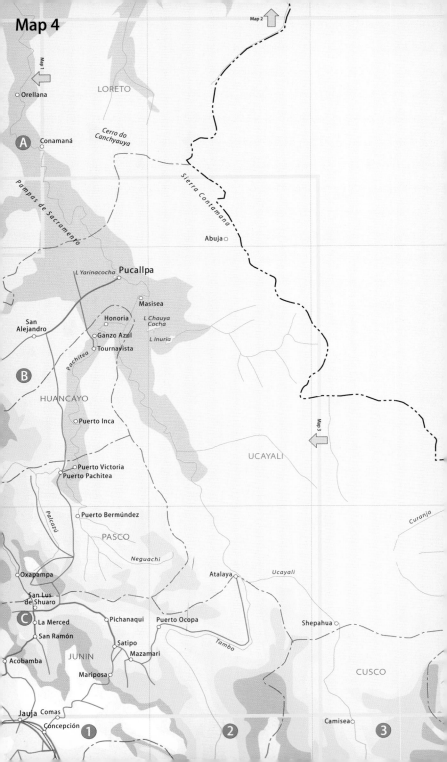

Map 4

Map 1
Map 2
Map 3

LORETO

Orellana

A Conamaná

Cerro do Canchyauya

Pampas de Sacramento

Sierra Contamana

Abuja

L Yarinacocha   Pucallpa

Masisea

San Alejandro

Honoria   L Chauya Cocha

Pachitea

Ganzo Azul   L Inuria

Tournavista

B

HUANCAYO

Puerto Inca

UCAYALI

Puerto Victoria
Puerto Pachitea

Palcazú

Puerto Bermúndez

Curanja

PASCO

Neguachi

Ucayali

Oxapampa

Atalaya

San Lus de Shuaro

C   La Merced   Pichanaqui   Puerto Ocopa   Shepahua

San Ramón

Acobamba   Satipo   Tambo

Mazamari

JUNIN   CUSCO

Mariposa

Jauja   Comas

Concepción   1   2   Camisea   3

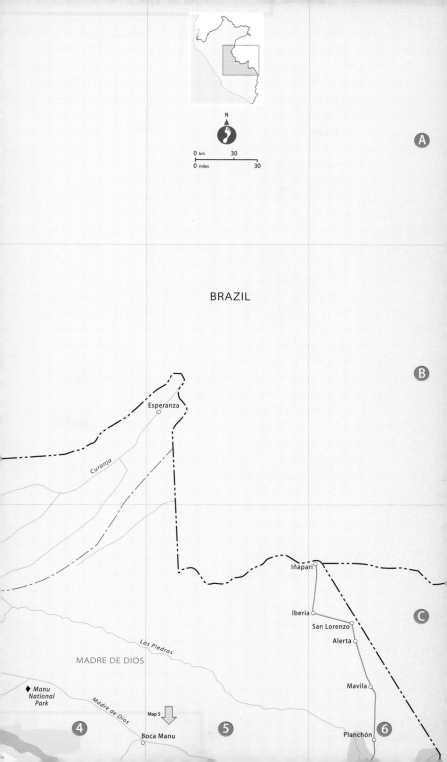

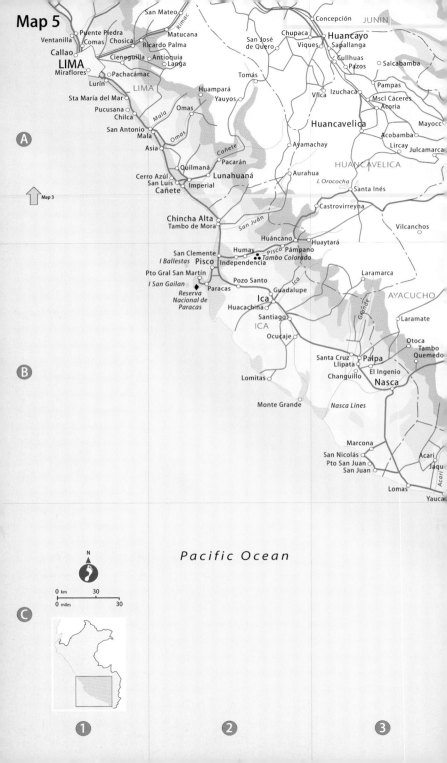

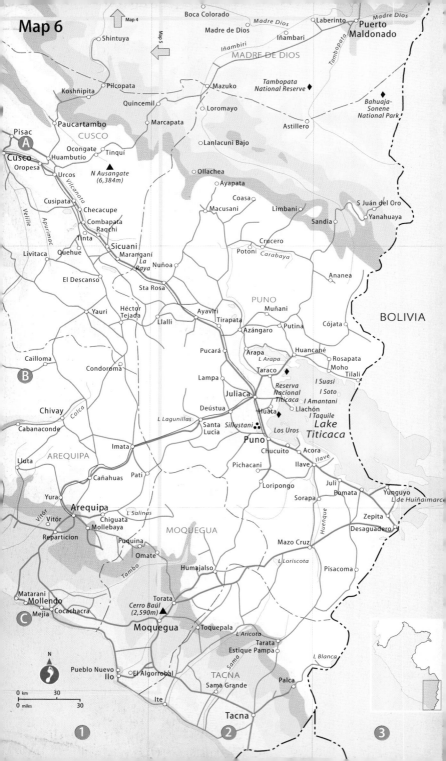